Gurban Singh

0343617

Small Gas Engines

11th Edition

Fundamentals
Service
Troubleshooting
Repair
Applications

by
Alfred C. Roth
Blake J. Fisher
W. Scott Gauthier

Publisher
The Goodheart-Willcox Company, Inc.
Tinley Park, IL
www.g-w.com

The Goodheart-Willcox Company, Inc. Brand Disclaimer: Brand names, company names, and illustrations for products and services included in this text are provided for educational purposes only and do not represent or imply endorsement or recommendation by the author or the publisher.

The Goodheart-Willcox Company, Inc. Safety Notice: The reader is expressly advised to carefully read, understand, and apply all safety precautions and warnings described in this book or that might also be indicated in undertaking the activities and exercises described herein to minimize risk of personal injury or injury to others. Common sense and good judgment should also be exercised and applied to help avoid all potential hazards. The reader should always refer to the appropriate manufacturer's technical information, directions, and recommendations; then proceed with care to follow specific equipment operating instructions. The reader should understand these notices and cautions are not exhaustive.

The publisher makes no warranty or representation whatsoever, either expressed or implied, including but not limited to equipment, procedures, and applications described or referred to herein, their quality, performance, merchantability, or fitness for a particular purpose. The publisher assumes no responsibility for any changes, errors, or omissions in this book. The publisher specifically disclaims any liability whatsoever, including any direct, indirect, incidental, consequential, special, or exemplary damages resulting, in whole or in part, from the reader's use or reliance upon the information, instructions, procedures, warnings, cautions, applications, or other matter contained in this book. The publisher assumes no responsibility for the activities of the reader.

The Goodheart-Willcox Company, Inc. Internet Disclaimer: The Internet resources and listings in this Goodheart-Willcox Publisher product are provided solely as a convenience to you. These resources and listings were reviewed at the time of publication to provide you with accurate, safe, and appropriate information. Goodheart-Willcox Publisher has no control over the referenced websites and, due to the dynamic nature of the Internet, is not responsible or liable for the content, products, or performance of links to other websites or resources. Goodheart-Willcox Publisher makes no representation, either expressed or implied, regarding the content of these websites, and such references do not constitute an endorsement or recommendation of the information or content presented. It is your responsibility to take all protective measures to guard against inappropriate content, viruses, or other destructive elements.

Library of Congress Cataloging-in-Publication Data

Roth, Alfred C., author.
    Small gas engines/by Alfred C. Roth, Blake J. Fisher,
    W. Scott Gauthier.—11th edition.
    pages cm
    Includes index.
    ISBN 978-1-63126-390-3
    1. Small gasoline engines. I. Fisher, Blake J., author. II.
    Title.

TJ789.R59 2017
621.43'4--dc23

2015034661

Preface

Small Gas Engines is an easy-to-understand, up-to-date textbook detailing the operation, diagnosis, service, and repair of small gasoline engines. It has been designed to help prepare aspiring technicians for exciting and productive careers in the small engine and outdoor power equipment service industry. It also provides the information needed to prepare for EETC certification tests.

The information provided in the book is applicable to a wide range of small engines, including overhead valve, overhead cam, and L-head designs from different manufacturers. Variations in basic engine design and the techniques needed to diagnose and service diverse engine types are clearly explained.

Because small engine technology continues to evolve, the new edition of **Small Gas Engines** has been carefully reviewed and revised to include recent technologies, like electronic fuel injection. At the same time, we realize that small engines tend to stay in service for an extended period. We carefully evaluated older technologies in the book, and eliminated those that have slipped into complete obsolescence while keeping those that a technician is likely to occasionally encounter on the job.

The 2017 edition of **Small Gas Engines** contains the information needed to pass EETC certification tests. The information on employment and workplace skills has also been greatly expanded.

Small Gas Engines has been painstakingly designed to provide a student-focused approach to learning. Short sentences, concise definitions, and thousands of color illustrations will help you learn quickly and easily. Information is presented using a building-block approach that starts with simple principles and general rules, and progresses gradually to more complex subjects.

As society transitions from printed textbooks to digital learning tools, we know it is important to provide the content you need in the format you need it in. The **Small Gas Engines** textbook and the accompanying workbook are available in both print and digital formats, and are supported with professionally developed, user-friendly online resources. These resources include electronic study tools and interactive activities designed to prepare you for success in your studies and career.

We congratulate you on your study of small engine technology and encourage you to take advantage of all the resources available as part of the **Small Gas Engines** learning solution.

About the Authors

Alfred Roth taught for more than 30 years at the college level and was a member of the Equipment & Engine Training Council (EETC) Certification Test Committee. He was also an inventor and holds six patents.

Blake Fisher is a technical editor and writer with over 15 years of experience. His areas of expertise include small engines, automotive technology, and welding.

W. Scott Gauthier has more than 20 years of experience as a technical editor and writer. He is a coauthor of the Goodheart-Willcox *Automotive Encyclopedia* and has written several educational supplements.

Acknowledgments

The authors and publisher would like to thank the following companies and individuals for their valuable input in the development of **Small Gas Engines**.

- **Briggs & Stratton Corporation**; Milwaukee, Wisconsin, for the illustrations used throughout the text.
- **Engine Service Association, Incorporated**; Exton, Pennsylvania, for their contribution of materials and illustrations.
- **Generac Corporation**; Waukesha, Wisconsin, for illustrations used throughout the text.
- **Honda**; Alpharetta, Georgia, for illustrations used throughout the text.
- **J & R Lawn and Garden**; Mokena, Illinois, for the use of much of the lawn equipment illustrated throughout this text.
- **Kawasaki Motors Corporation U.S.A.**; Irvine, California, for illustrations used throughout the text.
- **The L. S. Starrett Company**; Athol, Massachusetts, for the use of the precision measuring instruments illustrated throughout this text.
- **Mercury Marine**; Fon du Lac, Wisconsin, for illustrations used throughout the text.
- **Sears, Roebuck and Company—Orland Park Retail Store**; Orland Park, Illinois, for the use of many of the tools illustrated throughout this text.
- **Steve Olewinski**; Phoenix, Arizona, for providing technical illustrations.
- **Tecumseh Products Company**; Grafton, Wisconsin, for numerous illustrations used throughout the text.

Reviewers

The author and publisher wish to thank the following industry and teaching professionals for their valuable input into the development of **Small Gas Engines**.

Lonnie Prewitt
AST/SCT Instructor
Kiamichi Technology Centers,
    Poteau Campus
Poteau, Oklahoma

Jared Reeves
Transportation and Logistics Instructor
North Lamar High School
Paris, Texas

Larry Smith
Small Gas Engines I and Advanced
    Small Gas Engines Instructor
Jacksonville High School
Jacksonville, Texas

Laurent W. Soucie
High School Technology Education
    Instructor
Lodi High School, District of
    Lodi Schools
Lodi, Wisconsin

J R Watson
Automotive Instructor
Ford High School
Quinlan, Texas

Richard Westbrook
Small Engines/Automotive Instructor
Pine Tree High School
Longview, Texas

William Young
Small Engine Instructor
Lehigh Career & Technical Institute
Schnecksville, Pennsylvania

G-W Integrated Learning Solution

Together, We Build Careers

At Goodheart-Willcox, we take our mission seriously. Since 1921, G-W has been serving the career and technical education (CTE) community. Our employee-owners are driven to deliver exceptional learning solutions to CTE students to help prepare them for careers. Our authors and subject matter experts have years of experience in the classroom and industry. We combine their wisdom with our expertise to create content and tools to help students achieve success. Our products start with theory and applied content based upon a strong foundation of accepted standards and curriculum. To that base, we add student-focused learning features and tools designed to help students make connections between knowledge and skills.

G-W recognizes the crucial role instructors play in preparing students for careers. We support educators' efforts by providing timesaving tools that help them plan, present, assess, and engage students with traditional and digital activities and assets. We provide an entire program of learning in a variety of print, digital, and online formats, including economical bundles, allowing educators to select the right mix for their classroom.

Student-Focused Curated Content

Small Gas Engines features student-focused content built from standards and accepted curriculum coverage. This comprehensive text uses a building-block approach, with attention devoted to a logical teaching progression that helps students build upon their learning. All important components are introduced and operating principles are fully explained before troubleshooting, service, and repair are discussed. Written in clear, easy-to-understand language, **Small Gas Engines** provides concise explanations of engine fundamentals and common service procedures.

We call on industry experts and teachers from across the country to review and comment on our content, presentation, and pedagogy. Finally, in our refinement of curated content, our editors are immersed in content checking, securing, and sometimes creating figures that convey key information, and revising language and pedagogy.

Equipment & Engine Training Council (EETC) Certification

The Equipment & Engine Training Council (EETC) creates voluntary technician certification tests. EETC certification tests are carefully constructed to measure knowledge in basic skills, interpersonal relationship skills, engine fundamentals, theory, servicing, failure analysis, troubleshooting, and repair. These tests are available to anyone wishing to enhance their training, employment opportunities, and personal credibility.

Passing a certification test indicates that an individual has met industry standards of professionalism and has studied to obtain certification. Certification can be obtained in one or more of the following areas:

- Four-Stroke Engines.
- Two-Stroke Engines.
- Compact Diesel Engines.
- Electrical.
- Driveline/Hydraulics.
- Generators.
- Components Plus.
- Reel Technology.

Each certification area has its own certification test. Individuals passing one or more certification tests are granted EETC Technician Certification. Those passing six of the eight available tests are granted Master Technician Certification.

Small Gas Engines is an ideal resource for those preparing for the EETC certification tests. In addition, sample EETC certification tests for Four-Stroke Engines and Two-Stroke Engines can be found in the **Small Gas Engines Workbook**.

EETC certification can provide personal and professional benefits. Personal prestige and credibility are gained by individuals who have demonstrated interest by studying and meeting certification requirements to advance their professional qualifications. Employers who hire certified technicians are recognized by their customers as having qualified service personnel who are competent and will produce quality work.

Precision Exams Certification

Goodheart-Willcox is pleased to partner with Precision Exams by correlating **Small Gas Engines** to their Small Engines 1 Standards. Precision Exams Standards and Career Skills Exams™ were created in concert with industry and subject matter experts to match real-world job skills and marketplace demands. Students that pass the exam and performance portion of the exam can earn a Career Skills Certification™. Precision Exams provides:

- Access to over 150 Career Skills Exams™ with pre- and post-exams for all 16 Career Clusters.
- Instant reporting suite access to measure student academic growth.
- Easy-to-use, 100% online exam delivery system.

To see how **Small Gas Engines** correlates to the Precision Exams Standards, please visit www.g-w.com/small gas engines-2017 and click on the Correlations tab. For more information on Precision Exams, including a complete listing of their 150+ Career Skills Exams™ and Certificates, please visit https://www.precisionexams.com.

Features of the Textbook

Features are student-focused learning tools designed to help you get the most out of your studies. This visual guide highlights the features designed for the **Small Gas Engines** textbook.

Learning Objectives clearly identify the knowledge and skills to be obtained when the chapter is completed.

Key Terms list the vocabulary to be learned in the chapter.

Warnings identify hazards that may result in personal injury if the proper procedures and safety measures are not followed. If a warning is not understood, always consult a supervisor or instructor.

Notes include technical information and/or hints that provide detailed information about small gas engine systems, service procedures, or applications.

Green Tech features highlight key practices related to sustainability, energy efficiency, and environmental issues.

Cautions identify hazards that may result in temporary or permanent damage of equipment or tools if the proper procedures and safety measures are not followed. If a caution is not understood, always consult a supervisor or instructor.

Illustrations have been designed to clearly and simply communicate the specific topic.

368

Figure 19-1.
Use a seal driver or a socket to tap seals into place.
A—Using a seal driver. B—Using a socket.

Figure 19-2.
Compress the valve springs and install the keepers.
A—When using an L-head type compressor, place the retainers on the spring and then compress the assembly. B—Place the spring and retainers into position and then insert the valve stem through them. Reposition the retainer so it locks on the valve stem, and then open the valve spring com...

Installing Valves (L-Head Engine)

If the engine being serviced is an L-head engine, engine reassembly should continue with reinstallation of the valves. If an overhead valve engine is being reassembled, the valves are located in the cylinder head rather than the block. Overhead valves can be reinstalled toward the end of the reassembly process. Overhead valve installation is covered in a separate section later in this chapter.

After the valves and seats have been properly reconditioned, apply valve guide lubricant to the valve stems and then place each valve in its respective guide. Use a valve spring compressor to compress the spring and, then, install the keepers. See **Figure 19-2.**

When reinstalling the val... the coils are closer together o... than on the other. These are ... and they should be located... and retainers. See **Figure 1...**

Installing the Cr... Camshaft, and C...

Tape the crankshaft... the oil seals from being...

Summary features provide an additional review tool for you and reinforce key learning objectives.

Review Questions allow you to demonstrate knowledge, identification, and comprehension of chapter material.

411

Summary

Power mowers are manufactured in a variety of different sizes and designs. For the average yard, a rotary-type mower with a 22″ diameter blade is satisfactory. Mowers may be either push-type or self-propelled. There are several mechanical methods for starting small engines including the recoil starter and electric starter. Every mower manufactured today must be equipped with a blade brake.

After each use, the mower should be cleaned. Blades can be sharpened when they become dull or nicked. Spark plugs should be cleaned and gapped as recommended by the manufacturer. Air filters should be cleaned and oil should be changed after every twenty-five hours of operation.

Always follow safe operating procedures when using a gasoline-powered chain saw. Chain saws are manufactured in a variety of sizes for different cutting tasks. Safe operation of a chain saw comes from a thorough knowledge of correct operating procedures. Always stop the engine and make sure the chain is stopped before doing maintenance work on a chain saw. Follow all manufacturer's maintenance instructions.

Always keep safety devices in place when using a gas-powered string trimmer, brushcutter, or edger/trimmer. Never attempt to make adjustments on this type of equipment when the engine is running. Common maintenance procedures on string trimmers, brushcutters, or edger/trimmers include replacing broken strings, worn blades, and belts; changing oil; and lubricating moving parts. Special precautions should be taken when storing any engine-powered implement.

Review Questions

Answer the following questions using the information provided in this chapter.

1. How should accidental engine starting be prevented when working on an engine-driven implement?
2. What invisible, odorless, toxic gas (designated CO) is generated from running gasoline engines?
3. What explosive gas is generated when charging lead-acid storage batteries?
4. A(n) _____ mower has a helical blade that rotates around a horizontal shaft and a(n) _____ mower has a blade that rotates in a horizontal plane.
5. List the procedures for preparing and starting an engine.
6. Describe the two types of blade brakes found on mowers.
7. Describe two design features that prevent an engine from being damaged if a mower blade strikes a solid object.
8. When the unshielded nose of the chain saw hits a solid surface, it may jump toward the operator. This is called _____.
9. The device often built into the muffler of a chain saw to prevent sparks from causing a fire is called a(n) _____.
10. What does the abbreviation ANSI stand for?
11. True or False? You should hold a string trimmer in the upright position while starting it.
12. Describe the procedure discussed in this chapter for adjusting nylon string length on a trimmer.
13. List five maintenance tasks to perform on string trimmers and brushcutters.
14. The _____ should always be in place when you operate an edger/trimmer.
15. A standard edger/trimmer blade is _____ long.

Suggested Activities

1. Demonstrate proper safety precautions for preparing to work on an engine or implement.
2. Demonstrate the safe use of a compressed air blow gun for cleaning parts.
3. Perform preventative maintenance on a power lawn mower.
4. Sharpen and balance a lawn mower blade.
5. Demonstrate engine starting procedures.

Suggested Activities extend your learning and help you analyze and apply knowledge.

Student Resources

Textbook

The **Small Gas Engines** textbook provides an exciting, full-color, and highly illustrated learning resource. The textbook is available in both print and online versions.

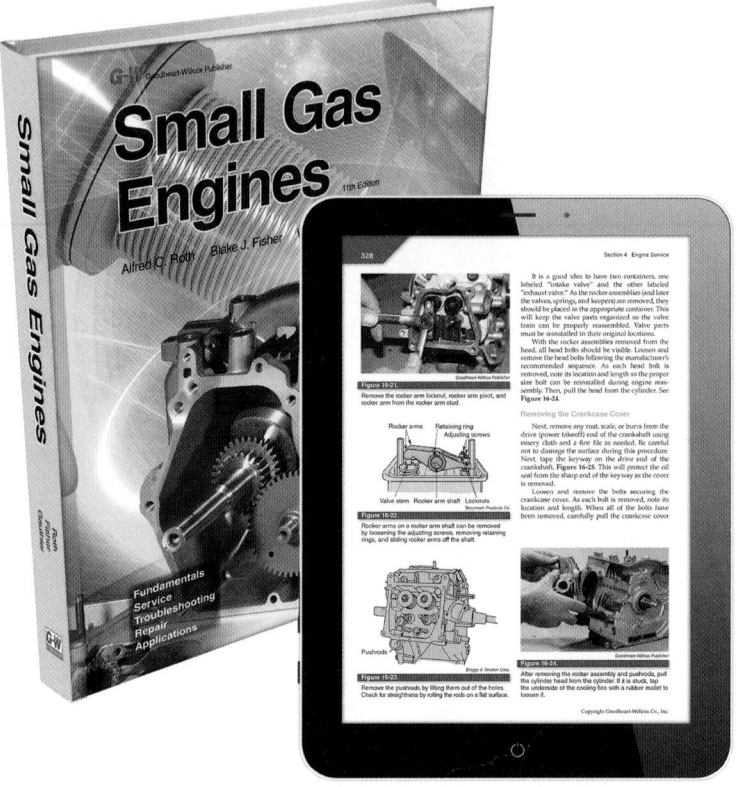

Workbook

The student workbook provides minds-on practice with questions. Each chapter corresponds to the text and reinforces key concepts and applied knowledge. Hands-on jobs in the workbook allow students to practice what they learn in the classroom.

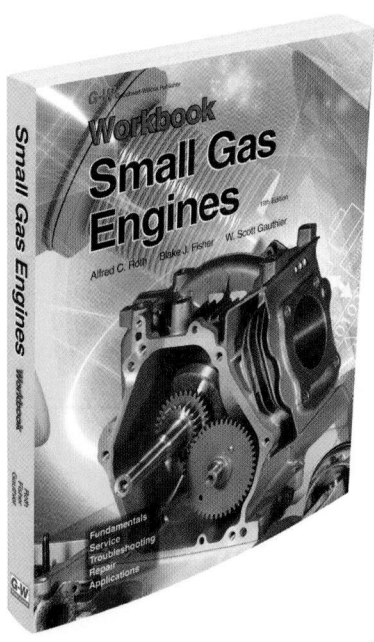

Online Learning Suite

Available as a classroom subscription, the Online Learning Suite provides the foundation of instruction and learning for digital and blended classrooms. An easy-to-manage shared classroom subscription makes it a hassle-free solution for both students and instructors. An online student text and workbook, along with rich supplemental content, brings digital learning to the classroom. All instructional materials are found on a convenient online bookshelf and are accessible at home, at school, or on the go.

Online Learning Suite/Student Textbook Bundle

Looking for a blended solution? Goodheart-Willcox offers the Online Learning Suite bundled with the printed textbook in one easy-to-access package. Students have the flexibility to use the print version, the Online Learning Suite, or a combination of both components to meet their individual learning style. The convenient packaging makes managing and accessing content easy and efficient.

Instructor Resources

Instructor resources provide information and tools to support teaching, grading, and planning; class presentations; and assessment.

Instructor's Presentations for PowerPoint®

Help teach and visually reinforce key concepts with prepared lectures. These presentations are designed to allow for customization to meet daily teaching needs. They include objectives, outlines, and images from the textbook.

ExamView® Assessment Suite

Quickly and easily prepare, print, and administer tests with the ExamView® Assessment Suite. With hundreds of questions in the test bank corresponding to each chapter, you can choose which questions to include in each test, create multiple versions of a single test, and automatically generate answer keys. Existing questions may be modified and new questions may be added. You can prepare pre-tests, formative tests, and summative tests easily with the ExamView® Assessment Suite.

Instructor's Resource CD

One resource provides instructors with timesaving preparation tools such as answer keys, lesson plans, correlations to certification standards, and other teaching aids.

Online Instructor Resources

Online Instructor Resources provide all the support needed to make preparation and classroom instruction easier than ever. Available in one accessible location, support materials include Answer Keys, Lesson Plans, Instructor's Presentations for PowerPoint®, ExamView® Assessment Suite, and more! Online Instructor Resources are available as a subscription and can be accessed at school or at home.

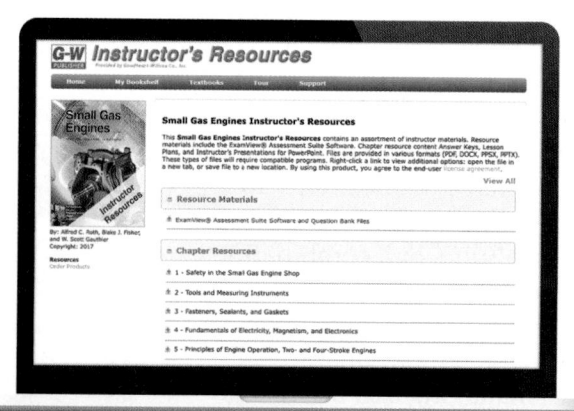

Brief Contents

Contents

C H A P T E R   4

Fundamentals of Electricity, Magnetism, and Electronics . . 63

S E C T I O N   2

Basics of Engine Operation

C H A P T E R   5

Principles of Engine Operation, Two- and Four-Stroke Engines 85

CHAPTER 24
Career Opportunities and Certification 475

SECTION 1
Shop Equipment, Supplies, and Safety

C H A P T E R 1

Safety in the Small Gas Engine Shop

Learning Objectives

After studying this chapter, you will be able to:

- Explain why a clean, well-organized shop is extremely important.
- List several dangers associated with working in a small engine shop.
- Explain the importance of maintaining and using tools properly.
- Describe methods for minimizing the risks involved in working with small engines.
- Explain the function of OSHA.

Key Terms

carbon monoxide
dead man switch
earplugs
eyewash station
face shield
fire extinguishers
flashpoint
hazardous wastes
headphone-type
  protectors
hydrogen gas
Occupational Safety
  and Health
  Administration
  (OSHA)
respirators
safety data sheets
safety glasses
safety goggles
safety shoes

Shop Safety

Small gas engine work can be rewarding and exciting. However, you may encounter dangerous situations whenever you work in a small engine shop. Special precautions should be taken when working with small engines. It is important to recognize potential hazards and to take the steps necessary to make sure your work area is safe.

Safety is the responsibility of everyone in the small engine shop. If you notice dangerous shop conditions or unsafe work practices, notify your instructor immediately. Never take unnecessary risks to complete a job. Safe shop practices can prevent serious injury or save a life.

Warnings and cautions appear throughout this textbook to point out the specific dangers encountered when working on small engines. Warnings identify practices that can result in serious injury or death if proper procedures or safety measures are not followed. Cautions signal situations that can result in serious damage to tools or equipment. See **Figure 1-1**.

Caution

Overfilling the crankcase with oil can foul plugs and cause the engine to use too much oil.

Warning

Be extremely careful when using compressed air. Never direct the air blast toward skin or clothing.

Goodheart-Willcox Publisher

Figure 1-1.

There are many safety hazards in the small engine shop. Warnings and cautions, such as those shown above, will be used throughout this text to signal potential dangers.

Proper Housekeeping

A clean, well-organized work area is very important to everyone in the shop. Floors should be free from oil and dirt. An oily floor is slippery and can cause serious falls. Always use spill control devices to capture leaks from any type of container. See **Figure 1-2**. Always clean up after working on a project. Pick up all tools and store them properly in a toolbox or workbench. Return all unused supplies to the proper storage area and discard all waste in appropriate containers. Aisles and doorways should be free from obstructions.

Keeping the shop area clean can also minimize fire hazards. When combustible materials are allowed to accumulate in the shop, the possibility of fire increases. Never store used rags in a closet or corner. Rags saturated with gasoline or solvent are highly flammable and can be easily ignited. An approved container for storing flammable waste is shown in **Figure 1-3**. A clean work area will increase safety and productivity.

Green Tech

Shop Rags

Used shop rags are a source of hazardous waste in small engine shops. If a rag has been contaminated with material considered to be hazardous waste, it must be handled properly. If thrown out, the contaminants on the used rag could do as much damage as the material itself. The Environmental Protection Agency expects shops to know how to deal with used shop rags. One option with used rags is to dispose of the rag in the same way as the hazardous waste. Another option is to have the rags taken to an industrial laundry so they can be used again.

Justrite Manufacturing Co.

Figure 1-3.

Oil-saturated or solvent-saturated waste is extremely flammable and should be stored in a proper container.

Some areas in the small engine shop are more dangerous than others. Areas where dangerous equipment is used or dangerous chemicals are stored are often identified by brightly colored floor markings or signs to alert employees to the potential hazards. When working in these marked safety areas, take extra precautions to prevent injury.

In the event of a fire, explosion, or toxic chemical spill, you must evacuate the shop quickly and calmly. Evacuation routes should be posted in prominent areas throughout the shop. These routes show you how to quickly exit the building in case of an emergency. Always study the evacuation routes and be aware of your location whenever you are working in the shop. Being able to exit the building in a timely manner could save your life.

Hazardous Materials

There are many dangerous chemicals used in the small engine shop. Always store chemicals in a safe place. Flammable liquids should be kept in closed safety containers when not in use. See

Justrite Manufacturing Co.

Figure 1-2.

Spill control pallets catch leaks or spills from containers in an easy-to-clean sump below.

Figure 1-4. These containers should be stored in safety cabinets to further minimize risks. Gasoline is extremely flammable, and its vapors can explode if exposed to sparks or flames. Never fill the fuel tank while the engine is running or hot. Heat from the engine could ignite the gasoline.

Some small gas engines are equipped with battery-operated ignition systems. The batteries used in these systems are similar to those used in automobiles. Handle batteries carefully to avoid splashing acid on clothes or skin, or in eyes. *Hydrogen gas* is produced when the battery is being charged or discharged. If the hydrogen gas is ignited, the battery can explode, throwing acid and fragments from its case in every direction. Always keep sparks and flames away from the battery.

Use chemicals for their intended purpose only. Gasoline should never be used as a cleaning solvent. Gasoline has a low flashpoint. *Flashpoint* is the lowest temperature at which a combustible material will produce an ignitable vapor. Materials with a low flashpoint can be ignited easily.

Many of the chemicals encountered in a small engine shop can cause serious burns. Avoid contact with skin. Wear rubber gloves and safety goggles when working with cleaning solvents.

Personal Protective Gear

Proper clothing should be worn when working with small gas engines. Avoid loose-fitting clothing, which can get caught in moving machine parts. Neckties and jewelry should never be worn when working near rotating machinery. Long hair should be worn up or secured under a cap. To avoid serious injury, keep hands, feet, hair, and clothing away from rotating engine parts. Never operate machinery with safety shrouds removed.

Safety glasses should be worn to protect eyes when using drills, grinders, hammers, chisels, or compressed air. Safety glasses look similar to regular glasses but have impact-resistant lenses designed to protect the eyes from flying debris. Some safety glasses have side shields to provide additional protection. Safety goggles or a face splash shield should always be worn when handling and working with chemicals. *Safety goggles* fit tightly against the face. They prevent debris and chemicals from being blown or splashed under the lens. A *face shield* covers the entire face to protect it from debris and chemicals. See **Figure 1-5**.

A pair of safety shoes is recommended to prevent foot and toe injury. *Safety shoes* are constructed of durable materials that prevent sharp objects from piercing the shoes. Soles are made of non-skid materials to help prevent falls when working on slippery surfaces. Some safety shoes have steel inserts in the toe area to protect feet from falling objects.

When working on small engines and related equipment, it is often necessary to kneel. Many times, kneeling is done on a hard, rough, and/or irregular surface. This can injure the knees if proper protection is not worn. Knee injury may

A

B

Justrite Manufacturing Co.

Figure 1-4.

A—Flammable liquids should be stored in closed containers. These safety cans are equipped with flame arrestors, which prevent flames or sparks from entering containers. B—Containers should be stored in safety cabinets.

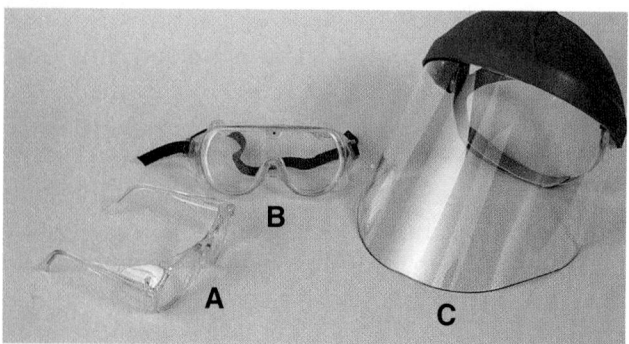

Figure 1-5.

Various types of eye and face protection. A—Safety glasses with side shields. B—Safety goggles. C—Face shield.

develop over a long period of time and show up as an arthritic condition. To avoid this, knee pads should be worn if kneeling for an extended period of time. Knee pads are readily available at hardware and building supply stores.

Hearing protection should be worn anytime you work in a noisy environment or operate loud equipment. Common sources of excessive noise include air tools, power tools, engines under load, and engines running in an enclosed space. Two effective forms of ear protection are *headphone-type protectors* and *earplugs*. See **Figure 1-6**.

Hearing loss often occurs slowly so that one is not aware that it is happening until later in life. This is when it becomes obvious that sounds and voices are not being heard distinctly or at all. A hearing aid may be the only recourse.

Respiratory protection should be worn when performing any operation that produces toxic fumes or dust. *Respirators* are used to protect against the inhalation of hazardous materials. See **Figure 1-7**. Be sure to choose a respirator designed for the type of contaminants present. For example, some respirators are designed to remove airborne particles, while others are designed to remove vapors and gases.

Proper Ventilation

The exhaust gases produced by gasoline engines contain carbon monoxide. *Carbon monoxide* is a colorless, odorless gas. Breathing small amounts of carbon monoxide can cause drowsiness and headaches. Large amounts of carbon monoxide can cause death.

If an engine must be operated in the shop, make sure that a properly maintained ventilation system is running and the doors and windows are open. A lethal amount of carbon monoxide can quickly accumulate in an enclosed space, such as a garage or shop. Adequate ventilation is extremely important in the small gas engine shop.

Solvents used to clean engine parts can release toxic fumes. Check warnings on solvent labels and follow instructions carefully. When working with any solvent for an extended period of time, make sure that there is plenty of fresh air.

Figure 1-6.

The two common types of ear protection are headphone-type protectors and earplugs. Two variations of earplugs are shown.

Figure 1-7.

A respirator should be worn when working with toxic solvents, or when working with equipment that may produce dust or dirt particles.

Hand Tool Safety

The safe use of hand tools is often taken for granted in the small engine shop. Many accidents, however, are caused by the improper use of common hand tools.

Keep tools clean. Greasy or oily tools are likely to slip from your hand and may fall into rotating engine parts. The rotating parts can throw the tool, causing serious injury.

Tools should only be used for the job they were designed for. Never, for example, use screwdrivers or files to pry items loose. These tools are not designed for this activity. Most screwdrivers and files are made from hardened steel and may crack or shatter if improperly used.

Keep tools in top shape. Sharpen tools periodically. Dull tools require greater effort to use. Make sure all tools are equipped with appropriate handles. When using a wrench, always pull the handle toward your body. This will help to prevent injury if the tool slips. See **Figure 1-8**. Hammer heads must be securely attached to the handle. If the head is loose, it could fly off during use.

Power Tool Safety

Before using a power tool, make sure it is in good condition and that all guards and shields are in place. Do not use any tool that is in poor condition or that has missing guards and shields. If you are not familiar with a tool, read the operating instructions carefully or ask for help before attempting to operate the unit.

Goodheart-Willcox Publisher

Figure 1-8.

To prevent injury, always pull a wrench toward your body.

Wear safety goggles when operating power tools. Never make adjustments on a power tool when it is running. Shut the tool off and wait for it to stop completely. Then, unplug the tool before attempting to service it in any way.

All power tools should be equipped with a *dead man switch*. This type of switch automatically shuts the tool off when the operator releases the control button.

Compressed Air Safety

Compressed air is used in the small engine shop to accomplish various tasks. Wear safety goggles when using compressed air. Regulate compressed air for cleaning to no more than 30 psi. Never use compressed air to clean your clothing or your hair. Flying particles can be blown into your eyes and can penetrate your skin.

Check all connections before turning on a compressed air system. Always hold the hose nozzle tightly when using compressed air. Never set the hose down without shutting off the air nozzle. Pressure in the hose can cause it to whip violently.

Lift Properly

Always lift heavy objects carefully. If necessary, ask for help when moving heavy items. Many shops are equipped with small overhead cranes to help move large objects.

To avoid unnecessary back strain, always lift with your legs, not with your back. Keep your back as straight as possible when lifting heavy objects. See **Figure 1-9**.

Avoid carrying items that will obstruct your view. Make several trips if necessary. When carrying long items, use two people so that the item is held level and both ends are attended. Never reach for heavy overhead items. The item may accidentally fall, causing severe head injury. Always use a good quality ladder.

Electrical Safety

Electrical hazards can be found in every small engine shop. Electricity is the most common cause of shop fires. Before using electrical equipment, check wires for fraying or cracking. Make sure all electrical equipment is properly grounded or double insulated. If equipment is not grounded,

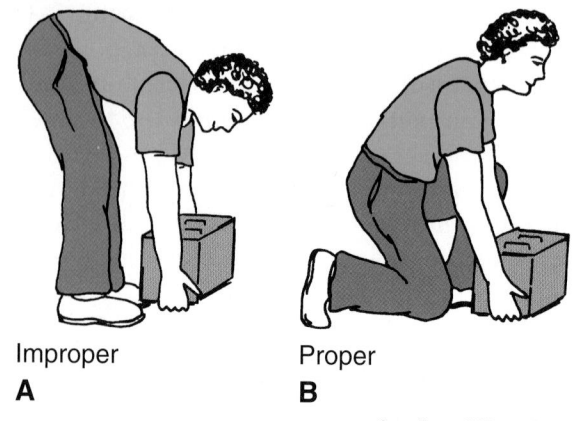

Improper
A

Proper
B

Goodheart-Willcox Publisher

Figure 1-9.

When lifting heavy objects, keep your back straight and use your legs to lift the weight. A—Improper lifting procedure. B—Proper way to lift heavy objects.

electrical shock can occur.

All outlets, switches, and junction boxes should be covered. Label the circuit breaker (fuse box) clearly so that it can be located in case of an emergency. Breaker switches should also be labeled.

Extension cords should not be used as permanent substitutes for fixed wiring. Extension cords should never run through holes in walls or floors.

Do not overload outlets. Too many components on one circuit can cause excess current to flow in the circuit. Overloaded circuits are a frequent cause of electrical fires.

Engine Operating Safety

Never operate a small engine at speeds greater than those recommended by the manufacturer. Excessive engine speed can cause parts to break loose from the engine. Severe personal injury can result from flying parts. Never tamper with the governor setting to increase maximum engine speed.

Keep hands, feet, and hair away from rotating engine parts. Small engines develop considerable speed and torque and can cause serious injuries. Never operate an engine with guards or shrouds removed.

Some small gas engine components get extremely hot. Avoid touching the engine when it is running. Let the engine cool before attempting repairs. In addition to causing burns, a hot engine may cause a fire if gasoline is accidentally spilled on hot surfaces.

Avoid touching an engine's electrical wires while the engine is running. The high voltage produced by ignition systems can cause electrical shock. Some systems produce more than 30,000 volts (V).

Do not operate an engine without a muffler. Wear ear protection when working on a running engine for a long period of time.

Be Prepared for Emergencies

In the event of an emergency, it is very important to be prepared. Emergency equipment should be stored in a highly visible place. List emergency numbers next to each telephone in the shop.

First aid kits should be properly stocked and placed in prominent locations. If someone gets hurt, notify your instructor or supervisor immediately. Always seek professional help for serious injuries.

If debris or chemicals accidentally get into your eyes, flush your eyes using an *eyewash station*. Some eyewash stations contain a bottle of sterile eyewash solution that can be used to flush debris from your eyes. Other stations are more elaborate. They are connected to the shop's water supply lines and provide a low-pressure stream of lukewarm water to flush from your eyes.

It is important that you locate the eyewash station(s) in your work area and know how to use them before you need them. If you wait until an emergency occurs, the time spent looking for and figuring out how to use the eyewash station might mean the difference between saving your sight and losing it.

All shop areas should be equipped with *fire extinguishers*. These extinguishers should be mounted in highly visible, unobstructed areas. All extinguishers should be inspected monthly. Always keep the area around the extinguisher free from obstructions.

Fire extinguishers are categorized according to the type of fire that each is designed to suppress or extinguish. See **Figure 1-10**. Class A fires involve ordinary combustibles such as wood, cloth, and paper. Class B fires involve flammable liquids such as gasoline and solvents. Class C fires are electrical fires. Be sure to use the proper type of extinguisher. Using the wrong extinguisher can be dangerous. Some fire extinguishers can be used for all types of fires.

While safety should be a priority whenever you are working in the shop, it is easy to overlook potential hazards. Therefore, it is important to perform periodic (weekly or monthly) shop safety inspections. Walk through your shop and take note of any unsafe conditions found. The shop should be neat and organized. Make sure that lighting is adequate, ventilation systems are functional, evacuation routes are clear, and hazardous materials are being handled and disposed of properly. Shop equipment must be in proper working order, with safety guards in place. Check to make sure electric equipment is properly grounded. Also, inspect all the fire extinguishers in the shop to ensure they are of the proper type and in good working condition. Finally, make sure that appropriate personal protective equipment (safety glasses, respirators, etc.) is available and in good condition. Report any unsafe conditions found to your instructor or supervisor.

Hazardous Wastes

There are many *hazardous wastes* generated during small engine maintenance and service procedures. Wastes are considered hazardous if they are on the EPA's list of hazardous material or if they have one or more of the following characteristics:

- Ignitability—has a liquid flash point below 140°F (60°C) or can spontaneously ignite.
- Reactivity—reacts violently with water or other materials; releases dangerous gases when exposed to low pH acid solutions; or produces toxic vapors, fumes, or flammable gases.
- Corrosivity—dissolves metals or burns skin.
- EP toxicity—leaches one or more of eight heavy metals in concentrations greater than 100 times the concentration found in standard drinking water.

The disposal of hazardous wastes is regulated by the Resource Conservation and Recovery Act. This federal act covers businesses that generate, transport, or manage hazardous wastes. Typical hazardous wastes generated from small engine service and repair include:

- Used motor oil and other discarded lubricants (contain toxic chemicals).
- Used oil filters (contain used motor oil and accumulated contaminants).
- Batteries (contain lead and acid/alkaline wastes).
- Antifreeze (contains heavy metals and chlorinated solvents).
- Cleaning solvents (combustible and toxic).

Disposing of Shop Wastes

The hazardous wastes generated during small engine maintenance and service should be disposed of according to state and federal regulations. Consult your regional EOA office for information on handling and disposing of hazardous wastes. The following are general guidelines for disposing of common wastes generated in the small engine shop.

- Used motor oil—Used motor oil must never be disposed of by pouring it on the ground or into a storm or sanitary sewer system. Instead, used oil should be stored in a labeled container until it can be sent to a recycling facility.
- Used oil filters—Used oil filters should be drained of all used oil before they are sent off for recycling. Holes can be punched in the top of canister-type filters to facilitate the draining process. Allow the oil to drain from the filters for several hours before disposing of the filter housings. The oil drained from the filters should be stored until it can be recycled.
- Used antifreeze—Antifreeze has a sweet odor and taste, and can be fatal if it is ingested by people or animals. Consequently, it is important that used antifreeze be stored in a closed container and recycled according to federal and state regulations.
- Batteries—Lead-acid batteries contain heavy metals and should be recycled when they reach the end of their useful service lives. If a battery is disposed of improperly, these metals can contaminate soil and ground water. Businesses that sell new batteries also accept used batteries and send them off to a recycler.

OSHA

The *Occupational Safety and Health Administration (OSHA)* is a governmental organization that establishes rules for safe work practices. All businesses and industries are required to follow OSHA regulations. It is very important to be familiar with OSHA rules and recommendations.

Safety Data Sheets

OSHA regulations require employers to provide employees access to safety data sheets for the hazardous chemicals used in the shop. *Safety data sheets* are available from chemical manufacturers. These sheets contain detailed information about a chemical, including its ingredients and characteristics, the type of protective equipment that should be worn when working with the substance, and the procedures to follow in case of an accident.

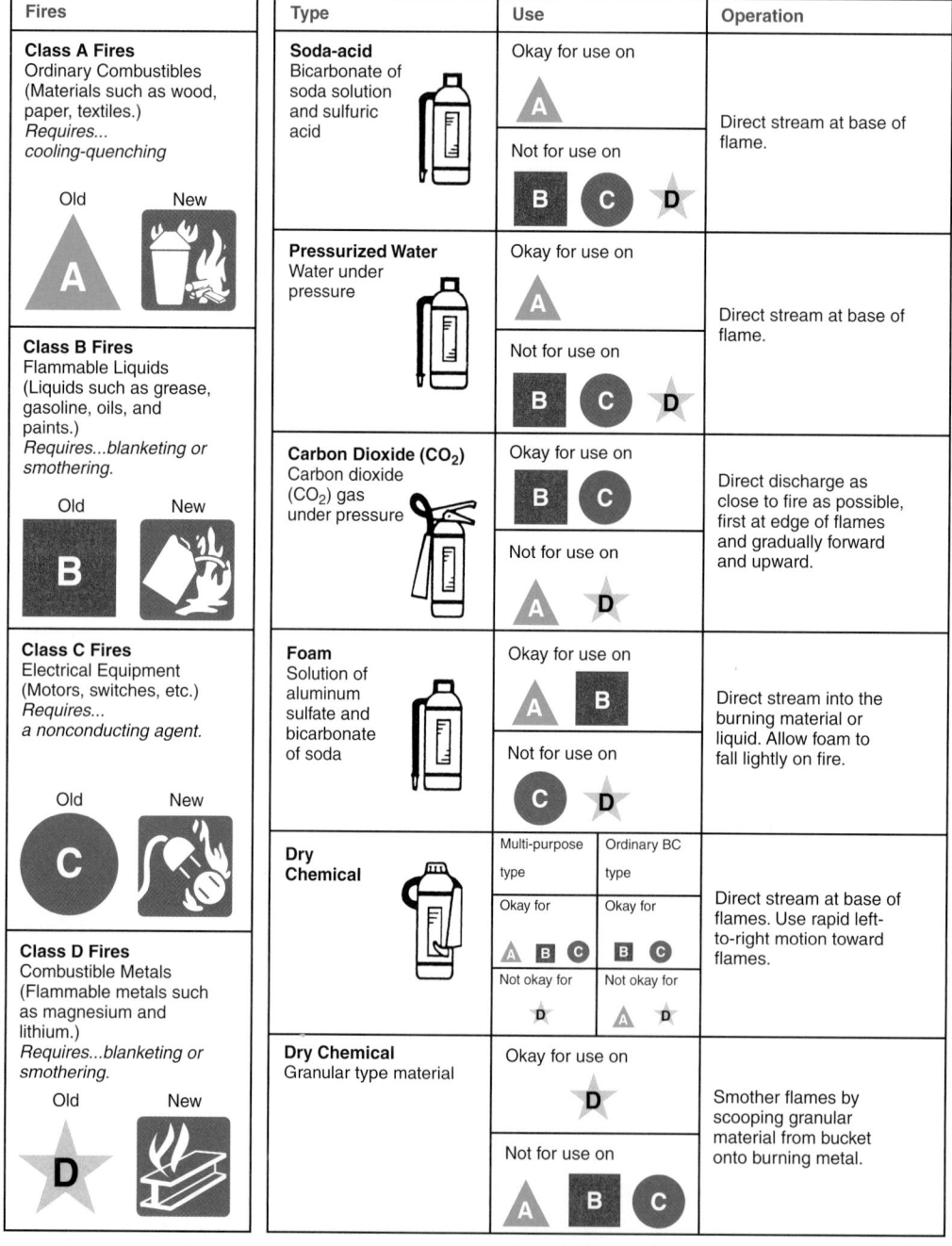

Goodheart-Willcox Publisher

Figure 1-10.

This chart illustrates the various fire extinguisher types and fire classifications. In the small engine shop, always use an extinguisher designed for use on electrical and chemical fires.

Summary

Certain precautions must be taken when working on small gas engines. Keeping the work area clean will increase safety and productivity in the shop. Hazardous materials must be handled with care to avoid fires or chemical burns. Dispose of rags that are saturated with solvents in a proper container. Areas where dangerous equipment is used or dangerous chemicals are stored are often identified by brightly colored floor markings or signs to alert employees to the potential hazards. Evacuation routes should be posted in prominent areas throughout the shop. These routes show you how to quickly exit the building in case of an emergency.

Proper clothing should be worn when working on small engines. Avoid loose-fitting clothing, which can get caught in rotating engine parts. Adequate ventilation is imperative when working in an enclosed area.

Use all tools properly. Read all instructions before using power tools. Never use compressed air to clean clothing.

Electrical malfunctions are the most common cause of shop fires. Do not overload electrical circuits.

Do not operate an engine at speeds greater than those recommended by the manufacturer. Keep hands and feet away from rotating engine parts. Avoid touching hot engine parts.

Be prepared for emergencies. List emergency phone numbers above each telephone. Keep fire extinguishers in highly visible areas. Make sure a first aid kit is properly stocked and easily accessible.

Employers must provide employees access to safety data sheets for the hazardous chemicals used in the shop.

The hazardous wastes generated during small engine maintenance and service should be disposed of according to state and federal regulations. Consult your regional EOA office for information on handling and disposing of hazardous wastes.

Review Questions

Answer the following questions on a separate sheet of paper.

1. *True or False?* There are many potential hazards in the small gas engine shop.
2. Oily or dirty floors can cause people to ____.
3. A flammable liquid frequently used in the small engine shop is ____.
4. *True or False?* Gasoline should always be stored in a closed container.
5. To prevent injury when working around small engines, avoid wearing ____.
   A. loose clothing
   B. jewelry
   C. neckties
   D. All of the above.
6. Carbon monoxide is ____ and ____.
7. *True or False?* Power tools should not be operated without proper safety shrouds.
8. Never use compressed air to clean ____ or ____.
9. Always lift with your ____.
   A. arms
   B. legs
   C. back
   D. All of the above.
10. *True or False?* Electrical malfunction is the most common cause of shop fires.
11. *True or False?* Small engine ignition systems can produce more than 30,000 volts.
12. Batteries produce ____ when charging or discharging.
13. *True or False?* Fire extinguishers are categorized by the type of fire they are designed to suppress.
14. OSHA establishes regulations for ____.
15. List the four characteristics of hazardous waste.

Suggested Activities

1. Make several safety posters warning of the potential dangers in a small engine shop and place them throughout your work area. Emphasize good housekeeping and proper storage of hazardous materials.

2. Check guards on all power tools and equipment and discuss the purpose for each guard. Make sure that all guards are correctly mounted and in proper condition.

3. Walk through the shop area and identify potential hazards. Discuss ways to minimize these hazards with your instructor.

4. Locate emergency equipment throughout your work area. Check fire extinguishers for sufficient charge. Make sure that they are designed for use on flammable liquids and electrical equipment. Make sure the first aid kit is properly stocked. Familiarize yourself with all the items in the first aid kit.

C H A P T E R 2

Tools and Measuring Instruments

Learning Objectives

After studying this chapter, you will be able to:

- Identify common hand tools.
- Use common hand tools properly.
- Identify common engine service tools.
- Identify power tools commonly used for small engine and outdoor power equipment service.
- Differentiate between common precision measuring instruments.
- Select and use the appropriate precision measuring instruments to accurately and precisely measure various engine components.

Key Terms

adjustable wrench
Allen wrench
box-end wrench
combination slip-joint
  pliers
combination wrench
compression testers
cylinder hones
diagonal side-cutting
  pliers
drift punch
feeler gauges
files
glaze breakers
hacksaws
lapping sticks
needle nose pliers
offset screwdriver

open-end wrench
Phillips screwdrivers
pin punches
reamers
ridge reamer
ring compressor
ring expanders
ring spreaders
safe files
socket sets
spark testers
tachometers
torque
torque wrench
tubing wrench
valve spring
  compressors
vise-grips

Introduction

High-quality tools should always be used when servicing a small gas engine. Quality tools allow you to service small engines easily and effectively. To avoid damage to engine parts, always use the tools recommended by the manufacturer. Keep tools clean and in proper working condition.

Some tools are common to most engine work, while others may have only one or two specific applications. Special-purpose tools may be designed by a manufacturer for limited use on only one engine make or model. The following sections will describe how to use common tools. Some special-purpose tools will also be examined, along with examples of their applications.

The tools and measuring instruments described in this chapter are available in US customary and metric sizes. A shop or technician should have sets of both.

Hand Tools

Small-engine technicians are required to use a number of common hand tools as they diagnose, service, and repair small engines and outdoor power equipment. In order to make their work as easy and safe as possible, technicians should purchase quality tools. They should keep those tools well organized, clean, and properly maintained.

Finally, they should use the tools properly. Tools should never be used for purposes other than those for which they were designed.

Wrenches

There are many types of wrenches available to suit practically every situation encountered when servicing small engines. These include box-end wrenches, open-end wrenches, adjustable wrenches, Allen wrenches, socket wrenches, and torque wrenches. The type of wrench used depends on the kind of fastener to be installed or removed. Box-end, open-end, adjustable, and socket wrenches are used on hexagonal bolt heads and nuts.

Open-End, Box-End, and Combination Wrenches

An *open-end wrench* is a wrench that grips a nut or bolt head on two sides. See **Figure 2-1A**. Because all of the tightening torque is applied to only two sides of the fastener, this type of wrench has a tendency to slip. For this reason, it should be used only when it is not possible to encompass the nut or bolt head with a box-end wrench or a socket.

A *box-end wrench* can be used where partial or full-turn clearance is available. Box-end wrenches are available in six- and twelve-sided versions and are less likely to slip around the bolt head corners than open-end wrenches or adjustable wrenches. See **Figure 2-1B**.

A *combination wrench* has a box-end wrench on one end and an open-end wrench on the other. See **Figure 2-1C**. A *tubing wrench* is similar to a box-end wrench, but has an opening so the wrench can be used on metal tubing connection fittings. See **Figure 2-1D**.

Adjustable Wrenches

An *adjustable wrench* should be used only as a last resort, such as when other wrenches are not available. Adjustable wrenches are used similarly to open-end wrenches. Due to the movable jaw in adjustable wrenches, they are prone to loosening and slipping around the corners of bolts and nuts. See **Figure 2-2**.

When applying force to a wrench, always pull the tool instead of pushing on it. See **Figure 2-3**. This will prevent hand and knuckle injury if the wrench accidentally slips from the bolt head.

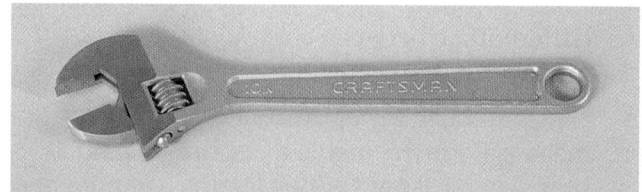

Goodheart-Willcox Publisher

Figure 2-2.

The jaws of an adjustable wrench can be opened and closed to fit various size fasteners. The jaws should be adjusted to fit the bolt or nut as tightly as possible.

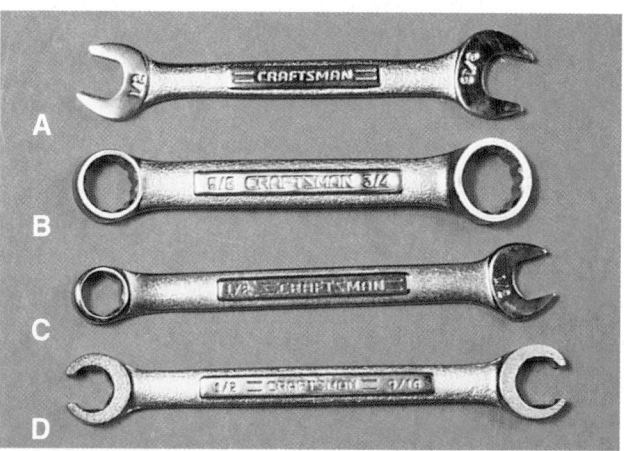

Goodheart-Willcox Publisher

Figure 2-1.

Always select the correct type of wrench for the job at hand. A—Open-end wrench. B—Box-end wrench. C—Combination box/open-end wrench. D—Tubing wrench.

Goodheart-Willcox Publisher

Figure 2-3.

A wrench should always be pulled in the proper direction to prevent it from slipping off a bolt or nut and rounding the corners. The movable jaw should face away from the direction the wrench is being pulled.

Socket Wrenches

Many varieties of *socket sets* are available. For small engine work, sets with standard and deep-well sockets, one ratchet wrench, one spark plug socket, and several extensions will meet most needs. See **Figure 2-4**. Sockets are extremely useful when bolts or nuts are recessed in counterbored holes. There are many occasions when, due to obstructions, other wrenches cannot be applied or turned very far. In these cases, a socket and ratchet wrench is the only way a bolt or nut can be removed or tightened. At other times, sockets can simply save time compared with other wrenches.

Allen Wrenches

An *Allen wrench* is used to remove or install hex socket-head screws. They may be the conventional right-angle style or straight with tee handles. See **Figure 2-5**. The correct size Allen wrench must be used, or the wrench can slip in the hex socket recess and damage the socket. Damage to the hex socket can make removing the screw difficult.

Some hex socket-head screws have metric size sockets. Never attempt to use metric Allen wrenches and US customary Allen wrenches interchangeably. This can deform the socket and render the screw difficult to remove. The proper size wrench will fit in the socket without any play.

Torque Wrenches

A *torque wrench* is used to tighten threaded fasteners to a specific torque setting. *Torque* is the turning force applied to the fastener. **Figure 2-6** shows how to use a preset, or click-type, torque

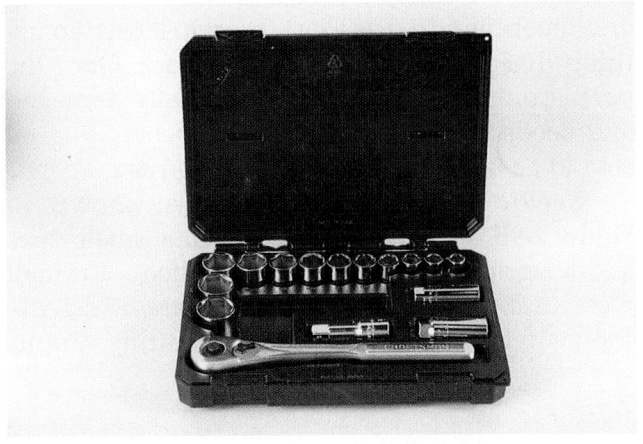

Goodheart-Willcox Publisher

Figure 2-4.

A socket set is almost a necessity for small engine work. It permits installation and removal of bolts in hard-to-reach places.

Support socket with one hand

Goodheart-Willcox Publisher

Figure 2-6.

The proper procedure for using a torque wrench is to support the socket with one hand and apply turning effort at right angles to the handle with the other hand.

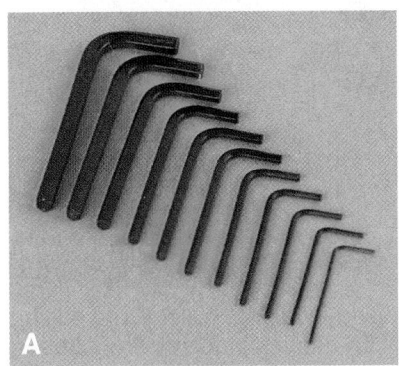

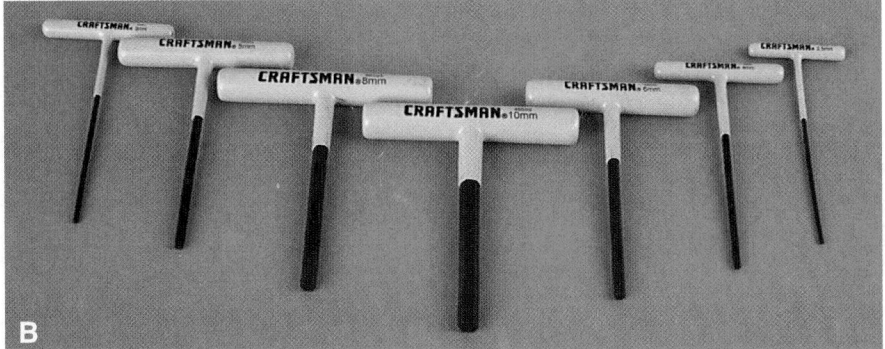

A

B

Goodheart-Willcox Publisher

Figure 2-5.

Allen wrenches are used on hex socket-head screws. A—Right-angle Allen wrenches. B—Tee-handle Allen wrenches.

wrench. After the desired amount of torque is set on the wrench handle, the socket is placed on the bolt head and the handle is pulled until a click is felt and heard. The socket should be held down firmly with one hand, while the handle is pulled with the other hand.

A beam-type torque wrench, like the one shown in **Figure 2-7**, has a pointer that moves across a scale as torque is applied. With this type of wrench, the mechanic pulls the wrench handle until the pointer reaches the correct torque reading. Another common type of torque wrench has a dial or digital readout on the handle that displays the torque being applied.

Torque data charts, like the one in **Figure 2-8**, supply the necessary data to correctly tighten critical parts. Most small engine torque charts specify both inch-pounds (in-lb) and foot-pounds (ft-lb) torque values. Torque wrenches may be calibrated in either of these units. The scale on the wrench will clearly indicate whether the reading is given in in-lb or ft-lb.

The torque reading is the product of the length of the wrench handle (in feet or inches) and the applied force. For example, applying one pound of force through a handle one foot long would produce 1 ft-lb or 12 in-lb of torque. In order to convert ft-lb to in-lb, multiply the ft-lb reading by 12.

Pliers

Pliers are useful tools for gripping, bending, pulling, and in some cases, cutting wire. They should *not* be used in place of wrenches. Because most pliers are not designed for loosening or tightening fasteners, they usually damage the surfaces of fasteners when used in this way.

A variety of pliers are helpful in small engine repair work. Locking pliers, or *vise-grips* are designed to apply great clamping pressure and have large gripping teeth. See **Figure 2-9A**. They use mechanical advantage to increase grip. They are sometimes used as a last resort to loosen something that is rusted or frozen in place. Once the part is removed, however, it is usually damaged and needs to be replaced. A good penetrating oil should be used to assist in removing rusted parts.

Needle nose pliers, like those shown in **Figure 2-9B**, are very useful for bending small wires and for gripping items that have fallen into small recesses. *Diagonal side-cutting pliers*, which are shown in **Figure 2-9C**, are used for cutting various

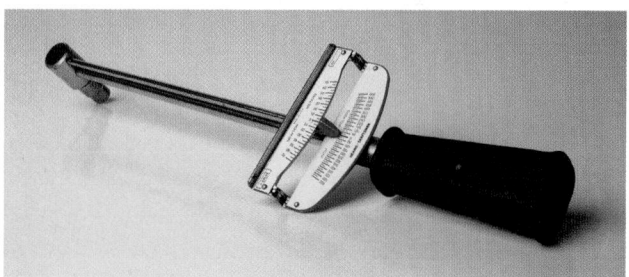

Goodheart-Willcox Publisher

Figure 2-7.

A beam-type torque wrench is shown here.

Four Cycle Torque Specifications

		in-lb	ft-lb
Cylinder Head Bolts		140–200	12–16
Connecting Rod Lock Nuts	1.5–3.5 H.P.	65–75	5.5–6
	4–6 H.P.	86–100	7–9
Cylinder Cover or Flange to Cylinder		65–110	5.5–9
Flywheel Nut		360–400	30–33

Goodheart-Willcox Publisher

Figure 2-8.

Torque specifications for all critical bolts and nuts are provided in engine manuals.

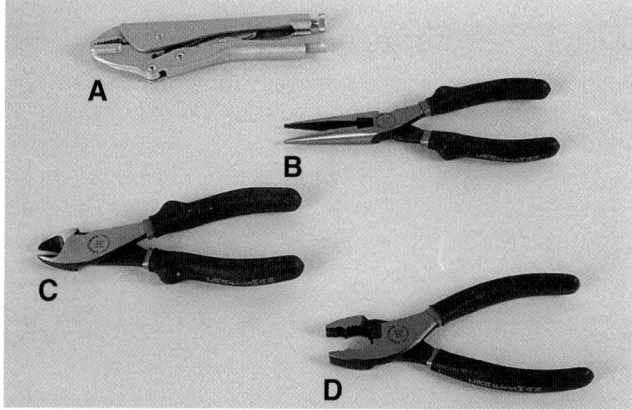

Goodheart-Willcox Publisher

Figure 2-9.

Pliers are used for gripping, bending, pulling, and cutting wires. They should not be used in place of wrenches on nuts and bolts. A—Locking pliers use mechanical advantage to increase grip. B—Needle nose pliers. C— Diagonal, side-cutting pliers. D— Combination slip-joint pliers.

types of electrical wire. These pliers are designed to cut soft metals, like copper, but should not be used to cut hard metals, like steel. *Combination slip-joint pliers* are general purpose pliers and are less expensive than other types of pliers. The jaws are adjustable so they can grip different size objects. They can also be used for cutting soft, solid wire.

Retaining Ring Pliers

Inside and outside retaining rings are used to keep a part from moving axially on a shaft (in a direction parallel to the centerline of a shaft). For example, a sliding gear may be limited from moving too far by a retaining ring set in a groove machined into a shaft. Retaining rings are made from spring steel and must be installed and removed with special retaining ring pliers, such as those shown in **Figure 2-10**.

To install an outside retaining ring, the nibs of the retaining ring pliers are inserted into the small holes in the ring and the ring is expanded by squeezing the handles of the pliers. The ring is then slid over the shaft to the machined groove, where it is released. For internal retaining rings, the ring is compressed to fit inside a bore when the handles are squeezed. The ring is then inserted into the bore and released into a machined groove. Some pliers are only for inside or outside rings, while others are designed to accommodate both types. Some types have replacement nibs.

Warning

Always wear safety glasses when using retaining ring pliers because retaining rings can slip off and fly with considerable velocity.

Screwdrivers

Several types of screwdrivers are frequently used when servicing small engines. Standard screwdrivers are available in a variety of shapes and sizes. See **Figure 2-11**. The proper size blade should be used to match the length and thickness of the screw head slot. See **Figure 2-12**. *Phillips screwdrivers* of various sizes are useful for installing and removing Phillips head screws and bolts, which have a cross-shaped recess. See **Figure 2-13A**. These screwdrivers are available in

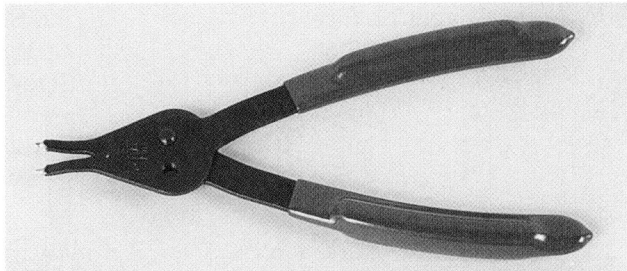

Goodheart-Willcox Publisher

Figure 2-10.

Retaining ring pliers are used to remove and install retaining rings on shafts or in bores. Retaining rings are made of spring steel and can fly off if they slip from the nibs of the pliers. Always wear safety glasses when using these pliers.

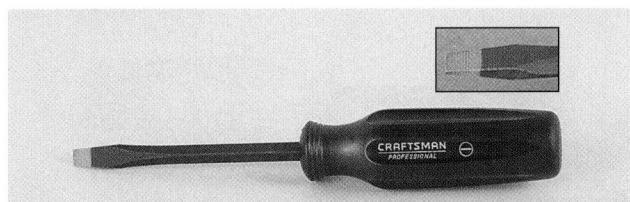

Goodheart-Willcox Publisher

Figure 2-11.

Standard screwdrivers have a flat blade.

a variety of sizes to accommodate various sizes of screws and bolts.

In tight situations, the length of a regular screwdriver may prohibit its use. When this occurs, an *offset screwdriver* can be very useful. See **Figure 2-13B**. Offset screwdrivers are available with standard and Phillips-type heads.

Hammers

Hammers are extremely useful for small engine work. They are available in a wide variety of designs, weights, and material compositions. The following paragraphs will describe the two types of hammers most commonly used by small engine technicians.

A ball peen hammer is a hammer with a cylindrical flat face on one end of the head and a hemispherical (half sphere) face on the other end of the head. Ball peen hammers are used for tapping things into place. They are often used in conjunction with other tools, such as punches and chisels. The ball peen hammer is considered to be a hard-faced

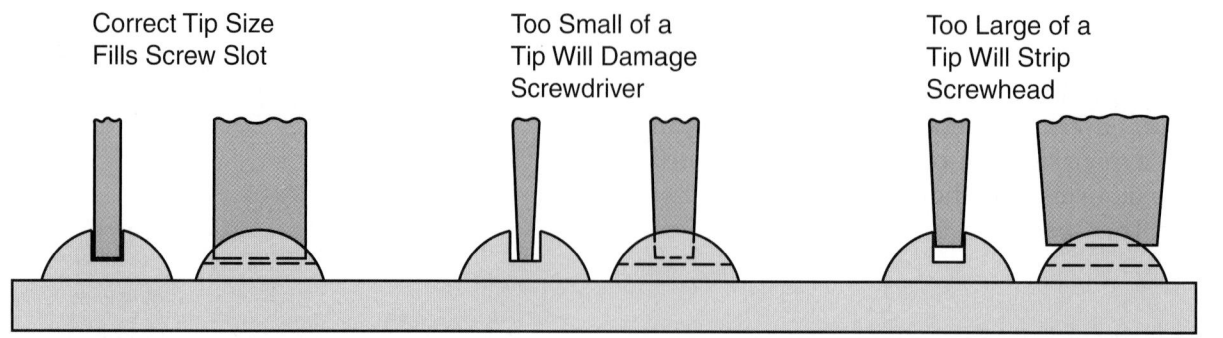

Correct Tip Size
Fills Screw Slot

Too Small of a
Tip Will Damage
Screwdriver

Too Large of a
Tip Will Strip
Screwhead

Goodheart-Willcox Publisher

Figure 2-12.

To avoid damaging the screw head, the screwdriver blade must fit the slot or recess in the screw properly.

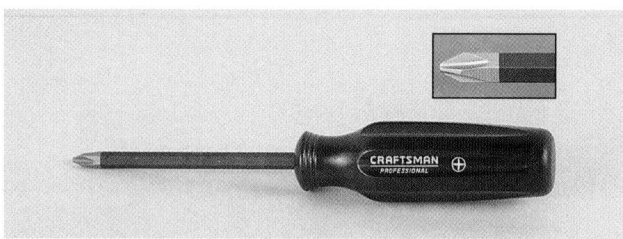

A

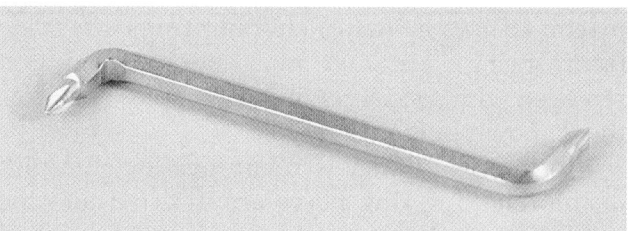

B

Goodheart-Willcox Publisher

Figure 2-13.

Other types of screwdrivers are also used for engine work. A—Phillips screwdriver. B—Offset screwdriver.

hammer because its head is made of steel. See **Figure 2-14**. When using a ball peen hammer for small engine work, care must be taken so that parts are not dented or deformed by the hard faces. A ball peen hammer can be used to tap on a wrench to loosen a stubborn bolt or nut. They can also be used with pin punches to install locking pins in holes or with cold chisels to shear bolts, pins, or sheet metal. Ball peen hammers are available in a

variety of sizes and are rated according to weight. A hammer's weight is usually stamped on the side of its head.

Soft-faced hammers are used to tap on parts that are easily damaged by hard-faced hammers. Soft-faced hammers are made from a variety of materials that are softer than steel. Lead, copper, brass, leather (rawhide), wood, rubber, and plastic are commonly used to make soft-faced hammers. **Figure 2-15** shows several soft-faced hammers.

Punches

Many types of punches are used for small engine work. A center punch has a hardened steel point and is used to make depressions in metal surfaces before drilling. The depression helps prevent the drill bit from wandering as the drilling is started. **Figure 2-16A** shows a center punch with a 90° point angle.

A prick punch is similar to a center punch. However, the point angle of a prick punch is 60°. A prick punch is used to make a very small depres-

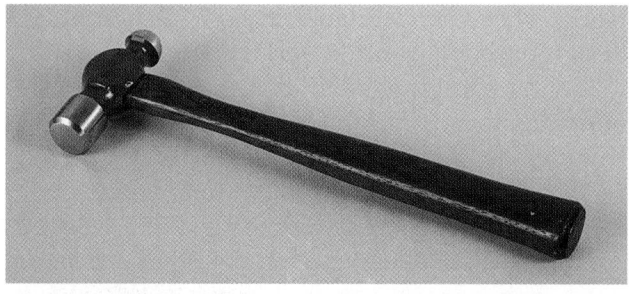

Goodheart-Willcox Publisher

Figure 2-14.

Ball peen hammers, like the one shown here, are frequently used in engine and power equipment service.

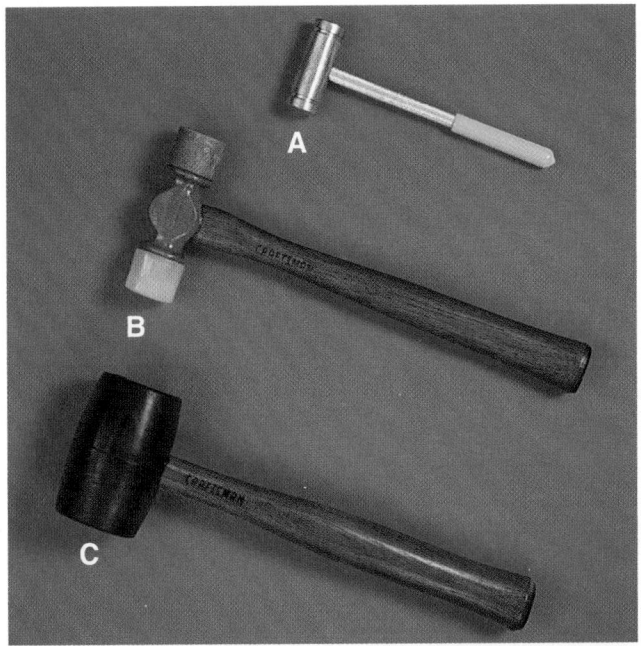

Goodheart-Willcox Publisher

Figure 2-15.

Soft-faced hammers have faces that are softer than the objects they are used on. A—Brass or lead hammer. B—Plastic-faced hammer. C—Rubber mallet.

sion prior to using the center punch to enlarge the depression for drilling. Center punches and prick punches are driven with a ball peen hammer.

Pin punches of various diameters and lengths are available for driving straight pins, tapered pins, and roll pins in and out of holes. See **Figure 2-16B**. A ball peen hammer is used to apply the driving force to the punch. A rusty and seized pin or bolt can often be driven out of a smooth bore with a pin punch.

A *drift punch* is tapered and is used to align holes in mating parts. This allows a bolt or pin to be passed through the mating parts. See **Figure 2-16C**.

Seal Drivers

Seal drivers are tools that equally distribute pressure over the entire surface of a seal as it is driven in place. This tool helps a technician drive a seal in squarely, without distorting or damaging it. A seal driver consists of a threaded shaft with interchangeable circular drive heads, **Figure 2-17**. To use this tool to install a seal, begin by selecting the proper size head for the seal and then thread it onto the driver shaft. Place the seal over its bore and place the seal driver's head squarely on the seal. Then, tap the end of the driver shaft with hammer to drive the seal into place.

Cutting and Forming Tools

Many common service tasks, such as sharpening blades and deburring sealing surfaces, require the removal of metal. The following sections describe the tools a service technician will commonly use to perform those tasks.

Hacksaws

Hacksaws are saws specifically designed to cut through metal. For example, a hacksaw can be used to cut through the sides of a nut that is frozen on a bolt or stud, allowing the nut to be removed. Hacksaws consist of a flexible blade fastened in a rigid frame. See **Figure 2-18**. The blade should be

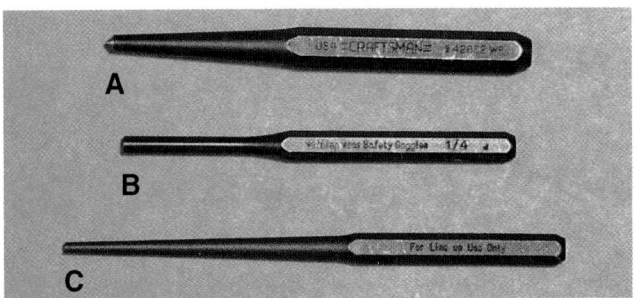

Goodheart-Willcox Publisher

Figure 2-16.

There are several types of punches available for small engine use. A—Center punch. B—Pin punch. C—Drift punch.

Goodheart-Willcox Publisher

Figure 2-17.

A seal driver kit includes different heads for different size seals.

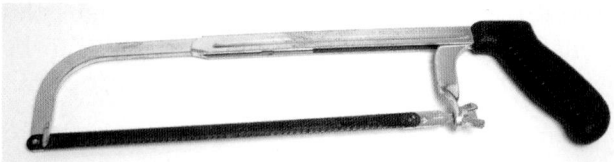

Goodheart-Willcox Publisher

Figure 2-18.

Typical hacksaws consist of a rigid frame and a replaceable flexible blade.

mounted in the frame so that the teeth of the blade point in the direction of the cut. If the teeth point toward the front of the frame, the saw cuts on the push stroke. If the teeth are pointed toward the frame handle, the saw cuts on the pull stroke.

Blades are available with 14, 18, 24, or 32 teeth per inch. The tooth count should correspond to the metal being cut. Coarser blades should be used to cut thicker metal and finer blades should be used to cut thinner metal.

The hacksaw should be grasped with one hand on the handle and the other hand at the front of the frame. The hand on the handle provides the cutting pressure and the hand at the front of frame guides the cut. A firm and steady downward pressure is applied during the cutting part of the stroke and released during the noncutting part of the stroke.

Reamers

Reamers are cylindrical cutting tools that are used to shave metal from the walls of a bore to enlarge it to a specific size. They are commonly used for tasks such as enlarging valve guides or bushings. Fixed-size reamers are used for precision work, like enlarging a valve guide bore for oversize valve stems, and adjustable reamers can be used for tasks that require less precision, like deburring a bore.

Reamers have multiple cutting edges, called flutes, that run lengthwise down the body of the tool. The size of the reamer is stamped on the tool body and is the major diameter of the tool, measured between the outer edges of the flutes. A square drive at the end of the shank allows the tool to be turned with a wrench, usually a tap wrench.

Files

Files are steel bars with rows of hardened shallow teeth used to deburr, smooth, shape, or sharpen metal. They are commonly used for tasks like dressing the ends of piston rings. Files can have a rectangular, square, round, half-round, or triangular cross section. They are available with single cut, double cut, or curved teeth. See **Figure 2-19**. Single cut teeth, which are cut in parallel diagonal rows across the file, produce the

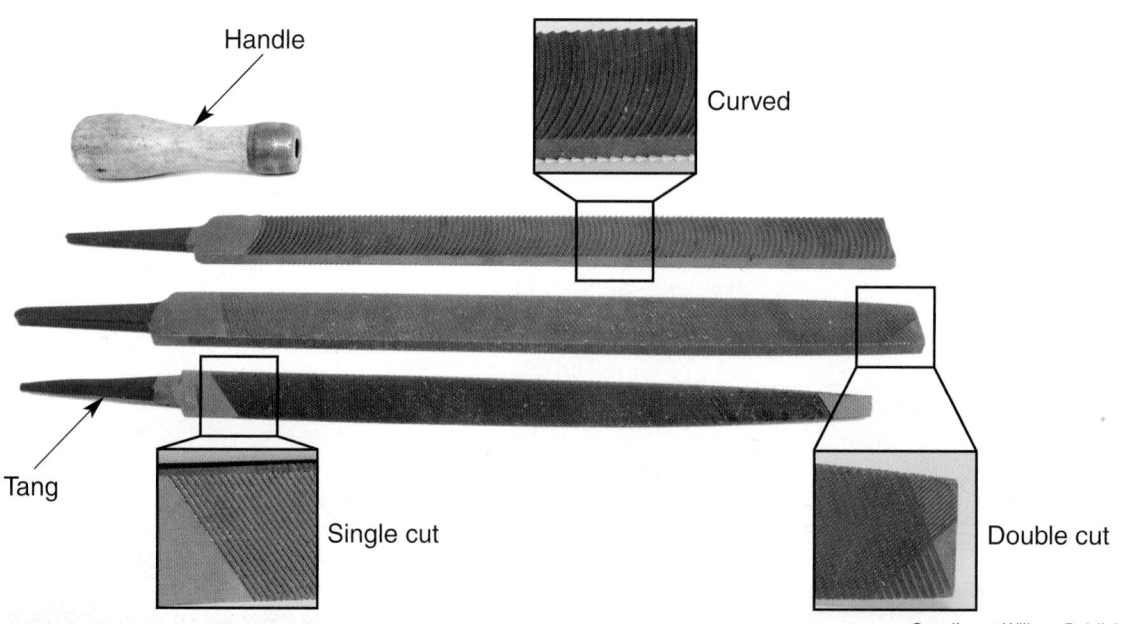

Goodheart-Willcox Publisher

Figure 2-19.

Files are available in a variety of shapes and tooth patterns.

smoothest finish. Double cut teeth, which are cut in crisscrossing diagonal rows across the file, provide a more aggressive cut, but do not produce as smooth a finish. Curved teeth, which are cut in parallel arcs across the file, remove material fairly quickly and produce a fairly smooth finish. However, curved teeth are best suited for soft metals like aluminum and brass.

Files are commonly available in three levels of tooth coarseness. From most coarse to finest, the levels are bastard, second cut, and smooth cut. Standard rectangular files have teeth cut in the edges of the file as well as the top and bottom surfaces. These edges of the files can be used to notch metal or to file very small areas. *Safe files* do not have teeth cut into the edges.

In use, a file is grasped at both ends. The front part of the file is placed on the metal to be smoothed. A steady, light downward pressure is applied as the file is pushed forward. If a large area is being filed, it can be moved laterally across the metal as it is pushed forward. The pressure is lifted on the return part of the stroke. See **Figure 2-20**.

Rat tail files are tapered round files especially useful for smoothing bores. Tapered square files are commonly used to sharpen saw teeth, like those on a chainsaw. Mower blade files are flat rectangular files with an integrated handle and the right tooth configuration for sharpening mower blades.

Cold Chisels

Cold chisels are cutting tools that can shear bolts, pins, rivets, sheet metal, rods, and other materials. See **Figure 2-21**. Cold chisels are made of special tool steel, which is hardened and tempered by heat-treatment. See **Figure 2-22**. The cutting edge is very hard and sharpened to an angle between 60° and 90°. A 60° angle is used for shearing sheet metal. A 90° angle is for shearing bolts and rivets. The cutting edge can be sharpened when it becomes dull and may need heat treatment after several grindings. It should have a slightly curved edge for shearing and a straight edge for cutting flat surfaces. See **Figure 2-23**.

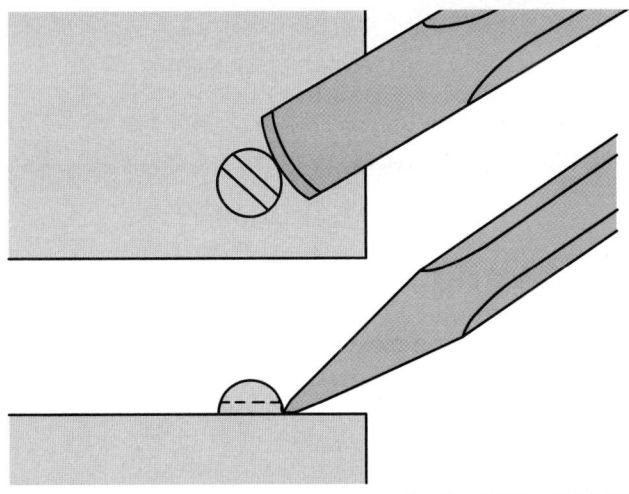

Goodheart-Willcox Publisher

Figure 2-21.

Cold chisels are used for shearing bolts, screws, rivets, sheet metal, rods, or other materials.

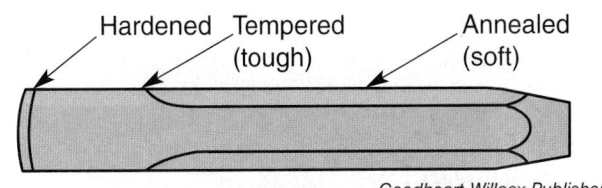

Hardened   Tempered (tough)   Annealed (soft)

Goodheart-Willcox Publisher

Figure 2-22.

The cold chisel is a heat-treated tool with a hardened and tempered cutting edge and an annealed shank.

Goodheart-Willcox Publisher

Figure 2-20.

This technician is using proper filing technique.

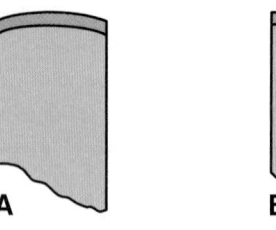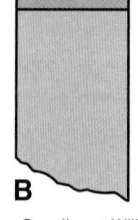

Goodheart-Willcox Publisher

Figure 2-23.

Cold chisels with different edges are used for different tasks. A—The cutting edge of a cold chisel should be slightly curved for shearing. B—The cold chisel's edge should be straight for cutting flat materials.

Although the portion immediately behind the cutting edge is tempered for toughness, the chisel's shank portion is annealed (made soft) to prevent it from shattering. When the shank end of the chisel becomes flared, it should be reground to remove the flared portion. See **Figure 2-24**. The flared part becomes work hardened and highly stressed from being hammered.

Warning

Safety glasses should always be worn when using punches or chisels. Pieces from the flared end of a chisel can fracture and fly at high velocity.

Probe and Pickup Tools

The probe and pickup tools shown in **Figure 2-25** assist when bolts, screws, washers, or other small items are dropped into crevices where fingers will

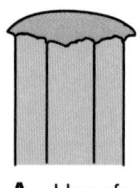 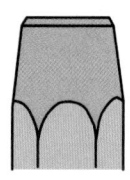

A Unsafe　　　　　**B** Safe

Goodheart-Willcox Publisher

Figure 2-24.

The hammered end of a cold chisel should be checked before each use for signs of mushrooming. A—The hammered end of a cold chisel becomes work hardened and flared after extended use. A flared or mushroomed end on a cold chisel is very dangerous. B—The end of a cold chisel should be ground to a slight taper anytime flaring is evident.

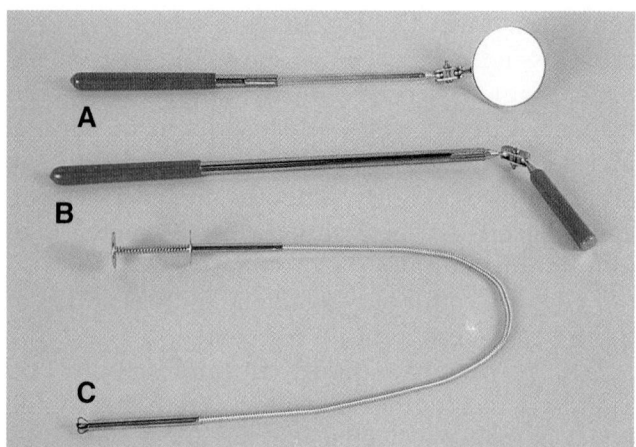

Goodheart-Willcox Publisher

Figure 2-25.

Probe and pickup tools are helpful in locating small parts that may drop into crevices or hard-to-reach places. A—Mirror probe. B—Magnetic pickup tool. C—Finger pickup tool.

not fit. A mirror probe can help locate items that are blocked from view. Ferrous (iron-based) items can be removed with a magnetic probe. Nonferrous (nonmagnetic) items can be gripped and removed with a finger pickup tool.

Vises

A machinist's vise is extremely useful for holding parts while they are being worked on. See **Figure 2-26**. Some vises can be swiveled for convenient positioning of the workpiece. The jaws of a vise are hardened steel and typically have a rough gripping surface. If parts that must not be scratched need to be clamped in a vise, soft jaw covers should be placed over the steel jaws. Sheet copper, soft aluminum, or wood can be used to pad the jaws. Always be careful not to distort or damage parts by overtightening the vise. Never clamp critical engine components, such as pistons, in a vise. Many engine parts are extremely delicate and the slightest distortion will render them useless.

A machinist's vise can also be used for holding parts or materials that need to be drilled, filed, formed, or sawed. When filing or sawing an object in a vise, adjust the piece so that the work is done close to, but not in contact with, the vise jaws. This minimizes vibration. The anvil portion of the vise can be used to flatten sheet metal or to straighten bent parts.

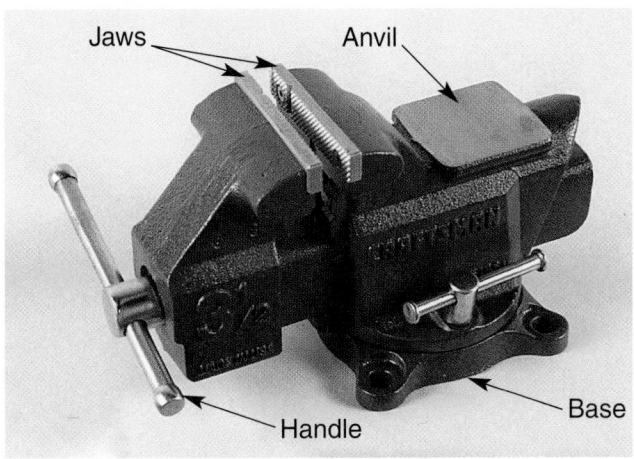

Goodheart-Willcox Publisher

Figure 2-26.

A machinist's vise can be a helpful third hand for holding parts while they are being worked on. Soft copper or aluminum jaw covers can be placed over the steel jaws to protect delicate parts.

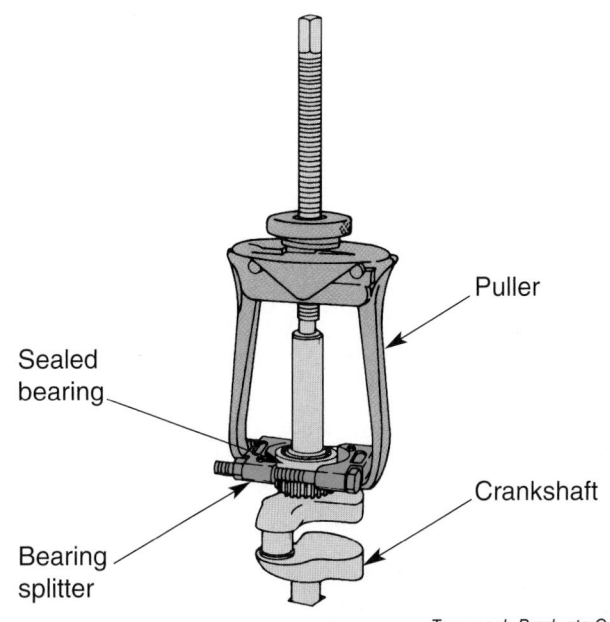

Tecumseh Products Co.

Figure 2-27.

Pullers are used to remove gears and bearings from shafts. When pulling bearings, a tool called a bearing splitter should be used to avoid damaging the bearing while force is being applied.

Engine Tools

A variety of specialized tools are required to disassemble, recondition, and rebuild a small engine. The following sections provide some general information about these tools. More specific information about the use of these tools will be provided in the engine service chapters of this book.

Gear and Flywheel Pullers

A gear puller is used for pulling gears and bearings from shafts. Gears and bearings are often press fit onto shafts and have to be pulled with considerable force to be removed. The gear puller is designed to provide this pulling force. Gear pullers can be adapted for many applications and are often used to remove flywheels from small gas engines. Also, timing gears can be removed from crankshafts with a gear puller. When sealed bearings are pulled, a tool called a bearing splitter must be used to avoid damage to the bearings and the outer race, **Figure 2-27**. More detailed information about using these tools will be presented in the engine service chapters of this book.

Flywheel Holders

A flywheel holder is essentially a spanner wrench designed to slide over the cooling fins on the flywheel. Once in place, the flywheel holder prevents the flywheel from rotating as the flywheel nut is loosened. If a flywheel holder is not available, a strap wrench can be used around the flywheel. See **Figure 2-28**.

Ridge Reamers

As an engine's piston moves up and down in the cylinder, the piston rings wear away a tiny amount of metal from the cylinder walls. The piston rings expand to compensate for the wear. However, over the life of the engine, a noticeable ridge forms in the cylinder above the area contacted by the piston rings.

A *ridge reamer* is an adjustable cutting tool designed to shave away the ridge that forms due to cylinder wear. This is done so that the new piston rings installed in the rebuild will not be damaged or quickly worn by coming into contact with the ridge. In cases of severe engine wear, the rings may catch on the ridge during disassembly, preventing piston removal. It may be necessary to cut the ridge in order to remove the piston.

A typical ridge reamer consists of a cylindrical tool body, three adjustable supports that center the

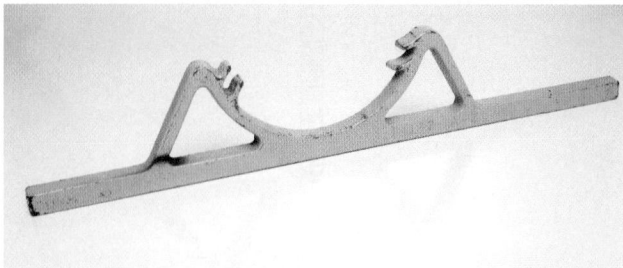

A

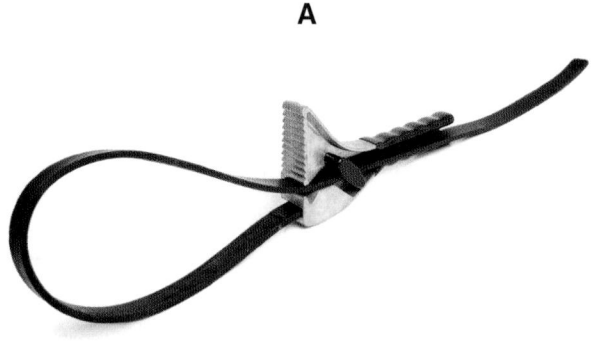

B

Goodheart-Willcox Publisher

Figure 2-28.

Methods of holding a flywheel so the retaining nut can be removed. A—A flywheel holder. B—A strap wrench.

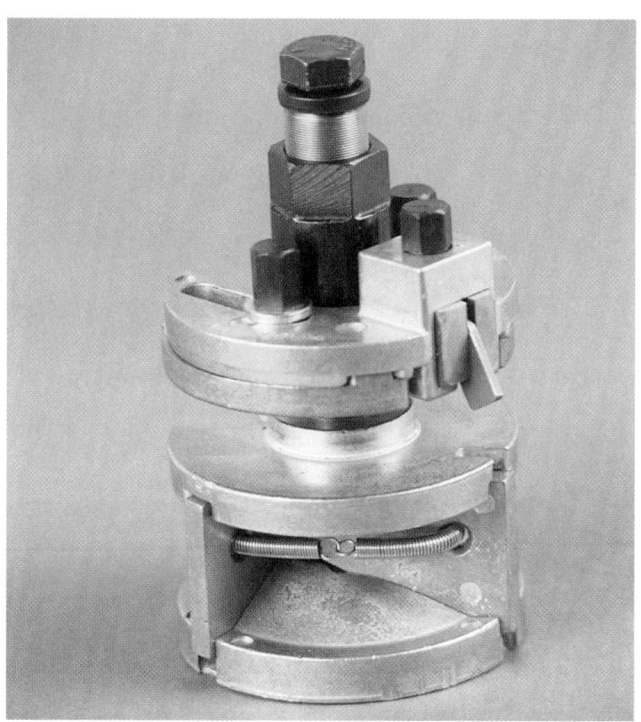

Goodheart-Willcox Publisher

Figure 2-29.

A ridge reamer is used to remove the ridge at the top of the cylinder on a badly worn engine. This is necessary so the piston can be removed and reinstalled without damaging the rings.

tool in the cylinder, an adjustment screw that is used to move the supports in and out, a cutting blade, and a hexagonal drive so the reamer can be turned with a wrench. The reamer is inserted into the cylinder and the adjustment screw is turned until the supports contact the cylinder walls. The reamer is then slowly turned with a wrench. This causes the cutter to shave away the ridge. See **Figure 2-29.**

Caution

Always follow the instructions provided by the ridge reamer manufacturer. Improper use of this tool can severely damage a cylinder.

Ring Spreaders

In order to install or remove piston rings, a technician must expand the piston rings so they can pass over the piston. The rings should be expanded as little as possible, just enough to clear the piston. Piston rings should not be pried open by hand, or they may become distorted or scratch or gouge the piston. *Ring spreaders*, also called *ring expanders*, are tools that uniformly expand a

piston ring so it can pass over the piston for installation or removal. See **Figure 2-30**. Ring spreaders apply force to the ring evenly so it does not become distorted.

Ring Compressors

A *ring compressor* is a tool that is tightened around a piston to compress the rings so the piston can be installed in the cylinder. They are made from a rectangular piece of thin spring steel that is overlapped at the ends to form a tube. Most have a worm-type adjuster, similar to that on a hose clamp, which is used to adjust the diameter of the tool.

The tool is placed over the piston, and then tightened until the rings are compressed and the inner surface of the tool is in light contact with the sides of the piston. See **Figure 2-31**. The piston and rod assembly is then inserted into the cylinder from the top until the bottom edge of the ring compressor is flush against the cylinder block deck. Then, a wooden dowel is used to push the piston assembly out of the ring compressor and into the cylinder.

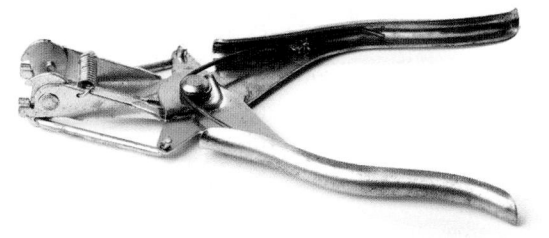

Goodheart-Willcox Publisher

Figure 2-30.

A ring spreader expands the rings so they can be installed over the piston without being damaged.

Glaze Breakers and Cylinder Hones

Glaze breakers are abrasive tools used to roughen the finish of a cylinder to promote proper ring seating. They typically consist of a flexible shaft around which a large number of spring-loaded abrasive balls are arranged to form a cylindrical brush. The balls are generally made from 220-grit abrasive. If used properly, a glaze breaker provides just enough cutting action to roughen the cylinder wall without resizing it. Glaze breakers are used only to recondition lightly worn cylinders. They cannot be used to resize a moderately or heavily worn cylinder or correct cylinder problems like taper or out-of-round.

Cylinder hones are tools used to recondition moderately worn or freshly bored cylinders. Cylinder hones usually consist of a rigid shaft, to which

two or three replaceable flat cutting stones are attached. On a flex hone, the cutting stones are mounted on spring-loaded arms that keep the stones in contact with the cylinder walls, **Figure 2-32.** Because the stones conform to the shape of the cylinder, a flex hone cannot be used to correct taper or out-of-round. On a rigid hone, the cutting stones are set to a certain diameter and then remain fixed until manually adjusted again. Because a rigid hone keeps its shape once it is set, it can be used to correct small amounts of taper and out-of-roundness in a cylinder. However, if the taper or out-of-roundness is excessive, the cylinder must be bored.

The cutting stones on a hone are typically replaceable. They are available in various grits, from coarse to superfine. If a cylinder requires extensive honing, the stones should be used progressively, usually beginning with coarse grit and finishing with fine grit. The ring manufacturer will specify the recommended finish for the rings selected.

Valve Spring Compressors

Valve spring compressors are tools that compress a valve spring so the spring retainer can be removed. Different styles of ring compressors are available. One type consists of two arms, connected at a pivot at one end. The other end of each arm has a slotted jaw. The slotted jaws are placed at either end of the spring, and then the adjusting screw is

Ring compresser

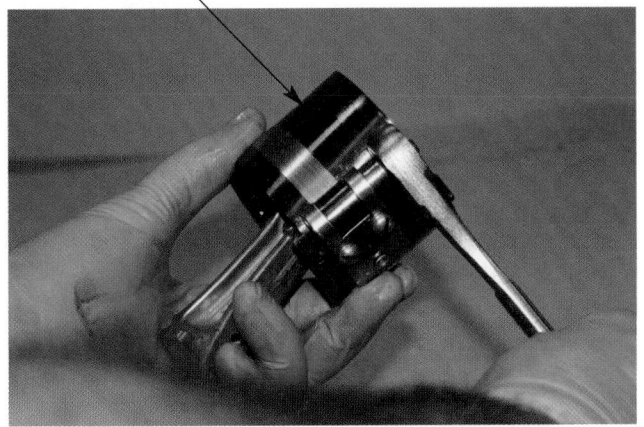

Goodheart-Willcox Publisher

Figure 2-31.

Ring compressors compress the piston rings so the piston and rod assembly can be installed into the cylinder.

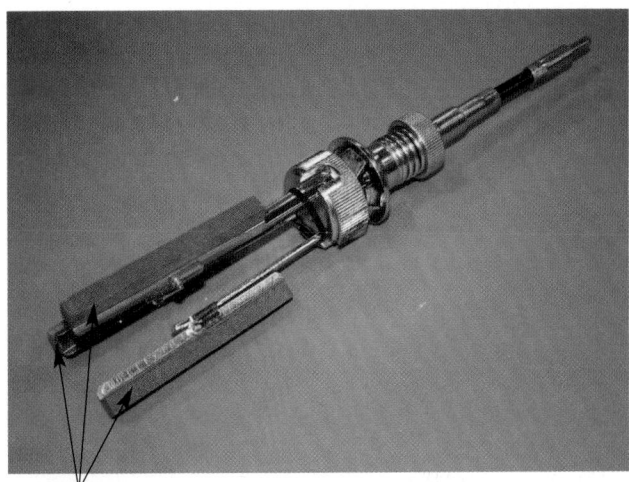

Replaceable stones

Goodheart-Willcox Publisher

Figure 2-32.

Flexible cylinder hones are used to recondition moderately worn and freshly bored cylinders.

tightened, drawing the arms together and compressing the spring. This type of spring compressor is suitable only for L-head (flat head) engines.

Another common type of spring compressor is simply a lever. This type of spring compressor is suitable only for overhead valve engines. It is attached to a rocker stud at one end. There is a hole in the lever that is positioned over the valve retainer. The loose end of the tool is pushed downward to compress the valve spring so the retainer can be removed.

The third type of valve spring compressor is similar to a C-clamp. It has a C-shaped frame with a slotted jaw at one end of the frame and a screw with a pivot at the other end. The slotted jaw is placed on the retainer end of the valve spring, and the pivot end of the screw is positioned above the flat side of the head of the valve. The screw is then tightened to compress the valve spring. See **Figure 2-33**. Some variations of this type of valve spring compressor use a lever to apply the pressure to compress the spring. A C-clamp type valve spring compressor can be used on most L-head and overhead valve engines.

> **Note**
>
> Special valve spring compressors are required to remove the valves from overhead cam engines. These types of valve spring compressors are designed for specific engines and must be purchased through the engine manufacturer.

Lapping Sticks

Lapping sticks are simple tools used to spin valves during a valve reconditioning procedure known as valve lapping. Lapping sticks are generally wooden dowels with a rubber suction cup attached to one or both ends, **Figure 2-34**. In the lapping procedure, an abrasive compound is applied to the valve seat. The valve is then reinserted into the valve guide, but not secured. The suction cup end of the lapping stick is stuck onto the valve head, and the dowel is spun back and forth between the technician's palms to rotate the valve.

Engine Test Instruments

Tachometers are instruments that measure engine speed. There are various types of tachometers available, ranging from simple mechanical tachometers to digital optical tachometers. Simple mechanical tachometers measure engine speed based on engine vibration. Optical tachometers require that reflective material be put on a rotating engine component. Then, optical sensors can be used to measure engine rotation across a distance up to several feet.

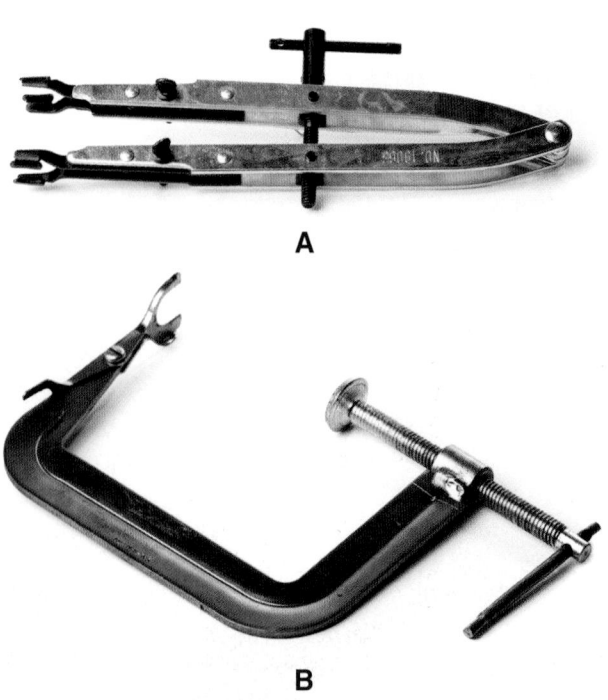

A

B

Goodheart-Willcox Publisher

Figure 2-33.
Valve spring compressors compress the valve spring so the valve retainer can be removed. A—Valve spring compressor suitable for L-head engines. B—C-clamp style valve spring compressor.

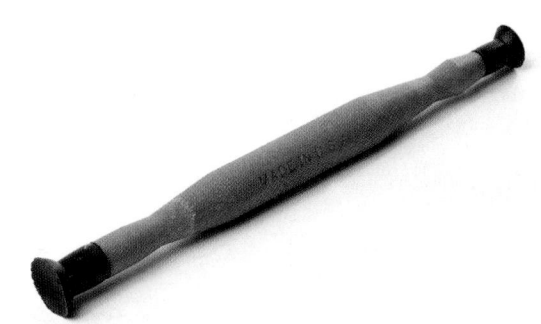

Goodheart-Willcox Publisher

Figure 2-34.
Lapping sticks are simple tools used to spin valves within their guides.

Spark testers are test instruments used to determine whether the ignition system is producing enough voltage to create a spark at the spark plug. The spark tester is connected to the spark plug wire and a grounded part of the engine, like a cooling fin. The tester itself is similar to a spark plug, having two electrodes with a small air gap between them, **Figure 2-35**. The gap area of the tester can be seen through a glass or plastic window in the tester body. If the ignition system is functioning properly, a spark will jump the gap when the starter is engaged.

Compression testers are gauges that measure the maximum air pressure in a combustion chamber. To use the gauge, the spark plug is replaced with the compression gauge and the engine is turned over several times. If the pressure reading is below specifications, air-fuel mixture is escaping during the compression stroke. This typically indicates a problem with the valves, piston rings, or cylinder head.

Power Tools

Most service and repair tasks that a technician faces are accomplished with basic hand tools. However, certain tasks require power tools. The power tools that technicians will use most often are drills, drill presses, and bench grinders.

Drills and Drill Presses

Electric drills are handheld, electric motor–driven tools that turn a twist drill or other type of bit. They have an adjustable chuck that can grip the shank of different size bits. The two most common drill sizes are 3/8″, which have chucks that can

Goodheart-Willcox Publisher

Figure 2-35.

A spark tester, like the one shown here, can reveal if there is a problem with the engine's ignition system.

accept shanks up to 3/8″ in diameter, and 1/2″, which can use bits with shanks up to 1/2″ in diameter. Most drills have a variable speed drive, which speeds up or slows down the rotational speed of the bit based on trigger position. Most drills have a maximum speed of 1000–2000 rpm.

A wide variety of bits and accessories can be attached to the drill for various tasks. Some of the most commonly used include twist drill bits, screwdriver bits, nut-driving bits, wire brushes, grinding stones, and sanding disks.

Drill presses are similar to handheld electric drills, but are larger and more powerful. Drill presses typically have several preset speed settings. The desired speed is typically selected using a multiposition switch on the front or side of the drill press. Turning the feed lever on the side of the drill press moves the chuck and bit toward the work, ensuring that the bit remains perpendicular to the drill press table.

Warning

Always wear eye protection and gloves when using a drill or drill press. Before drilling a bore, secure the work. If the work is not firmly clamped to a workbench or drill press table, the drill bit can bind in the bore. This causes the unsecured part to spin, which can cause significant injury.

Bench Grinders

Bench grinders are essentially double-shaft electric motors with a circular grinding stone attached to each shaft. Bench grinders are also equipped with tool rests to support the tools or part being ground. A wheel guard covers the unused portion of each grinding wheel, minimizing the risk of snagging. An adjustable spark guard should be present above the tool rest on each wheel. They should be positioned to deflect any sparks or metal fragments flying from the grinding wheel.

A bench grinder's grinding wheels are replaceable and are available with different finishes. Always use the right type of grinding wheel for the task being performed. Lower grit wheels are coarser, remove more metal, and result in a rougher finish than higher grit wheels. Wire wheels can be installed in place of the grinding stones for cleaning jobs, and buffing wheels can be installed for polishing jobs.

As with all tools, certain precautions must be observed in order to safely use a bench grinder. Before using a bench grinder, make sure that it is securely fastened to a pedestal or workbench. Adjust the tool rests so they are approximately 1/16″ from the face of the grinding wheel, and set to the desired angle. Make sure that the spark guards are in place. Turn on the bench grinder and let it reach operating speed. Place the object to be ground on the tool rest and hold it firmly. Slowly feed the object until it contacts the face of the grinding wheel. Keep the object in firm contact with the tool rest at all times during the grinding process.

Warning

Always wear a face shield and gloves when operating a grinder.

Cleaning Tools and Equipment

A small engine technician must use a variety of tools to clean engine, equipment, and parts. Scrapers are thin blades used to remove carbon buildup, gasket material, and built-up grime from engine parts or equipment. Brass or plastic scrapers should be used to clean critical or soft metal surfaces. Scraper blades should be kept nearly parallel to the surface being cleaned to avoid digging into the surface. Wire brushes are used to remove carbon buildup from heads and pistons. They can also be used to remove oxidation from metal parts. Emery cloth or scuff pads are used to remove built-up carbon at the top of cylinder walls. Wooden or plastic toothpicks can be used to clean small passages, like those in carburetors, without damaging them. Because they could score the passages, small drill bits or wire should not be used.

A cleaning tank is used to safely clean small engine parts. See **Figure 2-36**. A nontoxic, nonflammable solvent should be used to scrub engine parts after old gaskets and excess grease have been removed. The tank has a pump to recirculate and filter the solvent and direct it through a flexible tube. The tube can be directed at the parts for flushing. After the parts are clean, a low-pressure safety blowgun can be used to remove excess solvent.

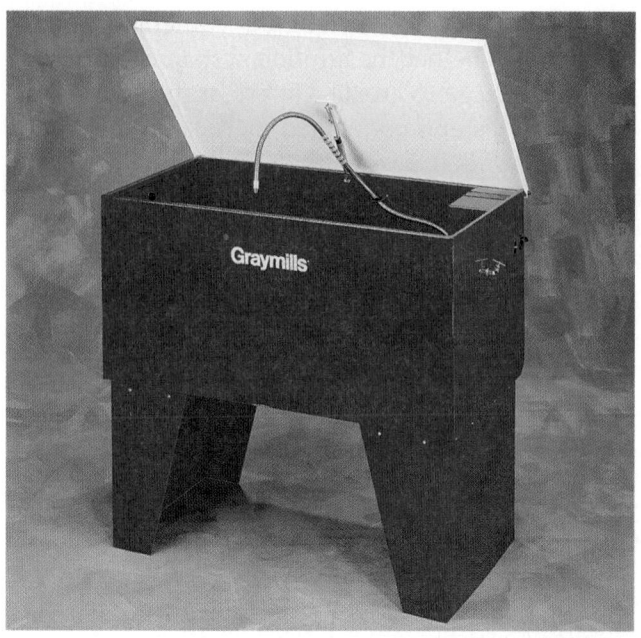

Graymills Corp.

Figure 2-36.

A cleaning solvent tank is used to clean engine parts. This tank is fitted with a fusible link, which will automatically close the lid in case of fire. It also has a built-in pump and filter system for cleaning the solvent.

Measuring Instruments

High-quality measuring instruments should always be used when servicing a small gas engine. Many dimensions are critical to proper engine operation. Therefore, it is extremely important to be able to measure various engine parts and clearances accurately. When making engine repairs, a technician must take measurements to determine if parts are within specified limits or if replacements and adjustments must be made. Quality measuring instruments allow you to service small engines easily and effectively. Keep instruments clean and in proper working condition.

Some measuring instruments are common to most engine work, while others have only one or two specific applications. Special-purpose tools may be manufacturer-designed for limited use on only one engine make or model. The following sections describe how to use common measuring instruments.

Micrometers

Micrometers are precision instruments designed to accurately measure pistons, crankshafts, valve stems, and other small engine components. You must be able to read a micrometer correctly to make judgments about the condition of various engine parts.

There are several varieties of micrometers available. Each type is designed for a specific purpose. The outside micrometer is used to measure thicknesses and outside diameters. See **Figure 2-37**. The inside micrometer is designed for taking measurements of internal dimensions. See **Figure 2-38**. A blade micrometer, such as the one shown in **Figure 2-39**, is used to take measurements in narrow slots. **Figure 2-40** illustrates the use of an inside micrometer and an outside micrometer.

Because micrometers are made of metal, they expand when heated and contract when cooled. Micrometers *should not* be held in the hand for long periods of time. Because of the instrument's level of precision, the expansion due to body heat is enough to cause inaccuracy in the instrument. Always hold the micrometer properly. **Figure 2-41** shows the proper one-hand method for measuring a valve stem diameter with a micrometer. **Figure 2-42** shows a micrometer being held with two hands. Note the minimal contact between the hands and the micrometer. Measuring instruments are quite expensive and should always be handled with care.

Micrometers are available in several sizes. Most micrometers have the capability to take measurements only within a 1″ range. For example, a 0–1″ micrometer can be used to measure objects smaller than 1″. A 2–3″ micrometer, on the other hand, is designed to measure objects that are between 2″ and 3″.

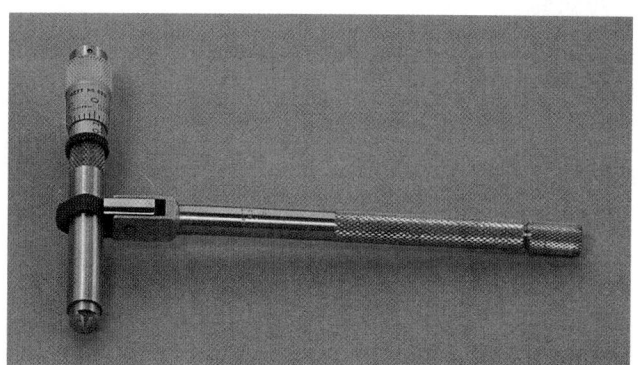

Goodheart-Willcox Publisher

Figure 2-38.

The inside micrometer is designed to measure internal dimensions.

Goodheart-Willcox Publisher

Figure 2-39.

The blade micrometer is designed to enable the spindle and anvil to measure in narrow grooves.

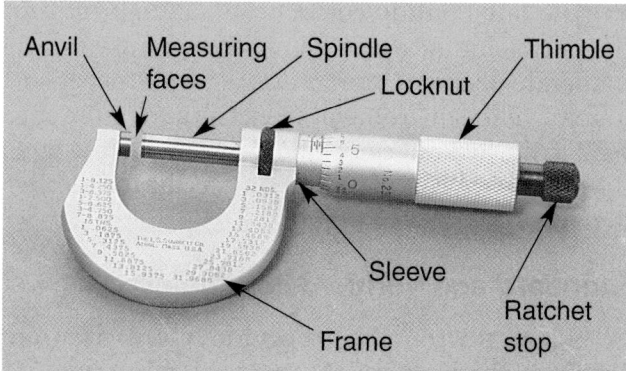

Goodheart-Willcox Publisher

Figure 2-37.

Note the parts of an outside micrometer with ratchet stop. This particular micrometer is graduated in thousandths of an inch (.001″).

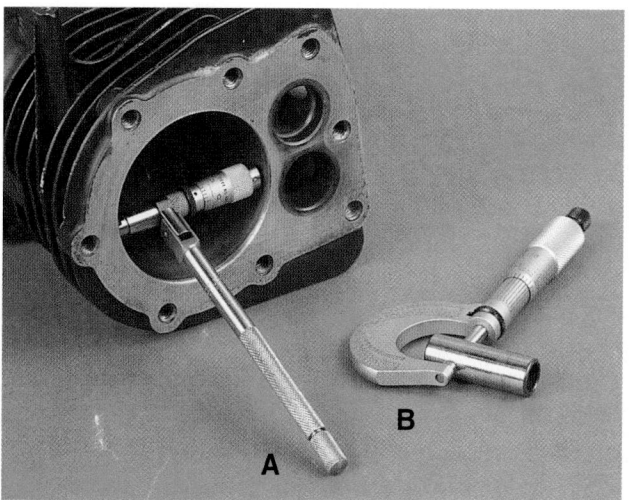

Goodheart-Willcox Publisher

Figure 2-40.

A—An inside micrometer being used to measure the internal diameter of a cylinder. B—An outside micrometer being used to measure a piston pin.

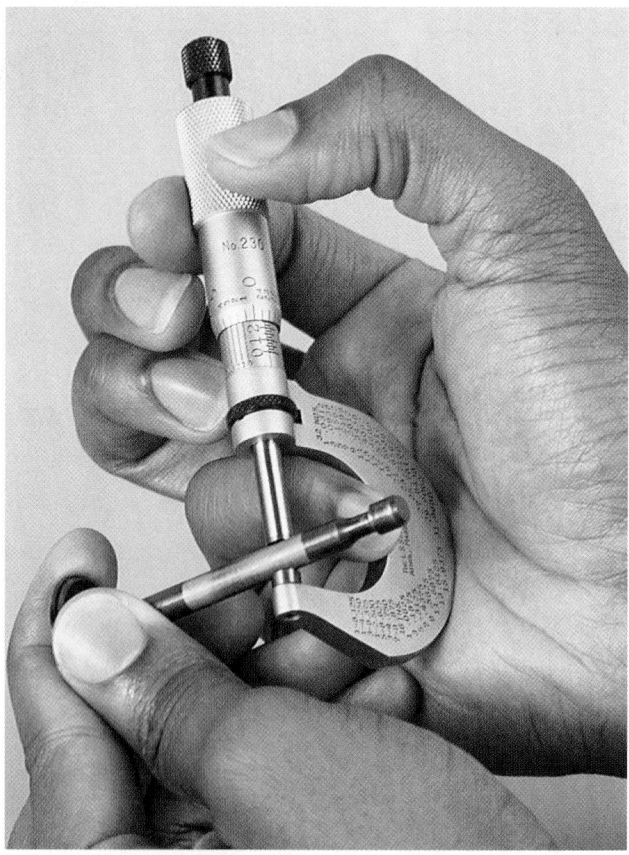

Goodheart-Willcox Publisher

Figure 2-41.

A micrometer should be held in one hand while the other hand holds the piece to be measured. Note the small finger in the frame of the micrometer.

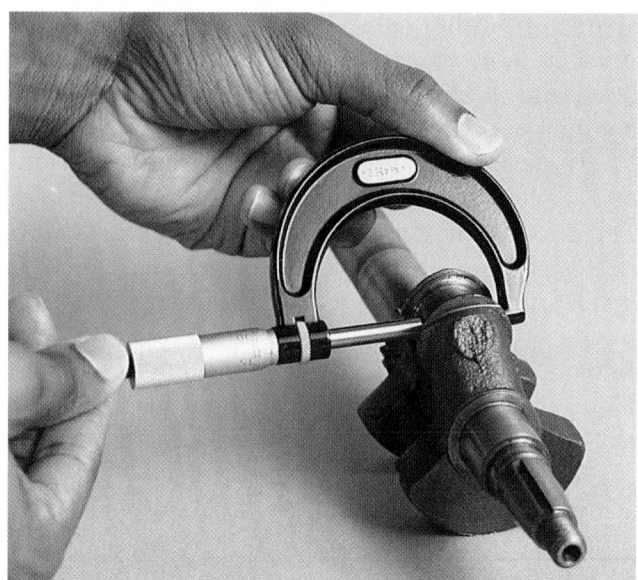

Goodheart-Willcox Publisher

Figure 2-42.

The proper technique for measuring with a micrometer when two hands are necessary. Use very light pressure when turning the thimble of the micrometer.

Cleaning and Calibrating a Micrometer

Before attempting to measure any object, make sure that the micrometer's anvil and spindle faces are clean. If necessary, clean the faces by gently closing the micrometer on a piece of clean, white paper and drawing the paper from between the faces. To ensure accuracy, the micrometer should always be checked for proper calibration before use. A 0–1″ micrometer can be checked by simply closing it and observing the reading on the sleeve and thimble. If the reading is not zero, clean the anvil and spindle again and retest the micrometer. If it still does not read zero, check the manufacturer's instructions for adjusting the instrument. Micrometers larger than 0–1″ require the use of a gauge block, cylindrical gauge, or gauge pin to verify calibration. These gauges are precision ground to exact dimensions and are used to check the micrometer for accuracy. For example, a 1″ gauge block can be used to check the calibration of a 1–2″

micrometer by simply measuring the block. The micrometer should read exactly one inch. If it does not, it must be recalibrated.

Using a Micrometer

To use a micrometer, simply place the object to be measured against the anvil and turn the thimble until the spindle touches the object. If the micrometer has a ratchet-stop, **Figure 2-37**, click it just once after making contact with the work surface. If the micrometer does not have a ratchet-stop, the thimble must be turned very gently so the anvil and spindle faces lightly contact the outer surfaces of the part being measured. Overtightening can permanently damage the micrometer. If it is necessary to remove the micrometer from the part in order to read it, the locknut can be tightened, which secures the spindle so that it does not turn as the micrometer is removed.

Standard and Vernier Micrometers

Some micrometers provide more accurate readings than others. A standard micrometer is graduated in thousandths of an inch (.001″). A Vernier micrometer, on the other hand, is graduated in ten-thousandths of an inch (.0001″). A Vernier micrometer has an additional scale on its sleeve.

See **Figure 2-43**. Part tolerances are specified in three or four decimal place numbers. A Vernier micrometer can be used for either measurement, but the standard micrometer is accurate to only three decimal places.

Reading a Standard Micrometer

The first step in reading any micrometer is to familiarize yourself with the divisions (graduations) on the sleeve and the thimble. The micrometer's sleeve graduations reflect the fact that the spindle moves 1/40″ (0.025″) for each revolution of the thimble. Therefore, the micrometer's sleeve is divided into 40 equal spaces. Each line on the sleeve represents 1/40″ (0.025″). Every fourth line is numbered. These numbers represent 1/10″ (.100″). See **Figure 2-44**.

The micrometer's thimble is divided into 25 equal parts. Each line on the thimble represents 0.001″. **Figure 2-45** illustrates a typical micrometer thimble. Looking at the example in **Figure 2-46A**, the thimble has been rotated four turns, or 1/10″ (4 × .025″ = .100″). **Figure 2-46B** shows a thimble that has been rotated ten full turns (.250″), plus .008″ more, totaling .258″. Now, read the micrometer scale in **Figure 2-46C**.

Reading a Vernier Micrometer

To obtain readings to four decimal places, a Vernier micrometer must be used. The Vernier micrometer has an additional scale, called the

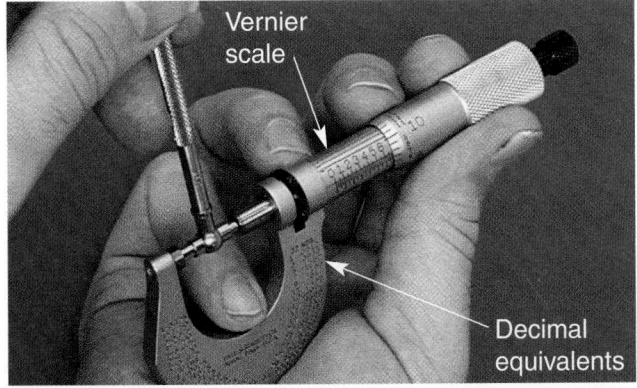

Goodheart-Willcox Publisher

Figure 2-43.

A Vernier micrometer can measure to four decimal places with the special scale that is located on its sleeve. The fourth decimal place is determined by the line on the thimble and line on the Vernier scale that coincide with each other.

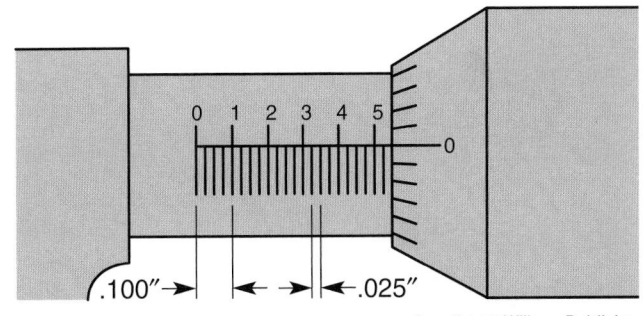

Goodheart-Willcox Publisher

Figure 2-44.

Each of the small spaces on the micrometer's sleeve is equal to 1/40″ (.025″). Since there are four small spaces between each of the numbers printed on the sleeve, the distance between numbers is equal to 1/10″ (.100″). The reading on this micrometer is .550″.

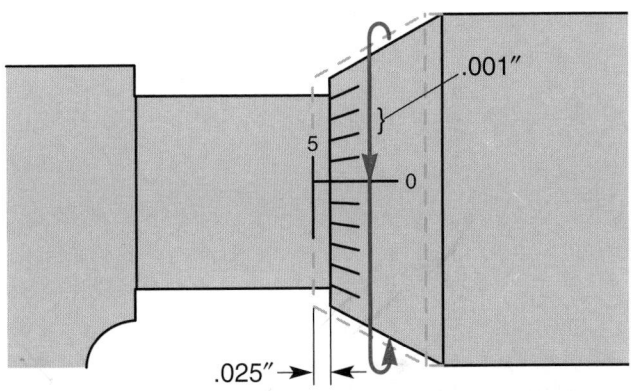

Goodheart-Willcox Publisher

Figure 2-45.

Each small space on the thimble of the micrometer is equal to 1/1000″ (.001″). One complete rotation of the thimble moves the spindle 25/1000″ (.025″), or one small space on the sleeve.

Vernier scale, located on the top of its sleeve. See **Figure 2-47**. The first three decimal places on a Vernier micrometer are read in the same way as they are on the standard micrometer. The fourth decimal number, however, is obtained from the Vernier scale. Unless the zero line on the thimble is aligned with the sleeve's horizontal reference line, only one line of the Vernier scale will be perfectly aligned with one of the lines on the thimble. If the sixth line of the Vernier scale is aligned with one of the lines on the thimble, the fourth decimal place number would be six. **Figure 2-47A** illustrates a 0–1″ Vernier micrometer displaying a reading of .2586″. Can you read the measurements in **Figures 2-47B** and **2-47C**?

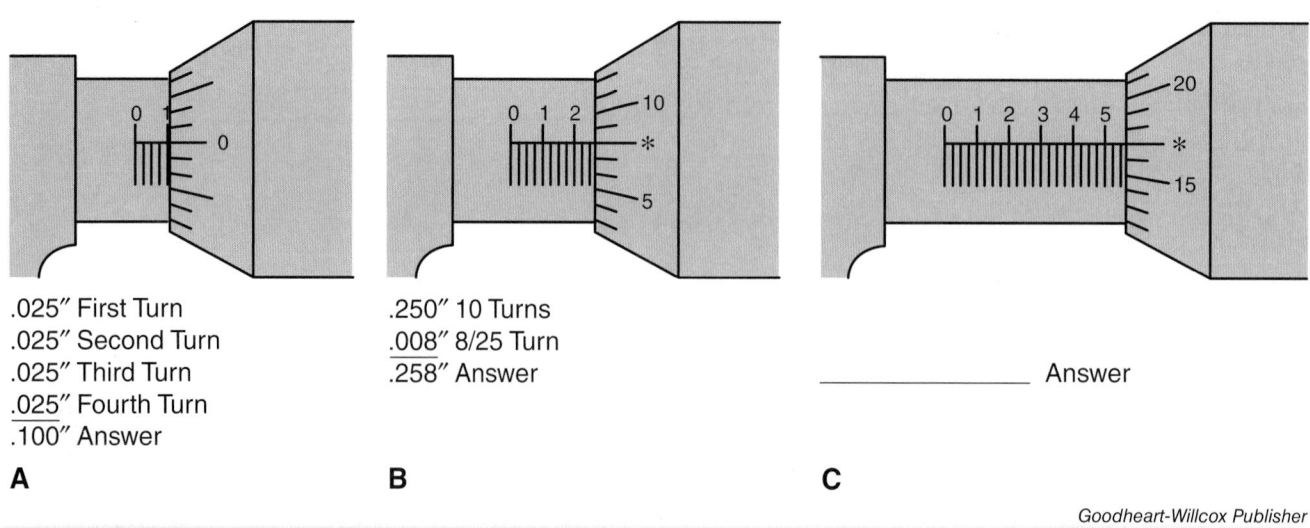

.025" First Turn
.025" Second Turn
.025" Third Turn
.025" Fourth Turn
.100" Answer

A

.250" 10 Turns
.008" 8/25 Turn
.258" Answer

B

_____ Answer

C

Goodheart-Willcox Publisher

Figure 2-46.

Study the micrometer readings on the 0–1" micrometers in A and B. Can you read the micrometer in C? (Answer = .567")

Remember, always handle measuring instruments carefully and keep them clean to maximize accuracy and reliability. Once you have practiced a few readings, you will see how easily and how quickly micrometers can be used.

Digital Micrometers

Digital micrometers simplify the measuring process by displaying the measurement on a digital readout. See **Figure 2-48**. Although the measurement appears in the window, it can also be read from the barrel and thimble. These types of micrometers typically have the same precision as standard micrometers.

Reading a Metric Micrometer

Metric micrometers closely resemble standard and Vernier micrometers. The only difference is the markings on the thimble and sleeve. The metric micrometer is marked to measure hundredths of a millimeter. Each line on the thimble equals 0.01mm, and each line on the sleeve equals 0.5mm. Two full revolutions of the thimble, equals 1.00mm on the sleeve.

To read a metric micrometer, note the number of marks between the zero line and the thimble to determine the measurement to the nearest half millimeter. Then, locate the line on the thimble that coincides with the horizontal line on the sleeve. Add these numbers, and this is the reading. See **Figure 2-49**.

Micrometer Depth Gauges

The micrometer depth gauge is a measuring device used to measure the depths of bores. See **Figure 2-50**. A micrometer depth gauge is read using almost the same steps as were used for reading the standard and Vernier micrometers. The main difference is the numbers on the sleeve that are under the thimble are used for the reading. It is necessary to see which numbers and spaces are visible on the sleeve and deduce those that are under the sleeve.

For example, if a number 4, a space, and a partial space are visible, then a 3, two full spaces, and a partial space is under the thimble. Therefore, the reading to this point is .350". Now a reading from the thimble is taken. So, if the twelfth line on the thimble is aligned with the reference line, .012" is added to .350" to get a reading of .362".

Vernier Calipers

The Vernier caliper is a measuring device used to take both internal and external measurements. See **Figure 2-51**. To take a measurement, slide the assembly until the jaws almost contact the part being measured. Lock the clamping screw, and adjust the fine adjusting nut. The contact between the jaws and the part must be firm but not tight. Now, lock the slide on the beam, carefully remove the caliper, and make your reading.

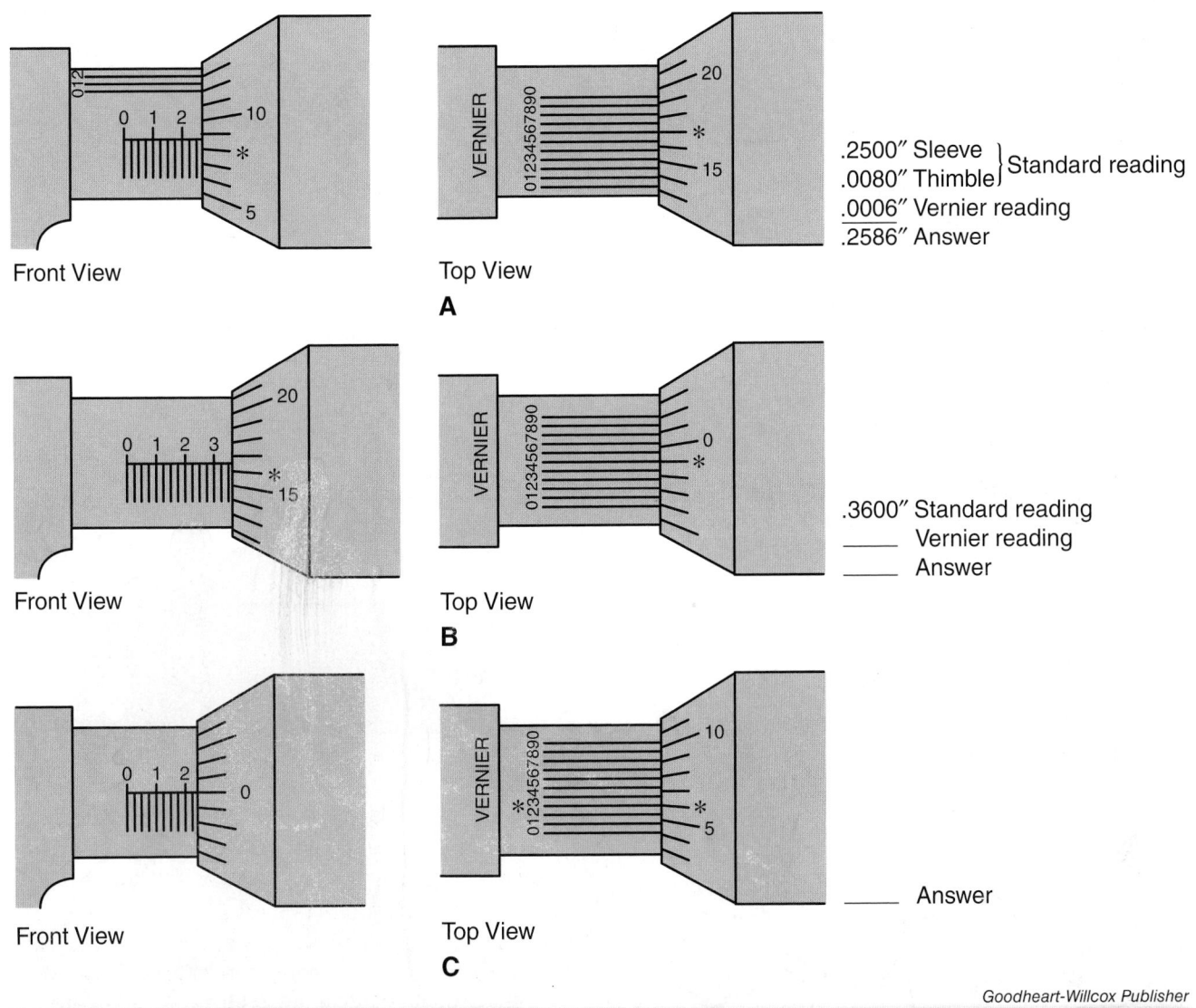

.2500″ Sleeve ⎫
.0080″ Thimble ⎬ Standard reading
.0006″ Vernier reading
.2586″ Answer

.3600″ Standard reading
_____ Vernier reading
_____ Answer

_____ Answer

Figure 2-47.

Study the Vernier micrometer reading in A. Complete the reading for B (.3665″). Read C (.2253″). Assume that these are 0–1″ micrometers.

Reading a Vernier Caliper

Vernier calipers are available in either 25- or 50-division Vernier scale. Both types of scales are graduated in thousandths of an inch (.001″).

25-Division Scale

On a 25-division Vernier caliper, each inch on the beam is graduated into 40 equal parts. Each graduation is .025″ (1/40″). So, every fourth one is numbered and is .100″ (1/10″). On the Vernier scale, there are 25 divisions numbered 5, 10, 15, 20, and 25.

To read a 25-division Vernier caliper, note how many inches (1, 2, 3, etc.), tenths (.100, .200, .300, etc.), and fortieths (.025, .050, or .075) there are between

the zero line on the Vernier scale and the zero line on the beam. Add these numbers together. See **Figure 2-52A**.

Now count the number of graduations (each being .001″ or 1/1000″) that are between the zero line on the Vernier scale and the line that lines up exactly with a line on the beam. Only one will exactly line up. Add this number to the total previously found. This is the reading.

50-Division Scale

On a 50-division Vernier caliper beam, every other graduation between the inch lines are numbered and are equal to .100″ (1/10″). The unnumbered

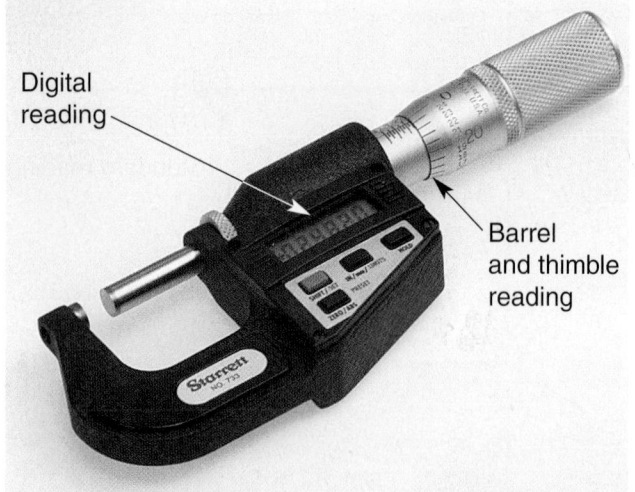

Goodheart-Willcox Publisher

Figure 2-48.

Today, digital micrometers are becoming more and more common.

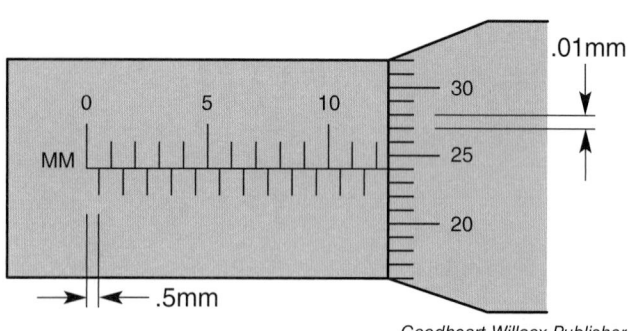

Goodheart-Willcox Publisher

Figure 2-49.

The metric micrometer measures to the hundredths of a millimeter. (Answer = 12.24mm)

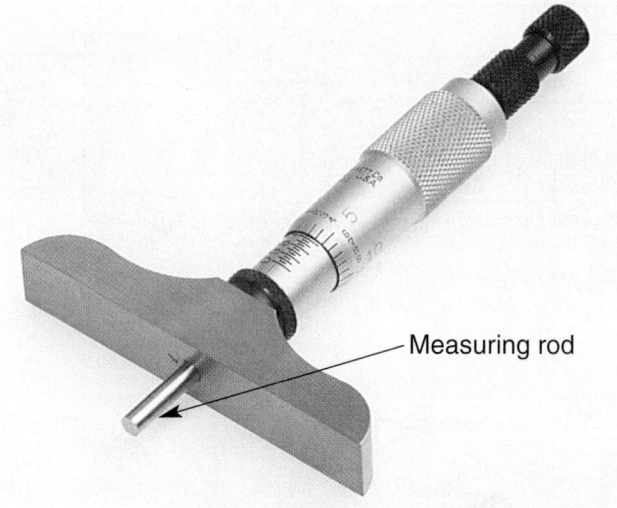

A

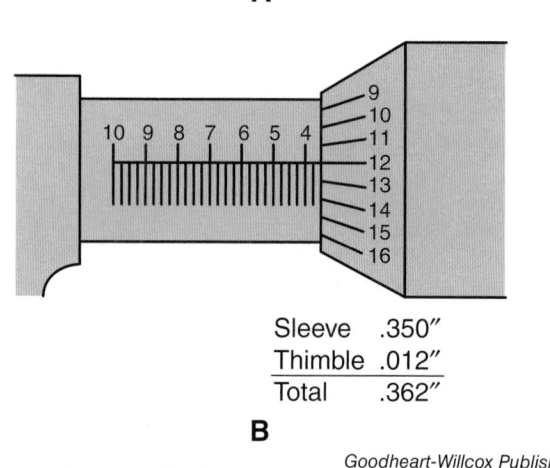

Sleeve .350″
Thimble .012″
Total .362″

B

Goodheart-Willcox Publisher

Figure 2-50.

Micrometer depth gauges are used to measure the depths of bores and recesses. A—The length of a depth micrometer's measuring rod determines the range of measurement. Many depth micrometer's have interchangeable rods for making measurements in different ranges. B—The depth micrometer reading is based on the sleeve lines and numbers hidden by the thimble.

ones are equal to .050″ (1/20″). The Vernier scale is graduated into 50 parts, each representing .001″ (1/1000″). Every fifth or tenth line is numbered (5, 10, 15, etc., or 10, 20, 30, etc.).

To read 50-division Vernier caliper, note how many inches (1″, 2″, 3″, etc.), tenths (.100″, .200″, .300″, etc.), and twentieths (.050″) there are between the zero line on the Vernier scale and the zero line on the beam. Add these three numbers together. See **Figure 2-52B**.

Now count the number of graduations (each being .001″ or 1/1000″) that are between the zero line on the Vernier scale and the line that lines up exactly with a line on the beam. Only one will exactly line up. Add this number to the total previously found. This is the reading.

Reading a Metric Vernier Caliper

The metric Vernier caliper closely resembles the standard type. Like the standard types, the metric Vernier calipers are available in 25- or 50-division scales.

Metric 25-Division Vernier Caliper

On a metric 25-division Vernier caliper, there are 25 equal divisions on the Vernier plate. Each division is equal to 0.02mm. Every fifth line is numbered (0.10mm, 0.20mm, etc.). The beam is graduated in

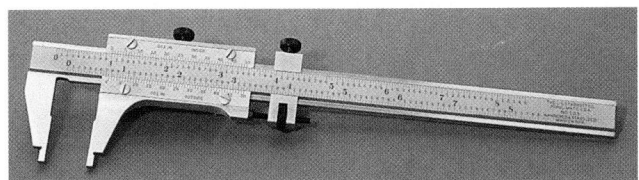

Figure 2-51.

Vernier calipers can be used to make internal and external measurements.

0.5mm divisions. Every twentieth division is numbered (10mm, 20mm, etc.).

To read the metric 25-division Vernier caliper, note the number of millimeters between the zero line on the beam and the zero on the Vernier plate. Then, locate the line on the Vernier plate that coincides with one of the lines on the beam. Note the value of this line as indicated on the Vernier plate. Add these numbers, and this is the reading. See **Figure 2-53A**.

Metric 50-Division Vernier Caliper

On a 50-division Vernier caliper, there are 50 equal divisions on the Vernier plate. Each division is equal to 0.02mm. Every fifth line is numbered (.10mm, .20mm, etc.). The beam is graduated in 0.1mm divisions. Every tenth division is numbered (10mm, 20mm, etc.).

To read a 50-division Vernier caliper, note the number of millimeters between the zero line on the beam and the zero line on the Vernier plate. Locate the line on the Vernier plate that coincides with one of the lines on the beam. Note the value of this line as indicated on the Vernier plate. Add these numbers, and this is the reading. See **Figure 2-53B**.

Digital Slide Caliper

Digital slide calipers eliminate the need to read anything but the digital readout. See **Figure 2-54**. This type of caliper has simplified the measuring

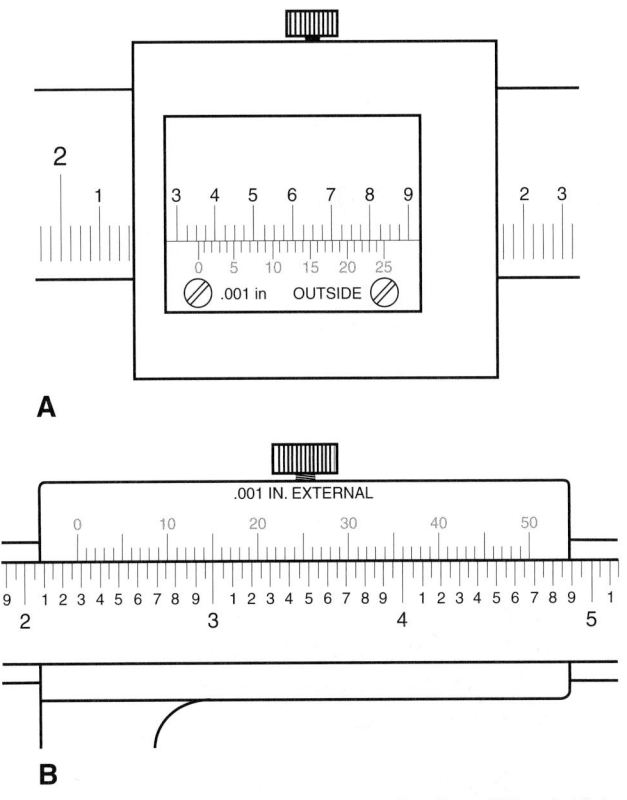

Goodheart-Willcox Publisher

Figure 2-52.

A Vernier caliper can have a 25-division (A) or 50-division (B) scale. (Answers A = 2.359″, and B = 2.265″)

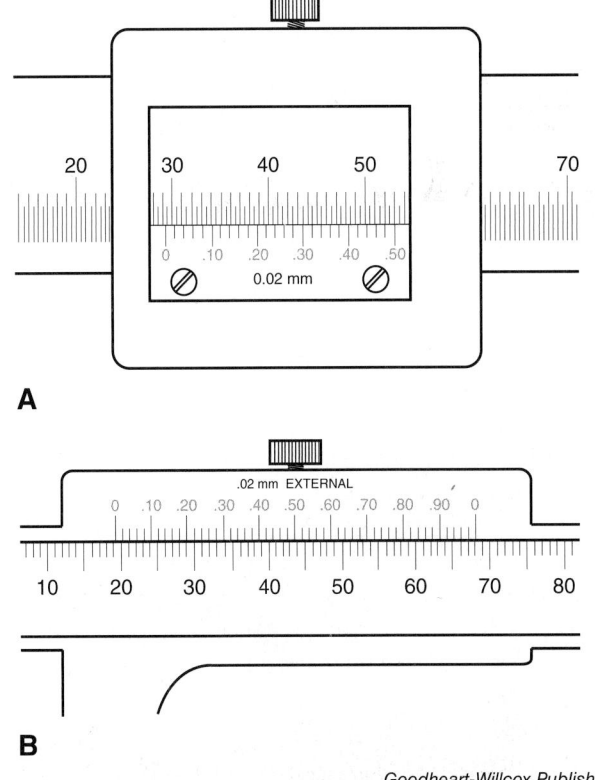

Goodheart-Willcox Publisher

Figure 2-53.

A metric Vernier caliper can have a 25-division (A) or a 50-division (B) scale. (Answers A = 29.28mm, and B = 19.20mm)

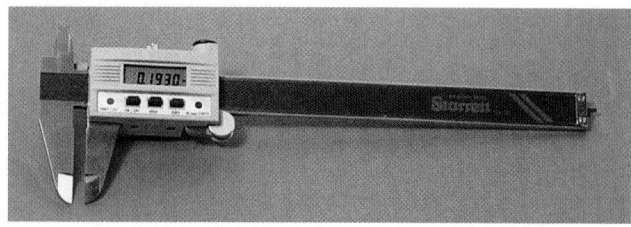

Goodheart-Willcox Publisher

Figure 2-54.

Digital slide calipers are becoming increasingly common.

procedure. Unlike digital micrometers, these instruments typically do not have markings that can be read manually.

Dial Caliper

A dial caliper is quite easy to read and will perform the same measuring operations as Vernier calipers. A dial caliper can quickly make inside, outside, and depth measurements. Its dial is simple to read and provides clear measurements. See **Figure 2-55**. To calibrate the dial, clean and close the jaws, loosen the dial lock, and rotate the dial until the zero is directly under the needle. Now tighten the dial lock. Place the jaws into, or over, the part to be measured. Adjust the roll knob until the jaws just lightly touch the surface and then tighten the lock screw to hold the measurement. Look at inches and tenths on the bar scale adjacent

to the jaw. Add to that the reading under the dial needle to get the total dimension of the part. Dial calipers are available in English and metric styles and are generally less expensive than the Vernier and electronic digital calipers.

Telescoping Gauges

Telescoping gauges are transfer-type measuring instruments. They do not provide a direct dimensional reading. A telescoping gauge, like the one in **Figure 2-56**, can be used to transfer the distance from A to B to a micrometer. See **Figure 2-57**.

Telescoping gauges can be purchased singly, **Figure 2-58**, or in sets, providing a wide range of sizes to accommodate a variety of measurements. See **Figure 2-59**. The spindle faces are curved so that each end has only one point of contact when curved surfaces are being measured. See **Figure 2-60**. To use a telescoping gauge to determine the diameter of a cylinder, loosen the lock screw on the end of the handle so that the telescoping spindles can be retracted. After the spindles are retracted, tighten the lock screw, and place the gauge in the cylinder. Once the gauge is located in the cylinder, release the lock screw to allow the telescoping ends to extend. The handle must be held perfectly in line with the centerline of the cylinder being measured. Also, it is essential that the telescoping ends be aligned exactly across the true diameter of the cylinder. The general practice to obtain this position

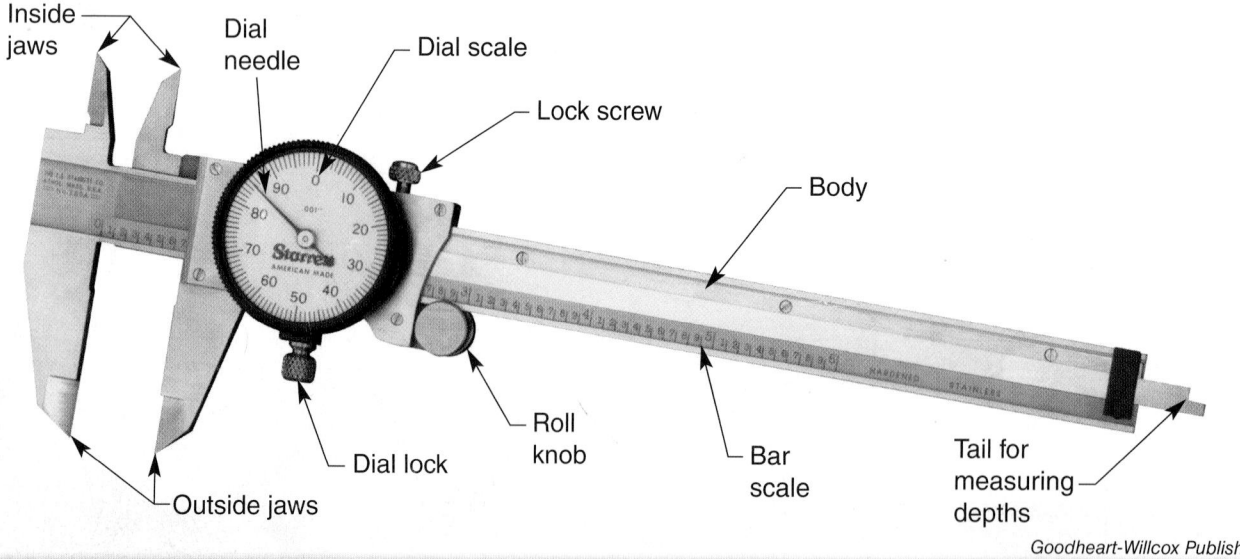

Goodheart-Willcox Publisher

Figure 2-55.

A dial caliper performs the same readings as a Vernier caliper.

is to hold the handle gently with the thumb and forefinger while sliding the gauge up and down the cylinder walls. Spring tension will cause the gauge to seek the true diameter of the cylinder.

When the true diameter has been located, use the opposite hand to gently tighten the lock screw, securing the telescoping ends. When removing the gauge from the cylinder, tilt the handle so the gauge can be removed without changing the setting. See **Figure 2-61**. After the gauge is removed, measure the distance between the telescoping ends with a micrometer. See **Figure 2-57**.

Small Hole Gauge

A small hole gauge is similar to the telescoping gauge. It is intended for measuring holes that are too small for the smallest telescoping gauge. Small hole gauges are usually provided in sets to accommodate a variety of hole sizes. See **Figure 2-62**. A small hole gauge is expanded by turning a knurled screw on the end of its handle until the split ball touches the inner walls of the hole. See **Figure 2-63**. Test for correct fit by moving the gauge back and forth in the hole until you feel a slight drag. Remove the gauge and measure across the ball with a micrometer. See **Figure 2-64**.

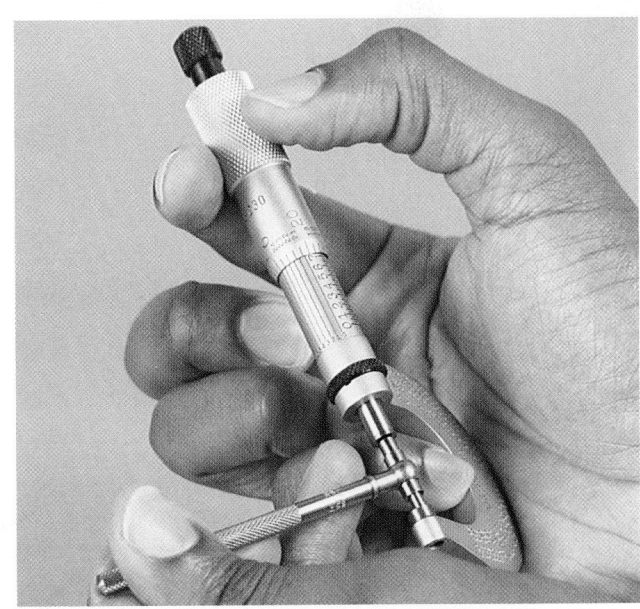

Goodheart-Willcox Publisher

Figure 2-57.

After removing the telescoping gauge from the cylinder, measure the gauge with a micrometer.

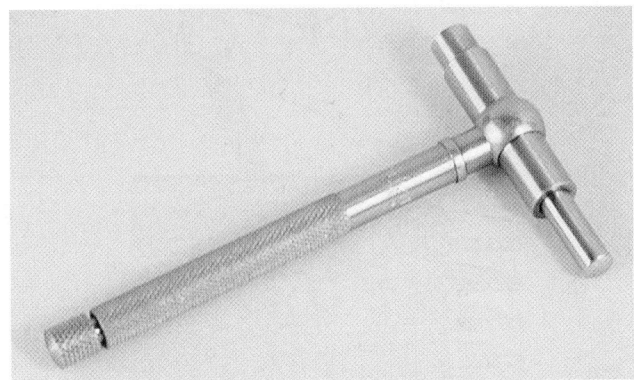

Goodheart-Willcox Publisher

Figure 2-58.

A single telescoping gauge.

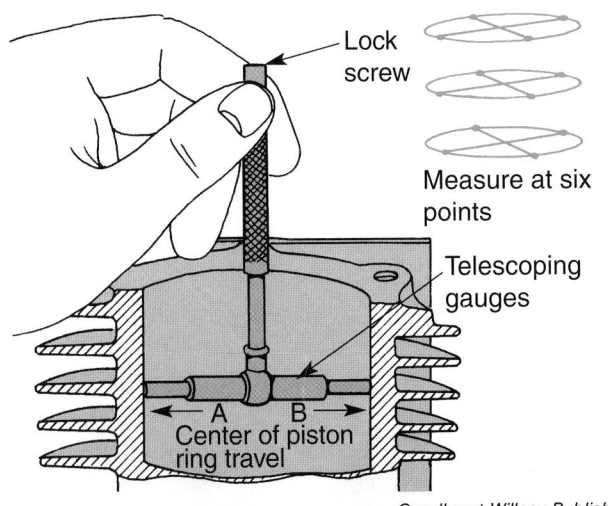

Goodheart-Willcox Publisher

Figure 2-56.

A telescoping gauge can be used to measure the inside diameter of a cylinder. 1—Depress the spindle and tighten the lock screw. 2—Place the gauge in the cylinder and release the lock screw. The spindle will spring out to touch walls of the cylinder. 3—Tighten the lock screw. 4—Tilt the gauge handle and remove the gauge. 5—Measure across the spindle faces with an outside micrometer.

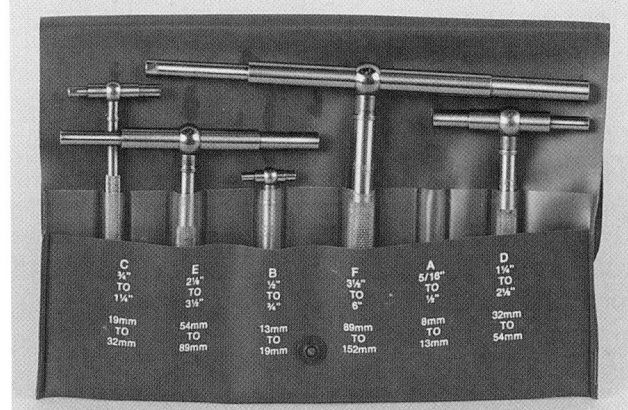

Goodheart-Willcox Publisher

Figure 2-59.

A telescoping gauge set.

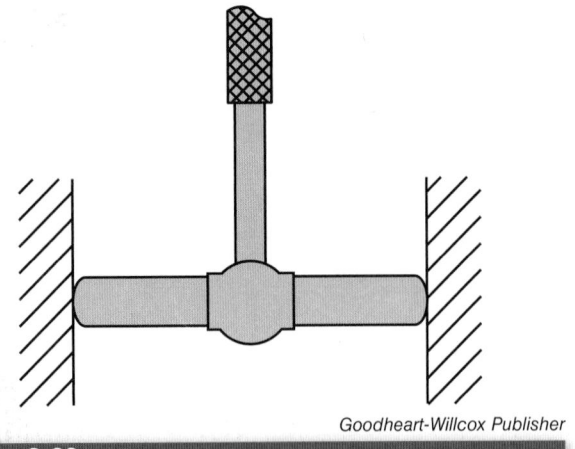

Goodheart-Willcox Publisher

Figure 2-60.

The spindle faces of telescoping gauges are curved so the spindle touches the cylinder at only one point.

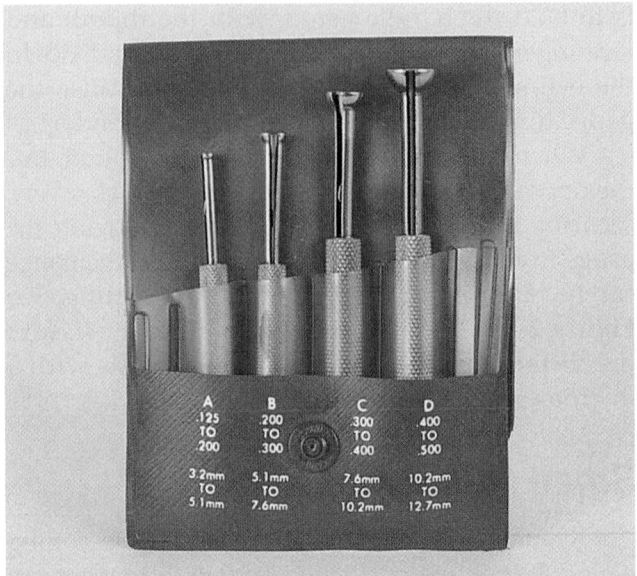

Goodheart-Willcox Publisher

Figure 2-62.

Small hole gauges are used to measure the diameter of holes that are too small for telescoping gauges.

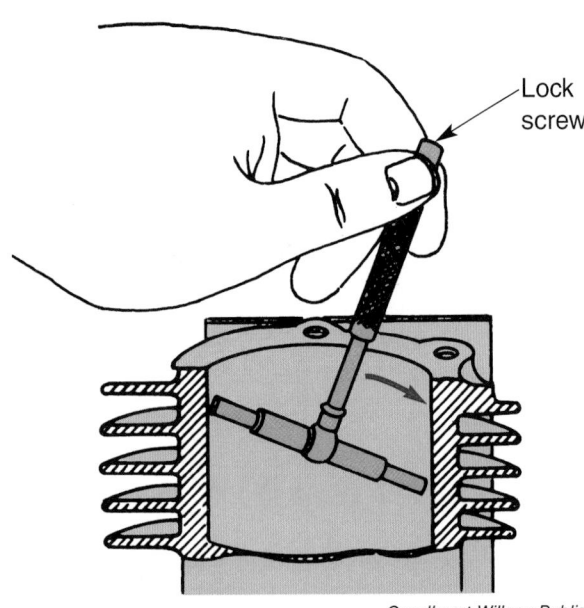

Goodheart-Willcox Publisher

Figure 2-61.

Tilting the telescoping gauge allows easy removal and will not change the position of the spindles.

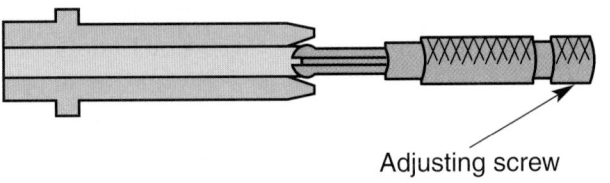

Deere & Co.

Figure 2-63.

A small hole gauge used to measure the inside diameter of a valve guide. Insert the gauge and expand the split ball end by turning the adjusting screw until contact is felt. Move the gauge up and down in the hole as the adjustment is made.

Thickness Gauges

Thickness gauges are sometimes called *feeler gauges* because they rely on the user's sense of feel for accuracy. They are used to measure small spaces and gaps between surfaces. Thickness gauges are used to take measurements such as crankshaft endplay, spark plug gap, and piston ring gap.

Thickness gauges consist of a set of metal leaves that vary in thickness. Each leaf has its decimal and metric thickness etched onto its surface. See

Figure 2-65. Some leaves are as thin as .0005″ and may be damaged if not handled carefully. It is sometimes necessary to select several leaves to equal a desired thickness.

To achieve an accurate reading with a thickness gauge, the leaves must be perfectly clean. Avoid bends and distortions. These conditions will increase the total thickness of the leaves and cause measurement errors.

Leaf-type feeler gauges should not be used to measure spark plug gaps. Instead, wire-type feeler gauges are used. Wire-type feeler gauges consist of a number of wires, each with a specific diameter. See **Figure 2-66**.

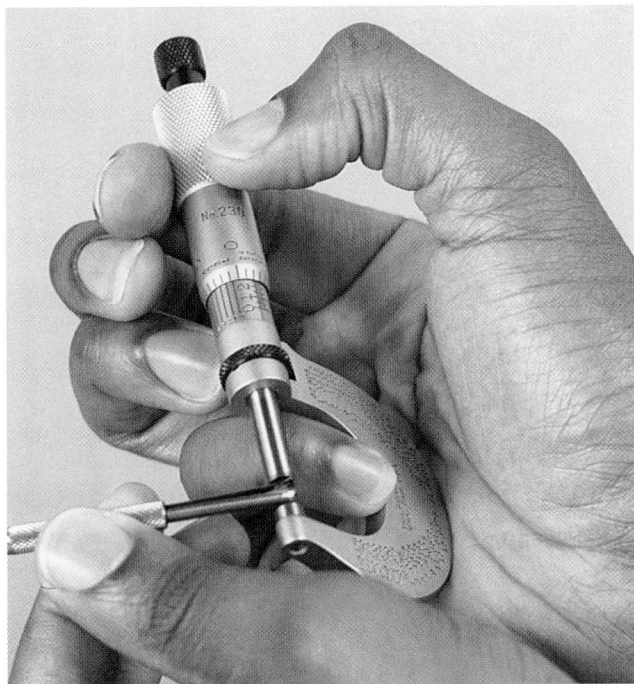

Goodheart-Willcox Publisher

Figure 2-64.

Measuring a small hole gauge with a micrometer.

Combination Square

A combination square has many uses. It is often used to measure the length of valve springs and check them for straightness. See **Figure 2-67**. For accuracy, always place spring and square on a flat, machined surface.

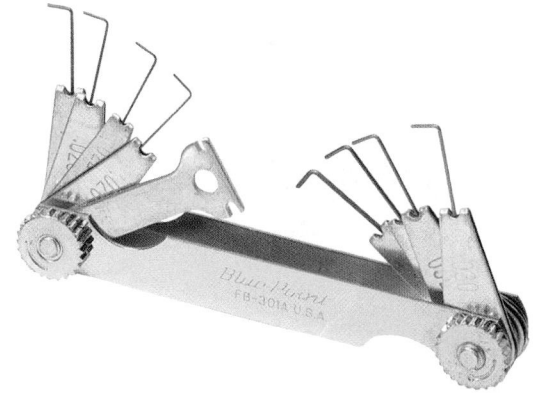

Snap-on Tools Corp.

Figure 2-66.

A set of wire-type feeler gauges. Note that the wire diameter is stamped on each blade.

Dial Indicator

A dial indicator is a precision instrument that is very useful for measuring the movement of various parts. See **Figure 2-68**. It is also used to check for surface irregularities and run-out.

A dial indicator is equipped with a spring-loaded spindle, which is placed against the part to be measured. A needle on the instrument's dial indicates the amount of movement made by the part being tested. The needle rotates over the dial indicator's face, which is calibrated in thousandths

Goodheart-Willcox Publisher

Figure 2-65.

The leaves of a thickness gauge are marked with their exact thickness. When several leaves are used to obtain a desired thickness, each must be flat and clean. Dirty or bent leaves will cause inaccurate readings.

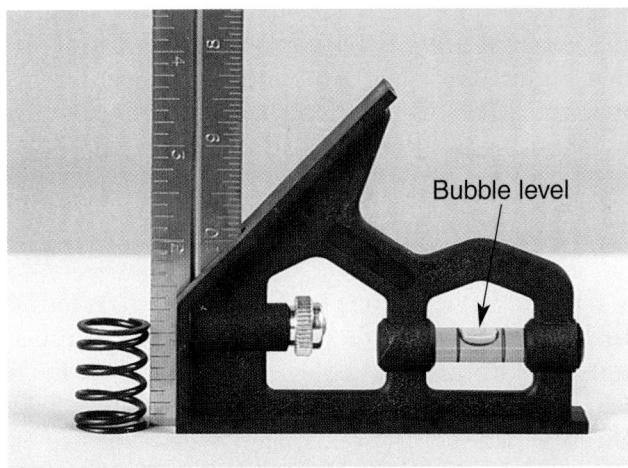

Bubble level

Goodheart-Willcox Publisher

Figure 2-67.

Straightness and length of valve springs can be measured on a flat surface with a combination square. The bubble level is used to check that the base surface is flat and level. The extended base ensures that the measuring scale is not angled or cocked.

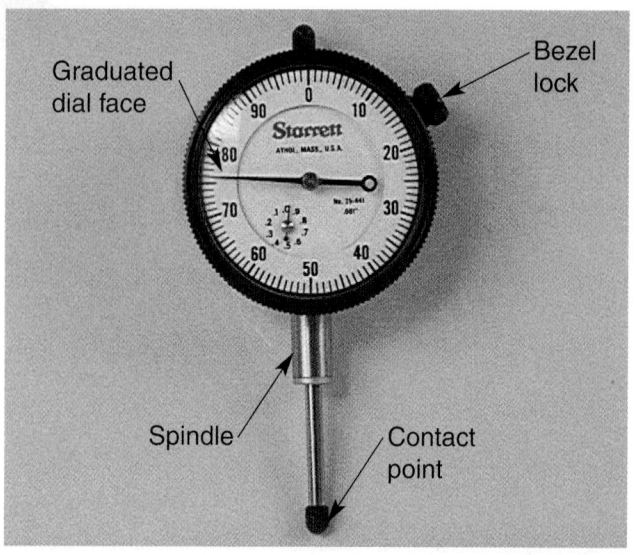

Figure 2-68.

The dial indicator can be used to measure linear movement. Each space on this dial indicator represents one one-thousandth of an inch (.001″).

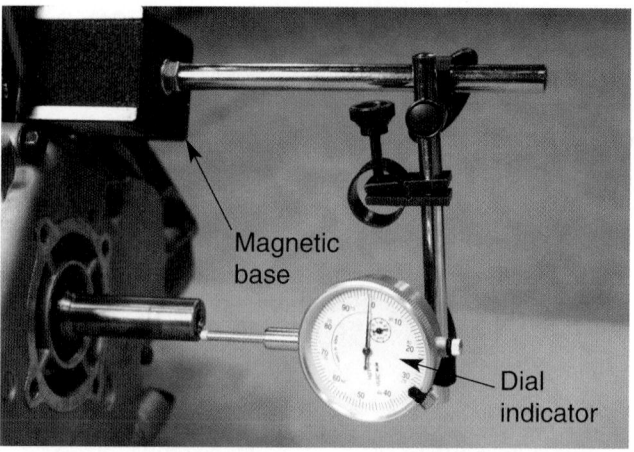

Goodheart-Willcox Publisher

Figure 2-69.

This dial indicator is held in position by a magnetic base.

of an inch, ten-thousandths of an inch, or hundredths of a millimeter. The instrument is set to zero by rotating the indicator's bezel until the zero line on the dial face is located under the needle. The zero line coincides with the initial position of the needle and serves as a reference point when checking for movement.

The dial indicator can be mounted on a variety of devices that are designed to hold it in the desired location. One convenient holding device has a magnetic base that can be turned on and off. See **Figure 2-69**. If the mounting surface is nonmagnetic, however, a clamp-type holding device must be used.

Screw Pitch Gauge

A screw pitch gauge is a tool used to determine the number of threads per inch on bolts, screws, nuts, and in threaded holes. See **Figure 2-70**. Each leaf of the gauge is marked with the number of threads per inch it will match when the leaf is placed onto the screw, bolt, etc. See **Figure 2-71**. Keep trying leaves until one fits exactly into the threads. Read the number on the leaf to determine the number of threads per inch on the item being checked. Screw pitch gauges are available for both standard and metric threads.

Goodheart-Willcox Publisher

Figure 2-70.

A screw pitch gauge has many blades. Each blade is marked with the number of threads per inch or threads per millimeter that it matches.

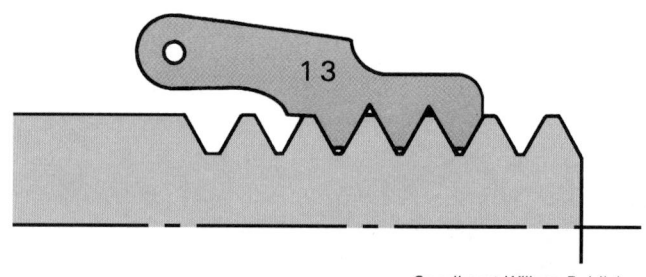

Goodheart-Willcox Publisher

Figure 2-71.

A screw pitch blade matched to the threads of a screw. Threaded bolts must match the threads of a threaded hole to prevent damage. A bolt should never be forced to enter a threaded hole if it will not turn freely.

Summary

A variety of hand tools are necessary for small engine work. These include box-end wrenches, open-end wrenches, combination wrenches, tubing wrenches, adjustable wrenches, Allen wrenches, socket wrenches, and torque wrenches. Pliers are used for gripping, bending, pulling, or cutting. They should never be used for tightening purposes. Several types of screwdrivers are also required for small engine work, including the straight blade screwdriver, the Phillips screwdriver, and the offset screwdriver.

Hammers are used for tapping things into place. Hard-faced hammers have a head that is made of steel. The head on soft-faced hammers is made of lead, copper, brass, leather, wood, or plastic. Soft-faced hammers are used on parts that would be easily damaged by a hard-faced hammer. Punches are used to make depressions in metal surfaces before drilling, to drive pins from holes, and to align holes in mating parts. Seal drivers are used to drive seals squarely into their bores without damaging them.

Many service tasks require the technician to cut or remove metal. Hacksaws are used to cut through metal. Reamers are used to enlarge and smooth bores. Files are used to shave small amounts of metal from a surface. Cold chisels are used to shear bolts, pins, rivets, sheet metal, and other materials.

Other tools commonly used by service technicians include holding fixtures like vises and probe and pickup tools. Probe and pickup tools assist when small items are dropped into areas that cannot be reached with hands and fingers. A machinist's vise is useful for holding parts while they are being worked on. Sheet copper, aluminum, or wood can be used to pad the vise jaws when working on parts that must not be scratched.

Technicians must also use many specialized engine tools when rebuilding and servicing engines. Common engine tools include gear pullers, flywheel holders, ridge reamers, ring spreaders, ring compressors, glaze breakers, cylinder hones, valve spring compressors, lapping sticks, tachometers, spark testers, and compression testers.

Power tools such as electric drills, drill presses, and bench grinders are also commonly used in service work. Electric drills are handheld tools used to bore holes in materials. Specialized bits and accessories can be installed in electric drills so they can be used to perform cleaning, sanding, or grinding functions. Drill presses are stationary machines used to bore holes. Bench grinders are stationary machines that can be equipped with abrasive wheels for grinding operations, wire brushes for cleaning operations, or buffing wheels for polishing.

Technicians must use specialized tools to clean engines and parts both before and during repair procedures. Scrapers are thin blades used to remove old gasket material, carbon buildup, or grime. Plastic or brass scraper blades should be used to clean critical or soft metal parts. Wire brushes are used to remove oxidation or carbon buildup from metal parts. Wooden or plastic toothpicks can be used to clean small passages, like those in carburetors. A cleaning tank is often used to clean small engine parts.

A variety of precision measuring instruments are used to measure engine components to make sure they are not excessively worn. A micrometer is a precision instrument used to measure crankshafts, pistons, and other components. A standard micrometer measures to three decimal places. A metric micrometer measures to the hundredths of a millimeter. Vernier micrometers can be used to obtain readings to four decimal places.

A Vernier caliper is another precision measuring instrument. Vernier calipers are available to measure in either standard or metric units. A Vernier caliper can be used to take both internal and external measurements.

Telescoping gauges are used to transfer dimensions to an outside micrometer. A small hole gauge is used to measure holes that are too small for the telescoping gauge. Thickness gauges, often called feeler gauges, can be leaf-type or wire-type. They are used to measure small spaces and gaps between surfaces. A dial indicator is used to measure the movement of various parts. Many holding devices are available to hold the indicator in the desired location. A screw pitch gauge is used to determine the number of threads on a screw, bolt, or nut. They are available for both standard and metric threads.

Review Questions

Answer the following questions on a separate sheet of paper.

1. What type of wrench is open on one end and boxed on the other?

2. Which kind of wrench should be used only as a last resort if others are not available?

3. To remove a spark plug, what kind of wrench would be best to use to avoid damaging the plug during removal?

4. *True or False?* A torque wrench is used to measure the turning force applied to a threaded fastener.

5. Why must safety glasses be worn when using retaining ring pliers?

6. To locate a position to be drilled, a hammer and a(n) _____ should be used.

7. When using punches and cold chisels, it is very important to make sure the hammered end is not _____.

8. What is the purpose of a ring compressor?

9. A(n) _____ usually consist of a rigid shaft, to which two or three replaceable flat cutting stones are attached.

10. List two common types of engine test instruments.

11. *True or False?* Small drill bits or pieces of wire should be used to clean small passages in carburetors.

12. Name three types of measuring instruments used to determine if engine parts are within manufacturer's tolerance.

13. Each space on the thimble of a standard micrometer represents _____.
    A. .0001"   C. .01"
    B. .001"   D. .1"

14. Each space on the sleeve of a standard micrometer represents what part of an inch?
    A. .0025"   C. .050"
    B. .100"   D. .025"

15. The discrimination of a Vernier micrometer is _____.
    A. .01"   C. .0001"
    B. .001"   D. .000001"

16. A telescoping gauge is used for measuring _____.
    A. inside diameters
    B. outside diameters
    C. depths of cylinders
    D. valve angles

17. A telescoping gauge is used to transfer inside dimensions to an outside _____.

18. Which measuring instrument is similar to the telescoping gauge?

19. Dial indicators are used to check for _____, _____, _____ or _____.

20. An instrument called a(n) _____ is used to determine the number of threads per inch on bolts or nuts.

Suggested Activities

1. Identify the various types of wrenches, pliers, punches, chisels, screwdrivers, and other tools in your shop.

2. Demonstrate the proper way to use wrenches, chisels, screwdrivers, pliers, punches, and other tools in your shop.

3. Clean the anvil and spindle of a micrometer and check its calibration accuracy.

4. Practice measuring engine parts with a standard outside micrometer.

5. Practice measuring engine parts with a Vernier micrometer.

6. Measure a cylinder bore with a telescoping gauge and outside micrometer.

7. Measure a valve guide bore with a small hole gauge and outside micrometer.

8. Check the straightness and length of a small engine valve spring. Does it meet the manufacturer's specifications?

9. Check ring groove and piston ring clearance with a thickness gauge.

10. Check ring end clearance in a cylinder with a thickness gauge.

11. Check the thread pitch of several different size bolts or several different size screws with a screw pitch gauge.

12. Measure the endplay of a crankshaft with a dial indicator.

C H A P T E R 3

Fasteners, Sealants, and Gaskets

Learning Objectives

After studying this chapter, you will be able to:

- Identify fasteners used on small gas engines and implements.
- Remove and install various fasteners correctly.
- Repair or produce internal and external threads.
- Properly select and install fasteners.
- Remove, select, and install gaskets correctly.

Key Terms

acorn nuts
anaerobic sealants
antiseize compounds
bolt grades
bolt head size
bolt length
bolts
bolt size
cap screws
castle nut
die stock
flat washers
form-in-place sealants
gaskets
hexagon nuts
jam nut
kantlink washer
keys
lock nuts
lock washers
machine screws
metric (M) series
pins
retaining rings

room temperature
  vulcanizing sealant
  (RTV)
screws
self-tapping screws
set screws
square nuts
taper tap
tapping
tensile strength
thread
threading
thread length
thread pitch
through hole
toothed washers
Unified National
  Coarse (UNC) series
Unified National Fine
  (UNF) series
wide bearing lock
  washer
wing nuts

Threaded Fasteners

Small gas engines and the implements they power are held together by fasteners. There are many kinds of fasteners. See **Figure 3-1**. Some are common and others are designed to perform special functions. During engine operation, these fasteners may be exposed to conditions such as heating and cooling, cyclic loading, tensile and shearing loads, corrosion, and vibration.

Typical threaded fasteners include screws, bolts, and nuts. The helical portion of a screw or bolt, or the helical portion in the hole or nut that it fastens to, is called a *thread*. A thread is an inclined plane that circles the cylindrical bolt or hole. See **Figure 3-2**. The incline of the bolt or screw thread must be the same as the incline of the thread in the nut or threaded hole into which it is placed. The tightness (tension) of threaded fasteners is very important and will be discussed in the *Torque* section of this chapter.

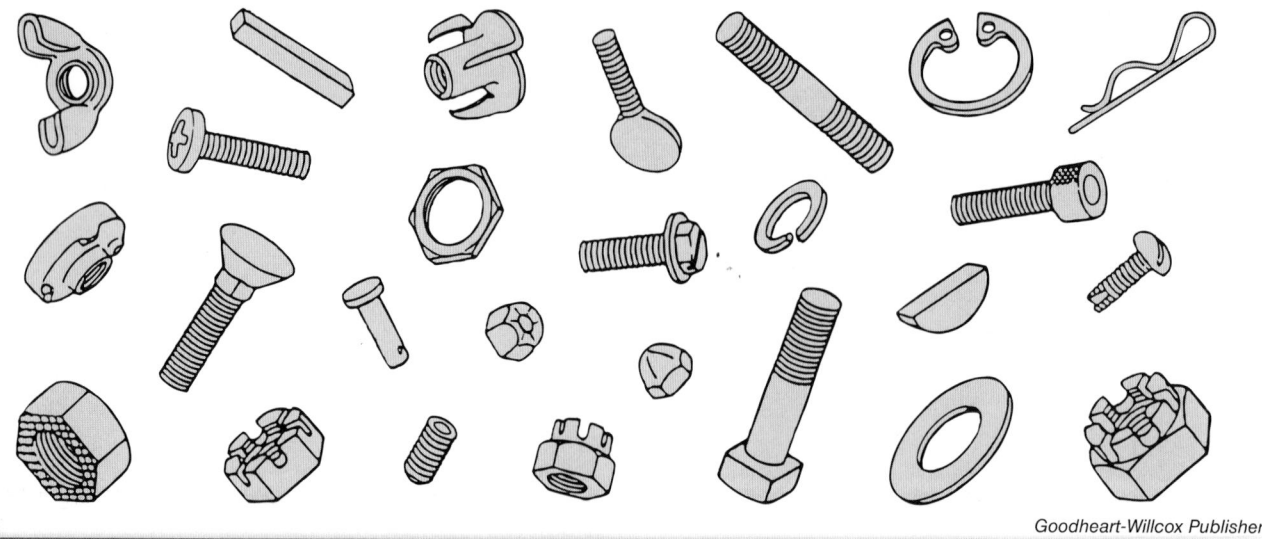

Goodheart-Willcox Publisher

Figure 3-1.

There are many kinds of fasteners used to hold parts together.

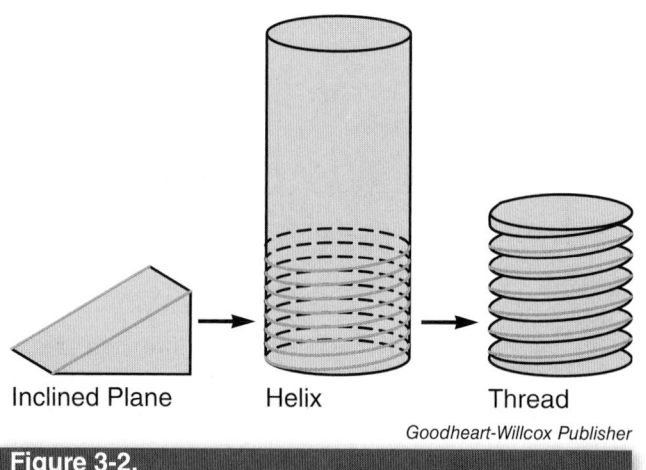

Inclined Plane   Helix   Thread

Goodheart-Willcox Publisher

Figure 3-2.

A thread is an inclined plane wrapped around a cylinder and is called a helix.

Note

When disassembling an engine, note the location of all parts, fasteners, and washers. Care should be taken during this process so that the parts, fasteners, and washers are put back in the correct locations during reassembly. When fasteners are badly damaged or worn, replace them with new ones. Lightly rusted fasteners should be cleaned with a wire brush or wire wheel and examined for damage.

Bolts

Bolts are threaded fasteners that hold parts together by squeezing them between the head on one end and a nut on the other end. See **Figure 3-3**. The hole the bolt passes through is not threaded. There should be a small amount of clearance between the bolt and the hole so the bolt does not have to be driven through the hole.

Some bolts have an unthreaded portion near the head. The unthreaded portion, or shank, of a bolt should pass through all of the top part

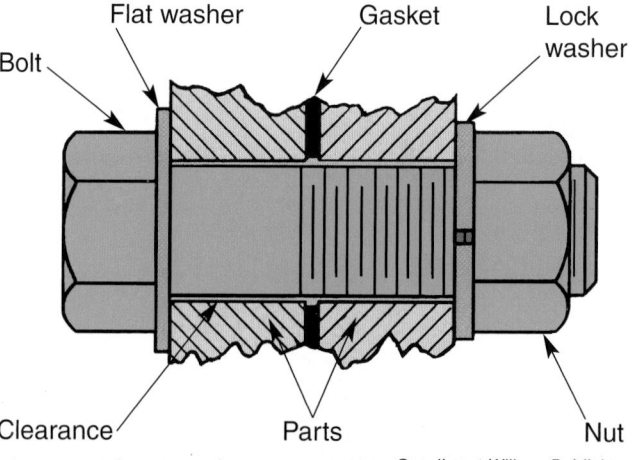

Flat washer   Gasket   Lock washer

Bolt

Clearance   Parts   Nut

Goodheart-Willcox Publisher

Figure 3-3.

A bolt and nut apply great clamping force. Washers are used with nuts and bolts. Note the gasket between parts.

and partially through the second component. See **Figure 3-4**.

A lock washer is often placed between the face of the nut and the part surface to prevent loosening caused by vibration. A flat washer is often used to provide a smooth and larger clamping surface. This is often necessary when fastening soft materials such as aluminum, plastic, or wood. Washers are covered in detail later in this chapter.

After being tightened, a bolt should be long enough to pass through the parts, any washers, and the nut, and protrude 1 1/2 –2 threads beyond the nut.

Nuts

Nuts vary in shape and size depending on their intended function. Plain *hexagon nuts* are most common type. These nuts have six vertical sides and can be loosened or tightened with standard sockets and box-end wrenches. Other types of nuts used include square nuts, jam nuts, castle nuts, acorn nuts, wing nuts, and various lock nuts. See **Figure 3-5**.

Square nuts are not commonly used, but can be found on old implements. A *jam nut* is used in conjunction with a plain hexagon nut. The jam nut is a thinner nut used with a plain nut to produce a locking condition of one nut tightening against the other. See **Figure 3-6**.

The *castle nut* is used on bolts that have a drilled hole through the threaded end. A cotter pin

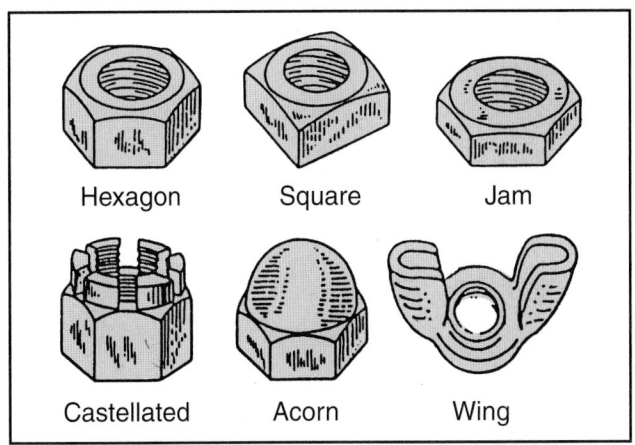

Goodheart-Willcox Publisher

Figure 3-5.

Various kinds of nuts apply clamping pressure on bolts.

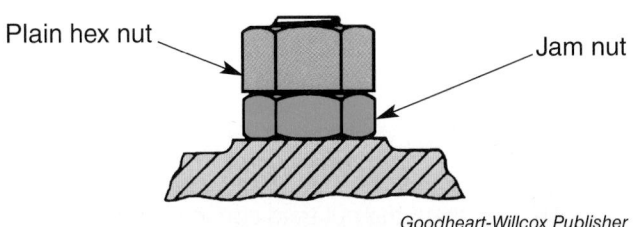

Goodheart-Willcox Publisher

Figure 3-6.

Two nuts can be used to prevent loosening of the bolt.

is used to prevent the castle nut from turning. Cotter pins should always be installed properly as shown in **Figure 3-7**. Castle nuts are used on bolts or shafts when a component turns or pivots on it. They are also used when axial clearance is required, such as with axle shafts having tapered roller or ball bearings. Proper adjustment is obtained by turning the nut until it makes light contact against the shoulder or flat washer. Back the nut off one slot aligning with the cotter pin hole. Install the cotter pin. Remember, coarse series threads will give greater axial clearance than the fine series threads.

Acorn nuts are used to tighten and also cover the sharp thread end of a bolt for safety. It is important when using acorn nuts to be certain that the bolt end does not bottom in the nut before it tightens. Acorn nuts get their name from their likeness in shape to oak tree acorns and are often used to provide a smooth, neat appearance.

Wing nuts are used when something needs to be frequently adjusted and can be tightened or loosened by hand. *Lock nuts* are designed to create friction to reduce the tendency for vibration or

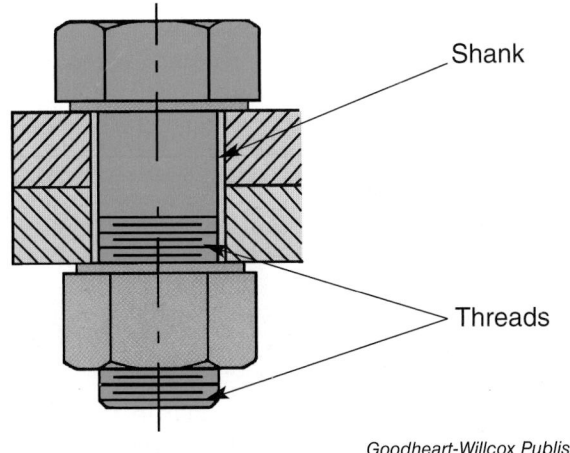

Goodheart-Willcox Publisher

Figure 3-4.

The unthreaded portion, or shank, of a bolt should pass through all of the top part and partially through the second component.

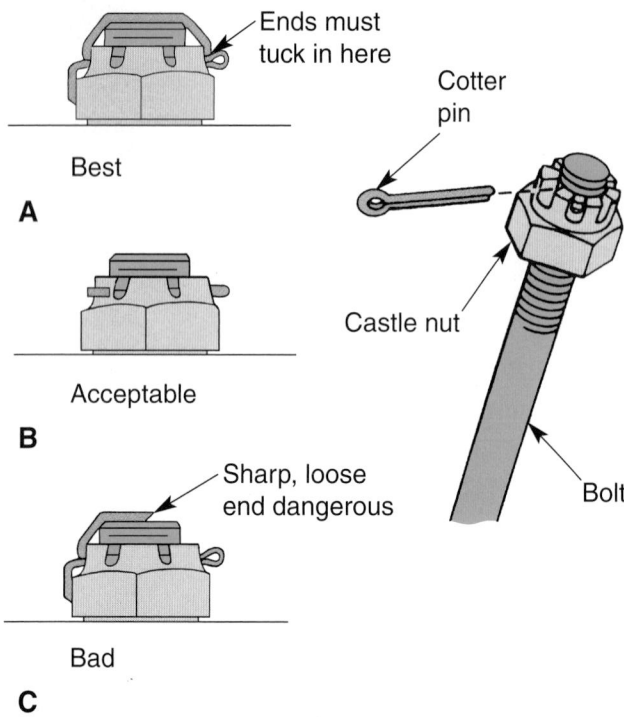

Ends must tuck in here

Best

A

Acceptable

B

Sharp, loose end dangerous

Bad

C

Cotter pin

Castle nut

Bolt

Goodheart-Willcox Publisher

Figure 3-7.

A cotter pin is placed through the castle nut and bolt hole to prevent the nut from coming off the bolt. Installation method A or B is acceptable. Method A is more difficult to produce, but eliminates sharp ends.

motion to rotate and loosen the nut. **Figure 3-8** illustrates some lock nuts.

Bolt and Nut Terminology

Bolts and nuts come in various sizes (lengths, diameters, and head size), grades (strengths), and thread types. Being familiar with these differences is important when the need arises to replace nuts and bolts. Important bolt dimensions are:

- *Bolt size*—The major (largest) diameter of the bolt threads.
- *Bolt head size*—The dimension across the flats of the hexagon. It is the same as the wrench size.
- *Bolt length*—The distance from the base of the bolt head to the threaded end of the bolt.
- *Thread pitch*—The number of threads per inch on U.S. customary fasteners. On metric fasteners it is the distance between each thread measured in millimeters.
- *Thread length*—The length of the portion of the fastener with threads.

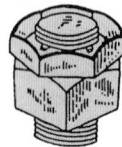
Palnut
A single-thread lock nut applied and tightened after the regular nut is in place

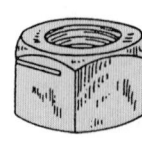
Self-retaining
Threads in the section above the slot are deformed to provide a friction grip

Anco
A pin impinges against the bolt to hold the nut in place

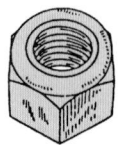
Esna
A fiber collar grips the bolt threads. Also available with a metallic collar

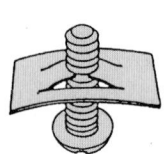
Tinnerman Speed Nut

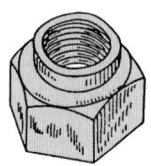
Lamson
The raised crown is distorted and heat-treated to give a spring grip on the bolt threads

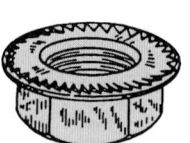
Spin-lock
Ratchet-shaped, serrated teeth embedded in the work provide a friction grip

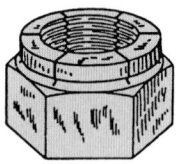
Flexloc
Segments press against the bolt threads because the inner diameter of the upper part is slightly less than the outside diameter of the bolt

Goodheart-Willcox Publisher

Figure 3-8.

Examples of common lock nuts.

Bolt Grades

Bolt grades are related to the minimum tensile strength specification of the bolt. *Tensile strength* is the amount of tension, or pulling, force a fastener can withstand before failing. **Figure 3-9** shows the tensile strength of various fasteners in pounds per square inch (psi).

SAE Standard/Foot-Pounds							Metric Standard					
Grade of Bolt	SAE 1 & 2	SAE 5	SAE 6	SAE 8			Grade of Bolt	5D	.8G	10K	12K	
Min. Ten. Strength	64,000 P.S.I.	105,000 P.S.I.	133,000 P.S.I.	150,000 P.S.I.			Min. Ten. Strength	71,160 P.S.I.	113,800 P.S.I.	142,200 P.S.I.	170,679 P.S.I.	
Markings on Head	⬢	◆	⬢	✳	Size of Socket or Wrench Opening		Markings on Head	5D	.8G	10K	12K	Size of Socket or Wrench Opening
U.S. Standard	Foot Pounds				U.S. Regular (in.)		Metric	Foot Pounds				Metric
Bolt Dia. (in.)					Bolt Head	Nut	Bolt Dia.	U.S. Dec. Equiv.					Bolt Head
1/4	5	7	10	10.5	3/8	7/16	6mm	.2362	5	6	8	10	10mm
5/16	9	14	19	22	1/2	9/16	8mm	.3150	10	16	22	27	14mm
3/8	15	25	34	37	9/16	5/8	10mm	.3937	19	31	40	49	17mm
7/16	24	40	55	60	5/8	3/4	12mm	.4720	34	54	70	86	19mm
1/2	37	60	85	92	3/4	13/16	14mm	.5512	55	89	117	137	22mm
9/16	53	88	120	132	7/8	7/8	16mm	.6299	83	132	175	208	24mm
5/8	74	120	167	180	15/16	1	18mm	.7090	111	182	236	283	27mm
3/4	120	200	280	296	1-1/8	1-1/8	22mm	.8661	182	284	394	464	32mm

Goodheart-Willcox Publisher

Figure 3-9.

General bolt torque chart. Torque values increase as bolt size and grade increases.

Bolt heads are often marked with a symbol indicating the grade of the bolt. For example, an SAE Grade 5 bolt has three marks on the head. A Grade 6 bolt has four marks on the head. In every case, the number of marks on the head is 2 less than the grade number. Grade 1 and 2 bolts have no marks on the head. Metric bolt heads are marked with 5D, 8G, 10K, 12K. See **Figure 3-9** for corresponding tensile strengths.

Note

The torque specifications listed in **Figure 3-9** are approximate guidelines only and may vary depending on conditions, such as amount and type of lubricant, type of plating on bolt, etc.

It should be understood that the load applied to the bolt due to tightening (primary load) coupled with the external (secondary) load exerted upon it could exceed the tensile limits of the bolt. An external load could be applied as a result of pulling, lifting a load, and/or heat expansion.

When a bolt reaches its load bearing limit it becomes weaker, exceeds its elastic limit, and begins to stretch plastically. When a bolt stretches plastically it does not return to its original length or shape when the load is released. A bolt that has been stretched may appear to be loose or show signs of leakage at a gasket. Unknowingly, one might try to retighten the bolt. This stretches it, weakens it more, and will result in the bolt failing in service or breaking during the tightening.

Thread Types

Figure 3-10 illustrates various parts of a thread. There are several types, or series, of threads of commercial importance. Only three are of significance for the purpose of this text. The first type is the *Unified National Coarse (UNC) series*. Fasteners with UNC threads are for general use where they are not subjected to vibration.

The second type is the *Unified National Fine (UNF) series*. Fasteners with UNF threads are for work where vibration is a considerable factor, such as automotive and aircraft applications.

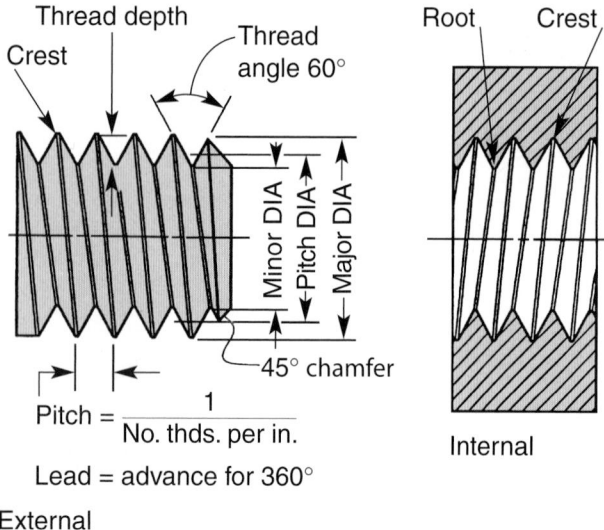

Pitch = $\dfrac{1}{\text{No. thds. per in.}}$

Lead = advance for 360°

Goodheart-Willcox Publisher

Figure 3-10.

Thread terminology for external and internal threads.

UNC and UNF refer to the number of threads per inch of length on threaded fasteners. Every bolt or nut diameter will have a specific number of threads per inch of length. For example, a 1/2″ diameter Unified National Coarse bolt or nut will always have 13 threads per inch of length. A Unified National Fine thread of the same diameter will always have 20 threads per inch. The diameter referred to in the thread specification is always the major (largest) diameter of the thread of the bolt or nut.

The third type is the *metric (M) series*. The metric thread is formed with a 60° angle, which is similar to the unified threads. The International Standards Organization (ISO) has attempted to standardize metric threads. The ISO metric thread series has 25 thread diameters ranging from 1.6 millimeters (mm) to 100mm.

Threads are either right-handed or left-handed. A fastener with right-handed threads must be turned clockwise to tighten it. A fastener with left-handed threads must be turned counterclockwise to tighten it. The letter *L* may be stamped on the fastener with left-handed threads.

Caution

The thread of a nut or threaded hole must always be the same series, size, and type as that of the bolt or screw entering it. If they are not the same, thread stripping or damage will occur.

Thread Fit

Some fastener applications can tolerate loose fitting threads. Other applications may require closer fitting, or tight threads. For example, the head on a gasoline engine may be held to the engine block with stud bolts, which are threaded on both ends. See **Figure 3-11**. One end of the stud bolt is threaded into the engine block. The other end receives a nut that tightens against the cylinder head. It is desirable to have the stud bolt remain in the engine block when the nut is removed. The block end requires a tighter fitting thread than the nut end. If the fit of the nut is too tight, the entire stud may be removed from the block when the nut is turned with a wrench. In some cases, a UNF thread is used in the block and a UNC thread on the nut end.

Unified threads are classified as external or internal, and according to classification of fit as follows:

- Class 1 Fit—Has the largest manufacturing tolerance. Used where ease of assembly is desired and a loose thread is not objectionable.

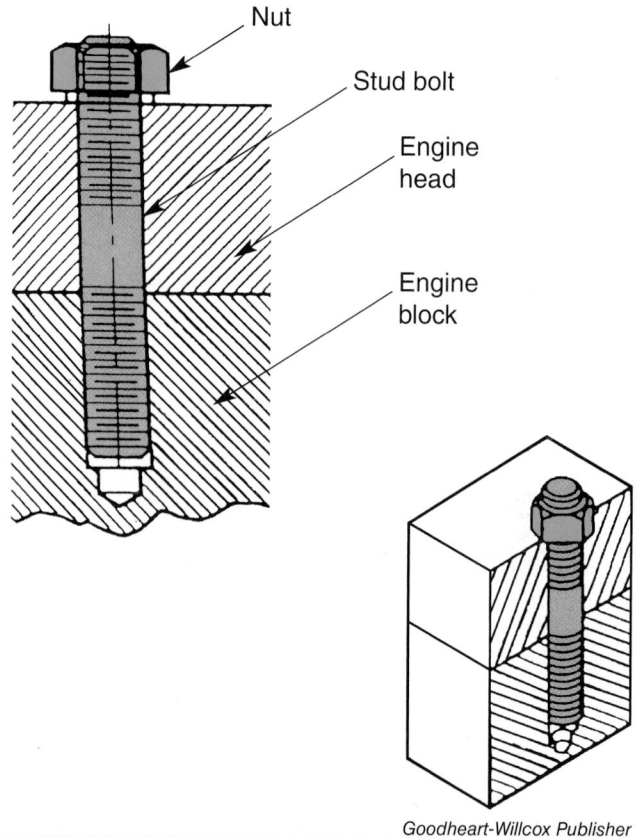

Goodheart-Willcox Publisher

Figure 3-11.

Stud bolts are threaded at both ends.

- Class 2 Fit—Used on the largest percentage of threaded fasteners.
- Class 3 Fit—Will be tight when assembled.

Thread Designations

The thread designation is a series of numbers and letters used to describe a bolt and thread. For example, the designation of *1/2-13 UNC-2A × 1* is defined as follows:

- *1/2*—Indicates the thread diameter. In this case, the diameter is 1/2″.
- *13*—Indicates the threads per inch. In this case, there are 13.
- *UNC*—Indicates the series of thread. In this case, it is a Unified National Coarse thread. The letters *UNF* specify a Unified National Fine thread.
- *2*—Indicates the class of fit. In this case, a **2** indicates a class 2 fit. The number **1** specifies a class 1 fit and **3** specifies a class 3 fit.
- *A*—Indicates that it is an external or internal thread. In this case, an **A** indicates an external thread. The letter **B** would indicate an internal thread, such as a nut or threaded hole.
- *1*—This number indicates the length of the fastener in inches. In this case, the fastener is 1″ long.

A letter *L* at the far right of thread designation indicates left-handed threads. For example, 1/4-20 UNC-2A L is a left-handed thread. If the L is not present, the thread is understood to be right-handed.

Metric thread designations are slightly different. For example, the metric designation of *M-10 × 1.5 × 25* is defined as follows:

- *M*—Indicates that the thread is metric.
- *10*—Indicates the diameter of the thread in millimeters. In this case, the diameter is 10mm.
- *1.5*—Indicates the distance between threads (pitch). In this case, the pitch is 1.5mm.
- *25*—Indicates the length of the fastener in millimeters. In this case, the length is 25mm.

Screws

Screws are threaded fasteners that hold parts together by passing through one part and threading into another. See **Figure 3-12**. The screws most commonly used in small engines and related implements have hexagonal heads that allow the use of hexagonal sockets and box wrenches for

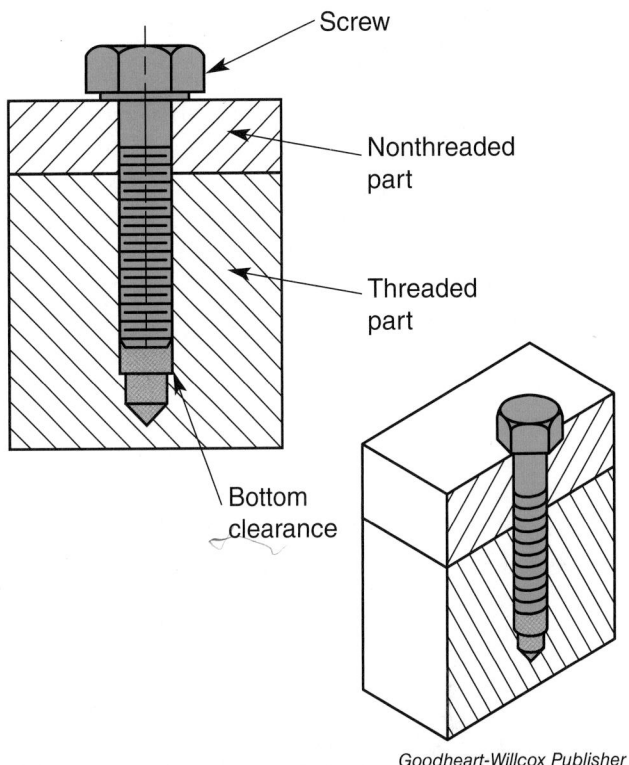

Goodheart-Willcox Publisher

Figure 3-12.

This screw passes through one part and threads into the mating part. Note the clearance at the bottom of the hole.

tightening and loosening. Screws with round heads require an appropriate screwdriver or Allen wrench to turn them.

The most common screw heads are shown in **Figure 3-13**. Notice that each head has a particular name that identifies the head type. Screws may be threaded all the way to the head.

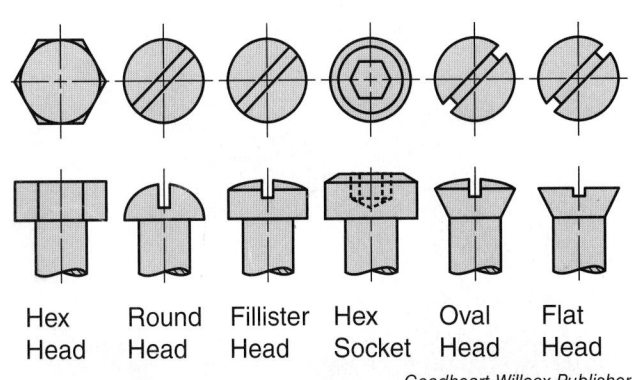

Hex Head   Round Head   Fillister Head   Hex Socket   Oval Head   Flat Head

Goodheart-Willcox Publisher

Figure 3-13.

Common types of screw heads.

Machine screws are externally threaded fasteners that are used in threaded holes, but they are also used with a nut. Most machine screws have round heads that accept a screwdriver or Allen wrench. *Cap screws* are similar to machine screws but they often have hexagonal heads. These screws are similar to bolts, but they are smaller in diameter and are often manufactured to tighter tolerances.

Set screws are heat-treated, hardened alloy steel fasteners that are used to secure rotating components, such things as pulleys and shafts, in relation to each other. See **Figure 3-14**. The common set screw head types are square, slotted hexagon socket, and fluted socket. The set screw points may be flat, cup, cone, half dog, or full dog. See **Figure 3-15**. Flat points are used when clamping friction alone is enough to hold the part without deforming its surface. Cup and cone point set screws cut into the surface of the shaft or part to

prevent motion or rotation. Dog point set screws are designed to positively lock into a predrilled hole in a shaft matching the diameter of the dog. See **Figure 3-16**.

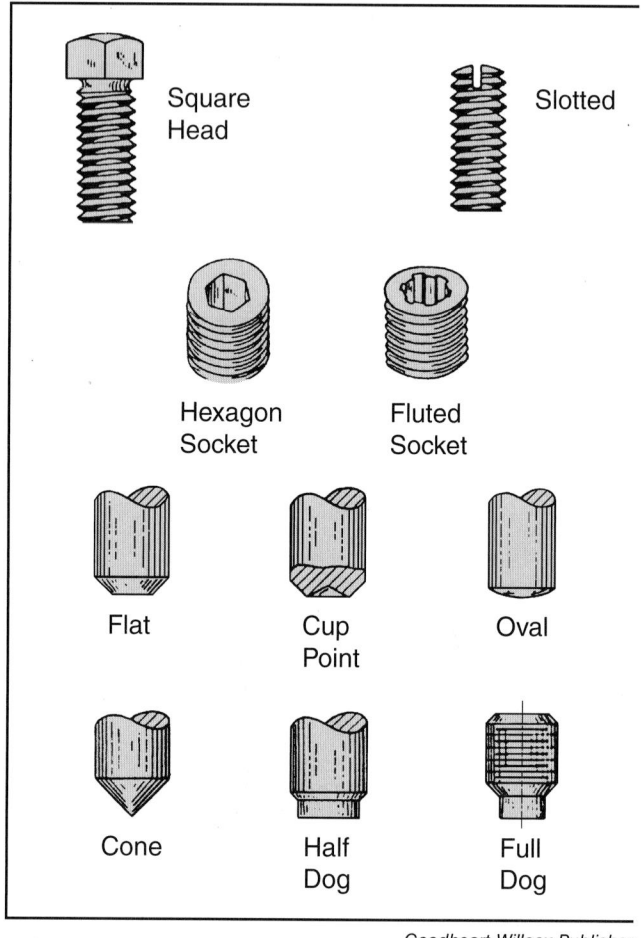

Goodheart-Willcox Publisher

Figure 3-15.

Common types of set screw heads and points. Set screws are made of hardened steel.

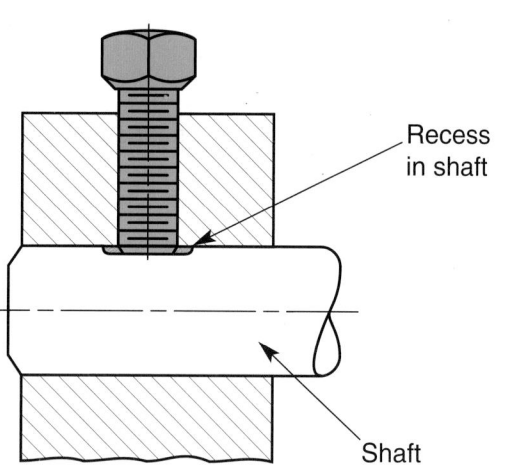

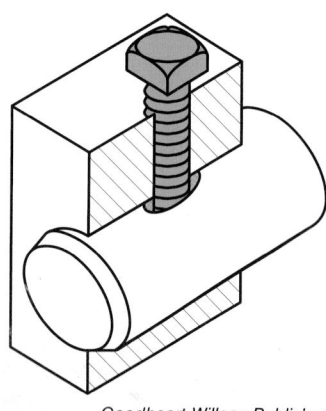

Goodheart-Willcox Publisher

Figure 3-14.

Set screws lock pulleys and gears to shafts to prevent rotation of the shaft in the hole. Note the recessed area on the shaft.

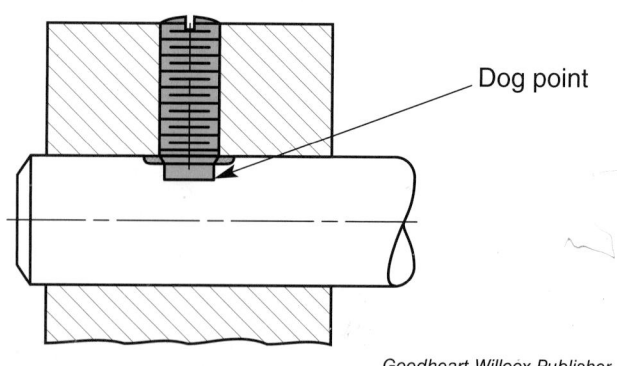

Goodheart-Willcox Publisher

Figure 3-16.

The dog point of this screw fits in a hole in the shaft.

A variety of *self-tapping screws* are shown in **Figure 3-17**. Self-tapping screws are fasteners that will cut their own threads in a predrilled hole of the appropriate size. Self-tapping screws have a grooved, tapered point that forms threads in the hole. Self-tapping screws are hardened steel because they perform as a cutting tool as well as a fastener.

Tightening and Loosening Threaded Fasteners

As previously mentioned, if a bolt, nut, or screw has right-handed threads, the direction for tightening is always clockwise and the direction for loosening is always counterclockwise. For beginners, this can be particularly difficult to understand if the bolt, nut, or screw is in the inverted (upside-down) position on an engine or implement. If the technician is not careful, the head of the fastener may be twisted off by attempting to turn it the wrong direction.

Tightening to Specific Torque Settings

Tightening bolts, nuts, and screws on engines should be done with a torque wrench. These fasteners should be tightened to specific torque (turning effort) settings. See torque charts for fractional and metric size bolts in **Figure 3-9**.

Removing Stubborn Fasteners

From time to time, you will encounter a threaded fastener that is difficult to remove. There are several methods of removing stuck fasteners.

In some cases, simply tapping the head of the fastener with a hammer will loosen the rust or corrosion between the threads, allowing the fastener to be removed. Be careful to strike the head of the fastener squarely, so you don't cause damage that would prevent removal. Never strike the threaded end of the faster, as this will distort the threads, making fastener removal even more difficult.

Another way to help free a stubborn fastener is to soak it with penetrating oil. Penetrating oil is a low-viscosity (very thin) oil designed to seep down between the treads on the fastener and the mating part, dissolving rust and corrosion and reducing tension holding the bolt in place. Allow the penetrating oil to work for several minutes before trying to remove the fastener. For extremely rusted or corroded fasteners, it is recommended that the penetrating oil be allowed to work for several hours (preferably overnight).

Heat can also be used to help free a stubborn fastener. Heating the area around the bolt will cause it to expand. If a nut is used, heat the nut rather than the bolt. Exercise caution when using heat so you do not damage nearby parts.

 For fastening all types and thickness of metal.

 For plastics. Note double slot.

 For metals and plastics. Note multiple slots.

 For plastics. Has coarse lead.

 For metals. Forms, rather than cuts, threads.

 For sheet metal up to 18 gage, plywood, asbestos, and composition materials.

 For sheet metal up to 6 gage, nonferrous castings, plastics, plywood, asbestos, and composition materials.

 For heavy gage sheet metal, castings, structural steel, plastics, and plywood.

Goodheart-Willcox Publisher

Figure 3-17.

Self-tapping screws cut, or form, their own threads.

In some cases, you can use a combination of these methods to remove extremely stubborn fasteners. For example, you may find that alternating between spraying the fastener with penetrating oil and tapping it with a hammer will do the trick.

Note

A breaker bar or an impact wrench can be used to help remove stubborn threaded fasteners. Caution must be exercised when using these tools to avoid damaging or breaking the fastener.

Removing Broken Fasteners

Occasionally, a bolt will break off during removal or installation. When this happens, the broken portion of the fastener that remains in the hole must be removed. If the broken fastener protrudes from the hole, it can sometimes be removed using vise grips or a small pipe wrench. In some cases, a bolt that breaks off flush with the hole can be backed out of the hole by driving it counterclockwise using a hammer and a small punch.

Fasteners that break off even with or below the surface of the hole are commonly removed using a screw extractor. Before the extractor is used, a hole approximately one-half the diameter of the bolt is drilled at the top center of the broken fastener. The extractor, which has many spirals, is then tapped into the hole with a hammer. The spirals on the extractor cause it to wedge tightly in the bolt. A wrench or socket is then applied to the hex head of the extractor and the broken bolt is backed out. See **Figure 3-18**.

Chasing Threads

When threads become damaged in a nut or threaded hole, it may be necessary to recut the threads with a tool called a threading tap. See **Figure 3-19**. This procedure is called chasing the thread. If the hole goes all the way through, it is called a *through hole*. The threaded hole in a nut is an example of a through hole. In the case of a nut, select a tap designated to fit the existing thread. If the existing thread is 1/2-13 UNC, then select a tap designated 1/2-13 UNC. This designation will be stamped on the tap shank of the tap.

For a through hole, a taper tap should be used. A *taper tap* has a slender taper at the beginning of the tap that makes it start easier in the threads. Select a tap wrench to turn the tap. Secure the

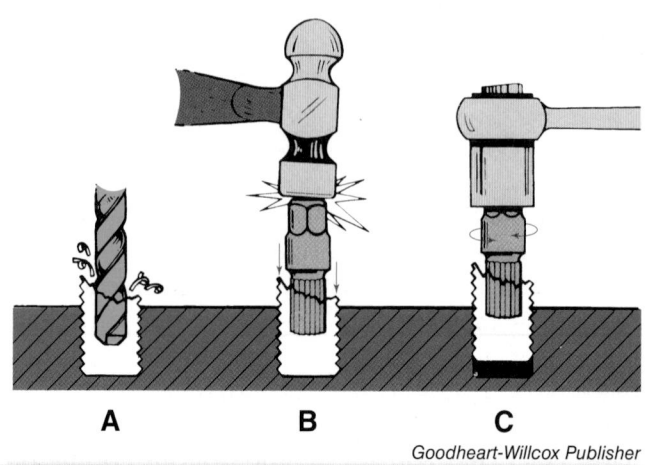

Goodheart-Willcox Publisher

Figure 3-18.

Removing a broken bolt. A—Drill a hole in the center of the broken bolt. B—Use a hammer to tap the extractor into the drilled hole. C—Use a wrench to turn the extractor. This will back the broken bolt out of the hole.

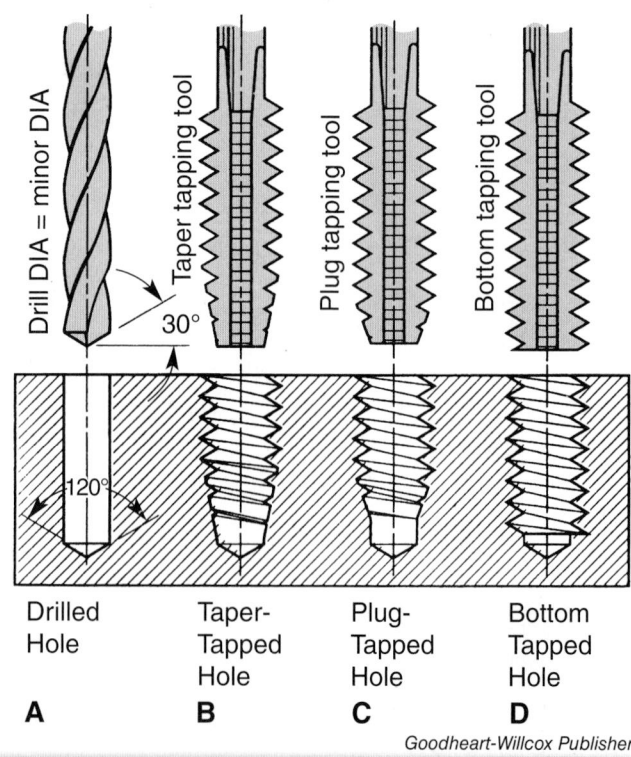

Goodheart-Willcox Publisher

Figure 3-19.

Taps are tools for cutting threads in holes. For blind holes, the taper tap should be used first, followed by the plug tap, and then the bottom tap.

square end of the tap in the wrench. You must decide whether the part can be secured in a vise or whether it can be done in place. A small item can be clamped in a vise to hold it. See **Figure 3-20**. Add a few drops of cutting oil on the tap before beginning. This will improve the cutting action and produce better threads. Align the tap with the hole and turn it clockwise (right-handed threads) until the tap turns freely. Then, reverse the rotation until the tap can be removed.

If bolt or screw threads are damaged, they can be chased with a threading die held in a die holder. Place the bolt head in a vise. Select the correct die that corresponds to the thread of the bolt. If the thread type is not known, determine it by measuring the major diameter of the thread, and counting the number of threads per lineal inch. If the bolt diameter is 3/8″ and there are 16 threads per inch, it is a 3/8-16 UNC thread. Select a corresponding die. Now, place the die in a die handle and secure it with the set screws. See **Figure 3-21**. The correct side of the die must face the threads when starting the die. The correct side has tapered teeth near the edge of the die. Using the correct side of the die makes starting easier and places the cutting edges of the teeth cut in the proper direction. Place some cutting oil on the die teeth and on the bolt threads. Place the die on the end of the bolt and begin turning

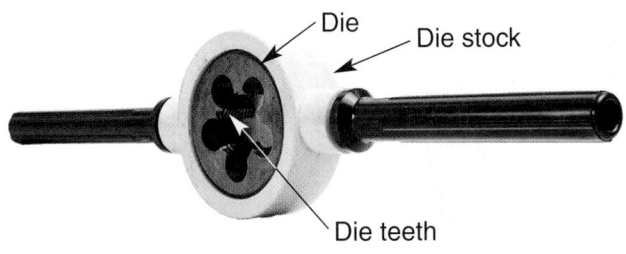

Die / Die stock / Die teeth

Fotos593/Shutterstock.com

Figure 3-21.

Threading dies are used to cut external threads. The die is inserted in a wrench called a die stock. The conical teeth of the die should be started on the rod or bolt.

it clockwise (right-handed threads) to cut and correct the threads. Now, reverse the die rotation until it can be removed from the bolt.

Internal Thread Repair

When internal threads are damaged, they can often be repaired using a tap. If the threads are severely damaged, other repair methods can be used. One method involves drilling out the old threads and tapping the hole to a larger thread size.

Another method involves using a patented helical insert to form new threads. First, the damaged threads are drilled out of the hole. Then the hole is tapped to accept the insert. Finally, the insert is installed in the tapped hole, restoring the threaded hole to its original size and condition. See **Figure 3-22**.

Tapping New Threads

Tapping is the process of cutting threads in a hole. The procedure of tapping new threads is similar to that of chasing threads. Prior to tapping, however, a new hole must be drilled to the proper diameter. The proper diameter is obtained using an appropriate tap drill chart. Tap drill charts for both standard and metric taps are included in the appendix of this textbook.

Rules for Hand Tapping

The following rules should be followed when tapping new threads.
- Use a good cutting fluid, except when tapping gray cast iron, which should be tapped dry.
- For through holes, start and end with a taper tap.

Keep tap square with hole / Tap wrench / Tap / Use lubrication when required

smuay/Shutterstock.com

Figure 3-20.

Taps fit into a special tap wrench. The tap must be held straight with the hole as it is turned into the work. Turn the wrench clockwise 2/3 of one turn, back it up 1/3 of one turn, and repeat the process. Use cutting fluid on the tap.

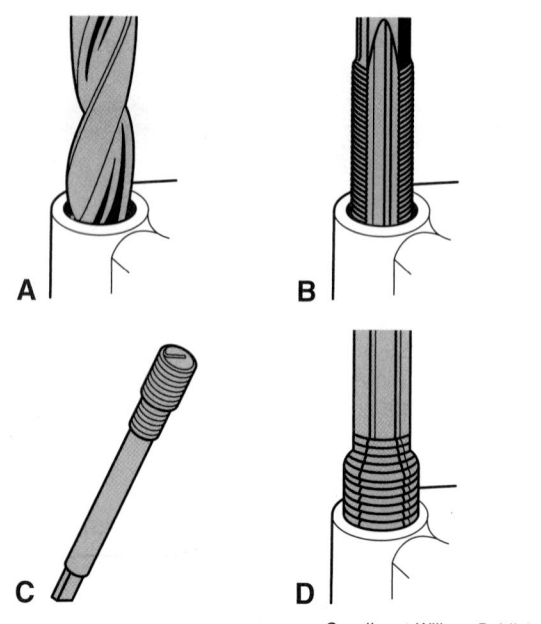

Figure 3-22.

Repairing damaged threads using a helical insert.
A—Drill out the damaged threads. B—Tap the hole.
C—Install the insert on the supplied mandrel.
D—Screw the insert into the tapped hole.

Goodheart-Willcox Publisher

- For blind holes (holes that do not go all the way through the material), start with a taper tap or a plug tap, followed with a bottom tap.
- Be careful to start the tap straight in the hole.
- The tap wrench should be turned clockwise two-thirds of a turn then reversed one-third of a turn to break and clear the chips. Continue this through, or to the bottom of, the hole.
- Never use excessive force to turn a tap.

Caution

Taps are very hard and brittle, and can break when forced. Removing a broken tap can be difficult, or impossible. The smaller the tap, the easier it will break.

Threading with a Die

Threading is the process of making external threads on an external cylindrical surface, such as a rod, bolt, shaft, or pin. A cutting tool called a die is used in a die handle called a *die stock*. See **Figure 3-21**. The threading procedure is the same as for tapping. The diameter of the rod must be the same as the major diameter of the thread.

Select the die. If the die is of the split type, it can be opened with the adjustment screw for the first cut and then adjusted down to the desired fit in the threaded hole. Place the die in the die stock so that the set screws align with the depressions along the edge of the die. Tighten the set screws. Start the die on the correct side and keep it perpendicular to the centerline of the rod. A good cutting fluid should be used on the die teeth.

Washers

Flat washers are used to provide a wider bearing surface for a bolt or screw head and/or nut. When tightening a bolt or screw against a relatively soft material such as wood, plastic, and soft metals (like aluminum, copper, or brass), the head may gradually become embedded in the surface. This may cause the fastener to become loose during use. A flat washer tends to prevent embedding and provides a harder surface for the bolt or screw head to pull against. See **Figure 3-23**.

Lock washers prevent loosening of bolts, screws, and nuts. There are many kinds to choose from. The most common lock washer used with nuts is the *kantlink washer*. It is made of spring steel and has beveled ends. The slight helix of the washer tends to cut into the mating surfaces of the nut and the component. When the nut is tightened, the washer is compressed flat. The tendency of the nut to reverse rotation causes the beveled ends of the washer to dig into the mating surfaces. This prevents further loosening of the fastener.

The *wide bearing lock washer* combines the characteristics of a flat washer and a kantlink lock

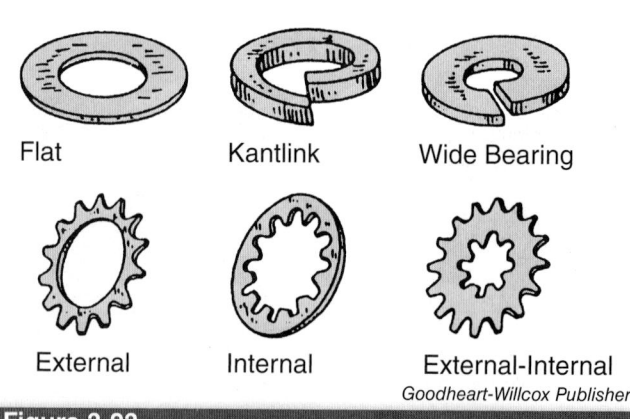

Flat   Kantlink   Wide Bearing

External   Internal   External-Internal

Goodheart-Willcox Publisher

Figure 3-23.

Common washers of several sizes and shapes.

washer. It provides the hard surface for the bolt or screw head to pull against, like a flat washer. It also provides beveled ends that are characteristic of the kantlink washer.

Multiple *toothed washers* are stamped from sheet metal and have internal, external, or external-internal teeth. This type of washer is used under the heads of screws to prevent them from backing out. The teeth are twisted to resist rotation in the direction that would cause loosening of the screw.

Pins

Pins are used to either retain parts in a fixed position or to preserve alignment of parts. **Figure 3-24** illustrates several types of pins that may be found on some gasoline engines or related implements.

Cotter Pins

Cotter pins are sized by a nominal dimension, such as 3/32". The hole size for a cotter pin should be slightly larger than the nominal size of the pin. Cotter pins are used to lock castle nuts and secure clevis pins. Cotter pins should be installed properly as shown in **Figure 3-7**.

Cotter pins may be made of steel, copper, brass, aluminum, or stainless steel. They can be cut to length with side-cutting pliers. They can be bent with combination, slip joint, or needle nose pliers. They can be tapped lightly with a soft hammer to form them.

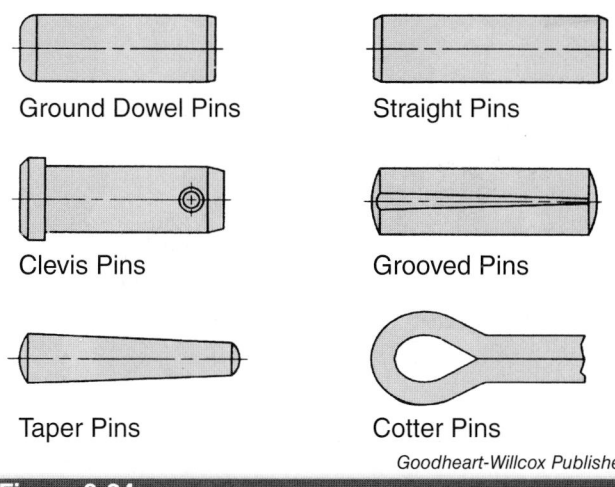

Ground Dowel Pins

Straight Pins

Clevis Pins

Grooved Pins

Taper Pins

Cotter Pins

Goodheart-Willcox Publisher

Figure 3-24.

Pins are used to hold parts together in an assembly.

> **Note**
> During reassembly, old cotter pins should be replaced with new ones.

Clevis Pins

Clevis pins function as an axle so a part can swivel on it. It requires a flat washer and cotter pin to prevent the part from sliding off the pin.

Dowel Pins

Dowel pins are used for alignment and usually fit very snugly. They are heat treated and hardened. The dowel pin is pressed into a hole with an interference fit. The mating part has a matching hole that fits closely to the pin but allows the part to be assembled or disassembled easily.

Straight Pins

Straight pins are also used for alignment. They fit closely, but are not usually an interference fit.

Grooved Pins

Grooved pins are driven into an interference hole. The groove cuts into the wall of the hole and secures the pin. There are several types of grooved pins. Each type has a different shape, and each has a different size and shape of groove. See **Figure 3-25**.

Taper Pins

Taper pins have a uniform taper along the entire length of the pin. Each end is rounded slightly. Taper pins are generally used to fasten pulleys and gears to shafts, preventing rotation of the component on the shaft. Taper pins fit into tapered holes that match the two mating parts. The taper pin is held in the hole by tapping it into the tapered holes, thus wedging it tightly in place. When tapped tightly into the mating parts, the taper pin does not extend beyond the holes. The taper pin can be removed by inserting a pin punch in the small end of the hole and striking the punch with a hammer to drive the pin out. Taper pins are designated by pin size number and standard lengths.

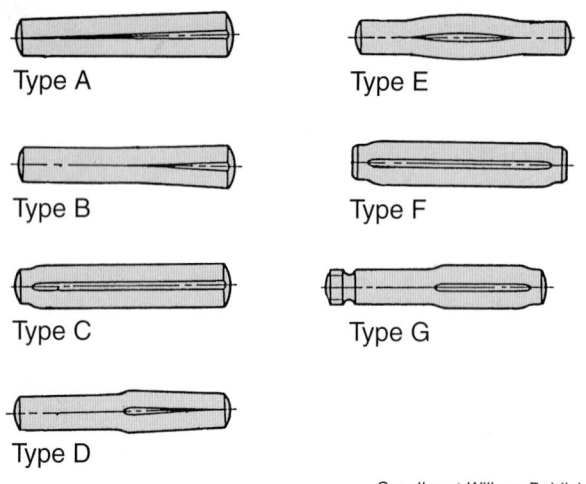

Type A
Type B
Type C
Type D
Type E
Type F
Type G

Goodheart-Willcox Publisher

Figure 3-25.

Groove pins come in several types.

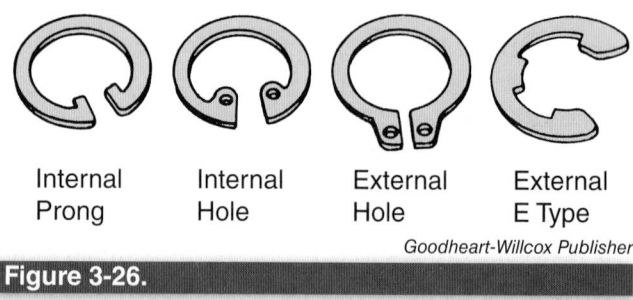

Internal Prong
Internal Hole
External Hole
External E Type

Goodheart-Willcox Publisher

Figure 3-26.

Retaining rings may be internal or external.

Rolled Pins

Rolled pins are used in similar fashion to grooved pins. Rolled pins are made of tough, spring steel. They are straight and available in various lengths and fractional diameters. A 3/16" rolled pin will provide a tight interference fit in a 3/16" diameter drilled hole. Rolled pins can be driven into place with an oversize pin punch and driven out with a punch equal to or slightly smaller than the pin diameter.

Retaining Rings

Retaining rings are circular spring steel fasteners that fit externally or internally into a groove in a part. An external retaining ring is placed in a groove that is machined into the surface of a shaft. An internal retaining ring fits into a groove cut in a cylindrical hole. There are several types of retaining rings. See **Figure 3-26**.

Retaining rings are used to prevent lateral (endwise) movement of shafts in a hole. At the same time, the retaining ring does not prevent the shaft from rotating in the hole.

Most retaining rings must be installed and removed with a retaining ring tool, also known as snap ring pliers. See **Figure 3-27**. The tool has nibs that fit into the small holes at the ends of the rings. When the handles of the plier-like tool are squeezed, internal rings are compressed inward and made smaller so they can be installed in the

cylinder and groove. External rings are forced open so they can be slid over the shaft and into the groove. The reverse action is used for removal. Retaining rings are very strong and require extreme care when installing and removing.

Warning

Safety glasses with side shields must always be worn when installing or removing retaining rings. Rings can easily slip off the nibs of the tool and can fly with considerable velocity.

Keys

Keys are used almost exclusively on shafts that have a component which fits and rotates with the

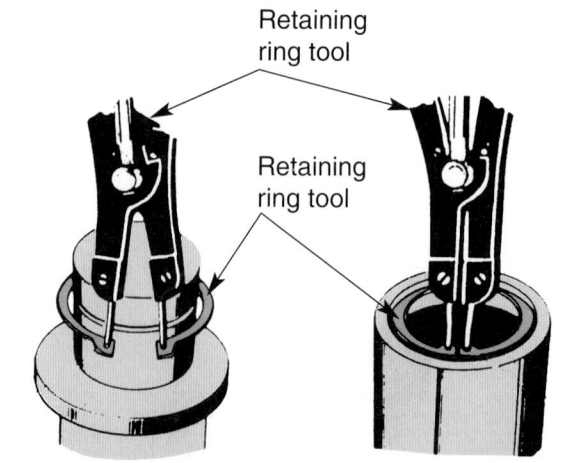

Retaining ring tool
Retaining ring tool

Goodheart-Willcox Publisher

Figure 3-27.

A special plier-like tool is required to install some retaining rings. The nibs are inserted in holes in the ring to expand or close the ring.

shaft. The recess in the shaft is called the *keyseat*. The groove in the pulley, gear, or collar is the *keyway*. See **Figure 3-28**.

An example is the flywheel on the crankshaft of a small gas engine. The key must fit the keyseat and keyway closely to prevent motion between them. Engine flywheel keys keep the engine timing correct. Several key types are used as shown in **Figure 3-29**.

Adhesives and Sealants

Many types of adhesives and sealants can be encountered when working with small engines.

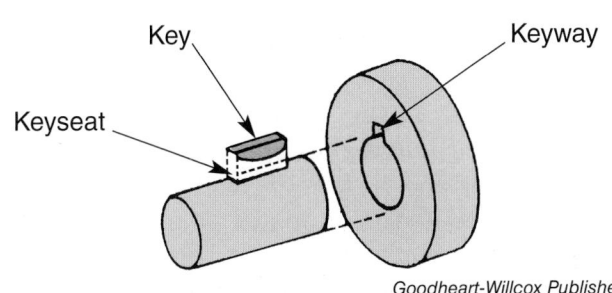

Goodheart-Willcox Publisher

Figure 3-28.

The key rests in keyseat of the shaft. The keyway is located in the surrounding part.

These products have varying properties. Both adhesives and sealants are either a liquid or semi-liquid material. They can be sprayed, brushed, or spread on. Some of these adhesives and sealants set up hard, while others remain pliable. The sections that follow detail some of these adhesives and sealants.

Thread Locking Compound

Thread locking compound, or thread adhesive, can be applied to the threads of nuts, bolts, or screws to prevent them from loosening during service. Compound strengths vary from low strength to high strength. Low-strength compound is generally recommended for fasteners that are 1/4″∅ or smaller. Fasteners secured with low-strength thread locking compound can be easily removed using hand tools. Medium-strength thread locking compound is recommended for use on fastener ranging from 1/4″∅ to 3/4″∅. Fasteners secured with medium-strength compound can also be removed using hand tools. High-strength thread locking compound is designed for use on fasteners ranging from 3/8″∅ to 1 1/2″∅. Fasteners treated with high-strength compound must be heated to about 500°F (260°C) before they can be removed using hand tools.

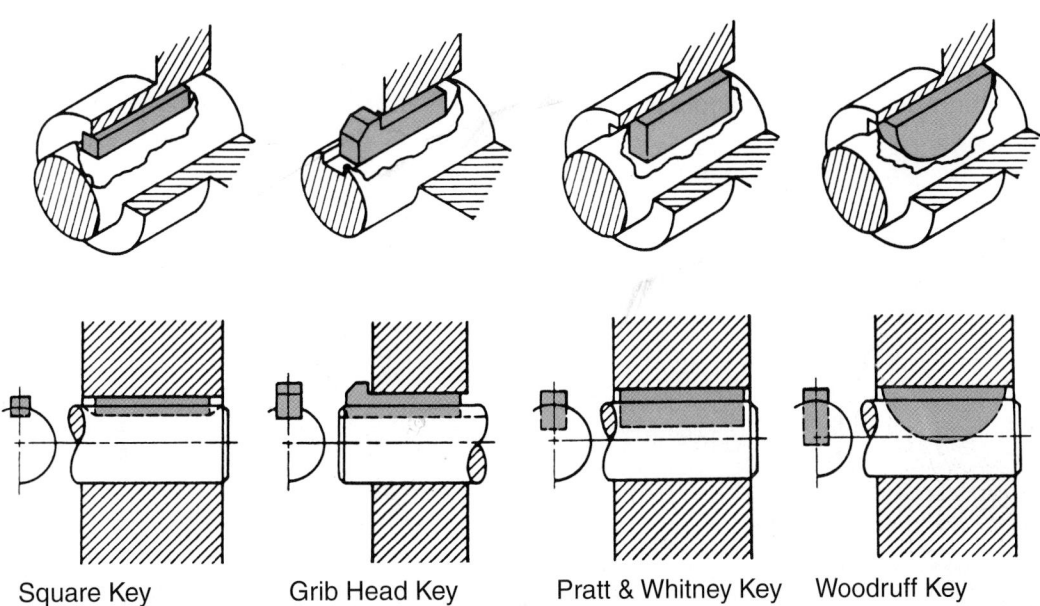

| Square Key | Grib Head Key | Pratt & Whitney Key | Woodruff Key |

Goodheart-Willcox Publisher

Figure 3-29.

Keys used to connect a shaft to a pulley, gear, or wheel.

Although there is no official color code for thread locking compound, most major manufacturers make their low-strength compound purple, their medium-strength compound blue, and their high-strength compound red. Green is reserved for wicking-type thread sealant, which can penetrate between the threads of preassembled fasteners. Care must be taken to use the proper type of compound for the job at hand. If in doubt, consult the service manual for specific information.

Only a drop of thread locking compounds on the thread prior to fastening is needed. See **Figure 3-30**. The compound cures once the threads are mated. This locks the mating threads together. Complete cure time may vary from 30 minutes to 24 hours. There are other uses for these compounds, such as fastening bearings, bushings, gears, and sleeves on shafts.

Warning

Always read health warning labels on adhesive containers. Adhesives may contain chemicals that can cause injury to eyes, lungs, and other parts of the body. Always follow the manufacturer's recommended procedures.

Sealants

Most sealants are resistant to oil, water, gas, grease, and salt solutions. Resistance to hot and cold conditions varies. Most sealants can be used for all applications except for use on the exhaust system. Special high-temperature sealants are used for exhaust systems.

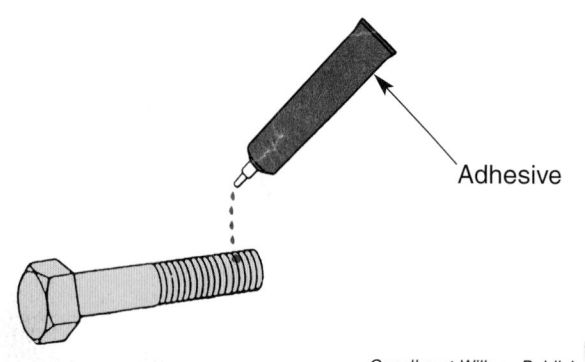

Goodheart-Willcox Publisher

Figure 3-30.

A drop of thread locking compound can be placed on the thread to lock a screw or nut.

Form-in-place sealants can be used in place of conventional gaskets (gaskets are covered later in this chapter). This type of sealant can be used when the exact replacement gasket is not available. *Room temperature vulcanizing sealant (RTV)* is a form-in-place sealant that is also referred to as silicon sealant. It can be used on both flexible and rigid mating surfaces.

Anaerobic sealants are similar to RTV, but they can cure in the absence of air. This type of sealant can be used as a thread locking material or between two machined surfaces.

Note

Become familiar with the sealants you use. Know the properties of the sealants and their recommended uses.

Antiseize Compounds

Antiseize compounds are applied to threaded fasteners and metal components that are exposed to constant heat. The compound is a lubricant that prevents the metal material from being cold welded together. If a threaded fastener and its connecting metal component are cold welded, then removal of the fastener will be impossible. The antiseize compounds should be applied to the threads or the connecting metal. These compounds can be used for the connection of the exhaust system.

Note

Remember, antiseize compounds are lubricants and not sealants.

Gaskets

Gaskets are used between engine parts to seal and prevent leakage of engine oil, coolant, compression, and vacuum. Gaskets are soft, pliable materials such as fiber, rubber, neoprene (synthetic rubber), cork, treated paper, thin steel, or laminated materials. Gaskets are manufactured to the shape of the surfaces between the mating parts with appropriate shapes and locations of holes. See **Figure 3-31**. The particular gasket material used

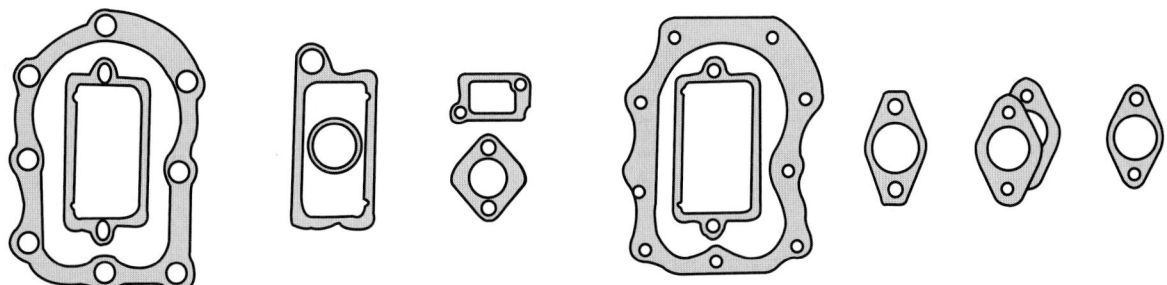

Goodheart-Willcox Publisher

Figure 3-31.
Engine gaskets vary in size, shape, and material. Some gaskets are delicate and should be handled carefully.

depends on the functions and conditions of the parts to be joined. This is specified by the engine manufacturer. Some replacement gaskets can be made by hand.

Caution

If gaskets are made by hand, make sure they are made of the same material and same thickness as the originals. Incorrect substitution will result in failure of the gasket. This may cause damage to the part and/or engine.

When a gasket is placed between parts and the bolts or screws are tightened, the gasket material is compressed and deformed. Any small dents, gaps, scratches, or other imperfections in the mating surfaces are filled by the gasket. This produces a leakproof seal between the parts.

Green Tech

Shop Waste Disposal

Small engine shops accumulate great amounts of different types of waste in daily operation. The used fluids, empty containers, and batteries must be disposed of. However, due to the potential danger these items can pose to the environment, it must be determined whether or not the refuse is considered hazardous waste. For paint and cleaning supplies, checking the SDS can help determine how to dispose of them. Some states now have organizations that will help shops decide what can be recycled and what can be thrown out. Be sure to find out how best to handle used materials before disposing of them.

Gasket Rules

The following are specific gasket rules. These rules should always be followed when working with gaskets.

- Inspect for leaks before disassembling the engine. Determine if only the gasket is leaking or whether the part is cracked or seriously deformed.
- Avoid damaging the parts during disassembly. Care must be taken while removing parts. Do not score, dent, or deform the mating surfaces.
- Remove the old gasket carefully. Remove all of the old gasket material from the part surfaces by scraping or wire brushing. Soft metals such as aluminum and brass are damaged easily and require extra care. Use a dull scraper and wire brush lightly.
- Wash and dry the parts thoroughly. Wash the parts in solvent after the gasket has been removed. Blow-dry with compressed air and wipe dry with a clean cloth.
- Check the new gasket fit. Compare the new gasket shape to the part surface shape. Lay the new gasket in place and inspect its fit. All holes and sealing surfaces must match precisely. Read any manufacturer's notices about the gasket. It may look symmetrical, but it really is not. It is common to install the gasket upside down or in reverse direction. This may cover or partly obscure a small hole in the part.
- Use gasket sealant as directed only. Some gaskets may need a gasket sealant, and others may not. Check the service manual for details about the recommended type(s) to use. Use sealant sparingly. Using large amounts of sealant may clog passages in the parts.

- Start all fasteners by hand before tightening. After the gasket and parts are in place, start the bolts by hand. This ensures proper alignment and threading of the bolts. Check for proper bolt lengths at this time.
- Tighten the bolts in small steps. Tighten each bolt a little at a time. Tighten the first one to about half its specified torque. Then tighten the others the same amount. Repeat to about three-fourths torque specification.
- Use a crisscross tightening pattern. Final torquing should follow either a basic crisscross pattern or the factory recommended pattern. This procedure produces even gasket compression and sealing, and prevents possible warping of parts. See **Figure 3-32**.
- Do not overtighten fasteners. Apply only the specified torque. It is easy to distort sheet metal or thin parts by overtightening. Instead of sealing, overtightening can create leakage between the fasteners.

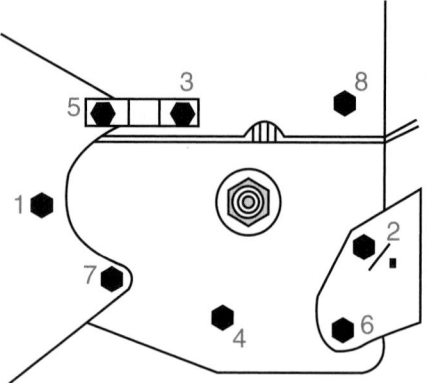

Goodheart-Willcox Publisher

Figure 3-32.

Bolts on an engine head should be tightened in a crisscross manner.

Summary

Many fasteners are used in the assembly of small gasoline engines and the implements they drive. Most, but not all, are threaded fasteners. Fasteners are exposed to conditions such as heating and cooling, cyclic loading, tensile and shear loads, corrosion, and vibration during engine operation. Helical portions of screws and bolts are called threads.

When disassembling an engine, all parts, fasteners, and washers should be noted so they can be replaced in proper locations. Damaged fasteners should be replaced with new ones. Lightly rusted fasteners may be cleaned and examined for reuse. All threaded fasteners should be lubricated before installing.

Bolts are threaded fasteners that hold parts together by squeezing them between the bolt head on one end and a nut on the other. A lock washer is often placed between the face of the nut and the part surface to prevent loosening caused by vibration. Nuts vary in shape and size, depending upon their intended function. Plain hexagon nuts are the most common. Other types are wing nuts, castle nuts, acorn nuts, jam nuts, and various self-locking nuts.

Bolt terminology includes major diameter, head size, length, and thread pitch. Bolt grades are related to the minimum tensile strength of the bolt. Bolt heads are marked with symbols to identify grade. Thread types of significance for small gas engines are Unified National Coarse (UNC), Unified National Fine (UNF), and metric (M). Threads of a bolt or screw must be the same as the mating thread in the hole or nut. Threads are identified by a thread designation such as 1/2–13 UNC–2A for standard threads and M10 × 1.5 × 25 for metric threads.

Screws hold parts together by passing through one part and threading into another. Machine screws and cap screws are commonly used on small engines. Set screws are heat-treated, hardened alloy-steel fasteners used to secure pulleys, gears, and shafts. They have a variety of heads and points. Self-tapping screws are hardened steel and cut their own threads in a predrilled hole of proper size. Tightening bolts, nuts, and screws on engines should be done with a torque wrench to a specified tightness obtained from a torque chart.

Threads can be repaired by chasing them with a threading tap for holes, or a threading die for bolts and screws. When tapping new threads, the proper size hole must first be drilled, as determined from a tap drill chart. Proper tapping and threading procedures must be applied to avoid breaking a tap in the hole.

Flat washers are used to provide a bearing surface for bolt and screw heads and nuts. Various types of lock washers prevent loosening of bolts and screws.

Cotter pins are used to secure castle nuts and clevis pins. Dowel pins and straight pins are used for alignment of parts and should fit quite snugly. Grooved pins are driven into interference fit holes. The grooves are cut into the walls of the hole to secure the pin. Taper pins have a taper along their entire length. They are used to fasten pulleys and gears to shafts to prevent slipping around the shaft. Retaining rings are circular spring steel fasteners that fit into a groove around a shaft or in a hole. They require a special plier-like tool to install and remove.

Keys are used on shafts that have a gear, pulley, or sleeve that fits and rotates with the shaft. The key rests in a keyseat and keyway.

Many types of adhesives and sealants are used on engines and implements. Thread locking compounds are used to prevent threaded fasteners from loosening due to vibration. Some liquid sealants are used to prevent leakage between the parts. It is important to use the correct sealant as specified by the manufacturer. Antiseize compounds are lubricants that prevent parts from locking together.

Gaskets seal between engine parts to prevent leakage of engine oil, coolant, compression, and vacuum. Gaskets are made of soft, pliable materials that are die cut to fit the shapes of surfaces they seal. Selecting the correct material, shape, and thickness is important when replacing a gasket. Following the proper procedures when installing gaskets will prevent gasket failure.

Review Questions

Answer the following questions on a separate sheet of paper.

1. The helical portion of a screw or bolt, or the helix in a hole that it fastens into, is called a(n) _____.

2. The unthreaded part of a bolt or screw is called the _____.

3. The helical portion of a bolt or screw is called the _____.

4. A type of hardened screw that makes its own threads, usually found in sheet metal, is a(n) _____ screw.

5. Name the four common head types for set screws.

6. Name the six types of points found on set screws.

7. The term bolt implies the use of a(n) _____.

8. Jam nuts are usually used with _____ nuts.

9. Answer the following about the thread notation given below:
3/8-16 UNC 1A
   A. The major diameter of the thread is _____".
   B. How many threads per lineal inch are there?
   C. Is the thread coarse or fine?
   D. Is the thread internal or external?
   E. Is the thread a loose, average, or close fit?

10. The proper thread notation for a 14 millimeter thread with a 1.5 millimeter pitch on a screw that is 40 millimeters long is _____.

11. The process of cutting new threads in a hole is called _____.

12. For cutting threads in a *through hole*, the proper tap to use would be a(n) _____ tap.

13. The cutting tool used to cut external threads is called a _____.

14. To provide a wider bearing surface for a bolt head or nut, a(n) _____ or _____ washer should be used.

15. If a 1/8" rolled pin is to be used in a shaft, the correct drill size to use for drilling the hole for this pin should be _____ diameter.

16. What fasteners are used to lock castle nuts?

17. Retaining rings are made of _____ steel.

18. _____ can be applied to the threads of nuts, bolts, or screws to prevent them from loosening during service.

19. _____ are used between engine parts to seal and prevent leakage of engine oil, coolant, compression, and vacuum.

20. When tightening bolts on an engine head, use a(n) _____ pattern unless a different pattern is specified by the manufacturer.

Suggested Activities

1. Make a collection of fasteners for a display board. Categorize and label each.

2. Explore the shop and identify as many different kinds of screws, bolts, nuts, and washers as you can. List them and the function of each kind.

3. Identify UNC and UNF taps and dies.

4. Identify the correct side to start a threading die.

5. Identify taper, plug, and bottom taps.

6. Chase threads on a damaged bolt. Chase threads on a nut.

7. Select the proper tap drill for a screw and drill a blind hole about 3/4" deep in a piece of mild steel. Tap threads to the bottom of the hole using the proper procedure and sequence of taps. If you have never tapped threads before, to avoid breakage, select a screw size 3/8" or more in diameter.

8. Make a display of keys and pins.

9. Display proper and improper installations of cotter pins.

10. Demonstrate proper installation of a gasket.

11. Demonstrate the proper technique for tightening engine head bolts. Demonstrate the proper way to torque engine head bolts.

Fundamentals of Electricity, Magnetism, and Electronics

Learning Objectives

After studying this chapter, you will be able to:

- Describe the structure of an atom.
- Explain the relationship between free electrons and current flow.
- Summarize the three basic units of electrical measurement.
- Describe the characteristics of series, parallel, and series-parallel circuits.
- Recall and apply Ohm's law.
- Explain the relationships between magnetism and electricity.
- Explain the construction and operation of diodes, transistors, and silicon controlled rectifiers.

Key Terms

alternating current (AC)
ammeters
ampere (A)
atom
base
bound electrons
circuit breakers
collector
conductors
direct current (DC)
domains
electronics
electrons
emitter
forward biased
free electrons
fuses
fusible link
insulator
jumper wires
magnetic field
multimeter

neutrons
ohmmeters
ohms (Ω)
Ohm's law
parallel circuits
peak inverse voltage
protons
relay
reverse biased
semiconductor diode
semiconductor material
series circuit
series-parallel circuits
silicon-controlled rectifier
solenoid
solid state
switch
test light
transformer
transistor
voltmeters
volts (V)

Introduction

Small gasoline engines rely on a spark produced by the ignition system to ignite a mixture of gasoline and air to provide power. Additionally, many small engine–powered implements contain electrical systems, such as lighting systems, starting systems, and charging systems.

To fully understand how these systems operate, as well as how to troubleshoot and repair them, a basic understanding of the principles of electricity, magnetism, and electronics is necessary. This chapter will provide you with the information needed to understand the material presented in later chapters of this textbook. It will also detail the most common electrical and electronic components encountered in small engine applications and describe the use of common electrical test equipment.

Atoms and Electricity

A basic understanding of the structure of atoms will help you understand how electricity works. Matter can be defined as anything that takes up space and has mass. All matter is composed of elements. An element is a material that cannot be changed into a simpler material by chemical means. An *atom* is the smallest particle of an element that can exist, alone or in combination. It is so small that it cannot be seen with the most powerful microscope; yet it consists of electrons, protons, and neutrons. See **Figure 4-1**.

Atoms can be broken down into types, determined by the number and arrangement of the electrons, protons, and neutrons. A few types of atoms are hydrogen, oxygen, carbon, iron, copper, and lead. There are many others, about 100 in all. The structure of the atom determines the weight, color, density, and other properties of an element.

Electrons travel in orbits around the center of the atom, **Figure 4-1**. They are very light and their number per atom varies from one element to another. Electrons have negative (–) electrical charges. The electrons, though varying in number, are identical in all elements. An electron from silver would be the same as an electron from copper, tin, or any other substance.

A nucleus is made up of protons and neutrons bound tightly together. *Protons* are large, heavy particles when compared with electrons and are positively (+) charged. *Neutrons* are electrically neutral.

The number of electrons in any atom is equal to the number of protons. Normally, atoms are electrically neutral because the negative electrons cancel the positive force of the protons.

Actually, an atom is held together because unlike electrical charges attract each other. The positively charged protons hold the negatively charged electrons in their orbits. Since like electrical charges repel each other, the negative electrons will not collide as they orbit the nucleus.

In most atoms, the nucleus is surrounded by closely held electrons that never leave the atom. These are called *bound electrons*. When the majority of atoms in an element or compounded material contain bound electrons, the material is called an *insulator*, or a nonconductor of electricity.

Other materials contain atoms in which the nucleus is surrounded by a group of electrons that can be freed to move from one atom to another when electricity is applied, **Figure 4-2**. Electrons of this kind are known as *free electrons*. Materials made up of atoms with free electrons are called *conductors* of electricity.

The flow of free electrons will take place only when there is a complete circuit and the source produces a difference in electrical potential in the circuit. A difference in potential is created when the positive terminal of the source of electricity lacks electrons, or is positively (+) charged, and the negative terminal has excess electrons, or is negatively charged. Since unlike charges attract, the free electrons move from the positive terminal of the source, through the circuit, and back to the

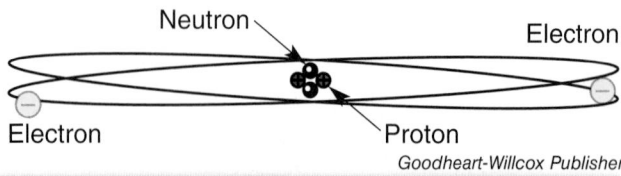

Neutron

Electron

Electron

Proton

Goodheart-Willcox Publisher

Figure 4-1.

All atoms consist of electrons, neutrons, and protons. Neutrons and protons form the nucleus. Neutrons have no electrical charge, but each proton carries a positive (+) charge. Electrons orbit the nucleus and carry negative (–) charges.

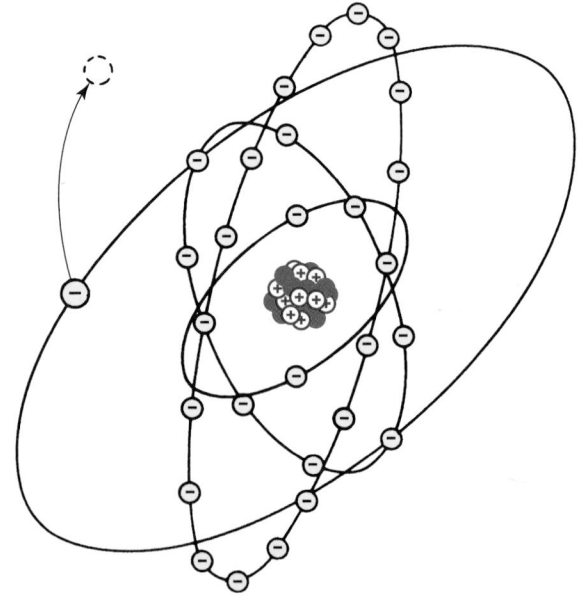

Goodheart-Willcox Publisher

Figure 4-2.

A copper atom consists of 29 electrons circling about its nucleus in four different orbits. Note that the copper atom has a free electron, making copper a good conductor.

negative terminal. This movement of free electrons is electric current. See **Figure 4-3**.

Electricity is produced in three ways:
- Mechanically.
- Chemically.
- Statically.

The electrical generator is a mechanical producer of electricity and can be run by water power, steam turbines, or internal combustion engines. A magneto used in small engine ignition systems is a type of generator. Mechanical energy from the crankshaft is used to rotate a permanent magnet.

Electricity used in homes and factories is produced mechanically. Batteries are chemical producers of electricity. Lightning is a result of static electricity.

Direct Current and Alternating Current

There are two types of electric current, direct current and alternating current. *Direct current (DC)* flows in one direction only. This is the type of current produced by a battery. DC is found in most small engine circuits. As its name implies, alternating current changes directions. *Alternating current (AC)* flows in one direction, stops, and then flows in the opposite direction. Alternating current is produced by alternators used in some charging systems. Both AC and DC voltage waveforms are shown in **Figure 4-4**.

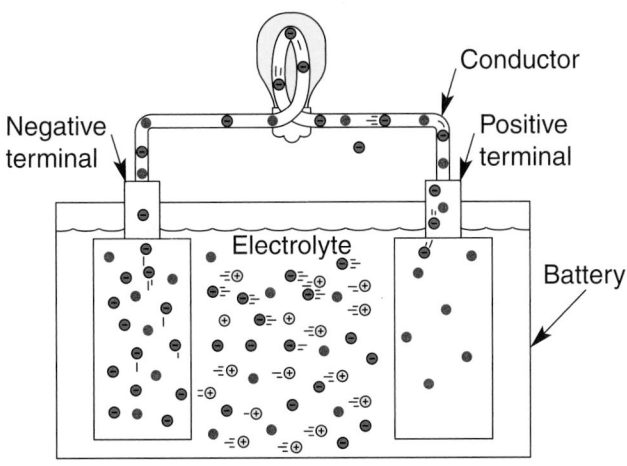

●Electron   ⊕Atom Minus Electron   ●Neutral Atom

Goodheart-Willcox Publisher

Figure 4-3.

A difference in potential exists if source of electricity lacks electrons and, therefore, is positively (+) charged. Electrons, being negatively (−) charged, are attracted to positive source.

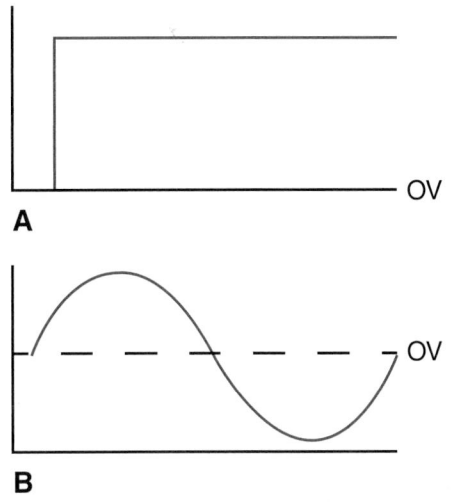

Goodheart-Willcox Publisher

Figure 4-4.

A—DC voltage. B—AC voltage.

Electrical Units of Measurement

The three basic units of electrical measurement are as follows:
- Amperes.
- Volts.
- Ohms.

An *ampere (A)* is a measurement of the number of electrons flowing past any given point in a circuit in a specific length of time. One ampere of current is equal to 6,240,000,000,000,000,000 (6.24×10^{18}) electrons flowing past a given point per second. Since electricity is generally transmitted through wires, the greater the number of electrons flowing, the larger the wire size must be.

The difference in electrical potential between two points in a circuit is measured in *volts (V)*. Voltage is the force, or potential, that causes the electrons to flow.

Resistance to electron flow is measured in *ohms (Ω)*. Some materials produce a strong resistance to electron flow; others produce little resistance. If a wire is too small for the amount of current produced by the source, the wire will create excessive resistance and will get hot.

Ohm's Law

Every electrical circuit operates with an exact relationship of volts, amps, and ohms. It is possible to work out their mathematical relationship through the application of *Ohm's law*. Ohm's law can be used to calculate an unknown circuit value when two other values are known. A basic understanding of Ohm's law will help you troubleshoot electrical circuits.

The formula for Ohm's law is as follows:

$$I = \frac{E}{R}$$

Where:

I = amperes
E = volts
R = ohms

A helpful visual aid for remembering Ohm's law is shown in **Figure 4-5**. To use this aid, simply cover the unknown value and perform the calculations indicated by the remaining values. For example, to find amperes, cover the I to get E over (divided by) R. To find ohms (unknown) when volts and amperes are known, cover the R to get E over (divided by) I. To find volts (unknown) when amperes and ohms are known, cover the E to get I next to (multiplied by) R. The following are examples of using Ohm's law.

If circuit voltage is 12V and resistance is 8Ω, the current would be found as follows:

$$I = \frac{E}{R}$$

$$I = \frac{12V}{8\Omega} = 1.5A$$

If amperage is 15A and voltage is 6V, resistance would be found as follows:

$$R = \frac{E}{I}$$

$$R = \frac{15A}{6V} = .4\Omega$$

If amperage is 3A and resistance is 10Ω, the voltage would be found as follows:

$$V = I \times R$$

$$V = 3A \times 10\Omega = 30V$$

Types of Electrical Circuits

All circuits, regardless of type, consist of a source of electricity (battery or generator), a load (one or more pieces of electrical equipment), and electrical conductors that connect the source to the load.

There are three basic types of electrical circuits:
- Series circuits.
- Parallel circuits.
- Series-parallel circuits.

Series Circuit

In a *series circuit*, **Figure 4-6**, the current passes from the power source (battery, in these examples) to each device in turn, and then flows back to the other terminal of the battery. When working with series circuits, remember that the sum of the voltage drops around a series circuit is equal to the source voltage.

Voltage drop is the decrease in voltage as current passes through a resistance. Ohm's law can be used to calculate voltage drop in different parts of the circuit. In **Figure 4-6**, assume that 1 ampere of current is flowing.

Goodheart-Willcox Publisher

Figure 4-5.

This learning tool is used to find formulas for Ohm's law.

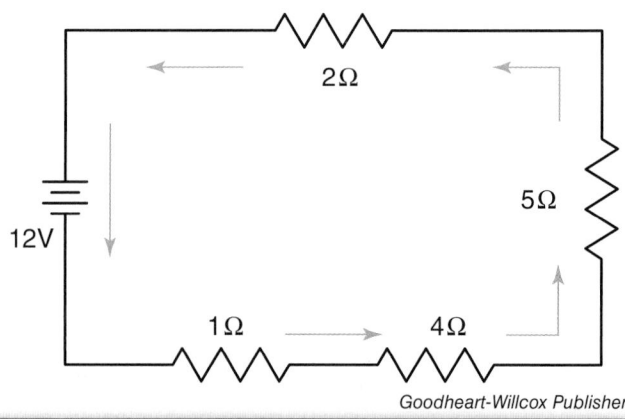

Goodheart-Willcox Publisher

Figure 4-6.

In a series circuit, total resistance is the sum of individual resistances, which are shown by Greek letter Omega (Ω).

$$\textit{Voltage drop (E)} = I \times R$$

First Part $\quad = 1 \text{ ampere} \times 1 \text{ ohm} \ = 1 \text{ volt}$

Second Part $\quad = 1 \text{ ampere} \times 4 \text{ ohms} = 4 \text{ volts}$

Third Part $\quad = 1 \text{ ampere} \times 5 \text{ ohms} = 5 \text{ volts}$

Fourth Part $\quad = 1 \text{ ampere} \times 2 \text{ ohms} = 2 \text{ volts}$

If you add these drops in voltage, you will have $1 + 4 + 5 + 2 = 12$ volts, which checks with the voltage impressed on the circuit.

- The current is the same in all parts of the circuit.
- The sum of the individual resistances in the circuit is equal to the total resistance of the circuit.

Parallel Circuit

In a *parallel circuit*, **Figure 4-7**, there is more than one path for the current to flow through in the circuit. In this type of circuit, one terminal of each device is connected to a common conductor, which leads to one terminal of the battery. The remaining terminals of each device are connected to another common conductor, which, in turn, is connected to the other terminal of the battery. When working with parallel circuits, keep the following rules in mind:

- Voltage is the same in all parts of the circuit. In other words, voltage at any point in the circuit will equal the source voltage.
- The total resistance is always less than the smallest resistance.

To calculate the total resistance of a parallel circuit, you can use the following formula:

$$\frac{1}{R_t} = \frac{1}{R_1} + \frac{1}{R_2} + \frac{1}{R_3} + \frac{1}{R_4}$$

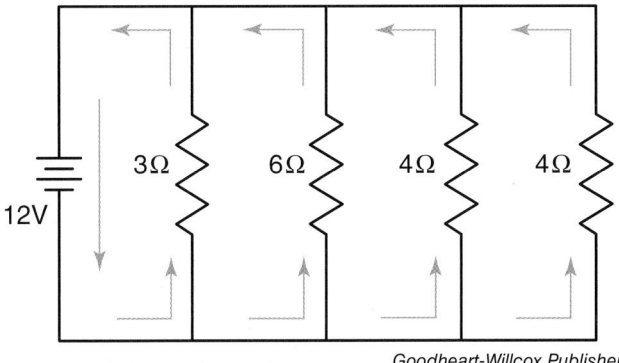

Goodheart-Willcox Publisher

Figure 4-7.

Note how current divides through different branches of the parallel circuit.

To calculate the total resistance of the parallel circuit shown in **Figure 4-7**, substitute the resistance values for the R factors into the equation.

$$\frac{1}{R_t} = \frac{1}{3} + \frac{1}{6} + \frac{1}{4} + \frac{1}{4}$$

$$\frac{1}{R_t} = \frac{4}{12} + \frac{2}{12} + \frac{3}{12} + \frac{3}{12} = \frac{12}{12}$$

Invert both sides of the equation:

$$R_t = \frac{12}{12} = 1 \text{ ohm}$$

- The total current is the sum of currents from each circuit branch.

The total current flowing through the circuit in **Figure 4-7** will be:

$$I_t = E \div R_t$$
$$I_t = 12 \text{ volts} \div 1 \text{ ohm}$$
$$I_t = 12 \text{ amperes}$$

The current flowing through any single branch of a parallel circuit can be found by dividing the voltage by the resistance of that particular branch. In **Figure 4-7**, the current flowing in each branch would be as follows:

First branch $\quad = 12 \text{ volts} \div 3 \text{ ohms} = 4 \text{ amperes}$

Second branch $= 12 \text{ volts} \div 6 \text{ ohms} = 2 \text{ amperes}$

Third branch $\quad = 12 \text{ volts} \div 4 \text{ ohms} = 3 \text{ amperes}$

Fourth branch $= 12 \text{ volts} \div 4 \text{ ohms} = 3 \text{ amperes}$

Adding these values gives 12 amperes, which checks with the value found for the total circuit.

Series-Parallel Circuit

Series-parallel circuits, **Figure 4-8**, have some electrical devices connected in series and others in parallel. When analyzing a series-parallel circuit, you must determine the resistance of each parallel element in the circuit. This resistance is then "plugged" into the circuit so the circuit can be treated as a series circuit.

In **Figure 4-8**, the resistance of the upper parallel circuit is 3 ohms. The parallel circuit on the right side of the diagram is 6 ohms. Adding these values (3 ohms + 6 ohms) to the 3 ohms of the series portion of the circuit gives you a total circuit resistance of 12 ohms.

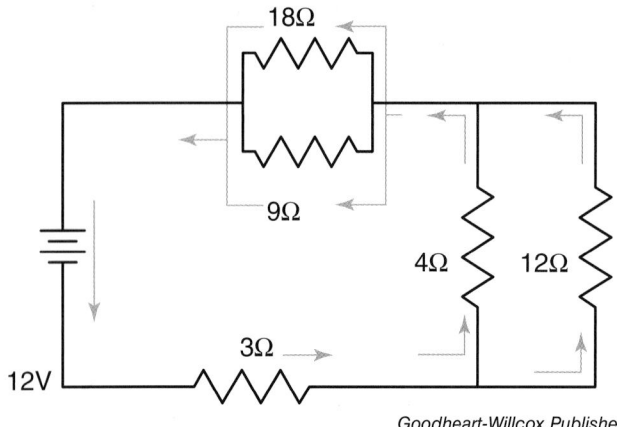

Goodheart-Willcox Publisher

Figure 4-8.

A series-parallel circuit has some electrical devices connected in series and others connected in parallel.

Magnetism

Magnetism plays an important role in the way electricity is generated and utilized in small engine applications. For example, the magneto ignition systems used in most small engines use magnets to generate the electricity needed to fire the spark plug. Therefore, it is important to have a basic understanding of the theories of magnetism and the relationship between magnetism and electricity.

The effects of magnetism were first discovered when it was found that pieces of iron ore from certain parts of the world would attract each other and also attract other pieces of iron. In addition, it was found that when suspended in the air, fragments of this iron ore would always point toward the North Star. The end of the ore that pointed toward the north was called the "north pole;" the other end was called the "south pole."

Magnetic Fields

All magnets produce a ***magnetic field***, which is evidenced by lines of force, or magnetic flux, around the magnet, **Figure 4-9**. The strength of the magnetic field varies. It is strongest close to the magnet and gets progressively weaker as it moves away from the magnet. Note how the lines of force leave the north pole of a magnet (and coil) and reenter at the south pole. Also note that the lines of force exerted by the horseshoe magnet are more concentrated between the two poles of the magnet.

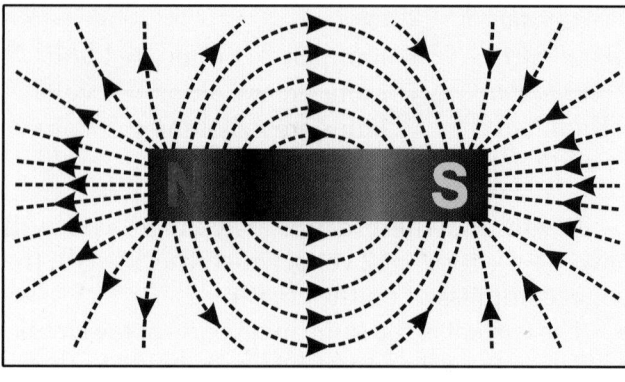

Bar Magnet

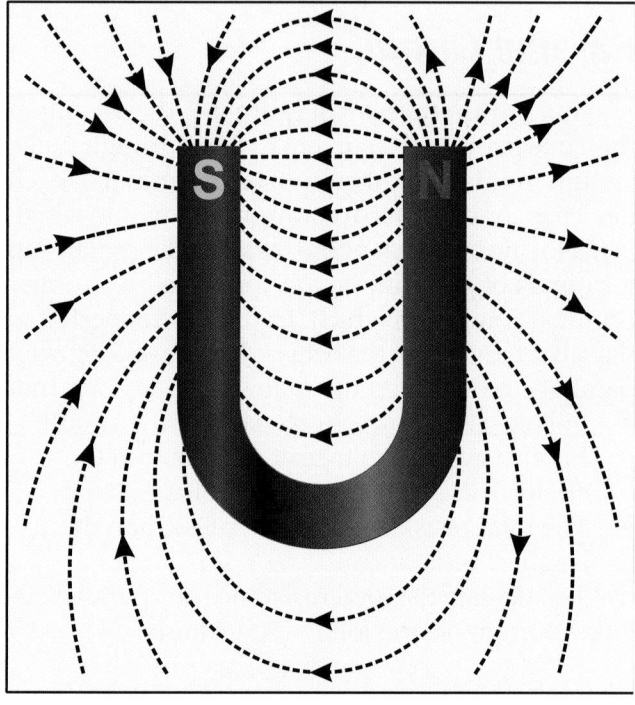

Horseshoe Magnet

Fouad A. Saad/Shutterstock.com

Figure 4-9.

Note that lines of force leave a magnet at the north pole and reenter at the south pole.

Theory of Permanent Magnets

The effects, direction, and extent of magnetic fields can be studied. However, there is no actual knowledge as to why certain materials have magnetic properties and others do not. The domain theory generally is accepted as the best explanation of magnetism.

According to this theory, an electron moving in a fixed circular orbit creates a magnetic field with the north pole on one side of the orbit and the south pole on the other side. When a number of magnetized orbiting electrons exist in a material, they interact with each other and form *domains*, or groups of atoms having the same magnetic polarity. However, these domains are scattered in random patterns throughout a material, and the material is, in effect, "unmagnetized." See **Figure 4-10**.

Under the influence of a strong external magnetic field, these domains become aligned and the total material is magnetized, **Figure 4-11**. The strength of the material's magnetic field depends on the number of domains that are aligned.

In magnetic substances (iron, cobalt, and nickel), the domains align themselves in parallel planes and in the same direction when placed in a magnetic field. This arrangement of the electron-created domains produces a strong magnetic effect.

It is also interesting to note that soft iron will lose virtually all of its magnetic effect as soon as it is removed from the magnetic field. Hard steel will retain its magnetic characteristics for an indefinite period. Special alloys of tungsten, chromium, and cobalt produce magnetic fields of considerably greater strength than other materials. They also retain their magnetism for a longer period. These alloys are used to form the magnets used in specialized electrical equipment, where a strong magnetic field is required.

Magnetic lines of force seem to penetrate all substances. They are deflected only by magnetic materials or by another magnetic field. There is no insulator for magnetism or lines of force.

Another interesting property of magnets is illustrated by the following experiment. Cut a magnet in two and check the individual pieces for north and south poles. You will find that each piece has north and south poles that are situated as they were in the original magnet. See **Figure 4-12**.

Magnetic Attraction and Repulsion

When two permanent magnets are placed so that the north pole of one is close to the south pole of the other, the magnets attract each other. Also, if the magnets are placed with similar poles close together, they repel each other, **Figure 4-13**. This attraction and repulsion of magnets forms a fundamental law of magnetism: Like poles of magnets repel each other; unlike poles attract each other.

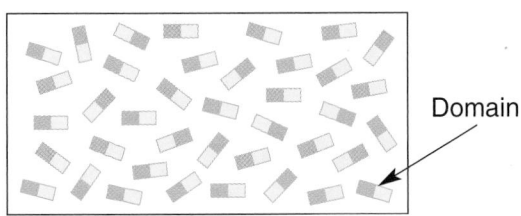

Domain

Unmagnetized Iron

Goodheart-Willcox Publisher

Figure 4-10.

An unmagnetized substance is made up of molecules whose poles are not aligned. Molecules have north and south poles, like bar magnets.

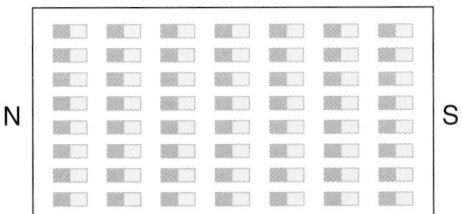

N   S

Magnetized Iron

Goodheart-Willcox Publisher

Figure 4-11.

A magnetized substance has all molecules in alignment, north to south. Individual molecules combine magnetic forces to produce a strong overall magnetic force.

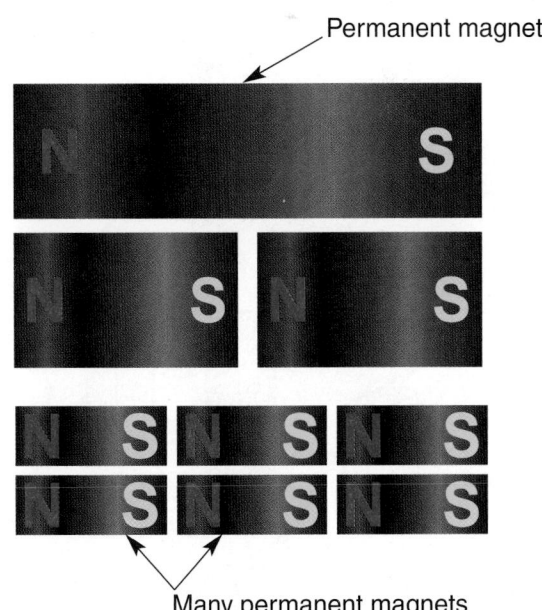

Permanent magnet

Many permanent magnets

Goodheart-Willcox Publisher

Figure 4-12.

If a permanent bar magnet is broken into subparts, each subpart has a north and south pole, like the parent magnet. If parts could be further broken into individual molecules, each molecule would be an individual magnet.

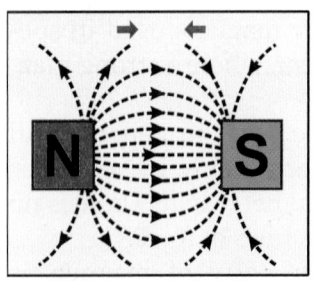 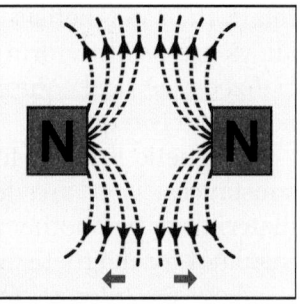

Unlike poles attract   Like poles repel

Fouad A. Saad/Shutterstock.com

Figure 4-13.

Lines of force leaving the north pole of one magnet will enter the south pole of an adjacent magnet, since all lines of force are in same direction. Lines leaving similar poles are repelled since they are in opposite directions.

Magnetism and Electricity

Over 100 years ago, Michael Faraday discovered that electricity could be produced from magnetism. One of his experiments showed that if a wire is moved past a magnet, the magnetic field is cut by the wire and current will flow in the wire. See **Figure 4-14**. When movement of the wire is stopped, the current flow also stops. Therefore, electricity will flow when the magnetic lines of force are being cut by the wire.

Another important principle in the study of magnetism and electricity is that when electrons flow through a conductor, a magnetic field is developed around the conductor. The lines of force are always at right angles to the conductor. This can be shown by placing a magnetic compass close to a conductor of electricity, **Figure 4-15**.

Not only are the lines of force at right angles to the conductor, but they also form concentric circles about the conductor, **Figure 4-16**. Also, when the current in the conductor increases, the strength of the magnetic field is increased. Doubling the current will double the strength of the magnetic field.

If the current-carrying conductor is formed into a loop, **Figure 4-17A**, the lines of force on the outside of the loop spread out into space; lines on the inside of the loop are confined and crowded together. This increases the density of lines of force in that area. A much greater magnetic effect is produced with the same amount of current flowing.

In this setup, one side of the loop will be a north pole and the other side will be a south pole. By increasing the number of loops to form a coil, **Figure 4-17B**, the magnetic field will be greatly increased. If a soft iron core is inserted in a coil, **Figure 4-17C**, the lines of force will be increased substantially.

Electrical Components

The following section describes the components commonly found in small engine electrical

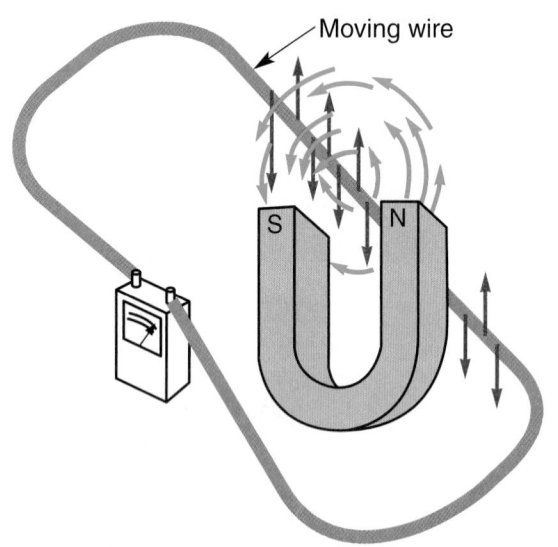

Moving wire

Goodheart-Willcox Publisher

Figure 4-14.

If a conductor, such as copper wire, is moved so that it cuts magnetic lines of force, electron flow is induced in the conductor. The flow of electrons (electricity) can be measured with a sensitive meter.

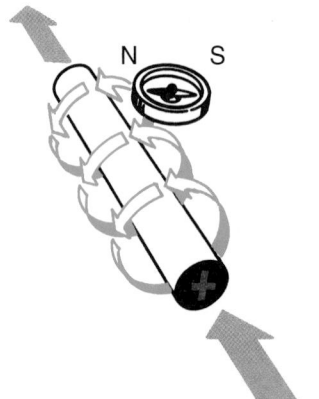

Goodheart-Willcox Publisher

Figure 4-15.

A magnetic field surrounds any conductor carrying an electric current. The magnetic field is at right angles to the conductor.

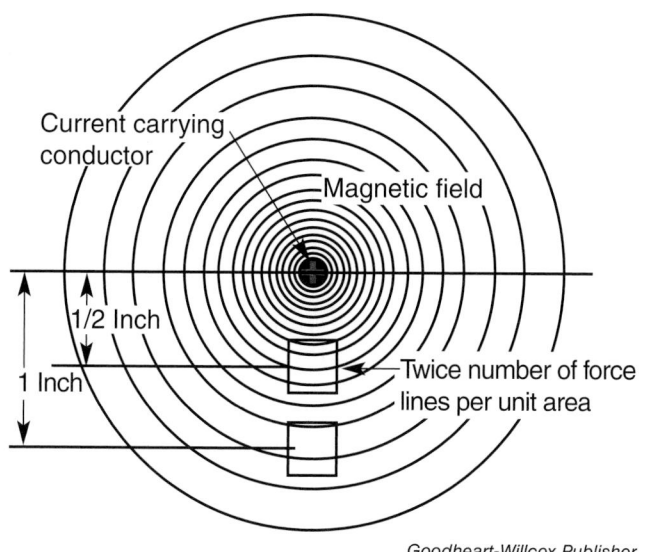

Goodheart-Willcox Publisher

Figure 4-16.

A magnetic field forms concentric circles around a conductor carrying an electric current.

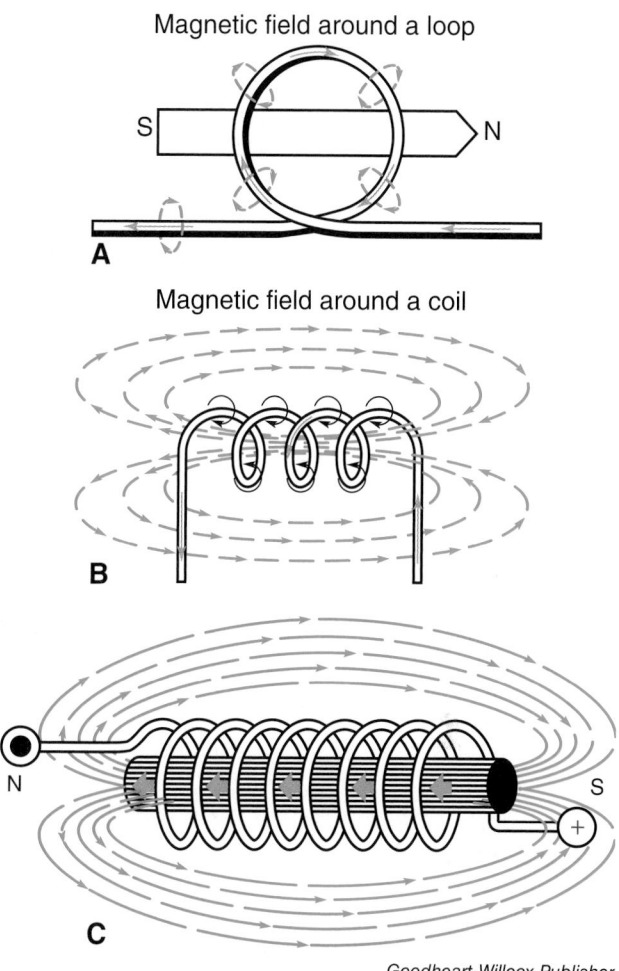

Goodheart-Willcox Publisher

Figure 4-17.

A—Magnetic field surrounding a single loop carrying current. B—Magnetic field surrounding a coil of wire. C—The magnetic field of a coil can be strengthened by winding the coil on a core of soft iron to form an electromagnet.

systems. There are many variations of these components and designs will vary from manufacturer to manufacturer.

Electrical Wire and Connectors

The wire and cable used in small engine applications generally consists of a metal conductor that is encased in plastic insulation. Most conductors are made of copper. The conductor can be solid or stranded. The benefit of using stranded conductors is that they are more flexible than solid conductors. This makes them ideal for use in high-vibration applications, which might weaken or break a solid conductor.

Secondary wire is used in the ignition system to carry high voltage, low current electricity generated by the ignition system to the spark plug. The conductor in this type of wire may be made of a carbon material that has more resistance than copper wire. Using this type of wire helps prevent radio interference caused by high voltage flowing through conventional copper wire.

The diameter of the copper conductor is determined by the amount of current it is intended to carry. Wire size and length determine the resistance of the wire. If the wire is too small in cross section or too long for its size, its resistance will be too

great and valuable voltage will be lost. This, in turn, will result in poor operation of the electrical devices in the circuit.

Wire and cable sizes are expressed by a gauge number, which indicates the cross-sectional area of the conductor. In **Figure 4-18**, the cross-sectional area of the wires is given in both metric size (mm²) and in circular mils. The diameter is given in decimals of an inch. A circular mil is a unit of area equal to the area of a circle one mil in diameter. A mil is a unit of length equal to 0.001″. Note that the larger the diameter of the wire or cable, the smaller the gauge number size. See **Figure 4-19**.

When comparing wires and cables, remember that the external diameter of the insulated wire or cable has nothing to do with its current carrying

Conductors			
SAE wire size (gauge)	Metric wire size (mm²)	Minimum cross-sectional area (circular mils)	Diameter (in.)
20	0.5	1072	.032
18	0.8	1537	.040
16	1.0	2336	.051
14	2.0	3702	.064
12	3.0	5833	.081
10	5.0	9343	.102
8	8.0	14810	.129
6	13.0	25910	.162
4	19.0	37360	.204
2	32.0	62450	.258
1	40.0	77790	.289
0	50.0	98980	.325

Goodheart-Willcox Publisher

Figure 4-18.

Wire and cable size given in gauge number, metric area, circular mils, and diameter in decimals of an inch.

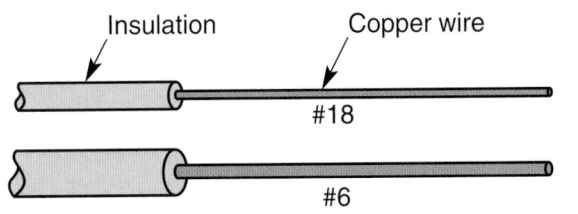

Goodheart-Willcox Publisher

Figure 4-19.

The larger a wire's gauge number, the smaller the wire.

capacity. Thick insulation will make a small gauge wire look much larger. It is important that only the size of the metal conductors be compared.

Connectors are used to attach wires to other parts of the circuit. They can also be used to attach wires together. Some of these connectors are designed to be attached to wires by soldering. Others are designed to be crimped to the wire to form a mechanical connection. Common crimp-type connectors used in small engine applications are shown in **Figure 4-20**. Regardless of the type used, connectors should be fastened securely to the wire.

Switches

A *switch* is used to control the flow of current in an electric circuit. There are many types of switches used in small engines and related implements. Many of these switches are shown and described in **Figure 4-21**.

Solenoids

A *solenoid* is a device that converts electrical energy into mechanical energy (motion). It consists of a coil of wire that surrounds a metal core, or plunger. As electricity flows through the coil, it creates a magnetic field to move the core. See **Figure 4-22**. Solenoids are commonly used to operate some mechanism or switch. One common application of a solenoid in the automotive field is to shift a starting motor drive into engagement with the flywheel ring gear.

Relays

Relays are used as electrical switches, allowing a relatively low current to be used to control a high current. A typical relay is shown in **Figure 4-23**. Note that the coil of wire surrounds an iron core. When current flows through the wire, a magnetic field is formed around the coil and the core. This magnetic field attracts the relay's arm, closing electrical contacts in the high-current portion of the circuit.

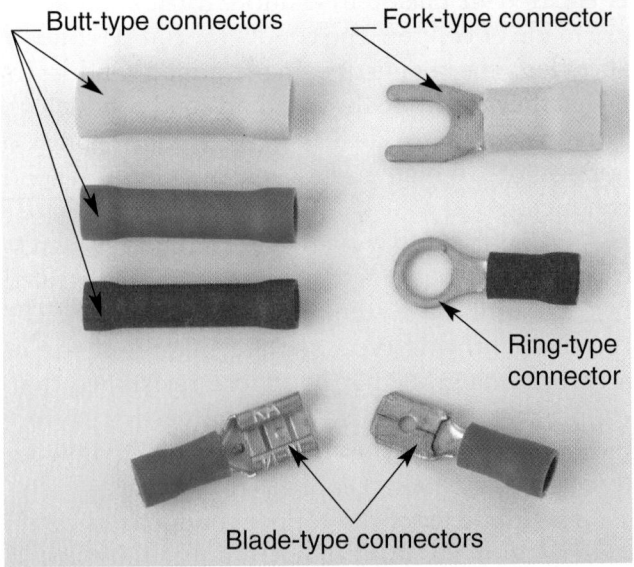

Goodheart-Willcox Publisher

Figure 4-20.

Typical connectors.

Transformers

A *transformer* is an electrical device designed to increase or decrease voltage or current levels. A transformer consists of two coils of insulated wire with an iron core inserted into each core. See **Figure 4-24**. When current passes through the first coil, a magnetic field builds around the coil. This field crosses the second coil of wire, inducing voltage and current in the second coil. When current to

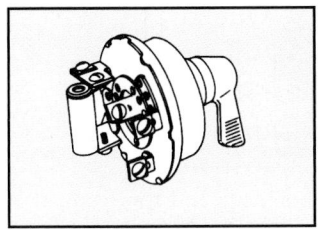

Multiple contact switches can be turned to different positions to open or close complex circuits (combination lighting and variable speed control circuits).

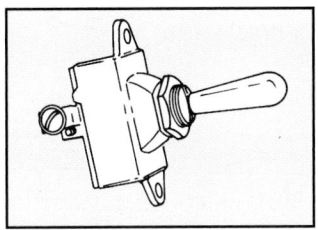

Toggle switches are simple on-offs switches used to control auxiliary circuits.

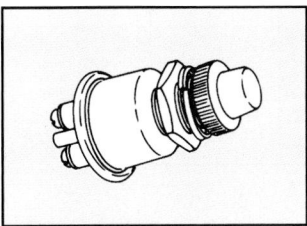

Push button switches are momentary switches that are pushed in one direction to open or close a circuit.

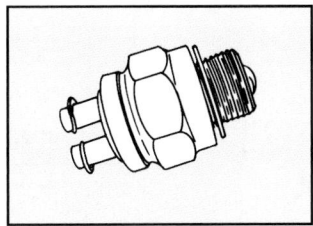

Pressure switches sense high or low pressure conditions and close a circuit to provide audible and/or visual warning signals.

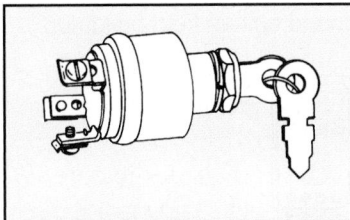

Ignition key switches must have a key inserted to turn them on and off.

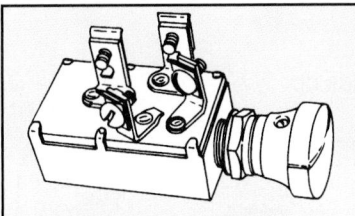

Push-pull switches are used for light switches and emergency switches.

Cutout switches are used to break electrical circuits during emergencies (if operator involuntarily leaves implement).

Deere & Co.

Figure 4-21.

These are some of the more common switches found on small engine–powered implements.

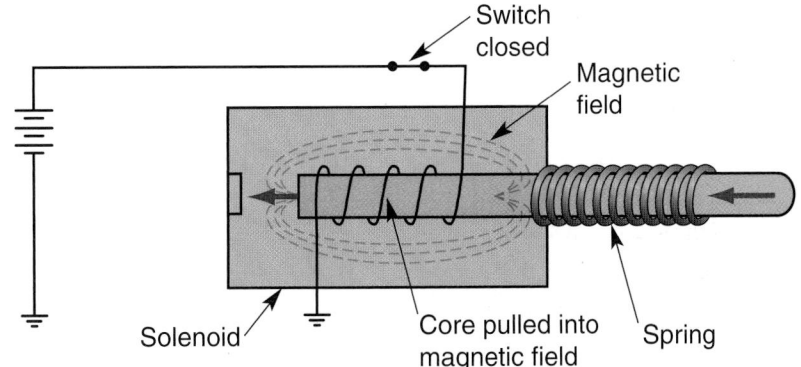

Goodheart-Willcox Publisher

Figure 4-22.

Study the construction of this solenoid. When the coil is energized, the resulting magnetic field pulls the core back against spring pressure. When current to the coil is stopped, the field collapses and the spring returns the core to its original position.

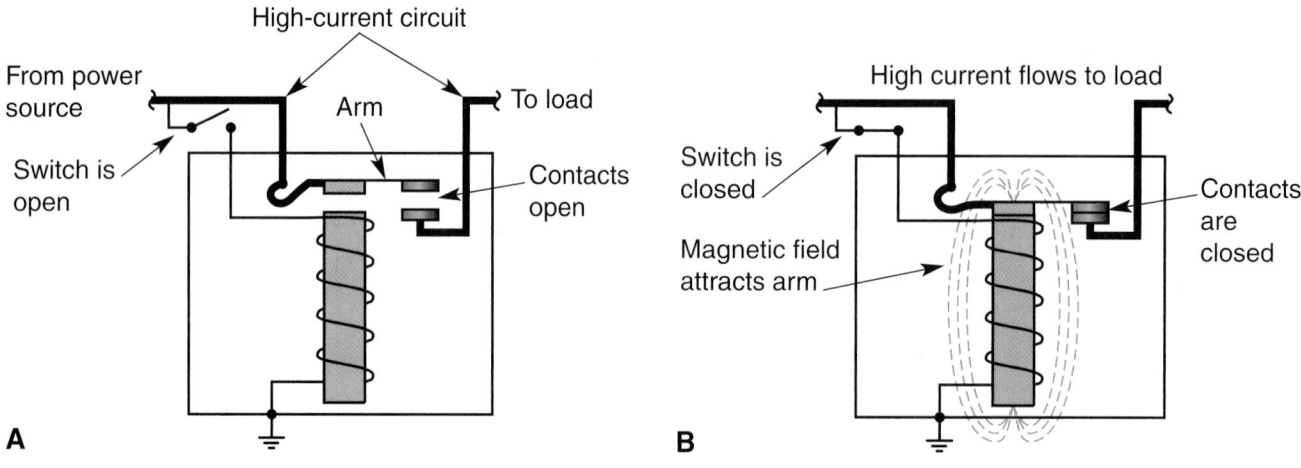

Figure 4-23.

Relay action. A—Power is not applied to coil, and the high-current contacts are open. B—When the coil is energized, the resulting magnetic field draws the contacts together, closing the high-current contacts.

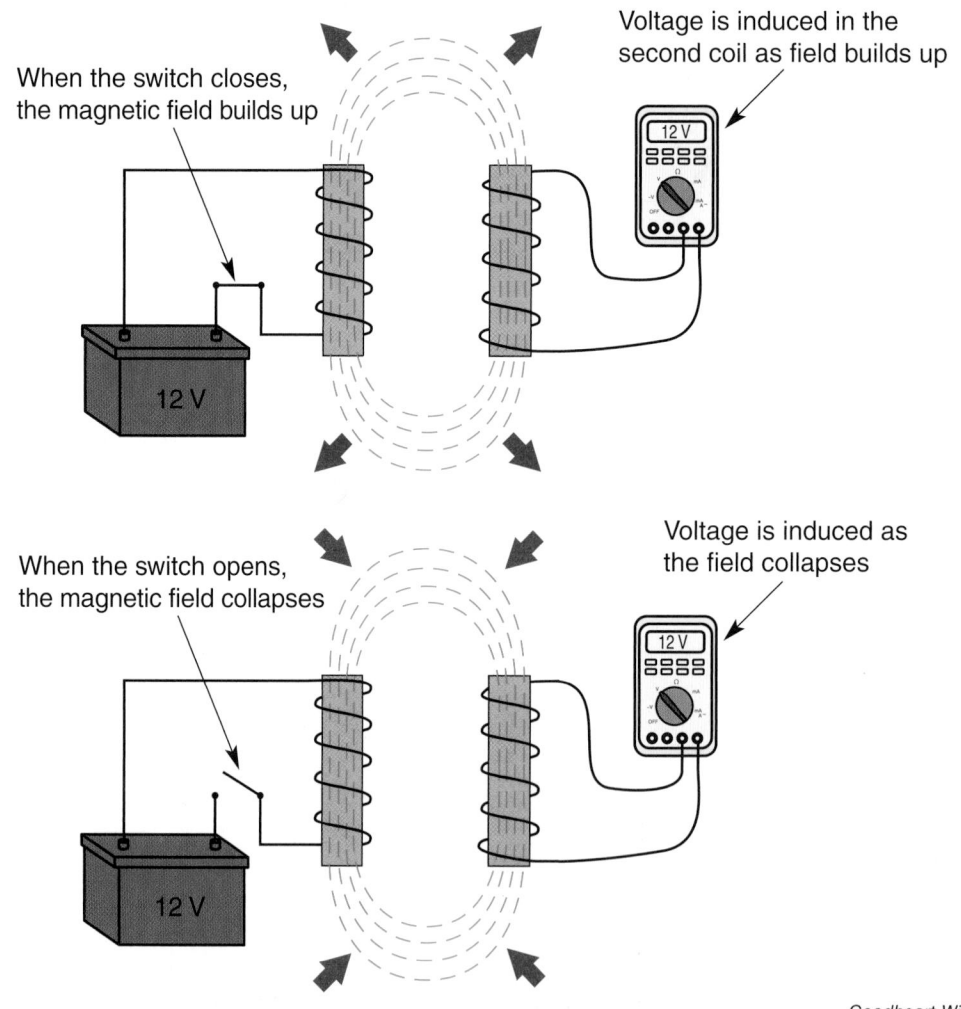

Figure 4-24.

Transformer operation. As the magnetic field around first coil builds and collapses, it induces voltage and current in the second coil.

the first coil is stopped, the magnetic field collapses and current is again induced in the second coil.

It is important to note that current is induced in the second coil only when the magnetic field in the first coil is building or collapsing. Once the magnetic field in the first coil reaches maximum strength, current stops flowing in the second coil.

The number of turns in each of the coils in a transformer determines the amount of voltage produced in the second coil. If the second coil has fewer windings than the first, the voltage produced in the second coil will be less than that applied to the first coil. If the second coil has more windings than the first coil, the voltage produced in the second coil will be more than that applied to the first coil. There is an inverse relationship between the voltage and current produced in the second coil of a transformer. As the voltage produced increases, the current will decrease.

Circuit Protection Devices

Circuit protection devices are used to protect a circuit from excessive current flow. Excessive current flow can generate excessive heat. This can damage electrical components and may lead to fire.

Fuses are the most common circuit protection devices used in small engine applications. Fuses contain an internal conductor that is designed to melt, or "blow," when current in the circuit exceeds the current rating of the fuse. See **Figure 4-25**.

Warning

When replacing a fuse, use one with the same current rating as the blown fuse. Replacing a fuse with one that has a higher current rating can allow too much current to flow in a circuit, potentially damaging the circuit and causing an electrical fire.

Another common type of circuit protection device is the fusible link. A *fusible link* is essentially a section of wire that is smaller than the rest of the wiring in the circuit, **Figure 4-26**. The fusible link wire is designed to melt when too much current is flowing through a circuit. This type of circuit protection device is generally used in circuits that carry large amounts of current. Like fuses, fusible links must be replaced when they are blown.

Circuit breakers are essentially switches that "trip," or switch to the open position, to stop excess

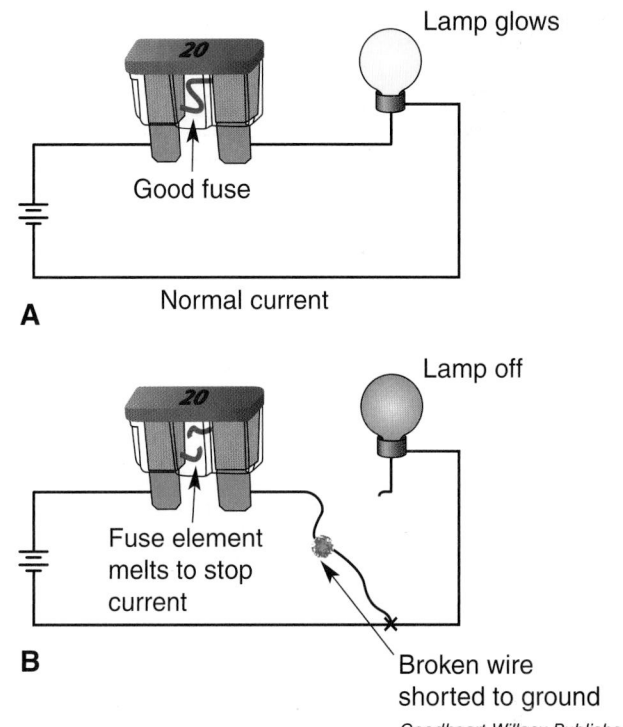

Lamp glows

Good fuse

Normal current

A

Lamp off

Fuse element melts to stop current

B

Broken wire shorted to ground

Goodheart-Willcox Publisher

Figure 4-25.

A fuse is designed to "blow" when excess current flows through a circuit. A—Fuse in a properly operating circuit. B—A broken wire shorts to ground, causing a short circuit. This results in high current flow in the circuit and causes the fuse element to melt.

current flow in a circuit. After a breaker trips, it can be reset to allow current flow through the circuit. Some circuit breakers reset automatically after they trip. They contain a bimetal strip that acts as a conductor in the circuit. When too much current flows through a circuit, the strip heat ups, distorts, and opens the circuit. When the strip cools down, it returns to its original position, completing the circuit. See **Figure 4-27**.

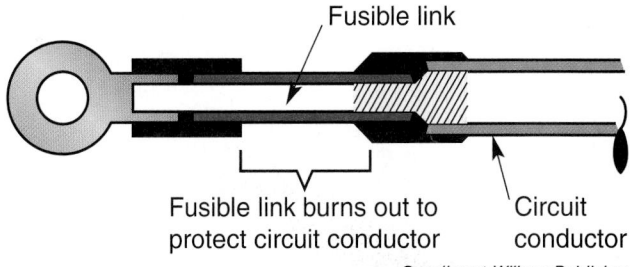

Fusible link

Fusible link burns out to protect circuit conductor

Circuit conductor

Goodheart-Willcox Publisher

Figure 4-26.

A typical fusible link. Note that the wire in the fusible link is smaller than that in the adjacent conductor.

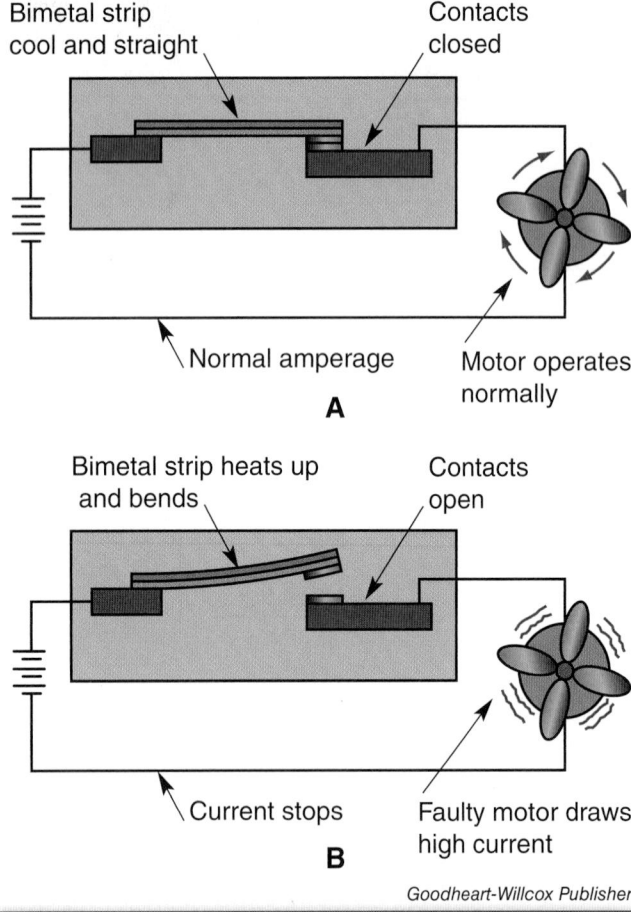

Bimetal strip cool and straight

Contacts closed

Normal amperage

Motor operates normally

A

Bimetal strip heats up and bends

Contacts open

Current stops

Faulty motor draws high current

B

Goodheart-Willcox Publisher

Figure 4-27.

This circuit breaker resets itself after it trips. A—Under normal circuit conditions, the circuit breaker is closed. B—When excess current flows through the circuit, the circuit breaker's bimetal strip heats up and bends to open the circuit. When the strip cools down, it returns to its original shape, closing the contacts.

Caution

After a circuit protection device blows or trips, it is important to identify and repair the cause of the excess current flow before replacing or resetting the device. If the circuit problem is not rectified, the new or reset device will blow or trip again.

Electronics

In the electrical portion of this chapter, you learned that conductors are materials that will pass an electric current. You also learned that nonconductors, or insulators, are materials through which it is difficult to pass an electric current. In this section, you will learn about semiconductor materials and the devices made from them.

The term *electronics* is used to refer to any electrical component, assembly, circuit, or system that uses semiconductor, or solid state, devices. *Solid state* devices have no moving parts, other than electrons. These devices are made from semiconductor materials. A *semiconductor material* can act as a conductor under certain conditions and an insulator under other conditions. Common semiconductor materials include silicon, germanium, and selenium. These semiconductor materials are combined with other materials to produce desirable characteristics. This process is called doping.

There are two types of semiconductor materials. A P-type semiconductor has excess protons, while an N-type material has excess electrons.

N-type and P-type semiconductor materials can be combined in various ways to produce semiconductor components. Common semiconductor devices include diodes, transistors, and SCRs (silicon controlled rectifiers).

Semiconductor Diodes

A *semiconductor diode* is a two-element solid state electronic device. It contains a piece of P-type material that is connected to a piece of N-type material. The union of the P and N materials forms a PN junction with two connections. The *anode* is the lead connected to the P material, and the *cathode* is the lead connected to the N material. See **Figure 4-28.**

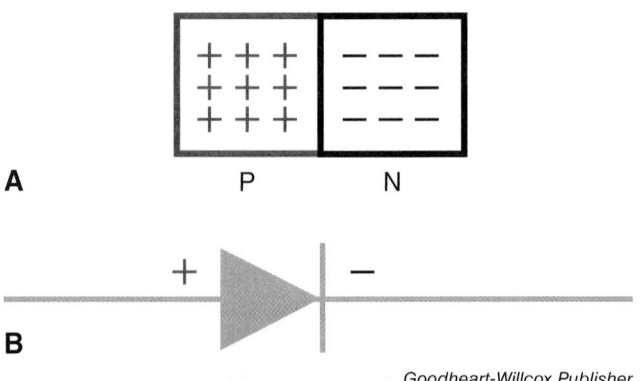

A

P   N

B

Goodheart-Willcox Publisher

Figure 4-28.

A—With P and N materials joined at the PN junction, the diode is ready to pass current in one direction only. B—Diode symbol.

A diode is, in effect, a one-way valve, **Figure 4-29**. It will conduct current in one direction and remain nonconductive in the reverse direction. When current flows through the diode, the diode is said to be *forward biased*. See **Figure 4-29A**. When current flow is blocked by the diode, the diode is *reverse biased*, **Figure 4-29B**. When a diode is placed in a circuit, the P-type material is connected to the positive side of the battery and the N-type material is connected to the negative side of the battery. See **Figure 4-30**. When the diode is connected in this manner, current will flow. If connections are reversed, current will not flow. *Peak inverse voltage* (PIV) is the amount of voltage a diode can take in the reverse direction (reverse bias) without being damaged.

Transistors

A *transistor* is a solid state device used as a switch or to amplify the flow of electrons in a circuit. Like a relay, the transistor uses a small current to control a relatively large current. The advantage of using a transistor in place of a relay is that the transistor is much smaller than a relay and has no moving parts to wear out.

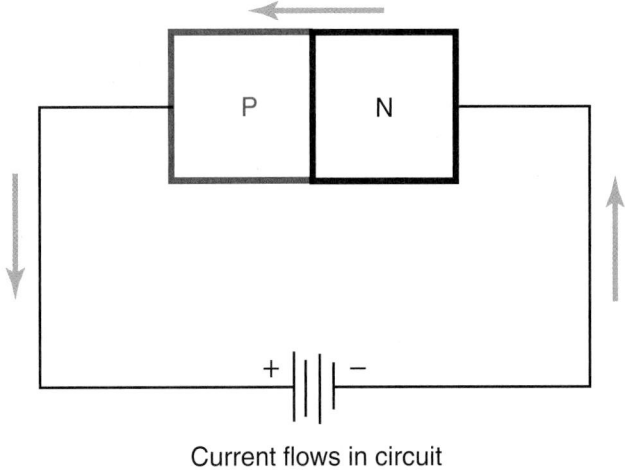

Current flows in circuit

Figure 4-30.

When a battery is connected to a diode with the positive side to the P material and the negative side to the N material, current will flow.

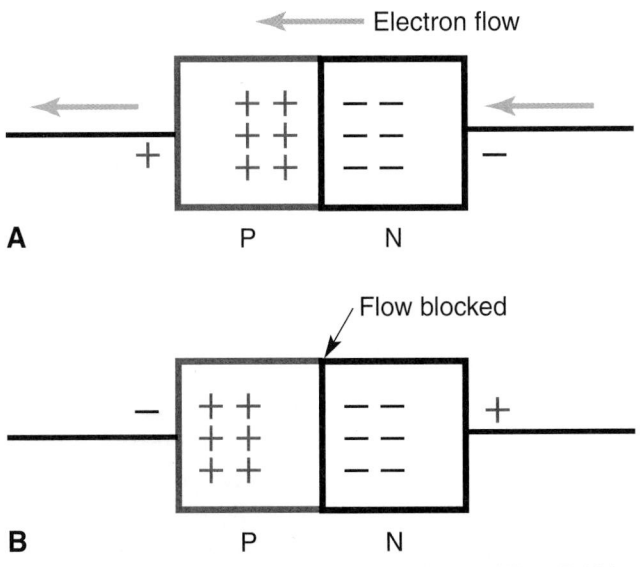

A — P   N

B — P   N

Figure 4-29.

A—With current flow from – to +, electrons in N material are repelled toward the PN junction. Current will flow through the diode. B—With current flow from + to –, electron flow will be away from PN junction. Current will not flow through the diode.

The transistor is a three-element device made of two types of semiconductor materials. See **Figure 4-31**. The three elements are called the *emitter*, the *base*, and the *collector*. The outer two elements (collector and emitter) are made of the same material. The other element (base) is made of a different material. Each element has a lead attached to it.

As shown in **Figure 4-31**, there are two types of transistors: PNP transistors and NPN transistors. Although their construction is different, they operate in basically the same way. In a PNP transistor, both the emitter and collector are made of P-type material and the base is made of N-type material. An NPN transistor has an emitter and base made of N-type material and a base made of P-type material.

The transistor leads (wires) are known as the emitter lead, the base lead, and collector lead. The PNP transistor will have its leads labeled as shown in **Figure 4-32**. Note that the emitter lead in the symbol always has an arrow. In order to identify the PNP symbol, think of the PNP as "pointing in" with reference to the arrow.

The NPN transistor leads will be labeled as shown in **Figure 4-33**. To identify the NPN transistor symbol, think of NPN as "not pointing in." Using these catchwords will be a help when working with transistors and transistorized circuit drawings.

When transistors are placed in a circuit, the emitter-base (E-B) junction is forward biased. The

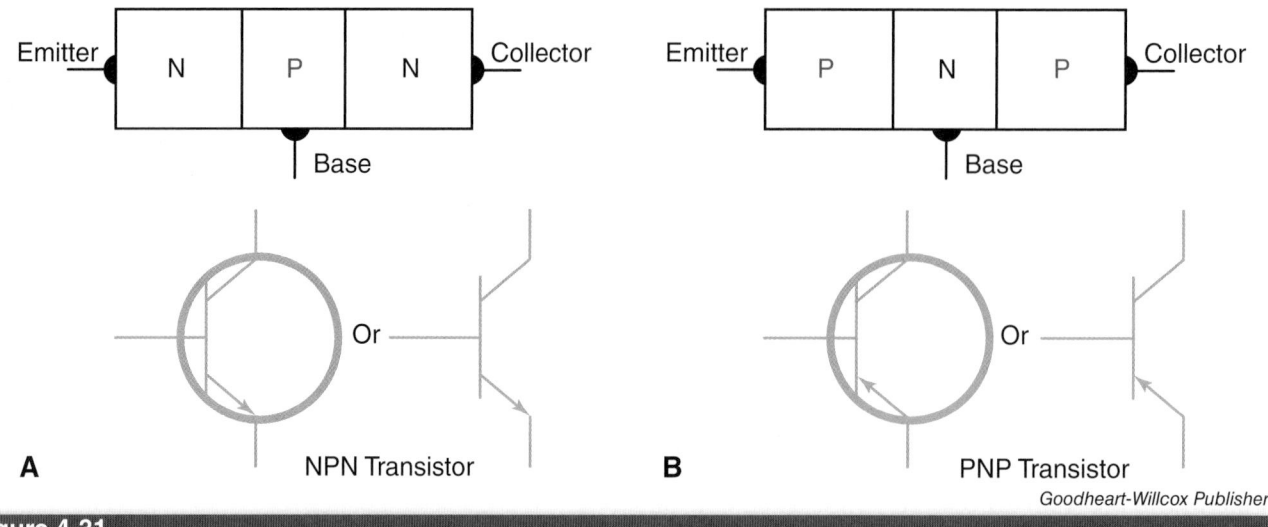

Figure 4-31.

Transistors are manufactured in two basic types. A—PNP transistor. B—NPN transistor. Symbols are shown below.

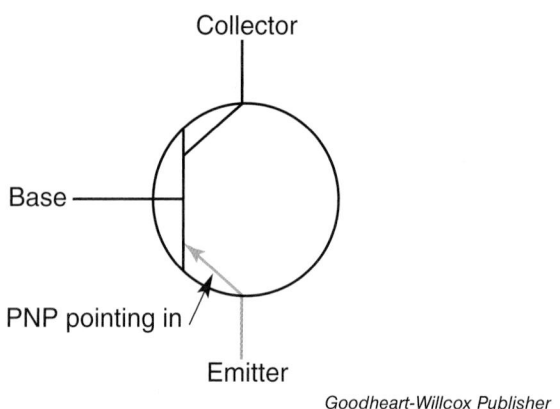

Figure 4-32.

On the PNP transistor symbol, the arrow is "pointing in."

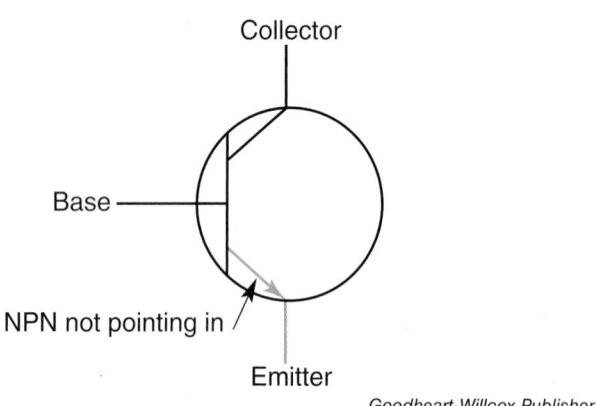

Figure 4-33.

On the NPN transistor symbol, the arrow is "not pointing in."

base of the transistor acts as the switch, controlling the flow of current through the resistor. In order to turn on a PNP transistor, **Figure 4-34**, a small negative signal must be applied to the base. When this happens, a comparatively large current can flow from the collector to the emitter. Note that direction of current flow is against the direction indicated by the arrow on the emitter, **Figure 4-35**.

With an NPN transistor, a positive signal must be placed on the base to make the transistor conduct. This will allow current to flow from emitter to collector, **Figure 4-35**. Again, the flow of electrons is against the direction indicated by the arrow on the emitter.

Silicon Controlled Rectifiers

A *silicon controlled rectifier* combines two diodes so that their junctions appear as shown in **Figure 4-36**. With this arrangement, junction 1 is forward biased, junction 2 is reverse biased, and junction 3 is forward biased.

The anode is positive in **Figure 4-36** and the cathode is negative, but the SCR will not conduct because one of the junctions will be reverse biased. A third connection made to the SCR is called the GATE. If dc is applied to the gate, it will trigger the SCR into conduction.

After initiating the conduction, the gate will lose control until the anode-cathode path to the source is broken momentarily. Then the gate is again in control for the next triggering action. The

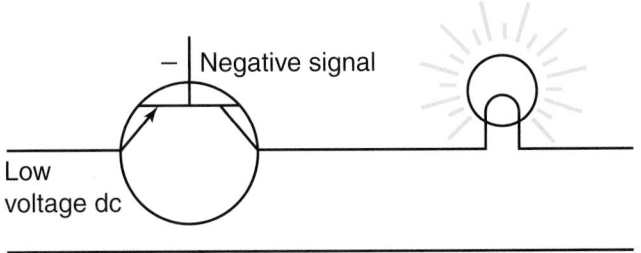

Goodheart-Willcox Publisher

Figure 4-34.

In a low-voltage DC circuit with a PNP transistor and a lamp, putting a negative signal on base of transistor will turn on the transistor and light the lamp.

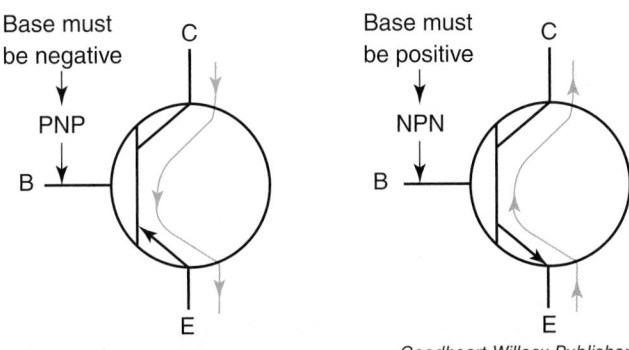

Goodheart-Willcox Publisher

Figure 4-35.

When transistor is forward biased, flow of electrons is against direction indicated by arrow on emitter.

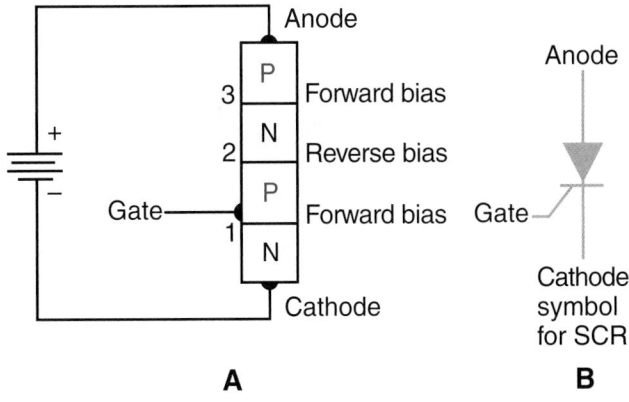

Goodheart-Willcox Publisher

Figure 4-36.

A—Schematic of silicon controlled rectifier construction and placement in a simple dc circuit. B—Symbol for SCR.

triggering capability of the SCR makes it suitable for use in electronic ignition systems and in battery chargers.

Electrical Test Equipment

There are a variety of devices available to help in the diagnosis of electrical system problems. Some are surprisingly simple; others are somewhat complex. However, a basic understanding of electrical system operation is required to effectively use any type of electrical test equipment. The following sections will describe the most common test instruments and explain how they are used to pinpoint electrical problems.

Jumper Wires

Jumper wires are the simplest devices used to pinpoint electrical system problems. A jumper wire is simply a length of wire with alligator clips attached to each end. The jumper wires can be used to bypass components. For example, a jumper wire can be used to bypass a switch that is suspected of being faulty. See **Figure 4-37**. A jumper wire can also be used to apply source voltage directly to a component to determine whether the component or the related circuit is faulty. If, for example, you suspect that the circuit providing voltage to a motor is faulty, a jumper wire can be used to supply voltage directly to the motor. If the motor runs when supplied with voltage from the jumper wire, there is a problem with the circuit feeding the motor. If the motor does not run, the problem is probably the motor itself.

Test Lights

A *test light* is used to check for continuity or the presence of voltage in an electrical circuit. There are two types of test lights—nonpowered test lights and powered test lights. Although both types look similar, they differ in function and the way in which they are connected in the circuit. The nonpowered test light is used to check for voltage in a circuit. It is connected between a ground and any point in a powered circuit. The nonpowered test light will glow if power is present in the circuit. See **Figure 4-38**.

A powered test light contains a battery and is used to check for continuity in a circuit. Power to the circuit must be disconnected when using a powered test light. After disconnecting the power from the circuit, the test light's leads are connected

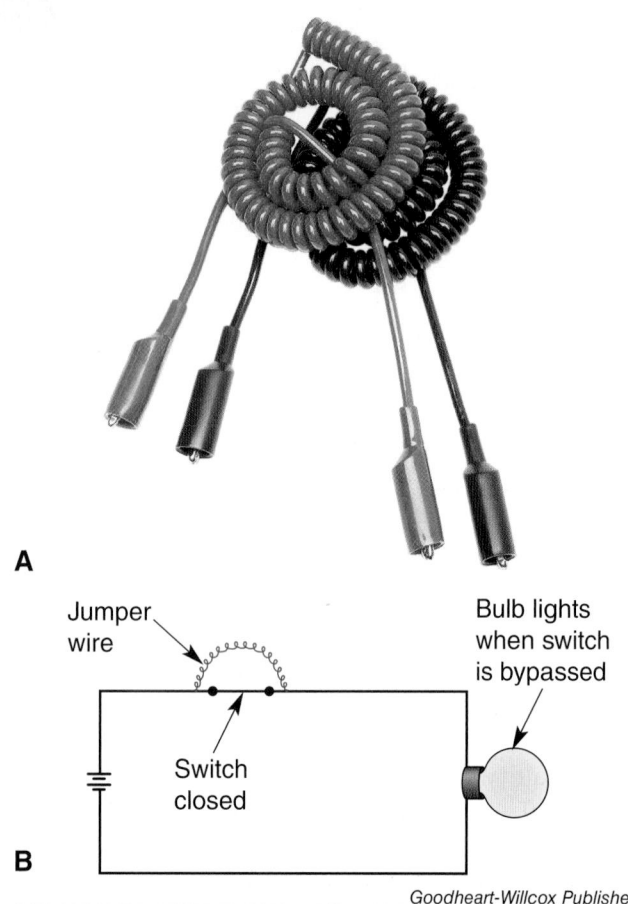

A

Jumper wire

Bulb lights when switch is bypassed

Switch closed

B

Goodheart-Willcox Publisher

A—Typical jumper wires. B—Jumper wire being used to bypass a switch.

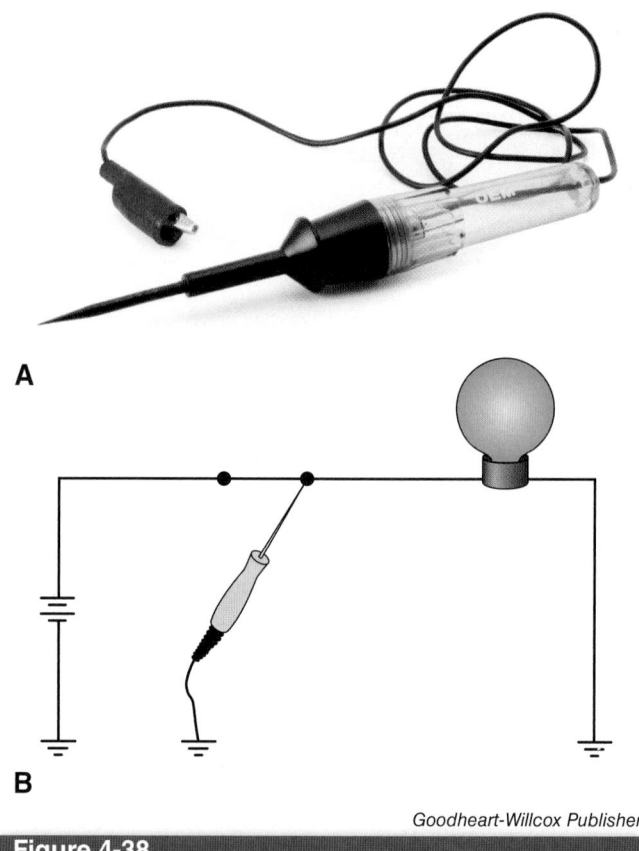

A

B

Goodheart-Willcox Publisher

A—A nonpowered test light. B—Nonpowered test light being used to check for voltage in a circuit.

between two points in the circuit. The test light will glow if there is continuity in the circuit between the two test points.

Meters

Meters are used to measure exact electrical values. *Voltmeters* are designed to measure voltage, *ammeters* are designed to measure current, and *ohmmeters* are designed to measure resistance. However, individual voltmeters, ammeters, and ohmmeters are rarely used when diagnosing small engine electrical systems. Instead, these three meters are generally combined in a single piece of test equipment called the *multimeter*. See **Figure 4-39**. Most multimeters have a digital display to provide a readout of test results, although some have an analog (dial and pointer) display. A continuity tester and a diode function test are also featured on many multimeters.

Measuring Voltage

The voltmeter function of the multimeter is used to measure voltage in an electrical circuit. To measure voltage, switch the multimeter to the appropriate voltage setting. Then connect the meter's leads in parallel with the terminals of the device or circuit being tested. See **Figure 4-40**.

A multimeter is generally designed to cover different ranges of voltage (0–2 volts, 0–20 volts, etc.). The voltage range is changed by means of a dial located on the face of the instrument. Some meters are autoranging, which means they can automatically select the correct voltage range when they are connected in the circuit.

Measuring Current

The ammeter function of the multimeter is designed to measure electrical current in amperes. When measuring current, switch the meter to the proper current range and connect the meter's leads in series with the circuit, **Figure 4-41**.

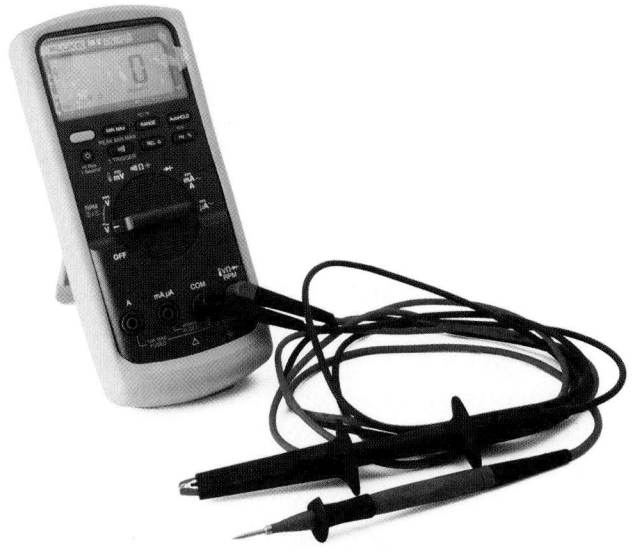

OTC

Figure 4-39.

This digital multimeter combines the functions of an ammeter, a voltmeter, and an ohmmeter, eliminating the need for separate test instruments.

When working with an ammeter, be sure to use the leads provided by the meter manufacturer. Leads having a different resistance will seriously affect the accuracy of the instrument.

Measuring Resistance

The ohmmeter function of the multimeter is designed to measure resistance of an electric circuit or unit in ohms. All ohmmeters contain batteries that serve as the voltage supply needed to force current through the circuit or unit being tested. The power must be off in the circuit being tested, or damage to the meter can occur.

Some analog ohmmeters must be calibrated before measurements are taken. This is done by joining the two leads together and adjusting the pointer to the "zero" mark on the calibrated dial.

To measure resistance, simply connect the meter's leads across the unit or the portion of the circuit to be tested. See **Figure 4-42**. Then read the resistance in ohms on the meter's display.

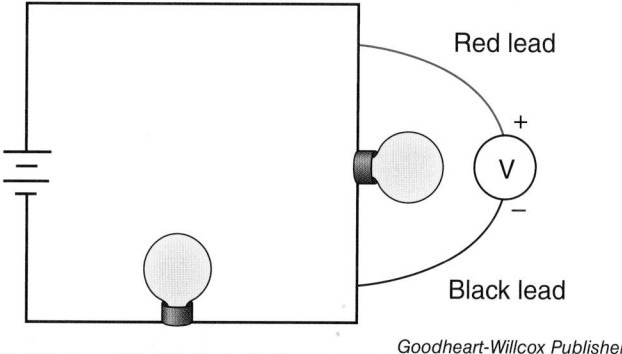

Goodheart-Willcox Publisher

Figure 4-40.

This schematic shows how to hook up a voltmeter across a circuit. Always connect the test leads so the meter is in parallel with the circuit.

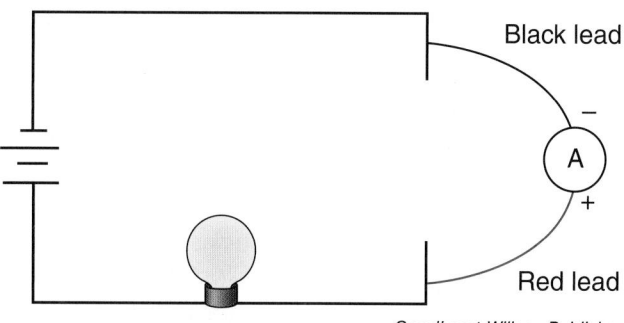

Goodheart-Willcox Publisher

Figure 4-41.

Schematic shows how to hook up an ammeter in series with a circuit. Break the circuit, connect the meter test leads, and then read the meter.

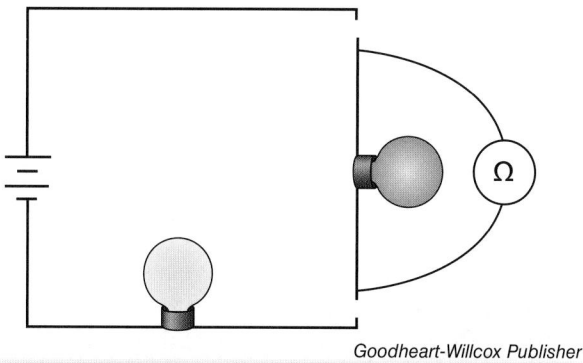

Goodheart-Willcox Publisher

Figure 4-42.

This schematic shows how to hook up an ohmmeter in a circuit. Note that power has been disconnected from the part of the circuit being tested.

Summary

An atom is the smallest particle of an element that can exist, alone or in combination. It is so small that it cannot be seen with the most powerful microscope; yet it consists of electrons, protons, and neutrons.

Electrons travel in orbits around the center, or nucleus, of the atom. Electrons have negative (–) electrical charges. A nucleus is made up of protons and neutrons bound tightly together. Protons are positively (+) charged. Neutrons are electrically neutral. The number of electrons is equal to the number of protons in any atom.

When bound electrons are in the majority of atoms in an element or compounded material, the material is an insulator. Materials that contain atoms with free electrons are conductors. The flow of free electrons will take place only when there is a complete circuit and the source produces a difference in electrical potential in the circuit.

There are two types of alternating current found in small engine applications. Direct current (DC) flows in one direction only. Alternating current (AC) flows in one direction, stops, and then flows in the opposite direction.

An ampere (A) is a measurement of the number of electrons flowing past any given point in a specific length of time. The difference in electrical potential between two points in a circuit is measured in volts (V). Resistance to electron flow is measured in ohms (Ω). Ohm's law can be used to calculate an unknown circuit value when two other values are known.

All circuits consist of a source of electricity, a load, and electrical conductors that connect the source to the load. There are three basic types of electrical circuits: series circuits, parallel circuits, and series-parallel circuits. In a series circuit, the current passes from the power source to each device in turn, and then flows back to the other terminal of the battery. In parallel circuits, there is more than one path for the current to flow in the circuit. Series-parallel circuits have some electrical devices connected in series and others in parallel.

All magnets produce a magnetic field. If a wire is moved past a magnet, the magnetic field is cut by the wire and current will flow in the wire. Similarly, a magnetic field is developed around a conductor when electrons flow through the conductor.

The electrical wire used in small engine applications generally consists of a metal conductor that is encased in plastic insulation. Wire and cable sizes are expressed by a gauge number, which indicates the cross-sectional area of the conductor. A switch is used to control the flow of current in an electric circuit. There are many types of switches used in small engines and related implements. A solenoid is a device that converts electrical energy into mechanical energy (motion). It consists of a coil of wire that surrounds a metal rod, or plunger. Relays are used as electrical switches, allowing a relatively low current to be used to control a high current. A transformer is an electrical device designed to increase or decrease voltage or current levels. Circuit protection devices are used to protect a circuit from excessive current flow. Common circuit protection devices include fuses, fusible links, and circuit breakers.

The term electronics is used to refer to any electrical component, assembly, circuit, or system that uses semiconductor devices.

A semiconductor diode is a two-element solid state electronic device that acts as a one-way valve. It will conduct current in one direction and remain nonconductive in the reverse direction. A transistor is a solid state device that can be used as a switch.

There are a variety of devices available to help in the diagnosis of electrical system problems. A jumper wire is simply a length of wire with alligator clips attached to each end. It can be used to bypass components or to apply source voltage directly to a component. A test light is used to check for continuity or the presence of voltage in an electrical circuit.

Meters are used to measure exact electrical values. Voltmeters are designed to measure voltage, ammeters are designed to measure current, and ohmmeters are designed to measure resistance. These three meters are generally combined in a single piece of test equipment called the multimeter.

Review Questions

Answer the following questions on a separate sheet of paper.

1. An atom contains _____.
   A. protons
   B. electrons
   C. neutrons
   D. All of the above.

2. Electrons have a(n) _____ electrical charge.

3. *True or False?* Bound electrons are closely held electrons that never leave the atom.

4. Name the three ways that electricity is produced.

5. *True or False?* Alternating current is produced by a battery.

6. The difference in electrical potential between two points in a circuit is measured in _____.
   A. amps
   B. volts
   C. ohms
   D. None of the above.

7. What is the formula for Ohm's law?

8. In a series circuit, _____ is the same in all parts of the circuit.

9. In a parallel circuit, _____ is the same in all parts of the circuit.

10. Define *voltage drop*.

11. *True or False?* The magnetic field that surrounds a magnet leaves the south pole of the magnet and reenters through the north pole.

12. Groups of atoms having the same magnetic polarity are called _____.

13. Explain what happens when a wire is moved past a magnet.

14. When electrons flow through a conductor, a(n) _____ is developed around the conductor.

15. What is the benefit of using a stranded conductor?

16. *True or False?* The larger the diameter of a wire or cable, the larger the gauge number size.

17. A(n) _____ is used to control the flow of current in an electric circuit.

18. A solenoid converts electrical energy into _____ energy.

19. Explain how the number of turns in each coil in a transformer affects the voltage produced at the output.

20. When replacing a fuse, why is it important to use a replacement with the same current rating as the blown fuse?

21. Solid state devices are made from _____ materials.

22. *True or False?* A diode acts as a one-way valve.

23. What advantages do transistors have over relays?

24. Powered test lights are used to check for _____ in a circuit.

25. When measuring current, the ammeter should be connected in _____ with the circuit.

26. When using a(n) _____ the power must be off in the circuit being tested.

Suggested Activities

1. Experiment with a coil of wire and a magnet to induce a current. Use a galvanometer to show the current flow.

2. With a dry cell, iron filings, copper wire, and a piece of paper, demonstrate the magnetic flux produced when the current flows through the wire.

3. Using copper wire, form it into a loose coil. Use a dry cell to pass a current through the wire and determine the polarity with a permanent magnet. Reverse the polarity.

4. Using the coil of wire from Suggested Activity number 3, wrap insulating tape around an iron bar and place it in the coil. Demonstrate how this can improve the magnetic strength of the coil when current is flowing.

5. Make a large Ohm's law pie chart (visual aid discussed in this chapter) and display it until it has been learned. Make up some problems that require the use of formulas.

Principles of Engine Operation, Two- and Four-Stroke Engines

Learning Objectives

After studying this chapter, you will be able to:

- Explain simple engine operation.
- Explain why gasoline is atomized in the small engine.
- Describe four-stroke engine operation and explain the purpose of each stroke.
- Explain the concept of valve timing.
- Compare the lubrication system in a four-cycle engine to the system in a two-stroke engine.
- Describe two-stroke engine operation and explain the principles of two-cycle operation.
- List the advantages and disadvantages of two-stroke and four-stroke engines.

Key Terms

atomization
bottom dead center
compression ratio
compression stroke
exhaust stroke
four-stroke engine
intake stroke
internal combustion engine

power stroke
scavenge loss
stroke
top dead center
two-stroke engine
valve overlap

Principles of Engine Operation

A gasoline-fueled engine is a mechanism designed to transform the chemical energy of burning fuel into mechanical energy. In operation, it controls and applies this energy to mow lawns, cut trees, propel tractors, and perform many other laborsaving jobs.

The small gasoline engine is called an *internal combustion engine* because an air/fuel mixture is ignited (fired) and burned inside the engine. See **Figure 5-1**.

For the engine to operate efficiently, the gasoline must be broken into small particles that will ignite easily and burn quickly. In addition, the energy produced by the burning gasoline must be controlled in some way so it can perform useful work.

Gasoline Must Be Atomized

The more surface area of gasoline exposed to the air, the faster a given amount will burn. Gasoline placed in a container and ignited will produce a hot flame, yet it will not burn fast enough to produce the rapid release of heat necessary to run an engine. Even though a considerable quantity of fuel may be involved, a large flame will not necessarily result. See **Figure 5-2**.

Warning

Under no circumstances should experiments illustrated in this chapter be performed. Gasoline can be a very dangerous fuel and must be handled with caution. Illustrations and examples discussed here are meant to demonstrate how gasoline is prepared and used in an engine.

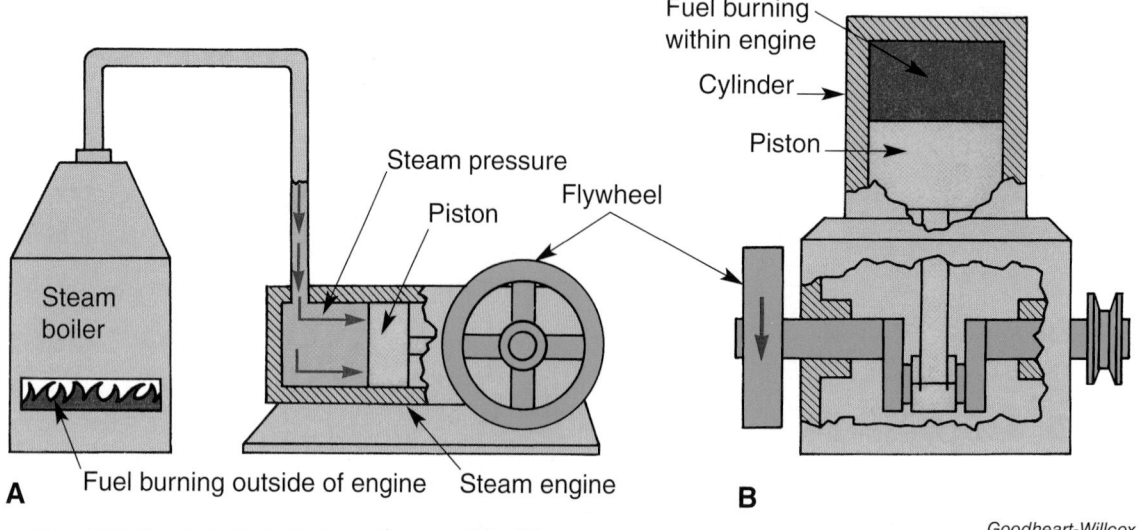

Goodheart-Willcox Publisher

Figure 5-1.

A—An external combustion engine burns fuel outside the engine. B—An internal combustion engine burns fuel within the engine.

In **Figure 5-2**, the surface area of the wick in the lighter is small. Vapor from the surface of the liquid, combined with oxygen, is what burns readily. If the surface of the liquid is small, relatively little vapor will be given off to provide combustion. Since the liquid must change to vapor before it is burned, it would take considerable time to use up the fuel at this rate.

By placing the same amount of fuel in a shallow, wide container, more surface area will contact air, more vapor will be given off, and the fuel will burn more rapidly. See **Figure 5-3**.

To produce the rapid burning required in an engine, gasoline must be broken up into tiny droplets and mixed with air. This is called *atomization*.

Once the entire surface of each droplet of the air-fuel mixture is exposed to the surrounding air, a huge burning area becomes available. Given a spark, the entire amount of gasoline will flash into flame almost instantly. In effect, atomization causes a sudden release of heat energy. See **Figure 5-4**.

Combustion Force Must Be Contained

To perform useful work, the force caused by the rapidly burning gas must be contained and controlled. To illustrate this point, imagine that a metal lid is suspended on a string and held several inches above the ground. If a mixture of gasoline and air (atomized) were sprayed under it and ignited, the lid would be raised a short distance by the force of the combustion. See **Figure 5-5**.

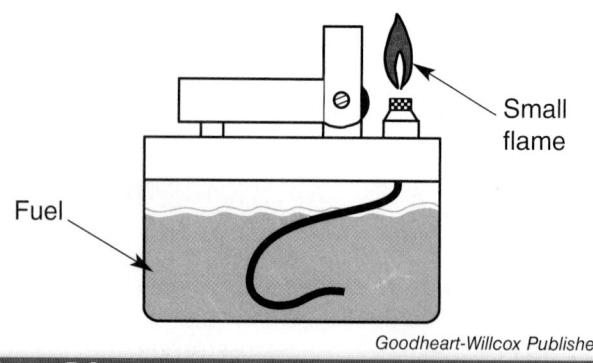

Goodheart-Willcox Publisher

Figure 5-2.

A small flame is produced, due to a small area of exposed fuel.

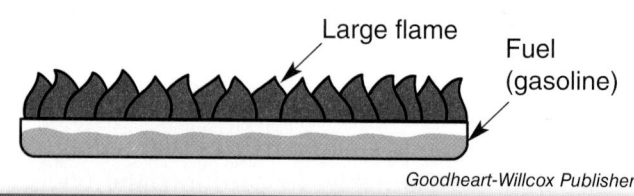

Goodheart-Willcox Publisher

Figure 5-3.

A large flame is produced by a large area of exposed fuel.

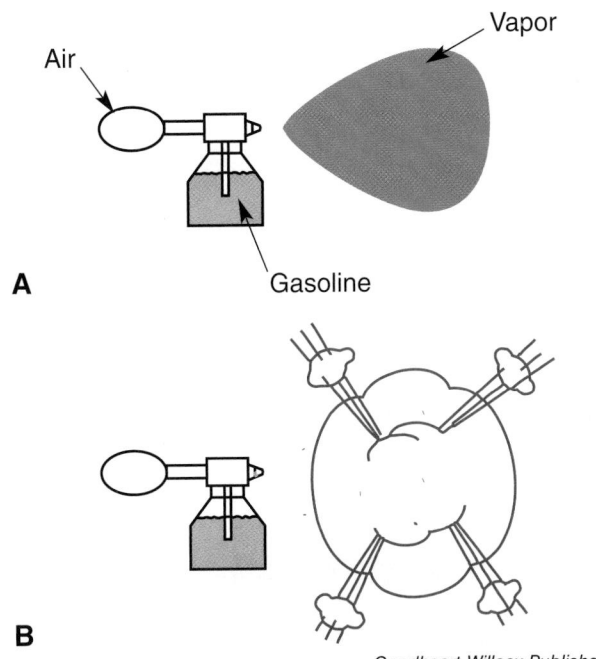

A

B

Goodheart-Willcox Publisher

Figure 5-4.

A—When atomized fuel is exposed to the surrounding air, a large burning area is available. B—When the atomized fuel is ignited, it will flash into flame almost instantly.

The reason the lid hardly moved is that the combustion force was not confined and directed toward the lid. Instead, the force was exerted in all directions, and much of the force was lost. If the air-fuel mixture is sprayed inside a metal container with a lid, the full force of combustion will be directed against the lid when the mixture is ignited. This will blow the lid high into the air. See **Figure 5-6**.

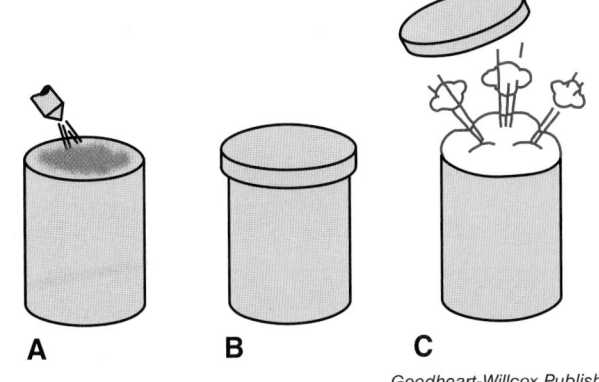

A   **B**   **C**

Goodheart-Willcox Publisher

Figure 5-6.

A—Mixture of fuel and air is sprayed into a container. B—A lid is placed on top. C—The full force of combustion is directed toward the base of the lid when the mixture is ignited, and the lid is driven high into the air.

Even though the burning air-fuel mixture is confined by the container, once the lid starts to lift, a large amount of the force escapes to the sides. To eliminate this loss, a long, cylindrical container may be used with the lid having a close, sliding fit. See **Figure 5-6**. With the fuel mixture slightly compressed in the bottom of the container by the weight of the lid, the fuel will burn and direct most of the pressure against the lid as it travels up through the container. When the lid reaches the top, it will be traveling at a high rate of speed. The expansion of the gas will be nearly complete and little force will be lost, even after the lid clears the container.

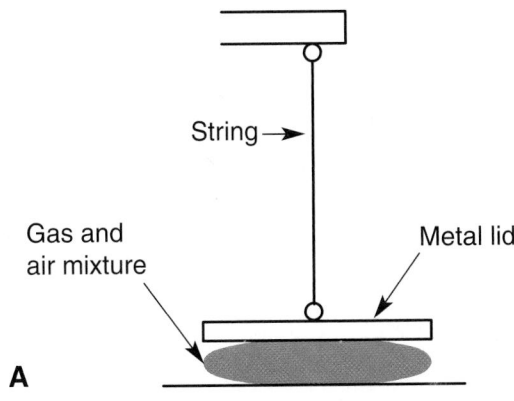

A

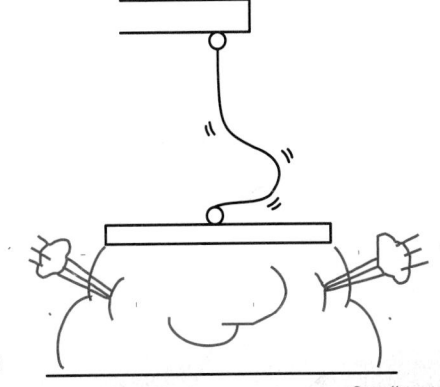

B

Goodheart-Willcox Publisher

Figure 5-5.

A—Atomized fuel is sprayed under a metal lid. B—When the fuel is ignited, the lid moves a short distance.

Constructing an Elementary Engine

An elementary engine can be formed by attaching a crankshaft and a connecting rod to the setup illustrated in **Figure 5-7**. The lid will serve as a piston and the container will act as a cylinder. See **Figure 5-8**. When the air-fuel mixture in the cylinder is ignited, it will drive the piston upward, causing the crankshaft to turn.

Although it is crude, this elementary engine illustrates the operating principles of a modern gasoline engine. Study the names of the various parts shown in **Figure 5-8**. Become acquainted with the parts and their application to engine design.

There are many shortcomings in the engine pictured in **Figure 5-8**. These are addressed in the following questions:

- How will a fresh air-fuel charge be admitted to the cylinder?
- How will the charge be ignited?
- What holds the various parts in alignment?
- How will the engine be cooled and lubricated?
- What will *time* the firing of the air-fuel mixture so that the piston will push on the crankshaft when the journal is in the correct position?
- How will the burned charge be removed (exhausted) from the cylinder?
- What will keep the crankshaft rotating after the charge is fired, and until another charge can be admitted and fired?

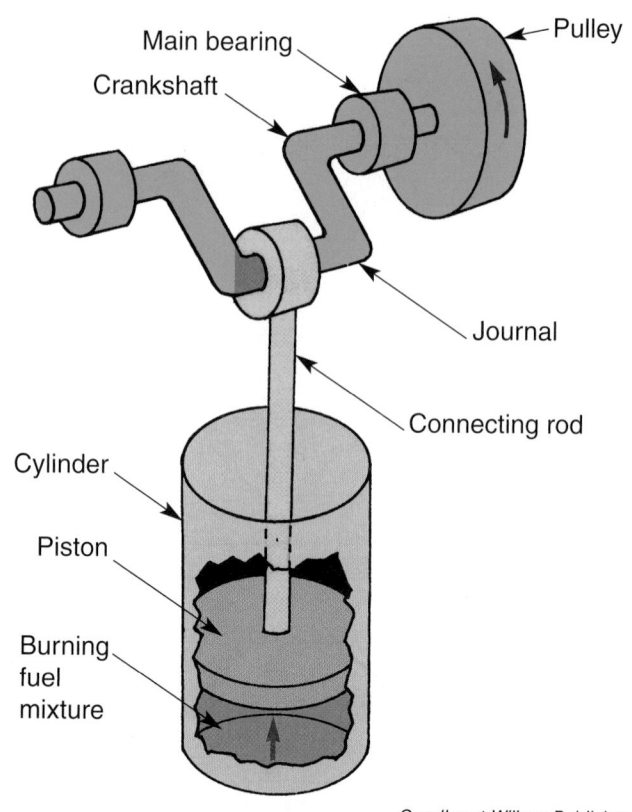

Goodheart-Willcox Publisher

Figure 5-8.

The principles of operation illustrated here are the same as those used in a modern gasoline engine. Note how the burning fuel mixture forces the lid (piston) upward to turn crankshaft and pulley.

The previous questions can be categorized into five basic areas:

1. *Mechanical* (engine design and construction)
2. *Fuel metering* (mixing gasoline and air, and admitting it to the cylinder)
3. *Ignition* (firing the fuel charge)
4. *Cooling* (heat dissipation)
5. *Lubrication* (oiling of moving parts)

For purposes of this chapter, we will assume that the gasoline and air are being mixed correctly, the fuel charge is being fired at the right time, and the engine is properly cooled and lubricated. Each of these areas will be covered in detail in later chapters.

Simple Engine in Operation

In its simplest form, an engine consists of a ported cylinder, piston, connecting rod, and crankshaft. See **Figure 5-9**. The piston is a close fit inside

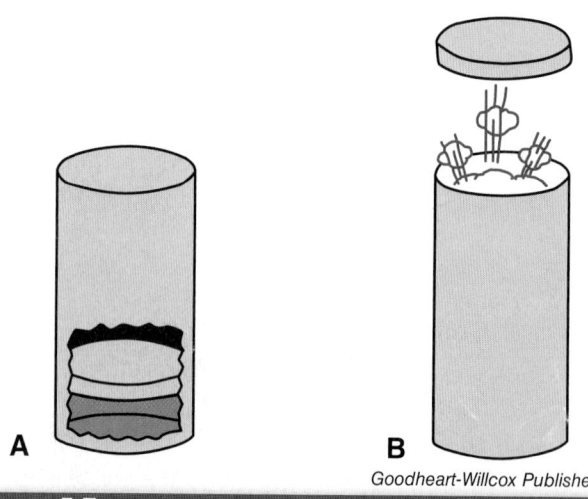

Goodheart-Willcox Publisher

Figure 5-7.

A—The lid is placed in a long container. B—Most of the energy of the burning fuel is absorbed by the lid, imparting greater speed to the lid when combustion occurs.

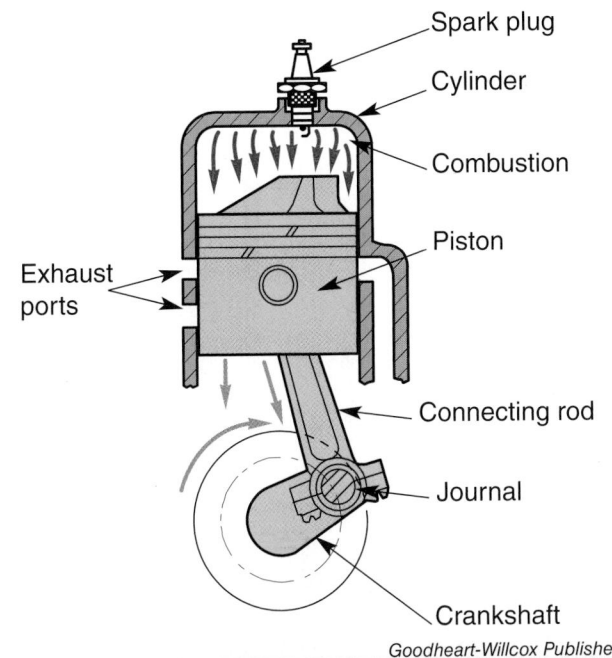

Goodheart-Willcox Publisher

Figure 5-9.

Combustion forces the piston down to rotate the crankshaft.

Two- and Four-Stroke Engines

A basic design feature that aids in small engine identification is the number of piston strokes required to complete one operating cycle. A four-stroke engine, for example, requires four strokes per cycle; a two-stroke engine requires two.

A *stroke* of the piston is its movement in the cylinder from one end of its travel to the other. When the piston is at the bottom of its travel, it is said to be at *bottom dead center* (BDC). When it is at the top of its stroke, it is at *top dead center* (TDC). Each stroke of the piston, then, is either toward the rotating crankshaft or away from it. Each stroke is identified by the job it performs (intake, exhaust, etc.).

Four-Stroke Engine

In a *four-stroke engine* (called a *four-cycle engine*), four strokes are needed to complete the operating cycle. The four strokes are as follows:

- intake stroke
- compression stroke
- power stroke
- exhaust stroke

Two strokes occur during each revolution of the crankshaft. Therefore, a four-stroke cycle requires two revolutions of the crankshaft to complete one operating cycle. **Figure 5-10** illustrates each of the four strokes taking place in proper sequence.

> **Note**
>
> Four-stroke engines use intake and exhaust valves to control the flow of gases into and out of the combustion chamber.

Intake Stroke

Figure 5-10A shows the piston traveling downward in the cylinder on the *intake stroke*. As the piston moves down, the volume of space above it is increased. This creates a partial vacuum that draws the air-fuel mixture through the intake valve port and into the cylinder.

With the intake valve open during the intake stroke, atmospheric pressure outside the engine forces air through the carburetor. This gives a

the cylinder, yet it is free to slide on the lubricated walls of the cylinder. One end of the connecting rod is attached to the piston; the other end is fastened to an offset journal, or crankpin, on the crankshaft. As the piston moves up and down, the connecting rod forces the journal to follow a circular path, rotating the crankshaft.

When the engine is cranked, gasoline is atomized and mixed with air. This mixture is forced through an intake port and into the cylinder, where it is compressed by the piston on the upstroke and ignited by an electrical spark.

Burning rapidly, the heated gases trapped within the cylinder (combustion chamber) expand and apply pressure to the walls of the cylinder and to the top of the piston. This pressure drives the piston downward, causing the crankshaft to turn. This downward movement of the piston is called the power stroke.

As the piston and connecting rod push the crankshaft journal downward, the pressure of the burned gases is released through an exhaust port. Meanwhile, a fresh air-fuel charge enters the cylinder and momentum pushes the crankshaft journal past the bottom of its travel, carrying it into the upstroke on another operating cycle.

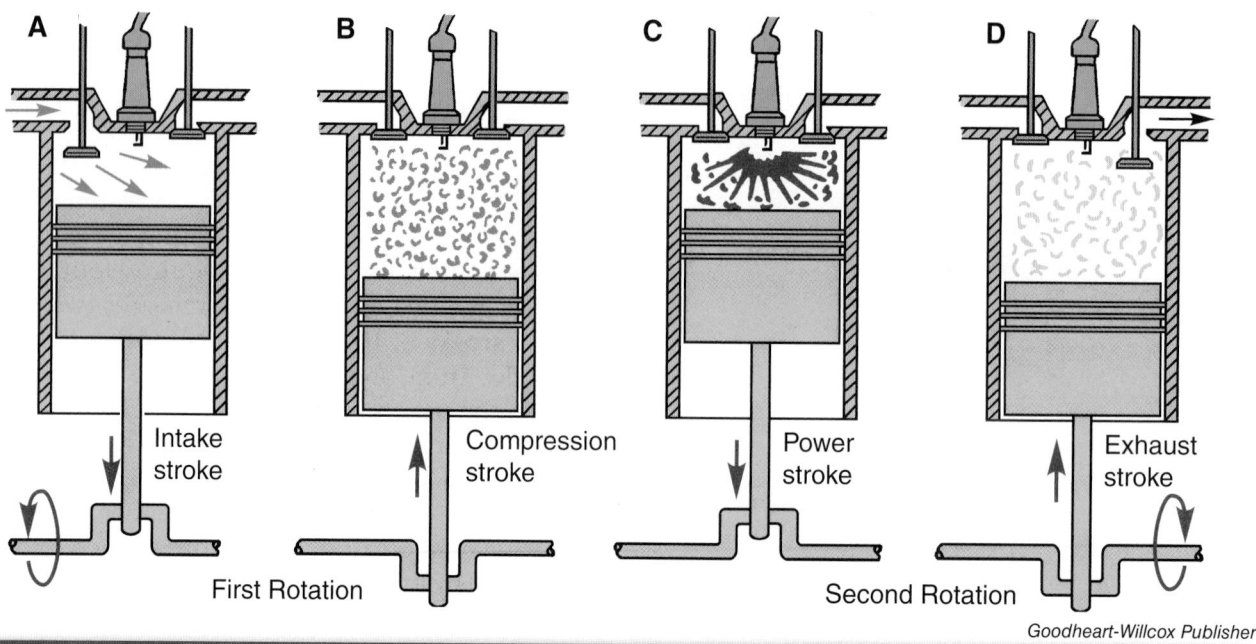

Figure 5-10.

Sequence of events in a four-stroke engine, requiring two revolutions of the crankshaft and one power stroke out of four.

large boost to the air-fuel induction process. With nature balancing unequal pressures in this manner, it follows that the larger the diameter of the cylinder and the longer the stroke of the piston, the greater the volume of air entering the cylinder on the intake stroke.

Bear in mind that the intake valve performs several key functions. These key functions are as follows:

1. It must open at the correct instant to permit intake of air-fuel mixture.
2. It must close at the correct time and seal during compression.
3. Its shape must be streamlined, so the flow of gases into the combustion chamber will not be obstructed.

The intake valves do not get as hot as the exhaust valves. The incoming air-fuel mixture tends to cool the intake valve during operation.

Compression Stroke

The *compression stroke* occurs as the piston moves upward in the cylinder. See **Figure 5-10B**. During this stroke, the valves are tightly closed.

As the piston moves upward, the air-fuel mixture is compressed into a smaller space. This increases the force of combustion for two reasons:

1. When atoms that make up tiny molecules of air and fuel are squeezed closer together, heat energy is created. Each molecule of fuel is heated very close to its flash point (point at which fuel will ignite spontaneously). When combustion does occur, it is practically instantaneous and complete for the entire air-fuel mixture.
2. The force of combustion is increased because tightly packed molecules are highly activated and are striving to move apart. This energy, combined with expanding energy of combustion, provides tremendous force against the piston.

Note

It is possible to run an engine on uncompressed mixtures, but power loss produces a very inefficient engine.

Power Stroke

During the *power stroke*, both valves remain in the closed position. See **Figure 5-10C**. As the piston compresses the charge and reaches the top of the cylinder, an electrical spark jumps the gap between the electrodes of the spark plug. This ignites the air-fuel mixture, and the force of combustion (rapid expansion of burning gases) pushes the piston downward.

Actually, the full charge does not burn at once. The flame progresses outward from the spark plug, spreading combustion and providing even pressure over the piston face throughout the power stroke.

The entire fuel charge must ignite and expand in an incredibly short period of time. Most engines have the spark timed to ignite the fuel slightly before the piston reaches top dead center (TDC) of the compression stroke. This provides a little more time for the mixture to burn and accumulate its expanding force.

Basically, the amount of power produced by the power stroke depends on the volume of the air-fuel mixture in the cylinder and the compression ratio of the engine. The *compression ratio* is the proportionate difference between the volume of cylinder and combustion chamber at bottom dead center and the volume of cylinder and combustion chamber at top dead center. If the compression ratio is too high, the fuel may be heated to its flash point during the compression stroke and ignite too early.

Exhaust Stroke

After the piston has completed the power stroke, the burned gases must be removed from the cylinder before introducing a fresh charge. This takes place during the *exhaust stroke*. The exhaust valve opens and the rising piston pushes the exhaust gases from the cylinder. See **Figure 5-10D**.

The exhaust valve has to function much like the intake valve. When closed, the valve must seal. When open, it must allow a streamlined flow of exhaust gases out through the port. The removal of gases from the cylinder is called *scavenging*.

The passageway that carries away exhaust gases is referred to as the exhaust manifold or exhaust port. The exhaust manifold must be designed for the smooth flow of gases.

The heat absorbed by the exhaust valve must be controlled or the valve will deteriorate rapidly. Some valve heat is carried away by conduction through the valve stem to the guide. However, the hottest part of the valve, the valve head, transfers heat through the valve seat to the cylinder block. See **Figure 5-11**.

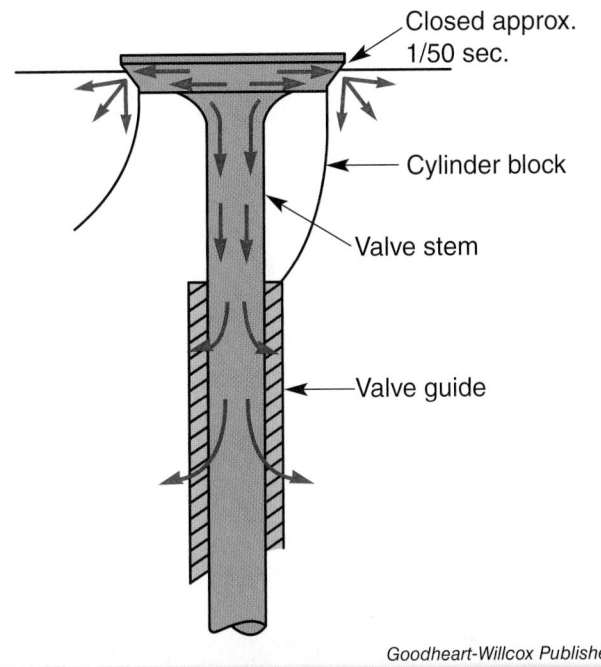

Goodheart-Willcox Publisher

Figure 5-11.

The exhaust valve must cool during an incredibly short period (1/50 sec. at 3600 rpm). Heat is conducted from the valve through the seat to the cylinder block. Some heat travels down the stem and to the valve guide.

Valve Timing

Valve timing is measured in degrees of crankshaft rotation. The point at which the valves open or close before or after the piston is at top dead center (TDC) or bottom dead center (BDC) varies with different engines.

Note

Engineers also specify the point at which the spark must occur. Chapter 9 of this text explores this in more detail.

Figure 5-12 shows one complete operating cycle of a four-stroke engine. Beginning at point A, the intake valve opens 10° before TDC and stays open through 235°. The exhaust valve closes 30° after TDC. *Valve overlap* occurs when both valves are open at the same time.

During the compression stroke, the intake valve closes and ignition occurs 30° before TDC. The power stroke continues through 120° past TDC. The exhaust valve opens 60° before BDC and stays open through 270°. During the last 40°, the intake valve is also open and the second cycle has begun.

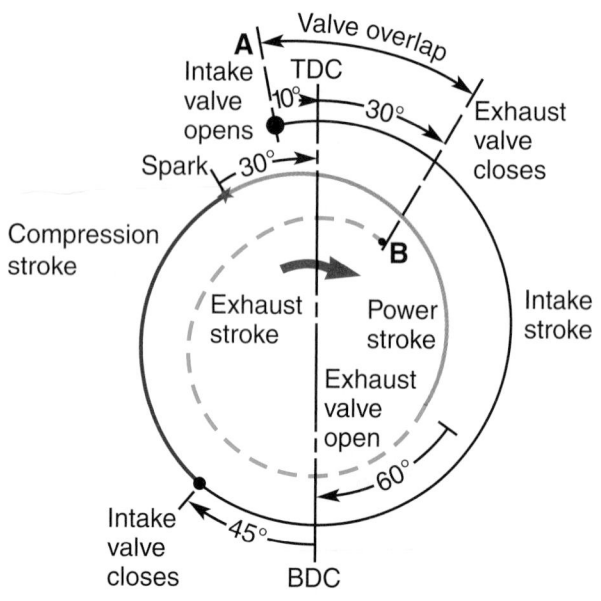

Figure 5-12.

The four-stroke cycle diagram shows the exact number of degrees each valve is open or closed and the time spark ignition occurs. Note that both valves are open (overlap) through an arc of 40°, permitting exhausting gases to create a partial vacuum in the cylinder and help draw a mixture of fuel into the cylinder.

Lubrication

Lubrication of the four-stroke engine is provided by placing the correct quantity and grade of engine oil in the crankcase. Several methods are used to feed the oil to the correct locations. The two most common methods are the splash system and the pump system. Some engines employ one or the other; others use a combination of both.

The oil in a four-stroke engine must be drained periodically and replaced with clean oil. Also worth noting, four-stroke engines must be operated in an upright position or the oil will flow away from the pump or splash finger, preventing lubrication.

Two-Stroke Engine

The *two-stroke engine* (commonly called *two-cycle engine*) performs the same cycle of events as the four-stroke engine. The main difference is that the intake, compression, power, and exhaust functions take place during only two strokes of the piston. The two strokes occur during each revolution of the crankshaft. Therefore, it takes only one revolution of the crankshaft to complete a two-stroke cycle.

A two-stroke engine has several advantages over a four-cycle unit. It is much simpler in design than the four-stroke engine because the conventional camshaft, valves, and tappets are unnecessary. See **Figure 5-13**.

Additionally, a two-stroke engine is smaller and lighter than a four-stroke engine of equivalent horsepower. Unlike the four-stroke engine, the two-stroke engine will get adequate lubrication even when operated at extreme angles. It receives its lubrication as fuel mixed with oil is passed through the engine.

Installing the correct mixture of fuel and oil is a critical factor in maintaining a two-stroke engine in good working condition. The prescribed type and grade of engine oil must be mixed with the fuel in proper proportion before being placed in the fuel tank.

Moving Parts—Four-Cycle Engine

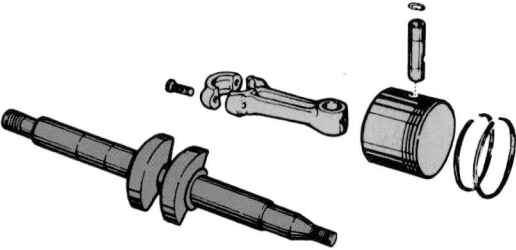

Moving Parts—Two-Cycle Engine

Figure 5-13.

The number of moving parts in a four-stroke engine is greater than in a two-stroke engine. Other differences are listed in the chart at the end of this chapter.

In this way, there is clean oil continuously supplied to all moving parts while the engine is running. The oil eventually burns in the combustion chamber and is exhausted with other gases.

Two-stroke engines are popular in string trimmers, leaf blowers, and other high-rpm applications.

Principles of Two-Stroke Operation

The location of the ports in a two-stroke engine is essential to correct timing of the intake, transfer, and exhaust functions, **Figure 5-14**. The cutaway cylinder in **Figure 5-14A** shows the exhaust port at the highest point, the transfer port next, and the intake port at the lowest point. Some engines have more than one transfer port. See **Figure 5-14B**. **Figure 5-15** illustrates the principles of two-stroke engine operation.

Intake into the Crankcase

As the piston moves upward in the cylinder of a two-stroke engine, crankcase pressure drops and the intake port is exposed. Because atmospheric pressure is greater than the crankcase pressure, air rushes through the intake port and into the crankcase to equalize the pressures. See **Figure 5-15A**.

While passing through the carburetor, the intake air pulls a charge of fuel and oil along with it. This charge remains in the crankcase to lubricate ball and needle bearings until the piston opens the transfer port on the downstroke.

Ignition-Power

As the piston travels upward, it also compresses the air-fuel charge brought into the cylinder during the previous cycle to about one-tenth of its original volume. See **Figure 5-15A**. The spark is timed to ignite the air-fuel mixture when the piston approaches TDC. See **Figure 5-15B**.

On some small engines, spark occurs almost at TDC during starting, and then automatically advances so that it occurs earlier. This is done to get better efficiency from the force of combustion at higher speeds.

Peak combustion pressure is applied against the piston top immediately after TDC. Driving downward with maximum force, the piston transmits straight line motion through the connecting rod to create rotary motion of the crankshaft. See **Figure 5-15C**.

Exhaust

The exhaust phase of the two-stroke cycle is shown in **Figure 5-15C**. As the piston moves to expose the exhaust port, most of the burned gases are expelled. Complete exhausting of gases from the cylinder and combustion chamber takes place when the transfer ports are opened and the new air-fuel charge rushes in.

Fuel Transfer

Figure 5-15C and **Figure 5-15D** show the piston moving downward, compressing the air-fuel charge in the crankcase. When the piston travels far enough on the downstroke, the transfer port is

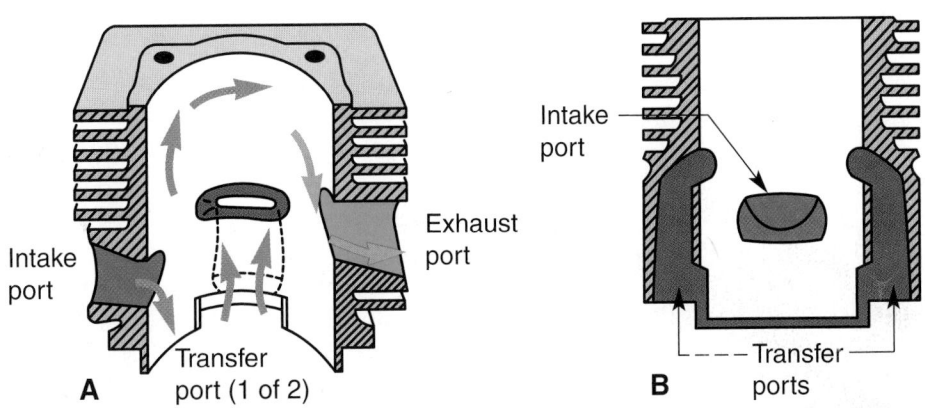

Intake port

Exhaust port

Intake port

Transfer port (1 of 2)

A

Transfer ports

B

Kohler Co.

Figure 5-14.

A cutaway cylinder block shows the location of the intake, exhaust, and transfer ports of a two-cycle engine. A—Due to the cutaway, only one of two transfer ports is shown. B—The section is revolved 90° to show both ports.

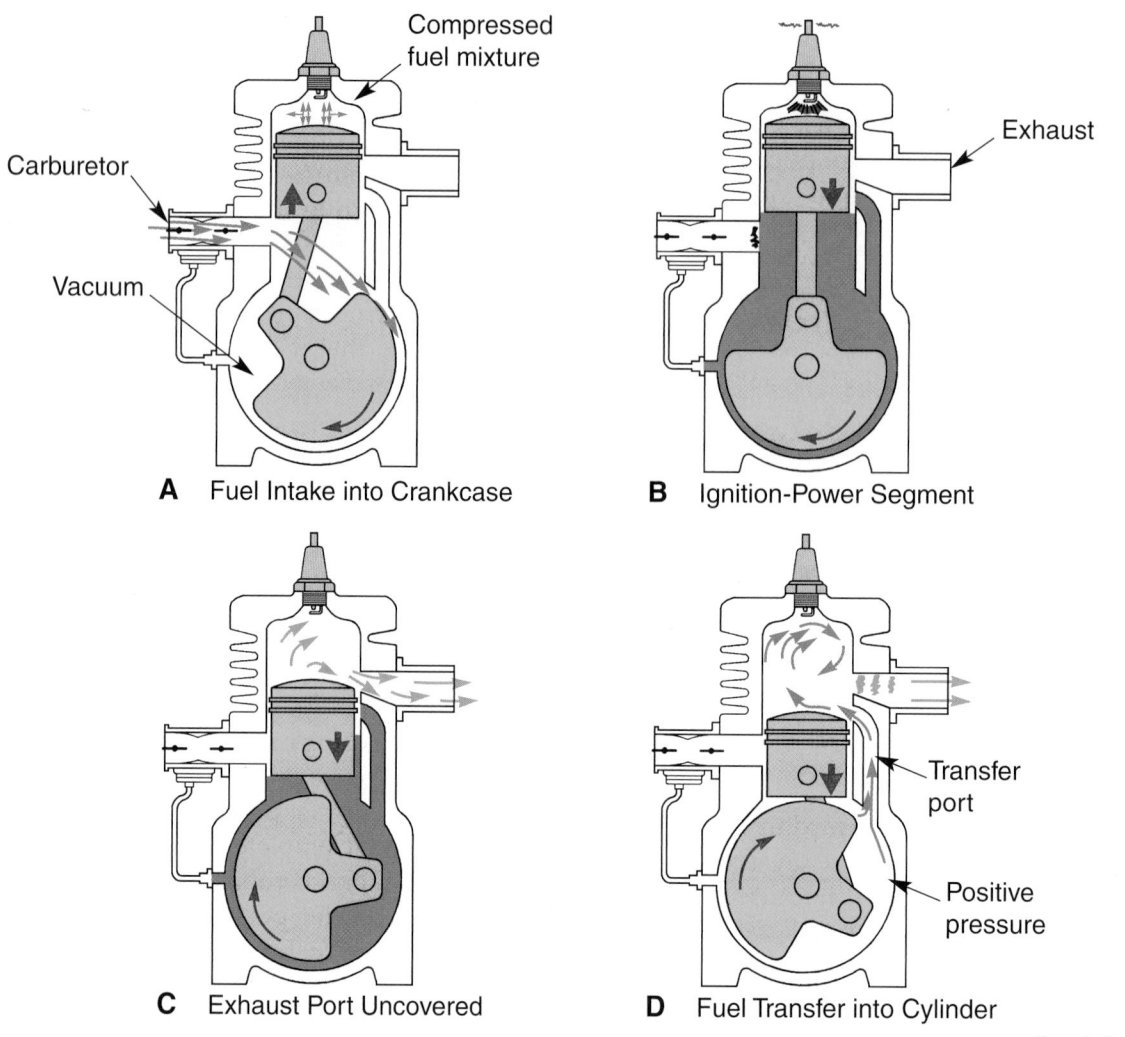

Rupp Industries, Inc.

Figure 5-15.

These illustrations show the sequence of events that take place in a two-stroke engine. Compression and intake occur simultaneously, and then ignition occurs. Exhaust precedes the transfer of fuel during the lower portion of the power stroke. The piston functions as the only valve in the engine.

opened and the compressed air-fuel charge rushes through the port and into the cylinder. The new charge cools the combustion area and pushes (scavenges) the remaining exhaust gases out of the cylinder. This completes one cycle of operation.

Scavenge Loss

In a conventional two-stroke engine, a significant portion of the air-fuel charge (in some cases, over 25%) flows out through the open exhaust port as it pushes the exhaust gases from the cylinder. This occurrence is called *scavenge loss*. Scavenge loss results in increased hydrocarbon emissions and reduced fuel economy.

Stratified Scavenge Engine

To reduce two-cycle engine emissions and increase fuel economy, manufacturers have designed a two-cycle engine that effectively eliminates scavenge loss of the air-fuel charge. This engine, called a stratified scavenge engine, uses an extra intake port and a specially shaped piston to introduce a small amount of fresh air into the transfer port ahead of the air-fuel charge. When the transfer port is uncovered during the fuel transfer phase of two-cycle operation, the fresh air flows into the cylinder before the air-fuel charge, pushing the spent exhaust gases from the cylinder. This prevents the unburned fuel in the air-fuel charge from escaping through the exhaust port.

Four-Stroke Engine vs. Two-Stroke Engine

The advantages and disadvantages of any engine are directly related to the purpose for which the engine is intended. It cannot be said that one type of engine is better than another without considering every aspect of its application.

The chart in **Figure 5-16** lists the differences between two- and four-stroke engines.

Characteristics	Four-Cycle Engine (equal hp) One Cylinder	Two-Cycle Engine (equal hp) One Cylinder
1. Number of major moving parts	Nine	Three
2. Power strokes	One every two revolutions of crankshaft	One every revolution of crankshaft
3. Running temperature	Cooler running	Hotter running
4. Overall engine size	Larger	Smaller
5. Engine weight	Heavier construction	Lighter in weight
6. Bore size equal hp	Larger	Smaller
7. Fuel and oil	No mixture required	Must be premixed
8. Fuel consumption	Fewer gallons per hour	More gallons per hour
9. Oil consumption	Oil recirculates and stays in engine	Oil is burned with fuel
10. Sound	Generally quiet	Louder in operation
11. Operation	Smoother	More erratic
12. Acceleration	Slower	Very quick
13. General maintenance	Greater	Less
14. Initial cost	Greater	Less
15. Versatility of operation	Limited slope operation (Receives less lubrication when tilted)	Lubrication not affected at any angle of operation
16. General operating efficiency (hp/wt. ratio)	Less efficient	More efficient
17. Pull starting	Two crankshaft rotations required to produce one ignition phase	One revolution produces an ignition phase
18. Flywheel	Requires heavier flywheel to carry engine through three nonpower strokes	Lighter flywheel

Kohler Co.

Figure 5-16.

This chart lists the differences between two-stroke and four-stroke engines.

Summary

A gasoline-fueled engine is a mechanism designed to transform the chemical energy of burning fuel into mechanical energy. A gasoline engine is an internal combustion engine. In an internal combustion engine, gasoline is combined with air and burned inside the engine. The more surface area of gasoline exposed to the air, the faster a given amount will burn. To produce the rapid burning required in an engine, gasoline must be broken up into tiny droplets and mixed with air. This is called atomizing.

The stroke of a piston is its movement in the cylinder from one end of its travel to another. Four-stroke engines need four strokes to complete the operating cycle: intake, compression, power, and exhaust. Lubrication of four-stroke engines is generally provided by a splash system or a pump system.

In a two-stroke engine, the intake, compression, power, and exhaust functions take place during two strokes of the piston. Two-stroke engines have many advantages over four-cycle units. They do not have conventional valves, tappets, or a camshaft, so they are simpler in design. Two-stroke engines are also smaller and lighter than four-stroke engines of equivalent horsepower.

The two-stroke engine receives its lubrication as a fuel-oil mixture is passed through the engine. Therefore, it will receive adequate lubrication even when operated at extreme angles.

Review Questions

Answer the following questions on a separate sheet of paper.

1. In a(n) _____ combustion engine, gasoline is combined with air and burned inside the engine.

2. Explain why gasoline is atomized before being burned in an engine.

3. Name the four strokes of a four-stroke engine in proper order.

4. Name three important intake valve functions.

5. Why is there a difference in temperature between the intake and exhaust valves?

6. How does compression increase the force of combustion?

7. The compression ratio must be limited in gasoline spark ignition engines, because _____.

   A. there is no power advantage after compressing the fuel to a certain point
   B. the engine becomes too difficult to start
   C. mechanically it is not possible to increase the compression ratio
   D. the heat of compression will ignite the air-fuel mixture too soon

8. Time during the four-stroke cycle when both valves are open is called _____.

9. What are the two methods employed for lubricating four-stroke engines?

10. What is the main difference between a four-cycle engine and a two-cycle engine?

Suggested Activities

1. Look up additional information about internal combustion engine development. Names to look up include Christian Huygens, Philip Lebon, Samuel Brown, William Barnett, Pierre Lenoir, Beau DeRochas, Dr. N. A. Otto, Atkinson, Gottlieb Daimler, Priestman and Hall, Herbert Akroyd Stuart, and Rudolph Diesel.

2. Begin a collection of engine repair and service manuals.

3. Make a bulletin board display that illustrates the principles of two- and four-stroke engines.

CHAPTER 6

Engine Components

Learning Objectives

After studying this chapter, you will be able to:

- Identify the basic components of a small engine and describe the function of each component.
- Describe engine block variations.
- Describe the construction and operation of the crankshaft.
- Explain piston design considerations and differentiate between types of piston rings.
- Describe connecting rod and bearing variations.
- Identify common valve train configurations.

Key Terms

antifriction bearings
automatic compression
  release
camshaft
compression rings
connecting rod
cooling fins
crankcase
crankcase seals
crankshaft
crankshaft throw
cylinder block
engine block
floating rings
flywheel
friction bearings
lands
oil control rings
overhead cam (OHC)
overhead valve (OHV)
pin boss
pinned rings

piston
piston pin
piston rings
piston skirt
poppet valve
pushrods
rewind starter
  assembly
ring tension
rocker arms
side clearance
slap
snap rings
sump
thrust surfaces
valve guide
valve lifter
valve spring
valve train
valve-in-block
wrist pin

Engine Components

Chapter 5 provided you with an explanation of two- and four-stroke engine operation and a general idea of how the major parts of a gasoline engine operate. This chapter will detail the design and construction of the various mechanical parts that are commonly used in small gasoline engines. Most of these parts are found on all engine types. A few of the parts are specific to either two- or four-stroke engine designs.

Engine Block

The *engine block* keeps all engine parts in alignment. See **Figure 6-1**. This critical engine component is usually a casting of iron or an aluminum alloy. The engine block consists of two sections: the cylinder block and the crankcase. The *cylinder block* is the portion of the engine block that contains the cylinder bore. It must be strong enough to contain the power developed by the expanding gases.

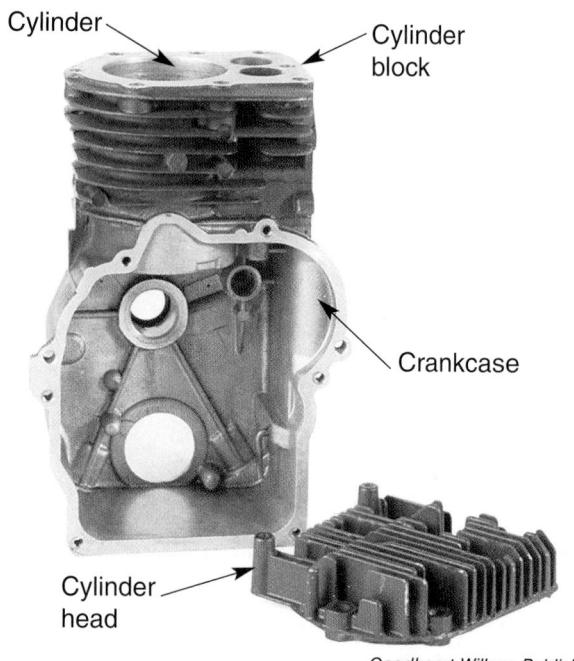

Goodheart-Willcox Publisher

Figure 6-1.

The engine block is important because it keeps all moving parts in alignment. This is a combined cylinder block and crankcase. The cylinder head and sealing gasket are bolted to the cylinder block.

The cylinder can be produced accurately by modern methods. It may be bored directly into the casting, or it may be a steel sleeve inserted into an oversize hole bored in the block.

The cylinder head may be bolted to the block or it may be cast as part of the cylinder block. The method employed depends on the intended application of the engine and the manufacturer's preference.

Aluminum cylinder blocks are often cast around a steel sleeve. Aluminum, being a soft metal, would wear out quickly due to the friction of the piston. Advantages of aluminum are its light weight and ability to dissipate heat rapidly.

All air-cooled engines have *cooling fins* on the outside of the cylinder block and cylinder head. The size, thickness, spacing, and direction of the cooling fins are carefully engineered for efficient air circulation and heat control.

The *crankcase* is the portion of the engine block that contains the crankshaft. It must be rigid and strong enough to withstand the rotational forces of the crankshaft, while keeping all parts in proper alignment. Oil for lubrication is contained in the crankcase on some engines. On others, a valve system in the crankcase is used that allows

a fuel, air, and oil mixture to enter. The crankcase must be designed to protect the internal parts. Gaskets and oil seals are used to keep out dirt and keep in the clean oil.

The crankcase and the cylinder block may be cast as a single unit or the two sections can be fastened together by bolts. Casting metal is the process of pouring molten metal into a form of a desired shape. **Figure 6-1** shows a one-piece engine block with a separate, bolted cylinder head. A two-piece engine block is shown in **Figure 6-2**. Note that the cylinder head is an integral part of the cylinder block.

Crankshaft

The *crankshaft* is the major rotating part of the engine. See **Figure 6-3**. It converts the reciprocating (back and forth) motion of the piston into rotary (circular) motion. The crankshaft transmits engine torque to a pulley or gear, so that some mechanism can be driven by the engine. It also drives the camshaft (on four-stroke engines), supports the flywheel, and, in many engines, operates the ignition system.

Crankshafts can be made of cast or drop-forged steel. One-piece and multipiece crankshafts are used. **Figure 6-4** shows a typical one-piece small engine crankshaft. Note the tapered end on the crankshaft, which receives the flywheel. The end of the crankshaft and the hole through the flywheel have matched tapers that provide good holding power. The flywheel is keyed to the end of the shaft with

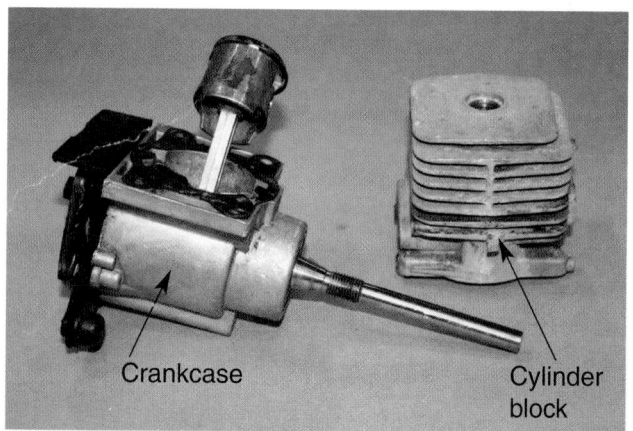

Goodheart-Willcox Publisher

Figure 6-2.

On this engine, the cylinder block is bolted to the crankcase. The cylinder head is cast as part of the cylinder block.

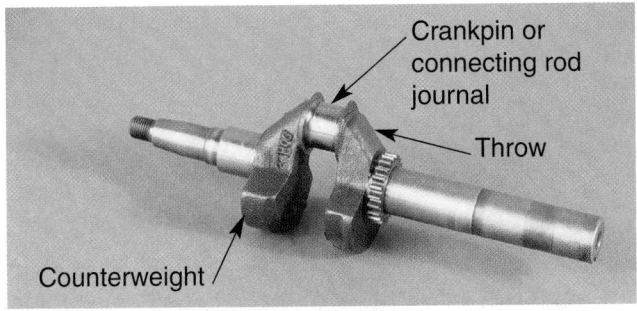

Goodheart-Willcox Publisher

Figure 6-3.

A crankshaft for a single cylinder engine. Large counterweights opposite the crank journal balance rotational forces.

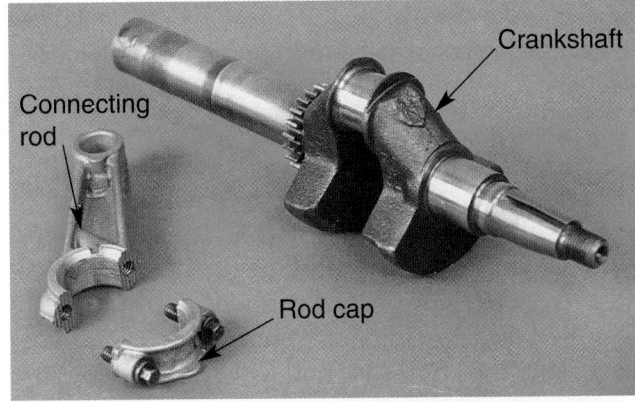

Goodheart-Willcox Publisher

Figure 6-4.

Single-piece crankshafts are most popular in small gasoline engine applications.

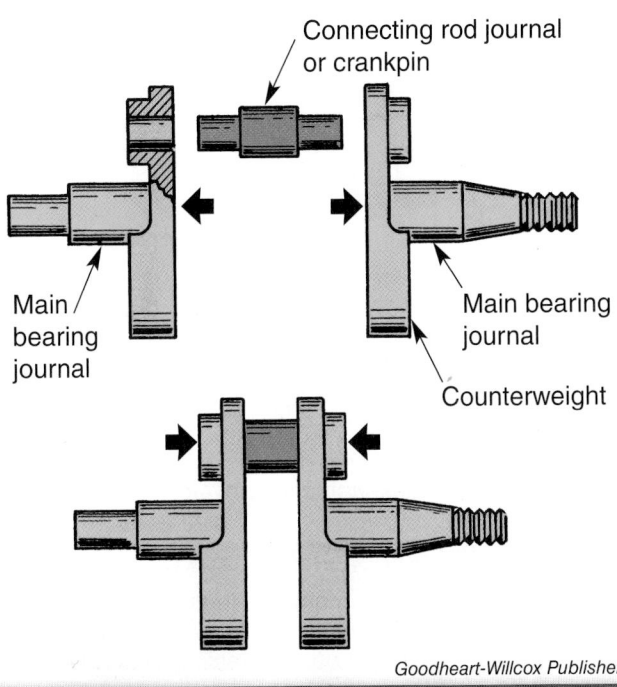

Goodheart-Willcox Publisher

Figure 6-5.

Multipiece crankshafts have various parts pressed together under heavy pressure.

Crankshaft Main Bearings

The crankshaft is supported by one or more main bearings. Often, the main bearing journal surfaces are hardened by an induction hardening process to provide long service life. The three types of main bearings used are:

- Sleeve or bushing. See **Figure 6-6**.
- Roller bearing. See **Figure 6-7**.
- Ball bearing. See **Figure 6-8**.

When roller bearings are used to support the crankshaft, highly polished, hardened alloy steel bearing races are pressed into the crankcase to reduce friction and provide good wearability.

Crankcase Seals

Crankcase seals prevent leakage of oil from the areas where the crankshaft and crankcase come together. The shell of the seal makes fixed contact with the crankcase, while the knife edge of the sealing lip rubs lightly against the crankshaft. A small coil spring keeps the sealing lip in constant contact with the shaft it seals. See **Figure 6-9**.

Seals are made of neoprene, leather, graphite, or other materials, depending on how they are used.

a Woodruff key. This type of key cannot slip out during operation. A lock washer and nut hold the flywheel in place. A multipiece crankshaft is shown in **Figure 6-5**.

The *crankshaft throw* is the offset portion of the shaft measured from the centerline of the main bearing bore to the centerline of the connecting rod journal. The connecting rod journal is commonly referred to as the *crank throw* or *crankpin*.

To help offset the unbalance created by the force of the reciprocating mass (connecting rod, piston, and crankpin), counterweights are added to the crankshaft. By placing these weights opposite the crankpin, engine vibration is greatly reduced. As shown in **Figures 6-4** and **6-5**, the counterweights are usually forged as an integral part of the crankshaft.

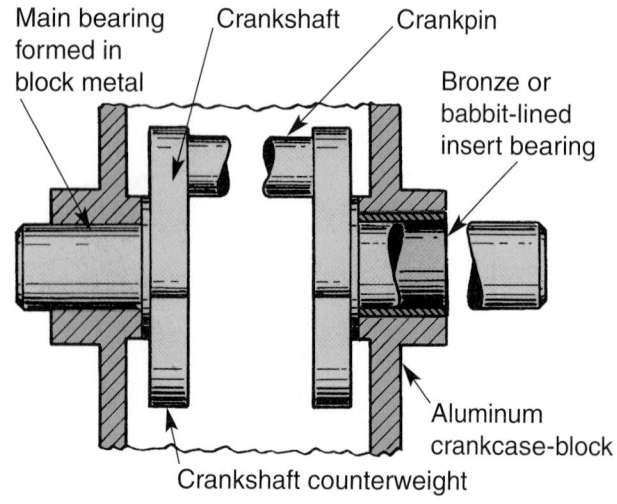

Main bearing formed in block metal — Crankshaft — Crankpin

Bronze or babbit-lined insert bearing

Aluminum crankcase-block

Crankshaft counterweight

Goodheart-Willcox Publisher

Figure 6-6.

Friction-type crankshaft main bearings. The shaft at left uses a bore in the aluminum crankcase as a bearing surface. The shaft at right uses a precision insert bearing.

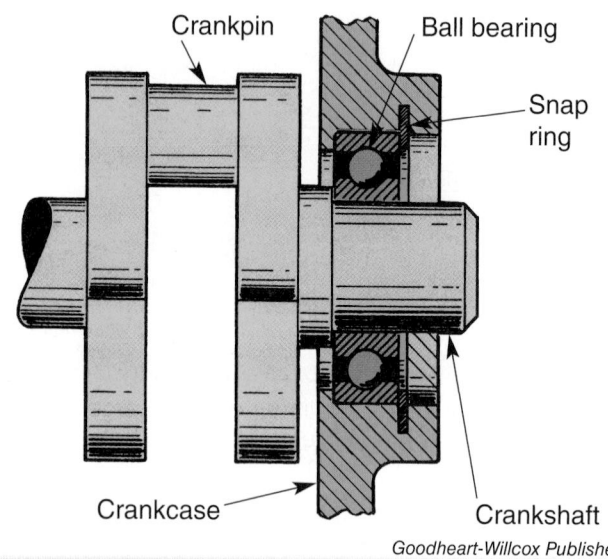

Crankpin — Ball bearing

Snap ring

Crankcase — Crankshaft

Goodheart-Willcox Publisher

Figure 6-8.

A ball bearing can also be used as a crankshaft main bearing.

Pistons

The *piston* is the straight line driving member of the engine. It is subjected to the direct heat of combustion and must have adequate clearance in the cylinder to allow for expansion.

The piston provides a seal between the combustion chamber and the crankcase. This is accomplished by cutting grooves near the top of the piston and installing *piston rings*. The piston rings fit the grooves with a slight side clearance, and exert tension on the cylinder wall. Properly installed, piston rings prevent blowby of exhaust gases into the crankcase and leakage of oil into the combustion chamber. The number of piston rings per piston depends on the type of engine and its design. Note the piston rings in **Figure 6-10**.

Piston Construction

Pistons can be made of aluminum or steel. Aluminum is by far the most popular metal for this application. The surface may be coated with a special break-in finish (tin or other coating). Sometimes pistons are chrome plated for installations where they operate directly on aluminum-alloy cylinder walls.

The type of piston often used in a four-stroke engine is shown in **Figure 6-11**. The head is quite thick, giving this hardworking part strength and resistance to overheating. The area below the head has grooves for the piston rings. The full-diameter ridges between the grooves are called *lands*. The wall or bottom of the oil ring groove is either slotted or pierced with holes. Oil wiped from the cylinder wall by the oil ring flows through these holes and back into the oil sump. The *sump* is the low area of the engine block where the oil collects.

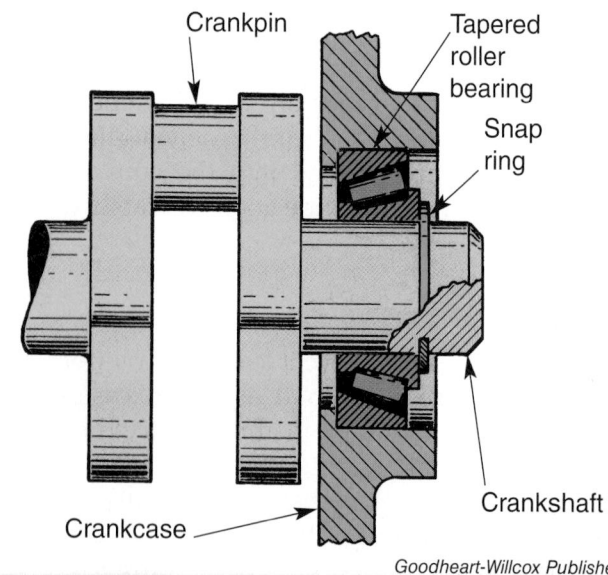

Crankpin — Tapered roller bearing

Snap ring

Crankshaft

Crankcase

Goodheart-Willcox Publisher

Figure 6-7.

Typical use of a tapered roller bearing as a crankshaft main bearing.

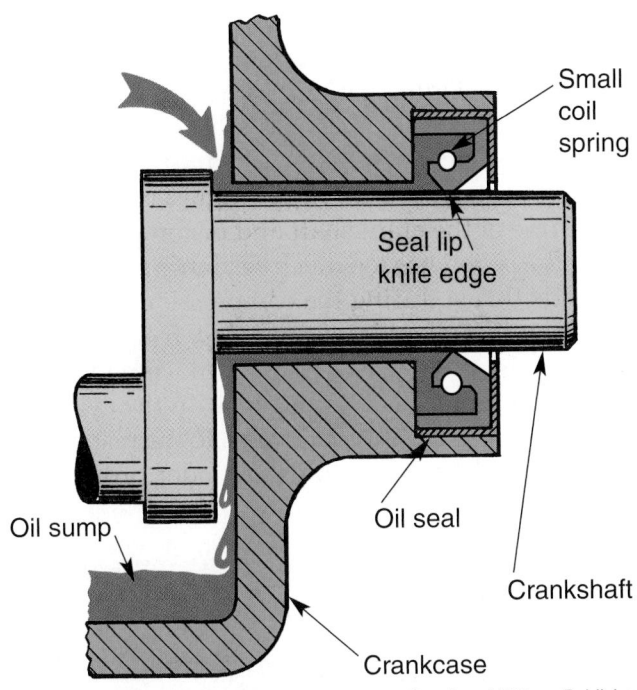

Figure 6-9.

A typical neoprene oil seal has a sealing lip with a sharp edge, providing increased pressure and reduced friction.

Pistons may have grooves for one to four rings. Generally, the two-stroke engine piston has one or two grooves. Both are compression ring grooves. Four-stroke engine pistons will generally have three grooves, two for compression rings and one for an oil control ring.

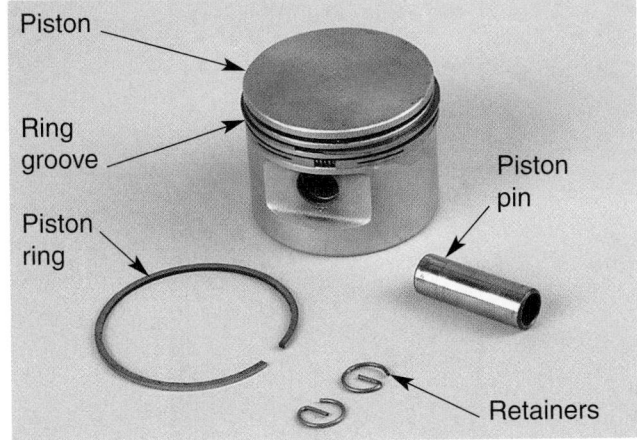

Figure 6-10.

The piston is the largest sliding-reciprocating part in an engine. Piston rings seal the combustion chamber from the crankcase and must fit properly.

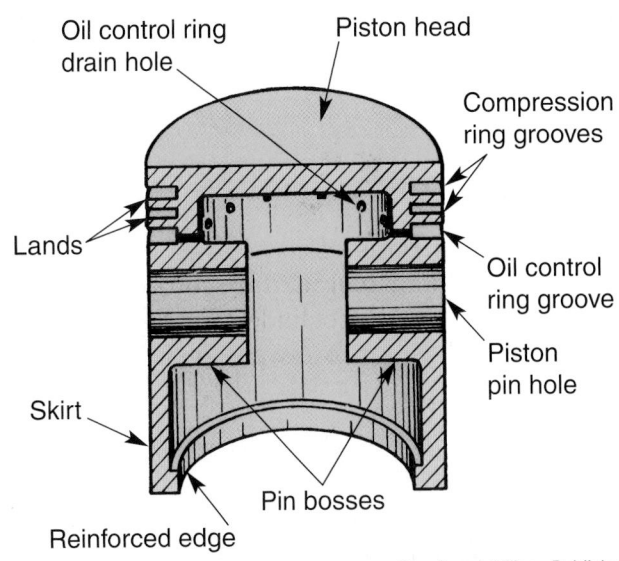

Figure 6-11.

This typical four-stroke engine piston is cut away to show construction details.

There is a hole in each side of the piston through which a *piston pin*, or *wrist pin*, is placed. This pin acts as a hinge between the connecting rod and piston and holds the two together. The section of the piston surrounding the piston pin hole is called the *pin boss*. It is thick and often reinforced with cast-in webs.

The *piston skirt* is the part of the piston below the bottom of the lower ring groove. The skirt is designed to be as light as possible to hold down the weight of the assembly.

The skirt actually guides the piston and keeps it from tipping from side to side. Portions of it may be cut away for lightness. Also, in some two-stroke engines, portions may be cut away to allow the air-fuel mixture to pass through the piston skirt into other parts of the cylinder.

Cam-Ground Pistons

When the designer wants the smallest possible clearance between the piston skirt and the cylinder wall, skirts are often cam ground to an elliptical (oval) shape. The oval shape of a cam-ground piston allows the thrust surfaces (sides of skirt forced against cylinder during compression and firing) to fit more closely, even when cold. As the piston heats up, the diameter across the thrust surfaces remains constant and the piston enlarges parallel to (in the same direction as) the piston pin. See

Figure 6-12. These exaggerated views illustrate how a cam-ground piston expands to a round shape as it becomes hot.

Piston Thrust Surfaces

During the compression stroke, the pressure of the confined air-fuel mixture forces the piston toward one side of the cylinder. See **Figure 6-13A**. When the crankshaft throw passes TDC, burning and rapidly expanding gases push hard on the piston, forcing it against the opposite side of the cylinder. See **Figure 6-13B**.

In each instance, the sides of the piston forced against the cylinder wall are called *thrust surfaces*. These surfaces are at right angles (90°) to the centerline of the crankshaft and piston pin.

If the piston has too much clearance in the cylinder, side thrust during the compression and firing strokes will make it move, or *slap*, from one side of the cylinder to the other. As it moves sideways, the piston will tend to tip, or cock, in the cylinder. This loose fit can be very harmful to the piston and rings. The piston must fit the cylinder properly to avoid slapping.

Piston Head Size

The piston head receives the brunt of combustion heat, so it runs hotter than the skirt and expands more. Because of this, the head of the piston often is made with a smaller diameter than the skirt. **Figure 6-14** shows an exaggerated view of a piston with the head smaller than the skirt. The actual difference is only a few thousandths of an inch.

Piston Head Shape

Piston heads are manufactured in many different shapes, depending on the type of small engine and its use. On four-stroke engines, the piston head

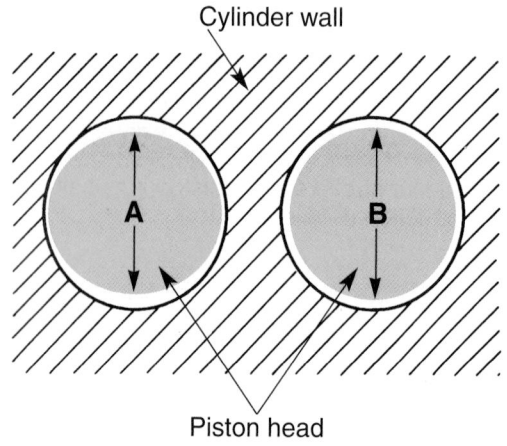

Cylinder wall

Piston head

Goodheart-Willcox Publisher

Figure 6-12.

Exaggerated top views of a cam ground piston as it would fit in a cylinder. A—Cold. B—Hot. Arrows indicate piston pin position.

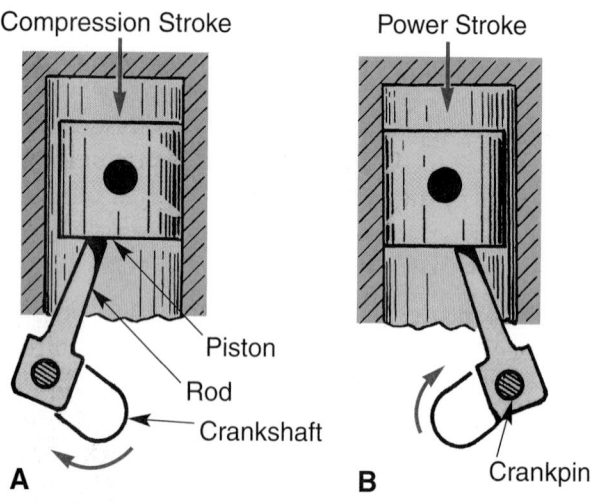

Goodheart-Willcox Publisher

Figure 6-13.

The thrust surfaces of a piston must resist heavy side pressure against the cylinder walls. A—Upstroke. B—Downstroke.

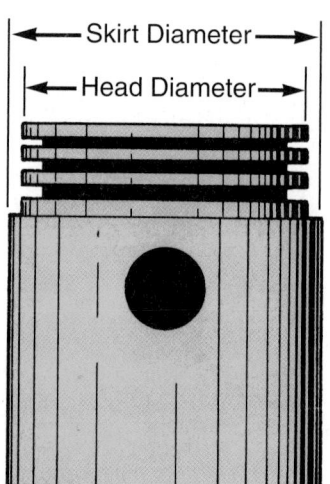

Goodheart-Willcox Publisher

Figure 6-14.

The piston head receives the greatest heat and is sometimes made smaller to compensate for expansion.

can be flat, domed, or wedge-shaped. Pistons used in two-stroke engines generally are flat when used with a loop-scavenging design. Cross-scavenging designs use a raised baffle or deflector head piston. See **Figure 6-15**.

Piston Rings

All small engine pistons must have clearance for lubrication and expansion. At the same time, they must have rings to help do the job of sealing the cylinder(s). Without piston rings, the piston could not compress the fuel charge properly. Also, burning gases would leak out between the sides of the piston and the cylinder wall.

In performing their job, the piston rings ride against the cylinder wall, separated from it only by a thin film of oil. The rings rub freely against the sides of the ring grooves, which hold the rings squarely to the bore and force them to slide up and down the cylinder with the piston. See **Figure 6-16**. Since the ring face is in steady contact with the cylinder walls an effective seal is formed.

Figure 6-17 shows a piston ring in its groove. The sides of the ring groove are flat, parallel, and smooth. In operation, expanding gases force the ring down against the lower side of the groove. At the same time, gases behind the ring force it against the cylinder wall. These forces help to form a good seal.

Piston Ring Types

Most pistons use three rings. These three rings consist of two ring types. Generally, the two upper rings are compression rings and the lower ring is an oil control ring. See **Figure 6-18**.

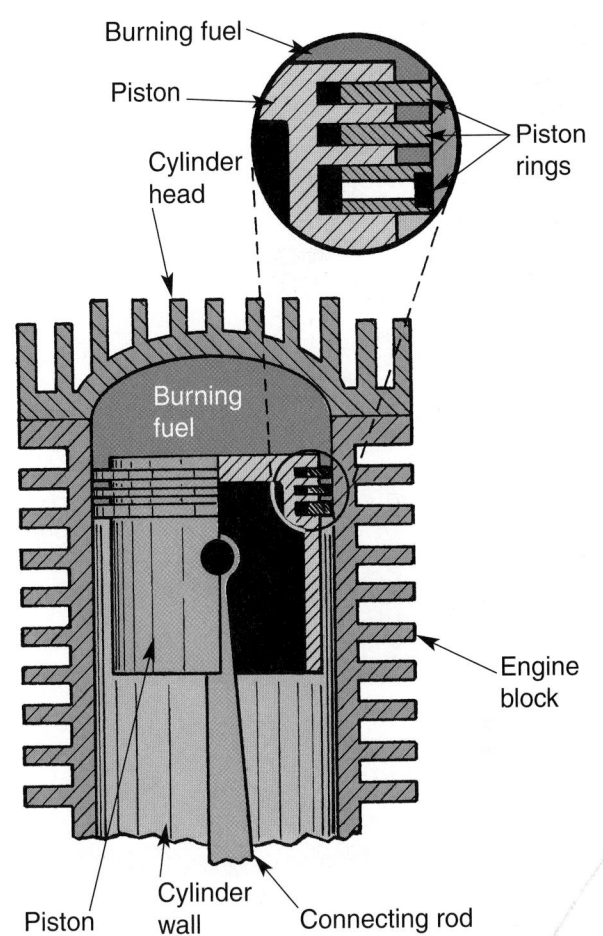

Goodheart-Willcox Publisher

Figure 6-16.

Piston rings form a seal between the piston and cylinder wall.

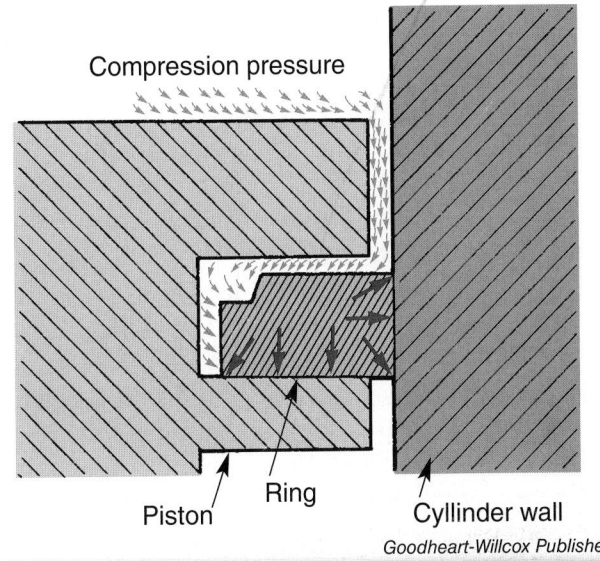

Goodheart-Willcox Publisher

Figure 6-17.

Combustion chamber pressure forces the ring against the cylinder wall and the bottom side of the groove.

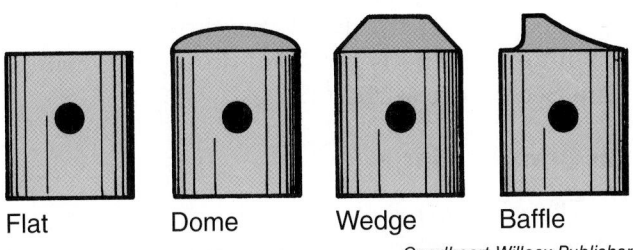

Flat   Dome   Wedge   Baffle

Goodheart-Willcox Publisher

Figure 6-15.

Small gasoline engine piston heads are manufactured in a wide variety of shapes.

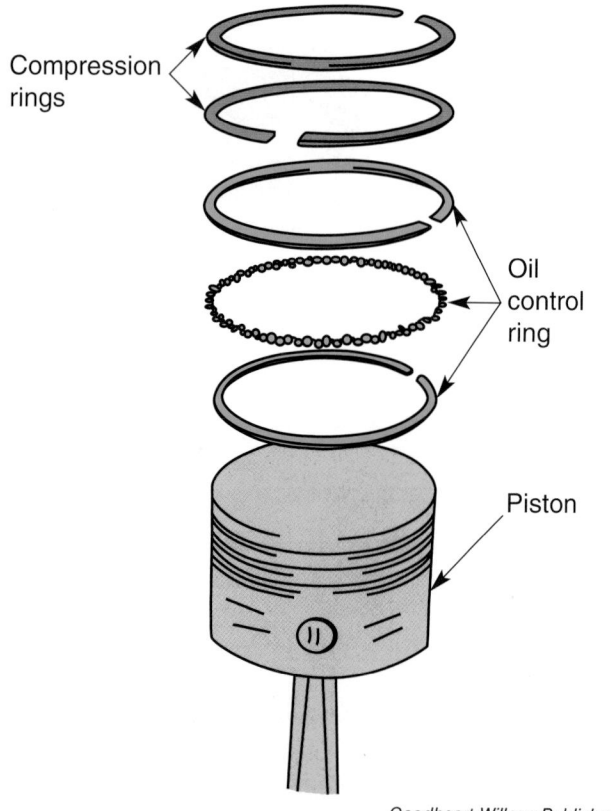

Goodheart-Willcox Publisher

Figure 6-18.

The two top piston rings are compression rings and the bottom ring is the oil control ring. They fit into the grooves cut into the piston.

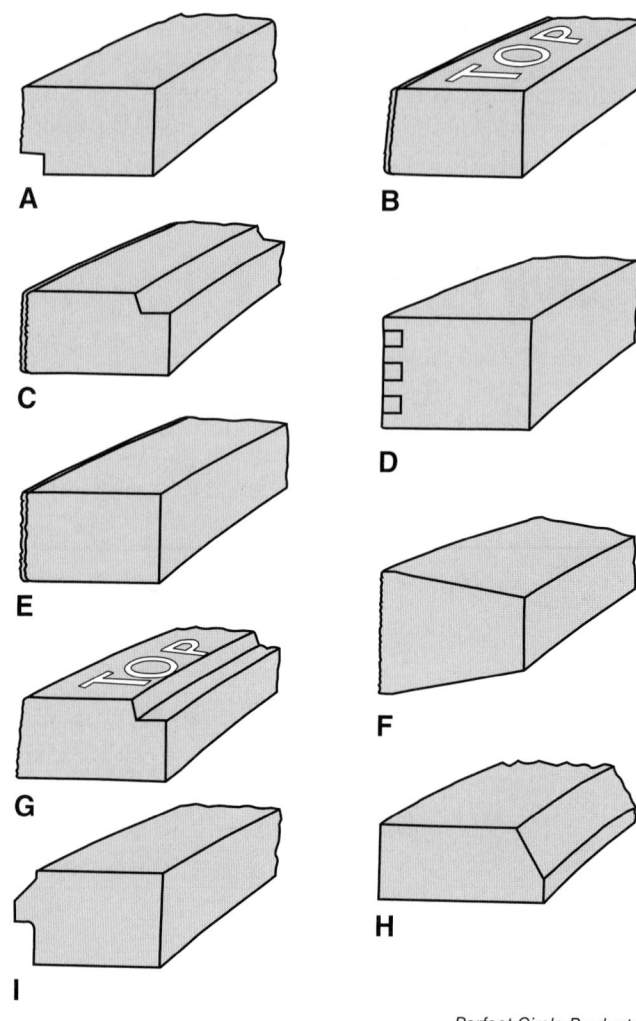

Perfect Circle Products

Figure 6-19.

Compression ring shapes. A—Outer groove. B—Chrome-plated, tapered face. C—Inner groove, chrome face. D—Ferrox-filled, grooved face. E—Plain chrome face. F—Keystone. G—Inner groove, tapered face. H—Inner chamfer, molybdenum-filled, grooved face. I—Scraper face.

Compression Rings

The first and second rings from the top of the piston are compression rings. *Compression rings* are designed to provide a strong seal, keeping the compressed air-fuel mixture and the burning gases above the piston by preventing passage between the piston and the cylinder wall. Compression ring shapes vary, with the scraper grooves, beveled faces, and grooves or bevels on the inner side of the ring. See **Figure 6-19**.

The various bevels and grooves are designed to create an internal stress in each compression ring. See **Figure 6-20**. The stress causes the ring to twist slightly in its groove during the intake stroke of the piston. The twisting action places the lower edge of the ring, rather than the face, in contact with the cylinder wall. This allows compression rings to act as a mild scraper to aid in oil control. See **Figure 6-20A**.

On the compression and exhaust strokes (four-stroke engine), the rings are in a tipped position

and tend to slip lightly over the oil film on the cylinder. See **Figure 6-20B**. On the power stroke, the pressure of the gases forces the ring flat so that the entire edge bears firmly against the cylinder wall. Maximum sealing is provided during this critical time. See **Figure 6-20C**.

Oil Control Rings

The *oil control rings* are designed to remove surplus oil from the cylinder walls. They do this through a light scraping action against the walls. Both the ring and the groove are slotted, or perforated (having holes). Oil trapped by the ring

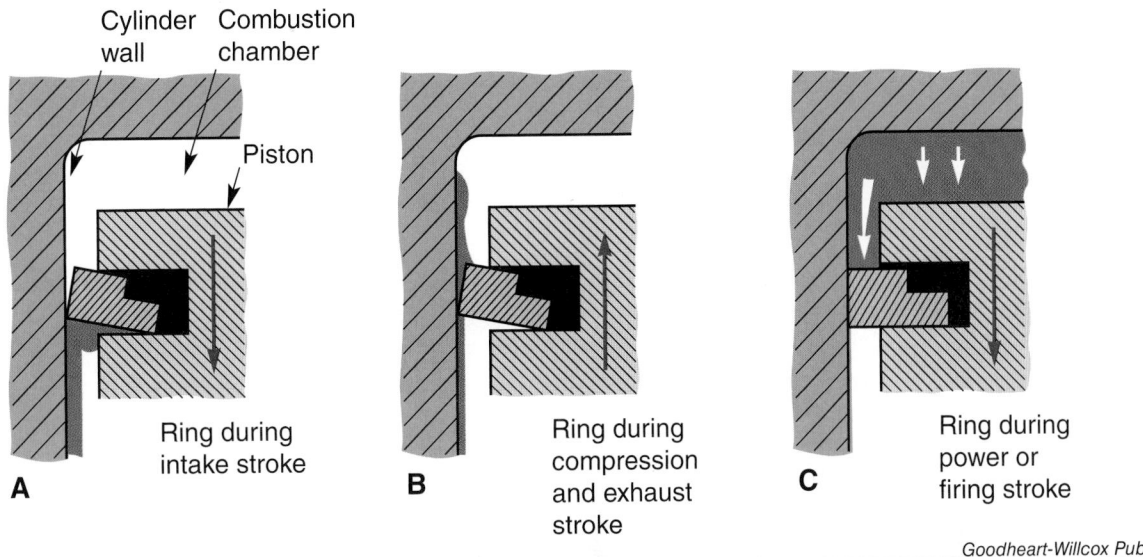

Cylinder wall   Combustion chamber

Piston

Ring during intake stroke

A

Ring during compression and exhaust stroke

B

Ring during power or firing stroke

C

Goodheart-Willcox Publisher

Figure 6-20.

The inner groove causes the ring to twist slightly, aiding oil control and compression. It also reduces wear.

passes through the slots or holes in the ring and the groove. See **Figure 6-21**. It then flows down inside the piston where it drops into the crankcase. A three-piece oil control ring with a hump-type, spring-steel expander is shown in **Figure 6-22**.

Piston Ring Construction

Piston rings are made of cast iron or steel. Both may be plated with chrome or other long-wearing materials. Most pistons use cast iron compression rings. Steel, when used, generally goes into the construction of the oil control ring. In some installations, a cast iron center spacer-scraper may be combined with steel side rails.

Ring Tension

To permit the piston rings to expand and contract under varied temperatures and operating conditions, the rings are cut through at one place at the time of manufacture. See **Figure 6-23**. The size of this opening between the ends of the ring (with piston and rings in the cylinder) is called the ring end gap. Although a great number of end gap designs have been used in an effort to seal against gas leakage, the plain butt joint is the most common.

In another design feature, the outside diameter of a piston ring is made slightly larger than cylinder bore diameter. This causes the ring to exert

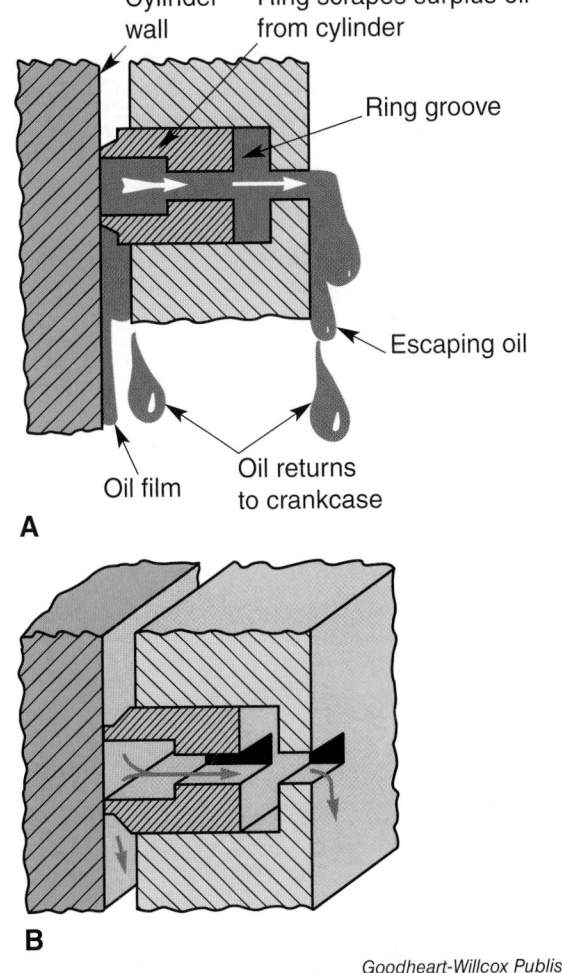

Cylinder wall   Ring scrapes surplus oil from cylinder

Ring groove

Escaping oil

Oil film   Oil returns to crankcase

A

B

Goodheart-Willcox Publisher

Figure 6-21.

An oil control ring removes surplus oil from the cylinder walls. A—Oil being removed. B—Path of oil during removal.

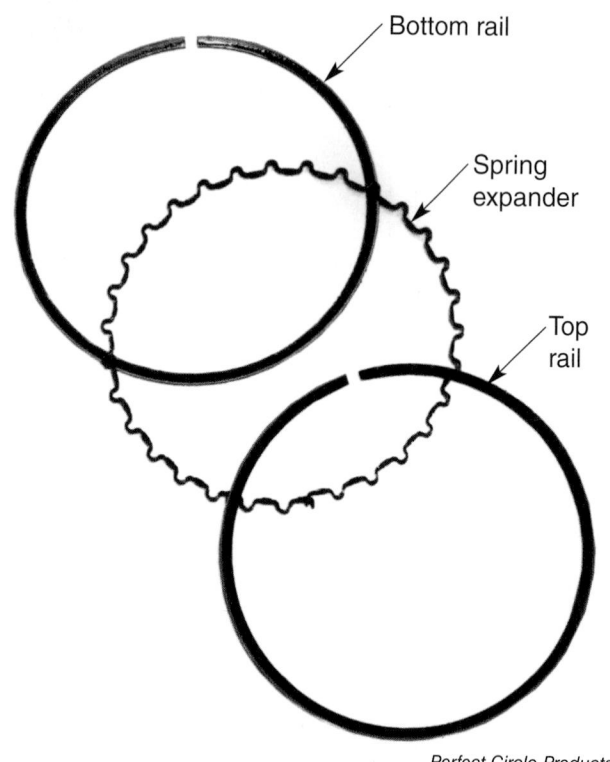

Figure 6-22.

Three-piece oil control ring with flat steel (hump-type) expander in place.

Perfect Circle Products

force on the cylinder wall when installed. This force is called *ring tension*.

Ring Movement

Piston rings must have the right amount of *side clearance*, which allows them to move in and out in the piston grooves while exerting tension on the cylinder wall. Side clearance also provides

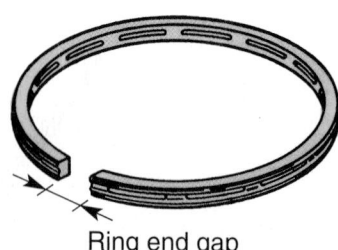

Figure 6-23.

An end gap is cut through the piston ring to permit the ring to enter the cylinder and still exert tension on the cylinder wall.

Goodheart-Willcox Publisher

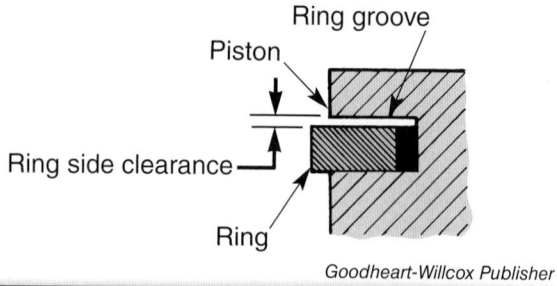

Figure 6-24.

Goodheart-Willcox Publisher

Ring side clearance allows movement, admits lubricating oil, and permits expansion of parts due to heat.

for adequate lubrication and heat expansion. See **Figure 6-24**.

Most four-stroke engines have *floating rings*, which will gradually work their way around (float) in the piston grooves. Floating rings should be installed with the ring end gaps staggered to prevent gap alignment and possible oil flow through the series of gaps to the combustion chamber. Some two-stroke engines are equipped with pinned rings. A *pinned ring* is held in position by a short pin manufactured into the piston ring groove. The pin prevents the ring from rotating in the groove and possibly catching on the edge of the intake or exhaust ports and cutting into the cylinder wall. As shown in **Figure 6-25**, the ring ends are cut out to straddle the pin.

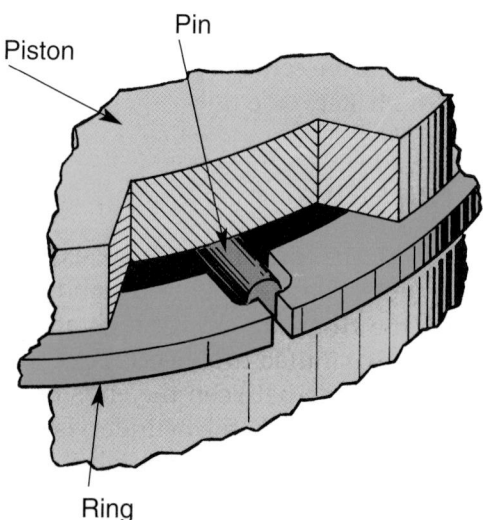

Figure 6-25.

Goodheart-Willcox Publisher

Many two-stroke engines have pinned rings to prevent ring rotation.

Piston Pins

A piston pin is used to secure the connecting rod to the piston. These pins are made of case-hardened steel and are ground to exact size. They may be hollow or solid. A typical solid piston pin is shown in **Figure 6-26**.

Many different piston pin assemblies have been used. The full-floating pin arrangement shown in **Figure 6-27** is free to turn in the rod as well as in the piston bosses. When both the connecting rod and piston are of aluminum alloy, the pin can operate directly against this material. If the rod is steel, either a bronze bushing or a needle roller bearing is used in the rod. The piston bosses may also have bronze bushing inserts for the pin.

Retaining *snap rings* are compressed and placed in grooves in the piston pin bosses. They prevent the pin from rubbing on the cylinder surface. See **Figure 6-28**. Some piston pins are a tight, press fit in the connecting rod. See **Figure 6-29**. The pin may turn in the piston bosses, bushings, or needle bearings, depending on the type of construction used.

Connecting Rods and Bearings

The *connecting rod* attaches the piston to the crankshaft. The upper end of the connecting rod has a hole through which the piston pin is passed. The lower end contains a large bearing that fits around the crankshaft journal. See **Figure 6-30**.

The lower end of the connecting rod is usually split when friction bearings are used. *Friction bearings* use smooth, sliding surfaces to reduce friction between moving parts. The place at which the halves separate is called the parting line. The bearing cap holds the assembly together with connecting rod bolts or screws. **Figure 6-31** shows the relative position of the connecting rod and cap. When needle or roller bearings are used, the rod end can be split or solid. See **Figure 6-32**.

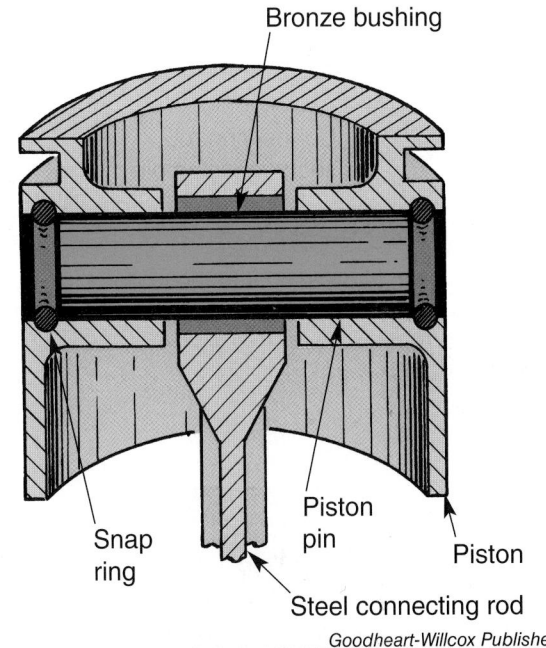

Goodheart-Willcox Publisher

Figure 6-27.

A full-floating piston pin used in a steel connecting rod requires use of a bushing.

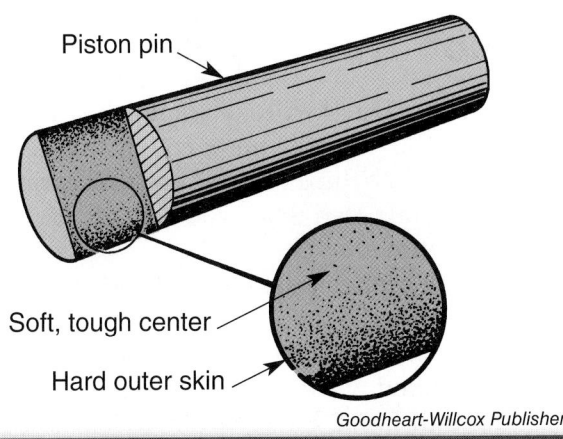

Goodheart-Willcox Publisher

Figure 6-26.

A solid piston pin has hardened and ground surfaces.

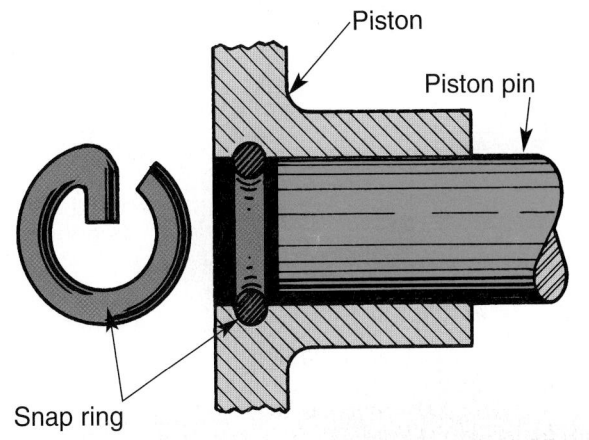

Goodheart-Willcox Publisher

Figure 6-28.

Snap rings keep a full-floating pin in place in the piston.

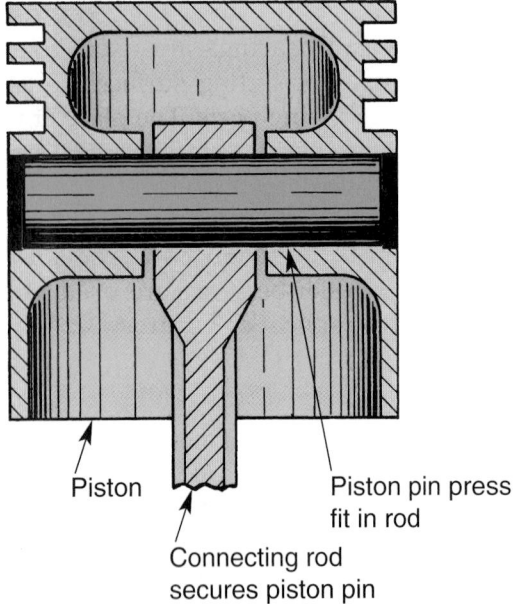

Piston

Piston pin press
fit in rod

Connecting rod
secures piston pin

Goodheart-Willcox Publisher

Figure 6-29.

This piston pin is pressed into the connecting rod, but
is allowed to turn in the pin bosses of the piston.

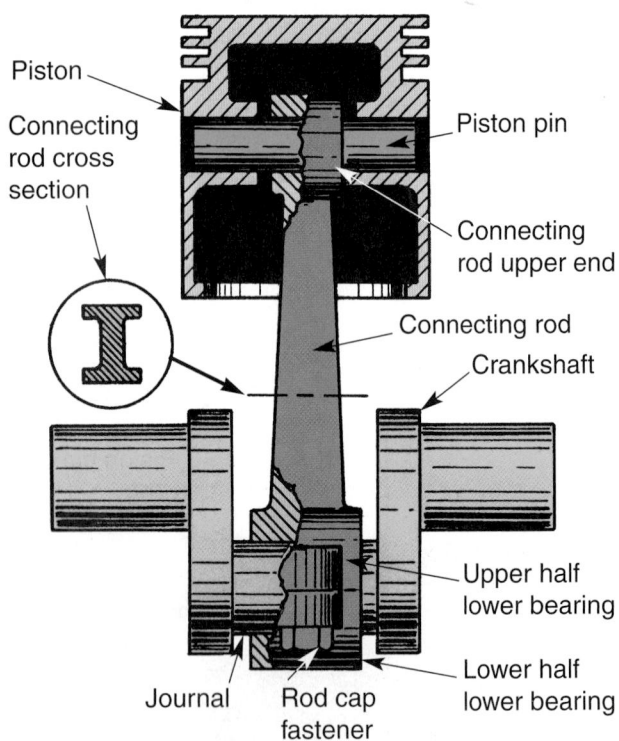

Piston

Connecting
rod cross
section

Piston pin

Connecting
rod upper end

Connecting rod

Crankshaft

Upper half
lower bearing

Lower half
lower bearing

Journal   Rod cap
fastener

Goodheart-Willcox Publisher

Figure 6-30.

A connecting rod attaches the piston to the crankshaft.
Bearings are used at both ends of the rod to reduce
friction.

Goodheart-Willcox Publisher

Figure 6-31.

Shown are the relative positions of connecting rod parts.

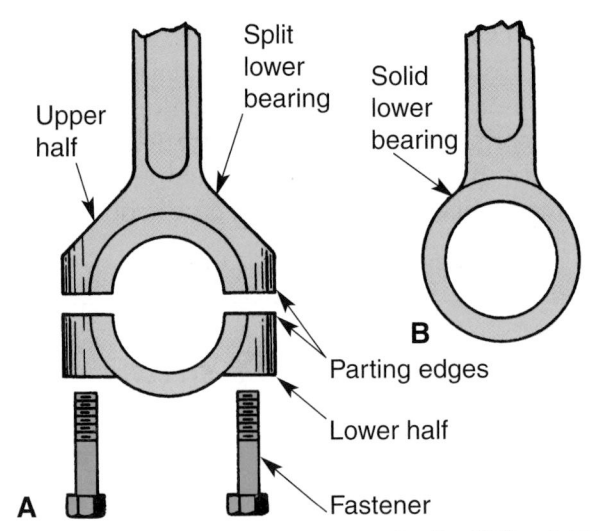

Split
lower
bearing

Solid
lower
bearing

Upper
half

Parting edges

Lower half

Fastener

A   B

Goodheart-Willcox Publisher

Figure 6-32.

Two types of connecting rod designs (crankshaft end).
A—Split construction. B—Solid construction.

Friction-Type Rod Bearings

There are three types of friction bearings commonly used in the big end of connecting rods. See
Figure 6-33. The three types of friction bearings are:

- Rod metal (used when rod is made of
  aluminum alloy).
- Bearing bronze (cast into rod end, bored,
  and finished).
- Removable precision insert bearings (steel
  shells lined with various materials).

The thin lining material on removable bearing
inserts can be lead-tin babbitt, aluminum, or copper-
lead-tin. **Figure 6-34** shows a steel-backed insert (1)

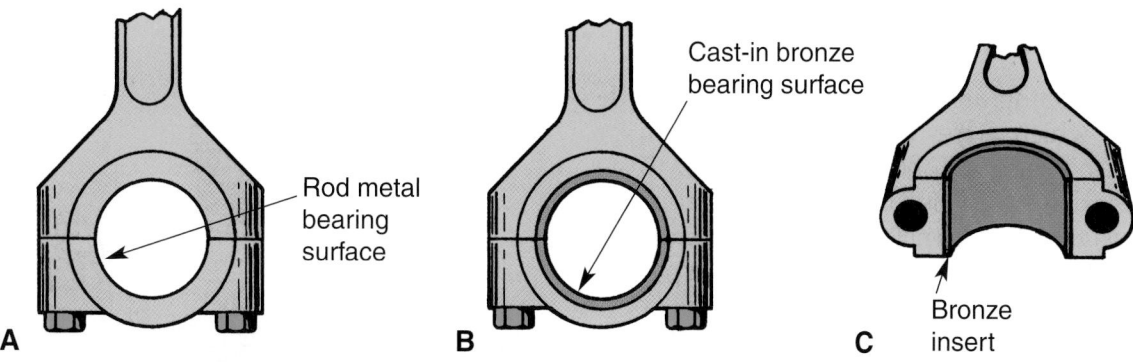

A

B

Cast-in bronze
bearing surface

Rod metal
bearing
surface

C

Bronze
insert

Goodheart-Willcox Publisher

Figure 6-33.

Friction-type connecting rod bearings. A—Rod metal forms the bearing surface. B—Bronze bearing is cast into the rod metal. C—Replaceable precision insert bearing.

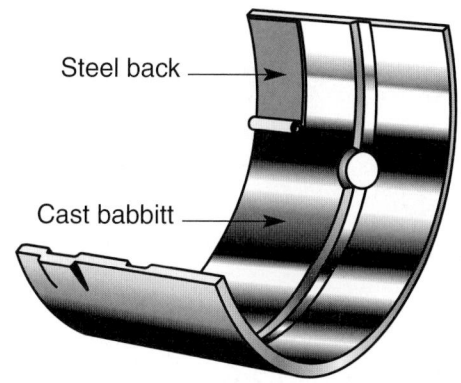

Steel back

Cast babbitt

Clevite Corp.

Figure 6-34.

Construction of a typical precision insert bearing.

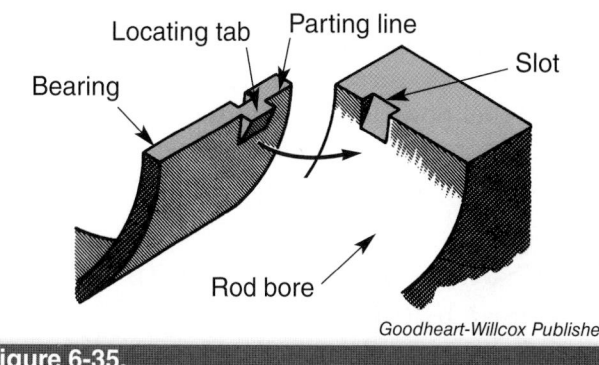

Locating tab   Parting line

Bearing

Slot

Rod bore

Goodheart-Willcox Publisher

Figure 6-35.

Locating tabs prevent precision inserts from turning.

that is coated with cast babbitt (2). This type of bearing is called a *precision* insert because it is made to an exact size for proper fit.

Bearing inserts are kept from turning in the rod end by a locating tab on the parting line edge of each insert. The tab fits into a slot in the rod itself. **Figure 6-35** illustrates this tab and slot arrangement.

Antifriction Bearings

Many small gasoline engines use an antifriction bearing in the big end of the connecting rod. *Antifriction bearings* use rollers or balls to reduce friction between moving parts. See **Figure 6-36**. These roller elements can be held together by a roller cage or separator. See **Figure 6-36A**. The rollers can also be left free as in **Figure 6-36B**. Antifriction bearing assemblies are hardened and ground to an exact size. They must fit accurately, but still have some clearance for expansion.

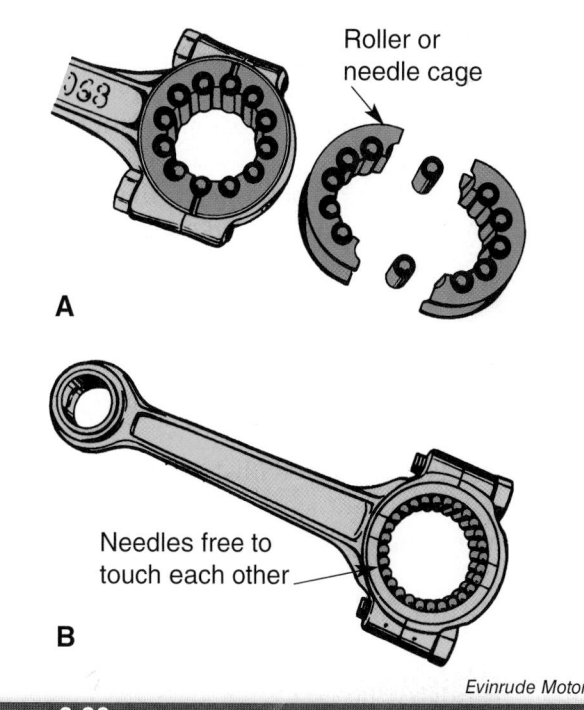

Roller or
needle cage

A

Needles free to
touch each other

B

Evinrude Motors

Figure 6-36.

Two types of connecting rod roller bearings. A—Caged rollers. B—Free needle bearings.

Intake and Exhaust Ports

In developing an engine, we need to provide a way in which a fresh air-fuel mixture can be admitted to the engine and, once burned, the waste products exhausted. This can be done by using ports (openings) that are alternately covered and exposed by the piston (two-stroke design) or by using poppet valves to open and close the port openings (four-stroke design).

Two-Stroke Engine Ports

Two-stroke engines use a piston port design. In this design, the intake and exhaust ports are alternately covered and exposed by the piston as it moves up and down in the cylinder. Some two-stroke engines use reed valves or rotary valves to control fuel flow directly into the crankcase. This allows room for additional transfer ports that promote better fuel transfer and scavenging.

Four-Stroke Engine Ports and Poppet Valves

In a four-stroke engine (see Chapter 5 for additional information on fundamentals), a *poppet valve* is installed in each port to control the flow of fresh fuel mixture into the cylinder and provide a means of exhausting the burned gases. During the period of expansion of the burning gases that drive the piston downward, both valves are tightly closed. See **Figure 6-37**.

The angled face of each valve will close tightly against a smooth seat cut around each port opening. To align the valve and ensure accurate raising and lowering in relation to the seat, the valve stem passes through a machined hole in the block. This hole is called a *valve guide*.

Poppet valves are subjected to tremendous heat. The normal operating temperature of the exhaust valve exceeds 1000°F. To withstand this heat, high-quality, heat-resistant steel must be used and the correct operating clearances must be maintained.

Valve Spring Assembly

A *valve spring* must be used on each valve to hold it firmly against the seat. Placed over the valve stem, the spring is compressed to provide tension. It is connected to the valve stem by means of a washer retainer and keeper (lock).

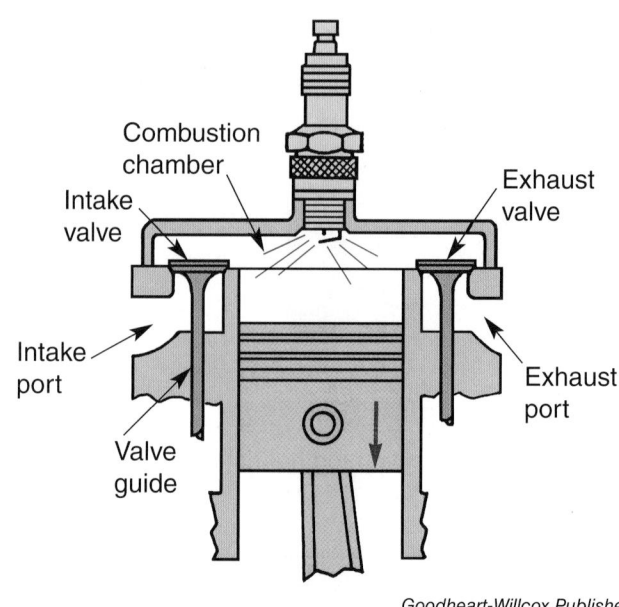

Goodheart-Willcox Publisher

Figure 6-37.

Poppet valves seal the intake and exhaust ports during the power stroke. Valve guides keep the valves aligned with the valve seats.

The spring allows the valve to be opened when necessary and will close it when pressure is removed from the valve stem. **Figure 6-38** shows the location of the spring and keeper assembled on the valve. An enlarged view of the horseshoe valve lock system is shown in **Figure 6-39**.

A valve in the open position is illustrated in **Figure 6-40**. When pressure is removed from the end of the valve stem, the spring will draw the valve down against the seat and seal off the port from the combustion chamber.

Camshafts and Gears

The *camshaft*, found in four-stroke engines, is designed to open the valves the right amount at the right time. It holds them open for a specific period and allows them to close at the correct instant. A single camshaft is used in most small engines, with a cam (lobe) for each valve. When the camshaft rotates, the lobe of the cam lifts the valve from its seat. This process is shown in **Figure 6-41**.

Camshafts are made of steel or cast iron. The surface of the shaft is hardened to improve wearability. The ends of the camshaft may turn in bearings or in the block metal. See **Figure 6-42**. Some small engine camshafts are hollow and have

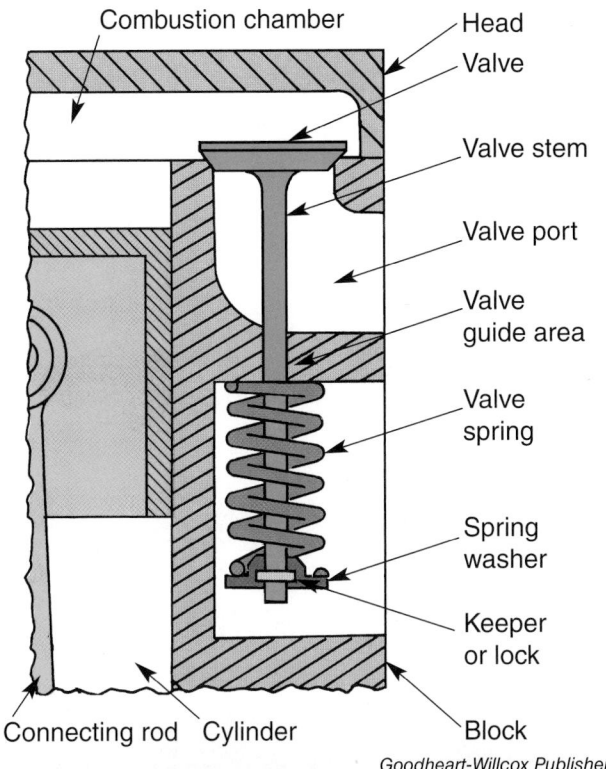

Figure 6-38.
The valve spring keeps tension on the valve to ensure proper seating. The valve spring keeper and washer hold the spring in place and permit removal when necessary.

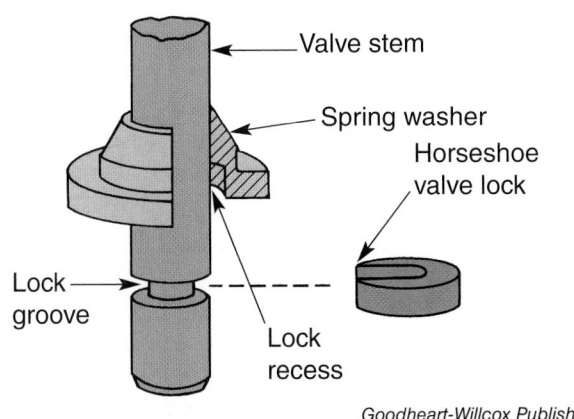

Figure 6-39.
Typical method of retaining the valve spring on the valve stem. A special tool generally is used to compress the spring prior to removing the horseshoe valve lock.

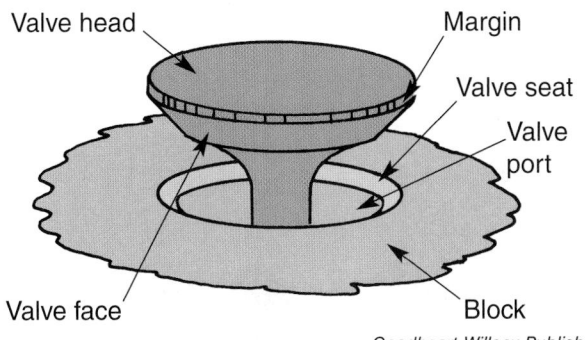

Figure 6-40.
The valve face and valve seat must be ground to correct angles, and concentric to the centerline of the guide, to seal properly.

with and drives a gear on the camshaft. Since the camshaft gear is exactly twice the size of the crankshaft gear, it runs at half crankshaft speed. See **Figure 6-44**.

Valve Lifter or Tappet

In actual practice, the cam lobe does not contact the valve stem directly. By locating the camshaft some distance below the valve stem end, it is possible to insert a *valve lifter* between the lobe and stem. See **Figure 6-45**. A hole in the block above the camshaft serves as a guide in which the lifter can operate. As the camshaft revolves, the lifter rises and falls, opening and closing the valve.

The valve lifter may have an adjustment screw in the upper end to provide a means of adjusting valve stem-to-lifter clearance. Without this adjustment, proper clearance must be obtained by grinding the end of the lifter or valve stem. The base of the lifter may be made wider than the body to provide a larger cam lobe-to-lifter contact area. See **Figure 6-46**.

Valve Train Configurations

The *valve train* consists of all of the components that work together to transform the rotation of the crankshaft into the opening and closing of the valves. There are three main types of valve train configurations used in modern small gas engines. See **Figure 6-47**.

a second shaft running through them, **Figure 6-43**. With this setup, the inner shaft is fixed and the hollow camshaft revolves on it.

Most small gasoline engines use gears to turn the camshaft. A gear on the crankshaft meshes

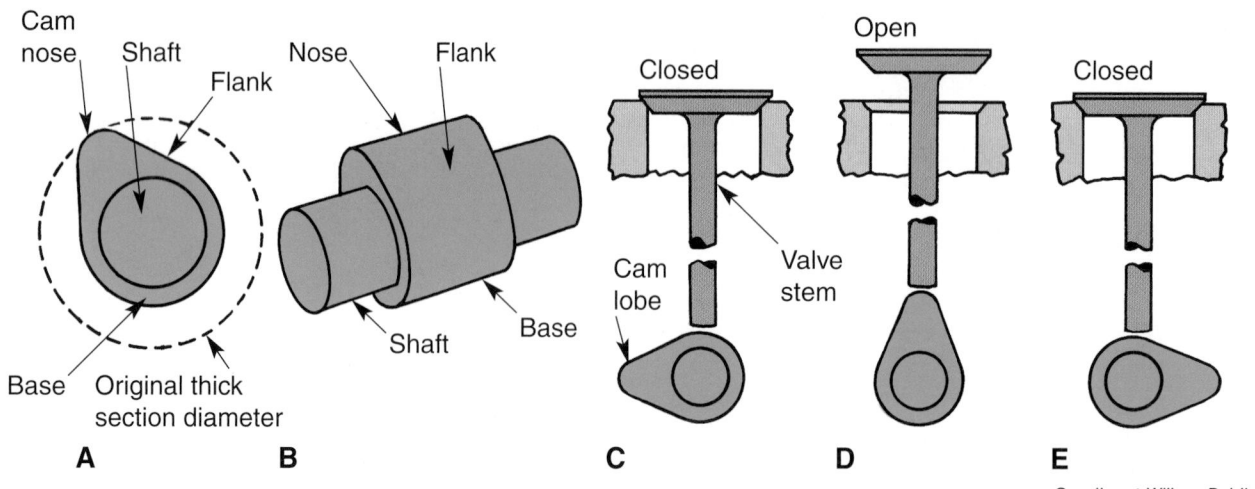

Goodheart-Willcox Publisher

Figure 6-41.

A, B—By grinding a round shaft into a cam shape, a camshaft is formed. C, D, E—When the camshaft is revolved, the cam lobe opens the valve.

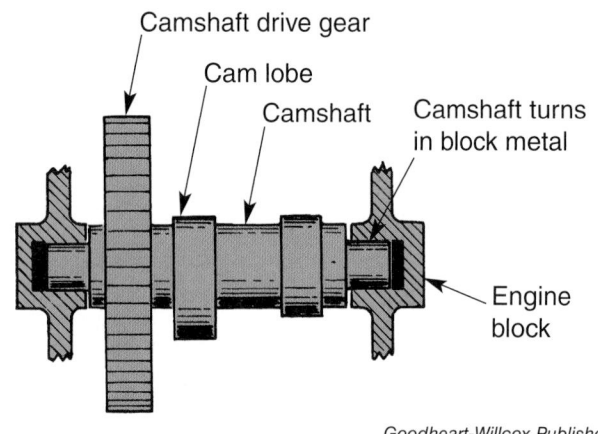

Goodheart-Willcox Publisher

Figure 6-42.

Solid camshaft.

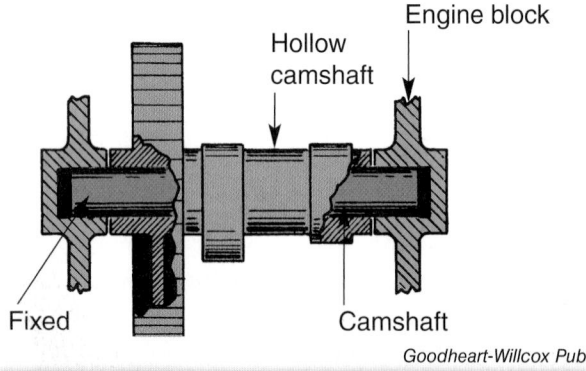

Goodheart-Willcox Publisher

Figure 6-43.

Hollow camshaft turning on a fixed shaft.

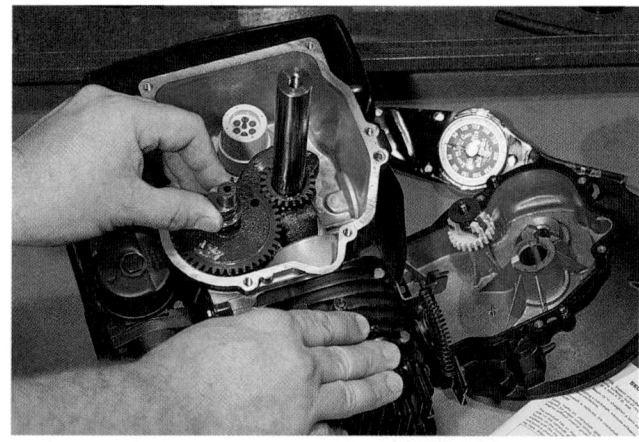

Goodheart-Willcox Publisher

Figure 6-44.

The camshaft gear is meshed with the crankshaft gear so that the timing marks are aligned. The camshaft turns at half crankshaft speed.

In the *valve-in-block* arrangement, **Figure 6-47A,** the camshaft is located in the crankcase and the valves are located in the cylinder block, directly above the camshaft lobes. As the camshaft rotates, the valve lifters act directly on the valve stems. Engines using this design are often referred to as flatheads, because the cylinder head is relatively flat and thin. This arrangement may also be referred to as an L-head or side-valve engine.

The *overhead valve (OHV)* arrangement has grown in popularity over recent years. In this

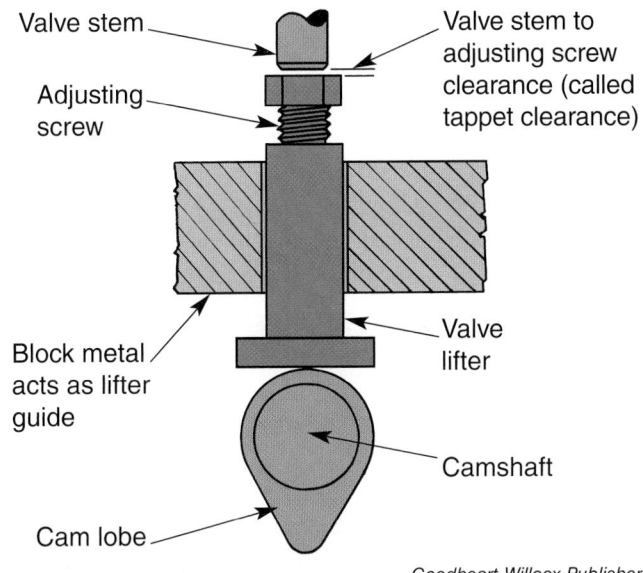

Goodheart-Willcox Publisher

Figure 6-45.

As the camshaft turns, the cam lobe will operate the valve lifter to open the valve and then allow it to close.

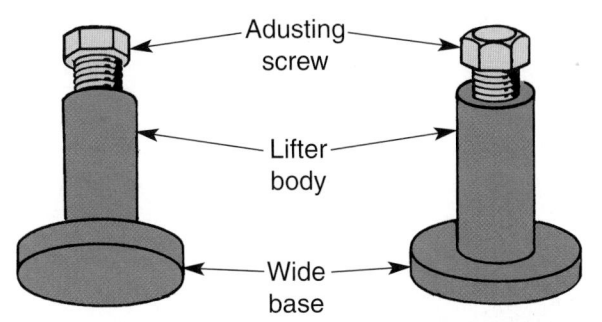

Goodheart-Willcox Publisher

Figure 6-46.

A valve lifter may be called a tappet or cam follower. An adjustment screw allows setting of the proper valve clearance. A wide base provides a larger contact area.

arrangement, the camshaft is installed in the crankcase, but the valves are installed in the cylinder head. *Pushrods* transfer motion from the valve lifters, which are in the block, to one end of the rocker arms, which are installed in the cylinder head. The *rocker arms* are basically levers. When the pushrod pushes up on one end of the rocker arm, the other end of the rocker arm pushes down on the valve stem. See **Figure 6-47B**.

Some manufacturers use an *overhead cam (OHC)* design, **Figure 6-47C**. In this valve train arrangement, both the camshaft and valve assemblies are installed in the cylinder head. There are

several variations of the overhead cam configuration. The camshaft may be positioned directly over the valves or offset. If the camshaft is offset, rocker arms are added to the design to transfer motion from the camshaft to the valves. Since the camshaft is located away from the crankshaft in all overhead cam designs, it is usually driven by a chain or belt rather than gears.

Starter Assembly

All small gasoline engines have some provision for spinning, or cranking, the engine during starting. Many small engines are equipped with a *rewind starter assembly*, which is mounted above the flywheel, **Figure 6-48**. When the rope is pulled, pawls in the starter assembly engage the flywheel clutch and the assembly turns the crankshaft. When the rope is released, the pawls retract, the assembly disengages from the flywheel clutch, and the rope recoils back into the unit. See **Figure 6-49**. Some engines are equipped with electric starters, which engage the flywheel to turn the crankshaft. These starters will be discussed later in this textbook.

Automatic Compression Release

To make hand cranking easier, some small engines have an *automatic compression release* mechanism on the camshaft. This device lifts the exhaust valve slightly during cranking and releases part of the compression pressure.

One manufacturer's compression release mechanism is pictured in **Figure 6-50**. In view A, the camshaft is at rest and springs are holding the flyweights in. In this position, the tab on the larger flyweight protrudes above the base circle of the exhaust cam, holding the exhaust valve partially open. In view B, the tab prevents the exhaust lifter from resting on the cam.

After the engine starts and its speed reaches about 600 rpm, centrifugal force overcomes spring pressure and the flyweights move outward. Movement of the flyweights causes the tab to be retracted, and the exhaust valve seats fully. See views C and D in **Figure 6-50**. The flyweights remain in this position until the engine is stopped.

A variation of this compression release mechanism is shown in **Figure 6-51**. This mechanism uses a single flyweight and a small pin to hold the exhaust valve open during starting.

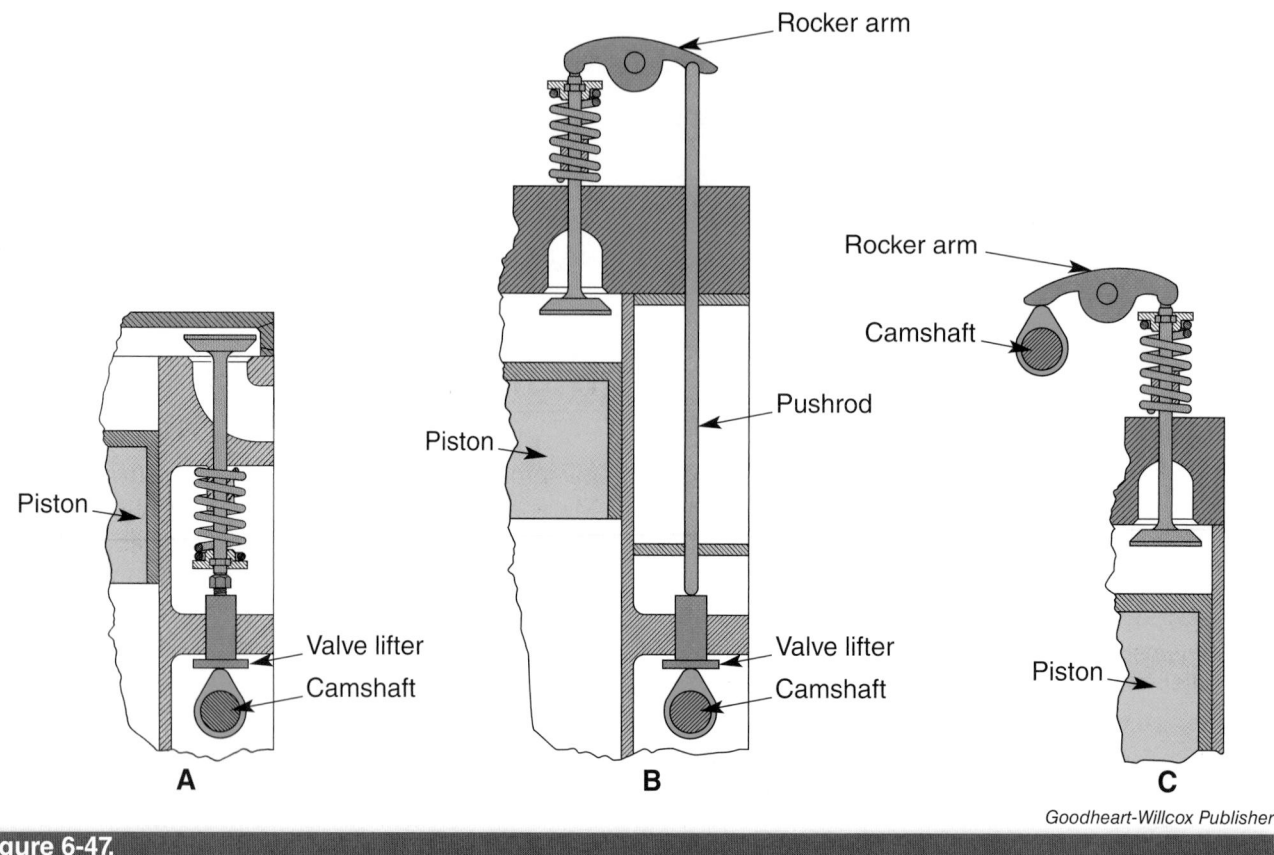

Goodheart-Willcox Publisher

Figure 6-47.

The three valve train configurations are shown here. A—Valve-in-block, or side valve configuration. B—Overhead valve (OHV) configuration. C—Overhead cam (OHC) configuration.

Goodheart-Willcox Publisher

Figure 6-48.

This rewind starter assembly is being removed from the engine, revealing the flywheel clutch.

Flywheel

To improve the running quality of the engine, an additional weight in the form of a round *flywheel* is fastened to one end of the crankshaft. See **Figure 6-52**. During the nonpower strokes, the inertia of the heavy flywheel keeps the crankshaft spinning and smoothes engine operation. Metal fins on the flywheel act as a fan that forces air over the cylinder to cool the engine. Magnets cast into the flywheel produce electrical current for the ignition system.

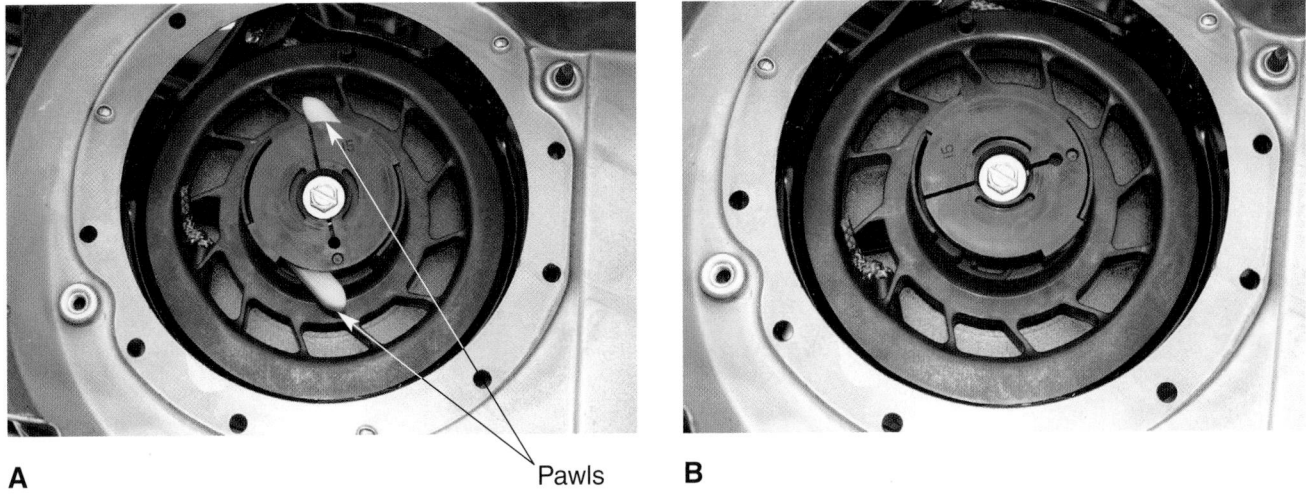

A   B

Pawls

Goodheart-Willcox Publisher

Figure 6-49.

Bottom view of a recoil-type starter assembly. When the starter rope is pulled, the pawls extend and engage the flywheel clutch. This locks the flywheel to the spinning starter assembly to turn the engine. B—When the rope is released, the pawls retract and the flywheel is free to spin independent of the starter assembly.

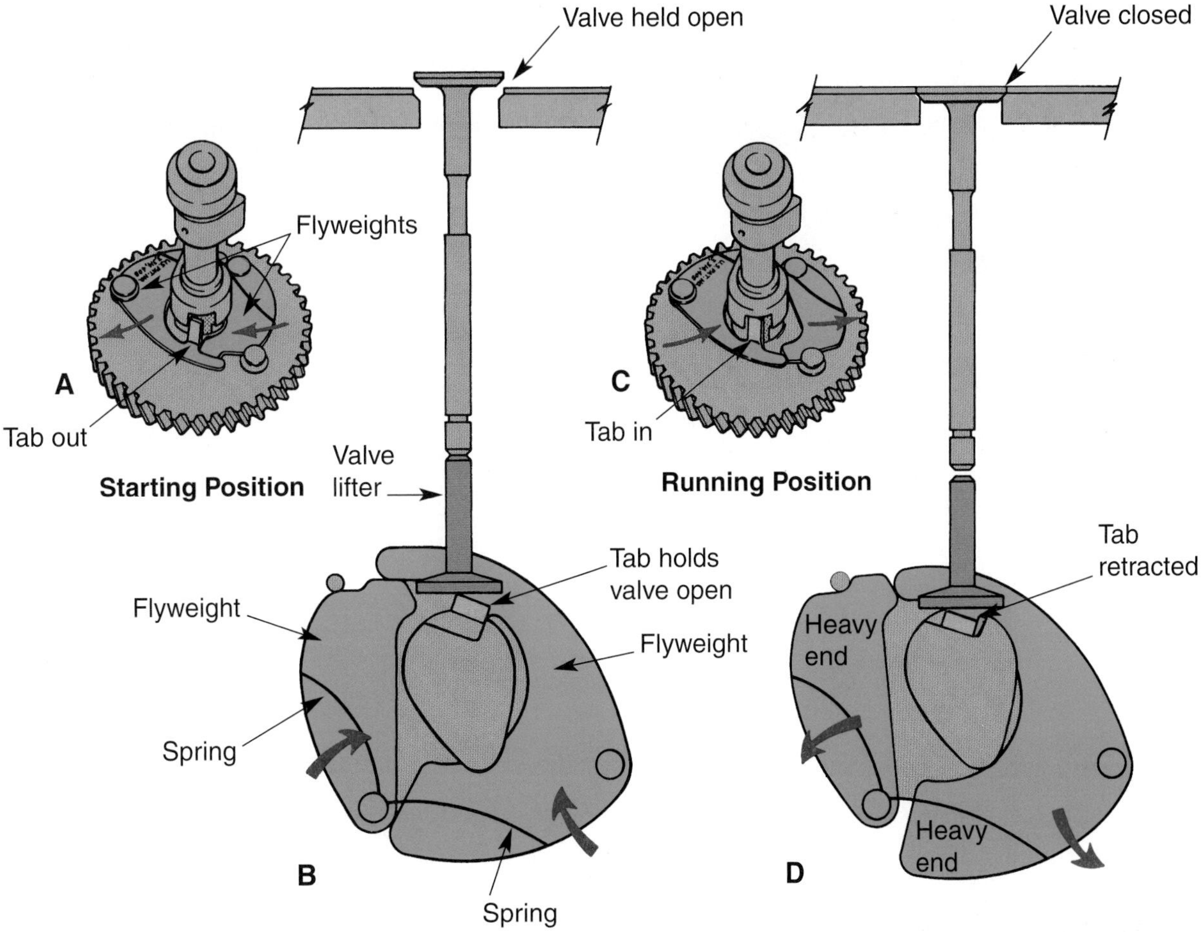

Valve held open   Valve closed

Flyweights

A   C
Tab out   Tab in
Starting Position   Valve   **Running Position**
                              lifter

                                                        Tab
                                                        retracted
Flyweight   Tab holds
                     valve open   Heavy
                              Flyweight   end

Spring

                                           Heavy
B   Spring   end   D

Kohler Co.

Figure 6-50.

An automatic compression release makes cranking easier. A and B—The tab is out, preventing the valve from closing completely. C and D—When the engine starts and reaches 600 rpm, the flyweights move out, the tab retracts, and the valve functions normally.

Pin   Flyweight

A

B

Goodheart-Willcox Publisher

Figure 6-51.

Automatic compression release. A—Starting position. The pin extends beyond the cam lobe to prevent the exhaust valve from seating. B—Running position. The pin retracts and the exhaust valve functions normally.

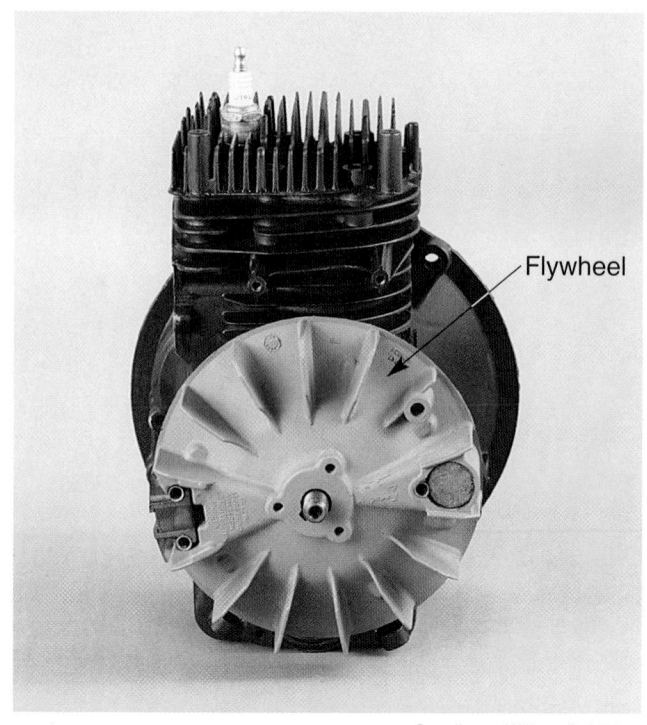

Flywheel

Goodheart-Willcox Publisher

Figure 6-52.

The flywheel is fastened to the crankshaft. When rotating, its weight smoothes engine operation.

Summary

The engine block keeps all engine parts in alignment. This component is usually a casting of iron or an aluminum alloy. The engine block consists of two sections: the cylinder block and the crankcase. The cylinder block is the portion of the engine block that contains the cylinder bore. The crankcase is the portion of the block that contains the crankshaft.

The crankshaft is the major rotating part of the engine. It converts the reciprocating (back and forth) motion of the piston into rotary (circular) motion. The piston is the straight line driving member of the engine. The piston provides a seal between the combustion chamber and the crankcase. This is accomplished by cutting grooves near the top of the piston and installing piston rings on the piston. Without piston rings, the piston could not compress the fuel charge properly. Also, burning gases would leak out between the sides of the piston and the cylinder wall. Most pistons use three rings. These three rings consist of two ring types. Generally, the two upper rings are compression rings and the lower ring is an oil control ring. The piston pin is used to secure the piston to the connecting rod.

The connecting rod attaches the piston to the crankshaft. The upper end of the connecting rod has a hole through which the piston pin is passed. The lower end contains a large bearing that fits around the crankshaft journal.

A fresh air-fuel mixture must be admitted to the engine and, once burned, the waste products exhausted. This can be done by using ports that are alternately covered and exposed by the piston (two-stroke cycle design) or by using poppet valves to open and close the port openings (four-stroke cycle design). The camshaft, found in four-stroke engines, is designed to open the valves the right amount at the right time. The valve train consists of all of the components that work together to transform the rotation of the crankshaft into the opening and closing of the valves. During the non-power strokes, the inertia of the heavy flywheel keeps the crankshaft spinning and smoothes engine operation.

All small gasoline engines have some provision for spinning the crankshaft during engine starting. This can be a recoil rope starter assembly or an electric starter. To make hand cranking easier, some small engines have an automatic compression release mechanism on the camshaft. This device lifts the exhaust valve slightly during cranking and releases part of the compression pressure.

Review Questions

Answer the following questions on a separate sheet of paper.

1. Name the two main sections of an engine block.
2. Why are aluminum cylinder blocks sometimes cast around a steel sleeve?
3. The crankshaft converts the _____ motion of the piston into rotary motion.
4. All of the following are used as crankshaft main bearings, except:
   A. bushings.
   B. roller bearings.
   C. lip bearings.
   D. ball bearings.
5. What type of material is most commonly used in piston construction?
6. The ridges between the piston grooves are known as the piston _____.
7. What is the purpose of the piston skirt?
8. Explain why pistons have both compression rings and an oil control ring.
9. *True or False?* Floating piston rings are installed with their end gaps aligned.
10. _____ are placed in grooves in the piston pin bosses to prevent the pin from rubbing on the cylinder surface.
11. A piston pin may turn in _____.
    A. piston bosses
    B. bushings
    C. needle bearings
    D. None of the above.
12. Name the three types of friction bearings used in the big end of the connecting rod.
13. _____ bearings use rollers or balls to reduce friction between moving parts.
14. In two-stroke engines, the intake and exhaust ports are alternately covered and exposed by the _____ as it moves up and down in the cylinder.

15. Four-stroke engines use _____ to open and close port openings.

16. Explain the function of a camshaft.

17. In some engines, a(n) _____ is located between the camshaft lobe and the valve stem.

18. Describe the three types of valve train configurations found in small engines.

19. What is the purpose of the starter assembly?

20. Automatic compression release mechanisms lift the _____ slightly during cranking to release part of the compression pressure.

Suggested Activities

1. Disassemble an engine and identify the parts discussed in this chapter. Carefully analyze the function of each part as it relates to the others.

2. Write to manufacturers of small gasoline engines requesting specifications for the models they produce. Write a report on the types of pistons, connecting rods, and crankshafts they use.

3. Prepare a display of the major components of a small gasoline engine. Use actual parts, photos, drawings, and cutaways to show the principal use of each part.

Measuring Engine Performance

Learning Objectives

After studying this chapter, you will be able to:

- Define engine performance.
- Define and compute bore and stroke.
- Understand the concept of energy and differentiate between kinetic and potential energy.
- Understand the concepts of force and pressure.
- Explain the concepts of work, power, and torque.
- Calculate an engine's displacement and compression ratio.
- Differentiate between the various types of engine horsepower.
- Define and calculate engine torque.
- Explain volumetric efficiency, practical efficiency, mechanical efficiency, and thermal efficiency.

Key Terms

bottom dead center (BDC)
brake horsepower (bhp)
corrected horsepower
crank offset
dynamometer
engine bore
frictional horsepower (fhp)
horsepower
indicated horsepower (ihp)
mean effective pressure (mep)
mechanical efficiency
over square
performance
power
practical efficiency
pressure
Prony brake
rated horsepower
square
stroke
tensile stress
thermal efficiency
top dead center (TDC)
under square

Basic Terminology

To better understand how a gasoline engine works and to appreciate the power it provides, you must learn certain basic terms. These terms will be defined here only as far as necessary to provide a background for further discussion of measuring engine performance. *Performance* can be defined as the work engines do and how well they do it.

Engine Bore and Stroke

Engine bore is the diameter or width across the top of the cylinder. *Stroke* is the up or down movement of the piston. The length of stroke equals the distance the piston moves from its uppermost position (*top dead center* or *TDC*) to its lowest position (*bottom dead center* or *BDC*).

The amount of crank offset determines the length of the stroke. *Crank offset* is the distance from the centerline of the connecting rod journal to the centerline of the crankshaft. A 2" offset would produce a 4" stroke. See **Figure 7-1**.

When the bore diameter is the same as the stroke, the engine is referred to as *square*. When the bore diameter is greater than the stroke, it is termed *over square*. Where bore diameter is less than the stroke, the engine is called *under square*.

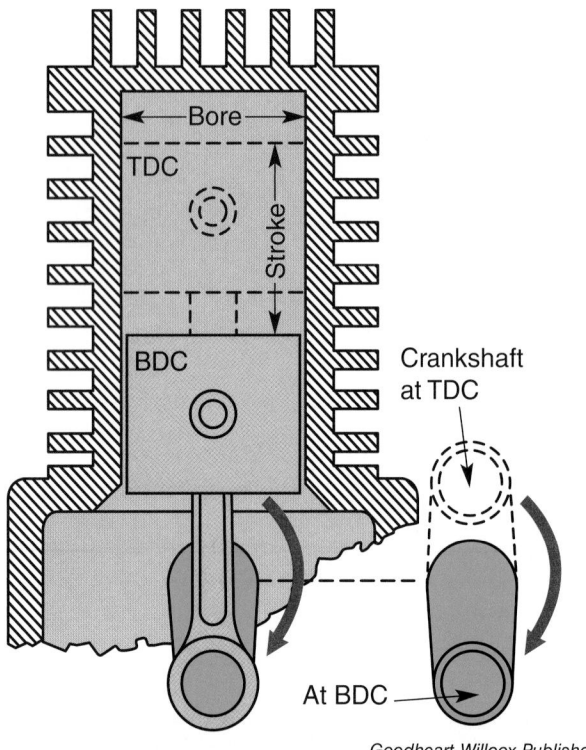

Goodheart-Willcox Publisher

Figure 7-1.

Engine bore refers to the diameter of the cylinder. Stroke indicates the length the piston travels as it moves from TDC to BDC.

Science of Engine Performance

In an engine, energy stored in fuel is converted into motion. In order to understand how an engine operates and the factors that affect engine performance, a technician must understand a few basic scientific concepts. The following sections explain the fundamental principles on which the design and operation of all internal combustion engines are based.

Energy

Energy is difficult to define. It puts *life* into matter, giving it warmth, light, and motion. Energy cannot be seen, weighed, or measured. It does not take up space. However, we know it is there, because we can observe and measure its effects. The warmth and light of a bonfire, the electrical spark that jumps the gap of a spark plug, or the turning of a wheel are things we can sense. They are all the effects of energy.

Energy is the capacity to perform work. It is grouped into two distinct classes, potential energy (PE) and kinetic energy (KE). Potential energy is energy that is stored, waiting to be released. A compressed spring or boulder at the top of a hill are common examples of potential energy. Kinetic energy is the energy of motion. Common examples are an expanding spring or a boulder rolling down a hill.

Energy can be further classified based on the way it is stored and transmitted. For example, mechanical energy (ME) is energy that results in the motion of matter. Chemical energy (CE) is energy that is stored or translated through chemical reactions. Thermal energy (TE) is energy that results in heat.

Matter and energy cannot be destroyed. Only the nature of matter and the forms of energy change. For example, when a piece of charcoal burns and disappears, we may think it is completely gone. However, the charcoal material has combined with air and formed a like quantity of ash, water, and gases. The energy that did this existed as flame (light energy) and heat (heat energy). All of this will continue until another change takes place.

Whenever a form of matter can be separated from other forms of matter so that a part or all of its energy can be released, it is said to contain potential energy. Examples of such matter include crude oil and the gasoline taken from it. We have learned different ways to release a part of the energy stored in these substances.

Engines are designed to release and change the potential energy of gasoline into mechanical power. Mechanical power does the work at hand.

Force

Forces are being applied all around us. Force is the pushing or pulling of one body on another. Usually two bodies must be in contact for force to be transmitted. For example, as you read this you are applying a force to a chair if you are sitting or to the floor if you are standing. The force is equal to the weight of your body. You can easily measure it with a scale. This is known as gravitational force and it acts on all materials on and around the earth.

Some forces are stationary (motionless); others are moving. For example, if you push against a wall, force is applied but the wall does not move. The use of force may or may not cause motion. Force

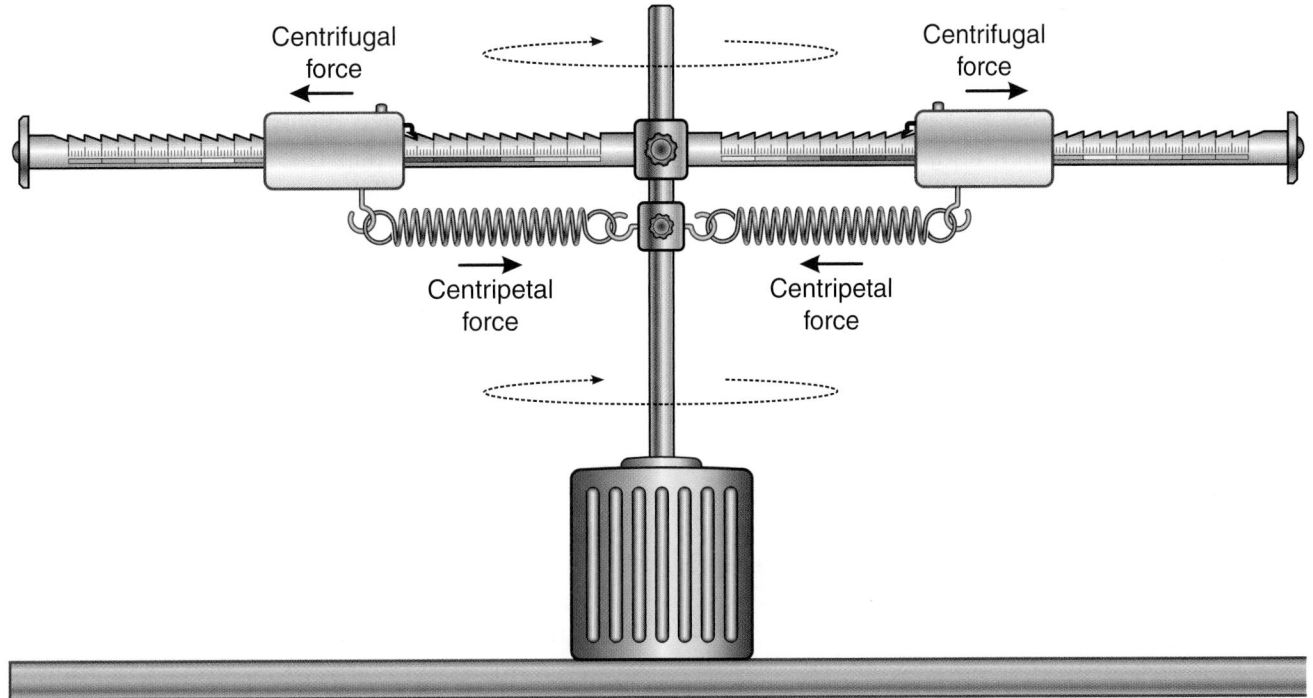

Fouad A. Saad/Shutterstock.com

Figure 7-2.

As the motor spins the horizontal bar, the weights are flung outward by centrifugal force. The springs exert a counteracting force (centripetal force). These forces are key to the operation of several engine components, including centrifugal governors and compression release mechanisms.

itself cannot be seen, but there are many ways of using it.

Centrifugal force acts on a body whenever it follows a circular or curved path. The body tries to move outward from the center of its path. Modern examples are the man-made satellites that orbit the earth. The circular path and speed of the satellite produces a centrifugal force outward that is equal to the earth's gravitational force inward so that each is opposed and balanced. Therefore, the satellite neither goes up nor comes down. This is one case where a force is applied without one body touching another body. The effect of centrifugal force can also be demonstrated by the device shown in **Figure 7-2**. As the motor spins the horizontal bar, the weights are flung outward by centrifugal force. The springs stretch until the force they exert on the weights perfectly balances the centrifugal force. The force that opposes centrifugal force is called centripetal force.

Many forces interact when a gasoline engine is operating. The rotational speed of the crankshaft and flywheel create centrifugal force, which causes *tensile stress* (tension or pull) within the materials making up these parts. If the outward

pulling force becomes greater than the strength of the material, the engine could fly apart. The rapid reciprocation (backward and forward or up and down motion) of the piston may put high forces on the connecting rod, crank journal, and piston pin.

One of the forces used efficiently in the gasoline engine is the one applied to the top of the piston by rapidly expanding gases in the combustion chamber. This force is produced by burning gasoline mixed with air. The greater the force applied to the piston, the greater the amount of power and work that can be done by the engine.

Force is measured in units of some standard weight such as pounds, ounces, or grams. For example, to support a shop vise weighing 16 lb, a person would have to apply a lifting force of 16 lb. Obviously, only half the lifting force would be needed to support an 8 lb vise.

Pressure

Force and pressure are often confused. It is important to understand the difference and to use the terms correctly. *Pressure* is a force applied to a given unit of area. For example, a piston with a face area of 5 square inches (in²) may have a total force of 500 lb applied to it by the expanding gases. However, the pressure being applied is 500 lb divided by 5 in², which equals 100 pounds per square inch (psi). This means that every square inch on the piston face has the equivalent of a 100 lb weight pushing on it.

The pressure formulas are as follows:

$$Pressure = \frac{Force}{Area}$$

$$or\ Force = Pressure \times Area$$

$$or\ Area = \frac{Force}{Pressure}$$

In order to use any of the formulas above, you must know any two of the three variables involved. In order to calculate the pressure acting on the piston, you must be able to calculate the surface area that the force is acting on. The most common application of the pressure formulas is determining the pressure or force acting on a piston, which has a circular head. The area of a circle can be found by multiplying pi (π = 3.1416) by the radius squared. The written formula is as follows:

$$Area = \pi r^2$$

Another method is to multiply the constant .7854 by the diameter squared. The written formula is as follows:

$$Area = .7854D^2$$

For example, calculate a force applied to a 3″ diameter piston, **Figure 7-3**, if the cylinder pressure is 125 psi.

$$
\begin{aligned}
Area &= \pi r^2 \\
&= 3.1416 \times (1.5'' \times 1.5'') \\
&= 3.1416 \times 2.25\ in^2 \\
&= 7.0686\ in^2
\end{aligned}
$$

You were given a pressure of 125 psi and you have determined the piston area equals: 7.0686 in². Next, you multiply the area by the pressure to determine the total force acting on the piston:

$$
\begin{aligned}
Force &= Pressure \times Area \\
&= 125\ psi \times 7.0686\ in^2 \\
&= 883.575\ lb
\end{aligned}
$$

This results in a total force of 883.575 lb.

Work

Work is accomplished only when a force is applied through some distance. If a given weight is held so that it neither rises nor falls, no work is done, even though the person holding the weight may become very tired. If the weight is raised some distance, then work is being done. The amount of work performed is the product or result of the force and the distance through which it is applied.

If a weight of 20 lb is lifted 3′, then 60 ft-lb of work is accomplished. The distance must always be measured in the same direction as the applied force. This results in the formula as follows:

$$Work = Force \times Distance$$

Because the formula calls for multiplying distance times force, common units in the US Customary system are foot-pounds (ft-lb) and inch-pounds (in-lb). The common unit in the SI system is Newton-meters (N•m).

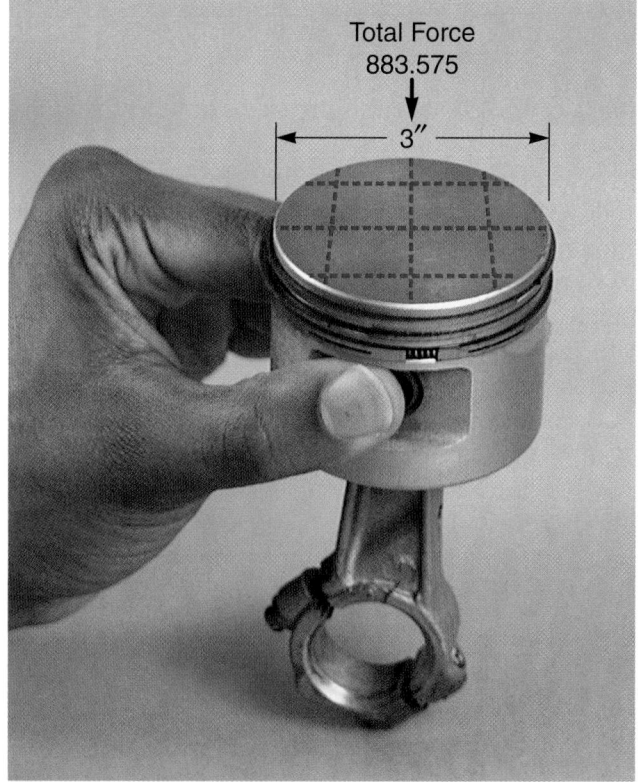

Goodheart-Willcox Publisher

Figure 7-3.

The total force applied to a piston face is equal to its area in square inches multiplied by the psi (pounds per square inch).

Levers and Mechanical Advantage

A gasoline engine utilizes the principles of a number of simple machines. One of the most common is the lever. The purpose of this simple machine is to change the amount of force required to perform a given amount of work. Since work equals force applied through a distance, the amount of force required to perform a given amount of work increases if the distance through which the force is applied is decreased. Similarly, the amount of force required to perform the work is decreased if the distance it is applied through is increased.

A lever produces a mechanical advantage, which allows a load to be moved with a reduced force. **Figure 7-4** illustrates how a heavy load can be moved a short distance by exerting a small force through a relatively great distance. The formula for computing leverage, as it applies to **Figure 7-4**, is as follows:

$$MA = \frac{ED}{RD}$$

Where

MA = mechanical advantage
ED = effort distance
RD = resistance distance

Imagine a 600 lb weight is being lifted. To lift the weight a foot in the air, a weightlifter would need to exert slightly more than 600 lb through a distance of one foot. The result would be 600 ft-lb of work.

A much weaker person could perform the same amount of work by using the mechanical advantage offered by a lever. For example, the lever shown in **Figure 7-4** provides a mechanical advantage of three to one.

$$MA = \frac{ED}{RD} = \frac{6'}{2'} = 3$$

This means that someone using the lever can lift the same 600 lb weight one foot up by exerting only 200 pounds of force through a distance of three feet.

$$E = \frac{R}{MA} = \frac{600\ lb}{3} = 200\ lb$$

Where

E = effort (force)
R = resistance (weight)
MA = mechanical advantage

Levers are commonly used to open and close valves in overhead valve engines. Since valves are equipped with heavy springs that keep them tightly sealed when the valve is closed, considerable force is required to open the valve. Simple levers convert the relatively large up and down motion provided by the camshaft lobe into a smaller, more forceful movement to open the valves.

Power

In studying the formula for work, note that it does not consider the time required to do the work. For example, if a small gasoline engine weighing 50 pounds is lifted 3′ from the floor to the workbench, 150 ft-lb of work is done. The same amount of work would be performed whether it took 50 seconds (sec) to lift the engine or only 5 seconds.

In order to evaluate the effectiveness of an engine for a given task, you must consider how quickly it can perform the required work. *Power* is the rate at

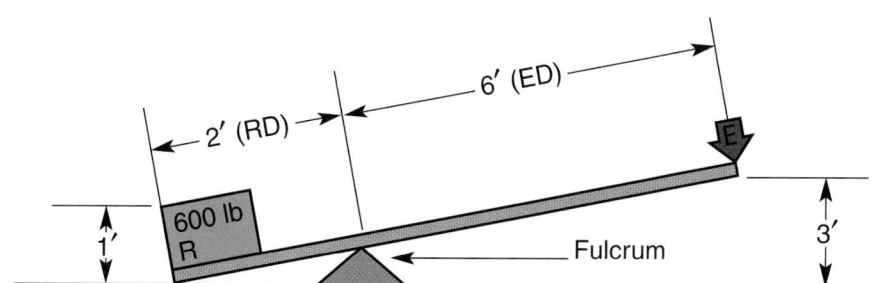

Goodheart-Willcox Publisher

Figure 7-4.

The mechanical advantage provided by a lever changes the ratio of force to distance required to perform a given amount of work.

which work is performed. The formula for power is as follows:

$$Power = \frac{Work}{Time}$$

$$or\ Power = \frac{(feet \times pounds)}{seconds}$$

$$or\ Power = ft\text{-}lb\ per\ second\ (ft\text{-}lb/sec)$$

When the engine is lifted in 5 seconds, 150 ft-lb of work is performed. Using the power formula, it can be seen that:

$$Power = \frac{Work}{Time}$$

$$= \frac{150\ ft\text{-}lb}{5\ sec}$$

$$= \frac{30\ ft\text{-}lb}{sec}$$

If the same engine is lifted in 50 sec, the formula shows the following:

$$Power = \frac{Work}{Time}$$

$$= \frac{150\ ft\text{-}lb}{50\ sec}$$

$$= \frac{3\ ft\text{-}lb}{sec}$$

Work is a force applied to an object that causes the object to move, and power is the rate at which the work is done. The standard unit of power is termed *horsepower*.

Horsepower

For hundreds of years, men used horses to perform work. It was only natural that when machines were invented, their ability to perform work would be compared to the horse.

In his work with early steam engines, James Watt wanted some simple way to measure their power output. In measuring the power of, or rate of work performed by, a horse, he found that most workhorses could lift 100 pounds a distance of 330′ in 1 minute.

If 1 pound is lifted 1′, 1 ft-lb of work is done. The horse lifted 100 pounds a distance of 330′. Using the work formula (Work = Distance × Force), Watt found that the horse performed 33,000 ft-lb of work.

In determining the *rate of power* developed by the horse, we use the following formula:

$$Power = \frac{Work}{Time}$$

$$= \frac{33,000\ ft\text{-}lb}{1\ min}$$

$$= \frac{550\ ft\text{-}lb}{sec}$$

$$= 1\ horsepower\ (hp)$$

The 550 ft-lb/sec (ability to lift 550 pounds a distance of 1′ in 1 second) was then established as 1 horsepower (hp). This standard is still in use today.

Torque

Torque refers to the ability of a force to cause an object to rotate. Therefore, any reference to engine torque refers to the turning force developed by the rotating crankshaft.

In order to find torque, we must know the force (in pounds) and the radius (distance, in feet, from the center of the turning shaft to the exact point at which the force is measured). The formula would read as follows:

$$Torque = Force \times Distance\ (Radius)$$

$$or\ Torque = pounds \times feet$$

$$or\ Torque = lb\text{-}ft$$

Figure 7-5 shows a torque wrench attached to a rotating crankshaft. If the handle of the torque wrench is supported so it cannot move, the torque applied by the engine would be registered on the torch wrench's scale. However, at some point the crankshaft would have too much resistance on it, and the engine would stop.

A Prony brake like the one shown in **Figure 7-6** can be used to measure torque on a running engine. A *Prony brake* is a friction device that grips an engine-driven flywheel and transfers the force to a measuring scale. One end of the Prony brake pressure arm rests on the scale and the other wraps around a spinning flywheel driven by the engine under test. A clamp is used to change the frictional grip on the spinning flywheel. As the clamp is tightened, more of the force generated by the engine is applied to the arm. This will allow the crankshaft to turn while still applying turning force to the scale. To measure the maximum torque

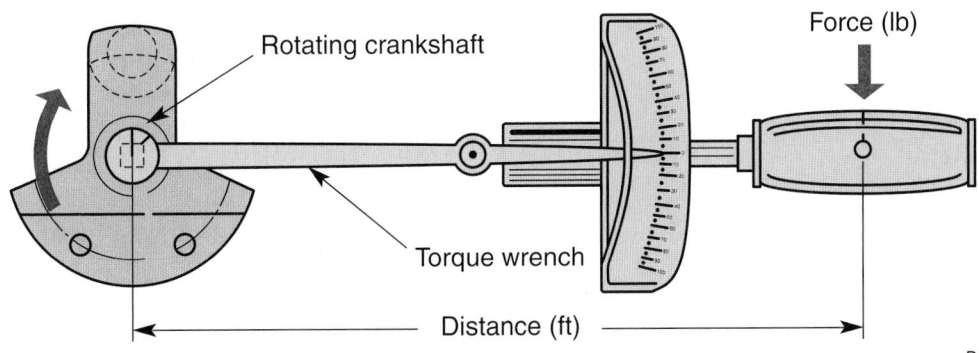

Dresser Industries Inc.

Figure 7-5.

Torque is determined by multiplying the turning effort in pounds by the distance from the shaft center to the point at which force is read.

applied by the engine, the friction band is tightened until the engine begins to bog down.

Suppose a scale is placed exactly 2′ from the center of the crankshaft. After the friction band is adjusted, the scale indicates a force of 100 lb. By using the formula for determining torque (*Torque = Force × Distance*, or *Torque = 100 lb × 2′*), we find that this engine is developing 200 lb-ft of torque.

If the scale is 3′ from the shaft center and the force is 50 pounds, the torque will be 150 lb-ft. When measuring torque, the reading is given in lb-ft. When measuring work, the reading is given in ft-lb.

Wheel and Axle

A wheel and axle arrangement can provide mechanical advantage like that provided by a lever.

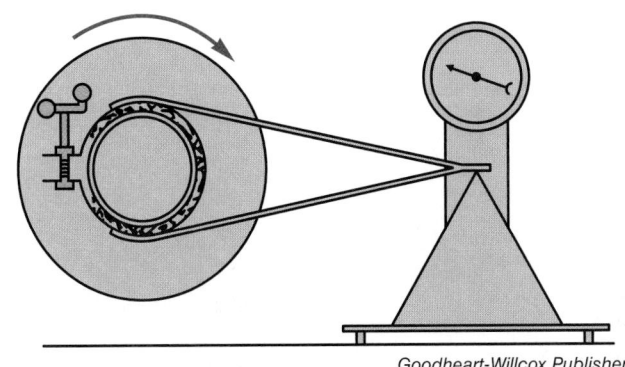

Goodheart-Willcox Publisher

Figure 7-6.

In a Prony brake setup, one end of the pressure arm surrounds a spinning flywheel driven by the engine. By tightening the friction device, torque is transmitted to and measured at the scale.

See **Figure 7-7**. The wheel is much larger than the axle. With each revolution of the wheel and axle assembly, a point on the outer edge of the wheel moves a much greater distance than a corresponding point on the axle. If the load is placed on the axle, and the wheel is turned, the force required to move the load is reduced. However, the distance that the load is moved is also reduced. On the other hand, if the load is placed on the wheel, the force required to move the load is increased, but the load moves farther with each rotation.

The mechanical advantage provided by a wheel and axle can be calculated by comparing the radius of the wheel to the radius of the axle:

$$ME = \frac{R_1}{R_2}$$

Where

ME = mechanical advantage
R_1 = radius of the load carrying member (wheel or axle)
R_2 = radius of the member to which force is applied (wheel or axle)

Pulley, Gear, and Chain Drive Systems

A pulley or gear installed on a shaft is essentially a wheel and axle system. If a large pulley is installed on the shaft, the force measured at a point on the outer edge of the pulley will be relatively low, but the point will travel a greater distance with each revolution of the shaft. If a smaller pulley is installed, the force at a point on the outer edge of the pulley will be greater, but the point will travel a shorter distance with each revolution.

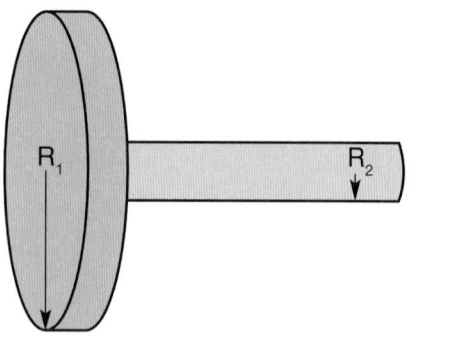

Goodheart-Willcox Publisher

Figure 7-7.

Wheel and axles systems can increase or decrease applied force. The factor by which the force is increased or decreased is determined by the radius of the wheel (R_1) compared to the radius of the axle (R_2). If force is applied to the axle and the load is on the wheel, force is decreased. If the force is applied to the wheel, and the load is on the axle, force is increased.

Pulley systems can be used between two shafts to increase the rotational speed or torque from one shaft to the other. The ratio of the diameter of the drive pulley to the driven pulley determines the factor by which the rotational speed and torque are changed. See **Figure 7-8A**. If the drive pulley is smaller than the driven pulley, torque is increased and rotational speed is decreased. If the drive gear is larger than the driven gear, the torque is decreased and the rotational speed is increased.

As an example, imagine an overhead cam engine where the crankshaft is fitted with a 2″ pulley that is connected by a belt to a 4″ pulley

on the camshaft. Two complete revolutions of the crankshaft are required for a single revolution of the camshaft. The camshaft turns at half the speed but twice the torque of the crankshaft.

Now, imagine an engine driving a low-pressure, high-volume air pump. The engine's crankshaft is equipped with a 9″ pulley, which is connected by a belt to a 3″ pulley on the pump. Every revolution of the crankshaft results in three revolutions of the pump. The pump's crankshaft turns at three times the speed, but with one-third of the torque of the engine's crankshaft.

The same concepts can be applied to sprocket and chain systems. In a sprocket and chain system, like the one shown in **Figure 7-8B**, the ratio of the number of teeth on the drive sprocket compared to the number of teeth on the driven sprocket determines the factor by which torque and rotational speed are altered.

Gear systems, like the ones shown in **Figure 7-8C**, produce similar results. Again, the ratio of the number of teeth on the drive gear to the number of teeth of the driven gear determine the factor by which rotational speed and torque are altered. It should be noted that the direct contact between the teeth of the input and output gears causes the output gear to turn in the opposite direction as the input gear. If an idler gear is placed between the drive gear and output gear, those gears will rotate in the same direction. The idler gear has no effect on the gear ratio between the input gear and output gear, no matter how large or small it is.

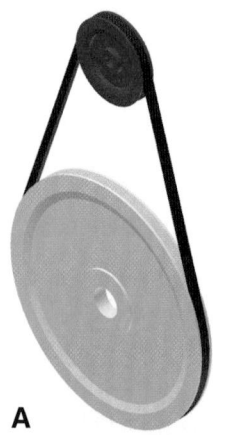  

A   B   C

Goodheart-Willcox Publisher

Figure 7-8.

Pulley systems, chain and sprocket systems, and gear systems can be used to multiply rotational speed or torque. A—A belt and pulley system. B—A chain and sprocket system. C—A gear system.

Measurements of Engine Performance

The term *engine performance* refers to a measurement of engine output. Engine performance is based on measurement of engine output in three areas: power, torque, and efficiency. Power is the measure of how much work an engine can perform in a given amount of time. Torque refers to how much of a load the engine can handle without bogging down. Efficiency is a measure of how well the engine uses its fuel and air resources to generate power.

Engine Displacement

Cylinder displacement is the change in the volume of a cylinder as the piston moves from the top to the bottom of its stroke. To determine cylinder displacement, use the volume formula for a cylinder (Volume = cross-sectional area of the cylinder × cylinder height). First, the cross-sectional area of the cylinder is determined by multiplying 0.7854 by the diameter cylinder squared (D^2). Next, that result is multiplied by the height of the cylinder, which (for the purpose of calculating engine displacement) equals the total length of the stroke (piston travel).

The formula is as follows:

$$Cylinder\ Displacement = 0.7854 \times D^2 \times Stroke$$

If the engine has more than one cylinder, multiply the answer to the above formula by the number of cylinders.

$$Engine\ Displacement = \frac{Cylinder\ Displacement \times}{Number\ of\ Cylinders}$$

For example, say that a two-cylinder engine has a bore of 3 1/4″ and a stroke of 3 1/4″. Using the displacement formulas, you would have the following:

$$
\begin{aligned}
Cylinder\ Displacement &= .7854 \times D^2 \times Stroke \\
&= .7854 \times 10.563\ in^2 \times 3\ 1/4″ \\
&= 26.96\ in^3
\end{aligned}
$$

$$
\begin{aligned}
Engine\ Displacement &= Number\ of\ Cylinders \times \\
&\quad Cylinder\ Displacement \\
&= 2 \times 26.96\ in^3 \\
&= 53.92\ in^3
\end{aligned}
$$

Figure 7-9 illustrates piston displacement. In drawing A, the piston is at TDC (top dead center). Green represents the space left between the piston and the cylinder head. The piston in drawing B is at the bottom of its stroke. Note the increased space above the piston now. In drawing C, red represents the piston displacement for this cylinder.

Compression Ratio

The compression ratio of an engine is a measurement of the relationship between the total cylinder volume when the piston is at the bottom of its stroke (BDC) and the volume remaining when the piston is at the top of its stroke (TDC). For example, if cylinder volume measures 6 in^3 when the piston is at BDC (**Figure 7-10A**) and 1 in^3 when at TDC, (**Figure 7-10B**), the compression ratio of the engine is 6 to 1. Many small gasoline engines have 5 to 1 or 6 to 1 compression ratios. Certain motorcycle engines have 9 to 1 or 10 to 1 compression ratios.

Compression ratios are commonly expressed by two values separated by a colon. For example, a 5 to 1 compression ratio would be expressed as 5:1. A 6 to 1 compression ratio would be expressed as 6:1.

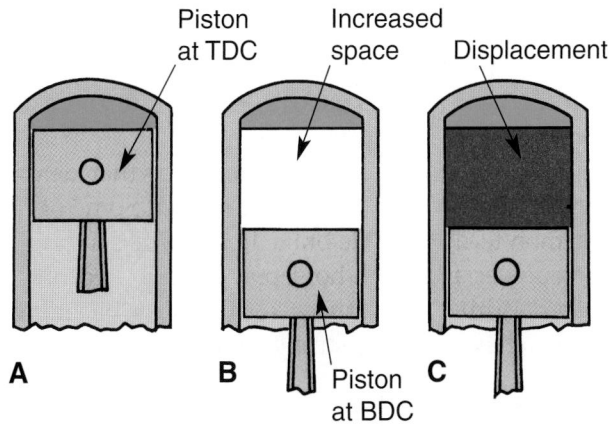

Goodheart-Willcox Publisher

Figure 7-9.

Engine displacement is the difference in the volume of the cylinder and combustion chamber above the piston when it is at TDC and at BDC. The red area shows displacement.

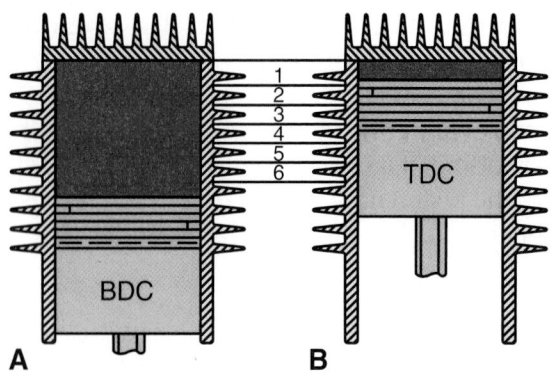

Briggs and Stratton Corp.

Figure 7-10.

A compression ratio is the relationship between the cylinder volume with the piston at BDC (A) and the piston at TDC (B). The volume has been compressed to one-sixth of its original size, which indicates a 6 to 1 compression ratio.

Engine Horsepower

Engine horsepower can be calculated by dividing the total rate of work (ft-lb/sec) by 550 ft-lb/sec. For example, if an engine lifted 330 pounds a distance of 100 feet in 6 seconds, its total rate of work would be as follows:

$$Horsepower = \frac{Rate\ of\ Work}{550\ \text{ft-lb/sec}}$$

$$= \frac{(100\ \text{ft} \times 330\ \text{lb})/6\ \text{sec}}{550\ \text{ft-lb/sec}}$$

$$= \frac{5500\ \text{ft-lb/sec}}{550\ \text{ft-lb/sec}}$$

$$= 10$$

You find that the engine is rated at 10 hp. This formula can also be used to determine the exact horsepower needed for other tasks.

The word *horsepower* is used in terms that identify various methods of measuring power. Some of the common terms include brake horsepower, indicated horsepower, frictional horsepower, and rated horsepower. While all of these terms describe engine power, they each measure it in different ways.

Brake Horsepower

Brake horsepower (bhp) indicates the actual usable horsepower delivered at the engine crankshaft. Brake horsepower does not remain constant with changes in engine speed. It increases with engine speed. At very high and generally unusable

engine speeds (depending on engine design), the horsepower output will drop off somewhat. **Figure 7-11** shows how horsepower increases with speed for two different engine models. However, the top speeds in this chart do not run high enough to show a drop in horsepower.

Measuring Engine Brake Horsepower

There are two common methods of measuring brake horsepower. It can be measured by using a Prony brake or an engine dynamometer. See **Figure 7-6**. To check brake horsepower, the engine under test is operated with the throttle wide open. Then engine speed is reduced to a specific number of revolutions per minute by tightening the pressure arm on the flywheel. At exactly the right speed, the arm pressure on the scale is read. By using the scale reading (W) from the Prony brake, the flywheel rpm (R), and the distance in feet from the center of the flywheel to the arm support (L), brake horsepower can be computed. The formula used to determine brake horsepower on the Prony brake is as follows:

$$bhp = \frac{2\pi \times R \times L \times W}{33,000\ \text{ft-lb/min}}$$

$$\text{or } bhp = \frac{R \times L \times W}{5252\ \text{ft-lb/min}}$$

Where

R = engine speed (rpm)
L = length from center of flywheel to point where beam presses on scale (ft)
W = weight as registered on scale (lb)

As with the Prony brake, the *dynamometer* loads the engine and transfers the loading to a measuring device. Instead of using a dry friction loading technique (clamping pressure arm to a spinning wheel), the dynamometer uses either hydraulic or electric loading. Several different types of dynamometers are shown in **Figure 7-12**.

Indicated Horsepower

Indicated horsepower (ihp) is a measure of the power developed by the burning fuel mixture inside the cylinder. It is essentially a measure of the total potential horsepower the engine is capable of developing. To measure ihp, you must determine the pressure inside the cylinder during the intake, compression, power, and exhaust strokes. A special

Horsepower		
	Engine Models	
RPM	ACN	BKN
1600	2.5	3.5
1800	2.9	4.0
2000	3.5	4.4
2200	3.7	4.9
2400	4.2	5.4
2600	4.5	5.8
2800	4.8	6.2
3000	5.2	6.5
3200	5.6	6.7
3400	5.8	6.9
3600	6.0	7.0

Wisconsin Motors Corp.

Figure 7-11.

Brake horsepower increases with engine speed. Note that these two example engines, bhp at 3600 rpm is about twice that developed at 1600 rpm.

measuring tool is used to continuously monitor cylinder pressure. This pressure information is placed on an indicator graph, like the one in **Figure 7-13**.

At this point, the *mean effective pressure (mep)* must be determined. To do this, subtract the average pressure during the intake, compression, and exhaust strokes from the average pressure developed during the power stroke. The mean effective pressure varies depending on engine type and design. After finding the mep, the following formula is used to determine the indicated horsepower:

$$ihp = \frac{P \times L \times A \times N \times K}{33,000 \text{ ft-lb/min}}$$

Where

P = mean effective pressure (psi)
L = length of piston stroke (ft)
A = cylinder area (in²)
N = number of power strokes per minute (rpm/2 for four-stroke engine)
K = number of cylinders.

Frictional Horsepower

Frictional horsepower (fhp) represents that part of the indicated horsepower lost because of the drag of engine parts rubbing together, **Figure 7-14**. Despite smooth contact surfaces and proper lubrication, a certain amount of friction (resistance to movement between two objects that are rubbing together) is always present and represents a sizable horsepower loss. Actual loss will vary with engine design and use, but will generally run about 10%. Friction loss does not remain constant. It increases with engine speed.

Frictional horsepower is determined by subtracting brake horsepower from indicated horsepower or by the following formula:

$$fhp = ihp - bhp$$

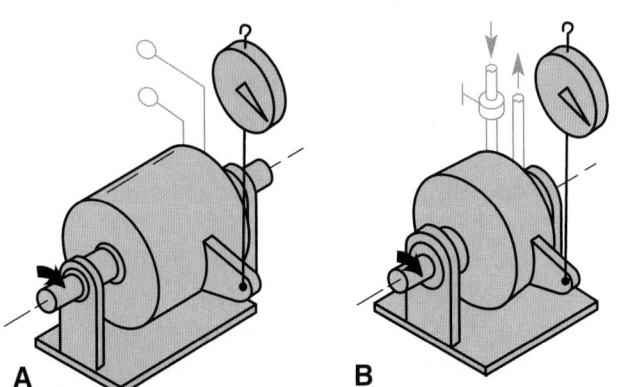
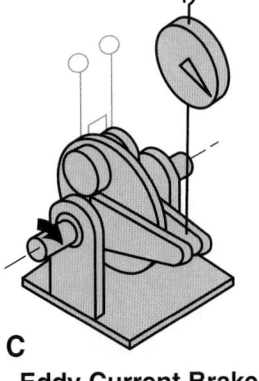
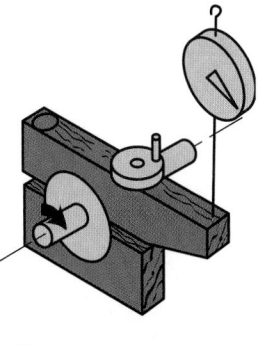

A	B	C	D
Cradled Electric Generator	**Hydraulic Water Brake**	**Eddy Current Brake**	**Prony Brake**

Go-Power Corp.

Figure 7-12.

The variety of dynamometers shown use different principles of construction. A—The engine drives an electric generator that is attached to a spring scale. When an electrical load is placed in the circuit, the generator housing (an enclosure holding the moving parts) attempts to spin, applying a force to the scale. B—A hydraulic water brake is attached to the scale. The engine is loaded by admitting more and more water into the brake, causing the housing to try to rotate, exerting a force on the scale. C—An eddy current brake. D—A Prony brake.

Rated Horsepower

An engine used under a load that is as great as the engine's highest brake horsepower rating will overheat. Excessive pressure on the bearings (loading) will seriously shorten the engine's service life. In

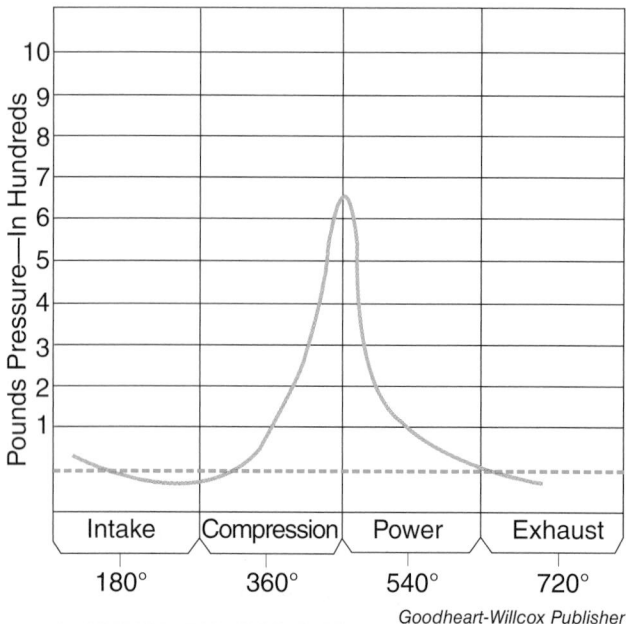

Figure 7-13.

This graph shows the simulated cylinder pressure developed in the cylinder of a specific four-cycle engine. Atmospheric pressure is shown by the dotted line. The graph makes it possible to establish a mean effective pressure (mep).

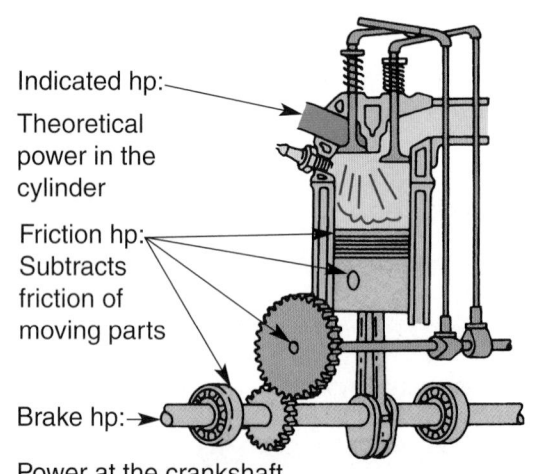

Figure 7-14.

Frictional horsepower is determined by subtracting crankshaft brake horsepower from indicated horsepower.

some cases, complete engine failure can occur in a very short period of time.

As a general rule, never load an engine to more than 80% of its highest brake horsepower rating. For example, if a job requires a horsepower loading of 8 hp, you would use an engine with at least a 10 hp rating. Then, the load would be no more than 80% of the engine's maximum hp.

An engine's *rated horsepower* generally will be 80% of its maximum brake horsepower. Note in **Figure 7-15** how the rated horsepower (recommended maximum operating bhp) is less than engine maximum bhp.

Corrected Horsepower

Standard brake horsepower ratings are based on engine test conditions with the air dry, temperature at 60°F, and a barometric pressure of 29.92 inches of mercury, or Hg (standard atmospheric pressure at sea level). Horsepower, however, can be greatly affected by changes in atmospheric pressure, temperature, and humidity (amount of moisture in the air).

Corrected horsepower is a *guess* at horsepower of a given engine under specific operating conditions that are not the same as those present during actual dynamometer testing. The following are some of the factors that may affect horsepower:

- S1   For each 1000' of elevation above sea level, horsepower will drop around 3 1/2%.
- S1   For each 1" drop in barometric pressure, horsepower will drop another 3 1/2%.
- S1   Each 10°F of temperature increase results in a horsepower loss of 1%.
- S1   New engines will develop somewhat less horsepower (due to increased friction) until they have been operated a number of hours.
- S1   An increase of 200°F–400°F in head operating temperature can lower horsepower by 10%.
- S1   Quality of fuel, mechanical conditions, and state of tune can also affect horsepower.

When horsepower tests are conducted under conditions varying from standard, corrections must be applied to establish true horsepower.

Correction Factor

The correction factor (a factor is a condition that would change an answer) is determined by using the following formula:

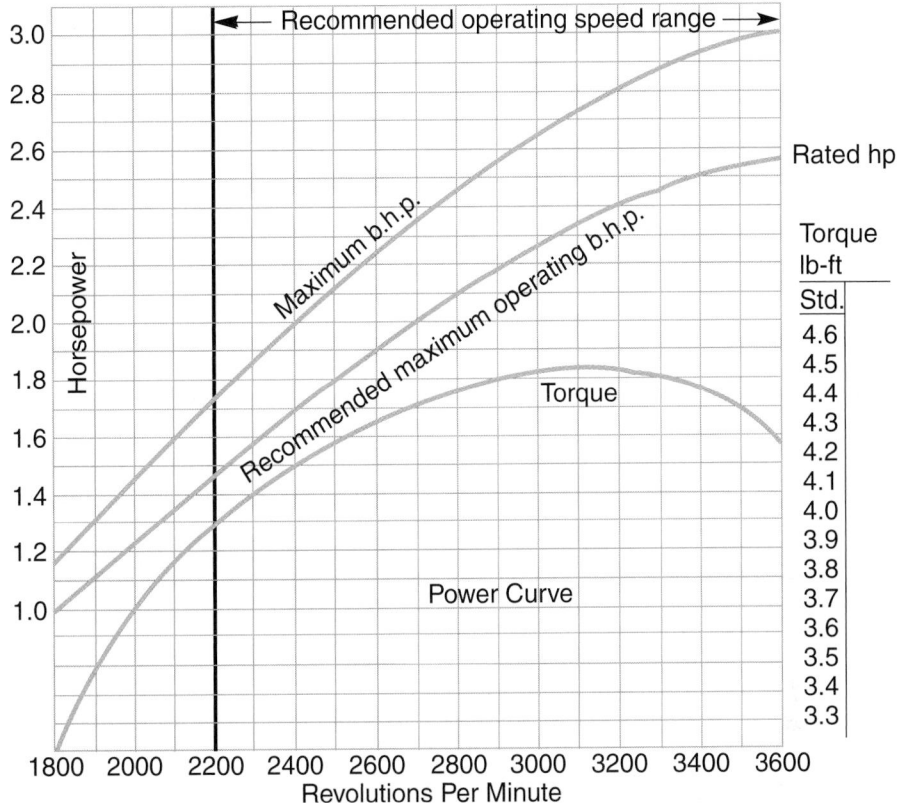

Figure 7-15.

The maximum operating brake horsepower loading is charted for a specific engine. At all speeds, the rated hp is about 80% of the maximum bhp.

$$Correction\ Factor = C_T \times C_P \times C_H$$

Where

C_T = temperature correction
C_P = pressure correction
C_H = humidity correction

For example, suppose that the dynamometer tests were carried out at a temperature of 90°F with an atmospheric pressure of 28.5″ Hg and a wet bulb temperature (determines humidity) of 73.5°F. First, see the chart in **Figure 7-16**. Follow dotted line A from top of chart (90°F temperature) down until it crosses the temperature line B. By moving left along the chart, you can see the dotted line shows a temperature correction factor of 1.028.

Now, follow dotted line C up from the 28.5″ Hg marking at the bottom of the chart until it crosses pressure line D. By moving left at this point, a pressure correction factor of 1.068 is shown.

To find the humidity correction factor, use the chart in **Figure 7-17**. Follow the dotted line up from the 90°F dry bulb temperature mark until it meets the 73.5°F dotted wet bulb temperature line. Move across to the right and note that the humidity correction factor is 1.0084.

Then, determine the overall correction factor using the following formula:

$$
\begin{aligned}
Correction\ Factor &= C_T \times C_P \times C_H \\
&= 1.028 \times 1.068 \times 1.0084 \\
&= 1.1071
\end{aligned}
$$

If the dynamometer test had shown 3.15 horsepower, this reading could be changed to standard test conditions by applying the correction factor of 1.1071 as determined earlier. Thus:

$$
\begin{aligned}
Corrected\ hp &= Correction\ Factor \times Test\ hp \\
&= 1.1071 \times 3.15\ hp \\
&= 3.4874\ hp
\end{aligned}
$$

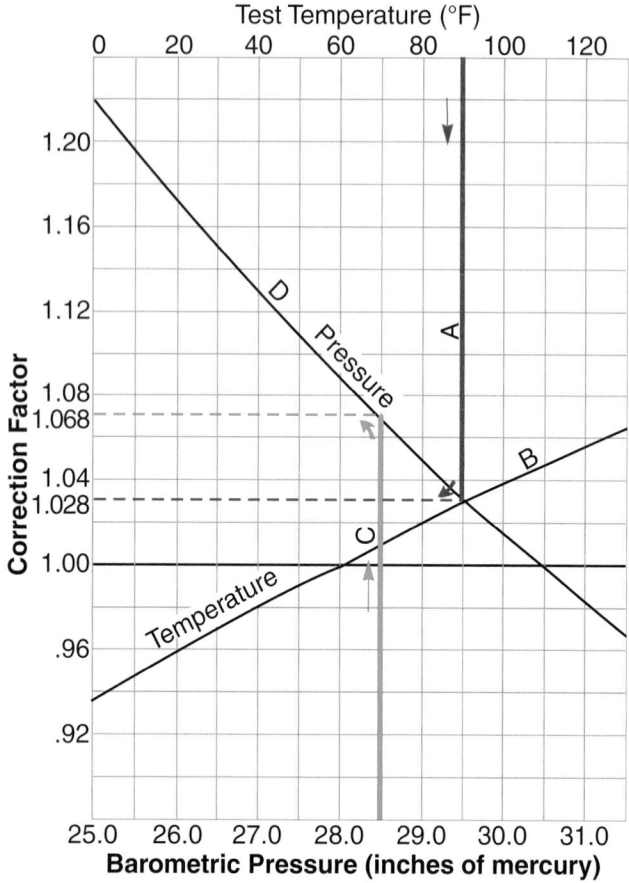

Test Temperature (°F)

Barometric Pressure (inches of mercury)

Go-Power Corp.

Figure 7-16.

A temperature and barometric pressure correction chart. Use this chart to determine the horsepower correction factor for temperature and pressure to 60°F and sea level pressure (29.92″ Hg). For example, if the actual temperature is 90°F, the correction factor (1.028) would be found by tracing line A from the scale at the top of the graph to the point at which it intersects with curve B, then following the dotted red line to the scale on the left. If the atmospheric pressure is 28.50″ Hg, the correction factor (1.08) is found by tracing line C from the scale on the bottom of the graph to the point at which it intersects with line D, and then following the dotted green line to the scale on the left.

Engine Torque

Engine torque, for any engine and set of test conditions, will change according to engine speed. The pressure of the burning air-fuel mixture against the piston is transferred to the crankshaft by the connecting rod. The greater the pressure, the more torque the crankshaft will develop.

The point where gas pressure will be highest is the speed at which the engine takes in the largest volume of air-fuel mixture. This point will vary according to engine design but will always be at a lower speed than that at which the greatest horsepower is reached. Horsepower generally increases as engine speed increases until the engine reaches a very high rpm, and horsepower finally begins to drop off. Torque, on the other hand, decreases at a much lower rpm.

As engine speed is increased beyond idle, its torque increases. As it continues to speed up, a point will be reached where the natural restriction to airflow through the carburetor, intake manifold, and valve ports begins to limit the speed at which the air-fuel mixture can enter the cylinder. At this point, the highest torque is developed.

When engine speed goes higher than this point, the intake valve will open but the piston moves far down on the intake stroke before the mixture can get into the cylinder. This cuts down the amount of air-fuel mixture entering the cylinder. As a result, burning pressure is lowered as well as the torque. Beyond this point, torque will decrease as speed increases.

Torque and Horsepower

Unlike torque (which drops off when engine revolutions per minute exceed the point of maximum volumetric efficiency), horsepower continues to increase until engine speed is very high. Beyond a certain speed, however, horsepower will actually decrease.

Keep in mind that torque measures the twisting force generated by the crankshaft while horsepower measures the engine's ability to perform work. Even though torque may decline at higher speeds, the shaft is turning much faster. Therefore, it is able to perform work at a greater rate.

Figure 7-18 shows the relationship between torque and horsepower curves for one specific engine. Note the arrow indicating the rated horsepower. This is the horsepower at which the engine can be operated continuously without damage.

Volumetric Efficiency

How well an engine breathes, or draws the air-fuel mixture into the cylinder, is referred to as its volumetric efficiency. It is measured by comparing the air-fuel mixture actually drawn in to the amount that could be drawn in if the cylinder were completely filled. See **Figure 7-19**.

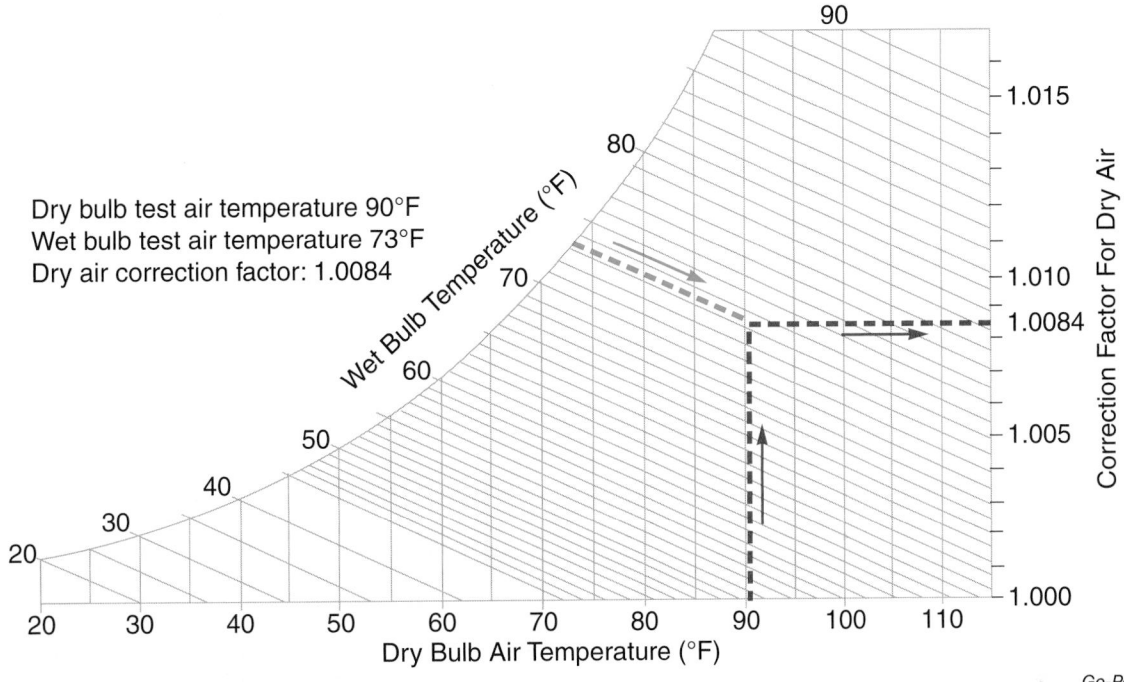

Dry bulb test air temperature 90°F
Wet bulb test air temperature 73°F
Dry air correction factor: 1.0084

Figure 7-17.

A chart for determining the humidity correction factor.

Volumetric efficiency changes with speed. At high engine speeds, it can be very low. The reason for this is simple. As engine revolutions increase beyond a certain point, the piston moves down (intake stroke) so rapidly that it travels far down the cylinder before the air-fuel mixture begins to flow into the cylinder. The intake cycle can be complete (piston moving upward on compression stroke) before the cylinder is much more than half full.

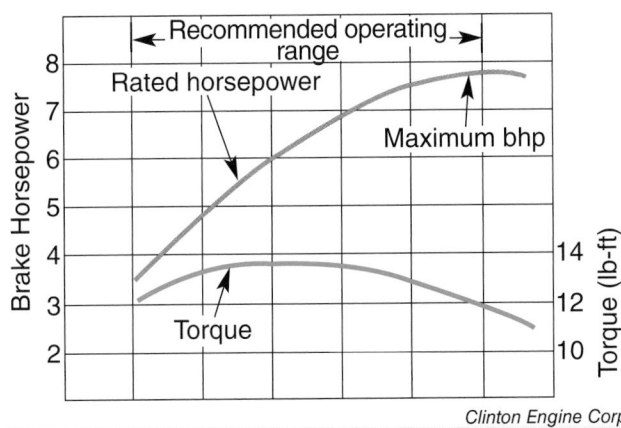

Figure 7-18.

An illustration of the relationship between torque and horsepower for one particular engine.

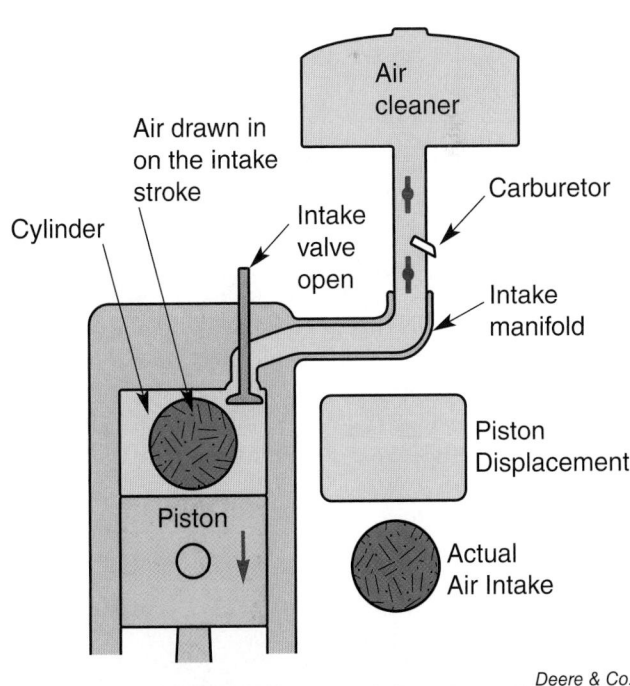

Figure 7-19.

Volumetric efficiency is the measurement of an engine's breathing ability. It compares the intake of air-fuel mixture with the piston displacement. Note that the actual air intake is considerably less than the piston displacement.

Other factors can change the volumetric efficiency, including atmospheric pressure; air temperature; air cleaner, carburetor and intake manifold design; size of intake valve; engine temperature; throttle position; valve timing; and camshaft design. Efficiency can be increased by using a larger intake valve, altering cam profiles (shapes) or cam timing, increasing the size of the carburetor air horn, straightening and increasing the diameter of the intake manifold, improving exhaust flow, and/or adding a supercharger.

Figure 7-20 illustrates how volumetric efficiency varies with speed. There is a gradual buildup to a certain rpm, followed by a rapid decline as speed is increased. Remember that the speed at which top volumetric efficiency is reached will vary with engine design.

Practical Efficiency

In theory, each gallon of gasoline contains enough energy to do a certain amount of work. This may be thought of as potential energy. Unfortunately, engines are not efficient enough to use all the potential energy in the fuel. Practical efficiency takes into consideration power losses caused by friction, incomplete burning of the air-fuel mixture, heat loss, etc. *Practical efficiency* is simply an overall measurement of how efficiently an engine uses the fuel supply.

Mechanical Efficiency

Mechanical efficiency is the percentage of power developed in the cylinder (indicated horsepower) compared to the power that is actually delivered at the crankshaft (brake horsepower). Brake horsepower is always less than indicated horsepower. The difference is due to friction losses within the engine. Mechanical efficiency runs about 90%, indicating an internal friction loss of about 10%. The formula for mechanical efficiency is as follows:

$$ME = \frac{bhp}{ihp}$$

Where

ME = mechanical efficiency
bhp = brake horsepower
ihp = indicated horsepower

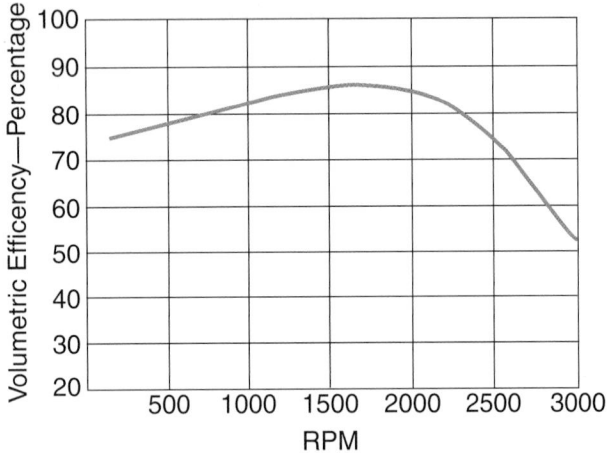

Goodheart-Willcox Publisher

Figure 7-20.

This graph shows the close relationship between volumetric efficiency and engine speed. As engine speed reaches a certain point, efficiency declines rapidly. Torque is also greatest at the point of highest volumetric efficiency.

Thermal Efficiency

Thermal efficiency (heat efficiency) indicates how much of the power produced by the burning air-fuel mixture is actually used to drive the piston downward. Much of the heat developed by the burning gas is lost to such areas as the cooling, exhaust, and lubricating systems. Thermal efficiency will run about 20% to 25%. Keep in mind that the percentages are only *about right* and will vary depending on engine design and operation. See **Figure 7-21**. The exhaust system siphons off about 35% of the heat. The cooling and lubricating systems combine to absorb a similar amount. The rest is lost through radiation and incomplete combustion. Use the following formula for computing brake thermal efficiency:

$$Thermal\ Efficiency = \frac{bhp \times 33,000\ \text{ft-lb/min}}{C \times FHV \times W}$$

Where

bhp = brake horsepower
C = 778 Btu/ft-lb
FHV = fuel heat value
W = weight of fuel burned per minute

The 778 Btu/ft-lb in the above formula is Joule's equivalent, a factor used to convert the units from Btus to foot-pounds. The fuel heat (calorific) value is based on the Btu (British thermal unit) per pound.

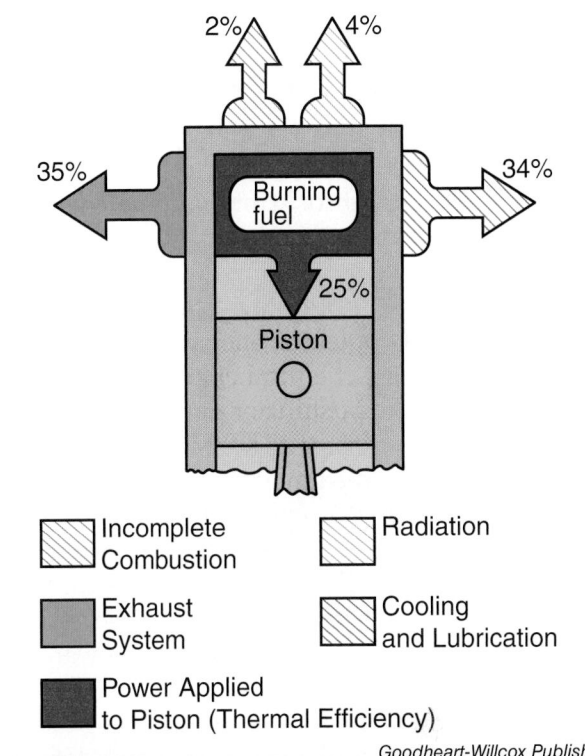

Goodheart-Willcox Publisher

Figure 7-21.

Thermal (heat) losses make thermal efficiency rather poor. Note that it is generally about 25%.

Summary

Engine bore is the diameter across the top of the cylinder. Stroke is the up or down movement of the piston. Length of stroke is determined by the distance the piston moves from its uppermost position to its lowest position.

Energy is the capacity to perform work. Types of energy include potential energy, kinetic energy, mechanical energy, chemical energy, and thermal energy. Force is the pushing or pulling of one body on another. The greater the force applied to the piston, the greater the amount of power and work that can be done by the engine. Pressure is a force per given unit of area. Work is accomplished only when a force is applied through some distance. Power is the rate at which work is performed. The standard unit of power is horsepower. The mechanical advantage provided by levers, belt-and-pulley systems, chain-and-sprocket systems, and gear systems can increase force and decrease distance or decrease force and increase distance components of any work input into the system.

Cylinder displacement is the volume increase in the cylinder as the piston moves from the top to the bottom of its stroke. Engine displacement equals the cylinder displacement times the number of cylinders in the engine. The compression ratio of an engine is a measurement of the relationship between the total cylinder volume when the piston is at the bottom of its stroke (BDC) and the volume remaining when the piston is at the top of its stroke (TDC).

Engine horsepower is calculated by dividing the engine's rate of work (in ft-lb/sec) by 550 ft-lb/sec. Brake horsepower indicates the actual usable horsepower delivered at the crankshaft. Brake horsepower increases with engine speed. Indicated horsepower refers to the power developed by the burning fuel mixture inside the cylinder. To measure indicated horsepower, you must determine the pressure inside the cylinder during the intake, compression, power, and exhaust strokes. Frictional horsepower represents the part of the indicated horsepower lost because of engine parts rubbing together. Frictional horsepower is determined by subtracting brake horsepower from indicated horsepower.

An engine's rated horsepower is generally 80% of its maximum brake horsepower. Standard brake horsepower ratings are based on ideal engine test conditions. Horsepower can be greatly affected by changes in atmospheric pressure, temperature, and humidity. Corrected horsepower is an estimation of the horsepower of a given engine under specific operating conditions. Engine torque refers to the turning force developed by the crankshaft. Engine torque will change according to speed.

Volumetric efficiency is the measurement of how well an engine draws the air-fuel mixture into the cylinder. Practical efficiency is an overall measurement of how efficiently an engine uses the fuel supply. Mechanical efficiency is the percentage of power developed in the cylinder (indicated horsepower) compared to the power that is actually delivered at the crankshaft (brake horsepower). Thermal efficiency indicates how much of the power produced by the burning air-fuel mixture is actually used to drive the piston.

Review Questions

Answer the following questions on a separate sheet of paper.

1. If a crankshaft offset is 2″, the piston would have a 4″ _____.
2. _____ force acts opposite to the direction of centrifugal force.
3. _____ is a force applied to a given area.
4. If a force of 35 lb is applied to an area of 5 sq in, the pressure generated is _____ psi.
5. If 48 foot-pounds of work is performed to lift an object 12 feet, the object weighs _____ lb.
6. Give the formula for *work*.
7. The top of a piston with a 2 1/2″ diameter would have an area of _____ sq in.
8. If 60 lb is lifted 5′ in 6 sec, the amount of power exerted is _____ ft-lb/sec.
9. What is the definition of *horsepower*? How much is 1 hp?

10. How do you compute engine displacement?

11. A measure of the horsepower delivered at the engine crankshaft is called _____.

12. A Prony brake with a 12″ arm is applied to an engine flywheel. At 1200 rpm, the scale registers 20 lb. Calculate the horsepower to two decimal places.

13. What is indicated horsepower?

14. What are the standard test conditions for testing an engine on the dynamometer?

15. An engine's rated horsepower is approximately _____% of its maximum brake horsepower.

16. What is the engine horsepower reduction for each 1000′ of elevation?

17. Explain the horsepower correction factor.

18. Volumetric efficiency reaches its maximum value at the same engine speed as _____ reaches its maximum value.

19. *True or False?* Horsepower of an engine is greatest at maximum rpm.

20. On the average, what percentage of the energy from fuel is used to produce power?

Suggested Activities

1. Using the principles studied in this chapter, determine the horsepower required of several individuals to walk up one flight of stairs. The following items will be needed: a stopwatch, tape measure, and bath scale.

2. Design and build a Prony brake for a small gasoline engine.

3. Use a dynamometer to develop a graph like the one in **Figure 7-18**. Compare the graph with the manufacturer's graph for the same model of engine.

4. On an engine with the head removed, measure the position of the top of the piston (in relation to the top of the block) at TDC and again at BDC. Determine the stroke of the engine.

5. On the same engine, measure the diameter of the piston and determine if the engine is square, oversquare, or undersquare.

6. Determine the cubic inch displacement of the engine from the facts learned in activities above.

SECTION 3
Engine Systems

Fuel Supply, Air Induction, and Emissions

Learning Objectives

After studying this chapter, you will be able to:

- Name various types of fuel that can be used in a small engine and list practical applications for each.
- Explain the importance of proper fuel-oil mixture in a two-cycle engine.
- Describe the purpose of fuel filters.
- Explain fuel pump operation.
- Describe the purpose of an air cleaner.
- Explain the importance of emission control.

Key Terms

California Air Resources Board (CARB)
diesel fuel
dry-type air cleaners
dual-element air cleaners
Environmental Protection Agency (EPA)
fuel pick-up line
fuel pumps
muffler
octane number
oil-wetted air cleaner
oxygenates
phase separation

Engine Fuels

Small gas engines can be designed to operate efficiently on gasoline, liquefied petroleum gas, natural gas, kerosene, or diesel fuel. Gasoline is the most popular small engine fuel. In addition to its power potential, gasoline is readily available and easily transported for refueling.

Gasoline

Gasoline is a hydrocarbon fuel (combination of hydrogen and carbon), refined from petroleum. Petroleum is a dark, thick liquid that is extracted from the earth by oil wells. Petroleum is the second most plentiful liquid in the world; only water is available in greater quantity. Gasoline, however, cannot be recycled as water can. Therefore, it is imperative that we conserve gasoline and use it wisely.

Gasoline contains a great amount of energy. Gasoline intended for use in engines must have the following characteristics:

- Ignites readily, burns cleanly, and resists detonation (violent explosion).
- Vaporizes easily, without being subject to vapor lock (vaporizing in fuel lines, impeding flow of liquid fuel to carburetor).
- Be free of dirt, water, and abrasives.

Gasoline is assigned an *octane number* that corresponds to its ability to resist detonation. Premium grade gasoline burns slower than regular gasoline. It has a high octane number and is used in engines with high compression. Regular grade gasoline has a lower octane number and burns relatively quickly. Generally, regular grade gasoline is used in small, low compression, one-cylinder and two-cylinder, gasoline engines.

Gasoline was once available in both leaded and unleaded varieties. The use of lead compounds was the most economical way to increase gasoline's octane number. For many years, most gasoline contained tetraethyl lead.

Since the mid-1970s, unleaded gasoline has replaced leaded gasoline. Instead of lead compounds, *oxygenates* (alcohols and ethers) are commonly added to these fuels to increase octane levels. The main reason that unleaded gas was introduced was to provide fuel for automobiles equipped with catalytic converters. These vehicles will not operate properly on leaded fuel.

Modern unleaded gasoline is a complex substance. Ongoing research is necessary to seek ways to produce fuels that offer efficient engine performance and meet air pollution standards.

The main drawback to these gasoline blends is their increased ability to absorb moisture, which can pass through the fuel filter and into the combustion chamber. These fuels should never be stored in high-humidity areas or used in engines that set idle for long periods of time. Gasoline containing alcohol can also corrode fuel tank linings, shrink carburetor floats and seals, increase carbon deposits, and pit metal parts. For maximum performance and engine life, use only the type of gasoline recommended by the engine manufacturer.

Most small engine manufacturers specify the use of regular grade, unleaded gasoline with an octane rating around 90. Occasionally, premium fuels are recommended for use in hot climates. This practice may prevent detonation or dieseling (after-run). However, a heavier buildup of solid materials in the combustion chamber can be expected from premium fuels because they contain more additives than regular grade fuels.

Caution

Gasoline should be clean, free from moisture, and reasonably *fresh*. After prolonged storage, especially in small quantities, gasoline tends to become *stale*. This is caused by oxidation that forms a sticky, gum-like material. This gum can clog small passageways in the carburetor and cause poor engine performance or hard starting.

Fuel-Related Problems

Modern fuel is the source of many small engine problems. Over time, fuel can break down, causing varnish to form within the fuel. This varnish can gum up carburetors and clog fuel filters. Aside from this chemical breakdown of fuel over time, the ethanol contained in most modern fuel can cause additional problems. Although modern small engines are designed to operate acceptably on fuels with an ethanol content as high as 10% (E10), fuel with higher ethanol content is becoming more common. Some suppliers offer fuels with an ethanol content of 15% (E15) and 85% (E85). These fuel formulations are *not* compatible with small engines and must not be used.

Ethanol is *hygroscopic*, meaning that it absorbs water. Over time, the ethanol in the fuel blend can absorb water and fall to the bottom of the fuel tank. This phenomenon is known as *phase separation*. When the ethanol and water mixture at the bottom of the tank is drawn into the engine, it has a corrosive effect and prevents the engine from running. The concentrated ethanol attacks rubber and plastic parts, and the water corrodes metallic parts.

The effects of phase separation can be minimized by keeping the fuel tank full during the operating season, and by draining the fuel system for long-term storage. Fuel stabilizers also combat phase separation. It is a good idea to treat fuel with a stabilizer as soon as you get it. This will help minimize phase separation.

Fuel Stabilizers

There are various fuel stabilizers available for all two- and four-stroke gasoline-powered engines. Particularly in small engines, a fuel stabilizer will keep fresh fuel fresh and promote quick, easy starts after the engine has been stored for an extended time. Fuel stabilizers delay fuel deterioration and protect engines from gum, varnish, rust, and corrosion. They also help prevent phase separation of ethanol-blended gasoline.

Fuel stabilizer can be added to the gasoline in the tank if the engine is likely to set idle for several weeks or longer. It is not necessary to drain the fuel before adding the fuel stabilizer. However, once fuel has been treated with stabilizer, additional stabilizer should not be added until the fuel in the tank is either used up or drained out.

Most fuel stabilizer containers have an automatic measuring design to aid in adding the stabilizer to the fuel tank or storage container. See **Figure 8-1**. The amount of stabilizer to use is relative to the quantity of fuel in the tank or container. Follow the recommendations on the label of the container.

Marked measuring device

Goodheart-Willcox Publisher

Figure 8-1.
A fuel stabilizer is used to keep fuel fresh and promote quick, easy starts after the engine has been stored for an extended time.

Fuel stabilizers contain petroleum distillate and should be used in accordance with the safety precautions on the label.

Two-Cycle Fuel Mixtures

Most two-cycle engines receive lubrication only from the oil mixed with the gasoline. Because of this, it is important that the correct quantity and proper quality of oil is thoroughly mixed with a specific amount of gasoline.

Note

Always follow the manufacturer's recommended specifications as to the type and quantity of oil to use.

Too little oil can cause the engine to overheat. Overheating, in turn, causes expansion of parts and possible scoring of machined surfaces. Eventually, the pistons may seize in the cylinders. Excessive oil, on the other hand, will cause incomplete combustion and rapid buildup of carbon, fouling the spark plugs and adding weight to the pistons.

Liquefied Petroleum Gas and Natural Gas

Liquefied petroleum gas (LPG), sometimes called autogas, may consist of propane, butane, or a mixture of both. Properly designed fuel systems allow the use of LPG with no appreciable loss of horsepower, when compared to a similar engine burning gasoline. LPG burns cleanly and leaves few combustion chamber deposits. Because they emit fewer noxious fumes, these engines are often used in warehouses, factories, etc. LPG also has a high anti-knock rating.

Unlike LPG, natural gas generally causes a horsepower loss of around 20% when compared with gasoline. Both LPG and natural gas require a different fuel system setup than the conventional type used for supplying gasoline.

Combustion of LPG

LPG burns slower than gasoline because it has a higher ignition temperature. For this reason, the timing is often advanced on LPG engines. Due to the higher ignition temperatures, greater voltage at the spark plugs may be needed for LPG combustion. *Colder* plugs or smaller spark plug gaps may solve this problem. Check the engine manual for recommendations.

Advantages of LPG

- Cheaper, especially when close to the source (refinery).
- Less engine wear because it will not wash oil from cylinder walls.
- Less oil consumption due to engine wear.
- Reduced maintenance costs—longer engine life between overhauls.
- Slow, even burning characteristics, which result in smoother power.
- Fewer noxious or poisonous exhaust gases, such as deadly carbon monoxide gas.
- Produces 20% fewer CO_2 emissions than gasoline combustion.

Disadvantages of LPG

- Initial equipment costs are high. Bulk fuel storage and carburetion equipment are costly.
- Fewer accessible fuel points (gas stations).
- Harder to start in cold weather—0°F (–18°C) or below.

Kerosene and Diesel Fuels

Some non-diesel–type small gas engines can be converted to operate on kerosene or fuel oil through the installation of a low compression cylinder head and a special carburetor. These engines are started and operated on gasoline until fully warm, then switched over to the kerosene or fuel oil. Such conversions are generally limited to heavy-duty, industrial engines.

A true diesel engine uses *diesel fuel* injected into the cylinder where it is ignited by the heat of compression. It is not unusual to have compression ratios as high as 20 to 1. Currently, however, small diesel engine use is somewhat limited. Small diesel engines are only practical for applications such as generators and pumps, where continuous use for long periods of time are common.

Fuel Systems

The fuel system consists of all of the components that work together to deliver fuel to the cylinder(s). On a small engine, the fuel system typically consists of a fuel tank, fuel line, fuel filter, and carburetor. Some engines are also equipped with a fuel pump.

Fuel Tanks

Small engine fuel tanks are made of metal or plastic. See **Figure 8-2**. Some fuel tanks are mounted away from the engine. Others are contoured to fit snugly around the engine. See **Figure 8-3**.

The tank filler cap is vented. If the vent becomes clogged, the engine will create enough vacuum in

Fuel tank

Goodheart-Willcox Publisher

Figure 8-3.

On this lawn mower, the plastic fuel tank is contoured to fit snugly around engine.

the tank to cause fuel starvation. Most filler caps have baffles and filters. See **Figure 8-4**. In some fuel tanks, a fuel strainer sits in the tank opening. This strainer captures large particles during refueling, preventing them from entering the fuel system. These strainers simply lift out of the tank, and should be checked and cleaned periodically. See **Figure 8-5**.

Fuel tanks used in all terrain vehicles (ATVs) and snowmobiles often have the *fuel pick-up line* inserted from the top of the tank. The pick-up line usually is very flexible and weighted at the bottom, so the line will always be where the fuel is deepest in the tank when the vehicle is at a steep angle.

Fuel tank

Carburetor

Generac Corp.

Figure 8-2.

On this portable engine-driven generator, the fuel tank is mounted on the top.

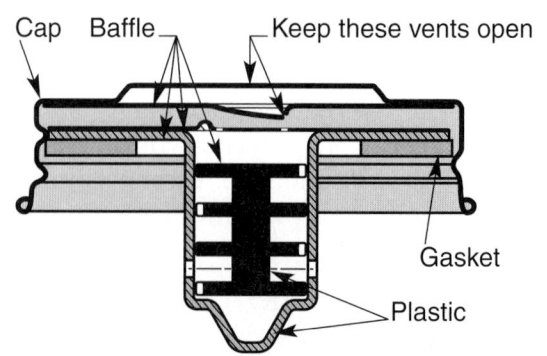

Cap   Baffle   Keep these vents open

Gasket

Plastic

Clinton Engine Corp.

Figure 8-4.

Vented fuel filler caps are baffled to prevent dirt and dust from entering fuel tank.

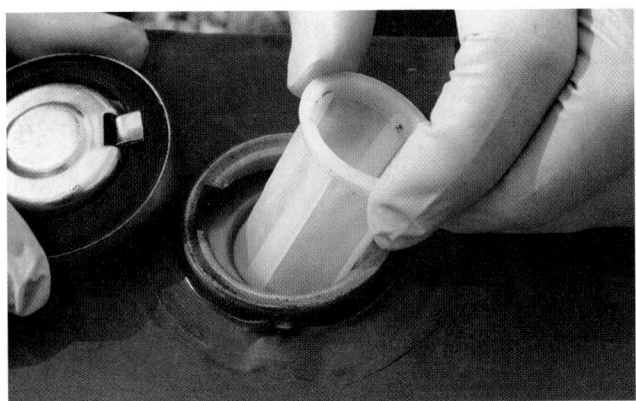

Goodheart-Willcox Publisher

Figure 8-5.

This fuel tank is equipped with a nylon mesh strainer. The strainer should be checked for contaminates periodically.

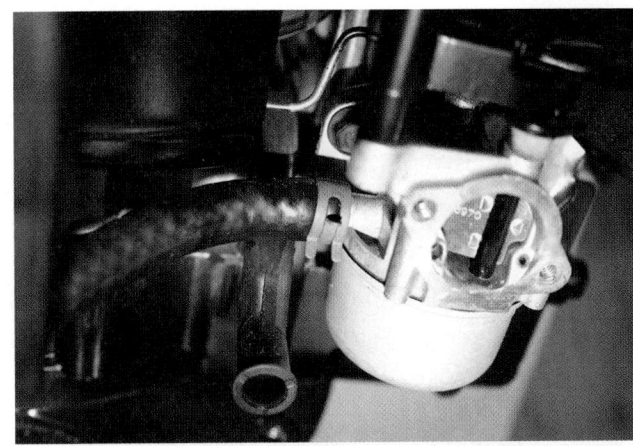

Goodheart-Willcox Publisher

Figure 8-6.

This fuel line is secured with a spring-type hose clamp.

Green Tech

Low-Permeation Fuel Tanks and Hoses

Special low-permeation fuel tanks and fuel hoses are used in some applications to reduce evaporative emissions. These low-permeation fuel tank and hoses cannot be replaced with conventional tanks and hoses, or the equipment may no longer be in compliance with emission regulations.

Fuel Lines and Fittings

Fuel lines are used to route fuel from the tank to the carburetor. On most small engines, the fuel lines are flexible rubber hoses. Fuel hoses are specially designed to minimize vapor emissions and to withstand constant exposure to fuel, which could swell and deteriorate a typical rubber hose. The ends of these hoses are typically connected to fittings and secured with hose clamps. See **Figure 8-6**.

Fuel Filters

Some engines have a pickup tube that extends down from the top of the tank. A filter screen is placed in the tank fitting or at the end of the pick-up line. See **Figure 8-7**. Other engines have a bottom mounted fuel fitting with a shutoff valve threaded into the tank. See **Figure 8-8**.

Older small engines were often equipped with a filter incorporated in a glass sediment bowl. The gasket, screen, and bowl could be removed for inspection and cleaning. Many modern small

engines have replaceable fuel filters installed in the fuel line between the fuel tank and the carburetor. These filters are typically unidirectional and must be installed so fuel flow passes through them in the correct direction. See **Figure 8-9**.

Fuel Pumps

Fuel pumps are mechanical devices that provide constant, pressurized fuel flow to the carburetor

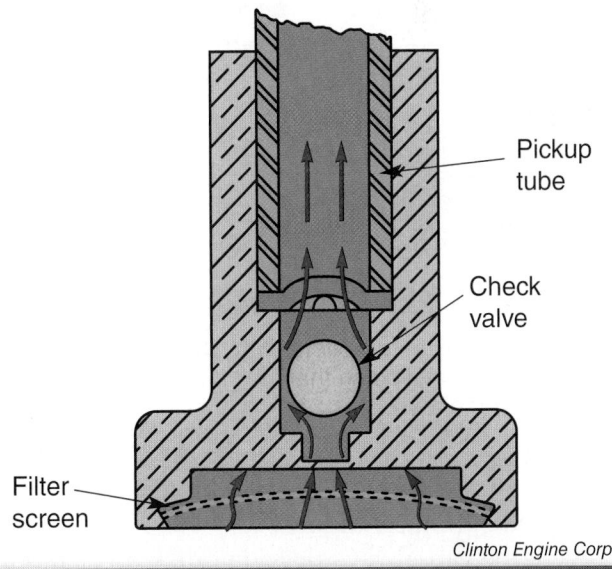

Clinton Engine Corp.

Figure 8-7.

Some fuel systems have a pickup tube that extends down from the top of the tank. A filter and check valve are attached to the end of the fuel pickup tube. The check valve prevents fuel from draining back into the tank when the engine is running.

Fuel tank

Fuel shutoff valve

Goodheart-Willcox Publisher

Figure 8-8.

A shutoff valve can block the flow of fuel from the tank, allowing parts of the fuel system to be removed for service.

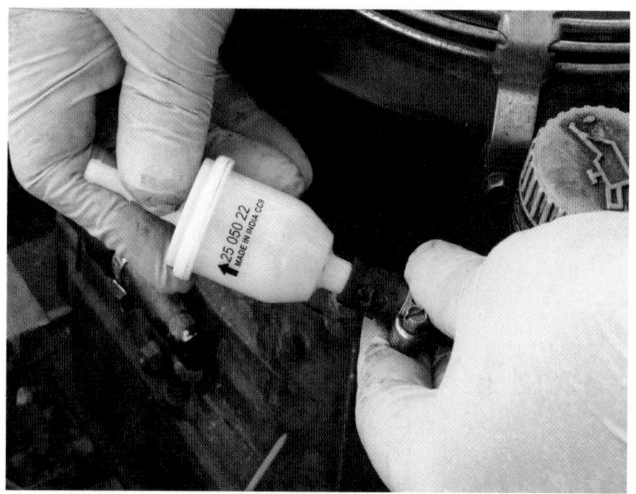

Goodheart-Willcox Publisher

Figure 8-9.

Replaceable inline fuel filters are typically unidirectional and must be installed so that fuel flows through them in the proper direction.

under changing conditions. They help ensure that the engine can always provide quick acceleration and sustained power.

Fuel pumps are used on engines in which a gravity-fed system cannot be relied on to supply fuel consistently. In these applications, the tank and fuel level may be lower than the carburetor, or

the fuel level may be above the carburetor at times and below the rest of the time. Fuel pumps are used on many types of handheld power equipment, such as chain saws, leaf blowers, and brush cutters. These types of equipment are moved into many different positions during operation, and there may be times when the carburetor is positioned above the tank. Fuel pumps are also used on many riding mowers and garden tractors, where the tank is mounted some distance away from the carburetor.

Mechanical Fuel Pumps

The type of mechanical fuel pump used on small engines is basically the same as the type used on automobile engines. **Figure 8-10** is a simplified drawing of a typical mechanical fuel pump. Trace the arrows to follow the flow of fuel.

Fuel Pump Operation

The typical mechanical fuel pump shown in **Figure 8-10** operates by means of a diaphragm and atmospheric pressure on the surface of the fuel in the tank. As the engine camshaft revolves, an eccentric actuates the fuel pump rocker arm. See **Figure 8-10A**. The rocker arm pivots, pulling the pull rod and diaphragm down against spring pressure, creating a depression in the pump chamber. Fuel is drawn from the tank through the pump intake and the inlet check valve into the pump chamber.

On the return stroke, pressure of the spring pushes the diaphragm upward. See **Figure 8-10B**. This forces fuel from the chamber through the outlet check valve and outlet to the carburetor. When the carburetor bowl is full, the carburetor float will seat the needle valve, preventing any flow from the pump chamber. This will hold the diaphragm down against the spring pressure. It will remain in this position until the carburetor requires additional fuel and the needle valve opens. The rocker arm will continue to follow the cam lobe, but will not actuate the pump. The spring on the rocker arm keeps the rocker arm in constant contact with the eccentric to eliminate noise.

Impulse Diaphragm Fuel Pumps

One type of diaphragm fuel pump sometimes used on small gas engines is activated by the pulsing vacuum in the intake manifold or crankcase. Four-cycle engines use the intake manifold vacuum; two-cycle engines use crankcase vacuum.

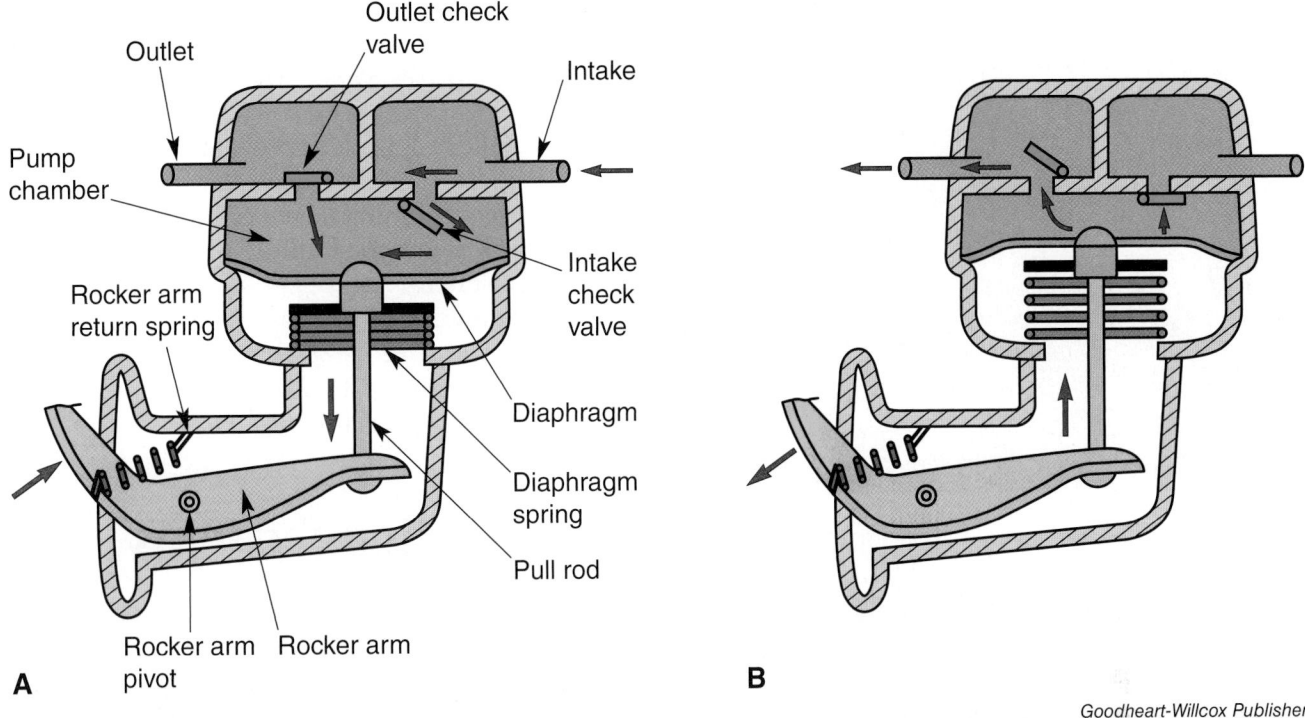

Goodheart-Willcox Publisher

Figure 8-10.

A simplified drawing of a mechanical fuel pump. A—The rocker arm moves up, pulling the diaphragm down and drawing fuel into the pump chamber. B—The rocker arm moves downward, pushing the diaphragm upward and pushing fuel out of the pump chamber.

A typical impulse diaphragm pump is shown in **Figure 8-11**. When vacuum draws the diaphragm upward against spring tension, the inlet check valve opens to allow fuel to flow in. When vacuum is relieved, the spring pushes the diaphragm downward to force fuel through the outlet check valve. This process is repeated as long as the engine is running.

In some cases, an impulse fuel pump is installed in the fuel line between the fuel tank and the carburetor, **Figure 8-12**. In other cases, an impulse diaphragm fuel pump is integrated into the carburetor itself. This type of carburetor will be explained in the next chapter.

Electric Fuel Pumps

Some engines with a battery-powered electrical system are equipped with electric fuel pumps. These are similar to automotive fuel pumps, but typically draw lower current. Electric fuel pumps are used in all fuel-injected small engines. They provide continuous flow at a steady pressure, regardless of engine speed.

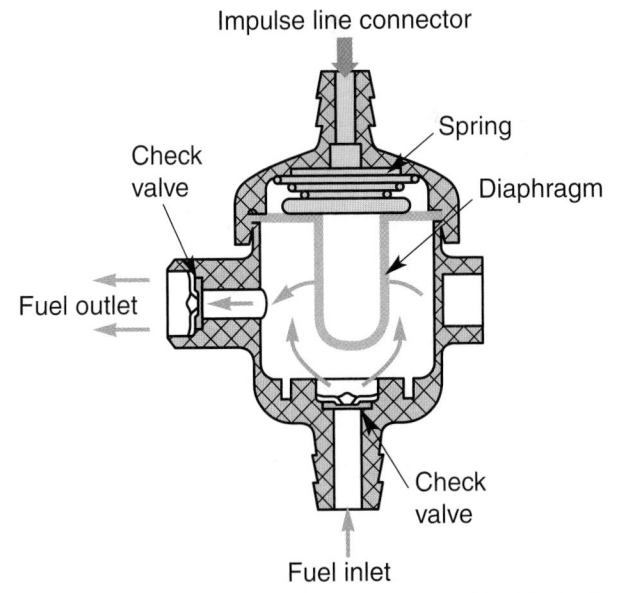

Clinton Engine Corp.

Figure 8-11.

This fuel pump is operated by vacuum pulses transferred from the engine crankcase. It can be mounted in any convenient location on the engine.

Diaphragm   Fuel inlet
fuel pump   hose

Fuel outlet   Vacuum   Fuel shutoff
hose   hose   valve

Goodheart-Willcox Publisher

Figure 8-12.

This impulse diaphragm fuel pump is installed between the fuel tank and carburetor on a riding mower. Note the vacuum line at the bottom of the pump.

Vapor Return Fuel Systems

If the temperature of the air around or inside a carburetor becomes high enough to vaporize the gasoline, pockets of vapor will stop all flow of fuel.

When this occurs, the engine will become vapor locked. It will not run until the temperature drops low enough for the vapor to condense (return to a liquid).

One of the best ways to prevent vapor lock is to use a carburetor with a vapor return line. In these systems, any vapor that forms is directed back into the fuel tank where the built-up pressure is vented to the atmosphere.

A diagram of a typical vapor return fuel system is shown in **Figure 8-13**. The carburetor in this system has a built-in diaphragm fuel pump. The impulse tube operates the pump.

Air Induction Systems

Air for combustion is brought into the carburetor through the induction system. Small gas engines typically have a very simple induction system, consisting solely of an air filter housing and filter. In most cases, the air filter assembly is attached directly to the carburetor. On some engines, the filter assembly is positioned a short distance from the carburetor. On these engines, an intake plenum carries clean air from the filter assembly to the carburetor.

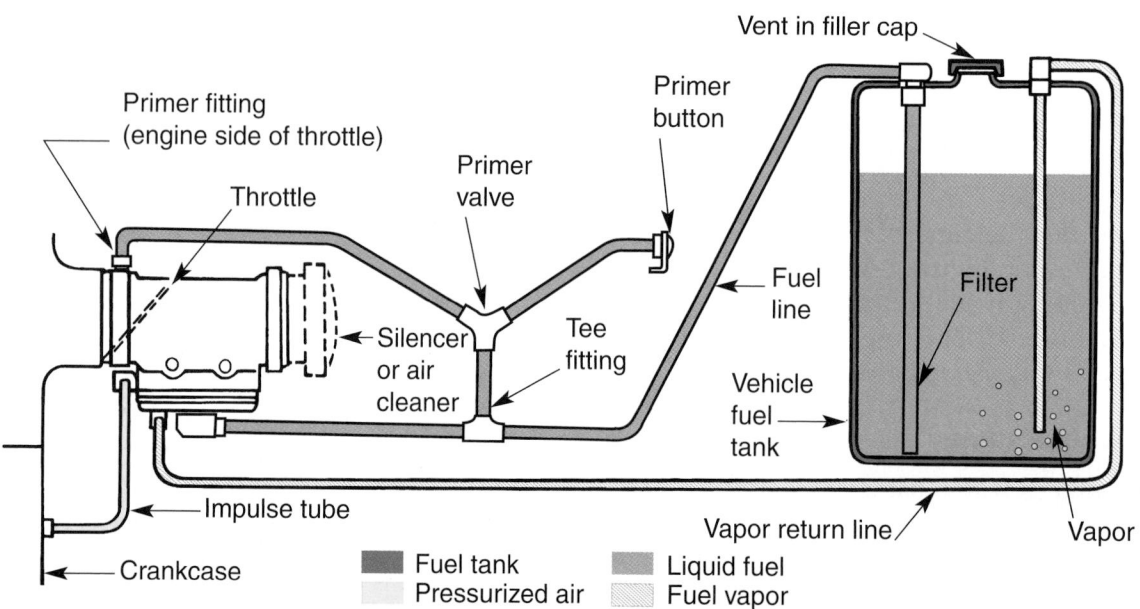

Kohler Co.

Figure 8-13.

A vapor return fuel system is one of the best methods for preventing a vapor lock. Vapors formed by heat are directed back to the fuel tank where they are cooled and condensed to liquid form.

Air Cleaners and Air Filters

An engine breathes a tremendous quantity of air during its normal service life. If the incoming air is not thoroughly cleaned by passing it through a filtering device, dirt and grit entering the cylinder would cause rapid wear and scoring of machined parts throughout the engine. Without a properly functioning air filter, engine life under severe dust conditions could be reduced to mere minutes.

The three types of air cleaners widely used in small gasoline engines are the oil-wetted, dry, and dual-element types.

Oil-Wetted Air Cleaner

An *oil-wetted air cleaner* has a filtering element (typically polyurethane foam) that is dampened with engine oil. There are many different designs of oil-wetted, foam air cleaners. A few common examples are shown in **Figure 8-14**. In operation, the air is drawn directly through the oil-wetted element where the damp material effectively filters out contaminants. This type of element can be reused by rinsing in soapy water, drying, and reoiling.

The air cleaner keeps dirt, dust, and gritty substances from entering the engine while it is running. In doing so, the dirt, dust, and grit become trapped on the external side and interior of the filter material. As the filter pores become filled with debris, less air can get through the filter, which creates a richer air-fuel mixture. When this happens, the engine runs as if the choke is partially closed. As a result, the engine runs poorly, uses more fuel, and generates less power. Carbon accumulates on the internal parts; lubricating oil becomes dirty and diluted; and internal engine wear increases.

When the air cleaner gets very dirty, the engine may become difficult to start. Black smoke from the rich mixture may show up in the exhaust. An air filter element is usually very easy to remove and clean. However, this simple task is sometimes neglected until engine damage is already done.

When to Service the Air Cleaner

Because engines are used in many different environments, the filter service intervals may vary considerably. However, for average applications, such as lawn mowing, the filter element should be cleaned after every 25 hours of operation or once a season, whichever comes first. In dustier conditions, the filter element should be cleaned more often. Inspecting the filter element at regular intervals is the best way to determine whether it should be cleaned or even replaced.

Removing a Foam Air Cleaner Element

Remove the screw, wing nut, or other fastening device to uncover the air cleaner foam element. **Figure 8-15** shows the filter receptacle with the cover

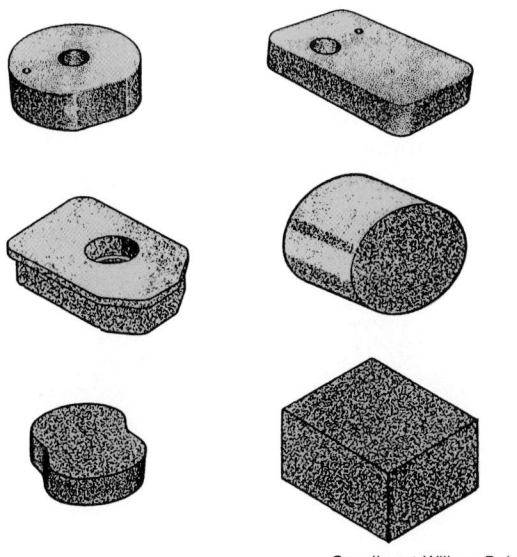

Goodheart-Willcox Publisher

Figure 8-14.

A few examples of common foam air cleaner shapes are shown here. Many special shapes are available for specific engines.

Goodheart-Willcox Publisher

Figure 8-15.

This polyurethane foam filter can be removed, cleaned, and reoiled.

open. The foam filter material is simply pulled from the receptacle, **Figure 8-16**. Care should be taken not to drop any dirt into the carburetor throat during this procedure.

Cleaning a Foam Air Cleaner Element

To clean a foam air cleaner element, do the following:

1. Wash the foam element in a solution of liquid detergent and water. See **Figure 8-17A**.
2. Wrap the foam element in dry cloth and squeeze the element dry. An absorbent towel works well for this procedure. See **Figure 8-17B**.
3. Saturate the foam with clean engine oil. See **Figure 8-17C**.

Goodheart-Willcox Publisher

Figure 8-16.

With the filter housing open, the foam element can simply be pulled from the housing. Note the debris captured by the filter. Without a filter, this material would have been drawn into the carburetor.

4. Squeeze excess oil out of the foam as shown in **Figure 8-17D**.
5. Reassemble the air filter unit. Follow any special instructions found in the owner's manual for the specific engine and filter.

Dry-Type Air Cleaner

Dry-type air cleaners pass the airstream through pleated paper, felt, fiber, or flocked screen. Some filter elements (flocked screen) can be cleaned, but most are designed to be thrown away when they become dirty.

An external pleated paper air cleaner element is shown in **Figure 8-18**. You can clean a filter element like this by tapping it on a flat surface to dislodge light accumulations of dirt. However, if it will not tap clean, the element must be replaced with a new element designed for the same engine.

Another style of dry-type filter cartridge is the rectangular pleated paper design shown in **Figure 8-19**. The paper filter material is a special treated paper with porosity of extremely small size to let air flow through while preventing fine particles of dirt and dust from penetrating. The pleated design provides a large surface area to collect particulates. This design is similar to the filters used in today's automobiles.

A flexible gasket material is molded all the way around the edges of the filter element, which creates a seal between the filter and the back of the filter housing when the element is installed. This prevents air from bypassing the filter element and being drawn into the carburetor from behind the filter.

The filter element is cleaned by tapping the cartridge with the front side down to shake off dirt. Care must be taken to prevent distortion of the pleated paper. If the dirt will not separate from

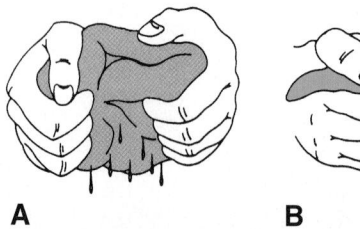 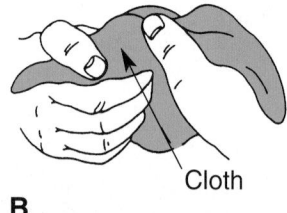 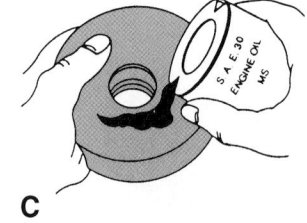 

A   B   Cloth   C   D

Briggs and Stratton Corp.

Figure 8-17.

Follow these steps when cleaning an oil-wetted foam element: A—Wash the element in a detergent and water solution. B—Wrap the element in a clean cloth and squeeze dry. C—Saturate the element in clean engine oil. D—Squeeze the excess oil out of the element.

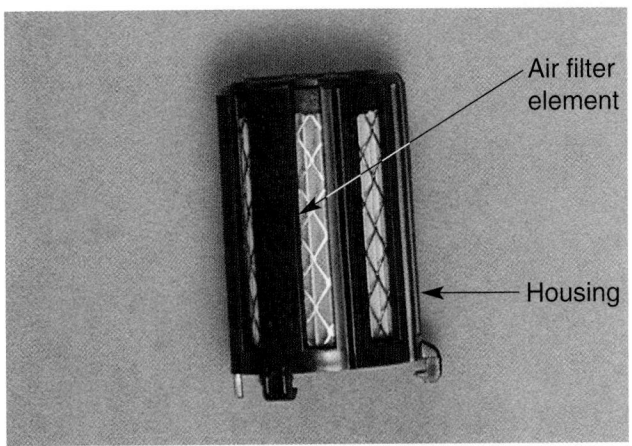

Goodheart-Willcox Publisher

Figure 8-18.

A dry-type filter element can be partially cleaned by tapping it gently. A new element should be installed as needed.

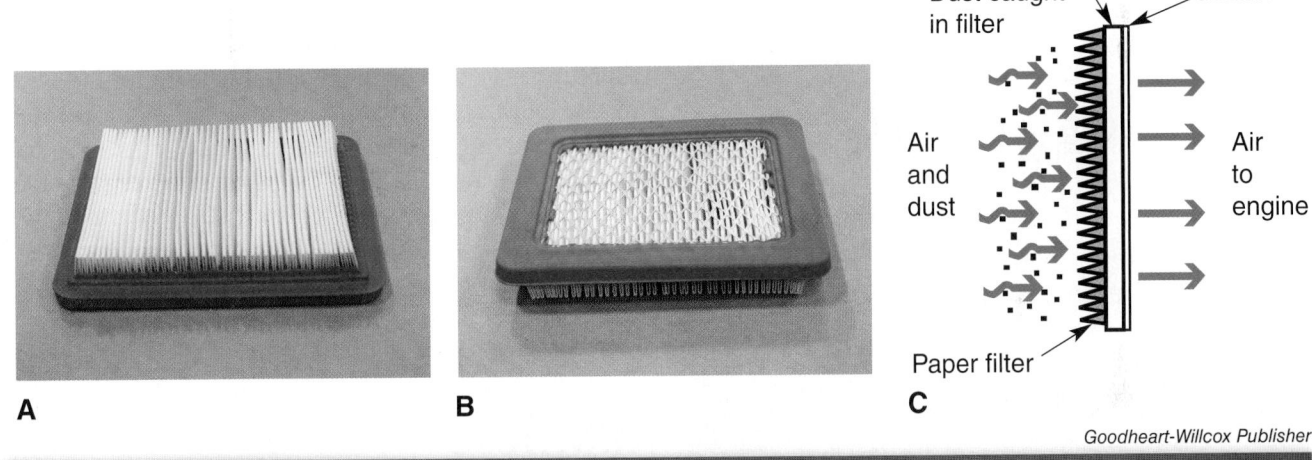

Goodheart-Willcox Publisher

Figure 8-19.

This is a typical pleated paper filter cartridge. Notice the thick foam rubber gasket surrounding the paper element. A—Front. B—Back. C—As air passes through the filter element, any dust is captured on the surface of the paper. The clean air continues to the engine.

the filter, throw the filter away and replace it with a new filter. A pleated paper filter element should be installed so that the loose pleats face outward. See **Figure 8-20**.

Caution

Never use compressed air to clean the paper filter. The high pressure air would enlarge the pores in the filter element. As a result, the filter would not prevent fine dirt from entering the engine.

Dual-Element Air Cleaners

Engines intended for use in dusty conditions may have *dual-element air cleaners* that provide more protection. Dual-element air cleaners contain a foam filter pre-cleaner ahead of a pleated paper-type cartridge. Some pre-cleaners are oiled and some are dry. See **Figure 8-21**.

Dual-element filters are contained in specially designed receptacles. See **Figure 8-22**. The cartridges and receptacles are found in a variety of designs, such as the cylindrical vertical mount, the front mount, and the horizontal mount. The pre-cleaner

Goodheart-Willcox Publisher

Figure 8-20.

When a pleated paper air cleaner element is installed, the loose folds of the pleats should face the external cover side of the receptacle.

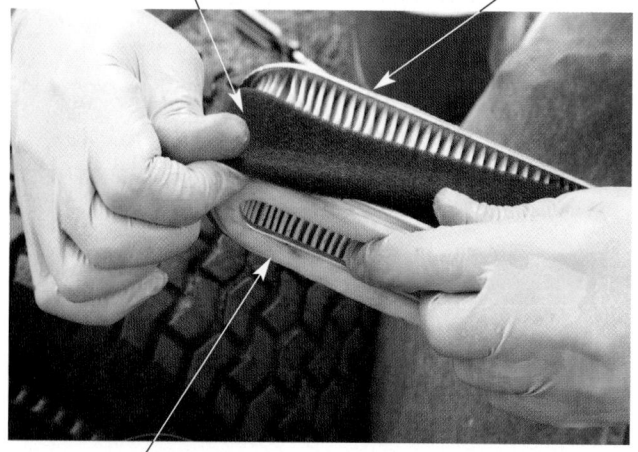

Foam pre-cleaner   Pleated paper cartridge

Air cleaner gasket

Goodheart-Willcox Publisher

Figure 8-21.

This dual-element air cleaner has a dry foam pre-cleaner installed on the outside of a pleated-paper filter cartridge.

can be washed clean with detergent and water and squeezed dry. The paper filter cartridge should be cleaned by shaking.

Every engine to be serviced or repaired should have the air cleaner examined. If the air cleaner element or pre-cleaner is damaged or shows signs of restriction, replace it. Worn or damaged mounting gaskets and air cleaner gaskets should be replaced to prevent dirt and dust from entering the engine through an improper seal around the filter.

Crankcase Breathers

Crankcase breathers are devices that prevent excessive pressure from building up in the crankcase. The open space in a crankcase is filled with air, vapors from hot oil, unburned gasoline, and small amounts of exhaust gas. Every time the piston moves down in the cylinder, the open space in the crankcase gets smaller and the pressure inside increases. Unless this positive pressure is vented, it can force oil out around the seals in the case.

A crankcase breather consists of a set of gaskets, a reed valve assembly, a filter, a cover, and a vent tube. When the pressure in the crankcase exceeds a certain level, the reed valves open and the vapors in the crankcase escape through the filter, to the vent tube.

In older engines, the cover has vent holes that release the crankcase vapors directly to the atmosphere. To decrease hydrocarbon emissions, newer engines are equipped with a vent tube that carries the vapors to the air filter housing, where they are mixed with fresh air and are drawn back into the engine during the next intake stroke.

On overhead valve engines, the crankcase breather is typically located in the top of the valve cover. In L-head engines, it is typically installed in the side of the crankcase, and serves the double purpose of a valve cover. See **Figure 8-23**.

Mufflers

As an engine runs, the combustion in the cylinder results in a large volume of hot exhaust gases. As these gases expand and escape through the exhaust valve, they produce a great deal of noise. A *muffler* is a component installed on the engine's exhaust port to reduce the exhaust noise while still allowing the gases to escape efficiently. The muffler also redirects the exhaust gas and traps any sparks carried by the gas. See **Figure 8-24**.

When the exhaust gas leaves the exhaust port, it enters a large chamber in the muffler. Here, the gas expands and cools, which lowers the pressure of the gas. The chamber must be large enough to accommodate all of the exhaust exiting the cylinder. If the chamber is too small, the exhaust gas is not able to expand sufficiently and excessive back pressure results. Excessive back pressure prevents additional exhaust from exiting the cylinder, which

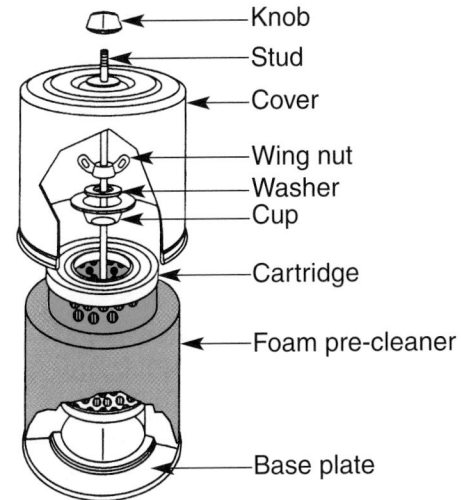

A   **Cylindrical, Vertical Mount**

- Knob
- Stud
- Cover
- Wing nut
- Washer
- Cup
- Cartridge
- Foam pre-cleaner
- Base plate

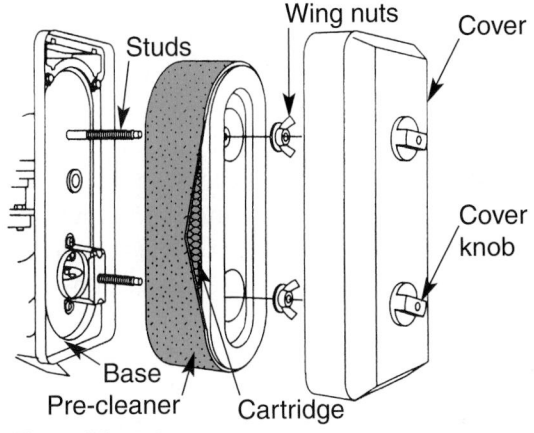

B   **Front Mount**

- Wing nuts
- Cover
- Studs
- Cover knob
- Base
- Pre-cleaner
- Cartridge

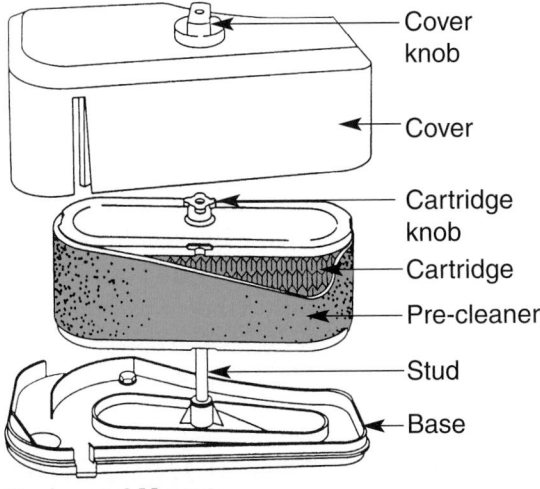

C   **Horizontal Mount**

- Cover knob
- Cover
- Cartridge knob
- Cartridge
- Pre-cleaner
- Stud
- Base

Briggs and Stratton Corp.

Figure 8-22.

Common types of dual-element air cleaners and housings are shown here. A—A cylindrical, vertically mounted dual-element air cleaner. B—A front-mounted dual-element air cleaner. C—A horizontally mounted dual-element air cleaner.

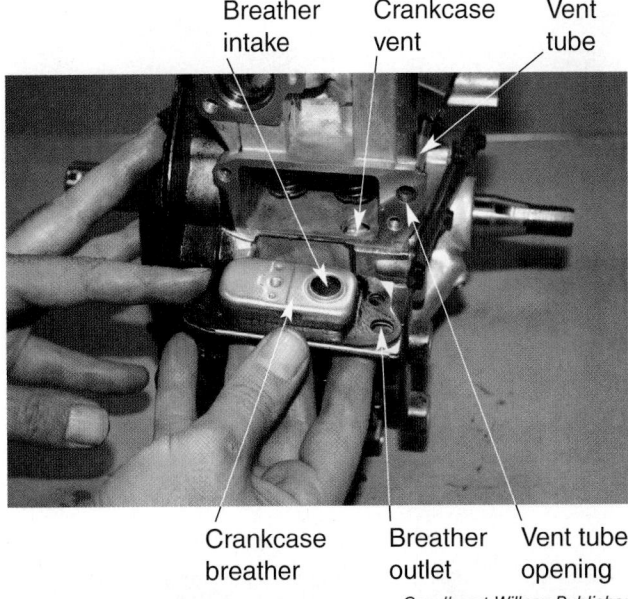

- Breather intake
- Crankcase vent
- Vent tube
- Crankcase breather
- Breather outlet
- Vent tube opening

Goodheart-Willcox Publisher

Figure 8-23.

Crankcase breathers act as check valves allowing crankcase pressure to vent while preventing air from entering the crankcase during the piston's upstroke.

in turn reduces the amount of air-fuel mixture that can be drawn into the cylinder during the next intake stroke, resulting in a power loss.

At the other end of the expansion chamber are baffles, which smooth and slow the exhaust flow, reducing exhaust noise. Most mufflers are also equipped with a metal screen to trap superheated pieces of carbon that are carried out of the engine along with the exhaust gas. These screens are commonly referred to as spark arrestors, and may be replaceable on some muffler designs. With other designs, the entire muffler must be replaced if the spark arrestor becomes clogged. After passing through the baffles and spark arrestor, the exhaust gas exits the muffler through the exhaust pipe.

The muffler may be threaded into the exhaust port, attached by bolts, or held in place by springs. There may be a heat shield on the exterior of the muffler. This prevents the operator from accidentally touching the extremely hot muffler shell. On certain equipment, there is a sheet metal exhaust deflector installed just beyond the end of the exhaust pipe. The deflector diverts the exhaust into the open air and away from heat sensitive equipment and the ground.

A

Heat shield

B

Thermostatic
choke mechanism

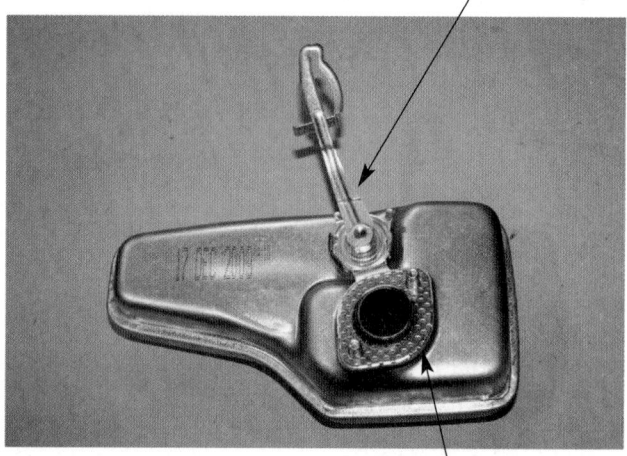

C

Exhaust gasket

Goodheart-Willcox Publisher

Figure 8-24.

Small engine mufflers come in many different designs. A—This type of screw-in muffler is frequently found on push mowers. B—This muffler is equipped with a heat shield. C—This muffler is equipped with a thermostatic choke linkage.

Warning

Heat shields and deflectors are important safety devices and should be in place any time the engine is operated.

Emissions

Emissions from lawnmowers, snowblowers, chainsaws, leaf vacuums, and similar outdoor power equipment are significant sources of pollution. In the United States alone, walk-behind lawnmowers, chainsaws, string trimmers, garden tractors, rotary tillers, and leaf blowers generate millions of tons of air pollution (the combined hydrocarbon, oxides of nitrogen, and carbon monoxide contribution) each year. Mowing a lawn for a half hour with a typical mower can produce as much pollution as driving a car 172 miles.

Engine exhaust emissions have come under considerable scrutiny. Today's small engines emit oxides of nitrogen (NO_x) and high levels of carbon monoxide (CO). CO is an odorless, colorless, and poisonous gas. These engines also emit hydrocarbons (HC), which contribute to the formation of ground-level ozone. Ground-level ozone, a component of smog, is a noxious irritant that impairs lung function and inhibits plant growth.

Although exhaust by-products are the major source of harmful small engine emissions, evaporative emissions also contribute to environmental and health problems. If spilled or uncontained, gasoline gradually evaporates into the air, where it contributes to the formation of ground-level ozone. Ozone is irritating to the eyes, damages the lungs, and aggravates respiratory problems. **Figure 8-25** shows a type of pouring device designed to eliminate gasoline spillage. The Sure Pour Nozzle® stops pouring automatically when the fuel tank is full. After use, the nozzle seals the container to prevent evaporation of fuel into the atmosphere.

Emission Control Regulations

In 1970, the U.S. government made a significant effort to combat the steadily increasing level of air pollutants. At this time, the Federal Clean Air Act was passed. This act was aimed at ridding the atmosphere of harmful road vehicle emissions.

| Rest Nozzle on Tank | Push Down to Pour | Stop Automatically | Closes When Removed |

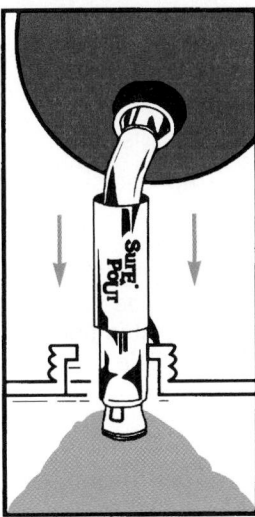 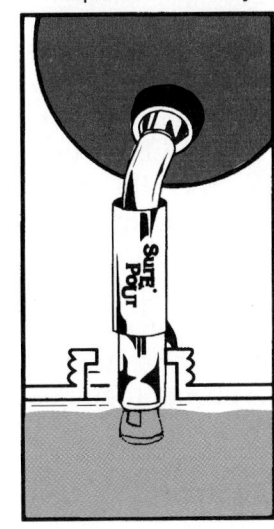 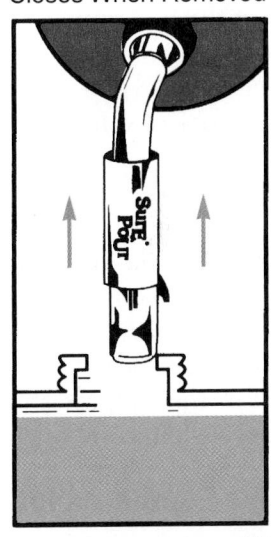

VEMCO, Inc.

Figure 8-25.

Products like this pouring device help prevent environmental and health hazards by reducing spillage.

Since that time, there has been an increased awareness of the harmful emissions generated by small gas engines. The 1990 amendment to the Clean Air Act initiated legal authority to regulate small engine emissions.

Small gas engine manufacturers have dedicated great amounts of time, money, and engineering expertise to make their engines perform more efficiently to meet demanding requirements. The *California Air Resources Board (CARB)* held a public hearing in 1990 to consider regulations regarding the California exhaust emission standards and test procedures for utility and lawn-and-garden equipment engines. This resulted in very detailed and extensive regulations for the testing and monitoring of manufactured engines.

The new regulations first took effect in California in 1995. The restrictions were met by engines manufactured during the 1995 model year. Most engine manufacturers claim to have accomplished this through combinations of better oil control, design of combustion chambers, carburetion, ignition systems, overhead valves, and valve timing. As stricter standards are implemented, widespread use of catalytic converters, fuel injection, and overhead valve arrangements will be necessary.

The *Environmental Protection Agency (EPA)* has become involved in reducing air pollution generated by small gasoline engines. In April, 1994, the EPA proposed the Federal Limits. In July of 1995, the EPA published the Phase 1 Standards for Small Spark-Ignition Engines to regulate air emissions from small engines used in residential and commercial equipment. Phase 2 Standards for Small Spark-Ignition Engines, which proposed even stricter emissions guidelines, were adopted in April of 2000 and phased in between the 2002 and 2007 model years. Phase 3 guidelines were proposed in May of 2007, and were completely phased in the 2012 model year.

In addition to pursuing regulatory emission controls, the EPA works with manufacturers, dealers and retailers, environmental and health groups, and consumers to promote pollution reduction. With the expected growth in the use of small engine–powered equipment, air pollution from these sources would continue to grow. Implementation of the EPA's emission standards is expected to slow (or reverse) the increase in air pollution over the next several decades.

The goal of emission control standards is to create low-emission engines that are both user friendly and environmentally friendly. Low-emission engines must be tuned precisely, which results in a finer margin of error when making repairs. Repairs or adjustments that put the engine out of compliance with the emissions regulations are prohibited. Service technicians must be especially precise in their repair and adjustment of ignition and fuel system components.

Phase 1 Standards for Small Spark-Ignition Engines

In 1995, the EPA, with input from engine and equipment manufacturers, developed the Phase 1 Standards for Small Spark-Ignition Engines. The regulations set down in this document were a first step toward reducing hydrocarbon, carbon monoxide, and nitrous of oxides emissions from nonroad spark-ignition engines with a gross power output at or below 19 kW (25 hp). Such engines are typically used in power lawn-and-garden equipment, small farm and construction equipment, commercial turf equipment, and utility equipment, **Figure 8-26**.

The emissions standards set forth in the Phase 1 regulations were chosen because they were demonstrated to be achievable and cost effective using the technology available at the time. The goal of the Phase 1 limits was to reduce emissions of hydrocarbon and oxides of nitrogen by roughly 32%. Manufacturers were given the flexibility to use any method to achieve the mandated emissions levels, as long as it was safe.

Engines Subject to Phase 1	
Non-handheld	**Handheld**
lawn mowers	trimmers
tillers	edgers
chippers	brush cutters
generator sets	leaf blowers
pumps	leaf vacuums
air compressors	chain saws
aerial lifts	shredders
lawn and garden tractors	augers
wood splitters	
commercial turf equipment	
pressure washers	
golf carts	
forklifts	
sweepers	

Goodheart-Willcox Publisher

Figure 8-26.

Several types of utility and lawn-and-garden equipment are regulated under the Phase 1: Small Spark-Ignition Engine Rule.

The limits set on emissions were based on five displacement classes—two for non-handheld equipment and three for handheld equipment. Non-handheld limits applied primarily to four-stroke engines, and handheld limits applied primarily to two-stroke engines. Because the manufacturers of two-stroke lawn mower engines demonstrated that it was prohibitively expensive and complicated to make their engines meet the same emissions requirements as four-stroke engines, they were granted special dispensation that allowed them to be regulated by the handheld equipment limits rather than the tighter, non-handheld equipment limits.

Phase 2 Standards for Small Spark-Ignition Engines

In April of 2000, the EPA established a new set of limits on emissions from small spark-ignition engines. These new limits were referred to as the Phase 2 Standards for Small Spark-Ignition Engines. The goal of the Phase 2 emission standards was to lower emissions of hydrocarbons and oxides of nitrogen by an additional 70%. The Phase 2 standards were phased in between the 2002 and 2007 model years.

In order to comply with the stricter emissions limits, many manufacturers of larger non-handheld equipment engines switched to overhead valve engine designs. Most manufacturers of smaller engines were able to adapt their existing designs to meet the requirements.

The Phase 2 standards also added two new non-handheld engine classifications, I-A for engines with displacement under 66cc and I-B for engines with displacements between 66cc and 100cc. The Phase 2 standards also instituted a program of certification, assembly line testing, and in-use testing to ensure that engines meet emissions requirements throughout their active service life.

Phase 3 Emissions Standards for New Nonroad Spark-Ignition Engines, Equipment, and Vessels

In April of 2007, the EPA proposed a new set of standards to regulate emissions from small engines. These new regulations were entitled Phase 3 Emission Standards for New Nonroad Spark-Ignition Engines, Equipment, and Vessels. Phase 3 standards are expected to further reduce emissions of hydrocarbons, oxides of nitrogen, and carbon monoxide from small (25 hp and under) spark-ignition engines, marine outboard engines, and personal watercraft engines.

In addition to further tightening the limits for exhaust emissions, the Phase 3 regulations also limit evaporative emissions. As the name implies, evaporative emissions result from the evaporation of fuel caused by fuel spills during refueling, fuel vapors permeating the fuel lines and tank, and venting of the fuel system. To meet the new emission limits, manufacturers of some engines employed technologies such as catalytic treatment of exhaust, low-permeation tanks and hoses, and fuel injection.

Impact of EPA Regulations on the Service Technician

As a small engine service technician, you should keep up to date on all applicable EPA regulations, which you can find in their entirety at the EPA's website. You have a legal responsibility when working on a small gas engine to make sure that your repairs or adjustments do not cause the engine's emissions to exceed the limits set forth by the EPA. For this reason, it is important to know which set of regulations apply to the engine you are working on. The set of regulations that are applicable to an engine are based on the engine size and date it was manufactured. In many cases, this data can be found on the engine's information sticker. See **Figure 8-27**.

Role of the Consumer

Both residential and commercial consumers must take an active role in preventing pollution from lawn-and-garden equipment. The type of equipment chosen and the way the equipment is used can have an impact on preventing pollution.

New technology is beginning to appear in the marketplace in the form of changes to traditional gasoline-powered engines, as well as alternative power sources, such as electricity and solar energy. As the new technology emerges, it will be increasingly important for the consumer to follow manufacturer's suggested maintenance procedures. This will result in reduced pollution, longer lasting and better performing engines, and a healthier environment. Operators of engine-powered equipment should also be mindful of spillage during refueling. By exercising a little care during refueling, operators can minimize the pollution caused by fuel spillage.

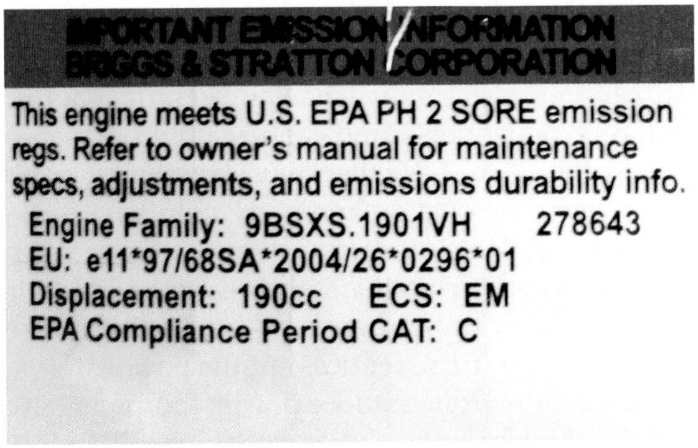

Goodheart-Willcox Publisher

Figure 8-27.

The information sticker on this engine indicates that it is subject to the EPA's Phase 2 regulations.

Summary

Small gas engines can be designed to operate on gasoline, LPG, natural gas, kerosene, or diesel fuel. Most manufacturers specify the use of unleaded gasoline with an octane rating around 90. Gas should be clean, free from moisture, and reasonably fresh. Two-cycle engines receive lubrication from oil that is mixed with fuel. Always follow the manufacturer's specifications for the type and quantity of oil to use. Small engine fuel tanks are made of metal or plastic. Various types of fuel filters are used in small engines.

Fuel pumps are used on engines that do not have a gravity-fed fuel supply system. Fuel pumps provide constant, pressurized fuel flow to the carburetor under changing conditions. Mechanical fuel pumps are usually driven by the camshaft. Diaphragm fuel pumps are activated by the pulsing vacuum in the intake manifold or the crankcase. Because electric fuel pumps are powered by the electrical system, their output is constant regardless of engine speed.

A filtering device is used to clean incoming air. If air is not properly filtered, dirt entering the cylinder will cause rapid wear and scoring of machined parts throughout the engine. Common types of filters used on small engines include oil-wetted foam filters, dry filters, and dual-element filters.

Engine breathers allow pressure inside the crankcase to vent during the downstroke of the piston. This prevents pressure from forcing oil out around the crankcase seals. The reed valves in the breather close during the piston upstroke to prevent air from being drawn into the crankcase.

Mufflers carry exhaust away from the engine, reduce exhaust noise, and capture any sparks carried by the exhaust. Mufflers must be properly sized to prevent excessive backpressure. Excessive backpressure prevents all of the exhaust from leaving the cylinder, which reduces the amount of fuel-air mixture that can be drawn in during the intake stroke. This, in turn, reduces engine power.

Emissions from outdoor power equipment are significant sources of pollution. Today's small engines emit oxides of nitrogen (NO_x), carbon monoxide (CO), and hydrocarbons (HC). Although exhaust byproducts are the major source of harmful emissions from small engines, evaporative emissions also contribute to environmental and health problems.

In 1970, the Federal Clean Air Act was passed. This act was aimed at ridding the atmosphere of harmful road vehicle emissions. The 1990 amendment to the Clean Air Act initiated legal authority to regulate small engine emissions.

The California Air Resources Board (CARB) held a public hearing in 1990 to consider regulations regarding the California exhaust emission standards and test procedures for utility and lawn-and-garden equipment engines. This resulted in very detailed and extensive regulations for the testing and monitoring of manufactured engines. The new regulations took effect in 1995.

Beginning in the mid-1990s, federal regulations were passed that established exhaust emission standards and test procedures for engines used in lawn-and-garden equipment, as well as those used in other utility equipment. The EPA emissions standards for small spark-ignition engines began with the Phase 1 standards in 1995. The Phase 2 standards tightened the limits on emissions and were phased in during the 2002 and 2007 model years. Many manufacturers switched to overhead valve designs to comply with the Phase 2 regulations. The EPA's Phase 3 standards were completely phased-in during the 2012 model year. Some manufacturers have adopted technologies such as catalysts, low-permeation fuel lines and tanks, and fuel injection to comply with the Phase 3 standards. It is the service technician's responsibility to know which set of regulations apply to the engine he or she is working on.

Review Questions

Answer the following questions on a separate sheet of paper.

1. In addition to the power available from gasoline, give two other reasons it is the most commonly used small engine fuel.
2. *True or False?* Most manufacturers specify regular grade, unleaded gasoline for small engines.
3. *True or False?* Premium fuels are sometimes recommended for use in hot climates.

4. *True or False?* Use of regular grade fuel results in greater buildup of solid materials in the combustion chamber than use of premium grade fuel.

5. *True or False?* Premium fuels contain more additives than regular grade fuels.

6. If excessive oil is mixed with the fuel for a two-cycle engine, _____.
   A. overheating may result
   B. spark plugs may become overheated
   C. incomplete combustion may occur
   D. seizing will result

7. LPG is either _____ or _____ or a mixture of both.

8. Natural gas used as a small engine fuel is generally accompanied by a horsepower loss of _____ percent.

9. The two types of fuel pumps discussed in this chapter are _____.
   A. atmospheric pressure and gravity vacuum
   B. impulse diaphragm and mechanical
   C. gravity vacuum and mechanical
   D. gravity vacuum and impulse diaphragm

10. Name three types of air cleaners.

11. Foam air cleaner elements should be washed in _____.
    A. low lead gasoline
    B. #1 kerosene
    C. detergent and water
    D. oil

12. The proper way to clean a pleated paper air filter cartridge is to _____.
    A. soak it in kerosene
    B. tap it with external side down
    C. blow it clean with compressed air
    D. wash it in a solution of detergent and water

13. Which of the following best describes the function of a crankcase breather?
    A. It sucks in air to cool internal engine components.
    B. It vents crankcase pressure to prevent oil being forced out around the seals.
    C. It injects air and oil vapor into the cylinder for better lubrication.
    D. It filters outside air being drawn into the carburetor.

14. *True or False?* A muffler quiets the noise made by moving parts inside the engine.

15. CARB stands for _____.

16. Stricter requirements in Phase 3 regulations caused some manufacturers to start equipping their engines with _____ converters and fuel _____.

17. What are the three major pollutants from exhaust fumes?

18. Spillage of gasoline contributes to ground level _____, a component of smog.

19. An engine manufactured in 2006 is subject to the EPA's Phase _____ regulations.

20. Why must a small engine technician know when an engine was manufactured?

Suggested Activities

1. Collect a variety of tank filler caps. Either cut them in half or disassemble them. Make a display board showing the baffle and the filter system.

2. Make a display board of cutaway drawings of fuel tanks with gravity feed fuel lines and top mounted pick-up lines.

3. Obtain and cut away some old fuel pumps so that internal parts can be seen and operated. Note the function and location of each internal component.

4. Cut away parts of an old fuel filter so that the fuel circuit can be traced.

5. Demonstrate proper methods of engine fueling that will minimize spillage of gasoline. Use a standard fuel can and filler nozzle. List equipment and/or methods of improving the procedure, such as those shown in **Figure 8-25**.

6. Remove the air cleaner from an engine and identify the type. Examine it, properly service it, and if needed, replace it.

A

B

Most people think of gasoline deterioration beginning when the fuel leaves the pump. However, fuel can begin to deteriorate and collect condensation even while stored in the tanks at the gas station. For this reason, it is best to purchase fuel from a station with a frequent turn over of its fuel stock (A). The fuel from a station that is less busy (B) has a greater chance of being contaminated.

Carburetion and Fuel Injection

Learning Objectives

After studying this chapter, you will be able to:

- List and explain the principles of carburetion.
- Distinguish between natural draft, updraft, and downdraft carburetors.
- Explain float-type carburetor operation.
- Explain the operation of diaphragm-type carburetors.
- Explain vacuum carburetor operation.
- Differentiate between wet-bulb and dry-bulb primers.
- Explain how manual throttle controls work.
- List the basic functions of a governor.
- Explain the operation of air-vane, centrifugal, electronic, and vacuum governors.
- Distinguish between open-loop and closed-loop electronic fuel injection (EFI).
- Explain the operation of open-loop and closed-loop EFI systems.
- Identify the components used in common open-loop and closed-loop EFI systems.

Key Terms

absolute vacuum
acceleration well
air-fuel mixture
air vane governors
anti-afterfire solenoid
atmospheric pressure
Bernoulli principle
carburetor
centrifugal governor
choke
closed-loop EFI system
downdraft carburetors
dry bulb primers
economizer circuit
electronic fuel injection (EFI)
electronic governor
engine control unit (ECU)
flash
fuel injector
hunting
idling circuit
load adjusting needle
natural draft carburetor
open-loop EFI system
sensitivity
stability
throttle
updraft carburetors
vacuum
vacuum carburetors
venturi
wet bulb primers

Principles of Carburetion

The primary purpose of a *carburetor* is to produce a mixture of fuel and air to operate the engine. This function, in itself, is not difficult. It can be done with a simple mixing valve.

The mixing valve, however, has limited efficiency. It cannot, for example, provide economical fuel consumption and smooth engine operation over a wide range of speeds. Meeting these performance goals requires a much more complex mechanism. This is the main reason why there are so many styles and designs of carburetors.

Gasoline engines cannot run on *liquid* gasoline. The carburetor must vaporize the fuel and mix it with air in the proper proportion for varying conditions:

- Cold or hot starting.
- Idling.
- Part throttle.

- Acceleration.
- High speed operation.

Basically, air enters one end of the carburetor and is mixed with liquid fuel, which is fed through carburetor passages and sprayed into the airstream. The *air-fuel mixture* that results is forced into the cylinder by atmospheric pressure and burned in the combustion chamber.

Figure 9-1 shows how a typical carburetor operates. In this drawing, the engine is at part throttle operation. Note that the choke valve is open, and the throttle valve is partly closed.

Air-Fuel Mixture

The amount of air needed for combustion is far greater than the amount of fuel required. During normal engine operation, the usual weight ratio is 15 parts of air to 1 part of fuel. One pound of air takes up a much greater space than one pound of fuel. Therefore, by volume, one cubic foot of gasoline needs to be mixed with 9000 cubic feet of air to establish a 15 to 1 weight ratio.

Small gasoline engines use varying air-fuel ratios, depending on engine speed and load. The chart in **Figure 9-2** shows how the mixture changes for various operating conditions.

Carburetor Pressure Differences

A carburetor relies on pressure differences to mix the fuel and the air and to keep the mixture moving in the right direction. When discussing pressure differences, several terms are commonly used. They are vacuum, atmospheric pressure, and venturi principle.

Vacuum

An *absolute vacuum* is any area completely free of air or atmospheric pressure. This condition is never reached in a small gasoline engine. Therefore, the term *vacuum* is generally used to describe any pressure less than atmospheric pressure. A vacuum is created in the cylinder when the piston moves down during the intake stroke. The pressure is reduced because the volume of area available in the cylinder increases. This draws air in through the carburetor to fill up the available volume in the cylinder.

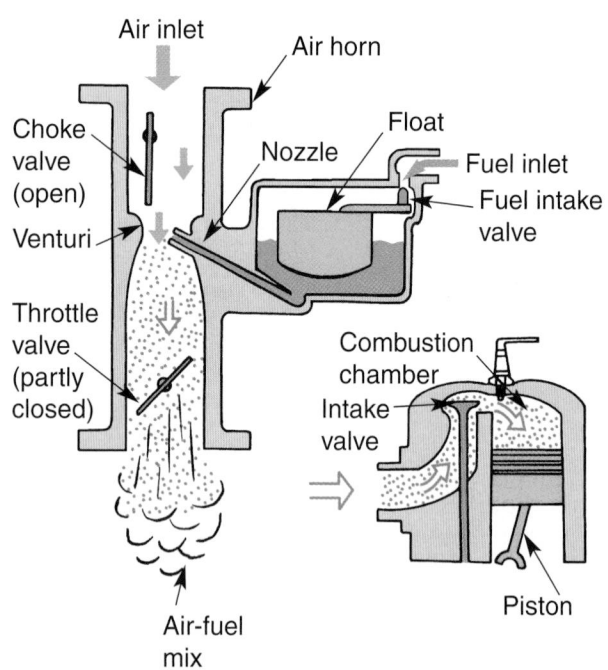

Deere & Co.

Figure 9-1.

Air entering the carburetor mixes with fuel in proper proportion, and the mixture flows into the combustion chamber.

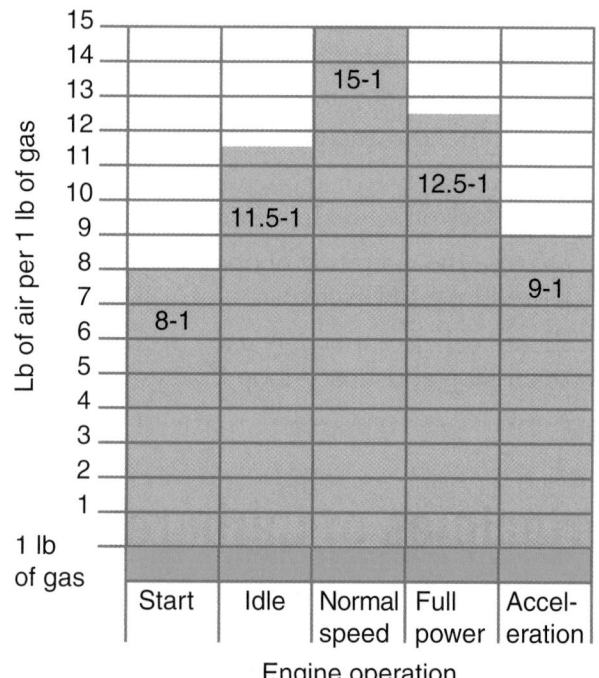

Goodheart-Willcox Publisher

Figure 9-2.

Air-fuel mixture requirements vary depending on operating conditions. This chart shows the approximate air-fuel ratios for various operating conditions.

Atmospheric Pressure

The pressure produced by the weight of air molecules above the earth is called *atmospheric pressure*. The amount of atmospheric pressure varies with altitude. A person standing on a beach at sea level, for example, would be under a taller vertical column of air than a person standing on a mountaintop. Therefore, the total weight of air molecules would be greater at sea level. See **Figure 9-3**.

Furthermore, any time air molecules are removed from a particular space, a vacuum is created. If conditions permit, this space quickly refills with air under atmospheric pressure. The air rushes into the space at a rate that is directly proportional to the pressure difference between the space and the surrounding atmosphere. As air is added to the space, the pressure increases in the space and the inflow of air slows down. The inflow of air stops when the pressure in the space equalizes with the surrounding air pressure.

The effect of atmospheric pressure can be related to small gasoline engines. As mentioned earlier, the downward movement of the piston creates a partial vacuum in the cylinder. As soon as the intake valve opens or the intake port is uncovered, atmospheric pressure forces air through the carburetor and into the cylinder to fill that vacuum.

Venturi Principle

The carburetor creates a partial vacuum of its own by means of a venturi for the purpose of drawing fuel into the airstream. A *venturi* is a restriction in a passage, which causes air to move faster (increased velocity). The increased velocity results in a drop in pressure. This phenomenon is known as the *Bernoulli principle*. At the top of the air horn shown in **Figure 9-4**, there is no change in velocity. Therefore, there is no change in pressure, and the gauge at the top port registers atmospheric pressure. The area in which the air is moving faster (middle gauge) develops a lower pressure. As a result, the vacuum gauge registers a higher vacuum.

Figure 9-5 shows a simple carburetor with fuel being drawn from the float bowl through the main discharge nozzle. This nozzle is located so that its outer end is in the low pressure area of the venturi section. Fuel coming from the discharge nozzle is still in relatively large liquid droplets that do not burn well.

To further atomize the fuel, an air bleed passage is built into the air horn. See **Figure 9-6**. A small portion of the air rushing through the carburetor is forced through the air bleed passage to the main

Mean Atmospheric Pressure at 68° F (20°C)	
Altitude (ft)	**Atmospheric Pressure (inches Hg.)**
9000	20.92
8000	21.92
7000	22.92
6000	23.92
5000	24.92
4000	25.92
3000	26.92
2000	27.92
1000	28.92
Sea level	29.92

Goodheart-Willcox Publisher

Figure 9-3.

The weight of air exerted on a given object is determined by the height and density of a column of air above the object. Air is less dense at higher altitudes. For every 1000′ above sea level, mercury column pressure is reduced by 1.0″ Hg.

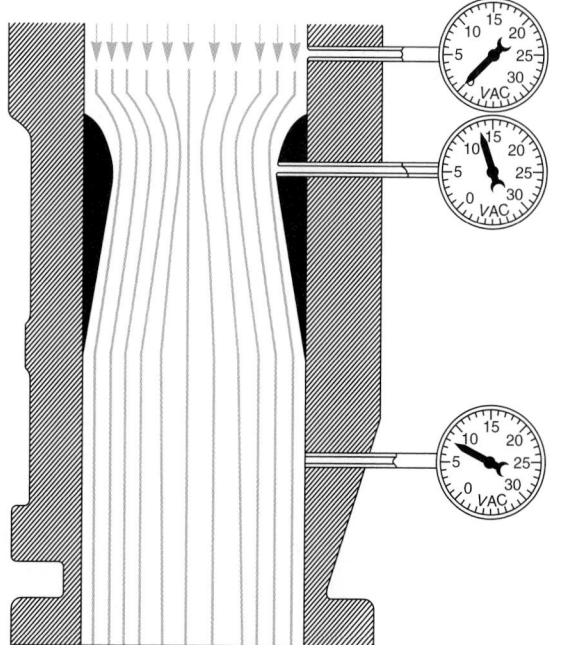

Goodheart-Willcox Publisher

Figure 9-4.

The venturi principle. A restriction in a passage causes incoming air to increase its velocity, reducing pressure. Reduction in pressure draws fuel into the airstream.

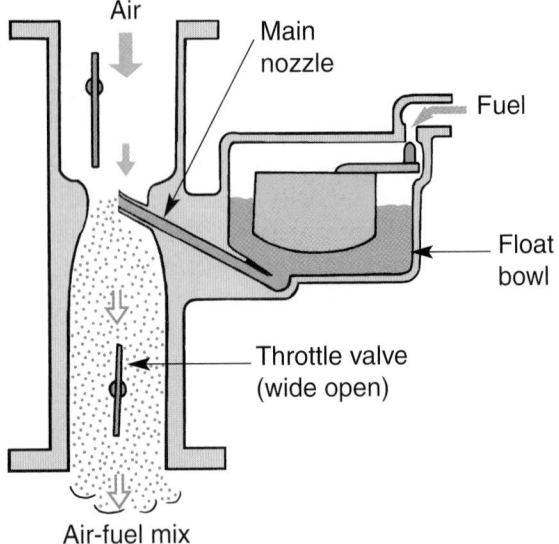

Deere & Co.

Figure 9-5.

Air flowing through the venturi has reduced the pressure around the nozzle. Fuel is drawn up the nozzle by vacuum and mixes in the airstream.

discharge nozzle. This air mixes with the stream of fuel, breaking it into small particles before it reaches the venturi. The small particles of fuel are broken into even finer particles by the air rushing through the venturi.

When the pressure on a fluid is lowered, that fluid's boiling point is also lowered. The pressure drop that takes place in the carburetor lowers the boiling point of the gasoline. As a result, many of the atomized fuel particles boil, or *flash*, into a vapor before they reach the cylinder. See **Figure 9-7A**. As the partially vaporized fuel moves toward the cylinder, it is warmed by engine heat. This causes further vaporization. See **Figure 9-7B**. When the mixture enters the combustion chamber, the swirling motion and the sudden increase in temperature due to the compression stroke complete the vaporization of the fuel.

Types of Carburetors

The three basic types of carburetors are named according to the direction that air flows through them. These types are the natural draft or side draft, the updraft, and the downdraft.

The *natural draft carburetor* is a carburetor in which the air flows horizontally through the air horn. This type of carburetor is used when there is little space on top of the engine. See **Figure 9-8**.

Updraft carburetors are placed low on the engine and use a gravity-fed fuel supply. See **Figure 9-9**. However, the air-fuel mixture must be forced upward into the engine. The air velocity must be high, so the carburetor must have small passages.

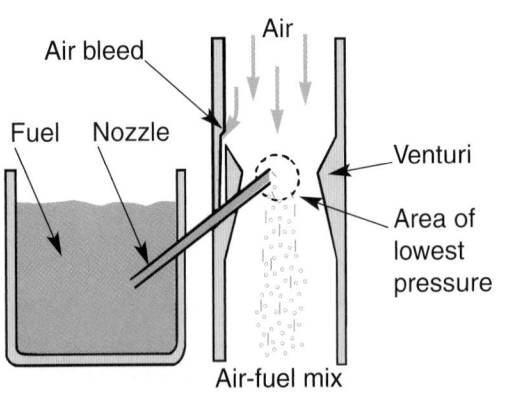

Goodheart-Willcox Publisher

Figure 9-6.

An air bleed is added to the air horn design to atomize fuel into finer particles. Higher pressure forces some air to enter the air bleed, which intersects the nozzle. This high-pressure air entering the nozzle partially atomizes the fuel before it leaves the nozzle.

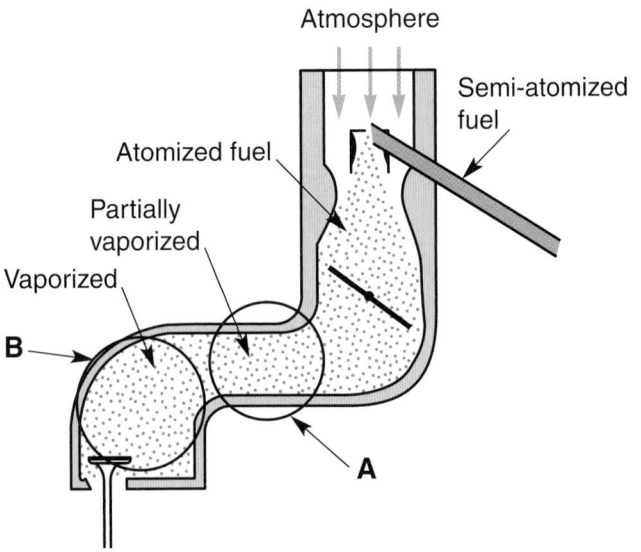

Goodheart-Willcox Publisher

Figure 9-7.

In addition to atomization caused by the air bleed and venturi, fuel is further vaporized by vacuum resulting from the restrictions of the venturi and the partially closed throttle valve (A) and by engine heat (B).

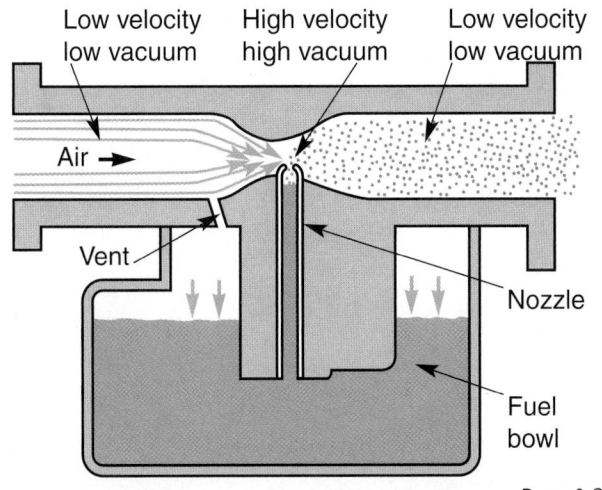

Deere & Co.

Figure 9-8.

Air flows horizontally through a natural draft carburetor.

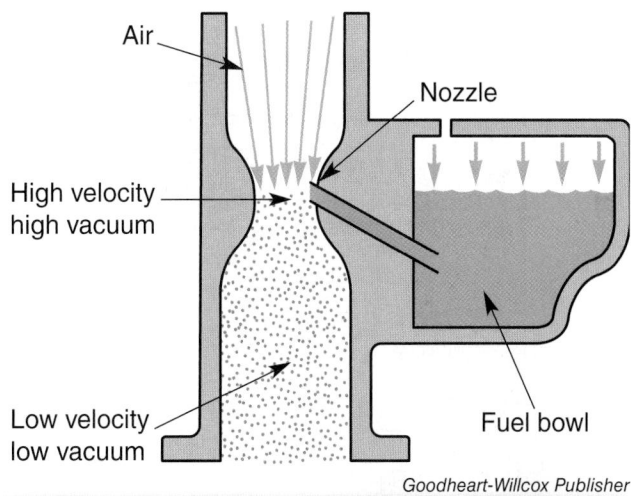

Goodheart-Willcox Publisher

Figure 9-10.

A downdraft carburetor has a downward flow of air through the venturi. Since it can operate with lower air velocities, it has larger passages.

Downdraft carburetors operate with lower air velocities and larger passages than either natural draft or updraft carburetors. See **Figure 9-10**. This is because gravity helps the air-fuel mixture flow into the cylinder. A downdraft carburetor can provide large volumes of fuel when needed for high-speed and high-power output.

Float-Type Carburetors

A carburetor float is a small vessel that rises and drops with the fuel level in the carburetor.

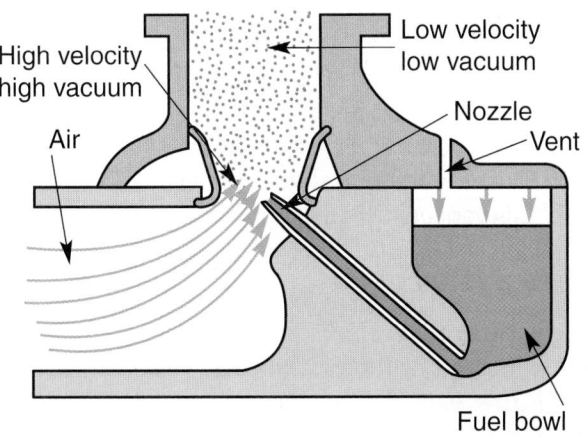

Goodheart-Willcox Publisher

Figure 9-9.

Air flowing through an updraft carburetor moves upward into the venturi. The passages must be smaller than those in a downdraft carburetor so that they can increase air velocity to carry fuel upward.

The purpose of the carburetor float is to maintain a constant level of fuel in the float bowl. As fuel is used from the float bowl, the float lowers and unseats a needle valve, which lets fuel enter the bowl, **Figure 9-11A**. This, in turn, raises the float, seating the needle valve and shutting off fuel supply to the bowl, **Figure 9-11B**. **Figure 9-12** shows the needle valve action in greater detail.

A typical float assembly is shown in **Figure 9-13**. The assembly consists of a float, a needle valve, a clip that holds the needle valve, and a hinge pin. Needle valves are typically made of brass. Many needle valves, including the one shown in **Figure 9-13**, are equipped with neoprene points. The neoprene needle point is soft and seats well in the valve. Also, it is less likely to wear out than a brass needle point.

Carburetor floats come in a wide range of shapes and materials, **Figure 9-14**. Many are hollow and made of thin brass or plastic. The problem with hollow floats is that they can spring a leak and become filled with gasoline. If a float becomes filled with gasoline, it will sink in the float bowl, and keep the fuel inlet valve open, even when the bowl is full. Other floats are made of solid buoyant materials, which eliminates the possibility of leakage. However, these materials can eventually break down and become saturated with fuel. If this happens, the float sinks just like a leaking hollow float.

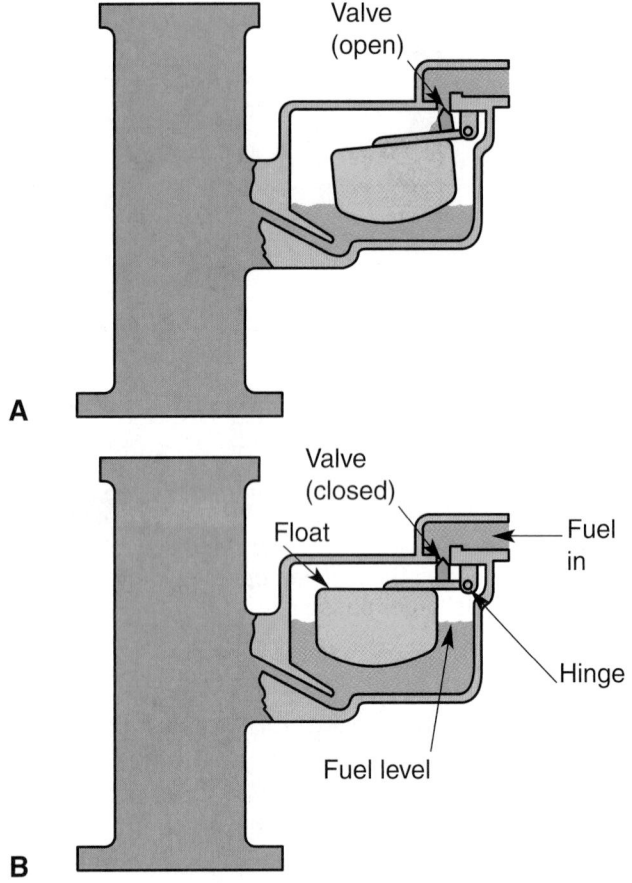

Figure 9-11.

The float in a float bowl maintains a constant fuel level. A—When the fuel level drops, the float unseats the needle and lets more fuel in. B—When the fuel level rises, the float closes the needle valve, stopping incoming fuel.

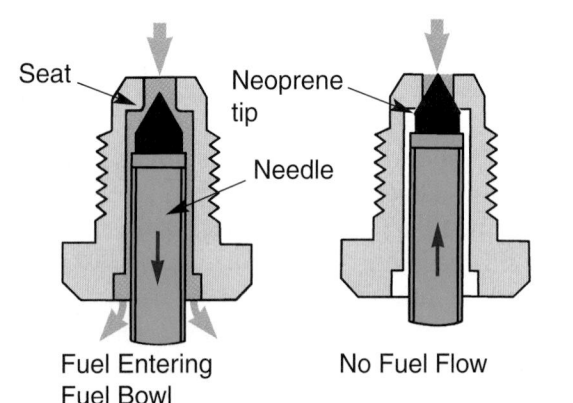

Figure 9-12.

The needle in a float bowl opens and closes the fuel passage into chamber. The needle is operated by the hinged arm of the float.

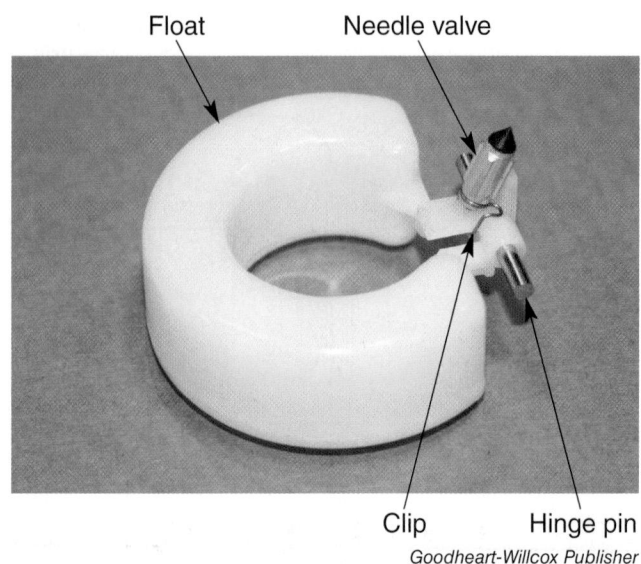

Goodheart-Willcox Publisher

Figure 9-13.

A typical float assembly is shown here. Notice that the tip of the needle valve is made of neoprene.

Caution

Although cork floats are not used in modern engines, many early carburetors were equipped with them. The shellac coating originally used on the floats dissolves when exposed to ethanol, which is found in most modern pump gas. When replacing a cork float in a vintage carburetor, you must ensure that the coating on the replacement is resistant to ethanol. Failure to use a cork float with the proper coating will result in rapid float failure.

Float Bowl Ventilation

Most carburetors are sealed and balanced to maintain equal air pressure. The air pressure above the fuel in the bowl and the air pressure entering the carburetor are equalized by a vent in the float bowl. This vent ensures a continuous, free flow of fuel.

Choke System

The carburetor *choke* is a thin disc mounted on a shaft located at the intake end of the carburetor. See **Figure 9-15**. When closed, the choke blocks intake air, resulting in a rich air-fuel mixture, which is necessary for starting a cold engine. The choke allows less air to enter the carburetor. This creates a deeper vacuum, which draws harder on the fuel nozzle. Therefore, more fuel and less air enters the combustion chamber.

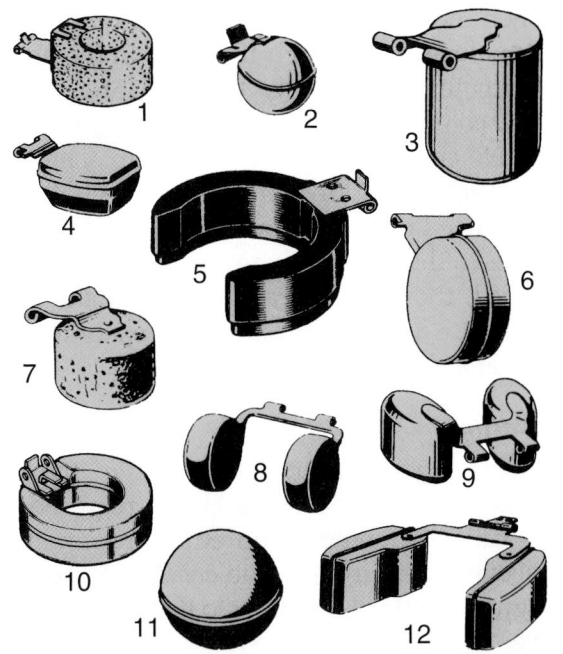

Figure 9-14.

Various float designs. 1—Doughnut-shaped cork. 2—Ball-shaped metal. 3—Cylindrical metal. 4—Rectangular metal. 5—Horseshoe-shaped plastic. 6—Cylindrical metal. 7—Round cork. 8 and 9—Twin-type metal. 10—Doughnut-shaped metal. 11—Ball-shaped metal. 12—Twin-type plastic.

Throttle System

Like the choke, the *throttle* is a thin disc mounted on a shaft. This valve, however, is located beyond the main fuel nozzle. See **Figure 9-16**.

The main purpose of the throttle valve is to regulate the amount of air-fuel mixture entering the cylinders. It also permits the operator to vary engine speed to suit conditions or to maintain a uniform speed when the load varies.

On many engines, a linkage connects the throttle valve to a governor. The governor, in turn, is connected to a speed control lever. When the speed control lever is set for a given speed, the governor will maintain that speed until the engine reaches its limit of power.

When the load on the engine increases, the governor automatically opens the throttle valve. This permits more air-fuel mixture to enter the engine, providing increased power to maintain a uniform speed. When the load decreases, the governor closes the throttle to reduce engine power. More details on governors are presented later in this chapter.

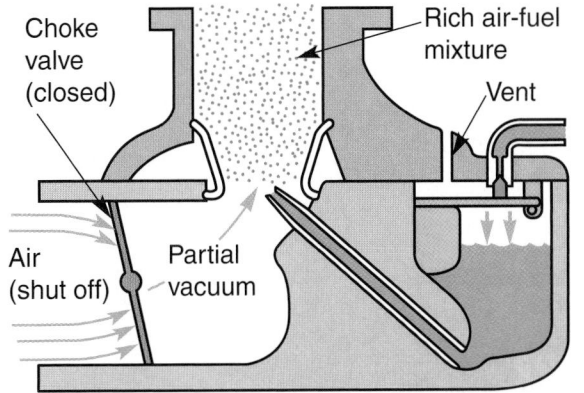

Figure 9-15.

The choke valve is closed and vacuum is high in the carburetor. The fuel mixture entering the intake manifold is extremely rich.

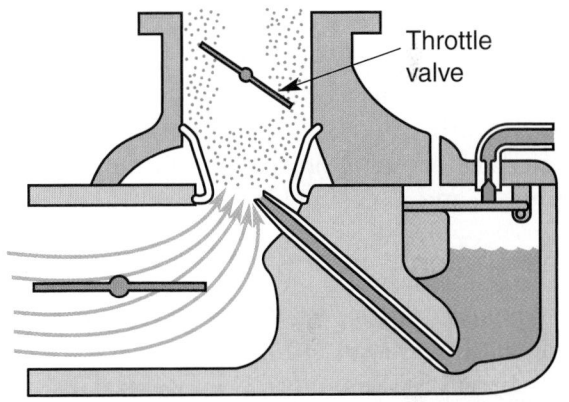

Figure 9-16.

The throttle valve is located downstream from the main fuel nozzle. The throttle regulates the amount of air-fuel mixture entering the engine.

Load Adjustment

The amount of fuel entering the main discharge nozzle is sometimes regulated by a *load adjusting needle*. See **Figure 9-17**. Many carburetors have a fixed jet or orifice, which is preset to allow proper fuel flow for maximum power and economy. Carburetors equipped with a fixed jet are nonadjustable.

Acceleration System

When the throttle valve is opened quickly for acceleration, a large amount of air is allowed to enter the carburetor. Unless some method is used to provide additional fuel to maintain a satisfactory air-fuel ratio, the engine will slow down and possibly

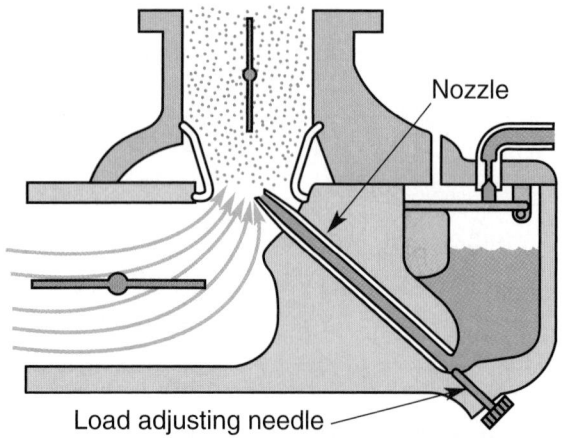

Goodheart-Willcox Publisher

Figure 9-17.

On some older, adjustable carburetors, a load adjusting needle regulates the amount of fuel entering the main nozzle.

stop. On larger engines and multi-cylinder engines, a mechanical plunger-type pump is connected to the throttle linkage. When the throttle valve is opened on acceleration, the pump automatically depresses and forces fuel into the carburetor.

Acceleration Well

An *acceleration well* is a reservoir of fuel. During idling, fuel rises inside the nozzle. The fuel flows through holes in the side of the nozzle and into the acceleration well. See **Figure 9-18.**

When the throttle valve is opened quickly, the stored fuel rushes through the holes in the nozzle without being metered by the adjusting needle. This fuel combines with the fuel in the nozzle, and the double charge enters the airstream. This provides a much richer air-fuel mixture when there is a sudden need for more power. As the fuel supply decreases in the accelerating well and the holes are uncovered, they become air bleeds for the main nozzle. These air bleeds help improve atomization of the fuel leaving the main nozzle.

Economizer Circuit

During operation at part throttle, the full capacity of the main nozzle is not required. To reduce capacity, some carburetors are equipped with economizer circuits. The *economizer circuit* is designed to retard fuel flow to the engine at part throttle.

The basic economizing process is the same for all carburetors. **Figure 9-19** shows an updraft carburetor with the bowl vent passage extended to a point near the throttle valve. When the throttle valve is partially open, the economizer passage is on the engine side of the plate. This permits the engine to draw air through the passage, reducing air pressure in the bowl and cutting down on fuel flow from the nozzle.

Idling Circuit

During idling operation, the throttle valve is closed. In this condition, the *idling circuit* of any

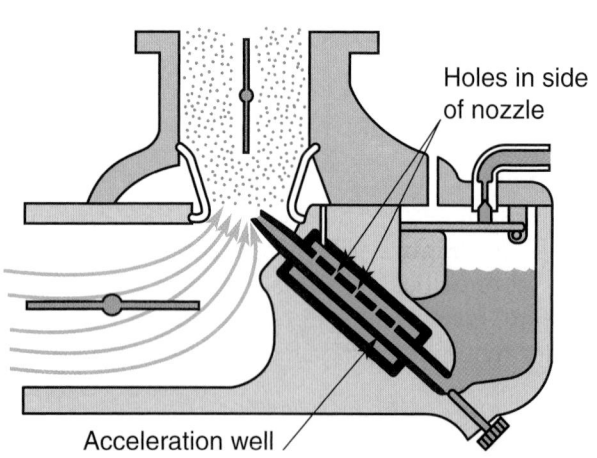

Deere & Co.

Figure 9-18.

An acceleration well stores fuel for use during rapid acceleration. When the fuel has been used from the acceleration well, the nozzle holes act as air bleeds.

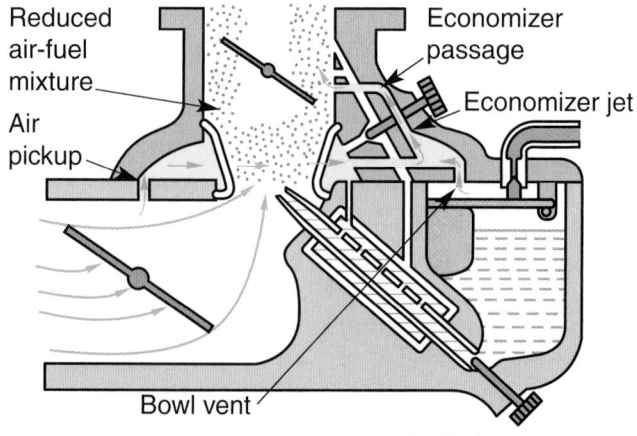

Goodheart-Willcox Publisher

Figure 9-19.

An economizer circuit (highlighted in yellow) creates a reduced pressure in the float bowl during part-throttle operation, which reduces the amount of fuel discharged from the main nozzle.

type of carburetor supplies just enough air-fuel mixture to keep the engine running. However, the idling circuit operation varies in updraft, downdraft, and natural draft carburetors.

The updraft carburetor in **Figure 9-20** is in the idling mode of operation. The choke is partially closed, directing airflow through the pickup. Since the throttle valve is closed, the air moves through a passage outside of the venturi to the idle orifice. At this point, the idle adjusting needle regulates the amount of air mixing with the fuel in the idle orifice. Less air provides a richer mixture, more air produces a leaner mixture.

At slow idle, the throttle valve is closed. Only the primary orifice is exposed to allow fuel to enter into the cylinder. At fast idle, the throttle valve opens slightly to expose both primary and secondary orifices. Remember, the speed and power of the engine is directly related to the amount of air-fuel mixture allowed to enter the cylinder. Note that at idling speed, the main discharge nozzle is inoperative due to lack of airflow through the venturi.

The downdraft carburetor in **Figure 9-21** is also in idling mode. The air bleed is located above the venturi and serves both the idling ports and main discharge nozzle.

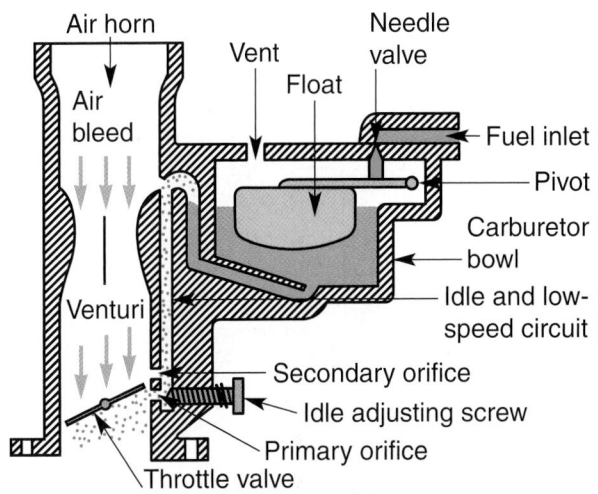

Deere & Co.

Figure 9-21.

In a downdraft carburetor, the incoming air enters in the air bleed above the venturi and travels with fuel to the idle orifice. The carburetor is in an idling state, since the throttle valve has uncovered the primary orifice only.

Note

The main discharge nozzle is not shown in **Figure 9-21** for purpose of clarity. It would be located as shown in **Figure 9-10**. The idle adjusting screw in this carburetor regulates flow of air-fuel mixture.

The natural draft carburetor in **Figure 9-22** is in the idling mode. The throttle valve is closed, and the engine is running from the primary idle discharge hole. The choke valve is wide open. The engine is idling.

Part-Throttle, Full-Throttle Sequence

Beyond idling speed, the carburetor has other circuits for part-throttle and full-throttle operation. In **Figure 9-23**, the throttle valve in this natural draft carburetor is partly open. The primary and secondary discharge holes are open, allowing more air-fuel mixture to enter. The engine is running at part throttle.

Figure 9-24 shows the full-throttle mode of operation for a natural draft carburetor. The throttle is wide open, and the maximum amount of air is flowing through the venturi. The main discharge nozzle is operating because of high vacuum in the nozzle area. The maximum air-fuel mixture is entering the cylinders, and the engine is developing full speed and power.

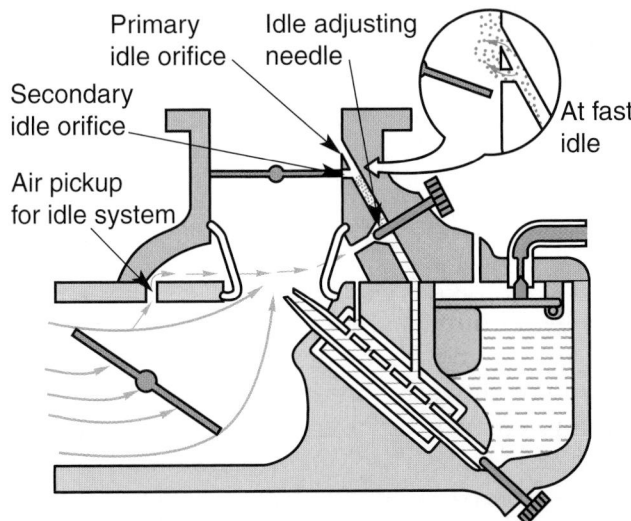

Goodheart-Willcox Publisher

Figure 9-20.

During idling, some incoming air is directed through a passage around the venturi. This air mixes with fuel and is drawn out the primary and secondary idle orifices. The throttle valve is closed for idle and slightly opened for fast idle.

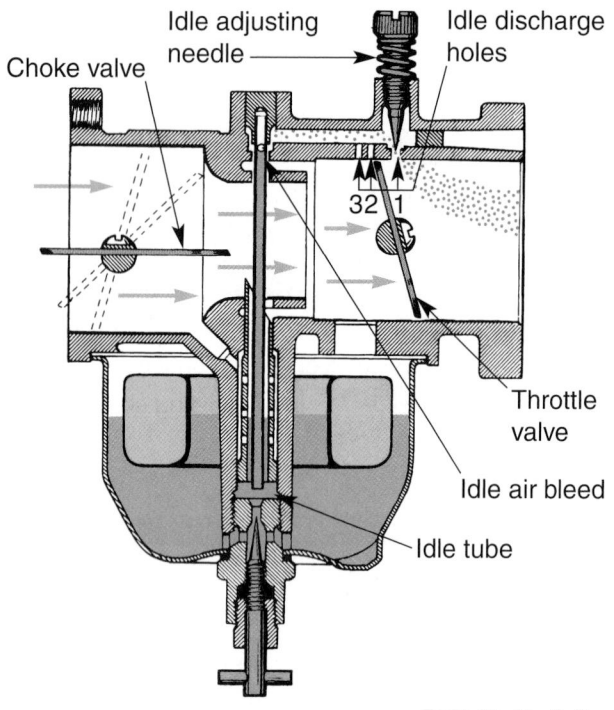

Figure 9-22.

This natural draft carburetor is idling. The throttle valve is closed, and the engine is operating on air and fuel from the primary idle orifice only.

Zenith Div., Bendix Corp.

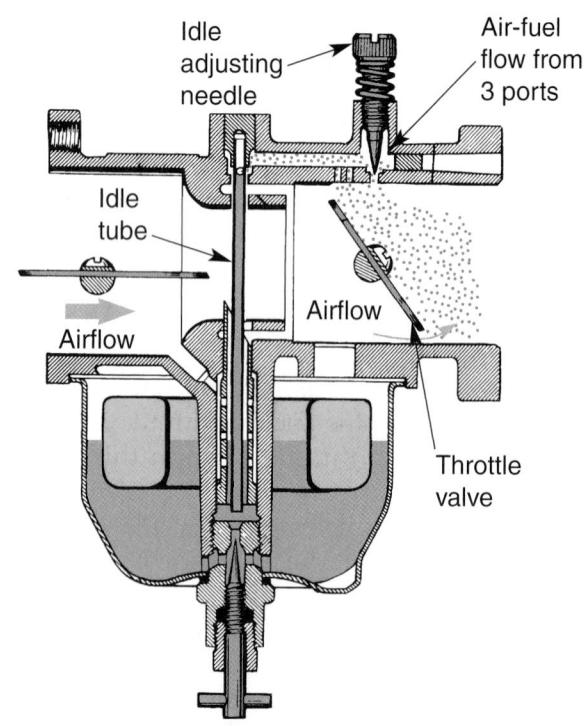

Figure 9-23.

This natural draft carburetor is at part throttle. The engine is running on air and fuel from the primary and secondary orifices.

Goodheart-Willcox Publisher

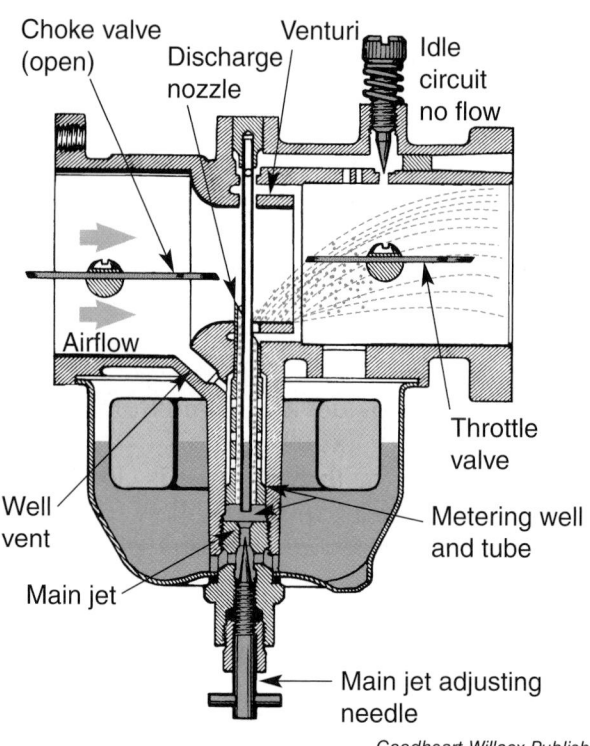

Figure 9-24.

This natural draft carburetor is operating at full throttle. The idle orifices have stopped feeding fuel due to the reduced vacuum in that part of the carburetor. A full flow of fuel is being drawn from the main nozzle.

Goodheart-Willcox Publisher

Note

Figure 9-25 shows an exploded view of the natural draft carburetor shown in **Figure 9-22** through **Figure 9-24**.

Diaphragm-Type Carburetors

A diaphragm carburetor is a carburetor with an integral impulse fuel pump. This type of carburetor does not have a float system. Instead, the difference between atmospheric pressure and the vacuum created in the engine pulsates a flexible diaphragm. The diaphragm draws fuel into a chamber of the carburetor, from which it is readily drawn into the venturi. The carburetor shown in **Figure 9-26A** is a diaphragm-type, natural draft carburetor. Views B and C illustrate the operation of the carburetor.

In **Figure 9-26B**, vacuum created in the manifold draws fuel from the upper chamber through the check valve into the venturi. Then, reduced pressure

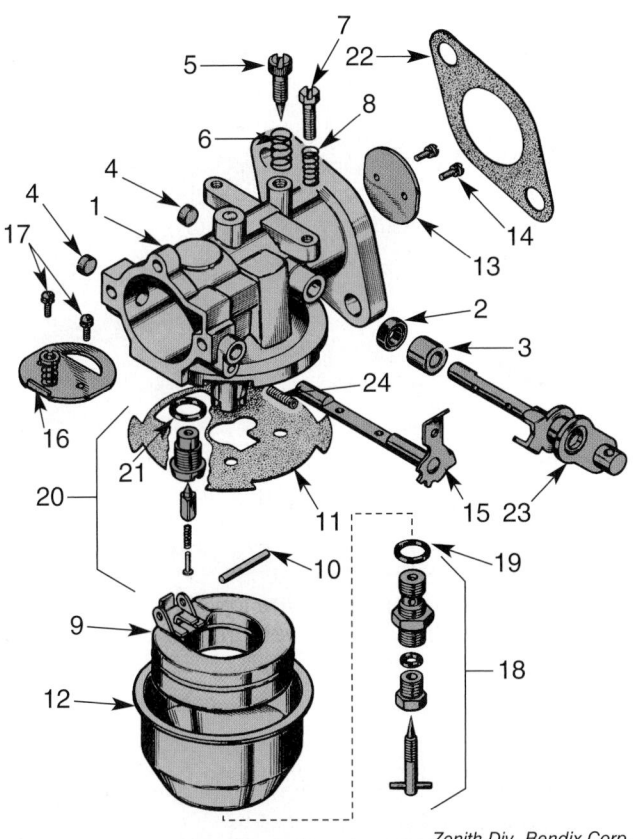

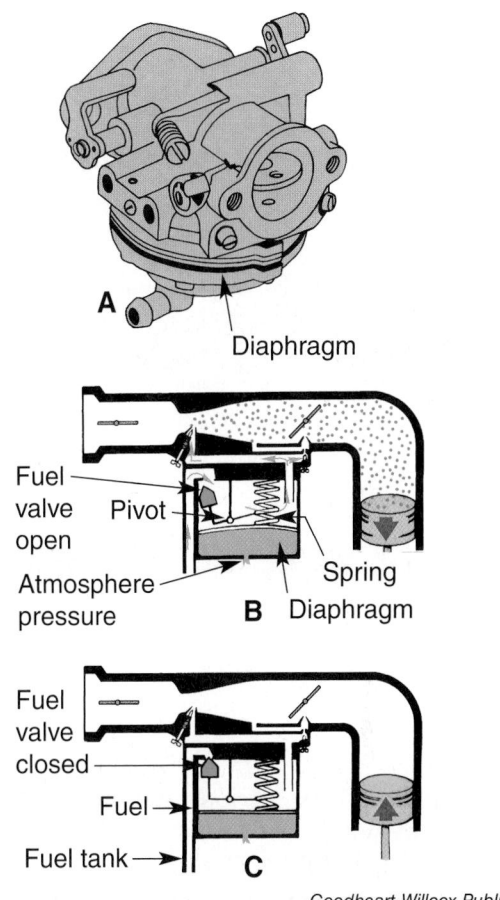

Figure 9-25.

An exploded view of a natural draft carburetor:
1—Throttle body. 2—Seal. 3—Retainer. 4—Cup rings.
5—Idle adjusting needle. 6—Spring. 7—Throttle stop
screw. 8—Spring. 9—Float and hinge assembly.
10—Float pin. 11—Gasket. 12—Fuel bowl. 13—Throttle
valve. 14—Screw. 15—Lever and shaft assembly for
choke. 16—Choke valve. 17—Screw. 18—Main jet and
adjustment assembly. 19—Washer. 20—Fuel valve
and seat assembly. 21—Gasket. 22—Flange gasket.
23—Throttle shaft and lever assembly. 24—Spring.

Zenith Div., Bendix Corp.

Goodheart-Willcox Publisher

Figure 9-26.

A—A diaphragm-type, natural draft carburetor.
B—The diaphragm is lifted by manifold vacuum while
fuel is being drawn from the jets. C—When the piston
moves up in the cylinder and vacuum is reduced,
diaphragm returns to normal, drawing new fuel into
upper fuel chamber.

in the upper chamber allows atmospheric pressure to lift the diaphragm, compressing the inlet tension spring. Finally, movement of the diaphragm opens the fuel valve, permitting fuel to flow into the upper chamber. Remember, this action takes place on the intake stroke of the piston.

In **Figure 9-26C**, manifold pressure increases to equal atmospheric pressure when the piston rises on the compression stroke. Since there is no difference in pressure between the upper chamber and the lower chamber, the inlet tension spring returns the diaphragm to a neutral position, closing the fuel valve.

The pulsation of the diaphragm takes place on every intake and compression stroke, regardless of the number of engine cylinders. On four-cycle engines, fuel is drawn into the cylinder on the downstroke of the piston. On two-cycle engines, fuel is drawn into the crankcase during the upstroke of the piston. In some carburetors, the diaphragm spring is adjustable (adjustment screw not shown) to balance the force of the inlet tension spring.

Another variation of diaphragm carburetor has two diaphragms. One diaphragm acts as a fuel pump, drawing fuel into the carburetor. The second diaphragm meters the flow of fuel into the venturi, **Figure 9-27**. A variation of this type of carburetor is used to explain carburetor operation in the following section. In the carburetor described in the following section, both diaphragms are on the same side of the carburetor, but the operating principles are the same.

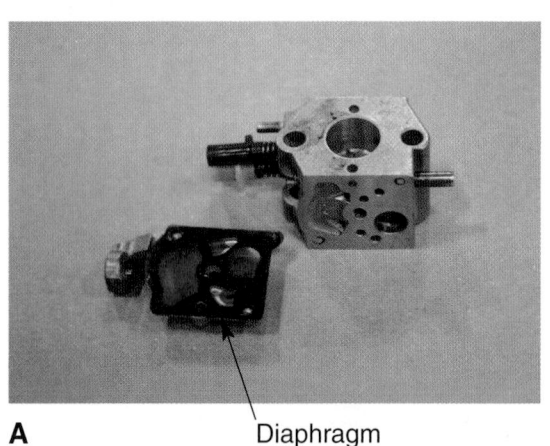

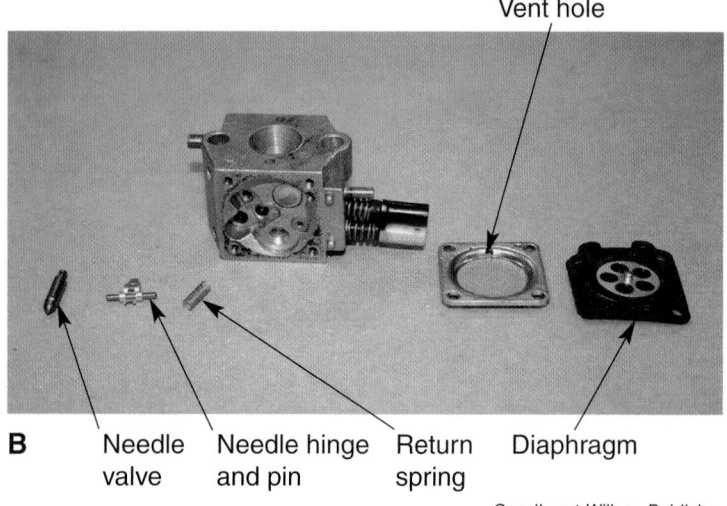

A Diaphragm

B Needle valve | Needle hinge and pin | Return spring | Diaphragm

Goodheart-Willcox Publisher

Figure 9-27.

This is a diaphragm carburetor from a small two-stroke brush cutter. A—The diaphragm on the top of the carburetor draws fuel from the tank. B—The diaphragm on the bottom side meters fuel flow into the venturi.

Diaphragm Carburetor Operation

A study of the various circuits of a typical diaphragm-type carburetor will help clarify operating principles. The carburetor shown in **Figure 9-28** is in the starting mode with the choke valve closed. The arrows indicate the direction of fuel flow.

Fuel is drawn from the idle discharge ports and main nozzle because manifold vacuum is high. The carburetor diaphragm is drawn upward during the intake stroke of the engine piston, unseating the fuel inlet needle to allow fuel to flow. High vacuum is supplied at the impulse channel, pulling the fuel pump diaphragm up. This draws fuel into the carburetor.

Figure 9-29 shows idling operation with the choke valve open and the throttle valve closed. Vacuum is in effect on the engine side of the throttle valve. Since only one of the three idle discharge ports is exposed to vacuum, a small quantity of fuel is being used, and the engine runs slowly.

Figure 9-30 shows the throttle partially open for intermediate speed. Airflow through primary venturi is still not great enough to draw fuel up the main nozzle. Three idle discharge ports are feeding fuel for medium speed. The two extra idle discharge ports are called "off-idle ports." They must supply more fuel than the single idle port, yet not as much as the main discharge port. The intermediate circuit must provide fuel for transition from idle to high-speed operation.

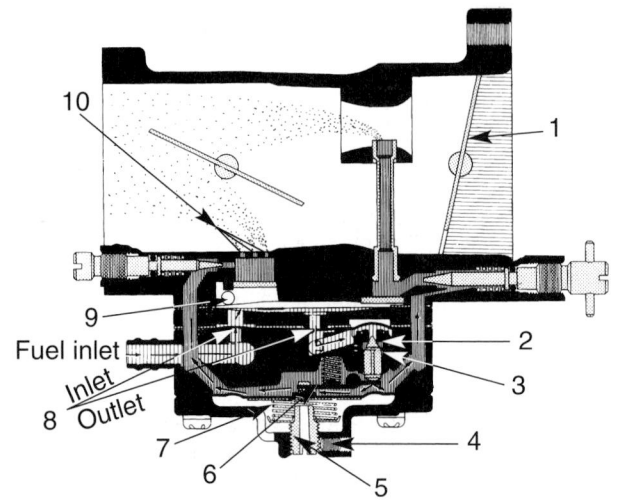

Starting (Choke) Operation

1-Choke valve.
2-Inlet control valve.
3-Valve seat.
4-Lock screw.
5-Adjustment screw.
6-Inlet control lever.
7-Diaphragm spring.
8-Check valve.
9-Impulse channel.
10-Idle discharge ports.

Rupp Industries, Inc.

Figure 9-28.

With the choke plate closed, a very strong vacuum is formed in the air horn. A large quantity of gasoline is sucked out of the idle jets and the main nozzle. A rich mixture results, which can support cold engine operation.

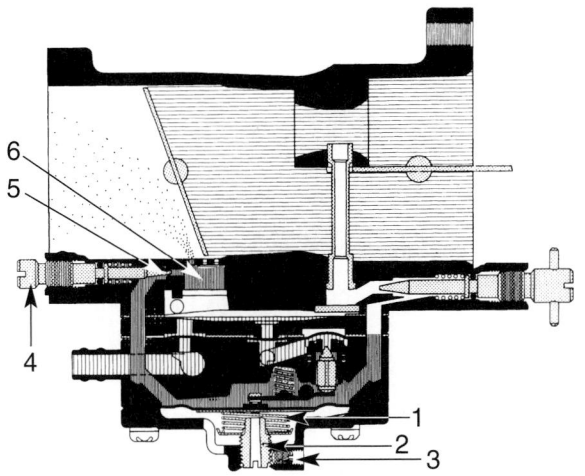

Idling Operation

1-Diaphragm spring.
2-Adjustment screw.
3-Lock screw.
4-Idle mixture screw.

5-Idle mixture
   screw orifice.
6-Idle fuel supply.
   channel.

Rupp Industries, Inc.

Figure 9-29.

During idling or very slow speed operation, only the idle fuel supply channel is feeding fuel to the engine. There is no vacuum to draw fuel out of the main nozzle. Remember, this circuit controls the fuel mixture when an engine is idling.

Figure 9-31 shows high-speed operation with maximum air and fuel flowing through the carburetor. The choke and throttle valves are fully open. All idle ports and the main nozzle are feeding fuel.

Vacuum Carburetors

Vacuum carburetors are simple carburetors that draw fuel directly out of the fuel tank. These carburetors are always mounted on the top of the fuel tank. They are equipped with a pickup tube that extends into the fuel tank. The fuel tank is vented, and therefore at atmospheric pressure. As air flows through the carburetor body, it creates a vacuum that draws fuel up the pickup tube. The fuel passes through an adjustable orifice and enters a small reservoir in the side of the carburetor body. See **Figure 9-32**.

Two small metering holes in the reservoir feed fuel into the airstream based on throttle position. When the throttle is wide open, fuel flows out of both holes. When the throttle is in the idle position, only one of the holes is exposed to vacuum, and fuel flows out of that metering hole only. This is similar to the way the throttle plate position affects fuel flow through idle discharge ports.

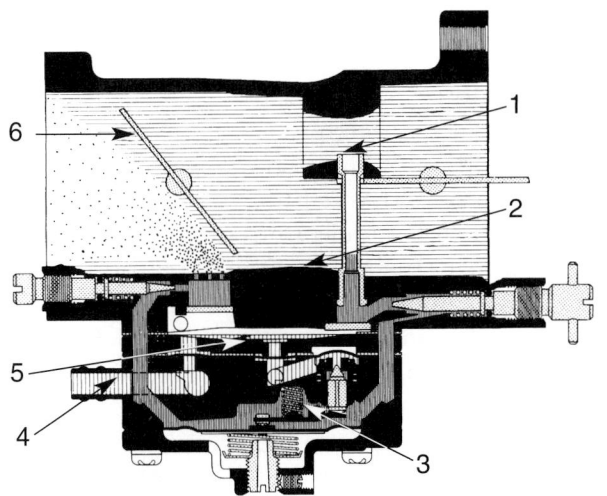

Intermediate Operation

1-Primary venturi.
2-Secondary venturi.
3-Inlet tension spring.

4-Fuel inlet.
5-Fuel pump diaphragm.
6-Throttle valve.

Rupp Industries, Inc.

Figure 9-30.

Fuel feeding from the idling discharge ports provides intermediate speed operation.

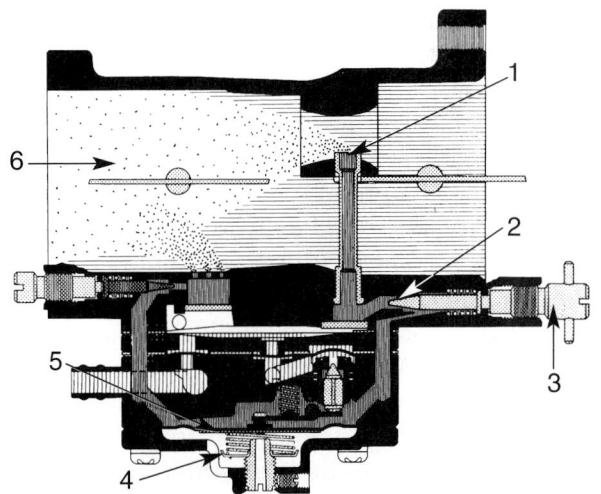

High-Speed Operation

1-Main fuel discharge port.
2-High-speed mixture screw orifice.
3-High-speed mixture screw.

4-Spring seat.
5-Main diaphragm.
6-Maximum airflow.

Rupp Industries, Inc.

Figure 9-31.

During high-speed operation, fuel flow from the main nozzle and idle jets combines with maximum airflow.

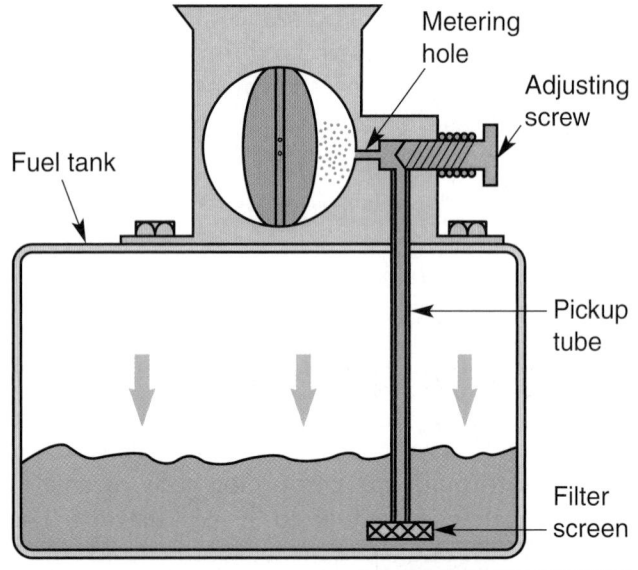

Goodheart-Willcox Publisher

Figure 9-32.

A simplified vacuum carburetor is shown here. Vacuum draws fuel up the pickup tube into a reservoir where it is mixed into the airstream through metering holes.

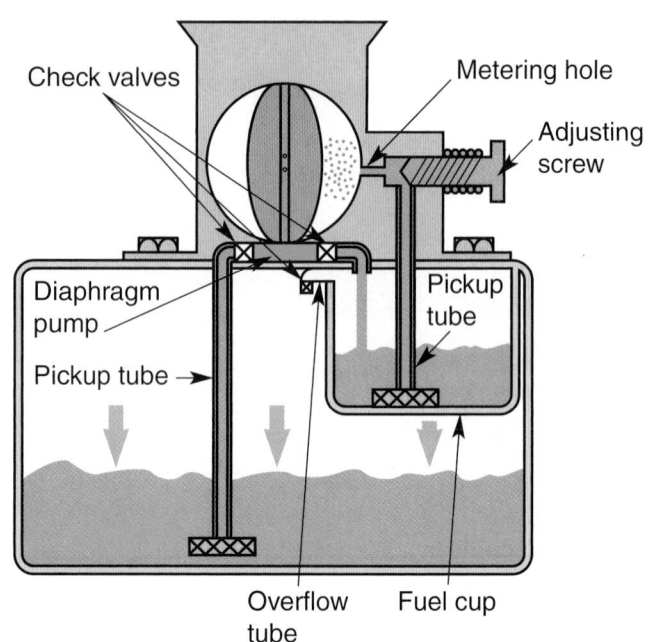

Goodheart-Willcox Publisher

Figure 9-33.

A vacuum diaphragm carburetor has an integral diaphragm fuel pump. The fuel pump draws fuel out of the tank through a pickup tube and transfers it to a fuel cup. There, the fuel is drawn up a second pickup tube and metered into the airstream.

Vacuum carburetor operation is affected by the level of fuel in the tank. As the fuel level in the fuel tank drops, the fuel must rise farther to enter the carburetor. Since the engine produces a limited amount of vacuum, this results in less fuel being delivered. As a result, as the fuel level in the tank drops, the carburetor produces a leaner mixture.

To counteract this effect, modern vacuum carburetors use a variation of the diaphragm fuel pump to provide a steady supply of fuel. These carburetors have two pickup tubes. The first is connected to a diaphragm pump. The pump draws fuel out of the tank, and delivers it to a cup inside the tank. A second pickup tube extends from the carburetor into the fuel cup. Vacuum inside the carburetor draws fuel through this shorter pickup tube, into the reservoir, and then through the metering holes into the airstream. See **Figure 9-33**.

The diaphragm pump delivers fuel continuously to the fuel cup. When the fuel tank is full, the diaphragm pump draws more fuel than is needed from the tank. This excess fuel gradually fills the fuel cup. When the fuel cup is completely full, the excess fuel is returned to the fuel tank through an overflow tube. As the fuel level in the tank drops, less fuel is delivered by the diaphragm pump. However, the fuel in the cup acts as a reserve, ensuring that a full charge is delivered to the carburetor.

Primers

Some carburetors are equipped with primers. A primer is a hand-operated plunger, which, when depressed, forces additional fuel into the carburetor for starting a cold engine. There are two types of primers commonly used on modern engines, dry bulb primers and wet bulb primers. *Wet bulb primers* act like a fuel pump, drawing fuel from the fuel tank or fuel reservoir in the carburetor and pumping it into the carburetor's air horn. The bulb of a wet bulb primer is always full of fuel. *Dry bulb primers* pump air into the float bowl, increasing air pressure and forcing fuel up the nozzle.

Primers may be installed on the carburetor or they may be remotely mounted. A primer bulb on a vacuum carburetor is shown in **Figure 9-34**.

Anti-Afterfire Solenoids

Some engines with a battery-powered ignition system are equipped with an *anti-afterfire solenoid*. The anti-afterfire solenoid is typically installed in the

Figure 9-34.

A wet-bulb primer on a vacuum carburetor.

Note

Many people mistakenly believe that the solenoid shuts off fuel supply to the carburetor. This is not the case, and this misconception can interfere with proper diagnosis of the fuel system. It is important to understand that the solenoid prevents fuel that is in the carburetor from entering the airstream.

Manual Throttle Controls

A basic manual throttle control consists of either mechanical linkage or a flexible cable. One end of the control is attached to the throttle shaft lever. The other end is connected to a lever, slide, or dial that is operated manually to open and close the throttle valve.

A manual throttle can be used as the sole control for positioning the throttle valve. Typical applications of this type of throttle are chain saws, motorcycles, snowmobiles, and outboard engines. In some installations, the manual control is used in conjunction with a governor. This setup permits governed speed to be changed when desired. See **Figure 9-36**.

Figure 9-37 shows a throttle control that varies governor spring tension, positions the throttle valve,

carburetor float bowl. See **Figure 9-35**. Its purpose is to cut off fuel supply to the venturi when the ignition is turned off to prevent run-on. A spring extends the solenoid plunger, sealing off the main jet orifice when battery power is cut off. This prevents fuel from entering the main nozzle.

When the ignition switch is turned on, battery power is applied to the solenoid, energizing the solenoid windings. The windings retract the plunger, compressing the solenoid's spring.

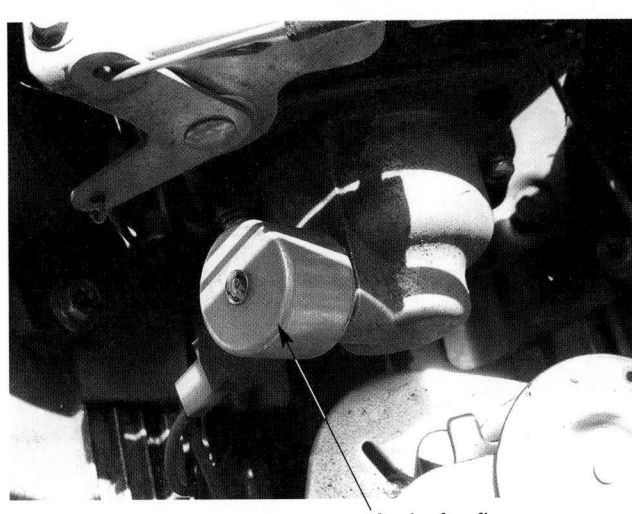

Anti-afterfire solenoid

Figure 9-35.

A carburetor equipped with an anti-afterfire solenoid.

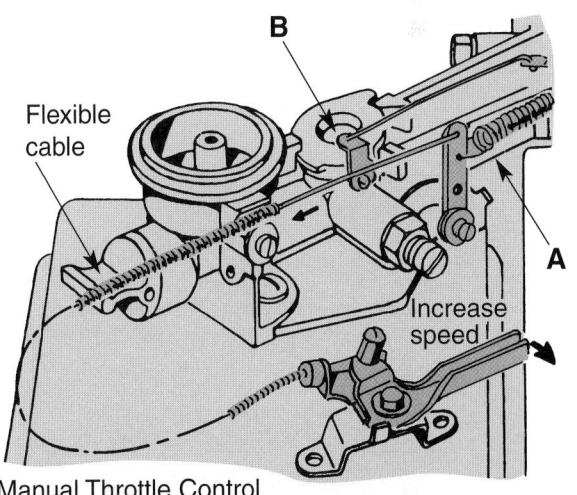

Manual Throttle Control

Figure 9-36.

This manual throttle control uses a flexible cable to transmit motion from the hand lever to the governor spring lever. A—The throttle cable changes position of an intermediate lever, which changes tension on the governor spring. B—The governor linkage is connected to a lever on the throttle shaft.

and actuates the choke for starting. In **Figure 9-37A**, the control knob is turned to *Start*, which rotates the choke valve shaft to the choked position. When the engine is started, the control knob is turned to *Run*, which opens the choke. To stop the engine, the knob is turned to *Stop*, as shown in **Figure 9-37B**. The stop switch grounds the ignition system, cutting off the flow of electricity to the engine.

Note

This type of switch is explained in detail in Chapter 10 of this text.

Governor Throttle Controls

In many small gasoline engine applications, such as lawn mowers, generators, and garden tractors,

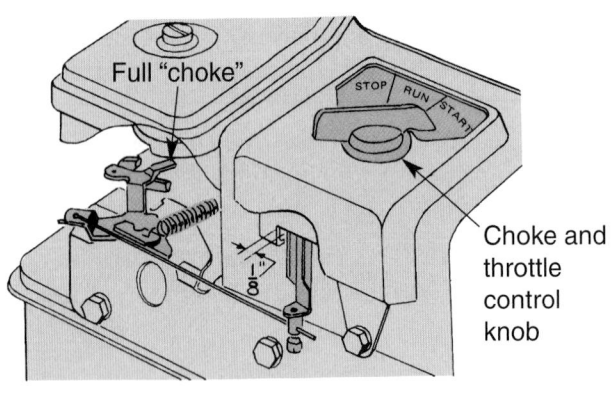

Full "choke"

Choke and throttle control knob

A

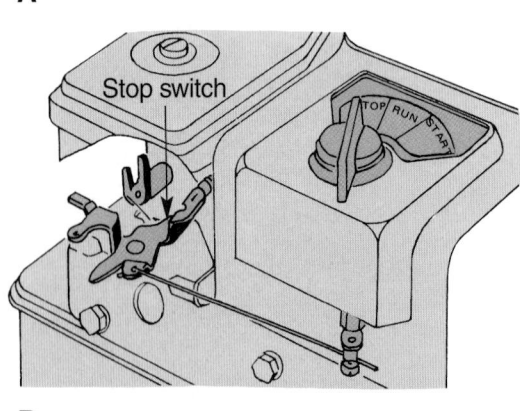

Stop switch

B

Goodheart-Willcox Publisher

Figure 9-37.
Combined manual throttle and choke control. A—The control knob turned to *Start* activates the choke. B—The knob turned to *Stop* closes the stop switch.

the load on the engine can change instantly. The change in load would require constant throttle changes on the part of the operator. Instead, governors are used to provide a smooth, constant speed, regardless of engine loading.

What an Engine Governor Does

Governors can be designed to serve three basic functions:

- Maintain a speed selected by the operator that is within range of governor.
- Prevent overspeeding, which can cause engine damage.
- Limit both high and low speeds.

Small engine governors are generally used to maintain a fixed speed not readily adjustable by the operator or to maintain a speed selected by means of a throttle control lever, see **Figure 9-38**. In either case, the governor protects against overspeeding. If the load is removed, the governor immediately closes the throttle. If the engine load is increased, the governor opens the throttle to prevent a reduction in engine speed.

For example, a lawn mower normally has a governor. When mowing through a large clump of grass, engine load increases suddenly. This tends to reduce engine speed. The governor reacts by opening the carburetor throttle valve. Engine power output

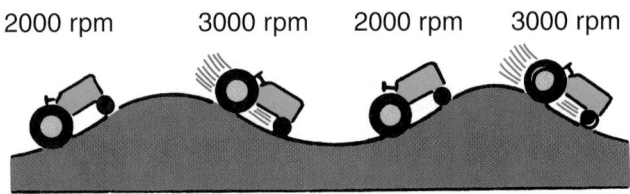

2000 rpm   3000 rpm   2000 rpm   3000 rpm

Without Governor (Fixed Throttle)

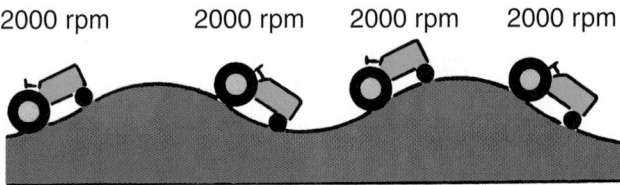

2000 rpm   2000 rpm   2000 rpm   2000 rpm

With Governor (Keeps Same Speed)

Deere & Co.

Figure 9-38.
Engine speed on the tractor without a governor varies with engine load as the tractor goes uphill and downhill. If the tractor is equipped with a governor, the engine speed remains constant under varying engine load.

increases to maintain the cutting blade speed. When the mower is pushed over a sidewalk (no grass or engine load), engine speed tends to go up. The governor reacts by closing the carburetor throttle valve. This limits the maximum cutting blade speed. As a result, the mower engine and cutting blade speeds stay relatively constant.

Types of Governors

There are several types of engine governors: centrifugal (also called mechanical), electronic, air vane (also called pneumatic), and vacuum. Most modern governors are centrifugal or electronic types. Pneumatic governors are common on older engines. Vacuum governors are usually found on farm and industrial engines. Basically, all governors perform the same functions. They protect the engine from overspeeding and maintain a constant engine speed, independent of load. However, the different types of governors use different methods of sensing engine speed.

Centrifugal (Mechanical) Governor

The purpose of a *centrifugal governor*, also called a mechanical governor, is to control engine speed. It uses pivoted flyweights that are attached to a revolving shaft or gear driven by the engine. With this setup, governor rpm is always directly proportional to engine rpm.

Figure 9-39 shows how centrifugal governors operate. When the engine is stopped, the heavy ends of the flyweights are held close to the shaft by the governor spring. The throttle valve is held fully open as illustrated in **Figure 9-39A**.

When the engine is started, the governor is rotated. As its speed increases, centrifugal force increases and causes the flyweights to pivot

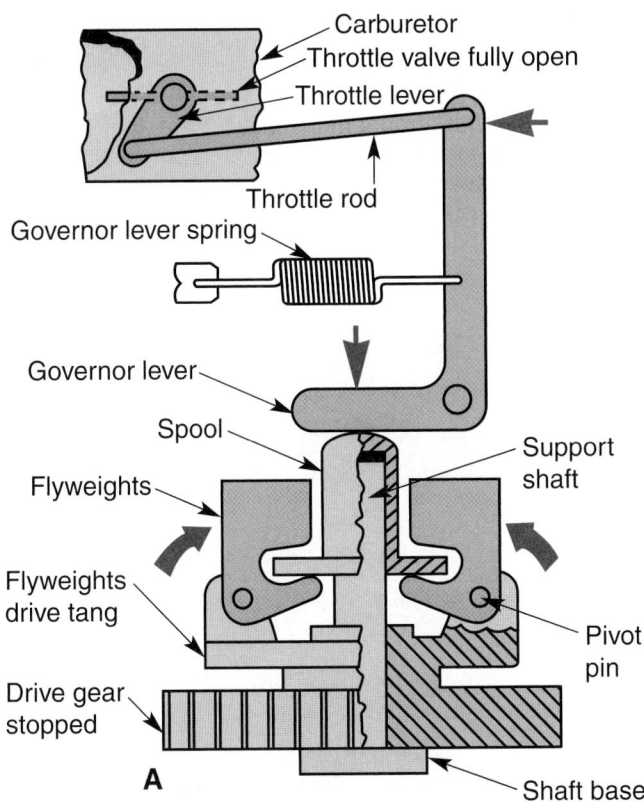
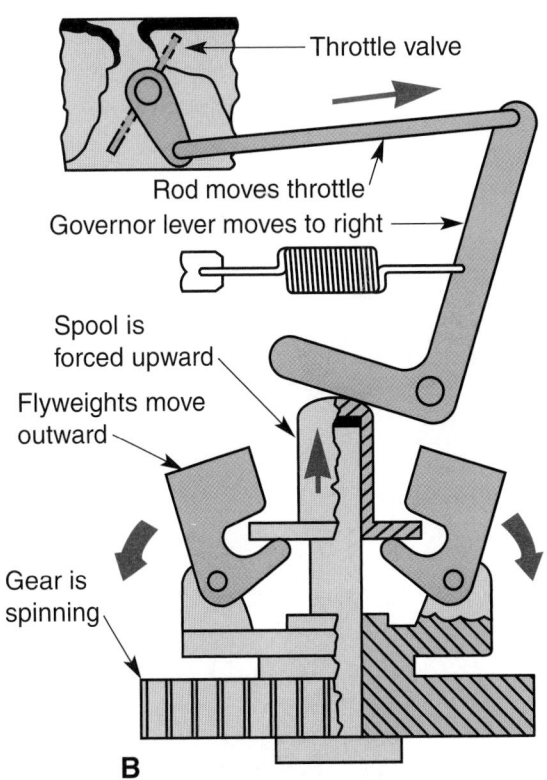

Tecumseh Products Co.

Figure 9-39.

Centrifugal governor operation. A—At low engine speed, there is very little centrifugal force generated by the drive gear, so the flyweights stay close to the center of rotation, keeping the throttle valve open. B—As the engine speeds up, centrifugal force throws the flyweights outward, raising the spool. The spool rotates the governor lever, which closes the throttle valve. The balance between centrifugal force and governor spring tension determines the throttle valve setting.

outward. This forces the spool upward, raising the governor lever until spring tension equals the centrifugal force on the weight. This action partially closes the throttle valve shown in **Figure 9-39B**.

If the engine is subjected to a sudden load that reduces engine speed, the reduction in speed lessens centrifugal force on the flyweights. The weights move inward, lowering the spool and governor lever. This series of actions opens the throttle valve and lost rpm is regained.

Changing the Governor Speed Setting

The centrifugal governor speed setting can be changed by turning a knurled adjusting nut on the end of the tension rod. See **Figure 9-40**. This system is used when the engine is expected to run at a constant speed setting for long periods of time.

Another type of governor speed adjusting arrangement is shown in **Figure 9-41**. Movement of the governor adjustment lever changes spring tension and engine rpm. The high-speed adjustment screw limits the range of motion of the governor adjustment lever.

A remote, hand-controlled cable that alters spring tension can also be used to set governor speed. See **Figure 9-42**. Movement of the control

handle increases or decreases spring tension, which speeds up or slows down the engine. The operator can quickly select any speed within the range of the governor.

Goodheart-Willcox Publisher

Figure 9-41.

On the governor arrangement shown here, the governor setting can be changed by moving the governor adjustment lever. The long spring on the throttle link removes any play in the governor linkage.

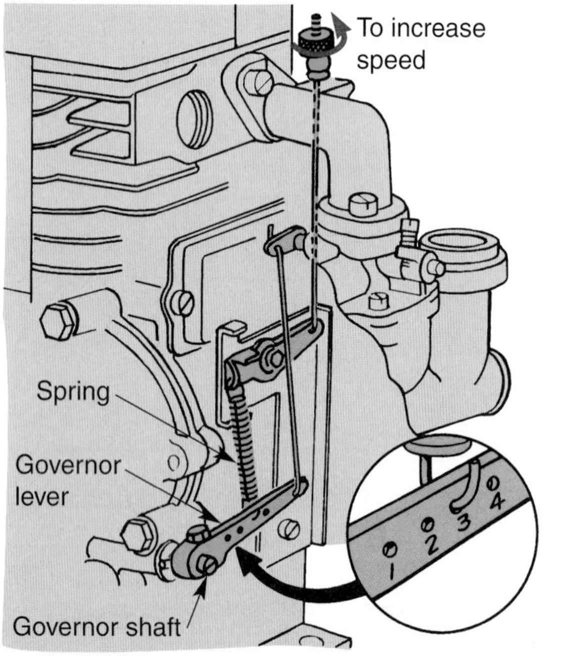

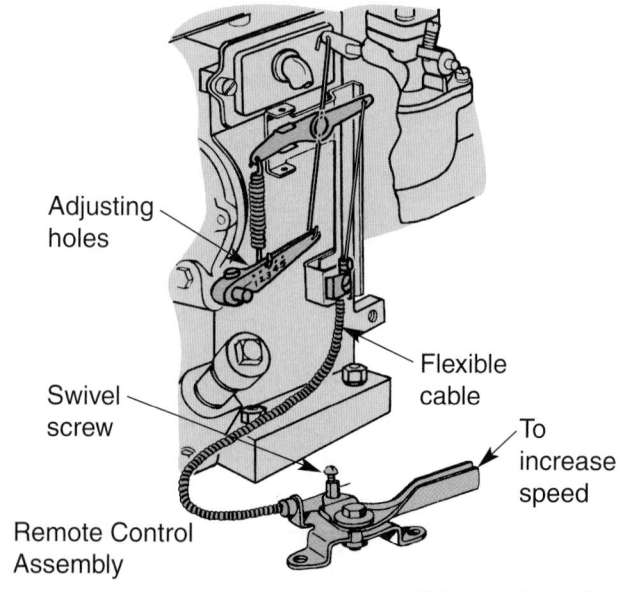

Briggs and Stratton Corp.

Figure 9-40.

A single speed arrangement, using a knurled nut to provide a limited governor speed range.

Briggs and Stratton Corp.

Figure 9-42.

An operator-controlled governor speed setting device allows quick, wide, governed speed changes.

Hunting of Centrifugal Governors

Frequently, when an engine is first started or is working under load, its speed becomes erratic or oscillates. The engine speeds up rapidly; the governor responds and engine speed drops quickly. The governor stops functioning and engine speed again increases. The governor responds and this action is repeated over and over. This condition is known as *hunting*.

Hunting is usually a result of improper carburetor adjustment. Leaning or richening the fuel mixture can often correct the problem. Also, the governor may cause hunting if it is too stiff or binds at some point. It must work freely. If there is a loose component on the engine, a vibration can result.

Occasionally, the engine vibration causes the governor spring to vibrate. As the spring vibrates, it stretches and contracts, improperly operating the throttle valve. If this happens, the loose part must be identified and tightened to eliminate the vibration.

Electronic Governor

Some late-model engines are equipped with an *electronic governor*. These engines are equipped with an electronic control unit (ECU) and a stepper motor that controls throttle plate position. The ECU receives a signal from the ignition pickup or a crankshaft position sensor, which varies with engine speed. Based on the engine speed, the ECU sends a signal to the stepper motor to open the throttle, close the throttle, or keep the throttle in the same position. Electronic governors are able to perform very quick and precise adjustments to the throttle and are not prone to hunting.

Air Vane (Pneumatic) Governor

Air vane governors, also known as pneumatic governors, are operated by the stream of air created by the flywheel cooling fins. The force developed by the airstream is in direct proportion to the speed of the engine.

A lightweight, thin strip of metal called an air vane is placed in the direct path of the airstream. It is pivoted on a pin or shaft set near one end. The vane is connected, with linkage, to the throttle shaft lever. When the engine is running, the airstream pivots the vane and attempts to close the throttle valve. See **Figure 9-43**.

The governor spring is attached to the throttle lever or to linkage from the vane. This spring is designed to pull the throttle valve to wide-open

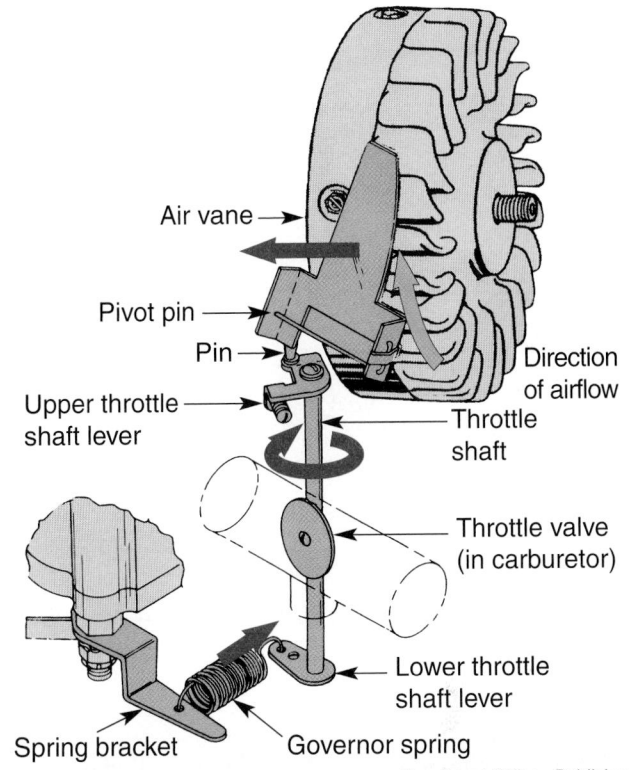

Goodheart-Willcox Publisher

Figure 9-43.

This schematic illustrates the operation of an air vane governor. The air vane tries to close the throttle valve, while the governor spring tries to open it. The balance between these two forces determines the throttle position. The governor is shown at a low engine speed position. The red arrows show the changes that will occur as engine speed increases.

position. The airflow (blue arrow) pivots the air vane, causing it to exert rotary pressure on the upper throttle shaft lever while the governor spring tries to pull the throttle valve open. The ratio of pressure developed by the vane, as opposed to the tension of the governor spring, determines throttle valve position. When the engine is stopped, the airstream ceases and the throttle valve is pulled to the wide-open position by the governor spring. The governor spring bracket can be moved to vary the amount of tension exerted by the spring. This will alter the vane spring pressure balance and establish a new throttle setting.

Governor spring tension is carefully calibrated by the manufacturer. If the spring is stretched or altered in any way, it should be replaced with a new spring designed for that make and model engine. If the linkage is bent, worn, or damaged, it should be straightened, repaired, or replaced. See **Figure 9-44**.

Air vane shaft   Governor spring

Throttle lever   Governor lever

Goodheart-Willcox Publisher

Figure 9-44.

The parts of a simple governor system for an actual engine.

Blade Length in Inches (millimeters)	Maximum Rotational (rpm)
18 (460)	4032
19 (485)	3820
20 (510)	3629
21 (535)	3456
22 (560)	3299
23 (585)	3155
24 (610)	3024
25 (635)	2903
26 (660)	2791

Goodheart-Willcox Publisher

Figure 9-45.

This table lists various lengths of lawn mower blades. For each length listed, the corresponding maximum rotational speed that will produce a blade tip speed of 19,000 feet per minute is also shown. It is recommended that top speeds be set 200 rpm less than shown.

Caution

If it is necessary to replace any component on an air vane governor, the top no-load rpm should be checked with an accurate tachometer. The top speed *must not exceed* the maximum recommended rpm for the implement being driven.

In the case of lawn mowers, blade tip speed should not exceed 19,000 feet per minute in a no-load condition. If necessary, change the governor spring or adjust the top speed limit device so the engine stops accelerating at the recommended rpm, which is based on blade length. See **Figure 9-45**.

Since blade tip speed is a function of blade length and engine rpm, longer blades require lower engine speeds. It is suggested that top governed engine speed be adjusted at least 200 rpm lower than the speeds shown in **Figure 9-45** to account for tachometer inaccuracy.

- **Fixed speed.** If the engine is designed to run at only one specific rpm setting, the tension of the governor spring is carefully adjusted until the speed is correct. Then, it is left at this setting, **Figure 9-46**. Fixed speed engines of this type have a limited range of governor spring adjustment. When the engine is started, the force of the airstream on the vane closes the throttle until that force is equal to spring tension.
- **Variable speed.** It is often desirable to have an engine operate at many different speeds that can be quickly and easily set by the operator.

In this case, a variable speed air vane governor is used. See **Figure 9-47**. Engine rpm is changed by pivoting the governor spring bracket. Remember, the throttle control adjusts governor spring tension. The spring is not connected directly to the throttle lever.

Vacuum Governors

Farm and industrial engines are often equipped with a vacuum governor for regulating maximum engine speed. A vacuum governor is located between the carburetor and the intake manifold. See **Figure 9-48**. It senses changes in intake manifold pressure (vacuum). There is no other mechanical connection between the governor and other parts of the engine.

As the engine speed and the suction (vacuum) increase, the governor unit closes the throttle butterfly valve. This causes a decrease in fuel flow and engine speed.

When engine speed and vacuum decrease, the spring opens the throttle valve. This action causes the fuel flow and engine speed to increase. An adjustment of spring tension is used to set the desired speed range.

Governor Features

The operating principles of the governor mechanism are quite simple and reliable. Governors provide accuracy and efficiency of operation

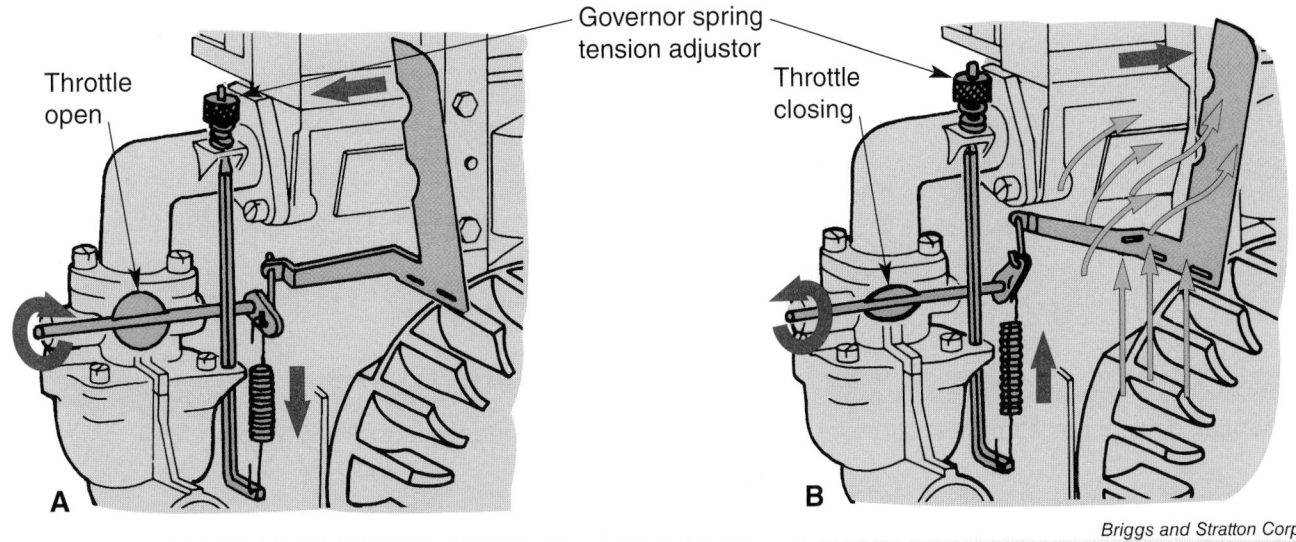

Briggs and Stratton Corp.

Figure 9-46.

Air vane governor. A—With the engine stopped, the spring holds the throttle open. B—With the engine running, air pressure pivots the vane of the fixed-speed governor and shuts the throttle valve until the spring pressure and the vane pressure are balanced. A knurled nut alters the spring tension and adjusts the speed.

combined with convenience and comfort for the operator. Two of the most important operating features of engine speed and power output governors are stability and sensitivity. *Stability* is the ability to maintain a desired engine speed without fluctuation. Instability results in hunting or oscillating due to over-correction. Excessive stability results in a dead-beat governor (one that does not correct sufficiently for load changes). *Sensitivity* is the percent of speed change required to produce a corrective movement of the throttle. The proper amount of governor sensitivity keeps the engine operating at a constant speed. Too much sensitivity can result in hunting, and too little sensitivity can result in inadequate speed correction.

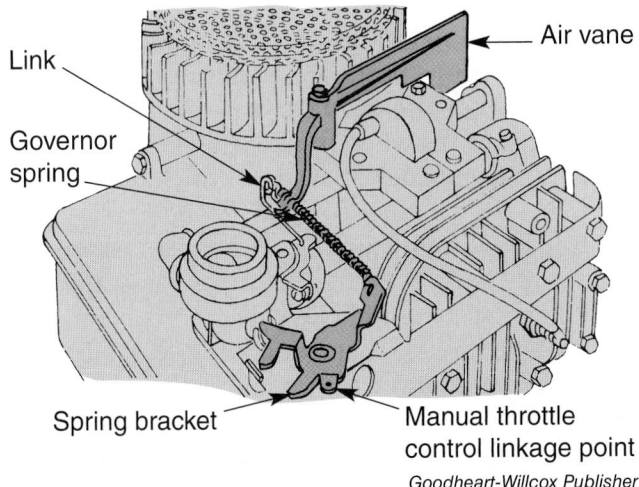

Goodheart-Willcox Publisher

Figure 9-47.

A variable speed air vane governor. To change rpm, the operator alters the governor spring tension by rotating the spring bracket. This is typically accomplished by a rod or cable linking the governor spring bracket to a throttle control.

Introduction to Electronic Fuel Injection (EFI)

As fuel prices increase and emission regulations become stricter, more and more manufacturers and commercial operators of small gas engines are turning to *electronic fuel injection (EFI)* technology. In an electronic fuel injection system, the operator controls air inlet into the system, but an onboard computer controls the amount of fuel added to the intake air. The amount of fuel injected into the intake air is based on input the computer receives from a variety of sensors. The sensors used in the system vary based on manufacturer and whether the system is an open-loop system or a closed-loop system.

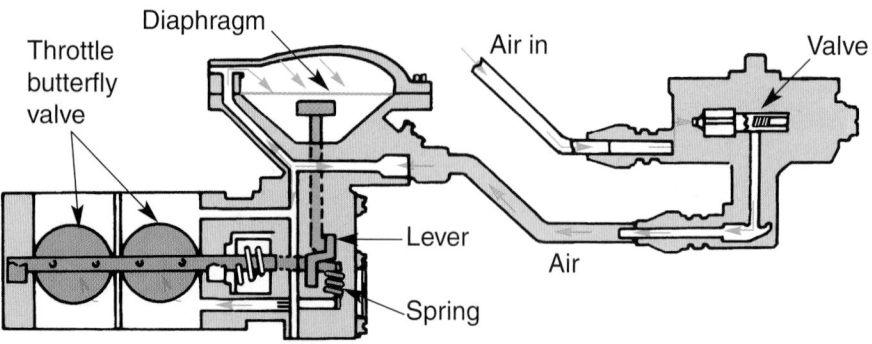

Throttle butterfly valve · Diaphragm · Air in · Valve · Lever · Air · Spring

Goodheart-Willcox Publisher

Figure 9-48.

A vacuum governor must maintain a preset maximum engine speed, independent of engine load.

Open-Loop and Closed-Loop EFI Systems

An *open-loop EFI system* relies on input from sensors and an algorithm programmed into the onboard computer to determine the proper fuel mixture. A *closed-loop EFI system* performs the same way, but the onboard computer receives feedback from the exhaust system that it uses to constantly adjust the mixture for maximum efficiency.

In both types of electronic fuel injection systems, the carburetor is replaced with a throttle body. The throttle body includes a throttle valve, like a carburetor. However, the fuel is injected into the throttle body or intake manifold by a *fuel injector* rather than being metered in by a carburetor. A sensor located in the throttle body monitors the amount of air entering the combustion chamber and sends the data to the onboard computer. This computer, referred to as an *engine control unit (ECU)*, or engine control module (ECM), also receives information about engine temperature, intake air temperature, and crankshaft position from other sensors in the system. It uses all of this information to calculate the proper charge of gasoline for the amount of air entering the cylinder. The ECU then sends a signal to the fuel injector, which sprays a metered stream of atomized fuel into the throttle body or intake manifold. This injection event is timed to coincide with the opening of the intake valve. This is where an open-loop injection cycle ends.

In a closed loop injection cycle, an oxygen (O_2) sensor in the muffler measures the level of oxygen in the exhaust gases and sends a signal to the ECU. The signal voltage will be high if the mixture is rich (relatively low oxygen level) and low if the mixture is lean (relatively high oxygen level). Based on this feedback, the ECU makes adjustments to the air-fuel mixture as needed. A simple diagram showing the difference between open-loop EFI and closed-loop EFI is shown in **Figure 9-49**.

Advantages of EFI

Electronic fuel injection provides many advantages over carburetors, including the following:

- **Improved fuel economy.** Because the ECU continually recalculates the proper air-fuel mixture as operating conditions change, the system maintains maximum efficiency.
- **Reduced exhaust emission.** Because the system injects the precise amount of fuel for the intake air charge, the amount of unburned hydrocarbons in the exhaust is minimized. The system also minimizes carbon monoxide, which results when the mixture is slightly rich, and nitrides of oxygen, which result when the mixture is slightly lean.
- **Improved cold starting.** The choke system on a carbureted engine is not a precise system. It generally has a choke valve with several preset positions that result in a rich mixture. As the engine warms up, the choke is opened to the next position, which increases airflow, leaning out the mixture. The EFI throttle body does not include a choke valve. Instead, input from system's sensors allow the ECU to precisely adjust the fuel mixture for the exact conditions at startup.
- **Improved reliability.** A carburetor has many small passages that can become clogged. In

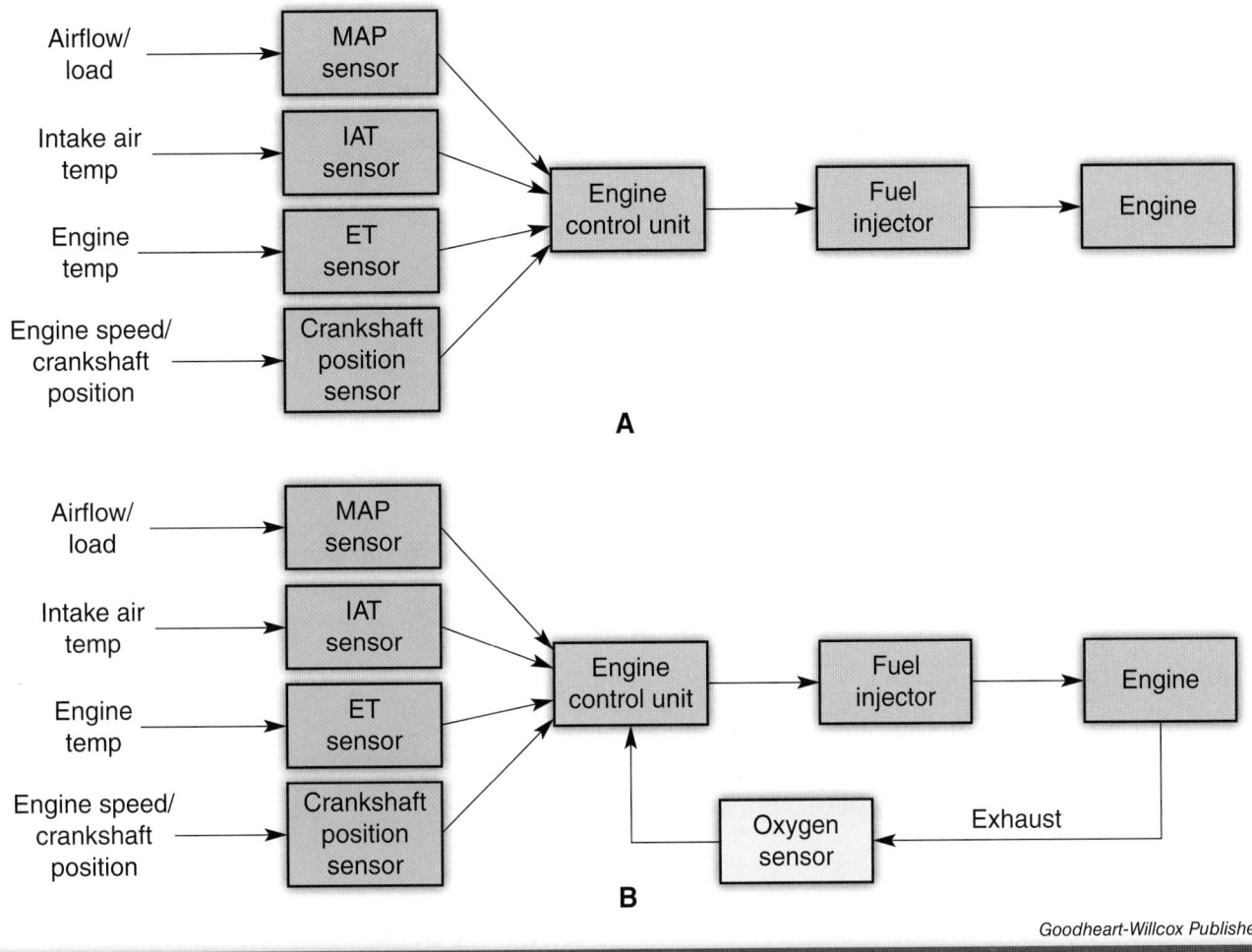

Figure 9-49.

A flowchart of EFI system operation. A—Open-loop EFI. B—Closed-loop EFI.

addition, the float system has moving parts that can fail. Most components of the EFI system are electronic. Aside from the fuel injector orifice, there are no small passages to become blocked. Because of the feedback provided by the oxygen sensor in a closed-loop system, the ECU is able to adjust for things like a partially clogged air filter, stale gasoline, or a small air leak around the throttle plate shaft.

- **Self-diagnostic capability.** The ECU constantly monitors the signals from the engine sensors. If a sensor sends a signal that is outside the expected range, the ECU will record the event and set a trouble code. The technician can use that information to diagnose problems with the system.

- **Programmability.** Fuel mixture in an EFI system is calculated using sensor input and a computer program, called *fuel mapping*. In many cases, the *fuel mapping* parameters can be modified by the technician to maximize efficiency, maximize power, or even adjust the system to work with alternative fuels, like E85 (gasoline-ethanol blend).

EFI System Components

As mentioned earlier, the specific components in an EFI system may vary from one engine to another. The following sections will describe the components commonly used in EFI systems and their functions within the system. See **Figure 9–50**.

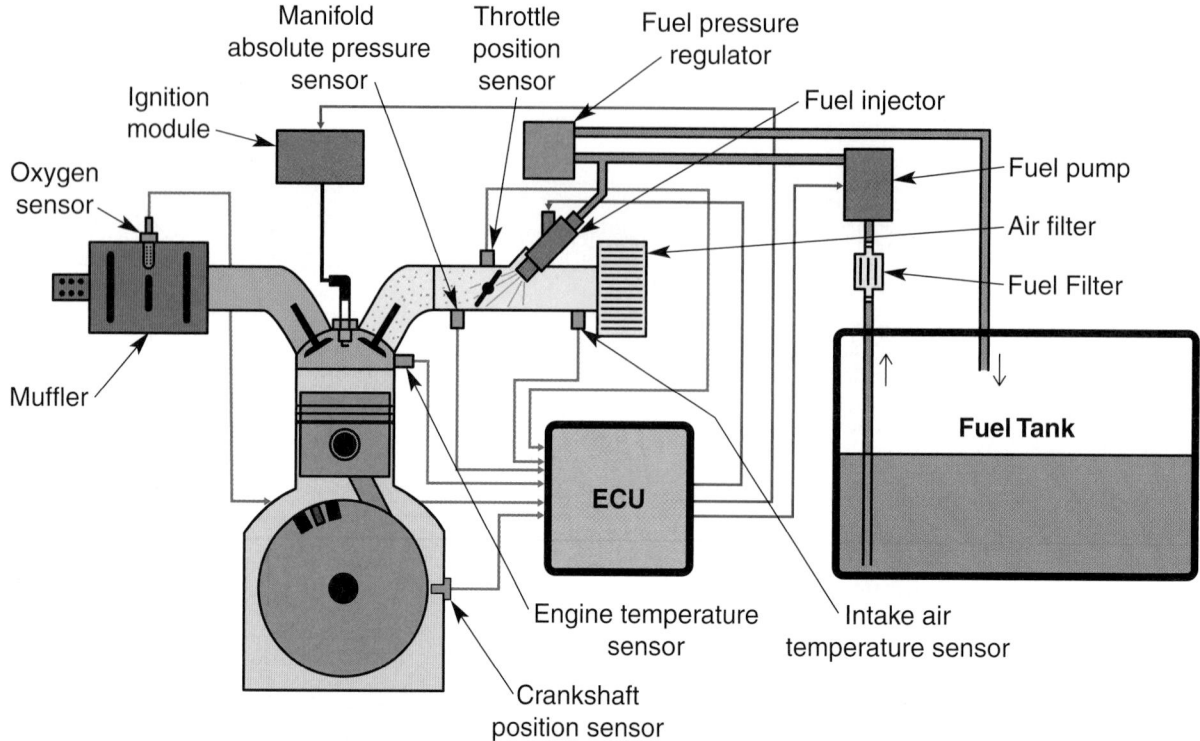

Figure 9-50.

The common components of a closed-loop EFI system.

Fuel Pump and Fuel Pressure Regulator

An EFI system relies on a steady supply of pressurized fuel at the fuel injector. These systems use a 12 V electric fuel pump to provide that fuel. The outlet of the fuel pump is connected to the fuel injector(s) and a fuel pressure regulator. The fuel pressure regulator maintains a steady pressure in the fuel line by returning excess fuel to the fuel tank.

The fuel pressure regulator may be separate from the fuel pump and connected by high-pressure fuel line, or the fuel pressure regulator may be integrated into the fuel pump. A combined fuel pump and fuel pressure regulator is commonly referred to as a fuel module.

Note

If the system is equipped with a high-pressure fuel pump, high-pressure (fuel injection) fuel line must also be used.

Fuel Injector

The fuel injector is a solenoid-operated device that sprays a measured amount of fuel into the intake airstream. When the fuel injector receives a signal from the ECU, the solenoid windings energize. This pulls in a plunger, which lifts a needle valve off its seat. The pressurized fuel from the fuel pump is allowed to pass through the orifice in the injector nozzle. As the fuel passes through the orifice, it is atomized and sprayed into the intake in a fine mist.

In EFI systems for single-cylinder engines, the fuel injector is typically mounted in the throttle body, downstream from the throttle valve. On multi-cylinder engines, there is typically an injector for each cylinder. They are usually mounted in the intake manifold, close to the engine's intake ports.

Throttle Body

The throttle body of an EFI system performs a very similar function to the throttle body of a carburetor. It contains an operator-controlled throttle valve that is used to vary the amount of air brought into the cylinders for combustion. It also houses the throttle position sensor (TPS).

On a single-cylinder engine, the throttle body bolts directly to the intake port. On single-cylinder systems, the throttle body will also house the fuel injector and MAP sensor. On a multi-cylinder engine, the throttle body is attached to the intake manifold. The fuel injectors and MAP sensor are typically separate from the throttle body.

Engine Control Unit (ECU)

The engine control unit can be thought of as the brain of the EFI system. It receives information about the amount of air being brought into the cylinders, the temperature of that air, the position of the throttle valve, and the temperature of the engine. Based on this information, it calculates the optimum amount of fuel to inject into the intake. The ECU also receives information about the position of the engine's pistons from the crankshaft position sensor.

Based on this information, the ECU sends a signal to the fuel injector just before the intake valve opens. The timing and duration of the signal are crucial. The injector must be held open just long enough to inject the precise amount of fuel needed, and at just the right time for the fuel to mix properly before it is brought into the cylinder. In closed-loop systems, the ECU receives feedback from the oxygen sensor. It uses this feedback to evaluate the effectiveness of the fuel-air mixture, and make adjustments as needed.

If the ECU receives sensor input that falls outside of the expected range, it records the event in the form of a diagnostic trouble code. When a technician connects the ECU to diagnostic software, the technician can review any diagnostic trouble codes that have been recorded. This aids in the troubleshooting of the system.

In many systems, the ECU also controls the timing of ignition events. Based on input from the crankshaft position sensor and throttle position sensor, it can advance or retard spark timing.

Sensors

As previously mentioned, EFI systems rely on input from a variety of sensors. Although EFI systems vary from engine to engine, there are a number of sensors that are found on most systems. The following sections will describe the function of those sensors.

Manifold Absolute Pressure (MAP) Sensor

The manifold absolute pressure (MAP) sensor measures the pressure of the intake air. This information, along with information about the engine speed and air temperature, is used by the ECU to determine the amount of air being drawn into the cylinder. Based on this information, the ECU determines the proper fuel charge.

Throttle Position Sensor (TPS)

The throttle position sensor is typically installed in the throttle body. It sends a voltage signal to the ECU, which varies depending on the position of the throttle plate. Based on this signal, the ECU determines not only the current throttle position, but also determines if the throttle is opening or closing, and the rate at which its position changes. The ECU uses this information to adjust fuel mixture and spark timing for acceleration, deceleration, and changes in load.

Intake Air Temperature (IAT)

The intake air temperature sensor is installed in the throttle body or the air filter housing. It sends a signal to the ECU based on the temperature of the air entering the intake. Because the temperature of the intake air will effect the air pressures in the throttle body, the ECU requires information from both the MAP sensor and the IAT sensor in order to accurately calculate the air-fuel mixture needed.

Engine Temperature (ET)

Some systems are also equipped with an engine temperature sensor. As its name implies, this sensor sends a signal to the ECU based on the temperature of the engine or, in the case of water-cooled engines, the temperature of the coolant. The ECU uses this information to richen the mixture for cold starts, and lean the mixture as the engine warms up. The ECU also uses the signal from this sensor to make adjustments to the air-fuel mixture and timing to keep the engine operating within the desired temperature range. This sensor is typically installed in the cylinder head.

Crankshaft Position (Hall-Effect) Sensor

The crankshaft position sensor sends a signal to the ECU as magnets on the flywheel rotate past a set location. The ECU uses this signal to determine engine speed, time injection events, and adjust ignition timing. The crankshaft position sensor is mounted on the engine, close to the flywheel.

Oxygen (O$_2$) Sensor

In closed-loop injection systems, the oxygen sensor provides the ECU with feedback regarding the effectiveness of the air-fuel mixture. The sensor detects whether there is excess oxygen or unburned hydrocarbons in the exhaust. Based on the feedback, the ECU adjusts the air-fuel mixture as needed. If the oxygen sensor detects unburned hydrocarbons, the ECU reduces the time that the fuel injector is kept open, resulting in less fuel in the mixture. If excess oxygen is detected, the ECU increases the time that the injector is held open, injecting more fuel into the airstream.

Oxygen sensors operate effectively only after they reach a high temperature. For this reason, the oxygen sensors typically have a heating element. The heating element brings them up to operating temperature quickly. Oxygen sensors are typically installed in the muffler or exhaust manifold.

Idle Air Control Valve

Some EFI systems are equipped with an idle air control valve. This valve provides a second passageway for air into the throttle body. A solenoid-operated plunger adjusts the amount of air allowed into the intake airstream when the throttle valve is closed. The ECU increases the amount of air allowed into the intake to increase idle speed, and decreases the amount of air to lower idle speed. If the system includes an idle air control valve, it is installed in the throttle body.

Summary

The main purpose of the carburetor is to produce a mixture of fuel and air to operate the engine. A gasoline engine cannot run on liquid gasoline. The carburetor must vaporize the fuel and mix it with air. More air than fuel is required for combustion. The average weight ratio is 15 parts air to 1 part fuel.

A carburetor is operated by pressure differences. A partial vacuum is created inside the carburetor by a venturi. A venturi is a restriction in a passage that causes air velocity to increase and pressure to decrease. Reduction in pressure draws fuel into the airstream.

Three basic types of carburetors include the natural draft, the updraft, and the downdraft. These carburetors are named according to the direction that the air flows from their outlets to the engine manifold.

Carburetors can be further classified by their operation. Some fuel systems are equipped with float-type carburetors. The purpose of a carburetor float is to maintain a constant level of fuel in the float bowl. A diaphragm carburetor does not have a float. Instead, the engine vacuum pulsates a flexible diaphragm. The diaphragm draws fuel into a chamber of the carburetor from which it is readily drawn into the venturi. A vacuum carburetor is a simple type of carburetor that draws fuel directly from the gas tank. A variation of the vacuum carburetor has an integral diaphragm fuel pump to compensate for performance problems that result from changing fuel level in the fuel tank. Some engines are equipped with an anti-afterfire solenoid, which seals off the main jet when the ignition is shut off.

A manual throttle control consists of mechanical linkage or a flexible cable that is operated manually to open and close the throttle valve. In many small engine applications, the load on the engine changes constantly. This change would require constant throttle changes on the part of the operator. Governors are systems that automatically operate the throttle valve to maintain a specific engine speed. Governors prevent overspeeding, and limit high and low speeds.

Electronic fuel injection (EFI) has replaced carburetors on some engines. In an EFI system, a variety of electronic sensors monitor engine conditions and send the data to a engine control unit (ECU). The ECU sends a signal to a fuel injector, which sprays a precise amount of fuel into the intake airstream. In a closed-loop EFI system, an oxygen sensor measures the condition of the exhaust and sends a signal back to the ECU. The ECU then adjusts the duration of injection in order to achieve proper air-fuel mixture.

Review Questions

Answer the following questions on a separate sheet of paper.

1. Starting is one operational condition that a carburetor must be able to supply the proper fuel mixture for. Name the other four.

2. During normal engine operation, the typical air-fuel mixture by weight is _____.
   A. 9 to 1
   B. 11 to 1
   C. 15 to 1
   D. 20 to 1

3. If barometric pressure on a standard day at 1500′ was 29.95″ Hg, then at 3500′ the barometric pressure would be _____. (See **Figure 9-3**.)
   A. 30.95″ Hg
   B. 31.95″ Hg
   C. 29.95″ Hg
   D. 27.95″ Hg

4. According to Bernoulli's principle, in a venturi, _____.
   A. air pressure is greatest where velocity is greatest
   B. air pressure is least where velocity is greatest
   C. velocity is least where air pressure is least
   D. air pressure is not affected by velocity

5. Name the three basic types of carburetors as defined by airflow through the carburetor.

6. Which type of carburetor would normally require a smaller air passage than the other two types?

7. Needle valve points in the carburetor float chamber are usually made from one of two materials. The two materials are _____ and _____.

8. The choke valve in the carburetor is always located _____.
   A. nearest the intake end of the carburetor
   B. nearest the engine side of the carburetor
   C. in the center of the carburetor
   D. above the float chamber level

9. The richest air-fuel mixture is created during
   _____.
   A. full throttle
   B. half throttle
   C. idle
   D. starting

10. On some carburetors, the amount of fuel that
    enters the main discharge nozzle is regulated
    by _____.
    A. the float level
    B. a load adjusting needle
    C. the idle adjustment needle
    D. a spray bar needle valve

11. The acceleration well fills when the engine is
    _____.
    A. running at steady high speed
    B. running at half throttle
    C. under heavy load
    D. idling

12. During idle and fast idle conditions, the main
    discharge nozzle is _____.
    A. discharging a small amount of fuel
    B. inoperative
    C. acting as an air bleed
    D. providing most of the fuel

13. The carburetor economizer circuit _____.
    A. reduces float bowl pressure
    B. reduces the amount of fuel discharged
       into the venturi
    C. operates only after the engine reaches part
       throttle
    D. All of the above.

14. The diaphragm in a carburetor _____.
    A. forces fuel through the main discharge
       nozzle
    B. operates only at high speed
    C. draws fuel under spring pressure
    D. draws fuel during a vacuum pulse from
       the manifold or crankcase

15. Describe the location of a vacuum carburetor
    in relation to the fuel tank.

16. *True or False?* A vacuum carburetor produces a
    leaner air-fuel mixture as the fuel level in the
    tank decreases.

17. Name the two types of primers commonly
    used on small engines.

18. The purpose of an anti-afterfire solenoid is to
    _____.
    A. prevent fuel from reaching the carburetor
       when the ignition is shut off
    B. prevent fuel from entering the main
       nozzle when the ignition is shut off
    C. drain fuel from the float bowl when the
       ignition is shut off
    D. close the throttle valve when the ignition
       is shut off.

19. Name the four basic types of small engine
    governors.

20. On a governor installation, the governor
    spring is attached to the throttle lever. The
    governor spring is intended to _____.
    A. have no effect on the throttle valve
    B. close the throttle valve
    C. open the throttle valve
    D. return the throttle lever to the off position

21. List three possible causes of hunting.

22. Briefly describe the difference between open-
    loop and closed-loop fuel injection systems.

23. In an EFI system, the volume of air intake is
    measured by the _____.
    A. mass airflow sensor
    B. oxygen sensor
    C. intake air volume sensor
    D. venturi airflow sensor

24. In an closed-loop EFI system, the ECU fine
    tunes the air-fuel based on feedback from the
    _____ sensor.

25. A(n) _____ valve has a solenoid that varies
    the amount of air allowed into the carburetor
    when the throttle valve is closed.

Suggested Activities

1. Make a venturi tube. Provide a connection so that air can be forced through the venturi. Install one pressure gauge before the restriction and one gauge in the restriction. Demonstrate what happens when the air is applied to the venturi.

2. Working with the same venturi used in activity number one, remove the pressure gauge in the restriction. Place a pickup tube in the restriction and draw water out of a beaker. Demonstrate the atomization of the water particles.

3. Make a cutaway of a float-type carburetor so that the float, needle, throttle valve, choke, and internal passages can be seen.

4. Make a working mock-up model of a variable speed centrifugal governor system that demonstrates governor principles.

5. Make a large cross-section of a float-type carburetor mounted on a board. Make the choke, throttle valve, float, and needle movable from the back. Paint the various parts, passages, and ports with bright colors. Give a demonstration to the class of choked, idle, part-throttle, and full-throttle carburetor functions.

Carburetors come in a wide variety of designs and capacities for varied applications.

Ignition Systems

Learning Objectives

After studying this chapter, you will be able to:

- Describe the primary purpose of the ignition system.
- Identify the components in a typical magneto system and describe the function of each part.
- Identify the three general classifications of magneto ignition systems and explain the operation of each.
- Describe the operation of a battery ignition system.

Key Terms

Alnico
capacitive discharge
   ignition (CDI) system
center electrode
condenser
dry-charged batteries
dwell (cam angle)
electronic switching
   devices
flashover
heat ranges
ignition advance
   system
ignition coil

insulator
magneto systems
mechanical breaker
   point ignition (MBI)
   system
mechanical breaker
   points
reach
spark plug
spark plug wire
transistor-controlled
   ignition (TCI) system
tungsten
wet-charged batteries

Basic Ignition System Operation

The primary purpose of the ignition system of a small gasoline engine is to provide sufficient electrical voltage to discharge a spark between the electrodes of the spark plug. See **Figure 10-1**. The spark must occur at exactly the right time to ignite the highly compressed air-fuel mixture in the engine's combustion chamber.

The ignition system must be capable of producing as many as 30,000 volts to force electrical current (electrons) across the spark plug gap. The intense heat created by the electrons jumping the gap ignites the air-fuel mixture surrounding the electrodes.

The rate, or number of times per minute, at which the spark must be delivered is very high. For example, a single cylinder, four-cycle engine operating at 3600 rpm requires 1800 ignition sparks per minute. A two-cycle engine running at the same speed requires 3600 sparks per minute. In multi-cylinder engines, the number of sparks per minute for one cylinder is multiplied by the number of cylinders.

Every spark must take place when the piston is at exactly the right place in the cylinder and during the correct stroke of the power cycle. Refer to *Chapter 5* of this text. Considering the high voltage required, the precise degree of timing, and the high rate of discharges, the ignition system has a remarkable job to do.

Most small gasoline engines use magneto systems to supply ignition spark. *Magneto systems* produce electrical current for ignition without any

Spark between electrodes ignites air-fuel mixture

Volodymyr Krasyuk/Shutterstock.com

Figure 10-1.

The ignition system of a small engine works hard to produce enough voltage to force electrons to jump the spark plug gap.

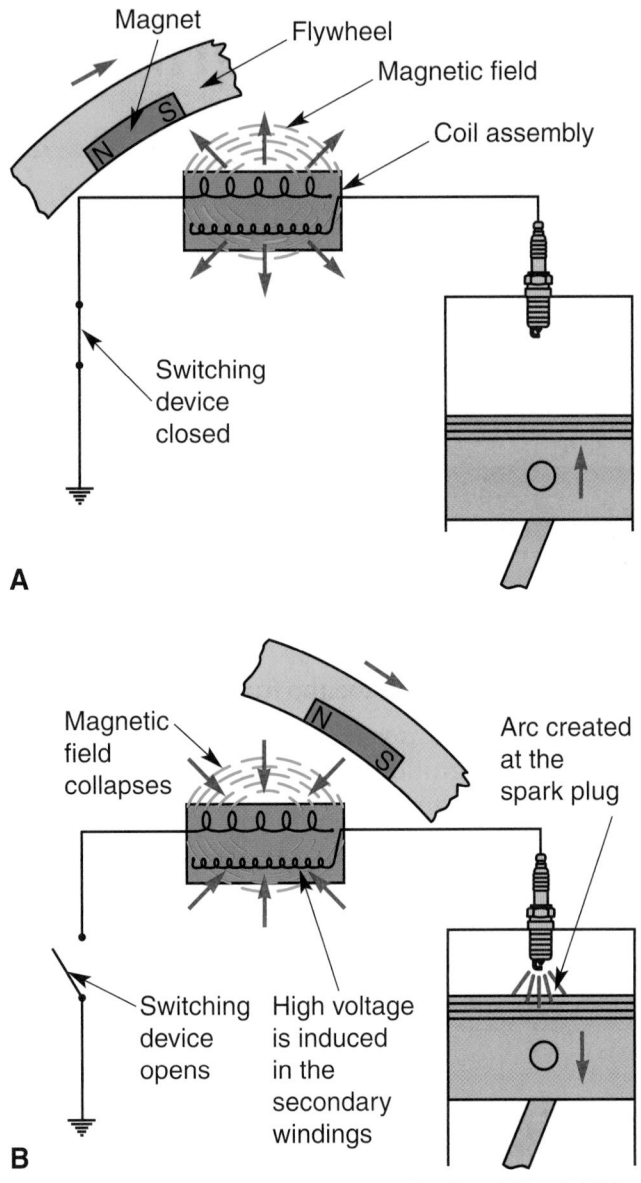

Goodheart-Willcox Publisher

Figure 10-2.

The major parts of this small engine magneto system are the switching device, coil, flywheel magnets, spark plug wire, and spark plug.

outside primary source of electricity. They serve as simple and reliable ignition systems. Basic parts of a magneto system include:

- Permanent magnets.
- Spark plug.
- Spark plug wire.
- Ignition coil.
- Switching device.

A simplified magneto ignition system is shown in **Figure 10-2**. Note that the magnets are mounted in the flywheel and rotate past the coil assembly as the flywheel spins. In **Figure 10-2A**, the switching device is closed. As the magnets move past the coil, current is induced in the coils primary windings. This current causes a magnetic field to form around the primary windings. As the engine's piston nears TDC on its compression stroke, the switching

device opens and the magnetic field in the primary windings collapses rapidly, inducing a high-voltage current in the secondary windings. The high voltage current travels to the spark plug, where it arcs across the spark plug gap and ignites the air-fuel mixture. See **Figure 10-2B**. An actual magneto ignition system is much more complex than the model shown here, but the basic operating principles are the same.

Ignition System Components

The following sections detail the components commonly used in small engine ignition systems. An understanding of the construction and operation of these individual components will help you better understand the various systems discussed later in this chapter.

Ignition Coil

The *ignition coil* used in a magneto system operates like a transformer. The coil contains two separate windings of wire insulated from each other and wound around a common laminated iron core. See **Figure 10-3**. The primary winding is heavy-gage wire with fewer turns than the secondary winding, which has many turns of light-gage wire.

When electrical current is passed through the primary winding, a magnetic field is created around the iron core. When the current is stopped, the magnetic field collapses rapidly, cutting through the secondary windings. This rapid cutting of the field by the wire in the coil induces high voltage in the secondary circuit. The high secondary voltage, in turn, causes a spark to jump the spark plug gap and ignite the air-fuel mixture.

Spark Plugs

A *spark plug* is a device inserted into the combustion chamber of an engine that ignites the compressed air-fuel mixture. At first glance, an assortment of spark plugs may look very much alike. Actually, there are many variations. Using the correct spark plug for a given engine application can greatly increase the efficiency, economy, and service life of the engine.

Figure 10-4 shows the major parts of a typical spark plug. The terminal nut is the external contact with the ignition coil. Some terminal nuts are removable, others are not. Many of the major parts of the spark plug are used to identify the actual type of the plug. Other considerations include construction, heat rating number, and firing end construction. To learn how to identify spark plug types, use the spark plug symbols chart in **Figure 10-5**.

The spark plug *insulator* is usually an aluminum-oxide ceramic material, which has excellent insulating properties. The insulator must have high mechanical strength, good heat conducting quality, and resistance to heat shock. Generally, ribs on the insulator extend from the terminal nut to the shell of the plug to prevent flashover. *Flashover* is the tendency for current to travel down the outside of the spark plug instead of through the center electrode.

The *center electrode* carries the high voltage current to the spark gap. If the electrical potential is great enough to cause the current to jump the plug gap, the side electrode will complete the circuit to ground.

The sillment seal is a compacted powder that helps ensure permanent assembly and eliminates compression leakage under all operating conditions. The inside gasket also acts as a seal between the insulator and the steel shell.

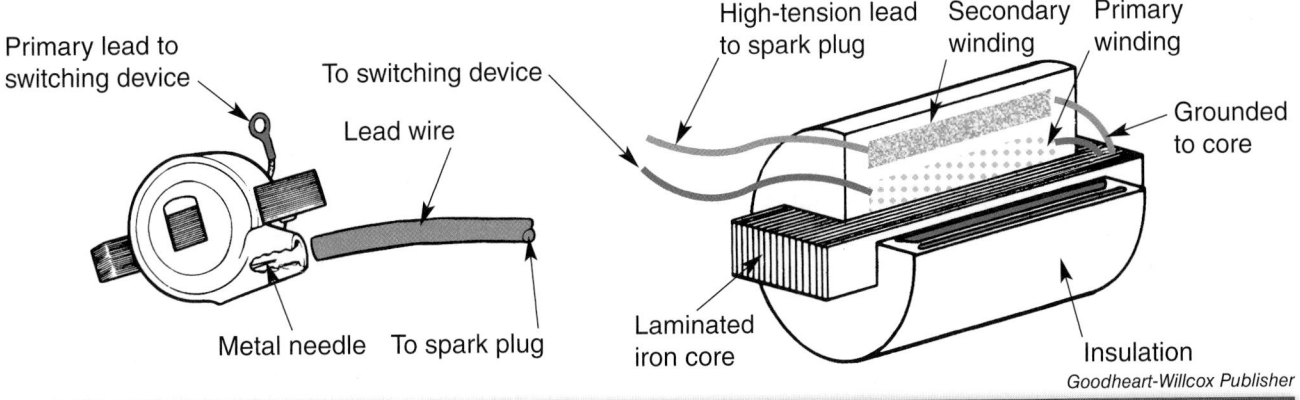

Goodheart-Willcox Publisher

Figure 10-3.

An ignition coil consists of two windings. The coil functions as a step-up transformer to produce high voltage and low amperage from low voltage and high amperage.

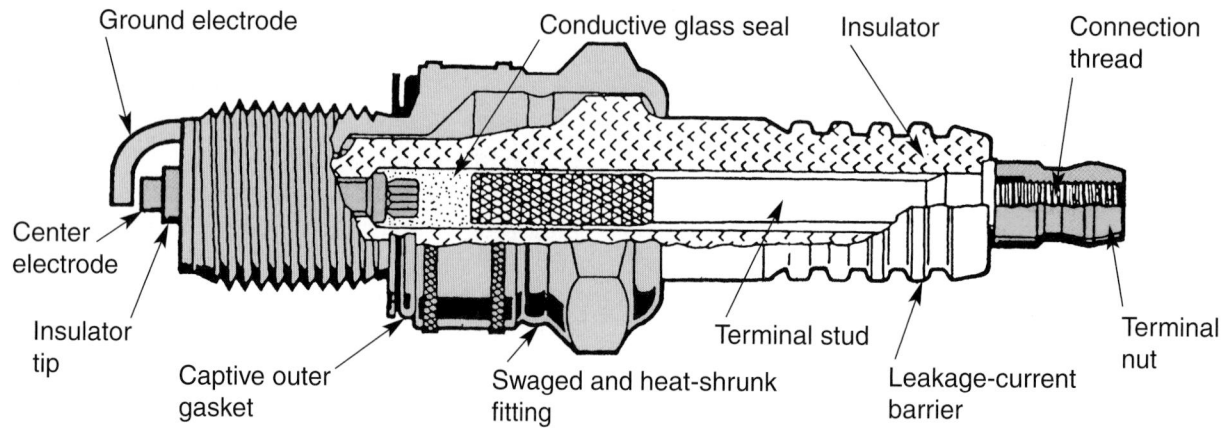

Ground electrode   Conductive glass seal   Insulator   Connection thread

Center electrode

Insulator tip

Captive outer gasket

Swaged and heat-shrunk fitting

Terminal stud

Leakage-current barrier

Terminal nut

Deere & Co.

Figure 10-4.

A spark plug carries high-voltage current produced by the ignition system. It also must withstand the high temperatures and shock of combustion, insulate the center electrode against current loss, and seal against compression leakage.

Spark plug *reach* varies with the type of spark plug. Some are long, others quite short. See **Figure 10-6**. Several standard thread sizes are commonly used. Threads on some spark plugs are metric sizes, usually 14mm.

Spark Plug Heat Transfer

Heat transfer in spark plugs is an important consideration. The heat of combustion is conducted through the plug as shown in **Figure 10-7**. Spark plugs are manufactured in various *heat ranges* from *hot* to *cold*. See **Figure 10-8**. Cold running spark plugs are those that transfer heat readily from the firing end. They are used to avoid overheating in engines having high combustion temperatures.

In figuring spark plug heat range, the length of the insulator nose determines how well and how far the heat travels. Spark plug A in **Figure 10-8**, for example, is a hot plug because the heat must travel a greater distance to the cylinder head. Spark plug D is comparatively colder than A. A cold plug installed in a cool running engine will tend to foul. Cool running usually occurs at low power levels, continuous idling, or in start/stop operation.

The tip of the insulator is the hottest part of the spark plug and its temperature can be related to preignition (firing of fuel charge prior to normal ignition) or plug fouling. Experiments show that if combustion chamber temperature exceeds 1750°F (954°C) in a four-cycle engine, preignition is likely to occur. If insulator tip temperature drops below

700°F (371°C), fouling or shorting of the plug due to carbon is likely to occur.

Spark Plug Wire

The *spark plug wire* connects the output of the ignition coil secondary windings to the spark plug. The spark plug wire is heavily insulated because it carries high voltage. If the insulation deteriorates, much of the voltage can be lost by arcing to nearby metallic parts of the engine.

Two common methods of spark plug wire connections are shown in **Figure 10-9**. Application A uses the exposed clip, which is satisfactory in uses where moisture, oil, or dirt will not get on the plug or can easily be wiped off. The boot type, shown at B, provides better plug protection.

Switching Devices

Switching devices are used in the ignition system to control the primary current to the ignition coil. The switching devices are either mechanical or electronic.

The ignition systems in some older engines use *mechanical breaker points* to control primary current to the coil. The breaker points generally consist of two tungsten contacts. One contact point is stationary, the other is movable. Each contact is fastened to a bracket. *Tungsten* is a hard metal with a high melting temperature. These characteristics

Spark Plugs
Spark Plug Code Interpretation

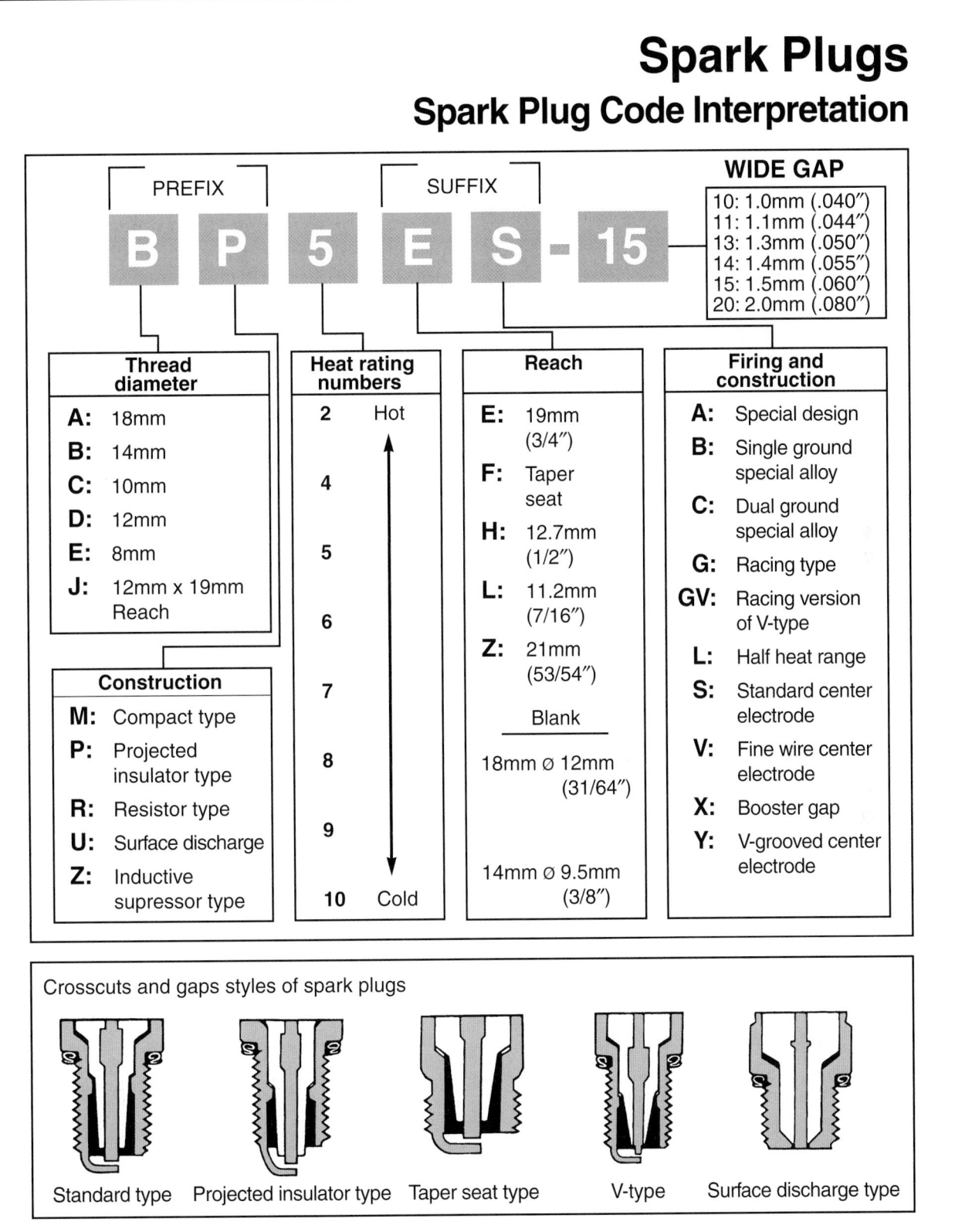

WIDE GAP

10: 1.0mm (.040″)
11: 1.1mm (.044″)
13: 1.3mm (.050″)
14: 1.4mm (.055″)
15: 1.5mm (.060″)
20: 2.0mm (.080″)

PREFIX · SUFFIX

B P 5 E S - 15

Thread diameter

A: 18mm
B: 14mm
C: 10mm
D: 12mm
E: 8mm
J: 12mm x 19mm Reach

Construction

M: Compact type
P: Projected insulator type
R: Resistor type
U: Surface discharge
Z: Inductive supressor type

Heat rating numbers

2   Hot
4
5
6
7
8
9
10 Cold

Reach

E: 19mm (3/4″)
F: Taper seat
H: 12.7mm (1/2″)
L: 11.2mm (7/16″)
Z: 21mm (53/54″)

Blank

18mm ⌀ 12mm (31/64″)

14mm ⌀ 9.5mm (3/8″)

Firing and construction

A: Special design
B: Single ground special alloy
C: Dual ground special alloy
G: Racing type
GV: Racing version of V-type
L: Half heat range
S: Standard center electrode
V: Fine wire center electrode
X: Booster gap
Y: V-grooved center electrode

Crosscuts and gaps styles of spark plugs

Standard type   Projected insulator type   Taper seat type   V-type   Surface discharge type

Goodheart-Willcox Publisher

Figure 10-5.

This chart explains how to identify spark plugs.

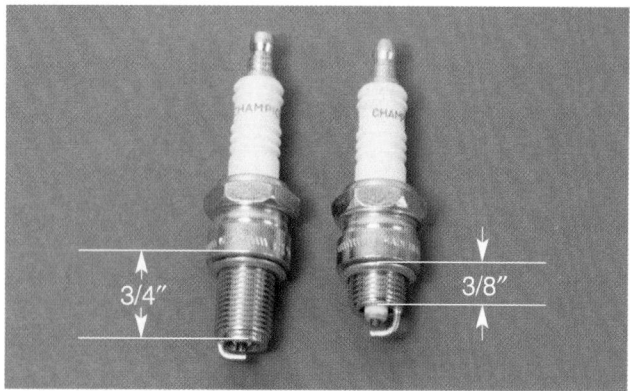

Goodheart-Willcox Publisher

Figure 10-6.

Spark plug reach (length of thread) can vary considerably from one plug to another. Too long a reach can damage a piston. Too short a reach provides poor combustion.

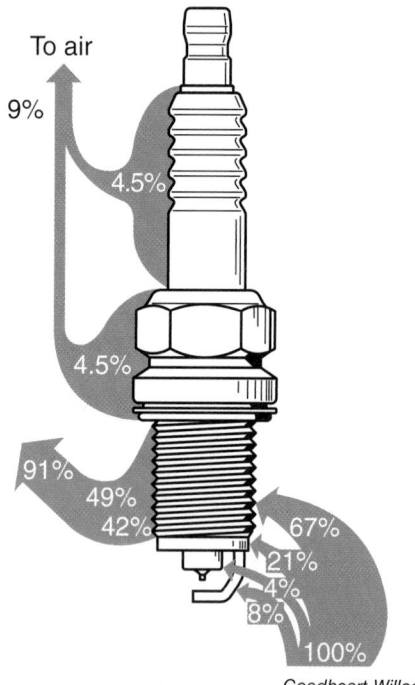

Goodheart-Willcox Publisher

Figure 10-7.

The heat of ignition and combustion must be conducted away from critical parts of the spark plug to prevent preignition and burning of the electrodes.

are needed to withstand the continual opening and closing that takes place and the eroding effect of the arc that occurs when the points *break* (start to open).

The ignition systems in most engines use *electronic switching devices* to control the primary current to the coil. An electronic switching device is

more dependable than a mechanical type because it has no moving parts to wear or burn out.

Magneto Ignition Systems

There are several types of magneto systems used on small engines. These systems are classified by the type of switching device they use to control primary current to the coil. Mechanical breaker point ignition (MBI) systems use mechanical breaker points to control current in the ignition coil. This type of system was used exclusively until the development of the solid state ignition system. Today, all ignition systems in late-model engines are of the solid state type. Solid state systems use electronic devices (transistors, capacitors, diodes, etc.) to control various ignition system functions. Solid state ignition systems provide many advantages over mechanical systems:

- Since there are no moving parts, mechanical adjustments are not required.
- No breaker points to burn, pit, or replace.
- Increase spark plug life.
- Easy starting, even with fouled plugs.
- Higher spark output and faster voltage rise.
- Spark advance is electronic and automatic. It never needs adjusting.
- Electronic unit is hermetically sealed and unaffected by dust, dirt, oil, or moisture.
- System delivers uniform performance throughout component life and under adverse operating conditions.
- Improves idling and provides smoother power under load.

The following are the three general classifications of magneto ignition systems.

1. A capacitive discharge ignition (CDI) system is a solid state (no moving parts) system that stores its primary energy in a capacitor and uses semiconductors for timing or triggering the system.
2. A transistor-controlled ignition (TCI) system is an inductive system that does not use mechanical breaker points. It utilizes semiconductors (transistors, diodes, etc.) for switching purposes.
3. A mechanical breaker point ignition (MBI) system is a flywheel magneto inductive system commonly used for internal combustion engines until the mid-1980s. It employs mechanical breaker points to time or trigger the system.

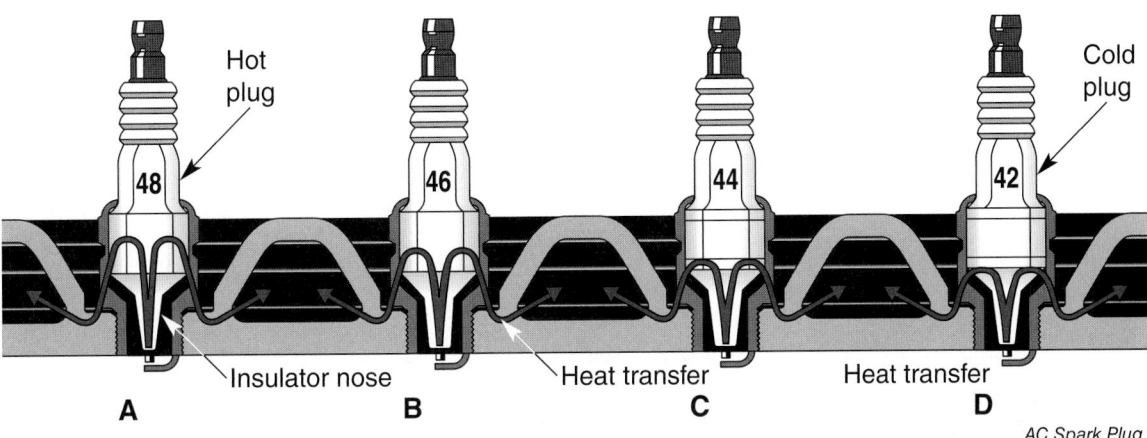

Figure 10-8.

Spark plug heat transfer determines whether the plug is hot or cold. Heat is controlled by the insulator nose.

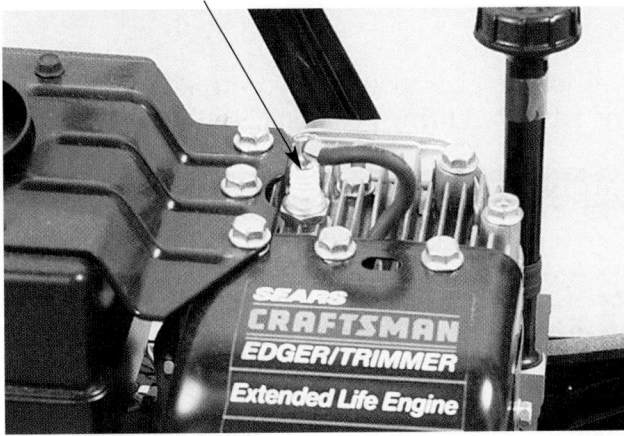

A

B

Goodheart-Willcox Publisher

Figure 10-9.

Two common spark plug wire connectors. A—Exposed type. B—Neoprene-boot type. An exposed clip connector can be used in conjunction with a metal strip stop switch.

Note

Figure 10-10 compares these three types of magneto ignition systems. Study them carefully!

Operation of Capacitive Discharge Ignition (CDI) System

The *capacitive discharge ignition (CDI) system* is a solid state ignition system. It is standard equipment in many applications and has improved the reliability of modern small gasoline engines. The only moving parts in a CDI system are the permanent magnets in the flywheel. **Figure 10-11** shows a CDI module installed on a small gasoline engine. Refer to **Figure 10-12** to progressively trace current flow through the various electronic components in a typical CDI system.

As the flywheel magnets rotate across the CDI module laminations, they induce a low voltage alternating current (ac) in the charge coil. The ac passes through a rectifier and is changed to direct current (dc), which travels to the capacitor, where it is stored.

When the silicon controlled rectifier is triggered, the 300V dc stored in the capacitor travels to the spark coil. At the coil, the voltage is stepped up instantly to a maximum of 30,000V. This high voltage current is discharged across the spark plug gap.

In **Figure 10-13**, the flywheel magnets rotate approximately 351° before passing the CDI module laminations and inducing a small electrical charge

Comparisons	Mechanical Breaker Ignition System	Transistor Controlled Ignition System	Capacitor Discharge Ignition System
Abbreviation	MBI	TCI	CDI
Circuit type	Conventional	Solid state	Solid state
Energy source	Primary current of ignition coil	Primary current of ignition coil	Stored in capacitor
Trigger switch	Breaker contacts	Power transistor	Thyristor
Secondary voltage	Standard	Standard	Higher
Spark duration	Standard	Standard	Shorter
Rise time*	Standard	Standard	Shorter
Maximum operating speed	Standard	Higher	Higher
Maintenance	Regap and retime	None	None

*Rise time–time required for maximum voltage to occur.

Goodheart-Willcox Publisher

Figure 10-10.

This chart compares mechanical breaker point, transistor-controlled, and capacitor discharge ignition systems.

in the trigger coil. At starting speeds, this electrical charge is just great enough to turn on the silicon controlled rectifier (SCR) in a retarded firing position (9° BTDC). This provides for easy starting.

In **Figure 10-14**, when the engine reaches approximately 800 rpm, advanced firing begins. The flywheel magnets travel approximately 331°, at which time enough voltage is induced in the trigger

coil to energize the silicon controlled rectifier in the advanced firing position (29° BTDC).

Note

On some small engines equipped with electronic fuel injection, the engine control unit (ECU) calculates the proper ignition timing based on engine operating conditions. In these systems, engine sensors feed information on engine operation to the ECU. The ECU then prompts the ignition module to fire the spark plugs at the proper time based on the sensor inputs. These systems provide precise control of spark timing for improved engine operating efficiency.

Operation of Transistor-Controlled Ignition (TCI) System

The individual components that make up the *transistor-controlled ignition (TCI) system* are given in a chart in **Figure 10-15**. Study the function of each part carefully.

There are a variety of transistor-controlled circuits. Each has its own unique characteristics and modifications. **Figure 10-16** illustrates a typical circuit for a transistor-controlled ignition. Refer to this circuit as its principles are described in the following section.

As the engine flywheel rotates, the magnets on the flywheel pass by the ignition coil. The magnetic

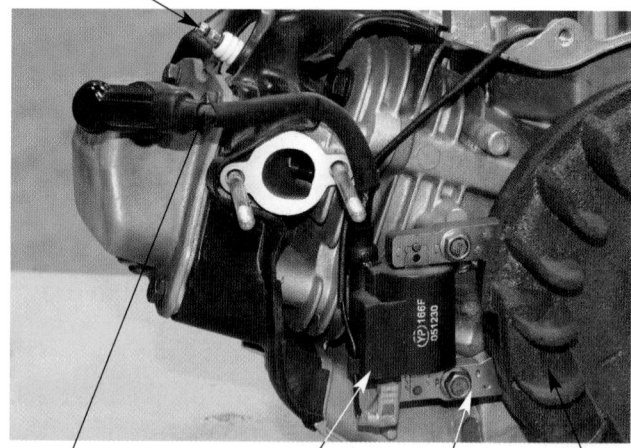

Spark plug

Spark plug wire   Module Laminations Flywheel

Goodheart-Willcox Publisher

Figure 10-11.

The CDI ignition module is compact and maintenance free. The only moving parts in a CDI system are the flywheel magnets.

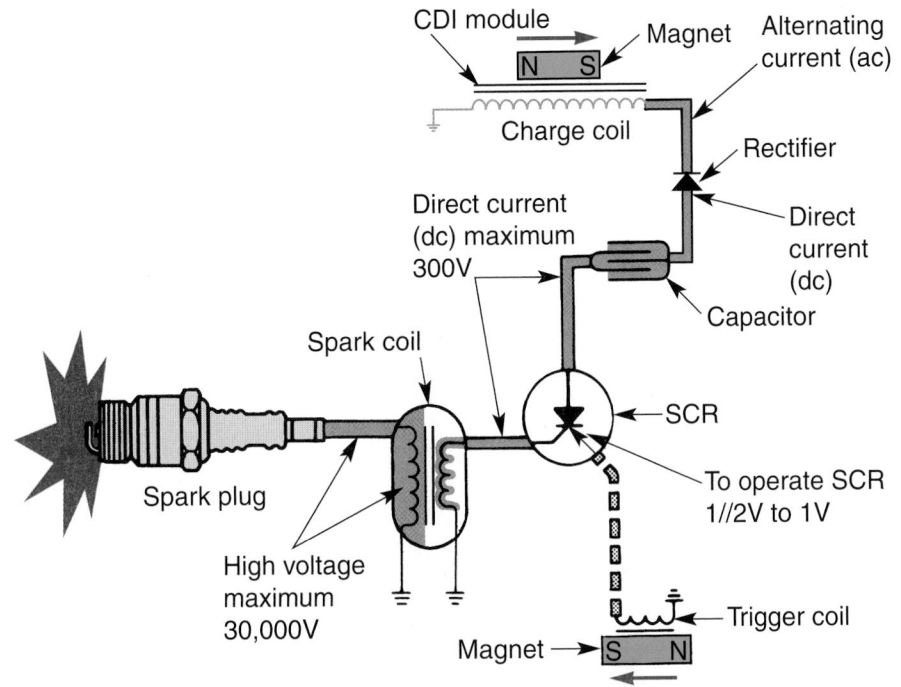

Goodheart-Willcox Publisher

Figure 10-12.

The flywheel magnets induce a low-voltage alternating current in the charge coil. As the alternating current passes through the rectifier, it is changed to direct current. The direct current continues to the capacitor, where it builds up a charge. When the capacitor nears its full charge, the flywheel magnets induce a small current in the trigger coil. The current briefly activates the silicon controlled rectifier (SCR), which allows the 300V stored in the capacitor to discharge through the primary windings of the spark coil. This induces a much higher voltage in the secondary windings, which fires the spark plug.

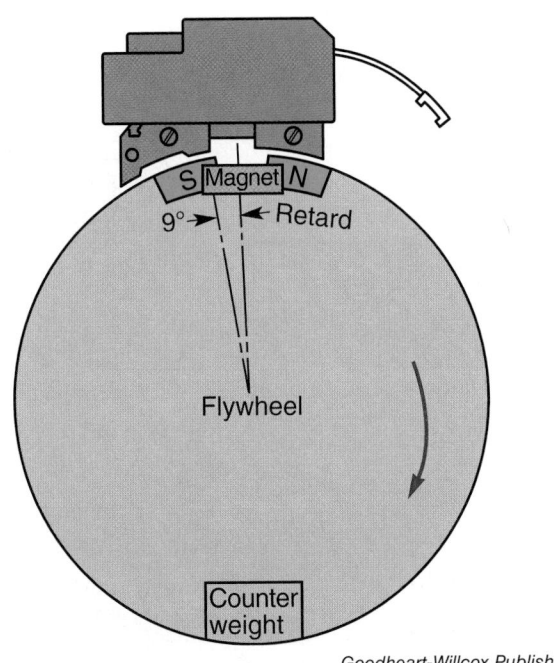

Goodheart-Willcox Publisher

Figure 10-13.

At low speeds, the flywheel magnets induce a small current in the trigger coil, which turns on a silicon rectifier at 9° BTDC for easy starting.

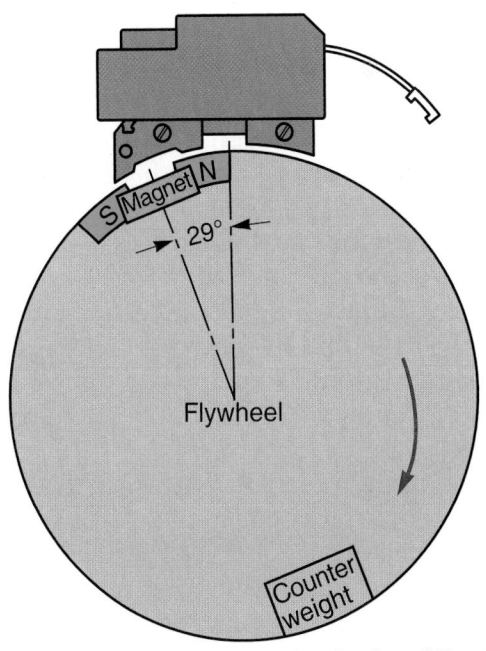

Goodheart-Willcox Publisher

Figure 10-14.

At 800 rpm, stronger trigger coil current turns on the silicon rectifier at 29° BTDC for satisfactory ignition during normal engine operation.

Diode (D1, D2)	A ▸|◂ K	Allows one way current from Anode "A" to Cathode "K" as rectifier.
Flywheel		Provides magnetic flux to primary windings of ignition coil.
High-tension lead		Conducts high voltage current in secondary windings to spark plug.
Ignition coil		Generates primary current, and transforms primary low voltage to secondary high voltage.
Ignition switch		No spark across gap of spark plug when switch is at "STOP" position.
Resistor (R1, R2)		Resists current flow.
Spark plug		Ignites fuel-air mixture in cylinder.
Thyristor (S)	A ▸|◂ K G	Switches from blocking state to conducting state when trigger current/voltage is on gate "G."
Transistor (T, T1, T2)	C B E	Very small current in the base circuit (B to E) controls and amplifies very large current in the collector circuit (C to E). When the base current is cut, the collector current is also cut completely.

Goodheart-Willcox Publisher

Figure 10-15.

Study the components of transistor-controlled ignition systems.

field around the magnets induces current in the primary windings of the ignition coil.

The base circuit of the ignition system has current flow from the coil primary windings, common grounds, resistor (R1), base of the transistor (T1), emitter of the transistor (T1), and back to the primary windings of the ignition coil.

Current flow for the collector circuit in **Figure 10-16** is from the primary windings of the coil, common grounds, collector of transistor (T1), emitter of transistor (T1), and back to the primary windings.

When the flywheel rotates further, the induced current in the coil primary increases. When the current is high enough, the control circuit turns on and begins to conduct current. This causes transistor (T2) to turn on and conduct. A strong magnetic field forms around the primary winding of the ignition coil.

The trigger circuit for this ignition system consists of the primary windings, common grounds,

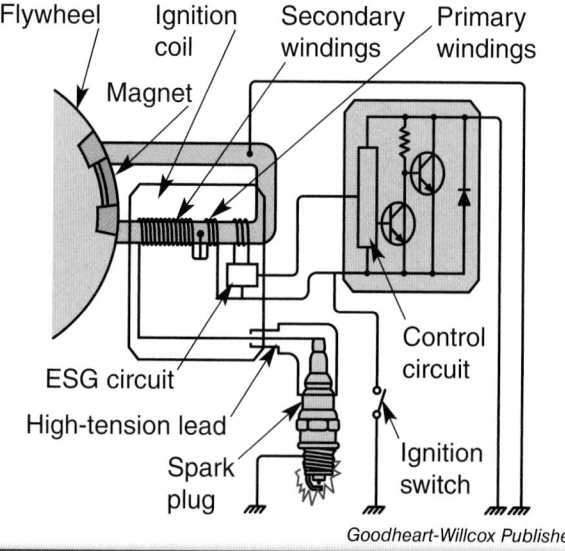

Goodheart-Willcox Publisher

Figure 10-16.

Study how this transistor circuit is used to operate the ignition coil. Note differences and similarities.

control circuit, base of transistor (T2), and emitter of transistor (T2).

When transistor (T2) begins to conduct current, the base current flow is cut. This causes the collector circuit to shut off, and the transistor (T1) stops conducting current.

When transistor (T1) stops conducting, current stops flowing through the primary of the ignition coil. This causes the primary magnetic field to collapse across the secondary windings of the ignition coil. High voltage is then induced into the secondary winding to fire the spark plug.

The secondary circuit includes the coil secondary windings, spark plug wire, spark plug, and common grounds returning to the coil secondary.

When the ignition switch is off, the primary circuit is grounded to prevent the plug from firing. Diode (D1) is installed in the circuit to protect the TCI module from damage.

The ESG circuit shown in **Figure 10-16** is used to retard the ignition timing. At high engine rpm, the ESG circuit conducts. This bypasses the trigger circuit and delays when the current reaches the base of transistor (T2).

Operation of the Mechanical Breaker Point Ignition (MBI) System

For many years, the *mechanical breaker point ignition (MBI) system* supplied the ignition spark on most small engines. Major components and operation of a typical MBI system are illustrated in **Figure 10-17**. The coil, condenser, and breaker points may be found inside or outside of the flywheel. This varies with engine type, but the principles of operation remain basically the same.

The *condenser* plays an important part in MBI system operation. Its primary purpose is to prevent current from arcing across the breaker point gap as the points open. If arcing were to occur, it would burn the points and absorb most of the magnetic energy stored in the ignition coil. Not enough energy would be left in the coil to produce the necessary high voltage surge in the secondary circuit. The condenser absorbs current the instant the breaker points begin to separate. Since the condenser absorbs most of the current, little is left to form an arc between the points.

Magnets are usually cast into the flywheel and cannot be removed. They are strong permanent magnets made of *Alnico* (aluminum, nickel, cobalt alloy) or a ceramic magnetic material.

The breaker points in the MBI system are mechanically actuated, opened by the cam and closed by the breaker point spring. As the flywheel turns, the magnets pass over the legs of the laminated core of the coil. When the north pole of the magnet is over the center leg of the coil, the magnetic lines of force move down the center leg through the coil, across the bottom of the lamination, and up the side leg to the south pole. See **Figure 10-17**.

As the flywheel continues to turn, the north pole of the magnet comes over the side leg and the south pole is over the center leg of the core. Now the lines of force move from the north pole down through the side leg, up through the center leg and coil, and to the south pole. At this point, the lines of force have reversed direction.

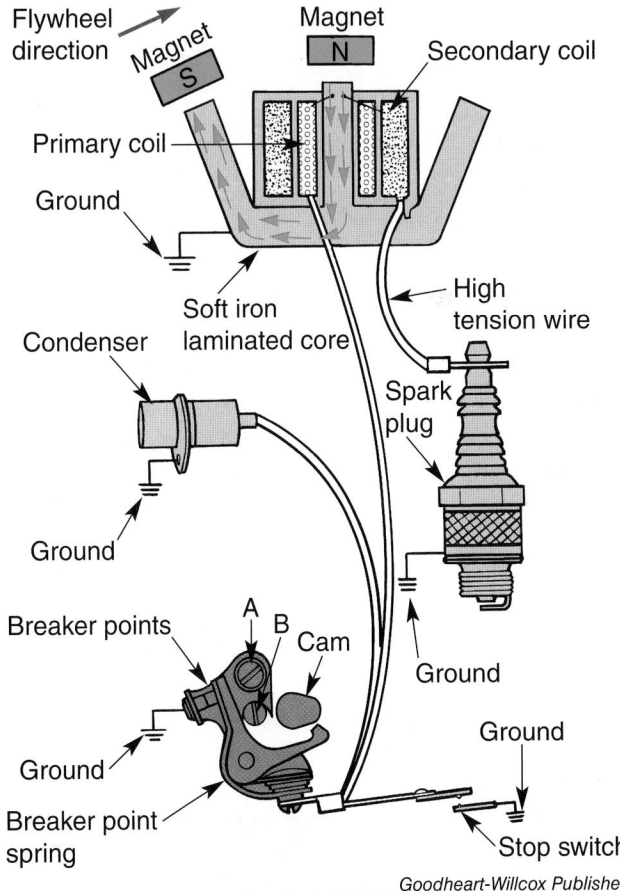

Goodheart-Willcox Publisher

Figure 10-17.

Typical MBI system. As the magnets on the flywheel align with the legs on the core, a magnetic field is established through the core.

Figure 10-18 shows the field reversal taking place in the center leg of the core and coil. The reversal induces low-voltage current in the primary circuit through the breaker points. Current flowing in the primary winding of the coil creates a primary magnetic field of its own, which reinforces and helps maintain the direction of the lines of force in the center leg of the lamination. It does this until the magnets' poles move into a position where they can force the existing lines of force to change direction in the center leg of the lamination. Just before this happens, the breaker points are opened by the cam.

Opening of the points breaks the primary circuit, and the primary magnetic field collapses through the turns of the secondary winding. See **Figure 10-19**.

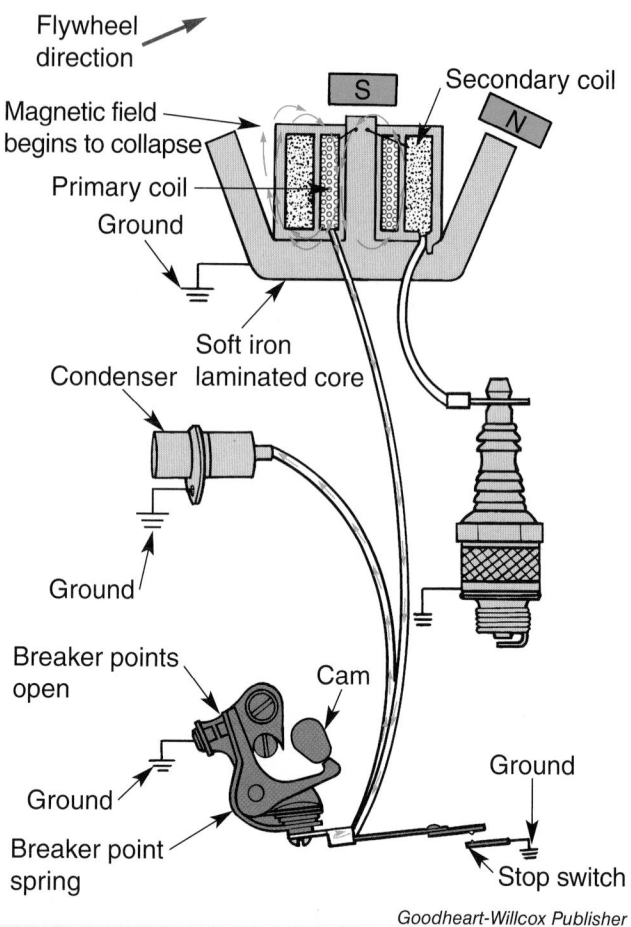

Goodheart-Willcox Publisher

Figure 10-19.

When the breaker points open, the magnetic field around the primary windings collapses quickly through the secondary windings. This induces high voltage in the secondary windings, which is required to fire the spark plug. The field collapse also cuts through the primary windings, where it induces a moderate voltage that is absorbed by the condenser.

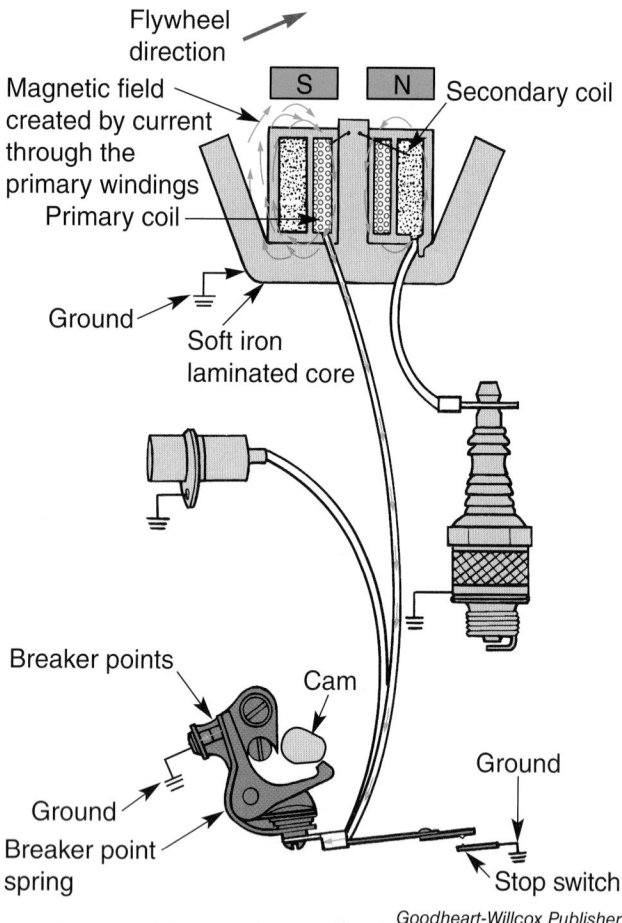

Goodheart-Willcox Publisher

Figure 10-18.

The change in the magnetic field through the core induces a voltage in the primary circuit. Since the breaker points are closed, the current is able to flow through the circuit. The current through the primary windings builds a magnetic field that passes through the secondary windings.

The condenser makes the breaking of the primary current as instantaneous as possible by absorbing the surge of primary current to prevent arcing between the breaker points.

As the magnetic field collapses through the secondary winding of the coil, high voltage is induced in the secondary winding. At exactly the same time, the charge stored in the condenser surges back into the primary winding, **Figure 10-20**, and reverses the direction of current in the primary windings. This change in direction sets up a reversal in direction of the magnetic field cutting through the secondary and helps increase the voltage in the secondary circuit. The high-voltage potential causes secondary current to arc across the spark plug gap.

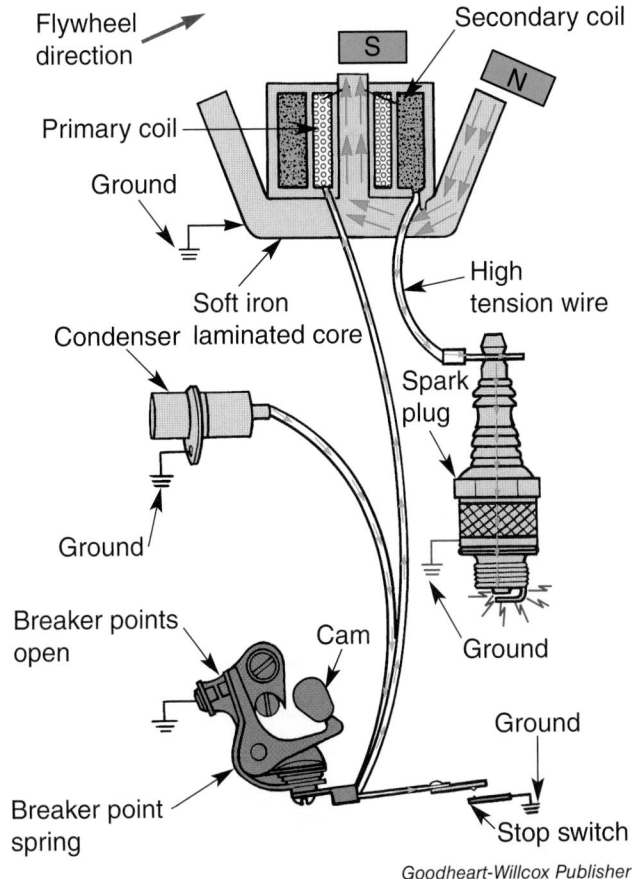

Flywheel direction

Secondary coil

S

N

Primary coil

Ground

Soft iron laminated core

High tension wire

Condenser

Spark plug

Ground

Ground

Breaker points open

Cam

Ground

Breaker point spring

Stop switch

Goodheart-Willcox Publisher

Figure 10-20.

The spark plug fires, and the condenser discharges voltage back into the primary circuit.

Dwell (cam angle) is the time the breaker points stay closed during one revolution of the cam. Dwell is measured in degrees of cam rotation from the point of closing to the point of opening. There is an inverse relationship between the breaker point gap setting and dwell time. With a wider breaker point gap setting, dwell decreases. A narrower gap setting increases dwell.

Remember that the cam is driven directly from the crankshaft. When the breaker points open, the spark plug fires. Obviously, then, changing the point setting can also change spark timing. The engine manufacturer specifies which gap setting is best (usually between .020″ to .030″) and the number of degrees before top dead center (BTDC) that the spark should occur.

Some MBI systems have mechanical *ignition advance systems* that retard occurrence of spark for starting. For intermediate- and high-speed operation, the system causes the spark to occur earlier in the cycle.

Magneto Ignition Systems for Two-Cylinder Engines

The magneto systems used in two-cylinder engines must fire the spark plug in each cylinder at the correct time. This is accomplished in one of two ways. Some systems use two coil assemblies to fire the plugs. These assemblies are mounted near the flywheel and are located 180° apart. As the magnets in the flywheel move past each assembly, the corresponding spark plug fires at the proper time.

Other two-cylinder engines use a waste-spark system to fire the spark plugs. In this type of system, the coil assembly has two secondary outputs and fires both spark plugs at the same time. The spark occurs when the piston in one cylinder is on its compression stroke and the piston in the other cylinder is on its exhaust stroke. The spark that occurs during a cylinder's exhaust stroke has no effect on engine operation and is, therefore, considered a "waste" spark.

Battery Ignition Systems

The battery ignition system has a low-voltage primary circuit and a high-voltage secondary circuit. Like the magneto system, it consists of a coil, solid state switching device (or points and condenser), and spark plug. The basic difference is that the source of current for the primary circuit is supplied by a lead-acid battery. See **Figure 10-21**.

When the ignition switch is turned on, current flows from the positive post of the battery to the ignition coil. Current traveling through the primary windings of the coil builds up a magnetic field. See **Figure 10-22**. During this time, the switching device is closed. Ignition at the plug is not required, so the current returns to the battery through the common ground.

Then, at the exact time when ignition at the plug is required, the switching device opens. Current flow stops abruptly, causing the magnetic field surrounding the coil to collapse. See **Figure 10-23**. This rapid change of magnetic flux causes voltage to be induced in every turn of the secondary windings.

The voltage built up in the secondary winding of the coil can become as high as 30,000V. The secondary windings have approximately 100 times as many turns of wire as the primary. Normally, the voltage does not reach this value. Once it becomes

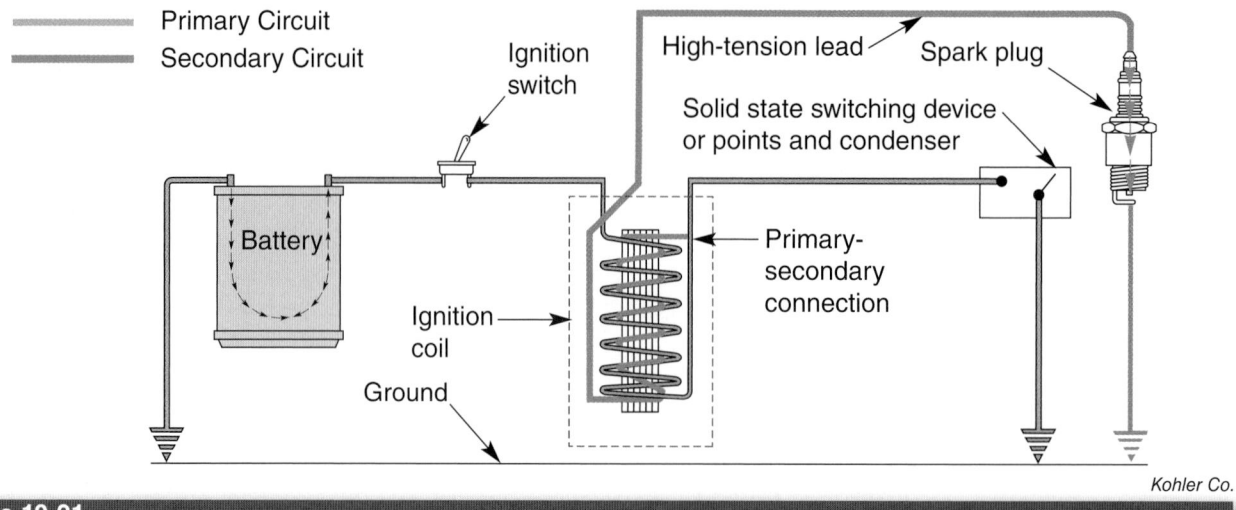

Kohler Co.

Figure 10-21.

A battery ignition system is similar to a magneto system, except that the battery replaces the flywheel magnets.

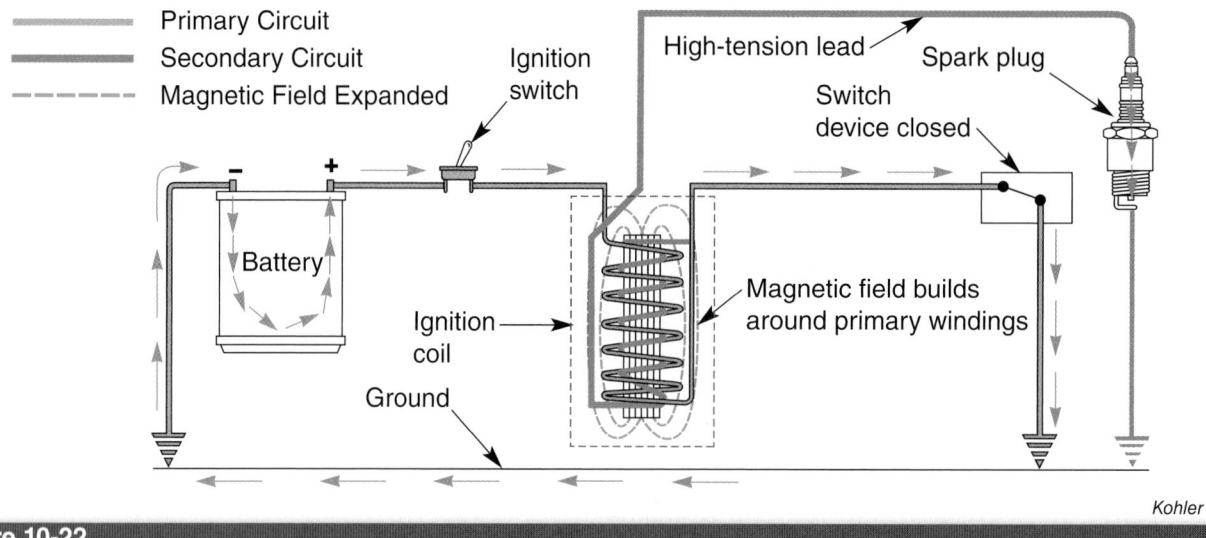

Kohler Co.

Figure 10-22.

When the switching device closes in a battery ignition system, primary current builds a magnetic field around the coil.

great enough to jump the spark plug gap, the voltage drops. Usually, the amount required to jump the gap is between 6000V and 20,000V. The actual amount of voltage required depends on variables such as compression, engine speed, shape and condition of electrodes, spark plug gap, etc.

Ignition Coil

The ignition coil used in battery ignition systems serves as a step-up transformer. It increases low-voltage primary current to the high voltage required to bridge the spark plug gap. The primary and sec-

ondary windings are connected, and the common ground of the battery and primary circuit is used to complete the secondary circuit.

With this type of coil, very little primary current can flow into the secondary circuit because the secondary circuit is normally open at the spark plug gap. Primary current is just not great enough to jump the gap. Therefore, the two circuits function separately.

The primary winding of the coil consists of about 200 turns of heavy copper wire. The secondary winding has approximately 20,000 turns of very fine copper wire. Because the magnetic field collapses

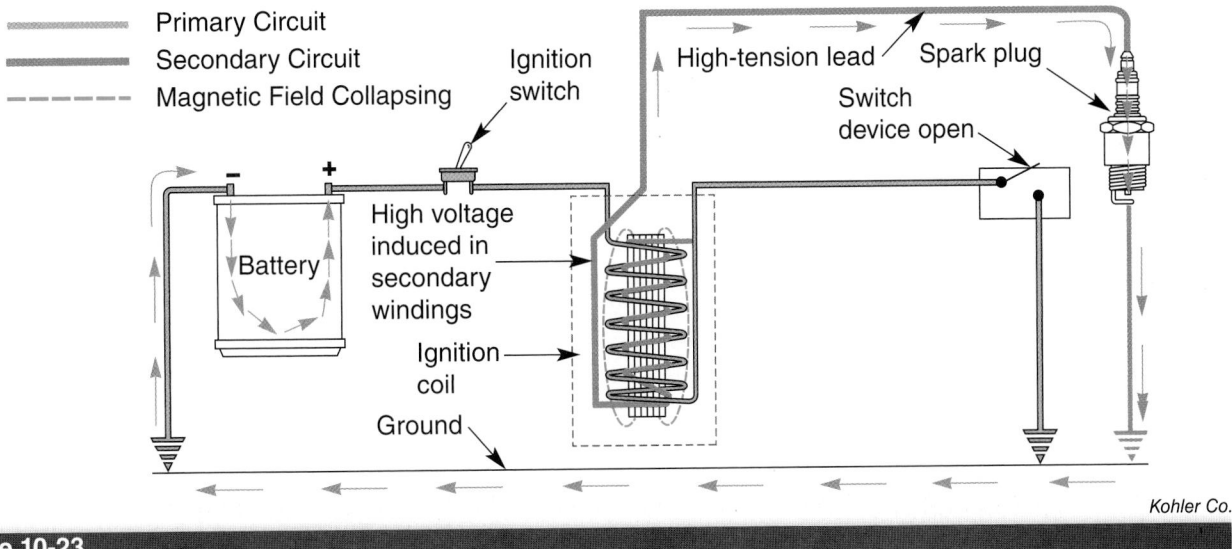

Kohler Co.

Figure 10-23.

The switching device opens and the field collapses, inducing high voltage in the secondary windings of the coil.

through such a great number of conductors in the secondary, a very high voltage is developed. The amperage, however, is proportionately low. This is a typical characteristic of any transformer.

Laminated iron is used as the center core of the coil. It also forms the outer shell of the inner assembly, providing maximum concentration of the magnetic field. The inner assembly is sealed in a coil case, and the remaining space inside is filled with a special oil to minimize the effects of heat, moisture, and vibration.

The top of the coil is provided with two primary terminals. They are marked positive (+) and negative (–). The positive terminal must be connected to the positive side of the battery. The negative terminal connects to the switching device. The center tower of the coil contains the high-tension terminal.

Lead-Acid Battery

The battery is the sole source of energy for the battery ignition system of a small gasoline engine. A generator is used to replenish energy in the battery. However, the generator does not supply energy directly to the ignition system.

Lead-acid type batteries are used in battery ignition systems. The cell plates are made of lead, and a sulfuric acid and water solution serves as the electrolyte. Wet-charged or dry-charged types are available. *Wet-charged batteries* are supplied

with the electrolyte in them, ready for use if the charge has been kept up. *Dry-charged batteries* must have electrolyte installed after purchase. Both types of batteries function in the same way.

Battery Construction

The typical 12V battery is constructed with a hard rubber case and six separate compartments called cells. See **Figure 10-24**. There are a specific

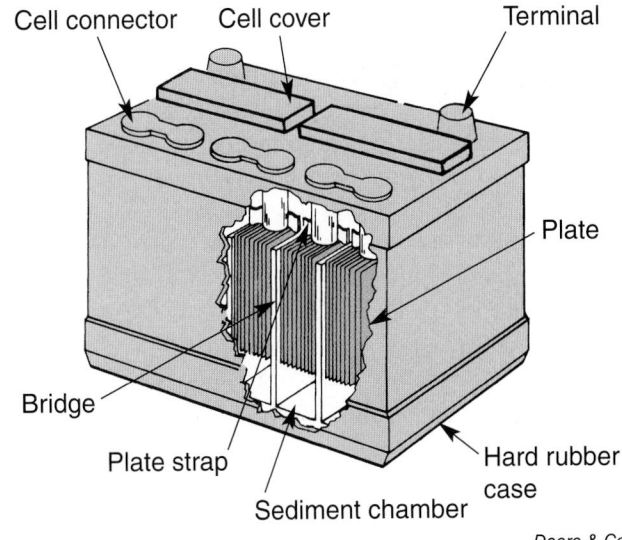

Deere & Co.

Figure 10-24.

A battery provides all the current for a battery ignition system. A 12V battery has six cells, each producing approximately 2V.

number of negative and positive plates in each cell. The greater the number of plates per cell, the higher the ampere-hour rating (capacity to provide current for a specific length of time) of the battery. The positive plates have a lead oxide covering. The negative plates have a porous or spongy surface.

Battery Voltage

In a charged battery, the lead oxide covering of the positive plate reacts with the electrolyte to generate a positive charge, and the pure lead of the negative plates reacts with the electrolyte to create a negative charge. This creates a potential difference (voltage) between the plates. All plates of a like charge are electrically connected, causing accumulative charges to be present at the positive and negative battery terminals.

Each cell of a battery in good condition contributes approximately 1.95V to 2.08V to the total charge of the battery. Six fully charged cells will produce at least 12V. If they do not, the battery must be recharged or replaced.

The Discharging/Charging Cycle

The charge in a battery remains relatively stable until a circuit is completed between the battery terminals. When this happens, current flows through the circuit and a chemical reaction takes place between plates and electrolyte as the battery attempts to equalize the potential difference between the plates.

The lead oxide (PbO_2) on the positive plates combines with the sulfuric acid (H_2SO_4) in the electrolyte to create lead sulfate ($PbSO_4$) and water (H_2O). In this reaction, each molecule of lead oxide must supply two electrons. This surrendering of electrons helps the plate stay positively charged, despite the influx of electrons through the circuit connecting the battery terminals.

A similar chemical reaction takes place at the negative plate, where the pure lead (Pb) combines with the sulfuric acid electrolyte (H_2SO_4) to form water (H_2O) and lead sulfate ($PbSO_4$). However, when this reaction is complete, there are two leftover electrons, which keep the plate negative despite the flow of electrons through the circuit to the positive plate.

As the process continues, more and more of the electrolyte is changed to water and the plates become more sulfated. Gradually, the chemical reaction becomes unable to keep up with the flow of electrons through the circuit. The voltage continues to drop as the charges on the plates equalize until the battery becomes fully discharged.

When a battery is recharged, a controlled direct current is passed through the battery in the reverse direction from normal operation. This causes a reversal in the chemical action and restores the plates and electrolyte to their original conditions.

Green Tech

Recycling Batteries

Today's lead-acid batteries typically contain a large percentage of recycled materials. This is because lead-acid batteries are recycled and some of their materials can be reused. As a result, less new material needs to go into a new battery. Automotive shops collect and send dead batteries to off-site recycling facilities. Used batteries can be stored for up to a year before being recycled. It is best to store used lead-acid batteries inside, away from the drainage system and any source of ignition. Cracked batteries should be contained, and any spills from a battery crack should be cleaned up as quickly as possible.

Summary

The primary purpose of the ignition system is to provide sufficient voltage to discharge a spark between the electrodes of a spark plug. Many small engines use magneto systems to supply ignition spark. Magneto systems are self-contained systems that produce electrical current for ignition without an outside primary source of electricity. Basic magneto system parts include permanent magnets, coil, switching devices, spark plug wire, and spark plug.

Using the correct spark plug can greatly increase engine efficiency and service life. Reach, heat range, and electrode type must all be considered.

Most small engines are equipped with solid state ignition systems that use electronic devices in place of one or more mechanical ignition components. These systems do not require mechanical adjustments. The two most common solid state systems are the capacitive discharge ignition (CDI) system and the transistor-controlled ignition (TCI) system.

The CDI system stores primary energy in a capacitor and uses semiconductor devices to trigger the ignition system. The TCI system is an inductive system that utilizes semiconductor devices (transistors, diodes, etc.) for switching purposes.

The mechanical breaker point ignition system is a flywheel magneto inductive system. It employs mechanical breaker points to time the triggering of the ignition system. Dwell (cam angle) is the amount of time that the breaker points stay closed during one revolution of the cam. Some small engines are equipped with mechanical systems that retard and advance timing.

Instead of a magneto, some ignition systems use a lead-acid battery to supply primary current. These systems generally employ an ignition coil. Because the battery is the only source of energy for battery ignition systems, a generator is used to replenish energy in the battery.

Review Questions

Answer the following questions on a separate sheet of paper.

1. Describe the two major tasks performed by an ignition system.
2. If a four-cycle engine runs at 3600 rpm, the number of sparks per minute required at the spark plug would be _____.
3. Name the main electrical components that make up the magneto ignition system.
4. The coil acts as a transformer that _____.
   A. steps down the voltage and increases the output amperage
   B. steps up the voltage and amperage
   C. steps down the voltage and amperage
   D. steps up the voltage and decreases the output amperage
5. In the ignition coil, the primary winding has _____.
   A. many turns of fine wire
   B. few turns of fine wire
   C. few turns of heavy wire
   D. many turns of heavy wire
6. What is the purpose of the ribs on the spark plug insulator?
7. Would a *cool* spark plug have a short or long insulator nose?
8. Define *preignition*.
9. When the switching device in the magneto is closed, _____.
   A. current is induced in the primary circuit by the flywheel magnets
   B. the spark plug fires
   C. a high voltage is induced in the secondary circuit
   D. All of the above.
10. *True or False?* Electronic switching devices are more dependable than mechanical switching devices.

11. Breaker point contacts are made of a very hard material called _____.

12. Name five advantages of a solid state ignition system.

13. The only moving parts in a CDI system are the _____ in the flywheel.

14. What is the purpose of the condenser used in an MBI system?

15. The ignition advance system causes spark to occur _____ in the cycle during intermediate- and high-speed operation.

16. When breaker points are set with a wider gap, the dwell _____.
    A. becomes greater
    B. becomes less
    C. does not change

17. Describe the operation of a waste-spark ignition system.

18. The amount of voltage required to jump the spark plug gap depends on _____.
    A. spark plug gap
    B. electrode condition
    C. engine speed
    D. All of the above.

19. When connecting the ignition coil in the circuit of a battery ignition system, the positive terminal of the battery must be connected to _____.
    A. the positive terminal of the coil
    B. the negative terminal of the coil
    C. either terminal of the coil
    D. None of the above.

20. A(n) _____ is used to replenish energy in the battery used in battery ignition systems.

Suggested Activities

1. Make a visible magneto mounted on a display board or built into a clear acrylic box so that it can be manually turned with a crank. Old, but usable, engine parts can be used.

2. A workable battery ignition system can be built and mounted as a display board. Demonstrate the operation and principles involved in this system.

3. Make a collection of various kinds of spark plugs.

4. Section an old ignition coil to show the primary and secondary windings around the core.

5. Carefully open a condenser to display the lamination of aluminum foil and insulation.

6. Disassemble a magneto and demonstrate how it works.

Lubrication Systems

Learning Objectives

After studying this chapter, you will be able to:

- Define friction and explain how it affects the internal engine components.
- List the functions of lubricating oil.
- Differentiate between the lubrication systems in two-cycle engines and four-cycle engines.
- Explain the operation of ejection pumps, barrel pumps, and positive displacement pumps.
- Explain the function of oil filter systems and differentiate between the three main types.

Key Terms

API engine oil service classification symbol
API engine oil service classification system
babbitt
barrel pump system
boundary lubrication
bypass filter system
constant level splash system
detergent/dispersant additives
dipper
ejection pump system
full-flow filter system
hydrodynamic lubrication
low-oil warning devices
lubrication
multigrade oil
multiviscosity oil
oil slinger
positive displacement oil pumps
pressurized lubrication system
shunt filter system
splash lubrication system
viscosity
viscosity index (V.I.)

Principles of Lubrication

Lubrication is the process of reducing friction between sliding surfaces by introducing a slippery or smooth substance between them. See **Figure 11-1**. Lubricants come in dry (powdered), semidry (grease), and liquid (oil) forms. Oil is the most important lubricant for small engine use, simply because it is often the only lubrication the engine needs.

Friction

Friction is the resistance to motion created when one surface rubs against another. Even highly polished metal surfaces have irregularities (when studied under a microscope) that will create a great

deal of friction if rubbed together. The microscopic roughness will resist movement and create heat.

As the relatively rough projections on the contact surfaces rub across each other, they eventually break off and become loose particles. These loose particles, in turn, work between the contact surfaces and gouge grooves in the metal. Then, as friction and heat increase, the metal parts expand, causing greater pressure between the surfaces and creating even greater friction. This condition of wear exists until the parts either weld themselves together or seize (expand so much that mating parts cannot move).

In some cases, the excessively worn parts lose so much material from their contact surfaces that they become too loose to function properly. When this happens, the scored part must be replaced.

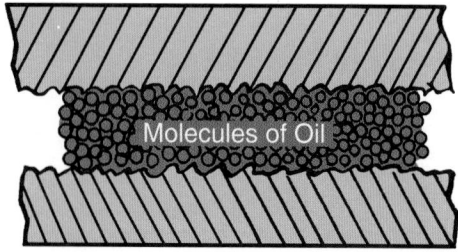

Figure 11-1.

A film of engine oil serves to separate and lubricate machined surfaces. When parts are in motion, oil molecules roll over one another like microscopic ball bearings.

Preventing Wear Due to Friction

In designing a small gasoline engine, the manufacturer selects suitable materials for parts that will be in moving contact with one another. For example, precision insert bearing shells are used in connecting rods and caps, and in main bearing saddles and caps. Rod and main bearing inserts must withstand reciprocating and rotational forces while fitting closely to the crank journal or throw. The steel backing of the bearing insert has a cast babbitt surface. *Babbitt*, an alloy of tin, copper, and antimony, has good antifriction qualities.

Regardless of the quality of the material used, all bearing surfaces in small gasoline engines must have oil separating moving parts that are in close contact. See **Figure 11-2**. A thin film of oil must

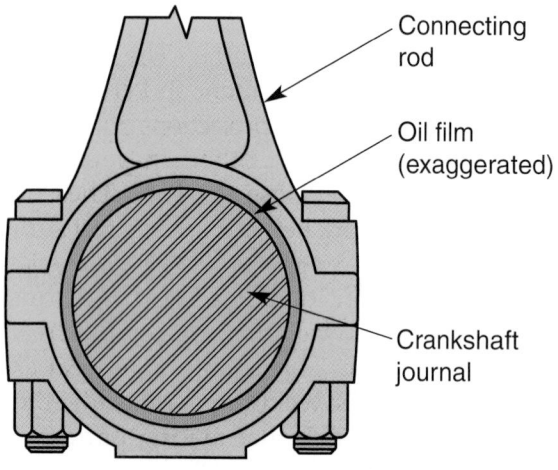

Connecting rod

Oil film (exaggerated)

Crankshaft journal

Figure 11-2.

An oil film between close fitting metallic parts prevents actual contact. Oil provides a relatively low-friction movement of parts.

coat the area between the piston/piston rings and the cylinder wall, the piston pin and the piston or connecting rod, the valve stem and the valve guide, the valve tappet and the guide, the main/rod bearing inserts and the crankshaft journals, etc.

The thin film of oil between the close-fitting parts may be only a few molecules thick, yet this is enough to prevent the two metal surfaces from actually touching. The molecules of oil then roll over one another, acting like microscopic ball bearings between the surfaces. See **Figure 11-1**.

Qualities of Lubricating Oil

Modern motor oil is a highly specialized product, which has been developed by engineers and chemists to perform many essential functions in an engine. In order to operate efficiently, engines depend on motor oil to do the following:

- Permit easy starting.
- Lubricate engine parts.
- Protect against rust and corrosion.
- Keep engine parts clean.
- Cool engine parts.
- Seal combustion pressures.
- Prevent foaming.
- Aid fuel economy.

Permits Easy Starting

The proper oil must be used if an engine is to start easily. If the oil is too thick, it will create so much drag between moving parts that the engine will not crank fast enough to start quickly and keep running.

Cold temperatures thicken oil. Oil for winter use must be thin enough to permit adequate cranking speeds at the lowest anticipated temperature. Once the engine is started, the oil must be fluid enough to flow quickly to the bearings to prevent wear. On the other hand, the oil must also be thick enough to provide adequate protection when the engine reaches normal operating temperatures.

Lubricates and Prevents Wear

Once an engine is started, oil must circulate quickly to prevent the metal-to-metal contact that can cause wear, scoring, or seizure of engine parts. Bearings and cylinder walls are particularly sensitive to movement, pressure, and oil supply.

Oil supplies to these components must be continually replenished by adequate flow and distribution.

Once the oil reaches the moving parts, it must lubricate and prevent wear of the moving surfaces. The oil is expected to establish a complete, unbroken film between surfaces. Lubrication engineers call this *hydrodynamic lubrication*, or full-film lubrication.

Under some conditions, it is impossible to maintain a continuous oil film between moving parts, and there is intermittent metal-to-metal contact between the high spots on sliding surfaces. Lubrication engineers refer to this as *boundary lubrication*. When this occurs, the friction generated by the contact can produce enough heat to cause the metals to melt and weld together.

Boundary lubrication always exists during engine starting and often exists during the operation of a new or rebuilt engine. Boundary lubrication is also found around the top piston ring where oil supply is limited, temperatures are high, and piston motion is reversed.

Protects against Rust and Corrosion

Normally, burning fuel forms carbon dioxide and water. Gasoline engines, however, do not burn all of their fuel completely. Some of the partially burned gasoline undergoes complex chemical changes during combustion and, under some conditions, forms soot or carbon. Some of this soot and partially burned fuel escapes through the exhaust in the form of black smoke. Part of the soot and fuel escapes past the rings and into the crankcase. They tend to combine with water to form sludge and varnish deposits on critical engine parts. Sludge buildup can clog oil passages, reducing oil flow. Varnish buildup interferes with proper clearances, restricts oil circulation, and causes vital engine parts to stick, resulting in rapid engine failure.

Water causes a considerable problem in the engine. For each gallon of fuel burned, more than one gallon of water is formed. Although most of this water is in vapor form and escapes with the exhaust, some condenses on the cylinder walls or escapes past the piston rings and is trapped temporarily in the crankcase. This occurs most frequently in cold weather, before the engine reaches its normal operating temperature.

In addition to water, other corrosive combustion gases get past the rings and are condensed or dissolved in the crankcase oil. Add to this the acids formed by the normal oxidation of oil, and the potential for rust and corrosive engine deposits becomes significant.

Engine life depends in part on the ability of motor oil to neutralize the effects of these corrosive materials. Due to extensive research by oil chemists, effective, oil-soluble, chemical compounds have been developed and are added to motor oil to provide protection for engine parts.

Keeps Engine Parts Clean

Engines are unable to tolerate excessive amounts of sludge and varnish on critical parts. Sludge can collect on oil pump screens and limit the flow of oil to vital engine parts. Accumulation of varnish can cause the piston rings to drag, preventing the engine from developing full power. Plugged oil-control rings prevent the removal of excess oil from the cylinder walls, resulting in excessive oil consumption.

Straight mineral oils have very limited ability to keep contaminants from forming masses of sludge in the engine. Therefore, various *detergent/dispersant additives* have been blended into modern motor oils. These additives keep engine parts clean by suspending fine particles of the oil contaminants until they can be trapped by the oil filter. See **Figure 11-3**.

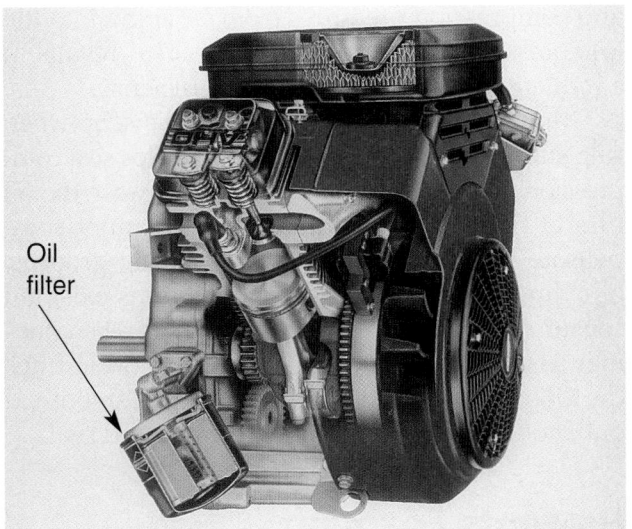

Briggs and Stratton Corp.

Figure 11-3.

An oil filter traps contaminants picked up by the engine oil. Most disposable filters are located on the side of the engine.

Detergent/dispersant additives are also effective at preventing varnish deposits within an engine. Varnish-forming materials react chemically with the oxygen in the crankcase to form complex chemical compounds. These compounds, which react with each other and with oxygen, are baked into a hard coating on hot engine parts. Piston rings and bearings are particularly sensitive to varnish deposits. When deposits are formed on these components, engine operation can be severely impaired.

Cools Engine Parts

The crankshaft, camshaft, timing gears, bearings, pistons, and other components in the lower part of the engine are directly dependent on the motor oil for cooling. Each of these parts has definite temperature limits that must not be exceeded. Some can tolerate fairly high temperatures, while others, such as the main and connecting rod bearings, must run relatively cool to prevent failure. These parts must get an ample supply of cool oil to absorb heat and transfer it back to the crankcase.

Seals Combustion Pressures

The surfaces of the piston rings, ring grooves, and cylinder walls are not completely smooth. When examined under a microscope, these surfaces consist of minute hills and valleys. Therefore, the rings cannot completely prevent high combustion and compression pressures from escaping into the low-pressure area of the crankcase. This results in a reduction in engine power and efficiency.

Motor oil fills in the hills and valleys between ring surfaces and cylinder walls, and helps seal compression and combustion pressures. Because the oil film at these points is quite thin, it cannot compensate for excessively worn rings, ring grooves, or cylinder walls. When such conditions exist, oil consumption may be high. New and rebuilt engines may also consume excessive amounts of oil until the hills and valleys on the surfaces have smoothed out enough to allow the oil to form a good seal.

Prevents Foaming

Modern engine oil has antifoaming additives to prevent it from whipping into bubbles that do not readily collapse. Oil foam does not cool well and does not provide adequate lubrication.

Aids Fuel Economy

Oils are available that have been formulated to improve fuel economy in gasoline-fueled engines. The fuel economy benefits are achieved by various means, including the use of friction-modifier additives.

Green Tech

Green Lubricants

Lubricants such as the motor oil used in small engines are necessary, but they are not environmentally friendly. Engine oil is not biodegradable, and in some states, it is considered a hazardous waste. However, alternatives to traditional motor oil are becoming available. Argonne National Laboratory has used nanotechnology to improve traditional motor oils. They combine extremely small particles of boric acid with motor oils. The resulting product is biodegradable, is not a health or environmental hazard, and does a better job of reducing friction than traditional motor oil. Engines that have less friction to overcome are more efficient and use less gasoline. Also, lowering friction can extend the life of the lubricated parts.

Oil Specifications

Specifications for engine oils are given in two ratings:
- Society of Automotive Engineers (SAE) Viscosity, referred to as viscosity grade.
- American Petroleum Institute (API) Engine Oil Service Classification, often referred to as the type of oil.

SAE Viscosity Grade

Viscosity must be considered when selecting engine oil. *Viscosity* is a measure of the oil's resistance to flow. This resistance keeps the oil from being squeezed out from between engine surfaces as they move under load or pressure. The resistance to flow is a function of the molecular structure of the oil. Because this resistance causes most of the drag during starting, it is important to use an oil with viscosity characteristics that ensure satisfactory cold cranking, good oil circulation, and adequate temperature protection.

The SAE has established a viscosity range classification system for engine lubricating oils. All engine oils are classified according to this system, which is used worldwide. Each oil is assigned an SAE grade (or grades) that signifies the viscosity range into which it falls. Single-grade motor oils commonly used today are SAE 5W, 10W, 15W, 20W, 20, 30, 40, and 50. Thick, slow-flowing oils have high numbers. Thin, free-flowing oils have low numbers. The W denotes oils suitable for use at low ambient (encompassing) temperatures. SAE numbered oils that do not have W designations are measured for viscosity at 212°F (100°C) to ensure adequate viscosity at normal engine operating temperatures.

Figure 11-4 compares the viscosity recommendations of five manufacturers for their four-cycle engines at various operating temperatures. Note that the higher viscosity oils (more resistant to flow) are recommended for higher temperatures. In low temperatures, a thick oil makes a cold engine very difficult to start and may deprive critical parts from adequate lubrication while the oil is gaining heat from combustion. Cold running can result in scored cylinder walls and engine bearings.

The temperature effect on viscosity varies widely with different types of oils. A standard has been developed for measuring the relationship between viscosity and temperature. This standard is called the *viscosity index (V.I.)*. Oil with a high viscosity index shows little change in viscosity over a wide range of temperatures. Today, through the use of selective crude oil stocks, new refining methods, and special chemical additives, there are many high viscosity index oils that are light enough to provide easy cranking at low temperatures and heavy enough to perform satisfactorily at high

temperatures. These oils, which meet the viscosity requirements of two or more SAE grades, are known as *multigrade*, or *multiviscosity oils*. Examples are oils labeled as SAE 5W-20, SAE 5W-30, and SAE 10W-30.

Note that some of the oils listed in **Figure 11-4** are single viscosity grade oils, such as SAE 20. Others are multiviscosity grade oils such as SAE 5W-20. Although multiviscosity oils can be substituted for single viscosity grades in four-cycle engines, they should *not* be used in two-cycle engines.

API Engine Oil Service Classification

The *API engine oil service classification system* is a dynamic method of rating an oil's suitability for use in various generations of engines. New categories are created as engine oil is reengineered to meet the growing demands placed on it by evolving engine designs. Currently, the classifications are divided into two types. The "C" categories classify oils that are suitable for use with compression-ignition (diesel) engines, and the "S" categories classify oils that are suitable for use with four-stroke, spark-ignition (gasoline) engines.

Since the focus of this book is on gasoline engines, only the "S" categories will be discussed in detail. Currently, there are 12 "S" categories, but only the SJ, SL, SM, and SN categories are considered current. The remaining categories are considered obsolete. Each successive "S" category of engine oil is a suitable replacement for all of the "S" categories that preceded it, **Figure 11-5**. It should be noted, however, that the same does not hold true for the "C" categories of engine oil.

Four-Cycle Crankcase Lubrication (Viscosity-Grade) Recommendations of Manufacturers

Manufacturer	Above 40°F	Above 32°F	Below 5°F	Below 0°F	Below -10°F
Briggs and Stratton	SAE 30 or 10W-30	5W-20 or 10W			
Kohler	SAE 30		SAE 10W	5W or 5W-20	
Tecumseh	SAE 30		10W-30		

Goodheart-Willcox Publisher

Figure 11-4.

A comparison of viscosity-grade recommendations by five engine manufacturers. Recommendations are for specific models only, not for full-line coverage.

API Engine Oil Categories for Spark-Ignition Automobile and Light Truck Engines

Category	Status	Description
SN	Current	For 2011 and older vehicles. Most recent category at the time of printing.
SM	Current	Suitable for engines manufactured in 2010 or earlier.
SL	Current	Suitable for engines manufactured in 2004 or earlier.
SJ	Current	Suitable for engines manufactured in 2001 or earlier.
SH	Obsolete	Suitable for engines manufactured in 1996 or earlier.
SG	Obsolete	Suitable for engines manufactured in 1993 or earlier.
SF	Obsolete	Suitable for engines manufactured in 1988 or earlier.
SE	Obsolete	*Do not use* in engines manufactured after 1979.
SD	Obsolete	*Do not use* in engines manufactured after 1971.
SC	Obsolete	*Do not use* in engines manufactured after 1967.
SB	Obsolete	*Do not use* in engines manufactured after 1951.
SA	Obsolete	*Do not use* in engines manufactured after 1979.

Note: Categories SI and SK have been intentionally left out by the API.

Goodheart-Willcox Publisher

Figure 11-5.

The American Petroleum Institute (API) has published oil service classifications in which oils are recommended for specific service conditions.

The API Engine Oil Service Classification Symbol

The *API engine oil service classification symbol* provides the consumer with information about an oil's characteristics and applications. See **Figure 11-6**. The symbol typically appears on the label of an oil container. It may also be found on the engine's oil fill cap or in the owner's manual. The symbol is divided into three parts, including:
- Top—Specifies the oil's service classification or recommended applications.
- Center—Describes the oil's viscosity.

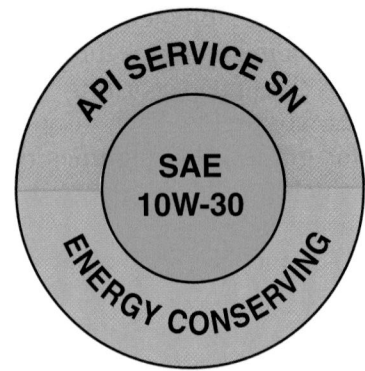

Goodheart-Willcox Publisher

Figure 11-6.

A typical API engine oil service classification symbol for one type of SAE 10W-30 oil.

- Bottom—Reserved for information on the oil's fuel saving properties. Oils labeled *energy conserving* offer better fuel-saving properties than oils that do not have this marking.

Selecting the Proper Engine Oil

The cost of oil for a small gasoline engine is relatively low. However, the particular oil selected for use in a small engine is extremely important to the life of the engine. See **Figure 11-7**. Always use the type of oil recommended by the engine manufacturer.

The oil recommended for use in a given engine may be shown on the engine nameplate, the oil filler cap, or a special label attached to the engine. The operator's manual also carries the manufacturer's recommendation, as does the lubrication guide provided by major oil companies.

The API engine oil service classification categories do not account for two-stroke engines or engines mated to a wet clutch. Special applications such as these require oils with special characteristics. For example, the friction-reducing additives in oils with the API's "Energy Conserving" label can cause the plates in wet clutches to slip. In short, when choosing an engine oil for any application, always follow the manufacturer's recommendation.

Since two-cycle engines are lubricated by mixing oil with the fuel, the oil eventually enters the combustion chamber and is burned. Some multi-viscosity and detergent-type oils have additives that do not burn completely and leave a residue

Figure 11-7.

Using the proper oil will help prevent premature engine failure. Always use the type of oil recommended by the engine manufacturer.

that fouls spark plugs and clogs exhaust ports. Two-cycle engine oils contain special additives to prevent unburned residues.

Engine Lubrication Systems

The way that moving parts are lubricated differs in two-cycle and four-cycle small gasoline engines. In preparing a two-cycle engine for use, oil is mixed with gasoline and poured into the fuel tank. As the engine operates, an oil mist is created that lubricates the cylinder wall and all internal engine parts. In a four-cycle engine, oil is poured into the crankcase. The oil in the crankcase supplies lubrication to all internal engine parts.

Two-Cycle Engine Lubrication

As previously mentioned, the two-stroke engine receives its lubrication as fuel mixed with oil passes through the engine. In this way, there is clean oil continuously supplied to all moving parts when the

engine is running. The oil eventually burns in the combustion chamber and is exhausted with other gases. The two-stroke engine will get adequate lubrication even when operated at extreme angles.

Installing the correct mixture of fuel and oil is a critical factor in maintaining a two-stroke engine in good working condition. The prescribed type and grade of engine oil must be mixed with the fuel in proper proportion before being placed in the fuel tank.

Mixing Fuel and Oil

In preparing a two-cycle engine for use, a specified amount of two-cycle engine oil is mixed with each gallon of gasoline to provide fuel for the engine. Refer to manufacturer's recommendations for the specific engine make and model.

The amount of oil required for a given amount of fuel is expressed as a ratio. For example, engines that require a fuel-to-oil ratio of 40:1 (40 to 1) require 1 part oil for every 40 parts of gasoline. **Figure 11-8** shows the amount of oil to add per gallon of gasoline to obtain a given ratio.

The oil and gasoline must be thoroughly mixed in a separate container before being poured into the fuel tank. The correct method to mix oil and gasoline is to first empty about half the fuel out of the fuel container. Then, add the appropriate amount of oil to the container, place the cap on the fuel container, and shake the container so the oil mixes thoroughly with the fuel. Add the fuel that was removed and shake the container thoroughly once more.

Two-Cycle Engine Fuel/Oil Ratio Chart						
Gallons of Gasoline	**16:1**	**20:1**	**24:1**	**32:1**	**40:1**	**50:1**
1	8	6	5	4	3	3
2	16	13	11	8	6	5
3	24	19	16	12	10	8
4	32	26	21	16	13	10
5	40	32	27	20	16	13
6	48	38	32	24	19	15

Figure 11-8.

This chart is used when mixing oil and gasoline. Note that 3 ounces of oil is mixed with 1 gallon of gasoline for both 40/1 and 50/1 ratios.

The mixing of oil with gasoline has been simplified by manufacturers by providing premeasured bottles of two-cycle oil like the small ones shown in **Figure 11-9**. By mixing one bottle of oil with one gallon of gasoline, a 40:1 ratio is obtained without having to measure out the oil. For other ratios, the oil can be added in accordance with the chart in **Figure 11-8**. Some bottles are calibrated in ounces for ratios other than 40:1.

> **Note**
>
> Some two-cycle engines use an oil injection system that meters the correct quantity of oil into the engine's crankcase, where it mixes with fuel before it enters the combustion chamber. These systems eliminate the need to mix oil with gasoline before adding the fuel to the tank. However, oil must be added to a separate reservoir to maintain proper engine lubrication.

It is convenient to mark the correct fuel-to-oil ratio on the fuel container with a permanent marker. This will prevent using the wrong fuel. For example, a person may have a chain saw, hedge trimmer, and leaf blower, each using a different mixture and each requiring a separate fuel container.

Four-Cycle Engine Lubrication

Lubrication of the four-stroke engine is provided by placing the correct quantity and grade of engine oil in the crankcase. In operation, the air-gasoline mixture is ignited in the combustion chamber. At the same time, the oil sump in the crankcase supplies lubrication for the cylinder wall and all of the internal engine parts.

Several methods are used to feed the oil from the crankcase to the correct locations. The two most common methods are the splash system and the pump system. Some engines employ one or the other; others use a combination of both. Four-stroke engines must be operated in an upright position or the oil will flow away from the pump or splash finger, preventing adequate lubrication.

Splash Lubrication System

Small, four-cycle, gasoline engines generally use some type of *splash lubrication system* to lubricate internal surfaces. The splash lubrication system shown in **Figure 11-10** features an oil dipper arm on the connecting rod cap. The *dipper* is designed to pick up oil from the crankcase on every revolution of the crankshaft, splashing oil on the various moving parts as it is carried around by the crank throw.

Some splash lubrication systems use an *oil slinger* rather than a dipper, **Figure 11-11**. The slinger, which is driven by a gear on the crankshaft or camshaft, has several blades, or fingers, that pick up oil and splash it onto the internal engine parts. Because the slinger has multiple blades, it provides a more consistent supply of oil to the moving engine parts than a dipper.

With the splash system, the cylinder wall receives a generous amount of oil. To avoid oil-burning problems, the oil control ring on the piston removes excess oil from the cylinder wall, returning it to the crankcase as illustrated in **Figure 11-12**. The connecting rod bearings and piston pin receive lubrication through oil passage holes. See **Figure 11-13**.

Briggs and Stratton Corp.

Figure 11-9.

Oil is the most important lubricant used for engine lubrication.

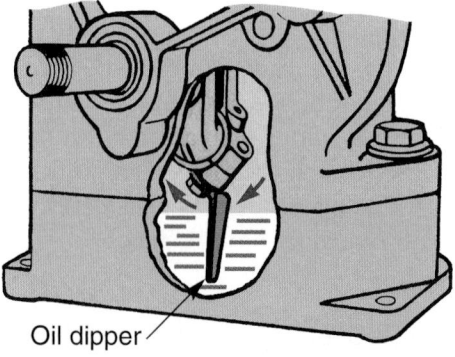

Oil dipper

Briggs and Stratton Corp.

Figure 11-10.

With a splash system, some oil dippers are cast onto connecting rod, others are bolted on. The oil level must be high enough for the dipping action.

Oil slinger   Camshaft gear

Blades

Goodheart-Willcox Publisher

Figure 11-11.

A slinger has several blades that pick up oil and sling it onto the internal engine parts.

Constant Level Splash System

The *constant level splash system* provides three major improvements over the simple splash system. These improvements include:

- An oil pump.
- A splash trough.
- A strainer.

A cam-operated pump supplies oil to the trough, where the oil dipper picks it up and distributes it to the cylinder wall and moving parts. The term *constant level* is used because the pump can supply more oil than the dipper can remove. Therefore, the trough is always full. Oil returning to the crankcase must pass through the strainer before it is pumped back to the trough. This keeps large contaminants in the crankcase.

The constant-level splash system will provide adequate lubrication as long as there is enough oil to supply the pump. Engines with constant-level systems can be operated at an angle while still providing adequate lubrication. However, if the oil level is low, the cooling effect of the oil is reduced.

Ejection and Barrel Pump Systems

The *ejection pump system* forces oil under pressure against the rotating connecting rod. Some oil enters the connecting rod bearings, while the remaining oil is deflected to other parts in the crankcase. The ejection pump system is similar to

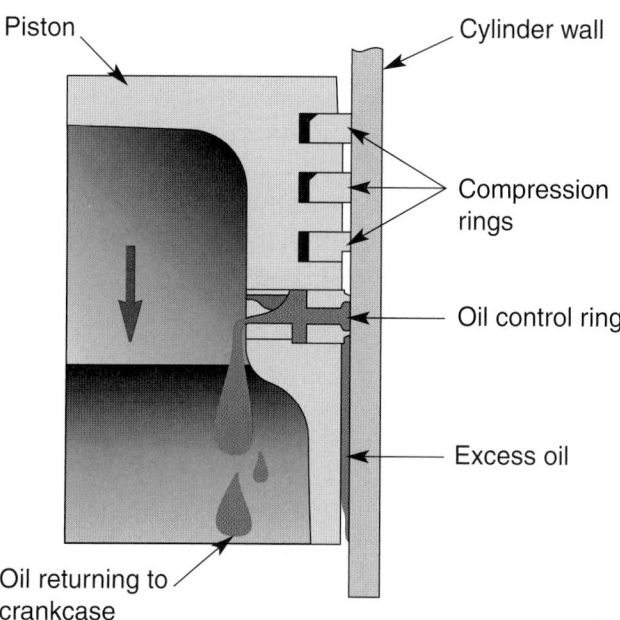

Piston   Cylinder wall

Compression rings

Oil control ring

Excess oil

Oil returning to crankcase

Goodheart-Willcox Publisher

Figure 11-12.

Oil splashed on cylinder wall lubricates the piston and piston rings. Excess oil is scraped from wall by oil control ring.

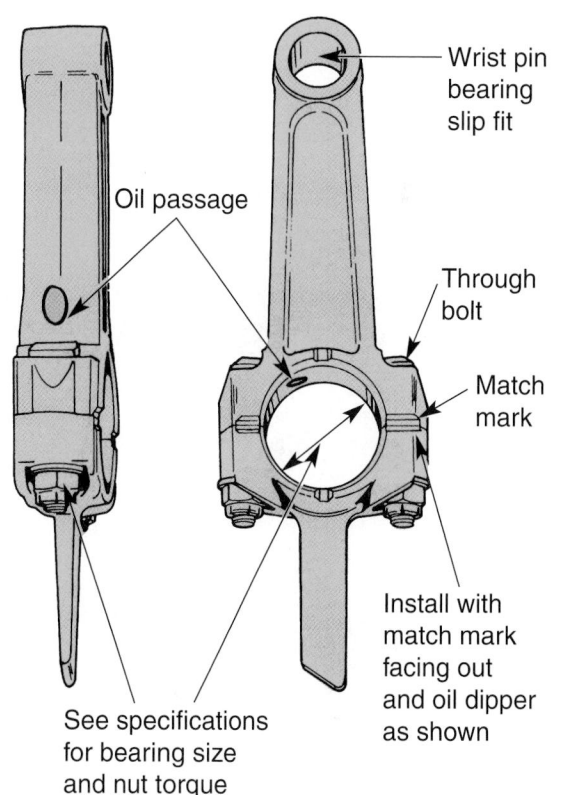

Wrist pin bearing slip fit

Oil passage

Through bolt

Match mark

Install with match mark facing out and oil dipper as shown

See specifications for bearing size and nut torque

Goodheart-Willcox Publisher

Figure 11-13.

Holes drilled in the connecting rod, bearing insert, and piston pin boss provide passageways for lubricating oil.

the constant level splash system, but it provides a more forceful spray of oil.

The *barrel pump system* uses a cylinder-and-plunger type lubrication pump. See **Figure 11-14**. By design, an eccentric on the camshaft moves the plunger in and out of the pump cylinder. The camshaft used in a barrel pump system is hollow and has holes that run from the center of the shaft to the eccentric.

In operation, the plunger is drawn out until a hole in the eccentric aligns with a hole in the plunger. This allows the cylinder to fill with oil. When the plunger is forced in, a different hole in the eccentric aligns with the plunger, and oil is forced through passages in the camshaft to the main bearings and crankshaft connecting rod journal.

Pressurized Lubrication Systems

Some larger small engines use a *pressurized lubrication system*, which is similar to the system used in an automobile engine. This type of system relies on a positive displacement gear pump or rotor pump to supply oil to moving engine parts. Passages for oil flow are drilled to all critical points, such as camshaft bearings, main bearings, connecting rod bearings, and piston pins. A splash

Barrel pump

Eccentric shaft

Goodheart-Willcox Publisher

Figure 11-14.

The plunger of a barrel pump is actuated by an eccentric shaft driven by the camshaft. A ball-shaped plunger end is held in a socket so that it can pivot as shaft turns.

system is used in conjunction with the pressurized system, particularly for lubricating cylinder walls.

Pressure relief valves are installed in all pressurized lubrication systems. Often they are an integral part of the oil pump.

Positive Displacement Oil Pumps

Several types of *positive displacement oil pumps* are used in pressurized lubrication systems. See **Figure 11-15**. One common type is the gear pump shown in **Figure 11-16**. The end cover has been removed to expose two meshed gears. One gear is shaft-driven from the engine. It drives the second gear.

Note that the driving gear in **Figure 11-16** is keyed to the driving shaft. As the gears turn, oil fills the spaces between the teeth and is carried around to the oil outlet. No oil passes between the gears where the teeth are meshed, because of the tight fit.

If, for some reason, oil flow is restricted somewhere in the engine, the increase in pressure would raise the ball against the spring in the pressure relief valve. When this happens, oil will pass through the valve and recirculate through the pump. Recirculation of the engine oil continues until the restriction to flow ceases and pressure declines, allowing the ball to seat and the relief valve to close. Without a pressure relief valve in the system, pressures would become excessively high during high engine speeds.

Oil Filter Systems

Oil filters are used on small engines with pressurized lubrication systems. Filters trap dirt, carbon, and other harmful materials, preventing them from circulating through the engine. The oil filter prevents very fine particles from circulating. The oil strainer, **Figure 11-17**, is usually attached to intake side of oil pump and prevents large particles from entering the filter. **Figure 11-18** shows one type of oil filter.

Three basic types of oil filter systems are in common use: bypass, shunt, and full-flow. Each of these systems uses a replaceable filter element that can be discarded when it becomes dirty.

Bypass Systems

The *bypass filter system*, shown in **Figure 11-17**, pumps part of the oil through the filter, while the

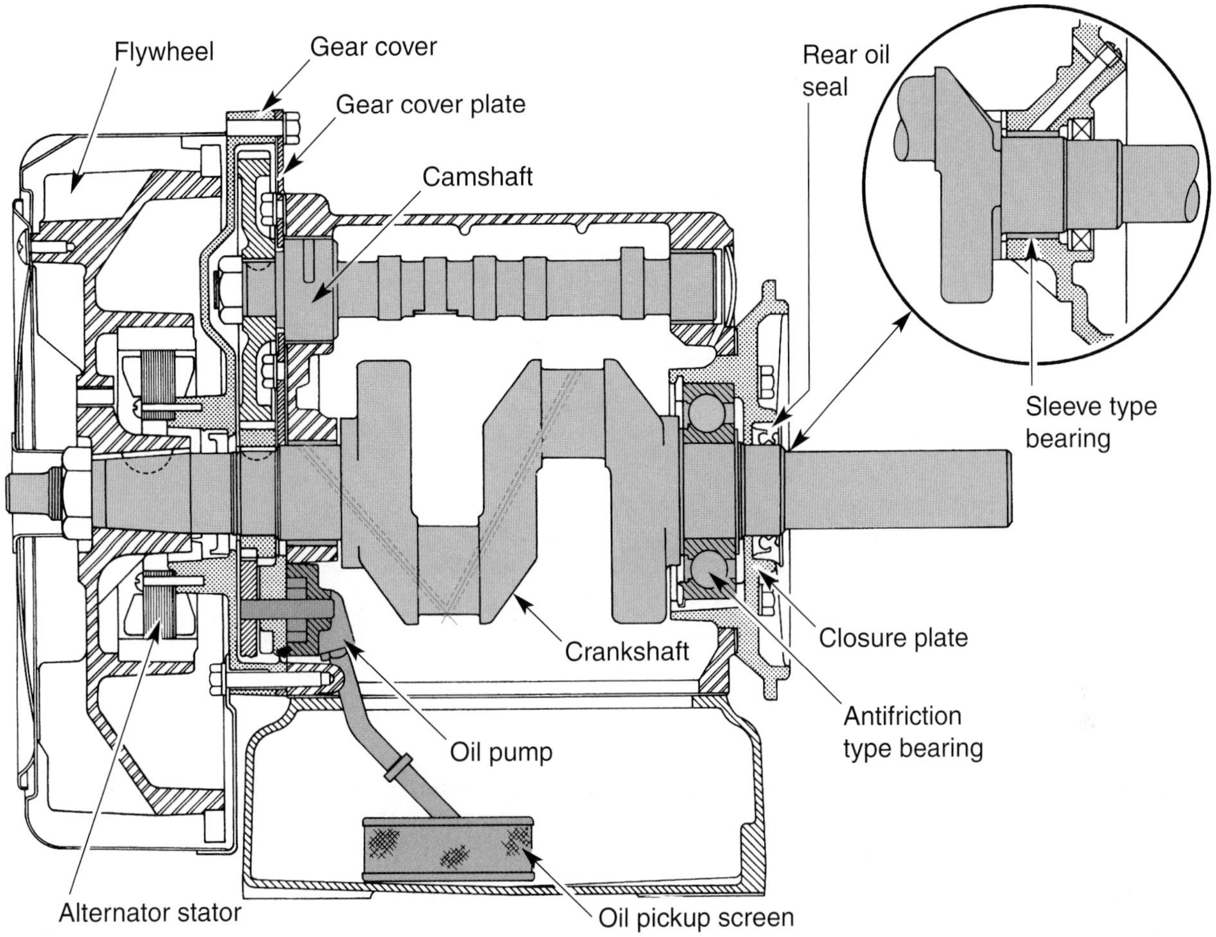

Flywheel Gear cover

Gear cover plate

Camshaft

Rear oil seal

Sleeve type bearing

Closure plate

Antifriction type bearing

Crankshaft

Oil pump

Alternator stator

Oil pickup screen

Figure 11-15.

The oil pump used in this two-cylinder engine supplies oil to the moving internal engine parts. Note drilled crankshaft.

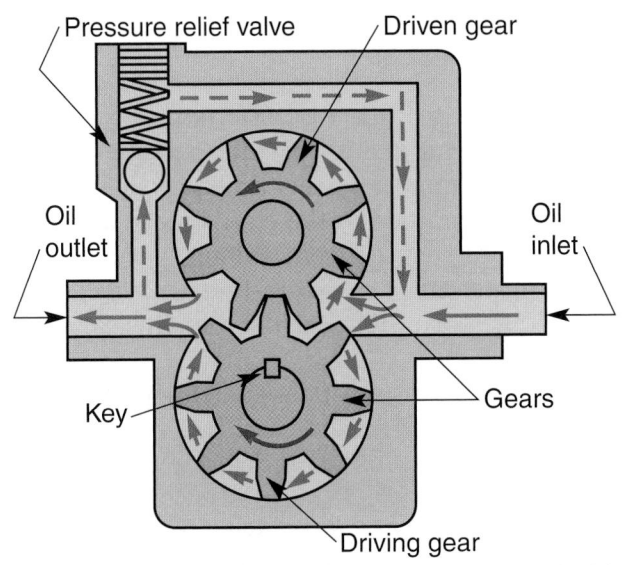

Pressure relief valve   Driven gear

Oil outlet

Oil inlet

Key

Gears

Driving gear

Figure 11-16.

In gear-type pump operation, the oil is carried between the teeth of matching gears. If the oil pressure is too high, a relief valve recirculates oil through pump.

remaining oil is pumped to the engine bearings. Oil pumped through the filter is returned directly to the crankcase. The primary purpose of the filter in the bypass system is to keep a clean supply of oil in the crankcase.

The pressure relief valve (regulating valve) in the bypass system controls the maximum allowable pressure in the system. If there is a restriction to oil flow, pressure buildup will overcome relief valve spring tension and the valve will open. When this occurs, oil pressure will be relieved and oil will flow through the valve and back to the crankcase.

Shunt Filter Systems

In the *shunt filter system*, part of the oil delivered by the pump is filtered and directed to the engine bearings. Some of the oil is shunted past the filter. The remaining oil is circulated through the pressure relief valve and back to the crankcase.

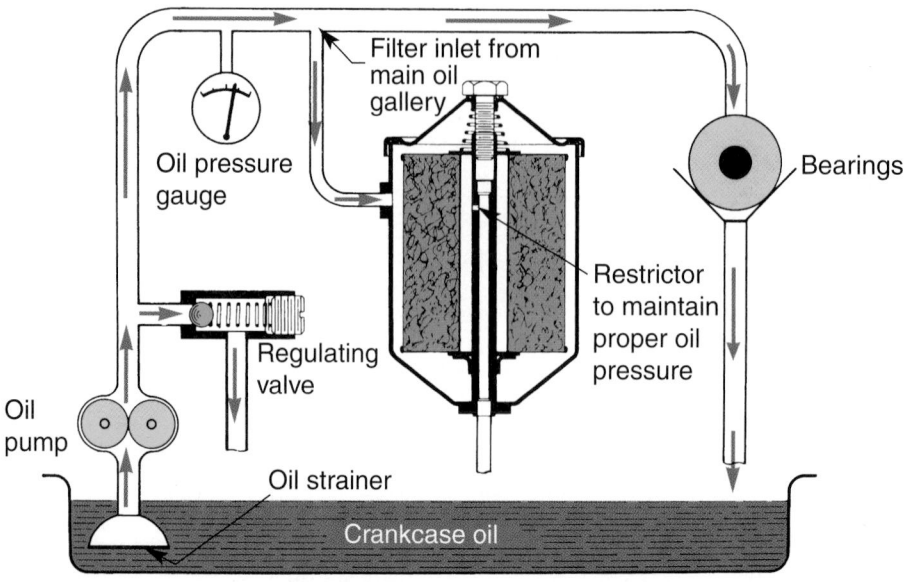

Wix Filters

Figure 11-17.

A bypass filter system pumps some engine oil through the filter. The remaining oil goes to the engine bearings.

Deere & Co.

Figure 11-18.

Filters, such as this one, trap unwanted materials and prevent those materials from circulating through the engine.

Full-flow Filter Systems

The *full-flow filter system* directs the entire volume of pumped oil through the filter to the bearings. See **Figure 11-19**. If the filter element becomes clogged with dirt, oil pressure will increase. The added pressure will open the relief valve, permitting the oil to flow. If the filter did not have a relief valve and the filter became clogged, serious engine damage would result.

The filter cartridge must correspond to the filter system on the engine. For example, a full-flow cartridge used in a partial-flow system will give longer service life, but initial efficiency will be poor due to its high-flow rate. On the other hand, a partial-flow cartridge used in a full-flow system would drastically reduce oil pressure. Proper oil filtration in modern gasoline engines cannot be overemphasized.

Low-Oil Warning and Shutdown Systems (LOS)

Because lubrication is essential to protecting the metal components of internal combustion engines, it is important that an adequate quantity of oil be maintained in the crankcase at all times. To protect the engine from a dangerously low oil level, some engines have *low-oil warning devices* installed to warn the operator when this condition exists.

One system uses a float switch located in the oil reservoir of the crankcase. See **Figure 11-20**. When the float reaches a predetermined low level, it closes the switch. When the switch closes, it completes a circuit from the primary windings of the ignition coil through the oil sensor, causing a warning light to flash. Primary ignition voltage is directed to ground and stops the engine before serious damage can occur. When oil is added to the correct level, the engine can be restarted.

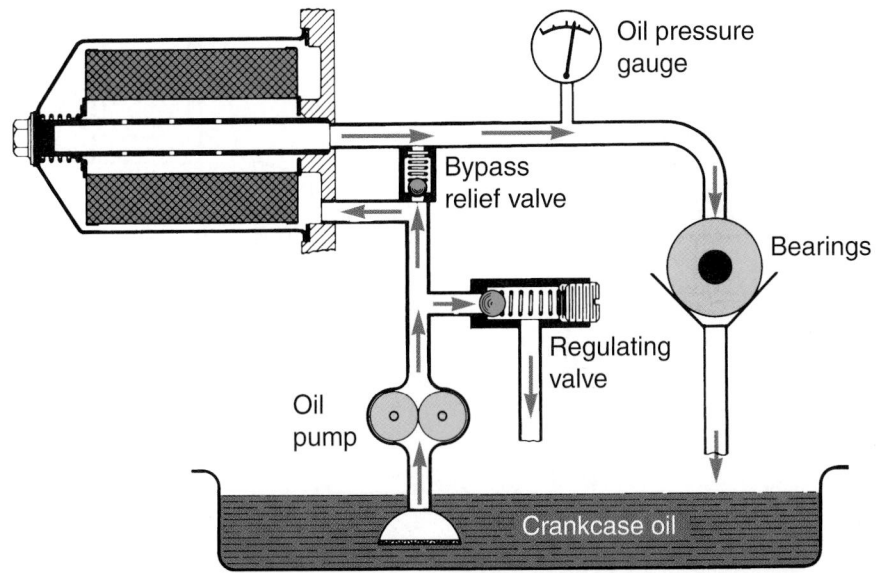

Goodheart-Willcox Publisher

Figure 11-19.

A full-flow filter system directs all engine oil through the filter. The relief valve opens if the filter becomes clogged.

Another type of low-oil shutdown method uses a sensor with a spark gap submerged in oil. See **Figure 11-21**. The sensor is connected to a lead from the ignition armature. When the quantity of oil is at the correct level, the submerged spark gap is filled with oil, which prevents a spark from jumping the gap. When the oil level is below the acceptable level, the spark gap is no longer submerged and is exposed to the air in the crankcase. The resistance of the spark gap in the sensor is lower than that of the spark plug gap. Therefore, the armature fires across the sensor spark gap instead of the spark plug gap and the engine stops running. When the oil level is brought to the correct level, the engine can be restarted.

The two methods of shutting down an engine when the oil level is low are limited to four-stroke engines. Two-stroke engines must have the proper amount of oil mixed with the fuel as previously mentioned in this chapter.

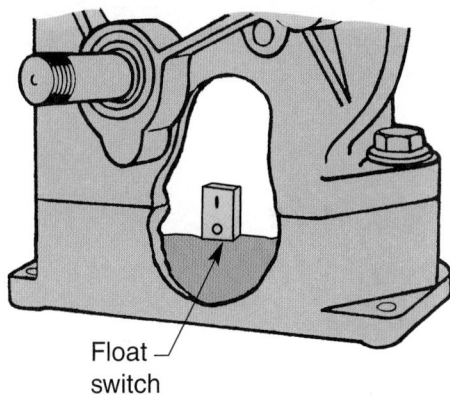

Goodheart-Willcox Publisher

Figure 11-20.

This LOS uses a float and switch located in the oil reservoir of the crankcase.

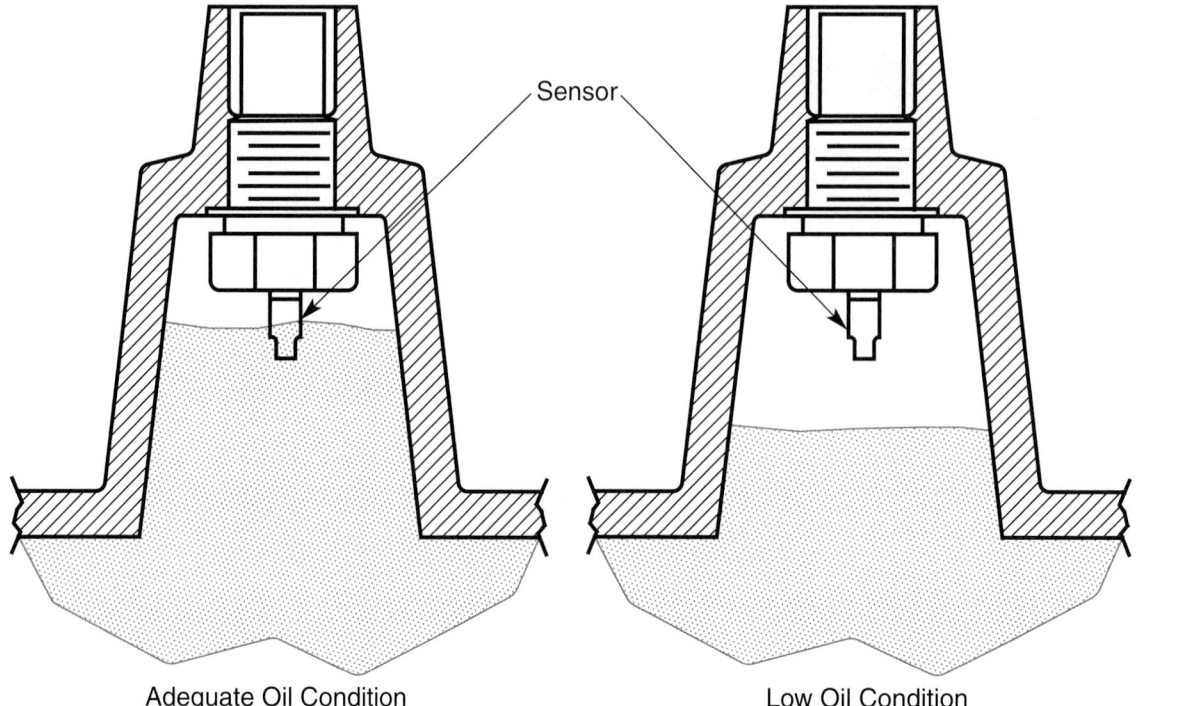

Sensor

Adequate Oil Condition   Low Oil Condition

Goodheart-Willcox Publisher

Figure 11-21.

This LOS system uses a sensor with a spark gap submerged in oil. This sensor is connected to a lead from the ignition armature and shuts down the engine when a low oil situation occurs.

Summary

Lubrication is the process of reducing friction by introducing a slippery substance between sliding surfaces. Friction is the resistance to motion created when one surface rubs against another.

All bearing surfaces in small gas engines must have oil separating any moving parts that are in close contact. The oil film between close-fitting parts may only be a few molecules thick, but it is enough to keep the metal surfaces from actually touching.

In addition to lubricating, oil cools and cleans the engine. The oil also provides a seal between the piston rings and the cylinder wall.

When selecting oil for use in a small engine, service classification and viscosity grade must be considered.

The way that moving parts are lubricated differs in two-cycle and four-cycle engines. Oil in a two-cycle engine is mixed with gasoline and poured into the fuel tank. In operation, an oil mist is created that lubricates all internal parts. In a four-cycle engine, oil is poured into the crankcase. The oil sump in the crankcase supplies lubrication to all internal engine parts.

Oil filters are used on many small engines. These filters trap dirt, carbon, and other harmful materials, preventing them from circulating through the engine. Three common types of oil filter systems include the bypass, shunt, and full-flow.

Review Questions

Answer the following questions using the information provided in this chapter.

1. Describe the three general types of lubricants.
2. Babbitt metal used as a bearing material is an alloy of three metals. Name them.
3. Name four important jobs performed by a good engine lubricant.
4. What is the purpose of detergent/dispersants in oils?
5. SAE stands for _____.
6. API stands for _____.

7. *Type of oil* refers to its _____.
   A. service classification
   B. viscosity
   C. grade
   D. maximum operating temperature
8. A high viscosity oil would _____.
   A. be thin
   B. be suitable for high temperature use
9. *True or False?* The lubricating oil recommendation for a particular make and model engine may be found on a special label on the engine.
10. Why are some oils with additives not suitable for two-cycle engine use?
11. Which engine lubrication system utilizes a trough in the crankcase?
    A. barrel type lubrication system
    B. ejection pump system
    C. constant level system
    D. splash system
12. Which small engine lubrication system is similar to the system used on automobiles?
    A. ejection pump system
    B. constant level splash system
    C. barrel type pump system
    D. full pressure system
13. *True or False?* Several types of positive displacement oil pumps are used in pressurized lubrication systems.
14. Name three types of oil filter systems in use.
15. *True or False?* Generally, the oil filter element is replaceable.

Suggested Activities

1. Demonstrate friction to the class by first rubbing two sheets of waste paper together, then rub two sheets of coarse abrasive together. Discuss how a lubricant could reduce friction in each case.
2. Make viscosity measurements of several engine oils with a viscosimeter.
3. Compare a multiviscosity oil with single viscosity oils, using a viscosimeter. Test the oils at various temperatures and make a chart of your results.

4. Create heat with friction. Place a dull, unwanted drill in a drill press. Try to drill a bar of metal. Show what happens to drill as a result of friction.

5. Demonstrate to the class how oil cleans. With engine grease and grime on your hands, wipe them clean in a container of clean engine oil. Compare the cleaning power with soap or a detergent.

6. Remove the end cover from a gear-type oil pump and demonstrate how it works. Reinstall the cover, place the pump in oil, and operate it by hand.

7. Demonstrate the proper and safe procedure of mixing oil in gasoline for two-cycle engine use.

Cooling Systems

Learning Objectives

After studying this chapter, you will be able to:

- Explain how air cooling systems work to lower engine operating temperatures.
- Describe the basic operation of pressurized liquid cooling systems.
- Explain the function of a thermostat and a radiator.
- Describe the basic operation of outboard water circulation systems.
- Define the basic function of a water pump and give examples of several common types.

Key Terms

centrifugal force
conduction
convection
coolant
cooling fins
plunger pump
pressure-vacuum water
    flow system
pressurized cooling
    system

radiator
radiator cap
radiator core
rotor-type pump
sliding vane pump
thermostat
vari-volume pumps
water jackets
water pump

Principles of Engine Cooling

The efficiency and life of an engine depend on how well it is cooled. The average temperature of burned gases in the combustion chamber of an air-cooled engine is about 3600°F (1982°C). About a third of the heat produced is converted to mechanical energy. The exhaust system carries away another third of the heat. The remaining third is carried away by the cooling system. See **Figure 12-1**.

Without a properly functioning cooling system, the engine oil can get so hot that it breaks down, leaving it unable to produce adequate lubrication. When this occurs, friction between moving parts increases. This generates even more heat. In extreme cases, internal engine parts can get so hot that they melt. Excessive heat can also lead to preignition. Preignition occurs when hot combustion

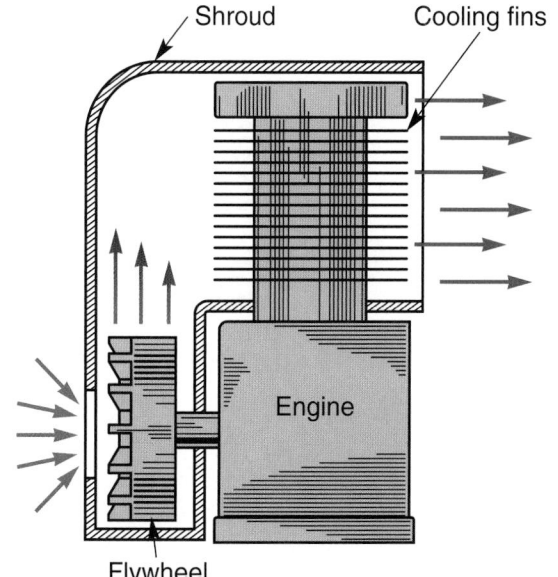

Goodheart-Willcox Publisher

Figure 12-1.

The air cooling system of a small gasoline engine consists of the shroud, screen, flywheel, baffles, and cooling fins. Airflow follows the path shown by arrows.

chamber parts ignite the air-fuel mixture before the spark plug fires.

There are two basic types of cooling systems used in small engines. Air cooling systems rely on the air surrounding the engine to carry excess heat away from the engine. Liquid cooling systems rely on a liquid coolant flowing through the engine to carry away heat.

Note

Engine oil also plays an important role in the cooling process. Oil circulating through the engine absorbs heat as it contacts the internal engine parts. It then draws off the heat as it leaves the engine (two-cycle engine) or transfers the heat through the crankcase to the outside air (four-cycle engine).

Air Cooling

Operating temperature is lowered as heat passes through the cylinder wall to the outer surfaces of the cylinder. See **Figure 12-2**. The heat of combustion (rapid burning and expansion of gas) travels from the cylinder through the cylinder walls by conduction. *Conduction* is heat transfer through a solid material.

When the heat reaches the outer surfaces of the cylinder, air forced over the surface carries the heat away by convection. *Convection* occurs when heat transfers through movement of a gas—in this case, air.

Thin *cooling fins* increase the surface area around the outside of the cylinder. See **Figure 12-3**. The greater the surface area in contact with the cooling air, the more rapidly the heat can be carried away. Cooling fins are necessary on air-cooled engines but not on water-cooled engines.

The flywheel has blades, which blow air around the cylinder and cooling fins. The flow of air is controlled and directed by a shroud and baffles surrounding the flywheel and cylinder. An engine should never be run without the shroud in place or it will quickly overheat. For safety, the flywheel is covered with a screen or perforated plate, which allows air to be drawn through it. See **Figure 12-4**. The screen should be kept clean to permit unrestricted airflow.

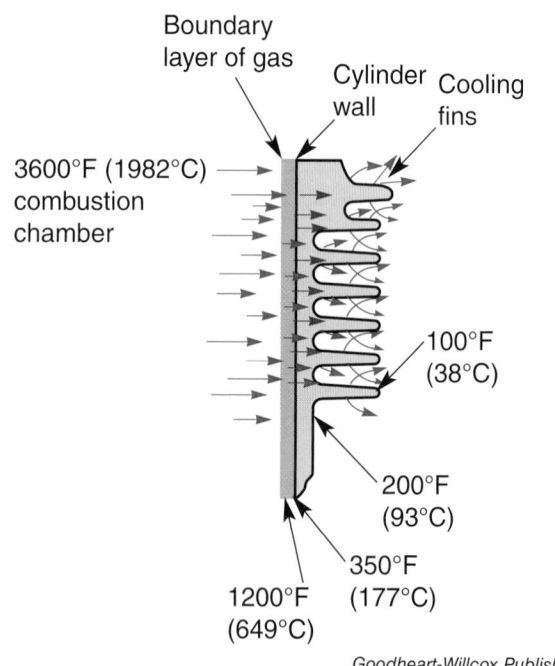

Goodheart-Willcox Publisher

Figure 12-2.

The high combustion chamber temperature is reduced by exhaust gases and the cooling system. The large area of the cooling fins controls heat dissipation from the cylinder.

Goodheart-Willcox Publisher

Figure 12-3.

Cooling fins are designed and placed to provide adequate cooling for each part of the cylinder. Thickness, surface area, and spacing are important considerations.

Figure 12-4.

The cooling air intake screen must be kept clean for unrestricted airflow. The screen must be kept in place to prevent clogging of the cooling fins.

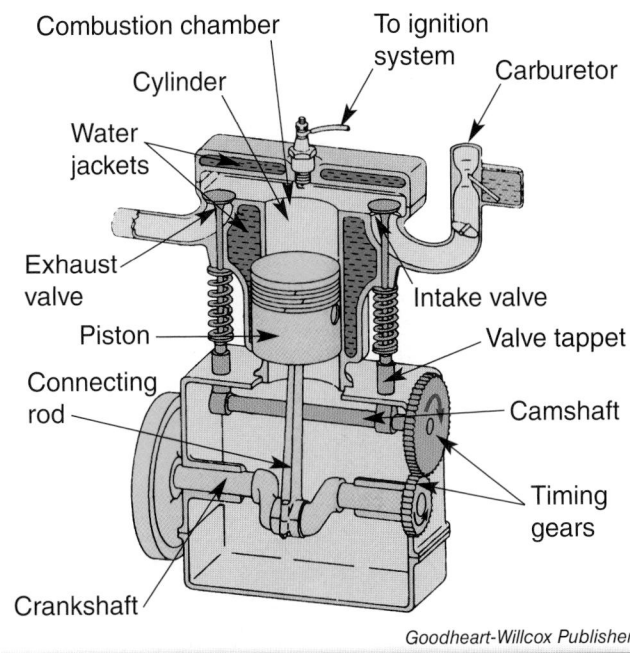

Figure 12-5.

Water is circulated around the cylinders through the water jacket, where it absorbs combustion heat.

Liquid Cooling

Water is an excellent medium for cooling engines. It is inexpensive, readily available, and absorbs heat well. Water is four times more effective than air for engine cooling. Liquid-cooled engines are generally made with coolant passages surrounding the cylinder. See **Figure 12-5**. These passages are called *water jackets.* As water (or a coolant mixture of water and antifreeze) circulates through the jackets, it absorbs some of the combustion heat and carries it away from the engine.

Pressurized Cooling Systems

Some liquid-cooled engines use a *pressurized cooling system*. The major components of a pressurized system include:

- Radiator.
- Water pump.
- Radiator cap.
- Hoses.
- Fan.
- Thermostat.

A basic pressurized cooling system is shown in **Figure 12-6**. The *radiator* is a water reservoir made from many thin copper or aluminum tubes. These tubes are connected at the top and bottom (or at each side) to water tanks. The tubes are held in place by thin metal fins. The fins increase the

cooling surface area of the tubes. The tube and fin assembly is called the *radiator core*. See **Figure 12-7**.

The liquid *coolant* used in a pressurized cooling system is a mixture of antifreeze and water. This mixture is designed to provide optimal performance under both cold and hot operating conditions. The antifreeze used in the coolant solution generally contains additives that prevent rust and corrosion from forming in the system. The formation of rust and corrosion can reduce the effectiveness of the cooling system.

The coolant, which is heated by the engine, is pushed into the top of the radiator core by an engine-driven *water pump*. The hot coolant travels downward or across through the tubes to the bottom tank. Cool air is forced between the fins in the core by an engine-driven fan. The air cools the water by conduction, radiation, and convection. The cooled water passes from the bottom tank to the engine water jacket, ready to absorb more heat.

In many liquid cooled engines, coolant temperature is carefully controlled by a thermostat. A thermostatically controlled engine will be kept at a constant temperature regardless of speed or outside temperature.

A *thermostat* is essentially a valve that stops circulation of engine coolant until the engine reaches the proper operating temperature. See **Figure 12-8**.

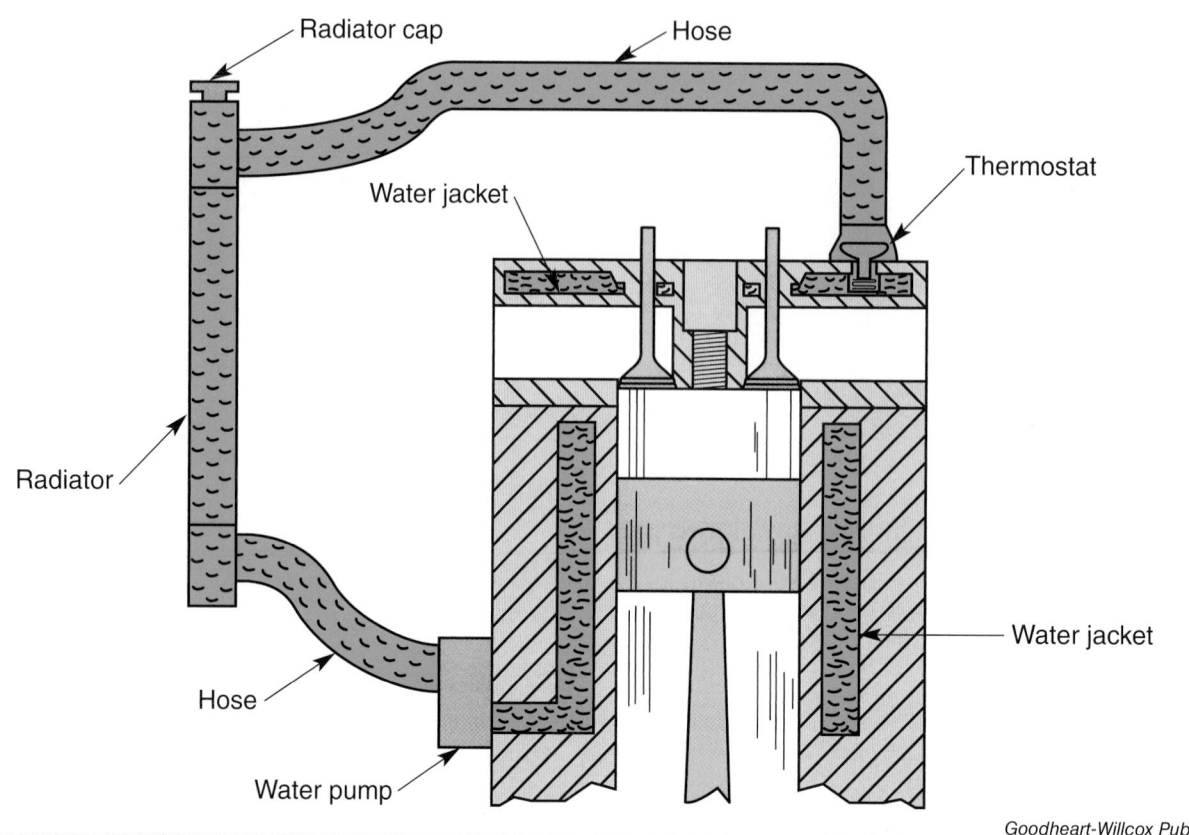

Figure 12-6.

Typical pressurized water cooling system. Note the location of the major components.

Goodheart-Willcox Publisher

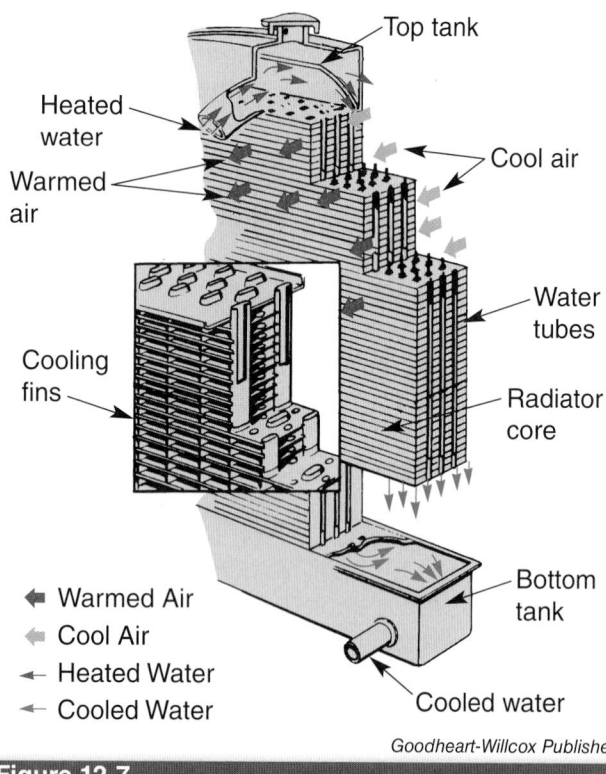

◄ Warmed Air
◄ Cool Air
◄ Heated Water
◄ Cooled Water

Goodheart-Willcox Publisher

Figure 12-7.

A radiator carries water through tubes in the core, where it is cooled by air forced across the cooling fins.

When engine temperature is below normal, the thermostat remains closed and the coolant is directed through a bypass channel. The coolant bypassing the radiator retains its heat and returns directly to the engine. This action delays forced cooling until the engine reaches its normal operating temperature. When the engine reaches normal operating temperature, the thermostat opens, allowing coolant to flow through the radiator. The fine balance of cooling maintained by the radiator and thermostat ensures that the engine will not overheat under loads in the hot summer or run too cold in the winter.

The *radiator cap* seals the radiator and allows pressure to build in the cooling system. This helps improve cooling efficiency and prevents evaporation of the coolant.

In many small-engine powered implements, the radiator is mounted directly above the flywheel and is connected to the engine with rubber hoses. See **Figure 12-9**. Blades formed on the top surface of the flywheel function as a fan to draw air in through the radiator as the flywheel spins. This air helps cool the engine coolant flowing through the radiator when the engine is running.

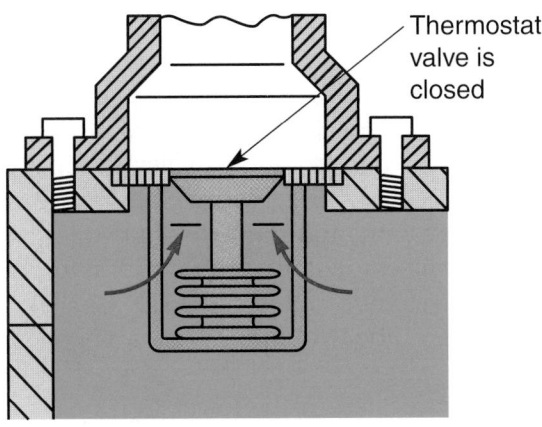

Thermostat valve is closed

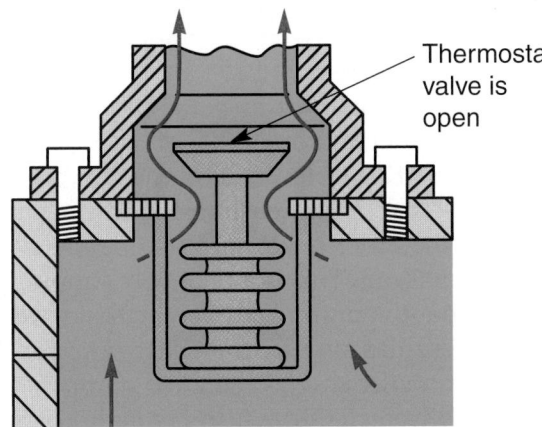

Thermostat valve is open

Goodheart-Willcox Publisher

Figure 12-8.

The thermostat is a valve that stops the flow of engine coolant until the engine reaches normal operating temperature.

Radiator

Radiator cap

Goodheart-Willcox Publisher

Figure 12-9.

This radiator is mounted above the flywheel. Cooling air is drawn through the radiator as the flywheel spins.

Outboard Engine Cooling Systems

Some small engines are water cooled because they are used in or around a water source. The outboard engine in **Figure 12-10** is typical of a relatively small water-cooled engine. Notice the absence of cooling fins, which are found only on air-cooled engines. Some small outboard engines use a simple cooling device called a *pressure-vacuum water flow system*. See **Figure 12-11**. The water

Evinrude Motors

Figure 12-10.

Outboard engines are frequently water cooled. Note the absence of cooling fins.

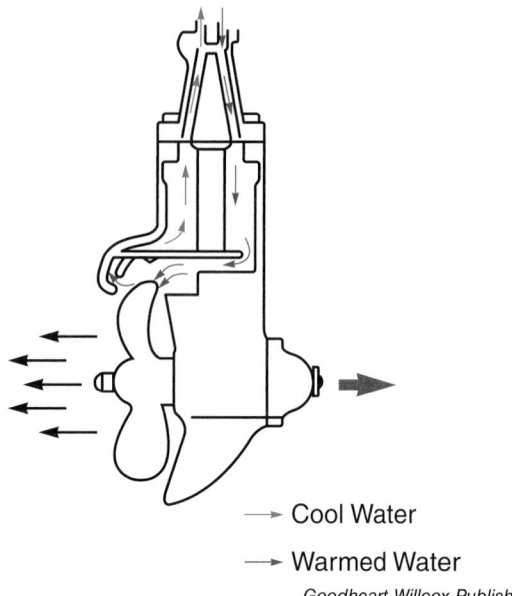

→ Cool Water

→ Warmed Water

Figure 12-11.

A pressure-vacuum cooling system utilizes the thrust of the propeller tips and venturi (narrowed section of a passage) vacuum, created by the forward motion of the engine, to circulate water.

flow from the propeller tips creates pressure against the intake port and vacuum at the outlet port, which is located immediately forward of the propeller. Propeller action and the forward motion of the boat provide water circulation.

At slow speeds, like those used for trolling, pressure of water from the propeller tips may not be enough to force water through the cooling system. Sufficient cooling is still maintained, however, by the siphon (sucking) effect of the discharge channels as the boat moves through the water. When starting an engine with a pressure-vacuum system, the engine should be given a short burst of speed to fill the channels and water jacket with water. See **Figure 12-11**.

Another type of pressure-vacuum water flow system has the discharge ports located in the propeller blades. The centrifugal force created by the turning propeller aids in discharging the water. *Centrifugal force* is the tendency of spinning matter to move away from the center of its path. Since there are no moving parts except for the propeller, the system will function as long as the water channels and jackets remain unobstructed.

With this system, vacuum must be maintained, particularly at low speeds. Therefore, all water connections in the system are airtight. Air seepage

into the cooling system would destroy the slow speed siphoning effect and cause overheating.

Worn propeller blades can also cause poor circulation. The propeller's reduced diameter puts the tips farther from the water scoop opening. This reduces water pressure. Saltwater corrosion, marine growth, and mud-clogged water channels are all causes of faulty water circulation in this type of system.

Some outboard engines use a water pump to circulate water through the system. The pump is generally located in the lower unit near or below the waterline. The main pump member is driven by the vertical drive shaft or horizontal propeller shaft. The pump must have an opening for water to enter and one for it to exit. These openings are called the inlet and outlet.

Figure 12-12 shows a pump-driven cooling system. Water is drawn into the intake, pumped through the water jacket surrounding the cylinders, and discharged. This is a relatively simple system. Notice that the pump is driven by the drive shaft.

In a similar system, the water pump is driven by the propeller shaft. When this pump location is used, the water is drawn in through ports in the propeller hub.

A *sliding vane pump* is illustrated in **Figure 12-13**. As the eccentric cam (an off-center enlargement

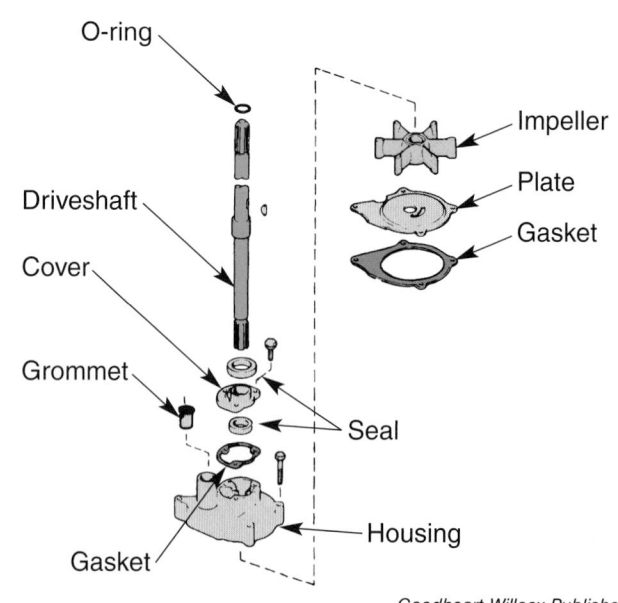

Figure 12-12.

This water pump for an outboard engine is driven by a vertical drive shaft. Some pumps are mounted on the propeller shaft.

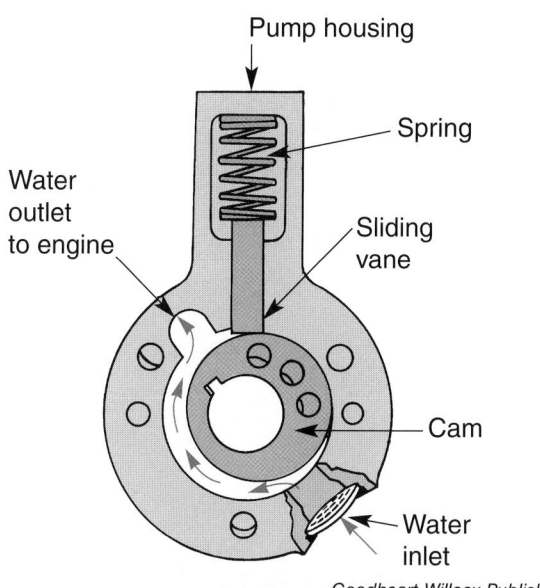

Goodheart-Willcox Publisher

Figure 12-13.

The revolving cam in a sliding vane water pump fills a large volume of space, and water is pushed through the outlet to the engine. The sliding vane prevents water from revolving with the cam.

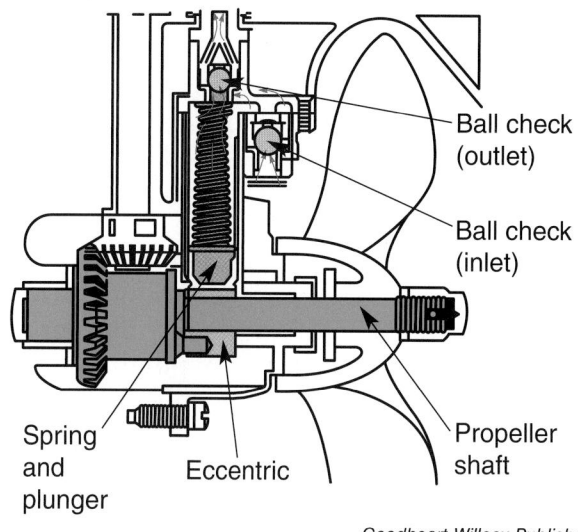

Goodheart-Willcox Publisher

Figure 12-14.

A plunger pump draws water in through one ball check valve and forces it out through a second valve. The plunger is operated by an eccentric.

on a shaft) is rotated in the sliding vane pump, the volume of space between the cam and pump housing constantly changes. Water enters the inlet and fills this space. The cam rotates and closes the inlet, pushing the water ahead of it toward the pump outlet.

The outlet is connected to the water jacket by suitable tubing. A second tube carries the heated water out of the engine. The sliding vane is kept in close contact with the cam by a spring. The vane provides a seal so water cannot continue past the outlet. However, during high-speed operation, water pressure may become high enough to lift the vane against the spring, allowing some water to recirculate through the pump. This action prevents too much pressure from building up in the cooling system.

The *rotor-type pump* operates much like the sliding vane pump. The vane and rotor are one piece, and the eccentric gyrates the rotor (rotates the rotor with a bobbing motion), causing a pumping action.

The *plunger pump* has a cylinder and plunger. See **Figure 12-14**. The plunger is raised and lowered in the cylinder by an eccentric on the propeller shaft. A spring keeps the plunger close to the eccentric.

When the spring forces the plunger down in the cylinder, water is drawn in through the inlet ball check valve while the outlet ball check valve is closed. As the eccentric lifts the plunger, the inlet check valve is closed by the increasing pressure in the cylinder and the outlet check valve is opened. Water in the cylinder is forced through tubing to the engine.

Vari-volume pumps use a synthetic rubber impeller. See **Figure 12-15A**. Since the impeller housing is off-center with the drive shaft, the impeller arms must flex as they revolve. The volume

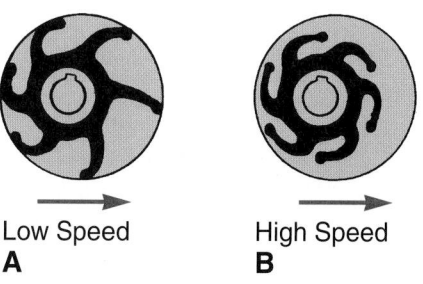

Low Speed
A

High Speed
B

Goodheart-Willcox Publisher

Figure 12-15.

A vari-volume pump has a flexible synthetic rubber impeller that is offset from the center of the impeller housing. A—Space between impeller arms varies as they rotate. B—At high speed, the increased water pressure forces the impeller arms inward to prevent overcooling of the engine.

between the arms increases and decreases with rotation.

The inlet port, or opening, is located where the volume is increasing and the water is drawn into the housing. The outlet is on the side where volume is decreasing and the water is forced out into the water jacket.

When a vari-volume pump is driven at high speeds, the back pressure of the water in the system becomes great enough to force the impeller arms inward. See **Figure 12-15B**. The pump loses some of its effectiveness and moves only enough water through the engine to maintain proper operating temperature in the cylinders. Overcooling of the cylinders of an outboard engine can happen at high engine speeds unless some sort of flow control, such as this, is designed into the cooling system.

A thermostatically controlled outboard cooling system is shown in **Figure 12-16**. Cold water enters the intake and passes through the pump to the water jacket. If the temperature of the water from the jacket is high enough to open the thermostat, the water is discharged from the engine. If the water is too cool to open the thermostat, it is recirculated through the pressure control valve and back to the pump. When water is recirculated, it retains some of its heat and eventually brings the cylinder head temperature up to thermostat temperature. This type of system can maintain a constant operating temperature and will automatically compensate for even slight changes in cooling water temperature.

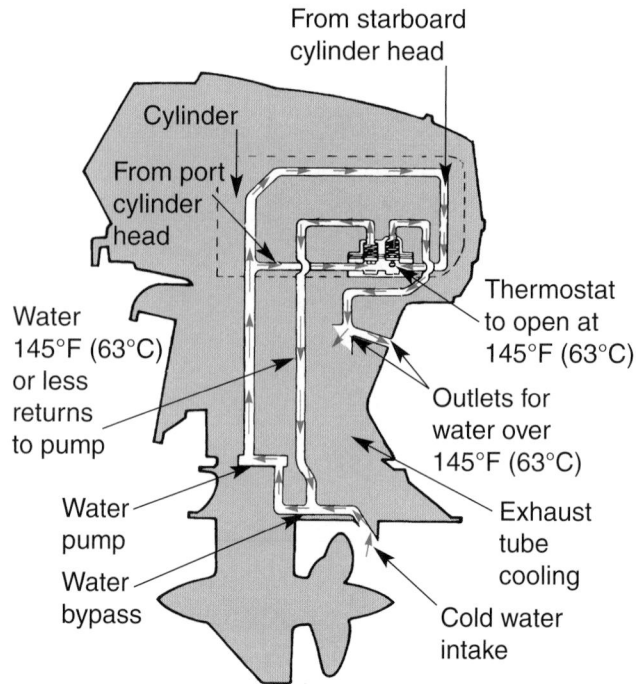

Kawasaki Motors Corp., U.S.A.

Figure 12-16.

Some outboard engines have a thermostatically controlled cooling system. Water recirculates until the thermostat opens, discharging heated water and allowing more cold water to enter the intake. This thermostatically controlled cooling system employs a double feed bypass.

Summary

The efficiency and life of an engine depend on how well it is cooled. About a third of the heat produced is converted to mechanical energy. The exhaust system carries away another third of the heat. The remaining third is carried away by the cooling system.

There are two basic types of cooling systems used in small engines. Air cooling systems rely on the air surrounding the engine to carry away excess heat. Liquid cooling systems rely on a liquid coolant flowing through the engine to carry away heat.

The heat of combustion travels from the cylinder through the cylinder walls by conduction. Conduction is heat transfer through a solid material. When the heat reaches the outer surfaces of the cylinder, air forced over the surface carries the heat away by convection. Convection occurs when heat transfers through movement of a gas. Thin cooling fins increase the surface area around the outside of the cylinder.

The major components of a pressurized system include the radiator, water pump, radiator cap, hoses, fan, and thermostat. The radiator is a water reservoir made from many thin copper or aluminum tubes. The liquid coolant used in a pressurized cooling system is a mixture of antifreeze and water. The coolant, which is heated by the engine, is pushed into the radiator core by an engine-driven water pump.

In many liquid-cooled engines, coolant temperature is carefully controlled by a thermostat. A thermostat is a valve that stops circulation of engine coolant until the engine reaches the proper operating temperature.

The radiator cap seals the radiator and allows pressure to build in the cooling system. This helps improve cooling efficiency and prevents evaporation of the coolant.

Some small engines are water cooled because they are used in or around a water source. Some small outboard engines use a simple cooling device called a pressure-vacuum water flow system. The water flow from the propeller tips creates pressure against the intake port and vacuum at the outlet port. Propeller action and the forward motion of the boat provide water circulation.

Some outboard engines use a water pump to circulate water through the system. The pump is generally located in the lower unit near or below the waterline. The main pump member is driven by the vertical drive shaft or horizontal propeller shaft.

Review Questions

Answer the following questions using the information provided in this chapter.

1. The average temperature of the burned gases in the combustion chamber is ____.
   A. 2400°F (1315.5°C)
   B. 3000°F (1649°C)
   C. 6200°F (3427°C)
   D. 3600°F (1982°C)

2. Approximately ____ of the heat produced by burning combustion gases is converted to mechanical energy.

3. What are the two basic types of cooling systems used in small engines?

4. What role does engine oil play in the cooling process?

5. The heat that reaches the cooling fins is carried away mainly by ____.
   A. convection
   B. conduction
   C. radiation

6. The ____ increase the surface area around the outside of the cylinder in air-cooled engines.

7. When used for engine cooling, water is about ____ times as effective as air.

8. Cylinders of water-cooled engines are surrounded by ____.
   A. insulation material
   B. a water reservoir
   C. a water jacket
   D. cooling water tubes

9. Name the six major components of a pressurized cooling system.

10. Explain the purpose of the radiator used in pressurized cooling systems.

11. A(n) _____ is a valve that stops circulation of engine coolant until the engine reaches proper operating temperature.

12. In a pressurized cooling system, air cools the coolant by _____.
    A. convection
    B. conduction
    C. radiation
    D. All of the above.

13. The _____ seals the radiator and allows pressure to build in the cooling system.

14. The _____ water flow system in outboard engines utilizes the tips of the propeller to circulate water.

15. *True or False?* Some outboard engines use a water pump to circulate water through the system.

Suggested Activities

1. Place a thermostat and thermometer into a beaker of water. Heat the water and check thermostat operation.

2. Operate an air-cooled engine and use a smoke generator to demonstrate the flow of air through the shroud and around the cooling fins.

3. Inspect a cutaway of a radiator and explain how it cools water.

4. Disassemble the lower unit of an outboard engine and study the pumping and circulation system.

5. Place the outboard engine in a tank and briefly operate it to observe the cooling system at work.

Kawasaki Motors Corp., U.S.A

This personal watercraft is powered by a three-cylinder, two-stroke, water-cooled engine.

SECTION 4
Engine Service

Preventive Maintenance and Troubleshooting

Learning Objectives

After studying this chapter, you will be able to:

- Perform preventive maintenance on various engine systems, including the crankcase breather, air cleaner, and muffler.
- Keep engines clean.
- Change the oil in a four-cycle engine.
- Prepare an engine for storage.
- Describe systematic troubleshooting.
- Use manufacturer's service manuals to determine engine specifications and explain why this information is necessary when servicing a small engine.

Key Terms

compression gauge
compression test
coolant hydrometer
differential pressure test
digital tachometer
filler plug
hot spots
loaded oil
optical tachometer
owner's manual
preventive maintenance
reverse flushing
service manual
systematic troubleshooting
thread chaser

Preventive Maintenance

Certain maintenance tasks must be performed regularly to keep an engine working properly. These tasks come under the heading of *preventive maintenance*, because they help prevent premature engine wear and other engine problems.

Engine Cleaning

Cleaning a small air-cooled engine periodically can help prevent overheating. For proper cooling action, air must pass across the extended metal surfaces (cooling fins) of the cylinder block and cylinder head. If the cooling fins are insulated by dirt, leaves, and/or grass clippings, engine parts will retain most of the combustion heat. Parts will expand, probably distort, and possibly seize. Therefore, all finned surfaces should be cleaned regularly.

Methods for cleaning small air-cooled engines vary. Begin by removing any shrouds or engine covers obstructing the cooling fins. You can then blow debris from the fins with compressed air and use a cleaning solvent to remove any remaining dirt and oil. See **Figure 13-1**. Alternately, you can scrape the dirty areas with a piece of wood and wipe them with a clean cloth. Various multipurpose spray cleaners are suitable for use on small engines.

> **Warning**
>
> When using compressed air, be extremely careful where you direct the blast of air. Wear safety goggles. Never direct the air blast toward skin or clothing.

In addition to cleaning cooling fins, be sure to clean the engine crankcase area. This area also transfers a great deal of engine heat to the surrounding air. A coating of dirt or oil will insulate the crankcase and may contribute to engine overheating.

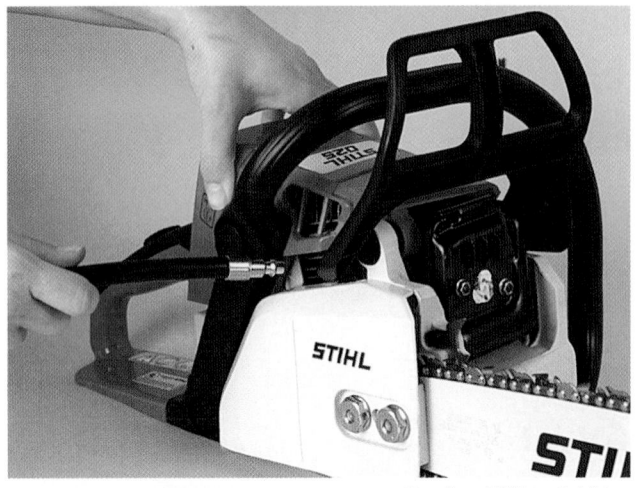

Goodheart-Willcox Publisher

Figure 13-1.

This chain saw engine is being cleaned with compressed air.

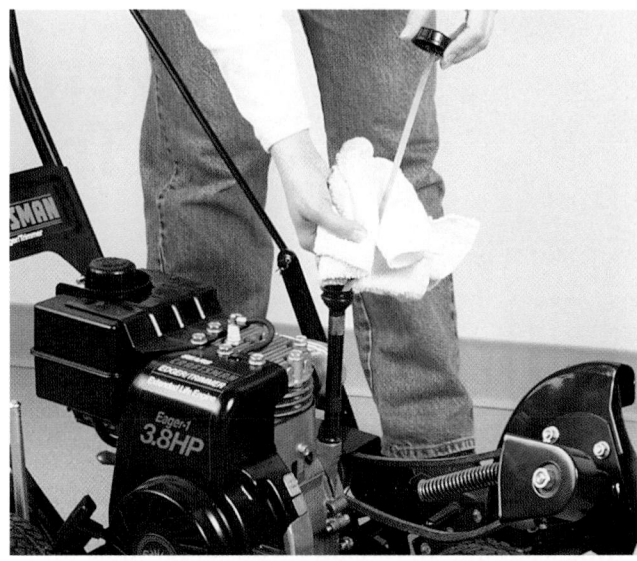

Goodheart-Willcox Publisher

Figure 13-2.

Checking the oil is an important part of preventive maintenance.

Checking Oil Level and Condition

Crankcase oil in four-cycle engines should be checked periodically. Preferably, it should be checked each time fuel is added. The engine manufacturer provides a means of visually inspecting the level and condition of the oil. Use the type and viscosity grade of oil recommended by the manufacturer and maintain it at the proper operating level.

To check the oil level in engines equipped with a dipstick, withdraw the dipstick and wipe it dry. Reinsert the dipstick as far as it will go. Withdraw it a second time and observe the oil level on the dipstick. See **Figure 13-2**.

The markings on dipsticks may vary, but all will have a *Low* (*Add*) mark and a *Full* mark. Add oil if the level is at or below the *Low* mark. Do not run the engine with oil showing above the *Full* mark on the dipstick. If the crankcase oil level is high, drain some oil.

Plug

Goodheart-Willcox Publisher

Figure 13-3.

A screwdriver can be used to remove the type of oil filler plug shown here.

Caution

Overfilling the crankcase with oil can foul plugs and cause the engine to use too much oil.

Some small gasoline engines do not have dipsticks. Instead, they have a *filler plug* that threads into the filler hole to seal out dirt and seal in the oil. **Figure 13-3** shows the proper method of loosening one type of filler plug. When the plug is removed,

the oil level should be at the top of the filler hole or to a mark just inside the filler hole.

If the engine oil level drops at an excessive rate (requires the addition of oil frequently), look for the cause. Refer to a troubleshooting chart for the particular engine at hand. Troubleshooting charts are covered later in this chapter. Typical causes of excess oil consumption are external leaks, worn oil seals around the crankshaft, worn valve guides, worn piston rings, or a hot running engine.

The color of used oil is not always an accurate indication of its condition. Additives in the oil may change its color without decreasing its lubricating qualities.

The small engine manufacturer will recommend oil changes at intervals based on hours of running time. A new engine should have the first oil drained after only a few hours of operation to remove any metallic particles from the crankcase. After that, the time specified may vary from 10–50 hours.

Engine oil does not wear out. It always remains slippery. However, oil used for many hours of engine operation becomes contaminated with dirt particles, soot, sludge, varnish-forming materials, metal particles, water, corrosive acids, and gasoline. These contaminants eventually render the oil useless. The harm they cause outweighs the lubricating quality of the oil.

The time interval for oil changes is selected so that the oil never reaches a *loaded* level of contamination. **Loaded oil** cannot absorb any more contaminants and still be an effective lubricant. When oil reaches a loaded condition, varnish deposits begin to form on the piston and rings, and sludge collects in the crankcase.

Changing Oil

Changing engine oil is not difficult. Begin by running the engine until it is thoroughly warmed up. Warm oil will drain more completely, and more contaminants will be removed if the oil is agitated.

Turn off the engine and disconnect the spark plug. The oil drain plug is located at a low point on the crankcase, usually along the outside edge of the base. See **Figure 13-4**.

Note
Some engines do not have an oil drain plug. Oil must be drained through the filler hole on these engines.

Clean the dirt from the drain plug area and then remove the plug with a proper wrench, **Figure 13-5**. Allow the oil to drain for approximately five minutes to remove as much contaminated oil as possible. See **Figure 13-6**. If the drain hole is located on the side or top of the engine, tilt the engine toward the drain hole if possible. When draining is complete, replace the drain plug.

If the engine is equipped with a disposable oil filter, replace the filter each time the oil is changed.

Drain plug

Goodheart-Willcox Publisher

Figure 13-4.

The oil drain plug is located at a low point in the crankcase to permit oil to drain completely.

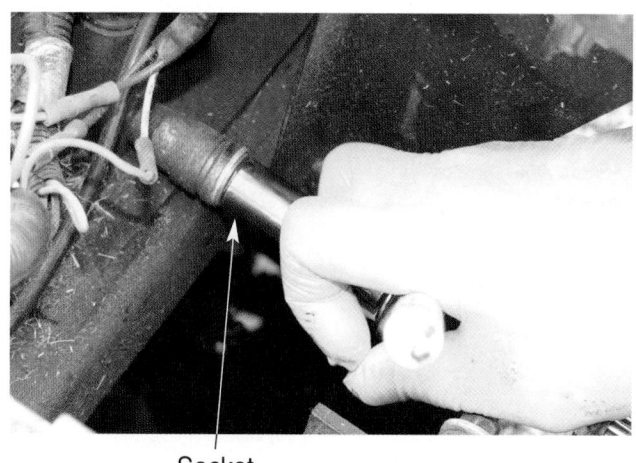

Socket

Goodheart-Willcox Publisher

Figure 13-5.

This technician is using a socket and ratchet to remove the drain plug. The plug should be turned counterclockwise for removal.

To prevent oil leaks, always coat the filter's O-ring seal with a light coat of clean oil before installing the filter. See **Figure 13-7**.

Before putting fresh oil in the engine, clean the filler opening, funnel, and the top of the oil container. Be sure to use the type, viscosity grade, and quantity of oil recommended by the manufacturer. Pour the oil in the engine's crankcase and then check the level. See **Figure 13-8**. If the oil level is correct, replace the filler cap and reconnect the spark plug lead to the spark plug.

Drain plug

Goodheart-Willcox Publisher

Figure 13-6.

It may take several minutes for all the old oil to drain from the engine.

Goodheart-Willcox Publisher

Figure 13-8.

Clean the area around the filler opening, as well as the funnel, before adding oil.

Gasket

Oil filter

Goodheart-Willcox Publisher

Figure 13-7.

A typical disposable oil filter. To prevent leaks, apply a light film of oil around the O-ring seal before installation.

If any oil is left in the oil container, cap the container tightly to prevent condensation or contamination.

Green Tech

Oil and Oil Filters

Engine oil must be changed regularly because of the impurities it collects while in use. Because of the hazardous nature of used petroleum products, the Environmental Protection Agency (EPA) has suggestions for how shops can handle used motor oil and oil filters. If you must dispose of used oil and oil filters, you must do so properly and contain the contaminants within the oil. Motor oil can be reused when properly refined. Often, offsite recycling facilities will accept both motor oil and oil filters. Oil filters must be properly drained before they are accepted for recycling. Be sure to properly contain used oil and do not mix it with other waste.

Start the engine and allow it to run for a few minutes. Then stop the engine and recheck the oil level. Add oil as necessary. Finally, inspect the drain plug and oil filter for oil leaks.

Caution

After changing the oil, wash oily rags or dispose of them properly. Storing them may cause spontaneous combustion. Spontaneous combustion occurs when combustible material self-ignites.

Lubricating Cables and Linkage

Engine cables and linkage should be lubricated periodically to ensure smooth operation and reduce the chances of binding and premature wear. Linkage (throttle linkage, governor linkage, etc.) can generally be lubricated by spraying it with an appropriate lubricant.

Note

Many manufacturers recommend silicone-based lubricants for use on cables and linkages. Unlike petroleum-based products, these lubricants will not attract dirt after they are applied.

To lubricate cables (throttle cable, engine bale, etc.), place a few drops of the recommended lubricant between the cable and its housing at the highest end of the cable. Allow the lubricant to run down between the cable and housing. Lubricant should flow out of the low end of the cable. If it does not, add a few more drops of lubricant and allow it to run down the cable. Continue this process until clean lubricant flows from the bottom end of the cable.

If desired, spray lubricant can be used to lubricate the cable. Simply spray the lube between the cable and the housing, and watch for it to exit at the low end of the cable. See **Figure 13-9**.

Some manufacturers produce a tool that provides a leak-proof connection between the tube from a can of spray lubricant and the cable. When this tool is used, the lubricant is forced under pressure through the cable, making lubricating cables fast and easy. This type of tool is especially helpful when lubricating cables that run horizontally rather than vertically.

Spark Plug Service

The spark plug should periodically be removed for inspection and cleaned or replaced. Begin by using compressed air to blow dirt away from the base of the spark plug. Remove the spark plug wire from the plug by pulling on the wire's insulating boot only. Do not pull on the wire itself. See **Figure 13-10**.

Install a deep spark plug socket on the plug and carefully turn the ratchet handle counterclockwise. Unscrew the spark plug and remove it from the cylinder head.

Carefully examine the electrode end of the plug. The electrodes and ceramic insulator should be dry. An insulator or electrodes that are wet with fuel or oil may be a sign of serious engine problems. A dry insulator that has a beige or gray/tan color indicates that the engine is in good condition. Next, examine the electrodes for any erosion, burning, or carbon fouling. Refer to *Spark Plug Condition* chart in the *Appendix* of this text.

If the spark plug insulator and electrodes appear to be good (no evidence of fouling or wear), the plug can be reinstalled. If not, install a new plug of the correct type. Refer to the manufacturer's technical service manuals for the proper replacement spark plug.

Cable   Housing

Spray lubricant

Goodheart-Willcox Publisher

Figure 13-9.

Lubricant can be sprayed between the cable and the housing.

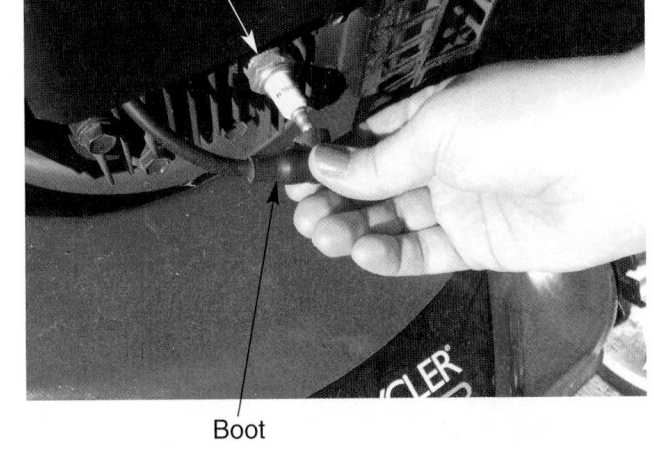

Spark plug

Boot

Goodheart-Willcox Publisher

Figure 13-10.

When removing a spark plug wire from the plug, pull on the boot only. Do not pull on the wire itself.

Check the electrode gap with a wire-type feeler gauge, **Figure 13-11**. The engine service manual will specify the proper gap setting. If the gap is too large, carefully bend the outer electrode toward the center electrode until the gap is correct. Use the gap setting tool.

Before installing the spark plug, clean the external ceramic insulator by wiping it with a clean cloth. Condensation can cause flashover (sparking externally) and erratic running if the insulator has a coating of dirt on it. If the metal base is rusty, clean it on a wire wheel or with a wire brush. If the threads are dirty, they should be wiped clean or wire brushed before inserting the plug back into the spark plug hole. The gasket should be in good condition or replaced with a new one.

Insert the spark plug in the spark plug hole and turn it clockwise by hand until it stops. Be careful not to cross thread the spark plug in the hole. If the plug will not turn, do not force it. Remove it and examine the threads in the hole. If they are damaged, a *thread chaser* (special thread tapping tool) may be needed to clean and correct the threads. If the spark plug turns smoothly by hand until it seats, tighten the plug with a torque wrench to 13–15 lb ft. Do not overtighten.

Examine the spark plug wire for deterioration before reinstalling it on the spark plug. Heat and dirt can make the insulation brittle and insulation cracking can occur. Cracked wire insulation can allow arcing to metallic parts of the engine and cause hard starting and erratic running. Oil- or fuel-soaked wires will leak current and cause weak firing of the plug. The insulating boot should be dry and in good condition.

Air Cleaner Service

The air cleaner should be cleaned before each season of operation and at regular intervals thereafter. Under severe dust conditions, air filters should be cleaned more often. A plugged air filter can cause hard starting, loss of power, and spark plug fouling.

Three types of air cleaners widely used in small gasoline engines are the oil-wetted (plastic foam element) type, the dry type (pleated paper element), and the dual-element type. Each has a different method of cleaning and servicing.

Begin by removing the screw, wing nut, or other fastening device to uncover the air cleaner element. See **Figure 13-12**.

When servicing an oil-wetted filter element, the element can be pulled from the receptacle after the cover is removed. See **Figure 13-13**. Be careful not to drop any dirt into the carburetor throat during this procedure.

To clean the element, wash it in liquid detergent and water. Then rinse the element in clear water. After washing the element, wrap it in dry cloth and squeeze it dry. Absorbent toweling works well for this procedure.

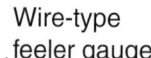
Wire-type
feeler gauge

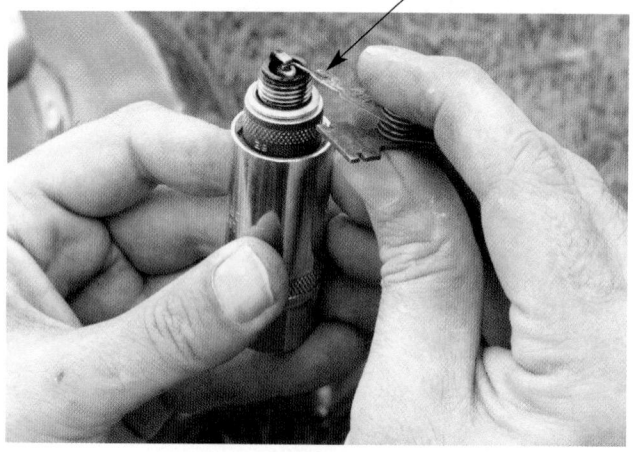
Goodheart-Willcox Publisher

Figure 13-11.

A wire-type feeler gauge is being used to check spark plug gap.

Air cleaner cover
Goodheart-Willcox Publisher

Figure 13-12.

The cover on this air cleaner housing is held in place by a screw.

Oil-wetted
air cleaner

Goodheart-Willcox Publisher

Figure 13-13.

After the cover is removed, the element can be pulled from the receptacle.

The plastic foam should be saturated with clean engine oil. After saturating the element, squeeze excess oil out of the foam. See **Figure 13-14**. Finally, reassemble the air filter unit. Follow any special instructions found in the owner's manual for the specific engine and filter.

Most dry-type air filter elements (pleated paper) are designed to be thrown away when they become dirty. Nevertheless, you can clean a pleated paper filter element by tapping it on a flat surface to dislodge light accumulations of dirt. However, if the element will not tap clean, it must be replaced.

Caution

Never use compressed air to clean the paper filter because the air can damage the filter element. The damaged filter may not prevent fine dirt from entering the engine.

When installing a pleated paper-type air filter element, the pleated paper should face the external side of the air cleaner receptacle. See **Figure 13-15**.

Engines designed to be used in dusty conditions may have dual-element air cleaners. Dual-element air cleaners use a plastic foam filter pre-cleaner that is mounted over a pleated paper filter element. See **Figure 13-16**. When servicing this type of filter, the pre-cleaner can be washed in detergent and water and squeezed dry, **Figure 13-17**. Some pre-cleaners must be oiled after they are cleaned. The paper filter element should be cleaned by shaking or replaced.

Every engine to be serviced or repaired should have its air cleaner examined. If the air cleaner element or cartridge is damaged or shows signs of restriction, replace it. Worn or damaged mounting gaskets and air cleaner gaskets should be replaced

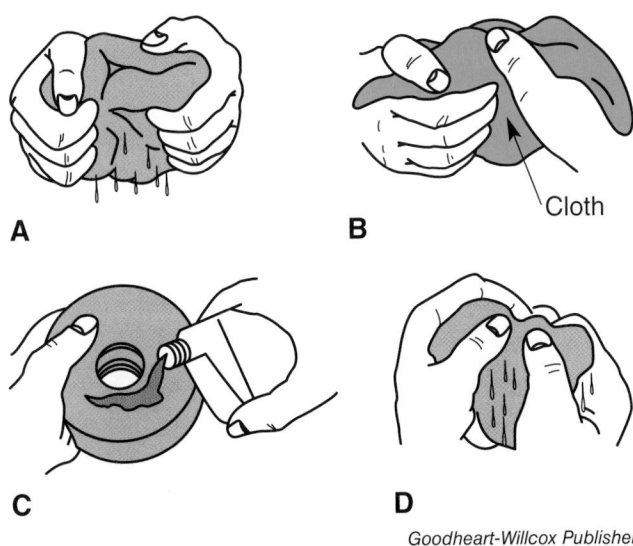

Goodheart-Willcox Publisher

Figure 13-14.

The sequence for servicing a foam-type filter element is shown. A—Wash the foam element thoroughly in liquid detergent and water. B—Wrap the foam in cloth and squeeze it dry. C—Saturate the foam with clean oil. D—Squeeze out the excess oil.

Air cleaner receptacle

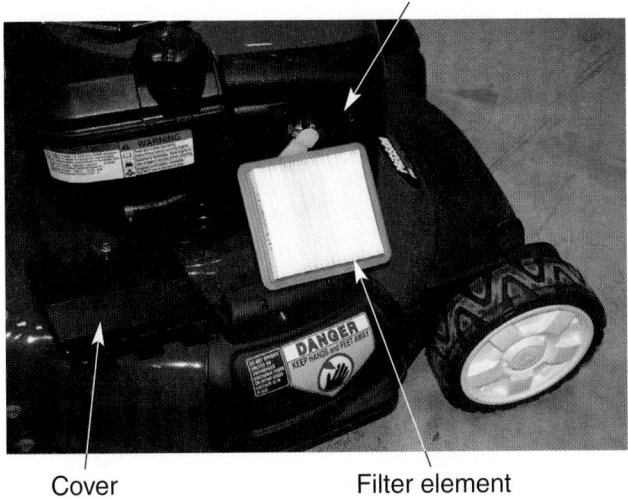

Cover

Filter element

Goodheart-Willcox Publisher

Figure 13-15.

The pleated paper should face the outside of the air cleaner receptacle (away from the engine).

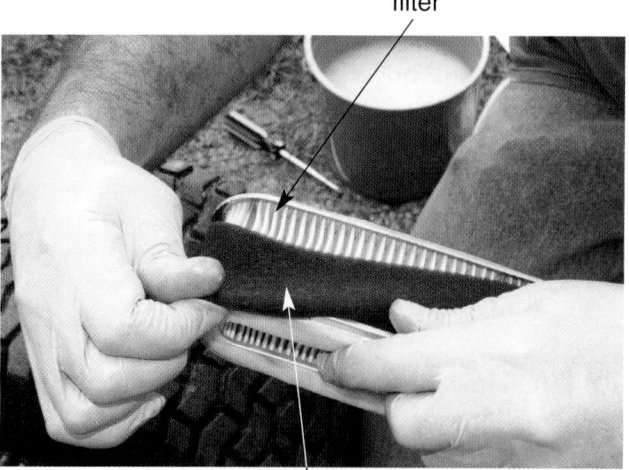

Pleated paper filter

Pre-cleaner

Goodheart-Willcox Publisher

Figure 13-16.

In a dual-element air cleaner, the pre-cleaner must be removed before the pleated paper filter can be serviced.

Goodheart-Willcox Publisher

Figure 13-17.

The foam pre-cleaner can be washed in detergent and water and squeezed dry.

to prevent dirt and dust from entering the engine through an improper seal around the filter.

Crankcase Breather Service

If the small gasoline engine has a crankcase breather, the breather assembly should be removed and cleaned periodically. The breather is located over the valve stem chamber. It is held in place with two or more screws.

To inspect the breather, remove the screws and the breather assembly. The breather contains a reed valve similar to the one shown in **Figure 13-18**. The valve allows outward airflow only.

Inspect the valve to make sure it is not damaged or distorted. If it is, the breather assembly must be replaced. If applicable, see that the drain hole in the body of the assembly is open. This hole permits accumulated oil to return to the engine. After all components have been inspected, replace damaged gaskets, reinstall the assembly on the engine, and tighten the screws.

Muffler Service

An engine takes in large quantities of air mixed with fuel, and then burns the mixture. Unless the engine readily rids itself of the by-products of combustion, its efficiency will be greatly reduced. This is the task of the exhaust system, which, in small gasoline engines, mainly consists of exhaust port(s) and a small muffler.

A muffler is designed to reduce noise and allow exhaust gases to escape. When it becomes clogged with carbon soot, gases cannot get out of the combustion chamber quickly enough to allow fresh air and fuel to enter. This causes a loss in engine power, along with a tendency to overheat.

If clogging is suspected with a sealed muffler, install a new muffler and check for improved engine efficiency. See **Figure 13-19**. If a muffler is designed to be taken apart, it can be disassembled and cleaned in a solvent to remove soot and other debris.

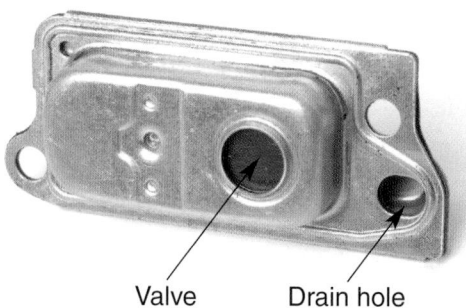

Valve   Drain hole

Goodheart-Willcox Publisher

Figure 13-18.

Crankcase breather elements need periodic inspection. The function of the reed valve is to allow air to leave the crankcase, but prevent it from entering.

Locking tab

A

B

Goodheart-Willcox Publisher

Figure 13-19.

Locking tabs are often used to prevent muffler fasteners from loosening. A—Before attempting to remove the fasteners, use a screwdriver to bend the tabs out of the way. B—Once tabs are bent down, a wrench can be used to remove the fasteners securing the muffler to the engine.

Battery Service

The battery in a small engine–powered implement may be either a maintenance-free battery or a conventional lead-acid battery. Check the manufacturer's service information to determine which type is being used.

The maintenance-free battery should not be replaced with a conventional lead-acid battery. The electrical system is designed exclusively for a maintenance-free battery and the electrical system will not work properly with a conventional lead-acid battery.

Conventional lead-acid batteries need occasional additions of distilled water to keep the electrolyte level above the plates. Fill to the level shown on the case of the battery. Use a bulb syringe to add water and do not overfill. Maintenance-free batteries *do not* need to have fluid added and should not have the sealed caps removed.

Removing, servicing, charging, or installing a battery must be done carefully to avoid spilling any electrolyte.

Batteries produce hydrogen gas, which is very explosive. Keep batteries away from sparks, flame, etc. Charging and using a battery should be done in a well-ventilated space. Battery electrolyte contains sulfuric acid, which can cause serious burns to the skin, eyes, or clothing if contact is made. Always wear eye protection when working with batteries.

Batteries are secured in a battery box, tray, or similar device and securely fastened to the implement. The battery is held in position to resist being thrown about during operation. A loose battery would quickly result in a cracked case. This could cause serious damage to the implement and possible injury to the user. When servicing the battery, make sure the battery hold-down is tight and in good condition.

Corrosion at the battery terminals and cable connectors is not uncommon. See **Figure 13-20**. The corrosion should be cleaned from the terminals. To clean the terminals, proceed as follows:

1. Remove the battery cable from the terminal.

Corroded terminal

Goodheart-Willcox Publisher

Figure 13-20.

This battery terminal and cable connection is extremely corroded.

2. Use a solution of baking soda and water to wash the cable connectors and battery terminals. (One teaspoon of baking soda to one cup of water.)
3. Use a stiff brush to remove the corrosion from the cable connectors and battery terminals, **Figure 13-21**.
4. Rinse the battery and connectors with clear water and dry the battery case and terminals with absorbent cloths, **Figure 13-22**.
5. Coat the terminals with a waterproof dielectric grease to prevent further corrosion.

6. Reinstall the battery cables on the battery terminals. In negative-ground systems, the positive cable should be connected before the negative cable.

Charge a battery only when it needs it. Normally, the alternator driven by the engine keeps the battery charged. If the battery is old and does not crank the engine, it should be tested and possibly replaced with a new one. A battery that is low on fluid will not take a full charge. This battery will eventually overheat the plates and fail completely. Sulfated plates will cause battery failure also. Refer to the *Batteries* section in Chapter 15 of this text for detailed information on charging batteries.

Pressurized Liquid Cooling System Service

The pressurized liquid cooling systems used in small engines require maintenance similar to that employed in the automobile engine. Because the combination of water and metal sometimes produces harmful chemical reactions that attack the water jacket, antifreeze containing a chemical rust inhibitor should be added whenever a system is drained and refilled. If rust and scale are allowed to form and accumulate, the walls of the water jacket will become insulated. This will cause engine heat to be retained rather than removed.

Scale settling to the bottom may plug water passages in the cylinder block and clog water tubes in the radiator. Without free circulation of water, the engine will run hot even when the thermostat is open. Local *hot spots* can occur in the engine when the passages in the block are obstructed.

In severe cases, water may boil inside the block, and the steam will prevent water from contacting and cooling inner walls. Then, serious overheating and damage to parts of the engine are bound to occur.

The cooling fins that surround the tubes of the radiator should be kept clean for efficient heat transfer. Compressed air or pressurized water will remove any accumulations that might prevent air from passing through the fins and across the tubes. To remove debris, direct the flow of air or water in the opposite direction of normal airflow.

Engine blocks and radiators may be cleaned periodically by *reverse flushing* the system with pressurized water. Disconnect the hoses from the radiator and the block. Force clean water through the block or the radiator in the direction opposite

Goodheart-Willcox Publisher

Figure 13-21.

A parts brush, old toothbrush, or other stiff-bristle brush should be used to remove the corrosion from the cable connectors and battery terminals.

Goodheart-Willcox Publisher

Figure 13-22.

After cleaning, rinse the battery, terminals, and cable connectors with clear water.

that of normal circulation. This will push loose sediment out. Continue flushing until the water runs clear. Flushing should be done with the engine stopped and cool. To remove additional rust clinging to inner surfaces, use a commercial cooling system rust remover. Follow the manufacturer's instructions.

When adding coolant, mix water and antifreeze as specified by the manufacturer. In most cases, a mixture that contains 50% water and 50% antifreeze is recommended. Never use just water. The 50/50 mixture will prevent the coolant from freezing in cold weather. It will also increase the boiling point of the coolant.

Always check the strength of the coolant before the cold season begins. Weak coolant can freeze, causing damage to the engine block and radiator. Coolant strength can be checked with a device known as a *coolant hydrometer*. See **Figure 13-23**. To use the hydrometer, simply place the pickup tube in the engine coolant and squeeze the bulb to draw coolant into the hydrometer. Most hydrometers contain small balls that float in the coolant. The number of balls that float indicates the strength of the coolant. Some hydrometers have a pointer that indicates coolant strength on a scale printed on the body of the tester.

Maintaining Outboard Cooling Systems

Outboard engine cooling systems can be clogged with dirt, sand, or other debris. Flushing the internal cooling system of an outboard engine is extremely important. Flushing is done by attaching a freshwater hose to the water scoop or by operating the engine in a barrel of freshwater for several minutes.

Engines operated in saltwater are exposed to extremely corrosive conditions. Exposed engine parts require careful maintenance. Flush the cooling system with fresh water after each use. Rinse the engine with freshwater and wipe all lower unit parts with a clean, oily cloth. Ignition leads and spark plug insulators should also be wiped frequently to prevent an accumulation of salt residue.

Note

Outboard engines used in saltwater should be removed from the water immediately after operation. If the engine cannot be removed, tilt the gearcase out of the water and rinse it with freshwater. (The gearcase must be removed from the water when not in use.)

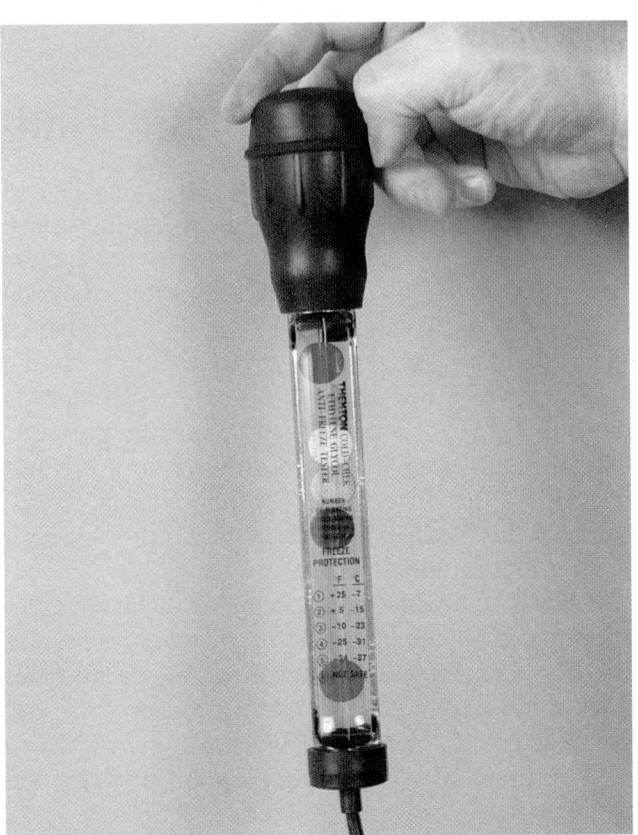

Goodheart-Willcox Publisher

Figure 13-23.

Coolant strength can be checked with a hydrometer.

Storing an Engine

Several precautions should be taken when storing an air-cooled engine for an extended period, such as when storing an implement for the winter season. Proper storage procedures will help ensure long engine life and easy starting the following season.

Begin by thoroughly cleaning the engine. Layers of dirt and debris tend to hold moisture, encouraging the formation of rust and corrosion.

Add fuel stabilizer to the fuel remaining in the tank and fill the tank with fresh gasoline. See **Figure 13-24**. Fuel stabilizer will help prevent fuel breakdown and the formation of gum, varnish, and corrosion in the fuel system. Start the engine and let it run for a few minutes so stabilized fuel flows through all parts of the fuel system. If fuel stabilizer is not available, run the engine dry of fuel.

Goodheart-Willcox Publisher

Figure 13-24.

Fuel stabilizer will help prevent fuel system problems.

Next, drain the oil from the crankcase. Do not refill it now. Place a tag on the engine that says *No Oil*.

Rotate the engine so the piston is at bottom of the cylinder. Remove the spark plug and squirt about one tablespoon of clean motor oil through the spark plug hole with an oil can. Rotate the engine slowly several times to distribute the oil on the cylinder walls. Then replace the spark plug.

With the spark plug wire disconnected, use the pull rope to rotate the engine slowly until compression resistance is felt. Then rotate the engine an additional one-quarter turn to close off its ports. This seals the cylinder and prevents moisture entry.

If possible, make sure the throttle is in the off position and the choke is closed. Then store the engine in a dry, clean area.

When removing the engine from storage, fill the crankcase with the recommended type and amount of fresh oil (four-stroke engine). Then remove the spark plug and use the pull rope or starter to spin the engine rapidly to remove excess oil from the cylinder. Clean or replace the spark plug. Then clean and oil the air filter or replace cartridge if necessary.

If necessary, fill the fuel tank. If you are servicing a two-stroke engine, make sure the proper fuel-oil mixture is added to the tank. See Chapter 11 for additional information on mixing oil and fuel.

Start the engine and let it idle until warm. Adjust the idle speed if necessary. Increase the engine speed in the normal manner. Make a brief test run while listening to the engine and watching the condition of all parts.

Storing Liquid-Cooled Engines

In addition to the storage precautions covered previously, storing liquid-cooled engines for lengthy periods, particularly during winter, calls for special maintenance procedures. If the engine has a pressurized system, the coolant must be strong enough to protect against freezing at the lowest possible temperatures.

If the engine will not be started at any time during storage, drain the cooling system completely. Then, tag the engine to indicate its drained condition.

When storing outboard engines, remove all plugs from the gearcase and drive shaft housing. This allows accumulated water in the gearcase and cooling system to drain off.

Failure to take this precaution when winterizing may result in a cracked cylinder block and/or gearcase, plus possible damage to water channels and tubes.

Rock the engine from side to side to make certain all water has drained. Refill the gearcase with the type of lubricant specified by the engine manufacturer. Attend to all other lubrication recommendations made by the manufacturer for care of the engine being stored.

Systematic Troubleshooting

Most small engine service and repair jobs can be done without taking the entire engine apart. If the engine will not start, is hard to start, runs rough, or lacks power, troubleshooting may be necessary. Troubleshooting is simply a number of tests and steps you go through to find a problem.

Sometimes the cause of an engine problem is easy to find. At other times, checking probable causes requires a certain amount of reasoning and the use of the process of elimination. Also, more than one fault can exist at the same time, making it harder to locate the trouble.

Always take a systematic approach when troubleshooting small engines. *Systematic troubleshooting* involves checking and/or testing one component after another component until the problem is located and corrected. There are two basic principles to keep in mind when trying to pinpoint small engine problems:

* Check the easiest things first.
* Verify the fundamental operating requirements.

Check the Easiest Things First

Always start troubleshooting by checking for the simplest, most probable problems first. If an engine will not start, the problem could be something as simple as an empty fuel tank or a disconnected spark plug wire. Do not start working on the carburetor or ignition system until you have made a few basic checks to determine that a simple remedy will not cure the problem.

Verify the Fundamental Operating Requirements

In order to start and run properly, an engine must meet five fundamental operating requirements. These requirements include:

- Proper carburetion—Clean, fresh fuel must be delivered in the correct proportion with combustion air.
- Correct ignition system operation—A strong ignition spark must be precisely timed for best performance and efficiency.
- Adequate lubrication—The proper amount of high-quality lubricating oil must reach critical engine components.
- Sufficient cooling—An ample supply of cooling air must reach engine.
- Proper compression—Compression should have 30–45 psi minimum for starting and 90 psi minimum for efficient operation and sufficient power.

Keep these operating requirements in mind when troubleshooting small gas engines. Through the process of elimination, you can easily isolate problems. For example, if an engine will not start but will spin normally, you can eliminate lubrication system problems because the engine is not locked-up. By spinning the engine, you can also determine whether or not it has sufficient compression. If the engine will not start after it has cooled down, the cooling system can be eliminated as a potential problem. In a matter of seconds, you have determined that your troubleshooting efforts should be concentrated in the areas of carburetion and ignition.

The engine's owner can also provide assistance with your troubleshooting efforts. Ask a few questions about the engine's performance before it stopped. Relate the answers to the operating requirements. For example, if an engine runs for 30–45 minutes and then stalls, you should ask if it restarts immediately after it stops. If the answer is yes, the problem is probably an ignition component that is intermittently experiencing heat-related breakdown. If the engine must cool before it will restart, vapor lock or sticking valves are possible problems. If a metallic snap is evident in the engine during the cooling period, the valves are likely to be the problem. The time you spend to ask a few pertinent questions can save a lot of time in the long run by eliminating additional problem possibilities.

Checking RPM

When servicing small engines, it is often necessary to test or set maximum idle rpm or governor rpm. One way to do this is by using a device that converts engine vibration from power pulses to rpm. See **Figure 13-25**. To use this tool, place the base of the instrument against the running engine. Using the dial on the tool, move the thin wire in or out of the instrument until the wire vibrates into a fan pattern. Continue to move the wire in or out until the fan pattern is as wide as possible. When fan pattern is as wide as you can make it, read the engine speed from the scale on the face of the instrument.

A *digital tachometer* can also be used to check engine rpm. See **Figure 13-26**. The lead from this particular tachometer is simply wrapped around

RPM scale

Vibrating wire

Figure 13-25.

You can measure the speed of an engine through the vibrations caused by power pulses of the piston.

Digital tachometer

Lead to spark plug wire

Goodheart-Willcox Publisher

Figure 13-26.

A digital tachometer can be used to check engine rpm.

Monarch Instrument

Figure 13-27.

This optical tachometer can measure rpm without contacting the engine by aiming it at a rotating part that has a reflective tape attached.

the spark plug wire. The tachometer will display engine rpm when the engine is running.

Another convenient and accurate method of measuring rpm is with a portable *optical tachometer* like the one in **Figure 13-27**. Before using this type of tachometer, a small piece of reflective tape is placed on a rotating part of the engine such as the crankshaft, flywheel, or pulley. The optical tachometer is aimed at the rotating part. The rpm is read on the digital display in the window. This tachometer can measure from 5–100,000 rpm at a distance up to 3′ and at an angle of 45°. These tachometers are small enough to fit in a pocket and weigh only 6 ounces. This is a safe method of measuring engine rpm, because contact with a hot engine is not necessary and a safe distance from moving parts can be maintained.

Testing Compression

A cylinder *compression test* can be a first step toward determining the condition of the upper major mechanical parts of the engine. This test is especially valuable if an engine lacks power, runs poorly, and shows little or no improvement after fuel system and ignition adjustments. To perform a compression test:

1. Run the engine until it is warm.
2. Disconnect all drives to the engine.

3. Open the choke and throttle valves wide.
4. Remove the air cleaner.
5. Remove the spark plug and insert the *compression gauge*. See **Figure 13-28**.
6. Crank the engine as fast as possible and read the gauge. Repeat the test to ensure accuracy.

Note

Engines equipped with compression release camshafts may have to be cranked in reverse rotation to obtain an accurate reading.

An engine producing a compression less than the minimum specified by the manufacturer usually has one or more of the following problems:

- Leaking cylinder head gasket.
- Warped cylinder head.
- Worn piston rings.
- Worn cylinder bore.
- Damaged piston.
- Burned or warped valves.
- Improper valve clearance.
- Broken or weak valve springs.

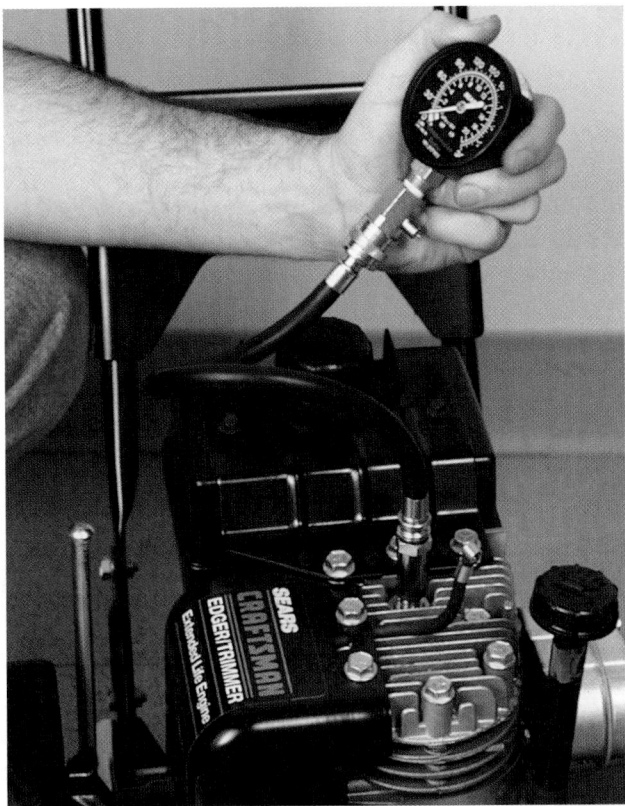

Goodheart-Willcox Publisher

Figure 13-28.

A compression test can indicate the condition of various mechanical components of an engine.

To determine whether the valves or rings are at fault, pour a tablespoonful of SAE 30 oil into the spark plug hole. Crank the engine several times to spread the oil and repeat the compression test. The heavy oil will temporarily seal leakage at the rings. If the compression does not improve, the leakage is due to problems with the valves, cylinder head, or piston. This does not disprove a problem with the rings; the engine may have worn rings *in addition to* its other problems. On the other hand, if the compression is much higher than the original test, the leakage is due solely to defective piston rings.

Testing Differential Pressure

A *differential pressure test* checks the condition of an engine by measuring leakage from the cylinder to other parts of the engine. This test device and procedure can identify a specific worn or damaged component in the engine that may or may not be directly related to the cylinder condition or rings. The device is designed so that specific leakages

can be detected and isolated before disassembling parts of the engine.

The differential pressure tester requires the application of air pressure to the cylinder being tested with the piston at top dead center on the compression stroke.

A schematic diagram of the differential pressure tester is shown in **Figure 13-29**. As the regulated air pressure is applied to one side tester with the air shutoff valve closed, both gauges will read the same. However, when the air shutoff valve is opened and leakage through the cylinder increases, the cylinder pressure gauge will record a proportionally lower reading.

The differential pressure test can be applied to single cylinder engines or multiple cylinder engines. Each cylinder is tested separately and in the same manner. Use the following procedure to test:

1. Run engine until it is warmed up to provide uniform lubrication to cylinder walls and rings.
2. Remove the spark plug wire(s) and spark plug(s).
3. Rotate the engine crankshaft until the piston of the cylinder being tested is at top dead center of the compression stroke. Both valves must be closed.
4. Install the holding fixture supplied with the tester to prevent the crankshaft from turning during the test.
5. Thread the adaptor into the spark plug hole.
6. Connect the adaptor on the rubber hose to the quick disconnect fitting on the tester.
7. Connect an air source of at least 90 psi to the tester adaptor.

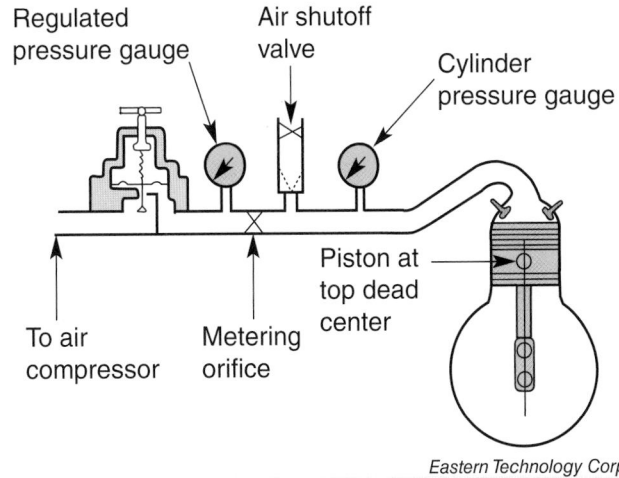

Eastern Technology Corp.

Figure 13-29.

This schematic diagram shows a differential pressure tester connected to an engine cylinder.

Warning

Make sure all personnel and objects are clear of the engine shaft, belts, pulleys, or other devices connected to the engine shaft.

8. Slowly adjust the regulated pressure gauge on the left with the regulator knob to read 80 psi.
9. The right-hand gauge indicates the relative pressure of the cylinder being tested. Due to standard engine clearances and normal wear, no cylinder is expected to maintain a perfect 80 psi. Generally, a reading of 60 psi or above is acceptable.

Note

It is important that all cylinders on multi-cylinder engines have a somewhat consistent reading. Good judgment should be used as to the allowable tolerance between cylinders. Recheck a cylinder that has a reading that is significantly lower (15 psi or more) than the other cylinder(s). If a second reading is still low, the cylinder should be suspected of being defective.

10. By listening for the sound of escaping air, you can determine leakage points in the engine and the cause of the low pressure reading. A hissing at the carburetor intake indicates a leaking intake valve, a hissing in the exhaust suggests a leaking exhaust valve, and hissing from the crankcase breather indicates leaking piston rings. See **Figure 13-30**.

Note

If the test indicates a valve problem, first check valve clearance to make sure the valve is not being held open due to inadequate clearance.

Air escaping from:	Indication:
carburetor intake	defective intake valve
exhaust system	defective exhaust valve
crankcase breather	defective piston rings

Goodheart-Willcox Publisher

Figure 13-30.

The chart shows the location of air leaks and the indicated defects.

Service Information

Before starting any maintenance, troubleshooting, or service procedures, the appropriate service information should be consulted. Basic maintenance and service information can often be found in the ***owner's manual*** provided with the implement or the engine itself. The owner's manual typically includes information on maintenance schedules, fluid capacities, and part numbers for maintenance components (filters, spark plugs, etc.). It may also include very basic maintenance and troubleshooting procedures. For example, the owner's manual may include instructions for changing an engine air filter or diagnosing a no-start condition.

Note

Many engine and implement manufacturers make copies of their owner's manual available online. These manuals can often be accessed free of charge.

A ***service manual*** contains more detailed information than the owner's manual. Service manuals are often published for each engine type a manufacturer produces. For example, one manufacturer publishes a manual for all variations of the single-cylinder engines it produces, and another manual for all two-cylinder engines it makes. Some companies publish service manuals for engines from a variety of manufacturers.

Service manuals can generally be purchased directly from engine manufacturers, as well as from aftermarket publishers. Often, you can purchase service manuals at shops that sell engines and engine parts.

Service manuals generally include comprehensive service procedures, detailed drawings of various engine assemblies, and troubleshooting charts, as well as a variety of tolerances, clearances, and specifications needed to properly troubleshoot and service a specific engine.

The service procedures found in most manuals list the steps to take in order to accomplish a task effectively. The detailed drawings of assemblies and systems are often exploded views that can help you disassemble and reassemble parts in the right order.

Troubleshooting charts list the most common engine troubles along with possible causes and suggested remedies. See **Figure 13-31**.

Engine Troubleshooting Chart

Cause	Remedy
Engine fails to start or starts with difficulty	
No fuel in tank.	Fill tank with clean, fresh fuel.
Shutoff valve closed.	Open valve.
Obstructed fuel line.	Clean fuel screen and line. If necessary, remove and clean carburetor.
Tank cap vent obstructed.	Open vent in fuel tank cap.
Water in fuel.	Drain tank. Clean carburetor and fuel lines. Dry spark plug and points. Fill tank with clean, fresh fuel.
Engine overchoked.	Close fuel shutoff and pull starter until engine starts. Reopen fuel shutoff for normal fuel flow.
Improper carburetor adjustment.	Adjust carburetor.
Loose or defective magneto wiring.	Check magneto wiring for shorts or grounds; repair if necessary.
Faulty magneto.	Check timing, point gap; if necessary, overhaul magneto.
Spark plug fouled.	Clean and re-gap spark plug.
Spark plug porcelain cracked.	Replace spark plug.
Poor compression.	Overhaul engine.
No spark at plug.	Disconnect ignition cutoff wire at the engine. Crank engine. If spark at spark plug, ignition switch, or safety switch, interlock switch is inoperative. If no spark, check magneto.
Crankcase seals and/or gaskets leaking (two cycle only).	Replace seals and/or gaskets.
Exhaust ports plugged (two cycle only).	Clean exhaust ports.
Engine knocks	
Carbon in combustion chamber.	Remove cylinder head and clean carbon from head and piston.
Loose or worn connecting rod.	Replace connecting rod.
Loose flywheel.	Check flywheel key and keyway; replace parts if necessary. Tighten flywheel nut to proper torque.
Worn cylinder.	Replace cylinder.
Improper magneto timing.	Time magneto.
Engine misses under load	
Spark plug fouled.	Clean and re-gap spark plug.
Spark plug porcelain cracked.	Replace spark plug.
Improper spark plug gap.	Re-gap spark plug.
Pitted magneto breaker points.	Replace pitted breaker points.
Magneto breaker arm sluggish.	Clean and lubricate breaker point arm.
Faulty condenser.	Check condenser on a tester; replace if defective.
Improper carburetor adjustment.	Adjust carburetor.
Improper valve clearance.	Adjust valve clearance to recommended specifications.
Weak valve spring.	Replace valve spring.
Reed fouled or sluggish (two cycle only).	Clean or replace reed.
Crankcase seals leak (two cycle only).	Replace worn crankcase seals.

(Continued)
Goodheart-Willcox Publisher

Figure 13-31.

Typical troubleshooting chart for small gas engines.

Engine Troubleshooting Chart *(Continued)*

Cause	Remedy
Engine lacks power	
Choke partially closed.	Open choke.
Improper carburetor adjustment.	Adjust carburetor.
Magneto improperly timed.	Time magneto.
Worn rings or piston.	Replace rings or piston.
Air cleaner fouled.	Clean air cleaner.
Lack of lubrication (four cycle only).	Fill crankcase to the proper level.
Valves leaking (four cycle only).	Grind valves and set to recommended specifications.
Reed fouled or sluggish (two cycle).	Clean or replace reed.
Improper amount of oil in fuel mixture (two cycle only).	Drain tank; fill with correct mixture.
Crankcase seals leak (two cycle only).	Replace worn crankcase seals.
Engine overheats	
Engine improperly timed.	Time engine.
Carburetor improperly adjusted.	Adjust carburetor.
Airflow obstructed.	Remove any obstructions from air passages in shrouds.
Cooling fins clogged.	Clean cooling fins.
Excessive load on the engine.	Check operation of associated equipment; reduce excessive load.
Carbon in combustion chamber.	Remove cylinder head and clean carbon from head and piston.
Lack of lubrication (four cycle only).	Fill crankcase to proper level.
Improper amount of oil in fuel mixture (two cycle only).	Drain tank; fill with correct mixture.
Engine surges or runs unevenly	
Fuel tank cap vent hole clogged.	Open vent hole.
Governor parts sticking or binding.	Clean and, if necessary, repair governor parts.
Carburetor throttle linkage or throttle shaft and/or butterfly binding or sticking.	Clean, lubricate, or adjust linkage and deburr throttle shaft or butterfly.
Intermittent spark or spark plug.	Disconnect ignition cutoff wire at the engine. Crank engine. If spark, check ignition switch, safety switch, and interlock switch. If no spark, check magneto. Check wires for poor connections, cuts, or breaks.
Improper carburetor adjustment.	Adjust carburetor.
Dirty carburetor.	Clean carburetor.
Engine vibrates excessively	
Engine not securely mounted.	Tighten loose mounting bolts.
Bent crankshaft.	Replace crankshaft.
Associated equipment out of balance.	Check associated equipment.

(Continued)
Goodheart-Willcox Publisher

Figure 13-31.

Continued.

Engine Troubleshooting Chart *(Continued)*

Cause	Remedy
Engine uses excessive amount of oil (four cycle only)	
Engine speed too fast.	Using tachometer, adjust engine rpm to specifications.
Oil level too high.	To check level, turn dipstick cap tightly into receptacle for accurate level reading. Drain excess oil as needed.
Oil filler cap loose or gasket damaged, causing spillage out of breather.	Replace ring gasket under cap and tighten cap securely.
Breather mechanism damaged or dirty causing leakage.	Replace breather assembly.
Drain hole in breather box clogged, causing oil to spill out of breather.	Clean hole with wire to allow oil to return to crankcase.
Gaskets damaged or gasket surfaces nicked, causing oil to leak out.	Clean and smooth gasket surfaces. Always use new gaskets.
Valve guides worn excessively thus passing oil into combustion chamber.	Ream valve guide oversize and install 1/32″ oversize valve.
Cylinder wall worn or glazed, allowing oil to bypass rings into combustion chamber. Piston rings and grooves worn excessively.	Bore, hone, or deglaze cylinder as necessary. Reinstall new rings, check land clearance, and correct as necessary.
Piston fit undersized.	Measure and replace piston as necessary.
Piston oil control ring return holes clogged.	Remove oil control ring and clean return holes.
Oil passages obstructed.	Clean out all oil passages.

Goodheart-Willcox Publisher

Figure 13-31.

Continued.

Engine specifications, tolerances, and clearances are also given in a service manual. See **Figure 13-32**. When tolerance specifications show two values, the actual dimension must be somewhere between the two values. In **Figure 13-32**, for example, the cylinder bore (diameter) must measure somewhere between 2.1260″ and 2.1265″.

Engine Identification

In addition to having the correct service information, it is important to identify the exact model engine you are servicing. This will allow you to locate the proper specifications for the engine. It will also help ensure that you order the correct repair parts.

Most engines have a model number displayed on a sticker affixed to the engine housing or to the engine itself. On some engines, the model number is stamped into the engine block, the metal shroud, or

Tolerances and Clearances for the J-321 Engine

Cylinder bore	Max.	2.1265″
	Min.	2.1260″
Piston skirt diameter	Max.	2.1227″
	Min.	2.1220″
Piston ring width	Max.	.0935″
	Min.	.0925″
Piston pin diameter	Max.	.5001″
	Min.	.4999″
Spark plug gap		.030″
Piston skirt to cylinder clearance	Max.	.0045″
	Min.	.0033″

Jacobsen Mfg. Co.

Figure 13-32.

Typical tolerance and clearance chart.

some other engine component. The model number will provide you with specific information about the engine at hand. For example, it will generally provide you with information on crankshaft orientation (vertical or horizontal), starter type (recoil start or electric start), carburetor type, etc.

In addition to the model number, some manufacturers use ID numbers, serial numbers, or other code numbers that convey additional information. See **Figure 13-33**. These numbers may identify unique features of the engine. For example, the engine used on a certain model of lawnmower may have a crankshaft with a special snout to accommodate the mower's blade. The numbers may also provide information on the date of engine manufacture, the location of the assembly plant, the engine warranty, emissions control compliance, etc. Information on interpreting model numbers, as well as other engine identification numbers, can be found in an appropriate service manual.

Goodheart-Willcox Publisher

Figure 13-33.

Identification numbers found on an engine provide valuable information. This sticker displays the engine's build date and serial number.

Summary

Preventive maintenance involves tasks that must be performed regularly to keep an engine working properly. Cleaning a small air-cooled engine periodically can help prevent overheating. For proper cooling action, air must pass across the metal surfaces of the cylinder block and cylinder head. If the cooling fins are insulated by dirt, leaves, and/or grass clippings, engine parts will retain most of the combustion heat. Parts will expand, probably distort, and possibly seize.

Crankcase oil in four-cycle engines should be checked periodically. The small engine manufacturer will recommend oil changes at intervals based on hours of running time. The time specified may vary from 10–50 hours.

Engine cables and linkage should be lubricated periodically to ensure smooth operation and reduce the chances of binding and premature wear. Many manufacturers recommend silicone-based lubricants for use on cables and linkages. Unlike petroleum-based products, these lubricants will not attract dirt after they are applied.

The spark plug should periodically be removed for inspection and cleaned or replaced. Carefully examine the electrode end of the plug. An insulator or electrodes that are wet with fuel or oil may be a sign of serious engine problems. If the spark plug insulator and electrodes appear to be good, the plug can be reinstalled. Examine the spark plug wire for deterioration before reinstalling it on the spark plug. Heat and dirt can make the insulation brittle and insulation cracking can occur.

The air cleaner should be cleaned before each season of operation and at regular intervals thereafter. A plugged air filter can cause hard starting, loss of power, and spark plug fouling. The three types of air cleaners widely used in small gasoline engines are the oil-wetted type, the dry type, and the dual-element type. Each has a different method of cleaning and servicing.

If the small gasoline engine has a crankcase breather, the breather assembly should be removed and cleaned periodically. The breather is located over the valve stem chamber.

A muffler is designed to reduce noise and allow exhaust gases to escape. When it becomes clogged, gases cannot get out of the combustion chamber quickly enough to allow fresh air and fuel to enter. This causes a loss in engine power, along with a tendency to overheat.

The battery in a small engine–powered implement may be either a maintenance-free or a conventional lead-acid battery. Conventional lead-acid batteries need occasional additions of distilled water to keep the electrolyte level above the plates. Fill to the level shown on the case of the battery. Corrosion at the battery terminals and cable connectors is not uncommon. The corrosion should be cleaned from the terminals.

The pressurized liquid cooling systems used in small engines require maintenance similar to that employed in the automobile engine. Because the combination of water and metal sometimes produces harmful chemical reactions that attack the water jacket, antifreeze containing a chemical rust inhibitor should be added whenever a system is drained and refilled. Outboard engine cooling systems can be clogged with dirt, sand, or other debris. Flushing the internal cooling system of an outboard engine is extremely important.

Several precautions should be taken when storing an air-cooled engine. Proper storage procedures will help ensure long engine life and easy starting the following season. Storing liquid-cooled engines for lengthy periods calls for special maintenance procedures. If the engine has a pressurized system, the coolant must be strong enough to protect against freezing at the lowest possible temperatures.

If the engine will not start, is hard to start, runs rough, or lacks power, troubleshooting may be necessary. Troubleshooting is simply a number of tests and steps you go through to find a problem. In order to start and run properly, an engine must meet five fundamental operating requirements. These requirements include proper carburetion, correct ignition system operation, adequate lubrication, sufficient cooling, and proper compression.

A cylinder compression test can be a first step toward determining the condition of the upper major mechanical parts of the engine. This test is especially valuable if an engine lacks power, runs poorly, and shows little or no improvement after fuel system and ignition adjustments. A differential pressure test checks the condition of an engine by measuring leakage from the cylinder to other parts of the engine. This test device and procedure can identify a specific worn or damaged component in the engine that may or may not be directly related to the cylinder condition or rings.

Before starting any maintenance, trouble-shooting, or service procedures, the appropriate service information should be consulted. Basic maintenance and service information can often be found in the owner's manual. A service manual contains more detailed information than the owner's manual. In addition to having the correct service information, it is important to identify the exact model engine you are servicing. This will allow you to locate the proper specifications for the engine. It will also help ensure that you order the correct repair parts.

Review Questions

Answer the following questions using the information provided in this chapter.

1. *True or False?* Preventive maintenance helps protect against premature engine wear.

2. Keeping an engine clean can help prevent _____.

3. *True or False?* Never run an engine if the oil level is above the *Full* mark.

4. Although oil does not wear out, excess _____ makes the oil useless.

5. When changing oil, the engine should be _____.
   A. cold
   B. warm
   C. running
   D. None of the above.

6. Many manufacturers recommend using _____ -based lubricants on cables and linkages.

7. *True or False?* Most manufacturers recommend replacing a carbon-fouled spark plug.

8. Name three problems caused by a plugged air filter.

9. Why should you refrain from using compressed air to clean a pleated paper air filter element?

10. What two problems can be caused by a clogged muffler?

11. *True or False?* All mufflers can be cleaned by soaking them in solvent.

12. When storing an engine for an extended period, _____ should be added to the gasoline to prevent fuel breakdown and the buildup of gum, varnish, and corrosion.

13. To prevent the formation of rust and scale, antifreeze containing a rust _____ should be used in the cooling system.

14. Outboard engines operated in saltwater are exposed to _____ conditions.

15. When storing outboard engines, all plugs should be removed from the _____ and _____ housing.

16. Systematic troubleshooting involves looking for the _____ possible problem first.

17. In order to run properly, an engine must have proper carburetion, correct ignition system operation, adequate lubrication, sufficient cooling, and _____.

18. *True or False?* A compression test can be used to determine the condition of the spark plug.

19. During a differential pressure test, air leakage heard at the crankcase breather is an indication of defective _____.

20. Manufacturer's service manuals contain _____.
    A. service procedures
    B. troubleshooting charts
    C. tolerance and clearance specifications
    D. All of the above.

Suggested Activities

1. Perform preventive maintenance procedures on several engines in your shop. Check the oil level and condition. If necessary, change the oil and the filter. Make sure the air filter element, crankcase breather (if applicable), and cooling fins are clean. If an engine is equipped with a water cooling system, check engine block and radiator for signs of rust and corrosion.

2. Locate several malfunctioning engines. Try to determine the cause of the problems using the systematic troubleshooting method. Remember the five fundamental operating requirements.

3. Perform a differential pressure test on an engine and determine the condition of the rings and valves.

4. Review several manufacturers' service manuals. Study troubleshooting charts and exploded-view assembly drawings. Check maintenance procedures for engines in your shop.

Fuel System Service

Learning Objectives

After studying this chapter, you will be able to:

- Identify and correct common fuel system problems.
- Summarize basic carburetor adjustments.
- Explain basic procedures for disassembling, cleaning, inspecting, and reassembling diaphragm and float-type carburetors.
- Describe the procedure for resetting the wide-open-throttle position on a centrifugal governor.
- Summarize the various methods used to adjust governor systems.

Key Terms

carburetor kits
diagnostic trouble code (DTC)
flooded engine
hunt
lean mixture

overhaul
rich mixture
vapor lock
vented
welch plugs

Troubleshooting the Fuel System

If symptoms of engine malfunction point to the fuel system, the problem could be located in several areas. It could involve the fuel pump, carburetor, fuel lines, filters, or air cleaner. Troubleshooting consists of systematically checking one part after another until the trouble is identified. Once the trouble has been identified, the proper service can be performed to restore proper engine operation. A systematic approach to troubleshooting can save time, reduce labor, and prevent unnecessary repairs.

The troubleshooting chart at the end of the chapter identifies common carburetor-related problems and lists the possible causes and corrective actions. In some cases, the carburetor must be overhauled. This consists of disassembling the carburetor, identifying and replacing all worn

components, and reassembling with new gaskets and O-rings. In other cases, a simple adjustment or relatively small repair is all that is needed.

The first step in troubleshooting the fuel system is to properly identify the symptoms. Is the engine hard to start? Does it idle rough? Does it run fine at idle but lack power and sputter off idle or at high speeds? The answers to each of these questions can give a small engine technician insight into the cause of the problem.

Hard Starts

If the engine is difficult to start, the first step is to ensure that the engine has spark and air. Perform a spark test and inspect the filter to make sure that it is not excessively dirty. When checking the air filter, remove the air filter housing and make sure that the choke is not stuck open. Once a clogged air filter and a malfunctioning ignition system have been eliminated as possible causes, the problem is likely in the fuel system.

Begin by making sure there is fuel in the tank. Next prime the carburetor and try to start the engine several times. If the engine does not fire, remove and examine the spark plug. If the end of the spark plug is wet with gas, fuel is getting into the cylinder. The problem may be that too much gas is being supplied or the gas is stale or contaminated. If the tip of the spark plug is dry, fuel is not being delivered to the cylinder.

If fuel is getting to the cylinder, the fuel may be stale or contaminated. This is especially true if the same fuel has been sitting in the tank for an extended period of time. Over time, fuel can break down and become contaminated with water. This causes it to burn less consistently, which results in poor performance and hard starting. Begin service by completely draining the tank and refilling it with clean, fresh gasoline.

To drain the tank, begin by clamping off the fuel line or turning off the fuel valve. Next, disconnect the fuel line at the carburetor if the fuel system is gravity fed, or at the fuel pump if the equipment has one, **Figure 14-1**. Place the loose end of the fuel line in a suitable container large enough to hold all of the gasoline, **Figure 14-2**. Then, remove the fuel line clamp or open the fuel petcock to let the fuel drain out.

Note

If the engine is equipped with a metal gas tank, it must be thoroughly inspected for rust after being drained. If rust is visible, the fuel tank should be replaced.

Once the tank is drained completely, replace any in-line fuel filter and inspect and clean or replace the filter screen in the tank outlet fitting. Reconnect the fuel line at the carburetor or fuel pump. Dispose of the old fuel in accordance with all local, state, and federal laws and regulations. Refill the tank with fresh, clean regular unleaded gasoline. Reformulated fuels containing no more than 10% ethanol, 15% MTBE, 15% ETBE, or premium gasoline can be used if regular unleaded gasoline is not available. Never use fuel containing methanol.

Once fresh gas has been added to the tank, prime the carburetor and try to start the engine. Let the engine run for a minute or two and note whether the fresh gas has restored proper engine operation. If it has, the equipment can be returned

Goodheart-Willcox Publisher

Figure 14-1.
The fuel petcock is turned off or the fuel line is clamped. Then, the fuel line is removed from the carburetor.

Goodheart-Willcox Publisher

Figure 14-2.
A container is placed under the end of the fuel line and the petcock is opened or the fuel line clamp is removed.

to the owner. If it has not, further diagnosis and service is required.

Checking Air-Fuel Mixture

An improper air-fuel mixture can result in hard starting and improper engine operation. If the engine is receiving too much fuel in the mixture, the condition is known as a *rich mixture*. The engine may be difficult to start. If too much gasoline enters the cylinder, there may not be enough oxygen available for combustion. This situation is referred to as a *flooded engine*, and can be compounded if the choke valve is closed (as is normal for cold-engine starting). If the engine is running rich, but does manage to start, it will often idle rough and produce black, sooty exhaust.

A rich mixture can be caused by either too much gas or not enough air in the air-fuel mixture. An excessive amount of gasoline can be caused by improper mixture screw adjustments, a leaking float, improper seating of the needle valve, or worn (enlarged) passages in the carburetor. Inadequate air in the mixture is commonly caused by a clogged air filter, a stuck choke valve, or clogged air bleeds.

If the engine is receiving too much air for the amount of fuel in the mixture, the condition is known as a *lean mixture*. A lean mixture can result if either too much air or not enough fuel is entering the cylinder. An insufficient amount of fuel in the mixture can be caused by improper mixture screw adjustments, a stuck float or needle valve, a restriction in the fuel system, an inoperative fuel pump, a clogged fuel tank cap vent, or clogged passages in the carburetor. Common causes of excessive air in the mixture include leaking intake gaskets, worn throttle or choke shafts, gaps at the fuel lines fittings, and leaking carburetor gaskets.

A visual inspection of the spark plug can reveal problems with the air-fuel mixture. If the tip of the spark plug is light tan in color, and does not have excessive deposits, the engine has been receiving the proper air-fuel mixture. However, if the tip of the spark plug is coated in fluffy black soot, the engine has been operating on a rich air-fuel mixture.

If the tip of the spark plug is white, the engine has been running on a lean air-fuel mixture.

Checking Gravity-Fed Fuel Supply

If fuel is not being delivered to the carburetor or a lean air-fuel mixture is evident in a gravity-fed system, check the following:
- Is there fuel in the gas tank?
- Is fuel flow blocked by a clogged filter or obstructions in the line?

Fuel delivery can be checked by clamping the fuel line or shutting off the fuel petcock and then disconnecting the fuel line from the carburetor. The fuel line is placed in a suitable container and the clamp is removed or the petcock is opened.

Fuel should flow freely from the end of the fuel line. The fuel stream should be approximately the same diameter as the inside diameter of the fuel line. If the fuel stream is weak or there is no fuel flow, there is an obstruction in the fuel system between the tank and carburetor.

To locate the restriction, begin by removing the gas tank filler cap. If fuel begins flowing when the gas cap is removed, the vent on the cap is plugged, and the vent should be cleared or the cap replaced. If fuel does not begin flowing, begin removing components one at a time until fuel begins flowing properly. See **Figure 14-3**. When fuel flows normally, you know that the last component removed was responsible for the blockage. Replace the faulty component and recheck engine operation.

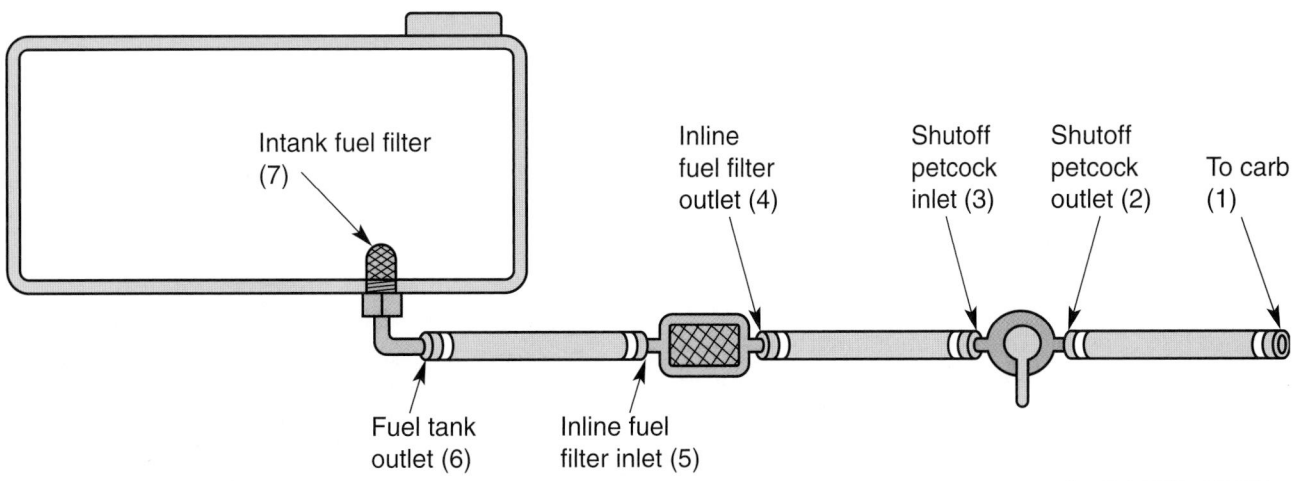

Goodheart-Willcox Publisher

Figure 14-3. Begin removing components in the order shown until proper fuel flow is established. Turn off the fuel valve or clamp the fuel line before removing each component to avoid spillage. Note: engines may not have all of the components shown.

Checking a Fuel Pump

If the engine is equipped with a fuel pump and fuel is not being delivered to the carburetor, check to see that:

- There is fuel in the gas tank.
- The fittings connecting the fuel line to the tank and the pump are tight. If these connections are not tight, the pump may be drawing air in around the connections.
- The fuel filter is not clogged.
- The pump is actually working.

To check whether the pump is working, disconnect the fuel line between the pump and carburetor. Place a metal container under the end of the fuel line. Turn the engine over with the starter. There should be a well-defined spurt of fuel at every stroke of the pump (every two revolutions of the engine).

If the fuel pump is not pumping sufficient fuel, check for a restriction in the fuel system leading to the pump. Remove components between the fuel tank and the fuel pump until proper fuel flow is established, as described in the previous section. Replace the faulty component and recheck engine operation.

Warning

Be careful when performing fuel checks. Ensure that there are no open flames or other potential ignition sources nearby. Use only metal containers to catch drained fuel. Dispose of any fuel or fuel soaked rags properly.

Other Checks

Sometimes an engine will start, but then die after a period of time or when operated off idle. Again, there are some simple checks that should be performed before the carburetor is blamed. First, squeeze each section of fuel line to make sure it is not hard and brittle. Any fuel line that is hard, brittle, or weather checked should be replaced. Hardened fuel line can allow fuel to leak out and air to enter around fittings. Tightening the hose clamps at the fittings will not fix the problem, and often make it worse. Also, a deteriorating fuel line may cause small particles of rubber to enter and clog the carburetor.

Note

Always shut off fuel flow at the tank before replacing fuel line. This will minimize fuel spillage.

Also, make sure that the fuel line is not too close to the hot surfaces of the engine. If the fuel line runs too close to the engine, heat from the engine can vaporize fuel in the line. The vaporized gasoline can form bubbles in the fuel line that prevent the proper flow of fuel. This condition is known as *vapor lock*. When the engine cools down, the gasoline vapor condenses back into liquid, and proper fuel flow is restored. To correct vapor lock, reroute the fuel line so there is adequate air space between it and the engine.

The next check is to make sure that the fuel tank filter screen is in good condition. Varnish from stale gasoline can impede flow through filter screens. A partially clogged fuel screen may allow enough fuel to pass to start the engine and allow it to run at idle. The same filter may collapse as the fuel draw increases. **Figure 14-4** shows a filter that allowed the engine to start and idle, but caused the engine to stall whenever the throttle was opened. A replacement filter solved the problem.

If the engine equipped with a diaphragm fuel pump operates properly at idle, but stumbles or dies under load, the problem may be a small vacuum leak at the diaphragm. When the engine is running at idle, high vacuum is produced. Even with the leak, there may be enough vacuum to provide adequate pumping action. However, as the throttle valve is opened and vacuum decreases, the leak may cause the pump to malfunction.

To check this, temporarily install a gravity-fed fuel system to the carburetor. Start the engine and

Goodheart-Willcox Publisher

Figure 14-4.
A damaged gas tank filter can block fuel flow.

operate it at full throttle. If the gravity-fed fuel system keeps the engine operating properly, the problem is a faulty fuel pump.

Carburetor Adjustments

If fuel is reaching the carburetor, but the engine still surges or lacks power, the cause may be poor carburetor adjustment or carburetor defects. Most carburetors have two needle valve adjustments: the high speed, or main, mixture adjustment and the idle mixture adjustment. A third adjustment that is found on carburetors is the idle speed stop screw. Needle valves are not always found in the same location on the carburetor body. It is good practice to refer to the manufacturer's manual for needle positions and instructions on proper settings.

Green Tech

Carburetor Adjustment

Today, most carburetors are factory preset and sealed. Other carburetors can be adjusted only by removing plugs and using the manufacturer's special tools. Both types of carburetors are not adjustable by the consumer. This ensures efficient performance. The purpose is to ensure a clean running engine and to minimize air pollution caused by exhaust emissions. Adjustable carburetors must be adjusted only by qualified technicians in strict adherence to the manufacturer's directions.

Before adjusting any mixture screws, reset the screws to the recommended carburetor presets. Check for proper governor adjustments as outlined in the appropriate manufacturer's manual. Identify the locations of your high speed and low speed RPM adjustment screws. Make sure that the throttle control brackets are adjusted properly to allow for full choke. Consult specifications to determine the proper RPM settings. Start the engine and allow it to warm up. The carburetor can then be adjusted for optimum performance using the information specified for the particular make and model of carburetor.

High Speed and Idle Mixture Adjustment

Each engine manufacturer will give *rough* settings for the high speed adjustment and idle

mixture adjustment. These settings will permit the engine to be started. It should then be warmed up before further adjustments are made.

The general adjustment procedure is to open the throttle wide and turn the high speed adjusting needle forward and backward slowly until maximum speed is reached. See the carburetor in **Figure 14-5** for the general location of external parts. After reaching the maximum speed, turn the needle counterclockwise very slightly so the engine is running a little rich.

To adjust the idle mixture needle, move the throttle to the slow running position. Turn the idle mixture needle slowly, first in one direction and then in the other. Continue turning the needle until the idle is smooth. If necessary, adjust the idle speed stop screw to obtain the idle speed recommended in the manual. Check the manufacturer's recommendations carefully. Each make and model is adjusted differently.

Unlike carburetor A in **Figure 14-6**, not all carburetors have two needle settings. Carburetor B has only a high speed needle adjustment, and carburetor C does not have fuel adjustment needles. Each carburetor has an idle speed adjustment screw. Some of the needle adjustments are omitted because the manufacturer has preset the adjustments and sealed them.

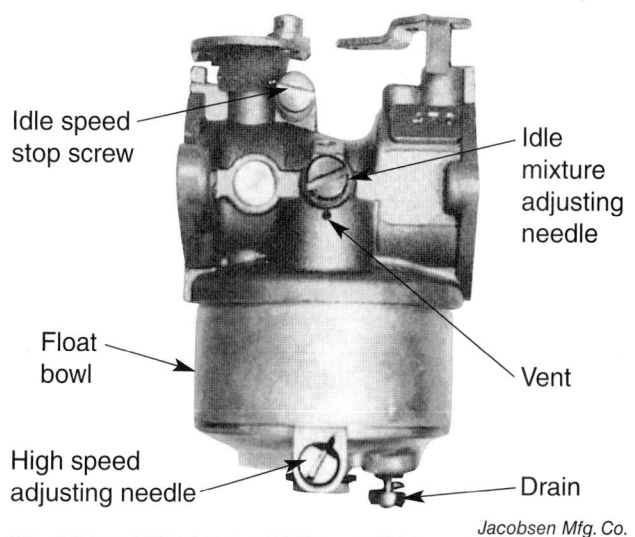

Idle speed stop screw

Idle mixture adjusting needle

Float bowl

Vent

High speed adjusting needle

Drain

Jacobsen Mfg. Co.

Figure 14-5.

External carburetor adjustments are made at the high speed mixture adjusting needle, the idle mixture needle, and the idle speed stop screw.

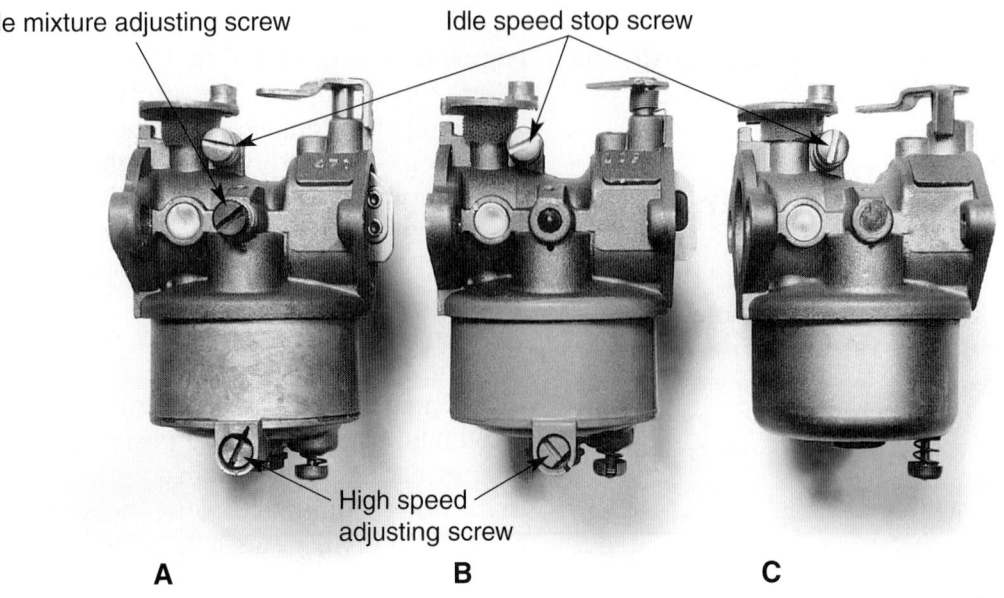

Idle mixture adjusting screw   Idle speed stop screw

High speed
adjusting screw

A   B   C

Goodheart-Willcox Publisher

Figure 14-6.

Depending on the make and model, carburetors may have one or several adjustments. A—Carburetor with high speed adjustment, idle mixture adjustment, and idle speed stop screw. B—Carburetor with two points of adjustment: high speed and idle speed. C—Carburetor with idle speed stop screw only.

Anti-Afterfire Solenoid Check

Some float-type carburetors on engines with battery-powered electrical systems are equipped with an anti-afterfire solenoid. If this solenoid sticks closed or malfunctions, it can prevent fuel from leaving the carburetor. If fuel is reaching the carburetor, but is not being delivered to the engine, this solenoid may be malfunctioning.

The solenoid typically threads into the float bowl. To check it, disconnect its electrical connector and then unthread it from the carburetor. Take the solenoid to a clean, dry work area, away from any fuel. Then, use jumper wires to connect one terminal of the battery to the solenoid's electrical connector and the other terminal of the battery to the body of the solenoid. When both connections are made, the solenoid plunger should retract. Because of the lower voltage, you may need to push lightly on the end of the plunger to get it started. At some point, the magnetic forces should take over and pull the plunger away from your finger.

If the plunger does not retract, double-check the electrical connections and try again. If the plunger still does not retract, it must be replaced.

Carburetor Overhaul

Carburetion problems that cannot be corrected by adjusting mixture needles are usually the result of gummed-up fuel passages or worn internal parts. The most effective solution to these problems is to overhaul the carburetor.

A carburetor *overhaul* generally consists of disassembling, cleaning, and replacing parts as recommended by the manufacturer. *Carburetor kits* are available from small engine repair shops or manufacturer's distribution centers. These kits contain all the parts needed for a typical carburetor overhaul.

Most carburetor kits also contain a detailed exploded view diagram of the carburetor for which the kit is intended. A typical carburetor diagram is shown in **Figure 14-7**. These diagrams are useful for identifying the parts in the kit and their locations on the carburetor being serviced. However, many kits are designed for multiple carburetors, so the kit may contain parts that are not used.

Warning

Do *not* allow flames, sparks, pilot lights, or arcing equipment near the fuel system. Ignition of fuel can result in severe personal injury or death.

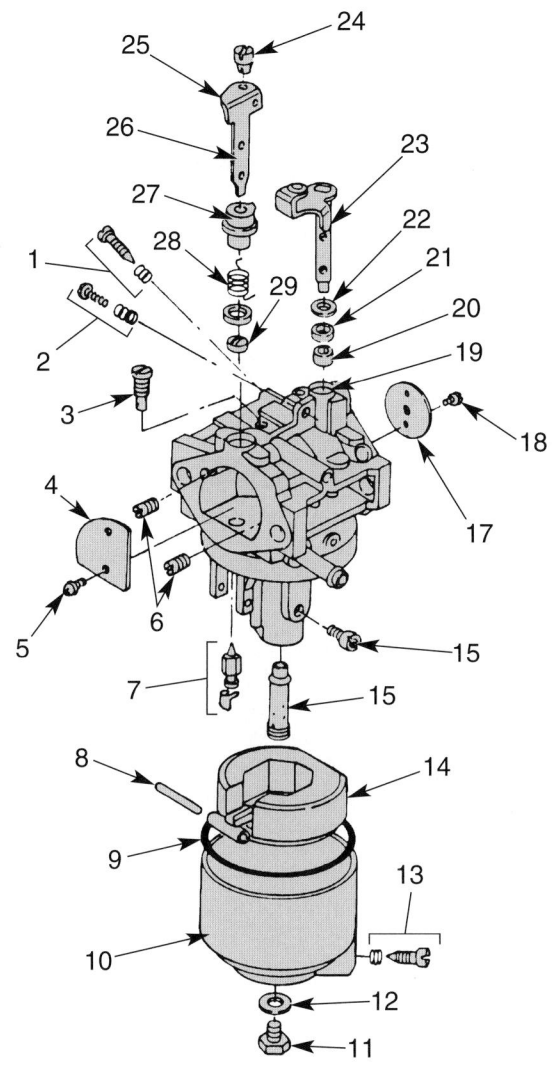

1. Carburetor idle valve assembly
2. Idle speed screw & spring assembly
3. Nozzle
4. Choke valve
5. (2) Choke valve screws
6. Carburetor nozzles
7. Fuel inlet needle valve
8. Float hinge pin
9. Bowl gasket
10. Bowl
11. Bowl mounting screw
12. Sealing gasket
13. Bowl drain
14. Float
15. Main jet
16. Nozzle
17. Throttle valve
18. (2) Throttle valve screws
19. Upper throttle shaft bushing
20. Lower throttle shaft bushing
21. Throttle shaft seal
22. Throttle shaft seal
23. Throttle shaft
24. Link retainer
25. Choke shaft
26. Upper choke shaft bushing
27. Choke shaft spring
28. Choke shaft seal
29. Lower choke shaft bushing

Briggs and Stratton Corp.

Figure 14-7.

Exploded view of a float-type carburetor, showing individual part locations.

The following are some basic things that should *not* be done when making carburetor repairs:

- Do *not* use drill bits to clean passages.
- Do *not* enlarge passages.
- Do *not* soak a carburetor in a cleaner for longer than 30 minutes.
- Do *not* reuse original choke and throttle shutter screws.
- Do *not* interchange bowl nuts.
- Do *not* reuse gaskets and O-rings.

Carburetor Removal

The following removal procedures are typical to most carburetor configurations:

1. Remove the air cleaner and air cleaner housing and set it aside for later use.
2. Turn off the fuel shut-off valve (located between the fuel tank and carburetor) or clamp the fuel line. See **Figure 14-8**.
3. Drain the carburetor bowl by removing the drain screw.
4. Loosen the hose clamp at the carburetor inlet fitting and disconnect the fuel line from the carburetor, **Figure 14-9**.

Caution

Never use a threaded fastener, like a bolt or screw, to plug a fuel line. This can damage the hose and allow small particles of rubber to enter the carburetor.

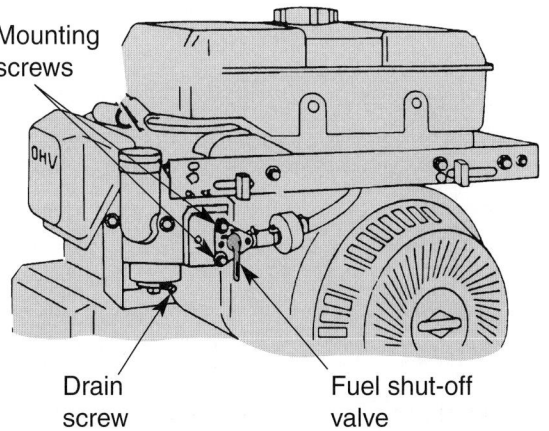

Briggs and Stratton Corp.

Figure 14-8.

The fuel shut-off valve is located between the fuel tank and the carburetor. If the engine does not have a fuel shut-off valve, clamp the fuel line ahead of the carburetor.

Goodheart-Willcox Publisher

Figure 14-9.

With the fuel shut off, remove the fuel line from the carburetor.

5. Sketch or take digital photos of the governor linkage. Governor linkages can be complicated and accurate reference sketches or photos may help during reassembly.
6. Disconnect governor linkage and spring. (Do not deform spring or linkage.)
7. Remove the throttle linkage from the throttle lever.
8. Remove the carburetor mounting screws. (Hold the body to prevent it from falling from the engine.) See **Figure 14-10**.
9. Remove the choke linkage from the choke lever. See **Figure 14-11**.
10. Lift the carburetor from engine (should be free from engine and linkage).

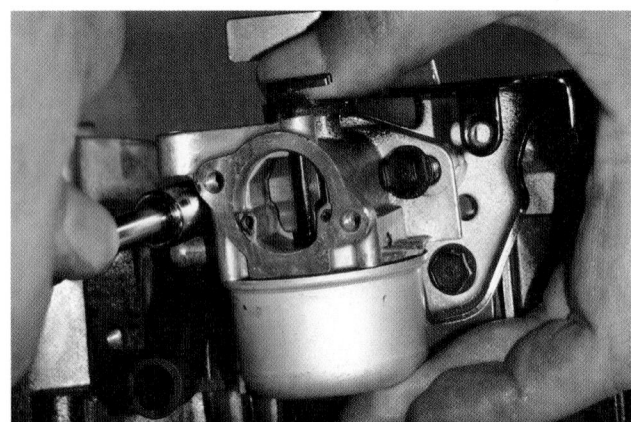

Goodheart-Willcox Publisher

Figure 14-10.

Hold the carburetor while removing the mounting bolts.

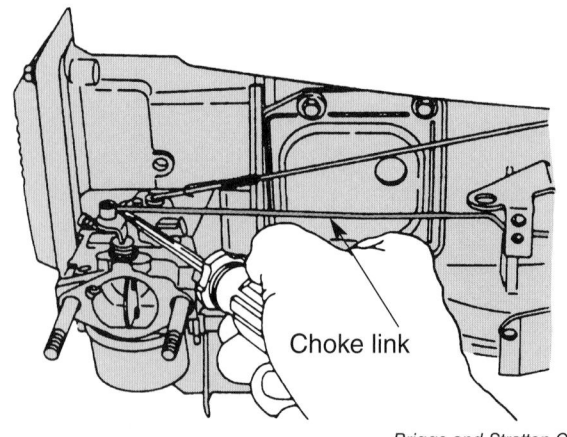

Briggs and Stratton Corp.

Figure 14-11.

Choke linkage can be removed from the choke lever by prying it with a screwdriver.

Carburetor Disassembly

Before disassembling the carburetor, familiarize yourself with its design by reviewing the appropriate service manual or the diagram included in the rebuild kit. It should be noted that many carburetors are designed for specific engine models. Similar carburetors may contain hundreds of significant variations in detail. The procedures presented in this chapter are general and may not pertain directly to the carburetor that you are attempting to service. However, if care is taken during the disassembly phase, no difficulty will be encountered during reassembly.

The carburetor must be carefully disassembled and all nonmetallic parts (gaskets, O-rings, etc.) must be removed prior to cleaning. As you disassemble the carburetor, carefully note each part removed and its orientation. This will help you reassemble the carburetor after it is cleaned.

Note

You may want to take digital photos of each part to refer to during reassembly.

Float Carburetor Disassembly

1. Remove the high-speed mixture adjustment and idle mixture adjustment screws, if the carburetor has them. Remove the idle speed stop screw. Take note of the number of turns required to remove each of the screws.

2. Remove the float bowl retaining nut and the float bowl. Remove the O-ring from the float bowl. See **Figure 14-12**.

3. Remove the float hinge pin and lift the float and needle valve from the carburetor. Some floats are equipped with a dampening spring. In such cases, note the position of the dampening spring hooks before removing the float hinge pin. See **Figure 14-13**.

4. Use a carburetor tool or small hook to remove the float needle seat.

5. On some carburetors, the main nozzle should be removed. On other carburetors, it should not be removed. Always consult the proper service information for the specific carburetor you are working on to determine whether the main nozzle should be removed.

6. Some carburetor models have *welch plugs* that must be removed to expose drilled passages. To remove welch plugs, sharpen a small chisel to a wedge point and drive the chisel into the plug. See **Figure 14-14**. Push down on the chisel and pry the plug out of position.

Note

Some carburetors have small ball- or cup-type plugs. These should not be removed unless the manufacturer specifically states to do so.

7. Note the orientation of the choke and throttle valves and the hooks on any shaft return springs. Remove the choke plate screws, remove the choke plate, and then pull the choke shaft from its bore. Repeat the process for the throttle valve assembly. See **Figure 14-15**.

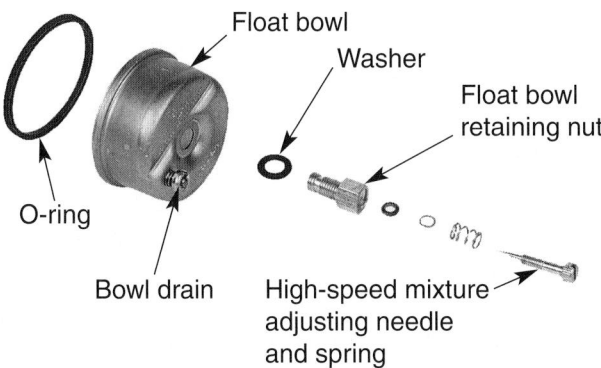

Goodheart-Willcox Publisher

Figure 14-12.

The float bowl assembly of an adjustable carburetor is shown here. Sealed carburetors will not have the high-speed mixture adjusting needle and spring.

Tecumseh Products Co.

Figure 14-13.

Remove the float hinge pin and lift the float and needle valve out of the carburetor.

A

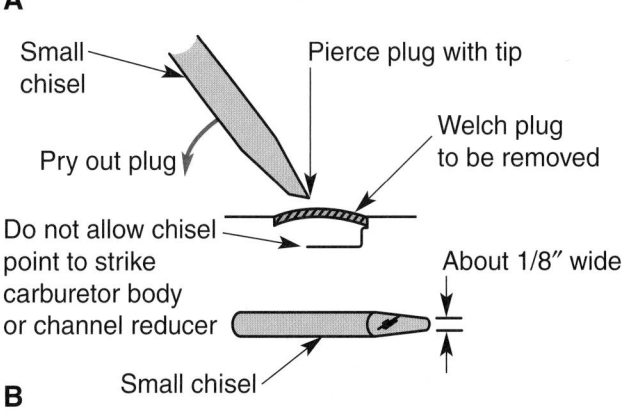

B

Tecumseh Products Co.

Figure 14-14.

Before soaking the carburetor in solvent, welch plugs should be removed from the carburetor body to expose the drilled passages. A—Welch plugs may be located on the side and bottom of the carburetor body. B—The welch plugs should be carefully removed with a small chisel.

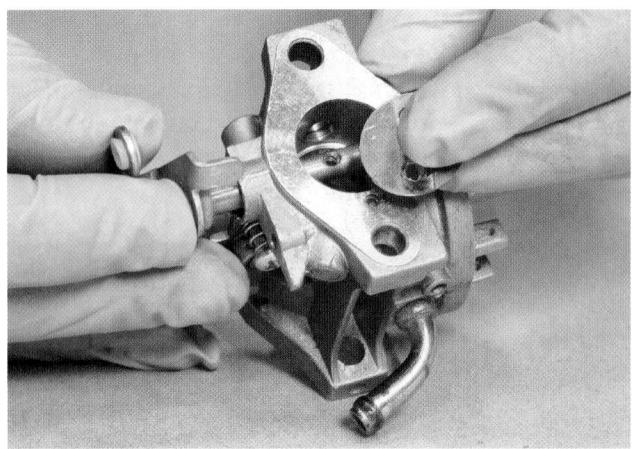

Goodheart-Willcox Publisher

Figure 14-15.
Remove the screws holding the choke valve plate to the choke valve shaft, remove the plate, and then pull the shaft from its bore. Repeat the process for the throttle valve.

8. If the carburetor is equipped with a primer bulb, it must be removed. Pry the retaining clip out of its seat with a thin screwdriver. Then, grip the bulb with pliers and twist while pulling the bulb free. Do not worry about destroying the bulb; it should be replaced any time the carburetor is overhauled.

Diaphragm Carburetor Disassembly

1. Remove the screws from the diaphragm cover, and then remove the cover, diaphragm, and gasket. Be sure to note the order in which they are removed.
2. Remove the fuel inlet needle assembly and the inlet needle seat.
3. Remove the high-speed mixture adjustment and idle mixture adjustment screws if present. Remove the idle stop screw. Note how many turns are required to remove each screw.
4. Remove welch plugs. Do *not* remove any cup or ball plugs unless specifically instructed to do so by the manufacturer.
5. Depending on the carburetor design, additional parts may need to be removed prior to cleaning. Consult the service manual for the carburetor you are working on to identify additional parts that must be removed.

Cleaning the Carburetor

After removing and disassembling the carburetor, inspect the parts for severe wear and contamination. Check the float bowl and the areas covered by welch plugs for particulates. These can give you some insight into problems with the carburetor. If there are black particulates in the carburetor, it indicates that rubber from a deteriorated fuel line is entering the carburetor. If there are bluish green particulates in the carburetor, it indicates that the copper from the carburetor body has leeched into the fuel. In these cases, the carburetor must be replaced. The carburetor must also be replaced if there is significant rust, excessively heavy varnish, or excessive wear.

After inspecting the carburetor components, wash all metallic parts in an appropriate solvent. If the carburetor is very dirty, the carburetor body and all metallic parts can be soaked in a commercial carburetor dip solution. It should be noted that some manufacturers recommend against using a harsh, dipping solution. For these carburetors and for lighter cleaning jobs, spray-type carburetor cleaners can be used. See **Figure 14-16**.

Warning

Be careful not to get any carburetor cleaning solution on hands or clothing. Wear safety glasses. Put only the metallic carburetor parts in the solution and let them soak. Nonmetallic parts can be damaged by harsh commercial cleaners.

Goodheart-Willcox Publisher

Figure 14-16.
Carburetor cleaning solutions. A—A dip-type cleaning solvent is aggressive and suitable for cleaning heavy contamination. Metallic parts are placed in the tray and lowered into the solution to soak. B—Spray-type carburetor cleaner is less aggressive.

After the parts have soaked for no more than 30 minutes, rinse them with a milder cleaning solvent and dry with compressed air. Do not dry the parts with a rag or paper towel. Lint from the rags may get into the passages. Never clean holes or passages with wires or similar objects. These will distort the openings and may prevent the engine from running properly.

Be careful not to plug the idle or main fuel ports. Dry all passages with low-pressure air (35 psi). Do not use wire, drill bits, or similar hard objects to clean passages. These items can remove metal and enlarge the diameter of the passages. However, the passages and orifices can be cleaned with a synthetic fiber, such as a section of heavy monofilament fishing line. See **Figure 14-17**.

Caution

Never soak parts in solvent for longer than 30 minutes. Nonmetallic parts should never be exposed to solvents. Safety goggles and rubber gloves should always be worn when working with solvents and commercial carburetor cleaners. Many commercial carburetor cleaners are extremely caustic and can cause serious burns to skin and eyes.

Green Tech

Volatile Organic Compounds (VOCs)

Volatile organic compounds (VOCs) are toxic substances that evaporate into the atmosphere, commonly as a by-product of drying. VOCs may develop into such environmental hazards as smog, but they are also harmful if kept indoors. VOCs are also associated with mild and severe health concerns. VOCs may be found in substances like carburetor cleaners. You can reduce your VOC output by choosing low-VOC-products.

Clean all carbon from the carburetor bore, especially where the throttle and choke plates seat.

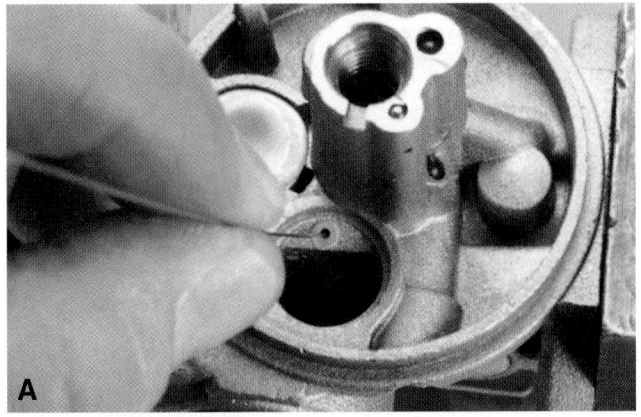

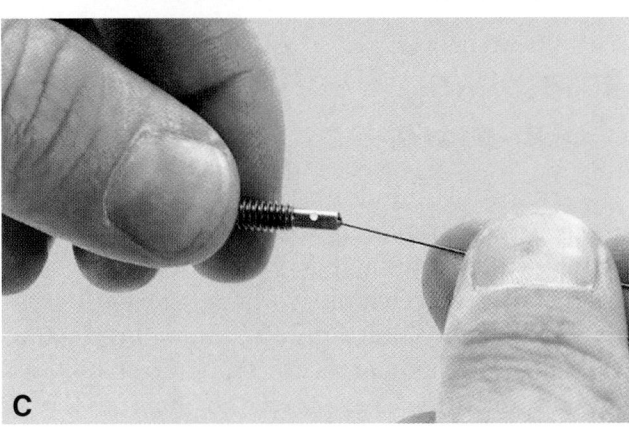

(Continued)

Tecumseh Products Co.

Figure 14-17.
Carburetor passages can be cleaned with a stiff synthetic fiber. A low-emissions (fixed jet) carburetor is being cleaned here. A—The extended prime well passage. B—Progression holes. C—Idle jet. D—Idle circuit fuel pickup passage.

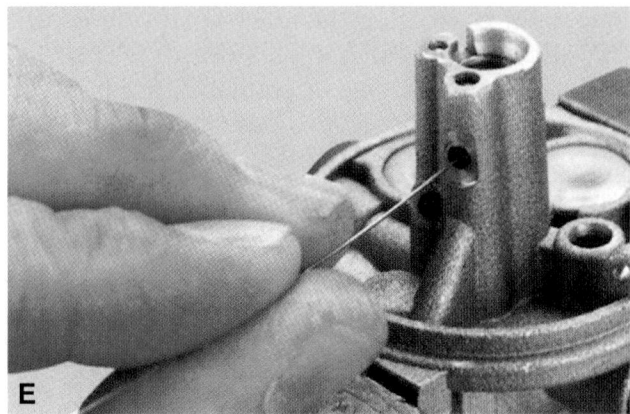

Tecumseh Products Co.

Figure 14-17. *(Continued)*

E—Secondary idle fuel pickup passage (bridged carburetor). F—Fuel pickup, main jet, and idle delivery hole in the bowl nut.

Inspecting Float Carburetor Parts

When all parts are clean and dry, organize them neatly on a clean white cloth. Inspect the parts for wear, material failure, or other damage. Check the carburetor body and crankcase for cracks and warped or worn mating surfaces. If the carburetor body is cracked, warped, or worn, the carburetor must be replaced. Carefully inspect each part of the carburetor for damage and wear. Some parts are replaceable, but wear or damage to other parts will require that the carburetor be replaced.

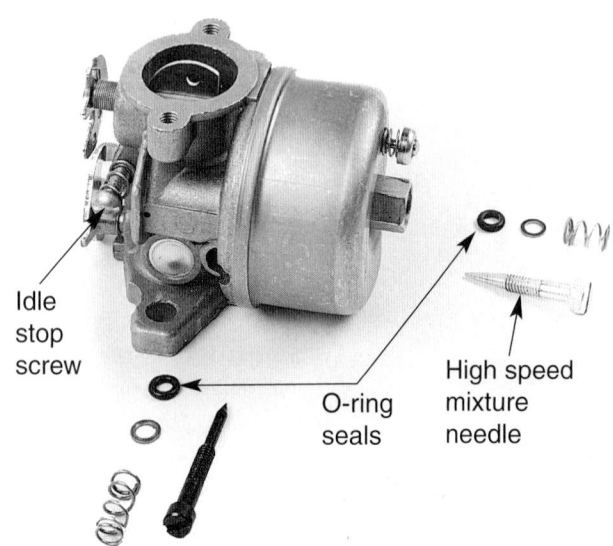

Idle stop screw

O-ring seals

High speed mixture needle

Tecumseh Products Co.

Figure 14-18.

Examine the adjustment needles and replace O-rings if they are deformed.

Examine the idle and high-speed adjusting screw needles. The points should be straight and smooth. O-ring seals should be replaced if they are damaged. See **Figure 14-18**. Check the choke shaft, throttle shaft, and their bores for wear. See **Figure 14-19**. If the shafts are worn, they should be replaced. If the shaft bores are worn, the carburetor must be replaced.

The fuel bowl must be free of dirt and corrosion. Examine the float for damage. Hollow, brass-type floats must be free from pinholes and dents. Check the float hinge bearing surfaces for wear. The tab that contacts the inlet needle should also be inspected for wear. See **Figure 14-20**. Check the condition of the spring clip that is used to attach the inlet needle to the float tab. Replace any worn or damaged parts.

Assembling Float-Type Carburetors

After all carburetor parts have been cleaned, inspected, and replaced (if necessary), they should be reassembled in the following order:
1. Install new welch plugs (if applicable). To install a new plug, apply an ethanol-resistant sealant to the plug if directed to do so by the manufacturer. Then, place the plug into the receptacle with the raised portion up and flatten it with a flat punch that is slightly larger in diameter than the plug itself. Do not dent the plug or drive the center of the plug below the top surface of the carburetor. See **Figure 14-21**.

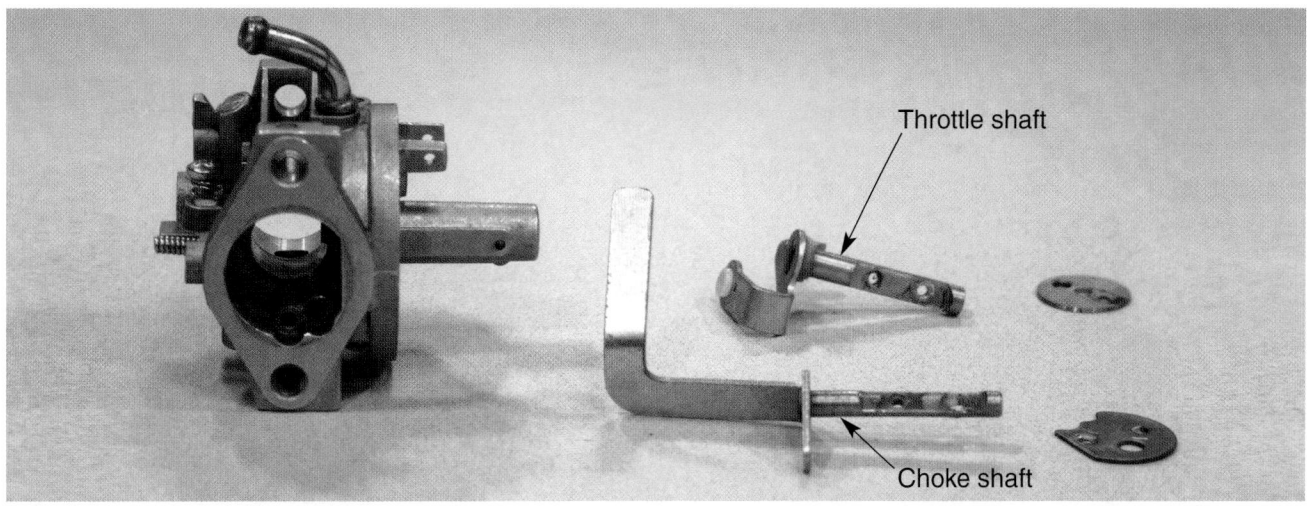

Goodheart-Willcox Publisher

Figure 14-19.

If the throttle or choke shaft exhibit wear, they must be replaced. If the bores are worn, the carburetor must be replaced.

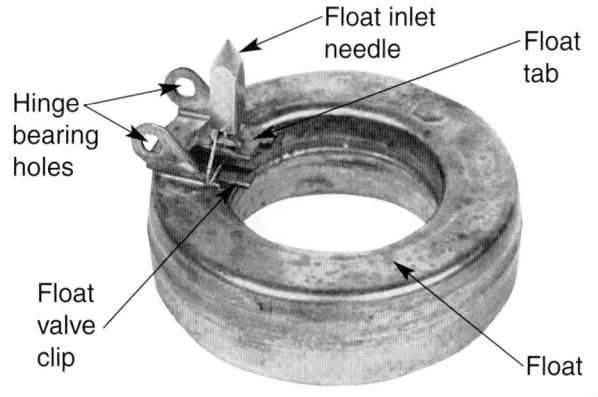

Tecumseh Products Co.

Figure 14-20.

The float hinge bearing holes should be examined for wear. The float tab is used to adjust float height per specifications.

Caution

Many of the sealants traditionally used to seal welch plugs are gradually dissolved by ethanol in the gasoline. Use of an improper sealant could gum up the carburetor or cause the welch plug to loosen. Apply sealant to the welch plugs only if directed to do so by the manufacturer's service literature. In such cases, use only the recommended sealant.

2. If necessary, install a new primer bulb in the carburetor body. Primer bulbs are typically installed by placing the bulb over the primer bulb socket with the retainer tabs sticking

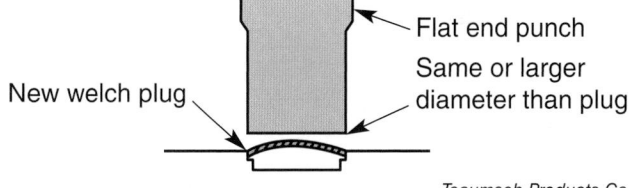

Tecumseh Products Co.

Figure 14-21.

Use a flat punch to install new welch plugs. Only flatten plug. Do not dent it.

out. An appropriately sized deep well socket wrench is then used to press the primer bulb and retainer into place.

3. Install the throttle shaft, bushings, seals, and washers.
4. Attach the throttle valve plate with new screws. Examine the choke and throttle plates for coded markings, which identify the way that they must be installed. See **Figure 14-22**. Always replace the old screws when installing the throttle and choke plates. The screws included with rebuild kits are treated with thread adhesive to prevent them from backing out during engine operation.
5. Install the idle-speed stop screw.
6. Install the choke shaft, spring, seal, washer, and bushing.
7. Attach the choke valve plate with new screws.
8. Install the main nozzles (if applicable).
9. Install the high-speed and idle mixture adjustment screw seats.

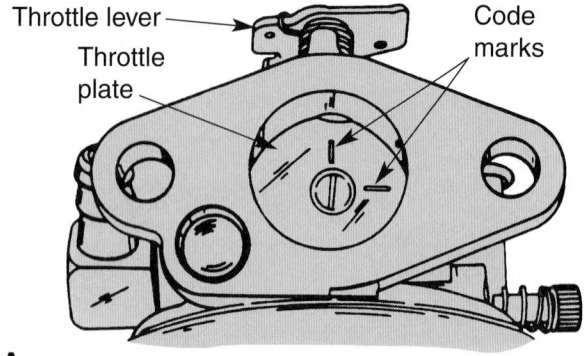

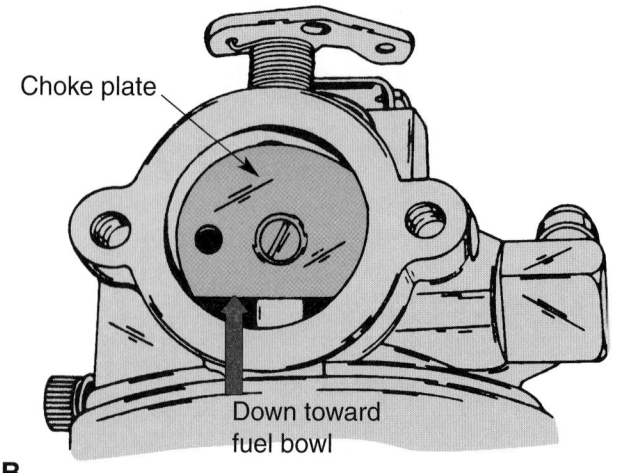

Tecumseh Products Co.

Figure 14-22.

A—This throttle plate must be installed with the code marks in the location shown. B—This choke plate must be installed with the flat side down toward the float bowl.

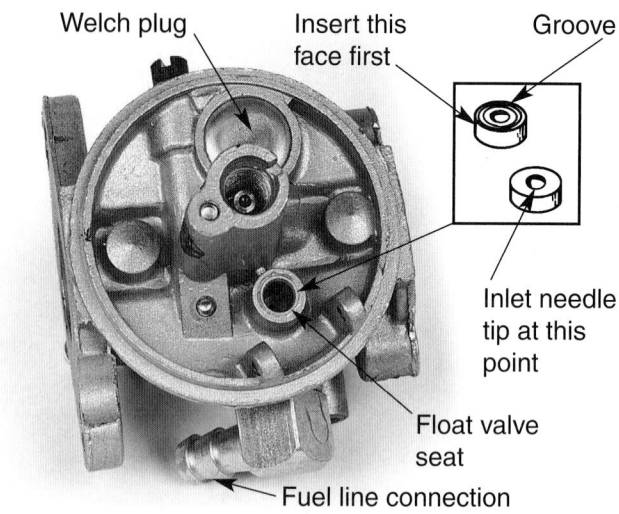

Tecumseh Products Co.

Figure 14-23.

This synthetic rubber needle seat must be installed with grooved face toward the bottom of the hole. The rubber seat is oiled before being pressed into the hole with a flat punch.

10. Install the idle mixture screw assembly.
11. Install the high-speed mixture screw assembly.
12. Install the inlet needle valve seat. Moisten it with oil and insert it into the carburetor body (smooth side toward the inlet needle). Press the seat into the cavity using a flat punch that is the same diameter as the seat. Make sure it is firmly seated. See **Figure 14-23**.
13. Attach the inlet needle to the float with a wire clip. See **Figure 14-24**.
14. Install the float on the carburetor with the hinge pin.
15. Adjust float height per manufacturer's specifications. See **Figure 14-25**.
16. Install the float-bowl over the float assembly with the mounting screw. Use a new gasket or O-ring to seal the bowl, **Figure 14-26**. Be aware that some fuel bowls will interfere with the float if not positioned correctly. See **Figure 14-27**.

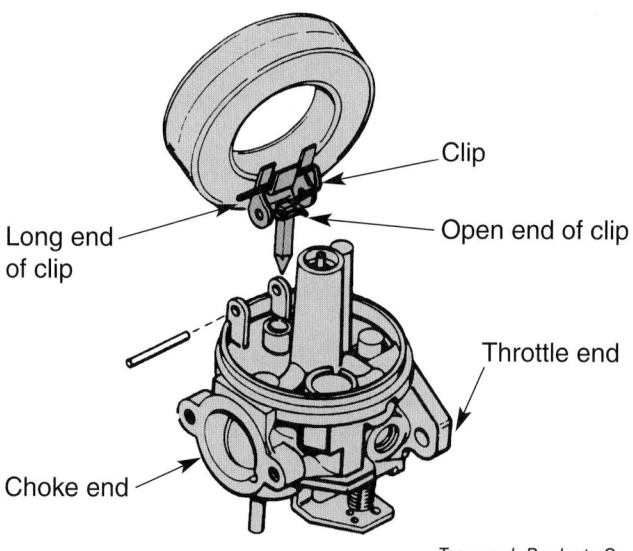

Tecumseh Products Co.

Figure 14-24.

The inlet needle is attached to the float with a specially shaped wire clip.

17. Install the carburetor on the engine. If a gasket is required, always use a new one.
18. Connect the throttle, choke, and governor linkage. On some engines, linkage is connected before bolting the carburetor to the engine.
19. Connect the fuel line.
20. Install the air cleaner.

Figure 14-25.
The float must rest on the needle at a specified height. If float is high, too much fuel will be used. If the float level is low, the lean mixture may cause overheating.

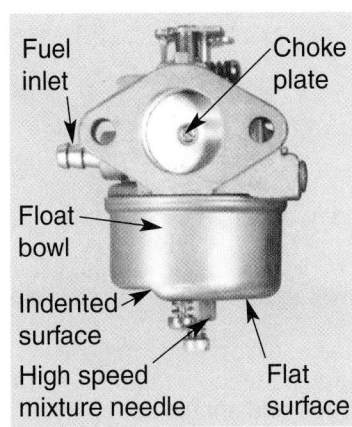

Fuel inlet

Choke plate

Float bowl

Indented surface

High speed mixture needle

Flat surface

Figure 14-27.
Some float bowls must be installed in a particular way to avoid interference with the internal float. Note the indented and flat surfaces on the bottom of this float bowl.

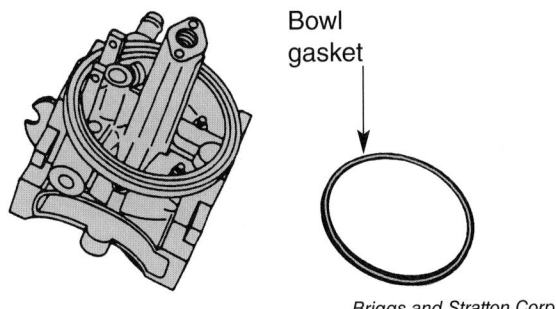

Bowl gasket

Figure 14-26.
When replacing a float bowl, always install a new gasket or O-ring.

21. Adjust the idle mixture and high-speed mixture adjustment needles to their initial starting settings, per manufacturer's instructions. Then, start the engine and make final mixture, idle, and governor adjustments.

Inspecting Diaphragm Carburetor Parts

The inspection process for diaphragm-type carburetors parts is similar to that used for float-type carburetors. Check the throttle and choke shafts. They must fit closely, but turn easily in their bearing holes. See **Figure 14-28**. If loose, they will cause poor engine performance.

The diaphragm should be checked for defects that would cause leakage. The diaphragm needle valve must be straight and fit the seat so that it seals

when closed. The high speed and idle mixture needles should have straight, smooth tapers. See **Figure 14-29**. The O-rings or seals around the needles should be replaced if they are cut or deformed.

Some manufacturers supply diaphragm carburetor repair kits that include items that would most likely need replacing. Other parts can be purchased as they are needed.

Assembling a Diaphragm Carburetor

Because of the many different carburetor designs, it is highly recommended that the manual

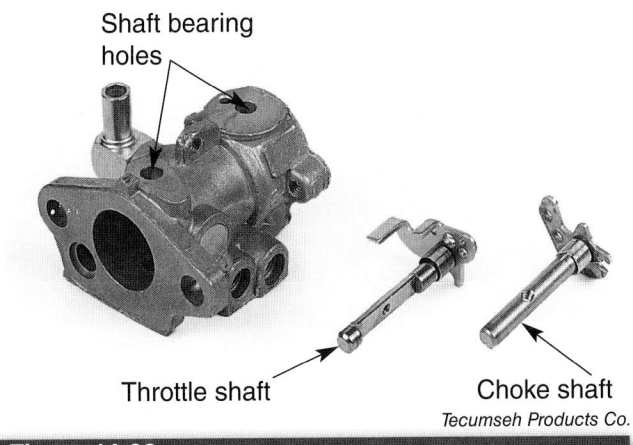

Shaft bearing holes

Throttle shaft

Choke shaft

Figure 14-28.
Throttle and choke shafts must fit their bores closely, but turn freely.

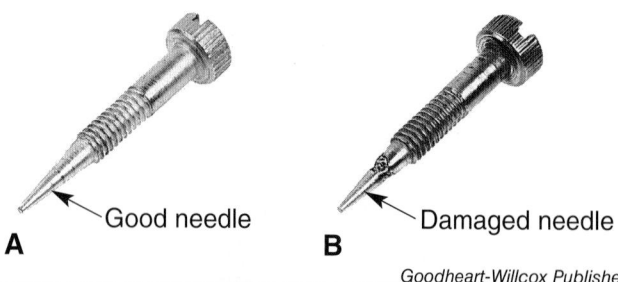

A Good needle   **B** Damaged needle

Goodheart-Willcox Publisher

Figure 14-29.

Check the needle valves for damage. A—This needle valve has a straight, smooth taper. B—This needle valve is damaged and should be replaced.

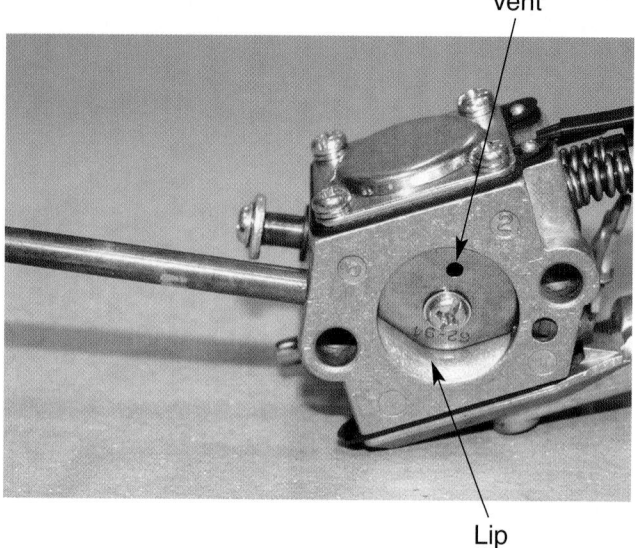

Vent

Lip

Goodheart-Willcox Publisher

Figure 14-30.

The choke plate shown here must be installed behind the lip. The lip stops the choke plate in the fully closed position.

be followed when assembling a carburetor. After all carburetor parts have been cleaned, inspected, and replaced (if necessary), the carburetor should be reassembled in the following order:

1. Replace any welch plugs that were removed for cleaning. Apply sealant to the plug as recommended by the manufacturer. Ensure that only an ethanol-resistant sealant is used.
2. If necessary, install a new priming bulb into the carburetor body.
3. Install the throttle shaft in its bore. Make sure that any seals, bushings, washers, or return springs are properly installed. Install the throttle plate on the throttle shaft. The throttle plate must be placed properly in the carburetor bore. Usually, identifying marks of some sort are put on the plate to assist the assembler. Be sure to use the new screws included in the rebuild kit.
4. Assemble the choke plate in the same way as the throttle. Choke plates are typically *vented*, which means that they have openings to allow some air to enter even when they are closed. There may be a small lip in the carburetor body that the plate must be positioned behind. This lip acts as a stop, limiting the choke valve's range of motion. See **Figure 14-30**.
5. Install the fuel inlet needle valve assembly. Follow the manufacturer's instructions to check and adjust the needle valve hinge lever position as needed.
6. Install the diaphragm, gasket, and diaphragm cover. The rivet head in the center of the diaphragm should face the needle valve.
7. Install high-speed and idle mixture needles.
8. Adjust the high-speed and idle mixture needles as prescribed by the carburetor's

service manual. This will get the engine started. Finer adjustments can be made when the engine is warmed up.
9. Install the idle stop screw.
10. Attach the carburetor to the engine. Be sure to use a new intake gasket.
11. Install the linkage.
12. Attach the air cleaner with new gaskets.

Engine Governor Service

Most small engines are equipped with either an air-vane governor or a centrifugal governor. A centrifugal governor is the most common. Before making any adjustments to the governor system, check the ignition system, air cleaner, and fuel systems for proper operation. Often, problems in these areas can be misinterpreted as governor problems.

If the governor system is suspected of causing the engine performance problem, check the system for binding and bent linkage. Replace any linkages or springs that are excessively rusty, bent, or broken. Inspect any bushings in the system for excessive wear. Make sure that the governor shaft rotates freely and does not have excessive side play. Check for loose brackets or levers and tighten as needed.

Resetting a Centrifugal Governor System

Proper centrifugal governor operation is dependent on maintaining the proper governor lever position relative to the position of the governor spool inside the engine. If the governor system is not functioning properly, or if the governor level has been loosened or removed, the governor's wide open throttle position must be reset. The following is a general procedure for reestablishing the proper governor lever position for wide-open throttle:

1. Loosen the clamp that holds the governor lever to the governor shaft.
2. Move the throttle lever to the idle position. Then, move it to the wide-open-throttle position and note which direction the governor lever rotates.
3. While holding the throttle in the wide-open position, use a screwdriver or special tool to turn the governor shaft the same direction that the governor lever rotated when the throttle was opened. See **Figure 14-31**.
4. When the governor shaft has turned as far as possible, tighten the governor lever clamp to the proper torque specifications (typically 35–45 lb•in or 4.0–5.0 N•m).

5. Before starting the engine, move the linkage manually to check for binding.

Caution

Never allow an engine to overspeed. When starting an engine after governor service, always be prepared to stop the engine immediately if the governor system malfunctions.

Governor Adjustment

If a centrifugal governor system still does operate properly after being reset, or if the engine is equipped with a malfunctioning air-vane governor system, additional adjustments can be made to the external linkage. Often, the method of adjusting the governor can be determined by good judgment and reasoning. When determining how to adjust the system, keep in mind that centrifugal force or air-vane action and spring pressure are opposed to each other. Spring pressure works to open the throttle and centrifugal force or air-vane action works to close the throttle.

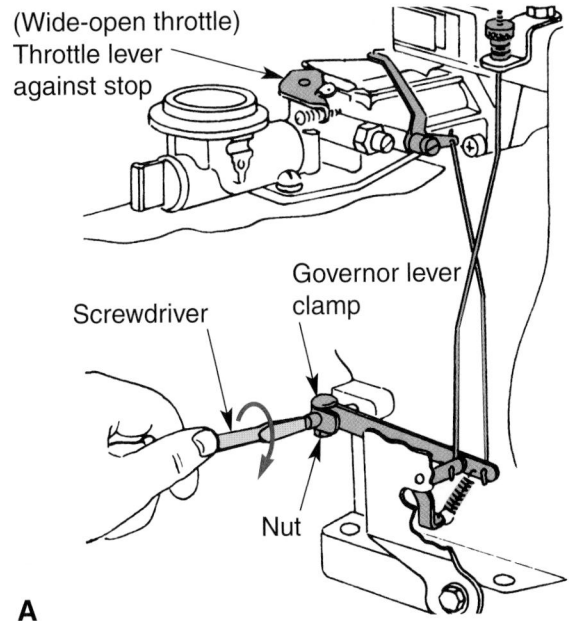 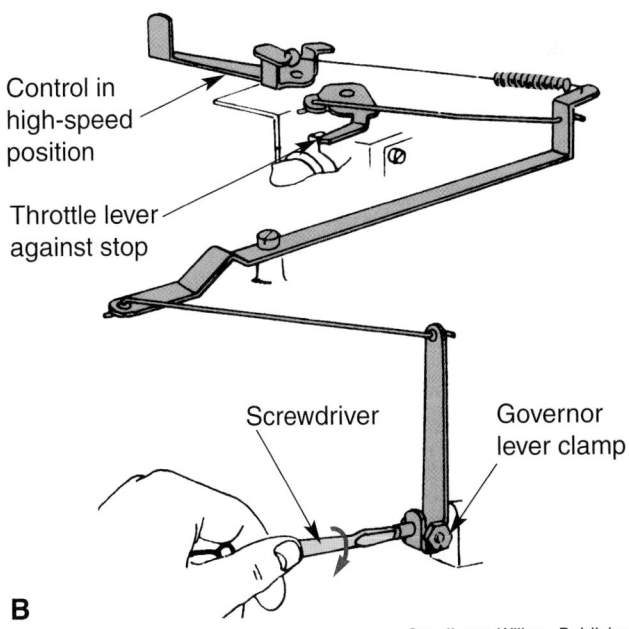

Goodheart-Willcox Publisher

Figure 14-31.

To adjust the governor, loosen the governor lever clamp, move the throttle to the wide-open position, rotate the governor shaft, and tighten the clamp. A—Typical governor system on a horizontal shaft engine. B—Typical governor system on a vertical shaft.

The sensitivity of the engine system can often be adjusted by changing the hole in the lever arm in which the governor spring is attached. In general, the closer the spring is to the pivot end of the lever, the smaller the difference between load and no-load engine speed. If the spring is brought too close to the pivot point, the engine will begin to *hunt* (engine speed increase and decrease). The farther the spring is from the pivot end, the less the tendency to hunt. However, there will be a greater speed drop under load. If the governed speed is lowered, the spring can usually be moved closer to the pivot.

Some governors are adjusted by turning a thumbscrew that adjusts governor spring tension at idle, thus changing engine speed. See **Figure 14-32**. Other governors are adjusted by bending the spring attach arm, as shown in **Figure 14-33**. Some governors are adjusted by repositioning the spring bracket to increase or decrease governor spring tension.

Fuel Injection Diagnosis

As with a carburetor fuel system, failure usually results in an incorrect air-fuel mixture. The basic diagnosis of fuel injection systems is the same as the diagnosis for a carburetor fuel system. Restrictions in the fuel delivery system, such as a faulty fuel pump, clogged fuel filter, or pinched fuel line, result in a lean mixture. If an insufficient volume of air is being delivered, check for a clogged air filter or a restricted air passage in the throttle body.

Fuel injection systems also have onboard diagnostic capability. These onboard diagnostic systems will produce a *diagnostic trouble code (DTC)* if a sensor reading is out of range. By interpreting the diagnostic trouble code, the technician can determine the component that is malfunctioning and the nature of the malfunction.

Some systems are equipped with a diagnostic connector. With these systems, a special cable can be connected to this diagnostic connector and to a dedicated code reader, diagnostic tablet, or laptop computer. The diagnostic software communicates

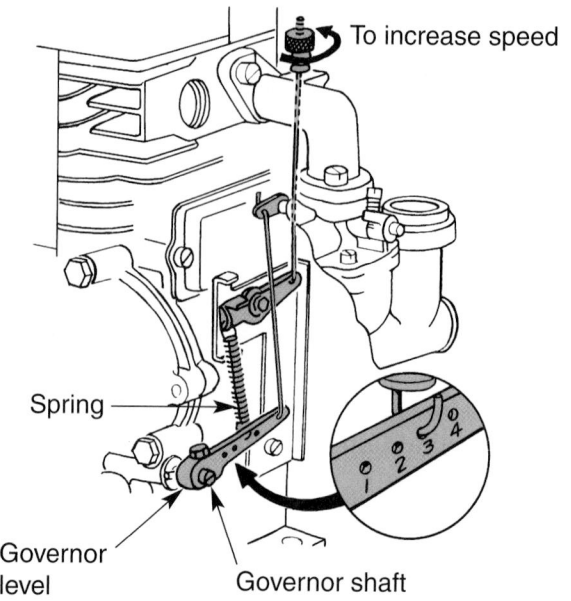

Briggs and Stratton Corp.

Figure 14-32.

The knurled thumbscrew on this governor is turned to adjust spring tension. Note that the spring is in hole number three of the governor lever. The spring position determines the governor sensitivity, and the thumbscrew sets engine speed.

with the ECU and displays any saved diagnostic trouble codes. On other systems, diagnostic trouble codes are displayed by LEDs flashing in a repeating pattern. The codes used and the method of retrieving them varies from system to system. Refer to the manufacturer's service literature for specific instructions.

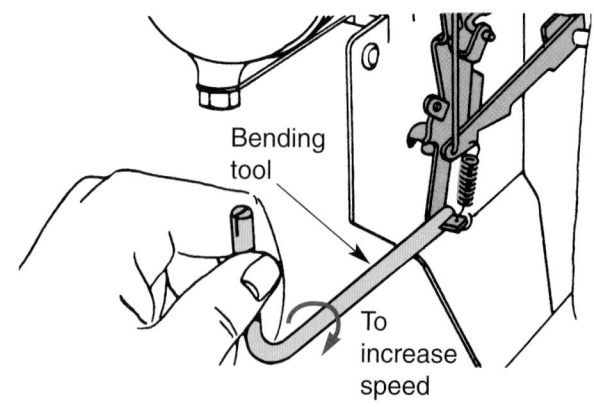

Goodheart-Willcox Publisher

Figure 14-33.

On this governor system, the governor spring attach arm is bent to increase or decrease spring tension and engine speed.

Summary

The first step in troubleshooting a fuel system is to make sure that poor engine performance is not being caused by an ignition system problem or clogged air filter. Troubleshooting the fuel system involves testing each component in the system until the problem area is located. Make sure that there is proper fuel flow through the fuel system. If fuel is getting to the carburetor, the poor engine performance may be caused by improper carburetor adjustments or a defective carburetor. Make high speed and idle mixture adjustments according to manufacturer's specifications.

If mixture adjustment does not resolve the performance problems, the carburetor can be overhauled. Carburetor repair kits are usually available from the manufacturer. Troubleshooting charts can be used to locate specific problems within the carburetor. Because of the many variations on the market, it is very important to use a service manual when disassembling a carburetor. Follow all instructions carefully. Never soak carburetor parts in solvent for longer than 30 minutes. Wires or similar objects should never be used for cleaning carburetor ports.

If the governor system is suspected of causing poor performance, check the ignition system, air filter, and carburetor before making adjustments. Inspect the governor system for binding, loose, or broken components. If the engine has a centrifugal governor, reset the wide-open-throttle position before making final adjustments. There are many different governor system configurations, and the different styles have various methods of adjustment. Often, the method of adjusting the governor can be determined by good judgment and reasoning. If you are unsure of the proper method of adjusting the governor, refer to the service manual for the engine being serviced.

Basic diagnosis of a fuel injection system is similar to diagnosis of a carburetor fuel system. If a sensor reading is out of range, the ECU will set a trouble code, which indicates the sensor that is malfunctioning and the nature of the malfunction.

Review Questions

Answer the following questions using the information provided in this chapter.

1. A customer brings in a lawnmower in early spring. The customer says the mower ran fine the last time he used it in the fall, but now will not start. The technician checks the mower and finds that it is producing spark, the air filter is clean, and fuel is getting to the carburetor. What should the technician do next?

2. The technician pulls a spark plug and finds the electrodes covered in dry, black carbon. What does this indicate?

3. A technician disconnects the fuel line from the carburetor on a gravity-fed fuel system, but no fuel comes out. What steps should the technician take to isolate the cause of the blockage?

4. *True or False?* A loose fuel line connection can disrupt proper fuel pump operation.

5. An engine starts and runs fine when it is cold, but begins running erratically and dies when it heats up. Which of the following is the most likely cause?
   A. Stale fuel.
   B. Vapor lock.
   C. A malfunctioning governor.

6. Name the three basic carburetor adjustments in the order in which they are performed.

7. Which of the following procedures would *not* be recommended in carburetor maintenance?
   A. Clean nonmetallic parts in a commercial carburetor cleaner.
   B. Wash metallic parts in commercial carburetor cleaner.
   C. Dry parts with compressed air.

8. *True or False?* Carburetor passages and holes should be cleaned by pushing a stiff wire of the proper size through them.

9. *True or False?* Paper towels are used to dry carburetor parts.

10. Never soak carburetor parts in solvent for more than _____ minutes.

11. *True or False?* Float bowl gaskets and O-rings are commonly reused when overhauling a float-type carburetor.

12. What two types of governor systems are most commonly used in small engines?

13. *True or False?* If the governor lever has been removed on a centrifugal governor system, the proper wide-open-throttle setting must be reset before other governor adjustments are made.

14. How is governor sensitivity typically adjusted?

15. *True or False?* All governor systems are equipped with a thumbscrew for adjusting governor spring tension.

Suggested Activities

1. Adjust a carburetor using the procedures described in the text. Check the service manual for specifications.

2. Rebuild a float-type carburetor.

3. Rebuild a diaphragm carburetor.

4. Look up governor adjustments in a service manual for a specific engine. Explain how the governor works and demonstrate the correct adjustment procedure.

5. Research different fuel injection systems and prepare a report detailing the methods of retrieving diagnostic trouble codes for those systems.

Troubleshooting Charts

The following pages include troubleshooting charts that are useful for diagnosing and correcting carburetor-related problems. Each chart lists common carburetor problems, the symptoms of those problems, and the corrective actions to take for those problems. Separate troubleshooting charts specifically for float-type carburetors and diaphragm carburetors are presented here.

Troubleshooting Float-Type Carburetors

Leaky Carburetor Gaskets

Symptoms:

Engine overspeeds
Idle speed is excessive
Carburetor runs lean with main adjustment needle shut off
Performance unsatisfactory after being serviced

Repair:

Replace with new gaskets on the intake and air cleaner end of the carburetor every time the gasket is disturbed.

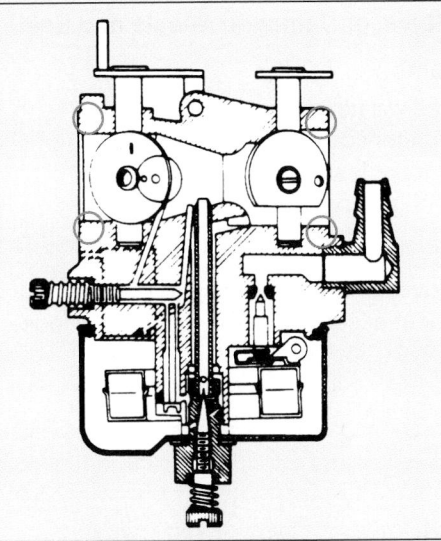

Throttle and/or Choke Shaft Worn, Throttle and/or Choke Springs Not Functioning

Symptoms:

Engine will not start
Engine hunts (at idle or high speed)
Engine will not idle
Engine lacks power at high speed
Idle speed is excessive
Choke does not open fully
Performance unsatisfactory after being serviced

Repair:

Replace all worn parts, springs, dust seals (when so equipped). If the shaft bores are worn out-of-round, causing the leak, a new service carburetor should be used.

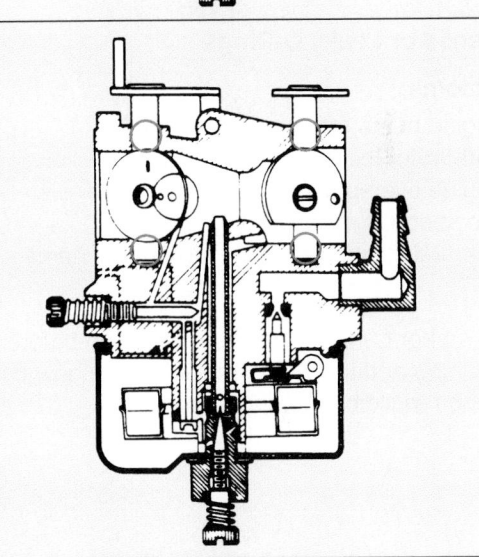

Fuel Inlet Is Plugged or Loose

Symptoms:

Engine will not start
Engine hunts (at idle or high speed)
Engine will not idle
Engine lacks power at high speed
Carburetor leaks
Engine starves for fuel at high speed (leans out)

Repair:

Clean fuel system completely. Refill with clean fresh fuel, as recommended. Replace loose clamps and fittings.

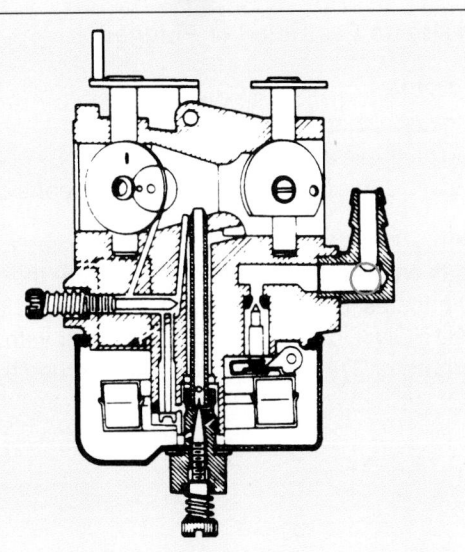

(Continued)
Tecumseh Products Co.

Troubleshooting chart for float-type carburetors.

Troubleshooting Float-Type Carburetors (Continued)

Dirty, Stuck, or Damaged Needle and Seat

Symptoms:

Engine will not start
Carburetor floods
Carburetor leaks
Poor engine performance

Repair:

Remove old needle and seat. Install a new needle and seat according to manual instructions.

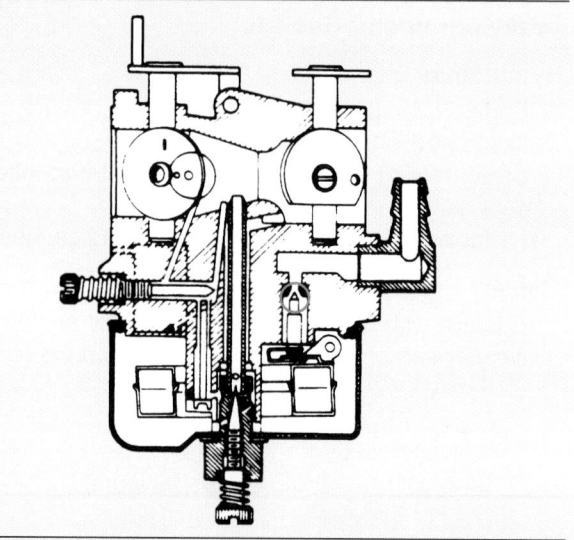

Damaged or Leaky O-Rings

Symptoms:

Engine hunts (at idle or high speed)
Carburetor leaks
Engine overspeeds
Idle speed is excessive
Carburetor runs with main adjustment needle shut off

Repair:

All rubber O-rings should be removed before cleaning and should be replaced with new ones when rebuilding the carburetor.

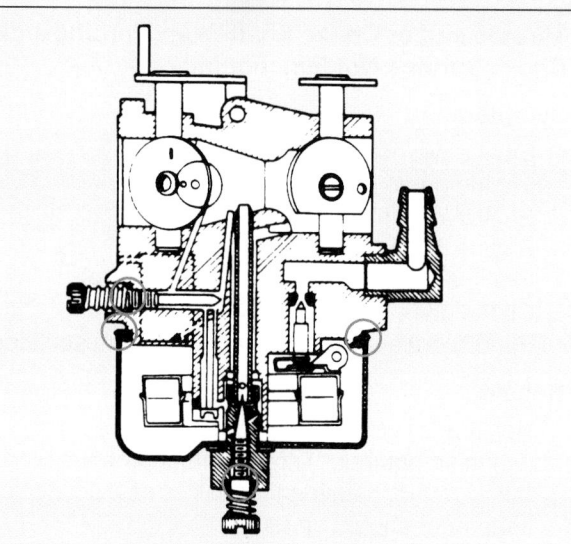

Main Nozzle Restricted or Plugged

Symptoms:

Engine will not start
Engine hunts at high speed
Engine starves for fuel at high speed (leans out)

Repair:

Soak carburetor in cleaner for no more than 30 minutes. Use compressed air to clean passages. CAUTION: Do not use compressed air with float on carburetor. The compressed air will crush the float.

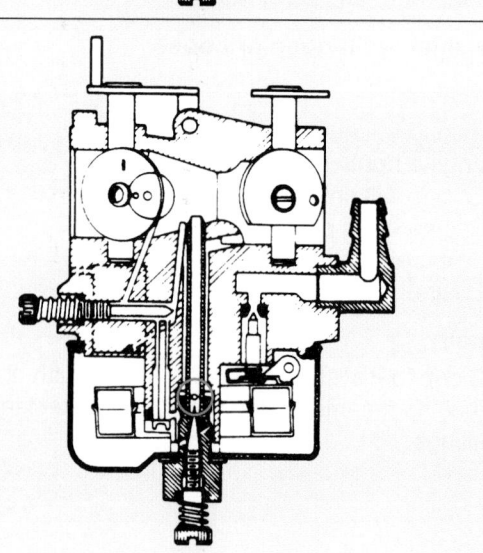

(Continued)

Troubleshooting Float-Type Carburetors *(Continued)*

Damaged and/or Worn Hinge Pin or Float, Improper Float Height

Symptoms:

Engine hunts (at idle or high speed)
Engine will not idle
Engine lacks power at high speed
Carburetor floods
Engine starves for fuel at high speed (leans out)
Carburetor runs with main adjustment needle shut off
Poor starting

Repair:

Replace float and axle. If hinge pin area of casting is worn, the carburetor body must be replaced. The float height is set using specified tool.

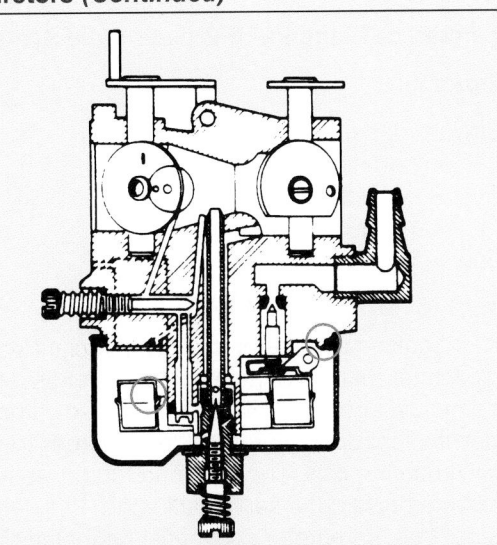

Fuel Pick-Up Restricted or Plugged

Symptoms:

Engine will not start
Engine hunts (at idle or high speed)
Engine will not idle
Engine starves for fuel at high speed (leans out)

Repair:

After soaking carburetor in a commercial cleaner (no longer than 30 minutes), use compressed air to clean passages. CAUTION: Do not use compressed air with float on carburetor. The compressed air will crush the float.

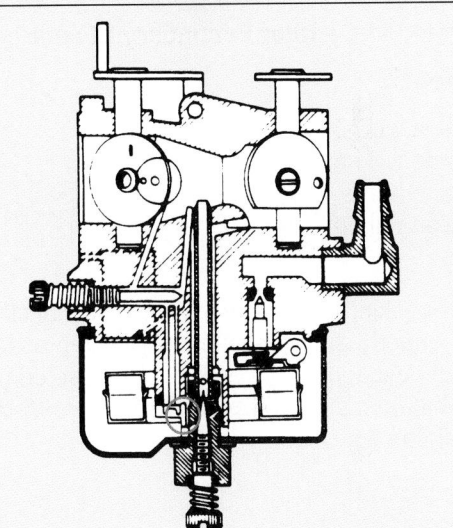

Damaged or Incorrect Fuel Adjustment Needles

Symptoms:

Engine will not start
Engine will not accelerate
Engine hunts (at idle or high speed)
Engine will not idle
Engine lacks power at high speed
Engine overspeeds
Engine starves for fuel at high speed (leans out)
Carburetor runs with main adjustment needle shut off
Performance unsatisfactory after being serviced

Repair:

Replace damaged needles with correct fuel adjustment needles. CAUTION: Do not over-seat needles.

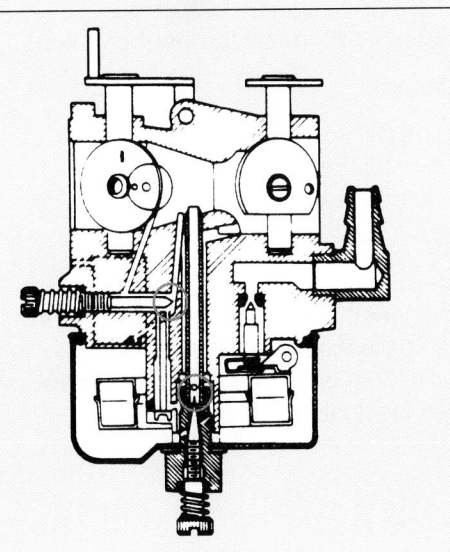

(Continued)

Troubleshooting Float-Type Carburetors *(Continued)*

Restricted or Plugged Air Bleed or Idle System

Symptoms:

Engine runs rich
Engine hard to start
Engine will not accelerate
Engine hunts
Engine will not idle

Repair:

After soaking carburetor in a commercial cleaner (no longer than 30 minutes), use compressed air to clean passages. CAUTION: Do not use compressed air with float on carburetor. The compressed air will crush the float. The metering rod on Series I carburetors is not a serviceable part. If metering rod is not free, carburetor body must be replaced.

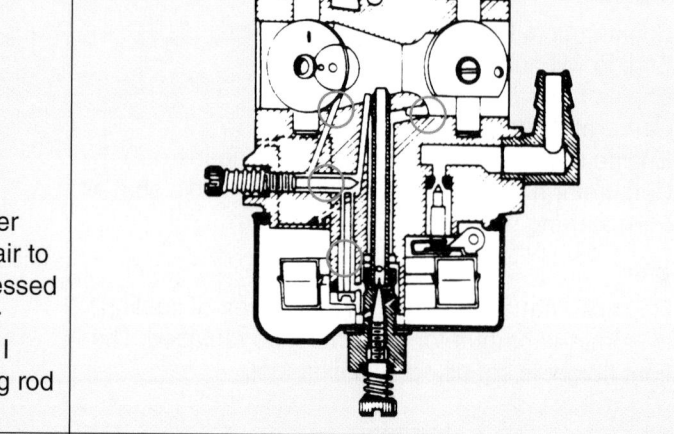

Restricted Idle and/or Secondary Discharge Ports

Symptoms:

Engine will not start at idle
Engine will not accelerate
Engine hunts
Engine will not idle

Repair:

After soaking carburetor in a commercial cleaner (no longer than 30 minutes), use compressed air to clean passages. CAUTION: Do not use compressed air with float on carburetor. The compressed air will crush the float.

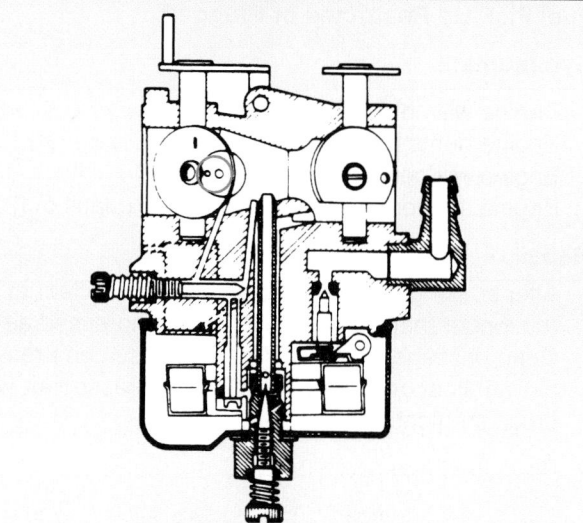

Restricted or Plugged Atmospheric Vent

Symptoms:

Engine will not start
Carburetor floods
Carburetor leaks

Repair:

After soaking carburetor in a commercial cleaner (no longer than 30 minutes), use compressed air to clean passages. CAUTION: Do not use compressed air with float on carburetor. The compressed air will crush the float.

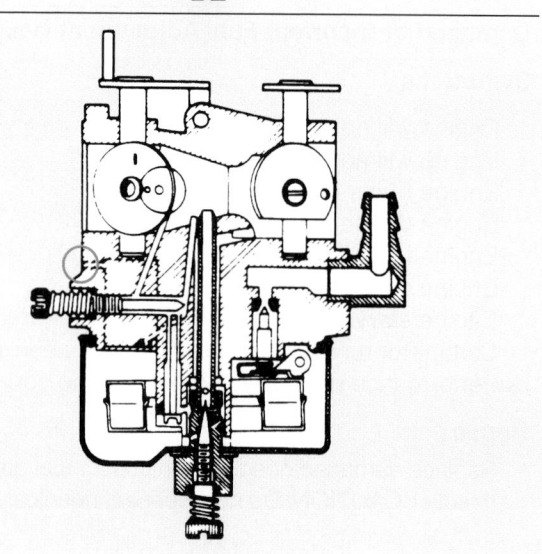

Troubleshooting Diaphragm Carburetors

Leaky Carburetor Gaskets
Symptoms:

Engine overspeeds
Idle speed is excessive
Carburetor runs lean
Performance unsatisfactory after being serviced

Repair:

Replace with new gaskets on the intake and air cleaner end of the carburetor every time the gasket is disturbed.

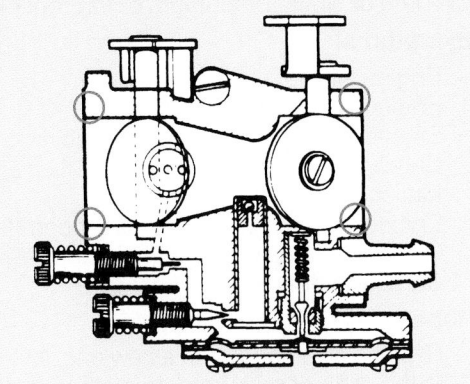

Throttle and/or Choke Shaft Worn
Throttle and/or Choke Spring Not Functioning
Symptoms:

Engine will not start
Engine will not accelerate
Engine hunts (at idle or high speed)
Engine will not idle
Engine lacks power at high speed
Idle speed is excessive
Choke does not open fully

Repair:

Replace all worn parts, springs, dust seals, (when so equipped). If carburetor body is worn out-of-round, causing the leak, a new service carburetor should be used.

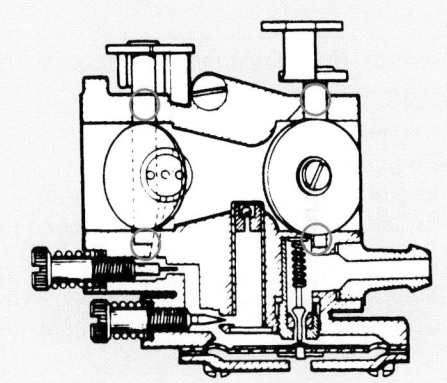

Fuel Inlet Is Plugged
Symptoms:

Engine will not start
Engine hunts (at idle or high speed)
Engine will not idle
Engine lacks power at high speed
Carburetor leaks
Engine starves for fuel at high speed (leans out)

Repair:

Clean fuel system completely. Refill with clean, fresh fuel as recommended. Replace loose clamps and fittings.

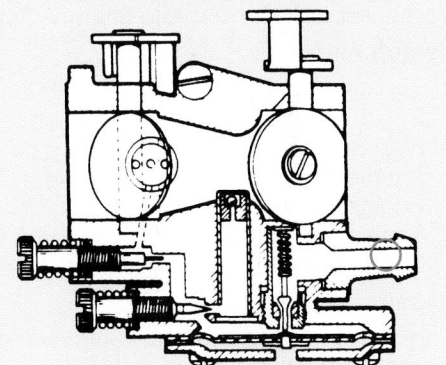

Dirty, Stuck, or Damaged Needle and Seat
Symptoms:

Carburetor floods
Carburetor leaks
Carburetor runs rich with main adjustment needle shut off

Repair:

Remove old needle and seat assembly. Install a new needle and seat assembly according to manual instructions.

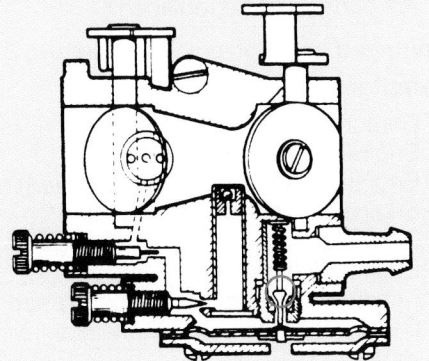

(Continued)
Tecumseh Products Co.

Troubleshooting chart for diaphragm-type carburetors.

Troubleshooting Diaphragm Carburetors *(Continued)*

Cracked or Brittle Diaphragm or Improper Positioning of Diaphragm

Symptoms:

Engine will not start
Engine will not idle
Engine lacks power at high speed
Carburetor floods
Idle speed is excessive
Engine starves for fuel at high speed (leans out)
Carburetor runs rich with main adjustment needle shut off
Carburetor leaks

Repair:

Replace diaphragm with a new one. Install a new gasket according to the style of carburetor body that you have. Check mechanic's manual for proper sequence of diaphragm and gasket.

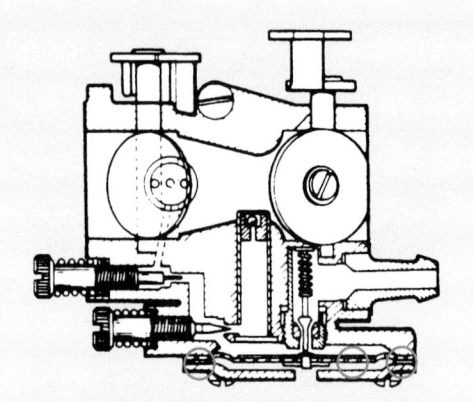

Fuel Pick-Up Restricted or Plugged

Symptoms:

Engine will not start
Engine will not idle
Engine hunts (at idle or high speed)
Engine starves for fuel at high speed (leans out)

Repair:

Soak in commercial carburetor cleaner (no longer than 30 minutes). Use compressed air to clean all passages.

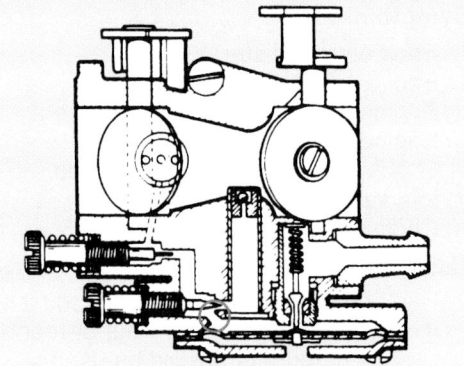

Damaged or Incorrect Idle Mixture Screw

Symptoms:

Engine will not start
Engine hunts (at idle or high speed) or will not accelerate
Engine will not idle
Engine lacks power at high speed
Engine overspeeds
Engine starves for fuel at high speed (leans out)
Carburetor runs rich with idle adjustment needle shut off

Repair:

Replace idle mixture screw and O-ring with new, clean passages. Do not overseat needle. If tip breaks off in carburetor, the body must be replaced.

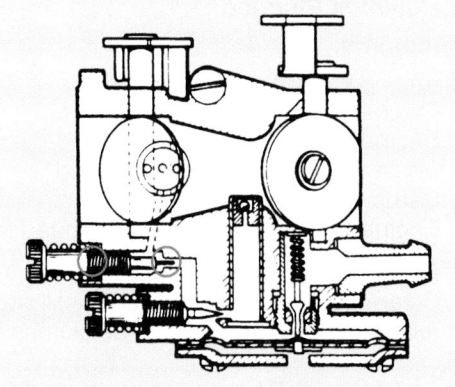

Damaged or Incorrect Main Mixture Screw

Symptoms:

Carburetor out of adjustment
Engine will not start
Engine hunts (at idle or high speed) or will not accelerate
Engine will not idle
Engine lacks power at high speed
Engine overspeeds
Engine starves for fuel at high speed (leans out)
Carburetor runs rich with main adjustment needle shut off

Repair:

Replace main mixture screw and O-ring with a new one. Clean passages. Do not over-seat mixture screw.

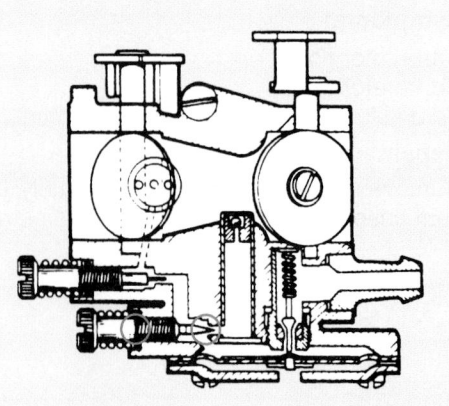

(Continued)

Troubleshooting Diaphragm Carburetors *(Continued)*

Restricted or Plugged Air Bleed

Symptoms:

Engine will not accelerate
Engine hunts (at idle or high speed)
Engine will not idle

Repair:

Soak carburetor body in commercial cleaner (no longer than 30 minutes). Use compressed air to clean all passages.

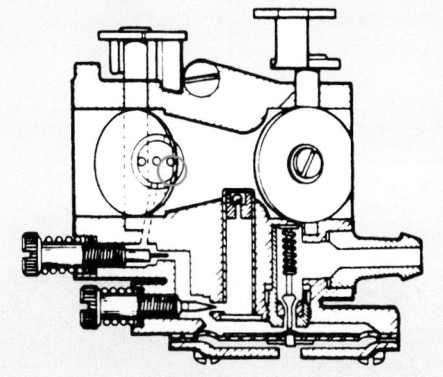

Restricted Idle and/or Secondary Discharge Ports

Symptoms:

Engine will not start at idle
Engine will not accelerate
Engine hunts
Engine will not idle

Repair:

Soak carburetor body in commercial cleaner (no longer than 30 minutes). Use compressed air to clean all passages.

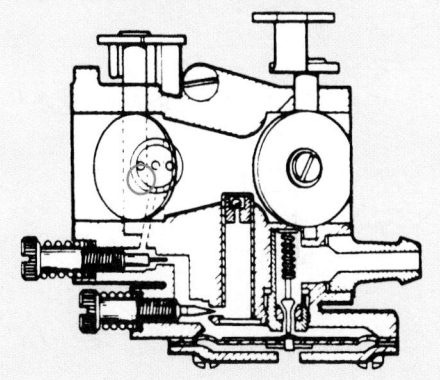

Stuck or Dirty Check Ball

Symptoms:

Engine will not idle
Engine will not run at high speed

Repair:

Soak carburetor in a commercial cleaner (no longer than 30 minutes). Use compressed air to free check ball. CAUTION: If check ball is damaged, carburetor body must be replaced. Check ball is not replaceable.

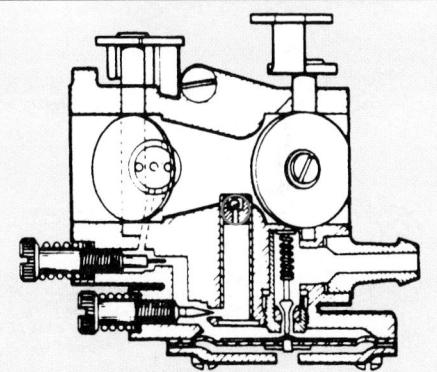

Restricted or Plugged Atmospheric Vent

Symptoms:

Engine will not start
Carburetor floods

Repair:

Atmospheric vent in cover should be cleaned, or diaphragm cover should be replaced.

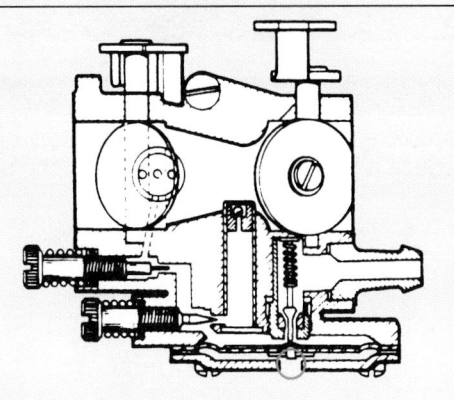

A spark test is one of the best indicators of ignition system condition. A properly functioning ignition system should produce a strong, bright arc between the spark plug's center and side electrodes.

Ignition and Electrical System Service

Learning Objectives

After studying this chapter, you will be able to:

- Examine spark plug deposits for signs of abnormal combustion.
- Clean, gap, and install spark plugs correctly.
- Explain the basic inspections and tests used to verify proper ignition system operation.
- Adjust breaker points, piston height, and ignition spark timing.
- Explain basic tests for breaker point and solid-state ignition systems.
- Explain typical service procedures for battery ignition systems.

Key Terms

diode
gapping tool
hydrogen
hydrometer
leaf-type feeler gauges
open-circuit voltage
overcharging
oxygen

spark test
spark tester
specific gravity
specific gravity tests
stator assembly
undercharging
wire-type feeler gauges

Ignition System Service

Although small engine ignition systems are durable, they do require periodic inspection and maintenance. Ignition system service involves the entire ignition system. The small engine technician will check or test part after part until the entire system is working well. In the process, worn or defective parts must be replaced.

Performing a Spark Test

A *spark test* can be performed to verify ignition system operation. During the spark test, a diagnostic tool known as a *spark tester* is connected in the ignition system and is used to observe the spark produced by the system. To perform a spark test:

1. Remove the spark plug wire from the spark plug and attach the wire to a spark tester.

Then, clip the spark tester to the spark plug as shown in **Figure 15-1**.

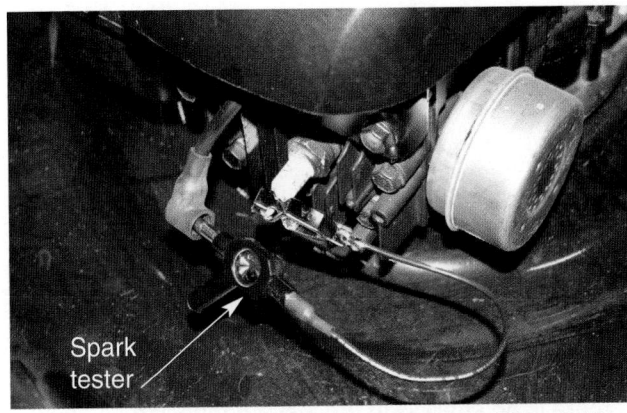

Spark tester

Goodheart-Willcox Publisher

Figure 15-1.

To check ignition system operation, connect the spark tester between the spark plug wire and the plug.

2. Pull the starter cord to spin the engine quickly while watching for spark between tester's electrodes. If a strong spark is present at the tester, the ignition system is working correctly.

Note

In many solid-state ignition systems, the engine must spin at 350 rpm or more to produce a spark.

3. If no spark occurs, remove the spark tester from the spark plug and clip it to the engine, **Figure 15-2**.

4. Pull the starter cord again and watch for spark at the tester. If there is a spark, the problem is most likely the spark plug. If there is no spark, an ignition system component other than the plug, such as the spark plug wire, the stop switch, or the module, is causing the problem. Further checks are necessary to pinpoint the faulty component. These checks will be detailed later in this chapter.

A variation of the spark test can help pinpoint the cause of engine performance problems. If the engine starts but runs rough or misses, connect the tester between the spark plug wire and the plug itself. Start the engine and watch the spark in the tester. If the spark is consistent even when the engine misses or stumbles, the performance problem is not ignition related.

Goodheart-Willcox Publisher

Figure 15-2.

If there is no spark with the tester connected as shown in Figure 15-1, connect the tester between the plug wire and a good engine ground and retest the system. If a spark occurs with the tester in this position, the spark plug may be faulty.

A similar test can be performed if the engine starts but dies when it warms up. Connect the tester between the plug wire and the plug, and start the engine. Watch the spark produced in the tester as the engine dies. If the spark remains strong as the engine coasts to a stop, the problem is likely not being caused by an ignition system malfunction.

Spark Plugs

When a small engine is difficult to start, a new spark plug may seem to solve the problem. However, the technician cannot assume that this is the only fault. Often, a less obvious problem has caused the plug to fail.

Although a magneto system may be able to supply 30,000 volts (V), it produces only enough voltage to jump the spark plug gap. Therefore, the condition of the spark plug determines the amount of voltage that other ignition parts must produce.

Spark plugs used in normal operation will wear out from erosion caused by combustion. A new plug may need only 5000V to fire. After many hours of operation, however, the same plug may require 10,000V to fire. If a pull on the starter cord produces less than 10,000V, an engine equipped with such a plug will not start. Certainly not all cases of hard starting are caused by a bad spark plug. Therefore, replacing the plug without further checking is not a good practice. The actual problem may lie in the malfunction of other ignition system components.

Changing the plug simply means that less voltage is needed to fire it. Carbon deposits will again build up in the cylinder and exhaust ports due to poor combustion. More carbon will form on the spark plug electrodes and cause further hard starting.

Spark Plug Removal

The following four steps for removing spark plugs are simple and should become a habit. They can prevent troublesome problems from occurring later. To remove a spark plug:

1. Gently rotate and pull the spark plug boot from the spark plug. Do not grab or pull on the spark plug wire. Pull on the boot only.
2. Before removing the spark plug, blast dirt away from the area around the plug with compressed air.
3. Install a correct-size spark plug socket on the plug and carefully turn the ratchet handle counterclockwise to loosen the plug.

Caution

Before removing spark plugs from engines with aluminum heads, allow the engine to cool. The heat of the engine, in combination with a spark plug that has run for many hours, may cause the spark plug to seize.

4. Remove the spark plug and check its appearance. Refer to the *Spark Plug Analysis Table* in the *Appendix* section of this text.

Analysis of Used Spark Plugs

Spark plugs can provide many hours of useful life in an engine. Spark plugs in two different engines of the same make and model may show a wide variation in appearance. Engine condition, carburetor settings, and operating conditions, such as sustained high speeds or continual low-speed, stop-and-start operation, are all variables that affect spark plug life.

You can analyze the quality of combustion that has been taking place in a cylinder by examining the deposits on the spark plug. See **Figure 15-3**. Deposits having a beige to gray-tan color indicate normal combustion of the air-fuel mixture at the proper operating temperature. **Figure 15-3A** shows how a normal, used spark plug looks. **Figure 15-3B** compares a normal plug with one that is extremely carbon fouled.

An oil-fouled plug, like the one shown in **Figure 15-3C**, is saturated with wet oil. The eroded plug pictured in **Figure 15-3D** got that way from many hours of use.

Study the situation carefully before changing the spark plug. Spark plug deposits are usually caused by weak magneto voltage, incorrect carburetor adjustments, poor air cleaner maintenance, incorrect gasoline or oil, or incorrectly mixed gasoline and oil.

Cleaning Spark Plugs

Note

Most manufacturers recommend replacing plugs that are fouled with oil, carbon, etc. Cleaning should only be done when a replacement plug is not available.

The following procedure should be followed when cleaning spark plugs:
1. Wipe all spark plug surfaces clean. Remove oil, water, dirt, and moist residues.

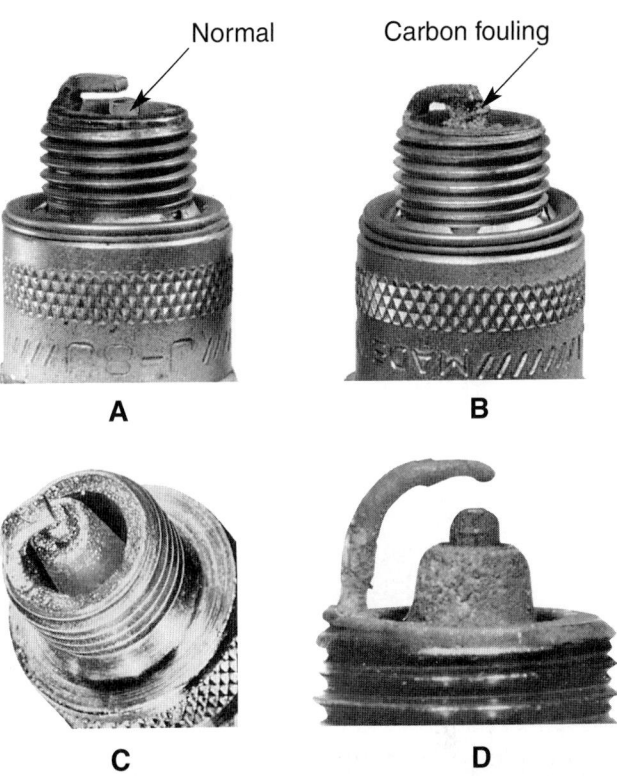

Normal   Carbon fouling

A   B

C   D

Jacobsen Mfg. Co.; Champion Spark Plug Co.

Figure 15-3.

A—A normal spark plug will be clean and dry, showing a light tan to gray-tan color on the porcelain shell insulator. B—A carbon-fouled plug. C—An oil-fouled spark plug can be an indication of a mechanical malfunction. D—After many hours of use, spark plug electrodes tend to erode from normal combustion.

2. Check the firing end or tip of the spark plug for oily or wet deposits. If the spark plug has deposits, brush the plug with a nonflammable, nontoxic solvent. Then, dry the plug with compressed air to prevent caking of the debris deep within the spark plug shell.
3. File the spark plug electrodes after cleaning to square them and to remove any oxide or scale from the surfaces. Open the gap so that a spark plug file will fit between the electrodes. See **Figure 15-4**.
4. Clean spark plug threads with a wire brush. See **Figure 15-5**. Take care not to damage the electrodes or insulator. If threads are nicked or damaged, discard the plug.

Before installing plugs, clean the spark plug seat in the cylinder head. Also, clean the plug's threads and make sure the gasket is in good condition. Not all plugs require gaskets. See **Figure 15-6**.

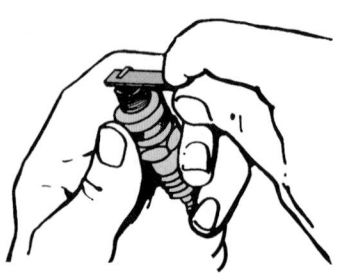

Goodheart-Willcox Publisher

Figure 15-4.

Oxides should be removed from electrodes with a spark plug file.

Goodheart-Willcox Publisher

Figure 15-5.

Threads can be cleaned with a power wire brush.

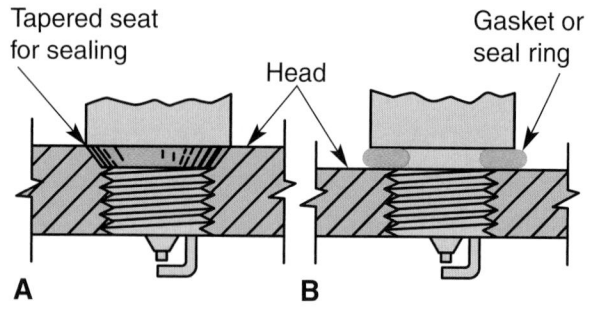

Goodheart-Willcox Publisher

Figure 15-6.

Two types of plugs. A—A plug with a tapered seat does not require a gasket. Clean the area around the plug hole for a good seal. B—Spark plug with gasket. Inspect plug gaskets carefully. A damaged gasket will not seal properly.

Gapping Spark Plugs

When gapping a spark plug, bend the outer electrode toward or away from the center electrode. For best results, use a *gapping tool*. See **Figure 15-7**.

Standard *leaf-type feeler gauges* may be used only if the plug is new. Otherwise, *wire-type feeler gauges* should be used. See **Figure 15-8**.

A   **B**

Goodheart-Willcox Publisher

Figure 15-7.

A—A common spark plug gapping tool. B—Use a spark plug gapping tool to bend the outer electrode toward or away from the center electrode.

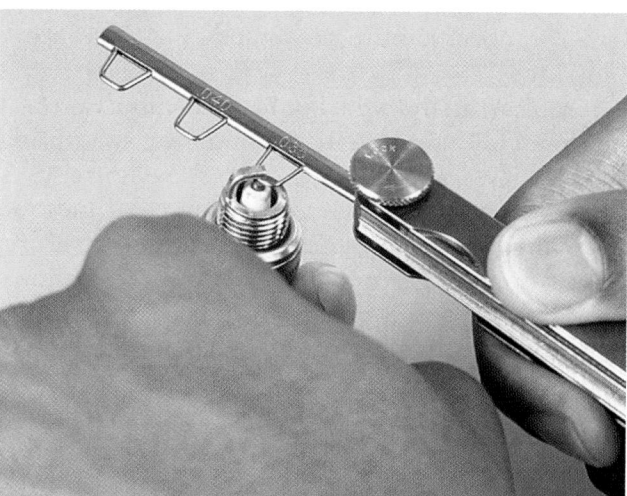

Goodheart-Willcox Publisher

Figure 15-8.

Gap should be carefully adjusted and measured with wire gauges.

The reason that wire-type feeler gauges are recommended for use on used spark plugs is shown in **Figure 15-9**. Note that the flat, leaf-type feeler gauge would leave an additional gap between the worn electrodes.

Spark Plug Installation

Spark plugs must be installed properly. The heat dispersing properties of the spark plug depend on correct plug seating. If the spark plug is tightened excessively, the gasket will be crushed. Internal leakage may result. Attempting to remove an overtightened spark plug can strip cylinder head

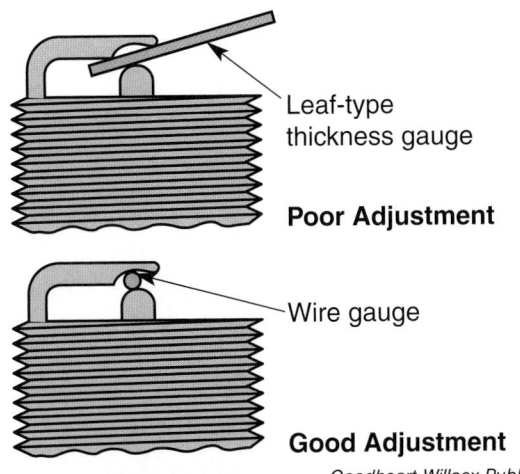

Goodheart-Willcox Publisher

Figure 15-9.

Leaf-type thickness gauges may not give an accurate measurement of gap if electrodes are not flat and parallel.

threads. Seating the spark plug too loosely can result in preignition and possible engine damage caused by spark plug overheating.

To install spark plugs:

1. Make sure the cylinder head and the spark plug threads are clean. If necessary, use a thread chaser and a seat cleaning tool.
2. Make sure the spark plug gasket seat is clean. Thread the gasket to fit flush against the gasket seat on the spark plug.
3. Make sure the spark plug has the correct gap.
4. Screw the spark plug finger-tight into the cylinder head. Then use a torque wrench to tighten the plug to 13–15 lb-ft. Do not overtighten.

Magneto System Service

The solid-state magneto ignition systems found in all late-model engines offer dependable service, with few moving parts to maintain or adjust. Most solid-state components (ignition coil, electronic triggering system, and mounting plate) are manufactured as an assembly, or module, that cannot be serviced.

Note

In most magneto systems, the module is mounted outside the flywheel. However, some magneto systems are completely contained under the flywheel. The flywheel must be removed from the crankshaft to service the ignition components in these systems.

Inspect the magneto system components. Check all parts for dents, cracks, and gouges. Make sure the insulation on all wire leads is in good condition, and that all connections are clean and tight.

Inspect the flywheel for damage. Remove the flywheel retaining nut, and make sure the key and keyway are in good condition. If the key has begun to shear or if it is too narrow for the keyway, the engine will be out of time. In either case, the key must be replaced. See **Figure 15-10**.

One way to test the flywheel magnet is to place a 1/2″ socket on the magnet. The socket should be held firmly in place. If not, the flywheel must be replaced. If the flywheel is in good condition, reinstall the retaining nut and tighten it to specifications.

The gap between the module's laminations and the flywheel magnets is adjustable. This adjustment must be made carefully or the voltage produced by the ignition system will be reduced. Begin by rotating the flywheel so its magnets are directly under the module laminations. Loosen the adjustment screws, pull the module away from the flywheel, and retighten one of the screws to hold the module in place. Insert a nonmagnetic feeler gauge or shim stock of the correct thickness in the gap between the module laminations and the magnets. Loosen the adjustment screw to allow the magnet to pull the laminations tightly against the gauge. Finally tighten both adjustment screws and rotate the flywheel to remove the feeler gauge. See **Figure 15-11**.

If a solid-state system fails to produce a spark when the spark tester is connected between the spark plug wire terminal and ground, disconnect the stop switch wire from the module and recheck system operation. If the system works after the wire is disconnected, the switch or the wire itself is

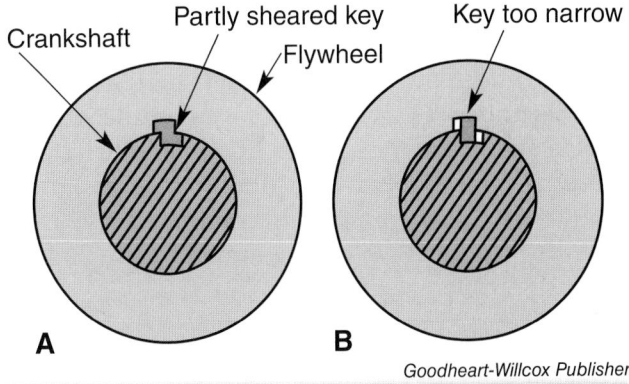

Goodheart-Willcox Publisher

Figure 15-10.

Partly sheared flywheel keys or keys that do not fit well can put the ignition system out of time.

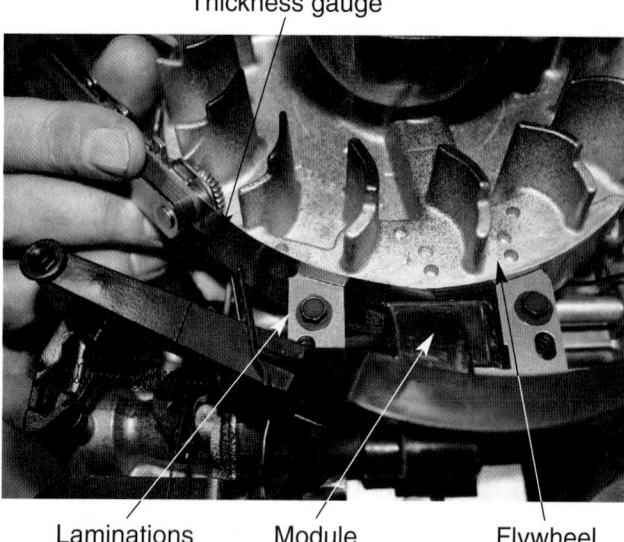

Thickness gauge

Laminations   Module   Flywheel

Goodheart-Willcox Publisher

Figure 15-11.

Magneto air gap can be set with a nonmagnetic thickness gauge.

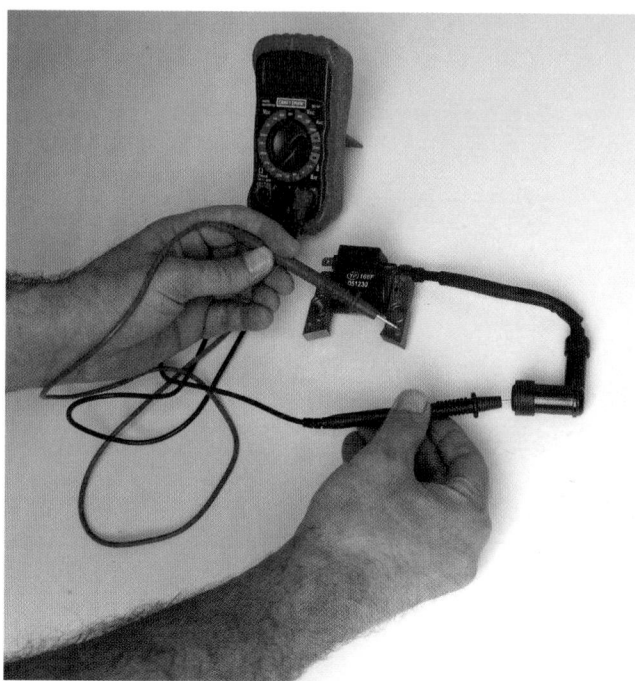

Goodheart-Willcox Publisher

Figure 15-12.

Some manufacturers recommend specific resistance tests to help detect a faulty module. Here, the resistance between the secondary wire and the laminated core is being checked.

faulty. If the system still does not produce a spark and all other ignition components are in good working condition, the module is most likely the cause of the problem and should be replaced or tested further.

Although most manufacturers suggest simply replacing the module if spark test results point to it as the most likely cause of a no-spark condition, some manufacturers provide instructions for checking the resistance between the module's core and its primary and secondary wiring. See **Figure 15-12**. Values that are not within the specifications verify that the module is faulty.

To replace the module, begin by disconnecting related wiring, including the spark plug wire, the primary wire (if necessary), and stop switch wire. Then remove the screws or bolts holding the module in place and remove the module from the engine. See **Figure 15-13**. Place the new module on the engine and install the screws or bolts loosely in their holes. Set the gap between the flywheel magnets and the module laminations as outlined previously. Finally, reconnect all wiring and start the engine to verify proper system operation.

Servicing Breaker Point Ignition Magneto Systems

If the magneto system is equipped with breaker points, check for improper alignment and pitted

contact surfaces. Refer to an appropriate engine manual for instructions for testing and adjusting breaker point systems.

Servicing Battery Ignition Systems

Many of the components in the battery ignition systems are the same as those in the magneto systems. Refer to magneto system section of this chapter for service information on these components. However, battery ignition systems have additional components that require maintenance and service. When servicing a battery ignition system, check for the following problems before beginning an extensive system analysis:

- Defective or undercharged battery.
- Corroded or loose terminals and connections.
- Wrong connections.
- Cracked insulation or broken wires.
- A wire grounding out in the system.
- A defective switch.
- Improperly functioning operator presence system.

A

B

Goodheart-Willcox Publisher

Figure 15-13.
A—Before removing the module, disconnect all wiring attached to it. B—Remove the bolts or screws securing the module, and then remove the module from the engine.

It is important to note that the presence of a battery and a starter does not mean the ignition system is battery operated. Some magneto ignition systems also use these parts. You can identify a battery ignition system by a can-shaped ignition coil, in addition to a battery and a generator or alternator.

Note

All lawn and garden tractors built after July of 1987 are required to have an operator presence system. Many implements were equipped with these systems prior to this date. If an engine will not start or is cutting out, check for a malfunction in the operator presence system.

Distributor Service

Older engines with more than one cylinder and a battery ignition system may use a distributor to deliver spark to the right cylinder at the right time. During service, the distributor cap should be removed and inspected for cracks, carbon tracking, and pitted contacts. The rotor also requires inspection. This is the small plastic arm that is mounted on top of the distributor shaft and revolves during engine operation. The metal tab on top of the rotor must make good contact with the metal inset in the center tower of the distributor cap. Additionally, the firing end of the rotor should not be worn or irregular.

Spark timing can be set by rotating the distributor. Usually, the distributor is clamped in place to lock in the ignition timing adjustment.

Distributors should be lubricated at several points. Put a small amount of oil or grease in the reservoir or cup provided for the shaft, a film of grease on the breaker cam, and a drop or two of oil on the pivot for the breaker points. Use care; too much lubricant can cause the points to burn.

Electrical System Service

The following sections will discuss the service of the non-ignition electrical systems found on some small gas engines.

Batteries

Storage batteries need regular maintenance to keep them in good operating condition. With proper setup and care, the battery will last for years. However, even when properly maintained, a battery can eventually fail.

Causes of Battery Failure

There are numerous causes for battery failure. *Overcharging*, or charging a battery in excess of what is necessary, can severely corrode the positive plate grids, weakening them and causing a loss of electrical conduction.

Overcharging also decomposes the water of the electrolyte into hydrogen and oxygen gas. The gas bubbles tend to wash active material from plates and carry moisture and acid from the cells as a fine mist. Decomposition of water also leaves the acid more concentrated and is harmful to cell components, particularly at high temperatures over a prolonged time period.

High internal heat created by overcharging accelerates the corrosion of the positive plate grids and damages the separators and negative plates. Overcharging alone, or in combination with a previous condition of undercharging, may cause severe buckling and warping of the positive plates with accompanying perforation of the separators.

Overcharging may also cause corrosion damage to the battery box, cables, and other critical electrical and engine parts by forcing liquid from the cells.

Undercharging a battery is harmful. A battery with insufficient charge over a prolonged period may develop a dense, hard, coarsely crystalline sulfate, which cannot be electrochemically converted to normal active material again. This condition can cause distortion and buckling of the positive plates.

An undercharged battery is unable to provide full power and is subject to freezing during severe winter weather. This may cause cracking of the case and leakage of acid.

Water is essential to a lead-acid storage battery and normally is the only component that is lost as a result of charging. Water should be added as soon as it falls to the top level of the separators. If water is not replaced, the plates become exposed and the acid reaches a very high concentration. This condition may char and disintegrate the separators and can permanently sulfate the plates and impair performance of the battery. The plates must always be completely covered by electrolyte.

Note

Maintenance-free, or sealed, batteries do not lose water during the charging process and, therefore, do not have to be periodically refilled. Never try to add water to a maintenance-free battery.

A battery that is not held down securely in an implement may vibrate excessively, causing a severe disarrangement of the plates and separators. If a battery bounces around, the case may be damaged, allowing acid to leak. Acid leaks will corrode terminals and cables, causing high resistance at the battery connections, weakening power, and shortening the life of the battery. Hold-downs that are too tight can distort or crack the battery case.

The temperature at which electrolyte will begin to freeze depends on the condition of the charge. During winter weather, a battery should be kept at least 3/4 charged. A 3/4-charged lead-acid battery is not in any danger of freezing. The freezing points of electrolytes are shown in **Figure 15-14**.

Warning

Never attempt to charge a frozen battery. It may explode.

Testing the Battery

There are several tests that can be performed to determine the condition of a battery. These tests include an open-circuit voltage test, a specific gravity test, and a load test. Before any of these tests are performed, the battery should be inspected for obvious problems. A visual inspection of the battery includes looking for the following:

- A broken or leaking cover.
- A broken case.
- Damaged post(s).
- Missing caps. See **Figure 15-15**.

Warning

Handle a battery with care. If a battery must be carried, use an approved battery carrier and wear rubber gloves and goggles. Keep the battery away from the body and clothing. A battery may be quite heavy depending on its size. Never test a battery by striking a cable or metal strap across the output terminals. An internally shorted battery could explode.

Freezing Points of Electrolytes

Specific Gravity	Freezing Point
1.265	−75°F (−59.5°C)
1.225	−35°F (−37°C)
1.200	−17°F (−27°C)
1.150	5°F (−15°C)
1.100	18°F (−7.8°C)
1.050	27°F (−3°C)

Goodheart-Willcox Publisher

Figure 15-14.

As the specific gravity of the electrolyte decreases, the temperature at which freezing begins increases.

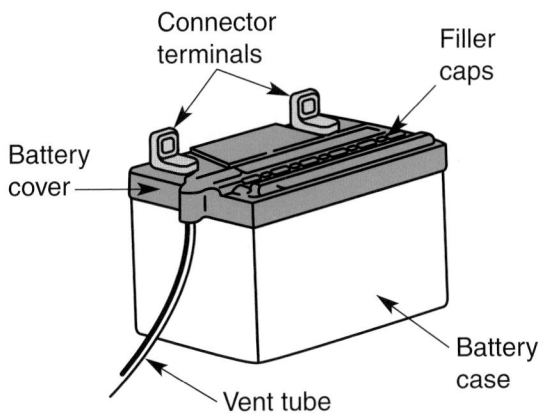

Figure 15-15.

Visual inspection of a lead-acid storage battery should include looking for a broken or leaking cover, a broken case, damaged posts, and missing caps.

Checking Open-Circuit Voltage

One way to check the general condition of a battery is to measure *open-circuit voltage* using a multimeter set on a voltage setting. The procedure for performing an open-circuit voltage test is as follows:

1. Disconnect the battery from the implement.
2. Connect the negative lead of multimeter to the negative terminal of the battery.
3. Connect the positive lead of the multimeter to the positive terminal of the battery.
4. Read the voltage displayed on the meter.

A fully charged battery will indicate 12.6V on the meter. A reading between 11.0V and 12.6V indicates that the battery needs charging. If the reading is less than 10.0V, the battery may not accept a charge and may need to be replaced.

Note

An open-circuit voltage test is a quick way to determine the general condition of the battery. If the open-circuit voltage indicates that the battery may be faulty, perform a hydrometer test or a load test before condemning the battery.

Checking Specific Gravity

A chemical reaction between the battery's electrolyte and plates, or electrodes, supplies electrical energy to an external circuit. When the battery is discharging, the positive plate (lead dioxide) and the negative plate (sponge lead) are both changed

to lead sulfate. At the same time, part of the electrolyte (diluted sulfuric acid) is changed to water. This conversion of diluted sulfuric acid to water reduces the *specific gravity* (density) of the electrolyte. By measuring the specific gravity with a *hydrometer,* a direct measure of how far the discharge process has progressed can be made. See **Figure 15-16**.

Specific gravity tests must be performed before adding water to the battery. In the event the electrolyte level is too low to test with the hydrometer, add water and charge the battery before testing.

A correct specific gravity reading can be measured only when the electrolyte temperature is 80°F. If the electrolyte temperature varies from this temperature, compensation must be made in the reading as follows:

    a. Add four gravity points (.004) for each 10° electrolyte temperature above 80°F.

    b. Subtract four gravity points (.004) for each 10° below 80°F.

The specific gravity test procedure is quite easy to perform. Remove the battery vent caps and squeeze the hydrometer's rubber bulb. Place the rubber tube from the hydrometer into the first cell and release the bulb. Electrolyte is drawn into the hydrometer until the float rises. Read the specific gravity at the level of the fluid on the float markings. Squeeze the rubber bulb to replace the electrolyte

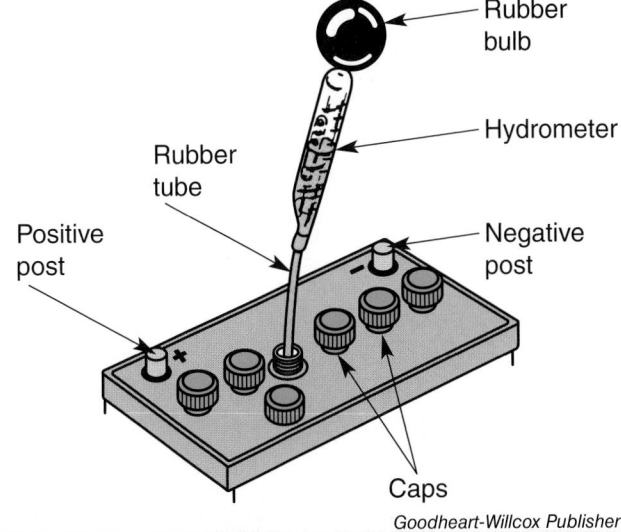

Figure 15-16.

This hydrometer reading shows a fully charged condition of the battery. Specific gravity reading is in the 1.260 to 1.280 range.

in the cell. Record the cell number and its reading. Repeat this step for each cell. If the readings between the highest and lowest cells vary 50 points (.050) or more, the battery should be removed from service and properly discarded. If there is less than a 50 point variation between the highest and lowest cell, and the specific gravity in one or more cells is below 1.235, recharge the battery.

After the battery is recharged, let it stand for at least 24 hours, and repeat the specific gravity test on all cells. If there is a 50 point variation or more between the highest and lowest cell, remove the battery from service. Inability to bring the specific gravity of any one cell up to 1.235 after charging indicates an unusable battery that should be removed from service.

Performing a Load Test

Maintenance-free batteries cannot be tested with a hydrometer because there is no way to access the electrolyte. These batteries are liquid filled or have a gel electrolyte and must be tested under load with a load tester. To perform a load test:

1. Connect the load tester directly to the battery posts. The positive clamp is connected to the positive battery terminal and the negative clamp is connected to the negative terminal. See **Figure 15-17**.

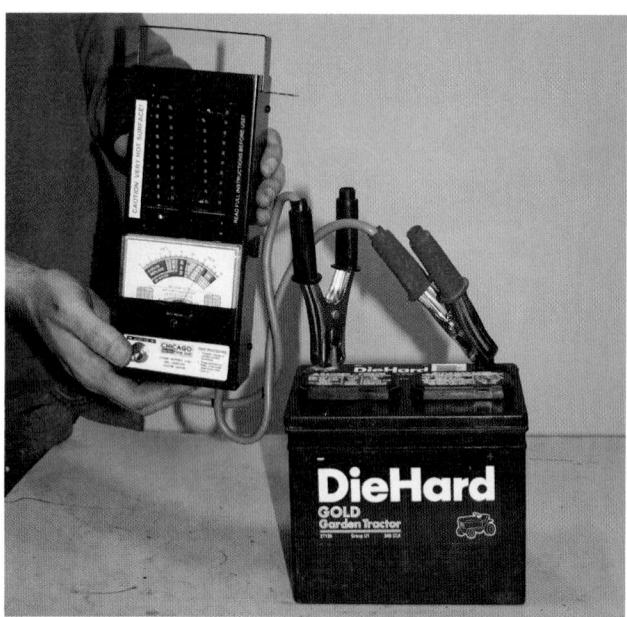

Goodheart-Willcox Publisher

Figure 15-17.

The load tester is used to evaluate a battery's performance under load.

2. Read the voltmeter on the tester's scale to determine the battery's voltage. If the battery voltage is less that 12V (6V on a 6-volt battery), recharge the battery before performing the load test.
3. If battery voltage is sufficient, press the load button on the tester for 5–10 seconds to simulate a load on the battery.
4. Read the meter on the tester to determine battery condition and then release the load button. In general, a voltage reading of 9.6 volts with the battery under load is acceptable for a 12V battery. If voltage is below 9.6 volts, the battery should be replaced.

Battery Maintenance and Service

The life of a battery can be greatly extended by proper maintenance and service. The following maintenance procedures should be performed monthly:

1. Clean the top of the battery case with a stiff bristle brush. Do not use a wire bristle brush. Wear safety goggles, a long-sleeve shirt, and rubber gloves, and be careful not to scatter corrosion particles. Wipe off with a cloth wetted with a solution of baking soda and water. Finish by wiping with a cloth wetted with clear water.
2. Inspect the cables. Replace the cables if they cannot be serviced. Inspect the battery terminals for damage.
3. Clean the battery terminals and cable clamps or connectors to bright metal. A wire brush can be used for this purpose. Coat the contact surfaces with dielectric grease or petroleum jelly before reconnecting the cables.
4. Examine the battery box and adjust the holddown bracket, clamps, or straps. Replace any components that are damaged or severely corroded.
5. Check the level of electrolyte (if battery is not the maintenance-free type). Add clean distilled water if the level is below the plates, or below the *Upper* and *Lower* level indicators on the case.
6. Make an open-circuit voltage test, a specific gravity test, or a load test. Remember, a voltage test alone will not give an accurate indication of battery condition. Even a partially discharged battery will display correct voltage under a no-load condition.

7. Make sure the vent tube is free of kinks and obstructions.

Battery Charging

Charging a battery is necessary when the battery becomes discharged, such as when it has been out of use an extended period of time. Charging a 12V battery should be done with a 12V automotive-type charger. Charging 6V battery should be done with a 6V charger. Chargers are also available with a switch to charge either 6V or 12V batteries.

Charging current for 6V or 12V batteries should not exceed manufacturer's recommendations. Exceeding the recommended charging rate can cause warping of the plates and will affect the life of the battery.

If batteries are used in temperatures below 32°F (0°C), it is important to keep them fully charged. A full charge can prevent the electrolyte from freezing and cracking the battery case. In cold temperatures, battery power decreases while the need for engine cranking power increases. Sub-zero temperatures can reduce a fully charged battery's capacity to 30% of its normal power, while increasing the cranking load beyond the warm weather cranking requirements. See **Figure 15-18**.

Only direct current can be used to recharge a battery. The battery charger automatically rectifies (converts) the alternating current (ac) available from electrical receptacles to direct current (dc).

Batteries generate *hydrogen* and *oxygen* during charging. These gases combine to form a highly explosive mixture. Always observe the following rules when charging a battery:
- Never check a battery fluid level with a flame.
- Do not attach a battery charger to a battery unless the ignition wiring is disconnected from the battery.
- Connect the negative cable last and disconnect it first (in negative ground systems).

Before charging a battery, add water if necessary to bring the electrolyte in the battery cells up to the right level. Make sure the outside of the battery is clean. Connect the positive charger lead to the positive battery terminal and negative lead to negative terminal. See **Figure 15-19**. Do not turn on the charger until the leads are connected to the battery. Charging times will vary, depending on battery condition and charging rate. Follow manufacturer's instructions.

Warning

To prevent sparks, do not disturb the connections to the battery while charging.

Badly sulfated batteries can sometimes be reclaimed by recharging them very slowly. This converts the sulfate to electrolyte.

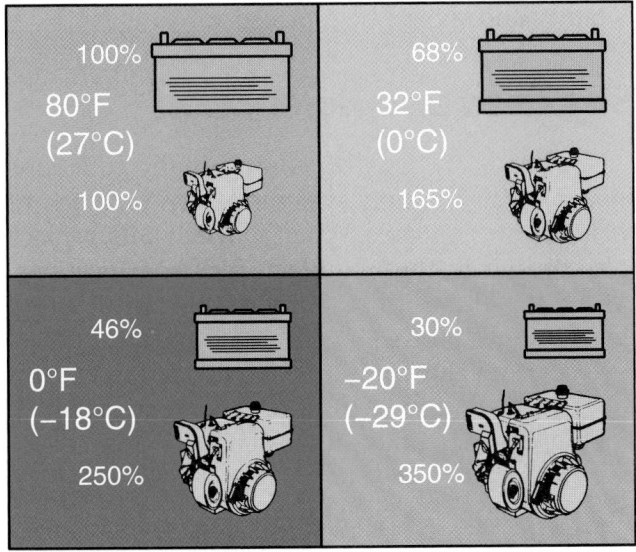

Goodheart-Willcox Publisher

Figure 15-18.

Cold temperatures can reduce the cranking power of a battery, while increasing the cranking load.

Goodheart-Willcox Publisher

Figure 15-19.

The positive charger cable must be attached to the positive battery terminal, and the negative cable must be connected to the negative terminal.

A battery that is dormant for a period of time may be connected to a "trickle charger" to keep it ready for use. Trickle chargers provide very low current and are available with an automatic shut-off to prevent overcharging.

Storing a Battery

There are several precautions that should be taken when storing a battery for an extended period. These include:

1. If the installed battery is to be left standing for a long time, disconnect the negative (–) terminal until the implement is to be used again.
2. Store a battery only with a full charge. A discharged battery can become sulfated and/or freeze.
3. Batteries should not be allowed to set on damp concrete. Place dry wood under a battery to be stored on the floor for any extended period of time.
4. Carefully inspect and recharge the battery at the beginning of each working season.

New Battery Installation

Most new batteries are dry-charged. To place this type of battery in service, add the electrolyte solution according to manufacturer's instructions. Some newly activated batteries require a short period of charging; others can be placed in service immediately. The following is the procedure for installing a new battery:

1. Remove the old battery. Note which cable is connected to the positive (+) terminal and which cable is connected to the negative (–) terminals. The positive cable is usually red and the negative is usually black.
2. Clean the cable connectors with a wire brush to remove oxidation.
3. If necessary, fill the new battery with acid and charge it (following manufacturer's instructions).
4. Install the new battery. Connect the cables to the proper terminals, positive cable to positive terminal (+) and negative cable to negative terminal (–).

Caution

Always connect negative cable last. Also, make sure you connect the cables to the correct battery terminals. Reversing polarity by connecting the positive cable to the negative terminal and the negative cable to the positive terminal can seriously damage the electrical system. Diodes in the system may be destroyed.

5. Check the vent tube for crimping or obstruction.
6. Securely fasten the battery to the unit with the battery hold-down clamp. A shaking or vibrating battery can be damaged.

Wiring

Electrical system wiring must have good insulation between all points of connection. Wires should be securely fastened and connecting points should be free of corrosion, rust, and oil. Loose and corroded connections can severely diminish battery potential.

A pinhole in a wire's insulation can cause electricity to leak and *ground out* on the engine or the implement. This condition can be amplified if water or oil is present on the insulation. A wire that is grounding out can make starting impossible. It can also cause an engine to run erratically.

Ammeters

Some battery ignition systems are equipped with an ammeter, which is used to measure the rate of current flow from the alternator to the battery. If no current flow is indicated by the ammeter, remove the meter from the circuit and check all components in the system. If the system is operating properly, use a multimeter set on an ohms setting to check continuity across the ammeter terminals. If continuity does not exist, the ammeter is faulty and should be replaced.

Switches and Solenoids

Switches are used to control many functions in a battery ignition system. Many varieties of switches are available. When a switch fails, replace it according to the manufacturer's specifications. Never substitute an automotive switch for small engine applications.

Most switches and solenoids can be tested with a standard multimeter set on an ohm setting or another type of continuity tester. See **Figure 15-20**.

Checking the Charging and Starting System Circuits

The following sections provide some guidelines for troubleshooting charging and starting systems.

TEST #1 (Switch A)
Probe terminal S (starter terminal of solenoid) and G (ground terminal of the solenoid). Continuity should exist only when the key is in the start position. When the key is in this position, the solenoid will snap closed. Current will flow from the battery to the starter, allowing the engine to crank over.

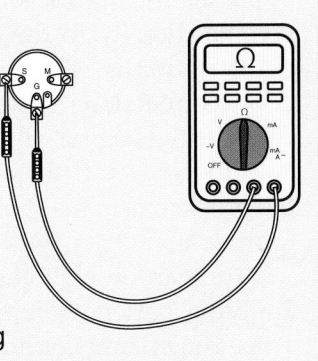

TEST #2 (Switch A)
Probe terminal M (magneto) and G (ground). Continuity should exist only when the key is in the off position. In this position, current flow from the ignition system is diverted to ground, killing the engine.

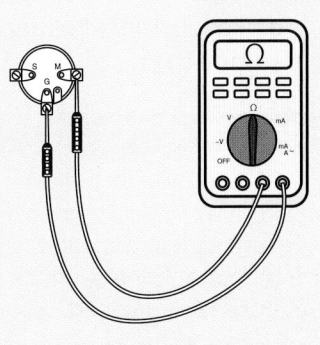

TEST #3 (Switch A)
Probe terminal M (magneto) and S (starter). Continuity should not exist in any switch position. Continuity would cause current flow from the battery to the ignition system, causing damage to the ignition system.

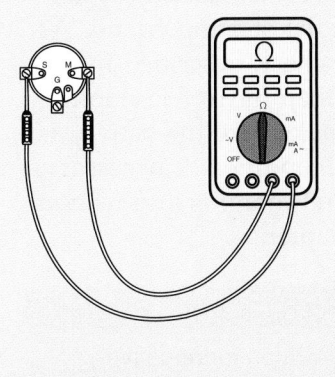

Tecumseh Products Co.

Figure 15-20.

This switch is being checked for continuity with a multimeter. Follow manufacturer's instructions when testing switches and solenoids.

There are many variations in charging and starting circuits. For example, some manufacturers may use a combination starter/generator while others use a separate alternator and starter motor. Some starter solenoids are incorporated into the starter unit while others are separate. The following procedures are only general guidelines; you should always follow the manufacturer's instructions for testing and troubleshooting your specific charging and starting systems.

Checking Charging System Output

If you are experiencing a problem that results in a discharged battery, the problem may be that the generator or alternator is not producing sufficient output to charge the battery. You can quickly check the output by checking that you have a fully charged battery, placing the equipment transmission in neutral (if applicable), and turning on the ignition switch.

With the ignition on and the engine not running, the charging warning light should be illuminated or the ammeter should show a discharge condition. Next, try to crank the engine. If the engine starts but the warning light remains on or the ammeter continues to show a discharge condition, there is likely a problem in the charging circuit. Refer to the later sections in this chapter to measure the charging system output, and to pinpoint and correct the problem. If the engine will not turn over or cranks slowly, check the starting system circuit.

Checking the Starting System Circuit

Battery starting circuits consist of the following components:
1. A battery is the source of electrical energy.
2. A starter solenoid transfers high starting current from the battery to the starter (starter relay).
3. A key start switch or other switch that energizes the starter solenoid.

4. A series-wound, low-resistance, high-current, direct-current starting motor that turns the engine over.

Note

If the starter will not activate, make sure a circuit breaker has not disconnected the circuit. If the circuit breaker has disrupted the circuit, it will not allow the starter to crank. Also, check diode wires to see if they are crossed. If crossed, reverse the diode wires.

The following procedures are used to isolate and identify a problem in the starting circuit. As with the charging system check described in the previous section, the first step in troubleshooting the starting system is to make sure the battery is fully charged and in good condition. If necessary, refer to the battery testing and charging information presented earlier in this chapter.

Note

The following procedures are written for negative-ground systems. If the engine you are working on is a positive-ground system, attach the test leads to the opposite battery terminal from the one described in the procedure. Be aware that the multimeter may show negative voltages.

Perform a voltage drop test to check the ground connections at the starter and battery. Begin by setting a multimeter for voltage measurements. Disconnect the spark plug wire and ground it against the block so you can turn the engine over without starting it. Attach the positive meter lead to the starter mounting frame and clip the negative meter lead to the negative terminal of the battery. Activate the starter switch and observe the meter reading. If the meter shows a voltage drop of less than .5V, move on to the next step. A reading of .5V or greater indicates a poor ground. Clean and tighten all ground connections and replace the ground cable if it is worn or corroded. Operate the starter switch and recheck the voltage.

Next, a quick check of the starter motor can eliminate the motor as a potential cause of the problem. Make sure the spark plug wire is disconnected and grounded against the block. Then, connect one end of a jumper cable to the positive terminal of the battery. Next, firmly touch the other end of the cable to the terminal on the starter. This bypasses the starter solenoid and applies battery voltage directly to the starter. The starter should crank normally. If it does not, make sure you have good connections with the jumper cable and try again. If the engine still will not crank, the problem is in the starter. If the engine turns over normally, the problem is in the starter solenoid, safety switches, ignition switch, or the wiring between them.

You can quickly check the starter solenoid by applying battery voltage directly to the solenoid. Trace the wiring coming from the ignition switch and note the solenoid terminal that it connects to. Leave one end of the jumper cable connected to the positive terminal of the battery and touch the other end of the jumper cable to the solenoid terminal you just located. This bypasses the ignition switch and safety switches and completes the circuit through the windings of the starter solenoid. The contacts between the battery and the starter motor should close and the starter should turn over. If not, the starter solenoid is bad and must be replaced.

If the engine turns over when you bypass the ignition and safety switches, you know the problem is in one of these components or the wiring between them. Refer to Chapter 19, *Lawn and Garden Tractors* for detailed procedures for testing these systems.

Starter and Generator Maintenance

All dc starters and generators have commutators and brushes, which occasionally need service. Start by cleaning the unit's metal housing. Avoid getting cleaning solvent on insulated wiring.

Check for worn bearings at both ends of the armature shaft. (You can feel play with your hands, and worn bearings are usually noisy when operating.)

If there is a cover band, remove it. A ring of solder along the inside of the band indicates that the unit has overheated. Further repair must be done by an experienced technician.

If the unit has no cover band, remove the long bolts running through the housing and pull off the end plate nearest the commutator. The commutator consists of a group of bars arranged in a cylinder-like fashion inside the generator or starter. Spring-loaded brushes rub on the commutator. See **Figure 15-21.** Check the brushes for wear. They should move freely and press firmly against the commutator.

A generator will have either two or three brushes. A starter-generator will have two. If the

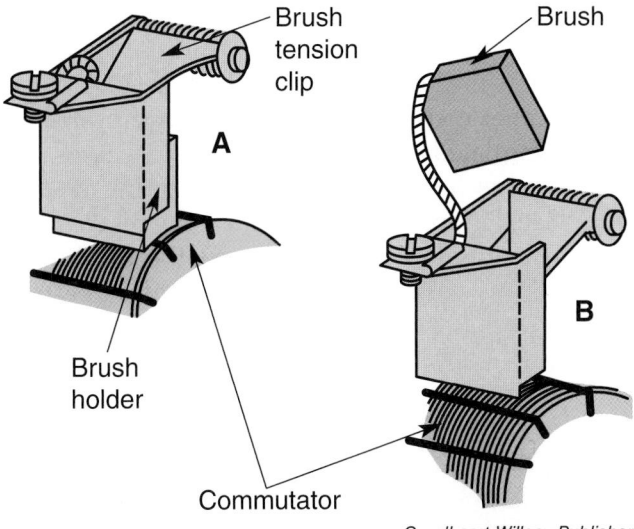

Goodheart-Willcox Publisher

Figure 15-21.

Brushes are held against the commutator by a brush clip. A—The brush is worn down so the clip rides on the holder. B—The brush is removed for replacement. Never pull on brush leads.

brushes are worn to half of their original length or the clips are resting on the brush holders, replace the brushes. If brushes are binding in the holders, wipe the holders with a clean, dry rag.

Check and tighten all electrical connections. Inspect the commutator for damage and/or wear. If the bars are rough and out of round, the armature will have to be chucked in a lathe and turned to a smooth finish. After turning, the mica (insulating material) between the commutator bars should be undercut. Follow all of the manufacturer's specifications.

If the commutator is only dirty and glazed, clean it with fine sandpaper. Never use emery cloth or solvent. Emery will cause arcing. Solvents will soften the insulation between the bars.

If necessary, install new brushes. If they do not seat squarely, pull sandpaper back and forth between brush and the commutator. Let the sandpaper work the brush down to the shape of the commutator. Blow out the dust and replace the band.

Polarize the generator at the regulator by placing one end of a jumper wire on the battery terminal. Momentarily, touch the other end of the wire to the generator terminal. This is only necessary if you have disconnected any of the wire leads to the generator.

If you do not do this and the polarity has reversed, you may burn out the generator, damage

the cutout relay points in the regulator, or run down the battery.

Alternator Maintenance

Small engine alternators come in many different sizes. Maintenance generally involves lubrication (on some units, but not on others) and inspection. Periodically, check that brushes, slip rings, and bearings are in good condition. If the battery is run down, test alternator output and, if necessary, test the individual parts of the alternator. Check battery polarity first. Is the proper terminal going to ground? If not, reverse them.

Caution

Never reverse polarity when servicing the battery. It could burn out alternator diodes and damage wiring by overheating. Do not try to polarize an alternator. It is *not* necessary. Polarity of an alternator cannot be lost or reversed.

Most small engine alternator systems use permanent magnets that are attached to the inner rim of the flywheel. These magnets are similar to the magneto magnets. The *stator assembly* consists of a series of coils that are mounted on a circular plate and attached to the engine inside the flywheel. The alternator produces alternating current (ac), which is converted to direct current (dc) to charge the battery. This is accomplished through the use of a rectifier, or diode arrangement, located in the circuit between the alternator and the battery. The size of the magnets and stator coils determines the output current of the alternator. **Figure 15-22** illustrates an alternator ring and a regulator-rectifier.

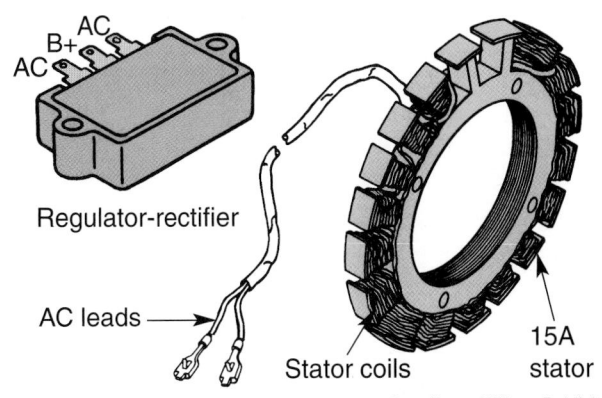

Goodheart-Willcox Publisher

Figure 15-22.

One type of alternator ring and a regulator-rectifier.

Dual, unregulated alternator systems charge the battery with dc current and provide ac current for operating the lights and other accessories. **Figure 15-23** shows a wiring diagram for a dual, unregulated alternator system using a diode in the direct current circuit. The current output is limited by the construction of the coils in the stator. Therefore, no regulator is used. Current to the electrical accessories is available only when the engine is running, and the brightness of the lights varies with the speed of the engine. The ac and dc units are separate, so the load on one does not affect the other.

Another common type of alternator system is the unregulated ac-only type. In these systems, the alternator is used to operate the lighting system only. See **Figure 15-24**. Current is available only when the engine is running, and the brightness of the lights varies with engine speed. A battery

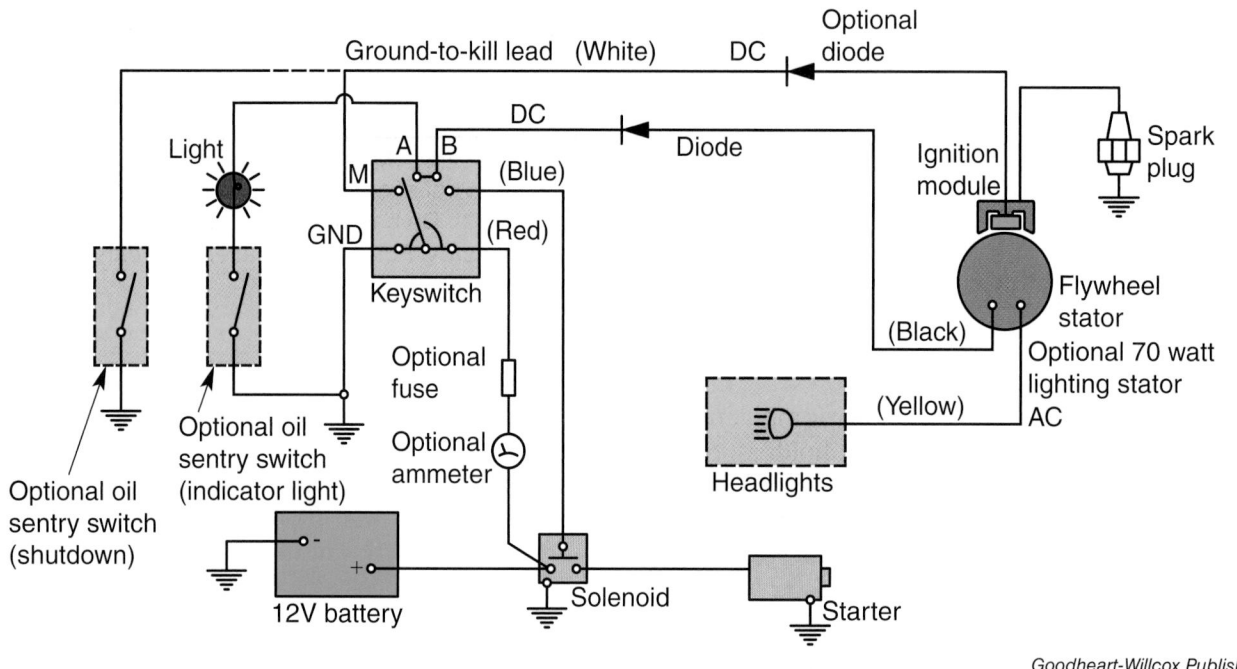

Goodheart-Willcox Publisher

Figure 15-23.
This wiring diagram is for a dual-purpose alternator. It provides ac for headlights and dc for battery charging.

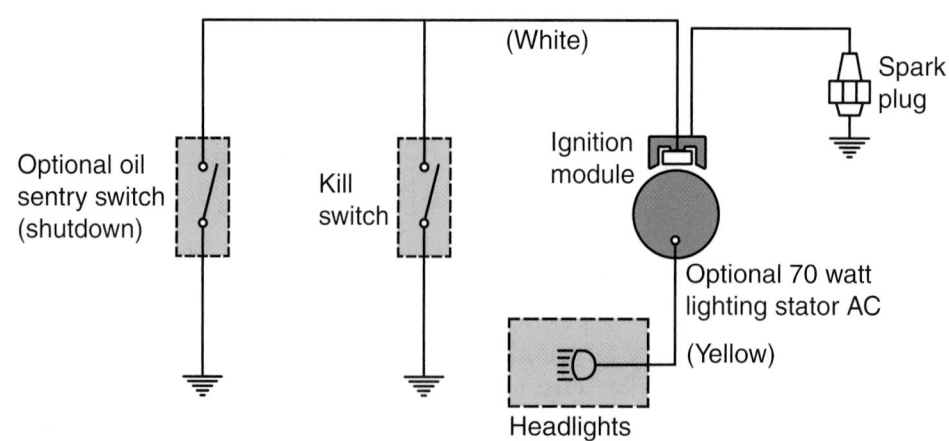

Kohler Co.

Figure 15-24.
A wiring diagram for a manual-start engine with an ac-only lighting stator for the headlights. A battery is not used in this system.

is not used in these systems. The troubleshooting chart in **Figure 15-25** points out common alternator system problems.

Alternator Output Tests

A few common tests can be performed to determine the output of most small engine alternators. A multimeter is recommended for carrying out these tests. See **Figure 15-26**. When checking alternators, make the tests in the following sequence:

1. Test alternator output.
2. Test diode(s) or regulator-rectifier (if equipped).

Most meter receptacles and test lead connector ends are color coded to ensure correct test lead attachment. See **Figure 15-27**. Before testing the alternator's output (volts, amps), use an accurate tachometer to temporarily adjust the engine speed to the rpm specified in the test instructions.

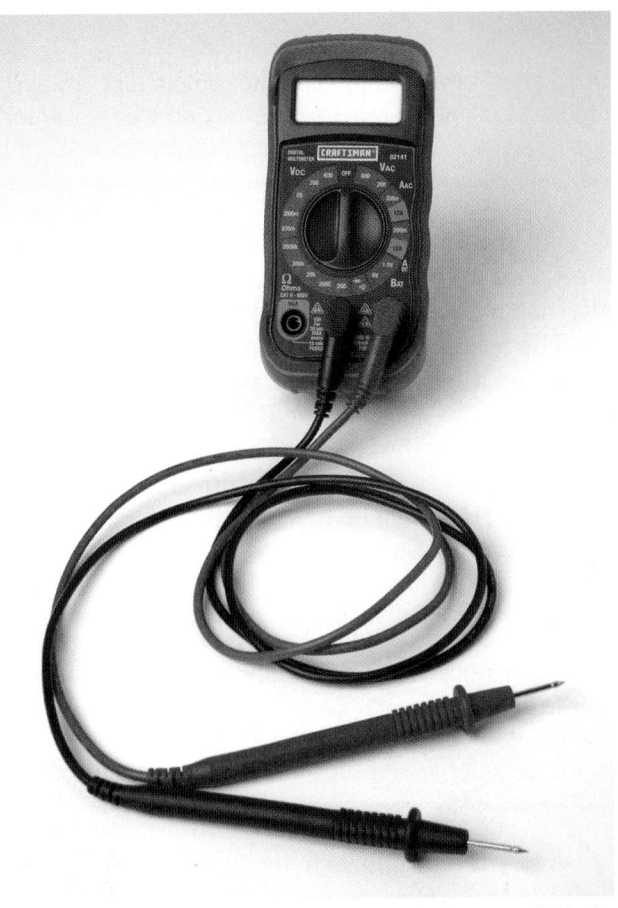

Kohler Co.

Figure 15-26.

A multimeter can be used for performing alternator tests. Note color-coded test leads.

Alternator System Troubleshooting

Battery Not Charging

Engine RPM too low.
Inline fuse "blown" (if equipped).
Defective battery.
Loose, pinched, or corroded battery leads.
Open, shorted, or grounded wires between output connector and battery.
Defective diode (open or shorted).
Defective or improperly grounded regulator-rectifier.
Diode installed incorrectly (reversed).
Damaged battery (shorted battery cells).
Excessive current draw from accessories.
Low magnetic flux or damaged alternator magnets.

Battery in State of Overcharge

Severe battery vibration (missing or broken tie-down straps).
Battery rate of charge not matched to alternator output.
Damaged battery (shorted battery cells).
Defective regulator.

Headlamps Not Working

Inline fuse "blown" (if equipped).
Defective headlamps.
Loose or corroded wires.
Open, shorted, or grounded wires between output connector and headlamps.
Low magnetic flux or damaged alternator magnets.

Goodheart-Willcox Publisher

Figure 15-25.

Alternator system troubleshooting chart.

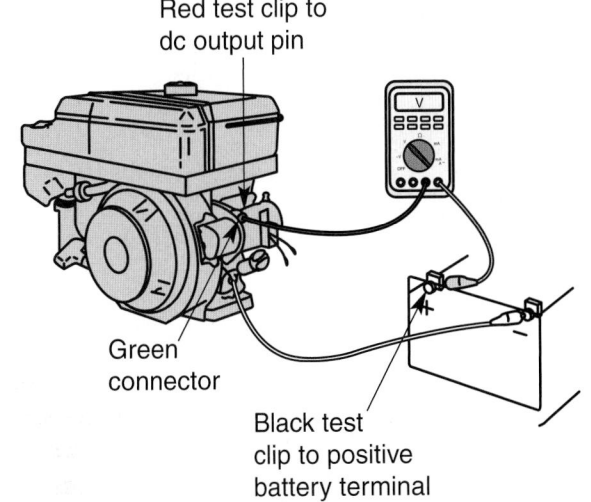

Red test clip to dc output pin

Green connector

Black test clip to positive battery terminal

Briggs and Stratton Corp.

Figure 15-27.

Typical test connections for checking the output of a 9A, regulated alternator. Output for this particular model should not be less than 40V.

Note

Upon completion of the alternator output test, always readjust the engine rpm to its correct no-load governed speed as specified in the engine service manual.

Figure 15-27 illustrates a typical output test for a 9A regulated alternator. This system provides alternating current to a regulator-rectifier.

The regulator-rectifier converts the ac to dc and regulates the current to the battery. The charging rate will vary with engine RPM and temperature. When testing the regulator-rectifier for output, a 12V battery with a minimum charge of 5V is required. There will be no charging output if battery voltage is below 5V. See **Figure 15-28**.

Note

When testing a regulator-rectifier, connect test leads before starting engine. Be sure connections are secure. If a test lead vibrates loose while the engine is running, the regulator-rectifier may be damaged.

A dc-only and dual-circuit alternator system uses a *diode* to convert ac to dc. The diode is located in the output wire on most alternators. A typical test hookup for one type of diode is shown in **Figure 15-29**. After the test is made in one direction,

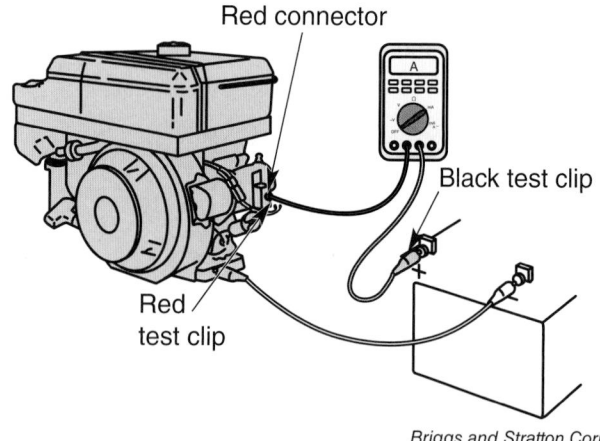

Briggs and Stratton Corp.

Figure 15-28.

Typical test connection for checking the output of one type of regulator-rectifier. Typical output should range from 3A to 9A, depending on battery voltage.

Note: It may be necessary to pierce the wire with a pin if the connections are not in the open.

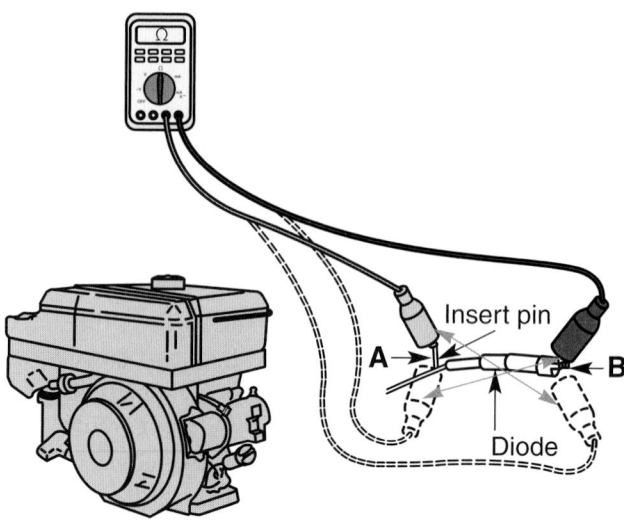

Briggs and Stratton Corp.

Figure 15-29.

Testing a diode for proper operation. The meter should show a reading in one direction only.

the leads are reversed and the diode is tested again. The meter should show continuity in one direction only. If the meter shows continuity in both directions, the diode is defective (closed). If the meter does not show continuity (needle movement) in either direction, the diode is defective (open).

Note

Replacement diode harnesses are available. When installing a new harness, use rosin-core solder. Use shrink tubing or electrician's tape on connections. Do not use crimp connectors.

Voltage Regulator Service

Most modern voltage regulators are solid-state units that cannot be adjusted. If the regulator is malfunctioning, it must be replaced. However, electro-mechanical voltage regulators, which are found in older engines, require periodic service and adjustment as their contact points wear. Refer to an appropriate service manual for more information on service electro-mechanical voltage regulators.

Summary

Although small engine ignition systems are durable, they do require periodic inspection and maintenance. A spark test can be performed to verify ignition system operation. During the spark test, a diagnostic tool known as a spark tester is connected in the ignition system and is used to observe the spark produced by the system.

Although a magneto system may be able to supply 30,000 volts (V), it produces only enough voltage to jump the spark plug gap. Therefore, the condition of the spark plug determines the amount of voltage that other ignition parts must produce.

You can analyze the quality of combustion that has been taking place in a cylinder by examining the deposits on the spark plug. Spark plug deposits are usually caused by weak magneto voltage, incorrect carburetor adjustments, poor air cleaner maintenance, incorrect gasoline or oil, or incorrectly mixed gasoline and oil.

Most manufacturers recommend replacing plugs that are fouled with oil, carbon, etc. Cleaning should only be done when a replacement plug is not available. When gapping a spark plug, bend the outer electrode toward or away from the center electrode. The heat-dispersing properties of the spark plug depend on correct plug seating. If the spark plug is tightened excessively, the gasket will be crushed. Internal leakage may result. Attempting to remove an overtightened spark plug can strip cylinder head threads. Seating the spark plug too loosely can result in preignition and possible engine damage caused by spark plug overheating.

In most magneto systems, the module is mounted outside the flywheel. However, some magneto systems are completely contained under the flywheel. The flywheel must be removed from the crankshaft to service the ignition components in these systems.

The gap between the module's laminations and the flywheel magnets is adjustable. This adjustment must be made carefully or the voltage produced by the ignition system will be reduced. Although most manufacturers suggest simply replacing the module if spark test results point to it as the most likely cause of a no-spark condition, some manufacturers provide instructions for checking the resistance between the module's core and its primary and secondary wiring.

Storage batteries need regular maintenance to keep them in good operating condition. With proper setup and care, the battery will last for years. However, even when properly maintained, a battery can eventually fail. There are several tests that can be performed to determine the condition of a battery. These tests include an open-circuit voltage test, a specific gravity test, and a load test.

Charging a battery is necessary when the battery becomes discharged, such as when it has been out of use an extended period of time. Batteries generate hydrogen and oxygen during charging. These gases combine to form a highly explosive mixture.

Electrical system wiring must have good insulation between all points of connection. Wires should be securely fastened and connecting points should be free of corrosion, rust, and oil.

Switches are used to control many functions in a battery ignition system. Most switches and solenoids can be tested with a standard multimeter set on an ohm setting or another type of continuity tester.

A voltage drop test can be performed to check the ground connections at the starter and battery. You can quickly check the starter solenoid by applying battery voltage directly to the solenoid.

All dc starters and generators have commutators and brushes, which occasionally need service. If the brushes are worn to half of their original length or the clips are resting on the brush holders, replace the brushes. If brushes are binding in the holders, wipe the holders with a clean, dry rag.

Inspect the commutator for damage and/or wear. If the bars are rough and out of round, the armature will have to be chucked in a lathe and turned to a smooth finish. If the commutator is only dirty and glazed, clean it with fine sandpaper.

Alternator maintenance generally involves lubrication (on some units, but not on others) and inspection. Periodically, check that brushes, slip rings, and bearings are in good condition. If the battery is run down, test alternator output and, if necessary, test the individual parts of the alternator.

Review Questions

Answer the following questions using the information provided in this chapter.

1. A spark test is being performed. There is no spark when the spark tester is connected between the spark plug wire and the plug tip. However, a spark does occur when the tester is connected between the spark plug wire and an engine ground. The problem lies with the _____.
   A. magneto
   B. spark plug wire
   C. flywheel
   D. spark plug

2. Which of the following determines the amount of voltage produced by the magneto when the engine is running?
   A. breaker points
   B. spark plug
   C. condenser
   D. spark plug wire

3. What color should the internal porcelain insulator be on a normal, used spark plug?

4. What five conditions cause spark plug deposits?

5. A(n) _____-type feeler gauge should be used when gapping a used spark plug.

6. If the key that positions the flywheel is deformed or partly sheared, the engine will most likely _____.
   A. lose the flywheel
   B. be out of time
   C. run exceptionally fast
   D. burn fuel excessively

7. The gap between a module's laminations and the flywheel magnet can be measured with a _____ feeler gauge.

8. What are the seven basic things to check for before starting an extensive battery ignition system analysis?

9. Name the single component that indicates for certain that an engine has a battery ignition system.
   A. battery
   B. distributor
   C. can-shaped coil
   D. starter

10. *True or False?* Undercharging can lead to distortion of a battery's positive plates.

11. Why is it important to keep batteries fully charged in below-freezing temperatures?

12. What is included in a visual inspection of a battery?

13. Which test will determine the condition of each cell of a battery?

14. If one or more battery cells shows a specific gravity of less than 1.235, the battery should be _____.
    A. discarded
    B. recharged
    C. discharged, then recharged
    D. None of the above.

15. If the fluid level in a battery is below the separators, _____ should be added, but never add _____.

16. In cold weather, battery power _____ while the need for engine cranking power _____.

17. What two gases are generated during battery charging?

18. Which cable should be connected last when installing a battery?

19. What kind of testing unit can be used to test switches?

20. What are the four components of a battery starting circuit?

21. Explain why emery cloth should not be used to clean a commutator of a generator or a starter.

22. Under what conditions would you polarize an alternator?

23. What is the type of current generated by an alternator?

24. Two electronic components that convert alternating current to direct current are _____ and _____.

25. *True or False?* When being tested, a diode should show continuity in one direction only.

Suggested Activities

1. Perform a spark test. Summarize the test results and explain what they mean.

2. Examine some old spark plugs. Attempt to analyze engine condition by their appearance. Clean, gap, and test them.

3. Place a bad plug in an engine. Test for spark at the plug tip and, then, at the base. Explain the difference.

4. Demonstrate a hydrometer test.

5. Demonstrate proper maintenance procedure for a battery.

6. Demonstrate proper installation procedure of a battery.

7. Demonstrate the proper procedure for charging a battery. Be sure to follow all safety rules when working with batteries and chargers.

8. Perform continuity tests on several types of switches.

9. Test several electrical system components with the test equipment described in this chapter. If other equipment is available, follow manufacturer's instructions for the equipment at hand.

With extended use, carbon can build up on the heads of pistons. This carbon can result in hot spots on the piston, engine overheating, and preignition. Carbon deposits should be carefully removed when the engine is reconditioned.

Engine Disassembly and Inspection

Learning Objectives

After studying this chapter, you will be able to:

- Inspect engines for problems.
- Describe the procedure for removing an engine from an implement.
- List the steps involved in disassembling an engine.
- Inspect various engine parts for damage and wear.

Key Terms

preignition
service manual
starter clutch wrench

Introduction

When repairing an engine, it is best to work in a clean, well-lighted area. Tools should be clean and close at hand.

Warning

When using tools, safety rules should be observed. For example, safety glasses should be worn to protect the eyes. Oily and gasoline-soaked rags should be placed in flameproof containers. Heat or flames should never be allowed near solvents or other materials that will burn. A workplace is not safe unless good judgment is used while working in it.

Some engines are easier to work on if they are mounted on an engine stand. Other engines in need of major repairs can be removed from the implement and torn down right on the workbench. See **Figure 16-1**.

Every engine make and model is built to certain dimensions and specifications that are different from other engines. You will need a *service manual* for the engine you are working on. The service

Goodheart-Willcox Publisher

Figure 16-1.

Small gasoline engines are easier to work on when removed from the implement.

manual provides detailed service procedures and specifications for a particular model or series of engines. Quality repair work depends a great deal on carefully and accurately following the instructions provided in the engine service manual.

Note

The disassembly and inspection procedures described in this chapter provide a general overview of the steps required, but are not intended to take the place of the detailed and specific instructions found in the proper service manual.

Engine Inspection

It is good practice to look for causes of engine problems even before removing the engine from the implement. Identifying the potential causes of engine failure can help you estimate the extent of service that will be required. It may also identify improper maintenance so you can advise the owner of the steps he or she can take to avoid similar problems in the future.

Begin the inspection process by visually checking the exterior of the engine before it is cleaned. Check for excessive debris or dirt buildup on and between the cooling fins of air-cooled engines, **Figure 16-2**. Even a small amount of debris trapped in the cooling

Goodheart-Willcox Publisher

Figure 16-2.
Grass clippings and other debris can obstruct airflow across the cooling fins. In severe cases, like the one shown here, the debris can interfere with proper air-vane governor operation.

fins can result in engine overheating. Also, look for loose or broken engine mounts, misaligned pulleys, or unevenly worn drive belts, which can cause excessive vibration. Wet oil on the outside of the engine may indicate that there are loose parts, leaking gaskets, leaking oil seals, or a cracked casting. Once the exterior of the engine has been carefully inspected, disconnect the spark plug so that it cannot fire accidentally. When working on lawn mowers, snow throwers, and other implements with exposed moving parts, never touch the blades or any driven parts until the spark plug has been disconnected. See **Figure 16-3**. Next, clean the engine to remove as much external grime as possible.

Green Tech

Aerosol Spray Cans

Aerosol spray cans are used in various areas of small engine–driven implement repair, such as for paint touch-ups or for degreasing. Many aerosol sprays use chlorinated compounds, which emit volatile organic compounds (VOCs) into the atmosphere. Another concern with aerosol spray cans is the product contained within. These cans must be completely empty for disposal, or they will be considered hazardous waste. The containers themselves also pose a threat to the environment if they are not recycled. To combat the dangers caused by aerosol spray cans, green shops use water-based products over chlorinated products whenever possible. An option to help with the empty cans is to use refillable spray bottles for aqueous solutions.

Remove and inspect the air filter. If the back side of the filter is dirty, it indicates that abrasive particles may have entered the engine. Check the back of the filter housing and the carburetor throat for dust. See **Figure 16-4**. Even small quantities of dust or other abrasive particles can cause severe wear if they enter the engine.

Remove and inspect the spark plug. Compare the condition of the spark plug electrode against a spark plug condition chart, like the one found in the appendix of this book. The condition of the spark plug can reveal a great deal of information about the engine's condition. You may want to leave the spark plug out after inspecting it.

Next, drain the fuel system into a clean metal container. Check the fuel for water contamination, rust and other particulates, and chemical breakdown. Over time, water vapor can condense in the fuel tank and contaminate the gasoline. This water

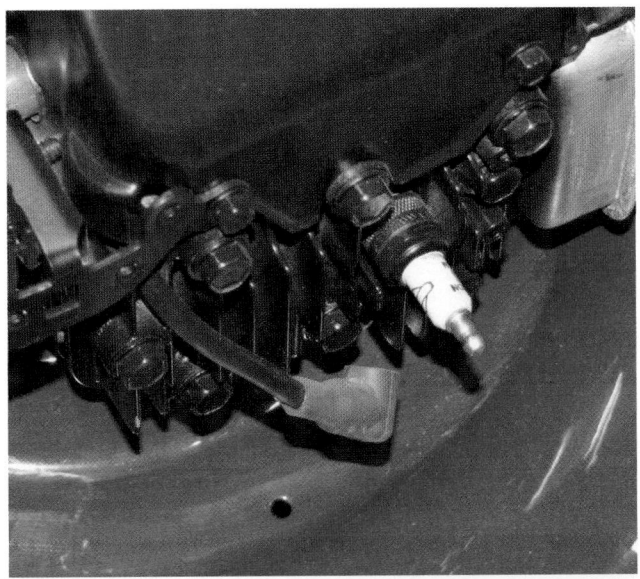

Goodheart-Willcox Publisher

Figure 16-3.

Always begin the disassembly process by disconnecting the spark plug.

can rust some carburetor and internal engine components and cause the engine oil to break down. Rust or other particulates in the fuel indicate a rusty or dirty fuel tank. If the fuel is dark, it has begun to break down chemically. The varnish created when the gasoline breaks down can clog passages in the carburetor, resulting in an incorrect fuel mixture.

Drain all the oil from the engine into another clean container and inspect it. If the oil is excessively thick or dirty, it is a sign of improper maintenance. If the oil is milky, water has entered the engine. If the oil has a strong gasoline smell, the engine is running rich or fuel has leaked into the engine. The presence of any metal particles suspended in the oil indicates severe wear inside the engine.

Engine Removal

Wires may need to be disconnected before the engine can be removed. If so, make flags of masking

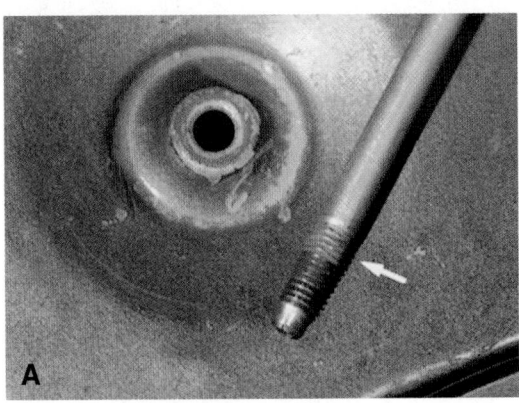

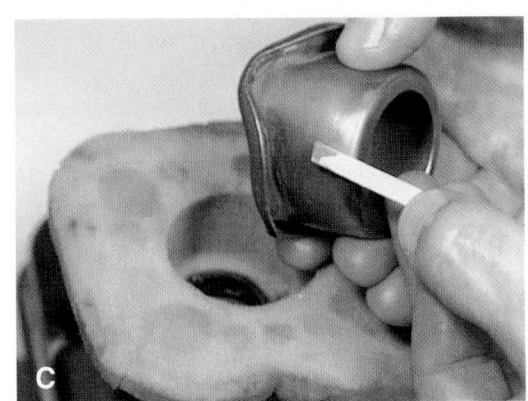

Goodheart-Willcox Publisher

Figure 16-4.

Check the back of the air filter, the filter housing, and the carburetor throat for signs of dirt infiltration. The presence of dirt in any of these areas indicates that the filter was not properly maintained, allowing abrasive particles to enter the engine. A—Check the threads on the end of the air filter housing bolt. B—Check the bottom of the filter cup. C—Check the lip on the underside of the filter cup. Also, check the back of the filter. D—Check the carburetor intake.

tape for the wire ends. Identify them with matching numbers. See **Figure 16-5**. This will prevent damage from wrong connections and will save time during reassembly.

Next, identify and remove any cables or linkages that will prevent engine removal. Cables that must typically be removed include remote throttle or governor control and flywheel brake cables. Be sure to make note of the way any wires or cables are connected so that they can be reinstalled in the same manner. See **Figure 16-6**.

Depending on the type of equipment the engine is attached to, it may be necessary to disconnect the equipment drive system prior to removing the engine. On most equipment, this involves removing the drive belt. On push mowers, the blade and blade adapter should be removed. Next, remove any fasteners holding the engine to the implement, lift the engine from the implement, and set it on a stable workbench.

Warning

Always lift an engine using your legs rather than your back. Engines can be heavy, and lifting them improperly can cause back injury.

Engine Disassembly

Once the preliminary inspection is complete, you should have a better idea of the condition of the engine. If the crankcase, cylinder block, or cylinder head is cracked or damaged, or if the engine shows signs of severe abuse, engine replacement may be a better option than engine overhaul. If the engine can be rebuilt, the next step is disassembly. There are two general phases to engine

A

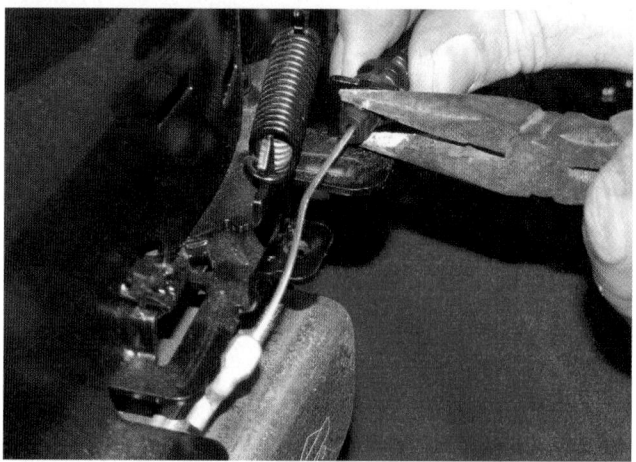

B

Goodheart-Willcox Publisher

Figure 16-6.

Throttle, governor control, and flywheel brake cables must be disconnected prior to engine removal. A—Disconnect the flywheel brake cable from the brake lever. B—Tabs on the end of this brake cable must be compressed so the cable can be freed from the engine bracket.

disassembly: removal of exterior components and disassembly of internal engine components.

Removal of Exterior Engine Components

If the engine is covered with a plastic or metal shroud, it should be removed to expose other engine parts. Next, the starter unit can be unbolted. It may be a retractable rope starter or an electric starter. Usually, only a few bolts fasten the starter unit to the engine. See **Figure 16-7**.

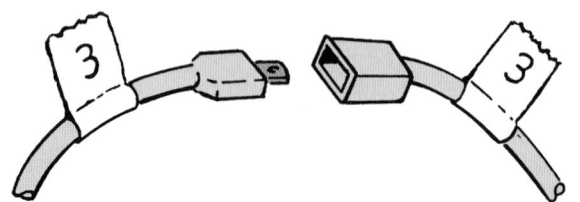

Goodheart-Willcox Publisher

Figure 16-5.

Identify mating wires before disconnecting them so they can be easily identified and reconnected.

Goodheart-Willcox Publisher

Figure 16-7.

With the engine out of the implement, the starter unit can be removed.

If the engine is equipped with an extended oil filler tube, pull it free from the crankcase, **Figure 16-8**. Inspect the condition of the O-ring. The exhaust manifold pipe and muffler can be taken off next. Set them aside and out of the way.

The carburetor and intake manifold pipe can also be removed. See **Figure 16-9**. It often helps to sketch or photograph the carburetor and linkage locations. This can save time and aggravation during reassembly. Check all gasket surfaces for defects. On some engines, the fuel tank is fastened

Goodheart-Willcox Publisher

Figure 16-8.

If the engine is equipped with an extended oil filler tube, pull it free from the crankcase.

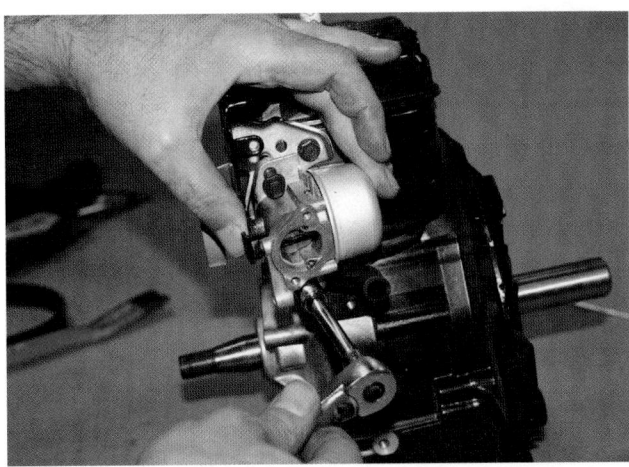

A

B   Intake manifold

Goodheart-Willcox Publisher

Figure 16-9.

Prior to disconnecting linkages and removing the carburetor, sketch or photograph the linkage hookup for later reference. A—Removing the carburetor. B—Removing the intake manifold. Note: Not all engines have intake manifolds.

to the carburetor. In any case, the tank can be removed, and the fuel lines can be disconnected. Next, sketch or photograph the various governor linkages, levers, and brackets, and remove them from the engine.

Remove and inspect the crankcase breather and breather tube. Follow the procedure in the service manual to check the breather. Some engines have a breather passage cast into the engine block. Remove the cover over the passage and inspect the condition of the passage and the cover. See **Figure 16-10**.

Goodheart-Willcox Publisher

Figure 16-10.

Remove the crankcase breather.

If the engine was equipped with an electric starter, there may still be an air shroud, blower housing, and baffles blocking access to the flywheel. Those components should be removed next. Check and record the air gap between the ignition module armature and the flywheel, and then remove the ignition module. See **Figure 16-11**.

Removing the Flywheel

The flywheel is mounted on the tapered end of the crankshaft. A keyway in the crankshaft is keyed for alignment. See **Figure 16-12**. To remove the flywheel, hold it stationary while the flywheel retaining nut is removed. See **Figure 16-13**. Some engines have a threaded starter clutch rather than

Goodheart-Willcox Publisher

Figure 16-11.

Remove the ignition module.

a flywheel retaining nut. A *starter clutch wrench* is used to remove these starter clutches. Starter clutch wrenches are special tools designed to grip indentations in a starter clutch so it can be turned.

Once the flywheel retaining nut is removed, the flywheel must be pulled from the crankshaft taper. One method of loosening the flywheel is to use a knock-off tool on the crankshaft. Thread the tool all the way onto the crankshaft and tap it with a hammer while applying pressure to the underside of the flywheel with a pry bar. See **Figure 16-14**. The sudden jolt will loosen the flywheel. Never use the flywheel nut as a knock-off tool or the crankshaft threads will be damaged.

Another way to remove the flywheel is to use a flywheel puller. After installing the puller, tighten the center bolt snugly. If the flywheel does not break loose from the crankshaft when the center bolt is tightened, tap the bolt with a hammer. Use extreme care when removing aluminum flywheels.

Inspecting the Flywheel

When the flywheel is removed, inspect it. Make sure that it is not cracked and that the mounting hole and keyway are not damaged. Inspect the key. If it has begun to shear or if the key is too narrow, the engine will be out of time. In either case, the key must be replaced.

Over time, the flywheel magnet can lose its magnetism. To check the strength of the flywheel magnet, place a 1/2″ socket on the magnet and shake the flywheel. The socket should remain in place on the magnet. See **Figure 16-15**. If the engine is equipped with internal breaker point ignition, the ignition components can be disassembled after the flywheel is removed.

Organizing the Job

Organizing the job saves time and effort. At this point, the outer parts have been taken off the engine. They should be set aside in their own groups. Magneto, flywheel shroud, and starter parts should be in one group; carburetor, fuel tank, and exhaust manifold in another.

Keeping the work clean is part of good organization. Outside surfaces can be cleaned at this point of tear-down. See **Figure 16-16**. Inside surfaces will be cleaned later. Grass clippings and other debris should be removed by scraping and brushing the fins and housings before cleaning fluid is used.

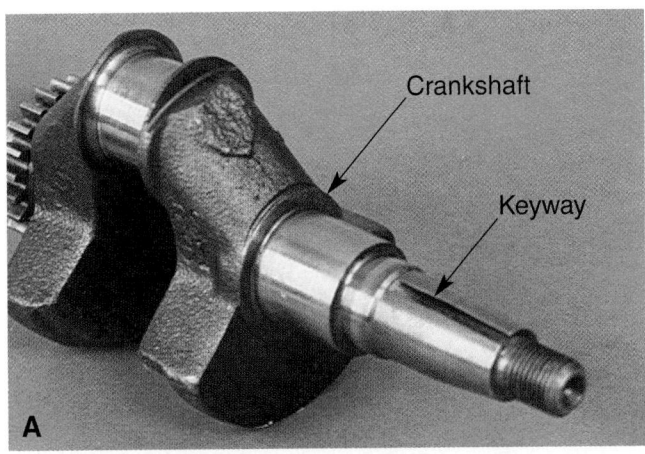

Goodheart-Willcox Publisher

Figure 16-12.

The crankshaft is keyed to hold the flywheel in an exact position. A—The crankshaft end is tapered and has a keyway. B—The crankshaft is keyed to hold the flywheel in an exact position. A special tool is often needed to remove the flywheel from the taper.

Goodheart-Willcox Publisher

Figure 16-13.

A variety of methods can be used to hold a flywheel stationary while the flywheel retaining nut is removed. The two most common are shown here. A—A flywheel holder. B—A strap wrench.

A safe engine cleaning solvent should be used to remove grease, oil, and grit. Some parts, such as the coil and condenser, may be cleaned by wiping with a clean cloth moistened with solvent. This is better than total immersion. Never use solvents that burn easily or those that may be harmful to humans.

As each part is washed, wipe it with a clean cloth and set it aside to dry. If the workbench is oily and greasy, clean it before doing disassembly work on it. Hands should be washed often to keep dirt off the cleaned parts.

Disassembling the Engine's Mechanical Systems

After all of the exterior components of the engine have been removed, measure crankshaft endplay. To measure endplay, set up a dial indicator to measure the forward and backward movement at the drive (power take off) end of the crankshaft. See **Figure 16-17.** Grasp the flywheel end of the crankshaft and pull it back as far as it will move. Then, zero the dial indicator, and push the crankshaft forward as far as it will go. Record the endplay

Figure 16-14.
A knock-off tool is often used to remove a flywheel. The tool must be tight on the shaft before being hit. A pry bar provides a valuable assist.

Figure 16-16.
Grass and other debris should be removed from cooling fins before the engine is cleaned with solvent.

Figure 16-15.
Test flywheel magnets by placing a socket on them and shaking the flywheel. The socket should remain in place.

Figure 16-17.
Set up a dial indicator as shown, zero the indicator, and move the crankshaft forward and back to check endplay.

and compare it to the specification in the service manual. If the endplay exceeds the specification, you will need to correct the endplay when you reassemble the engine.

The next step in disassembly is to remove the cylinder head.

Removing and Inspecting the Cylinder Head on an L-Head Engine

On an L-head engine, the head bolts should be loosened in a crisscross pattern. Remove each

head bolt one at a time and record its location and its length, **Figure 16-18.** The cylinder head may be secured with different length head bolts, and it is very important that the proper length bolt be reinstalled in each bore. A bolt that is too short may fail during engine operation. A bolt that is too long may bottom out and prevent the cylinder head from being properly tightened. After the cylinder bolts have been removed, the cylinder head and head gasket can be removed from the cylinder.

The cylinder head should be thoroughly cleaned and inspected for cracks and warpage. Carbon

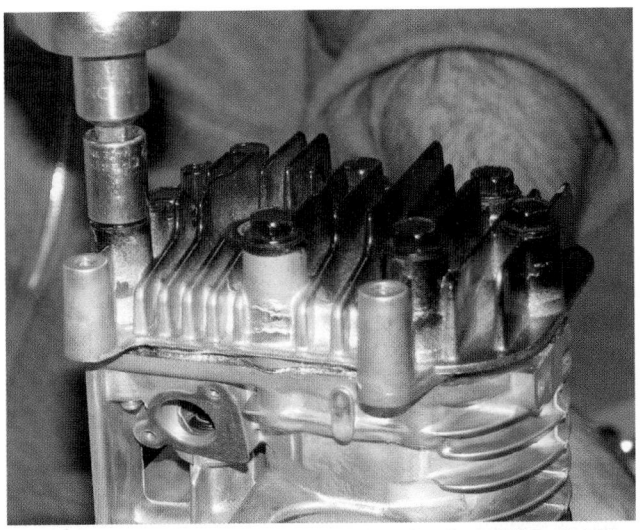

Goodheart-Willcox Publisher

Figure 16-18.
Loosen the head bolts in a crisscross pattern before removing them. Note the location and the length of each bolt as it is removed.

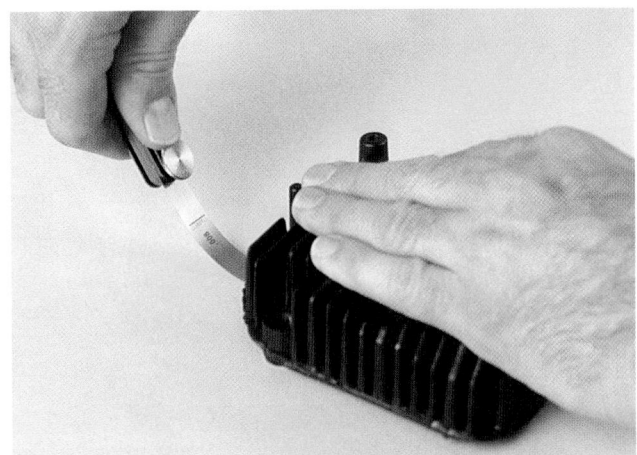

Goodheart-Willcox Publisher

Figure 16-19.
The cylinder head should be placed on a surface plate and tested for flatness with a feeler gauge.

buildup on the cylinder head can be loosened by soaking the head in parts cleaner. The carbon can then be removed with a parts brush.

When the head is clean, inspect it closely for cracks and broken cooling fins. If any cracks or broken fins are found, the cylinder head should be replaced. Inspect the mating surfaces for nicks and gouges, and have the head resurfaced if any are found.

Check the cylinder head for warpage by placing it on a surface known to be flat. Try to slide a .002″ feeler gauge between the cylinder's mating surfaces and the flat surface, **Figure 16-19**. Work all the way around the cylinder head. If the feeler gauge slips between the head and the flat surface at any point, the cylinder head is warped and must be resurfaced or replaced.

Caution

Never use a wire brush to clean an aluminum cylinder head. The wires can score the combustion chamber, which could result in hot spots when the engine is put back into service.

Removing the Cylinder Head on an Overhead Valve Engine

If an overhead valve engine is being serviced, the first step in removing the cylinder head is to remove the valve cover. See **Figure 16-20**. This should expose the rocker assembly. Remove the rocker arms as shown in **Figure 16-21**. Some engines have rocker arms that pivot on a rocker arm shaft. See **Figure 16-22**. To remove, loosen the adjusting screws, remove the retaining rings, and slide the rocker arms off the shaft.

After removing the rocker arms, pull the pushrods out of their guides. See **Figure 16-23**. Clean the pushrods and then check them for straightness by rolling them on a flat, machined surface. If they are bent, replace them. Do not try to straighten pushrods.

Goodheart-Willcox Publisher

Figure 16-20.
Remove the valve cover to expose the rocker assembly.

Goodheart-Willcox Publisher

Figure 16-21.
Remove the rocker arm locknut, rocker arm pivot, and rocker arm from the rocker arm stud.

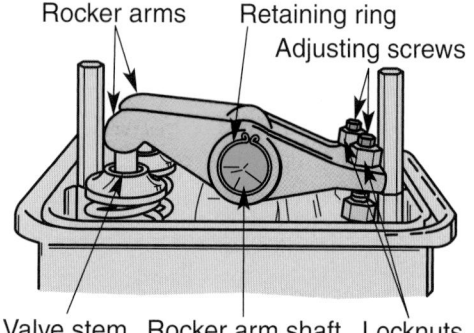

Tecumseh Products Co.

Figure 16-22.
Rocker arms on a rocker arm shaft can be removed by loosening the adjusting screws, removing retaining rings, and sliding rocker arms off the shaft.

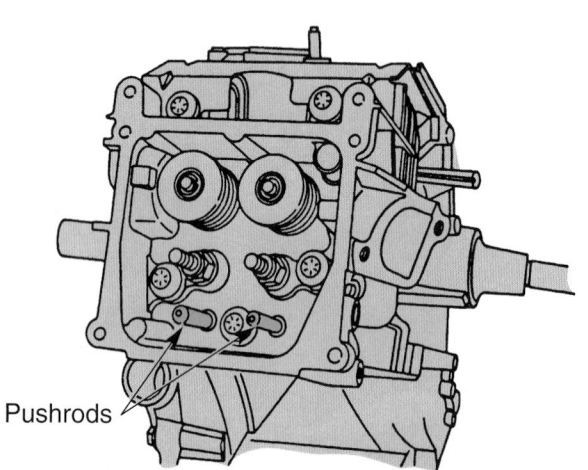

Briggs & Stratton Corp.

Figure 16-23.
Remove the pushrods by lifting them out of the holes. Check for straightness by rolling the rods on a flat surface.

It is a good idea to have two containers, one labeled "intake valve" and the other labeled "exhaust valve." As the rocker assemblies (and later the valves, springs, and keepers) are removed, they should be placed in the appropriate container. This will keep the valve parts organized so the valve train can be properly reassembled. Valve parts must be reinstalled in their original locations.

With the rocker assemblies removed from the head, all head bolts should be visible. Loosen and remove the head bolts following the manufacturer's recommended sequence. As each head bolt is removed, note its location and length so the proper size bolt can be reinstalled during engine reassembly. Then, pull the head from the cylinder. See **Figure 16-24**.

Removing the Crankcase Cover

Next, remove any rust, scale, or burrs from the drive (power takeoff) end of the crankshaft using emery cloth and a fine file as needed. Be careful not to damage the surface during this procedure. Next, tape the keyway on the drive end of the crankshaft, **Figure 16-25**. This will protect the oil seal from the sharp end of the keyway as the cover is removed.

Loosen and remove the bolts securing the crankcase cover. As each bolt is removed, note its location and length. When all of the bolts have been removed, carefully pull the crankcase cover

Goodheart-Willcox Publisher

Figure 16-24.
After removing the rocker assembly and pushrods, pull the cylinder head from the cylinder. If it is stuck, tap the underside of the cooling fins with a rubber mallet to loosen it.

Goodheart-Willcox Publisher

Figure 16-25.

Tape the keyway on the crankshaft so the oil seal will not be damaged by the sharp edges of the keyway when the crankcase cover is removed.

away from the crankcase. See **Figure 16-26**. If the crankcase cover hangs up, recheck the crankshaft for scoring or burrs and use emery cloth to smooth any damage found.

Note

On some engines, the oil seal and a retaining ring must be removed prior to pulling the crankcase cover.

Removing the Engine's Internal Components

With the crankcase cover removed, the engine's internal components are visible. Rotate the crankshaft

until it is at top dead center (TDC) on the compression stroke. Remove the oil slinger or centrifugal governor gear. The oil slinger or centrifugal governor gear is usually mounted on the camshaft. It may be held in place with a spring clip. See **Figure 16-27**.

Look for timing marks on the camshaft and crankshaft timing gears. If the gears are covered in sludge, wipe them clean with a lint-free rag. If no time marks can be found, scribe aligning marks on the crankshaft and camshaft timing gears with a sharp awl. Next, pull the camshaft from the engine. You may want to set the engine on its side when pulling the camshaft. This will prevent the valve lifters from falling out, which could scratch them. See **Figure 16-28**.

Note

If the engine is equipped with balance shafts, they should also have timing marks that align with the marks on the camshaft and crankshaft.

Next, remove the valve lifters, **Figure 16-29**. Keep track of which valve the lifter operates. You should have two separate containers, one labeled for the intake valve parts and one labeled for exhaust valve parts. As each part of the valve assembly is removed, it should be placed in the appropriate container. This will help to ensure that the valve parts are installed in their proper locations when the engine is reassembled. If the

Goodheart-Willcox Publisher

Figure 16-26.

Pull the cover free from the crankcase.

Governor gear/oil slinger

Goodheart-Willcox Publisher

Figure 16-27.

Remove the oil slinger or centrifugal governor gear.

Goodheart-Willcox Publisher

Figure 16-28.

After ensuring that there are visible timing marks, remove the camshaft from the engine.

Goodheart-Willcox Publisher

Figure 16-29.

Remove the valve lifters. Be sure to keep track of which lifter was removed from the exhaust valve and which was removed from the intake valve. The lifters must be reinstalled in the proper location.

engine is equipped with balance shafts, they should be removed at this point.

With the camshaft and lifters removed, check the piston rod and cap for alignment marks. These marks indicate how the cap fits on the piston rod, and how the piston rod should be installed on the crankshaft. If no marks are visible on the rod and cap, use a sharp punch to put small marks on matching sides of the rod and cap. After ensuring that the cap and rod are marked, remove the fasteners holding the cap to the rod, **Figure 16-30**, and remove the rod cap.

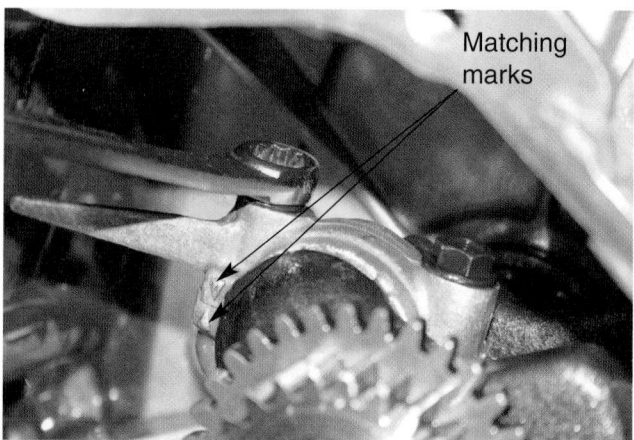

Matching marks

Goodheart-Willcox Publisher

Figure 16-30.

Make sure the rod and cap are clearly marked so they can be reinstalled properly. Then, remove the fasteners holding the cap in place.

Next, check the top of the cylinder for a wear ridge or carbon buildup that will interfere with piston removal. If there is a heavy ridge around the inside top of the cylinder, the piston rings will not pass the ridge without damage. See **Figure 16-31**. If the ridge is the result of carbon buildup at the top of the cylinder, it can be removed with emery cloth.

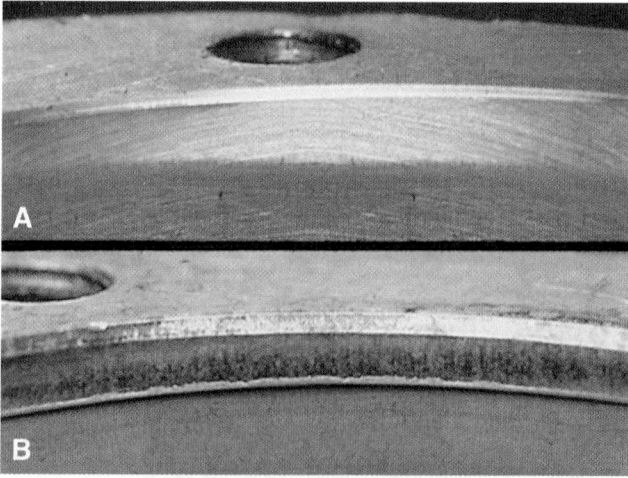

A

B

Goodheart-Willcox Publisher

Figure 16-31.

Check the top of the cylinder for a wear ridge. A—An engine with light or normal wear has a relatively smooth transition between the top of the cylinder and the ring travel area. B—Extreme cylinder wear results in a ridge that will interfere with piston removal. A ridge such as this must be reamed before the piston can be removed.

If the ridge is the result of extreme wear, a ridge reamer can be used to shave the ridge. Use extreme care when removing the ridge not to damage the cylinder. After every two or three revolutions of the reamer, stop and feel the cylinder wall. Stop reaming the ridge when the top portion of the cylinder blends smoothly with the lower portion.

Inspect the top of the piston for marks that can be used to ensure that the piston is reinstalled in the proper orientation. If there are no marks visible on the piston, use a felt-tip marker to draw an arrow pointing at the valves. Rotate the crankshaft to separate the rod from the crankshaft journal, then push the piston and rod assembly out through the top of the cylinder. See **Figure 16-32**.

Next, check the tapered end of the crankshaft for rust and burrs. Use emery cloth to clean up any roughness found. Remove the flywheel key and tape the keyway. Pull the crankshaft free from the main bearing. If the engine is equipped with a centrifugal governor, remove the governor follower arm.

Piston Damage and Its Causes

Pistons can be damaged in many ways. They should be cleaned, examined, and measured after removal. The type of damage and wear on the piston can indicate the cause of the engine failure. Steps can then be taken to ensure that the underlying cause of engine failure is corrected during the overhaul. **Figure 16-33** shows the most common types of damage found. Sometimes, pistons will have multiple types of damage in various combinations.

Most piston and cylinder damage can be traced to one or more of the following causes: lack of oil, use of the wrong oil or oil-fuel mixture, use of the incorrect type of gasoline, foreign particles in the cylinder, overheating caused by clogged cooling fins, excess carbon buildup in the cylinder exhaust ports, and improperly fitted rings and pistons.

Figure 16-33A shows scoring and light scuffing of both a piston and rings due to overheating. This occurs when high friction and combustion cause temperatures to approach the melting temperature of the piston materials. This type of damage can be caused by dirty cooling shroud and cylinder head fins, lack of cylinder lubrication, lean air-fuel mixture, improper bearing or piston clearance, or an overfilled crankcase causing fluid friction.

Figure 16-33B shows a piston with rings stuck and broken from lacquer, varnish, and carbon buildup, caused by abnormally high operating temperatures. This type of damage can result from overloading the engine, improper ignition timing, lean fuel mixture, clogged cooling fins, inadequate lubrication, or stale fuel.

Figure 16-33C shows vertical scratches on the ring faces and the piston, caused by the presence of abrasive particles. These particles can enter the engine through a damaged or improperly installed air cleaner, air leaks between the air filter and carburetor, or leaks in the gasket between the carburetor and block. They can also enter through air leaks around the carburetor's throttle or choke shafts or missing welch plugs in the carburetor body. In a newly overhauled engine, this type of damage can result if the cylinder is not properly cleaned after being bored or honed.

Compare the oil ring (bottom ring) in **Figure 16-33D** with the one in **Figure 16-33C**. The rails of the oil ring in **Figure 16-33D** are worn down to the drain holes, and the ring surface is flat. This type of wear results from extended use and possibly from abrasives in the engine.

The piston in **Figure 16-33E** has a burned top land resulting from detonation. Detonation is abnormal combustion which causes too much pressure and excessively high temperatures in the combustion chamber. Detonation is sometimes referred to as carbon knock, spark knock, or timing knock. It occurs when the air-fuel mixture ignites spontaneously and interferes with the normal combustion flame front. Detonation can result from

Goodheart-Willcox Publisher

Figure 16-32.

Push the piston and rod assembly out through the top of the cylinder. Note the notch on the flywheel side of the piston head.

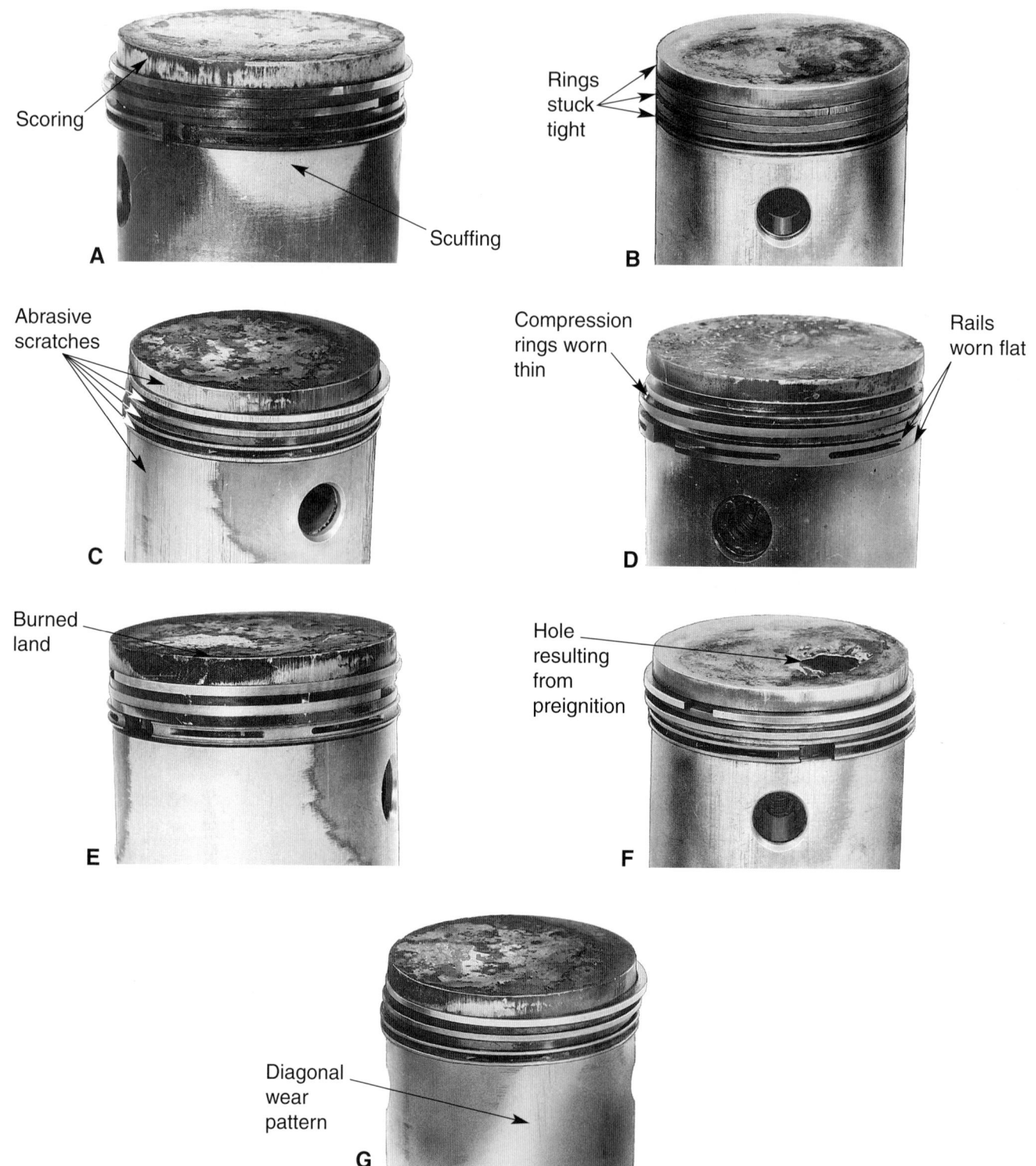

Tecumseh Products Co.

Figure 16-33.

Common types of piston damage. A—Piston scored and scuffed due to overheating. B—Piston rings are stuck due to lacquer, varnish, and carbon buildup, resulting from high temperatures. C—Vertical scratches on ring faces and piston are caused by abrasive materials entering the engine. D—This piston has extremely worn rings because of long use and possible abrasives. E—A burned top land results from detonation. F—The hole burned through this piston head was caused by preignition. G—A diagonal wear pattern indicates improper alignment of the connecting rod and piston.

a lean fuel mixture, low octane fuel, overly advanced ignition timing, or engine lugging. It can also be caused by excessively high compression resulting from carbon deposits on piston and cylinder head or a milled cylinder head.

Damage resulting from preignition is shown in **Figure 16-33F**. *Preignition* is the burning of the air-fuel mixture before normal ignition occurs. Preignition creates a pinging sound, resulting from a severe internal shock. It is accompanied by vibration, detonation, and power loss. If allowed to continue, it could cause severe damage to the piston, rings, and valves.

Preignition can result from internal carbon deposits that remain red hot and ignite the air fuel as it is brought into the cylinder. It may also be the result of a spark plug with too hot of a temperature range or a spark plug with a cracked insulator. If the valve margins are too narrow, the thin edges of the valves can heat up and cause preignition.

If the connecting rod and piston are not aligned, a diagonal wear pattern will show on the piston skirts, **Figure 16-33G**. This condition can occur, along with poor ring contact, if the cylinder is bored at an angle other than 90° to the crankshaft. The misalignment can also result in rapid piston wear, uneven piston wear, and excessive oil consumption.

Severe piston damage can be caused by foreign objects carelessly left inside an engine during reconditioning or objects that enter the engine through the carburetor, such as a throttle or choke plate screw. Always work carefully. Make sure all fasteners are tightened to the proper torque specification and thread lock is applied where appropriate.

Removing the Valve Assemblies on an L-Head Engine

The engine valve assembly includes the valve, valve spring, and one or more retainers, **Figure 16-34**. Once the cylinder head has been removed, remove the valve by compressing the valve spring with a compressor. See **Figure 16-35**. Remove the valve spring retainer from the groove in the valve stem using a pair of pliers. See **Figure 16-36**. Then, slowly release pressure on the spring and remove the compressor. The valve can be pulled out the top and the spring taken from the side. Keep the parts for each valve separated so

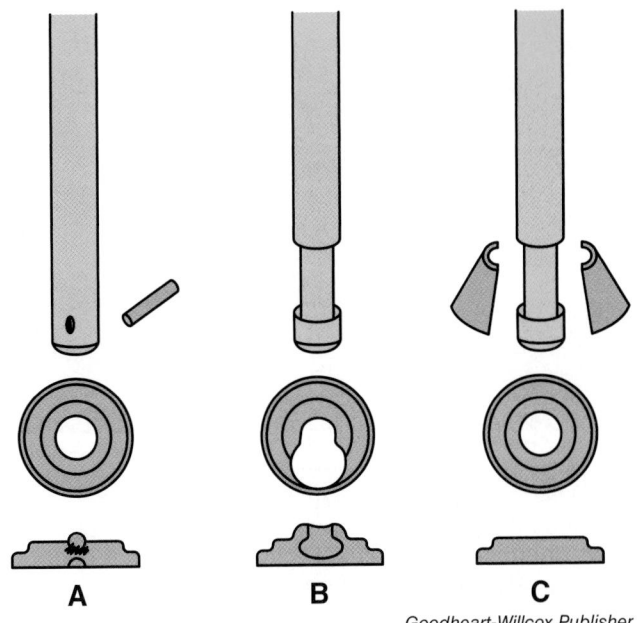

Goodheart-Willcox Publisher

Figure 16-34.
Three common types of valve spring retainers are shown here. A—Pin-type. B—Washer-type. C—Split keeper-type.

they can be reinstalled in the proper location during engine reassembly.

Warning

Always wear safety glasses when removing valves. The spring-loaded parts can fly apart unexpectedly during disassembly, causing eye injury.

Goodheart-Willcox Publisher

Figure 16-35.
A valve spring compressor squeezes the spring to uncover keepers in the valve stem.

Goodheart-Willcox Publisher

Figure 16-36.

When spring is fully compressed, use pliers to remove valve keepers. Then, release valve compressor and remove valve, spring, and retainers.

Removing the Valve Assemblies on an Overhead Valve Engine

To remove the valves in an overhead valve system, place the cylinder head on a workbench and place small wooden blocks under the valve faces to hold them in place. If there are wear buttons or caps on the valve stems, remove them.

Note

When removing valves and valve springs, identify the parts to prevent interchanging them during reassembly.

On some engines, you can compress the valve springs by pressing on the spring retainers with your thumbs. Push the spring retainer toward the large end of its slot and release pressure. See **Figure 16-37**. Remove the retainer, spring, and valve stem seals. Discard the seals.

If the valve springs cannot be compressed with your thumbs, a special valve spring compressing tool may be necessary. See **Figure 16-38**. In this illustration, split-type retainers are used to secure the valve springs to the valve stems.

After the valve assemblies have been removed from the cylinder head, the head should be thoroughly cleaned and inspected. The head is cleaned

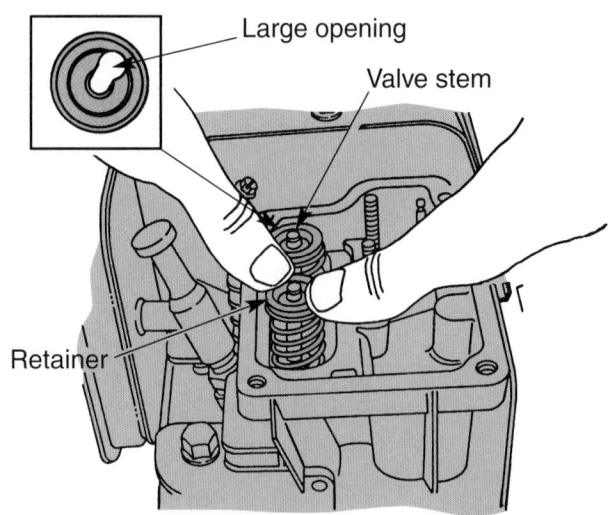

Briggs & Stratton Corp.

Figure 16-37.

Compress the valve spring and move the retainer to the large opening to release. A wooden block placed under the valve head prevents valve movement.

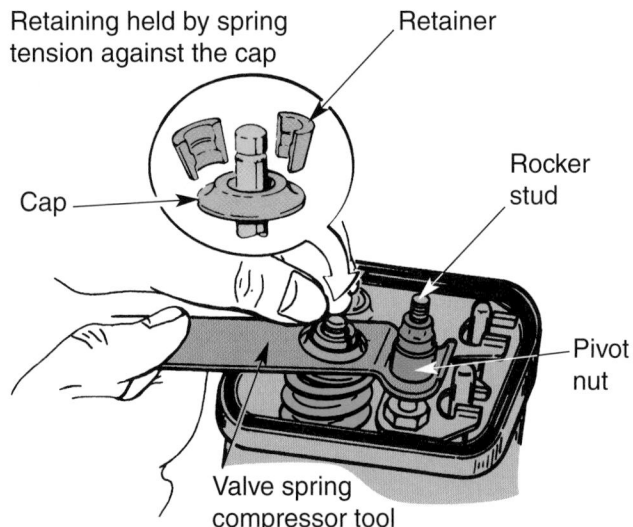

Tecumseh Products Co.

Figure 16-38.

Compressing the valve spring with a valve spring compressor to remove the split-type retainers.

and inspected the same way as an L-head, which was explained earlier in the chapter. When inspecting an overhead valve cylinder head for cracks, check the area around the valve seats very closely. Many cracks start in this area.

Summary

Engine work should be performed in a clean, well-lighted area. An engine stand can be used if necessary. Always refer to a manufacturer's service manual for exact dimensions and specifications.

Before removing the engine from an implement, look for causes of engine problems. If wires need to be disconnected before removing the engine, flag the ends of the wires with masking tape. Remove the spark plug to avoid accidental firing.

After the engine has been removed, unbolt the starter unit, exhaust manifold pipe, muffler, carburetor, intake manifold pipe, fuel tank, and fuel lines. Check all gasket surfaces for defects. Sketch or photograph the governor linkages and then remove them. Remove the air shroud, blower housing, and baffles to expose the flywheel. Remove the flywheel retaining nut and starter clutch, then use a proper puller to remove the flywheel.

Clean the outer engine parts by scraping off loose debris and soaking the components in solvent. Some parts, such as the ignition module, should not be immersed in solvent.

Remove the cylinder head. If the engine has overhead valves, remove the rocker arms and pushrods before removing the head. Next, loosen the bolts holding the crankcase cover. Tape the crankshaft keyway, and pull the cover off the engine. Remove the governor gear or oil slinger. Align the timing marks on the camshaft and crankshaft timing gears. Pull the camshaft free and then remove the lifters. Check the piston rod and cap for alignment marks, and then remove the cap. Make sure that the top of the piston is marked for alignment and then push the piston and rod assembly out through the top of the cylinder. Remove the valve assemblies to complete the disassembly.

Review Questions

Answer the following questions using the information provided in this chapter.

1. Why should a service manual always be referred to during an engine overhaul?

2. Excessive vibration could be caused by _____.
   A. loose engine mounts
   B. pulleys out of line
   C. worn drive belts
   D. All of the above.

3. Before removing an engine from an implement, you must always _____.
   A. drain the oil
   B. disconnect the ignition switch
   C. remove the spark plug
   D. crank the engine slowly to remove all the fuel from the cylinder(s)

4. Milky oil is an indication that_____.
   A. the engine has overheated
   B. the wrong viscosity oil has been used
   C. the engine is running rich
   D. water has gotten into the oil

5. Before a carburetor is removed from an engine, what step should be taken to help you remember how the linkage is reattached?

6. *True or False?* The best way to remove a flywheel is to strike the flywheel nut with a hammer while applying upward force with a pry bar.

7. *True or False?* Rocker arms and pushrods should be removed from an overhead engine before the cylinder head is removed from the cylinder block.

8. How is crankshaft endplay measured?

9. Explain how the piston is removed if there is a heavy ridge at the top of the cylinder in an integral cylinder block and crankcase type engine.

10. Which of the following parts should be marked so they can be reinstalled in the proper orientation?
    A. The piston head and connecting rod.
    B. The camshaft timing gear and crankshaft timing gear.
    C. The connecting rod and rod cap.
    D. All of the above.

Suggested Activities

1. Design a well-organized workbench and tool panel for repairing small engines.
2. Completely disassemble an engine that has been in service for many hours and is in need of reconditioning.
3. Inspect disassembled parts for wear or damage. Discuss possible causes.
4. Ream a cylinder ridge.

Cylinder, Crankshaft, and Piston Service

Learning Objectives

After studying this chapter, you will be able to:

- Describe how to inspect a cylinder for damage and measure a cylinder for wear, taper, and out-of-roundness.
- Explain the difference between boring and honing and identify when each process should be used.
- Summarize the steps in inspecting a crankshaft for damage and measuring it for wear.
- Describe the steps in main bearing service.
- Summarize the steps involved in piston, rod, and ring service.

Key Terms

boring machine
cylinder taper
inside micrometer

out-of-roundness
reboring
telescoping gauge

Cylinder Reconditioning

Cylinder reconditioning is an important part of restoring an engine to good operational condition. Reconditioning consists of inspection, measurement, and honing of the cylinder. If the cylinder is damaged, the reconditioning process includes the additional step of reboring the cylinder to a larger diameter.

Cylinder Inspection

With the piston out of the engine, inspect the cylinder block. Look for areas of scuffing or scoring on the cylinder wall. Inspect the cylinder wall and block for signs of overheating. Hot spots in the cylinder can result in discolored areas on the cylinder wall. Severe overheating can cause valve seat inserts in the block to loosen. See **Figure 17-1**.

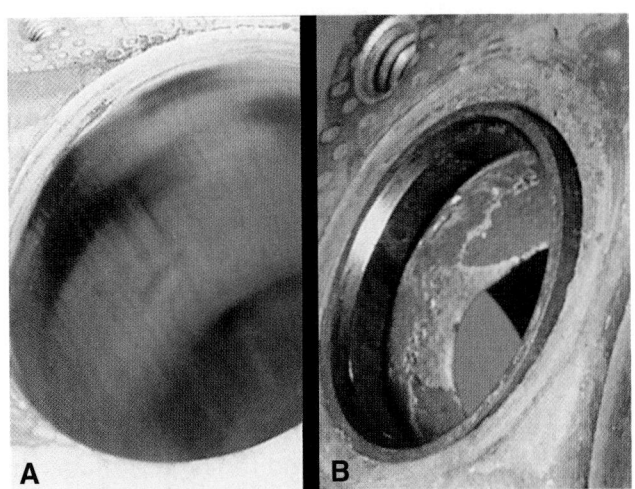

A   **B**

Goodheart-Willcox Publisher

Figure 17-1.

Inspect the cylinder for signs of overheating. A—Hot spots can cause discoloration on the cylinder wall. B—Extreme overheating can loosen valve seat inserts.

Next, check for nicks or grooves in the crankcase cover and cylinder head gasket surfaces. Inspect the exterior of the cylinder for cracks and chipped or broken cooling fins. Examine the head bolt holes and spark plug holes for damaged or stripped threads. Depending on the extent of damage found, the engine block or cylinder head may need to be replaced.

A worn cylinder has a narrow, unworn ridge at the top. The bottom of this ridge indicates the extent of the top piston ring travel. Right below the ridge is the area where most cylinder wear occurs. The wear will be the greatest on two opposite sides of the cylinder, 90° from the crankshaft centerline. The cylinder, therefore, wears into an oval shape, known as *out-of-roundness*. This increased wear is due to several things:

- Less lubrication at this portion of the cylinder wall.
- The diluting effect of raw gas on the engine oil.
- The pressure that builds up behind the rings at their highest position.

Below the point where cylinder diameter is the greatest, cylinder wear lessens rapidly. Because of this wear pattern, there is a gradual taper toward the bottom of the ring travel. This is known as *cylinder taper*. Below ring travel there is almost no wear. This lack of wear results because this area is well lubricated and only receives light wall pressure from the piston skirt.

Cylinder Measurement

If the cylinder wall looks smooth and free of scuff and score marks, you are ready to measure the cylinder for wear and out-of-roundness.

Finding the amount of cylinder taper is the first important measurement in determining cylinder condition. Cylinder taper is the difference in diameter at top of the cylinder and bottom of cylinder. To determine taper, measure the cylinder diameter below the bottom of ring travel. Then, measure it at the top of ring travel, just below the ring ridge. The difference between the largest diameter reading at the top of the cylinder and the largest diameter reading at the bottom of ring travel is an accurate indication of the amount of cylinder taper. The taper measurements should be taken both parallel and at right angles to the crankshaft to determine the greatest amount of wear and out-of-roundness. See **Figure 17-2**.

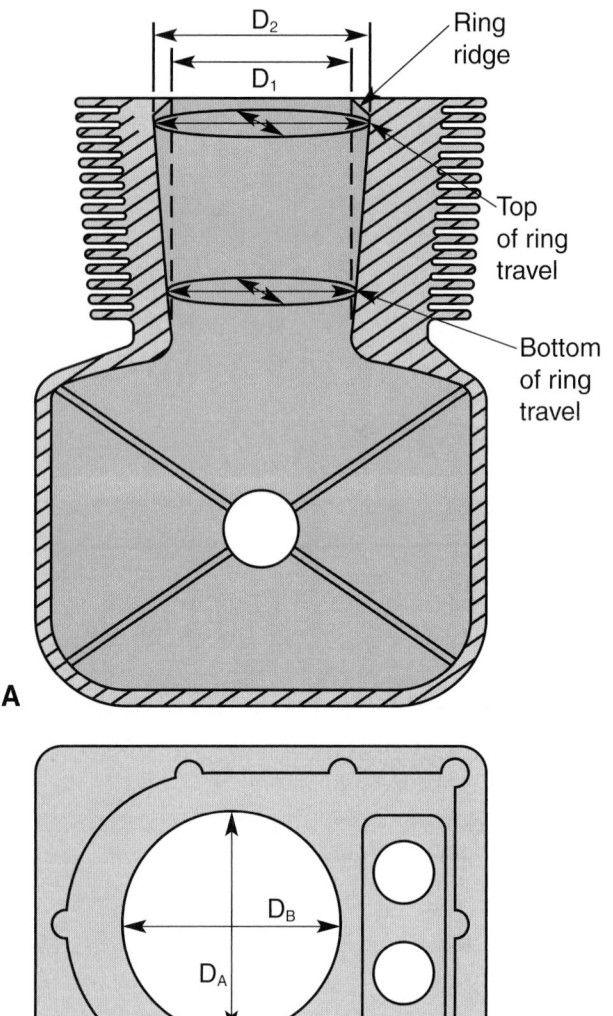

Goodheart-Willcox Publisher

Figure 17-2.

The cylinder must be measured at the top and bottom of ring travel to determine cylinder out-of-round and taper. The measurements should be made parallel to the crankshaft and perpendicular to the crankshaft. A—The difference between D_2 and D_1 represents the cylinder taper. B—The difference between D_A and D_B represents the cylinder out-of-round.

The amount of acceptable taper depends on engine design, its general condition, and the type of service in which it is used. There are no rules that apply to all engines regarding cylinder taper. The manufacturer, however, may set a limit. Beyond a certain point, the engine manufacturer will advise reboring the cylinder or cylinder replacement.

Out-of-roundness for small engines is generally limited to .005″ or .006″. Beyond this limit, engine performance is greatly reduced. The cylinder out-of-roundness is equal to the largest difference between any two of the diameter measurements.

Several methods can be used to measure cylinders. **Figure 17-3** shows an *inside micrometer* equipped with an extension handle. This precision instrument must be carefully adjusted to cylinder size to provide the exact diameter of the cylinder.

Figure 17-4 shows a *telescoping gauge* being used to measure cylinder size. The gauge head is spring loaded to expand when the thumbscrew is released. Once positioned in the cylinder, the gauge is locked in place by tightening the thumbscrew. Then, it is removed from the cylinder. An outside micrometer is used to measure the length of the telescoping head. This measurement represents the cylinder size (diameter).

The steps required to recondition the cylinder are determined by its condition. If the surface of the cylinder is not damaged, and if taper and out-of-round readings are within specified limits, only a light deglazing with a flexible hone may be needed. The engine block must be thoroughly washed afterward.

Reboring the Cylinder

There are several ways to repair a cylinder that shows too much wear. Repair procedures depend

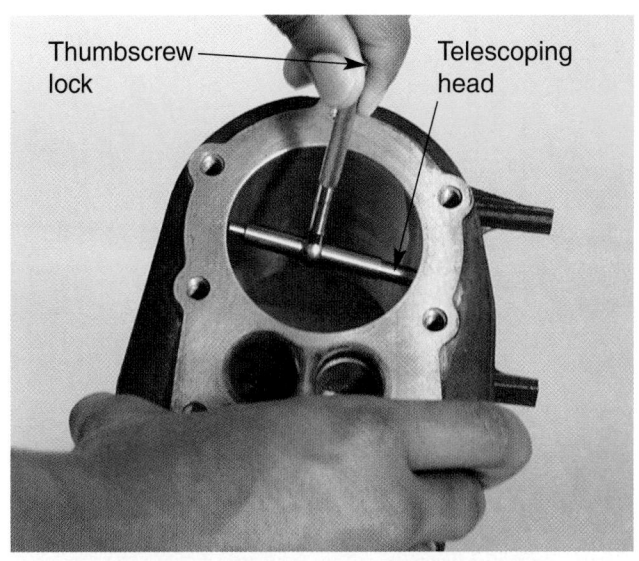

Goodheart-Willcox Publisher

Figure 17-4.

A telescoping gauge can also be used to measure cylinder diameter. The gauge is adjusted to cylinder size and is measured with an outside micrometer.

on engine type. Some engines have chrome-plated, aluminum cylinders. See **Figure 17-5**. Worn or damaged cylinders of this type should be replaced with a new cylinder. Other engines have a pressed-in, flanged, cast-iron cylinder sleeve that can be removed and replaced with a new sleeve. See **Figure 17-6**. A cast-in sleeve or a solid cast iron or uncoated aluminum cylinder can usually be rebored to a larger size. See **Figure 17-7**.

Two problems must be solved when *reboring* a cylinder. The first is to resize and maintain original

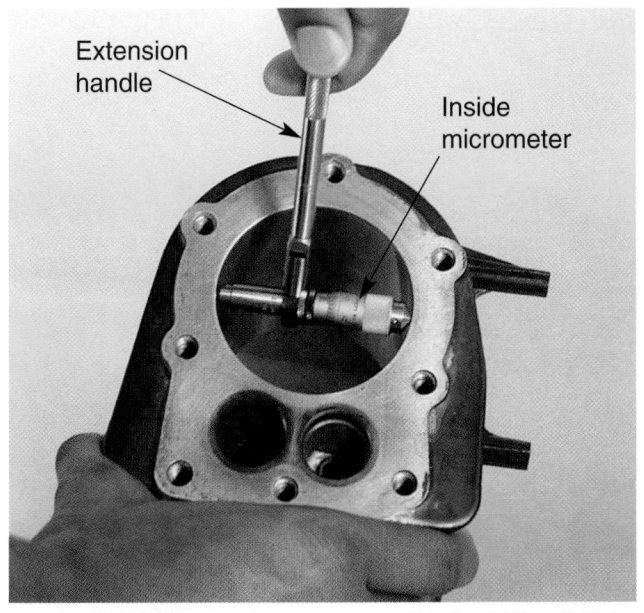

Goodheart-Willcox Publisher

Figure 17-3.

An inside micrometer can be used to measure cylinder diameter.

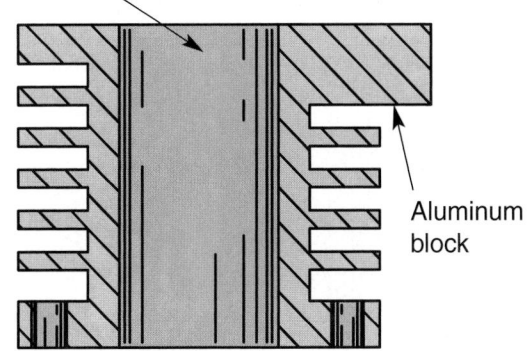

Goodheart-Willcox Publisher

Figure 17-5.

Special cylinder construction with a chrome-plated surface is shown.

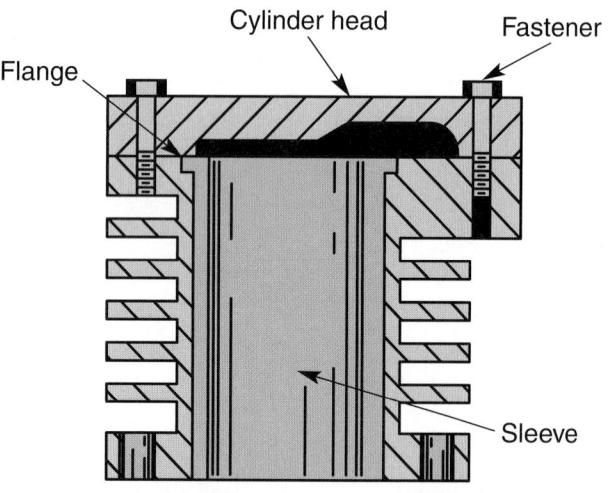

Figure 17-6.

A pressed-in sleeve are typically secured by a flange on the upper end. The cylinder head holds the sleeve in place.

alignment while producing a round, straight bore. The second is to produce the correct cylinder wall finish.

Cylinders are usually rebored in .010″ increments. If the cylinder is being rebored for the first time, its diameter will be increased .010″ over the standard size. If this does not *clean up* the cylinder (remove imperfections), the next step is .020″ over the standard size. When replacing pistons and rings, order .010″ or .020″ over standard size to match the new cylinder bore.

Note

Ensure that an oversize piston and rings are available before reboring a cylinder.

A *boring machine* can be used to resize the bore on a small engine. In setting up the machine, the engine block or cylinder block is clamped in place below the boring head. The cutter is adjusted to the correct diameter for the new bore.

An electric motor drives the spindle to rotate the cutter. The feed rate controls the distance the cutter advances into the bore during each cutter revolution and can be changed by moving the feed dial.

Boring the cylinder will produce a straight, round bore. However, the boring operation does not produce a satisfactory surface finish. The boring tool leaves microscopic furrows and surface fractures, so it is recommended that the new bore be a minimum of .0025″ smaller than the desired final cylinder size. This additional material will be removed when the cylinder is honed to the desired finish.

Honing the Cylinder

Honing is an abrasive finishing process that removes the boring tool marks and surface fractures. Honing also produces the desired cylinder wall finish. The honing process is used to refinish the cylinder wall after boring, or if new rings are

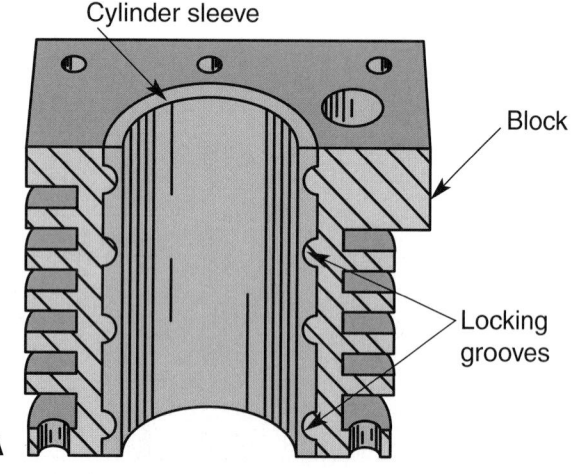
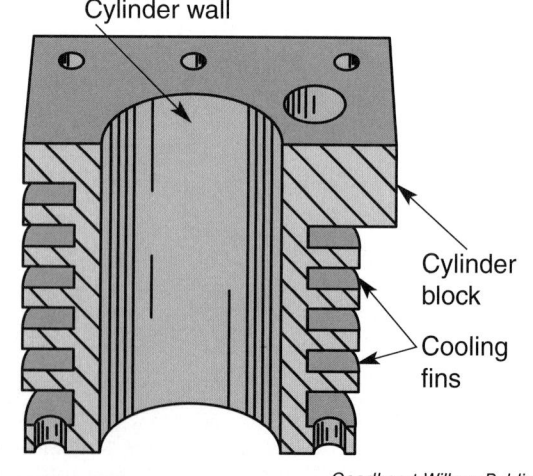

Figure 17-7.

Cast iron cylinders can typically be rebored. A—Some cast iron cylinders are cast in place in an aluminum block. B—Most cast iron or aluminum cylinders are part of the engine block.

going to be installed. The smoothness of the finish depends on the grit size of the stones used.

The purpose of honing is to create a surface in the cylinder that promotes ring break-in. The process scratches shallow crosshatch lines in the cylinder wall. As the engine operates, these lines trap oil, providing additional lubrication to the rings during the crucial break-in period.

> **Note**
>
> Some rings are coated with materials like chromium or molybdenum that alter their break-in characteristics. In these cases, honing may not be recommended. Likewise, some aluminum cylinders should not be honed. Always check the piston ring and engine manufacturer's recommendations before honing a cylinder.

Ideally, a newly honed cylinder will wear smooth at just about the same rate the new piston rings wear in. When this break-in process is complete, both the cylinder walls and the piston rings will be smooth and should last for hundreds of hours of engine operation.

To hone a cylinder, begin by installing the hone in an electric drill. The drill should be held perfectly in line with the cylinder's centerline so the stones contact the cylinder wall squarely. An electric drill is used to rotate the cylinder hone. In operation, the assembly is slowly and steadily moved in and out of the cylinder. See **Figure 17-8**. Stones should not be permitted to extend out of the cylinder end, as uneven wearing of the stones may occur. For best results, the honing process should produce a fine surface pattern, like that shown in **Figure 17-9**.

> **Note**
>
> The honing process cannot correct out-of-round or taper in a cylinder. For this reason, the honing process should *not* be used to resize a cylinder.

After reboring and honing a two-stroke engine cylinder, use a piece of fine emery cloth to remove any burrs that may have developed around the ports. After honing any cylinder, wash the cylinder walls and the block thoroughly with soapy water and a brush (do not use a rag). Dry the block with compressed air. To prevent cylinder rusting, apply a light coat of SAE 10 oil.

> **Caution**
>
> Be sure to wash the cylinder and crankcase thoroughly. Any metal or abrasive particles carelessly left in the engine from the boring or honing process can damage the newly rebuilt engine quickly.

Crankshaft and Main Bearing Service

Tremendous forces are placed on the crankshaft and main bearings during engine operation. These forces can lead to wear and damage that can result

Goodheart-Willcox Publisher

Figure 17-8.

The abrasive stones of the cylinder hone are spring loaded, and stay in constant contact with the cylinder wall as the hone is rotated.

Goodheart-Willcox Publisher

Figure 17-9.

A fine cross-hatched surface pattern is created by the in-and-out motion of the revolving hone.

in engine failure. The next step in engine reconditioning is to inspect the crankshaft and main bearings to determine whether they can be reused or must be replaced. If these parts are not properly reconditioned, the newly overhauled engine will fail quickly.

Inspecting the Crankshaft

If ball bearings or tapered roller bearings are installed on the crankshaft, they should be removed using the procedure recommended by the manufacturer. Usually this is done using a bearing separator and puller to pull the bearing from the shaft or an arbor press to press the bearing from the shaft.

With any bearings removed, inspect the crankshaft journals for signs of discoloration, metal transfer, scoring, and wear. The pattern of wear can provide vital clues about the cause of engine failure. Discoloration indicates that the surfaces have overheated. This is commonly caused by a lack of lubrication. Scoring or metal transfer on multiple bearing surfaces typically indicate that the engine was operated with insufficient lubrication, **Figure 17-10**.

If the damage is limited to a single bearing surface, it may have been caused by a defect in the bearing or crankshaft or improper engine assembly. If the damage is limited to the main bearing journal on the power-take-off end of the crankshaft, it may

have been caused by excessive loading, such as that resulting from an improperly aligned or over tensioned drive belt. See **Figure 17-11**.

In some cases, light metal transfer can be cleaned up by polishing the journal with a strip of fine emery cloth. Use only a light pressure and rotate the strip around the entire journal to avoid creating a flat spot on the journal. Polish the journal just enough to remove the transferred metal.

Run your thumbnail over the entire bearing surface of the journal. If there are any imperfections that are deep enough to catch your thumbnail, the crankshaft must be replaced or sent to a machine shop to be reconditioned. To recondition the crankshaft, the machine shop will grind down and polish the crankshaft journals to a smaller diameter. The reconditioned crankshaft must be used with undersize bearings, so make sure that undersize bearings are available for the engine before having the crankshaft reconditioned.

Note

In certain cases, a machine shop can weld a layer of metal to the journals and then machine the journals down to their original size. However, this process is expensive and not cost-effective in most cases.

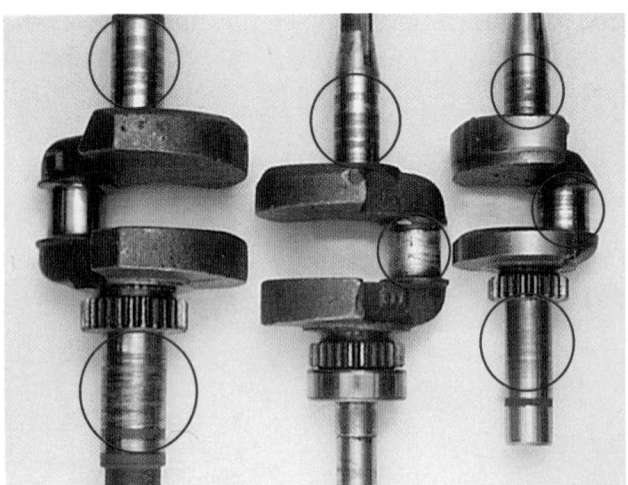

Goodheart-Willcox Publisher

Figure 17-10.

Scoring or metal transfer on multiple bearing surfaces is typically caused by operating the engine with insufficient lubrication.

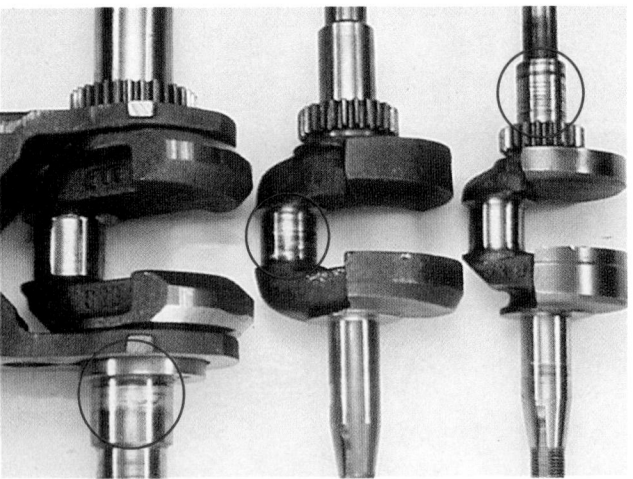

Goodheart-Willcox Publisher

Figure 17-11.

Scoring or metal transfer on a single bearing surface can be caused by a defect in the bearing or crankshaft, bearing failure, or improper assembly. Damage on the main bearing journal on the power-take-off side of the crankshaft (far right) may have been caused by improper loading, such as an overtensioned drive belt.

Make sure that the keyways in both ends of the crankshaft are not damaged, deformed, or excessively worn. If the crankshaft has keyway damage, it must be replaced. Carefully use a fine file to remove any minor burrs on the edges of the keyway.

If any defects are found during the initial inspection of the crankshaft, the crankshaft must be either replaced or reconditioned. In many cases, it is more cost-effective to simply replace the crankshaft than to recondition it. Before deciding to recondition the crankshaft, make sure that undersize bearings are available for that engine. If the crankshaft passes the initial visual inspection, it must be measured for wear to determine whether it can be reused.

Green Tech

Recycling

Shops generate many solid wastes, such as paper cartons, plastic oil containers, and used parts. Paper and plastic can be recycled at local recycling drop-off sites. Many municipalities pick up recyclable paper and plastic. Used metal parts can be sent to scrap recyclers for the value of their metal content. This is especially true of iron and steel, aluminum, and copper.

Measuring Crankshaft Journals

The forces placed on crankshaft by the reciprocating piston assembly and loads placed on the crankshaft itself cause wear on the crankshaft journals. The force applied to crankshaft by the rod assembly is typically greatest at the top of the journal during the downstroke and greatest at the bottom of the journal during the upstroke. These forces cause the crankshaft journals to wear. Because the forces are nonuniform, they can wear the journals out-of-round.

The crankshaft journals must be measured to determine their overall wear, but also to make sure that they are not tapered or out-of-round. **Figure 17-12** illustrates the method of measuring the bearing surfaces on a crankshaft with a micrometer. Measurements must be taken in at least two positions on each journal, 90° to each other. If any of the dimensions are smaller than specified by the manufacturer, or if there are any score marks, the crankshaft must be reconditioned or replaced.

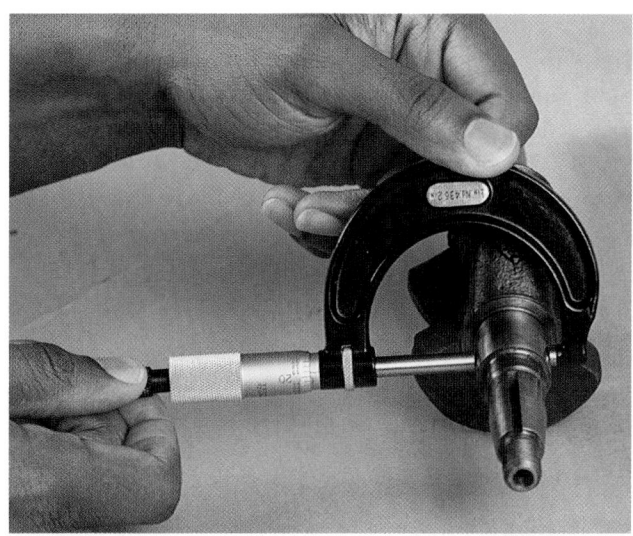

Goodheart-Willcox Publisher

Figure 17-12.

A micrometer is required to accurately measure bearing surface diameter on a crankshaft.

Inspecting the Main Bearings

Engines may be equipped with plain (integral friction-type), renewable bushing, caged needle, tapered roller, or ball bearings. Because the different bearing types have different loading capacities, some engines are equipped with one type of main bearing on the flywheel side of the crankshaft and a different type on the power take off side of the crankshaft. Caged needle bearings, tapered roller bearings, and ball bearings should be replaced during an engine overhaul. Plain and bushing-type bearings should be inspected for wear and damage, and reconditioned or replaced as needed.

Caged Needle Bearings

Caged needle bearings are used as main bearings on some small two-stroke engines. These bearings are typically held in place in the crankcase or cover by a press fit or retainers. These bearings should be removed and replaced any time the engine is overhauled. The bearing assembly is typically removed from the crankcase or cover by driving it out with a bushing driver or by pressing it out. Keep the old bearing assembly so it can be compared with the replacement bearing.

Tapered Roller Bearings

Tapered roller main bearings are typically used in engines that are designed to operate under heavier loads. Usually, the outer race, or cup, is held in the crankcase or cover by a press fit or retainers. The bearing cone (consisting of the inner race, cage, and bearings) is pressed onto the crankshaft. The outer race is removed by removing the retainers or by pressing the cone out of the cover or crankcase. The bearing cone is removed from the crankshaft using a bearing separator and puller or an arbor press. Keep the old bearing to compare to the replacement.

Note

The outer race and the bearing cone must always be replaced as a matched set. Never reuse either part of the bearing assembly.

Roller Bearings

Ball bearings are found on many engines. This type of bearing may be pressed onto the crankshaft, pressed into crankcase or cover, or held in the crankcase or cover with retainers. Use a bearing separator and puller to remove a ball bearing from a crankshaft. To remove a ball bearing from the crankcase or cover, press it out with an arbor press or remove the retainers, depending on the design. Always keep the old bearing so it can be compared to the replacement bearing.

Plain and Bushing-Type Bearings

On many small engines, the main bearings are simply machined bores or pressed-in bushings in the crankcase halves. The surface of these bores or bushings must be inspected for signs of metal transfer, scoring, and abrasive wear. See **Figure 17-13**. If any damage is found, the surfaces will need to be reconditioned. In the case of integral plain bearings, reconditioning consists of reaming the bearing bore and installing a new bearing bushing. If the crankshaft journal was ground during the reconditioning process, an undersize bushing must be installed. In the case of bushing-type main bearings, the old bushing must be driven out and a new bushing installed. Again, if the crankshaft was reconditioned, an undersize bushing must be installed.

If the bearing surface appears to be free from damage, it must be measured for excessive wear. Measure the inside diameter of the main bearing with a telescoping gauge. See **Figure 17-14**. Lock the

Goodheart-Willcox Publisher

Figure 17-13.
Check the bearing surface for scoring and metal transfer.

gauge, remove it from the bearing, and measure the telescoping head with a micrometer. Write down the reading and compare it to the bearing reject size listed in the manufacturer's service manual. If the bearing measurement is larger than the reject size, a bushing will need to be installed to restore proper clearance.

If the bearing measurement does not exceed the manufacturer's reject size, the bearing may not require service.

Note

If a manufacturer specifies a main bearing clearance specification rather than a bearing reject size, the bearing clearance can be determined by subtracting the diameter of the crankshaft journal measurement from the bearing measurement.

Piston Assembly Service

Proper piston, ring, and rod condition are absolutely essential to proper engine operation. If the engine is being reconditioned because of compression problems, reboring and/or honing of the cylinders is usually necessary. This should be followed by a thorough inspection of all parts in the piston assembly.

To do the job well, the small engine technician must understand the stresses to which a piston and its rings are subjected. A technician must also

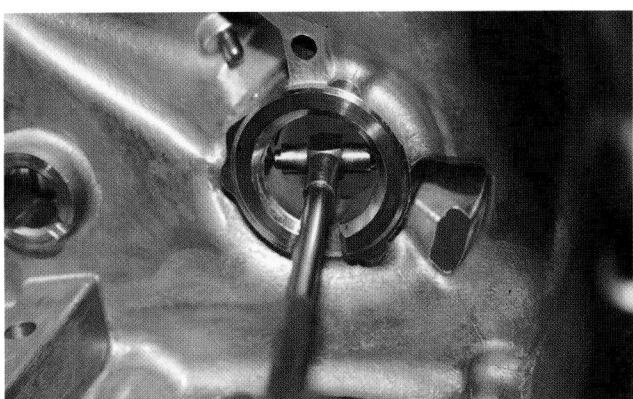

Goodheart-Willcox Publisher

Figure 17-14.

Measuring the diameter of a plain main bearing with a telescoping gauge.

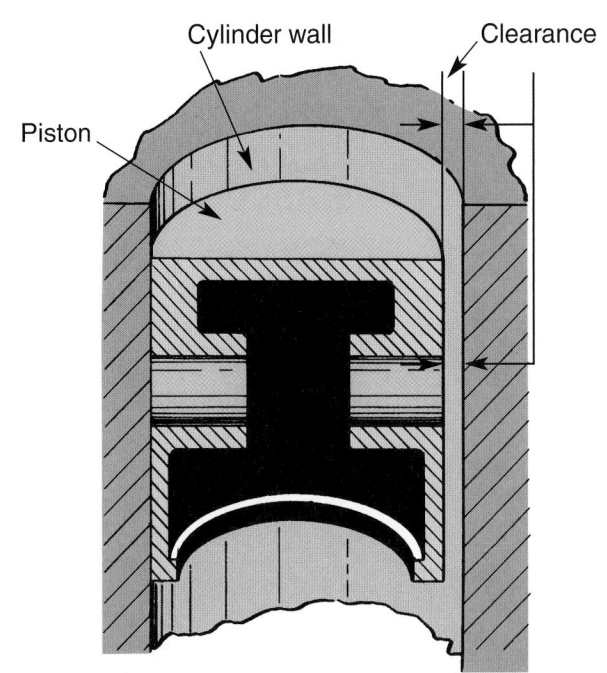

Cylinder wall   Clearance

Piston

Goodheart-Willcox Publisher

Figure 17-15.

Sufficient clearance must be allowed between the piston skirt and cylinder wall to permit adequate lubrication and to allow for expansion of parts due to high temperatures.

know the kinds of materials they are made from. Lastly, a technician must know what to do to put these parts back into top shape and to reassemble them for efficient, long-lasting engine operation.

The condition of the rings and pistons can be determined by inspecting the parts during disassembly of the engine. Any damage or excessive wear in these parts can result in low compression, blow-by, oil pumping, and fouled plugs. If the cylinder was not resized in the overhaul process, pistons and rods that are not damaged or excessively worn can be reused. However, piston rings should always be replaced during an overhaul. If the cylinder was resized by boring or honing, the piston and rings must be replaced with an oversize piston and rings.

Checking Piston Clearance

The piston is subjected to high temperatures, causing it to expand during operation. To allow for this increase in size, there must be a specific amount of clearance between the piston skirt and cylinder wall.

The cylinder also expands, but not as much as the piston. Normal clearance must be great enough to allow for lubrication and piston expansion. Different engines have different clearances. The amount depends upon engine design and use. Most small engines call for .003″ to .005″ piston-to-cylinder wall clearance. See **Figure 17-15**.

Piston clearance is determined by measuring the diameter of the piston skirt with a micrometer

and subtracting the value from the measured diameter of the cylinder. The piston should be measured at 90° to the piston pin bore, and about 1/2″ up from the bottom of the piston skirt. See **Figure 17-16**. If the piston clearance is too great, the piston must be replaced. If the piston clearance is

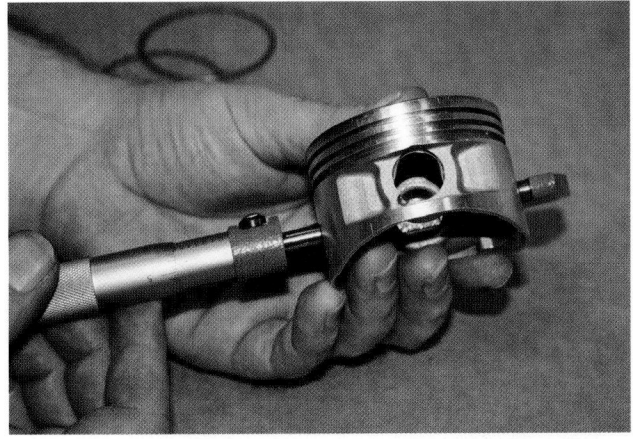

Goodheart-Willcox Publisher

Figure 17-16.

Measure piston skirt diameter 90° from the piston pin bore and 1/2″ from the bottom of the skirt.

too small (after reboring and oversizing the piston) the cylinder must be rehoned to provide the proper clearance.

Ring Side Clearance

The ring grooves must be carefully examined for wear and carbon buildup. If the grooves are worn, the ring will not seat properly, therefore the piston must be replaced. Also inspect the piston ring grooves for carbon buildup. Make sure that the oil return holes in the oil control ring groove are clear. See **Figure 17-17**.

Piston ring grooves are typically cleaned with a special tool having different size scrapers that are pulled around the grooves. The grooves can also be cleaned with a broken section of old ring. The end of the ring segment should be filed to a point so that it can effectively remove carbon buildup. Be careful not to gouge the groove.

Piston rings must have the right amount of side clearance, which permits them to move in and out in the groove while exerting tension on the cylinder wall. Side clearance also provides space for adequate lubrication and heat expansion. After cleaning any buildup from the ring grooves, check ring side clearance.

Side clearance is checked by inserting a new ring into the ring groove, and then inserting a feeler gauge into the gap between the side of the groove and the ring, **Figure 17-18**. The largest

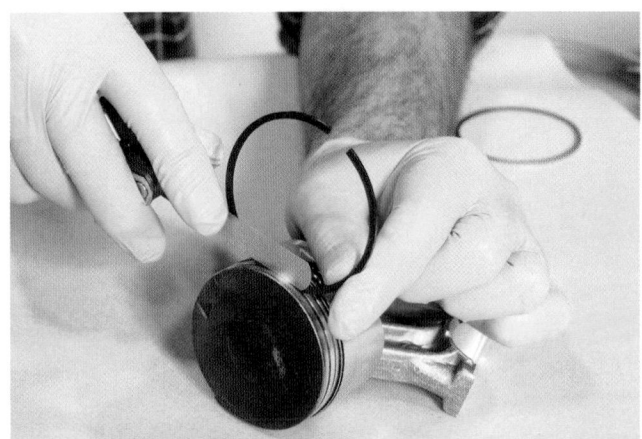

Goodheart-Willcox Publisher

Figure 17-18.

Ring side clearance is checked with a piston ring and a feeler gauge. The thickest feeler gauge blade that will fit between the walls of the ring groove and the ring equals the side clearance.

feeler gauge blade that will fit between the ring and groove wall is equal to the ring side clearance. If the side clearance is too great or the groove is damaged, the piston must be replaced.

Removing Piston Pins

Most piston pins fit snugly in the piston. If the pin turns by hand, inspect it for wear. If snap rings or other retainers are used to hold the piston pin in place, they must be removed. Some piston pin retainers are formed spring-steel wire; others are stamped flat spring steel. The two common methods of removing the wire-type snap rings are with a screwdriver or with needle nose pliers. See **Figure 17-19**. Removal of stamped snap rings usually requires specially designed snap ring pliers.

Warning

Wear safety glasses when removing or replacing snap rings. They can slip out of the pin boss or the jaws of the pliers and cause severe eye injuries.

If the piston pin is full floating and somewhat worn, it may slide out easily. On the other hand, it may be quite snug. A soft-faced mallet and a dowel rod can be used to tap the pin out. Be careful not to hit the piston. Let the pin fall into a soft cloth.

Press-fit pins must be removed with a mechanical or hydraulic press. Refer to the engine manual for the

Oil return holes

Goodheart-Willcox Publisher

Figure 17-17.

Check the ring grooves for signs of wear and carbon buildup. Make sure the oil return holes are clear.

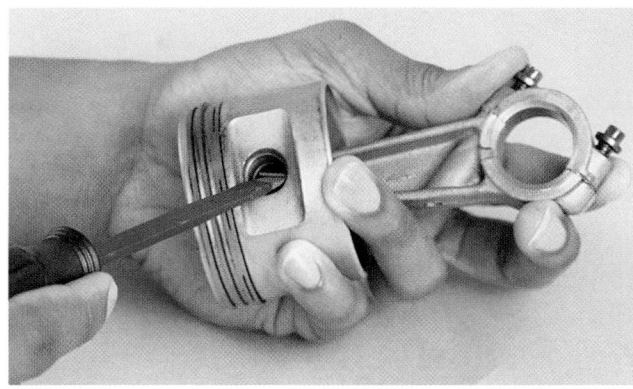

A

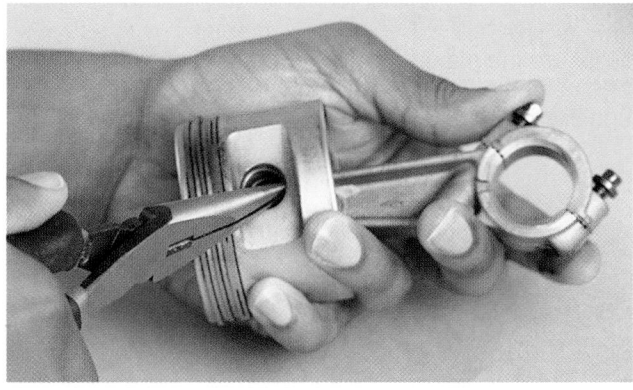

B

Goodheart-Willcox Publisher

Figure 17-19.

A—Some snap rings can be removed from their grooves using a screwdriver. B—Some snap rings can be removed using needlenose pliers. Always wear safety glasses for this operation.

If the pin-to-boss clearance is excessive, a new pin and bushing or an oversize pin and reaming of the bosses are needed. In some cases, oversized pins are not available, and a new piston and pin will need to be used.

Inspecting Connecting Rods

With the connecting rod removed from the piston, inspect the connecting rod saddle and piston pin boss for scoring, metal transfer, or other damage. See **Figure 17-20.** If the connecting rod uses precision bearing inserts, check the condition of the locking grooves. Check the connecting rod for evidence of warpage or cracks. If damage is found, the connecting rod must be replaced. If the connecting rod appears to be in good shape, it must be measured for wear and out-of-round conditions.

To measure connecting rod wear, begin by installing the rod cap. Before installing the cap bolts, check the matching marks on the rod and cap to make sure the cap is installed correctly. Install the rod cap bolts and tighten the bolts to specification. Use a telescoping gauge to measure the large connecting rod bore. Take the first measurement in line with the connecting rod centerline. Write down the measurement, and then take a second measurement at 90° from the first. The difference between the two measurements equals the out-of-roundness. The largest of the two values equals the connecting

proper support of the piston. If needle bearings are used, be careful not to lose them or misplace them.

Measuring Piston Pins and Bosses

When the piston pin has been removed, measure its outside diameter with a micrometer. Make a note of the measurement. Next, measure the inside diameter of the rod and piston bosses using a small hole gauge. Expand the gauge in the boss until it gently contacts the inner surfaces. Withdraw the gauge and measure it with the micrometer. Then, subtract the pin diameter from the boss diameter. The difference must be within the limits specified for the engine being serviced.

Goodheart-Willcox Publisher

Figure 17-20.

Check the connecting rod saddle surfaces for wear. This saddle has only light wear.

rod's wear size. If either the out-of-round or wear exceeds manufacturer specifications, the connecting rod must be replaced.

Next, measure the wear in the connecting rod's piston pin bore with a small hole gauge or telescoping gauge, **Figure 17-21**. Compare the measurement to the manufacturer's specification. If the pin bore diameter exceeds the manufacturer's specification, the connecting rod must be replaced or an oversize pin installed. If the connecting rod is undamaged and wear and out-of-round are within specification, the connecting rod can be reused.

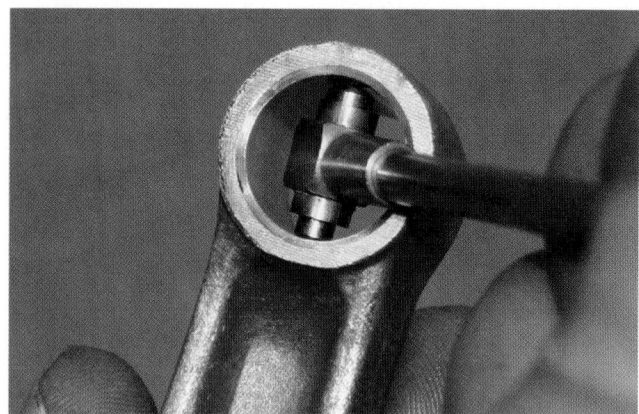

Goodheart-Willcox Publisher

Figure 17-21.

Measure the piston pin bore with a telescoping gauge or small hole gauge and compare the reading to specifications.

Summary

The condition of the piston and the rings can be observed by inspecting the parts during disassembly of the engine. Low compression, blow-by, oil pumping, and fouled plugs all signal the need for piston and ring service.

Pistons expand during operation. Therefore, a specific amount of clearance between the piston skirt and the cylinder wall must be present.

Pistons can be damaged in many ways. They should be cleaned, examined, and measured after removal. A piston pin is used to secure the piston to the connecting rod. The pin may be held in place by a snap ring or can be press fit in the connecting rod.

When the piston is removed, inspect the cylinder walls for scuffing and scoring. Check gasket surfaces for nicks and grooves. Examine the head bolt holes and spark plug holes for damaged threads.

If the cylinder wall looks smooth, measure it for wear and out-of-roundness. Check for excessive cylinder taper.

Cylinder service is determined by the cylinder condition. If the bore is within specifications, only a light deglazing is necessary.

If the cylinder is worn excessively, repair will depend on engine type. Chrome-plated aluminum cylinders must be replaced. Cast-in sleeve and solid cast iron cylinders can be rebored. Cylinders are usually rebored in steps of .010″. The cylinder must be honed after boring. Honing is an abrasive finishing process that removes boring tool marks and produces a desirable cylinder wall finish.

Review Questions

Answer the following questions using the information provided in this chapter.

1. The greatest amount of cylinder wear occurs _____.
    A. at the top of the cylinder
    B. in the center of the cylinder
    C. at the bottom of the cylinder
    D. about two inches from the bottom of the cylinder

2. Cylinder diameter is measured using a(n) _____.
    A. a telescoping gauge and outside micrometer
    B. an inside micrometer
    C. Either A or B.
    D. Neither A nor B.

3. Cylinder diameter measurements should be taken _____.
    A. at the very top and bottom of the cylinder, at two points 90° to each other
    B. at the center of the cylinder, at two points 90° to each other
    C. just below the ridge and at the bottom of ring travel, at two points 90° to each other
    D. only below the ridge, at two places 90° to each other

4. Explain how cylinder out-of-roundness is measured.

5. After a cylinder is rebored, it must be _____.
    A. honed
    B. lapped
    C. reamed
    D. deglazed

6. What parts of a crankshaft should be measured for wear?

7. Explain how an integral main bearing that is worn beyond specification can be repaired.

8. *True or False?* Damaged tapered roller bearings can often be reconditioned by polishing the bearing elements.

9. Ring side clearance is measured by _____.
    A. measuring the diameter of the piston skirt and subtracting that value from the cylinder diameter
    B. placing a ring in the groove and finding the thickest feeler gauge blade that will fit between the side of the groove and the ring
    C. placing the ring at the bottom of the cylinder and measuring the ring gap with a feeler gauge
    D. None of the above.

10. Explain how to measure a connecting rod's large bore for wear and out-of-roundness.

Suggested Activities

1. Measure a worn cylinder with an inside micrometer or other measuring tool. Record readings for taper and out-of-round.

2. Rebore and hone or deglaze a cylinder.

3. Remove the rings from a piston, clean the piston, and measure it.

4. Measure ring side clearance.

5. Recondition piston bosses by reaming, and replace the worn piston pin with an oversize pin.

Camshaft and Valve Train Service

Learning Objectives

After studying this chapter, you will be able to:

- Explain how to inspect and service the camshaft.
- Summarize service procedures for in-block and overhead valve assemblies.
- Describe the steps in inspecting and reconditioning valve seats.
- Explain how to inspect and recondition valve lifters and valve guides.

Key Terms

interference angle
peening

poppet valves
valve seat width

Introduction

The valve train performs several vital functions. It allows air-fuel mixture to enter the cylinder during the intake stroke, seals the combustion chamber during the compression and power strokes, and allows hot combustion gases to escape during the exhaust stroke. In order for the engine to function efficiently, each part in the valve train must be in good condition and functioning properly. If any one part in the system is worn or damaged, it will quickly wear related components, resulting in rapid engine failure.

For this reason, every part must be carefully inspected and measured for wear. If a worn or damaged part is found, it should be reconditioned or replaced. All other parts in physical contact with the worn part will also likely need to be reconditioned or replaced.

Camshaft Service

Begin valve train service by inspecting the camshaft for wear or damage, especially on the bearing surfaces, cam lobes, and timing gear. Look for chips, nicks, and worn edges on the timing gear teeth. If any damage is found, the camshaft timing gear must be replaced. Any other gears in contact with the damaged gear, such as the crankshaft timing gear, oil slinger gears, or governor gears, must be closely reinspected. Any gear in contact with a worn camshaft gear likely has matching wear. If a new camshaft or timing gear is installed without replacing the other worn gears it contacts, the new gear will quickly wear out.

Note

The timing gears on many crankshafts and camshafts are not serviceable. In these cases, the entire camshaft or crankshaft must be replaced if the timing gear is damaged.

Next, use an outside micrometer to measure the camshaft journal surfaces for wear. Compare the camshaft journal diameter to the reject size specified by the manufacturer. Use an inside micrometer, telescoping gauge, or small hole gauge to measure bearing bores in the crankcase cover and crankcase, **Figure 18-1**. If either of the diameters is greater than the manufacturer's reject size, a new bushing must be installed, or the crankcase or cover replaced.

Next, use a micrometer to measure the distance from the bottom of the cam lobes to the top. See **Figure 18-2**. Compare these values to the manufacturer's reject sizes. If either measurement is smaller than the reject sizes specified, replace the camshaft. Bearing clearance can be determined by subtracting the camshaft bearing journal measurement from camshaft bearing bore measurement.

Many small engines are equipped with centrifugally operated compression release systems.

Goodheart-Willcox Publisher

Figure 18-2.

Measure the camshaft lobe length from the bottom of the cam lobe to the top.

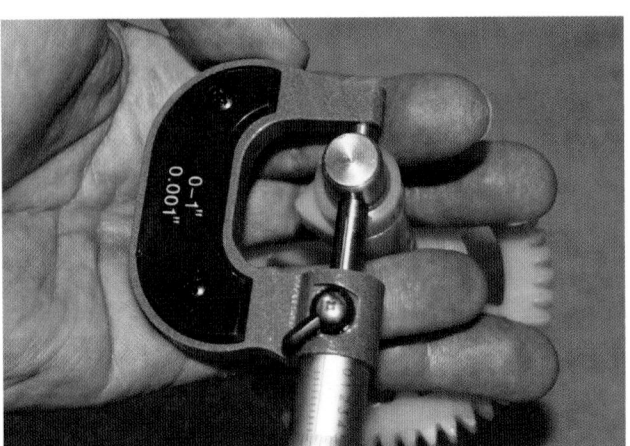

A

B

Goodheart-Willcox Publisher

Figure 18-1.

Check the camshaft bearing journals and bores for wear. A—Measure the camshaft bearing journals with an outside micrometer. B—Measure the camshaft bores in the crankcase and crankcase cover with a telescoping gauge or small hole gauge.

These typically consist of a weighted, spring-loaded lever that moves a pin in the cam lobe. When the engine is stationary, the pin holds the exhaust valve open. As the camshaft rotates more quickly, the weighted lever overcomes spring pressure and moves outward. When the lever moves outward, the pin in the cam lobe drops, allowing the exhaust valve to close fully.

If the camshaft is equipped with one of these systems, ensure that the weighted lever can move freely. Make sure that the spring action returns the lever to proper position, and that the pin moves freely. See **Figure 18-3**. If there is a problem with the

Valve lifting pin

Goodheart-Willcox Publisher

Figure 18-3.

Make sure that the compression release system operates properly.

compression release system, sometimes a thorough cleaning will fix it. If not, replace the compression release mechanism.

Valve Service

Four-cycle engines contain *poppet valves*, which are subjected to tremendous heat. The normal operating temperature of the exhaust valve exceeds 1000°F. To withstand this heat, high-quality, heat-resistant steel must be used and the correct operating clearances must be maintained.

Inspecting Valves and Seats

When the valves have been removed, clean them with a power-operated wire brush and inspect them for the following defects:

- Eroded, cracked, or pitted valve faces, heads, or stems.
- Warped valve head. See **Figure 18-4**.
- Worn or improperly ground valve stems. See **Figure 18-4**.
- Bent valve stems.
- Margin less than 1/64″.
- Partial seating.

Heavy carbon deposits on intake valves sometimes cause faulty valve operation by restricting the flow of fuel into the cylinder. If any serious defects are observed, the valve should be replaced. If a valve is to going to be reused, the valve face should be machined to a smooth, true finish.

Inspecting Valve Springs

Through overheating and extensive use, valve springs can lose their elasticity and become distorted (warped or bent). Check each spring for squareness and proper length with a square and a surface plate. See **Figure 18-5**. Replace all springs that are badly distorted or reduced in length.

Valve Guides

Valve guides align the valves with the valve seats so that they can open fully and close completely. Guide-to-valve stem clearance must not exceed tolerances, since this would permit the valve to tip. Tipping causes the valve face to strike

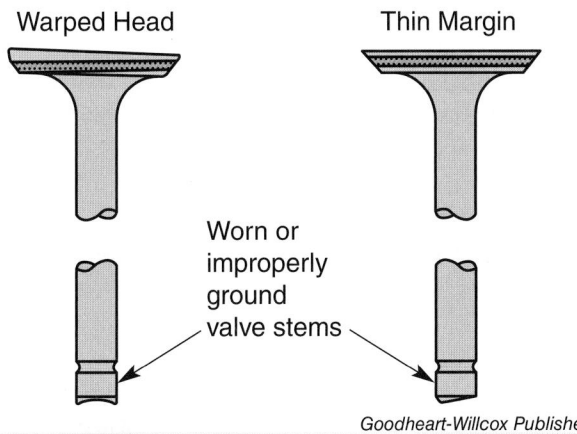

Goodheart-Willcox Publisher

Figure 18-4.

A warped valve head, thin margin, or worn stem indicates the need for valve reconditioning or replacement.

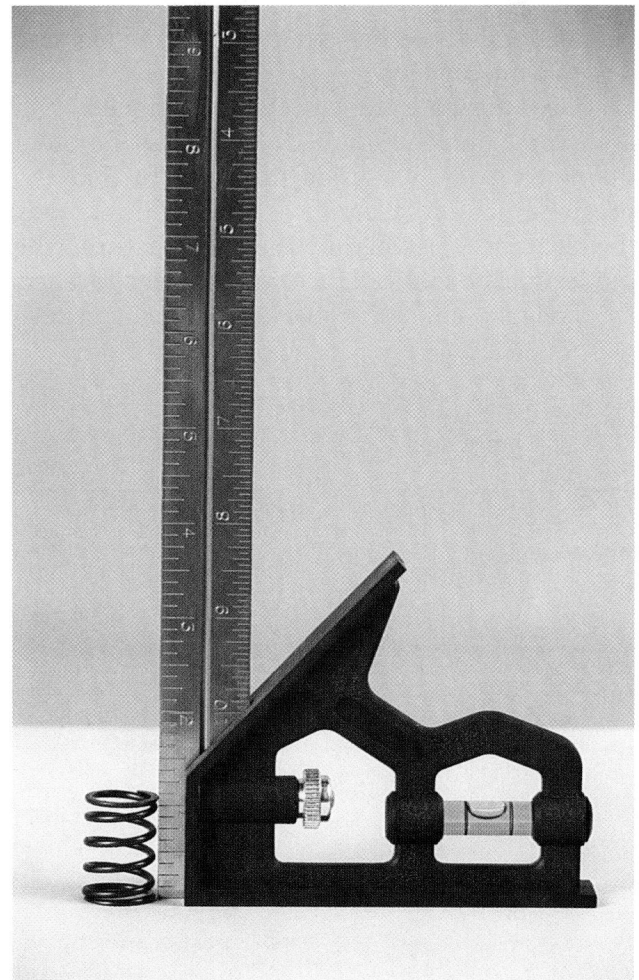

Goodheart-Willcox Publisher

Figure 18-5.

Use a square and a surface plate to check a valve spring for proper length and squareness.

the seat at an improper angle, resulting in a gap that allows hot combustion gases to escape. Some clearance is required, however, to allow for heat expansion and lubrication. Generally, guide-to-valve stem clearance should run about .002″ to .003″.

Valve guides can be a replaceable insert or an integral part of the block. See **Figure 18-6**. Most replaceable guides are cast iron. Worn replaceable guides can be replaced by driving the old guide out and driving in a replacement guide. Worn integral guides can be reconditioned by reaming the guide oversize so it can be fitted with a new valve with an oversize stem.

Inspecting Valve Guides

Valve guides must be cleaned before inspection. A special cylindrical wire brush, driven by a power drill, is made for this job. After cleaning the guide, measure the bore with a small hole gauge. See **Figure 18-7**. Expand the gauge until it lightly touches the sides of the bore. Remove the gauge and measure it with a micrometer.

Next, measure the valve stem diameter with a micrometer. See **Figure 18-8**. Subtract the stem diameter from the guide diameter to find the precise amount of clearance. If the value exceeds the clearance specified by the manufacturer, the guide must be serviced to restore proper clearance.

Some manufacturers have special plug gauges

for checking guide clearance. If this special tool can be inserted into the valve guide a specified distance, the valve guide is worn and should be replaced.

Correcting Worn Integral Aluminum Guides

If the clearance between the valve stem and an integral aluminum valve guide exceeds the allowable limit, two different methods can be used to correct the clearance, depending on the engine make and model. If valves with oversize stems are available for the engine, enlarge the guide to the next oversize dimension with an adjustable reamer. Next, select and install a replacement valve with the correct oversize stem.

If valves are not available for the engine being overhauled, thin-walled valve guide bushings may be available. In such cases, the following procedure should be used to correct valve clearance.

Note

When using either procedure to correct valve clearance, do *not* enlarge the lifter guides. Lifters with oversize stems are seldom available.

1. Measure the guide clearance with a small hole gauge or plug gauge, **Figure 18-9A**.
2. If the clearance exceeds manufacturer specifications, lubricate the counterbore reamer with cutting oil and place it into the valve guide. Push the pilot bushing over the counterbore reamer until the bushing is in solid contact with the valve seat.
3. Set the replacement bushing on the pilot bushing. Mark the reamer 1/16″ above the top of the replacement bushing. See **Figure 18-9B**.
4. Turn the reamer clockwise slowly and smoothly to ream the valve guide. During the reaming operation, periodically lubricate the guide with cutting oil. Stop when the mark on the counterbore reamer is even with the top of the pilot bushing. See **Figure 18-9C**.
5. When the guide is reamed to size, pull the reamer back out of the guide, while continuing to turn it clockwise.
6. Place the replacement bushing in the valve guide and press it in with a bushing driver. The bushing should be driven until it is flush with the top of the valve guide. See **Figure 18-9D**.

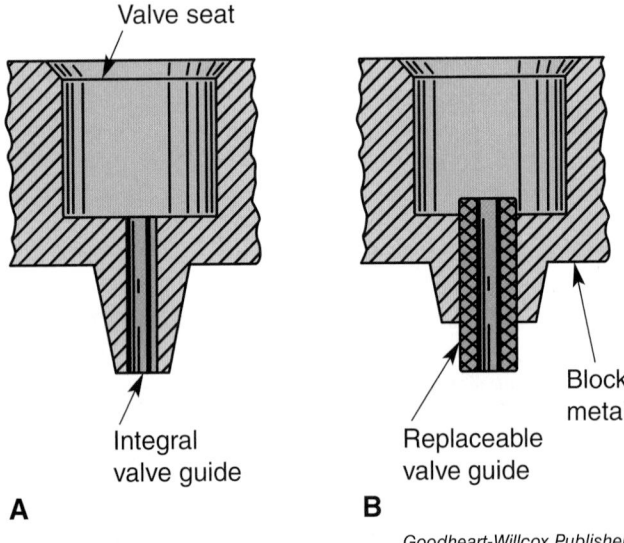

Valve seat

Block metal

Integral valve guide

Replaceable valve guide

A   B

Goodheart-Willcox Publisher

Figure 18-6.

There are two types of valve guides. A—Integral valve guides are part of the block. B—Guides that are pressed into the block can be replaced.

Valve guide

A

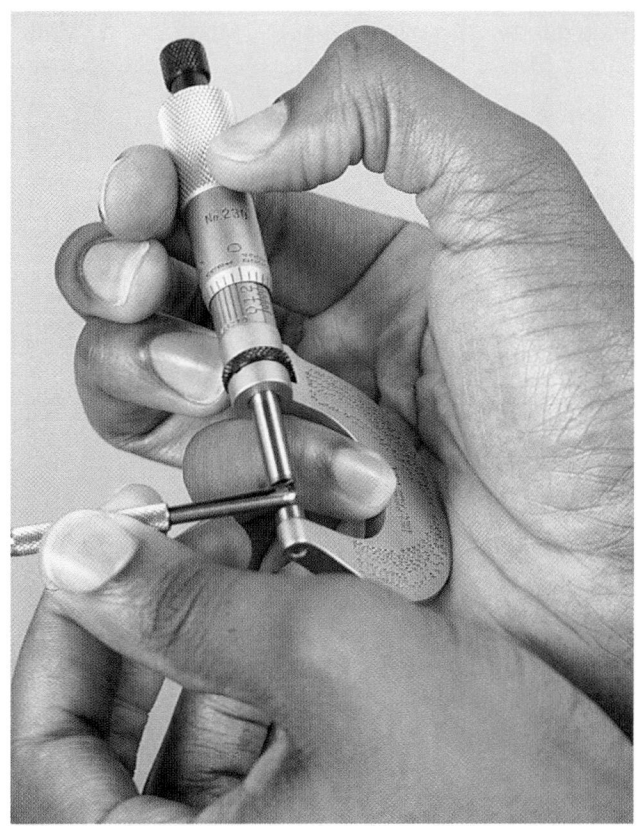

B

Goodheart-Willcox Publisher

Figure 18-7.

Valve guides must be measured for wear. A—Valve guide diameter can be measured with a small hole gauge. B—The small hole gauge measurement is transferred to a micrometer.

7. Use a proper-size finishing reamer to finish ream the bushing all the way through. Apply smooth pressure while turning the reamer handle clockwise to ream the bushing. Periodically lubricate the bushing with cutting oil during the process. See **Figure 18-9E**.

8. Spray penetrating oil into the top of the guide to wash away all metal filings before removing the reamer. Pull the reamer out of the guide while turning it clockwise.

Note

The procedure shown in **Figure 18-9** is one example of a method used for several engine models. The engine being serviced may require slightly different techniques. Always follow the manufacturer's service procedure.

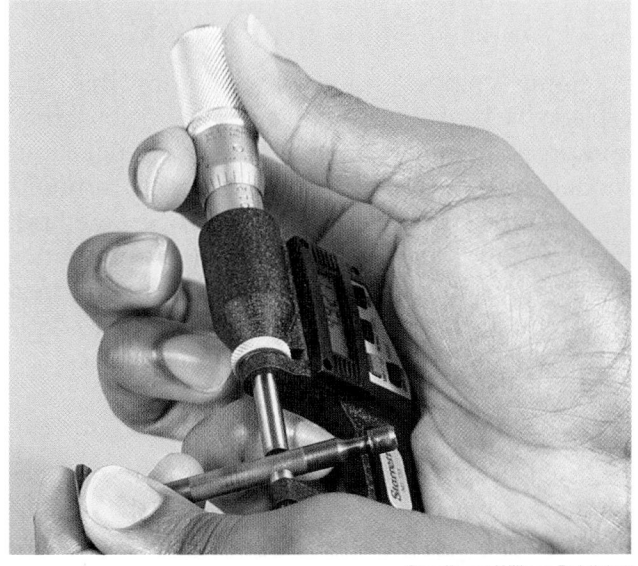

Goodheart-Willcox Publisher

Figure 18-8.

Measure the valve stem diameter and subtract the valve guide diameter to determine the valve stem-to-guide clearance.

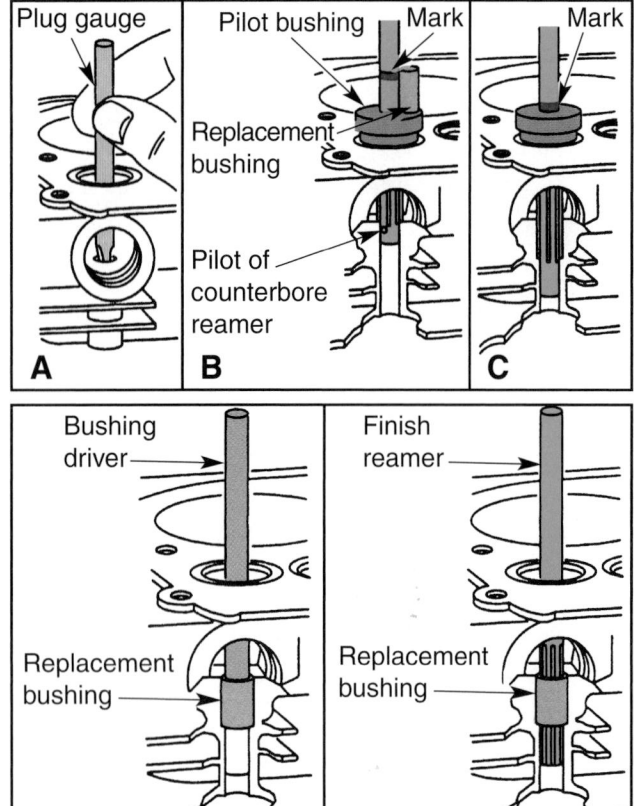

Figure 18-9.

Replacing worn aluminum valve guides with new valve guide bushings.

top of their bores. See **Figure 18-10**. The depth of the bushing must be measured before the worn bushing is removed. The replacement guide bushing is then driven or pressed into the bore to the same depth as the old bushing.

Refacing Valves

Valve refacing can be done on a specially designed grinder. The valve is revolved while being fed over an abrasive wheel. The collet that holds the valve is adjusted to achieve the desired face angle. Coolant flows over the valve head during grinding to reduce heat and produce a good surface finish. The feed wheel is used to precisely control the amount of material being ground from the valve face. In some cases, a specially designed lathe called a valve cutter can be used to reface valves. See **Figure 18-11**.

Valve refacing can also be done using a manual valve refacer. See **Figure 18-12**. The valve is placed tightly into a machinist's vise. Then, the valve refacer is placed on the valve. The crank lever turns the 45° (or 30°) cone against the stationary valve face. The cone has carbide blades that cut the valve face to the desired angle. The crank lever provides enough leverage to make the job effortless. The second lever is used to control the feed rate of the blades.

Valve Guide Bushing Replacement

Some engines have valve guides that are replaceable by driving out the worn guide bushings and pressing in new bushings. For each make and model, the manufacturer's service manuals should be examined to determine the proper method, bushings, and tools to use. Typically, iron guides are driven out through the bottom of their bores. Guides made of brass or other soft metals are typically pulled out through the top of their bores.

Replacing Worn Brass or Sintered Iron Guides

Replaceable valve guides that require replacement are typically driven out through the bottom of their bores with a bushing driver if they are iron. If they are brass or other soft metal, driving the bushing out could fracture the guide and cause damage to the bore. These types of guide bushings are typically tapped and pulled out through the

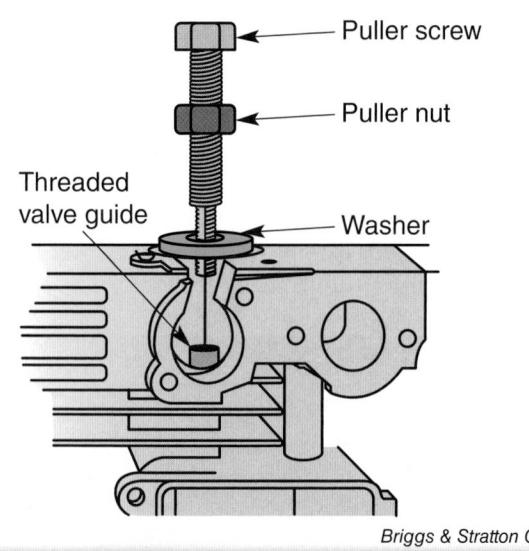

Briggs & Stratton Corp.

Figure 18-10.

Often, a soft metal guide is removed by tapping threads in the bushing, which is then extracted out of the top of its bore with a puller setup like the one shown here.

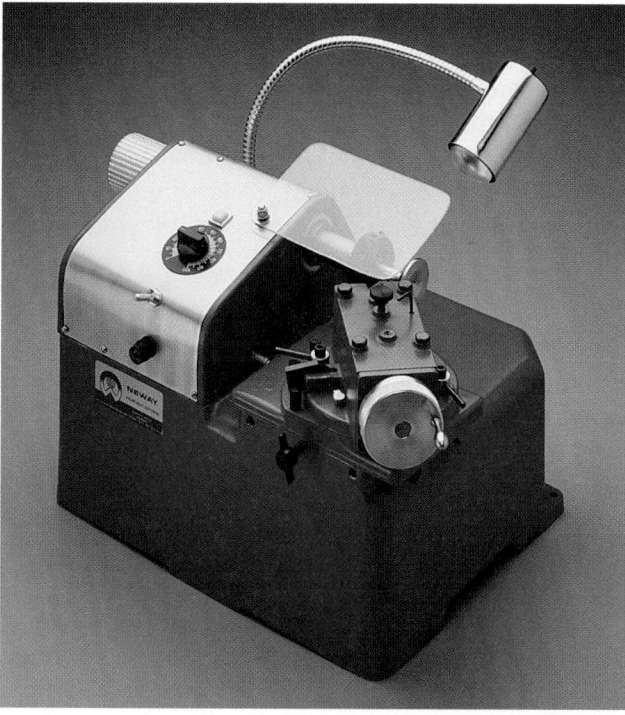

A

B

Neway Mfg. Co.

Valve cutters can be used to reface valves. A—A valve cutter is a lathe specially designed to cut and true the valve face with a carbide cutting tool. B—Closeup of a valve face being turned and trued on a valve cutter.

Neway Mfg. Co.

The handle of the manual valve refacer is turned by hand until the desired face angle is achieved.

Valve Lifter Service

Inspect valve lifters to ensure that the cam lobe contact area is not excessively worn. See **Figure 18-13**. If the cam lobe contact surfaces are concave or deformed in any other way, the surfaces must be ground flat on a grinding wheel or the lifters replaced. If a lifter appears to be in good shape, install it into its guide and check for excessive play. The lifter should move up and down in its guide without resistance and without excessive side play. Refer to the manufacturer's service manual for the corrective steps to take if the lifter hangs up in its bore or has excessive side play.

Valve Seat Service

Valve seats should always be reconditioned or replaced during an engine overhaul. Begin by inspecting the valve seat to make sure it is not loose or damaged. If a replaceable valve seat insert is burned, pitted, or otherwise damaged, it should be replaced. If an integral valve seat is damaged, in some cases it may be possible to bore out the old seat and install a valve seat insert. In other cases, the most economical solution is to replace the block. If the valve seat is in good condition, the only service that may be required is a light cutting to remove small surface imperfections.

Peening a Valve Seat Insert

Peening refers to displacing metal just outside the edge of the valve seat insert to lock the insert in

A

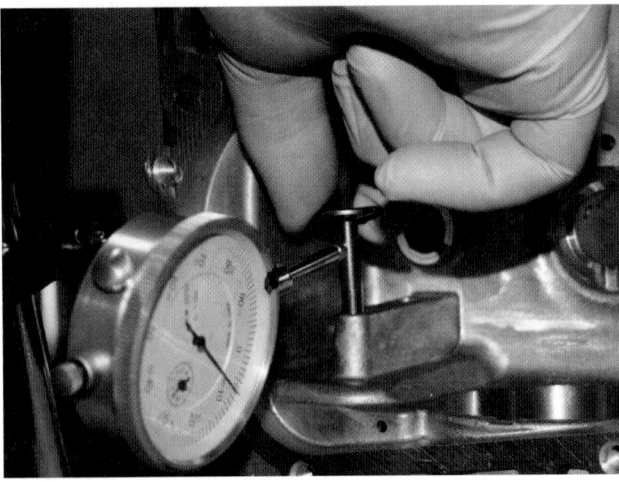

B

Goodheart-Willcox Publisher

Figure 18-13.

Inspect the valve lifters. A—Check the cam lobe contact surfaces for wear. B—Put the lifter in its bore and make sure it moves freely, without excessive side play.

place. If a valve seat insert is loose, it may be possible to secure the insert by peening it. However, be aware that a loose valve seat insert may have damage that makes it unsuitable for reuse. Always make sure the old valve seat insert is in good condition before securing it.

To secure a loose valve seat, place the insert squarely in its bore. Then, use a center punch and hammer to tap the insert at three equidistant points around its rim. This ensures the insert is fully seated. Next, use a small flat-ended drift punch or pin punch to make small indentations in the block metal just outside of the insert's rim. Work around the insert in a star pattern, peening points directly

across from each other to ensure the insert does become tilted in its bore as it is secured.

The small indentations created by peening flatten the metal, forcing it outward so it overlaps the top of the insert, locking the insert in place. It also bulges the block metal under the punch outward, forcing it into contact with the side of the insert. See **Figure 18-14**.

Valve Seat Angle and Width

Anytime an engine is overhauled, the valve seats should be cut to ensure that they are smooth and have the proper angle and width. The correct valve seat angle is necessary for proper valve seating. Valve seats are generally cut to a 45° angle, although 30° seat angles are used in a few engines. Follow all of the manufacturer's recommendations.

The *valve seat width* is important for effective valve system operation. The seat must be wide enough to prevent cutting into the valve face. It must also provide enough contact area for adequate heat dissipation. On the other hand, the seat must not be too wide. If it is, carbon will pack between the seat and the valve face, holding the valve off the

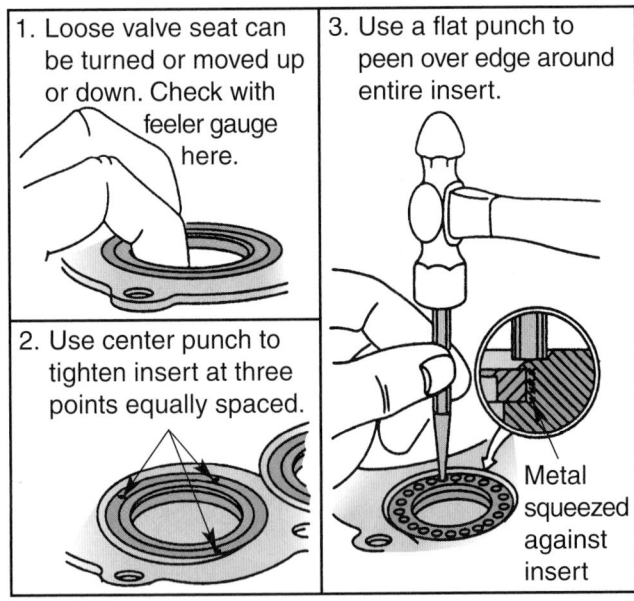

Briggs & Stratton Corp.

Figure 18-14.

Steps for securing a valve seat insert. 1—If the space between the insert and cylinder is more than .005", a new insert must be installed. 2—A center punch is used in three equally spaced locations to hold the insert for the peening operation. 3—A flat end punch about 1/8" diameter is used to force metal against the insert to hold it tightly in place.

seat. A valve that fails to seat results in a rough-running engine and will quickly warp and burn. Seat widths typically range from .030″ to .060″ (1/32″ to 1/16″). See **Figure 18-15**.

Some valve seats are finished to an angle 1° greater or less than the valve face. The 1° variation produces a hairline contact that results in fast initial seating. Some manufacturers believe that, upon heating, the valve will form a perfect seal. The difference in the angle between the valve face and the valve seat is called an *interference angle*. See **Figure 18-16**. Valve seat contact must be near the center of the valve face. See **Figure 18-17**.

Refacing (Cutting) Valve Seats

Valve seats should be cut with a special valve seat cutting tool that has sharp carbide blades, such as the one shown in **Figure 18-18**. These tools can be purchased separately or in a kit like the one in **Figure 18-19**. If the carbide cutter blades become dull, they can be easily replaced. The cutting blades

have angular teeth to give a smooth shearing cut as they are turned. See **Figure 18-20**.

The amount of cutting required depends on valve seat condition. If the valve seat is in good condition and has the correct seat angle and width, a single turn of the cutter may be all that is required to remove any minor imperfections. If the valve

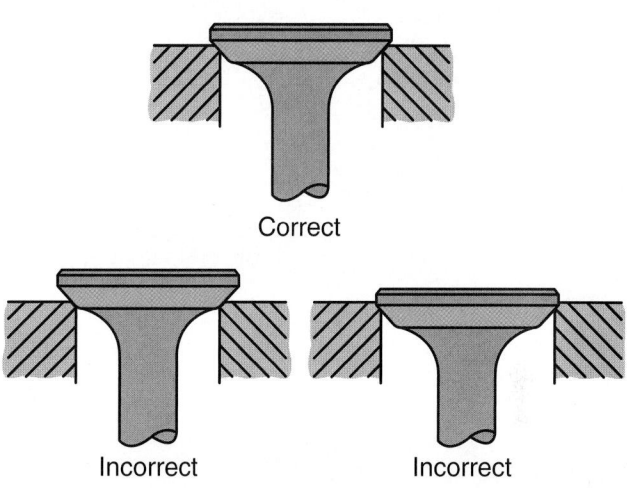

Correct

Incorrect   Incorrect

Deere & Co.

Figure 18-17.

Comparison of correct and incorrect location of the seating area on a valve face.

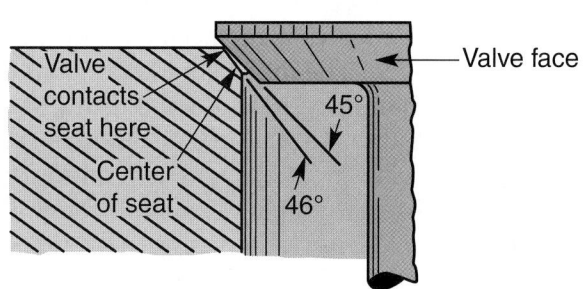

.030″–.060″   45°

Valve seat   Valve seat

Goodheart-Willcox Publisher

Figure 18-15.

A typical integral valve seat is shown here. The hole for the seat is bored in the block metal. Note the typical valve seat angle and valve seat widths.

Valve contacts seat here
Center of seat
Valve face
45°
46°

Goodheart-Willcox Publisher

Figure 18-16.

A 1° difference between the valve face and the valve seat provides better seating.

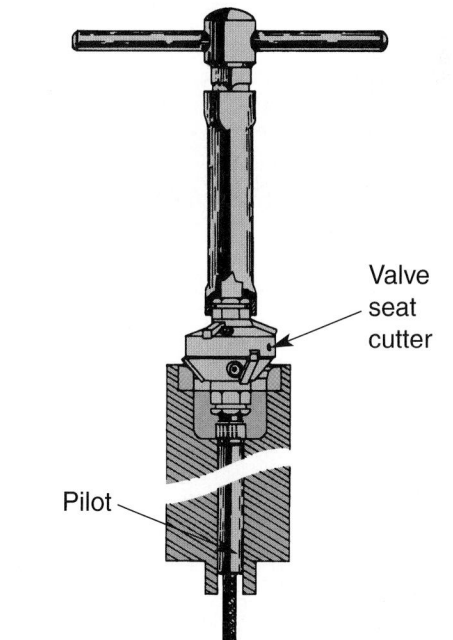
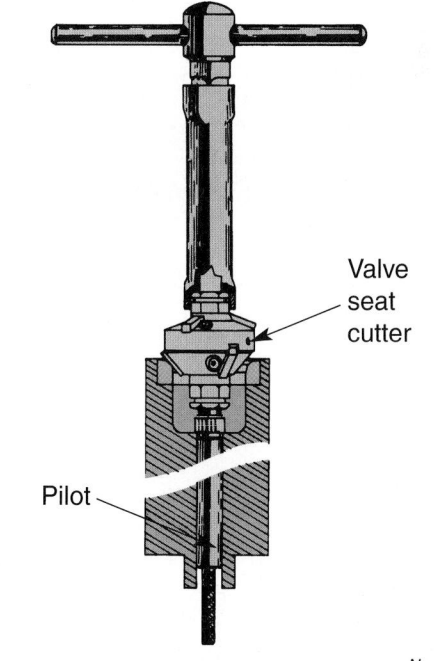

Valve seat cutter

Pilot

Neway Mfg. Co.

Figure 18-18.

A valve seat cutting tool with carbide cutting blades. This tool is used to recondition valve seats by hand.

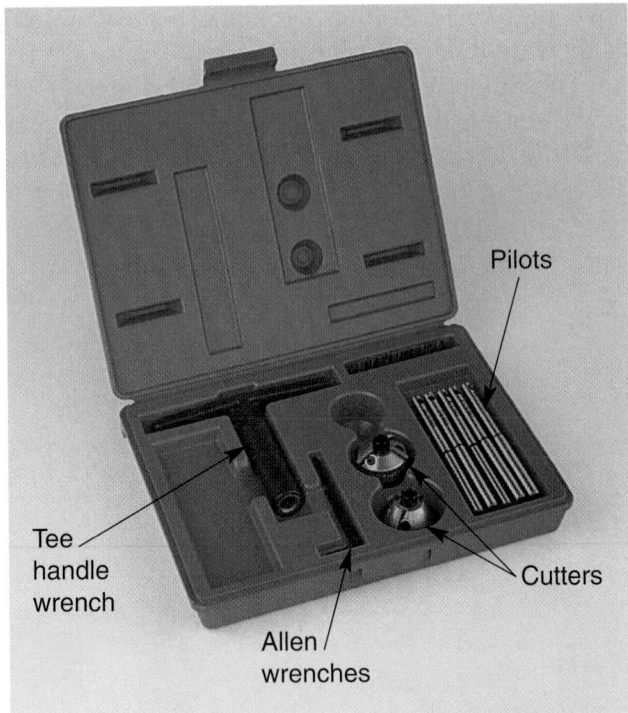

Neway Mfg. Co.

Figure 18-19.
A valve seat cutting tool kit. The cutter heads have carbide cutter blades that are very hard and will cut smooth and precise angles. Pilot rods accommodate various valve guide sizes.

Neway Mfg. Co.

Figure 18-20.
Valve cutter heads have angled cutting edges that provide a chatterless shearing cut for smooth valve seat surfaces.

inspection revealed evidence of improper valve seating or the valve seat angle or width is incorrect, more seat material will need to be removed.

Before cutting a valve seat, use a black felt tip marker to completely color the seat area. As the seat is cut, the black marker ink will be shaved away, revealing the clean metal underneath. This will make it easier to judge the progress of the cut. After marking the valve seat, place the pilot rod in

the valve guide, and then slide the valve seat cutter over the pilot. The tee handle wrench is used to turn the cutter. Apply moderate downward pressure and turn the cutter clockwise only. Cutting action is controlled by steady pressure and smooth turning of the handle.

After every one or two turns, remove the cutter and check the progress of the cut. Clean metal should be visible in the seat area. Any area still covered by black ink remains uncut. When the seat is cut to the proper width and has no irregularities, stop cutting. **Figure 18-21** illustrates the correct procedure to follow when using a valve cutter and pilot. Follow the cutter manufacturer's instructions for correcting various problems with seat geometry.

Caution

After a cutting operation, such as reaming valve guides or cutting valve seats, any chips or grit must be thoroughly washed away.

Replacing Valve Seat Inserts

If valve seat inserts are damaged or worn, they can be removed and replaced with new inserts. The procedures described in this section are general in nature, and may not be suitable for all engines. Always follow the procedures in the manufacturer's service manual for the specific engine being serviced.

Typically, the old valve seat insert is removed using a puller like the one shown in **Figure 18-22**. The puller nut is positioned under the valve seat insert. Then, the slotted puller body is slid around the puller bolt and centered over the insert. The bolt is tightened to pull the insert from its bore. A slide hammer with a special adapter or a pry bar can also be used to remove most valve seat inserts. Care must be taken not to damage the insert bore.

One outside edge of a replacement valve seat insert is chamfered. The insert should be set in the bore with the chamfered side down, **Figure 18-23**. Then, the old insert is turned upside down and set on top of the replacement insert. The pilot shaft of the valve seat insert driver is installed through the opening in the old insert, the opening in the new insert, and into the valve guide. See **Figure 18-24**. Next, make sure that the inserts are properly aligned over the bore, and drive the new insert until it bottoms in the bore. Finally, peen the metal

Valve Seat Cutter Kit
GENERAL INSTRUCTIONS

SELECTION AND USE OF PROPER PILOT
A. SOLID PILOTS.

1. Select a pilot same diameter (fractional or metric) as valve guide.
2. Insert pilot in valve guide, twisting slightly, until very snug. Pilot shoulder should not touch valve guide. (Fig. 1)
   - If small, try next size larger.
   - If too large, try next smaller size.

DETAILED CUTTING INSTRUCTIONS

A. Slowly lower cutter to valve seat. DO NOT DROP CUTTER.

B. Turn clockwise and apply very light pressure. Release the down pressure at end of each cut. Make one or two turns with no pressure.

C. BOTTOM NARROWING CUT.

1. Cut lightly with narrowing cutter (usually 60°).
2. Cut until a fine continuous line is formed with valve seat. (Fig. 2)

D. TOP NARROWING CUT.

1. Cut lightly with narrowing cutter (usually 15°). For engines with hemispheric combustion chambers, use 30°/31°.
2. Cut until seat width is slightly less than required. (This operation LOWERS THE SEAT.)

E. FINAL SEAT CUT.

1. Cut lightly, with seat cutter (usually 31° or 46°).
2. Cut seat to proper width. This should take only a few turns. (Fig. 3)

F. INSPECT SEAT.

1. Remove pilot, using pilot puller. (Fig. 4)
2. Insert valve in valve guide.
3. Tap valve slightly up and down in the guide (holding it with fingers top and bottom—above and below the cylinder head). Do this until seat contact ring shows on the **valve face**.

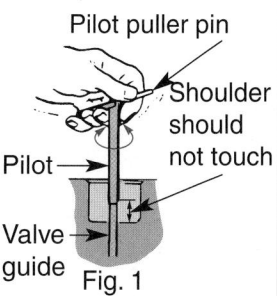
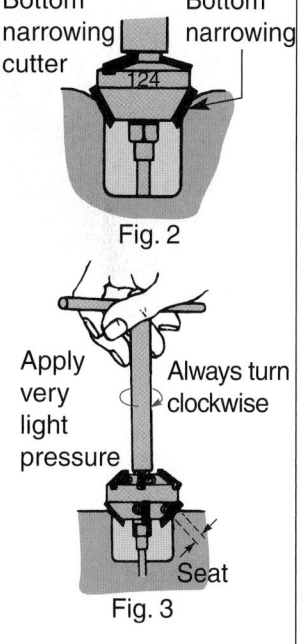
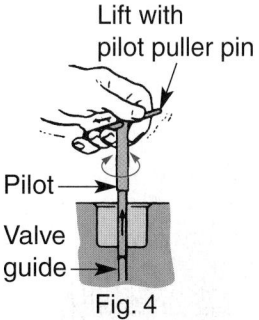
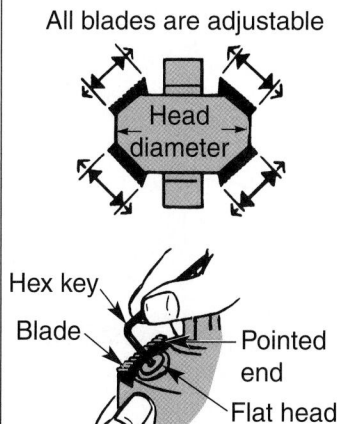

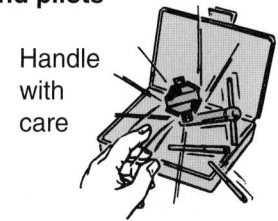

All blades are adjustable

Head diameter

Hex key, Blade, Pointed end, Flat head screw

Proper care of cutting blades

Serrations on the blades should be cleaned regularly with the brush provided with each kit. (A toothbrush could also be used.)

Proper care of cutters and pilots

Handle with care

The tools should be kept in tool case. When removed from case, they should be placed on a cloth or pad. These precision instruments will last a long time if reasonable care is used.

Neway Mfg. Co.

Figure 18-21.

Proper procedures for using a valve seat cutting tool.

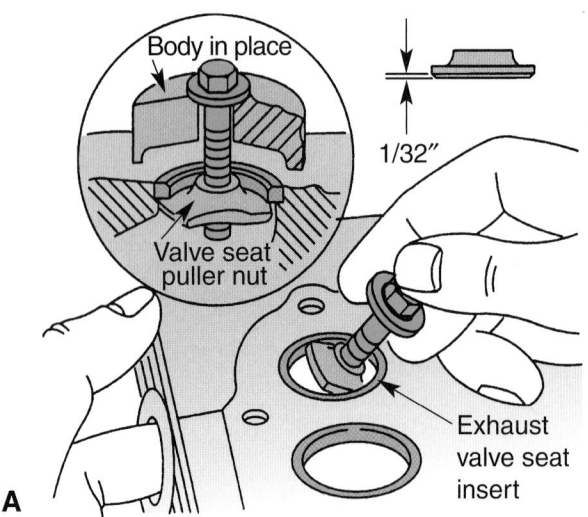

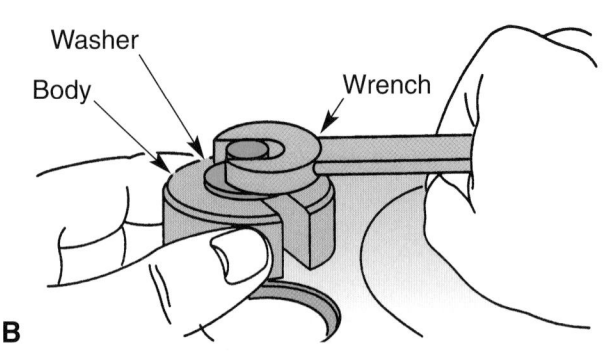

Briggs & Stratton Corp.

Figure 18-22.

A valve seat puller tool removes old valve seat inserts. A—The puller nut is inserted through the hole and held in place with a finger in the port. The puller body is placed on the bolt and over the insert. B—When the nut on the puller is tightened with a wrench, the insert is pulled up and out.

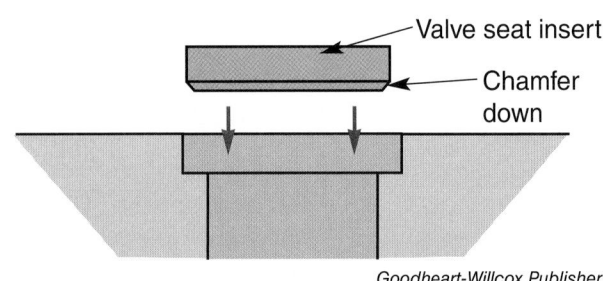

Goodheart-Willcox Publisher

Figure 18-23.

When installing the insert, the chamfered edge should be placed down in the bore.

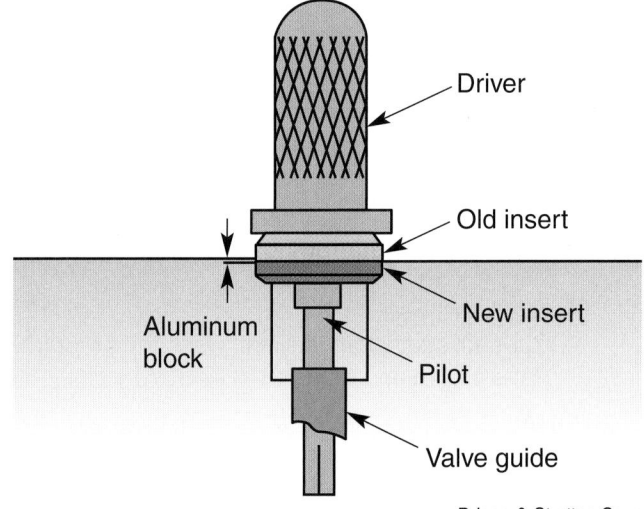

Briggs & Stratton Corp.

Figure 18-24.

The old insert is used to drive in the new insert and seat it so that it will be slightly below the surface.

around the insert to secure it and then reface the insert as described earlier.

If the engine has integral valve seats, it may be possible to counterbore the valve seats so valve seat inserts can be installed. A special cutter is used to enlarge the valve seat bore to a specified depth. The insert is installed in the bore with the chamfered edge down. Then, the valve seat insert is driven into place and secured by peening the metal around the insert. See **Figure 18-25**. Reface the seat as previously described in this chapter.

Lapping Valves

Some engine manufacturers recommend hand lapping of the valve seats. Lapping compound is available from engine parts distributors. Lapping compound consists of silicon carbide abrasive combined with a special grease. It is generally available in course grade and fine grade. The course grade removes more metal than the fine grade. The condition of the valve will dictate which grade to use.

If the coarse lapping compound is used, follow up with the finer compound. Apply the lapping compound to the valve face only, **Figure 18-26**.

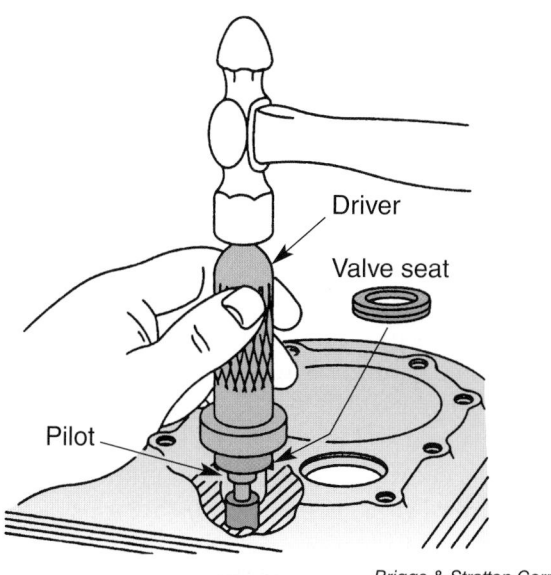

Figure 18-25.

Driving the valve insert into place with a driver tool and ball peen hammer. A pilot guides the driver tool.

The compound should not be allowed to contact the valve stem or guide. Next, a lapping tool is attached to the valve head by means of a suction cup. See **Figure 18-27**. With the tool attached, the valve is placed in the guide and twirled back and forth. See **Figure 18-28**.

The lapping process is complete when a dark gray, narrow band, which is equal to the seat width, can be seen all the way around the valve face. Do not lap more than is necessary to create a properly sized seat.

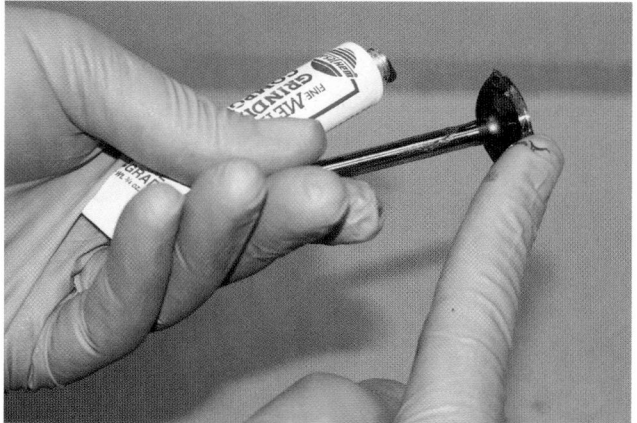

Figure 18-26.

Apply lapping compound to the valve face before lapping the face to the seat.

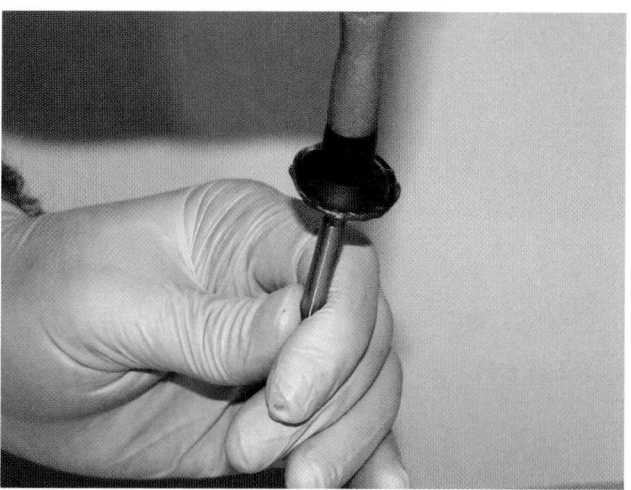

Figure 18-27.

To use a lapping stick, attach the stick to the valve head with a suction cup.

After lapping, thoroughly clean the valve and valve seat chamber so that none of the abrasive finds its way into the engine. The best way to clean the seat area is to turn the engine upside down and wash the chamber with solvent, from the bottom.

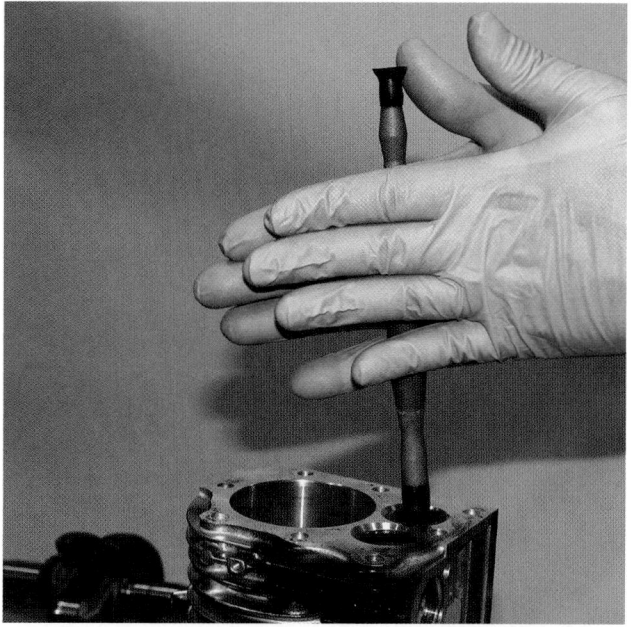

Figure 18-28.

Lap the valve to the seat by twirling the lapping stick between the palms of the hands. Lift the lapping stick and valve occasionally to increase the cutting action of the compound.

Adjusting Valve Lifter-to-Stem Clearance

Valve clearance refers to the space between the end of the valve stem and the top of the valve lifter when the valve is closed. The amount of clearance needed depends on engine design and use. Due to hotter operation, the exhaust valve often requires more clearance than the intake valve. Clearances of around .008" for the intake valve and .012" for the exhaust valve are fairly common. Always refer to the manufacturer's specifications.

When there is too little valve clearance, the valve may be held open when the valve stem heats up and lengthens (expands). As a result, engine performance is poor and both the valve face and valve seat will burn. See **Figure 18-29**. Insufficient clearance can also alter valve timing, making it too far advanced.

Too much valve clearance, on the other hand, will make valve timing late and reduce valve lift. This results in sluggish engine performance. It can also cause rapid lifter wear because of the pounding action involved. Under these conditions, the engine will be noisy and the valve could break. **Figure 18-30** shows a complete small L-head engine valve train.

After a valve has been refaced, it rides lower in the guide, and, therefore, the valve lifter-to-stem clearance is reduced. If the engine does not have adjustable lifters, the end of the valve stem must be ground to obtain correct clearance. To check clearance, turn the camshaft until the lobe is away from the lifter. Hold the valve against its seat while testing clearance with a thickness gauge, **Figure 18-31**. If there is too little clearance, remove the valve and grind .001" or .002" off the end of the stem. Repeat the clearance check and grinding operation until the clearance is correct.

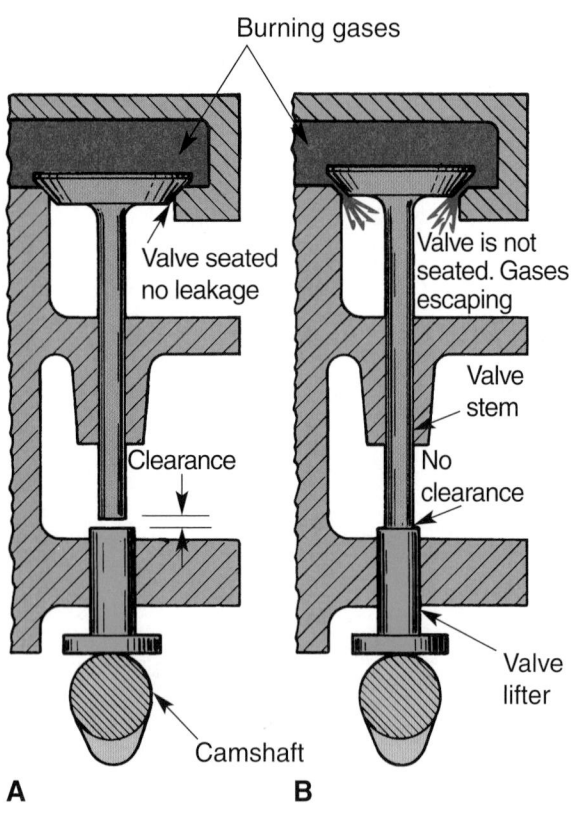

Goodheart-Willcox Publisher

Figure 18-29.

Valve clearance setting is essential to good engine performance. A—Correct clearance permits valve to seat. B—Lack of clearance keeps valve open.

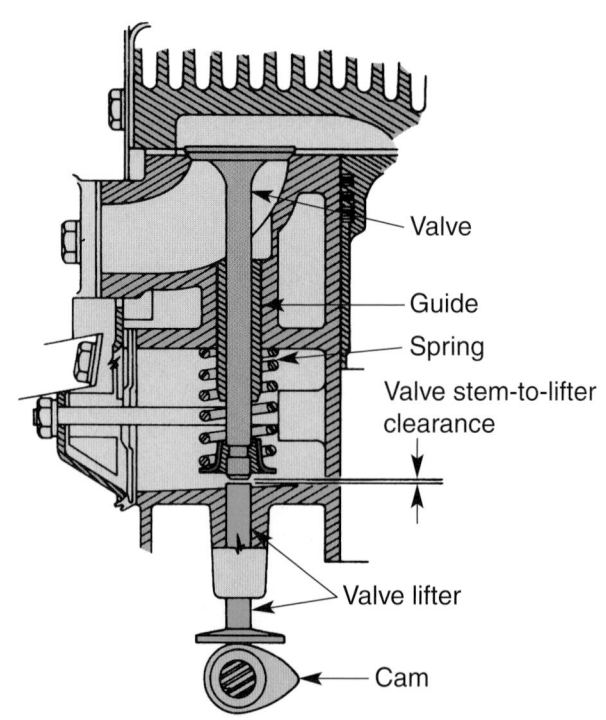

Kohler Co.

Figure 18-30.

Components of a complete L-head engine valve train.

Goodheart-Willcox Publisher

Figure 18-31.

Hold the valve against its seat and slide a feeler gauge blade between the valve stem and lifter. The clearance is equal to the thickest blade that will fit.

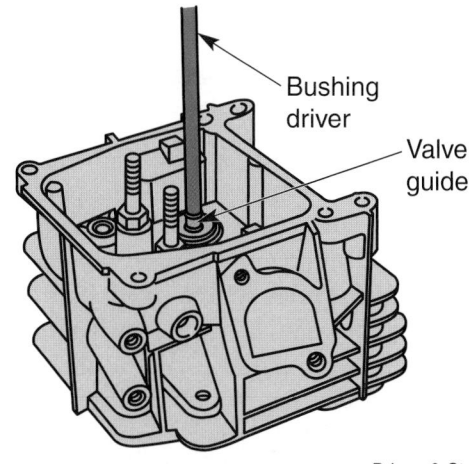

Briggs & Stratton Corp.

Figure 18-32.

Pressing a valve guide out of a cylinder head with a bushing driver or a flat punch.

Servicing Overhead Valves, Seats, and Guides

The valves, seats, and guides used in overhead valve systems are serviced in the same way as those in L-head engines (also called flat head or side valve engines). Valves should be cleaned and resurfaced to a 45° angle (or a 30° angle) on a valve grinding machine.

Valve seats can be reconditioned with a valve seat cutting tool. Valves should be lapped if recommended by the manufacturer. Thoroughly clean lapping compound from valve seats and faces. Inspect and measure valve springs. Replace any parts that do not meet specifications.

Measure the intake and exhaust valve guides. If dimensions are not within specifications, the guides must be replaced. To remove worn guides, use a bushing driver or flat-ended pin punch. Support the cylinder head and press the guides out. See **Figure 18-32**. When pressing new guides into a cylinder head, press only to the specified depth. See **Figure 18-33**. This dimension will vary from one engine model to another.

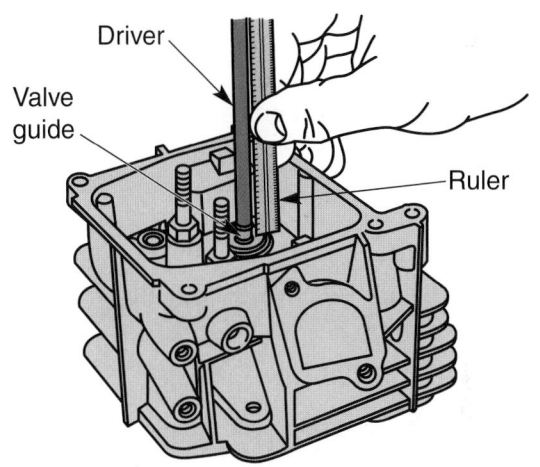

Briggs & Stratton Corp.

Figure 18-33.

Drive the replacement valve guide to the specified height above the hole, as shown.

Summary

After valves are removed, clean and inspect them for defects. Valves with serious defects must be replaced. Valve springs should be checked for squareness, length, and tension. Replace all springs that are not within specifications.

Check valve guides with a small hole gauge. If the clearance between the guide and stem exceeds the allowable limit, enlarge the guide with an adjustable reamer. A new valve with an oversize stem must be installed.

Valve seats are generally cut to a 45° angle. Seat contact must be near the center of the valve face. A valve seat cutter is used to recondition seats. Good used valves can be reseated by a hand-lapping process.

Valve clearance refers to the space between the end of the valve stem and the top of the lifter. Valves must be closed when measuring clearance. If there is too little clearance, the valve may be held open when the stem expands.

Valve refacing can be done on a specially designed grinder or with a manual valve refacer. Valve clearance is reduced when a valve is refaced. Therefore, the lifters must be adjusted or the valve stem end must be ground to obtain the correct clearance.

Review Questions

Answer the following questions using the information provided in this chapter.

1. A camshaft timing gear is inspected and found to be severely worn. In addition to replacing the camshaft, what further actions should the technician take and why?
2. How is a centrifugally operated compression release checked?
3. Valve margins should not be less than _____".
   A. 1/64
   B. 1/32
   C. 1/16
   D. 3/32
4. After reaming a valve guide, bushing, or cutting a valve seat, it is important to immediately _____.
5. Why is it important to select the correct valve guide bushing before reaming the block?

6. Valve seats that are too wide will _____. *Select correct answer(s).*
   A. cause valves to stick closed
   B. cause valves to stick open
   C. transfer too much heat to the block
   D. warp and burn
7. What is the 1° difference between the valve face angle and the valve seat angle called?
8. How is a valve seat insert secured in the cylinder head bore?
   A. It is tack welded in place.
   B. It is held in place by peening metal surrounding the insert.
   C. It is held in place with a snap ring.
   D. It is threaded into place.
9. Name the process of placing abrasive compound on the valve face and twirling the valve back and forth in the valve seat.
10. Too little valve clearance will cause the valve to _____.
    A. break
    B. be noisy
    C. burn
    D. open late

Suggested Activities

1. Grind valves on a grinding machine or turn and true valve faces on a valve cutter.
2. Recondition old valve seats with a valve seat cutter.
3. Lap valves into seats after the valve faces and seats are reconditioned by grinding.
4. Ream new valve guides in an aluminum block engine having aluminum guides.
5. Remove old valve guide bushings and install new guide bushings.
6. Demonstrate removing an old valve seat insert.
7. Demonstrate counterboring a cylinder for a new valve seat insert.
8. Demonstrate peening a valve seat on an aluminum engine block.
9. Ream valve guides to fit oversize valve stems with proper clearance.
10. Adjust lifter-to-valve clearance by grinding valve stems.

Engine Reassembly and Break-In

Learning Objectives

After studying this chapter, you will be able to:

- Summarize the steps in reassembling L-head and overhead valve engines.

- Explain how crankshafts and camshafts should be reinstalled.

- Summarize the steps in reassembling a piston and rod assembly and installing rings.

- Explain the purpose of ring end gap.

- Describe methods of adjusting crankshaft endplay.

- Summarize what happens during piston ring wear-in.

Key Terms

assembly lube
bearing crush
bearing spread

break-in
dampening coils

Introduction

After the engine has been disassembled and all the parts have been cleaned, inspected, and reconditioned as needed, the engine must be properly reassembled. Always reassemble the engine in a clean work area. If dirt or other abrasives get into the engine during reassembly, it can undo all of the hard work that went into the engine rebuild.

Have all of the necessary repair parts, supplies, and instructions handy and well organized. Read through the manufacturer's instructions for reassembling the engine and be sure you understand them before beginning. The instructions provided in this chapter are general in nature, and may not apply to the engine you are servicing.

Reinstalling Internal Engine Components

The steps followed to reassemble an engine are essentially the reverse of the steps used to disassemble it. Begin by making sure that all bearings or bushings are properly installed in the crankcase and crankcase cover. Next, install replacement oil seals in the crankcase and crankcase cover. Apply sealant around the outside of the shell of the seal before pressing it in place. Often, seals can be replaced by tapping them into the bore with a seal driver. If a seal driver is not available, a socket of the appropriate size can be used. See **Figure 19-1**.

If the engine is equipped with a centrifugal governor, the governor shaft should be installed next.

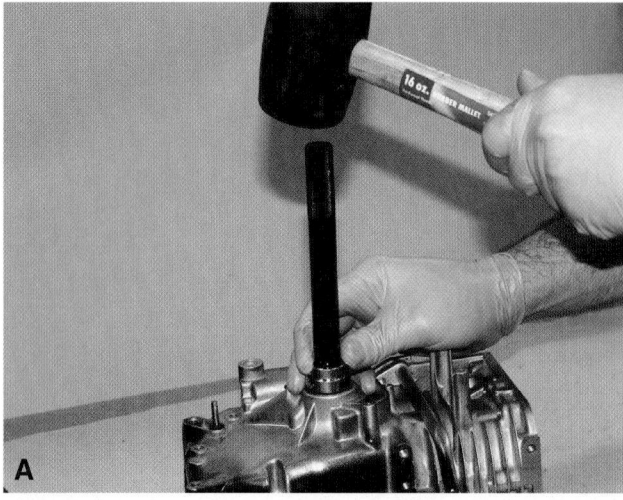

Goodheart-Willcox Publisher

Figure 19-1.

Use a seal driver or a socket to tap seals into place. A—Using a seal driver. B—Using a socket.

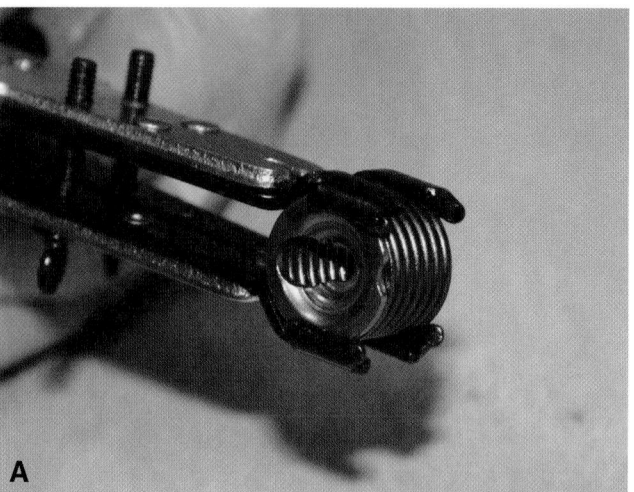

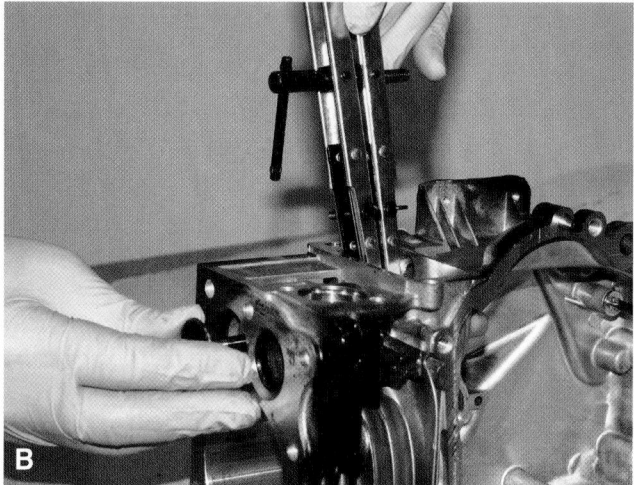

Goodheart-Willcox Publisher

Figure 19-2.

Compress the valve springs and install the keepers. A—When using an L-head type compressor, place the retainers on the spring and then compress the assembly. B—Place the spring and retainers into position and then insert the valve stem through them. Reposition the retainer so it locks on the valve stem, and then open the valve spring compressor.

Installing Valves (L-Head Engine)

If the engine being serviced is an L-head engine, engine reassembly should continue with reinstallation of the valves. If an overhead valve engine is being reassembled, the valves are located in the cylinder head rather than the block. Overhead valves can be reinstalled toward the end of the reassembly process. Overhead valve installation is covered in a separate section later in this chapter.

After the valves and seats have been properly reconditioned, apply valve guide lubricant to the valve stems and then place each valve in its respective guide. Use a valve spring compressor to compress the spring and, then, install the keepers. See **Figure 19-2**.

When reinstalling the valve springs, note that the coils are closer together on one end of the spring than on the other. These are called *dampening coils* and they should be located opposite the valve cap and retainers. See **Figure 19-3**.

Installing the Crankshaft, Camshaft, and Governor Gear

Tape the crankshaft keyways. This will protect the oil seals from being damaged by the sharp edges

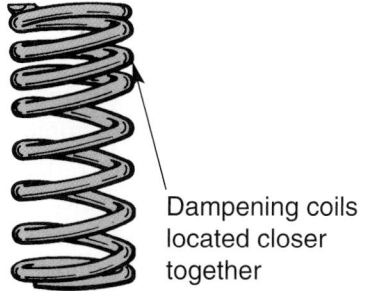

Dampening coils located closer together

Tecumseh Products Co.

Figure 19-3.

Valve spring with dampening coils.

Goodheart-Willcox Publisher

Figure 19-5.

Tilt the engine so the valve lifters will not fall out of their guides.

of the keyways when the crankshaft is installed. Next, lubricate the crankshaft main bearing journals and timing gear with assembly lube and then install the crankshaft. See **Figure 19-4**. *Assembly lube* is a heavy oil that protects parts from wear during initial start up. Install the crankshaft with the tapered end positioned on the flywheel side of the crankcase.

Next, position the engine so the valve lifters can be installed in their guides without falling out. Lubricate the lifters with assembly lube before installing them. Be sure to install each lifter in the proper guide. See **Figure 19-5**.

Lubricate the camshaft's bearing journals, cam lobes, and timing gear. Rotate the crankshaft so the timing mark on the crankshaft is pointing toward the lifters. Next, align the timing mark on camshaft timing gear with the timing mark on the crankshaft gear and install the camshaft, **Figure 19-6**.

Timing marks

Goodheart-Willcox Publisher

Figure 19-6.

Lubricate the bearing journals and cam lobes and align the timing marks before installing the camshaft.

If the engine is equipped with an oil slinger or centrifugal governor gear, they should be installed next. See **Figure 19-7**.

Installing the Piston and Rod Assembly

Lubricate the piston pin with assembly lube. Place the piston on the connecting rod. Refer to the marks on the piston and the connecting rod to ensure the piston is installed in the proper direction. Push the piston pin through the piston and connecting rod and secure it with new retainers. See **Figure 19-8**.

Goodheart-Willcox Publisher

Figure 19-4.

Install the crankshaft carefully to avoid damaging bearing surfaces and seals.

Oil slinger/governor

Goodheart-Willcox Publisher

Figure 19-7.

Some engines have a centrifugal governor gear or oil slinger installed on the camshaft.

Checking Ring End Gap

The inside diameter of a piston ring is always made smaller than the piston's diameter. This being the case, each ring must be expanded to get it over the piston head and into the ring groove. The amount of end gap is critical and should match the manufacturer's specifications. As a rule of thumb, however, allow .004″ of end gap for every inch of cylinder diameter. For example, the minimum end gap for a 2.5″ cylinder is .010″.

Too much end gap will allow the gases to leak between the ring ends. Too little gap is even more serious. When the rings heat up in service, they will expand and close up. If the rings continue to heat and expand, they will break and score the cylinder wall.

To measure ring end gap, place the ring in the cylinder. Then, turn a piston upside down and push the ring to the lower end of the cylinder. When the ring reaches the proper depth, remove the piston.

Select a feeler gauge blade that is thinner than the gap to be measured and place it in the gap. See **Figure 19-9**. Progressively use thicker leaves until you can feel a slight contact or drag from the gap's edge surfaces. At this point, compare the leaf thickness with the amount of gap specified. If the

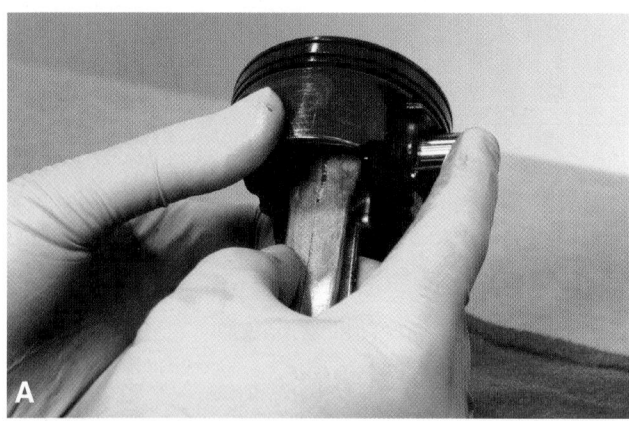

Goodheart-Willcox Publisher

Figure 19-8.

Check the marks on the piston head and connecting rod to ensure that the piston head is reinstalled in the proper orientation. A—Install the piston pin. B—Install the piston pin retainer.

Goodheart-Willcox Publisher

Figure 19-9.

Ring end gap is measured by pushing the ring into the cylinder with an inverted piston. Then, the piston is removed and a thickness gauge is used to measure the gap.

gap is too small, it can be corrected by carefully filing the ring ends. See **Figure 19-10**. If the gap is too wide, a new ring is required.

Installing Rings

Next, check the ring side clearance as described in Chapter 17. If the piston ring end gaps and side clearances are satisfactory, install the rings on the piston. Refer to the instructions that came with the ring set to determine how the rings should be installed. Generally, if the rings have a chamfer on the inside edge, the ring is installed with the chamfered edge up.

The oil control ring is installed first, into the bottom groove of the piston. The oil control ring may be a one-piece unit or a three-piece unit consisting of two thin rails and an expander. One-piece oil control rings are installed using a ring expander, and three-piece rings are installed by hand. The expander is installed first, then the rails are installed one at a time. The rails are installed in the top ring groove, and then twisted down, one groove at a time until they are in position on either side of the expander. See **Figure 19-11**.

The two compression rings are installed next. See **Figure 19-12**. The rings should be rotated so the ring gaps are staggered 120°. Next, lubricate the rings and piston skirt heavily with clean engine oil. Do *not* apply assembly lube to the rings and piston skirt.

Goodheart-Willcox Publisher

Figure 19-11.

If the oil control ring is a three-piece design, install the expander first. Then, twist the rails into place one at a time.

Installing the Piston and Rod Assembly in the Cylinder

Next, tighten a piston ring compressor around the piston head to compress the rings flush with the grooves. See **Figure 19-13**. Hold the compressor firmly against the top of the block and use a wooden dowel or hammer handle to tap the piston out of the compressor and into the cylinder. Once free

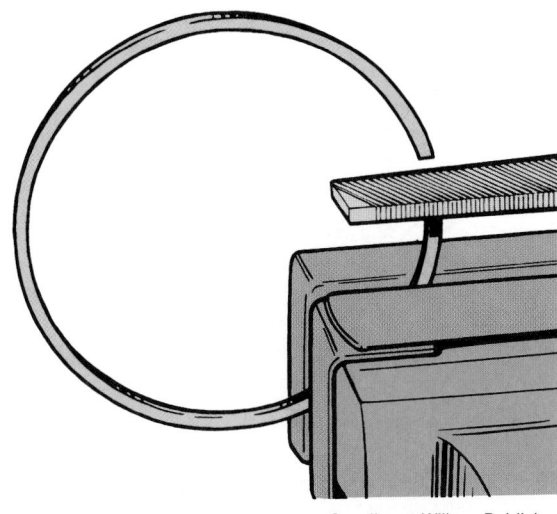

Goodheart-Willcox Publisher

Figure 19-10.

Ring ends can be dressed with a file if the end gap is too small. Use copper vise jaws to protect the ring.

Goodheart-Willcox Publisher

Figure 19-12.

Install the compression rings. Stagger the ring gaps by 120° to prevent blowby.

Goodheart-Willcox Publisher

Figure 19-13.
A ring compressor is used to squeeze the ring ends together while the piston is pushed into the cylinder.

of the compressor, the rings will maintain firm contact with the cylinder wall, even if the cylinder is slightly tapered. See **Figure 19-14**.

If the rod has integrated bearings, the saddle should be guided into place on the crankshaft journal as the piston is pushed into the cylinder. If the rod uses bearing inserts, they must be installed before the saddle is brought into contact with the crankshaft journal.

Installing Insert-Type Rod Bearings

The diameter across the parting surfaces of insert bearing halves is slightly larger than the diameter across the curve machined into the rod and rod cap. This condition is called *bearing spread*. The correct amount of bearing spread gives tight insert-to-bore contact around the entire bearing and provides support and alignment. It also helps to carry heat away through the rod and bearing cap and holds the bearing in place during assembly.

To seat the insert, the ends must be forced down and snapped into place. Never press down in the center of the insert to seat it in the rod bore. When precision inserts are snapped into the rod bore, the ends will protrude slightly above the parting surface. See **Figure 19-15A**. This built-in design feature is called *bearing crush*. Generally, bearing crush varies from .001″ to .002″.

When the rod cap is installed and drawn into place, the insert ends meet first and force the insert halves tightly against the rod bore. This provides firm support for the insert. The forced fit makes the insert round and, through close metal-to-metal contact, allows heat to be carried away through the rod. **Figure 19-15B** shows how radial pressure is exerted against the rod bore.

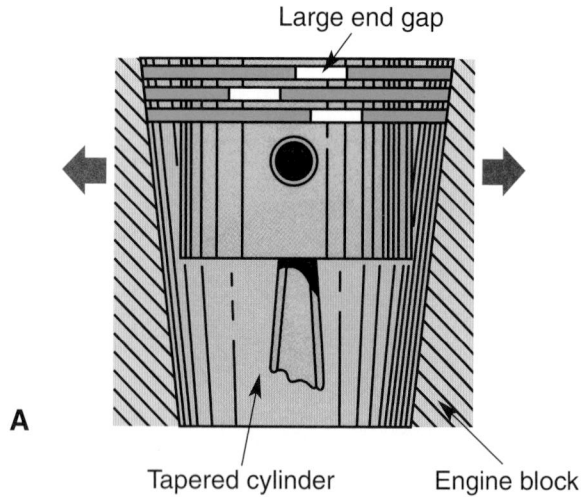

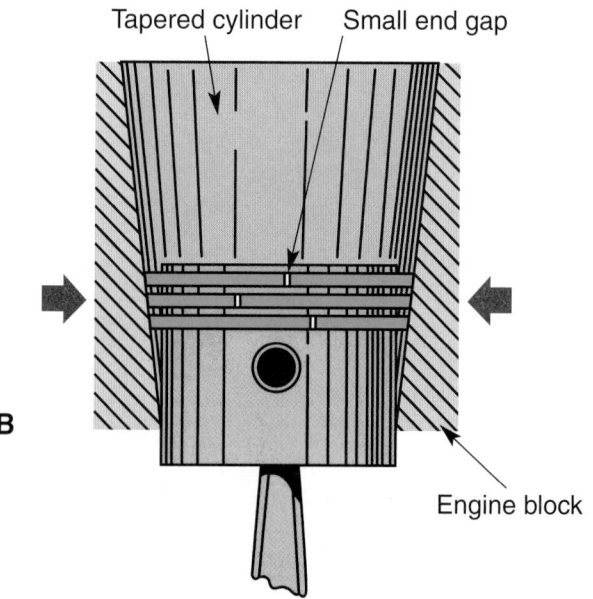

Goodheart-Willcox Publisher

Figure 19-14.
The ring end gap allows the ring to expand and contract so they can stay in constant contact with the cylinder wall, even when the cylinder becomes tapered due to wear. The taper of the cylinder in this drawing is extremely exaggerated for illustrative purposes. A—At the top of piston travel, the rings expand outward. B—At the bottom of piston travel, the rings are forced into their grooves.

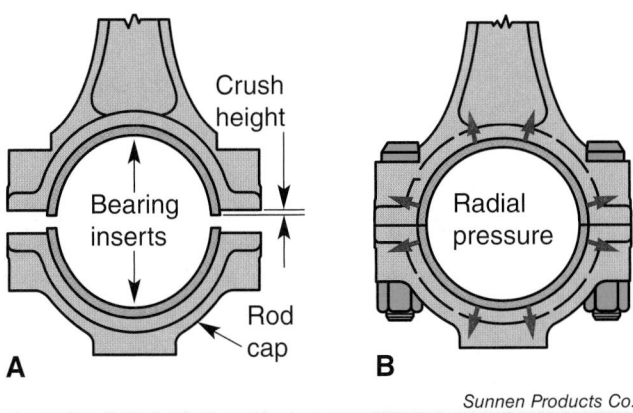

Sunnen Products Co.

Figure 19-15.

The effect of bearing crush. A—Rod and cap separated. B—Rod and cap drawn together, creating radial pressure on the inserts.

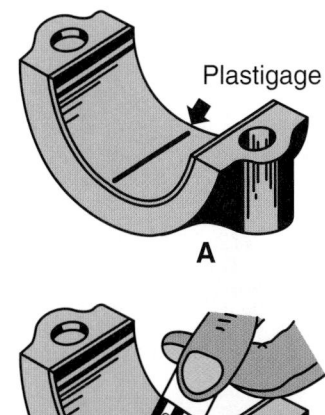

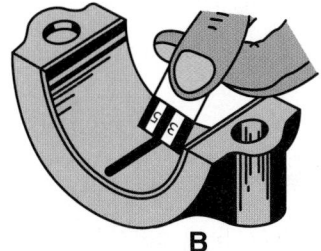

Goodheart-Willcox Publisher

Figure 19-16.

Plastigage is used to check bearing clearance. A—A strip of Plastigage is placed across the bearing surface of the rod cap. B—The cap is tightened to specification and then removed. The width of the flattened strip is compared to the scale on the package.

Precision inserts must be kept in matched pairs. Never mismatch bearing inserts. Always use the exact size needed. For most engines, standard sizes and various undersizes are available. Bearings *cannot* be made larger or smaller in the shop.

Checking Rod Bearing Clearance

Bearing clearance is the space between the inner bearing surface and the crankshaft rod journal. When checking bearing clearance, use a special compressible plastic material called Plastigage. This material is color coded and selected according to the recommended clearance range. It comes in a thin, round strand, which is stored in a paper package.

To use Plastigage, select the correct color for the specified clearance. Cut a piece of plastic equal to the width of the bearing and lay it across the bearing surface, **Figure 19-16A**. Next install the cap and tighten it to the proper specification. Be careful to install the rod cap in the proper orientation.

Torque the bearing cap in place. Then, remove the cap and compare the compressed width of the plastic with the scale printed on the Plastigage package. See **Figure 19-16B**. The number within the graduation on the package (envelope) indicates the bearing clearance in thousandths of an inch or in millimeters depending on which side of the package is used. Taper is indicated where one end of the Plastigage is flattened wider than the other end. Measure each end of the flattened Plastigage and the difference between reading is the approximate

amount of taper. Excessive amount of taper indicates that a new or reground crankshaft is required. In effect, the wider the plastic, the less clearance there is.

If bearing clearance is too great, undersize inserts will have to be used. If the crank journal is worn, it will require grinding to clean it up. After grinding the journal, recheck the clearance with a Plastigage, and select the proper undersize inserts.

Installing the Connecting Rod Cap

After measuring the bearing clearance, scrape the Plastigage from cap bearing surface with a fingernail. If the clearance and taper were within specifications, lubricate the connecting rod bearing surfaces and the crankshaft journal with assembly lube. Next, install the rod cap and tighten the bolts to the proper torque specification. See **Figure 19-17**.

When the engine is manufactured, the rod cap is bolted into position on the rod. Then, the assembly is bored to an exact size. It is important, therefore, that the rod cap is always put back in its original position. If the cap is turned 180°, the upper and lower halves will be offset. This error in assembly will eventually result in bearing and shaft failure. See **Figure 19-18**.

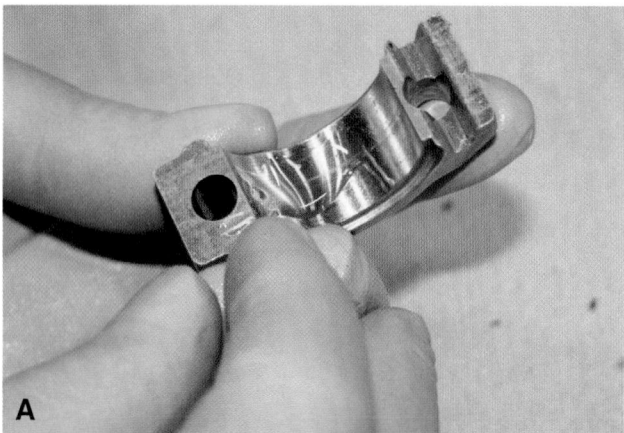

Goodheart-Willcox Publisher

Figure 19-17.
Lubricate the connecting rod bearing surfaces and the crankshaft journals with assembly lube before installing the rod cap. A—Assembly lube being applied to rod cap. B—Rod cap installed on rod.

Caution

Caps must never be switched from one rod to another.

Frequently, locking devices are installed on the rod cap to stop connecting rod bolts or cap screws from loosening in service. One common device is a thin sheet metal strip with locking tabs. See **Figure 19-19**. The cap screw is inserted through holes in the locking strip, holding it in place against the rod. After the cap screw is tight, the metal tabs are bent up against the flat sides of the screw head.

Self-locking nuts, lock washers, and specially shaped cap screws are also used to prevent loosening. The final tightening of the cap screws is especially important. Always use a torque wrench to tighten rod fasteners to the exact torque specified by the manufacturer.

Installing Overhead Valves

Before starting assembly of an overhead valve cylinder head, inspect valve stems for foreign material and burrs, which can cause sticking and damage the new stem seals. Coat the valve stems with valve guide lubricant. Do not allow the lubricant to contact the valve face, valve seat, or end of the valve stem. Install the valves in the cylinder head, being careful to install the intake and exhaust valves in their respective guides.

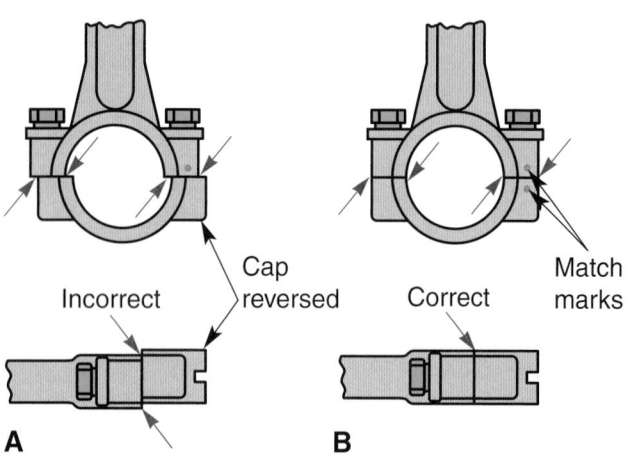

Figure 19-18.
Connecting rod cap installation. A—If the cap is turned 180°, the rod bore will be offset. B—The match marks on the rod and cap signal correct assembly.

Goodheart-Willcox Publisher

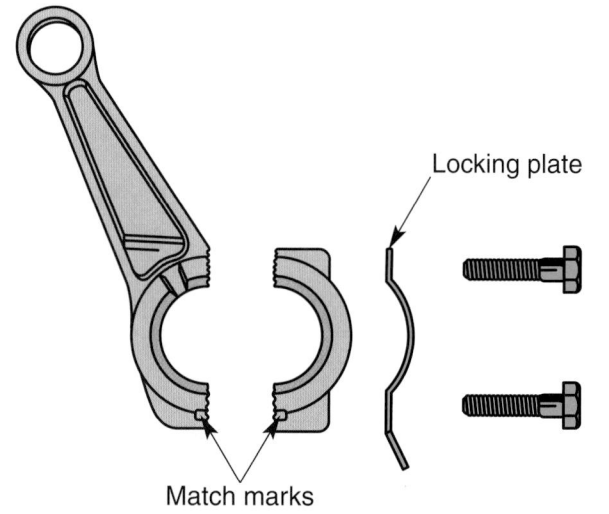

Tecumseh Products Co.

Figure 19-19.
A locking plate is often used between the connecting rod cap and cap screws.

Place the cylinder head on a workbench and support the valve faces with wooden blocks. If stem seals are used, place them over the stems. Place the valve springs over the valve stems and set the retainers on the springs. Compress the springs and install the retainers. See **Figure 19-20**.

Installing the Cylinder Head

The mating surfaces of the cylinder and the cylinder head should be completely clean. Install a new head gasket on the cylinder block and then align and place the cylinder head on the cylinder. See **Figure 19-21**. Never use gasket cement or sealer on a head gasket. Install the bolts through the head and into the cylinder block holes. Do *not* apply oil or anti-seize compound to the bolts unless specifically recommended by the manufacturer's service manual.

Tighten the bolts evenly by hand in a crisscross pattern. Then, use a torque wrench to tighten the bolts to the proper torque specifications. See **Figure 19-22**. Torque the head bolts in sequential increments in the pattern specified by the manufacturer to avoid causing the cylinder head to warp. If the engine being serviced is an L-head engine, the cylinder head installation is complete. If the engine is an overhead valve engine, the pushrods and rocker arms must be installed and valve clearance must be checked and adjusted if needed.

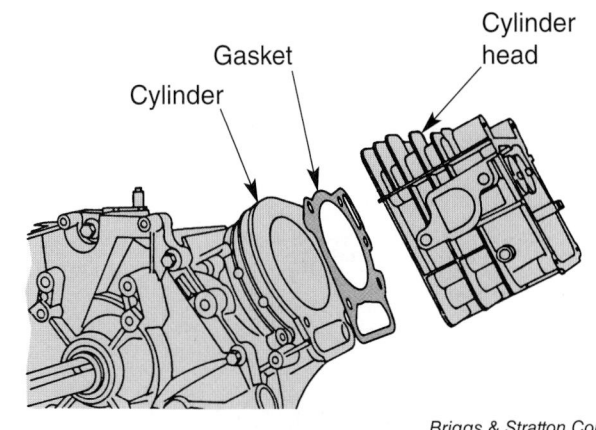

Briggs & Stratton Corp.

Figure 19-21.
Use a new gasket when installing the cylinder head on the block. Head and block surfaces must be clean.

Installing Pushrods and Rocker Arms

Place the pushrods into their respective guides. Place the rocker arms on the studs and install the rocker arm nuts. Turn the nuts until they just touch the rocker arms. Carefully rotate the crankshaft to verify proper pushrod operation.

Adjusting Overhead Valve Clearance

Proper clearance between the rocker arm and the valve stem is essential. Too much clearance will reduce volumetric efficiency. Too little clearance can cause valve burning or warpage.

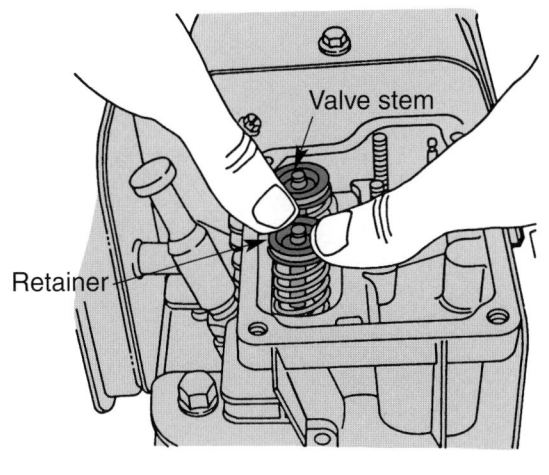

A

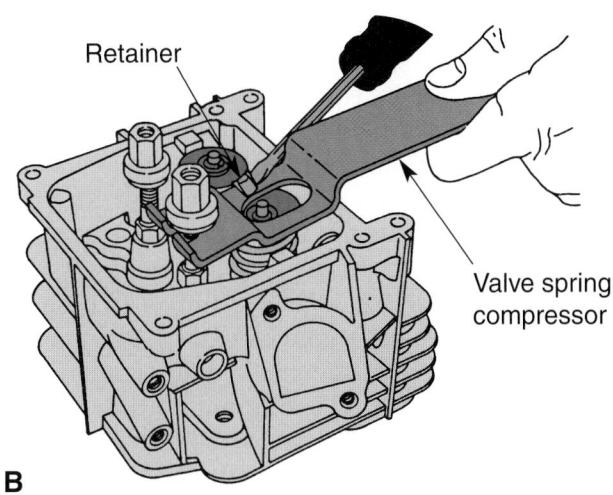

B

Briggs & Stratton Corp.

Figure 19-20.
Valves must be installed in an overhead valve cylinder head before the head is installed on the engine. A—Installing valve spring retainers. B—Replacing split-type retainers. A magnetized screwdriver or a bit of grease helps to place the retainer onto the valve stem recess.

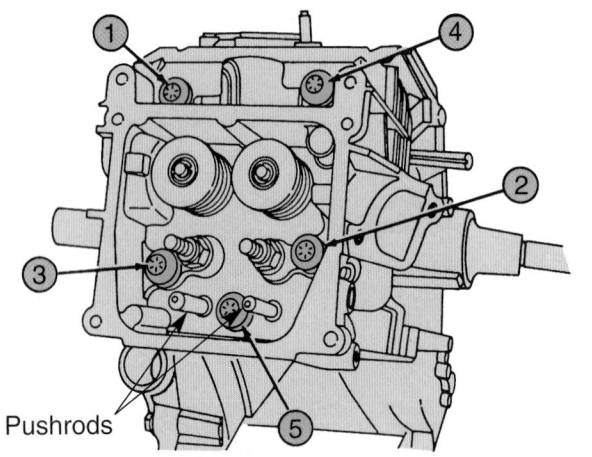

Figure 19-22.

Goodheart-Willcox Publisher

Tighten the cylinder head bolts with a torque wrench in the proper sequence and in gradual increments to avoid head warpage.

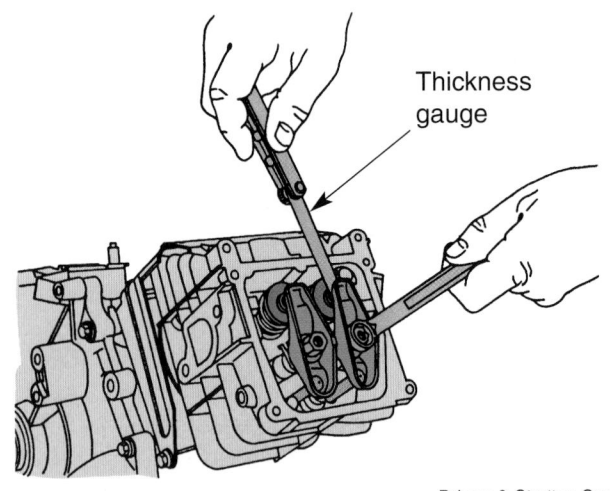

Briggs & Stratton Corp.

Figure 19-23.

Adjust rocker arm-to-valve stem clearance until very slight drag is felt on the thickness gauge.

Before checking valve clearance, position the piston as recommended by the manufacturer. To accomplish this, simply rotate the crankshaft until the piston reaches the position specified. Top Dead Center is the correct piston position for some engines; others may require the piston to be a certain distance beyond Top Dead Center. Always check specifications. If necessary, the distance past Top Dead Center can be measured through the spark plug hole with a ruler, dial indicator, or similar tool.

Once the piston is set at the correct position, place the proper feeler gauge leaf between the rocker arm and the valve stem. See **Figure 19-23**. Check engine specifications for the required clearance. Some engines require equal clearance for both intake and exhaust valves. However, some engine manufacturers use a different metal for exhaust valves than intake valves, so the coefficient of thermal expansion is not the same for each valve. Therefore, clearances must be different for each valve.

Turn the locking/adjusting nut clockwise to reduce clearance or counterclockwise to increase clearance. The feeler gauge should drag slightly when pulled out. Hold the adjusting nut with a wrench and tighten the locking screw slightly. Recheck clearance with the feeler gauge. If necessary, readjust until correct clearance is obtained. Tighten the locking screw.

Installing the Crankcase Breather and Valve Cover

If an L-head engine is being reassembled, make sure the oil drain back holes are clear, and then bolt the crankcase breather assembly in place. If there is a breather passage cast into the block, replace the cover on the passage as well.

If an overhead valve engine is being reassembled, replace the crankcase breather, valve cover, and gaskets. See **Figure 19-24**. Tighten the valve

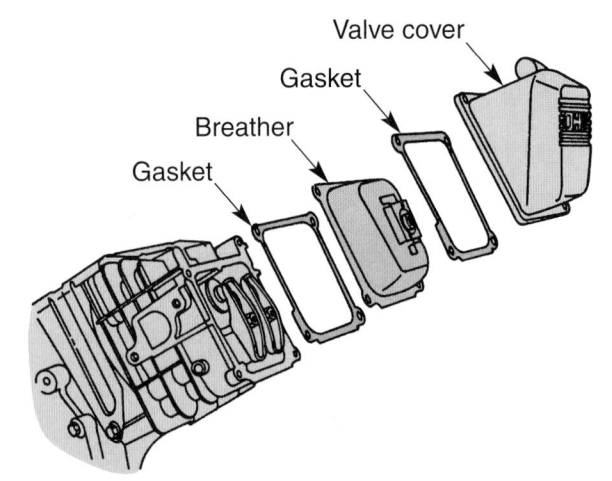

Briggs & Stratton Corp.

Figure 19-24.

When a valve cover and breather assembly is installed, all mating surfaces should be clean and new gaskets should be used.

cover bolts to the recommended torque setting. See **Figure 19-25**.

Adjusting Crankshaft Endplay and Installing the Crankcase Cover

The next step in reassembly is to reinstall the crankcase cover. Crankshaft endplay should have been measured before the engine was disassembled. If the endplay was greater or less than specification, any necessary endplay adjustments must be made before the crankcase cover is bolted on.

Endplay will vary with engine type, design, and use. Endplay, along with bearing clearance, allows room for thermal expansion during engine operation. See **Figure 19-26**. For this reason, endplay must be held to the exact tolerances specified by the manufacturer.

The method of adjusting endplay varies depending on engine design. Typically, endplay is adjusted by installing thicker or thinner gaskets on the crankcase cover or by installing different thickness thrust washers on the crankshaft. A thicker gasket or thrust washer effectively moves the main bearings farther apart, increasing endplay. Installing a thinner gasket or thrust washer decreases endplay. Always follow the manufacturer's instructions for adjusting endplay.

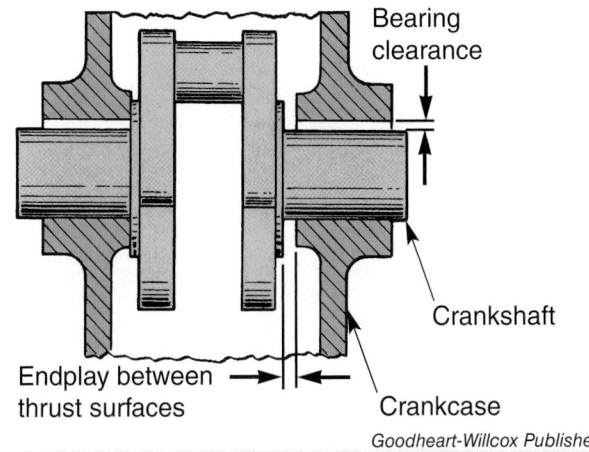

Goodheart-Willcox Publisher

Figure 19-26.

Crankshaft bearings and thrust surfaces must have some clearance (endplay) to provide space for lubricant and for heat expansion.

When the necessary endplay adjustments are made, make a final inspection of the engine's interior. Make sure that the timing marks are properly aligned and the oil slinger and governor shaft and gear are installed. If the power-take-off end is keyed, put tape over the keyway to protect the oil seal when the cover is installed. Then, install the proper gasket on the crankcase cover and insert two or three bolts through the cover to hold the gasket in place. Align the cover with the crankcase, slide it over the crankshaft, and tighten the cover bolts.

Reinstalling External Engine Components

Next, the flywheel can be reinstalled. To reinstall the flywheel, turn crankshaft until the keyway is in the 12 o'clock position, and then insert the key. If the shaft uses a Woodruff key, install it as shown in **Figure 19-27**. Make sure that the key seats properly in the keyway before starting the flywheel on the shaft.

Next, align the flywheel keyway with the crankshaft key and install the flywheel. Install the starter clutch and crankshaft nut. Tighten the crankshaft nut to the correct torque.

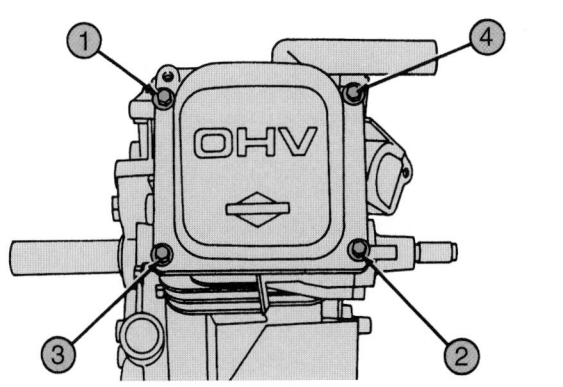

Briggs & Stratton Corp.

Figure 19-25.

When installing the valve cover bolts, tighten them in the proper sequence. Tighten to the specified torque to avoid warping the cover flanges.

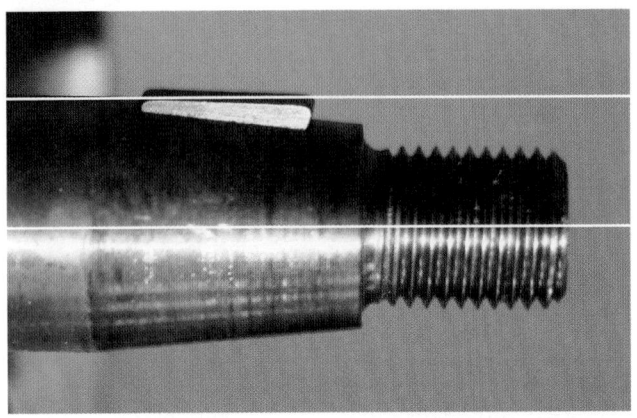
Goodheart-Willcox Publisher

Figure 19-27.

If a Woodruff key is used on a crankshaft, it should be placed so that the top of the key is parallel to the centerline of the crankshaft.

Note

Use a strap wrench or a spanner wrench to hold the flywheel when torquing the crankshaft nut.

Install the ignition module, set the proper air gap, and then tighten the mounting bolts. Then, install any brackets or shrouds on the engine. Reinstall the intake manifold, carburetor, and air filter assembly, using new gaskets. Make sure the breather hose is reconnected to the air filter or carburetor intake.

Reinstall the governor linkages. Refer to sketches or photos taken during engine disassembly to ensure that the governor linkages are reassembled properly. Make sure there is no binding by operating the governor linkages by hand.

Install any remaining engine components, including oil filler tube, throttle and choke linkages, gas tank, starter, muffler, and drive pulley. Install a new fuel line and filter. Refill the engine with the required amount of fresh motor oil and make sure there is fresh gasoline in the tank. The final step in engine reassembly is to gap and install a new spark plug. The spark plug wire should not be attached to the spark plug until you are ready to start the engine. This will prevent the engine from firing accidentally.

Engine Break-In

Secure the engine on a test stand or reinstall it on the implement before starting it for the first time. Although some engines can be bench tested, push lawn mower engines are often equipped with a lightweight flywheel, and require the added mass of a mower blade to operate properly. These engines should be remounted on the mower and the blade should be reinstalled before the engine is started.

Before starting the engine, check for and fix any fuel or oil leaks. Several attempts may be required to start the engine for the first time. Be prepared to stop the engine quickly if the governor malfunctions or if there are any indications of severe engine problems. After starting the engine and letting it warm to operating temperature, make any necessary carburetor and governor adjustments. The engine may smoke excessively when first started. The smoking should diminish as the oil applied to the piston and rings burns away and the rings are broken-in.

After a reconditioned engine is started, a short break-in period occurs. *Break-in* is the process in which the face of each ring wears off until it fits perfectly against the cylinder wall. To help the rings seat quickly, the face is covered with microscopic grooves. During the first few hours of operation, these grooves rub against the cylinder wall and all high spots are worn off. As the grooves wear away, the faces of rings and the cylinder wall become very smooth. Under normal operating conditions, very little wear occurs beyond this point.

Ring break-in varies from engine to engine, but may take as many as ten hours of operation. During this period, the engine oil level should be checked frequently. The engine oil should be changed after the first hour of operation. The greatest wear occurs during this period, and changing the oil removes the metal particles resulting from the wear. The engine can be operated normally during the break-in period, but should not be subjected to heavy loads until the break-in period is over.

Some manufacturer's require the cylinder head to be retorqued after a certain number of hours of operation. Additional service measures may be required during or following the break-in period. Always consult the manufacturer's service manual for proper break-in procedures.

Summary

An engine is essentially reassembled in the reverse of the order in which it was disassembled. First, bearings and seals are installed in the crankcase and the crankcase cover. In an L-head engine, the valve assemblies are reinstalled in the block. In an overhead valve engine, the valves will be reinstalled in the cylinder head before the head is reinstalled.

The journals of the crankshaft are then coated with assembly lube and the crankshaft is installed in the crankcase. The valve lifters are installed in their bores, and then the timing marks on the crankshaft and camshaft are aligned and the camshaft is installed. The governor gear or oil slinger is installed next.

The piston is reinstalled on the connecting rod. Check the marks on the rod and piston to ensure that the piston is installed in the right orientation. Next, the piston rings are installed on the piston. The oil control ring is installed first, and then the two compression rings are installed. The piston and rings are lubricated with engine oil, and then the piston and rod assembly is installed in the cylinder. If the rod uses insert-type rod bearings, they are installed next. Rod bearing clearance is checked using Plastigage, and then the connecting rod cap is installed on the rod. Matching marks on the rod and cap should be aligned to ensure that the cap is put on in the right orientation.

Next, the cylinder head is installed on the cylinder block. Always use a new cylinder head gasket and tighten the head bolts in the manufacturer's recommended pattern. On an overhead valve engine, the valve assemblies must be installed in the cylinder head before the head is installed on the cylinder block. Then, the pushrods and rocker arm assemblies can be installed and the proper valve clearance can be set.

The crankcase breather is reinstalled next. Then, any needed crankshaft endplay adjustments are made and the crankcase cover is reinstalled. Before the cover is installed, the keyway in the crankshaft should be taped in order to prevent the oil seal from being damaged by the sharp edges of the keyway.

Next, all of the engine's external components are reinstalled, including the carburetor, intake manifold, muffler, gas tank, air filter, governor linkages, shrouds, ignition module, and starter. Mount the engine on a test stand or reinstall it in the implement. Gap, install, and connect the spark plug.

Check the engine for leaks, and then start it. Be prepared to stop the engine immediately if there is any indication of over-speeding or engine troubles. Allow the engine to reach operating temperature and then make any necessary carburetor or governor adjustments. Change the oil after the first hour of operation and retorque the cylinder head as directed by the manufacturer.

Review Questions

Answer the following questions using the information provided in this chapter.

1. *True or False?* Valves should be installed so the dampening coils are on the same side as the valve caps and retainers.

2. Briefly list the results of excessive ring end gap and a lack of ring end gap.

3. Piston rings can be one of two basic types. Can you name them?

4. Name the tool used to squeeze the piston rings together so the piston assembly can be installed in the cylinder.

5. Properly fitted friction bearing ends protrude slightly above the parting surface of the connecting rod cap. This characteristic produces what is commonly called _____.
   A. bearing crush
   B. bearing spread
   C. bearing seat
   D. bearing swell

6. Bearing caps must never be _____ when being replaced on the rods.

7. What tool must always be used to tighten rod caps?

8. What is the name of the special plastic substance used to measure bearing clearance?

9. When new or reconditioned valves are being installed in guides, what should be placed on the valve stems first?

10. How is valve clearance checked on an overhead valve engine?

11. Why should valve cover screws never be tightened excessively?

12. What two methods are typically used to adjust crankshaft endplay?

13. Why should lawn mower engines be reinstalled in the equipment before they are test run?

14. *True or False?* Engine oil should be changed after the first hour of operation following an engine overhaul.

15. Some manufacturers require the _____ to be retorqued after a certain number of hours of operation following an engine overhaul.

Suggested Activities

1. Replace oil seals in the crankcase.

2. Time the camshaft to the crankshaft.

3. Measure crankshaft bearing clearances with Plastigage and telescoping gauges.

4. Install new main and rod bearing inserts. Observe rules of cleanliness and torque rod bolts to specified value.

5. Using an old ring, demonstrate the method of dressing ring ends with a file to increase ring end gap.

6. Replace piston rings with a ring expander.

7. Using ring compressor, replace a reconditioned piston assembly in the cylinder.

8. Adjust valve clearances in an overhead valve assembly.

Christina Richards/Shutterstock.com

Small gas engines are used in a wide range of construction equipment, such as this power tamper.

SECTION 5
Applications

Lawn and Brush Equipment

Learning Objectives

After studying this chapter, you will be able to:

- List and follow safe work practices.
- List the features available in different lawn mower designs and their advantages.
- Summarize basic lawn mower maintenance procedures and safety precautions.
- Describe the proper method for storing a lawn mower for long periods of time.
- List the different features available on chain saws, leaf blowers, string trimmers, and edger/trimmers.
- Summarize the maintenance, safety, and storage procedures for chain saws, string trimmers, brushcutters, and edger/trimmers.
- Identify a variety of cutting blades for trimmers and brushcutters.

Key Terms

bail
blade guard
brushcutters
chain guard (scabbard)
dethatcher blade
edger/trimmers
electric starters
extended rope starter
grass discharge chute
   guard

kickback
kickout
push mowers
reel-type mower
rotary mowers
self-propelled mowers
spark arrestors
string trimmers

Working Safely

Safety is of primary importance when working on small gas engines and the implements they power. The safety rules presented in this section pertain to a wide variety of implements that may occasionally need adjustment or service. The list is only partial because it is impossible to predict every possibility that might cause accident or injury. The rules listed are broad. It is expected that persons servicing their own equipment, or the equipment of others, should always use good judgment and be familiar with safety precautions provided in manufacturer's technical service manuals relating to the specific piece of equipment being serviced.

To prevent the engine from accidentally starting, always remove the spark plug wire from the spark plug before servicing and/or adjusting the machine. If possible, ground the spark plug wire and tie it so it is out of the way. See **Figure 20-1**. Keep children or bystanders away from equipment while it is being serviced.

Do not wear jewelry or loose fitting clothing when working on engines or equipment. Wear good quality work boots and make sure the laces are properly tied whenever servicing lawn equipment. The blades of the equipment can throw rocks and loose debris and loose laces could become tangled in moving parts.

Goodheart-Willcox Publisher

Figure 20-1.

Always pull the spark plug wire off the spark plug before servicing the equipment or engine.

Inspect the power cords on power tools for damage. Do not use any tool that has a damaged cord. Make sure all power tools are properly grounded. Always wear safety glasses when operating equipment that can create flying chips or debris.

When using compressed air to clean or dry parts, wear safety glasses and do not point the airstream at yourself or others. If the work area or the part being blown off is dirty or dusty, be sure to wear a dust mask. Similarly, if a power washer is used to clean an engine, be sure not to point the high-pressure spray at yourself or other people. The high-pressure water stream can cause serious injury.

Special precautions must be taken if a portable heater is used to heat the work area. Do not use a portable heater around gasoline, paint, or other volatile materials. Keep the heater a minimum of four feet from flammable materials. If a propane or kerosene heater is used, make sure the work area is well ventilated.

Be careful when working with gasoline. Gasoline is highly volatile and gasoline fumes are highly explosive. Use only approved containers for storing gasoline. Do not smoke or perform any action that produces sparks when working around gasoline. If gasoline is spilled, clean up the spill immediately. Store any fuel- or oil-contaminated rags in a fire can until they can be properly disposed of. See **Figure 20-2**.

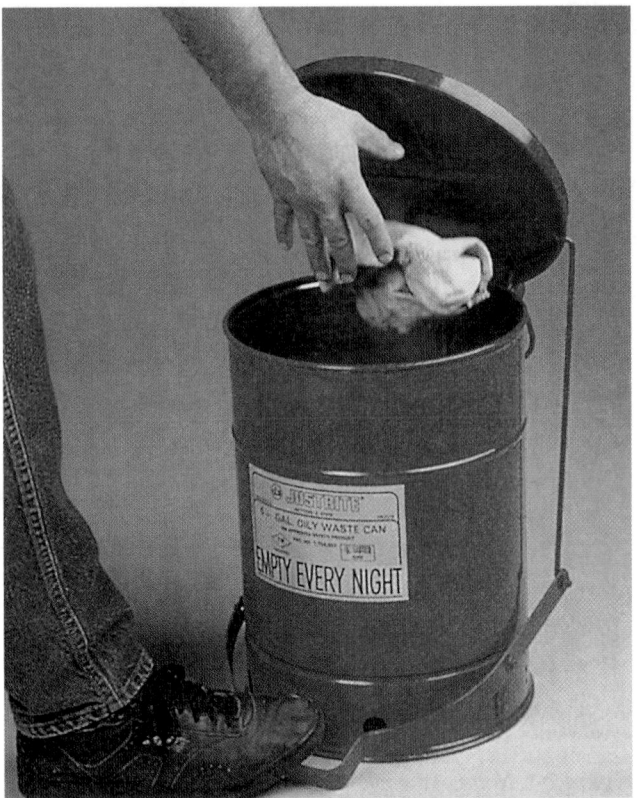

Justrite Manufacturing Company

Figure 20-2.

Store oil- or fuel-contaminated rags in a fire can until they can be properly disposed of.

Running engines produce carbon monoxide (CO), which can be deadly. For this reason, engines should not be operated in an enclosed area, such as a shop or garage, longer than needed to move the equipment outdoors. Simply opening doors and windows may not provide adequate ventilation.

Batteries release hydrogen gas, especially during charging. Hydrogen gas is explosive, so it is important not to allow sparks or open flame near a battery. Always disconnect the battery before working on equipment. This prevents accidental short circuits, which can damage wiring, destroy electronic components, and cause sparking.

Hydraulic systems operate under high pressure. A leak in the hydraulic system can release a high pressure stream of hydraulic fluid that is capable of piercing the skin. Never put your hands near a suspected hydraulic leak. Use a piece of cardboard or wood to locate the leak instead. Always cycle hydraulic controls to relieve pressure from the system before performing any service, including tightening hoses and lines. Make sure all hoses are in good condition and all connections are tight before pressurizing the system.

After completing service on an engine or equipment, make sure all parts are reinstalled, all fasteners are properly tightened, and all tools are removed. Any loose parts or tools could fly off when the equipment is operated, causing damage or injury.

Lawn Mowers

This chapter will examine a few of the more common types of lawn mowers available. It will discuss purchasing considerations, safety features, service warnings, and maintenance methods. Since there are many variations of mowers on the market, you should always study the owner's manual before operating and servicing these devices.

Lawn mowers have caused a great number of injuries. Severe lacerations to hands and feet can be caused by objects thrown from under the mower housing or out of the discharge opening. Recently, laws have been enacted forcing manufacturers to provide certain safety devices on lawn mowers to help prevent accidents. A *grass discharge chute guard* is an important safety device that can prevent lawn mower injuries.

As with many other types of equipment, there is no age, skill, or intelligence requirement for using a lawn mower. However, young children should never be allowed to operate a mower. The human body is no match for a sharp steel blade rotating at hundreds of revolutions per minute.

Rotary and Reel Mowers

A wide range of power mowers are available. Each type of mower has certain advantages over other designs. *Rotary mowers* (those with blades that rotate in a horizontal plane) for large areas have large diameter blades with large, heavy engines and housings. Also, safety and accessory items may add to mower weight. Remember, a mower may roll easily on a smooth floor. However, it may be difficult to push on a deep, rough lawn when the grass catcher is loaded with grass.

A *reel-type mower* (with helical blades that rotate around horizontal shaft) is the type commonly used on golf course greens. See **Figure 20-3**. They produce a clean and consistent cut but may be more difficult

Deere & Co.

Figure 20-3.

This walk-behind greens mower is a reel-type mower.

and expensive to maintain. Special equipment is needed to sharpen the reel. Adjustments of the reel blades to the cutter bar are critical, and occasional readjustments are necessary as the blades wear. Cutter height is controlled by raising or lowering the rollers.

For the average size yard, a rotary-type mower with blade diameter of 22″ is usually satisfactory. For small yards, a 20″ mower is more maneuverable and takes less storage space. On a typical rotary mower, the height that grass is cut to is controlled by raising or lowering the entire mower by adjusting the wheels. See **Figure 20-4**.

Push-Type and Self-Propelled Mowers

Push mowers rely on the operator to push them. These mowers are generally simpler and less expensive than self-propelled mowers. *Self-propelled mowers* are equipped with engine-driven wheels. Engines for self-propelled mowers have to rotate the blade and the drive mechanism to the wheels. This requires additional engine horsepower. In some mowers, power is transmitted to the wheels through shafts and gears. Others use a belt and pulley system. See **Figure 20-5**. Commercial self-propelled mowers may be equipped with a hydro-static drive. Depending on which type of drive

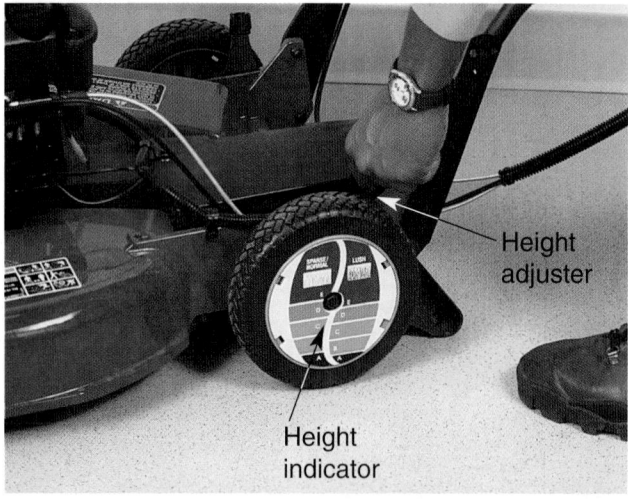

Goodheart-Willcox Publisher

Figure 20-4.

Each wheel on this mower has an adjuster to raise or lower the housing and blade for the desired length of grass. Always stop the engine before making these adjustments.

mechanism is used, the additional maintenance that is required may include greasing bearings and gears or replacing drive belts.

Optional Features

One optional feature for mowers is side-bagging or rear-bagging. Grass bags may be fabric or molded plastic containers. Side-bagging mowers tend to extend the width of the mower but may be a little easier to remove and install. If mowing in narrow quarters, a rear bag may be slightly more maneuverable, particularly if the mower must be backed out of the space.

Most manufacturers try to make bag removal and replacement as easy as possible. Typically a bag must be removed a number of times during a mowing session. This means stopping the mower, removing the bag, emptying the bag, replacing the bag, and restarting the mower. This is enough work without having to wrestle with a clumsy bag connection. The bag should also be durable and not wear on chaffing points.

Using either a side or rear bag reduces thatch (compacted dead grass cuttings) in the lawn. Thatch, if allowed to accumulate, tends to smother the lawn and create growth problems.

A

B

Goodheart-Willcox Publisher

Figure 20-5.

Self-propelled mowers are commonly driven by a belt and pulley system. A—The drive pulley is typically located above the cutting blade. B—The belt drives the rear axle of the mower.

Warning

To prevent serious injury, always stop the engine or blade when emptying the grass catcher. Never start the engine or blade without the grass catcher in place. See **Figure 20-6**.

Grass cuttings are excellent additions for the compost pile or garden. Some people prefer to use a bagless mower and rake the grass cuttings after mowing. Some mowers have blades and housings designed to cut and mulch (cut into fine particles) grass and leaves for composting.

Another optional accessory is a *dethatcher blade*. See **Figure 20-7**. This can be purchased to fit any mower and is installed in place of the cutting blade. There are spring-like fingers attached to the blade that reach down into the lawn. As the blade turns, the fingers rake the thatch up to the surface. The thatch is then collected in the grass bag or hand raked later.

Engine Starting

Various mechanical means have been devised for starting small engines. The recoil starter is still used today. It utilizes a rope, a ratchet mechanism, and a rewind spring. When the rope is pulled, the ratchet engages the flywheel and rotates the crankshaft. When the engine starts, the ratchet disengages from the flywheel. The rewind spring retracts and recoils the rope for the next starting. The proper technique for starting is shown in **Figure 20-8**.

Because of convenience and safety concerns, the *extended rope starter* has become very common today. The advantage to this system is that the operator does not have to bend over as far and feet are clear of the blade housing. See **Figure 20-9**. Also, the blade brake must be released with one hand while the opposite hand pulls the rope.

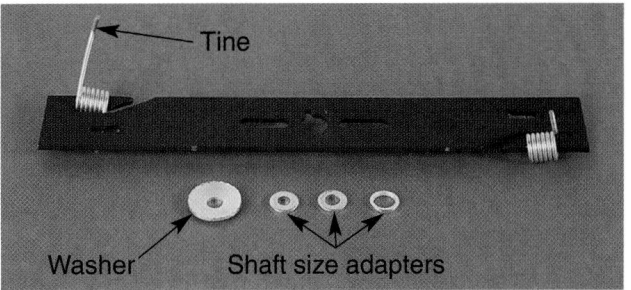

Goodheart-Willcox Publisher

Figure 20-7.

A dethatcher blade uses spring tines (pointed prongs) to rake out dead grass. Adapters with various hole sizes permit bar to fit on any mower shaft diameter.

Goodheart-Willcox Publisher

Figure 20-6.

Never allow the blade to run as the grass catcher is removed. On this mower, a blade brake and clutch stop the blade while allowing the engine to continue running.

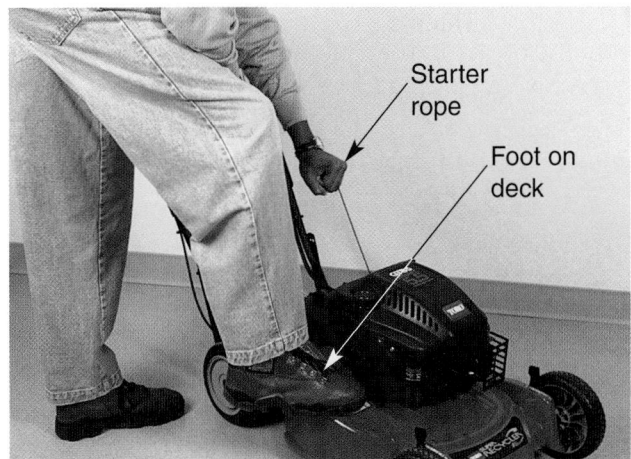

Goodheart-Willcox Publisher

Figure 20-8.

When hand starting a vertical-pull engine, place one foot on the deck and the other foot away from the mower. Pull the rope briskly.

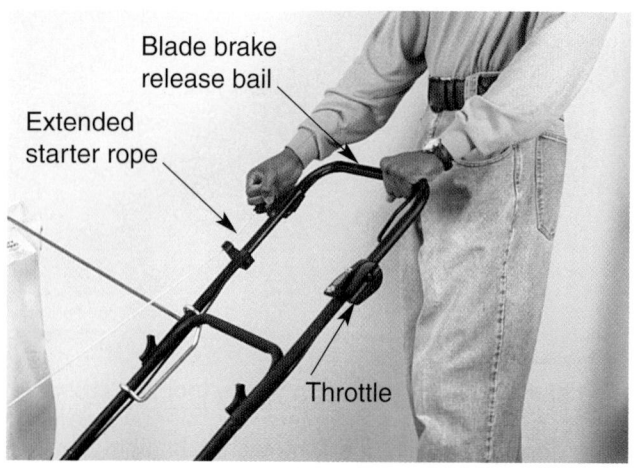

Blade brake
release bail

Extended
starter rope

Throttle

Goodheart-Willcox Publisher

Figure 20-9.

An extended rope starting system helps keep hands
and feet away from the mower while starting.

Electric starters are becoming more common.
The electric start mower has the additional
components of a starter motor, switch, battery, and
wiring. A key is required to turn on the switch.
See **Figure 20-10**.

Procedure for Starting an Engine

The following is a basic procedure for starting
a cold engine:

1. Fill the fuel tank with the proper fuel for the
   engine type.

2. Check the oil level and condition of the oil. Add
   or change the oil if necessary. See **Figure 20-11**.
3. Close the choke and/or prime the engine with
   fuel. See **Figure 20-12**.
4. Turn the key on and/or advance the throttle
   to the *Start* position. See **Figure 20-13**.
5. Start the engine:
   a. **Vertical or Horizontal Rope Start:** Place a
      foot on mower deck and pull the rope. See
      Figure 20-8.

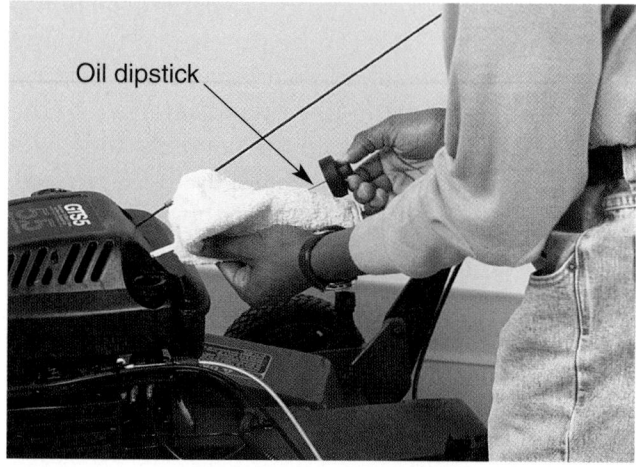

Oil dipstick

Goodheart-Willcox Publisher

Figure 20-11.

This engine has a dipstick for checking the oil level. Oil
is added through the dipstick opening.

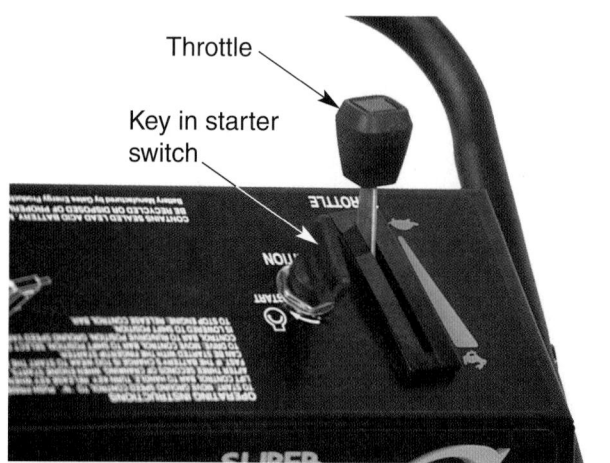

Throttle

Key in starter
switch

Goodheart-Willcox Publisher

Figure 20-10.

An electric start system has an electric motor, battery,
and switch, like an automobile. Most of these mowers
have a hand start backup system in case the battery
is discharged.

Goodheart-Willcox Publisher

Figure 20-12.

Depressing the primer forces fuel into the cylinder
for quickly starting a cold engine. Engines without a
primer have a choke, which is closed to richen the air-
fuel mixture.

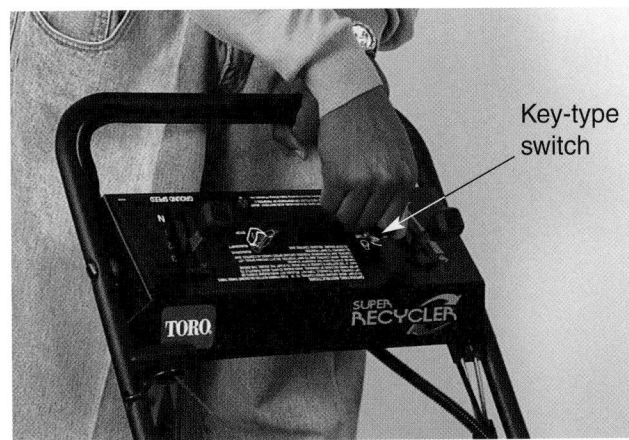

Goodheart-Willcox Publisher

Figure 20-13.

Electric start mowers have a key-type switch. To start, insert the key and turn it to the start position until the engine begins to run. Release the key immediately on starting.

b. **Extended Rope Start:** Hold the bail to the handle and pull the rope. See **Figure 20-9**.
c. **Electric Start:** Turn the key in the switch to *Start*. Release the key as soon as the engine starts. See **Figure 20-10**.
6. When engine starts, open the choke and adjust the throttle to operating speed (about 1/2 to 2/3 maximum speed).

Note

For restarting a warm engine, priming or choking should not be necessary. A cold two-cycle engine may need several prime pump strokes after the engine starts to keep it running.

Blade Brakes

One of the major safety features of every mower manufactured today is a brake that stops the blade within three seconds after the operator's hands leave the handle. This requires a highly efficient braking system. There are basically two kinds of blade brakes.

In one system, a brake pad or band rubs against the flywheel to stop the engine and the blade. See **Figure 20-14**. The second system type of system has a clutch release that allows the engine to remain running while a brake stops the blade. Both systems utilize a *bail* (hand lever) hinged to the handle. In the position shown in **Figure 20-15**, the brake is

A Brake shoe

B Brake shoe

Goodheart-Willcox Publisher

Figure 20-14.

To stop the engine and blade within three seconds of the release of the handle, this engine has a flywheel brake. A—When bail is held against the handle, the flywheel brake is pulled away from the flywheel. B—When the bail is released, spring pressure pulls the brake into contact with the flywheel.

engaged and the blade will not turn. When the bail is pulled into the handle, the brake is released and the blade is free to turn.

Note

In all cases, operators should thoroughly study the owner's manual and be familiar with all safety precautions and operating procedures before using a power mower.

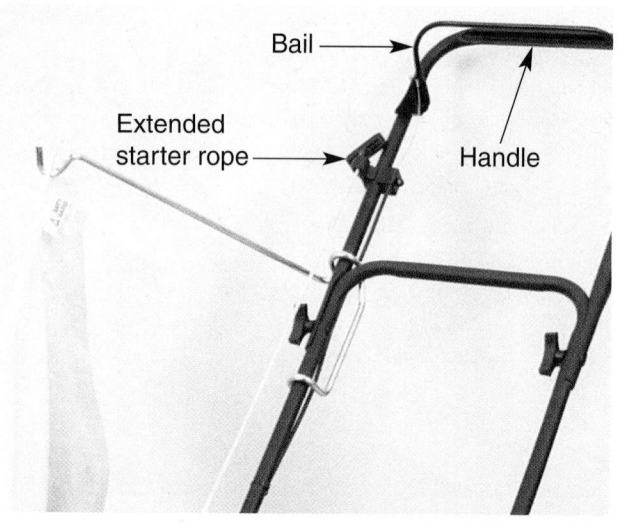

Goodheart-Willcox Publisher

Figure 20-15.

The bail must be held against the handle to release the engine or blade brake.

Goodheart-Willcox Publisher

Figure 20-16.

The bottom of a mower should be kept clean for efficient cutting. Steel housings should be cleaned and painted occasionally to prevent rust.

Minor Checks

If an engine idles too fast or too slow, refer to the manufacturer's service manual. In most cases, the idle speed can be adjusted with the idle speed screw on the carburetor. The engine should idle slowly and smoothly. If the engine will not start, test the spark plug as described in Chapter 15, *Ignition System Service*. If there is no spark, service or replace the spark plug. If the engine still does not start, refer to the troubleshooting chart near the end of this chapter.

General Maintenance

Mowers must be cleaned periodically. It is good practice to let the mower cool after mowing; then tip it on its side (crankcase down) and wash out the residue with a garden hose. See **Figure 20-16.** If grass is allowed to build up on the blade and in the housing, it will dry and become very difficult to remove. Also, cutting efficiency will be reduced. The upper parts of the mower and engine should also be kept clean to maintain engine cooling and proper functioning of the carburetor and governor parts.

The business end of the mower is the cutting blade. After prolonged use, it will become nicked and dull. There are many styles of blades. To remove the blade for sharpening, the mower is tipped on its side (crankcase down) and several bolts are removed.

See **Figure 20-17.** The mower should be properly supported when it is set on its side so that it cannot fall over.

Warning

Always remove the spark plug wire and tie it back before tipping the mower. Wear gloves to protect your hands from the blade's sharp edges.

Goodheart-Willcox Publisher

Figure 20-17.

Before removing a blade, always remove the spark plug wire and tie it away from the plug. Hands and knuckles should be protected with gloves while loosening or tightening bolts.

Blade Sharpening

When mower blades become dull and nicked, it makes the engine work harder and the lawn is cut poorly. Blades can be sharpened by clamping them to a table or in a vise and filing. Always retain the same edge angle. Blades can also be sharpened on a grinding wheel. When grinding a blade, always wear safety goggles or glasses with side shields.

When sharpening the blade, balance it at the same time. Grind or file a small amount off the heavy end until the blade balances horizontally. Test the blade by using a blade balancer, **Figure 20-18,** or balance the blade on a sharp edge, as in **Figure 20-19**. An unbalanced lawn mower blade will create damaging engine vibration.

Hitting solid objects with the blade, such as large rocks, cement edges, pipes, etc., can be very damaging to a mower. Besides damage to the blade, the engine crankshaft can be bent, crankcase housings distorted, connecting rods bent, and flywheel keys sheared. Some blade adapters have shear lugs that are designed to break if the blade strikes a solid object. This allows the blade to slip on the blade adapter, which prevents engine damage.

In another type of design, a friction washer is placed on each side of the blade. The blade is held tightly to the blade adapter during normal operation. However, if the blade strikes a solid object, crankshaft torque overcomes friction and the blade slips, preventing damage.

V-Belts

V-belts are widely used to transfer power on self-propelled mowers. V-belts may look very much alike, but there are many unseen differences that may affect their quality and life span.

Some belts have a fabric cover; others do not. The cords embedded inside the belt may be rayon, polyester, or Kevlar. Rayon will not last as long as the tremendously strong Kevlar. Polyester tends to shrink as it gets hot. The shrinking of the polyester could present a danger, causing unintentional engagement due to shrinkage. Always use only the type and size belt specified by the manufacturer.

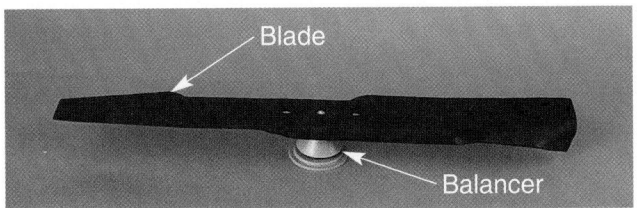

Goodheart-Willcox Publisher

Figure 20-18.

This blade balancer is being used to test blade balance. An unbalanced blade can cause vibration and shorten engine life.

Warning

Always keep hands and objects away from any exposed belts when the engine is running. Remove the spark plug wire when servicing belts. Always keep belt guards in place when operating implements.

Storing a Power Mower

Proper preparations must be made before storing a lawn mower for extended periods. Proper preparation will help ensure long mower and engine life. It will also ensure easy starting the following season.

1. Clean the grass bag and hang it in a dry location.
2. Clean the mower of grass cuttings, mud, etc.
3. Avoid storing gasoline for long periods of time. Store gasoline only in approved *safety* containers. Never store fuel or a mower in an enclosure where there is an open flame. If fuel must be stored, add a stabilizer to it. Fuel stabilizer is available from implement dealers.
4. Try to plan ahead and run the engine dry of fuel at the last use.

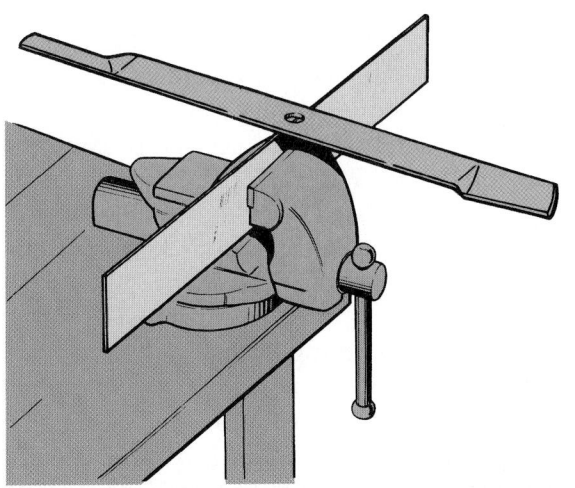

Goodheart-Willcox Publisher

Figure 20-19.

A sharp-edged object can also be used for blade balancing. Center the blade hole over the sharp edge.

5. Drain the oil from the crankcase. Place a tag on the engine that says *No Oil.*

6. Rotate the engine so the piston is at bottom of the cylinder. Remove the spark plug. Spray fogging oil through the spark plug hole, or squirt about one tablespoon of clean motor oil through the spark plug hole with an oil can. Rotate the engine slowly several times to distribute the oil on the cylinder walls. Replace the spark plug.

7. Leave the spark plug lead disconnected. Using the pull rope, rotate the engine slowly until compression resistance is felt. Then rotate the engine an additional one-quarter turn to close off its ports. This seals the cylinder and prevents moisture from entering.

8. Leave the throttle in the off position (closed) and close the choke.

9. Lubricate the mower as described by the manufacturer.

10. Coat the cutting blade with chassis grease to prevent rusting.

11. Store the mower in a dry, clean area.

Removing a Mower from Storage

1. Replace the grass bag.

2. Fill the crankcase with new oil, or make new mixture for a two-cycle engine.

3. Remove the spark plug. Using the pull rope or starter, spin the engine rapidly to remove excess oil from the cylinder. Clean or replace the spark plug.

4. Clean and oil the air filter or replace cartridge if necessary.

5. Fill the fuel tank with fresh fuel.

6. Reconnect the spark plug wire. Start the engine and let it idle until warm. Adjust the idle speed if necessary.

7. Increase the engine speed in the normal manner.

8. Make a brief test run while listening to the engine and watching the condition of all parts.

9. If the engine does not start, review the troubleshooting chart in **Figure 20-20** and the other chapters of this text.

Chain Saws

Small gasoline-powered chain saws are very popular for cutting firewood and trimming trees. Like any cutting tool, they work best when properly maintained. To avoid hazards, all safety devices should be in place and safe operating procedures must be carefully followed. The parts and controls of a typical chain saw are shown in **Figure 20-21**.

Chain Saw Designs

Chain saws are manufactured in a number of sizes from about 10″ to over 40″ of blade length. A smaller saw works well for cutting branches, small trees, and fireplace logs. A large professional model is good for cutting big trees and continuous rugged work.

The lighter a chain saw is, the easier it is to handle, control, and carry. Chain saws range in weight from less than 10 lb to over 25 lb. Heavier models are typically more rugged and more powerful. However, when trimming tree branches from a ladder, a lighter saw will be less tiring.

Some states have laws that require certain safety devices to be used on every chain saw. Check which devices are required and be sure the saw is properly equipped.

Safety Features

Safe operation of a chain saw comes from a good knowledge of correct operating procedure. However, there are a few safety features on many chain saws that are very important.

When the unshielded nose of a chain saw hits a solid surface, the spinning chain may cause the saw to fly back toward the operator. This is known as *kickback* and can be very dangerous. Some chain saws have a tip guard device that is attached to the end of the blade that helps prevent kickback. It can be installed or removed very quickly.

Another safety feature on chain saws is the quick-stop device, **Figure 20-22**. This device stops the chain to reduce the possibility of injury. With a sudden kickback, the operator's left hand moves forward to make contact with the front hand guard and the chain is stopped. The front hand guard is the quick-stop activating lever.

Some chain saws come with a case that protects the saw during transportation and storage. See **Figure 20-23**. Another safety feature is the *chain guard (scabbard)* shown in **Figure 20-24**. The chain guard protects the operator from the sharp blade when not in use and protects the blade from moisture and rust.

Chapter 20 Lawn and Brush Equipment

Troubleshooting Chart

Problem	Cause	Remedy
1. Engine fails to start.	A. Blade control handle disengaged. B. Check fuel tank for gas. C. Spark plug lead wire disconnected. D. Throttle control lever not in the starting position. E. Faulty spark plug. F. Carburetor improperly adjusted, engine flooded. G. Old, stale gasoline. H. Engine brake engaged.	A. Engage blade control handle. B. Fill tank if empty. C. Connect lead wire. D. Move throttle to start position. E. Spark should jump gap between center electrode and side electrode. If spark does not jump, replace the spark plug. F. Remove spark plug. Dry the plug. Crank engine with plug removed, and throttle in off position. Replace spark plug and lead wire and resume starting procedures. G. Drain and refill with fresh gasoline. H. Follow starting procedure.
2. Hard starting or loss of power.	A. Spark plug wire loose. B. Carburetor improperly adjusted. C. Dirty air cleaner.	A. Connect and tighten spark plug wire. B. Adjust carburetor. See separate engine manual. C. Clean air cleaner as described in separate engine manual.
3. Operation erratic.	A. Dirt in gas tank. B. Dirty air cleaner. C. Water in fuel supply. D. Vent in gas cap plugged. E. Carburetor improperly adjusted.	A. Remove the dirt and fill tank with fresh gas. B. Clean air cleaner as described in separate engine manual. C. Drain contaminated fuel and fill tank with fresh gas. D. Clear vent or replace gas cap. E. Adjust carburetor. See separate engine manual.
4. Occasional skip (hesitates) at high speed.	A. Carburetor idle speed too slow. B. Spark plug gap too close. C. Carburetor idle mixture adjustment improperly set.	A. Adjust carburetor. See separate engine manual. B. Adjust to .030″. C. Adjust carburetor. See separate engine manual.
5. Idles poorly.	A. Spark plug fouled, faulty, or gap too wide. B. Carburetor improperly adjusted. C. Dirty air cleaner.	A. Reset gap to .030″ or replace spark plug. B. Adjust carburetor. See separate engine manual. C. Clean air cleaner as described in separate engine manual.
6. Engine overheats.	A. Carburetor not adjusted properly. B. Airflow restricted. C. Engine oil level low.	A. Adjust carburetor. See separate engine manual. B. Remove blower housing and clean as described in separate engine manual. C. Fill crankcase with the proper oil.
7. Excessive vibration.	A. Cutting blade loose or unbalanced. B. Bent cutting blade.	A. Tighten blade and adapter. Balance blade. B. Replace blade.

Goodheart-Willcox Publisher

Figure 20-20.

This engine troubleshooting chart lists common problems, their causes, and the actions required to fix them.

Copyright Goodheart-Willcox Co., Inc.

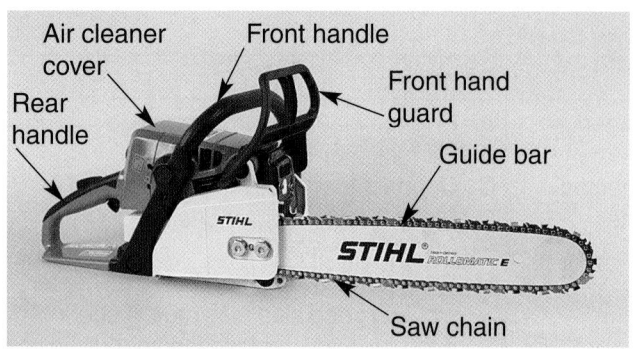

A

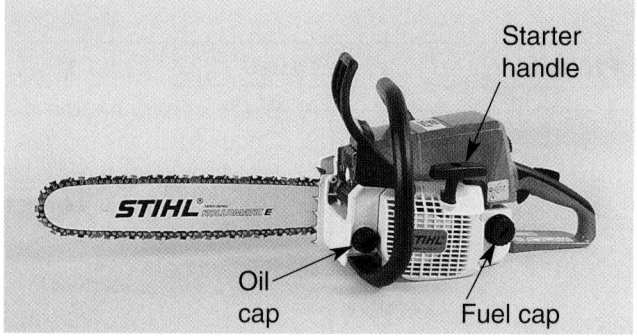

B

Goodheart-Willcox Publisher

Figure 20-21.

Study the parts of a gasoline-powered chain saw.

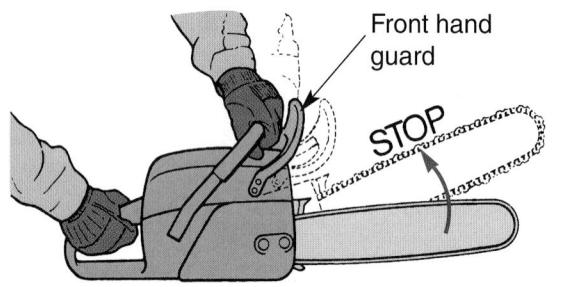

Goodheart-Willcox Publisher

Figure 20-22.

When the operator's left hand makes contact with the front hand guard, it will activate the quick-stop to stop the chain and reduce the risk of injury.

Spark arrestors are another safety feature required by some states. A spark arrestor is a device built into the exhaust system to prevent sparks from exiting through the exhaust and catching dry grass or wood chips on fire. These devices are sometimes known as fire arrestor screens.

Rules for Safe Operation

When carrying the chain saw by hand, the engine must be stopped and the saw must be in the proper position. Grip the front handle and place the muffler to the side away from the body. The chain guide bar should be behind you. Hold the chain saw with both hands when cutting. See **Figure 20-25**. You should also wear heavy gloves to protect your hands and dampen vibration.

When operating a chain saw, obey the following safety rules:

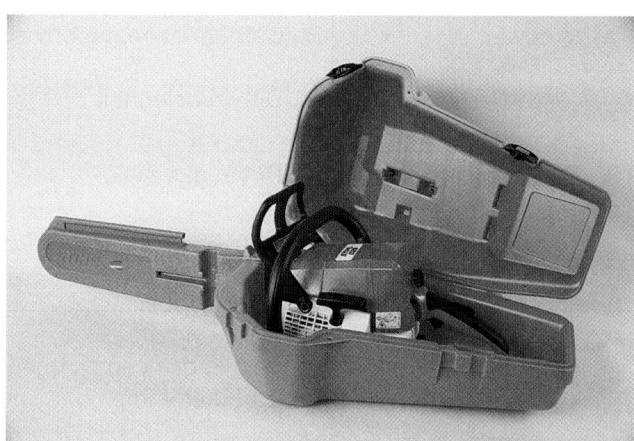

Goodheart-Willcox Publisher

Figure 20-23.

This chain saw is well protected in a tough, plastic carrying case.

1. Never operate a chain saw when you are tired.
2. Use safety footwear; snug-fitting clothing; and eye, hearing, and head protection devices.
3. Always use caution when handling fuel. Move the chain saw at least 10′ (3 m) from the fueling point before starting the engine.
4. Do not allow other persons near the chain saw when starting or cutting. Keep bystanders and animals out of the work area.
5. Never start cutting until you have a clear work area, secure footing, and a planned retreat path from the falling tree.
6. Always hold the chain saw firmly with both hands when the engine is running. Use a firm grip, with thumb and fingers encircling the chain saw handles.

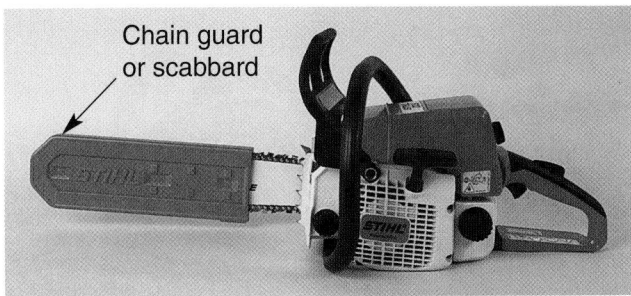

Goodheart-Willcox Publisher

Figure 20-24.

A chain guard (scabbard) protects the saw blade during transportation and storage.

Goodheart-Willcox Publisher

Figure 20-25.

Hold the chain saw with both hands when cutting. Wear heavy gloves for protection.

7. Keep all parts of your body away from the saw chain when the engine is running.
8. Before you start the engine, make sure the saw chain is not contacting anything.
9. Always carry the chain saw with the engine stopped, with the guide bar and saw chain to the rear, and the muffler away from your body.
10. Never operate a chain saw that is damaged, improperly adjusted, or is not securely assembled. Be sure that the saw chain stops moving when the throttle control trigger is released.
11. Always shut off the engine before setting the chain saw down.
12. Use extreme caution when cutting small brush and saplings because slender material may catch the saw chain. This could fling the saw toward you or pull you off balance.

13. When cutting a limb that is under tension, be alert for springback so that you will not be struck when the tension in the wood fibers is released.
14. Keep the handles dry, clean, and free of oil or fuel mixture.
15. Do not operate the chain saw with a deteriorated or removed muffler system. Fire-preventing mufflers (those with fire arrestor screens) should be used in dry areas.
16. Operate the chain saw only in well-ventilated areas.
17. Do not operate a chain saw in a tree unless you are specially trained to do so.
18. Guard against kickback. Kickback can lead to severe injuries.

Avoiding Kickback

1. Hold the chain saw firmly with both hands. Do not reach too far.
2. Do not let the nose of the guide bar contact a log, branch, ground, or any other obstruction.
3. Keep the engine at high engine speeds while cutting.
4. Do not cut above shoulder height.
5. Follow manufacturer's sharpening and maintenance instructions for the saw chain.

Chain Saw Maintenance

Careful maintenance of the engine and chain are necessary to keep the chain saw in good running condition and safe to use. Never operate a chain saw that is damaged, improperly adjusted, or not completely assembled.

Warning

Always stop the engine and be sure that the chain is stopped before doing any maintenance or repair work on the saw.

Fuel and Carburetor

Always use the correct gasoline and oil mixture for a two-cycle engine as recommended by the manufacturer. Before refueling, carefully clean the filler cap and the area around it to ensure that no dirt falls into the tank.

Do not adjust the carburetor unless it is necessary. The high speed and low speed carburetor adjustments on a chain saw engine are very critical. Incorrect settings of these speeds can cause serious damage to the engine. If adjustments become necessary, carefully follow the manufacturer's adjustment procedures.

If the engine stops while idling, there is excessive smoke in the exhaust, or engine does not run smoothly, try adjusting the idle. Normally, you must turn the adjusting screw clockwise when the idle setting is too rich and counterclockwise when the setting is too lean. See **Figure 20-26**.

Apart from minor adjustments, carburetor repairs should be made by a trained technician who has all the necessary service tools, equipment, and experience.

Cylinder Fins

Check the cylinder fins periodically. Clogged fins result in poor engine cooling. Remove the dirt and sawdust from between the fins so cooling air can pass freely. This can be done with a small stick, brush, or compressed air. See **Figure 20-27**.

Air Cleaner (Filter)

The function of the air filter is to catch dust and dirt in the inlet air and reduce wear on engine components. Clogged air cleaners cut down on engine power, increase fuel consumption, and make starting more difficult. The air cleaner should be cleaned every day in very dusty operating conditions.

Goodheart-Willcox Publisher

Figure 20-27.

Cylinder fins can be cleaned with a compressed air.

Before removing the air cleaner, close the choke valve so that no dirt can get into the carburetor. See **Figure 20-28**. Remove the air cleaner cover and remove the element. See **Figure 20-29**. Lightly brush dust off the filter element or wash it if it is extremely dirty. It should be dried completely before replacing it on the engine.

Fuel Filter

Check the fuel filter periodically. A clogged fuel filter will cause engine trouble, such as hard starting. Remove the fuel filler cap and fish for the flexible pick-up tube with a hook. Pull the fuel pick-up

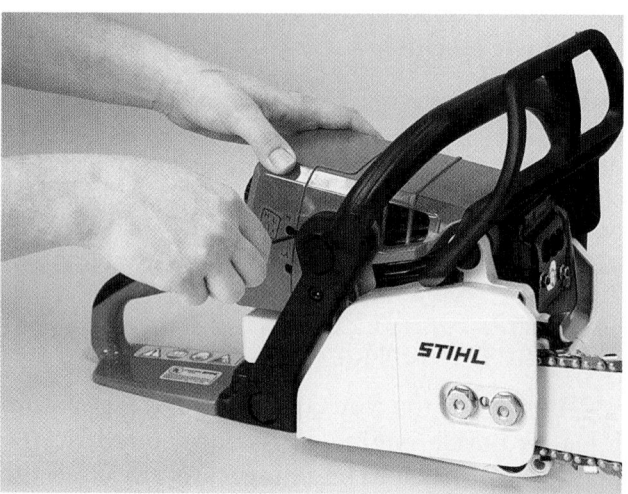

Goodheart-Willcox Publisher

Figure 20-26.

Turn the idle adjusting screw with a screwdriver to obtain the correct idle.

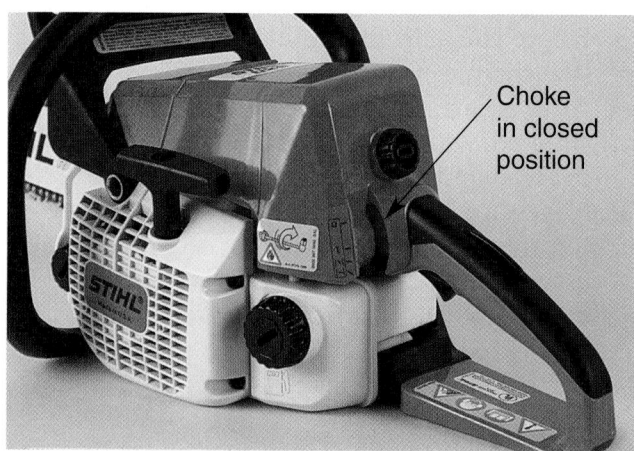

Choke in closed position

Goodheart-Willcox Publisher

Figure 20-28.

Move choke into closed position so dirt cannot enter carburetor.

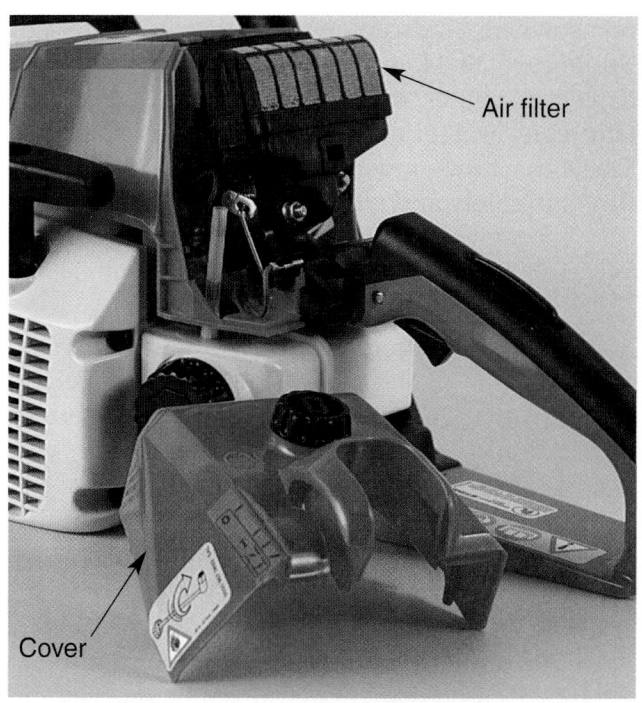

Goodheart-Willcox Publisher

Figure 20-29.

This air filter cover was removed and the air filter is ready for cleaning.

out. See **Figure 20-30**. Remove the old filter sleeve and slide a new sleeve in place. Return the flexible pick-up tube to the gas tank.

Lubrication

The saw chain and guide bar must be continuously lubricated during operation to protect them from excessive wear. An automatic chain oiling system provides the necessary lubrication. Clean the lubricating oil supply hole daily. It is located at the base of the blade. Always fill the oil tank with chain oil each time the engine is refueled. See **Figure 20-31**. *Never* use waste oil for this purpose.

Muffler

The muffler should be kept clean and open. Do not run a chain saw without the muffler. See **Figure 20-32**. If local laws or regulations require the use of a spark arrestor, check its condition periodically. Carbon deposits in the muffler and cylinder exhaust port will cause lower engine power output and sparking from the muffler. If needed, remove the muffler and clean the cylinder exhaust port. Be careful not to damage the metal surfaces.

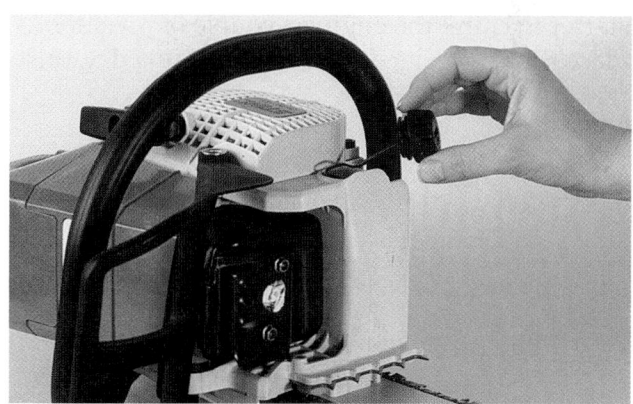

Goodheart-Willcox Publisher

Figure 20-31.

Removing the oil tank cap to fill the tank with chain oil.

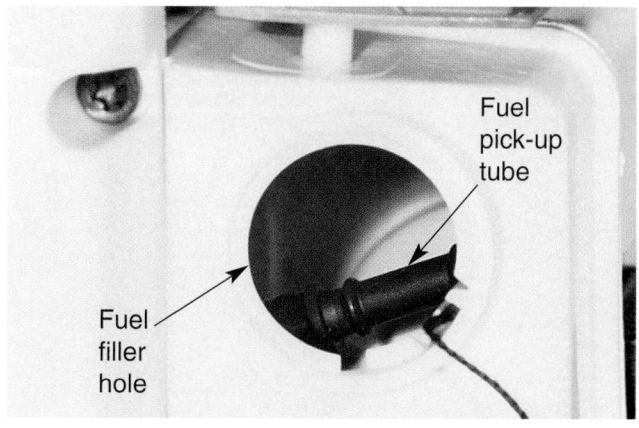

Goodheart-Willcox Publisher

Figure 20-30.

A flexible fuel pick-up tube is removed through fuel filler hole.

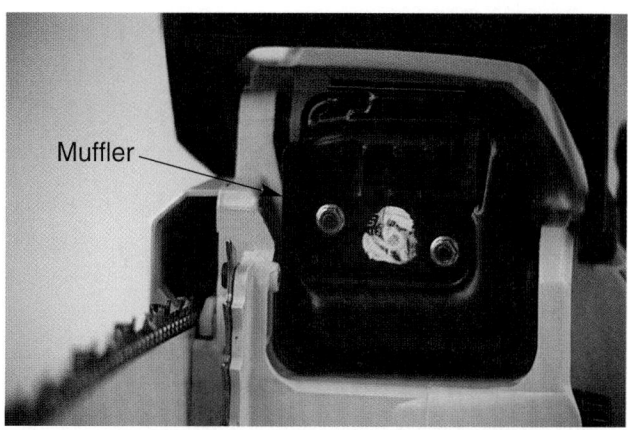

Goodheart-Willcox Publisher

Figure 20-32.

Do not run a chain saw without the muffler.

Guide Bar

Clean the guide bar daily or before each use of the chain saw. Remove any burrs that are found along the bar rails. On most chain saws, the roller nose bearing must be lubricated. Place the chain saw on its side so that the bar nose is firmly supported. Clean the grease hole and pump grease in as shown in **Figure 20-33**.

Storage

Inspect and make adjustments of every part of the chain saw before storage. Clean all parts and apply a thin coat of oil to all metal surfaces to prevent rust. Remove the chain and the guide bar. Apply a sufficient oil coat and wrap them in a plastic bag. Drain the fuel tank and pull the starter a few times to drain the carburetor.

Pour a small amount of oil in the spark plug hole and replace the spark plug. Slowly pull the starter to crank the engine a couple of revolutions. Place the saw in its case and store it in a dry, dust-free area.

String Trimmers and Brushcutters

String trimmers and *brushcutters* are hand-held, engine-powered machines for cutting brush and weeds. String trimmers spin a nylon filament at high speed to cut weeds. Brushcutters spin a solid metal saw blade to cut through heavy weeds and brush. These machines are very popular items for homeowners, landscaping contractors, and foresters. See **Figure 20-34**. As with any type of small gas-driven machines, safety and proper use of string trimmers and brushcutters are major concerns. These machines must be properly maintained to function safely and efficiently.

Design Features

A variety of different string trimmer and brush-cutter designs are available. Each design has certain features that make it better suited for certain applications:

- Engine power should be adequate for the kind of work. Brushcutting requires more power than grass cutting for example. The manufacturer determines proper power for each model.
- Construction should be durable, yet lightweight. If use will be for long periods, weight becomes very important and a shoulder harness may be needed.
- Some models have an interchangeable head that allows the operator to switch from nylon string to circular saw blade cutters for different tasks.
- Antivibration systems reduce operator fatigue.

Goodheart-Willcox Publisher

Figure 20-33.

Lubricate the roller nose bearing with a grease pump as shown.

Stihl

Figure 20-34.

Shown is a person wearing proper safety gear and operating a string trimmer properly.

Handles and Cutters

The string trimmers and brushcutters may have a straight shaft or one that is curved at the end. String trimmers most commonly have a loop-type handle. See **Figure 20-35**. Bike- and J-type handles are available for brushcutters with interchangeable cutting blades.

Warning

A loop-style handle should never be used on a machine equipped with cutting blades.

The versatility of string trimmers and brushcutters is due to the great variety of cutters that can be installed on the cutting head of the machine. See **Figure 20-36**. Available cutters range from nylon string cutters for grass and weeds to circular saw blades for cutting small trees.

Grass Cutting

The most basic cutting end is the rotating string cutting head. The cutting head contains nylon string, which is available in various strengths and rigidity. The nylon string cutting heads are intended to supplement a lawn mower. They are used primarily for trimming grass around obstacles where a lawn mower will not cut, such as around flower beds, shrubbery, and fences. When replacing the string, always use the manufacturer's recommended type for the specific make and model of trimmer.

A deflector is mounted behind the cutting head to protect the operator's feet and legs. The deflector has a small chopper blade on one edge, which cuts the string if it gets too long. See **Figure 20-35**.

Brush Cutting

A brushcutter may be fitted with a brush knife. A brush knife is suitable for applications ranging

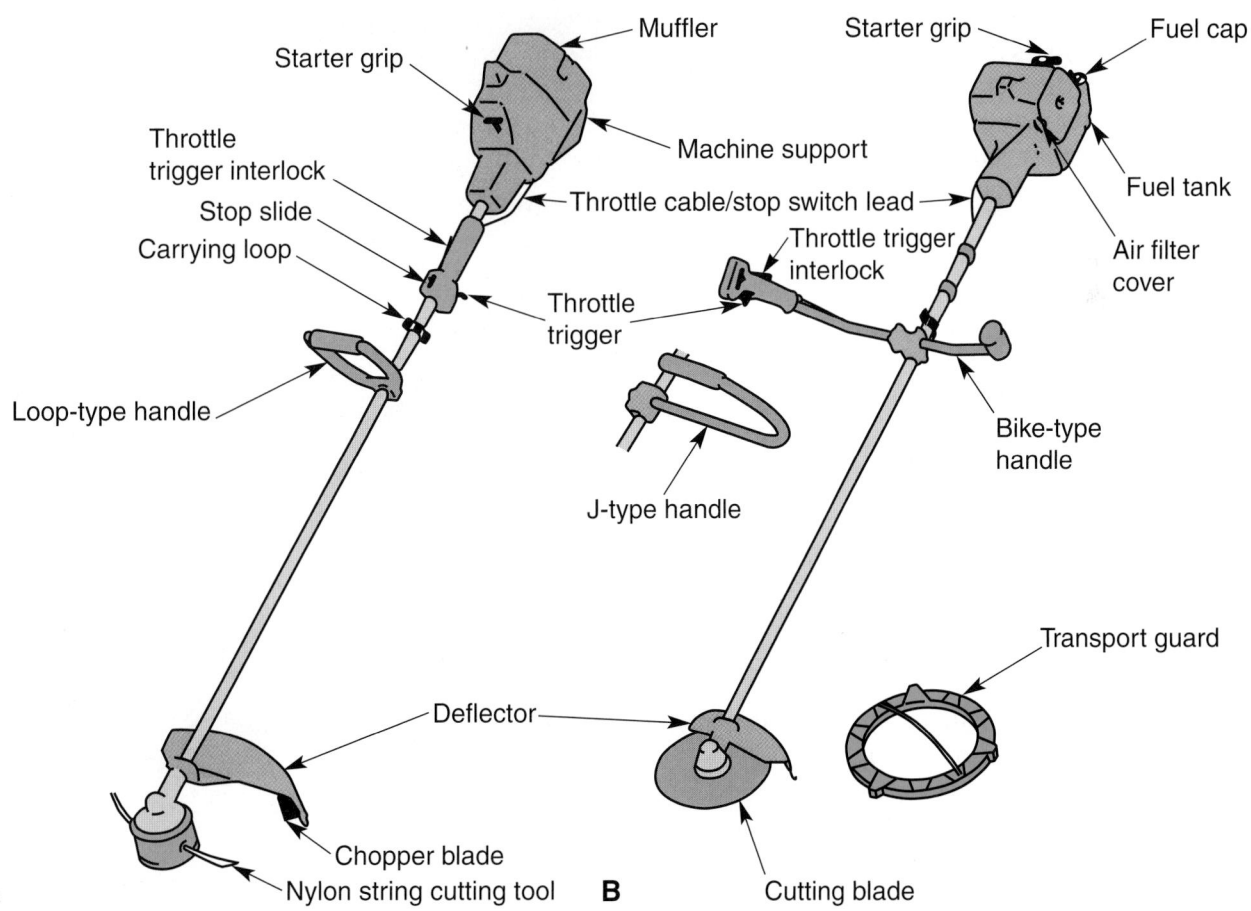

Stihl

Figure 20-35.

Major parts of a string trimmer. A—This string trimmer is equipped with a loop-type handle. B—This brushcutter is equipped with a bike-type handle. The J-type handle is shown between the A and B views.

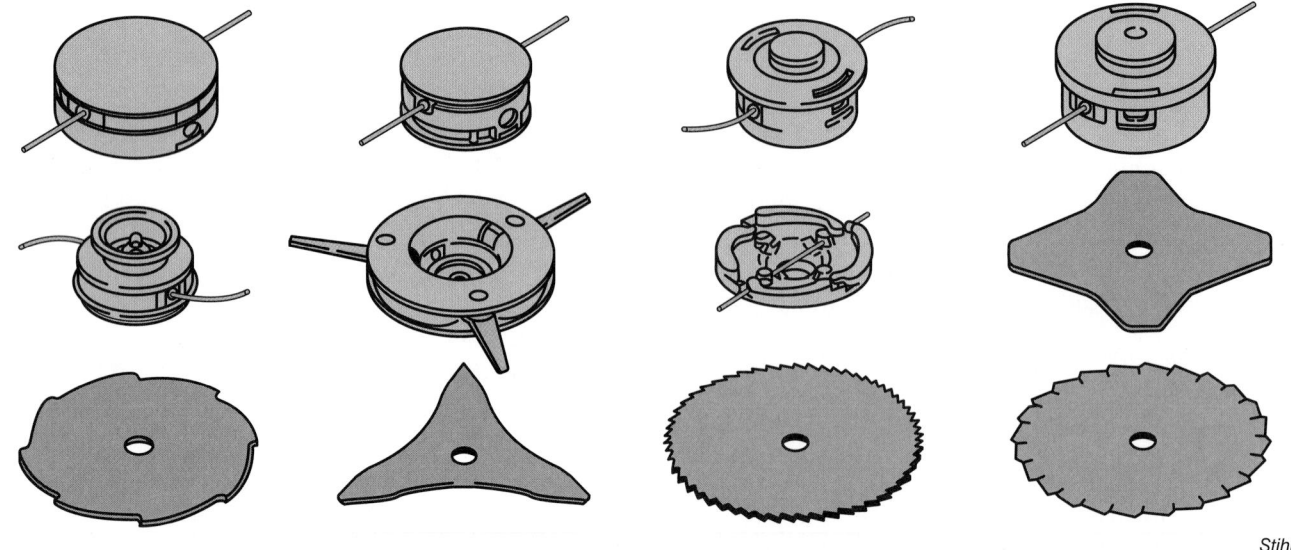

Stihl

Figure 20-36.

Samples of the many kinds of cutting heads for string trimmers and brushcutters.

from cutting matted grass to clearing weeds, wild growth, and scrub. Brush knives can also be used to cut young saplings or other woody materials up to 3/4″ (2 cm) in diameter.

A brushcutter may also be fitted with a circular saw blade. Circular saw blades are suitable for thinning brush and cutting small trees up to a diameter of 2 3/4″ (7 cm). Do not attempt to cut trees with larger diameters, since the blade may catch or jerk the brushcutter forward.

Operator Safety

String trimmers and brushcutters are high-speed cutting tools. Special precautions must be practiced to reduce the risk of personal injury. Careless use can cause serious or even fatal injury.

Basic safe clothing consists of leather work boots, heavy fabric work pants, leather work gloves, hearing protection, safety goggles or glasses, and a shoulder harness. In some instances additional safety clothing such as chaps or leggings, face shield, and hard hat are required. See **Figure 20-37**.

Because string trimmers and brushcutters are held close to the body, noise from the engine can cause hearing loss over a period of time if hearing protection is not used. The soft, padded, earphone-type ear protector should be worn. See **Figure 20-38**. The ear protector should have a headband that maintains consistent pressure and is comfortable to wear. The ear protector should provide a high noise

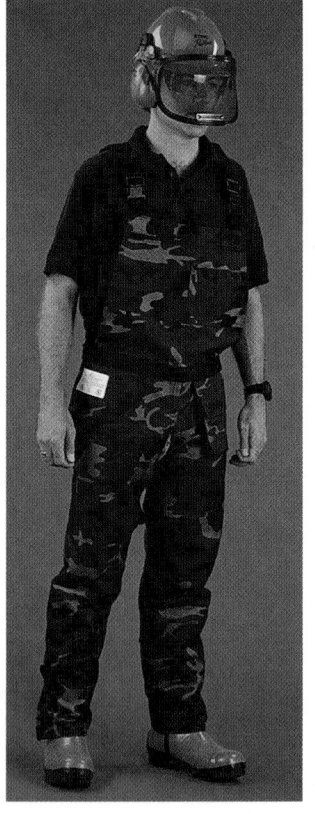

A   **B**

Stihl

Figure 20-37.

Proper clothing for string trimmer and brushcutter operation is shown here. A—Basic safe work apparel includes heavy work clothes, work boots, safety goggles or glasses, work gloves (not shown). B—Wrap-around chaps.

Goodheart-Willcox Publisher

Figure 20-38.

Earphone-type hearing protection should be worn to protect against loud engine noise.

Homelite

Figure 20-39.

To start the engine, lay the trimmer on a flat bare surface. For right-handed people, hold the trimmer down with the left hand and pull the starter cord with the right hand. For left-handed people, hold the trimmer down with the right hand and pull the starter cord with the left hand.

reduction of 22 decibels (dB) and meet *ANSI (American National Standards Institute) S3.19* standards.

Operators of handheld machines should be alert and in good health. If the operator becomes fatigued, he or she should take a break before resuming. Prolonged use of a trimmer or brushcutter, which exposes the operator's hands to vibrations, may result in white finger disease (Raynaud's phenomenon) or carpal tunnel syndrome. These conditions impair the hands' ability to feel and regulate temperature, produce numbness and burning sensations, cause nerve and circulation damage, and cause tissue necrosis (deadening).

Starting and Safe Operation

Two-cycle trimmer and brushcutter engines run on and are lubricated by an oil and gasoline mixture. Refer to the manufacturer's technical service manuals for proper oil/fuel mixing amounts. Once mixed, the fuel should be poured into the fuel tank well away from any flame or sparks. After the equipment is fueled up, it is ready for operation. The following is the procedure for starting, operating, and shutting down a string trimmer or brushcutter:

1. Place the machine on the ground in the starting position. See **Figure 20-39**.
2. Press the primer 5 to 6 times.
3. Move the choke lever to the *Full Choke* position.
4. While holding the unit down with your left hand, also hold the throttle in the open position.
5. With your right hand, pull the starter until the engine starts. If the engine does not start in 7 pulls, or starts and then stops, proceed as follows:
   a. Move the choke lever to the *Partial Choke* position.
   b. While holding the throttle in the open position, pull the starter until engine runs.
6. After allowing the engine to warm up for 5 to 45 seconds, move the choke lever slowly to the *Run* position.
7. When using a string trimmer, follow the guidelines shown in **Figure 20-40**.
8. When using a brushcutter to cut grass, sweep it left and right in an arcing motion. See **Figure 20-41A**. When using a brushcutter equipped with a brush knife to cut wild growth and scrub, lower the rotating brush knife down onto the growth to achieve a chopping effect. Keep the cutting attachment below waist level. See **Figure 20-41B**.

   When using a brush knife to cut young saplings or other woody materials up to 3/4" (2 cm) in diameter, or when using a circular saw blade for thinning brush and cutting small trees up to a diameter of 2 3/4" (7 cm) in diameter, use the left side of the blade to avoid kickout, **Figure 20-42**. *Kickout* is the sudden and uncontrolled motion toward the operator's right or rear. Kickout can occur if rotating blade comes in contact with a solid object like a tree, rock, bush, or wall; or if it snags, stalls, or binds.

   Also, do not attempt to cut material that has larger diameters than recommended for the cutter. The blade may catch or jerk the brushcutter forward. This can cause damage to the blade or brushcutter, or loss of control of the brushcutter, which can result in personal injury.

9. When using a string trimmer, you must occasionally adjust the string to the correct length. The following is the procedure for extending and trimming the string to the correct length.

    a. The engine should be running at high speed.

    b. Hold the rotating cutting head horizontal above the ground and tap it on the ground.

    c. The blade on the deflector will trim the string to the correct length. Avoid tapping the head more than once.

    d. If the string does not extend, stop the engine and examine the spool to see if it is out of string. A new nylon string can be installed. See the *Spool Replacement* section in this chapter.

Operating Do's and Don'ts

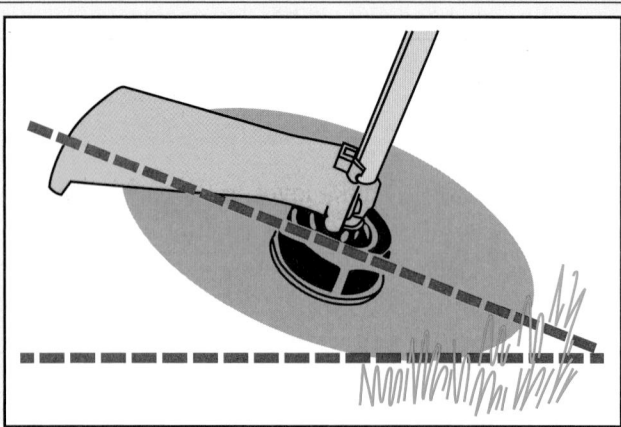

Hold the string trimmer at a slight tilt so string contact occurs at one point away from you. This provides the best cutting and minimum string wear.

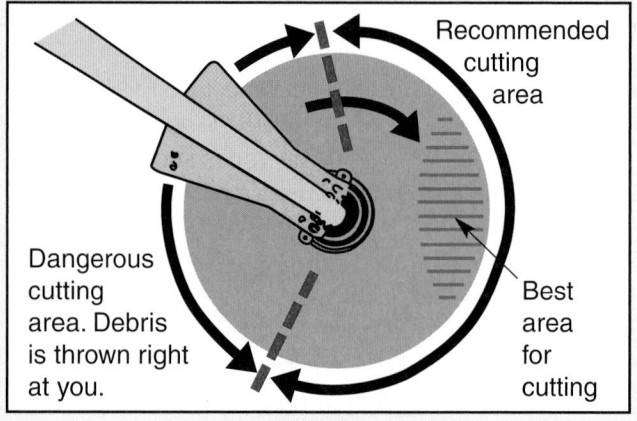

Keep the string trimmer head tilted so the trimming action occurs away from you. The recommended cutting area is illustrated. The best point of contact is also shown. If you do not cut using the recommended area, debris will be thrown toward you.

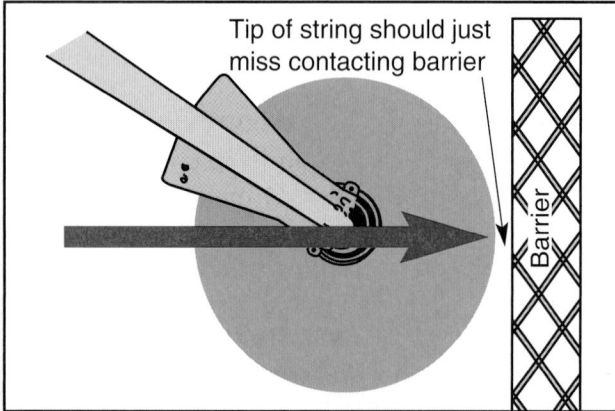

Approach your target position gradually so that you will cut only with the tip of the string and not smash it broadside into a barrier.

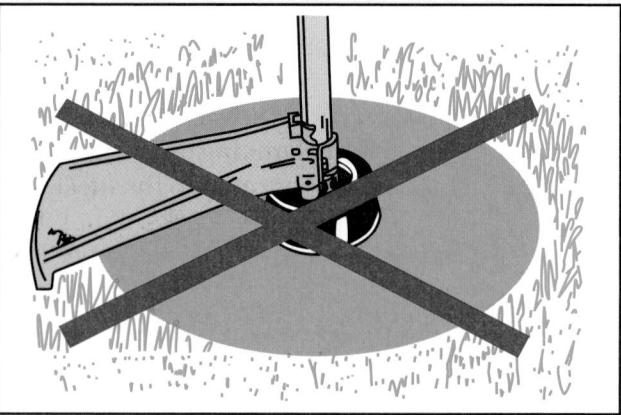

Do *not* use the whole 360° string circle to cut. If you do, you will use up too much string.

(Continued)

Homelite

Figure 20-40.

General guidelines for operating a string trimmer or brushcutter are shown here.

Operating Do's and Don'ts *(Continued)*

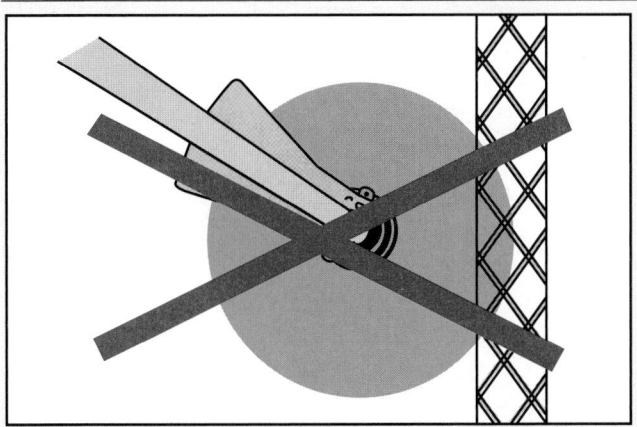

Do *not* overfeed string. Overfed string will break off.

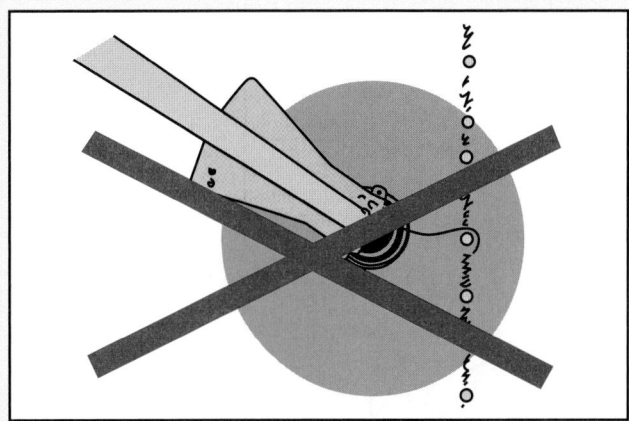

Wire and picket fences are hard on string. Learn to feed slowly. Every time you catch the string around a wire or picket, the string will break off.

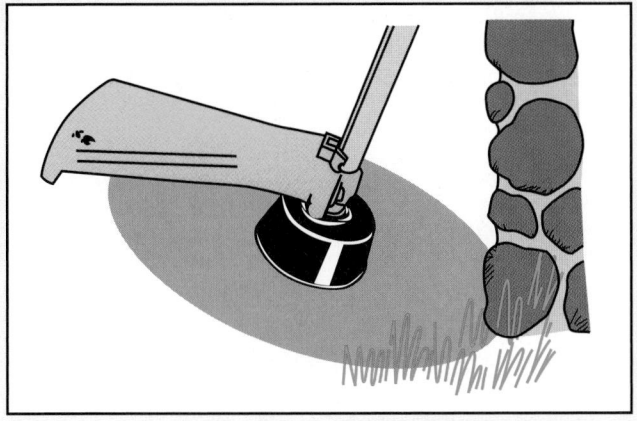

Stone and brick walls and curbs wear string rapidly. Be sure not to overfeed. Even with minimum exposure of the string tip to the barrier, string wear will be high during this kind of trimming.

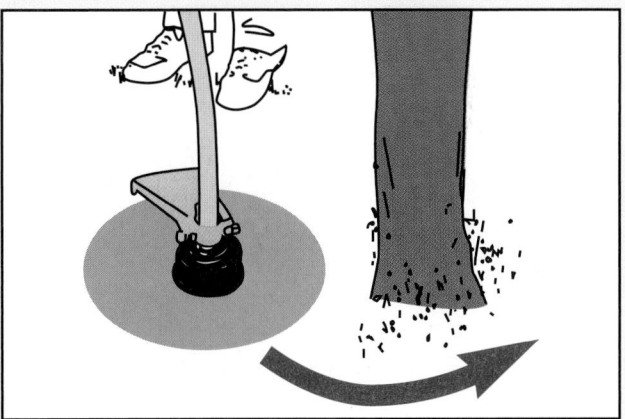

Trim around trees. Take your time. Walk around the tree. Do *not* whip the bark with an excessive length of string.

Homelite

Figure 20-40.

(Continued)

10. To stop the engine, press the stop button or turn off the ignition switch. Allow the engine to cool before storing the equipment.

String Trimmer and Brushcutter Maintenance

Careful maintenance of a string trimmer or brushcutter will extend its service life and keep it safe to use. There are a number of parts that need periodic inspection and maintenance. *Never* operate a string trimmer or brushcutter that is damaged, improperly adjusted, or not completely assembled.

Warning

Always stop the engine and be sure that the cutter is stopped before doing any maintenance or repair work on a string trimmer or brushcutter.

Because of the shape of string trimmers and brushcutters, they can be difficult to hold during service. The device shown in **Figure 20-43** is designed

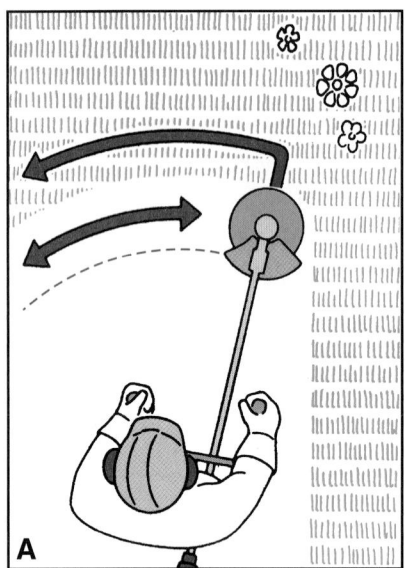

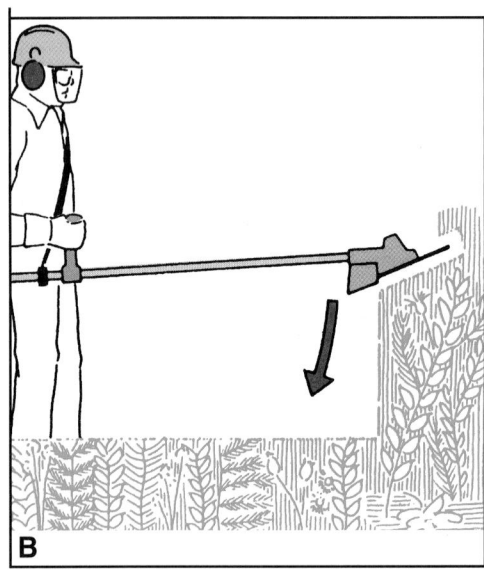

Stihl

Figure 20-41.

Different techniques are used for different cutting operations. A—A brushcutter can be used for cutting grass by sweeping it left and right in an arcing motion. B—To cut wild growth with a brush knife, lower the blade down onto the growth to achieve a chopping effect. Always keep the attachment below waist level.

to securely hold a string trimmer or brushcuttter while servicing it.

String Trimmer Spool Replacement

Before starting a string trimmer, always visually check the spool and string. When using a string trimmer, you must occasionally lengthen the cutting string. If the string does not extend properly, stop the engine and examine the spool. It may be out of

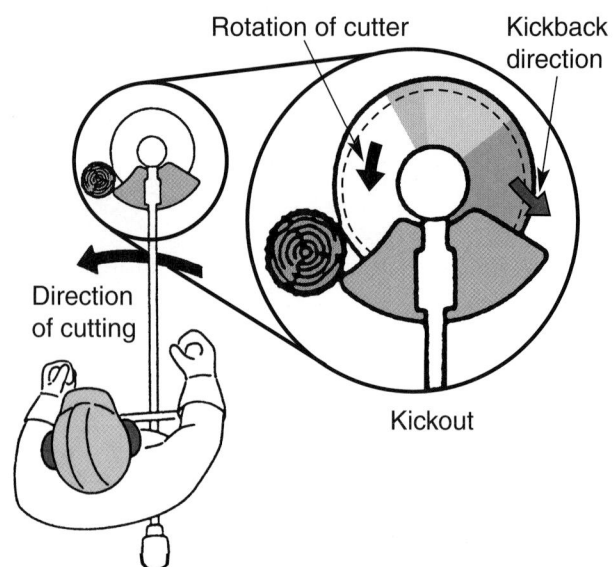

Goodheart-Willcox Publisher

Figure 20-42.

When cutting young saplings up to 3/4″ (2 cm) in diameter, use the left side of blade to avoid kickout.

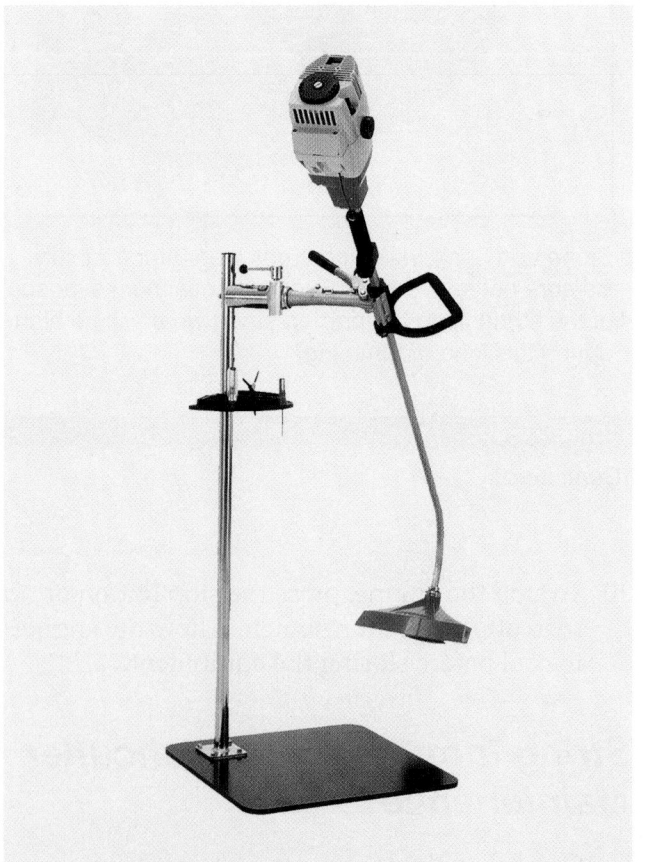

Park Tool Co.

Figure 20-43.

This device holds a string trimmer or brushcutter so it can be serviced.

string. A new nylon string can be installed. Refer to the manufacturer's technical service manuals for installation procedures for the specific make and model. The following is the method for installing new string or new spool for one particular type of cutting head:

1. Remove retainer cap by turning it clockwise. Lift out the spool and string. See **Figure 20-44A**.

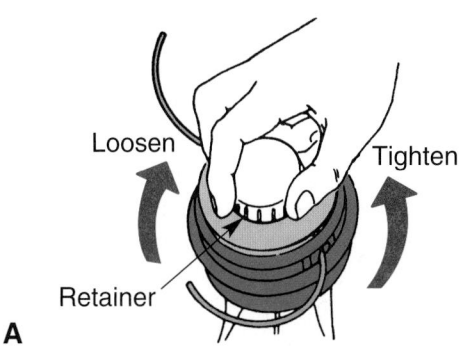

Loosen   Tighten

Retainer

A

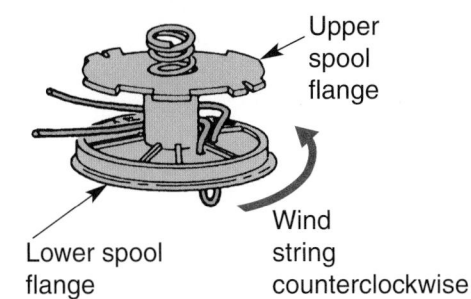

Upper spool flange

Lower spool flange

Wind string counterclockwise

B

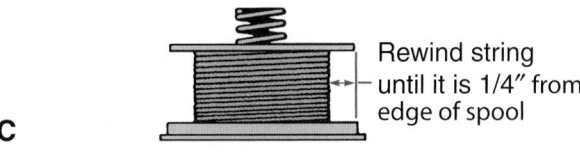

Rewind string until it is 1/4" from edge of spool

C

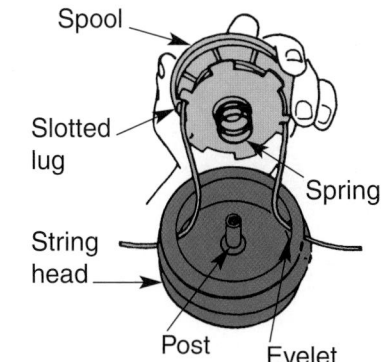

Spool

Slotted lug

Spring

String head

Post   Eyelet

D

Homelite

Figure 20-44.

Procedure for rewinding new nylon string on a string trimmer spool.

2. The spool will hold a maximum of 20' (6.1 m) of string. Insert one end of the string into one of the small holes in the spool flange and center the spool on the length of the string. Thread the string back through the closest hole. See **Figure 20-44B**.

3. Pull the loop tight and wind the string counterclockwise on the spool. Wind tightly and evenly. After the string is wound on the spool, there should be 1/4" clearance between the wound string and the outer edge of the spool. See **Figure 20-44C**.

4. Place the ends of the string into slots in the spool lugs. Leave 5" to 6" of string protruding from the lugs. See **Figure 20-44D**.

5. Reinstall the retainer. Once a year, lightly grease the threads on the retainer.

6. To test the operation, pull on the string while alternately pressing down on and releasing the retainer.

Carburetor Adjustment

On some models, the high speed and idle speed carburetor needles may need adjustment. Newer models have factory adjusted and sealed carburetors. No adjustment can be made on these carburetors. The carburetor is replaced if it is a suspected cause of poor performance.

Lubrication

Other than the engine, which is lubricated by the fuel mixture if equipped with a two-cycle engine or crankcase oil if equipped with a four-stroke engine, the flexible drive shaft and gearbox on some models may need greasing. The shaft must be removed from the shaft housing, cleaned, coated with molybdenum disulfide grease. Reinstall the shaft in the reverse direction to extend the service life of the shaft.

Straight shaft machines have a gearbox at the cutter end with a filler plug for grease. Check the grease level after every 50 hours of operation. See **Figure 20-45**.

Spark Plug

If the engine does not start, it may be due to a wet, fouled, or faulty spark plug. Check the spark plug periodically and clean or install a new one as necessary. Adjust the spark gap if it is wider or narrower than the standard gap. Be sure the stop-start switch is in the *Off* position when checking the spark plug.

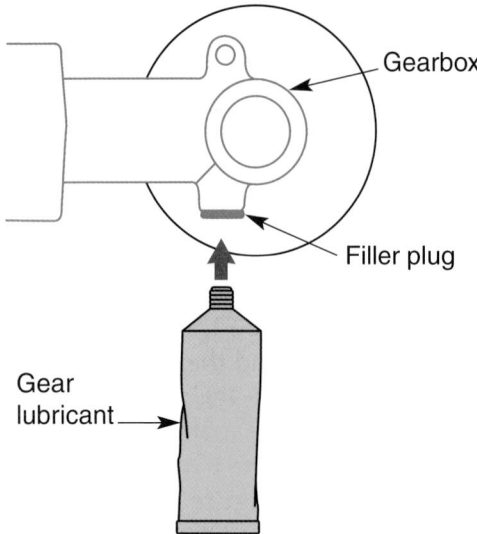

- Check the grease level after every 50 hours of operation.
- Unscrew the filler plug.
- If no grease can be seen on the inside of the filler plug, screw the tube of gear lubricant into the filler hole.
- Squeeze grease into the gear housing—about 5–10g (1/4 oz).

  Do not completely fill the gear housing with grease.

- Refit the filler plug and tighten it down firmly.

Goodheart-Willcox Publisher

Figure 20-45.

Trimmers and brushcutters with straight shafts have a gearbox. The gearbox should be greased at specified intervals. Do not completely fill the gearbox.

Air Filter

The function of the air filter is to catch dust and dirt in the inlet air to reduce wear on engine components. Clogged air cleaners cut down on engine power, increase fuel consumption, and make starting more difficult. The air cleaner should be cleaned after every operation in very dusty operating conditions.

Muffler

The muffler on most models is located to the rear of the engine. It is usually shielded. The muffler should be kept clean and open. Check the condition of the muffler periodically and change it as needed. Do not run a string trimmer or brushcutter without the muffler.

Starter Rope/Spring Breakage

After extensive use, it is not uncommon for a starter rope or the flat coil spring to break. Either of these items can be repaired. Because there are variations in recoil starters, refer to the manufacturer's technical service manuals for the procedure for a specific make or model.

Edger/Trimmers

Gasoline-powered combination *edger/trimmers* are versatile implements equipped with a blade that can be adjusted for vertical trimming or horizontal trimming operations. When the blade is oriented vertically, the machine functions as an edger. When the blade is oriented horizontally, the machine functions as a trimmer. Edger/trimmers are very popular for lawn care maintenance. See **Figure 20-46**.

Since an edger or trimmer has an exposed, fast-spinning blade, it is very important that the safety devices designed for the unit are always in place. Use proper operating procedures to assure safe, dependable service.

Goodheart-Willcox Publisher

Figure 20-46.

This is a combination edger/trimmer set for edging operation.

Edger/Trimmer Features

Edgers come in a variety of sizes with respect to the construction and power of the unit. Small engines in the range of two to five horsepower are generally used to drive a belt to the blade.

The most popular edgers are the small units designed for home lawn care and weed cutting. Commercial edgers for heavy-duty work are built to be more rugged. They incorporate a larger, more powerful engine and are considerably more expensive.

Some edgers are single-purpose units designed for edging along sidewalks and driveways. Others are designed so the blade can be tilted from vertical to horizontal for trimming long grass or weeds under fences and close to buildings.

Safety Features and Adjustments

The blade of an engine-driven edger is belt-driven from the engine. You should always disengage the blade clutch when starting the engine or when doing maintenance work on the unit. See **Figure 20-47**. This loosens the belt drive to the blade and allows the engine shaft to turn freely.

Warning

Never attempt to make adjustments on an edger/trimmer while the engine is running. Serious injury could result.

The guide wheel can normally be adjusted horizontally by loosening the knob, or lever, on the front of the frame and moving the wheel to either side of the frame as needed. See **Figure 20-48**. The lever should then be tightened to hold the wheel firmly in place.

With some designs, the depth of the edger blade can be controlled by raising and lowering the guide wheel. The wheel is raised and lowered by adjusting a lever on the right of the frame in the desired notch. See **Figure 20-49**.

Goodheart-Willcox Publisher

Figure 20-48.

This operator is locking the front guide wheel in a newly adjusted position.

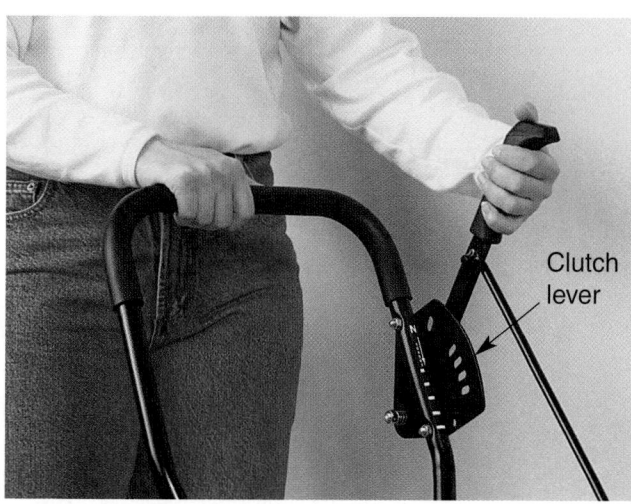

Clutch lever

Goodheart-Willcox Publisher

Figure 20-47.

Disengage the clutch lever when you are not trimming or edging.

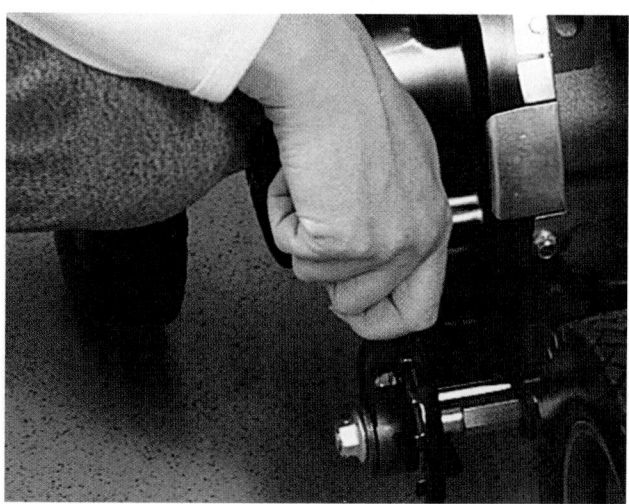

Goodheart-Willcox Publisher

Figure 20-49.

Raising front guide wheel by placing the adjusting lever in the correct notch.

One lever, either on the handle or on the engine, may operate the choke, regulate engine speed from slow to fast, and stop the engine. See **Figure 20-50**. When starting the engine, place this lever in the choke position, or run position, and pull the starter handle rapidly. See **Figure 20-51**. Grip the handle firmly and place your foot behind the rear wheel so that the unit will not move during starting. In order to start a cold engine or one that has been off for an extended period, you may need to prime the carburetor. Depending on the type of priming

system, you may have to turn a knob or press a plunger to prime the carburetor. See **Figure 20-52**.

The *blade guard* should always be in place during use. The adjusting arm releases the blade guard and blade, so the guard can be rotated to cover the blade in any edging or trimming position.

For edging along a sidewalk or driveway, the blade is in the vertical position. See **Figure 20-53**. When the unit is to be used for trimming, the blade is set horizontally. It can also be set at an angle for special edging jobs. See **Figure 20-54**. The notches in the bracket will hold the blade firmly in a variety of positions.

Goodheart-Willcox Publisher

Figure 20-50.

The speed adjustment and stop lever is located on the engine on this model.

Rules for Safe Operation

1. Thoroughly inspect the area where the equipment is to be used and remove all stones, sticks, wire, and other foreign objects.
2. Do not operate the edger/trimmer while barefoot or when wearing sandals. Always wear substantial footwear when operating an edger/trimmer.
3. Check the fuel level before starting the engine. Do not fill the gasoline tank indoors, when the engine is running, or while the engine is still hot. Wipe off any spilled gasoline before starting the engine.
4. Disengage the blade clutch before starting the engine.
5. Never attempt to make a wheel adjustment while the engine is running.

Goodheart-Willcox Publisher

Figure 20-51.

Pull the starter handle to start the engine. The drive clutch should be disengaged, keeping the drive belt loose.

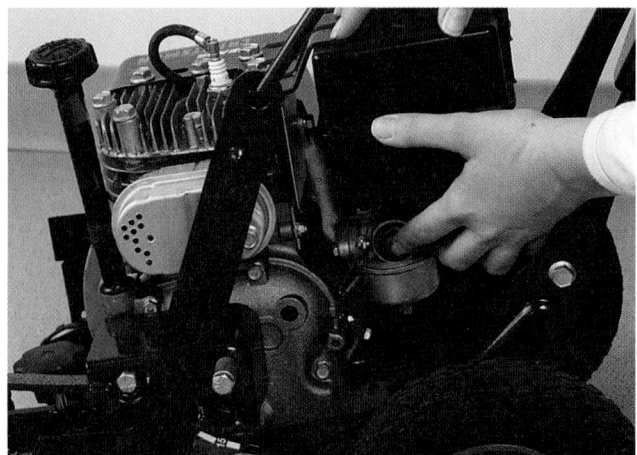

Goodheart-Willcox Publisher

Figure 20-52.

The carburetor may need to be primed before starting the engine.

A

B

Goodheart-Willcox Publisher

Figure 20-53.

An edger/trimmer blade position can be adjusted for different tasks. A—The blade is set vertical for edging jobs. B—The blade is set horizontal for trimming jobs.

Goodheart-Willcox Publisher

Figure 20-54.

The blade is set at an angle for special trimming jobs.

6. Never operate the equipment in wet grass. Always be sure of your footing. Keep a firm hold on the handle.
7. Do not change the engine governor settings or overspeed the engine.
8. Do not put hands or feet near or under rotating parts. Keep clear of the discharge opening at all times.
9. Stop the blade when crossing a gravel drive, walk, or road.
10. After striking a foreign object, stop the engine. Remove the wire from the spark plug. Thoroughly inspect the edger/trimmer for any damage and repair the damage before restarting and operating the edger/trimmer.

11. If the edger/trimmer starts to vibrate abnormally, stop the engine and check for the cause. Vibration is generally a warning of trouble.
12. Stop the engine whenever you leave the equipment, before cleaning the guard assembly, and when making any repairs or inspections.
13. When cleaning, repairing, or inspecting the edger/trimmer, make certain the blade and all moving parts have stopped. Disconnect the spark plug wire, and keep the wire away from the plug to prevent accidental starting.
14. Do not run the engine indoors.
15. Shut the engine off and wait until the blade comes to a complete stop before unclogging the guard assembly.
16. Always wear safety glasses or other eye protection when operating an edger.

Edger/Trimmer Maintenance

The standard edger blade is 10″ long and is notched on the ends. Since the blade scrapes the edges of driveways or sidewalks during operation, it wears down quickly. Edger blades are never sharpened. They are just replaced when they become too short to make good contact with a surface being edged.

To change the blade, raise the front wheel and loosen the nut on the drive shaft. Remove the old blade, and replace it with a new one. Be sure the blade nut is tightened properly. Always wear a glove to hold the blade to prevent injury to your hand. See **Figure 20-55**.

To replace a worn belt, remove the belt guard on the engine pulley and the belt guard on the spindle housing. Remove the belt. Replace with a proper size V-belt and secure the belt guards.

Lubrication

Check the engine oil level before starting the engine and after every six hours of use. Add oil as necessary to keep level on full. Before removing the filler plug, clean the area around the plug to prevent dirt from entering the oil fill opening.

Check the oil before operating. See **Figure 20-56**. Change the oil after 30 hours of operation by draining the oil through the lower oil drain plug. Refill with the correct amount and weight of fresh oil.

Lubricate all moving parts of the edger with engine oil periodically. Check and clean or replace the spark plug each operating season. Remove and clean the air filter at recommended intervals.

Edger/Trimmer Storage

The following steps should be taken to prepare edgers and trimmers for storage:
1. Clean and lubricate the unit thoroughly.
2. Loosen the belt so it will not stretch during extended storage.
3. Coat the cutting blade with oil to prevent rusting.
4. Remove the spark plug and spray fogging oil into the cylinder or pour a tablespoon of clean engine oil into the spark plug hole. Rotate the crankshaft a few times and replace the spark plug.
5. Check the blade and engine mounting bolts for proper tightness.
6. Never store the edger with gasoline in the tank if it going to be stored inside a building where fumes may reach a spark or open flame.
7. Store the edger in a dry, clean area.

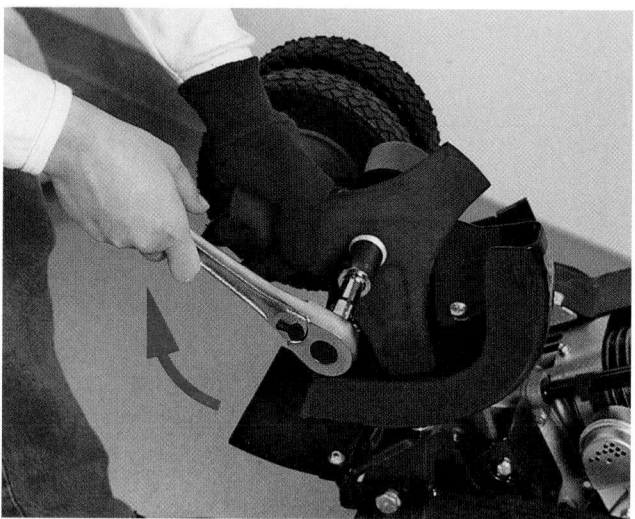

Goodheart-Willcox Publisher

Figure 20-55.

Hold the blade while loosening the blade nut on the drive shaft. Be sure to wear a heavy glove to protect your hand.

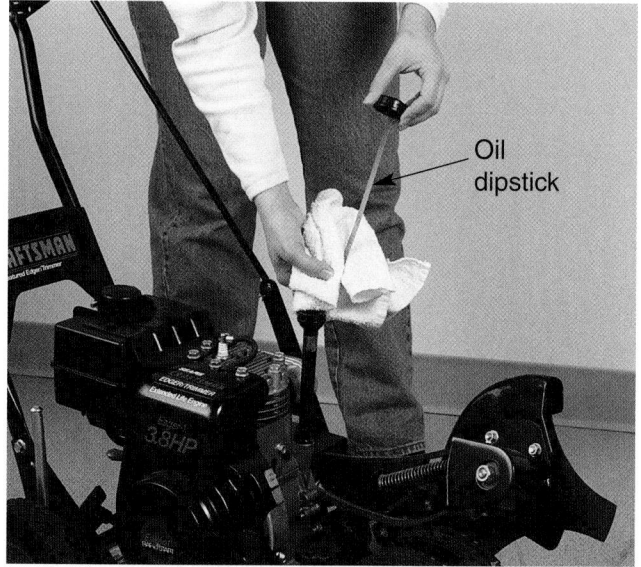

Oil dipstick

digitalreflections/Shutterstock

Figure 20-56.

Check the oil before operating. Change the oil after 30 hours of operation by draining the oil through the lower oil drain plug.

Summary

Power mowers are manufactured in a variety of different sizes and designs. For the average yard, a rotary-type mower with a 22″ diameter blade is satisfactory. Mowers may be either push-type or self-propelled. There are several mechanical methods for starting small engines including the recoil starter and electric starter. Every mower manufactured today must be equipped with a blade brake.

After each use, the mower should be cleaned. Blades can be sharpened when they become dull or nicked. Spark plugs should be cleaned and gapped as recommended by the manufacturer. Air filters should be cleaned and oil should be changed after every twenty-five hours of operation.

Always follow safe operating procedures when using a gasoline-powered chain saw. Chain saws are manufactured in a variety of sizes for different cutting tasks. Safe operation of a chain saw comes from a thorough knowledge of correct operating procedures. Always stop the engine and make sure the chain is stopped before doing maintenance work on a chain saw. Follow all manufacturer's maintenance instructions.

Always keep safety devices in place when using a gas-powered string trimmer, brushcutter, or edger/trimmer. Never attempt to make adjustments on this type of equipment when the engine is running. Common maintenance procedures on string trimmers, brushcutters, or edger/trimmers include replacing broken strings, worn blades, and belts; changing oil; and lubricating moving parts. Special precautions should be taken when storing any engine-powered implement.

Review Questions

Answer the following questions using the information provided in this chapter.

1. How should accidental engine starting be prevented when working on an engine-driven implement?
2. What invisible, odorless, toxic gas (designated CO) is generated from running gasoline engines?
3. What explosive gas is generated when charging lead-acid storage batteries?
4. A(n) _____ mower has a helical blade that rotates around a horizontal shaft and a(n) _____ mower has a blade that rotates in a horizontal plane.
5. List the procedures for preparing and starting an engine.
6. Describe the two types of blade brakes found on mowers.
7. Describe two design features that prevent an engine from being damaged if a mower blade strikes a solid object.
8. When the unshielded nose of the chain saw hits a solid surface, it may jump toward the operator. This is called _____.
9. The device often built into the muffler of a chain saw to prevent sparks from causing a fire is called a(n) _____ _____.
10. What does the abbreviation ANSI stand for?
11. *True or False?* You should hold a string trimmer in the upright position while starting it.
12. Describe the procedure discussed in this chapter for adjusting nylon string length on a trimmer.
13. List five maintenance tasks to perform on string trimmers and brushcutters.
14. The _____ should always be in place when you operate an edger/trimmer.
15. A standard edger/trimmer blade is _____ long.

Suggested Activities

1. Demonstrate proper safety precautions for preparing to work on an engine or implement.
2. Demonstrate the safe use of a compressed air blow gun for cleaning parts.
3. Perform preventative maintenance on a power lawn mower.
4. Sharpen and balance a lawn mower blade.
5. Demonstrate engine starting procedures.

6. Make a list of maintenance tasks to be done before placing a chain saw in storage.

7. Check and change, if necessary, the gas line filter in a chain saw fuel tank.

8. Check the muffler of a chain saw to see if it has a spark arrestor device.

9. Remove a string trimmer spool and install a new nylon string.

10. Disassemble a trimmer drive shaft and demonstrate how it should be greased and reassembled. Demonstrate how to lubricate the gearbox on a string trimmer.

11. Replace a worn out blade on an edger/trimmer.

Lawn and Garden Tractors

Learning Objectives

After studying this chapter, you will be able to:

- Describe guidelines for operating a tractor safely.
- List different features available in lawn and garden tractors.
- List the various kinds of work done with lawn and garden tractors.
- Identify principles of good design for lawn and garden tractors.
- Describe the kinds of accessories that can be used with lawn and garden tractors.
- Identify several transmission systems used for lawn and garden tractors.
- Describe electrical systems and components used on lawn and garden tractors.

Key Terms

ANSI (American National Standards Institute)
ball piston pump
cavitation
chassis
compost
differential gears
four-wheel steering
grease fittings (zerks)
movable sheave
mulching
multimeter (continuity tester)
operator presence switch
power-take-off (PTO)
reservoir
reverse safety switches
single-stage snow throwers
speed ranges
spontaneous combustion
spring-loaded check valves
swash plate
transaxles
two-stage snow blowers

Tractor Safety

Lawn and garden tractors, compared to heavy farm-type tractors, are smaller in physical size and weight. They are designed to do the kinds of jobs associated with residential homes or light commercial work. See **Figure 21-1**. Before attempting to operate a lawn or garden tractor, all safety instructions provided by the manufacturer should be read and understood. Safety signs and labels placed on the machine and implements should be read and understood before use.

Learn how to properly operate the tractor and controls. Keep the machine in proper operating condition. Do not let anyone operate the tractor who has not had proper instruction about its use.

The Toro Co.

Figure 21-1.

Garden tractors are smaller in size and weight than farm tractors. They can do many jobs required with residential homes and light commercial work.

Protect Children

When operating a tractor and approaching blind corners, shrubs, trees, or other objects that may block vision, be alert for children. Never carry children or let children ride on the tractor or any attachment.

While a tractor is being operated, children should be kept in the house under supervision. If children enter a work area, turn the tractor off. Take the children out of the area to a safe location where they can be supervised.

Protective Clothing

When operating a lawn or garden tractor, be sure to wear clothing appropriate for the job. Full length denim jeans, a long-sleeve work shirt, and steel-toed work boots are recommended. Leather work gloves can provide added protection for the hands and improve gripping some items. An orange safety vest or other highly visible clothing is recommended if the tractor will be operated near a work zone or traffic area.

Wear protective safety glasses or goggles. Hearing protective earphone-type protectors or earplugs can lessen noise and make work more comfortable. Prolonged exposure to excessive noise can cause serious hearing impairment.

Depending on the type of work being done, protective masks or respirators may be required. Also depending on the location of the work area, a hard hat may be required.

Warning

Safety requires full attention of the operator. Do not wear radio or music headphones while operating a machine.

Operating a Tractor Safely

Rotating mower blades can cut off arms or legs. The following are a number of safety considerations to follow while mowing:
- Clear the mowing area of objects that might be thrown by mower blades.
- Keep people and pets out of the mowing area.
- Study the area to be mowed. Determine a safe mowing pattern. Avoid conditions where traction or stability is questionable.

- First, test drive area with the *power-take-off (PTO)* disengaged and the mower deck lowered.
- Slow down when traveling over rough ground.
- *Do not* mow in reverse unless it is absolutely necessary.
- Back up very carefully:
  Disengage the mower.
  Then, look carefully over the entire area behind the tractor, especially for children.
- Drive forward very carefully:
  People, especially children, can move quickly into the mowing area.
  Be alert at all times when driving forward.
- Keep hands, feet, and clothing away from the mower when the engine is running. *Never* place fingers or feet under the mower deck.
- Stop the mower blades when not mowing.

Safely Adjusting Mower Blades

Before getting off the tractor to disconnect or adjust the mower, follow these steps to prevent possible injury:
1. Shift to *Neutral*.
2. Disengage the PTO.
3. Engage the parking brake.
4. Stop the engine.
5. Remove the ignition key.
6. Wait for the mower blades to stop.

Avoid Tipping the Mower

If operated improperly, mowers may tip. To avoid tipping a mower, follow these rules:
- Do not operate the tractor in places where it could slip or tip.
- Be alert for holes, rocks, roots, and other terrain hazards. Stay clear of drop-offs.
- Slow down before making sharp turns.
- Do not stop or start suddenly when going uphill or downhill.
- If the machine stops going forward uphill, back down slowly. Do not attempt to turn around to descend the hill.

Parking a Tractor Safely

The following is the procedure for parking a tractor safely:
1. Shift to *Neutral*.
2. Disengage the PTO.
3. Lower the equipment to the ground.
4. Engage the parking brake.
5. Stop the engine.
6. Remove the ignition key.

Transporting a Tractor

Occasionally, you may need to transport a tractor. The tractor should be transported on a heavy-duty trailer or a truck. If you are not careful, you can be severely injured while loading and unloading a tractor. Always obey the following safety rules for transporting a tractor:

- Do not tow a lawn or garden tractor without a trailer.
- When loading a mower on a truck or trailer that does not have a tilting bed, use sturdy ramps secured to the truck or trailer bed. See **Figure 21-2**. Ramps should be adequately wide to accommodate the tractor's wheels.
- Lower the deck completely and block the wheels.
- Engage the parking brake.
- If using a truck, close the tailgate and secure the tractor to the bed of the truck. If using a trailer, fasten the tractor to the trailer with straps, chains, or cables.
- Ensure the trailer has all lights and signs required by law.
- Be sure the trailer is properly secured to the tow vehicle with safety chains.

Tractor Uses

A wide variety of different tractor designs are available. The size and design of the tractor will determine the work that the tractor is capable of performing. The following are some of the most common uses of lawn and garden tractors:

- Mowing and mulching lawn.
- Collecting leafs.
- Plowing, throwing, and blowing snow.
- Grading soil and gravel.
- Preparing soil for planting.
- Pulling a trailer for hauling.
- Sweeping walks and driveways with a rotary broom.
- Performing specialized grass care (golf course maintenance).
- Pulling heavy items, such as stumps and rocks.

Mowing and Mulching

If mowing a lawn is the only job to be done and the lawn is not more than about one-half acre, a riding mower may be more appropriate and economical than a larger tractor-type mower. However, for larger areas and a variety of jobs, a tractor should be considered.

Easy-Up Industries, Inc.

Figure 21-2.

Sturdy ramps must be used to load a tractor into a truck or onto a trailer. A—Loading a tractor safely on a truck. B—Loading a tractor safely on a trailer.

A mower deck should be easy to install and remove from the tractor. When purchasing a tractor, ask for a demonstration of this procedure. The area to be mowed is again an important factor. The width of the mower deck should be wider for larger areas so that fewer trips around, or back and forth, will be necessary. Fewer trips means less time on the tractor and engine, less fuel consumption, and less time required to get the work completed.

Options for mowing include cutting and letting the cuttings lie, cutting and collecting the cuttings, or cutting and mulching the cuttings to re-fertilize the earth. Cutting and *mulching* requires specially designed blades that will cut and chop the cuttings into very fine particles and deposit them evenly over the path being cut. **Figure 21-3** shows a tractor equipped with mulching blades. The small grass particles filter into the lawn and decompose organically into natural nitrogen fertilizer to enrich the soil and stimulate thicker growth and a healthier lawn. Depositing long cuttings without mulching may cause a smothering effect as they blanket the shorter blades of grass, preventing sunlight and moisture from penetrating very deeply.

If the grass is not to be mulched, the cuttings should be collected in some sort of container connected to the tractor. See **Figure 21-4**. To move the cuttings from the mower deck to the container, which is usually located at the rear of the tractor, there must be a strong blower and a pathway tube to the container. This pathway tube should be resistant to clogging. The container should have a

Pathway tube

Containers   Blower

Deere & Co.

Figure 21-4.

Cuttings can be collected for composting. A blower forces cuttings into containers that can be emptied.

large capacity, but should be easy to empty when it is full.

Figure 21-5 shows grass cuttings traveling through the pathway to the containers at the rear of the tractor. The grass cuttings can be discharged and used as *compost* for future fertilizer.

Proper Mowing

Each parcel of land is different and will require different procedures when mowing. When mowing a parcel of land for the first time, use the following as a guide:

- Travel slow and with cut height on high until the terrain is learned. This gives you the opportunity to learn the best mowing pattern while avoiding terrain hazards and hidden objects in the grass.
- For best performance, operate the engine at full throttle while mowing.
- Travel at a speed that fits the conditions: Mow slower in thick, tall grass. Mowing too quickly will result in stripes or an uneven cut.
- Before making a turn, slow down. Short, fast turns may cause the blades to skim the ground and pull grass out by roots.
- Mow grass only when it is dry.
- Mow grass often. Short clippings decay more quickly than long clippings.
- Cutting grass too short may kill the grass and let weeds grow easily.

MTD Products, Inc.

Figure 21-3.

Special mulching blades cut grass into fine particles and return it to the soil to become fertilizer.

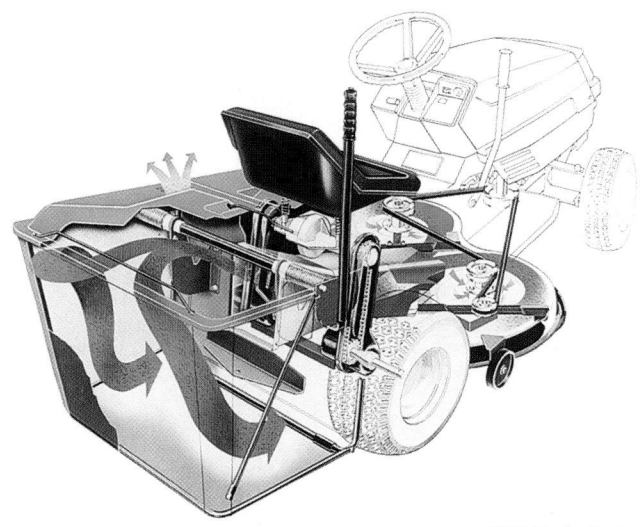

Figure 21-5.

An unrestricted pathway is provided for grass cuttings to travel easily to containers.

- Turn to the left when trimming around trees, bushes, and other obstacles. Drive slowly.
- To avoid scalping ground that slopes, approach trees or bushes head on.
- Keep the blades sharp. Dull blades tear grass, causing the tips of the grass to turn brown.
- If the cut is uneven, make sure the mower deck is level and make adjustments if necessary. Slow down before making turns, sharpen the blades often, and check wheels for needed adjustments.

Mower Deck and Blade Adjustment

The mower deck must be level from side to side to obtain an even cut. From front to rear it should be *almost* level. A better cut is obtained if the deck slants *forward* so it is 1/8″ to 1/4″ lower in front than in the back. See **Figure 21-6**.

As mowing progresses, the blade tip (A) cuts a forward arc through the grass. Tip (A) then swings to the rear cutting little grass. Tip (B) follows tip (A) and cuts a forward arc of grass also. The grass is therefore cut only once.

Note

The blades should never be level or slant toward the rear.

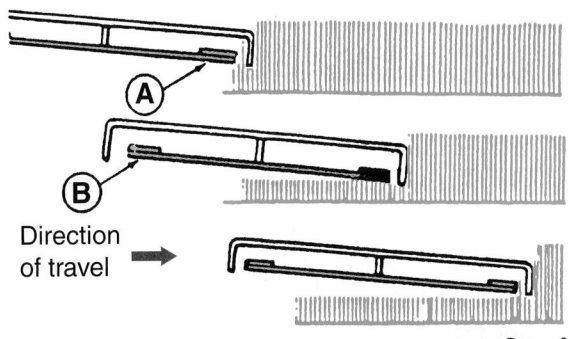

Direction of travel

Figure 21-6.

Blades should slant slightly toward direction of travel for best cutting action. The drawing is exaggerated for illustration purposes.

Proper Mulching

When mulching, there are a number of rules to follow. The following is a list of these rules:
- Cut only about 1/3 of the blade of grass when using a mulcher.
- Mulch only when the grass and leaves are dry.
- Mow a different direction each time you mow.
- Overlap mowing paths 2″ to 4″.
- Slow the mower's travel speed. Mulching requires more power.
- Keep the underside of the mower deck clean. Clean the deck after each use with a garden hose.

Leaf Collecting

Leaf collecting is similar to collecting grass. Leaves are shredded and blown into the container at the rear of the tractor mower. The leaves can be mixed with grass cuttings and other organic materials. This mixture can then be composted into fertilizer.

Plowing, Throwing, and Blowing Snow

Plowing snow with a tractor requires a concave blade attached to the front of the tractor. See **Figure 21-7**. The blade is typically raised, lowered, and angled to either side hydraulically or mechanically. The tractor must have enough horsepower to move heavy snow without lugging or stalling. Chains and wheel weights can often be installed on

The Toro Co.

Figure 21-7.
A curved plow blade is used for snow plowing. The blade is raised and lowered mechanically or hydraulically.

Deere & Co.

Figure 21-9.
A plow blade can be used for moving and grading operations.

the rear drive wheels for better traction on slippery, icy surfaces. See **Figure 21-8**. A blade can also be used to spread and level gravel for driveways. See **Figure 21-9**. Blade edges wear quickly when leveling gravel, and a metal edge is recommended for this task.

Single-stage snow throwers of varying widths can be attached to the front of tractors. These throwers have a horizontal auger that gathers and throws the snow through an adjustable deflector. Typically, the operator can direct the deflector to the right or left without leaving the tractor seat.

Two-stage snow blowers are snow blowers that incorporate a high-speed blower in conjunction with the auger of the single stage type. The auger draws the snow in where the blower then discharges the snow through the deflector chute. A two-stage snow blower is a more efficient system and can handle larger quantities and heavier snow than the single-stage thrower. A two-stage snow blower may require more horsepower. See **Figure 21-10**.

The Toro Co.

Figure 21-8.
Chains and wheel weights may be needed to increase traction for some jobs, such as plowing snow.

The Toro Co.

Figure 21-10.
Snow blowers can be attached to the front of some tractors. Note the tire chains, wheel weights, and enclosure to protect the driver.

Preparing Soil for Planting

Tractors are excellent for tilling, or preparing, soil for gardens. Rotary garden tillers are available that connect to the rear of the tractor and the tines, or blades, are driven mechanically from a power-take-off (PTO) from the rear drive unit of the tractor. See **Figure 21-11**. Tines should be replaced when they become worn too short to be effective. A three-point hitch allows the tiller to be raised and lowered mechanically or hydraulically. The hitch is controlled with a lever located so the driver can easily reach it. Cultivators, harrows, and discs are available, but generally can only be used with tractors that produce at least 18 horsepower (hp).

Hauling a Trailer

A trailer for hauling can be a very economical and useful accessory. See **Figure 21-12**. Trailers can be easily attached to the tractor to carry all types of equipment and materials. Logs, dirt, gravel, mulch, and garden tools are just a few of the items that can be hauled. There are trailers available to accomplish specific jobs such as collecting grass clippings. Most trailers will tilt and dump the load by releasing a lever located on the tongue. Some trailers have hinged tailgates that make the trailer easy to load or unload. Trailers may be constructed from steel or plastic.

Deere & Co.

Figure 21-12.

A trailer is a very useful accessory for hauling behind a tractor. They may be made of metal or plastic.

Rotary Broom Sweeping

Rotary bristled brooms are available for some tractors. These brooms are useful for sweeping sidewalks and driveways. See **Figure 21-13**. The rotary broom is fitted to the front of the tractor. The broom can be angled to the right or left so debris can be cleared to either side. The broom rotates so that debris is pushed forward and to the side of the tractor's path. Rotary brooms can also be used for clearing light, dry snow.

Warning

A rotary broom can create a large amount of dust. A dust mask should be worn when using a rotary broom.

The Toro Co.

Figure 21-11.

Soil can be prepared for planting with a tiller attachment.

Deere & Co.

Figure 21-13.

A rotary broom can be used to sweep debris and light, dry snow. The broom can be directed to the right, straight, or to the left.

Engine Components

Nearly all yard and garden tractor engines are four-cycle, electric start engines with overhead valves and electronic ignition systems. Electronic ignition systems are essentially trouble free. Electric starter motors require a 12V battery and alternator battery charging system. Engines in typical lawn and garden tractors range from 12 hp to 22 hp. Engine horsepower for a tractor depends on the size and weight of the tractor, any accessories it must drive, and the kind of work the tractor is designed to do. For example, less horsepower is required to operate a dual-bladed mower deck for lawn care than is needed for tilling land or pulling a trailer full of gravel.

Single-cylinder engines are frequently used on light-duty tractors. These engines typically range from 12 hp to 14 hp and have a cast-iron cylinder sleeve or a solid cast-iron block. If the engine has a cast-iron sleeve, the sleeve can be replaced with another standard size sleeve during an engine overhaul. Standard size pistons and rings are used. Cast-iron engine blocks require boring and honing to the next larger standard size and a corresponding oversize piston and rings must be installed. Refer to Chapter 17, *Cylinder, Crankshaft, and Piston Service.*

Tractor engines from 14 hp to 22 hp generally have two cylinders. They are either the vee, or opposed cylinder configuration. They may have a vertical or horizontal output shaft. The engine type depends on the manufacturer and their decision on the best way to drive the tractor and its accessories. Overhead valves and hydraulic valve lifters are used on all tractor engines, because of their greater efficiency and service life.

Most tractor engines are easy to maintain. Some tractors have a hood that covers the entire engine. The hood protects the engine from external elements. Other tractors have partial hoods over the top of the engine compartment leaving the sides open for better cooling and ease of access. As the tractor is used, dirt and debris can accumulate on the engine. This may hamper engine cooling and clog air filters. Be sure to clean the engine compartment, and check and service the air filter regularly.

Tractor hoods are hinged so they can be opened forward to expose the engine compartment. Locate the oil dipstick. Become familiar with oil level markings on the dipstick. Check the oil regularly. Locate the oil filler tube and cap, and the oil filter. Oil should be poured without spillage, and the filter should be changed every time the oil is changed.

Locate the in-line fuel filter. Check the filter periodically and replace it if needed. Most tractors have fuel tanks that can be reached easily with the spout of the fuel container. The majority of these tanks are located at the rear so that if there is an accidental spill, the fuel will not run onto a hot portion of the engine.

Locate the air filter housing. Become familiar with the air filter replacement procedures. Refer to the manufacturer's technical service manual for this information.

Make sure the muffler and exhaust system are in good condition. The engine should run comfortably quiet. The system should direct the exhaust away from the operator. The exhaust system normally gets very hot. It should be located so that the operator is protected from accidental burns. Spark arresting mufflers are available for most tractors. These types of mufflers are required by law in some areas to prevent accidental fires.

Some tractor engines are liquid cooled. The coolant level needs to be checked periodically. It is good practice to flush and add new coolant seasonally. Locate the coolant drain point. It will be located at a low point on the engine. Check the coolant and the thermostat regularly. Replace thermostat and coolant as needed. Check the manufacturer's service manual for recommendations. Clean the radiator cooling fins occasionally to prevent dirt or debris from clogging them.

Become acquainted with the engine controls, such as the throttle, choke, and ignition switch. On most tractors these controls are within easy and comfortable reach of the operator. Gauges and system indicators should also be visible to the operator. See **Figure 21-14.**

Chassis and Steering

The *chassis* is the main framework of the tractor around which the entire tractor is assembled. The chassis must be strong and rigid enough to withstand bending and torsional forces imposed on it during operation. The engine, transmission, and work accessories must all be held in exact proper alignment regardless of terrain. Heavy steel components secured with high quality welds and locking-type threaded fasteners are indicators of a well designed chassis. Sheet metal components that are secured to the chassis should be smooth and made from heavy gauge sheet metal. The sheet metal

The Toro Co.

Figure 21-14.

The throttle, choke, ignition switch and other controls and instruments should be easy to reach and see.

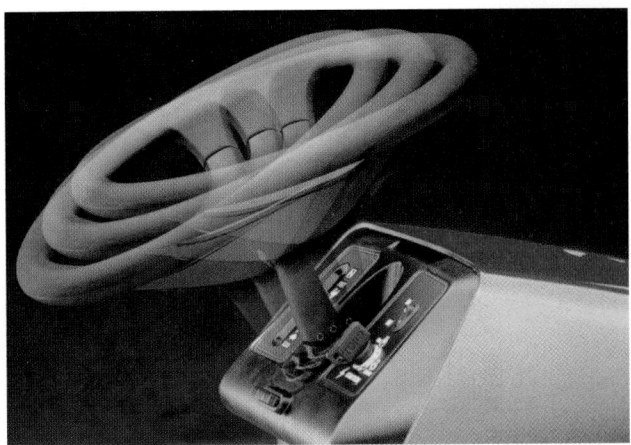

The Toro Co.

Figure 21-15.

An adjustable, tilting steering wheel tilts to provide comfortable steering for the driver.

should protect the operator from contact with any moving parts.

The steering components must function smoothly and easily in all driving configurations. Strength in the front axle is essential, because it must be able to pivot up and down laterally to conform to changing terrain while allowing controlled steering of the front wheels. In many cases, cast-iron is used for front axles. Heavy cast-iron is an excellent material for this application, because of its inherent strength and rigidity. *Grease fittings (zerks)* are used where lubrication is required for king pins and tie rods. The recommended type of grease should be applied at recommended intervals using a hand-operated grease gun. Excess grease should be wiped away to prevent it from mixing with dirt.

The steering wheel should be of such a size, angle, and location that the operator can easily reach it without straining arm or back muscles. Some steering wheels can be tilted for comfort. See **Figure 21-15.**

Steering linkage between the steering column and front wheels should be free of excess looseness and provide positive directional control at all times. Easy steering on a smooth display room floor may not be representative of how it will react on an irregular terrain. Customers should thoroughly test drive a tractor outdoors on irregular terrain before making a purchase.

Four-wheel steering is available on some tractors to provide greater maneuverability around obstacles. See **Figure 21-16.** When the front wheels are turned less than 45°, the rear wheels remain straight

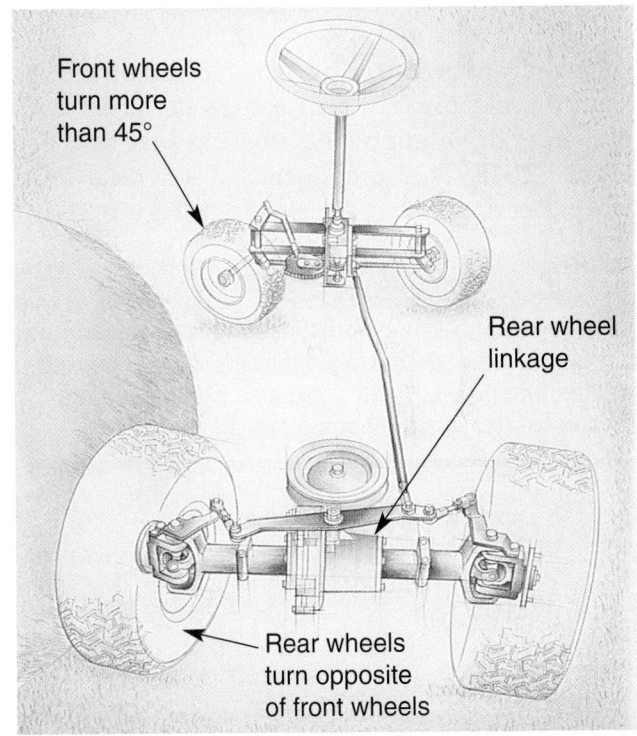

Front wheels turn more than 45°

Rear wheel linkage

Rear wheels turn opposite of front wheels

MTD Products, Inc.

Figure 21-16.

Four-wheel steering can increase maneuverability around trees and shrubbery. Notice the additional linkage and joints at the rear wheels.

ahead. For tight turning, when front wheels are turned more than 45°, the rear wheels will turn the opposite direction but at a slower rate than the front wheels. See **Figure 21-17.** The difference in angle between the front wheels and rear wheels

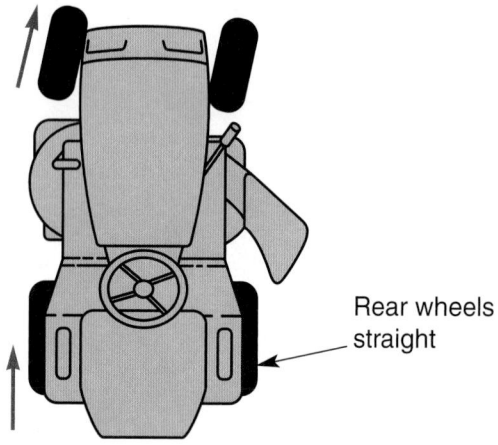
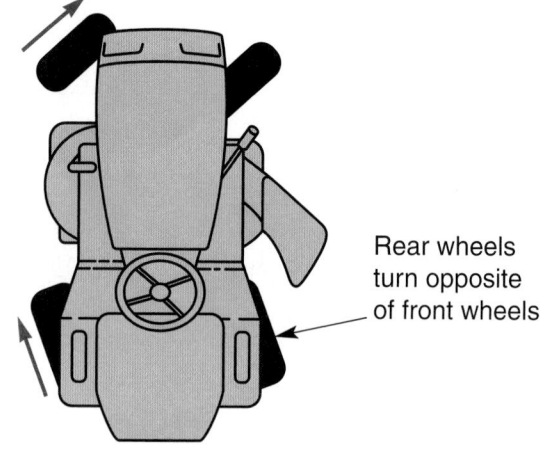

Less Than 45° Turn of Steering Wheel

More Than 45° Turn of Steering Wheel

Rear wheels straight

Rear wheels turn opposite of front wheels

MTD Products, Inc.

Figure 21-17.

Front wheels turn 45° before rear wheels begin to turn the opposite direction.

helps prevent oversteering, which could otherwise lead to accidents. The rear axle is designed with universal drive joints and steering brackets. See **Figure 21-18**. The components of a typical four-wheel steering system are shown in **Figure 21-19**.

Warning

When operating a four-wheel steering lawn tractor near a drop-off in the ground, *do not* turn sharply. The rear wheels turn outward and could lose ground contact. This could result in the tipping over of the tractor.

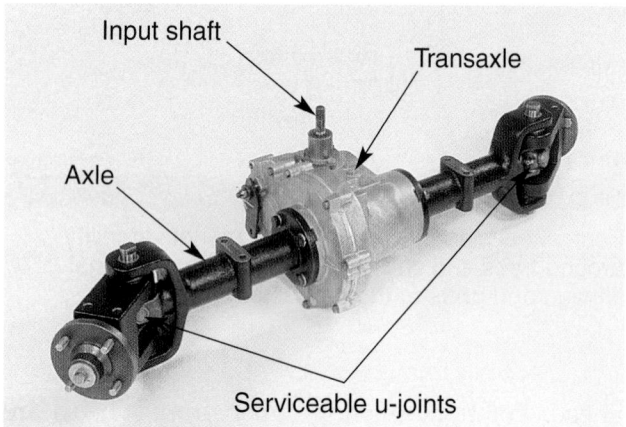

Input shaft

Transaxle

Axle

Serviceable u-joints

MTD Products, Inc.

Figure 21-18.

Rear-wheel drive for four-wheel steering consists of axles, serviceable universal-joints, transmission, input shaft.

Transmissions

The transmission and rear axles are very important, hard working components of any tractor. They are called *transaxles*. The transaxle unit may be driven by the engine from a V-belt, a series of V-belts and pulleys, or a direct driveshaft. See **Figures 21-20** and **21-21**. The major function of the transmission is to allow the operator to control motion and power from the engine to the rear wheels.

Mechanical, geared transaxles produce greater pulling power and slower tractor speed by gearing down (low-speed gear). They produce less pulling power with greater tractor speed by gearing up (high-speed gear). Mechanical transmissions contain a variety of gear sizes and ratios. The operator can shift gears with a lever to apply the necessary driving force at the rear wheels without slowing the engine excessively. For example, heavy pulling requires a lower gear ratio than mowing, so the operator would shift to a lower gear.

A clutch mechanism is used to disconnect the engine from the transmission while gears are shifted. The clutch is operated by pressing a foot pedal. A reverse gear and brake are also a part of the transmission. They allow the operator to back up or stop the tractor. Often, the brake is linked to the clutch and is engaged when the clutch pedal is depressed.

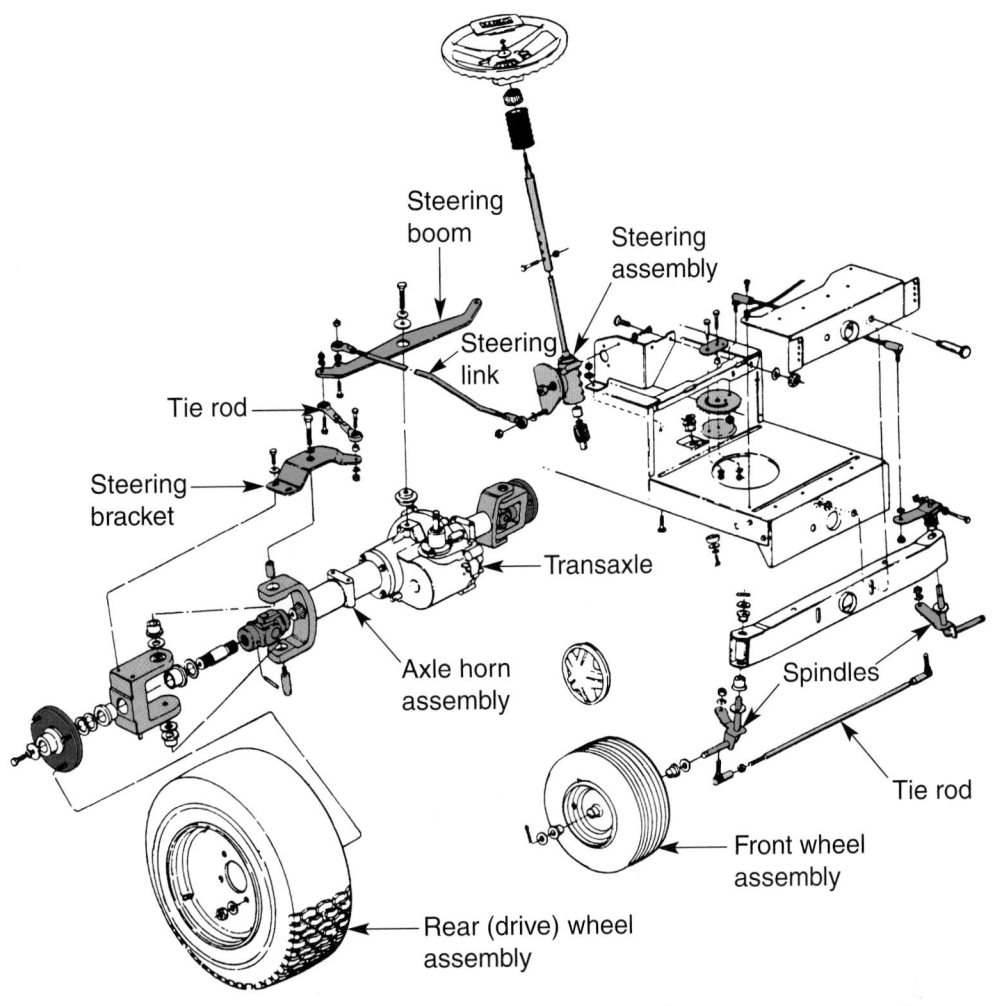

Steering boom

Steering assembly

Steering link

Tie rod

Steering bracket

Transaxle

Axle horn assembly

Spindles

Tie rod

Front wheel assembly

Rear (drive) wheel assembly

MTD Products, Inc.

Figure 21-19.

Four-wheel steering assembly.

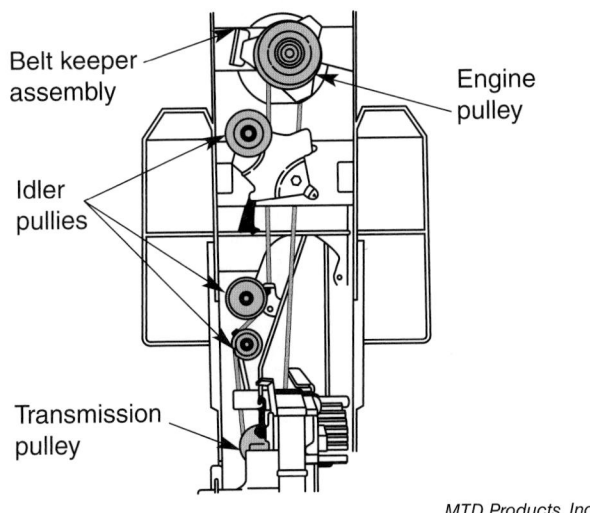

Belt keeper assembly

Engine pulley

Idler pullies

Transmission pulley

MTD Products, Inc.

Figure 21-20.

Single V-belt drive system from engine to transmission pulley. A series of idler pulleys route and maintain tension on the belt.

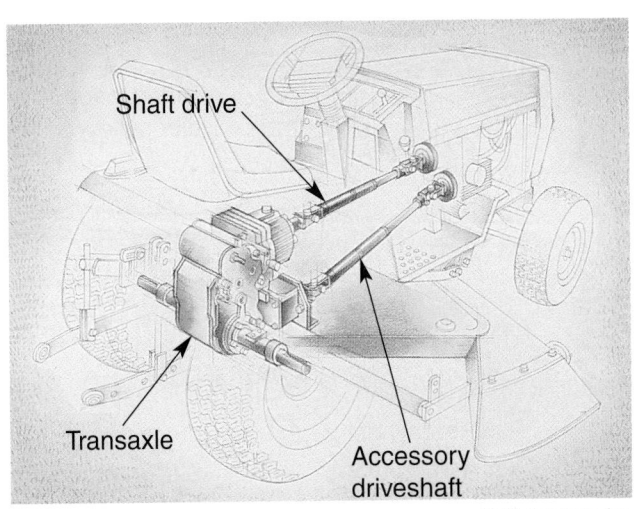

Shaft drive

Transaxle

Accessory driveshaft

MTD Products, Inc.

Figure 21-21.

A driveshaft from engine drives the hydrostatic transaxle. A power-take-off (PTO) unit is driven by the second drive shaft.

Variable-Speed Transmission

A variable-speed pulley is a torque converter used on some tractors, riding mowers, and rotary tillers. A variable-speed pulley allows the operator to vary the tractor speed while maintaining a constant engine speed. A variable drive pulley system coupled with the transaxle allows the operator to select a base speed with the speed selector lever, but also slow the tractor down for a turn by depressing the clutch/brake pedal. See **Figure 21-22**. The tractor automatically resumes speed when the pedal is released. This enables the operator to match the tractor speed to various mowing conditions without slowing the speed of the engine or mowing blades.

As the variable-speed pulley changes position, the pulley ratios are changed, which alters the speed of the driven pulley. See **Figure 21-23**. The center part of the pulley, called a *movable sheave*, is free to move up and down. Remember, V-belts normally do not stretch or change length. When the speed control pedal is pressed, it mechanically pulls the movable sheave toward the engine pulley and the engine's V-belt runs outward on the variable-speed pulley. At the same time, the transmission

V-belt runs closer to the center of the variable-speed pulley. Because the large driving pulley is now turning slower, the belt on the smaller pulley is also running slower. To speed up, the pedal is released.

The speed selector lever provides a variety of *speed ranges*. See **Figure 21-24**. The clutch pedal must be depressed and the clutch disengaged when changing the speed selector lever. The speed control pedal controls the speed in each range. If the transaxle is the single-speed type, the tractor speeds are controlled only by the variable-speed belt drive system. See **Figure 21-25**. The transaxle provides forward, neutral, and reverse direction only. The shift lever will have forward, neutral, and reverse positions. Internal components of a heavy-duty, single-speed transaxle are illustrated in **Figure 21-26**.

A two-speed transaxle, coupled with a variable-speed drive, will provide a high-speed gear range and a low-speed gear range. The high-speed and low-speed ranges are selected using the transmission shift lever. See **Figure 21-27**. Within each range are a fixed number of variable-speeds, which are

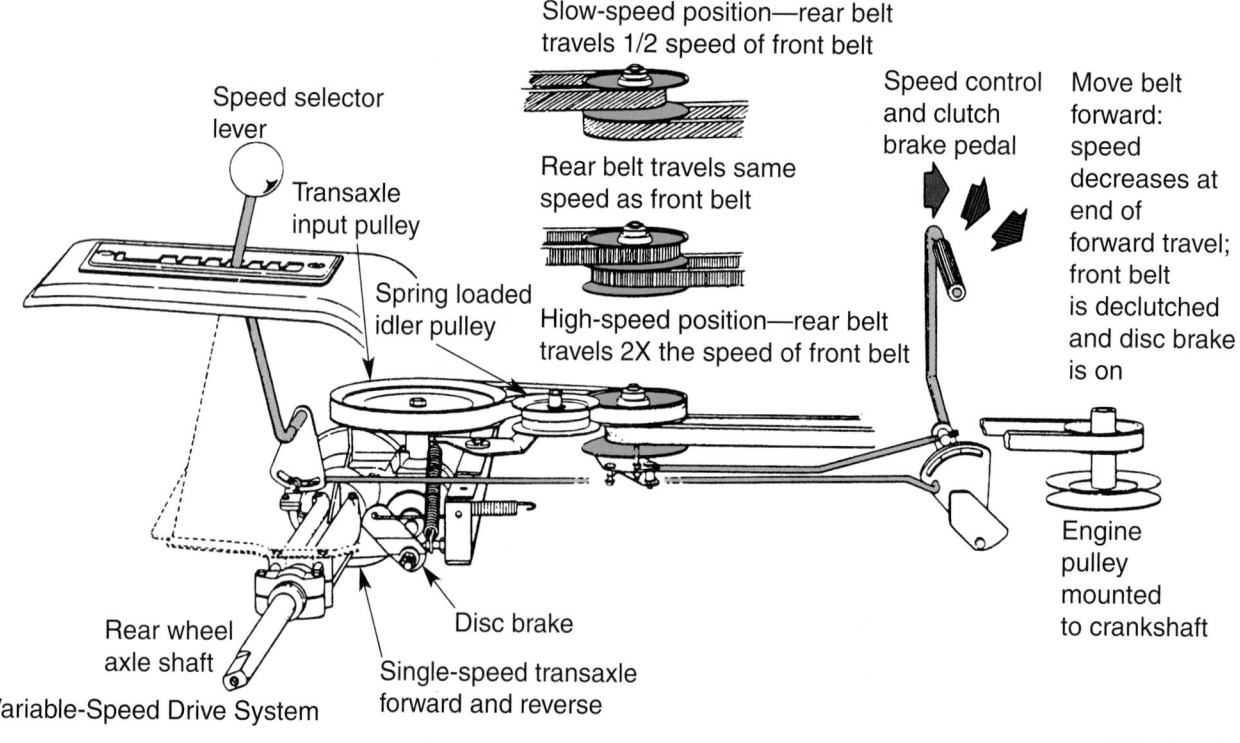

Figure 21-22.

A variable-speed drive system. The speed selector lever selects speed range. The tractor must be stopped when shifting the speed selector lever. The speed control pedal varies speed through variable-speed pulleys.

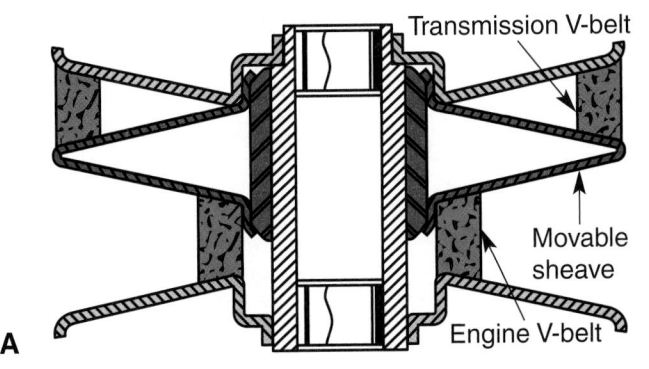
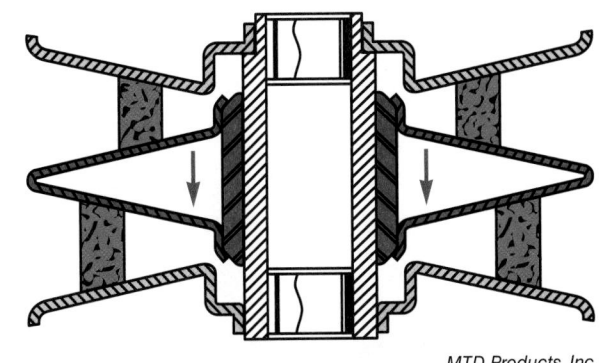

A — Transmission V-belt, Movable sheave, Engine V-belt

B

MTD Products, Inc.

Figure 21-23.

Variable-speed drive pulleys. A—Under normal operating conditions, the engine V-belt rides close to the center of the variable-speed pulley. This causes the variable-speed pulley to spin at the maximum speed. B—When the pedal is depressed, the movable sheave is moved downward, forcing the engine V-belt to ride outward in the pulley. This causes the pulley to turn more slowly.

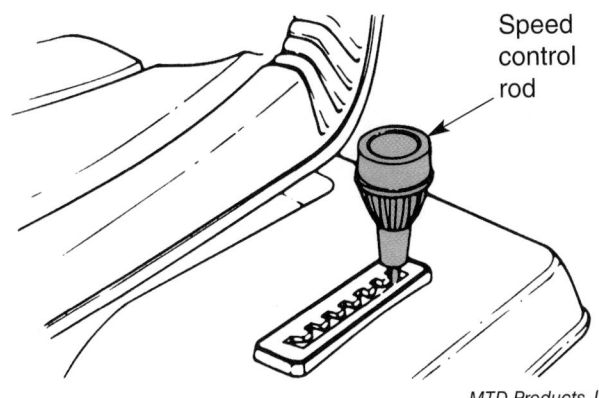

Speed control rod

MTD Products, Inc.

Figure 21-24.

The speed control lever is moved to the desired location and held in place by notches. On many tractor models, it is located on the rear fender.

selected using the speed control lever. For example: the number of speeds may be seven high speeds plus seven low speeds. The clutch pedal must be depressed and the tractor not moving when shifting gears. The two-speed transaxle shift lever will have high, low, neutral, and reverse positions. See **Figure 21-28**.

Hydrostatic Transmissions

Hydrostatic transmissions consist of a variable-displacement hydraulic pump, a fixed-displacement hydraulic motor, and a system of check valves, all contained within one housing. See **Figure 21-29**. Hydrostatic transmissions can be used in various

types of applications where variable output speed is required. This type of transmission has many advantages over other variable-speed drives and gear-type transmissions. The advantages of the hydrostatic transmission are as follows:

- **Precise speed.** Hydrostatic transmissions are capable of maintaining precise speed under varying load conditions.
- **Ease of operation.** Simple controls allow the operator to control direction and speed smoothly, without gear change.
- **Low maintenance.** Simple design keeps maintenance minimal.
- **Increased productivity and versatility.** Hydrostatic transmissions allow complete matching of power to load.
- **Completely self contained.** There are no external hydraulic lines, separate drive components, etc.
- **Simple design.** Hydrostatic transmissions have fewer mechanical drive components.
- **Positive braking action.** The one lever that controls speed and direction also controls braking. As the control lever is moved toward neutral the output shaft slows until it finally stops at the neutral position. Equalized hydraulic pressure prevents the output shaft from turning freely.
- **Self lubricating.** The system is completely filled with oil at all times and all internal parts move in a bath of oil.

The difference in performance between the hydrostatic transmission and a geared transmission is shown with a graph in **Figure 21-30**. The smooth

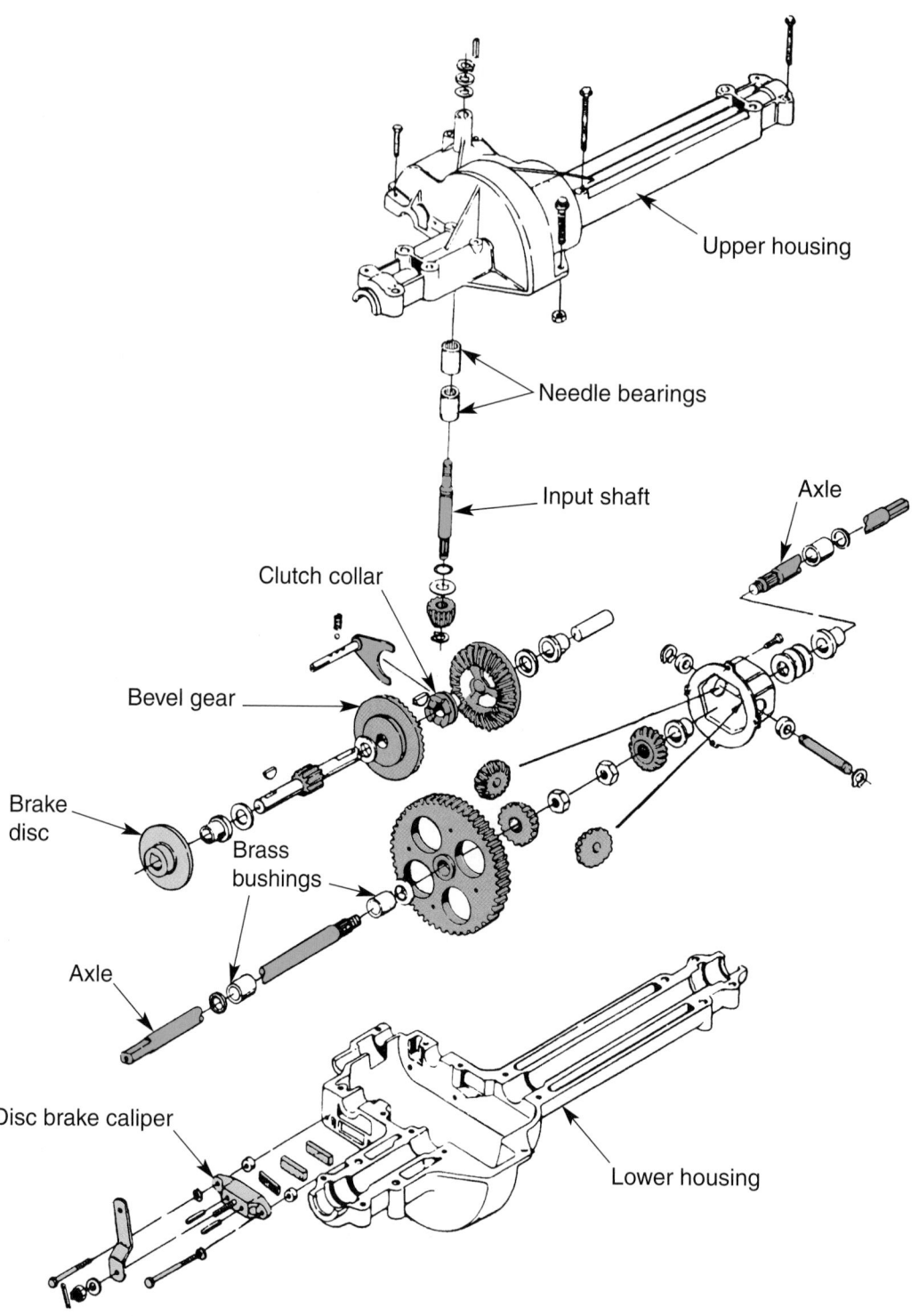

Upper housing

Needle bearings

Input shaft

Axle

Clutch collar

Bevel gear

Brake
disc

Brass
bushings

Axle

Disc brake caliper

Lower housing

MTD Products, Inc.

Figure 21-25.

The inner components of a single-speed transaxle. Note that there are no provisions for changing gear ratio inside the transmission. The transaxle is very similar to a rear differential in a car or truck. With this setup, tractor speeds are controlled only by the variable-speed belt drive system.

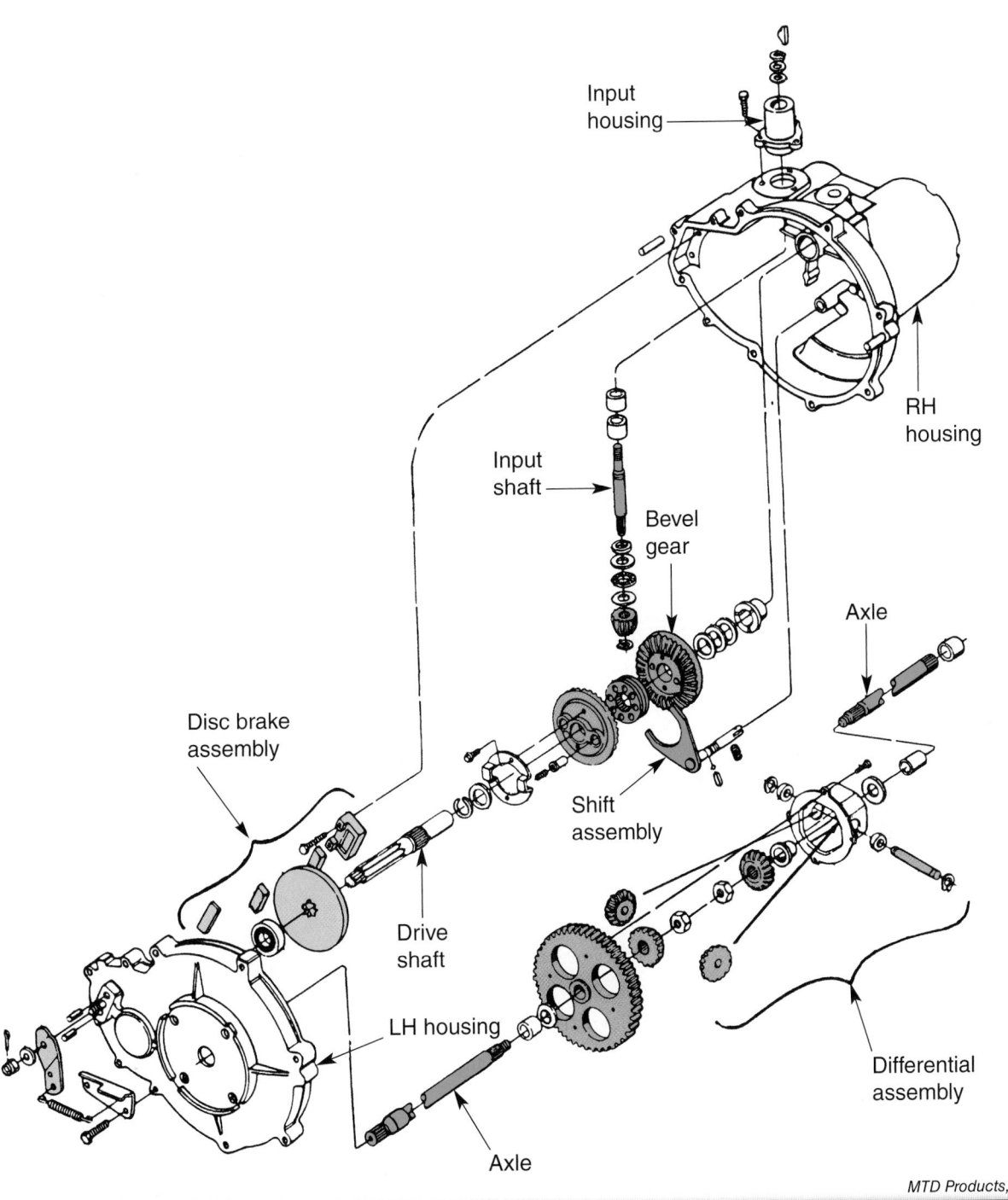

Input
housing

RH
housing

Input
shaft

Bevel
gear

Axle

Disc brake
assembly

Shift
assembly

Drive
shaft

LH housing

Differential
assembly

Axle

MTD Products, Inc.

Figure 21-26.

Heavy-duty, single-speed transaxle.

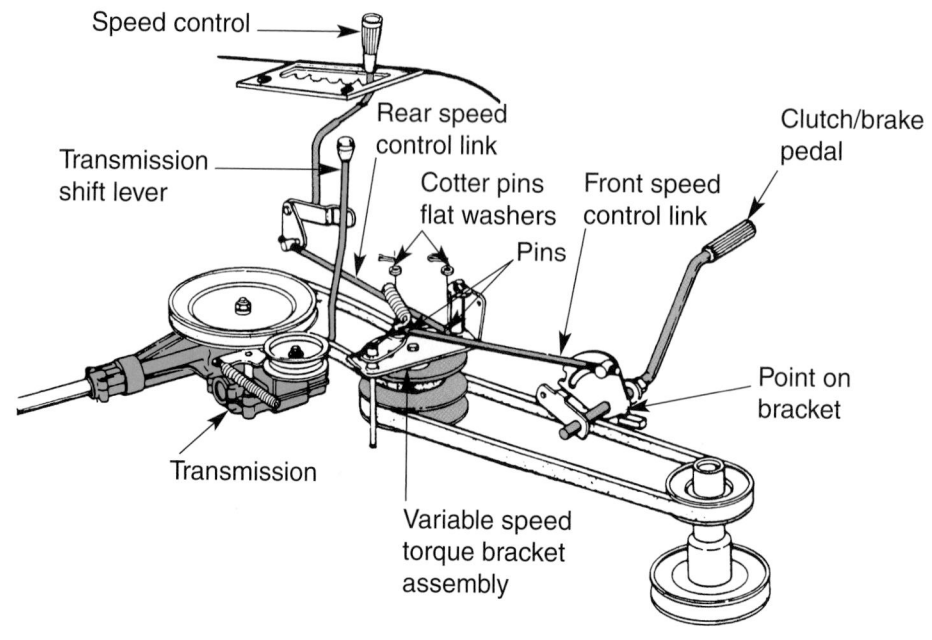

MTD Products, Inc.

Figure 21-27.

A two-speed transmission system with variable-speed drive.

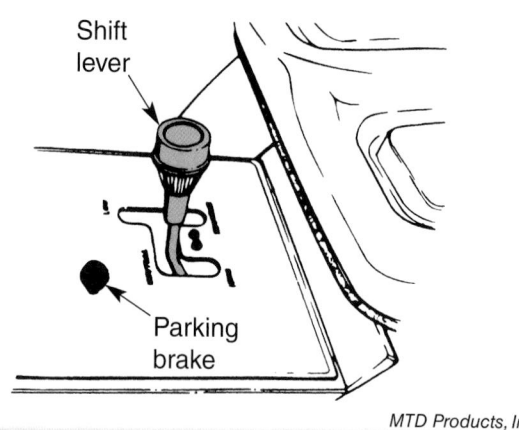

MTD Products, Inc.

Figure 21-28.

A shift lever with *High*, *Low*, *Neutral*, and *Reverse* positions.

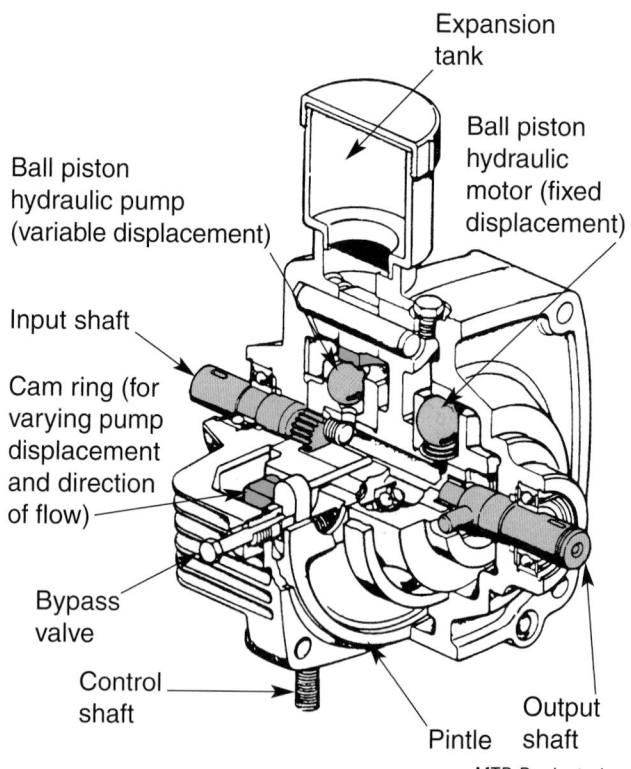

MTD Products, Inc.

curve shows the uniform matching of torque and speed requirements by the hydrostatic transmission. As speed increases, torque decreases smoothly. The geared transmission has three peaks and valleys requiring manual shifting between each of them.

The pump section of the transmission controls speed and direction of the output shaft by a single lever. See **Figure 21-31**. By varying the displacement ratios between the pump and motor, infinite speed control is achieved. Speed increases as the lever is moved farther from neutral. From neutral to

Figure 21-29.

A hydrostatic transmission is a variable-displacement hydraulic pump driving a fixed-displacement hydraulic motor. The input shaft is driven by the engine, the output shaft drives the axles.

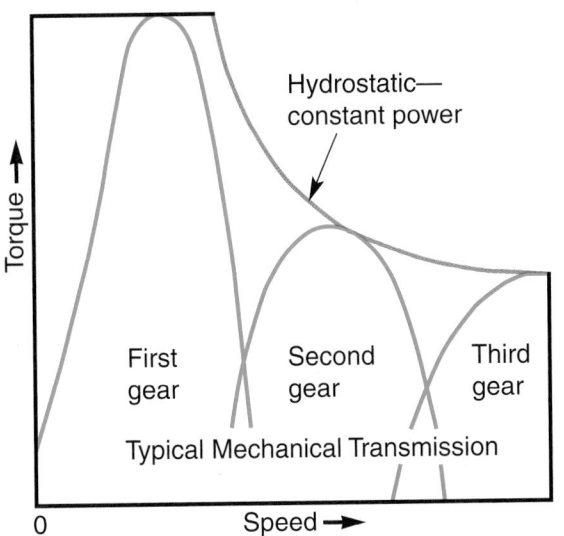

Hydrostatic/Mechanical Transmission Performance Graph

MTD Products, Inc.

Figure 21-30.

Unlike the mechanical gear-type transmissions, hydrostatic transmission provides constant smooth power.

forward produces one direction of rotation of the output shaft. When the lever is in the neutral position, the output shaft stops, producing an effective braking action. To produce opposite rotation of the output shaft the lever is moved from neutral to reverse.

Hydrostatic Transmission Fluid Flow

The variable displacement *ball piston pump* is driven by the engine at a constant speed. See **Figure 21-31**. The ball pistons rotate and roll within a close fitting circular housing. When the control lever places the cam ring in a position that causes the balls to reciprocate in their cylinders, they draw in oil from one port and force it out the opposite port to the motor (lever in forward position). When the cam ring is centered so the balls do not reciprocate and only roll in a concentric circle (lever in neutral position), no oil is moved to the motor. This causes an effective braking action at the motor output shaft. When the control lever is moved to the reverse position, the cam ring causes the balls to reciprocate. This causes the fluid to be pumped in the opposite direction to the motor, resulting in reversing of the output shaft.

During use, hydraulic oil gets warm and expands. A *reservoir* is necessary to accommodate the oil expansion without overflowing. See **Figure 21-32**. When the oil is cold, the pump and motor cavities must be full of oil. If they are not full, air occupies the space that should contain oil. Because air is compressible and oil is not, any air in the system will cause erratic running, noise, and eventual serious damage to the pump and motor. This condition is called *cavitation* and should not be tolerated for any lengthy period of time. It is important

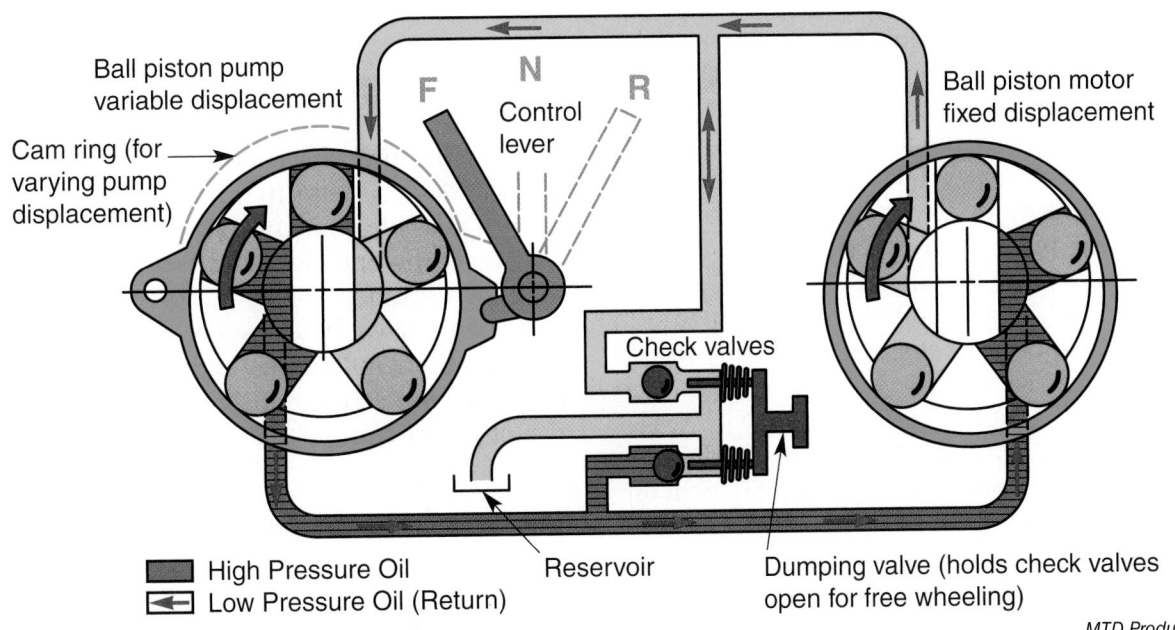

MTD Products, Inc.

Figure 21-31.

Fluid flow diagram for a hydrostatic transmission system. Notice the function of the check valves.

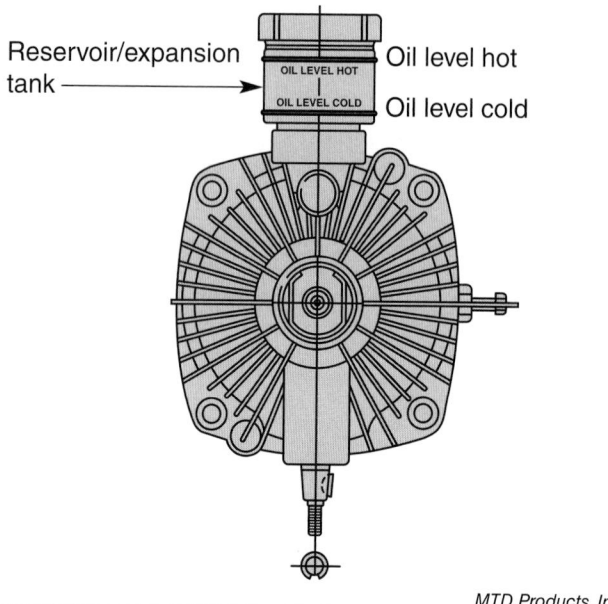

Reservoir/expansion tank

OIL LEVEL HOT
OIL LEVEL COLD

Oil level hot

Oil level cold

MTD Products, Inc.

Figure 21-32.
The oil level should be checked and maintained when the unit is cold. The reservoir allows the oil to expand due to heat without overflowing.

that the hydraulic oil level be checked frequently and oil added as needed. If the transmission is cold, add oil only to the cold level indicated on the reservoir. Overfilling will cause fluid to spill out at operating temperature.

Rather than using a ball piston pump, some hydrostatic transmissions pump hydraulic fluid using a variable-displacement *swash plate* pump. The pistons and the cylinder assembly, called a barrel, rotate together. Shoes on bottoms of the pistons slide on the swash plate as the barrel rotates. See **Figure 21-33**. As the swash plate is tilted, the pistons travel a greater distance in their cylinders and more oil is pumped. As the swash plate tilt is lessened, the pistons travel less, and less fluid is drawn in and pumped out to the motor. When the swash plate angle reaches 0°, no oil is pumped, and the motor output shaft stops. Both pump systems function in the same basic way but vary in their mechanical makeup.

Spring-loaded check valves are used in the hydrostatic fluid flow system to permit flow in one direction and prevent flow in the opposite direction. See **Figure 21-31**. If the tractor is pushed or towed, both check valves must be opened to allow fluid to flow freely in either direction in the system. This overrides the normal neutral braking action. When the pump is in neutral, both check valves are

closed preventing fluid flow in either direction in the system. The tractor will not move in this case. Usually, there is a lever at the back of the tractor that will open a bypass valve so the tractor can be pushed or pulled. See **Figure 21-34**. Zero-turn models have two hydraulic pumps and two bypass valves.

To prevent overheating of the system, a cooling fan is placed on the input shaft of the transmission. See **Figure 21-35**. The input shaft and fan are driven from a V-belt between the engine and transmission. The differential and transmission housing have cooling fins to aid in cooling. See **Figure 21-36**. The *differential gears* permit each rear axle to turn at different speeds as is necessary when turning corners. See **Figure 21-37**.

There are many different makes and models of hydrostatic transmissions. The troubleshooting chart in **Figure 21-38** is general in its scope and may not be adequate for certain makes and models. Refer to the manufacturer's technical service manuals for the particular make and model in need of service or repair.

Caution

Hydrostatic transmissions should be serviced only by properly trained technicians. Hydraulic systems are sensitive to contamination and improper service procedures can lead to catastrophic failure.

Electrical Safety Systems

Manufacturers have incorporated safety devices and interlock systems in tractors to protect against certain possible accidents. These systems are used to protect the operators and those people around them. Children and pets are often unpredictable and should never be allowed near tractors or other work equipment that may cause them injury. Even adults have been seriously injured by improper use of power equipment.

Safety Interlocks

Safety interlocks are two or more devices that are connected in such a way that none of them can be operated independently. Safety interlock systems are used to provide added safety on lawn and garden

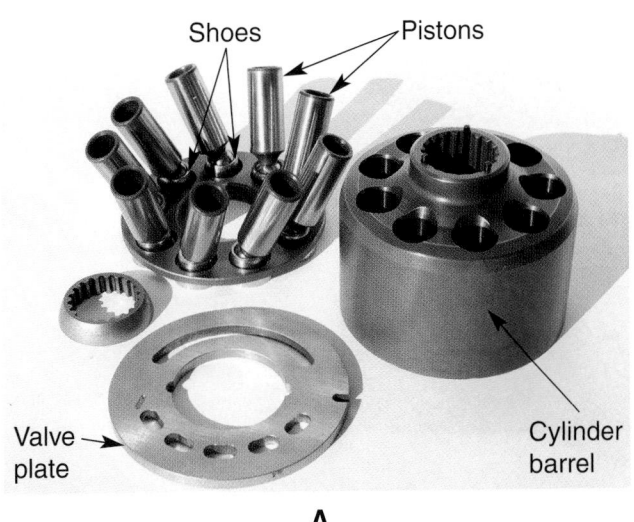

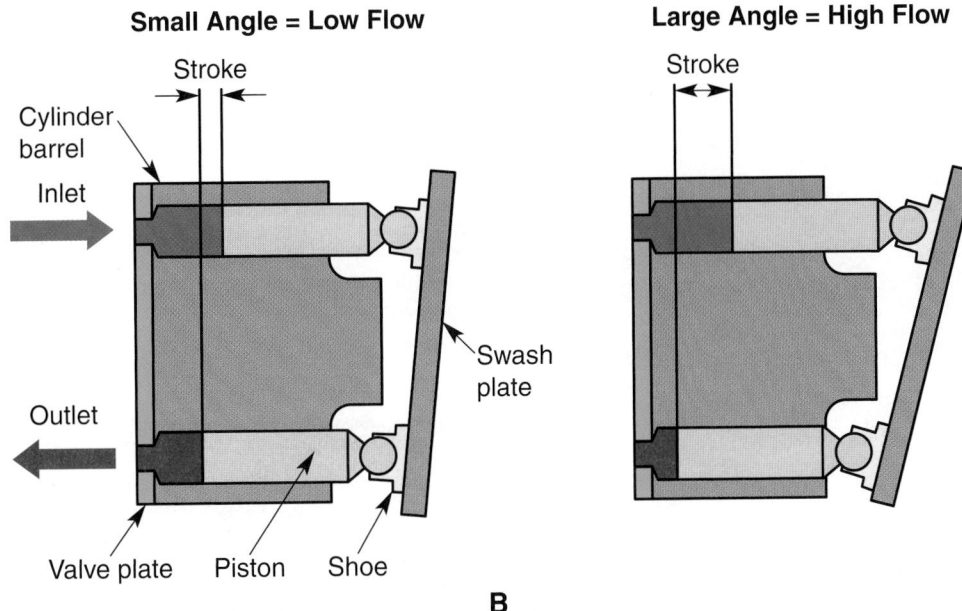

Figure 21-33.

In a swash plate variable-displacement pump, the angle of the swash plate determines the stroke of the pistons within their cylinders. A—The pistons and cylinder barrel of a swash plate pump. B—Basic operation of a swash plate pump.

M.Khebra/Shutterstock.com; Goodheart-Willcox Publisher

tractors. This arrangement of devices may be mechanical, hydraulic, electronic, or any combination of the three. They are arranged so the functioning of one device is controlled by the functioning of another. Examples of safety interlocks are the reverse safety switch and the seat-activated switch.

Reverse safety switches are safety interlocks that require the cutting deck (mower unit) to be disengaged before the unit can be shifted into reverse. In one variation of the reverse safety switch, the tractor is equipped with a lever for lifting and

lowering the cutting deck to set cutting height. Pulling the lever all the way back and locking it disengages the blades. The lift and disengage lever must be all the way back and the blades disengaged in order to start the engine or shift into reverse.

As an added safety feature, *ANSI (American National Standards Institute)* requires that all lawn and garden tractors produced after July, 1987 have an operator present for the tractor to be operational. The engine must stop if the operator leaves the seat while the blades or PTO (power-take-off) is

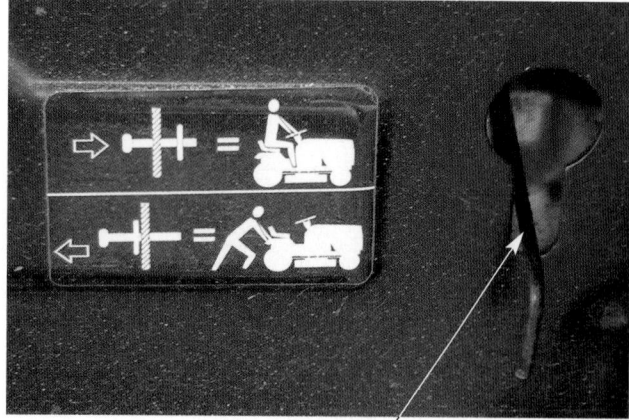

A   Bypass valve lever

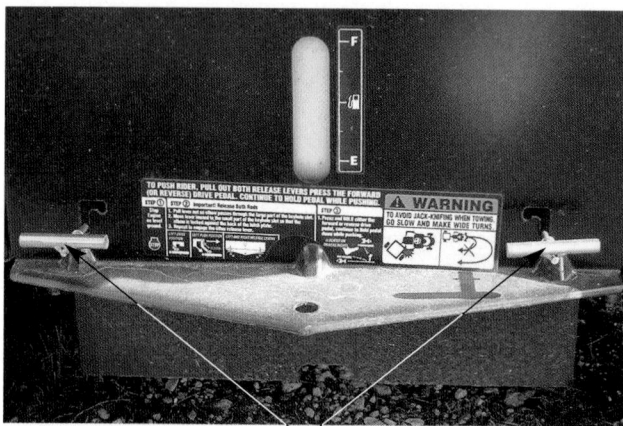

B   Bypass valve levers

C   Bypass valve

Goodheart-Willcox Publisher

Figure 21-34.

On a mower or tractor with a hydrostatic transmission, a bypass valve must be opened so the tractor can be pushed or pulled. The location and appearance of the bypass lever varies from tractor to tractor. A—A single lever at the back of the tractor. B—Zero-turn models have two bypass levers. C—This zero-turn model has a bypass valve on each pump.

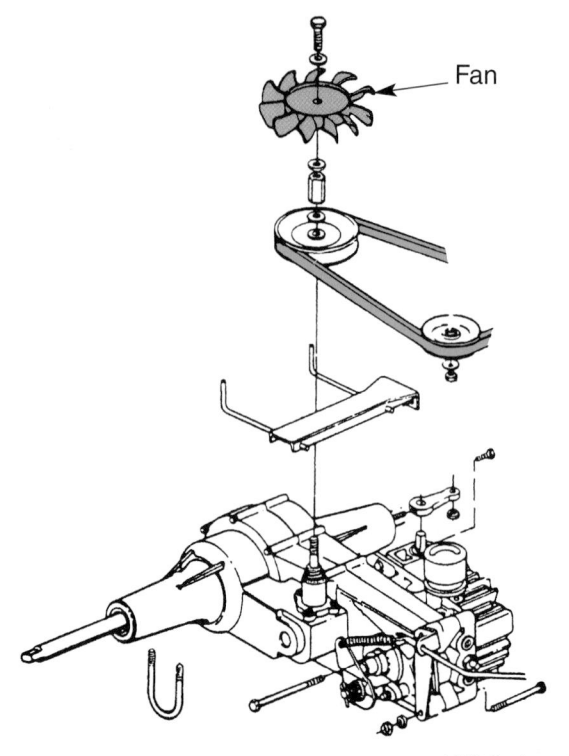

Fan

MTD Products, Inc.

Figure 21-35.

A cooling fan on the input shaft cools the transmission system.

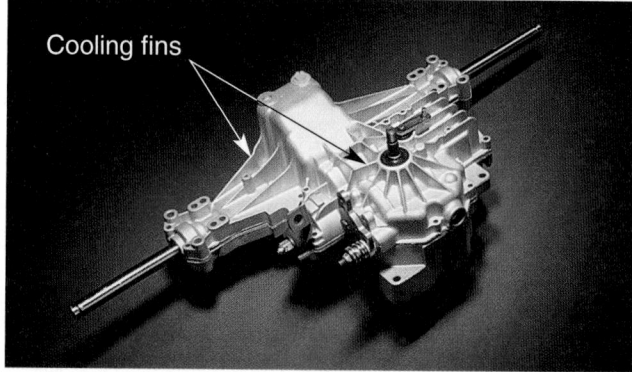

Cooling fins

MTD Products, Inc.

Figure 21-36.

Cooling fins on the differential and transmission housing disperse heat.

engaged. An *operator presence switch* is the safety device used for this protection. The seat is mounted on a pivot bracket. As long as the operator's weight is on the seat, the switch remains closed. When the operator gets off the seat a spring raises the seat, opens the switch, and shuts off the engine. See **Figure 21-39**.

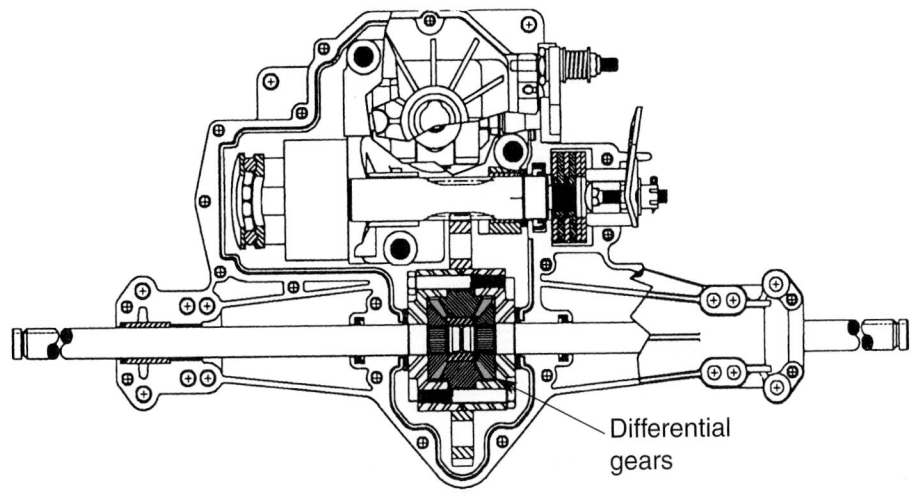

Differential gears

MTD Products, Inc.

Figure 21-37.

Differential gears allow each rear axle to turn at a different speed when cornering.

Electric Start Systems

A typical electric start system including safety interlocks is shown in **Figure 21-40**. To start the engine with this system, the ignition key must be turned on, and the clutch and blade safety switches must be closed. The clutch safety switch is closed when the clutch is depressed. The blade safety switch is closed when the blade is disengaged. The circuit is complete between the battery and the coil primary of the solenoid when the safety switches are closed. The solenoid switch will close allowing the starter motor to crank the engine. The safety switches are wired in series in the ignition circuit of an electric start tractor. If any one switch is not activated, the tractor will not start.

Note

Tractors with hydrostatic drives often have a parking brake interlock that prevents the engine from starting unless the parking brake is engaged. This is necessary because vibration can cause the drive to engage, propelling the tractor.

Testing an Interlock Electrical System

The following is a general test procedure for an electrical interlock system like the one shown in **Figure 21-40**.

1. Attempt to start the engine:
   a. Make sure the blade or PTO is disengaged.
   b. Make sure the clutch pedal is depressed, disengaging the clutch.
   c. Set the throttle to the wide open or run position. Close the choke if the engine is cold.
   d. Turn the ignition key to the *Start* position. If the engine turns over or the starter solenoid clicks, the interlock system is not at fault. If the engine does not turn over, the problem may be in the interlock system. The components should be checked systematically to identify the problem.
2. Make sure that the blade safety switch closes when the blade is disengaged. The plunger on the switch should be depressed a minimum of 1/8″. Make sure that depressing the clutch pedal operates the clutch safety switch. Again, the plunger should be depressed a minimum of 1/8″.
3. Check for a blown fuse or tripped circuit breaker between the positive battery terminal and the ignition switch.
4. Check the battery terminals to ensure that all wiring is tightly connected and that the connections are free of corrosion. Also, make sure all ground connections are tight.
5. Check all wiring to the ignition switch, clutch and blade safety switches, starter solenoid, and coil to make sure there are no broken wires and all connections are all tight.
6. Check the condition and state of charge of the battery.

Hydrostatic Transmission Troubleshooting

No output torque (power) in either direction, cold start.	1. Recheck relief valve position, control linkage, input drive. 2. Oil level in reservoir. 3. Broken control shaft dowel pin. Transmission must be repaired or replaced.
Loss of output torque, continuous load.	1. Operating at conditions approaching hydraulic stall. The transmission fluid has exceeded 180°F. 2. Internal leakage due to wear. Transmission should be repaired or replaced. 3. Water in transmission fluid. Purge system of all fluid and replace with new transmission fluid. Replacement of the transmission is generally not necessary.
No output torque in one direction.	1. One of the directional valves is stuck. Transmission should be repaired or replaced. 2. Low oil level.
Riding mower cannot be pushed with engine off.	1. Relief valve control not set. 2. Relief valve travel not adjusted. 3. Motor piston or rotor seized. Transmission must be repaired or replaced.
No neutral.	1. Recheck linkage. Loose linkage creates an adjustment problem. Note: The hydraulic neutral band is very narrow. Deflection in the linkage may make it difficult to obtain neutral from both directions. It is recommended that neutral should be positive from forward drive.
Oil leakage at the relief valve.	1. Check O-ring for damage. Apply Loctite PST5924 to threads and torque to 13 to 17 ft-lbs.
Oil leakage at the control shaft seat.	1. Spillage when fluid has been added to the reservoir. 2. Spillage at the vent in the reservoir at operating temperatures due to cold level being too high or water in the fluid. Reduce fluid level or replace fluid in the event there is water in it (milky color). 3. Loose oil reservoir. 4. Loose vent bolt. 5. Damaged control shaft seal. Transmission should be repaired.
Noisy operation.	1. Operating at part throttle. Hydrostatic transmission is designed to operate with the engine running at full throttle. 2. Water in transmission fluid. Replace transmission fluid. 3. Air in transmission fluid. Bleed air from vent.
Output shaft rotates in the opposite direction.	1. The transmission body is 180° out of position. Transmission has to be removed and reassembled correctly.

MTD Products, Inc.

Figure 21-38.

A sample hydrostatic transmission troubleshooting chart.

7. Use a *multimeter (continuity tester)* to check for opens in the wiring between each component of the interlock system.

Warning

To test the interlock system further, the safety switches must be bypassed. To perform these tests safely, make sure the blade drive and clutch are disengaged and shift the transmission to the neutral position. Disconnect the spark plug wire and ground it against the engine block. The following tests may cause the engine to turn over.

8. Run a jumper wire from the battery's positive terminal to the coil primary terminal on the starter solenoid. If the engine turns over, the problem lies between the positive terminal of the battery and the coil primary terminal of the solenoid. Perform the following tests to pinpoint the problem.

Caution

Make sure the jumper wire is heavy enough gauge to handle the current.

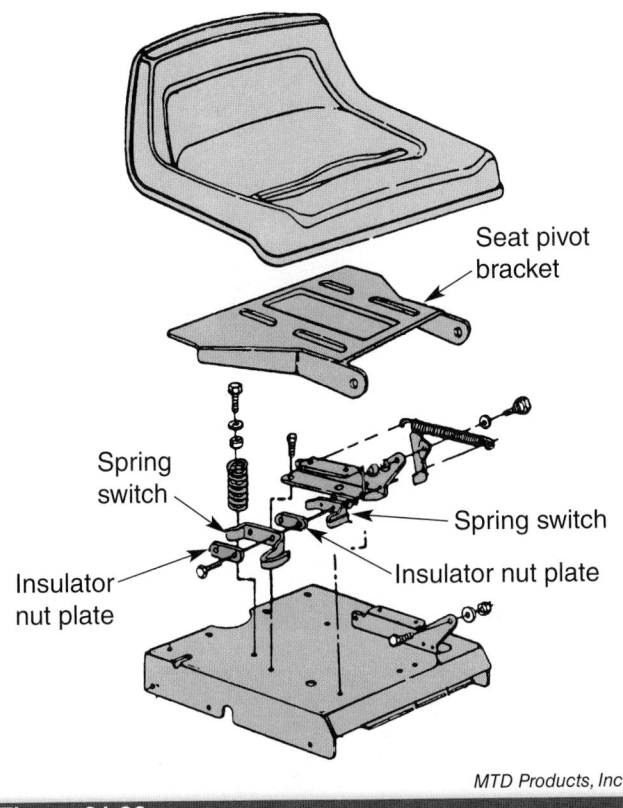

Seat pivot bracket

Spring switch

Spring switch

Insulator nut plate

Insulator nut plate

MTD Products, Inc.

Figure 21-39.

Operator present safety seat.

a. Run a jumper wire from the battery's positive terminal and the starter terminal on the ignition switch. If the engine turns over, the problem is in the wiring between the battery and the ignition switch or in the ignition switch itself. Move the jumper to the battery terminal of the ignition switch. If the engine does not turn over, the problem is in the ignition switch.

b. Run a jumper from the starter terminal on the ignition switch to the coil primary terminal on the solenoid. If the engine turns over, the problem is in the wiring between the ignition switch and the solenoid. To find the exact cause of the problem, keep one end of the jumper wire connected to the starter terminal on the ignition switch, and move the other end of the jumper wire back through the circuit, one terminal at a time, until the engine fails to turn over.

c. Run a jumper wire between the two main terminals on the solenoid. Use only wire that is at least as heavy as the wire from

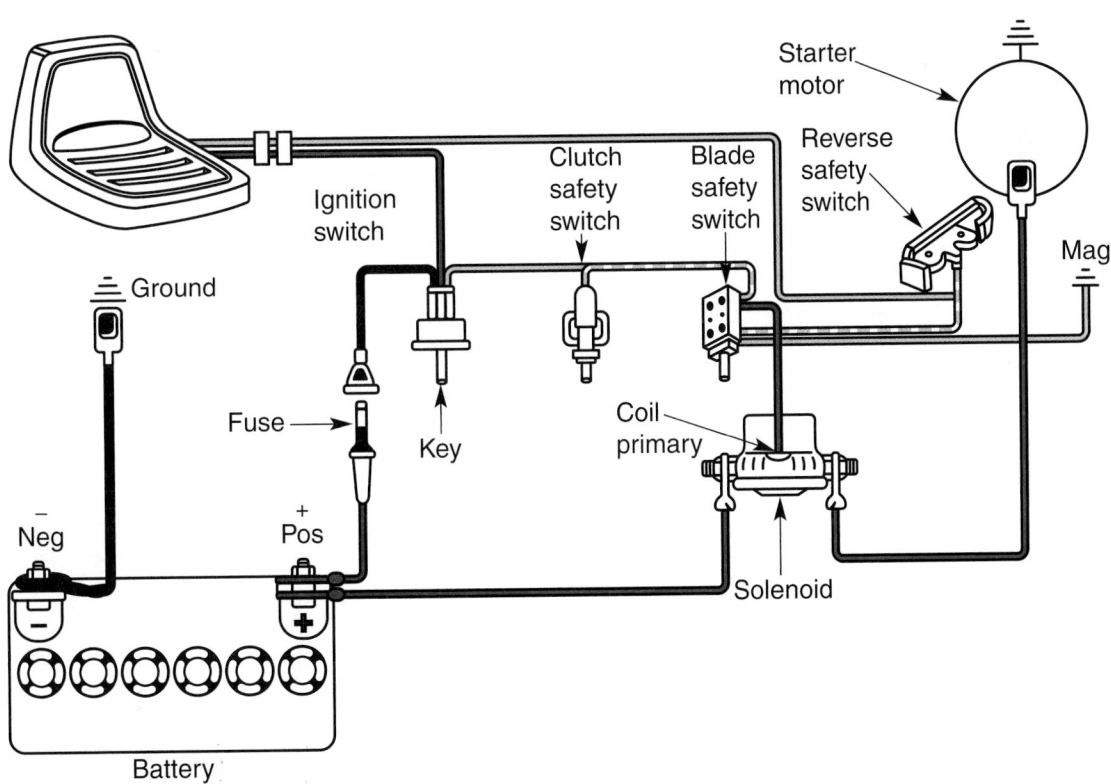

Starter motor

Reverse safety switch

Clutch safety switch

Blade safety switch

Ignition switch

Mag

Ground

Coil primary

Fuse

Key

Neg

+ Pos

Solenoid

Battery

MTD Products, Inc.

Figure 21-40.

Typical electric start system with safety interlock switches wired in series.

the solenoid to the starter. In some cases, you may be able to short between the terminals with a screwdriver. If the engine turns over when a short is created across the two main solenoid terminals, the problem is in the solenoid. Make sure the base of the solenoid has a good ground to the frame of the tractor. If the solenoid has a good ground, but still will not operate, replace the solenoid.

The following list contains possible solenoid problems. If the solenoid exhibits any of these conditions, it must be replaced.

- **Solenoid is stuck.** The engine turns over when the ignition key is in the *Off* position.
- **Coil wire (inside solenoid) is bad.** The solenoid will not function.
- **Bad washer (inside solenoid).** The solenoid clicks, but starter motor does not turn.

Testing Procedure for Operator Presence System (Safety Seat)

To check the operation of the safety seat, proceed as follows:

1. Start the engine as instructed in the owner's guide.
2. Set the parking brake.
3. Place the shift lever in neutral gear.
4. Engage the PTO or blades.
5. Raise up off the seat (this will activate the seat's kill switch).

At this point the engine should stop running. If unit continues to run, check wire lead and seat plug for proper connection. If this connection is good, then the seat switch and wiring should be inspected for electrical shorts. See **Figure 21-41**.

Disassembly Procedure

To disassemble the safety seat, proceed as follows:

1. Remove the molding clip on the lower front of the seat. Remove the molding.
2. Remove the seat covering and foam padding. The covering and padding are likely bonded together.
3. Remove the screws, metal plate, bushings and foam pad. See **Figure 21-42**.
4. Check the wiring harness for a broken terminal end or frayed plug wire. Tape the wiring harness to the bottom of the seat pan.

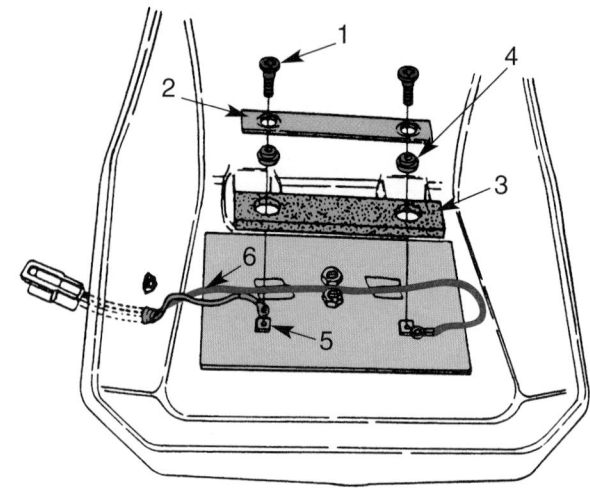

1. Shoulder screw	4. Shoulder spacer
2. Seat switch base	5. Push-in nut
3. Foam insert	6. Wire harness

MTD Products, Inc.

Figure 21-41.

Safety seat electrical system.

Assembly Procedure

Assemble the seat in reverse order. Note the position of the nylon bushings. The shoulders of the bushings must be placed upward through the plate. Once assembled, check by pushing downward on metal plate. The distance between metal plate and screws must be maintained for proper switch operations.

Some lawn and garden tractors have different seat safety switch types and locations. One such variation is shown in **Figure 21-43**.

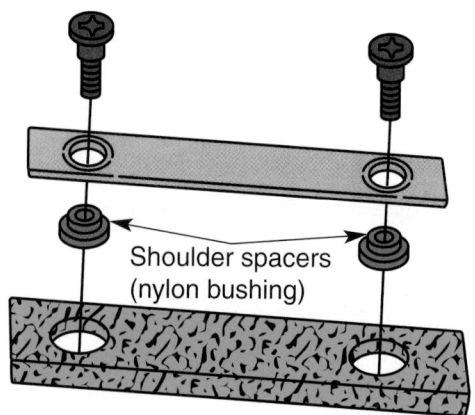

Shoulder spacers (nylon bushing)

MTD Products, Inc.

Figure 21-42.

Safety seat disassembly.

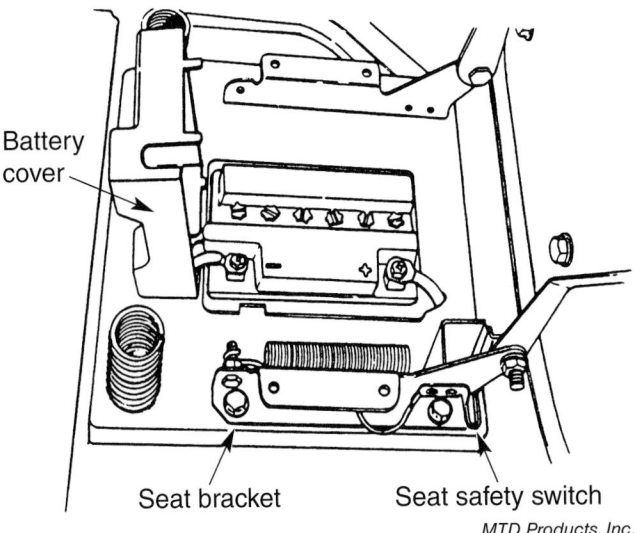

Battery cover

Seat bracket   Seat safety switch

MTD Products, Inc.

Figure 21-43.

Safety switch location.

Circuits for Study

The electrical circuits in **Figure 21-44** through **Figure 21-48** are for 600 Series MTD tractors with Briggs & Stratton Vee Twin-Cylinder, Vanguard, OHV engines. The electrical circuit in **Figure 21-49** is for 800 Series MTD tractors with Briggs & Stratton Vee Twin-Cylinder, Vanguard, OHV engines. They all are included for further study and practice. You should be able to identify and trace circuitry for components previously presented. On these circuit diagrams, you will find additional circuitry for headlights and headlight switch, bulb monitors, PTO (power-take-off) switch, and oil pressure switch.

Note

The information on electrical systems in this chapter is presented for educational purposes only. It is not intended to be directly applicable to all products, though there may be some similarities. Always consult the manufacturer's technical service manual for the specific make and model when troubleshooting and servicing engine-powered equipment.

General Maintenance

Maintenance is an important part of working with small gas engines and the machines they power. Lawn and garden tractor engines should be maintained regularly to keep them in good operating condition. A regular maintenance schedule will extend the life of the engine. The following is a list of guidelines for performing tractor maintenance safely:

1. Keep the maintenance area clean and dry.
2. *Never* lubricate or service a machine while it is moving or the engine is running.
3. Keep hands, feet, and clothing away from power driven parts.
4. Disengage all power and operate hydraulic controls to relieve pressure. Lower the equipment to the ground. Stop the engine. Remove the key. Allow the machine to cool.
5. Securely support any parts that must be raised for service work.
6. Disconnect the battery ground, or negative, cable (–) before making adjustments on electrical systems or welding on the machine.
7. Dispose of waste materials safely. Used oil, fuel, brake fluid, and batteries are harmful to the environment. Refer to local recycle center for disposal information.
8. Dispose of cleaning rags in a safe manner. Never leave used cleaning rags lying around. *Spontaneous combustion* (self ignition) can occur and result in a serious fire. Keep fire extinguishers available and fully charged. Consult with the local fire department for information.

Note

Refer to Chapter 1 of this text for more safety information.

Engine Lubrication

Using the manufacturer-recommended engine oil ensures that the internal parts are properly lubricated under all operating conditions. Changing the oil and oil filter at specified intervals will greatly extend the service life of the engine. Draining the oil removes the contaminated oil and any particles from the crankcase that might cause internal wear.

The manufacturer's technical service manual will specify the recommended oil change intervals. A new engine must have the oil changed after 5 to 8 hours of operation to remove any residual manufacturing contaminants and break-in material. The oil filter should also be replaced at the first oil change.

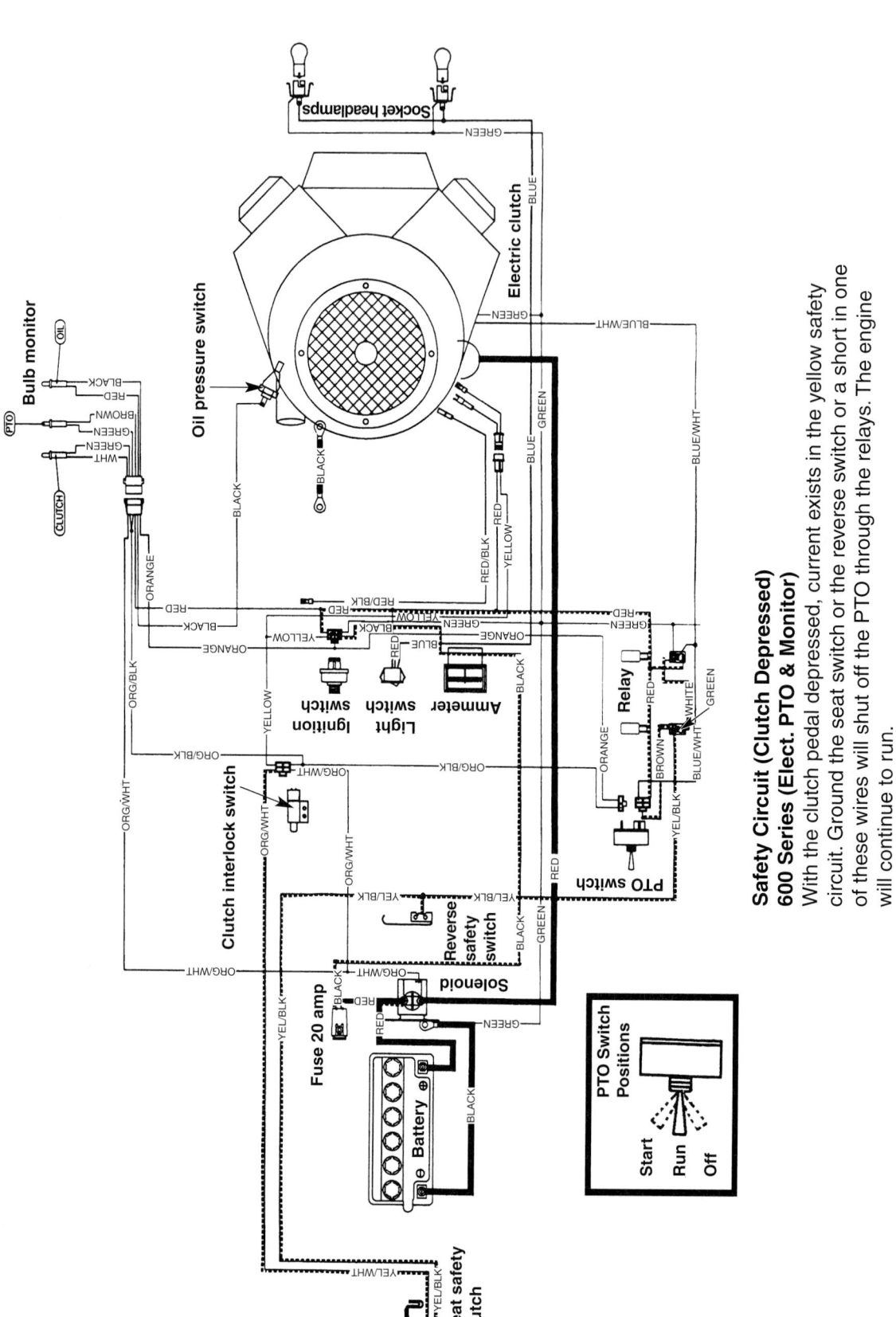

**Safety Circuit (Clutch Depressed)
600 Series (Elect. PTO & Monitor)**
With the clutch pedal depressed, current exists in the yellow safety circuit. Ground the seat switch or the reverse switch or a short in one of these wires will shut off the PTO through the relays. The engine will continue to run.

Figure 21-44.
Electrical circuit for 600 Series MTD tractors with Briggs & Stratton Vee Twin-Cylinder, Vanguard, OHV engines.

MTD Products, Inc.

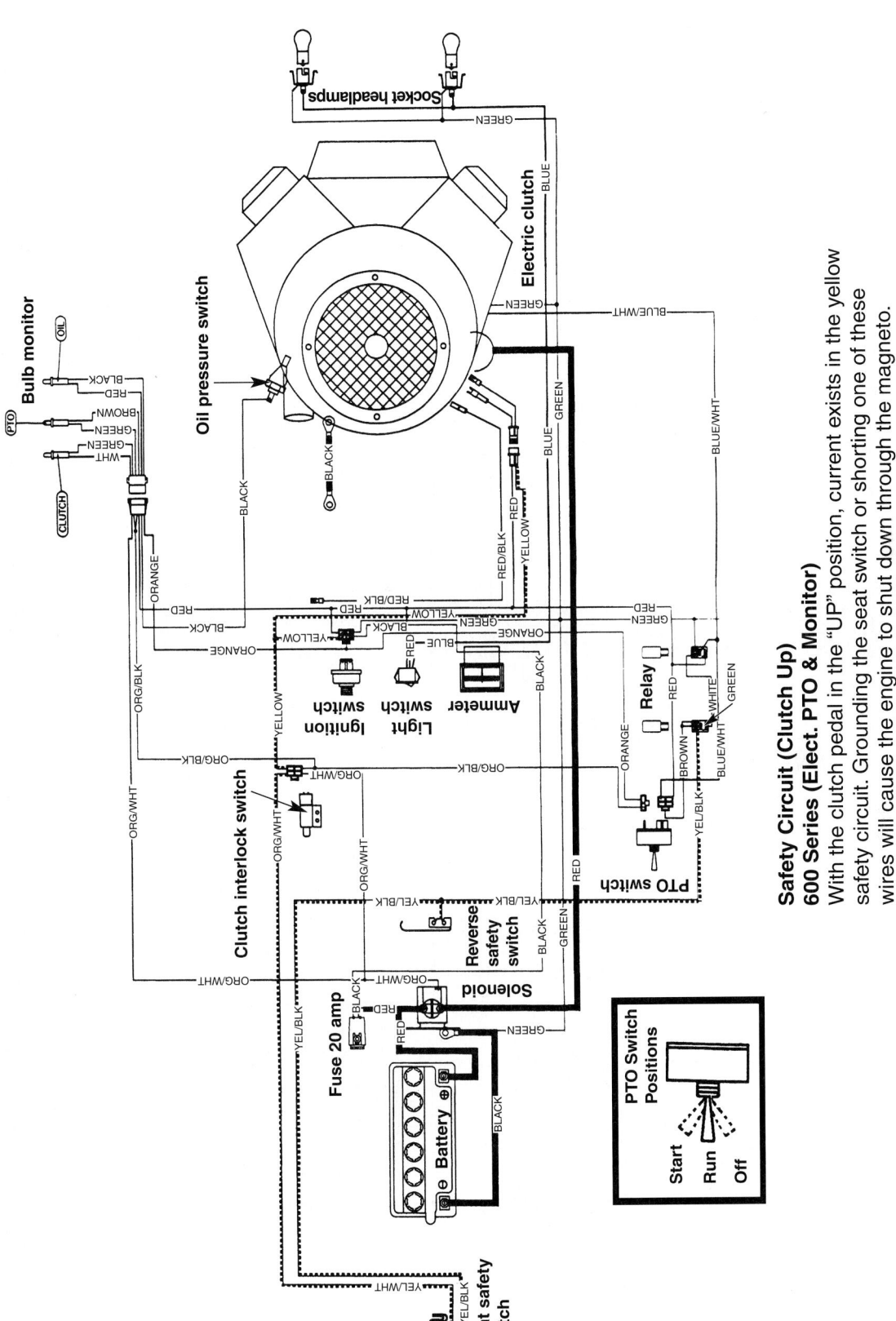

Safety Circuit (Clutch Up) 600 Series (Elect. PTO & Monitor)

With the clutch pedal in the "UP" position, current exists in the yellow safety circuit. Grounding the seat switch or shorting one of these wires will cause the engine to shut down through the magneto.

MTD Products, Inc.

Figure 21-45.
Electrical circuit for 600 Series MTD tractors with Briggs & Stratton Vee Twin-Cylinder, Vanguard, OHV engines.

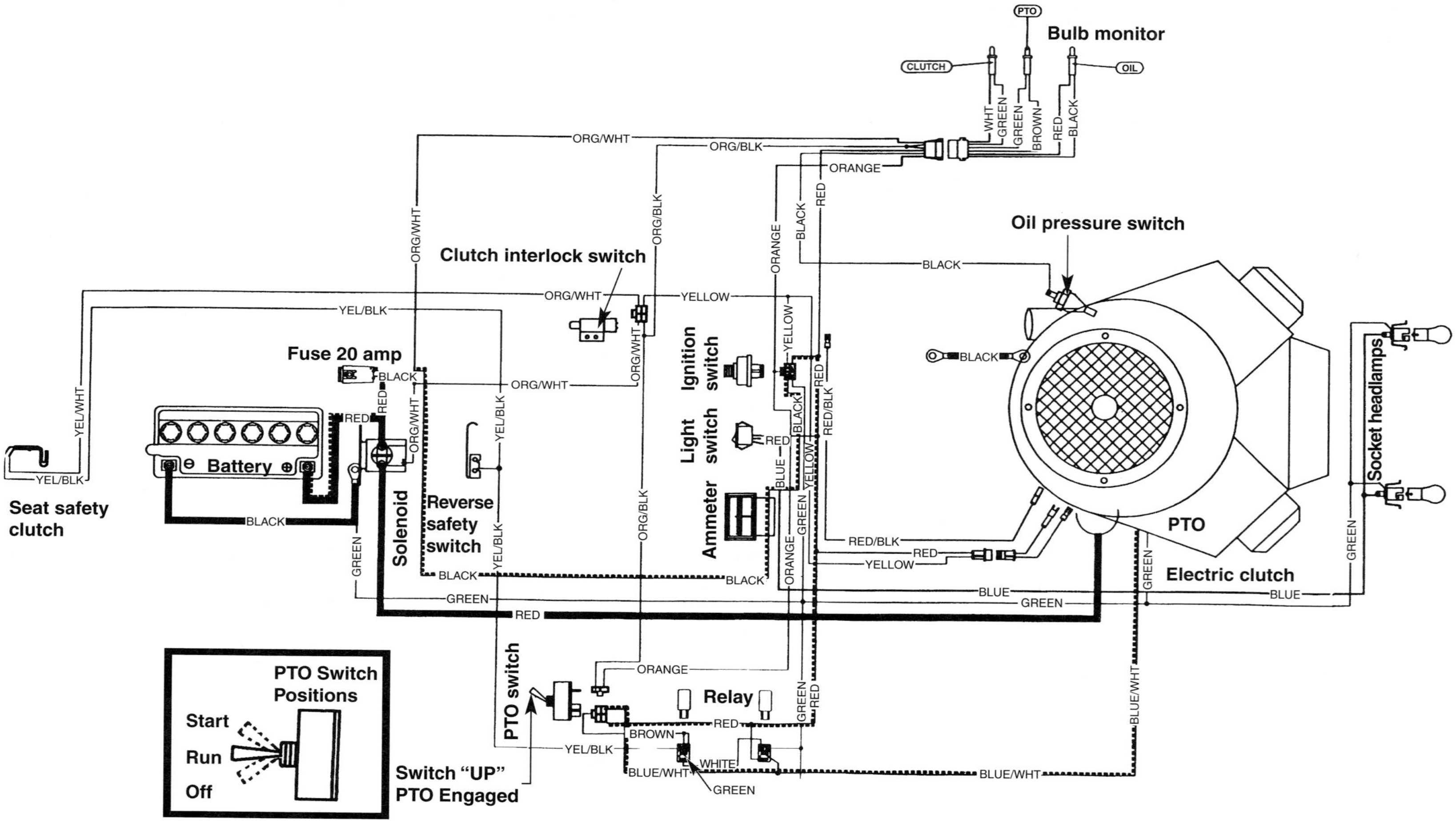

Figure 21-46.

Electrical circuit for 600 Series MTD tractors with Briggs & Stratton Vee Twin-Cylinder, Vanguard, OHV engines.

Safety Circuit (PTO Engaged Switch Up) 600 Series (Elect. PTO & Monitor)

With PTO switch in "up" position, relays block out the safety switches and engage the PTO.

MTD Products, Inc.

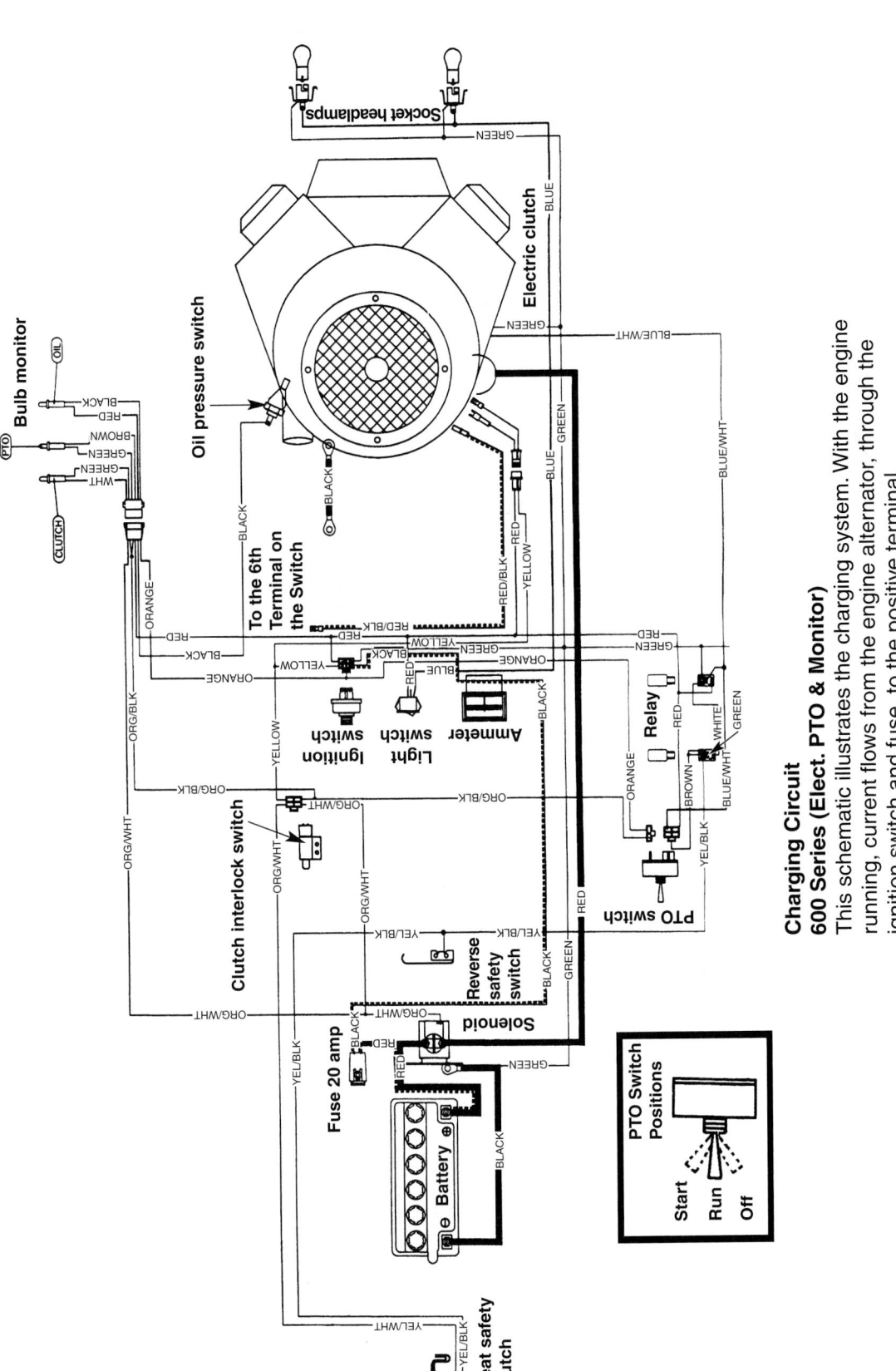

**Charging Circuit
600 Series (Elect. PTO & Monitor)**
This schematic illustrates the charging system. With the engine running, current flows from the engine alternator, through the ignition switch and fuse, to the positive terminal.

Figure 21-47.
Electrical circuit for 600 Series MTD tractors with Briggs & Stratton Vee Twin-Cylinder, Vanguard, OHV engines.

MTD Products, Inc.

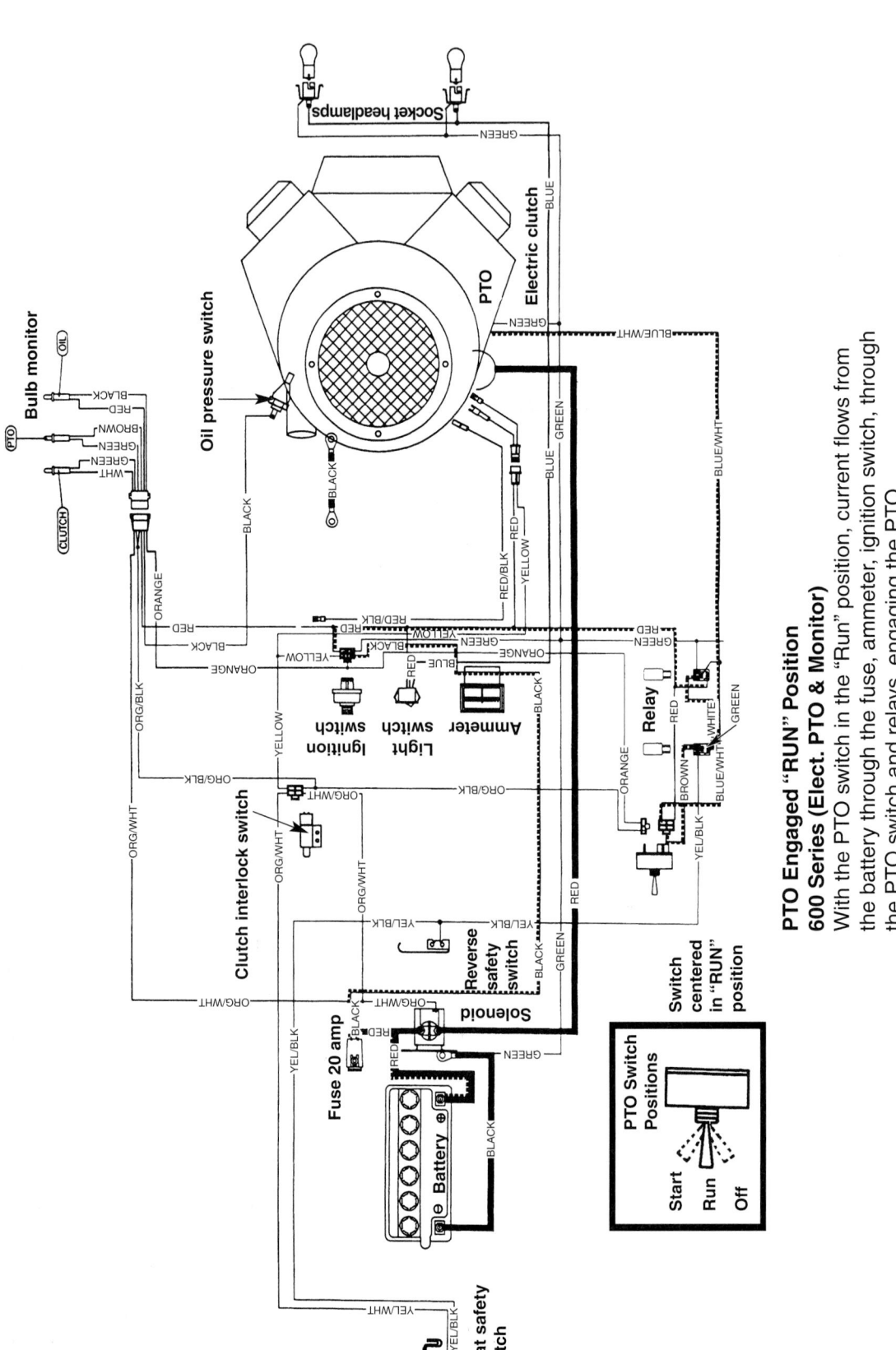

PTO Engaged "RUN" Position
600 Series (Elect. PTO & Monitor)
With the PTO switch in the "Run" position, current flows from the battery through the fuse, ammeter, ignition switch, through the PTO switch and relays, engaging the PTO.

MTD Products, Inc.

Figure 21-48.
Electrical circuit for 600 Series MTD tractors with Briggs & Stratton Vee Twin-Cylinder, Vanguard, OHV engines.

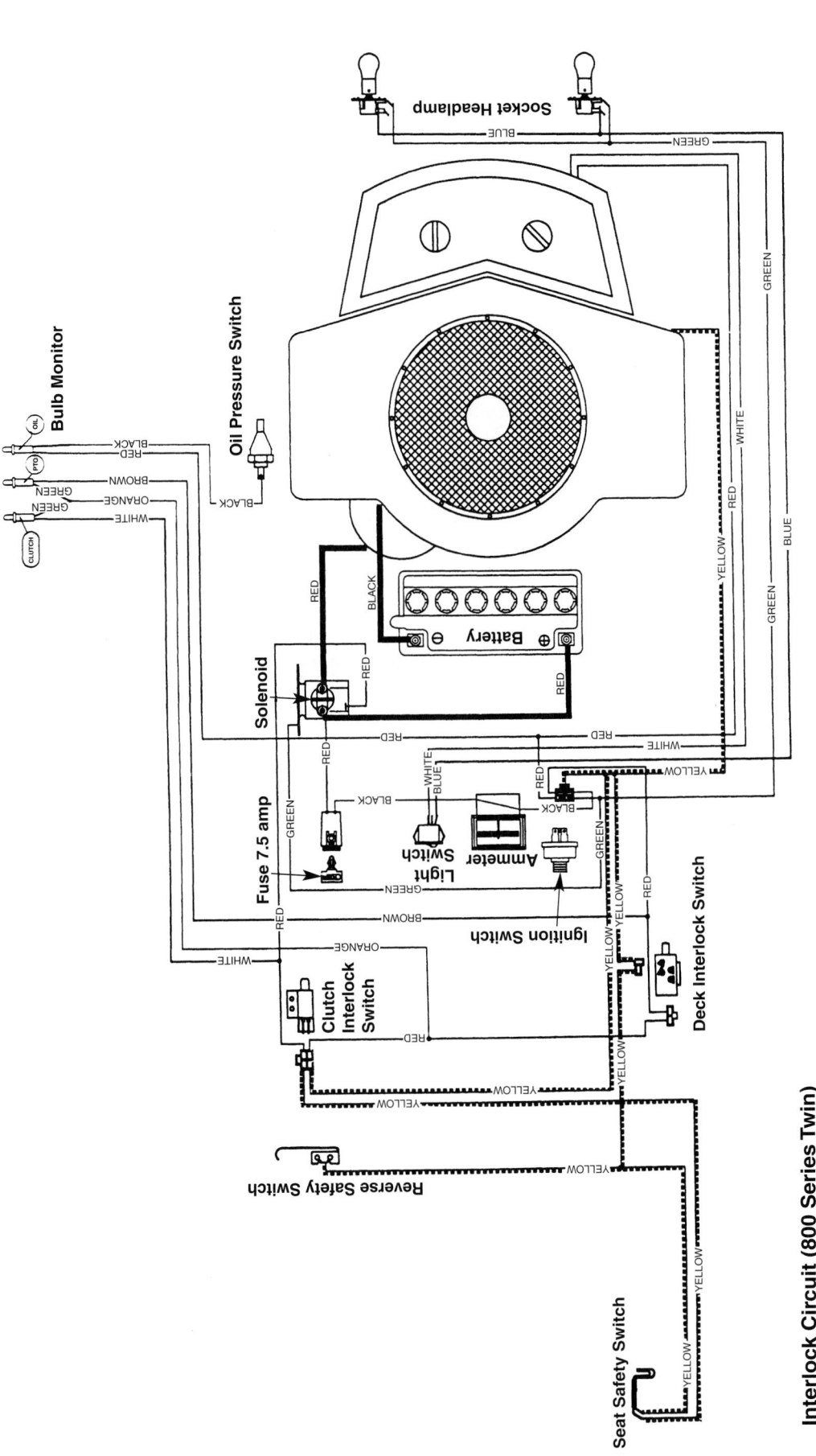

Interlock Circuit (800 Series Twin)
With the engine running, current exists in the safety circuit.
Grounding the reverse switch or the seat switch, or a short
to ground in the yellow wires, will shut down the engine.

Figure 21-49.
Electrical circuit for 800 Series MTD tractors with Briggs & Stratton Vee Twin-Cylinder, Vanguard, OHV engines.

The oil should be drained after the engine has been run long enough to heat the oil. A drain plug is located at the lowest point in the crankcase. Drain the oil into a metal or plastic pan and inspect it for metal particles. Save the old oil in a sealed container and take it to a recycling center. Never pour oil into a drain or onto the ground.

Select the correct oil filter cartridge for replacement. Remove the old filter with an oil filter wrench. Apply a film of clean engine oil to the rubber gasket and thread the new cartridge onto the engine until it is hand tight. Use the oil filter wrench to turn the cartridge another 1/2 to 3/4 turn to seal it. Do not overtighten the cartridge.

Replace the oil plug. Remove the oil filler cap and dipstick and pour in the recommended type and quantity of engine oil. Do not overfill with oil. Excess oil can cause spark plug fouling and other internal problems. Wipe and check the dipstick until the oil level shows full. Run the engine for 30 seconds, stop the engine, and check the oil level again. Add oil if necessary. Check oil level before each use of the tractor.

Optional Oil Accessories

The engine may have an oil pressure switch with a warning light on the instrument panel. If the engine runs low on oil, the switch will activate the warning light or stop the engine. An oil level light may also be located on the instrument panel to indicate a low level condition. If the level is low, the light flickers when the engine is started. The engine should be stopped and oil added to the Full mark on the dipstick.

Air Filter

Internal combustion engines consume a far greater volume of air than fuel. The air filter prevents dirt and abrasive particles in the air from entering the carburetor and engine. The air filter is installed on the intake side of the carburetor. The filter material is contained in a metal or plastic case. The air filter may be a single or dual element, dry-type filter.

To service the air filter, remove the cover and take out the filter element. Examine the element for dirt accumulation. Clean the element by tapping it on a flat surface to shake off any dirt particles. Do not use compressed air or solvents. Replace the ele-

ment if it still appears to have dirt on it. Air filters should be serviced after every 25 hours of use. However, the interval may vary, depending on the conditions in which the tractor is used. Operating the tractor in very dusty conditions will require the air filter to be serviced more frequently.

Mufflers

The muffler is a sound-deadening device, but it also affects engine efficiency. Mufflers are designed to control the amount of back pressure generated by the exhaust gases. Check the muffler periodically to see that it is not rusting and leaking exhaust around the flanges or gaskets. If the inside baffles corrode away, the sound emitted will change and become louder. This is an indication that a new muffler is needed. Sulfuric acid is one of the by-products of combustion and causes corrosion inside the muffler. Mufflers get very hot when the engine is running. Let the engine cool down before touching or making any examination of the exhaust system. If an exhaust spark arrestor is required, it should also be removed and inspected periodically.

Engine Cleaning

Tractor engines can get very dirty, which greatly reduces cooling efficiency. Remove any grass or other materials that have become lodged in the cooling fins. If necessary, wash the cold engine to remove soil; use water from a garden hose. If leaking oil has mixed with dirt and is caked on the engine, use a degreasing solvent. Spray the solvent on the cold engine and then wash it off. Follow the instructions on the solvent container

Radiator Cleaning

Some tractors have water-cooled engines with a radiator like those found in automobiles. Clean the radiator cooling fins by directing low-pressure water from a garden hose through the fins. Do this from the back side of the radiator.

The coolant inside of the radiator and engine block should be drained each year. After draining the radiator, flush the cooling system with a flushing compound and refill the system with new coolant. The coolant should be a mixture of 50% water, and 50% ethylene glycol antifreeze. The 50/50 mixture should have a freezing point of about –34°F (–38°C). This mixture is also used in warm climates because the boiling point of the liquid is about 265°F (129°C). If the antifreeze does not contain a rust inhibitor, one should be added to the cooling system. Rust inhibitors help keep the cooling system clean.

Warning

Dispose of used coolant properly. Do not allow it to enter drainage systems. Do not pour it into sink drains. Ethylene glycol is poisonous to animals and humans if ingested.

Battery Maintenance

The battery may be maintenance-free or a conventional lead-acid type. If the battery is a conventional lead-acid type, the fluid (electrolyte) should be checked each time the tractor is used. Add only distilled water to bring the electrolyte to the proper level. The electrolyte should always be kept above the lead plates.

After the specified electrolyte has been installed at the initial service of a maintenance-free battery, the sealed caps should never be removed. Checking the electrolyte level or adding distilled water is not necessary when servicing maintenance-free batteries.

Clean the battery terminals for both the maintenance-free and conventional lead-acid type. If a white, pasty, corrosive substance is found on the battery terminals, it must be removed. Mix 1/4 cup of baking soda with 1 quart of water and then pour some of the solution on each of the terminals. The solution should begin to dissolve the corrosion on the terminals. Next, scrub the terminals with a parts brush and then rinse with clear water. Dry the terminals and battery top and then apply a thin film of petroleum jelly or white lithium grease on the terminals.

Warning

Wash your hands thoroughly after touching or handling a lead-acid battery to prevent acid burns. Protect your eyes with safety glasses.

If the tractor is not used for long periods, keep the battery charged with a trickle charger. A trickle charger provides a very low charging current. It

can be left connected to the battery indefinitely without harm.

If a battery no longer will hold a charge, it should be replaced. If this is the case, a maintenance-free battery should never be replaced with a conventional lead-acid battery. The electrical system is designed exclusively for a maintenance-free battery. The electrical system will not work properly with a conventional lead-acid battery substituted for a maintenance-free battery.

Sharpening and Balancing Mower Blades

A sharpened and balanced mower blade results in an even cut. To sharpen and balance mower blades, proceed as follows:
1. Wear goggles and gloves when removing and sharpening blades.
2. Sharpen blades with a grinder, hand file, or electric blade sharpener. Maintain the original bevel angle of the blade.
3. Balance the blade as follows:
   a. Clean debris from the blade.
   b. Put the blade on a nail held in a vise. See **Figure 21-50**.
   c. Turn the blade to the horizontal position. The heavy end will drop.
   d. Remove metal from the heavy end by grinding or filing the cutting edge until the blade remains horizontal.

Note

Other methods of balancing mower blades are covered in Chapter 20 of this text.

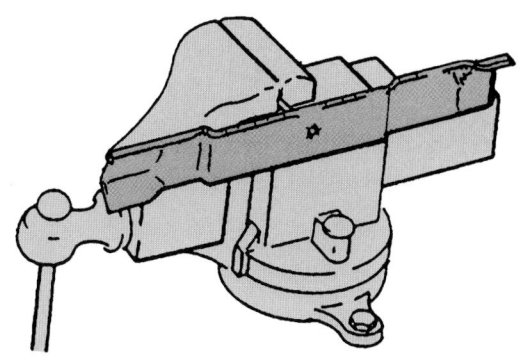

Deere & Co.

Figure 21-50.

Balancing a mower blade.

Fueling and Refueling

The following are guidelines for refueling a tractor safely:
- *Do not* fuel or refuel the machine:
  While smoking.
  When the machine is near an open flame or sparks.
  When the engine is running. *Stop* the engine.
- Refuel outdoors.
- Keep a first aid kit and fire extinguisher close by.
- Have emergency phone numbers readily accessible.

Storing a Tractor

When storing a tractor, add a fuel stabilizer to the fuel to prevent carburetor varnish from forming or partial plugging of the carburetor jets. Either condition can cause the engine to run lean and hot with possible piston seizure and engine failure. To prepare a tractor for storage, proceed as follows:

1. Run the engine for at least 10 minutes to distribute the stabilizer throughout the fuel system.
2. Change the engine oil while it is warm.
3. Repair any worn or damaged parts. Install new parts as necessary.
4. Service, or replace the air cleaner.
5. Lubricate all grease fittings and wipe clean.
6. Wash the tractor with mild soap and water. Wipe dry.
7. Start the engine and engage the PTO for a couple minutes to remove water. *Stop* the engine.
8. Remove any oil, grease, or dirt around the engine.
9. Apply grease or paint to bare metal areas, as appropriate, to prevent rust.
10. Remove the battery:
    a. Clean the battery.
    b. Check electrolyte level.
    c. Charge the battery.
    d. Store the battery in a cool, dry place where children cannot reach it.
11. Clean belts with a damp rag. Do not use petroleum-based solvents on belts. *Lock* the parking brake to relieve transmission drive belt tension.
12. Close the fuel shut-off valve.
13. Remove and clean the mower deck.
14. Check the mower belts and relieve drive belt tension.
15. Remove, sharpen, balance, and then reinstall mower blades.
16. Reinstall the mower deck.
17. Store the tractor in a dry, protected location. If stored outside, place a waterproof cover over it.
18. Take weight off the tires by placing blocks or stands under the tractor. Let about one-third of the air out of the tires.

Removing a Tractor from Storage

To remove a tractor from storage and put it back into service, proceed as follows:

1. Inflate the tires to the correct pressures.
2. Remove any blocks or chocks from under the tractor.
3. Clean and gap the spark plug(s).
4. Check the fluid level in battery. Install and charge the battery if necessary.
5. Adjust the transmission drive belt.
6. Lubricate all grease fittings.
7. Ensure all shields and guards are in place.
8. Move the mower drive belt tension lever *in* to tighten the belt.
9. Check the engine oil level.
10. Check the coolant level.
11. Open the fuel shut-off valve.
12. Fill the fuel tank with fresh fuel.
13. Run the engine 5 minutes with no load. Make sure the area is well ventilated.

Summary

Working with a tractor requires the operator to have a good understanding of safety. Like other engine-powered machines, there is inherent danger when used carelessly. All safety instructions provided by the manufacturer should be studied before attempting to use an unfamiliar machine and its attachments. Children should be kept out of the work area and under supervision. Mowing in reverse can be very dangerous and should always be avoided. If done, extreme caution and vigilance should be maintained. Remember, older machines may not have the safety interlock systems that are provided in modern equipment.

Lawn and garden tractors are very versatile machines but they are generally smaller with less horsepower than farm-type tractors. Lawn and garden tractors can accomplish a wide variety of jobs with the appropriate accessories. Lawn mowing and mulching, leaf collection, plowing and throwing or blowing snow, soil preparation, pulling loads, and rotary sweeping are some of the types of work that can be done.

Nearly all engines used in lawn and garden tractors are four-cycle, electric start, overhead valve engines with electronic ignition systems. They are trouble-free if proper care and maintenance is followed. Engine horsepower may vary from tractor to tractor from about 14 hp to 22 hp. Some engines are the single cylinder type and others have two opposed or vee configured cylinders. Some engines have a cast-iron block, others may have aluminum blocks with cast-iron cylinder sleeves. Overhead valves with hydraulic valve lifters are most efficient and provide greatest service life.

External components of the engine should be easy to access and service as needed. Fuel level; oil level and condition; air filter condition, and fuel filter condition are items that need attention periodically. Battery fluid level and condition also need regular inspection and attention. Exhaust should be directed away from the operator at all times and under all conditions.

The chassis and steering portions of a tractor must be strong enough to withstand twisting and torsional load imposed on them while holding all other parts in proper alignment. Steering should be smooth and positive in action even when running over rough ground. Zerk fittings are provided at lubrication points and can be lubricated with a hand-operated grease gun. The steering wheel should be of such size, angle, and location that it is comfortable for the driver to operate without straining muscles. Four-wheel steering turns the front and rear wheels for better maneuvering around trees and other sharp turns. This is available on some tractors.

The transmission, usually called a transaxle, is a hard working part of the tractor and is driven by the engine with either a V-belt or driveshaft. Variable-speed pulley systems are often used with a single- or two-speed geared transmission. This allows smooth and gradual speed changes within a particular selected transmission gear ratio. A clutch mechanism is used to disengage the engine from the transmission during gear changes.

Hydrostatic transmissions consist of a variable-displacement hydraulic pump and a fixed displacement hydraulic motor. Both of these units, the differential, and the axles are all contained in one housing. This type of transmission has many advantages over other types of transmissions. Hydrostatic transmissions can be driven from the engine by belts or a driveshaft. In the neutral mode, the transmission provides braking, which eliminates the need for a separate disc-type braking system. Cooling is provided by fins on the housing and a fan attached to the input shaft.

Tractor electrical systems incorporate safety interlocks. One type of interlock requires mower decks to be disengaged before a tractor can be shifted into reverse. Another interlock switch shuts off the engine if the operator leaves the seat when the blades or PTO (power-take-off) is engaged.

An electric start system may have interlocks that require the clutch pedal to be depressed and the blade disengaged to start the engine with the key switch. The safety switches are wired in series in an electric start system so that any one switch can prevent starting.

Review Questions

Answer the following questions using the information provided in this chapter.

1. List five kinds of work that can be done with garden tractors.
2. What three things can be done with the clippings when a lawn is mowed?
3. List four engine design features that are common on nearly all garden tractor engines today.
4. A chassis is subjected to _____ and _____ forces during tractor operation.
5. _____ is a strong and rigid material commonly used for front axles.
6. Grease fittings are also referred to as _____ fittings.
7. Describe how the rear wheels turn in relation to the front wheels in a four-wheel steering system.
8. The transaxles of tractors may be driven from the engine by _____ or a(n) _____.
9. A low speed gear ratio will have _____ pulling power than a high speed gear ratio.
10. The center portion of a variable-speed pulley is called a movable _____.
11. A(n) _____ pulley allows the operator to slow or speed-up the tractor.
12. The hydrostatic transaxle is a self-contained unit consisting of what four primary components?
13. How is reverse obtained with the hydrostatic transmission?
14. Before pushing or pulling a tractor equipped with a hydrostatic transmission, the _____ in the hydraulic circuit must be opened.
15. Electric start systems have interlock switches wired in _____.

Suggested Activities

1. Visit a store or tractor dealership and examine the various tractor models available. Ask questions about them.
2. Demonstrate proper procedures for normal tractor maintenance of: oil, air filter, fuel filter, coolant (if used), battery, fuel, and tire pressures.
3. Practice proper engine starting and stopping procedure.
4. Examine tractor drive belts. Replace belts if needed.
5. Lubricate a tractor chassis.
6. Show how a variable-speed drive pulley operates.
7. Practice some electrical tests following instructions in a tractor technical service manual for the make and model being tested.
8. Locate the safety interlock switches on a new model tractor.
9. Demonstrate safe procedure for attaching and removing a lawn cutting deck or other implement to a tractor.
10. Test drive a tractor to see if all systems are working properly. Note any problems and take corrective action.

CHAPTER 22

Snow Throwers

Learning Objectives

After studying this chapter, you will be able to:

- Safely operate and service snow-throwing equipment.
- List important purchasing considerations for snow throwers.
- Identify major parts of walk-behind snow throwers.
- Make adjustments to snow throwers.
- Properly maintain snow-throwing machines.

Key Terms

augers
fuel stabilizer
grease (zerk) fittings
operator presence
  controls
rubber tracks
scraper bar

shear bolt
shear pin
single-stage snow
  throwers
skid shoes
two-stage snow
  throwers

Operating Safely

When servicing small engine driven implements, use good judgment at all times. Before attempting to service a snow thrower, review all safety instructions provided by the manufacturer and make sure you understand them. Learn how to properly operate the machine and its controls. See **Figure 22-1**. Never let anyone operate the snow thrower who has not had proper instruction about its use. The following is a list of rules to adhere to when servicing a snow thrower:

- Never attempt to make adjustments while the engine is running.
- Disengage all clutches (release drive levers) before starting the engine.
- Inspect the machine and be sure all hardware is tight. Damaged or badly worn parts should be repaired or replaced. Guards and shields should be in good condition and in place.
- Examine and clear the work area of objects that may be thrown. People should be well away from the work area. If a person or pet does enter the work area, stop the machine.

Deere & Co.

Figure 22-1.

Gasoline-powered snow throwers are an effective way of removing snow. Well-maintained equipment can make the work safe and efficient.

- If an object is hit, stop and inspect the machine. Make any repairs before resuming operation. Properly maintain the machine.
- Adjust the skid shoes to clear gravel or crushed rock surfaces. See the *Skid Shoe Adjustment* section in this chapter for the adjusting procedure.
- Do not leave a running machine unattended.
- Make sure to have good footing. Operate machinery slower on a slippery surface. It is important to be especially careful when pulling a running machine backward.
- Avoid sudden starts and stops. Keep a firm grip on the machine handles.
- Do not run the engine in a confined space, such as a shop or garage. Dangerous carbon monoxide from exhaust fumes can accumulate in such places.
- Keep hands and feet away from rotating parts. Stay clear of the discharge chute opening at all times.
- Always use a grounded, 3-wire plug receptacle for electric starting.
- Do not overload the machine capacity by clearing snow at too fast of a ground speed.
- Disengage the auger drive when transporting the unit, or when the unit is not in use.
- Do not change engine governor speed settings or overspeed the engine.

Note

As a reminder to the operator of the most important precautions, safety and warning decals are placed at strategic locations on the snow thrower. They must be read and obeyed. If any decals are lost, damaged, or worn off, replace them. Replacement decals are available at a local snow thrower dealer.

Machine Types and Features

Walk-behind snow removal equipment is available in various sizes and with a wide range of features to meet varying snow removal requirements. Engines for snow throwers are designed for easy starting in low temperatures.

Small Snow Throwers

Small machines ideal for locations where snow-falls are generally light and the area to be cleaned is relatively small, such as steps, walks, and small driveways. The cleaning width of the machine may be 16"–20". Engine size is about 3 horsepower (hp). Almost all small machines have a recoil starter (rope pull). The handle on recoil starter pull ropes should be large enough to grasp easily with a gloved hand. See **Figure 22-2**. Electric start is sometimes an option for this size of snow thrower. See **Figure 22-3**.

The Toro Co.

Figure 22-2.

The recoil start rope handle on snow throwers should provide for an easy, secure grasp with a gloved hand. The engine should start quickly with one or two pulls, even in cold weather.

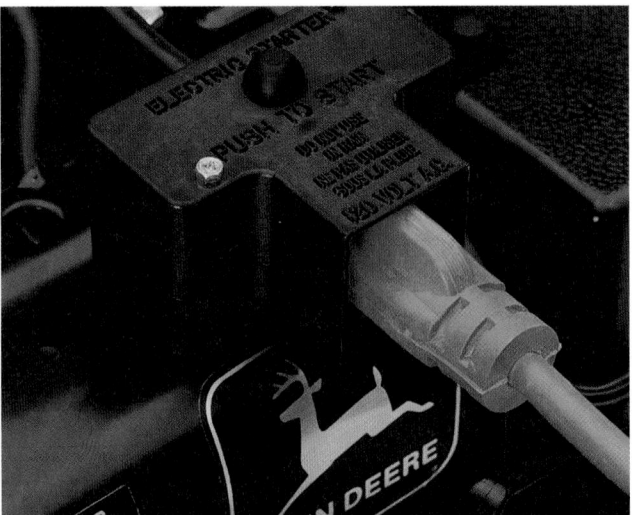

Deere & Co.

Figure 22-3.

In addition to the recoil start, electric starters may also be installed for convenience where an electric source is readily available from an extension cord.

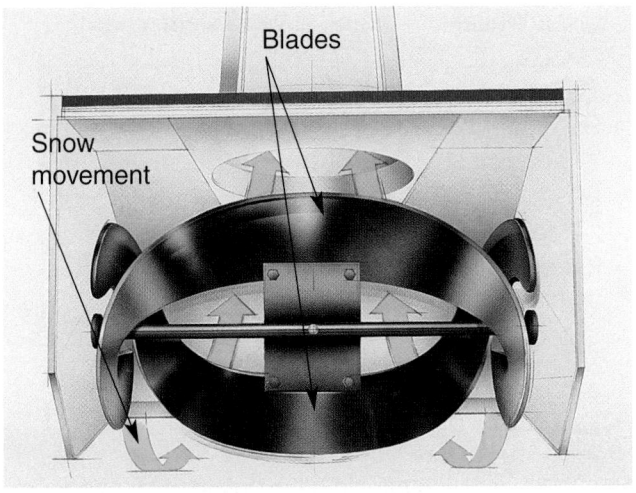

The Toro Co.

Figure 22-4.

Some smaller snow throwers have paddle-like impellers that throw the snow upward and out the discharge chute. Various designs exist.

Small snow throwers are single-stage type. *Single-stage snow throwers* have steel or rubber blades that rotate like paddles and throw the snow upward and forward. See **Figure 22-4**. The direction of snow throwing is controlled by a discharge chute located above the housing. The chute can be rotated to the left, right, or straight ahead. See **Figure 22-5**. The direction and distance of snow throwing may be more limited on small machines than with larger snow throwers. The maximum quantity of snow removal for small snow throwers is about 1000 lb per minute.

Small snow throwers are pushed manually through the snow. They have small wheels with hard plastic tires. These tires should be checked every season. These tires can crack and make it difficult to push the equipment. If needed, replacement tires can be found at a local dealer.

Midsize Snow Throwers

Midsize snow throwers are heavier than small snow throwers and have engines ranging from 3–8 hp. Midsize machines may be either a single-stage or a two-stage type. **Figure 22-6** illustrates a two-stage type. In *two-stage snow throwers*, the auger feeds the snow into a high-speed blower fan that ejects the snow out of the chute. Two-stage snow throwers are generally more effective than single-stage snow throwers.

Midsize snow throwers have a chute and deflector to direct the snow and control the height and distance to which it is thrown. The chutes can be rotated as much as 230°. See **Figure 22-5**.

Some midsize snow throwers are self-propelled. Three or four forward speeds, and one or two reverse speeds are available on most self-propelled

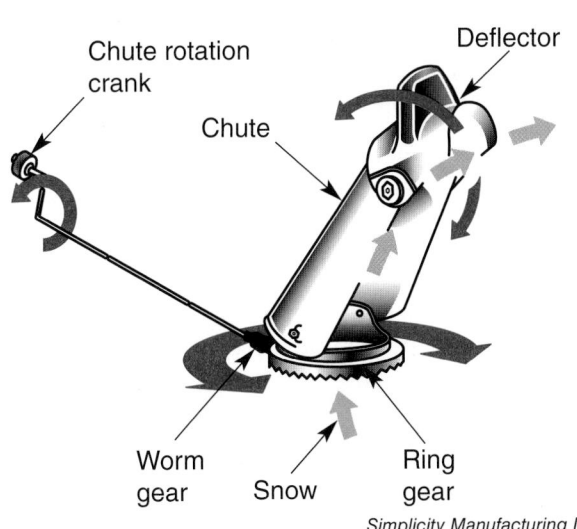

Simplicity Manufacturing Inc.

Figure 22-5.

By turning the chute rotation crank, the discharge chute can be rotated left, right, or straight ahead. The deflector can be raised or lowered to establish throwing distance.

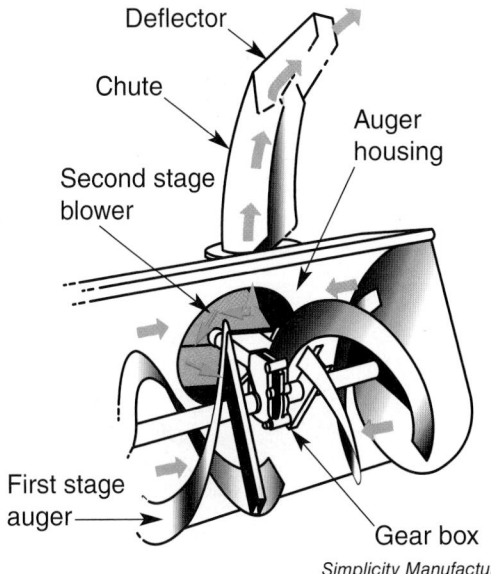

Simplicity Manufacturing Inc.

Figure 22-6.

Two-stage snow throwers have an auger to draw snow into a high-speed, second stage blower fan. Single-stage snow throwers do not have a blower fan.

snow throwers. Pneumatic rubber tires with heavy treads help increase traction. See **Figure 22-7**. With the traction engagement knob, the wheels can be adjusted to provide one- or two-wheel traction. A freewheeling feature allows for easy transporting. Tire pressure should be periodically checked. Proper air pressure in the tires helps with traction and eliminates improper wear of the tire tread. See **Figure 22-8**.

Electric start can be found on most midsize units. Ignition systems are electronic, and alternators are available for powering a sealed beam headlight for night snow removal. See **Figure 22-9**.

Helical-shaped steel *augers* rotate and pull the snow into the machine. See **Figure 22-10**. Some augers have serrated edges to help break ice and snow into finer particles before it enters the high-speed blower. See **Figure 22-11**.

Heavy-Duty Snow Throwers

Heavy-duty snow throwers range from 8–20 hp. The additional horsepower allows larger quantities of snow to be removed. Heavy-duty machines have all the same features as midsize machines, but they are heavier and clean wider paths.

Deere & Co.

Figure 22-7.

Heavy treads on rubber pneumatic tires provide good traction in snow. Chains can be installed to increase traction on ice. The traction knob is used to provide traction to one, or both wheels.

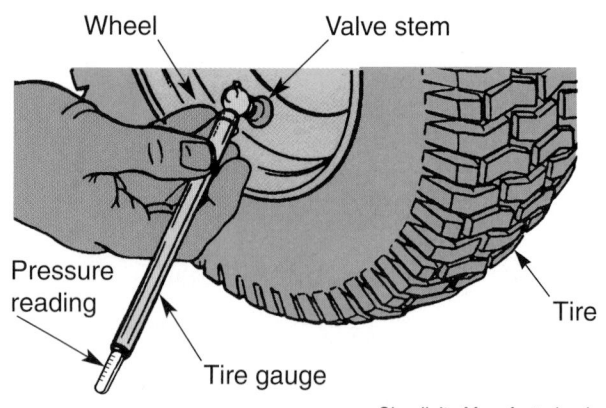

Simplicity Manufacturing Inc.

Figure 22-8.

Proper tire inflation should be maintained by checking with a tire gauge.

Deere & Co.

Figure 22-9.

This model has a sealed beam headlamp for night work. Unless the electrical system is voltage regulated, the light will brighten and dim as engine speed varies.

Heavy-duty snow throwers are self-propelled, two-stage machines. The distance snow is thrown may be as far as 40′, but this is controllable by a deflector at the top of the chute. Plastic (polymer) chutes are often used so snow will not stick in the chute, causing an obstruction.

Large pneumatic tires are common heavy-duty snow throwers. Correct tire inflation is important. Pneumatic tires can have chains installed to increase traction in icy conditions.

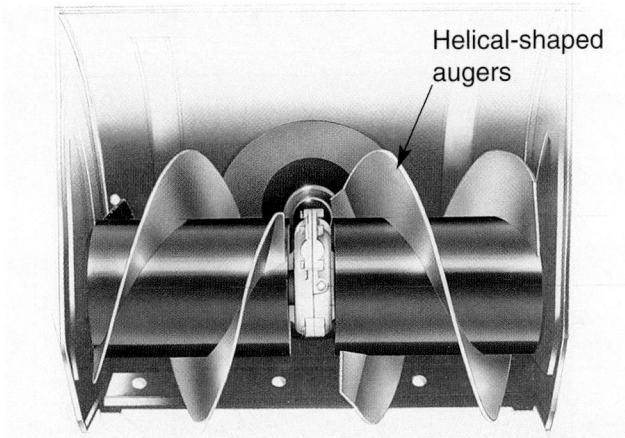

Helical-shaped augers

Figure 22-10.
A helical steel auger for pulling the snow into the machine.

The Toro Co.

The Toro Co.

Figure 22-12.
Weight shifting is accomplished by moving the wheels forward or backward.

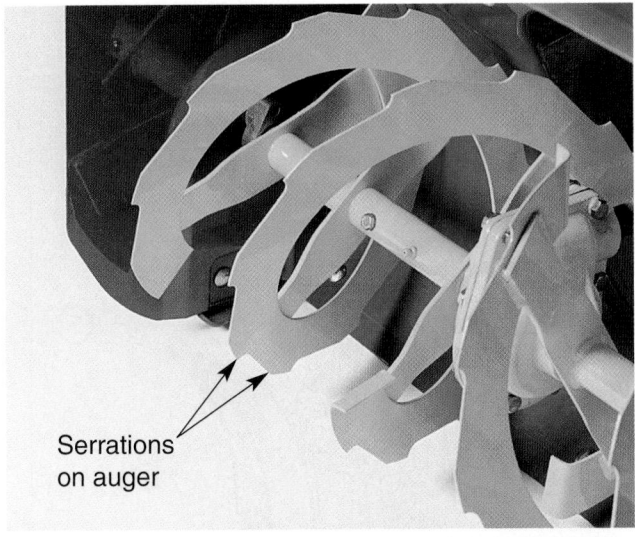

Serrations on auger

Deere & Co.

Figure 22-11.
An auger with serrated edges can break up ice and snow into finer particles before it enters the second stage blower.

Available on some models are features such as weight shifting by moving the wheels forward or backward; and raising, tilting, and lowering the auger housing. See **Figure 22-12**. These features should be considered, depending on the terrain and snow conditions to be encountered.

Engine Controls

Engine controls will vary from one make and model to another. **Figure 22-13** illustrates the basic

controls that are quite common on snow throwers with four-cycle engines. Read the manufacturer's service manuals for specific details about engine controls.

Operator Presence Controls

To provide additional safety, **operator presence controls** automatically stop the auger from rotating when the drive (traction) lever is released. The auger (impeller) is engaged by depressing a spring-loaded auger control lever on top of the right handle. See **Figure 22-14**. When the drive control lever on the left handle is engaged, traction is established and the snow thrower moves forward. When the drive control lever is engaged, the impeller lever will stay engaged without holding it down. When the drive control lever is released, the auger control lever will also be released and the auger stops. This allows one-hand guidance of the snow thrower, but stops all movement when the drive control lever is released. In an emergency, all one has to do is let go of the drive control lever and all movement stops but the engine continues to run.

Some snow throwers have two spring-loaded control handles. One handle (right handle) engages the auger when depressed. The second handle (left handle) engages the drive wheels when depressed. When both handles are released, all motion stops but the engine continues to run. See **Figure 22-15**. This requires the operator to hold both handles down while removing snow.

Engine Controls

A	Electric start button (optional)	Activates electric starter.
B	Fuel valve	Turns fuel supply on or off.
C	Starter handle	Used to start engine.
D	Primer button	Primes carburetor for faster cold starting.
E	Throttle lever	Controls engine speed.
F	Engine key	Prevents starting of engine without key. Stops engine when removed.
G	Choke knob	Adjusts air/fuel mixture.

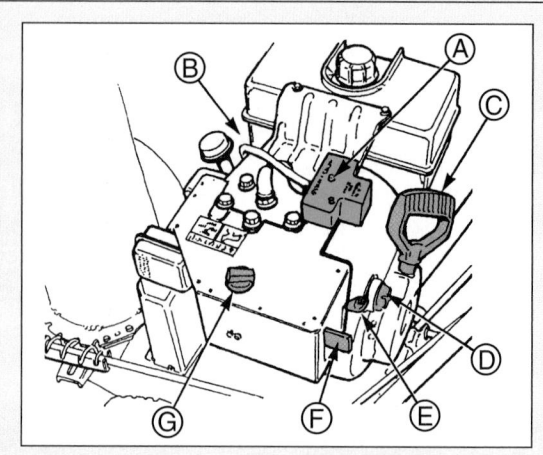

Simplicity Manufacturing Co.

Figure 22-13.

Basic engine controls vary from one make and model to another.

Snow Thrower Controls

1	Speed selector	Selects forward speeds 1-5, reverse speeds 1-2.
2	Drive control	Engages drive to wheels as it is depressed; disengages when released.
3	Auger control	Engages auger/impeller as it is depressed; disengages when released.
4	Chute direction control	Rotates discharge chute to desired direction.
5	Chute deflector	Controls vertical angle snow is thrown.
6	Chute deflector knob	Locks chute deflector at desired angle.
7	Skid shoes	Controls height of scraper bar.
8	Traction lock pins	Engages and disengages for drive or free-wheeling.

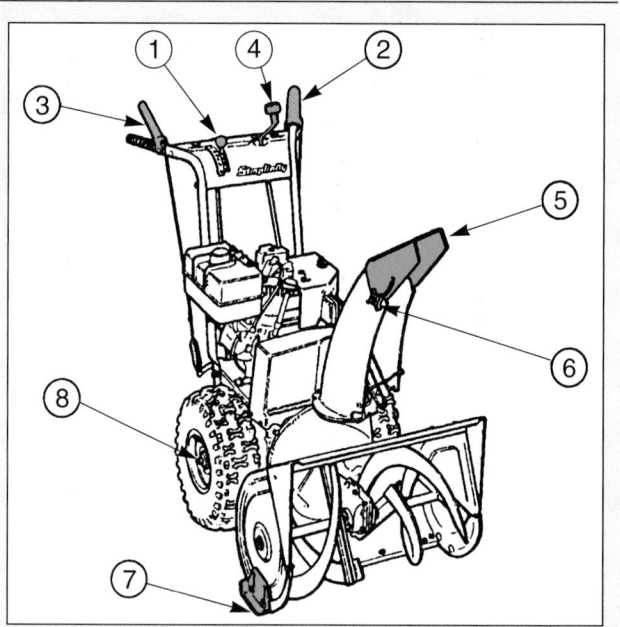

Simplicity Manufacturing Co.

Figure 22-14.

Controls 2 and 3 require the operator to be present at the controls during operation. If the drive control lever 2 is released, auger control lever 3 also releases. The wheels and auger stop.

Warning

Never reach into the chute or auger housing without stopping the engine, and removing and grounding the spark plug wire.

Electric Start Systems

Electric starters may be provided as standard or optional equipment. Snow throwers with electric starters also have recoil starters. When supplemental

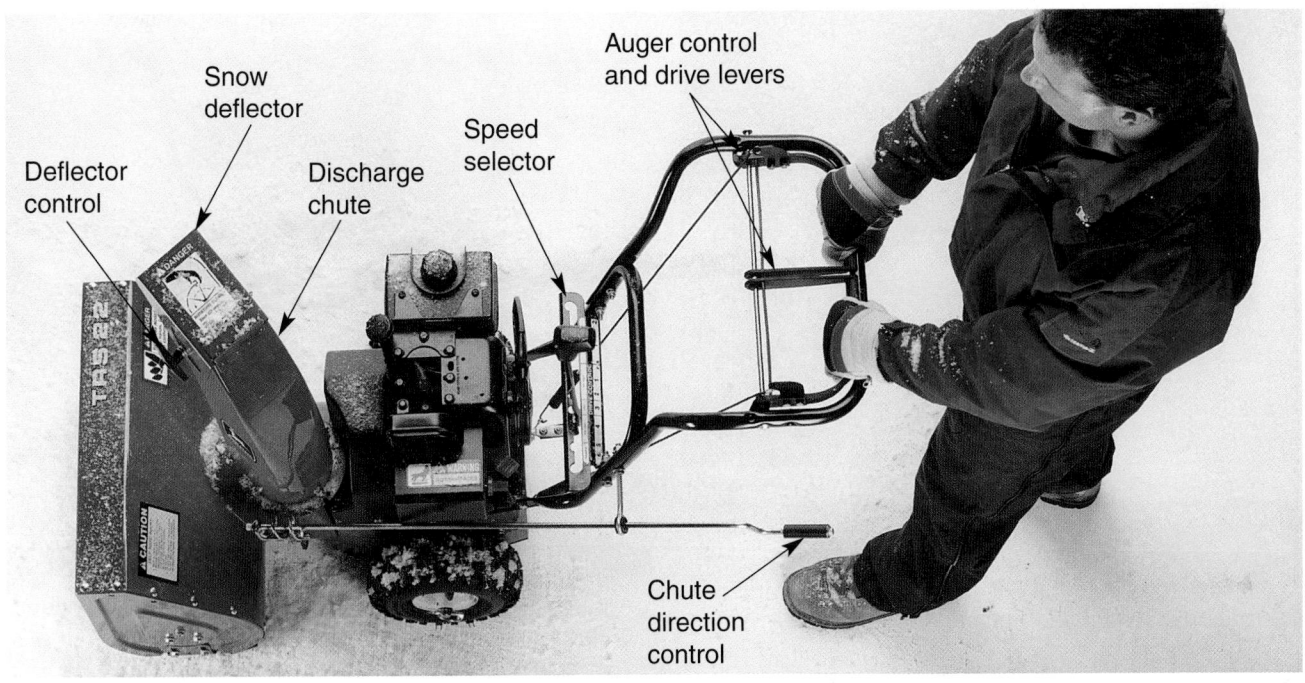

Snow
deflector

Auger control
and drive levers

Speed
selector

Deflector
control

Discharge
chute

Chute
direction
control

Deere & Co.

Figure 22-15.

Two handles must be held down to operate this snow thrower. When both are released, the wheels and auger stop. The engine continues to run.

electrical power is not available, the recoil starter can be used for starting.

Electric starting is convenient due to the size of the larger engines and cold conditions that may be encountered. The snow thrower is connected to a 110V ac grounded outlet using a 3-wire extension cord. The ac current is reduced to 12V dc current for the starter motor. With some models, the cord is plugged into the receptacle on the snow thrower and a button on the receptacle is depressed to start the engine. See **Figure 22-16.** With other models, after the cord is plugged in, the engine is started by depressing the start button on the control panel. See **Figure 22-17.**

Drive Systems

There are basically two drive system types. The first system drives the auger in single-stage machines or the auger and blower in two-stage machines. For models that are self-propelled, a second drive system is for the wheels or tracks. There are many drive designs and each manufacturer may utilize different ones for different models. Transmissions may consist of gears, belts, chains, or combinations of these components.

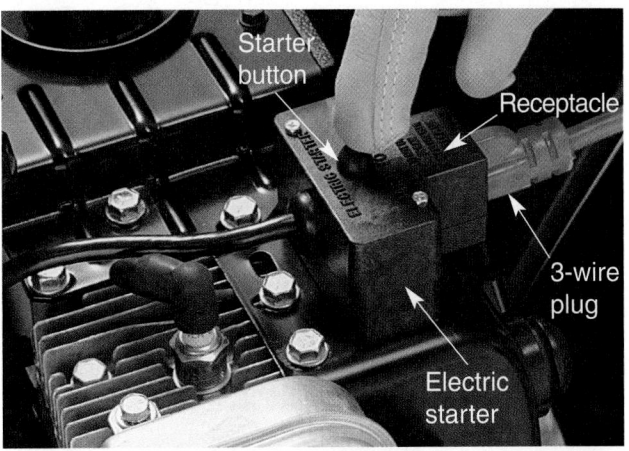

Starter
button

Receptacle

3-wire
plug

Electric
starter

The Toro Co.

Figure 22-16.

The 3-wire extension cord is plugged into the electric starter receptacle on the snow thrower. A button on the electric starter is depressed to start the engine.

Figure 22-18 shows a portion of the chains and belts used in a wheel-driving system. **Figure 22-19** shows the location of the reduction gearbox transmission that drives the auger and blower from the engine. The internal parts of a typical gearbox utilizing a ring gear and pinion gear are shown in

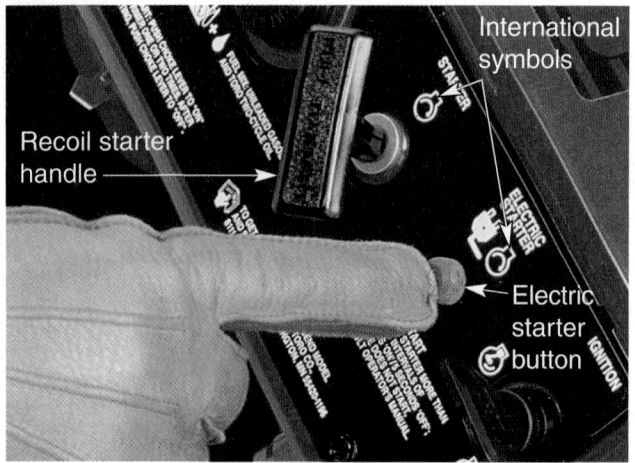

The Toro Co.

Figure 22-17.

Electric start button on a control panel. Notice the recoil start handle to the left of the start button and the international symbols for the various controls.

Gear box

Deere & Co.

Figure 22-19.

An auger reduction gearbox reduces the rotation speed of the auger.

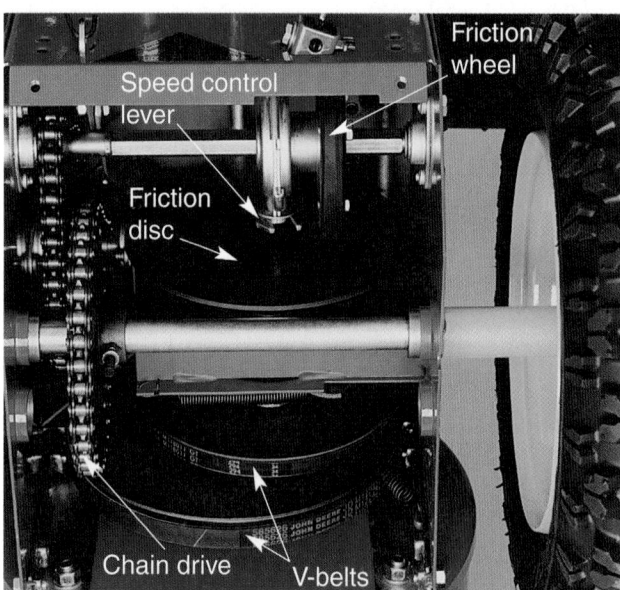

Deere & Co.

Figure 22-18.

Belts and chains are used to transmit motion from the engine to the wheels and auger. The friction wheel drives the friction disc and changes speeds when it is moved right or left by the operator. Moving to the right slows down the wheels and moving left speeds the wheels up.

Figure 22-20. Before beginning any service requiring disassembly and reassembly of parts, refer to the manufacturer's service manuals for the exact make and model being serviced.

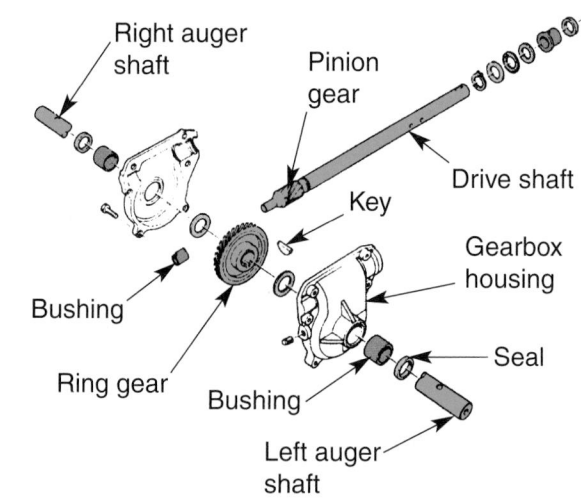

The Toro Co.

Figure 22-20.

Auger gearbox components. The pinion and ring gear reduce the rotation speed of the auger and increase auger torque.

Track Systems

Rubber tracks are found on some heavy-duty models and provide exceptional traction on ice and snow. See **Figure 22-21.** The tracks can be engaged singularly for steering, or together for maximum traction. Clutch levers are provided on each of the handles to control the direction of travel. See **Figure 22-22.** The tracks can be disengaged for ease of transporting.

Cleated track

Deere & Co.

Figure 22-21.

Rubber tracks provide exceptional traction on ice and snow and can be engaged singly, together, or disengaged entirely.

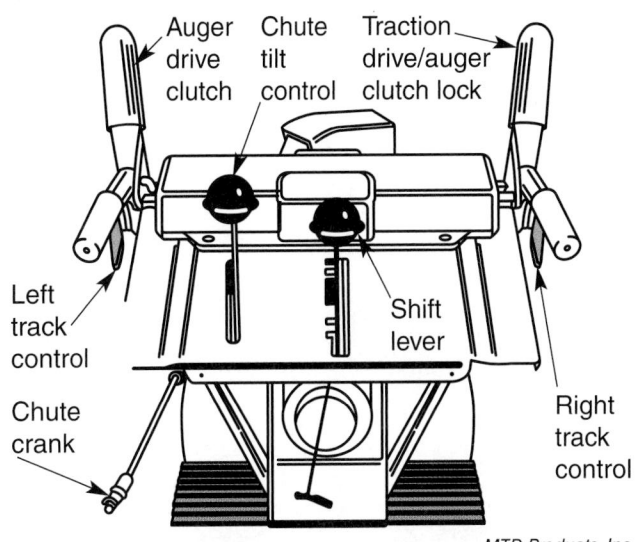

Auger drive clutch | Chute tilt control | Traction drive/auger clutch lock

Left track control

Chute crank

Shift lever

Right track control

MTD Products, Inc.

Figure 22-22.

Right and left track clutch levers permit responsive direction control. All controls are within easy reach of driver.

With extensive use, the tracks may wear out or become damaged. Also, the chain drive that powers the track may need to be replaced. Track adjusters allow loosening or tightening of the tracks by moving the idler wheel assembly forward or backward. This is done by loosening a nut or bolt. **Figure 22-23** is an exploded view of a track drive system for one model of snow thrower.

Track Chain Replacement

To replace the track chain, proceed as follows:
1. Block up the frame of the unit so the tracks are off the ground.
2. Loosen the nut on the track tension adjusters.
3. Roll the track off the idler and drive wheel assembly as shown in **Figure 22-24**.
4. Remove the chain by disconnecting the master link. See **Figure 22-25**. A master link and chain assembly is shown in **Figure 22-26**. The keeper is pried open with a screwdriver and removed so the link can be removed. The open end of the keeper should trail the direction of chain rotation. It is best to replace the keeper on the outer side of the chain so it can be removed more easily.

5. Reassemble in reverse order with a new chain and/or track. When reassembling the track, be certain the tread of the track is running in the proper direction. See **Figure 22-27**.

Track Tension Adjustment

It is important that the track tension on both sides be adjusted properly and equally. There are track adjusters for adjusting the tension. To adjust track tension, proceed as follows:
1. Disconnect the spark plug wire and ground it against the engine.
2. Drain the fuel from the fuel tank.
3. Tip the snow thrower forward so that it rests on the auger housing.
4. Loosen the track adjuster bolt.
5. Insert a screwdriver between the tab on the track adjuster to tighten or loosen the track. See **Figure 22-23**. The track is adjusted properly when it can be deflected about 1/2" (12.7 mm).
6. Tighten the track adjuster bolts.

Track Lock Lever

The track lock lever assembly, shown in **Figure 22-23** on the right side of the snow thrower, is used to select the position of the auger housing and the method of track operation. The lever positions are used to meet the following operating conditions:

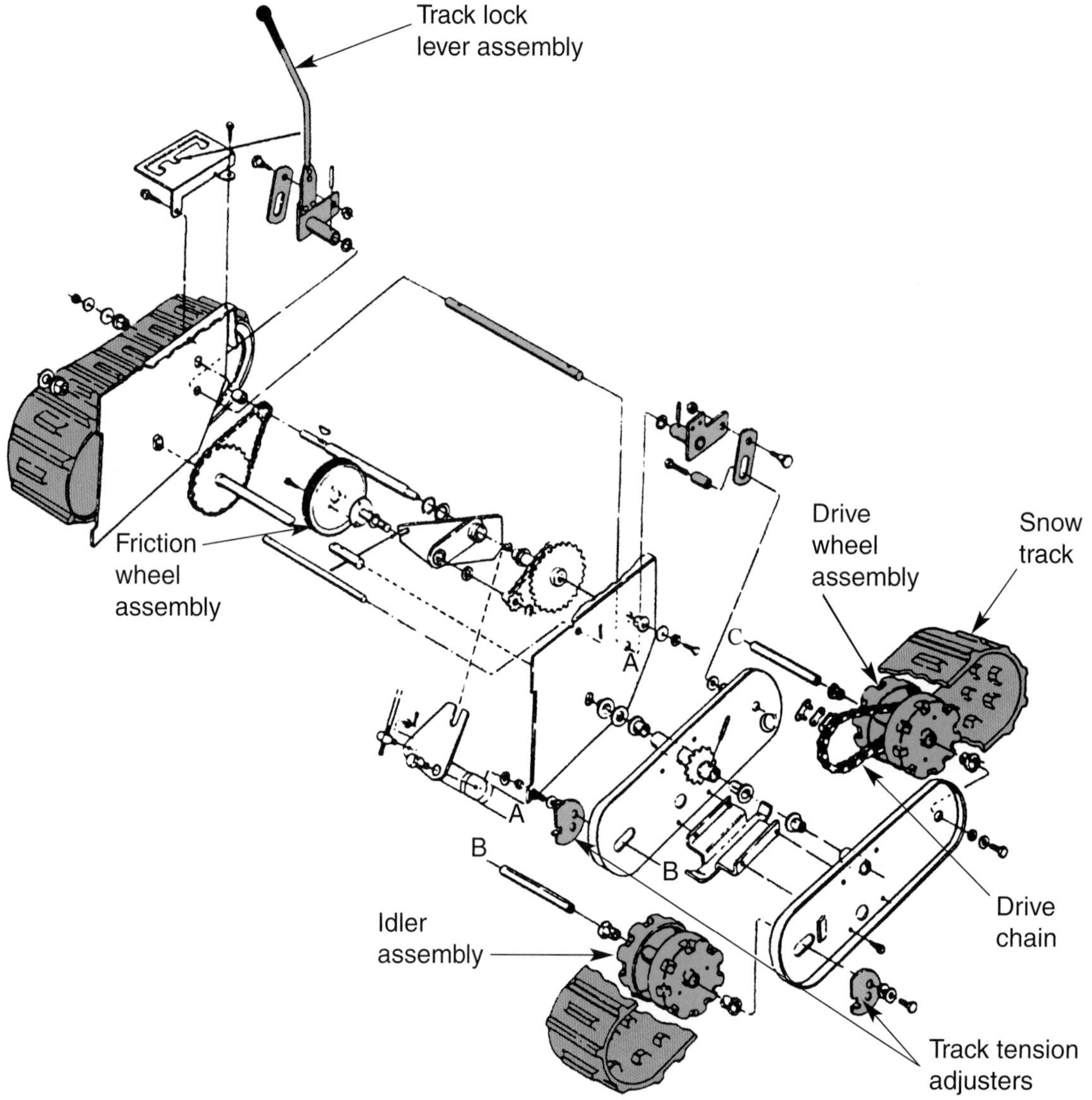

Track lock
lever assembly

Friction
wheel
assembly

Drive
wheel
assembly

Snow
track

A

C

A

B

C

B

A

Idler
assembly

Drive
chain

Track tension
adjusters

MTD Products, Inc.

Figure 22-23.

The track lock lever is used to select the position of the housing and method of track operation. It moves tracks forward or backward relative to the housing.

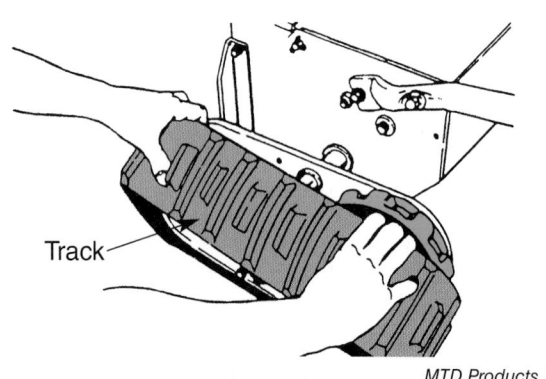

Track

MTD Products, Inc.

Figure 22-24.

Rolling the track off the idler and drive wheel assembly after releasing tension.

- *Transport.* Raises the front end of the snow thrower for easy transporting or to clear snow from gravel driveways without disturbing the gravel.
- *Normal snow.* Allows tracks to be suspended independently for continuous ground contact.
- *Packed snow.* Locks the front end of the snow thrower down to the ground for hard-packed or icy snow conditions.

Skid Shoes

Skid shoes establish the height of the scraper bar above the surface. The shoes are located at the

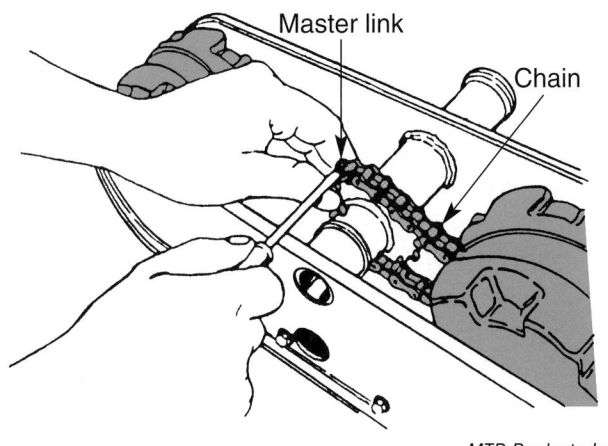

Master link

Chain

MTD Products, Inc.

Figure 22-25.

Removing drive chain by disconnecting the master link with screwdriver.

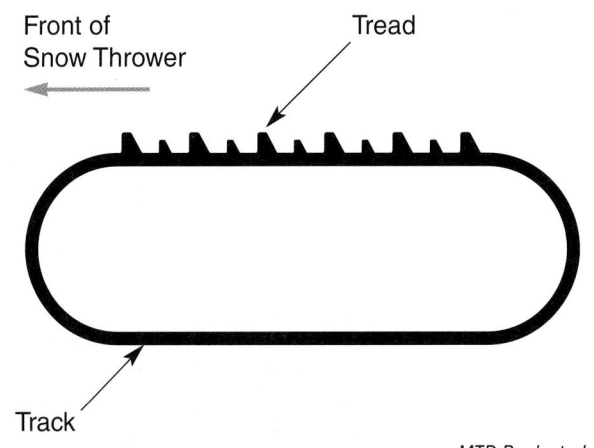

Front of
Snow Thrower

Tread

Track

MTD Products, Inc.

Figure 22-27.

Direction of track tread must be as shown when installing the track on the idler and drive wheels.

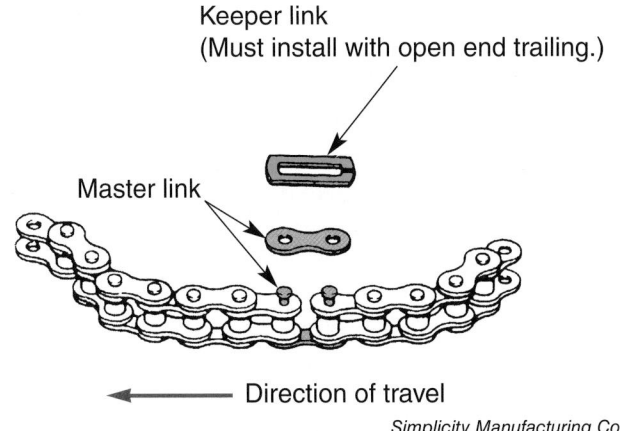

Keeper link
(Must install with open end trailing.)

Master link

Direction of travel

Simplicity Manufacturing Co.

Figure 22-26.

Details of a roller chain and master link with keeper.

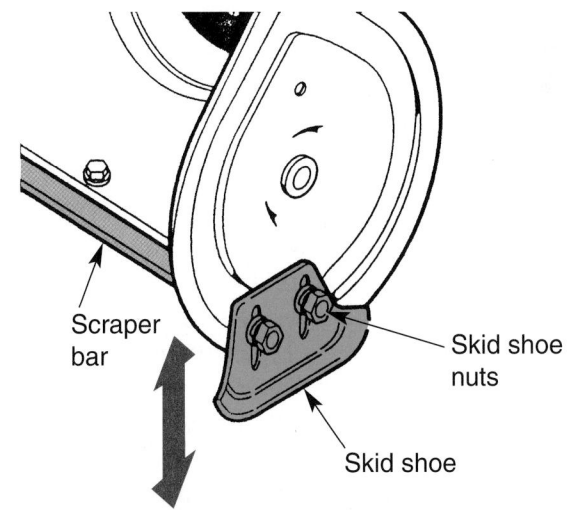

Scraper
bar

Skid shoe
nuts

Skid shoe

Deere & Co.

Figure 22-28.

Skid shoes establish height of scraper bar above the surface.

bottom edges of the auger housing and absorb the wear during operation. Fasteners fitted into slotted holes on the skid shoes allow easy adjustment and replacement. See **Figure 22-28**. The *scraper bar* is a metal bar fastened along the bottom edge of the auger housing intake. The scraper bar adds stiffness to the sheetmetal housing and can be replaced when it becomes worn.

On smooth surfaces such as concrete or asphalt, the scraper bar should lightly scrape the surface or clear the surface by about 1/8″ (3 mm). On gravel surfaces, the scraper bar should be high enough so that it will not pick up gravel or debris (about 1 1/4″ or 30 mm). If the scraper bar is damaged or worn excessively, replace it before adjusting the skid shoes.

Skid Shoe Adjustment

The skid shoes shown in **Figure 22-29** are adjusted in the following manner:
1. Park the snow thrower on a hard, smooth surface.
2. Stop the engine, remove the key, and wait for all moving parts to stop.
3. Remove the wire from the spark plug and ground it to the engine to prevent accidental start up.

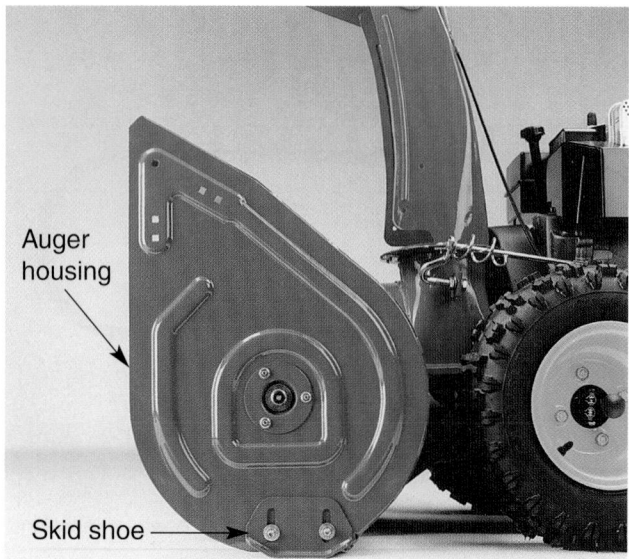

Deere & Co.

Figure 22-29.
On a level surface, place two pieces of wood of desired thickness under the scraper bar. Loosen the skid shoe nuts, lower the skids to surface, and tighten the nuts; 1/8″ (3mm) for smooth surfaces and 1 1/4″ (30mm) for gravel surfaces.

4. Check tire pressure with a tire gauge:
   a. Air pressure should be equal in both tires. Recommended tire pressure may be printed on the side wall of the tire or printed in the manufacturer's service manuals.
   b. Each tire must be resting on a hard surface, not a cross-link of the tire chain.
5. Put a block of the desired height under the scraper bar of the auger housing.
6. Inspect the skid shoes. If the shoes have excessive wear, replace them.
7. Loosen the adjustment nuts, lower the skid shoes to the surface, and tighten the nuts.

Snow Thrower Operation

There are a variety of models of snow throwers, but starting and using them is similar. Always refer to the manufacturer's technical service manuals for instruction for the specific model being used.

Engine Starting

The procedure for starting a cold engine is slightly different from the procedure for warm engine restarting. See **Figure 22-30** for the location of parts and controls for one particular snow thrower. Since snow thrower models differ, refer to the manufacturer's manual for the implement at hand. To start an engine, proceed as follows:

1. Turn the fuel valve on. Fuel valves are located where the fuel exits the bottom of the fuel tank.
2. Insert the engine ignition key into the switch and turn it to the *Run* or *Start* position. This switch may be located on a control panel.
3. Move the throttle lever to the *Fast* position. The throttle lever may be located on a control panel.
4. Close the choke knob. Do not choke a warm engine to restart.
5. Press the primer button several times if the engine is cold. Do not prime a warm engine for restarting.
6. Pull starter handle rapidly or push the starter button if the snow thrower is equipped with electric starter. Do not let the starter handle snap back. Let the starter rope rewind slowly, while keeping a firm grip on the starter handle.
7. As the engine starts and begins to operate evenly, turn the choke knob to the *Off* position and set the throttle lever to *Slow*. If the engine begins to slow down and run roughly, turn the choke knob until the engine runs smoothly. Let the engine warm up more and return the choke knob setting to *Off*.

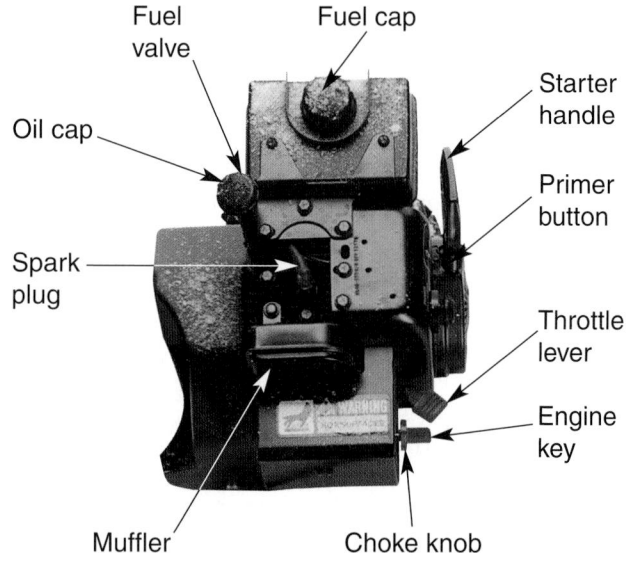

Deere & Co.

Figure 22-30.
Shown are many of the parts and controls for this snow thrower engine.

Allow the engine to warm up at *Slow* throttle before operating the snow thrower at full speed. The engine must reach operating temperature before it can develop full power. For best performance, run the snow thrower engine at full operating speed once it reaches operating temperature. Use the throttle lever to set the engine speed.

Snow Throwing

The procedure for snow throwing may vary from model to model. Refer to the manufacturer's manuals. To start snow throwing with the model shown in **Figure 22-15**, proceed as follows:

1. Use chute direction control to rotate the snow discharge chute to the desired direction.
2. Set the speed selector to the desired forward speed.
3. Fully press and hold the auger control lever to begin auger rotation. To disengage the auger, completely release the lever.
4. Fully press and hold the traction drive control lever to engage the traction drive and begin moving the snow thrower. To disengage the traction drive, release the lever.
5. To select the forward or reverse speed as needed, use the speed selector lever. Release the drive control lever, and change to the desired speed or direction.

General Maintenance

Maintenance is an important part of working with small gas engines and the machines they power. Small gasoline engines in snow throwers are similar to the engines in other kinds of implements. Snow thrower engines are designed to start easily and run under moderate to extremely cold working conditions. In addition to the preventive maintenance procedures outlined in Chapter 15 of this textbook, there are a number of components that need checking, service, and periodic adjustments when working with snow throwers. Performing these on a regular basis will result in a properly operating snow thrower.

Preventing Freeze-Up

Normal use of a snow thrower may result in a build-up of snow packed in and around the starter cord housing and engine controls. Engine heat will melt the snow and prevent the resulting water from freezing solid while the machine is running. After the engine is stopped and the engine cools, some snow may continue melting and later freeze around moving parts. To prevent freeze-up around engine controls and external parts, it is good practice to do the following after each use:

1. Before stopping the engine, pull the starter rope out several times and allow it to rewind slowly. This will help clear packed snow from the starter cord area.
2. Stop the engine by moving the throttle lever to the *Stop* position or by removing the ignition key.
3. Disconnect the spark plug wire and ground it on the engine away from the spark plug. Tie it away with string or tape if necessary.
4. Brush snow and ice from the snow thrower. Be sure to clear the engine and snow thrower controls, discharge chute, worm and chute rod gears, clutch rod areas, and anywhere snow has accumulated.
5. Reconnect the spark plug wire.

Servicing Augers

The augers are made in two halves. The center driving members of the augers are hollow tubes installed over the solid shafts on each side of the gearbox. A *shear bolt* or *shear pin* is installed through each hollow tube and the solid shaft to connect them together. Should something become lodged in the auger housing and stop the auger, the bolt(s) or pin(s) will shear to protect the auger and gearbox from more serious damage. See **Figure 22-31**. After removal of the obstruction and the sheared bolts or pins, new bolts or pins can be installed.

Replace sheared bolts or pins with the exact same kind of bolts or pins. Replacements must have the proper shear strength. Stronger bolts or pins may not shear. This can cause serious damage to the gears in the auger gearbox.

Lubrication

There are various places on snow throwers that need periodic lubrication to extend the useful life of the machine. Some parts require application of oil, while others require grease. Where contact

Shear bolt

Grease fitting

Deere & Co.

Figure 22-31.

The shear bolt or pin protects the auger gearbox from damage resulting from an obstruction in the auger housing. The grease fitting allows the auger shaft to be lubricated.

between moving metal parts is made, oil should generally be applied. External parts can be oiled with a medium weight (10W) oil. When oiling parts, it is important not to over oil. Excess oil might drip on floors or on parts that should be kept dry, such

as the traction drive or friction disc. Visible, excess oil generally provides no lubricating value. It mixes with dirt.

Figure 22-32 shows most of the parts that need oiling and greasing. Oil locations are shown by an orange oil can, and grease locations are shown by a green grease gun. Use a grease gun to apply grease directly to the *grease (zerk) fittings*. See **Figure 22-31**.

It is very important that grease fittings on the auger shaft be lubricated regularly. If the auger rusts to the shaft, damage to the worm gear may occur if the shear bolts or pins do not break. There are two grease fittings on the auger shaft. Wipe the fittings clean and apply grease, using a grease gun. Wipe away any excess grease from fittings or seepage between parts. If there are no grease fittings, the parts must be disassembled and water-proof grease must be applied liberally to the auger shafts during reassembly to prevent corrosion and seizing of parts.

The auger shaft is driven from a gearbox that requires lubrication. A filler plug may be located near the top of the case as in **Figure 22-33**, or at a lower level on the gearbox housing. If the filler plug is at the top of the case, it may be necessary

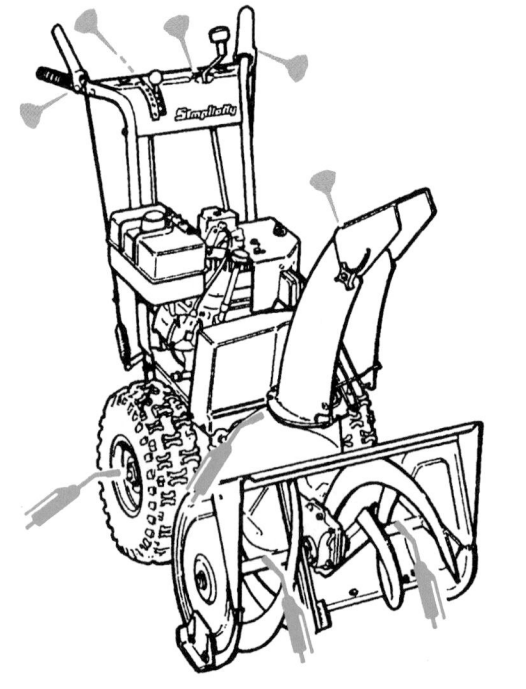

A

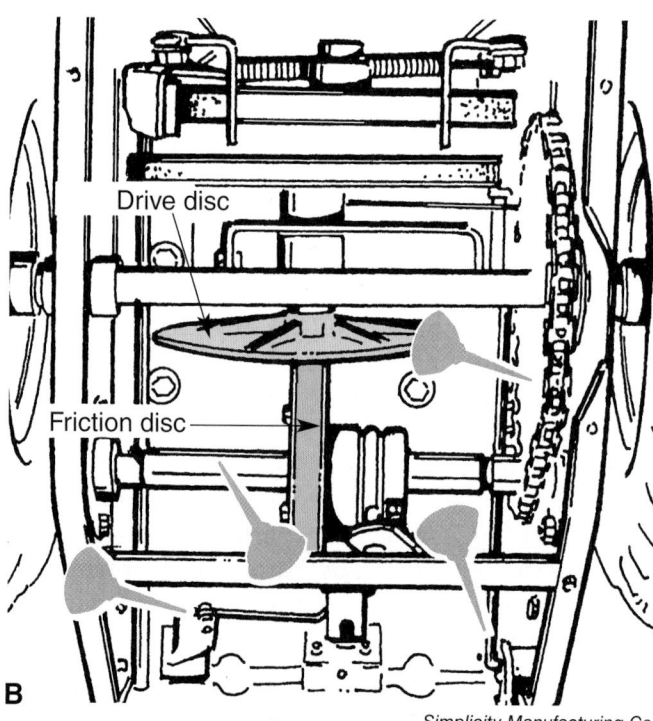

Drive disc

Friction disc

B

Simplicity Manufacturing Co.

Figure 22-32.

A—General lubrication points on a snow thrower. B—Lubrication points of a drive area with the bottom cover removed from the snow thrower.

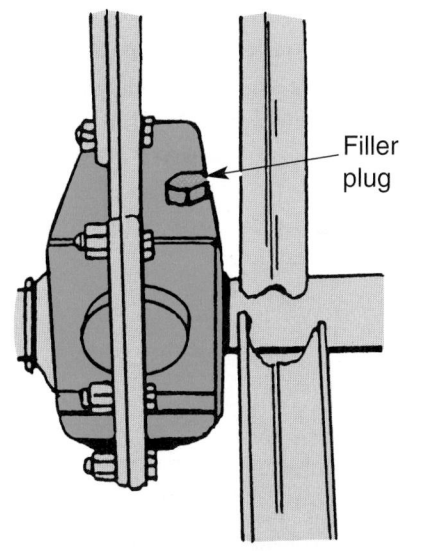

MTD Products, Inc.

Figure 22-33.

When the filler plug is located at the top of the auger gearbox, oil must be measured out before filling.

to drain the oil from the gearbox and then refill it with the correct amount of recommended oil. If the filler plug is at a level below the top of the gearbox, it is only necessary to fill oil to the lower edge of the plug. See **Figure 22-34**. See the manufacturer's service information for amount and type of oil to add.

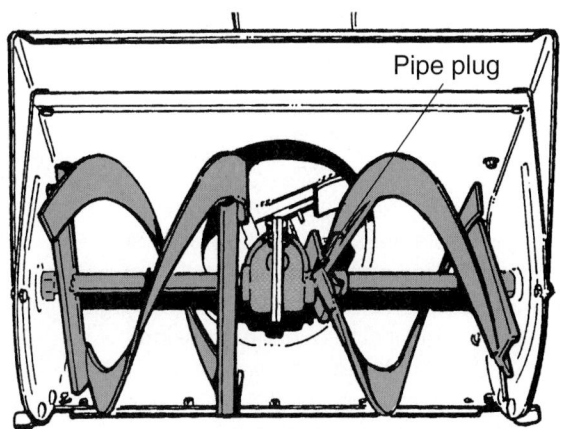

Simplicity Manufacturing Co.

Figure 22-34.

If the filler plug is located on the side of the auger gearbox, remove the plug and fill to the lower edge of the plug hole.

Off-Season Storage

When preparing to store a snow thrower for an extended period of time, refer to the manufacturer's service information for any specific instructions about the make and model being stored. If storing the unit outside, a weather resistant cover may be placed over the snow thrower to protect it against severe weather conditions.

Caution

Gasoline may develop gummy deposits if left in the tank unused for more than 30 days. This can adversely affect the carburetor and filter, causing the engine to malfunction. To prevent this condition, add a *fuel stabilizer* to the fuel in the tank or drain all fuel from the system. To drain fuel for the system, empty the fuel tank and then start and run the engine until it uses all the remaining fuel.

Remove the spark plug and spray a fogging oil into the spark plug hole while cranking the engine slowly with the recoil starter. This will allow the fogging oil to enter between the valve seats and faces, and will help prevent corrosion. Then replace the spark plug.

Clean the snow thrower thoroughly with a clean cloth. Protect any bare metal surfaces from corrosion by coating with paint, oil, or grease.

Store the snow thrower in its normal position. This prevents any oil from the crankcase from entering into the cylinder head of the engine.

Starting after Storage

After being stored for an extended period of time, there are some important steps to take when starting a snow thrower. To start a snow thrower after storage, proceed as follows:

1. Remove the spark plug, wipe it dry and inspect it for excess carbon, burned electrodes, and proper gap. Replace the plug with a new one if necessary.
2. If the fuel tank was emptied before storing, fill the fuel tank with fresh gasoline. Skip this step if a fuel stabilizer was used before storing.
3. Make sure the cooling fins are clean and no airflow obstructions exist.

4. Check the engine oil level and lubricate the snow thrower. Change the oil if necessary. If an oil filter is used on the engine, change it when changing the engine oil.
5. Belts that are worn or loose should be adjusted or replaced.
6. Start the engine outdoors. Warm up the engine by running at *Slow* speed for a few minutes before running at *Fast* speed or removing snow.

7. Check the operating condition of all controls. Make any adjustments that may be needed.
8. If the engine or snow thrower does not perform as expected, refer to a troubleshooting chart such as the one in **Figure 22-35**.

Troubleshooting Guide—Snow Thrower

Trouble	Possible Cause(s)	Corrective Action
Engine fails to start	1. Fuel tank empty, or stale fuel. 2. Blocked fuel line. 3. Key not in switch on engine. 4. Spark plug wire disconnected. 5. Faulty spark plug.	1. Fill tank with clean fresh gasoline. 2. Clean fuel line. 3. Insert key. 4. Connect wire to spark plug. 5. Clean, adjust gap or replace.
Engine runs erratically	1. Unit running on choke. 2. Blocked fuel line or stale fuel. 3. Water or dirt in fuel system. 4. Carburetor out of adjustment.	1. Turn choke knob to *Off* position. 2. Clean fuel line; fill tank with clean fresh gasoline. 3. Use carburetor bowl drain to drain fuel tank. Refill with fresh fuel. 4. Adjust carburetor.
Loss of power	1. Spark plug wire loose. 2. Gas cap vent hole plugged.	1. Connect and tighten spark plug wire. 2. Remove ice and snow from cap. Be certain vent hole is clear.
Engine overheats	1. Engine oil level low. 2. Carburetor not adjusted properly.	1. Fill crankcase with proper oil. 2. Adjust carburetor.
Excessive vibration	1. Loose parts or damaged impeller.	1. Stop engine immediately and disconnect spark plug wire. Tighten all bolts and nuts. Make all necessary repairs. If vibration continues, have unit serviced by authorized service dealer.
Hard to shift, or will not shift	1. Shift rod misadjusted.	1. Adjust drive clutch.
Unit fails to propel itself	1. Incorrect adjustment of drive clutch. 2. Drive belt loose or damaged.	1. Adjust drive clutch. 2. Replace drive belt.
Unit fails to discharge snow	1. Auger shear bolt broken. 2. Discharge chute clogged. 3. Foreign object lodged in auger. 4. Incorrect adjustment of auger drive clutch. 5. Auger drive belt loose or damaged.	1. Replace auger shear bolt. Refer to Maintenance section. 2. Stop engine immediately and disconnect spark plug wire. Clean discharge chute and inside of auger housing. 3. Stop engine immediately and disconnect spark plug wire. Remove object from auger. 4. Adjust auger clutch. 5. Replace auger drive belt.

MTD Products, Inc.

Figure 22-35.

Troubleshooting guide for a snow thrower.

Summary

Before attempting to service a snow thrower, all safety instructions provided by the manufacturer should be read and understood. The appropriate owner's manual and manufacturer's service information should be consulted whenever there is a question regarding safe repair, maintenance, or operating procedures.

Snow throwers are available in various sizes and work capacities. Engines for snow throwers are designed for easy starting in low temperatures.

Small machines are ideal for locations where snowfalls are generally light and the area to be cleaned is limited. Small snow throwers are single-stage type. Single-stage snow throwers have steel or rubber blades that rotate like paddles and throw the snow upward and forward.

Midsize snow throwers are heavier and have engines ranging from 3–8 hp. Midsize machines may be either a single-stage or a two-stage type. In two-stage snow throwers, the auger feeds the snow into a high-speed blower fan that ejects the snow from the chute. Two-stage snow throwers are generally more effective than single-stage snow throwers.

Heavy-duty snow throwers range from 8–20 hp. They have the same features as midsize machines, but are heavier and clean wider paths.

To provide additional safety, operator presence controls automatically stop the auger from rotating when the drive (traction) lever is released.

Snow throwers with electric starts also have recoil starters. When supplemental electrical power is not available, the recoil starter can be used for starting.

There are basically two drive systems. The first system drives the auger in single-stage machines or the auger and blower in two-stage machines. For models that are self-propelled, a second drive system is for the wheels or tracks. Rubber tracks are found on some heavy-duty models and provide exceptional traction on ice and snow. See **Figure 22-21**. The tracks can be engaged singularly for steering, or together for maximum traction. It is important that the track tension on both sides be adjusted properly and equally.

Skid shoes establish the height of the scraper bar above the surface. The shoes are located at the bottom edges of the auger housing and absorb the wear during operation. Fasteners fitted into slotted holes on the skid shoes allow easy adjustment and replacement. On smooth surfaces, the scraper bar should lightly scrape the surface or clear the surface by about 1/8" (3mm). On gravel surfaces, the scraper bar should be high enough so that it will not pick up gravel or debris (about 1 1/4" or 30mm).

Allow the engine to warm up at slow throttle before operating the snow thrower at full speed. The engine must reach operating temperature before it can develop full power.

Maintenance is an important part of working with small gas engines and the machines they power. There are a number of components that need checking, service, and periodic adjustments when working with snow throwers.

Normal use of a snow thrower may result in a build-up of snow packed in and around the starter cord housing and engine controls. Engine heat will melt the snow and prevent the resulting water from freezing solid while the machine is running. After the engine is stopped and the engine cools, some snow may continue melting and later freeze around moving parts. Precautions should be taken to prevent freeze-up around engine controls and external parts.

The augers are made in two halves. The center driving members of the augers are hollow tubes installed over the solid shafts on each side of the gearbox. A shear bolt or pin is installed through each hollow auger tube and the solid shaft to connect them together. Should something become lodged in the auger housing and stop the auger, the bolt(s) or pin(s) will shear to protect the auger and gearbox from more serious damage.

There are various places on snow throwers that need periodic lubrication to extend the useful life of the machine. Some parts require the application of oil, while others require grease. When oiling parts, it is important not to over oil. It is very important that grease fittings on the auger shaft be lubricated regularly. If the auger rusts to the shaft, damage to the worm gear may occur if the shear bolts or pins do not break.

The auger shaft gearbox requires lubrication. A filler plug may be located near the top of the case or at a lower level on the gearbox housing. See the manufacturer's service information for amount and type of oil to add.

When preparing to store a snow thrower for an extended period, refer to the manufacturer's service information for specific instructions about the make and model being stored. Gasoline may develop gummy deposits if left in the tank unused for more than 30 days. To avoid this condition, add a fuel stabilizer to the fuel tank or drain all fuel from the system before storing the unit.

Review Questions

Answer the following questions using the information provided in this chapter.

1. List five basic rules that should be followed when servicing a snow thrower.

2. The engines used in snow throwers are designed for easy starting in _____.

3. *True or False?* Small snow throwers are generally self-propelled units.

4. Midsize snow throwers have engines that range in size from _____ horsepower.
   A. 3–8
   B. 6–10
   C. 8–12
   D. 15–24

5. Snow throwers are of two basic types. They are either _____-stage or _____-stage units.

6. Snow is drawn into a snow thrower by a device called a(n) _____.

7. All heavy-duty snow throwers are of the _____-stage type.

8. Operator presence controls stop the _____ from rotating when the drive lever is released.

9. What is the advantage of the track systems found on some large snow throwers?

10. _____ are used to establish the height of the scraper bar above the surface.
    A. Lock levers
    B. Skid shoes
    C. Idler arm
    D. None of the above.

11. After a cold engine is started, it should be allowed to warm up at _____ throttle before the snow thrower is operated at full speed.
    A. slow
    B. medium
    C. full

12. List three precautions that can be taken to present freeze-up around a snow thrower's engine controls and external parts.

13. A _____ is used to protect the auger and gearbox from damage if something becomes lodged in the auger housing and stops the auger from turning.
    A. fluid coupling
    B. shear bolt or pin
    C. key
    D. All of the above.

14. Explain why it is important to avoid applying too much oil when lubricating the external parts of a snow thrower.

15. What must be done to lubricate the auger shaft if the auger does not have grease fittings?

16. To prevent the formation of gummy deposits, a fuel _____ should be added to the tank before a snow thrower is stored for an extended period of time.

Suggested Activities

1. Identify and point out all the external parts of a snow thrower.

2. Check a snow thrower for proper condition of all visible parts.

3. Demonstrate and/or describe lubrication procedures for a snow thrower.

4. Check tire condition and pressure. If there are tracks, check condition and tension. Adjust track tension, or show how it is adjusted.

5. Demonstrate skid shoe adjustment.

6. Demonstrate safe and proper engine starting procedures, and start the engine.

Personal Watercraft

Learning Objectives

After studying this chapter, you will be able to:

- Understand the major components of personal watercraft.
- Maintain and make adjustments to personal watercraft.
- Properly store and remove from storage a personal watercraft.

Key Terms

bilge
bow line
drain plug
fuel vent check valve
identification numbers
jet pump
jet pump intake grate
jet pump outlet nozzle

personal watercraft
pitch
pop-off pressure
reverse bucket
ride plate
sediment bowl
stator vanes
water inlet screen

Introduction

The term *personal watercraft* is used in this chapter to describe a particular type of popular small boat, which is propelled and guided by a high-velocity jet of water. For clarity, the abbreviation *PWC* will be used to refer to these small jet-driven vessels. Many manufacturers produce PWC. The term *Jet Ski*, though used frequently for all types of PWC, is a registered trademark of the Kawasaki Motors Corp., U.S.A., and relates only to their brand of PWC. See **Figure 23-1**.

PWC are powered by an inboard engine that has an axial jet pump mechanism. See **Figure 23-2**. The capabilities and limitations are somewhat different from those of propeller-driven boats. PWC can operate in shallower water and are quickly and easily maneuvered. Acceleration is rapid, but the PWC is affected more by waves, turbulence, and obstructions than larger boats. It is important to take extra precautions when operating PWC in boat traffic conditions, because operators of other boats may not understand the capabilities of the smaller jet-type PWC. Those who service or operate

Kawasaki Motors Corp., U.S.A.

Figure 23-1.

This is a personal watercraft (PWC). This particular one is a Jet Ski made by Kawasaki.

PWC should be aware of the serious nature of the equipment. PWC service requires persons to be responsible and knowledgeable about the unique rules and safety requirements that govern this type of watercraft.

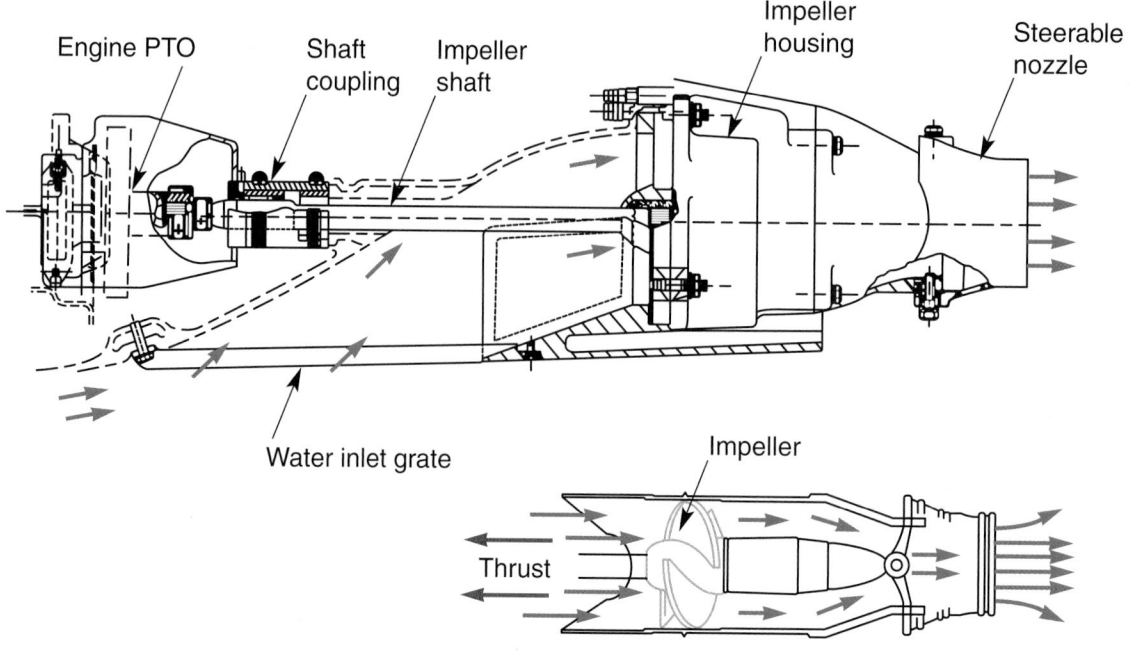

Sea-Doo

Figure 23-2.

An axial jet pump can operate in shallow water and can maneuver the craft quickly and easily. The engine-driven impeller draws water through the inlet and pumps it out the nozzle at high velocity. The reaction creates thrust to push the boat ahead.

Identification Numbers and Placards

The engine and hull *identification numbers* are used to register a PWC. These numbers are the only way of positively identifying one PWC from another. They are unique numbers and may also be needed when ordering parts.

The hull identification number is placed on the hull by the manufacturer. It is usually located near the stern (back) of the boat. The engine identification number will be stamped somewhere on the engine block by the manufacturer. See the manufacturer's service manuals for the exact location of the numbers.

Warning label decals are located in appropriate and readily readable locations. All labels should be read, understood, and followed carefully by anyone servicing or operating a PWC. If any label becomes illegible or comes off, it should be replaced as soon as possible. The PWC dealer will provide the proper decals, usually at no cost. Special procedures are required to remove and replace old decals. Some of the typical warning label decals are shown in **Figure 23-3**.

Types of PWC

PWC are available in several types. They vary in performance, stability, and the amount of skill necessary to operate them. Some are operated in a sitting position, and others are operated in a kneeling or standing position. See **Figure 23-4**. Passenger-carrying capacity can vary from one-person boats to those that can carry up to three people.

All PWC are designed to allow the operator to fall safely overboard. The reduced risk is due to the jet propulsion system that replaces the rudder and propeller on the outside of the hull, which is common in other power boats. Also, the lanyard on the PWC stops the engine immediately if the operator falls overboard. This prevents the PWC from running away out of control. See **Figure 23-5**. If safety and manufacturer's instructions are followed, reboarding the PWC can be done with minimal risk.

Hull shapes and lengths vary from one type of PWC to another. The variations depend on the purpose for which the PWC was designed, such as racing, water stunts, or pleasure cruising.

⚠ DANGER
HIGH VOLTAGE ELECTRICAL SHOCK HAZARD!
7073713

Located on the electrical box.

⚠ WARNING
DO NOT REMOVE ELECTRICAL PARTS WHEN STARTING OR DURING OPERATION. 7073712

Located on the engine water manifold.

RECOMMENDED OIL: POLARIS PREMIUM TWO-CYCLE LUBRICANT OR NMMA CERTIFIED TC-WIII OIL.
7074959

Located on the engine (water out manifold).

FIRE EXTINGUISHER CONTAINER LOCATED INSIDE   7073467

Located near fire extinquisher container (on top of storage compartment cover).

Push to Reset
7073734

Located on the electrical box (inside engine compartment).

GREASE LUBRICANT FITTING LOCATED BELOW SHROUD.
SEE OWNER'S MANUAL FOR INSTRUCTIONS.   7074963

Located on shroud.

→
PUSH ROD FORWARD TO RELEASE
7073717

Located near support for storage compartment.

⚠ CAUTION

RIGHTING CAPSIZED BOAT

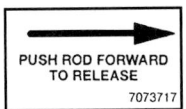

• To prevent injury, do not place hands or objects into pump inlet.
• To prevent major engine damage: Make sure engine is stopped by pulling lanyard from engine stop switch and turn boat to upright position in a clockwise direction.   7073865

Located at rear of watercraft and positioned upside down allowing the operator to read it when the boat is in the capsized position.

Polaris

Figure 23-3.

Decal labels such as those shown are positioned to warn and instruct riders about important information. Labels should be replaced if they are removed or unreadable.

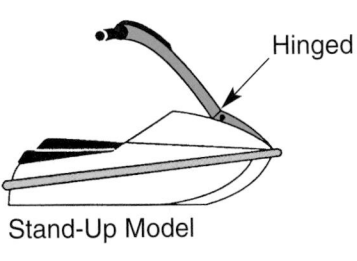
Hinged

Stand-Up Model

Sit-Down Model

Goodheart-Willcox Publisher

Figure 23-4.

The stand-up model is ridden in a kneeling or standing position. The sit-down model is ridden with the rider sitting down.

Lanyard stops engine

PFD

Lock plate and stop switch

Goodheart-Willcox Publisher

Figure 23-5.

A lanyard is attached to the rider's wrist and the engine stop switch. If the operator falls from the craft, the lanyard stops the engine, the PWC stops, and the rider can reboard from the rear of the craft.

PWC Main Components and Parts

Before servicing a PWC, you should be familiar with the common components and parts. **Figure 23-6** shows the components found on most PWC. The following is a list of those components:

• Seat strap—A seat strap is available on PWC designed to carry more than one person. It provides the passenger with a handle to hold while riding.

• Seat/engine compartment—The seat is molded to a comfortable shape and should be made of a material that resists chaffing. Removing the seat provides access to the engine, battery, electrical box, muffler, and other mechanical components.

• Handlebars—Handlebars are used to steer and control a PWC by turning the steerable jet nozzle at the stern. Turning the handlebar left turns the nozzle left and the boat turns left. A starter button, stop button with lanyard key, and trim adjust switch are located on the left handlebar. Before starting the PWC, the operator must always attach the lanyard cord to their left wrist or a personal floatation device (PFD), making sure it is secure.

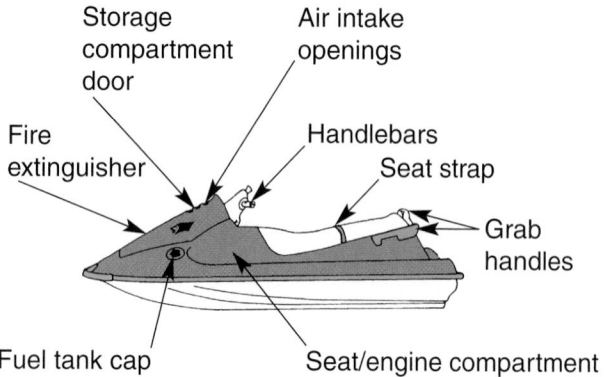

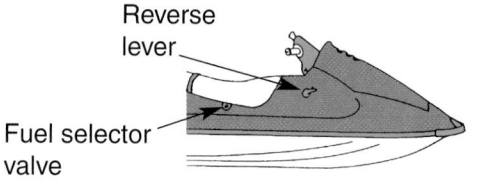

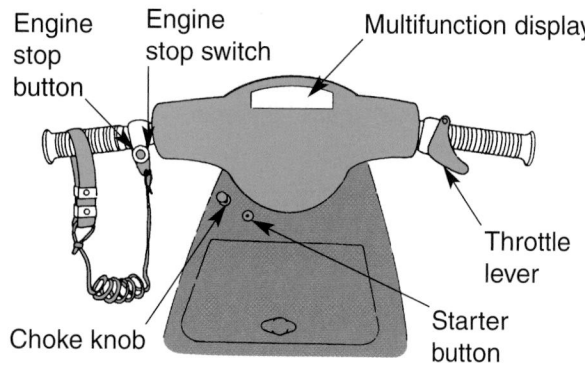

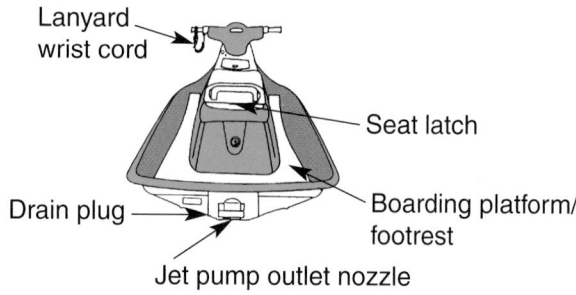

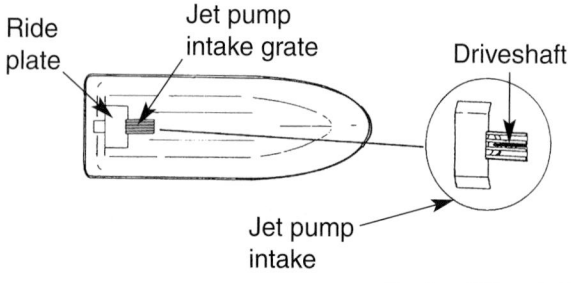

Goodheart-Willcox Publisher

Figure 23-6.

These illustrations show the main components that are typically found on a PWC.

- Fire extinguisher—The fire extinguisher should be securely held in the storage compartment. The U.S. Coast Guard requires that a class B-1 fire extinguisher in working condition be readily accessible aboard boats. Class B-1 extinguishers are charged with carbon dioxide for extinguishing class B fires, or flammable liquid fires. The *1* indicates the size of fire that the extinguisher can be used against. The larger the number, the larger the fire the extinguisher can be used for. Locking pins and sealing wires should be in place.
- Storage compartment door—Opens to provide access to the fire extinguisher and other items being carried.
- Air intake openings—The air intake openings allow air to enter the engine compartment to supply the engine with air and ventilate the compartment.
- Fuel tank cap—Turn the cap counterclockwise to remove and clockwise to replace. The cap must be tight before operating the PWC.
- Grab handles—Assist riders when boarding from the water.
- Fuel selector valve—The fuel valve knob or lever has three positions: *On*, *Off*, and *Res* (reserve). The fuel must be turned *On* before starting the engine and turned *Off* after stopping the engine. If the PWC runs low on fuel with the fuel selector in the *On* position, the low fuel warning light will come on. Switching to *Res* will allow a specific amount of additional running time to get to shore. The rider should know the amount of time and approximate distance that can be covered after switching to *Res*. After refueling, the fuel selector should always be set to the *On* position, not *Res*, for the next ride. Refueling should be done as soon as possible to avoid being stranded in open water. Being stranded in open water is very dangerous.
- Reverse lever—A reverse lever is used to engage a reverse bucket over the jet pump outlet nozzle. The reverse lever has a lock button that must be pressed before the lever can be turned to the reverse position. The *reverse bucket* causes the jet stream to flow toward the bow of the boat. This causes the PWC to back up. This is very useful in docking or close quarter maneuvering situations. The boat should always be allowed to slow down before attempting to shift into reverse.

The reverse bucket should *never* be used as a brake. This action can cause the PWC to dive into the water throwing the occupants forward and possibly causing injury.

- Multifunction display—The multifunction display is similar to the instrument panel on an automobile. The display may contain such things as the oil level warning light, low fuel warning light, fuel level lights, cooling water temperature warning light, engine tachometer, and trim position indicator.
- Starter button—To start the engine, the starter button is pressed until the engine starts. The button should be released as soon as the engine starts. *Never* press the button longer than 5 seconds. If the engine does not start after holding the button down for 5 seconds, release the button, wait 15 seconds, and try again. If the engine does not start after several attempts, refer to the troubleshooting guide in the manufacturer's service manuals.

Note

The lanyard and lock plate must be attached to the engine stop switch or the engine will not crank or start.

- Choke knob—When starting a cold engine, turn on the choke knob to help the engine obtain a rich mixture of fuel. This will make the engine start easier. As soon as the engine has started and runs a few seconds, the choke knob should be slowly turned off. Choking should not be necessary when starting a warm engine.
- Throttle lever—The throttle lever is located on the right-hand side of the handlebar. The engine increases speed when the throttle lever is squeezed. When the lever is released, spring pressure returns the engine to idle speed. The throttle lever should move freely and return to idle quickly when released. This should always be checked before starting the engine.
- Engine stop button—The stop button is red for easy identification. It is located on the left-hand side of the handlebar. The stop button will stop the engine when pressed.
- Engine stop switch—The lock plate end of the lanyard cord attaches to the stop switch on the left-hand side of the handlebar. Should the rider be dislodged from the PWC, the lanyard connected to the operator's wrist will pull the lock plate out and stop the engine.

Note

On some PWC, disconnection of the lanyard slows the engine to idle speed and automatically turns the craft in a left circle. The PWC will then return to the operator.

- Jet pump outlet nozzle—High-velocity water is pumped out through the *jet pump outlet nozzle* by an axial-flow jet pump driven from the engine. An impeller blade, like the propeller on an outboard engine, is housed inside a tubular pump housing. The rotating impeller draws water in through the grate on the hull bottom. It forces the water out through the jet nozzle at high velocity. This drives the craft ahead similar to the operation of an aircraft jet engine. The jet pump outlet nozzle is hinged to allow it to control the direction of the PWC. The nozzle is directed by turning the handlebars right or left. Control cables connect the handlebars to the nozzle.
- Lanyard wrist cord—The lock plate end is fastened to the stop switch on the left-hand side of the handlebar. The wrist end is fastened to the operator's wrist or a PFD. If the rider is dislodged, the lanyard lock plate is pulled from the stop switch and the engine automatically stops or slows to idle speed.
- Seat latch—Holds the seat in place. When the latch is released, the seat can be raised to provide access to the engine compartment.
- Boarding platform/footrest—The place for the rider's feet while riding. It also provides footing for boarding the PWC.
- Drain plug—When water gets into the bilge (bottom of hull), it can be drained by removing the PWC from the water and removing the *drain plug*. Some watercraft have an automatic bilge system that removes water from the engine compartment while the craft is being used. A venturi vacuum is created by the jet pump. This vacuum draws water from the engine compartment through a hose to a nozzle in the jet pump. A siphon breaker (check valve) is installed in the hose to prevent water from entering the hull when the engine is not running.
- Jet pump intake grate—The *jet pump intake grate* prevents large debris from entering the jet pump and damaging the impeller or driveshaft. Riders, who may suddenly become swimmers, should stay clear of the intake

grate when the engine is running. Long, loose items such as hair can be drawn into the shaft and impeller. Loose articles of clothing or jewelry should be kept safely inside a wet/dry suit. PWC should never be used in water less than 2′ (60 cm) deep. This will prevent small debris from entering the pump, which could severely damage the impeller blades.

- Driveshaft—The driveshaft transmits power from the engine to the impeller. The driveshaft is located under the intake grate.
- Jet pump intake—The impeller draws water through the grate and into this opening.
- Ride plate—The *ride plate* covers and protects the jet pump. It provides leveling control for the PWC. Some PWC have electric trim control. Pressing a trim switch on the left-hand side of the handlebar energizes an electric motor that raises or lowers the jet pump nozzle. Pressing the switch down directs the nozzle down and lowers the bow of the PWC. Pressing the switch up raises the nozzle and raises the bow of the PWC. A trim indicator on the panel shows the position of the nozzle. The electric trim motor provides subtle changes in the boat's attitude for a more efficient and comfortable ride.

PWC Engines

Engines used in PWC are precision built machines. These engines are multi-cylinder, two- or four-cycle, water-cooled, high-speed engines. See **Figure 23-7**. A service technician should become familiar with these engines and their function, as well as the cooling and jet propulsion systems.

PWC Engine Cooling Systems

There are a number of cooling systems used with PWC engines. They all work by circulating water or coolant (a mixture of water and antifreeze) around engine parts. The engine cylinders and cylinder heads are jacketed to allow water or coolant to circulate.

In open cooling systems, engine cooling is achieved as water drawn from the body of water the craft is operated in is circulated through the engine. See **Figure 23-8**. This water is taken from a pressurized area between the impeller and venturi in

A

B

Kawasaki Motors Corp., U.S.A.

Figure 23-7.
PWC engines are precision machines. The engine in A has two cylinders and the one in B has three cylinders. These engines are specifically designed for jet propelled watercraft.

the jet pump. It passes through a tee, where a small amount is diverted directly into the exhaust gas for noise reduction and performance improvement.

Most of the water passes into the exhaust system and is warmed. The water enters the water jacket on the tuned exhaust pipe and travels into the water jacket around the exhaust manifold. Next, it enters the water jackets around the cylinders through small passages under the exhaust ports. The water surrounding the cylinders moves upward through calibrated holes in the cylinder head, exiting the engine at the intake side of the cylinder head. The hot water is returned to its source through a hose and calibrated, limited-flow fittings at the stern

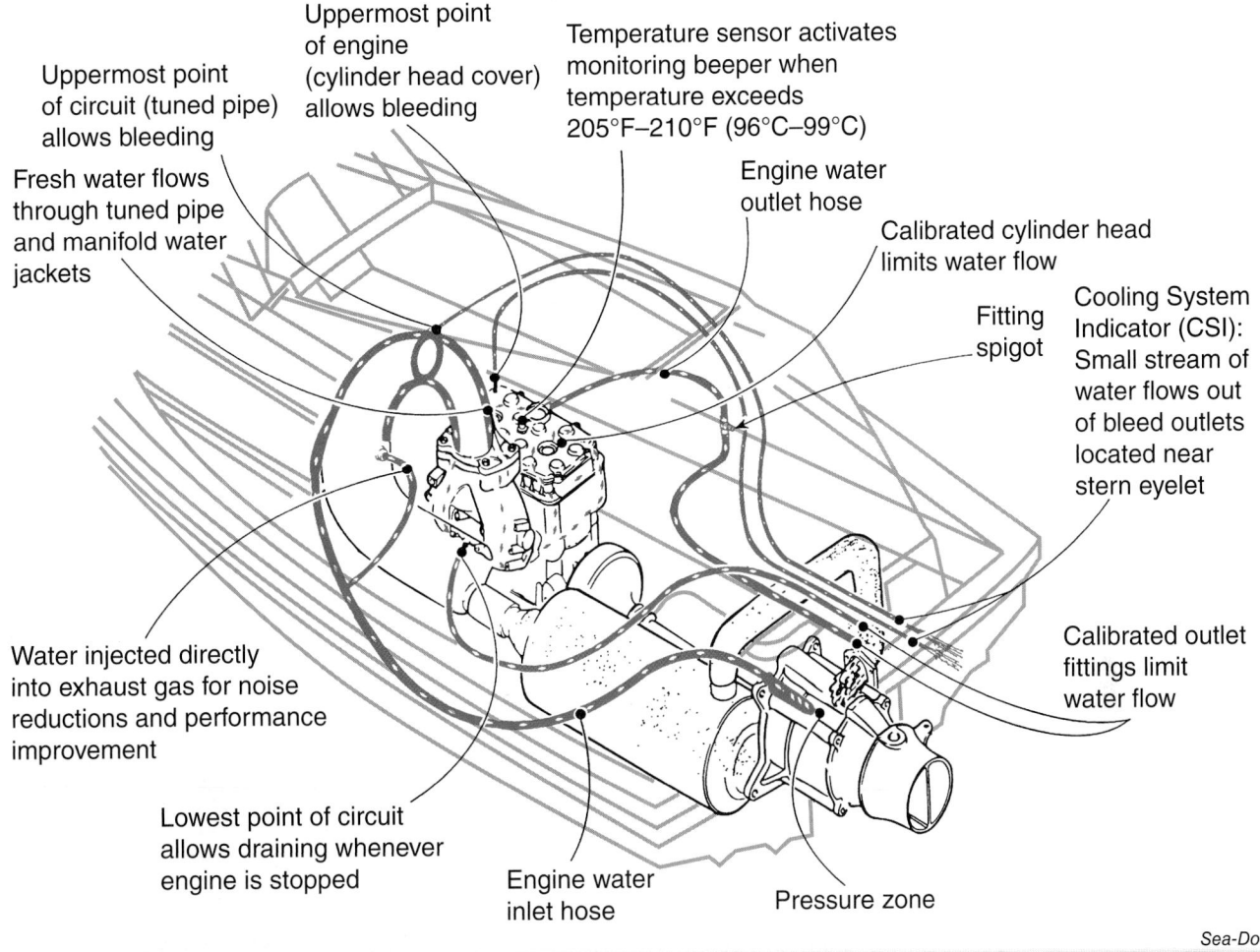

Uppermost point
of circuit (tuned pipe)
allows bleeding

Uppermost point
of engine
(cylinder head cover)
allows bleeding

Temperature sensor activates
monitoring beeper when
temperature exceeds
205°F–210°F (96°C–99°C)

Fresh water flows
through tuned pipe
and manifold water
jackets

Engine water
outlet hose

Calibrated cylinder head
limits water flow

Fitting
spigot

Cooling System
Indicator (CSI):
Small stream of
water flows out
of bleed outlets
located near
stern eyelet

Water injected directly
into exhaust gas for noise
reductions and performance
improvement

Calibrated outlet
fittings limit
water flow

Lowest point of circuit
allows draining whenever
engine is stopped

Engine water
inlet hose

Pressure zone

Sea-Doo

Figure 23-8.

This is one example of an engine cooling system used in PWC.

of the PWC. Bleed valves and lines prevent air entrapment in the uppermost parts of the engine. If bleeding is not done, hot spots can occur.

Many late-model PWC engines use a closed cooling system, or pressurized cooling system. In this type of system, liquid coolant is routed through the engine and then through a radiator, where excess heat is removed. Pressurized cooling systems were covered in detail in Chapter 12. Advantages to pressurized cooling systems include the fact that they circulate coolant through the engine instead of the water the PWC is being operated in. This eliminates the possibility of saltwater or debris being drawn into the engine and causing corrosion or clogging. Additionally, pressurized cooling systems can more accurately control engine temperature, which leads to more efficient engine operation and better fuel economy.

Jet Pump Propulsion System

The *jet pump* is an axial flow device, which means it has a single impeller driven by a centrally located shaft. See **Figure 23-9**. Other than the engine, it is the major component that drives the PWC. It provides thrust in water similar to the way a jet engine produces thrust in air. The impeller draws water in through the grate screen on the bottom of the hull and forces it out through a discharge nozzle at great velocity. The reaction of the water being forced out the stern forces the boat forward. Essentially, the engine provides the rotational force transmitted to the shaft and impeller. The motive force is provided by the difference in pressures between the front and rear of the impeller blades. See **Figure 23-10**. The low-pressure side draws water in, and the high-pressure side forces water out.

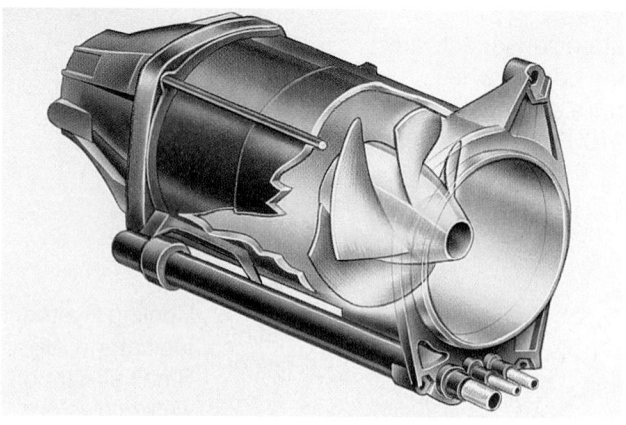

Polaris

Figure 23-9.

An axial flow jet pump with single impeller that is driven by a centrally located shaft is the major driving unit of the PWC.

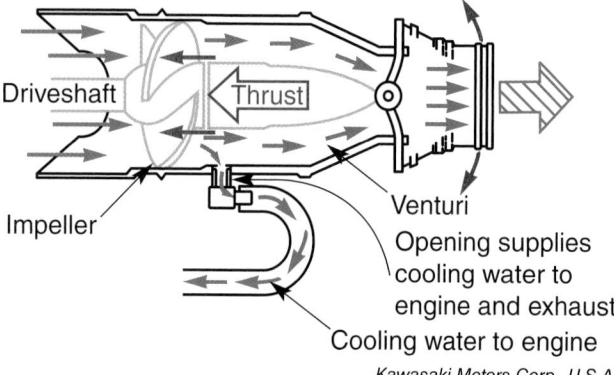

Kawasaki Motors Corp., U.S.A.

Figure 23-10.

The impeller draws water in and forces water out through the venturi, where velocity is increased before water jets out through the steering nozzle. The reactionary force, which is opposite the water direction, therefore forces the craft forward.

Performance of the PWC is closely related to the amount of pitch in the impeller blades and the horsepower of the engine The *pitch* of the impeller is the angular relationship of the blades to a line perpendicular to the shaft it is mounted on. See **Figure 23-11**. Racing craft have higher pitch impellers with high-horsepower engines to rotate them. Blade area and shape are also factors in attaining proper efficiency. To achieve both acceleration and top speed, blades may have low-pitch leading edges and high-pitch trailing edges. Impellers are precision machined, and foreign materials passing through them can cause minor to severe damage to their blades. See **Figure 23-12**.

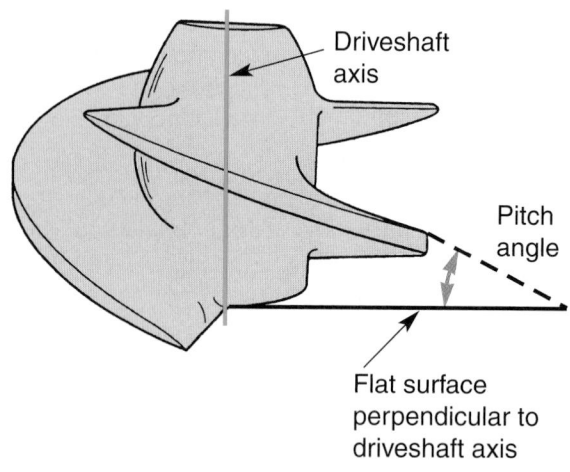

Sea-Doo

Figure 23-11.

The pitch of the impeller blades is the angle measured from the blade to a line perpendicular to the axis of the driveshaft.

Polaris; Sea-Doo

Figure 23-12.

Impellers are precision machined and can be damaged if abrasive materials such as sand or stones pass through them.

Figure 23-13 shows the internal components of an axial flow pump. *Stator vanes* reduce the tendency of the water to revolve as it enters the venturi. The venturi restriction causes the water to increase in velocity as it exits through the steering nozzle. The blade ends of the impeller rotate close to, but do not touch, the wear ring. Clearance is about .020″ (.5 mm). This clearance should be checked with a long feeler gauge at assembly.

In addition to providing propulsion for the PWC, the pump may provide cooling water circulation for the engine, as shown in **Figure 23-10**. Likewise, on some PWC, a bilge draining system is installed by creating a venturi vacuum to draw water out with water in the discharge nozzle. See **Figure 23-14**.

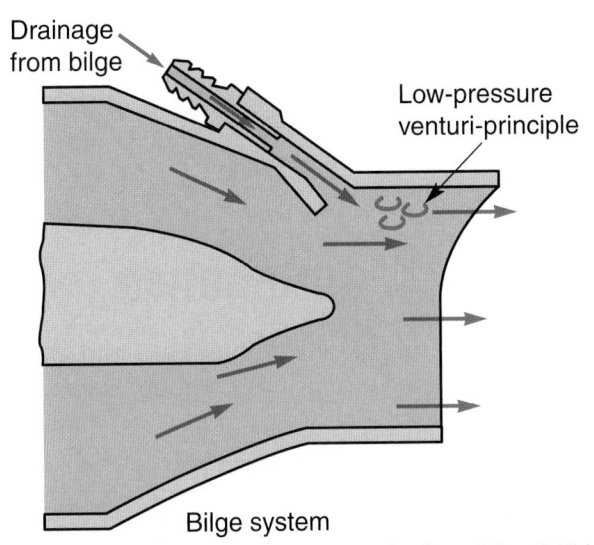

Goodheart-Willcox Publisher

Figure 23-14.

A low-pressure area in the venturi of the pump can be used to drain water from the bilge.

Note

The general relationship of parts for a PWC jet pump is shown in **Figure 23-15**. Study this Figure to become familiar with the jet pump parts.

New Engine Break-In

New PWC need a careful break-in period for the engine parts to wear in to each other to produce smooth, long-wearing surfaces. Overheating during this period due to improper use can do extreme damage to engine parts and shorten the engine's useful life.

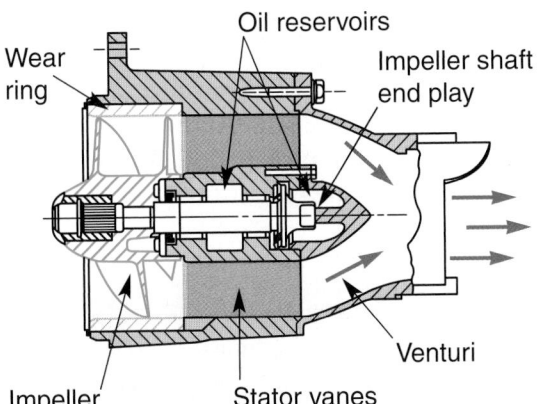

Sea-Doo

Figure 23-13.

The components of a jet pump are precisely fitted to each other and must be in exact alignment. Stator vanes in the housing reduce the rotational tendency of the water as it leaves the impeller. Lubrication is essential. Leaks cannot be tolerated in the shaft area.

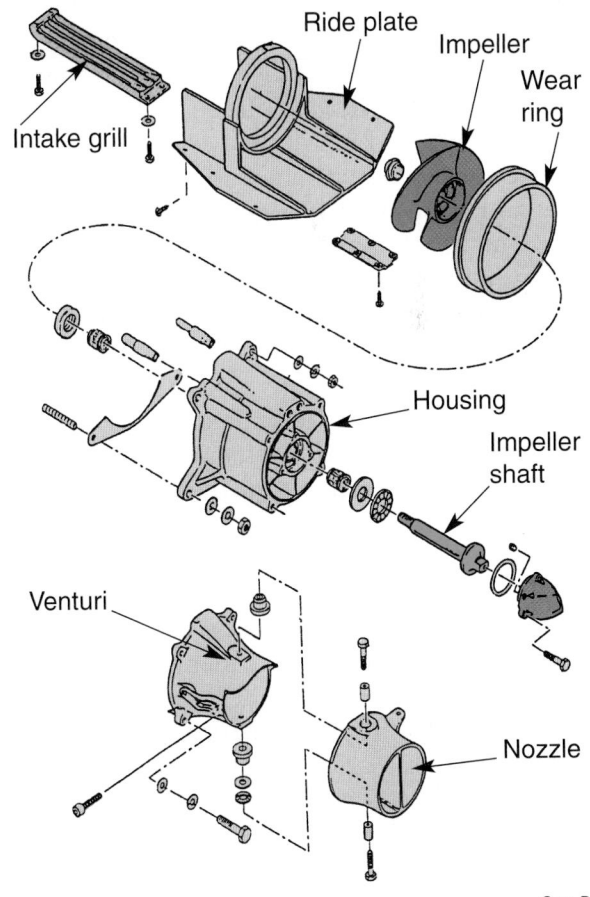

Sea-Doo

Figure 23-15.

Parts of a PWC jet pump and their general relative positions to one another. Engine driveshaft and coupling are not shown.

PWC engines vary and require the operator to follow the manufacturer's recommendations for the specific make and model engine in the watercraft. Break-in information is provided in the manufacturer's service manuals.

General Maintenance

PWC require proper maintenance and care to keep them in good operating condition. Even under ideal conditions, a certain amount of wear and deterioration of parts should be expected.

If extensive engine work is to be done, it will be necessary to have, or obtain, special tools designed by the manufacturer to properly do the job. Some of the tools are mandatory, others are recommended. Special pullers, drivers, installers, and gauges may be necessary. Of course, the type and extent of the work will determine the tools needed. If engine disassembly is needed, the engine will have to be removed from the PWC. This means all hoses and electrical connections must be removed. It also means the engine will have to be separated from the jet pump. The engine should be removed from the PWC and placed in a cradle in the shop. Never attempt engine removal while the PWC is in the water. Lifting the engine from the hull may require an engine hoist. Eye bolts or lifting lugs on the engine may be needed. Trying to manually lift an engine out of the hull could be dangerous. If the engine is dropped, damage may be caused to the engine, the hull, and the person lifting.

The most important information to have at hand when doing any kind of engine work is the manufacturer's service manuals for the PWC make and model. They will provide invaluable information about general PWC service, engine components, fuel and carburetion, electrical systems, lubrication system, cooling system, propulsion and drive system, steering system, hull and body maintenance, storage, and inspection.

In addition to the maintenance procedures outlined in Chapter 13 of this textbook, the following maintenance procedures should be performed when servicing a PWC.

Fuel Filter

The fuel filter for a PWC is usually an inline type. The location of the fuel filter may vary from one PWC to another. However, the filter will be installed in the fuel line between the fuel tank and the carburetor. Before removing the fuel filter, turn off the fuel valve at the fuel tank to prevent spillage. See the manufacturer's technical service manuals.

The fuel filter is designed to prevent water or dirt particles from entering the carburetor or injectors and engine. If foreign particles and/or water accumulate in the filter, replaced the filter with a new one.

Note

Inline fuel filters are sealed and are not serviceable.

Fuel Filter Screens

There may be fuel filter screens located at the fuel outlet of the fuel tank. The screens can be removed and cleaned or replaced. Always shut off the fuel tank valve before removing screens for inspection.

Fuel Vent Check Valve

A rubber vent hose is connected from the fuel tank to a sediment bowl. A *fuel vent check valve* mounted in the vent hose allows air to enter the fuel tank but minimizes fuel spillage if the PWC is overturned.

To examine the check valve, remove it from the system and test it by blowing through each end. Air should pass easily in one direction, and none should pass through in the opposite direction. If the valve fails either of these tests, it should be replaced. See **Figure 23-16**. An arrow on the valve indicates the direction of airflow. When installing the check valve in the line, this arrow should point toward the tank.

Warning

The fuel filler cap should be loosened to relieve tank pressure before disconnecting any lines in the system.

Sediment Bowl

The *sediment bowl*, located in the vent hose, prevents water from entering the fuel tank. The

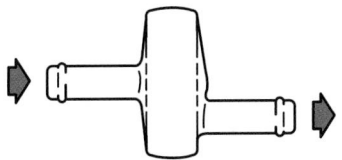

Air Should Pass This Direction

Air Should Not Pass This Direction

Kawasaki Motors Corp., U.S.A.

Figure 23-16.

Test the fuel vent check valve by blowing into it from each end. Air should pass through one direction only. If it fails, replace the valve. Install the valve with the arrow pointing toward the fuel tank.

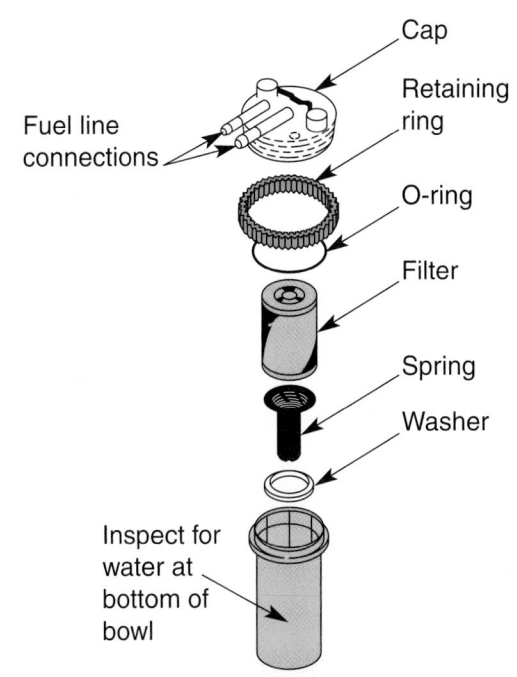

Polaris

Figure 23-17.

The sediment bowl retaining ring must be unscrewed to remove the bowl. Check the filter and clean the bowl. O-ring must be seated properly when assembling to avoid leakage.

sediment bowl can be disassembled, drained of any water, and cleaned. The sediment bowl retaining ring is unscrewed and the bowl removed. The bowl is sealed with an O-ring. The O-ring must be in place when the bowl is reassembled and the retaining ring is tightened. See **Figure 23-17**.

Carburetors

Idle speed is the lowest speed at which the engine will run slow and smoothly. An idle adjust screw is used to adjust the idle speed. If the screw is turned clockwise, the idle speed increases. If the screw is turned counterclockwise, the idle speed decreases. A good idle speed is about 250 rpm in the water and 700 rpm out of the water. To read the rpm, use a tachometer. Most PWC are equipped with a tachometer.

Carburetors for PWC engines are adjusted at the factory for best performance under most sea level conditions. It is recommended by the manufacturers that these settings not be changed. If the PWC is to be used at high altitudes, the air/fuel mixture will become richer due to the less dense air in the atmosphere. If the watercraft is to be used at altitudes above 3000' (914 m) mean sea level (MSL), the carburetor should be adjusted accordingly. For this operation, refer to the manufacturer's service information.

Figure 23-18 shows the external components of a PWC carburetor. There are a number of carburetor types. The type depends on the size and kind of engine the carburetor is used with.

Figure 23-19 shows the internal features of a carburetor. In this carburetor, fuel flow is divided between the main jet and the low-speed jet. In the low-speed circuit, fuel is routed by the bypass holes (transition circuit). Some of this fuel is drawn through the bypass holes as the throttle is opened and the throttle plate (butterfly valve) exposes the holes to the airflow. Fuel flowing to the low-speed outlet is metered by the low-speed adjuster. The ability for fuel to pass through the low-speed circuit and transition is controlled by *pop-off pressure* (lifting of the needle from its seat) at the needle valve assembly and then by the size of the low-speed jet. If the low-speed jet is changed, it affects the mixture at idle and speeds other than idle.

In the high-speed circuit, fuel flow is divided at the main jet. This means even if the high-speed adjuster is fully closed, fuel would still pass through the jet.

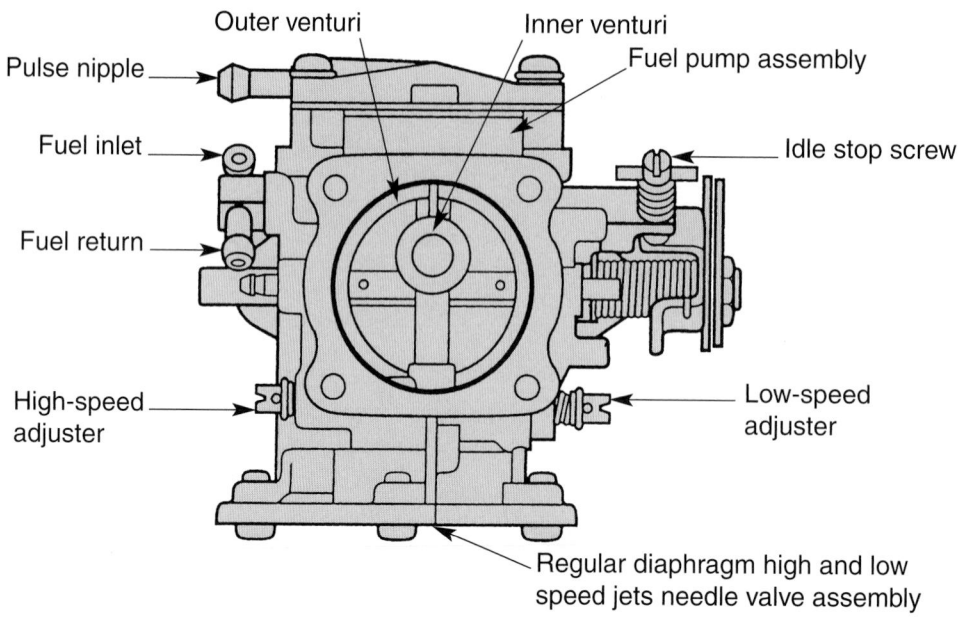

Pulse nipple

Fuel inlet

Fuel return

High-speed adjuster

Outer venturi

Inner venturi

Fuel pump assembly

Idle stop screw

Low-speed adjuster

Regular diaphragm high and low speed jets needle valve assembly

Sea-Doo

Figure 23-18.

Shown are the external parts of one type of PWC carburetor.

There is a relationship between the arm spring and the needle in the needle valve assembly. The spring exerts a pressure through the arm onto the needle. The size of the hole in the valve seat contributes to the performance of the carburetor in several ways. First, and most importantly, the hole size helps determine pop-off pressure. Four things combine to create the pop-off pressure:

- Vacuum created within the carburetor body (manifold pressure).
- Atmospheric pressure.
- Arm spring pressure.
- Fuel pressure acting on the needle valve.

Fuel pressure acts against the exposed end of the needle valve. For example, with a 2.0 size needle valve, the fuel pressure pushes against the needle with a certain force. If a larger 2.5 needle is used with the same spring, the fuel has a larger surface to push against and can move the needle more easily. Therefore, increasing needle valve size effectively decreases pop-off pressure; decreasing needle valve size will increase pop-off pressure.

Note

The principles of hydraulics apply when figuring the changes in needle size and its relationship to the change in pop-off pressure.

The arm spring can also be changed to accommodate adjustment. The manufacturer of the carburetor in **Figure 23-19** provides four springs with different gram ratings of stiffness. It also provides a reference chart to obtain approximate pop-off pressures with spring pressure and needle valve combinations.

Study the carburetor diagram in **Figure 23-19**. Examine how the fuel flow is affected by the varying throttle settings. Airflow through the carburetor is from right to left.

Cooling System Service

Open cooling systems must be protected from accumulating salt deposits and sand. To prevent this, the system must be thoroughly flushed with fresh water. This should be done after every use in saltwater. If used in fresh water, the system should be flushed as directed or whenever there appears to be reduced water flow from the bleed outlets. See **Figure 23-8**. These outlets are located on the hull of the craft at the stern. An open cooling system should be flushed clean before any extended storage period. The procedure for flushing is also used for providing auxiliary cooling water during out-of-water maintenance checks.

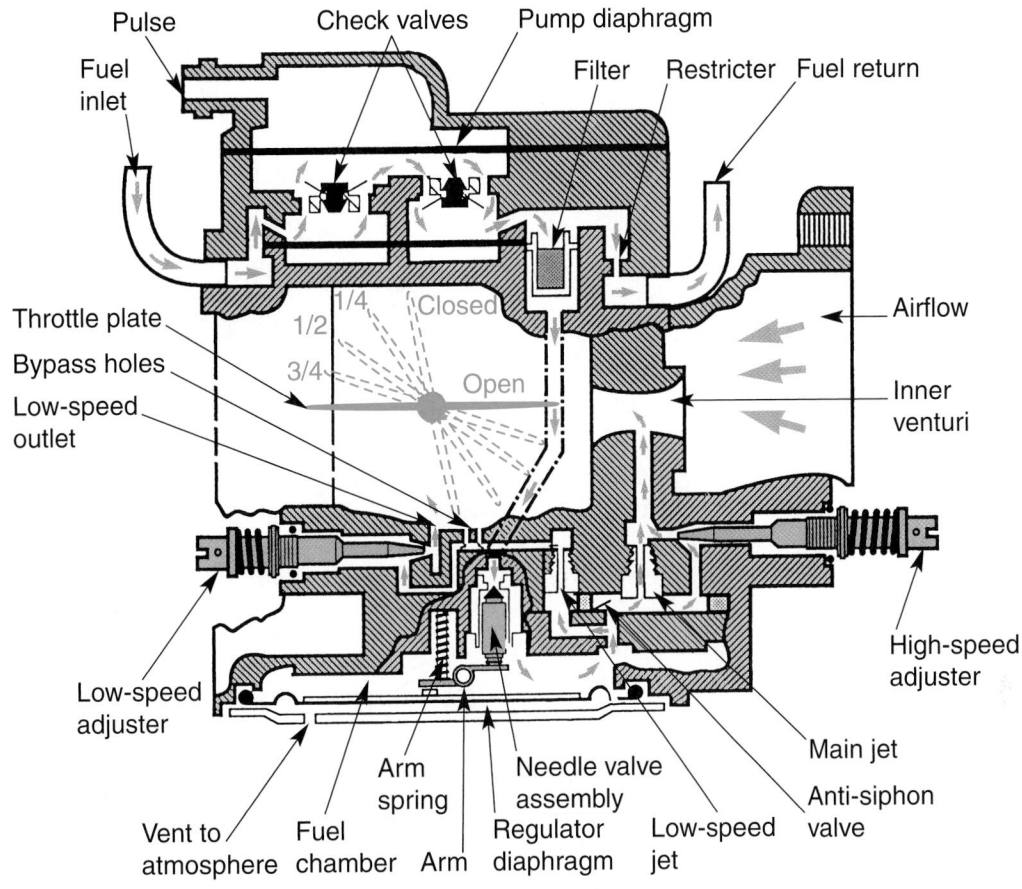

Pulse   Check valves   Pump diaphragm

Fuel inlet   Filter   Restricter   Fuel return

Throttle plate   Airflow

Bypass holes

Low-speed outlet   Inner venturi

1/4   Closed
1/2
3/4   Open

High-speed adjuster

Low-speed adjuster

Main jet

Anti-siphon valve

Arm spring   Needle valve assembly

Vent to atmosphere   Fuel chamber   Arm   Regulator diaphragm   Low-speed jet

Sea-Doo

Figure 23-19.

Shown are the internal features of one type of PWC carburetor. Airflow is from right to left. Internal features of carburetor showing fuel flow at idle speed setting. Notice bypass holes in relationship to the position of throttle plate; closed through full throttle settings.

Operating in shallow or dirty water will require more frequent flushing than operating in deep, clear fresh water. Beaching a PWC with the engine running should always be avoided. If the PWC is beached, the cooling system must be flushed before the engine is run again or severe engine damage will result.

To flush the open cooling system of a PWC, proceed as follows:

Caution

Always follow the manufacturer's recommended procedure for flushing the watercraft cooling system to avoid engine damage. Never flush a hot engine. Severe engine damage could result.

Warning

Do not touch any electrical part when the engine is running. Severe injury or death could result.

1. Remove the seat.
2. Locate the inlet for auxiliary cooling water. Refer to manufacturer's service manuals for this location.
3. If a special adapter is required, install it and fasten a garden hose as directed in the manufacturer's service manuals. If a fitting is already installed for attaching a garden hose, follow the prescribed procedure in the manufacturer's service manuals.
4. Start the engine, allowing it to idle *before* turning on the water.

5. Turn the water on immediately (within 10 seconds) after the engine is started. Remember, the engine should never be run longer than 15 seconds without cooling water.
6. Adjust the water flow so that a small trickle of water discharges from the bypass outlet of the hull.
7. Slightly *rev* the engine (increase engine speed) intermittently for one or two minutes to flush the system completely.
8. Turn off the water. Turn off the engine within 10 seconds.
9. Remove the garden hose and reassemble hoses and clamps, or install the plug in accordance with the instructions in the manufacturer's service manuals.

Closed, or pressurized, cooling systems must be periodically drained, flushed, and refilled with the correct mixture of water and antifreeze. The general procedure for servicing a pressurized cooling system is covered in Chapter 12. Refer to the manufacturer's service information for specific instructions.

Flushing the Bilge

The **bilge** is the inside bottom of the hull of a PWC. Some PWC have a drain plug in the stern to drain water that may accumulate in the bilge. See **Figure 23-20**. To flush and drain the bilge, the PWC should be removed from the water, the plug removed, and bilge water allowed to drain completely. Flush the bilge with fresh water and continue to drain the remaining water. The bilge should be wiped dry with towels or shop cloths. Reinstall the plug securely before launching the PWC.

Some PWC have automatic bilge draining systems. These systems also need flushing with fresh water and will require certain hoses and fittings to be disconnected. A garden hose is connected to the hoses and fresh water turned on for flushing of the system. During this procedure, water may flow into the engine compartment. Do not allow a large amount of water to enter the engine compartment. Remove the drain plug in the stern of the watercraft and drain *all* the water from the engine compartment.

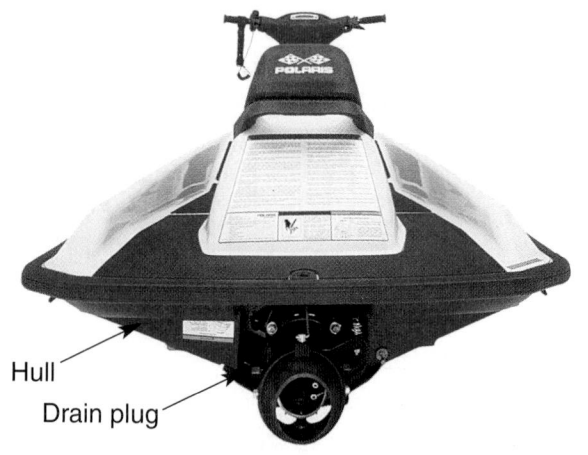

Hull

Drain plug

Polaris

Figure 23-20.

The drain screw or plug must be secured to avoid taking on water during riding.

Jet Pump Water Inlet Screen

The purpose of the **water inlet screen** is to prevent grass and debris from entering the engine cooling system. See **Figure 23-21**. The water inlet screen is located inside the stationary nozzle of the jet pump. The screen should be visually inspected for buildup of any contaminants and debris. Clean the screen as needed by flushing the engine and

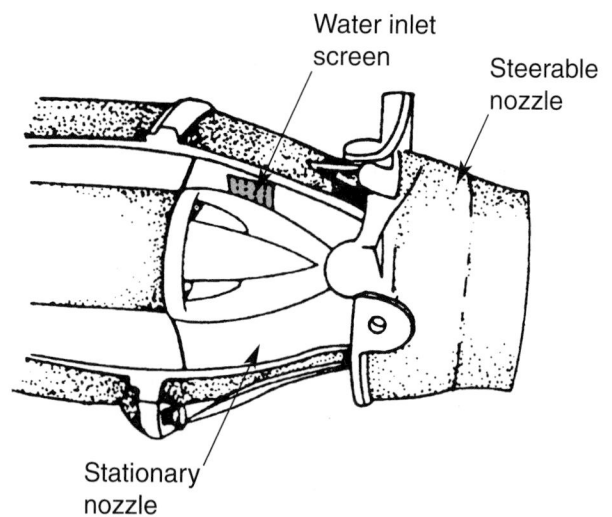

Water inlet screen

Steerable nozzle

Stationary nozzle

Polaris

Figure 23-21.

The jet pump water inlet screen must be inspected for foreign materials. If cooling water to the engine cannot pass through this screen, the engine will overheat and seize, causing severe damage.

screen. If the water inlet screen becomes plugged with contaminants, the engine will overheat. In such a case, the PWC should be stopped immediately to avoid serious internal engine damage.

External Lubrication Points

Because of exposure to corrosive elements in water and atmospheric conditions, proper lubrication of all moving parts is essential to maintain good performance and extend the useful life of the PWC. Grease used for PWC is special marine grease that is water and salt resistant. At points where grease should be applied, always use the type specified for the particular PWC being treated. The following are common locations on the PWC that require periodic lubrication:

- Throttle cable and choke cable—Special cable lube is used to lubricate the inner cables. The throttle lever should be depressed and cable lube squirted onto the cable. The lubricant is worked down the cable by pushing and releasing the throttle several times. The choke cable is lubricated similarly. See **Figure 23-22**.
- Steering cable joints and inner wire— Lubricate the same way as the throttle cable and choke cable. Lubricate the steering nozzle ends and handlebar ends. Seals can be moved to allow oil to enter into the cables. Replace the seals after oiling.

- Steering nozzle pivot shaft—Lubricate the pivot connections.
- Steering handle pivot shaft—Lubricate the shaft and bushing. Tighten the shaft if it has loosened.
- Seat latch and hooks—Grease the locking mechanism.
- Carburetor—Grease springs, exposed portions of cable, and shafts at the carburetor. If the PWC is used in saltwater, grease more often.
- Electrical connections—Apply dielectric grease to battery posts and exposed cable connections.

Depending on the make and model of the PWC, additional components may need lubrication. Refer to the manufacturer's technical service manuals for procedures and the specific kinds of lubricants to use.

Transporting PWC

It is common practice to transport PWC on trailers. Trailers are commercially available to handle one PWC or two PWC side by side. See **Figure 23-23**. All-aluminum trailers are corrosion resistant, light, and easy to handle. The trailer should be equipped with greasable, sealed wheel bearings to prevent water from entering the bearings. See **Figure 23-24**. If the wheel bearings are not sealed and water enters them, they will corrode and eventually fail. Grease fittings on the axle hub caps permit pressure

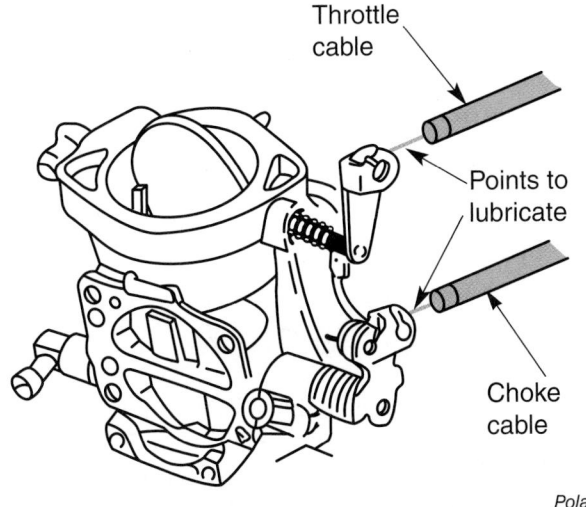

Polaris

Figure 23-22.
Grease springs and exposed portions of cable and shafts at the carburetor. Use the specified waterproof grease.

Featherlite Trailers

Figure 23-23.
Trailers are available for towing one or two PWC. The trailers should have proper supports and tie-down equipment. Running lights and license illumination are required.

Dutton-Lainson Co.

Figure 23-24.

The trailer should be equipped with greasable, sealed wheel bearings to prevent water from entering the bearings. Grease fittings on the axle hub caps permit pressure greasing with waterproof wheel-bearing grease.

greasing with a hand grease gun without removing the wheels and wheel bearings from the axles. Waterproof wheel-bearing grease should always be used.

PWC trailers are often backed down a launch ramp and the wheels are submerged until the PWC floats off the trailer. To put the PWC on the trailer, the trailer is lowered down the ramp, and the PWC floated up to it. The bow of the PWC is hooked to the trailer, and the PWC is pulled onto the trailer. The trailer and PWC can then be pulled out of the water.

The watercraft should be securely fastened to the trailer. A *bow line*, usually a cable or line (rope) attached to the trailer or winch, holds the bow in place. See **Figure 23-25**. Manufacturers provide a tie-down at the bow of the PWC for this purpose.

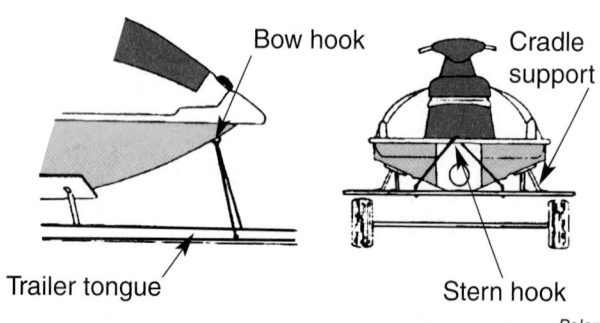

Bow hook   Cradle support

Trailer tongue   Stern hook

Polaris

Figure 23-25.

Fore and aft tie downs secure the PWC for towing, while the hull rests on cradle pads.

The stern of the craft should also be tied down to the trailer. Tie-downs, or boarding handles, at the stern may be used to fasten a line to the trailer frame. Additional tie-down lines may be used between the bow and stern for additional security. Study the manufacturer's service manuals for the recommended method of securing the craft to a trailer.

It is important that the trailer cradle supports be located properly so the weight of the craft and road bumps do not damage the hull. It may be important to avoid supporting the hull at particular places to prevent exceeding strength limits. A cracked hull can surely spoil a long anticipated day of recreation for the owner. To protect the overall appearance and keep the craft clean while trailering over long distances, an opaque fitted cover can be used.

When transporting a PWC, the fuel valve should always be turned to the *Off* position. The seat should be latched and compartment doors secured. The trailer should be matched to the PWC weight and hull configuration. Adjustments to the trailer cradle, rollers, and/or pads are possible to conform to the hull shape and length. Abide by the trailer laws and regulations for the area in which it will be used. Proper trailer licensing and lights are mandatory.

Running lights, stop lights, and turn signals are required. These must be functioning any time the trailer is being towed on the road. A locking trailer hitch on the trailer tongue must conform to the weight of the trailer and include safety chains. The ball hitch on the towing vehicle must also be securely attached and conform to the weight of the trailer and PWC being towed. Electrical connections for the trailer lights should have a quick-disconnect receptacle with a ground wire to the vehicle ground. Grounding through the ball hitch is not proper due to grease, corrosion, and constant movement between the ball and the hitch. If this is done, lights will be dim, flash intermittently, and may be entirely out of service at times.

Towing PWC to Shore

It is entirely possible that a PWC might need to be towed to shore by another watercraft. Running out of reserve fuel, engine problems, a dead battery, or other complications could necessitate such towing. To accomplish this, tie one end of a 20' (6 m) line to the bow of the dead PWC. Attach the other end to the towboat. Towing must be done slowly at idle speed. Do not exceed 5 mph (8 km/h).

PWC Storage

When preparing a PWC for off-season storage, some preventive maintenance is recommended to preserve the PWC and its components. By taking a few precautions at the time of storage, the PWC will be ready to ride the next season with minimum preparation. The following are the steps for preparing the PWC for storage:

1. If the PWC is equipped with an open cooling system, flush the entire system with fresh water and dry. See the *Cooling System Service* section in this chapter.
2. Inspect and clean the jet pump intake, outlet, and impeller area. These components should receive service at this time if any damage is observed.
3. Make sure the exhaust system is drained and dry. Do this by starting the engine and briefly rev the engine.

Warning

Gasoline fumes are highly flammable and can be explosive under certain conditions. Do not smoke. Make sure the area is well ventilated and free from any source of flame or sparks; including appliance pilot lights.

4. If it is desired to leave gasoline in the fuel tank during storage, add fuel stabilizer to the fuel in the tank, fill the tank with gasoline, and replace the cap. The stabilizer will prevent varnish from forming. Filling the fuel tank will prevent condensation of water in the tank. After adding stabilizer and filling the tank with gasoline, run the engine briefly to circulate the stabilizer through the carburetor. An alternate method is to starve the engine of gas. To do this, add the stabilizer to the fuel tank and then shut off the fuel from the tank with the shut-off valve. Now, run the engine at low speed until it starves of fuel. Because it may take longer than 15 seconds to starve the engine of fuel, this procedure must be done with cooling water circulating in the engine. If cooling water is not used, stop the engine

after 10 seconds, let it cool 5 minutes, and repeat the process until the engine starves and stops by itself. When the engine has stopped, leave the fuel shut-off valve in the Off position. This method removes all fuel from inside the carburetor(s) and prevents varnish buildup during storage.

If it is desired that the fuel tank be completely emptied for storage, drain the tank with a fuel siphon, or hand-operated pump. Leave the fuel tank cap loose. This will allow air to circulate in the tank and prevent water condensation. Fogging the engine with rust-preventive oil and drying out the carburetors can be done simultaneously.

5. Fog the engine with a rust-preventive oil by following the procedures on the can. Fogging oil is available from the PWC dealer or an automotive service store. The fogging oil will protect the internal components of the engine, such as cylinders and rings, bearings, crankshaft, etc.

Note

Instead of fogging the engine, you can remove the spark plugs and pour about one tablespoon of two-cycle engine oil into each cylinder.

6. Inspect the spark plug condition. Spread a small quantity of antiseize grease on the spark plug threads and reinstall old plugs or replace with new plugs as needed. Tighten plugs with a torque wrench to 13 lb-ft to 15 lb-ft. Do not overtighten.
7. Lubricate the choke, throttle, and steering cables. See *External Lubrication Points* section in this chapter.
8. Lubricate all other areas described in *External Lubrication Points* section in this chapter.
9. Drain the bilge and engine area by removing the drain plug. Cleaning may be done with hot water and mild detergent (dish soap). Rinse and drain. Dry remaining water with clean, absorbent towels. Leave the drain open and prop up the seat 1″ to 2″ during storage. This prevents condensation from forming in the engine compartment.
10. Coat the engine and engine compartment with a protective spray and lubricant. These are available for use on the engine and in the engine compartment.

11. Wash the exterior of the PWC with fresh water and mild detergent. Rinse thoroughly. Protect and shine the exterior with a nonabrasive silicone wax. The seat and other vinyl surfaces can be protected with a vinyl protector.

Caution

Never use strong detergents, abrasives, degreasers, paint thinner, acetone, window cleaners, ammonia, or products containing alcohol for cleaning the PWC. They can cause damage to finishes, decals, vinyl and plastics and accelerate UV breakdown. This breakdown can cause color change and early deterioration of parts.

12. Place an opaque cover over the PWC during storage to keep it clean. Store it in a cool, dry place.

Summary

The term *personal watercraft* is used to describe a particular type of popular small boat that is propelled and guided by a high-velocity jet of water. PWC are powered by an inboard engine that has an axial jet pump mechanism.

The engine and hull identification numbers are used to register a PWC. These numbers are the only way of positively identifying one PWC from another. They are unique numbers and may also be needed when ordering parts.

PWC are available in several types. They vary in performance, stability, and the amount of skill necessary to operate them. Some are operated in a sitting position and others are operated in a kneeling or standing position. Before servicing a PWC, you should be familiar with the common components and parts.

Engines used in PWC are precision-built machines. These engines are multi-cylinder, two- or four-cycle, water-cooled, high-speed engines. A service technician should become familiar with the parts of these engines and their function, as well as the cooling and jet propulsion systems. There are a number of cooling systems used in PWC engines. They all work by circulating water around engine parts.

The jet pump is an axial flow device, which means it has a single impeller driven by a centrally located shaft. Other than the engine, it is the major component that drives the PWC. It provides thrust in water similar to the way a jet engine produces thrust in air. The impeller draws water in through the grate screen on the bottom of the hull and forces it out through a discharge nozzle at great velocity. The reaction of the water being forced out the stern forces the boat forward.

Performance of the PWC is closely related to the amount of pitch in the impeller blades and the horsepower of the engine. The pitch of the impeller is the angular relationship of the blades to a line perpendicular to the shaft the impeller is mounted on.

New PWC need a careful break-in period for the engine parts to wear in to each other to produce smooth, long wearing surfaces. Overheating during this period due to improper use can do extreme damage to engine parts and shorten the engine's useful life.

PWC require proper maintenance and care to keep them in good operating condition. Even under ideal conditions, a certain amount of wear and deterioration of parts will occur.

If extensive engine work is to be done, it will be necessary to have, or obtain, special tools designed by the manufacturer to properly do the job. The most important documents to have at hand to do any kind of engine work are the manufacturer's service manuals for the engine make and model.

The fuel filter is designed to prevent water or dirt particles from entering the carburetor and engine. If foreign particles and/or water accumulate in the filter, it should be replaced with a new one. There may be fuel filter screens located at the fuel outlet of the fuel tank. The screens can be removed and cleaned or replaced. A fuel vent check valve mounted in the vent hose allows air to enter the fuel tank but minimizes fuel spillage if the PWC is overturned. The sediment bowl, located in the vent hose, prevents water from entering the fuel tank. The sediment bowl can be disassembled, drained of any water, and cleaned.

Open cooling systems must be protected from accumulating salt deposits and sand. To prevent this, the system must be thoroughly flushed out with fresh water. This should be done after every use in saltwater. If used in fresh water, the system should be flushed as directed or whenever there appears to be reduced water flow from the bleed outlets. Operating in shallow or dirty water will require more frequent flushing than operating in deep, clear fresh water. Closed cooling systems must be periodically drained, flushed, and refilled.

The bilge is the inside bottom of the hull of a PWC. Some PWC have a drain plug in the stern to drain water that may accumulate in the bilge. The purpose of the water inlet screen is to prevent grass and debris from entering the engine cooling system. The screen should be visually inspected for buildup of any contaminants and debris.

Because of exposure to corrosive elements in water and atmospheric conditions, proper lubrication of all moving parts is essential to maintain good performance and extend the useful life of the PWC.

When transporting a PWC, the fuel valve should always be turned to the *Off* position. The seat should be latched and compartment doors secured. The trailer should be matched to the PWC weight and hull configuration.

When preparing a PWC for off-season storage, some preventive maintenance is recommended to preserve the PWC and its components.

Review Questions

Answer the following questions using the information provided in this chapter.

1. A personal watercraft is propelled and guided by a high-velocity jet of _____.
2. What is the significance of the engine and hull identification numbers?
3. A(n) _____ on the PWC stops the engine immediately if the operator falls overboard.
4. What is the purpose of the reserve setting on the fuel selection valve?
5. Explain the purpose of the reverse bucket.
6. The drain plug can be used to remove water that accumulates in the _____.
7. The _____ prevents large debris from entering the jet pump.
   A. outlet nozzle
   B. intake grate
   C. bilge pump
   D. None of the above.
8. The _____ draws water into the jet pump intake.
9. The engines used in PWC are _____.
   A. two-cycle
   B. four-cycle
   C. air-cooled
   D. Either A or B.
13. PWC engine cylinders and cylinder heads are _____ to allow cooling water to circulate.
14. The _____ of the impeller is the angular relationship of the blades to a line perpendicular to the shaft the impeller is mounted on.
15. What is the purpose of the stator vanes on an axial flow pump?
16. Why must a new engine be broken in?
17. The most important documents to have on hand when performing engine work are the _____.

18. The _____ is located at the fuel outlet of the fuel tank.
    A. fuel filter
    B. sediment bowl
    C. fuel filter screen
    D. None of the above.
19. *True or False?* An open cooling system should be flushed every time the PWC is used in saltwater.
20. The _____ is the inside bottom of the hull of a PWC.
21. What will happen if the water inlet screen becomes clogged with contaminants?
22. Why must the cradle supports be located properly when fastening a PWC to a trailer?
23. When storing a PWC for an extended period, fuel _____ should be added to the tank to prevent varnish from forming.
24. What is the purpose of fogging oil?
25. The exterior surface of the PWC should be cleaned with a(n) _____ before it is put into storage.
    A. abrasive cleanser
    B. ammonia-based cleaner
    C. alcohol-based product
    D. None of the above.

Suggested Activities

1. Identify the major parts of a PWC.
2. Demonstrate proper cooling system flushing procedures.
3. Demonstrate proper engine and systems maintenance.
4. Demonstrate how to launch or remove a PWC from the water and secure it and a trailer for towing.

Career Opportunities and Certification

Learning Objectives

After studying this chapter, you will be able to:

- Identify several career opportunities in the small gas engine field.
- Discuss the factors that should be taken into account when exploring career options.
- Prepare a letter of application and résumé.
- List qualities that are essential for anyone pursuing a career in small engines.
- Identify the benefits of EETC certification.

Key Terms

abilities
apprenticeship
aptitude
critical-thinking skills
engine service technicians
engineers
entrepreneurs
Equipment & Engine Training Council (EETC)
ethical behavior
general manager
internship
job application form
job interview
job shadowing
leadership
letter of application
letters of recommendation
lifelong learning
manufacturer's technicians
mentor
networking
reference
résumé
sales managers
service managers
service representatives
transferable skills

Career Opportunities in the Small Gas Engine Field

The small gas engine field offers career opportunities in three different areas: service, sales, and manufacturing. Through training, study, and work experience, you can become an engine service technician, service manager, sales manager, or general manager of a small engine service center. You can also be a manufacturer's technician, service representative, or engineer.

Engine Service Technician

Implement sales facilities and equipment rental centers need *engine service technicians* to do tune-ups, service equipment, and make repairs. Often,

the quality of workmanship and reliability of the technician who services the customers' equipment directly affects the reputation and sales volume of the business.

Small gas engine service technicians must be able to diagnose engine troubles and make appropriate repairs and/or part replacements. See **Figure 24-1**. They should be able to analyze the mechanical condition and performance of an engine and make proper recommendations to the owner. A service technician should also be competent in the use of test equipment and thoroughly familiar with manufacturers' technical service manuals.

Good service technicians keep their tools and equipment in first-class condition and organized for convenient use. They must have specialty tools (pullers, drivers, etc.), which are available from the engine manufacturers or tool manufacturers. Small

Goodheart-Willcox Publisher

Figure 24-1.

A small gas engine service technician must know engine construction and principles of operation. Technicians must be proficient in troubleshooting, maintenance, service, and repair. Notice the certified EETC technician arm patch.

gas engine technicians must know how to use micrometers and dial indicators. Basic machining and welding experience is also desirable.

Engine service technicians generally receive their training at technical career centers or vocational schools. Most engine manufacturers have their own training programs for service personnel. Certification tests are available. See the *Certification* section in this chapter for more information.

Service Manager

There are numerous opportunities as service managers in small gas engine shops with more than one service technician. *Service managers* are responsible for quality workmanship and satisfactory shop operation. They must plan and supervise the activities of all service department employees.

Service managers discuss service problems with customers, make recommendations, write job tickets, and assign work to the technicians. They handle customer complaints, are responsible for the training of apprentices, and inspect all finished repair work. They report directly to the general manager or the owner of the service facility.

Sales Manager

Sales managers are needed to sell or rent implements and vehicles that utilize small gasoline engines. Some sales managers handle a variety of products, such as yard and farm equipment, marine and sports vehicles, construction equipment, and emergency repair or rescue equipment. Others specialize in one field or sell a few closely related products such as personal watercraft, motorcycles, all-terrain vehicles (ATVs), and snowmobiles.

The geographical location of a sales or rental business often determines the type of vehicle or equipment that is most in demand by the consumer. Gasoline engine applications are numerous, and new uses are being developed each year.

General Manager

Managing a successful small engine sales and service business requires experience and education. Keeping accurate sales and service records, budgeting, promoting sales, and maintaining adequate tools, parts, supplies, and accessories are just a few of the responsibilities of the *general manager.*

The general manager must have a sincere, personal commitment to provide fair, quality service to customers. Often, a mechanic or salesperson works up to this position through years of work experience and college courses in business and management.

Manufacturer's Technician

Small gas engine manufacturers need people to develop prototype engines or engine parts and test new design theories. See **Figure 24-2.** *Manufacturer's technicians* need to be skilled in the use of tools, materials, and machine processes in order to produce a special part or engine unit. They are usually required to run exhaustive tests using dynamometers and other specialized testing equipment, observing and recording test results.

Technicians are generally involved with experiments, tests, and analysis of various engine systems and designs in the plant and in actual field use. When testing is completed, they present the test results and recommend changes to engineers and others involved in the project. Their observations and recommendations may be presented orally or in writing. Therefore, they must be able to

Briggs & Stratton Corp.

Figure 24-2.
Manufacturer's technicians help small gas engine manufacturers develop prototype engines or engine parts and test new design theories.

communicate in clear, technical language. This requires adequate communicative skills combined with technical talents.

Many colleges, technical institutes, and universities offer programs for technicians. Engine mechanics can become technicians if they have the desire to further their education through evening courses and service training programs.

Service Representative

Small gas engine manufacturers may train certain employees with broad service experience to become *service representatives*. These representatives are required to work closely with service managers and mechanics in the field to catch and correct chronic service problems. In some cases, service representatives write and distribute service bulletins concerning these problems. They also meet with and report findings to company engineers involved in engine design.

Engineer

Manufacturers need *engineers* to design engines that will perform satisfactorily under specific environmental conditions. For example, a small gas engine designed for use in a garden tractor is quite different from one intended for use in a chain saw.

Engineers must use their knowledge of scientific principles to design and create engines that will meet all the specified operating requirements.

Engineers usually have college engineering degrees. Sometimes, however, an engineer's license can be obtained by passing special examinations. Engineers must have a strong background in science, mathematics, and many specialized technical subjects, such as electronics, drafting, or fluid power. They must be analytical and creative, with a practical knowledge of manufacturing processes and materials.

Executive

Any of the careers outlined in this chapter can serve as stepping stones to high-level management positions in the small gas engine field. Many of the successful executives in this field began their careers in engine production, design, sales, or service. Almost invariably, the key to their success is learning to do the job at hand to the best of their ability.

Entrepreneur

Many people in the small gas engine field start their own business. These people are called *entrepreneurs*. See **Figure 24-3**. Entrepreneurs must have a total understanding of the managerial,

Goodheart-Willcox Publisher

Figure 24-3.
The entrepreneurs who own this lawn and garden shop sell, service, and repair small gas engine–powered equipment. In addition to technical knowledge about small gas engines, they must have a complete understanding of the managerial and financial aspects of the business.

financial, and technical aspects of the small engine business.

There are several advantages associated with owning a business. As the owner, you have total control over the way a business grows and develops. You have the opportunity to hire and train people as you desire. Additionally, your income is only limited by the success of your business.

On the other hand, owning a business can be extremely difficult. Entrepreneurs work very long hours trying to establish and maintain a profitable business. They also take many risks to get the new business started. Most entrepreneurs spend years repaying loans that were taken to go into business. Entrepreneurs are responsible for these loans even if their business fails.

Teacher

Teaching is a rewarding career choice for many individuals. The industrial technology and vocational education teaching field can use qualified teachers with knowledge of small gas engines. To teach at the high school or vocational school level, a college degree with a specialization in teaching is required. Teaching certification is obtained in the state in which one wishes to teach at one of these levels. This type of teaching is a rewarding career for individuals who enjoy working with young people.

In addition to hiring certified teachers, many community colleges hire teachers that have extensive industry-related experiences, as well as the aptitude for teaching. Manufacturers also hire teachers to come to their facility and teach service courses to mechanics and technicians.

Considering Career Options

Preparing for a meaningful career requires advance planning. This involves setting goals, which are aims or targets a person tries to achieve. Before you can set career goals, you must consider your values, which are beliefs or ideas about what is important. You also need to identify your interests, abilities, and aptitudes. You can then determine which occupations match your aptitudes, abilities, and interests.

Once you decide which careers interest you, begin to evaluate other important factors. Among these are the kind of wages you might earn and the education or training you would need. Knowing the job duties and responsibilities will also impact your decision.

Examining Career Interests

Few people entering the workforce know exactly what career they want. Sometimes adults who have prepared for one career decide they want to pursue another. As you grow older, you may notice that your interests change. This is normal. Active people are constantly developing new interests.

Usually a person's interests parallel his or her likes. If you enjoy working with your hands and enjoy diagnosing problems, you may enjoy a career as a small engine technician. However, if you dislike that type of work, a job involving these tasks is definitely not for you. By reviewing your likes and dislikes, you will get a better picture of the tasks you would enjoy in a career. See **Figure 24-4**.

Determining Aptitudes and Abilities

Career planning cannot take place until you know what you can do well. An *aptitude*, or natural talent, is an ability to learn something quickly and easily. Are some of your subjects in school much easier than others? Knowing this can help determine some of your talents. You may not be aware of all of your aptitudes if you have never been challenged to use them. A school counselor can give you an aptitude test to help reveal your strengths.

Abilities are skills you develop with practice. As you prepare to handle a new responsibility, you will learn that it requires certain skills. It is impossible to excel at every skill, so find out what you can do well.

Considering Earning Levels

You will want to check average earnings before choosing a career. What is the average beginning pay? What does it take to achieve higher earnings? Are additional degrees or training generally required?

When checking pay levels for various careers, you can expect professional positions to get higher pay. Entry-level employees make the least. As you work your way up from entry-level, your pay generally increases. This is because your knowledge and skills also increase, and they are worth more to your employer.

Grandpa/Shutterstock.com

Figure 24-4.
Small engine and equipment repair can be a rewarding career choice for those who enjoy working with their hands.

Investigating Education and Training

You will need to consider what educational level is necessary for entering each career you investigate. How much training or experience is needed? Can people enter the field with less training and acquire expertise while working on the job? Are special certificates, licenses, or credentials needed?

Before deciding on a specific career, you may wish to shadow someone who holds the type of job you desire. *Job shadowing* is the process of observing a person in the workplace to learn more about his or her job and its requirements. In addition, you may seek to have a mentor's assistance. A *mentor* is someone with greater experience and knowledge who guides you in your career.

You might also consider assisting someone who knows how to do the job tasks well, such as working in an internship or apprenticeship. An

internship is an arrangement with an educational institution whereby a student is supervised while working with a more experienced jobholder. An *apprenticeship* involves learning a trade under the direction and guidance of an expert worker. You also gain valuable experience through working at a part-time job or volunteering at community or charitable organizations.

Perhaps your plan of study leads you to acquire a license or become certified. Other programs may require a college degree.

Learning about Job Duties and Responsibilities

It is important to find out exactly what a job entails. Remember, you will be fulfilling these duties every day for many years. If they do not sound appealing now, it is unlikely that you will enjoy them in a few years' time. When exploring different occupations, look carefully at what each involves and what is expected of the jobholder. Also study the qualifications for entering that field.

Considering Your Personal Traits

Some people have personality traits that are in conflict with the requirements of certain occupations. Choosing one of these occupations would not lead to career satisfaction or success. For instance, if you are outgoing, you may not enjoy work that requires a more reserved person. If you prefer a routine, you may resent a job that involves constant change. Think carefully about your personality while you are exploring career choices and keep your strongest characteristics in mind.

Thinking about Lifestyle

The career you choose affects your lifestyle in many ways. It affects your income, which determines how much you can spend on housing, clothing, food, and luxury items. Your career choice may also affect where you live. You will want to locate where the work is plentiful. If you prefer not to live in a large city, you should be sure to choose work that is available in other areas.

Your friendships are affected by your career choice, too. You are likely to become friends with some of your work associates. You may meet other friends through the people you know from work.

Your leisure time is affected by the hours and vacation policies of your job. If you prefer to work weekdays from 9 to 5, you should avoid jobs that require overtime, late shifts, or working weekends.

Researching Employment Outlook

In 10 years, will the need for a certain career increase, stay the same, or decrease compared to average employment trends? Are too many people flocking to a field that is not growing? If the employment outlook for a career is poor, you will have fewer employment choices. It is best to focus on career areas that are growing. They will offer you greater employment options when you are ready to begin your career. You can research job trends when investigating other career information.

Sources of Career Information

When you are ready to find employment, you can get job leads through a variety of sources. You can check the Internet or the newspaper for want ads and job fairs. Good information is also available in libraries. The professional journals in your career field and the leading professional organizations often announce job openings. Family members and neighbors can provide help, too.

Internet Sites

Today, one of the best ways to find jobs is using the Internet. You can search for open positions, and many sites also offer tips for job hunting. You can start at the U.S. Department of Labor's website. You can also explore the following helpful sources:

- The *Occupational Outlook Handbook* describes the major U.S. jobs and their working conditions, requirements, average salaries, and future outlook. This publication is available in most libraries and on the Internet.
- The *O*Net (the Occupational Information Network)* website provides tools for exploring careers, examining job trends, and assessing personal abilities and interests. It also includes options for finding jobs related to specific skills.

- The *CareerOneStop* website has components for exploring careers, salaries, benefits, education, training, and other resources.

One part of CareerOneStop is *America's Career InfoNet*. You can use this site for exploring careers, including occupational trends, wage information, and state resources.

America's Service Locator is another component of CareerOneStop. This site helps users find jobs and job-related resources in their local area. These resources include One-Stop Career Centers offer assistance in job-seeking skills, such as résumé writing. They also offer help with various types of job training.

Networking

Many people find employment through networking. *Networking* is the exchange of information or services among individuals or groups. As a newcomer to the career field, the goal of your networking is to learn about possible job leads.

Social networking sites have become popular places to find information on companies and their available positions. Many companies network on these sites because it is an additional source of advertising for them. Users find that these sites expand their job search possibilities. In addition, these sites allow a personal exchange between users and company representatives.

Applying for a Position

When you are ready to apply for employment, you will need to know the appropriate steps to take. Having a well-prepared résumé is an important first step. Knowing how to write an acceptable letter of application is another goal. Finally, you will want to practice your interviewing techniques.

Your Résumé

A *résumé* is a brief outline of your education, work experience, and other qualifications for work. A well-written résumé can definitely help you get an interview. Make sure that your résumé is precise and without errors, **Figure 24-5**. Print your résumé on high-quality, neutral-colored paper (white, gray, or cream colors). Use your printed résumé when an employer requests a résumé sent via traditional mail.

Ron Johnson

1407 W. Gasoline Alley
Speedway, IN 12345
rjohnson@speedy.net
Phone: 1-317-555-3272, Cell 1-317-555-4094

Objective

To obtain a challenging position utilizing my training and experience in outdoor power equipment technology.

Education

Allied Technical College—Indianapolis, IN
- Associate's Degree in Outdoor Power Equipment Technology
  - Specialized in two- and four-stroke engines

Speedway High School—Speedway, IN
- Graduated with Academic Honors
- Two years of small engine technology instruction

Experience

July 2014-Present

Spritle's Lawn and Garden Equipment Repair, Indianapolis, IN—Maintenance Technician
- Performed preventive maintenance tasks, including oil changes and cooling system service.
- Diagnosed and repaired a variety of outdoor power equipment.

September 2012–July 2014

Ray's Motors, Speedway, IN—Helper, Detailer
- Detailed vehicles that were sold on used car lot
- Performed minor vehicle repairs
- Performed lot and office maintenance

References:

Ms. Jennifer Davis, Instructor, Allied Technical College, (317) 555-5077
Mr. James Lemon, Manager, Spritle's Lawn and Garden Equipment Repair, (317) 555-4304
Mr. Ray Andres, Owner, Ray's Motors (317) 555-4551

Goodheart-Willcox Publisher

Figure 24-5.

A résumé provides a quick way for employers to learn about the applicant.

Some employers request an electronic résumé that is sent via e-mail or posted to the employer's job site. You can also post an electronic résumé to a number of online job-search sites. To create one, save your résumé as "text only" without any formatting. Then review the text only résumé to make sure lines and headers break properly. Be sure to save this in a separate file from your formatted résumé. Employers may use the electronic file to search for key terms that match their descriptions of an ideal job candidate.

Along with the résumé, you need to develop a list of references. A *reference* is an individual who will provide important information about you to a prospective employer. A reference can be a teacher, school official, previous employer, or any other adult outside your family who knows you well.

You will need at least three references. Always get permission from each person to use his or her name as a reference before actually doing so. Your list of references, along with their titles, phone numbers, and addresses, should be kept private. Share this list only with an employer who has interviewed you and asks for your references.

You can have your references write *letters of recommendation* for you. These give an employer a more in-depth look at your skills. Choose people who know you well. Make sure you choose references who are good writers, since they will be representing you. Ask as many people as possible. Then you can choose the best letters to submit to employers.

Letter of Application

The *letter of application* is often the first contact you have with a potential employer. It can make a lasting impression. It should be neat and follow a standard form for business letters. The paper should be ivory, white, or a neutral color and free of smudges and mistakes. Use a standard font to give the letter a professional look. Written communications skills are a trait employers are looking for, so be sure to check spelling and punctuation. Have several people read the letter and offer advice for improving it. You should mail your résumé with your letter of application.

The letter of application should be brief and to the point. It should include the following items:
- Title of the job you seek.
- Where you heard about the job.
- Your strengths, skills, and abilities for the job.
- Reasons you should be considered for the job.

- When you are available to begin work.
- Request for an interview.

Job Application Forms

A prospective employer may ask you to complete a *job application form* before having an interview. The job application form highlights the information the employer needs to know about you, your education, and your prior work experience. Employers often use these forms to screen applicants for the skills needed on the job—skills such as written communications and following directions. You might complete a form in a personnel or employment office. Sometimes you may get the form by mail.

The overall appearance of the application form can give an employer their first opinion about you. Fill out the form accurately, completely, and neatly. How well you accomplish this can determine whether you get the job. When asked about salary, write *open* or *negotiable*. This means you are willing to consider offers.

Be sure to send or give the form to the correct person. The name of the correct person often appears on the form.

Online Application Forms

Many employers now request electronic applications, either through their company websites or independent job-search websites, **Figure 24-6**. When filling out an online application, it is extremely important to include key terms for which the employer may search. This will help you stand out from the many other applications the employer will receive.

When preparing your application, be sure to save it in the appropriate format. If a preferred format is not given, it is best to save the application in document file format or PDF file format. This will enable the employer to search for specific terms in your document.

The ability to follow directions and accomplish the task at hand is a quality all employers seek, so be sure to complete all the fields of the application. At work, you will be expected to communicate effectively with customers and coworkers. By submitting an application that is written in a clear and concise way, you show potential employers that you may have the communications skills they are looking for. Many job-search sites have sample forms on which you can practice before attempting a real application.

bdstudio/Shutterstock.com

Figure 24-6.

When filling out a job application form, be sure to complete all fields of the application.

The Job Interview

The *job interview* gives you the opportunity to learn more about a company and to convince the employer that you are the best person for the position. An employer wants to know if you have the skills needed for the job, and the interview is your chance to prove it. Adequate preparation is essential for making a lasting, positive impression. Here are some proven ways to prepare for an interview.

- Research the employer and the job: Know the mission of the employer and specifics about the job. Also, try to learn what the company looks for when hiring new employees. Often, this kind of information is readily available on the company's website.
- Be prepared to answer questions.
- List the questions you want answered. For example, do you want to know if on-the-job training is offered? Are there any opportunities for advancement?
- List the materials you plan to take to the interview. This seems simple enough. However, if you wait to grab items at the last minute, you will likely forget something important.
- Decide what to wear. Dress appropriately, usually one step above what is worn by your future coworkers. For instance, casual clothing

is acceptable for individuals who will do manual labor or wear a company uniform. Always appear neat and clean.
- Practice the interview. Have a friend or family member interview you in front of a mirror until you are happy with your responses.
- Know where to go for the interview. Verify the address of the interview location by checking the site beforehand, if possible. Plan to arrive ready for the interview at least 10 minutes early.

Good preparation will make you feel more confident and comfortable during the interview. Be polite, friendly, and cheerful during the process. Use a firm handshake. Maintain eye contact at all times. Answer all questions carefully and as completely as you can. Be honest about your abilities. Avoid chewing gum and fidgeting. Also be aware of questions you legally do not have to answer, such as those related to age, marital status, religion, or family background. See **Figure 24-7**.

A prospective employer may ask you to take employee tests. Some employers administer tests to job candidates to measure their knowledge or skill level under stress. Since all employers support a drug-free workplace, most will require you to take a drug test if hired.

Sjale/Shutterstock.com

Figure 24-7.

Adequate preparation is essential for making a positive impression during an interview. Always greet the interviewer with a firm handshake, and answer questions politely and thoroughly.

After the interview, send a letter to the employer within 24 hours, thanking him or her for the interview. If you get a job offer, respond to it quickly. If you do not receive an offer after interviewing for several positions, evaluate your interview techniques and seek ways to improve them.

Evaluating Job Offers

When considering a job offer or comparing two or more positions, you should explore the following work factors:

- Physical surroundings—Where is your workspace located? Is the atmosphere conducive to your style of working? Is parking provided? Is public transportation close by?
- Work schedule—Will the workdays and work hours mesh with your lifestyle? Is occasional overtime work required?
- Income and benefits—Is the proposed salary fair? Will you receive benefits that are just as valuable as extra income? How much sick leave is granted during the year? Is personal or emergency leave available? What is the vacation policy? Are there medical and life insurance benefits? Is there a credit union? Will the company pay tuition for college courses or special programs related to your job?
- Job obligations—Will you be expected to join a union or other professional organization? If so, what are the costs? Will you be expected to attend meetings after work?
- Advancement potential—Is there opportunity for advancement? After demonstrating good performance, how soon can you seek a position with more responsibilities? Before you can advance, are there special expectations such as additional training or a higher degree? Are training programs provided?

Talking about advancement requires considerable diplomacy. After all, you should not appear too eager to leave the job for which you are interviewing. Many employers expect a new employee to remain at least one year at that job. If you place undue emphasis on getting some other job, you will appear uninterested in the current opening.

You may also want to explore the transportation options to and from work. Can you get to work in reasonable time by taking public transportation? Are carpools available? You must report to work daily and on time. How much effort it takes to get to work will greatly affect your satisfaction with the job.

Succeeding in the Workplace

It goes without saying that a thorough understanding of small engine operation, service, and repair is necessary to succeed as a small engine technician. However, there are many other traits that will help you get and keep a job in any field. How to behave in the workplace is an important lesson all employees should learn.

Maintain a Professional Appearance

As an employee, you are a representative of your company. Therefore, your employer expects you to be neat and clean on the job. Taking care of yourself gives the impression that you want people to view you as a professional.

Employers expect workers to dress appropriately. Many places of work have a dress code. If your workplace does not, use common sense. Always wear clean work clothes. A professional appearance is especially important for employees who have frequent face-to-face contact with customers. See **Figure 24-8**.

Work Habits

Employers want employees who are punctual, dependable, and responsible. They want their employees to be capable of taking initiative and working independently. Other desirable employee qualities include organization, accuracy, and efficiency.

A punctual employee is always prompt and on time. This means not only when the workday starts, but also when returning from breaks and lunches. Being dependable means that people can rely on you to fulfill your word and meet your deadlines. If you are not well, be sure to call in and let the employer know right away. If there are reasons you cannot be at work, discuss them with your employer and work out an alternate arrangement. Many people have lost jobs by not checking with their supervisor before taking time off.

Taking initiative means that you start activities on your own without being told. When you finish one task, you do not wait to hear what to do next.

involves not wasting time. Time-wasting behaviors include visiting with coworkers, making personal phone calls, texting, sending e-mails, or doing other nonwork activities during work hours.

While it is important to complete all your work, you must also be able to gauge which assignments are most important. Avoid putting excessive efforts into minor assignments when crucial matters require your attention. Even though you are still accomplishing work, this is another way of wasting time.

Professional Behavior

You will be expected to behave professionally on the job. This includes showing respect for your boss and coworkers. Limit personal conversations and phone calls to break times or lunch. Act courteously; remember that others are focusing on their work. Interruptions can cause them to lose concentration.

Part of behaving professionally is responding appropriately to constructive criticism. Every employee, no matter how knowledgeable or experienced, can improve his or her performance. If you receive criticism from a supervisor or coworker, do not be offended. Instead, use the feedback to improve yourself. The more you improve, the more successful you will be in your work.

Stefanolunardi/Shuterstock.com

Figure 24-8.

As an employee, you are a representative of your company. Your employer expects you to dress appropriately, and to be neat and clean.

Decision Making and Problem Solving

The ability to make decisions and solve problems requires *critical-thinking skills*. These are higher-level skills that enable you to think beyond the obvious. You learn to interpret information and make judgments. Supervisors appreciate employees who can analyze problems and think of workable solutions.

Communication Skills

Communicating effectively with others is important for job success. Being a good communicator means that you can share information well with others. It also means you are a good listener.

Good communication is central to a smooth operation of any business. Communication is the process of exchanging ideas, thoughts, or information. Poor communication is costly to an employer, as when time is lost because an order was entered

Individuals who take initiative need much less supervision. They have self-motivation, or an inner urge to perform well. Generally, this motivation will drive you to set goals and accomplish them. All these qualities together show that you are capable of working independently.

You are expected to be as accurate and error-free as possible in all that you do. Complete your work with precision and double-check it to ensure accuracy.

Time Management

A good employee knows how to manage time wisely. This includes ability to prioritize assignments and complete them in a timely fashion. It also incorrectly. Poor communication can result in lost customers, too.

Types of Communication

The primary forms of communications are verbal and nonverbal. Verbal communication involves speaking, listening, and writing. Nonverbal communication is the sending and receiving of messages without the use of words. It involves body language, which includes the expression on your face and your body posture.

Listening is an important part of communication. If you do not understand something, be sure to ask questions. Also give feedback to let others know you understand them and are interested in what they have to say. Leaning forward while a person is talking signals interest and keen listening. Slouching back in a chair and yawning give the opposite signal—that you are bored and uninterested.

The message you convey in telephone communication involves your promptness, tone of voice, and attitude. Answering the phone quickly with a pleasant tone conveys a positive image for the company. Learning to obtain accurate information from the caller without interrupting that person's message is important.

Communication tools have advanced with the development of new technologies. To be an effective employee, you must know how to communicate well with the common tools of your workplace. For example, when sending e-mail communications, remember to think through each message as you would before sending a postal letter. Often messages are sent quickly without thought of how the recipient may interpret them. The same is true of voice mail.

The development of good communication skills is an ongoing process. Attending communication workshops and practicing often can keep your skills sharp.

Customer Relations Skills

Working with customers takes special communication skills. The most important aspect of customer relations is always remaining courteous. This may also require patience in some situations. When customers visit your business, you want them to have the best possible service and to leave happy. Remember that your behavior and skills at handling customers can determine if the customer will return to your business. The customer may spread the word about his or her experience with you to other potential customers. Make sure your customers know you appreciate their business.

Customer relations may also involve problem solving. If a customer needs help, you must provide answers as quickly and accurately as possible. When a situation becomes stressful, you must be able to control your own level of stress without letting it affect your performance. At the same time, you must be able to lessen the customer's stress and attempt to eliminate its source.

Ethical Workplace Behavior

Ethical behavior on the job means conforming to accepted standards of fairness and good conduct. It is based on a person's sense of what is right to do. Individuals and society as a whole regard ethical behavior as highly important. Integrity, confidentiality, and honesty are crucial aspects of ethical workplace behavior. Integrity is firmly following your moral beliefs.

Unfortunately, employee theft is a major problem at some companies. The theft can range from carrying office supplies home to stealing money or expensive equipment. Company policies are in place to address these concerns. In cases of criminal or serious behavior, people may lose their jobs. If proven, the charge of criminal behavior stays on the employee's record. Such an employee will have a difficult time finding another job.

Interpersonal Skills

Interpersonal skills involve interacting with others. Some workplace activities that involve these skills include teaching others, leading, negotiating, and working as a member of a team. Getting along well with others can require great effort on your part, but it is essential for accomplishing your employer's goals.

Teamwork

Employers seek employees who can effectively serve as good team members. Due to the nature of most work today, teamwork is necessary. A team is a small group of people working together for a common purpose. If someone is uncooperative, it takes longer to accomplish the tasks. When people do not get along, strained relationships may occur, which get in the way of finishing the tasks.

A big advantage of a team is its ability to develop plans and complete work faster than individuals working alone. In contrast, a team usually takes longer to reach a decision than an individual worker does. Team members need some time before they become comfortable with one another and function as a unit. You will be more desirable as an employee if you know how to be a team player.

Leadership

Leadership is the ability to guide and motivate others to complete tasks or achieve goals. It involves communicating well with others, accepting responsibility, and making decisions with confidence. Those employees with leadership skills are most likely to be promoted to higher levels.

Leaders often seem to carry the most responsibility in a group. Other group members look to them for answers and direction. The most important role of leaders is to keep the team advancing toward its goal. Leaders do this by inspiring their groups and providing the motivation to keep everyone working together.

Good leaders encourage teamwork, because a team that is working together well is more likely to reach goals. Leaders listen to the opinions of others and make sure all team members are included in projects. Leaders also want to set a good example by doing a fair share of the work. In these ways, leaders cultivate a sense of harmony in the group.

Belonging to Organizations

Leading others may not be easy for some people, but everyone can improve their leadership skills with practice. Becoming involved in a school club or organization can help. Taking a role as an officer or a committee chair will give you even more practice.

Belonging to an organization can also help you develop your teamwork skills. You will learn how to work well in a group as you plan events, create projects, and accomplish goals together.

Lifelong Learning

No matter what career you enter, you will be expected to keep pace with the changes in your field. Continually updating your knowledge and skills is known as *lifelong learning*. The term implies that your need for learning will never end. You cannot assume that the skills you have will be all you ever need during your career. Technology and other advances mean you must continue to learn to keep up with changes in the field. Employers usually provide some training. However, employees are often expected to use time outside the job to stay up-to-date in their field of expertise. People who enjoy their work will view lifelong learning as an exciting challenge.

Possessing *transferable skills* can help you succeed in whatever job you choose. The transferable skills useful in all jobs include reading, writing, speaking, and basic math. The essential skills identified for a given career cluster, however, are transferable across the careers within that cluster.

Transferable skills can help employees during career transitions. Many people today do not stay in one career their entire lives. They may change career directions at some point and pursue other interests. If there is a decline in their industry, jobs may be eliminated. These employees may need additional training or education to succeed in a new career area. Having transferable skills can help smooth career transitions.

Certification

The *Equipment & Engine Training Council (EETC)* is an organization that creates voluntary technician certification tests. These tests are available to anyone wishing to enhance their training, employment opportunities, and personal credibility. Employers having certified technicians are recognized by their customers as having qualified service personnel who are competent and will produce quality work.

Why Get Certified?

Certification can provide personal and professional benefits. Personal prestige and credibility are gained by individuals who have demonstrated interest by studying and meeting certification requirements to advance their professional qualifications.

Individuals who pass one of the certification tests will receive an arm patch bearing the certified EETC technician emblem and an 8" × 10" certificate. Wearing the official emblem, obtained by passing a certification test, shows customers that service will be performed by a competent person who can proficiently diagnose and repair equipment. See **Figure 24-1**. Passing a certification test indicates that an individual has met industry standards of professionalism and has studied to obtain certification. This accomplishment can increase one's chances for advancement and monetary awards.

Dealerships that advertise they employ certified technicians can increase their sales of equipment. The service dealer who employs certified technicians can ensure customers that any service problems that occur during or after the warranty period will be taken care of in a fair and equitable manner.

What Is on a Certification Test?

EETC certification tests are carefully constructed to measure knowledge in basic skills, interpersonal relationship skills, engine fundamentals, theory, servicing, failure analysis, troubleshooting, and repair. Certification can be obtained in one or more of the following test areas:
- Four-Stroke Engines.
- Two-Stroke Engines.
- Compact Diesel Engines.
- Electrical.
- Drivelines.
- Generators.
- Reel Technology.
- Components Plus.

Each of the test areas has its own certification test. Sample certification tests for Four-Stroke Engines and Two-Stroke Engines can be found in the *Small Gas Engines Workbook*, which can be ordered directly from Goodheart-Willcox. Each certification test consists of 150–200 multiple choice questions. The questions are divided into four main categories:
- Fundamentals.
- Servicing Engine Systems.
- Failure Analysis.
- Troubleshooting.

There is a two hour time limit for taking a certification test. A minimum passing score is 70%.

Who Can Take the Test?

Anyone may take the test at any scheduled test session. Tests are administered at approved locations throughout the United States. EETC promotes the certification and schedules all testing locations and dates. The organization handles the registration, collection of fees, and certification-related questions. The registration fee is kept minimal, but it must be paid 30 days prior to the test date.

All registered participants will be provided with all pertinent details prior to testing and will be notified of scores after testing. EETC also handles the dissemination of arm patches, certificates, and maintains individual records on all applicants. Certification is valid for three years in each test area. For information on testing locations, registration, obtaining a study guide, or any other inquiries, visit the EETC website.

Summary

The small gas engine field offers career opportunities in several areas. The engine service technician diagnoses engine trouble and makes appropriate repairs. Service managers plan and supervise the activities of all service department employees. Sales managers sell implements and vehicles that utilize small gas engines. General managers oversee both the service and sales aspects of the business.

Small engine manufacturer's technicians develop prototype engines and test new design theories. Manufacturers often train employees with broad service experience to become service representatives. Service representatives work to solve chronic service problems. Manufacturers also need engineers to design new engines that will perform satisfactorily under specific conditions.

Any career in small engines can lead to high-level management positions. Most successful executives began their careers in production, design, sales, or service. Many individuals in the small engine field start their own business. These people are entrepreneurs.

The industrial technology and vocational education teaching field can use qualified teachers with the knowledge of small gas engines. Teaching can be a rewarding career choice.

Preparing yourself for a meaningful job in the workplace requires planning. Once you decide which careers interest you, you should begin to evaluate other important factors. Among these are the kind of wages you might earn and the education or training you would need. Knowing the job duties and responsibilities will also impact your decision.

When you are ready to find employment, you can get job leads through a variety of sources. Today, one of the best ways to find jobs is using the Internet. You can search for open positions, and many sites also offer tips for job hunting. Many people find employment through networking. Networking is the exchange of information or services among individuals or groups.

When you are ready to apply for employment, you will need to know the appropriate steps to take. Having a well-prepared résumé is an important first step. Knowing how to write an acceptable letter of application is another goal. Finally, you will want to practice your interviewing techniques.

A résumé is a brief outline of your education, work experience, and other qualifications for the job. A well-written résumé can definitely help you get an interview.

Along with the résumé, you need a list of references. A reference is an individual who will provide important information about you to a prospective employer. You can have your references write letters of recommendation for you. These give an employer a more in-depth look at your skills.

The letter of application is often the first contact you have with a potential employer. It can make a lasting impression. It should be neat and follow a standard form for business letters.

A prospective employer may ask you to complete a job application form before having an interview. The overall appearance of the application form can give an employer their first opinion about you. Fill out the form accurately, completely, and neatly. Many employers now request electronic applications, either through their company websites or independent job-search websites.

The interview gives you the opportunity to learn more about a company and to convince an employer that you are the best person for the position. Adequate preparation is essential for making a lasting, positive impression. Good preparation will make you feel more confident and comfortable during the interview.

Employers want employees who are punctual, dependable, and responsible. They want their employees to be capable of taking initiative and working independently. Other desirable employee qualities include organization, accuracy, and efficiency.

Communicating effectively with others is important for job success. Being a good communicator means that you can share information well with others. It also means you are a good listener.

Belonging to a school club or organization can also help you develop your teamwork skills. You will learn how to work well in a group as you plan events, create projects, and accomplish goals together.

The Equipment and Engine Training Council certification tests are available for anyone interested in improving their employment potential and credibility in the workplace. Passing the certification tests can bring personal and professional benefits.

Review Questions

Answer the following questions using the information provided in this chapter.

1. Small engine service technicians generally receive their training at _____.

2. The service manager _____ the activities of all service department employees.

3. General managers are often required to keep accurate _____ and _____ records.

4. *True or False?* Small engine manufacturer's technicians must have good oral and written communications skills.

5. The _____ works closely with service managers and service technicians to catch and correct chronic service problems.

6. *True or False?* Many successful executives in the small engine field began their careers in production, sales, or service.

7. *True or False?* An entrepreneur is an individual who starts his or her own business.

8. Before setting career goals, you should consider your _____, which are beliefs about what is important.

9. *True or False?* Most people entering the workforce know exactly what type of career they want.

10. A(n) _____ involves learning a trade under the direction and guidance of an expert worker.

11. List five items that should be included in a letter of application.

12. Why is it important to prepare well for an interview?

13. Why is it important to maintain a professional appearance on the job?

14. Taking _____ means that you start activities on your own without being told.

15. List four workplace activities that involve interpersonal skills.

16. Who is eligible to take the EETC certification tests?

17. What are the eight test areas available for EETC certification?

18. How many questions are on each of the EETC tests?

19. How much time is allotted to take each of the EETC tests, and what is the minimum passing score?

20. How long is EETC certification valid?

Appendix

Units of Measure

U.S. CUSTOMARY	METRIC
LENGTH	
12 inches = 1 foot	1 kilometer = 1000 meters
36 inches = 1 yard	1 hectometer = 100 meters
3 feet = 1 yard	1 dekameter = 10 meters
5,280 feet = 1 mile	1 meter = 1 meter
16.5 feet = 1 rod	1 decimeter = 0.1 meter
320 rods = 1 mile	1 centimeter = 0.01 meter
6 feet = 1 fathom	1 millimeter = 0.001 meter
WEIGHT	
27.34 grains = 1 dram	1 tonne = 1,000,000 grams
438 grains = 1 ounce	1 kilogram = 1000 grams
16 drams = 1 ounce	1 hectogram = 100 grams
16 ounces = 1 pound	1 dekagram = 10 grams
2000 pounds = 1 short ton	1 gram = 1 gram
2240 pounds = 1 long ton	1 decigram = 0.1 gram
25 pounds = 1 quarter	1 centigram = 0.01 gram
4 quarters = 1 cwt	1 milligram = 0.001 gram
VOLUME	
8 ounces = 1 cup	1 hectoliter = 100 liters
16 ounces = 1 pint	1 dekaliter = 10 liters
32 ounces = 1 quart	1 liter = 1 liter
2 cups = 1 pint	1 deciliter = 0.1 liter
2 pints = 1 quart	1 centiliter = 0.01 liter
4 quarts = 1 gallon	1 milliliter = 0.001 liter
8 pints = 1 gallon	1000 milliliters = 1 liter
AREA	
144 sq. inches = 1 sq. foot	100 sq. millimeters = 1 sq. centimeter
9 sq. feet = 1 sq. yard	100 sq. centimeters = 1 sq. decimeter
43,560 sq. ft. = 160 sq. rods	100 sq. decimeters = 1 sq. meter
160 sq. rods = 1 acre	10,000 sq. meters = 1 hectare
640 acres = 1 sq. mile	

TEMPERATURE

FAHRENHEIT		CELSIUS
32° F	Water freezes	0° C
68° F	Reasonable room temperature	20° C
98.6° F	Normal body temperature	37° C
173° F	Alcohol boils	78.34° C
212° F	Water boils	100° C

Conversion Table: Metric to U.S. Customary

WHEN YOU KNOW:	MULTIPLY BY: * = Exact		TO FIND:
	VERY ACCURATE	APPROXIMATE	
LENGTH			
millimeters	0.0393701	0.04	inches
centimeters	0.3937008	0.4	inches
meters	3.280840	3.3	feet
meters	1.093613	1.1	yards
kilometers	0.621371	0.6	miles
WEIGHT			
grains	0.00228571	0.0023	ounces
grams	0.03527396	0.035	ounces
kilograms	2.204623	2.2	pounds
tonnes	1.1023113	1.1	short tons
VOLUME			
milliliters	0.20001	0.2	teaspoons
milliliters	0.06667	0.067	tablespoons
milliliters	0.03381402	0.03	fluid ounces
liters	61.02374	61.024	cubic inches
liters	2.113376	2.1	pints
liters	1.056688	1.06	quarts
liters	0.26417205	0.26	gallons
liters	0.03531467	0.035	cubic feet
cubic meters	61023.74	61023.7	cubic inches
cubic meters	35.31467	35.0	cubic feet
cubic meters	1.3079506	1.3	cubic yards
cubic meters	264.17205	264.0	gallons
AREA			
square centimeters	0.1550003	0.16	square inches
square centimeters	0.00107639	0.001	square feet
square meters	10.76391	10.8	square feet
square meters	1.195990	1.2	square yards
square kilometers	0.386102	0.4	square miles
hectares	2.471054	2.5	acres
TEMPERATURE			
Celsius	*9/5 (then add 32)		Farenheit

Conversion Table: U.S. Customary to Metric

WHEN YOU KNOW:	MULTIPLY BY: * = Exact		TO FIND:
	VERY ACCURATE	APPROXIMATE	
LENGTH			
inches	* 25.4		millimeters
inches	* 2.54		centimeters
feet	* 0.3048		meters
feet	* 30.48		centimeters
yards	* 0.9144	0.9	meters
miles	* 1.609344	1.6	kilometers
WEIGHT			
grains	15.43236	15.4	grams
ounces	* 28.349523125	28.0	grams
ounces	* 0.028349523125	0.028	kilograms
pounds	* 0.45359237	0.45	kilograms
tons	* 0.90718474	0.9	tonnes
VOLUME			
teaspoons	* 4.97512	5.0	milliliters
tablespoons	* 14.92537	15.0	milliliters
fluid ounces	29.57353	30.0	milliliters
cups	* 0.236588240	0.24	liters
pints	* 0.473176473	0.47	liters
quarts	* 0.946352946	0.95	liters
gallons	* 3.785411784	3.8	liters
cubic inches	* 0.016387064	0.02	liters
cubic feet	* 0.028316846592	0.03	cubic meters
cubic yards	* 0.764554857984	0.76	cubic meters
AREA			
square inches	* 6.4516	6.5	square centimeters
square feet	* 0.09290304	0.09	square meters
square yards	* 0.83612736	0.8	square meters
square miles	* 2.589989	2.6	square kilometers
acres	* 0.40468564224	0.4	hectares
TEMPERATURE			
Fahrenheit	*5/9 (after subtracting 32)		Celsius

Millimeter Conversion Chart

mm	In.	mm	In.	mm	In.	mm	In.	mm	In.	mm	In.	mm	In.	mm	In.	mm	In.
0.25	.0098	15	.5905	30	1.1811	45	1.7716	60	2.3622	75	2.9527	90	3.5433	105	4.1338	120	4.7244
0.50	.0197	15.25	.6004	30.25	1.1909	45.25	1.7815	60.25	2.3720	75.25	2.9626	90.25	3.5531	105.25	4.1437	120.25	4.7342
0.75	.0295	15.50	.6102	30.50	1.2008	45.50	1.7913	60.50	2.3819	75.50	2.9724	90.50	3.5630	105.50	4.1535	120.50	4.7441
		15.75	.6201	30.75	1.2106	45.75	1.8012	60.75	2.3917	75.75	2.9823	90.75	3.5728	105.75	4.1634	120.75	4.7539
1	.0394	16	.6299	31	1.2205	46	1.8110	61	2.4016	76	2.9921	91	3.5827	106	4.1732	121	4.7638
1.25	.0492	16.25	.6398	31.25	1.2303	46.25	1.8209	61.25	2.4114	76.25	3.0020	91.25	3.5925	106.25	4.1831	121.25	4.7736
1.50	.0591	16.50	.6496	31.50	1.2402	46.50	1.8307	61.50	2.4213	76.50	3.0118	91.50	3.6024	106.50	4.1929	121.50	4.7885
1.75	.0689	16.75	.6594	31.75	1.2500	46.75	1.8405	61.75	2.4311	76.75	3.0216	91.75	3.6122	106.75	4.2027	121.75	4.7933
2	.0787	17	.6693	32	1.2598	47	1.8504	62	2.4409	77	3.0315	92	3.6220	107	4.2126	122	4.8031
2.25	.0886	17.25	.6791	32.25	1.2697	47.25	1.8602	62.25	2.4508	77.25	3.0413	92.25	3.6319	107.25	4.2224	122.25	4.8130
2.50	.0984	17.50	.6890	32.50	1.2795	47.50	1.8701	62.50	2.4606	77.50	3.0512	92.50	3.6417	107.50	4.2323	122.50	4.8228
2.75	.1083	17.75	.6988	32.75	1.2894	47.75	1.8799	62.75	2.4705	77.75	3.0610	92.75	3.6516	107.75	4.2421	122.75	4.8327
3	.1181	18	.7087	33	1.2992	48	1.8898	63	2.4803	78	3.0789	93	3.6614	108	4.2520	123	4.8425
3.25	.1280	18.25	.7185	33.25	1.3091	48.25	1.8996	63.25	2.4901	78.25	3.0807	93.25	3.6713	108.25	4.2618	123.25	4.8524
3.50	.1378	18.50	.7283	33.50	1.3189	48.50	1.9094	63.50	2.5000	78.50	3.0905	93.50	3.6811	108.50	4.2716	123.50	4.8622
3.75	.1476	18.75	.7382	33.75	1.3287	48.75	1.9193	63.75	2.5098	78.75	3.1004	93.75	3.6909	108.75	4.2815	123.75	4.8720
4	.1575	19	.7480	34	1.3386	49	1.9291	64	2.5197	79	3.1102	94	3.7008	109	4.2913	124	4.8819
4.25	.1673	19.25	.7579	34.25	1.3484	49.25	1.9390	64.25	2.5295	79.25	3.1201	94.25	3.7106	109.25	4.3012	124.25	4.8917
4.50	.1772	19.50	.7677	34.50	1.3583	49.50	1.9488	64.50	2.5394	79.50	3.1299	94.50	3.7205	109.50	4.3110	124.50	4.9016
4.75	.1870	19.75	.7776	34.75	1.3681	49.75	1.9587	64.75	2.5492	79.75	3.1398	94.75	3.7303	109.75	4.3209	124.75	4.9114
5	.1968	20	.7874	35	1.3779	50	1.9685	65	2.5590	80	3.1496	95	3.7401	110	4.3307	125	4.9212
5.25	.2067	20.25	.7972	35.25	1.3878	50.25	1.9783	65.25	2.5689	80.25	3.1594	95.25	3.7500	110.25	4.3405	125.25	4.9311
5.50	.2165	20.50	.8071	35.50	1.3976	50.50	1.9882	65.50	2.5787	80.50	3.1693	95.50	3.7598	110.50	4.3504	125.50	4.9409
5.75	.2264	20.75	.8169	35.75	1.4075	50.75	1.9980	65.75	2.5886	80.75	3.1791	95.75	3.7697	110.75	4.3602	125.75	4.9508
6	.2362	21	.8268	36	1.4173	51	2.0079	66	2.5984	81	3.1890	96	3.7795	111	4.3701	126	4.9606
6.25	.2461	21.25	.8366	36.25	1.4272	51.25	2.0177	66.25	2.6083	81.25	3.1988	96.25	3.7894	111.25	4.3799	126.25	4.9705
6.50	.2559	21.50	.8465	36.50	1.4370	51.50	2.0276	66.50	2.6181	81.50	3.2087	96.50	3.7992	111.50	4.3898	126.50	4.9803
6.75	.2657	21.75	.8563	36.75	1.4468	51.75	2.0374	66.75	2.6279	81.75	3.2185	96.75	3.8090	111.75	4.3996	126.75	4.9901
7	.2756	22	.8661	37	1.4567	52	2.0472	67	2.6378	82	3.2283	97	3.8189	112	4.4094	127	5.0000
7.25	.2854	22.25	.8760	37.25	1.4665	52.25	2.0571	67.25	2.6476	82.25	3.2382	97.25	3.8287	112.25	4.4193		
7.50	.2953	22.50	.8858	37.50	1.4764	52.50	2.0669	67.50	2.6575	82.50	3.2480	97.50	3.8386	112.50	4.4291		
7.75	.3051	22.75	.8957	37.75	1.4862	52.75	2.0768	67.75	2.6673	82.75	3.2579	97.75	3.8484	112.75	4.4390		
8	.3150	23	.9055	38	1.4961	53	2.0866	68	2.6772	83	3.2677	98	3.8583	113	4.4488		
8.25	.3248	23.25	.9153	38.25	1.5059	53.25	2.0965	68.25	2.6870	83.25	3.2776	98.25	3.8681	113.25	4.4587		
8.50	.3346	23.50	.9252	38.50	1.5157	53.50	2.1063	68.50	2.6968	83.50	3.2874	98.50	3.8779	113.50	4.4685		
8.75	.3445	23.75	.9350	38.75	1.5256	53.75	2.1161	68.75	2.7067	83.75	3.2972	98.75	3.8878	113.75	4.4783		
9	.3543	24	.9449	39	1.5354	54	2.1260	69	2.7165	84	3.3071	99	3.8976	114	4.4882		
9.25	.3642	24.25	.9547	39.25	1.5453	54.25	2.1358	69.25	2.7264	84.25	3.3169	99.25	3.9075	114.25	4.4980		
9.50	.3740	24.50	.9646	39.50	1.5551	54.50	2.1457	69.50	2.7362	84.50	3.3268	99.50	3.9173	114.50	4.5079		
9.75	.3839	24.75	.9744	39.75	1.5650	54.75	2.1555	69.75	2.7461	84.75	3.3366	99.75	3.9272	114.75	4.5177		
10	.3937	25	.9842	40	1.5748	55	2.1653	70	2.7559	85	3.3464	100	3.9370	115	4.5275		
10.25	.4035	25.25	.9941	40.25	1.5846	55.25	2.1752	70.25	2.7657	85.25	3.3563	100.25	3.9468	115.25	4.5374		
10.50	.4134	25.50	1.0039	40.50	1.5945	55.50	2.1850	70.50	2.7756	85.50	3.3661	100.50	3.9567	115.50	4.5472		
10.75	.4232	25.75	1.0138	40.75	1.6043	55.75	2.1949	70.75	2.7854	85.75	3.3760	100.75	3.9665	115.75	4.5571		
11	.4331	26	1.0236	41	1.6142	56	2.2047	71	2.7953	86	3.3858	101	3.9764	116	4.5669		
11.25	.4429	26.25	1.0335	41.25	1.6240	56.25	2.2146	71.25	2.8051	86.25	3.3957	101.25	3.9862	116.25	4.5768		
11.50	.4528	26.50	1.0433	41.50	1.6339	56.50	2.2244	71.50	2.8150	86.50	3.4055	101.50	3.9961	116.50	4.5866		
11.75	.4626	26.75	1.0531	41.75	1.6437	56.75	2.2342	71.75	2.8248	86.75	3.4153	101.75	4.0059	116.75	4.5964		
12	.4724	27	1.0630	42	1.6535	57	2.2441	72	2.8346	87	3.4252	102	4.0157	117	4.6063		
12.25	.4823	27.25	1.0728	42.25	1.6634	57.25	2.2539	72.25	2.8445	87.25	3.4350	102.25	4.0256	117.25	4.6161		
12.50	.4921	27.50	1.0827	42.50	1.6732	57.50	2.2638	72.50	2.8543	87.50	3.4449	102.50	4.0354	117.50	4.6260		
12.75	.5020	27.75	1.0925	42.75	1.6831	57.75	2.2736	72.75	2.8642	87.75	3.4547	102.75	4.0453	117.75	4.6358		
13	.5118	28	1.1024	43	1.6929	58	2.2835	73	2.8740	88	3.4646	103	4.0551	118	4.6457		
13.25	.5217	28.25	1.1122	43.25	1.7028	58.25	2.2933	73.25	2.8839	88.25	3.4744	103.25	4.0650	118.25	4.6555		
13.50	.5315	28.50	1.1220	43.50	1.7126	58.50	2.3031	73.50	2.8937	88.50	3.4842	103.50	4.0748	118.50	4.6653		
13.75	.5413	28.75	1.1319	43.75	1.7224	58.75	2.3130	73.75	2.9035	88.75	3.4941	103.75	4.0846	118.75	4.6752		
14	.5512	29	1.1417	44	1.7323	59	2.3228	74	2.9134	89	3.5039	104	4.0945	119	4.6850		
14.25	.5610	29.25	1.1516	44.25	1.7421	59.25	2.3327	74.25	2.9232	89.25	3.5138	104.25	4.1043	119.25	4.6949		
14.50	.5709	29.50	1.1614	44.50	1.7520	59.50	2.3425	74.50	2.9331	89.50	3.5236	104.50	4.1142	119.50	4.7047		
14.75	.5807	29.75	1.1713	44.75	1.7618	59.75	2.3524	74.75	2.9429	89.75	3.5335	104.75	4.1240	119.75	4.7146		

Useful Conversions

WHEN YOU KNOW:	MULTIPLY BY:	TO FIND:
⬇	⬇	⬇
TORQUE		
pound-inch	0.11298	newton-meters (N•m)
pound-foot	1.3558	newton-meters
LIGHT		
foot candles	1.0764	lumens/meters^2 (lm/m^2)
FUEL PERFORMANCE		
miles/gallon	0.4251	kilometers/liter (km/L)
SPEED		
miles/hour	1.6093	kilometers/hr (km/h)
FORCE		
kilogram	9.807	newtons (n)
ounce	0.278	newtons
pound	4.448	newtons
POWER		
horsepower	0.746	kilowatts (kw)
PRESSURE OR STRESS		
inches of water	0.2491	kilopascals (kPa)
pounds/sq. in.	6.895	kilopascals
ENERGY OR WORK		
btu	1055.0	joules (J)
foot-pound	1.3558	joules
kilowatt-hour	3600000.0	joules

Decimal Equivalents of 8ths, 16ths, 32nds, 64ths

8ths	32nds	64ths	64ths
1/8 = .125	1/32 = .03125	1/64 = .015625	33/64 = .515625
1/4 = .250	3/32 = .09375	3/64 = .046875	35/64 = .546875
3/8 = .375	5/32 = .15625	5/64 = .078125	37/64 = .578125
1/2 = .500	7/32 = .21875	7/64 = .109375	39/64 = .609375
5/8 = .625	9/32 = .28125	9/64 = .140625	41/64 = .640625
3/4 = .750	11/32 = .34375	11/64 = .171875	43/64 = .703125
7/8 = .875	13/32 = .40625	13/64 = .203125	45/64 = .671875
16ths	15/32 = .46875	15/64 = .234375	47/64 = .734375
1/16 = .0625	17/32 = .53125	17/64 = .265625	49/64 = .765625
3/16 = .1875	19/32 = .59375	19/64 = .296875	51/64 = .796875
5/16 = .3125	21/32 = .65625	21/64 = .328125	53/64 = .828125
7/16 = .4375	23/32 = .71875	23/64 = .359375	55/64 = .859375
9/16 = .5625	25/32 = .78125	25/64 = .390625	57/64 = .890625
11/16 = .6875	27/32 = .84375	27/64 = .421875	59/64 = .921875
13/16 = .8125	29/32 = .90625	29/64 = .453125	61/64 = .953125
15/16 = .9375	31/32 = .96875	31/64 = .484375	63/64 = .984375

Rules Relative to the Circle

To find circumference—
Multiply diameter by 3.1416... Or divide diameter by 0.03183

To find diameter—
Multiply circumference by 0.3183... Or divide circumference by 3.1416

To find radius—
Multiply circumference by 0.15915... Or divide circumference by 6.28318

To find side of an inscribed square—
Multiply diameter by 0.7071
Or multiply circumference by 0.2251 .... Or divide circumference by 4.4428

To find side of an equal square—
Multiply diameter by 0.8862 .... Or divide diameter by 1.1284
Or multiply circumference by 0.2821 .... Or divide circumference by 3.545

Square—
A side multiplied by 1.4142 equals diameter of its circumscribing circle.
A side multiplied by 4.443 equals circumference of its circumscribing circle.
A side multiplied by 1.128 equals diameter of an equal circle.
A side multiplied by 3.547 equals circumference of an equal circle.

To find the area of a circle—
Multiply circumference by one-quarter of the diameter
Or multiply the square of diameter by 0.7854
Or multiply the square of circumference by 0.07958
Or multiply the square of 1/2 diameter by 3.1416

Check Sheet for Four-Cycle Engine Reconditioning

Check List for Disassembly

_____ 1. Remove all gasoline from engine.
_____ 2. Inspect engine for broken or missing parts.
_____ 3. Record all important data.
_____ 4. Remove spark plug. Check gap and condition of electrodes.
_____ 5. Take and record compression reading.
_____ 6. Check ignition output with spark tester.
_____ 7. Drain oil from crankcase.
_____ 8. Disconnect all linkage from remote throttle assembly to engine.
_____ 9. Remove engine from mountings.
_____ 10. Clean engine housing or mounting area.
_____ 11. Remove blower housing from engine.
_____ 12. Remove carburetor and carburetor linkage.
_____ 13. Remove governor linkage.
_____ 14. Remove muffler.
_____ 15. Remove valve cover. Remove rocker arms and pushrods (OHV only).
_____ 16. Remove cylinder head and head gasket.
_____ 17. Measure and record bore and stroke.
_____ 18. Check and record valve clearance (L-head only).
_____ 19. Remove air deflector shields.
_____ 20. Check and record armature air gap.
_____ 21. Remove ignition module.
_____ 22. Remove starter clutch and flywheel nut.
_____ 23. Remove flywheel.
_____ 24. Remove all rust and burrs from end of crankshaft.
_____ 25. Remove mounting flange, if any.
_____ 26. Check timing marks.
_____ 27. Remove camshaft and governor gear/oil slinger.
_____ 28. Remove valve tappets.
_____ 29. Remove piston and rod assembly. Note: Mark rod first.
_____ 30. Remove piston rings from piston.
_____ 31. Check and record ring end gap.
_____ 32. Clean ring grooves in piston.
_____ 33. Check and record piston ring-to-land clearance.
_____ 34. Remove crankshaft and inspect it.
_____ 35. Remove intake and exhaust valves (L-head only).
_____ 36. Disassemble cylinder head valve train components (OHV only).
_____ 37. Wash and clean all parts that will not be damaged by solvent.
_____ 38. Inspect engine block for scores or imperfections.
_____ 39. Check all bearings and oil seals for possible damage.
_____ 40. Recondition or replace necessary engine components.

Check List for Reassembly

_____ 1. Clean valve seats with wire wheel and brush.
_____ 2. Have instructor check valve parts after they are cleaned.
_____ 3. Recondition the cylinder as needed.
_____ 4. Lap valves against valve seats, using lapping compound.
_____ 5. Install valve assemblies.
_____ 6. Install crankshaft.
_____ 7. Fit rings on piston in proper order.
_____ 8. Oil cylinder wall. Install piston and rod assembly in proper direction.
_____ 9. Torque rod bolts to specifications. Bend up retainer clips.
_____ 10. Install tappets, camshaft, and governor gear/oil slinger.
_____ 11. Align timing marks on camshaft and crankshaft.
_____ 12. Bolt mounting flange (crankcase cover) on engine. Check for proper fit.
_____ 13. Check and record valve clearance measurements (L-head only).
_____ 14. Assemble valve cover and breather and bolt to engine block (L-head only).
_____ 15. Install cylinder head and head gasket. Torque to specifications.
_____ 16. Install pushrods and rocker arms (OHV only).
_____ 17. Check valve clearance and install valve cover (OHV only).
_____ 18. Install ignition module.
_____ 19. Install flywheel key and flywheel. Torque flywheel nut.
_____ 20. Set armature air gap to specifications.
_____ 21. Install governor linkages.
_____ 22. Mount carburetor on engine block. Connect governor linkages.
_____ 23. Install muffler.
_____ 24. Install blower housing.
_____ 25. Connect fuel lines and valve breather tube.
_____ 26. Mount engine in implement or equipment.
_____ 27. Connect engine to drive train.
_____ 28. Connect all linkage between remote throttle and engine.
_____ 29. Tighten oil plug and fill engine with proper oil.
_____ 30. Clean and install air cleaner.
_____ 31. Check engine compression.
_____ 32. Clean and set gap of spark plug electrodes. Install spark plug.
_____ 33. Check to be sure all components are tight and properly adjusted.
_____ 34. Fill fuel tank with clean gasoline.
_____ 35. If indoors, turn on exhaust fan and wear goggles.
_____ 36. Engage carburetor choke and start engine.
_____ 37. Adjust carburetor.

V-Belt Failure and Correction Chart

Cause of Failure	Correction	Cause of Failure	Correction
1. Normal wear.	Replace belt.	6. Damaged or worn pulleys.	Align pulleys (except where an offset system is used with special pulleys).
2. Poor operating habits.	Do not engage and disengage clutch excessively.	7. Incorrect tensions.	Replace belt. Check idler spring tension. Lubricate idler brackets.
3. Damaged or worn idler pulleys.	Replace idler, frozen bearings, and belt.	8. Oil and grease damage.	Replace belts. Eliminate oil leakage. Use oil resistant belts if possible.
4. Incorrectly positioned belt guards.	Realign guards. Replace damaged guards.	9. Heat damage (140° or higher).	Use heat resistant belt. Avoid polyester belts. Shield belts from heat source.
5. Misaligned pulleys.	Replace pulleys.	10. Incorrect installation.	Install with care. Never use force. Recheck belts after 48 hours of use.

Spark Plug Condition Chart

Normal Appearance

A spark plug in a sound engine operating at the proper temperature will have deposits that range from tan to gray in color. If LPG is used, the deposits will be brown. Under normal conditions, the electrode should wear slightly, but there should be no evidence of burning.

Carbon Fouling

Carbon fouling (dry, black, sooty carbon deposits) can be caused by plugs that are too cold for the engine, an over-rich fuel mixture, a clogged air cleaner, a faulty choke, or sticking valves. Installing a hotter plug will temporarily solve this problem.

Oil Fouling

Oil fouling (wet, black deposits) is caused by excessive oil in the combustion chamber. Worn rings, valve guides, valve seals, and cylinder walls can cause oil fouling. Switching to a hotter spark plug may temporarily relieve the symptoms, but will not correct the problem.

Ash Fouling

Ash fouling is caused by the buildup of heavy combustion deposits. These deposits are formed by burning oil and/or fuel additives. Although ash fouling is not conductive, excessive deposits can cause a spark plug to misfire.

Splashed Fouling

Splashed fouling can occur after a long-delayed tune-up. When a new plug is installed in an engine with excessive piston and combustion chamber deposits, the plug will restore regular firing impulses and raise the combustion temperature. When this occurs, accumulated engine deposits may flake off and stick to the hot plug insulator.

Gap Bridging

Gap bridging (combustion deposit bridging the center and ground electrodes) is caused by a sudden burst of high speed operation following excessive idling. It can also be caused by improper fuel additives, obstructed exhaust ports (two-cycle engines), and excessive carbon in the cylinder.

High Speed Glazing

High speed glazing (hard, shiny, electrically conductive deposits) can be caused by a sudden increase in plug temperature during hard acceleration or loading. High speed glazing can cause the engine to misfire at high speeds. If high speed glazing recurs, a cooler plug should be used.

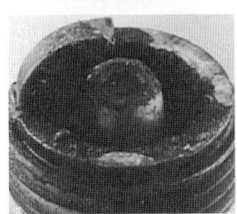

Preignition

Preignition (fuel charge ignited by a glowing combustion chamber deposit or a hot valve edge before the spark plug fires) can cause extensive plug damage. When plugs show evidence of preignition, check the heat range of the plugs, the condition of the plug wires, and the condition of the cooling system.

Detonation

Detonation can cause the insulator nose of a spark plug to fracture and chip away. The explosions that occur during heavy detonation produce extreme pressure in the cylinder. Detonation can be caused by low octane fuel, advanced ignition timing, or an excessively lean fuel mixture.

Overheating

Overheating (dull, white insulator and eroded electrodes) can occur when a spark plug is too hot for the engine. Advanced ignition timing, cooling system problems, detonation, sticking valves, and excessive high speed operation can also cause spark plug overheating.

Mechanical Damage

Mechanical damage can be caused by a foreign object in the combustion chamber. It can also occur if the piston hits the firing tip of a spark plug with improper reach. When working on an engine, keep spark plug hole(s) and carburetor throat covered to prevent foreign objects from entering the combustion chamber.

Worn Out

Extended use will cause the spark plug's center electrode to erode. When the electrode is too worn to be filed flat, the plug must be replaced. Typically, symptoms of worn spark plugs include excessive fuel consumption and poor engine performance.

SkillsUSA—Preparing Students for Leadership in the World of Work

Introduction to SkillsUSA

SkillsUSA is a national organization that brings together students, educators, and industry members dedicated to preparing students for excellence in career and technical occupations. The SkillsUSA Framework supports the acquisition of technical skills grounded in academics, personal skills, and workplace skills. Becoming involved in SkillsUSA is a commitment that can provide many lifelong rewards.

History

In 1965, the Vocational Industrial Clubs of America (VICA) formed to fill demand for a national skills organization that could connect industry professionals, educators, and youth in order to train students for future technical careers. While VICA began with just 200 members from 14 states, it grew quickly and expanded its membership to include college students. By 1969, VICA had more than 82,000 members.

VICA held its first competitive events in 1967, giving student competitors the chance to showcase their technical skill for peers, instructors, and professionals. In 1995, VICA changed the name of its national competition, the US Skill Olympics, to SkillsUSA Championships. In 1998, VICA was renamed VICA-SkillsUSA, and in 2004, the name of the organization was shortened to SkillsUSA.

Membership

SkillsUSA represents over 360,000 members in over 18,000 local chapters across the United States, with industry support from more than 600 corporations, trade associations, and labor unions.

Organization Colors & Relationships

The SkillsUSA colors illustrate the importance of the relationship between the national organization and the individual states and chapters. Red, white, blue, and gold represent the national organization itself. Within this color scheme, red and white represent the individual states and chapters while blue represents their common union. Gold represents the most important part of the organization, the individual member.

Motto, Creed & Pledge

The SkillsUSA organization lives by its motto, "Preparing for leadership in the world of work," and members follow its creed. In accordance with the creed, SkillsUSA members believe in the dignity of work, the American way of life, fair play, high moral and spiritual standards, and that satisfaction is achieved by good work.

SkillsUSA members also pledge to be productive members of their schools, chapters, and communities:

"Upon my honor, I pledge:
- To prepare myself by diligent study and ardent practice to become a worker whose services will be recognized as honorable by my employer and fellow workers.
- To base my expectations of reward upon the solid foundation of service.
- To honor and respect my vocation in such a way as to bring repute to myself.
- And further, to spare no effort in upholding the ideals of SkillsUSA."

SkillsUSA membership not only helps its members hone their technical skills, it helps them choose their futures. The organization recognizes the importance of diversity in the workforce and gives students from all backgrounds the opportunity to prove their skills and choose their careers. Championship contests are designed to evaluate career readiness, as well as preparedness for applying and interviewing for jobs. In addition to taking assessment tests and career interest inventories, members can try out potential careers in hands-on environments.

SkillsUSA Leadership Opportunities

SkillsUSA promotes good citizenship and expects its members to prepare to become leaders in their fields and their communities. SkillsUSA encourages all its members to contribute to their communities. Chapters can organize community service projects to give back to their communities and submit these projects to championship events.

Mentorship

SkillsUSA members can learn to lead by example through Student2Student mentoring. In these programs, chapters work with middle and elementary schools to help younger students explore future careers. Older students mentor younger students by going on field trips or working on hands-on activities together.

National Officers

Members can learn to lead a community by serving in the House of Delegates and as SkillsUSA National Officers. National officers are elected by vote from the House of Delegates and hold their positions for one year. Potential officers should study the SkillsUSA Leadership Handbook closely and meet the qualifications for candidacy, which include active membership in their chapter and past SkillsUSA leadership experience.

There are strict regulations about where, when, and how candidates may campaign for officership. Campaigning with social media is not allowed, and candidates do the bulk of their campaign work by interacting directly with the delegates. Candidates must give a brief speech, participate in question-and-answer sessions, and attend three Meet the Candidate sessions.

SkillsUSA Competitions

SkillsUSA competitions at the local, state, and national level test for more than a participant's technical skill. The definitive goal of SkillsUSA is preparing members to excel in the workplace. So, participants' preparation, appearance, and behavior are also thoroughly graded as part of a complete work performance. Competitions are held for both technical skills and leadership qualities.

The National SkillsUSA Championship is held annually in Louisville, Kentucky, and more than 6,300 students compete each year in order to earn Skill Point Certificates. Skill Point Certificates are awarded to participants who reach or exceed industry-defined cut scores, regardless of medal standing or contest ranking. The competition holds contests for more than a hundred concentrations in the technical, skilled, and service occupations as well as career and leadership skills. SkillsUSA also sponsors competitions on the local, state, regional, and international levels.

Professional Behavior

Each competition requires careful preparation, both before and during the contest event. Participants should study the regulations for their contest and observe all standards for dress, tools, and other preparations. Contest events have multiple parts. For each event, it is standard to have: a.) a professional development program (PDP) test, b.) a technical skills–related written test, c.) an oral professional assessment or interview, and d.) a submission of a hard-copy résumé. Contestants will then complete industry-defined challenges that are specific to their skill set.

The skills required to net the most points are also those required to do good work on the job. Contestants must know their task, tools, and skill set inside and out in order to perform the task proficiently. Often, projects must be prepared within a set time limit, which requires careful time management. Other events may call for teams that require excellent teamwork and communication to ensure all parts of the project are completed correctly.

Professional Ethics

Participants in SkillsUSA competitions are held to high standards of performance and sportsmanship. SkillsUSA will not tolerate unethical or disruptive behavior. Interrupting other contestants, tampering with other contestants' work, and other unethical behavior can be grounds for immediate disqualification.

Professional Dress

During the SkillsUSA ceremonies, meetings, and similar functions, students should dress professionally and follow SkillsUSA's guidelines for dress. Both genders are expected to wear black SkillsUSA jackets or red SkillsUSA blazers, windbreakers, or sweaters and dress in a business-formal style. For men, this means a white dress shirt, black dress slacks, black socks, black shoes, and black ties. For women, this means a white blouse or turtleneck with a collar that does not extend over the lapels or neck of her blazer or jacket. Women may wear a black dress skirt or slacks with black shoes. Black sheer (not opaque) or skin-tone seamless hose should be worn with skirts.

SkillsUSA is an organization that asks for a commitment from its members, but it provides many rewards. If you are interested in learning more about SkillsUSA, please see their website.

Glossary

A

abilities: skills developed with practice.

abrasion: wearing or rubbing away.

absolute vacuum: a complete absence of air or atmospheric pressure.

acceleration well: a fuel reservoir that provides additional fuel to the engine when the throttle valve is opened quickly.

acorn nut: a nut that has an integral cap to cover the sharp thread end of a bolt for safety; named for its resemblance to an acorn.

additive: a material that is added to the oil to give it certain properties.

adjustable wrench: a wrench with a movable jaw that can be adjusted to fit different size bolts or nuts.

aft: toward the rear of a PWC.

air: a gas containing approximately 4/5 nitrogen, 1/5 oxygen, and some carbonic gas.

air bleed: a tube in a carburetor through which air can pass into fuel moving through a fuel passage.

air cleaner: a device for filtering, cleaning, and removing dust from the air admitted to an engine.

air-cooled engine: an engine cooled by air.

air-fuel mixture: the combination of air and atomized fuel produced by the carburetor.

air-fuel ratio: the ratio, by weight, of fuel compared to air in carburetor mixture.

air gap: the space between the flywheel and magneto core poles.

air horn: the part of the air passage in carburetor that is on the atmospheric side of the venturi. The choke valve is located in the air horn.

air lock: a bubble of air trapped in a fluid circuit that interferes with normal circulation of the fluid.

air vane (pneumatic) governor: a governor that is operated by the stream of air created by the flywheel cooling fins.

alignment: an adjustment to bring related components into a line.

Allen wrench: a hexagonal (six-sided) wrench that fits into a recessed hexagonal hole. Used commonly with set screws.

alloy: a mixture of different metals.

Alnico: an alloy of aluminum, nickel, and cobalt used to make flywheel magnets.

alternating current (AC): electric current that alternately changes direction.

alternator: a generator that produces alternating current.

aluminum: a metal noted for its lightness. Aluminum is often alloyed with small quantities of other metals.

American National Standards Institute: an organization that establishes a variety of standards, including safety standards. Abbreviation is ANSI.

American Petroleum Institute: abbreviation is API.

American Society of Mechanical Engineers: abbreviation is ASME.

ammeter: an instrument for measuring the flow of electric current. See *ampere* and *multimeter.*

ampere: a unit of measurement for flow of electric current.

ampere-hour capacity: a term to indicate the capacity of a storage battery.

anaerobic sealant: a sealant similar to RTV, but can cure in the absence of air. This type of sealant can be used as a thread-locking material or between two machined surfaces.

anti-afterfire solenoid: a solenoid installed in float bowl of some carburetors that cut off fuel supply to the venturi when the ignition is turned off to prevent run-on.

antifreeze: a material, such as ethylene glycol, that is added to water to lower its freezing point.

antifriction bearing: a bearing constructed with balls or rollers between journal and bearing surfaces to provide rolling instead of sliding friction.

antiseize compound: a lubricant applied to threaded fasteners and metal components that are exposed to constant heat to prevent the metal from being cold welded together.

API engine oil service classification symbol: a symbol that appears on an oil container and provides the consumer with information about an oil's characteristics and applications.

API engine oil service classification system: a dynamic method of rating an oil's suitability for use in various generations of engines.

apprenticeship: a training opportunity that involves learning a trade under the direction and guidance of an expert worker.

aptitude: an ability to learn something quickly and easily.

arc: a discharge of electric current across a gap, such as between electrodes.

armature: the part of an electrical motor or generator that includes the main current-carrying winding.

assembly lube: a heavy oil that is applied to parts during reassembly to protect them from wear during initial start up.

atmospheric pressure: the weight of air at a given elevation (about 14.7 psi at sea level; less at higher altitudes).

atom: the smallest particle of an element that can exist, alone or in combination.

atomization: the process of breaking gasoline into tiny droplets and mixing it with air to produce the rapid burning required in an engine.

auger: a helical-shaped steel shaft that rotates to pull snow into a snow thrower.

automatic compression release: a mechanism on the camshaft designed to lift the exhaust valve slightly during cranking to release part of the compression pressure.

axial clearance: clearance that allows movement parallel to the axis of rotation.

B

babbitt: an alloy of tin, copper, and antimony having good antifriction properties. Used as a facing for bearings.

back pressure: a resistance to free flow, such as a restriction in the exhaust line.

backfire: ignition of the mixture in the intake manifold by a flame from the cylinder, such as might occur from a leaking or open intake valve.

backlash: the clearance or *play* between two parts, such as meshed gears.

baffle: an obstruction for checking or deflecting the flow of gases or sound.

baffle plate: see *baffle.*

bail: a hand lever on a mower handle that operates the blade or flywheel brake.

ball bearing: an antifriction bearing consisting of a hardened inner and outer race with hardened steel balls set between the two races.

ball piston pump: one type of variable-displacement pump used to transfer engine power to a fixed-displacement hydraulic motor in a hydrostatic transmission.

barrel pump system: a lubrication system that uses a cylinder-and-plunger lubrication pump. An eccentric on the camshaft moves the plunger in and out of the pump cylinder.

base: one of the three elements in a transistor.

battery: any number of complete electrical cells assembled in one housing or case.

Battery Council International: abbreviation is BCI.

bearing: a part in which a journal, pivot, or similar object turns or moves.

bearing crush: the distance that bearing inserts extend beyond the surface of the rod bore and cap prior to assembly.

bearing spread: the difference in diameter between the insert bearing halves and the diameter across the curve machined into the rod and rod cap.

Bernoulli principle: a principle of fluid dynamics that states that the pressure of a fluid decreases as its flow speeds up.

bevel: the angle that one surface makes with another when they are not at right angles.

bilge: the inside bottom of the hull of a personal watercraft.

blade guard: a sheet metal shield on an edger/trimmer that prevents objects from accidentally contacting the blade.

blow-by: a leakage or loss of pressure, often used in reference to leakage of compression, past the piston rings, between the piston and cylinder.

boiling point: the temperature at atmospheric pressure at which bubbles or vapors rise to the surface of a liquid and escape.

bolt: A threaded fastener that holds parts together by squeezing them between the head on one end and a nut on the other end.

bolt grade: a grade assigned to a bolt based on the minimum tensile strength specification of the bolt.

bolt head size: the dimension across the flats of the hexagon.

bolt length: the distance from the base of the bolt head to the threaded end of the bolt.

bolt size: the major (largest) diameter of the bolt threads.

bore: the diameter of a hole, such as a cylinder; also to create or enlarge a hole.

boring machine: a machine used to enlarge a cylinder bore.

boss: an extension or strengthened section that supports the piston pin or piston pin bushings.

bottom dead center: the lowest point of piston travel. Abbreviation is BDC.

bounce: in reference to engine valves, a condition where the valve is not held tightly to its seat when the cam is not lifting it. In reference to an ignition distributor, a condition where breaker points make and break contact when they should remain closed.

boundary lubrication: a noncontinuous oil film between moving parts allowing intermittent metal-to-metal contact between the high spots on sliding surfaces.

bound electron: a closely held electron that never leaves an atom.

bow: the front of the PWC.

bow line: a cable or rope attached to the trailer or winch to hold the bow of the watercraft in place on the trailer.

box-end wrench: a six- or twelve-sided wrench that completely encompasses a nut or bolt head.

brake horsepower: a measurement of power developed by an engine in actual operation. Abbreviation is bhp.

breaker arm: a movable part of a pair of contact points in an ignition distributor or magneto.

breaker cam: the lobed cam rotating in the ignition system that interrupts the primary circuit to induce a high tension spark for ignition.

breaker points: two separable points that interrupt primary circuit in a distributor or magneto for the purpose of inducing a high tension current in the ignition system.

break-in: the process of wearing into a desirable fit between surfaces of two new or reconditioned parts.

British Thermal Unit: a measurement of the amount of heat required to raise the temperature of 1 lb of water, 1°F. Abbreviation is BTU.

brushcutter: a handheld, engine-powered machine that cuts brush with a spinning blade.

brushes: bars of carbon or other conducting material that contact the commutator of an electric motor or generator.

bushing: a removable liner for a bearing.

bypass: an alternate path for a flowing substance.

bypass filter system: an oil filtration system that pumps part of the oil through the filter, while pumping the remaining oil to the engine bearings. Oil pumped through the filter is returned directly to the crankcase.

C

calibrate: to determine or adjust the graduation or scale of any instrument giving quantitative measurements.

California Air Resources Board (CARB): the agency responsible for setting emission limits for the state of California.

cam angle: the number of degrees of distributor shaft rotation during which contact points are closed.

cam-ground piston: a piston ground to a slightly oval shape, which, under the heat of operation, becomes round.

camshaft: a shaft containing lobes or cams that operate engine valves.

cap screw: an externally threaded fastener, similar to a machine screw but with a hexagonal head, that can be used in a threaded bore or with a nut.

capacitance: the property that opposes any change in voltage in all electrical circuits.

capacitive discharge ignition: a type of electronic ignition system that uses a silicon-controlled rectifier for switching. Abbreviation is CDI.

capacitor: a device that possesses capacitance (stores electricity). In simple state, consists of two metal plates separated by an insulator.

carbon: a common nonmetallic element that is an excellent conductor of electricity. It also forms in the combustion chamber of an engine during the burning of fuel and oil.

carbon monoxide: a gas, formed by incomplete combustion, that is colorless, odorless, and very poisonous. Chemical formula is CO.

carburetor: a device for automatically mixing fuel in proper proportion with air to produce a combustible gas.

carburetor icing: a term used to describe formation of ice on a carburetor throttle plate during certain atmospheric conditions.

carburetor kit: a kit that contain all the parts needed for a typical carburetor overhaul.

case harden: to harden the surface of steel.

castle nut: a hexagonal nut with a slot cut into the top of each side. Commonly used in conjunction with cotter pins, which prevent the nut from loosening.

cavitation: the formation of air pockets or bubbles in a fluid.

cell: part of a battery containing a group of positive and negative plates along with electrolyte.

cell connector: the lead bar or link connecting the pole of one battery cell to the pole of another.

Celsius: a measurement of temperature. Zero on Celsius scale is 32° on Fahrenheit scale.

center electrode: the conductor that carries the high voltage current to the spark gap. If the electrical potential is great enough to cause the current to jump the plug gap, the side electrode will complete the circuit to ground.

centrifugal force: a force that tends to move a body away from its center of rotation.

centrifugal (mechanical) governor: a governor that consists of pivoted flyweights that are attached to a revolving shaft or a gear driven by the engine.

chain guard (scabbard): a sheath placed over the chainsaw blade when the saw is not in use.

chamfer: a bevel or taper at the edge of a hole.

charge (or recharge): passing an electrical current through a battery to restore it to activity.

chasing: the procedure of recutting a thread with a threading tap.

chassis: the main framework of the tractor around which the entire tractor is assembled.

check valve: a gate or valve that allows the passage of gas or fluid in one direction only.

choke: a reduced passage, such as a valve placed in a carburetor air inlet to restrict the volume of air admitted.

circuit: the path of electrical current, fluids, or gases.

circuit breaker: a switch that trips to the open position to stop excess current flow in a circuit. After a breaker trips, it can be reset to allow current flow through the circuit.

clearance: the space allowed between two parts, such as between a journal and a bearing.

clevis pin: a pin that functions as an axle so a part can swivel on it.

clockwise rotation: rotation in same direction as the hands of a clock.

closed-loop EFI system: an electronic fuel injection system that continuously adjusts the air-fuel mixture based on feedback from an oxygen sensor.

coefficient of friction: a measurement of the amount of friction developed between two surfaces that are rubbed together.

coil: an electrical device made up of a helical conductor, which builds a concentrated magnetic field when current passes through it.

collector: one of the three elements in a transistor.

combination slip-joint pliers: pliers with adjustable jaws that are equipped with edges designed to cut soft metal wire.

combination wrench: a wrench that has a box-end wrench on one end and an open-end wrench on the other.

combustion: the process of burning.

combustion space or chamber: the portion of a cylinder above the piston with the piston at top dead center.

commutator: a ring of copper bars in a generator or electric motor that provides connections between armature coils and brushes.

components: the parts that constitute a whole.

compost: decomposing organic material used for fertilizer.

compound: a mixture of two or more ingredients.

compression: the reduction in volume or the *squeezing* of a gas. As applied to metal, such as a coil spring, compression is the opposite of tension.

compression gauge: see *compression tester*.

compression ratio: the volume of a combustion chamber at end of the compression stroke as compared to the volume of the cylinder and chamber with the piston at bottom dead center.

compression rings: piston rings designed to provide a strong seal, keeping the compressed air-fuel mixture and the burning gases above the piston by preventing passage between the piston and the cylinder wall.

compression stroke: occurs as the piston moves upward in the cylinder with both valves closed. During this stroke, the air-fuel mixture is compressed into a smaller space.

compression test: a test used to evaluate cylinder sealing.

compression tester: a gauge that measures the maximum air pressure in a combustion chamber.

concentric: term used to describe two or more circles having a common center.

condensation: the process of vapor becoming a liquid; the reverse of evaporation.

condenser: a device for temporarily collecting and storing a surge of electrical current for later discharge.

conduction: heat transfer through a solid material. Also, the flow of electricity through a conducting body.

conductor: a material along or through which electricity will flow with slight resistance; silver, copper, and carbon are good conductors.

connecting rod: a link that attaches the piston to the crankshaft.

constant level splash system: a lubrication system that contains an oil pump, a splash trough, and a strainer. Engines with constant-level systems can be operated at an angle while still providing adequate lubrication.

contact breaker: a device for interrupting an electrical circuit; often automatic and may be known as a *circuit breaker, interrupter, cut-out,* or *relay.*

contact points: two separable points used to open and close a circuit.

continuity tester: See *multimeter*.

contraction: a reduction in mass or dimension; the opposite of expansion.

convection: a transfer of heat by circulating heated air.

converter: when used in connection with liquefied petroleum gas, it is a device that converts or changes LPG from liquid to vapor state for use in the engine. See *liquid petroleum gas*.

coolant: a mixture of antifreeze and water used in a pressurized cooling system.

coolant hydrometer: a test instrument used to check coolant strength.

cooling fins: thin metal projections on the cylinder block that increase the surface area around the outside of the cylinder on air-cooled engines.

corrected horsepower: an estimate of the horsepower of a given engine under specific operating conditions that are not the same as those present during actual dynamometer testing.

corrode: to eat away gradually, especially by chemical action.

cotter pin: a pin used to lock castle nuts and secure clevis pins.

counterclockwise rotation: rotating in the opposite direction of the hands on a clock.

coupling: a connection that transfers movement from one part to another; may be mechanical, hydraulic, or electrical.

crankcase: the housing for the crankshaft and other related internal parts.

crankcase dilution: the thinning of engine lubricating oil resulting from unburned fuel.

crankcase seal: a seal that prevents leakage of oil from the areas where the crankshaft and crankcase come together.

crank offset: the distance from the centerline of the connecting rod journal to the centerline of the crankshaft.

crankshaft: the major rotating part of the engine. It converts the reciprocating (back-and-forth) motion of the piston into rotary (circular) motion.

crankshaft counter-balance: a series of weights attached to or forged integrally with the crankshaft and placed to offset the reciprocating weight of each piston and rod assembly.

crankshaft throw: the offset portion of the crankshaft measured from the centerline of the main bearing bore to the centerline of the connecting rod journal.

critical-thinking skills: higher-level skills that enable one to think beyond the obvious.

crude oil: oil as it comes from the ground, unrefined.

cubic inch: abbreviation is cu in.

current: the flow of electricity.

cylinder: a round chamber of some depth bored to receive a piston; also sometimes referred to as *bore* or *barrel*.

cylinder block: the portion of the engine block that contains the cylinder bore.

cylinder head: a detachable portion of an engine that sits atop the cylinder block and contains all or a part of the combustion chamber.

cylinder hone: a tool equipped with abrasive stones that is used to recondition moderately worn or freshly bored cylinders.

cylinder sleeve: a liner or tube placed between the piston and the cylinder wall or cylinder block to provide the wearing surface of the cylinder.

cylinder taper: a cylinder wear pattern in which the cylinder diameter is greater at the top than at the bottom.

D

dampening coils: valve spring coils that are progressively spaced closer together to provide additional tension as the valve closes.

dead center: the extreme upper or lower position of the crankshaft throw at which the piston is not moving in either direction.

dead man switch: a switch that automatically shuts the tool off when the operator releases the control button.

deck: any permanent horizontal covering over the hull.

degree: abbreviation is deg., or indicated by a ° symbol placed alongside of a figure; may be used to designate temperature readings or angularity, one degree being 1/360th of a circle.

demagnetize: to remove the magnetization of a pole that has previously been magnetized.

density: compactness; relative mass of matter in a given volume.

detergent/dispersant additives: oil additives that keep engine parts clean by suspending fine particles of the oil contaminants until they can be trapped by the oil filter.

dethatcher blade: a mower blade equipped with springlike fingers that rake up thatch as the blade rotates.

detonation: an excessively rapid burning or explosion of the mixture in the engine cylinders.

diagonal side-cutting pliers: pliers with cutting jaws for clipping soft metal wire.

diagnostic trouble code (DTC): a code that is created by and stored in the ECU in the event of an engine malfunction. The technician can retrieve the code for use in diagnosis of electronic fuel injection systems.

diaphragm: a flexible partition or wall separating two cavities.

die: a cutting tool used for cutting (threading) external threads on a rod, bolt, shaft, or pin. See *die-stock*.

die casting: an accurate and smooth casting made by pouring molten metal or material into a metal mold or die under pressure.

diesel fuel: fuel formulated specifically for use with diesel engines.

die stock: used to hold die while cutting external threads. See *die*.

differential gears: gears that permit each rear axle to turn at different speeds.

differential pressure test: a test that checks the compression of an engine by measuring leakage from the cylinder to other parts of the engine.

digital tachometer: an electronic test instrument used to check engine rpm. This type of tachometer has a digital readout that will display engine rpm when the engine is running.

dilution: adding one fluid to another fluid in order to thin or weaken it. See *crankcase dilution*.

diode: a solid-state device that will conduct current in one direction and remain nonconductive in the reverse direction.

dipper: an arm on the connecting rod that picks up and splashes oil on the moving parts within the crankcase during each crankshaft revolution.

direct current: electric current that flows continuously in one direction, such as that generated by a storage battery. Abbreviation is dc.

discharge: the flow of electric current from the battery.

displacement: see *piston displacement*.

distortion: a warpage or change in physical form.

domain: a group of atoms having the same magnetic polarity.

dowel pin: a pin inserted in matching holes in two parts to maintain those parts in fixed relation to each other.

downdraft carburetor: a carburetor type in which the mixture flows downward to the engine.

draft: the depth of the watercraft's hull below the waterline.

drain plug: a plug that is removed to allow water to drain from the bilge of a personal watercraft. Can also refer to the plug that is removed to drain oil from an engine.

drift punch: a tapered punch used to align holes in mating parts.

drop forging: shaping a piece of steel between dies while it is hot.

dry bulb primers: primers that pump air into the float bowl, increasing air pressure and forcing fuel up the carburetor's main nozzle.

dry-charged batteries: a type of storage battery that must have electrolyte installed after purchase.

dry-type air cleaner: an air cleaner in which the airstream passes through a pleated paper, felt, fiber, or flocked screen.

dual-element air cleaner: an air cleaner that consists of a foam filter pre-cleaner ahead of a pleated paper-type cartridge.

dwell: the number of degrees the breaker cam rotates from the time the breaker points close until they open again. Also known as *cam angle*.

dynamometer: A machine for measuring the actual power produced by an internal combustion engine.

E

ear plugs: hearing protection that fits inside the ear canal.

eccentric: one circle within another circle, each having a different center. Example: a cam on a camshaft.

economizer circuit: a carburetor circuit that provides reduced fuel flow when the engine operates at part throttle.

edger/trimmer: a versatile implement equipped with a blade that can be adjusted for vertical trimming or horizontal trimming operations.

ejection pump system: a lubrication system in which oil is forced under pressure against the rotating connecting rod. Some oil enters the connecting rod bearings, while the remaining oil is deflected to other parts in the crankcase.

electric starter: an electric motor that rotates the engine for starting.

electrode: usually refers to the insulated center rod of a spark plug. It is also sometimes used to refer to the rod attached to the shell of the spark plug.

electrolyte: a mixture of sulphuric acid and distilled water used in conventional lead-acid type storage batteries.

electromotive force or voltage: electrical pressure that results in current. Abbreviation is EMF.

electronic: term used to describe any electrical component, assembly, circuit, or system that uses semiconductor, or solid state, devices.

electronic fuel injection (EFI): a computer-controlled system that injects the proper amount of fuel into the air intake based on information received from a variety of sensor that monitor engine operation.

electronic governor: a governor system in which an electronic control unit (ECU) and a stepper motor control throttle plate position.

electronic switching device: a device used instead of breaker points to control the primary current to the coil. An electronic switching device is more dependable than a mechanical type because it has no moving parts to wear or burn out.

electrons: negatively (–) charged particles that travel in orbits around the center of the atom.

element: one set of positive plates and one set of negative plates complete with separators assembled together.

emitter: one of the three elements in a transistor.

energy: the capacity for doing work.

engine: the term applies to the prime source of power generation.

engine block: a casting of iron or an aluminum alloy designed to keep all engine parts in alignment.

engine bore: the diameter or width across the top of the cylinder.

engine control unit (ECU): a computer that receives and interprets data from sensors and controls engine operation by sending signals to actuators.

engine displacement: the sum of the displacement of all the engine cylinders.

engineer: an individual who designs engines that will perform satisfactorily under specific environmental conditions.

engine service technician: an individual who performs tune-ups, services equipment, and makes repairs to small engines and related implements.

entrepreneur: a person who starts his or her own business.

Environmental Protection Agency: a government-funded agency that regulates policies that deal with environmental issues. Abbreviation is EPA.

Equipment & Engine Training Council (EETC): an organization that creates and administers voluntary certification tests related to small engine repair.

ethical behavior: behavior that conforms to accepted standards of fairness and good conduct.

evaporation: the process of changing from a liquid to a vapor, such as boiling water to produce steam.

exhaust: the spent fuel after combustion takes place in an internal combustion engine.

exhaust pipe: the pipe connecting the engine to the muffler to conduct the exhausted or spent gases away from the engine.

exhaust stroke: the piston stroke during which the exhaust valve opens and the rising piston pushes the exhaust gases from the cylinder.

expansion: an increase in size.

extended rope starter: a recoil starter with a rope long enough that the operator can start the engine without bending over.

F

face shield: a shield, made from shatterproof plastic, that protects the entire face from debris and chemicals.

Fahrenheit (F): a scale of temperature measurement in which the boiling point of water is 212° and the freezing point of water is 32°.

Federal Clean Air Act: an act aimed at ridding the atmosphere of harmful road vehicle emissions.

feeler gauge: a metal strip or blade finished to an accurate thickness and used for measuring the clearance between two parts. Feeler gauges ordinarily come in a set of different blades graduated in thickness by increments of .001″.

ferrous metal: metals that contain iron.

field: in a generator or electric motor, the area in which magnetic flow occurs.

field coil: a coil of insulated wire surrounding the field pole.

file: a steel bar with rows of hardened shallow teeth used to deburr, smooth, shape, or sharpen metal.

filler plug: a plug that threads into the crankcase filler hole to seal out dirt and seal in the oil.

fillet: a rounded junction between two parts joined at an angle.

filter: a unit containing an element, such as a screen of varying degrees of fineness, that traps foreign material that is in a fluid, such as air, fuel, or oil.

fire extinguisher: a handheld device used to suppress fires.

fit: closeness of contact between surfaces.

flange: a projecting rim or collar on an object for keeping it in place.

flash: to vaporize.

flashover: tendency of current to travel down the outside of a spark plug instead of through the center electrode.

flash point: the lowest temperature at which a combustible material will produce an ignitable vapor.

flat washer: a washer that provides a wider bearing surface for a bolt or screw head and/or nut.

float: a hollow tank that is lighter than the fluid in which it rests. A float is ordinarily used to automatically operate a valve controlling the entrance of a fluid.

floating piston pin: a piston pin that is not locked in the connecting rod or the piston, but is free to turn or oscillate in both the connecting rod and the piston.

floating rings: piston rings installed with the ring end gaps staggered to avoid gap alignment and possible oil flow through the series of gaps to the combustion chamber.

float level: the predetermined height of the fuel in the carburetor bowl, usually regulated by means of a suitable valve.

flooded engine: a condition in which too much fuel enters the cylinder, resulting in combustion failure.

flutter: a condition arising from a valve not being held tightly on its seat when the cam is not lifting it.

flyweights: special weights that react to centrifugal force to provide automatic control of other mechanisms, such as accelerators or valves.

flywheel: a heavy wheel fastened to one end of the crankshaft to improve the running quality of the engine. The inertia of the flywheel keeps the crankshaft spinning and smoothes engine operation.

foot-pound: a measure of the amount of work performed by lifting 1 lb a distance of 1 ft. Abbreviation is ft-lb.

force-fit: also known as a press-fit, interference-fit or drive-fit. This term is used when a shaft is slightly larger than a hole and must be forced in place.

forge: to shape plastic or hot metal by hammering.

form-in-place sealant: a sealant that can be used in place of conventional gaskets when the exact replacement gasket is not available. See *gasket.*

forward: toward the bow of a watercraft.

forward biased: term used to describe a diode that is connected in a circuit in such a way that it acts as a conductor.

four-stroke engine: also known as *Otto cycle.* A combustion cycle that consists of an intake, a compression, a power; and an exhaust stroke.

four-wheel steering: a steering arrangement in which the rear wheels turn in the opposite direction as the front wheels in order to reduce turning radius.

free electron: an electron that can be freed to move from one atom to another when electricity is applied.

friction: resistance to motion created when one surface rubs against another.

frictional horsepower: the portion of indicated horsepower lost due to the drag of engine parts rubbing together. Abbreviated fhp.

friction bearing: a bearing that uses a smooth, sliding surface to reduce friction between moving parts.

fuel injector: a solenoid-operated device that sprays a measured amount of fuel into the intake air stream when it receives a signal from the ECU.

fuel knock: see *detonation.*

fuel pick-up line: a tube that draws gasoline from the fuel tank.

fuel pump: a device that provides constant, pressurized fuel flow to the carburetor under changing conditions.

fuel stabilizer: an additive that delays the deterioriation of gasoline.

fuel vent check valve: a valve mounted in the personal watercraft fuel tank vent hose to allow air to enter the fuel tank but minimize fuel spillage if a personal watercraft is overturned.

fulcrum: the support on which a lever turns in moving a body.

full-flow filter system: an oil filtration system that directs the entire volume of pumped oil through the filter to the bearings.

fuse: circuit protection device that contains an internal conductor that is designed to melt when current in the circuit exceeds the current rating of the fuse.

fusible link: a special type of wire that is designed to melt when too much current is flowing through a circuit. This type of circuit protection device is generally used in circuits that carry large amounts of current.

G

gapping tool: a tool used to bend the outer electrode toward or away from the center electrode when gapping a spark plug.

gas: a substance that can be changed in volume and shape according to the temperature and pressure applied to it.

gasket: a soft, pliable material, such as fiber, rubber, neoprene (synthetic rubber), cork, treated paper, thin steel, or laminated material, used between engine parts to seal and prevent leakage of engine oil, coolant, compression, and vacuum; acts as a seal.

gassing: the bubbling of the battery electrolyte that occurs during the process of charging a battery.

gear ratio: the number of revolutions made by a driving gear compared to the number of revolutions made by a driven gear of a different size.

general manager: an individual who oversees the overall operation of a business.

generator: a device consisting of an armature, field coils, and other parts, which when rotated, generates electricity. A generator is usually driven by a belt from the engine crankshaft.

glaze: an extremely smooth or glossy surface finish, such as the highly polished finish of a cylinder that develops over a long period of time due to the friction of the piston rings.

glaze breaker: a tool for removing the glossy surface finish in an engine cylinder.

glow plug: a device with a fine wire connected in series to an electrical circuit for the purpose of creating enough resistance and heat to ignite fuel in a combustion chamber.

governor: a mechanical, hydraulic, or electrical device that controls and regulates speed.

grass discharge chute guard: an important safety device on lawn mowers and tractors that prevents objects from being thrown out the discharge chute.

grease fitting: a fitting to which a grease gun can be attached in order to lubricate an otherwise inaccessible part.

grid: the metal framework of an individual battery plate in which the active material is placed.

grind: to finish or polish a surface by means of an abrasive material.

grip length: the distance from the base of the bolt head to the thread.

grooved pin: a type of pin driven into an interference hole; the groove cuts into the wall of the hole and secures the pin.

gum: oxidized petroleum products that accumulate in the fuel system, carburetor, or engine parts.

H

hacksaws: a thin-blade saw designed to cut through metal.

hazardous waste: waste that is on the EPA's list of hazardous material or has one or more of the following characteristics: ignitability, reactivity, corrosivity, and EP toxicity.

headphone-type protector: ear protection that surrounds the entire ear.

heat range: an indicator of a plug's ability to transfer heat from the firing end to the cylinder head.

heat treatment: a combination of heating and cooling operations timed and applied to a metal in a solid state in a way that will produce desired properties.

hexagon nut: a nut that has six sides and can be loosened or tightened with standard sockets and box-end wrenches.

high tension: the secondary or induced high-voltage electrical current; high tension is also used in reference to the wiring from the distributor cap to the coil and the spark plugs.

hone: an abrasive tool for correcting small irregularities or differences in the diameter of a cylinder.

horsepower: the rate of work performed by lifting 550 lb a distance of 1 ft in 1 second. Abbreviation is HP or hp.

hot spot: refers to a comparatively thin section or area of the wall between the inlet and exhaust manifold of an engine, the purpose being to allow the hot exhaust gases to heat the comparatively cool incoming mixture. Also used to designate local areas of the cooling system that have above average temperatures.

HP or hp: see *horsepower*.

hull: the body of the watercraft from bow to stern.

hunting: erratic or oscillating engine speed.

hydrocarbon: any compound composed entirely of carbon and hydrogen, such as petroleum products.

hydrocarbon engine: an engine that uses petroleum products, such as gas, liquefied gas, gasoline, kerosene, or fuel oil as a fuel.

hydrodynamic lubrication: a complete, unbroken film of oil between surfaces.

hydrogen gas: gas generated by batteries during charging. It combines with oxygen to form a highly explosive mixture.

hydrometer: an instrument for determining the state of charge in a battery by finding the specific gravity of the electrolyte.

I

identification numbers: numbers found on the engine and hull of personal watercraft that are used to register the craft.

idle: refers to the engine operating at its slowest practical speed.

idling circuit: a carburetor circuit that supplies just enough air-fuel mixture to keep the engine running during idle.

ignition advance system: a mechanical system used in MBI systems to cause the spark to occur earlier in the operating cycle during intermediate- and high-speed operation.

ignition coil: a device consisting of primary and secondary wire windings. As current passes through the primary windings, it builds an electric field. When current stops, the magnetic field collapses and induces high voltage current in the secondary windings.

ignition distributor: an electrical unit containing the circuit breaker for the primary circuit and providing a means for conveying the secondary or high-tension current to the spark plug wires as required.

ignition system: the means for igniting the fuel in the cylinders; includes spark plugs, wiring, ignition distributor, ignition coil, and source of electrical current supply.

impeller: a rotor or wheel with blades to pump water or propel objects through water or other fluids.

indicated horsepower: a measure of the total potential horsepower the engine is capable of developing. Abbreviation is IHP.

induction: the influence of different strength magnetic fields that are not electrically connected to one another.

induction coil: essentially a transformer that, through the action of induction, creates a high-tension current in the secondary windings by collapsing a magnetic field that surrounds the primary windings.

inertia: the tendency of a motionless body to remain at rest and also the tendency of a moving body to remain in motion.

inhibitor: a material to prevent or hinder some unwanted action, such as a rust inhibitor, which is a chemical added to a cooling system to retard rust formation.

inlet pipe: see *intake manifold*.

inlet valve: see *intake valve*.

inside diameter: the diameter of the inner circle in a tube or donut shape. Abbreviation is ID.

inside micrometer: a micrometer designed to measure the inside diameter of a bore.

insulation: any material that does not conduct electricity; used to prevent the flow or leakage of current from a conductor. Also, used to describe a material that does not conduct heat readily.

insulator: a nonconductor of electricity. Material in which the majority of atoms contain bound electrons. Cas also refer to the aluminum-oxide ceramic material that surrounds a spark plug's center electrode and forms top portion of the spark plug.

intake manifold: the tube used to conduct the gasoline and air mixture from the carburetor to the engine cylinders.

intake stroke: the piston stroke in which the piston travels downward in the cylinder with the intake valve open. This increases the volume above the piston and creates a partial vacuum that draws the air-fuel mixture into the cylinder.

intake valve: a valve that permits a fluid or gas to enter a chamber and seals against exit.

integral: formed as a unit with another part.

intensify: to increase or concentrate, such as to increase the voltage of an electrical current.

interference angle: the difference in angle between mating surfaces of a valve and a valve seat.

intermittent: motion or action that is not constant but occurs at intervals.

internal combustion: the burning of a fuel within an enclosed space.

internal combustion engine: a type of engine in which an air/fuel mixture is ignited and burned within the engine.

Internal Combustion Engine Institute, Inc: Abbreviation is ICEI.

internship: an arrangement with an educational institution whereby a student is supervised while working with a more experienced jobholder.

J

jam nut: a thin nut that is tightened against a plain nut to produce a locking condition.

jet pump: an impeller-type pump that provides the propulsion for a PWC.

jet pump intake grate: a screen or grate on a personal watercraft that prevents large debris from entering the jet pump intake and damaging the impeller or drive shaft.

jet pump outlet nozzle: a nozzle on a personal watercraft through which water is forced at high velocity. The jet pump outlet nozzle is hinged to allow it to control the direction of the personal watercraft. The nozzle is directed by turning the handlebars right or left.

job application form: a form that highlights the information an employer needs to know about you, your education, and your work experience. Employers often use job application forms to screen applicants for the skills needed on the job.

job interview: a face-to-face meeting that gives the prospective employee the opportunity to learn more about a company and to convince the employer that he or she is the best person for the position.

job shadowing: process of observing a person in the workplace to learn more about his or her job and its requirements.

journal: the part of a shaft or crank that rotates inside of a bearing.

jump spark: a high-tension electrical current that jumps through the air from one terminal to another.

jumper wire: a length of wire with alligator clips at each end used to bypass components or to apply source voltage directly to a component.

K

kantlink washer: the most common type of lock washer; made of spring steel with beveled ends.

key: a small block inserted between a shaft and hub to fasten a pulley or gear to the shaft.

keyseat: the recess in which the key rests. See *key* and *keyway*.

keyway: the groove in the pulley, gear, or collar where the key and the keyseat match. See *key* and *keyseat*.

kickback: the sudden, violent movement of a chainsaw blade toward the operator; often caused by the nose of the chain saw hitting a solid object.

kickout: the sudden and uncontrolled motion toward the operator's right or rear that occurs if a rotating brushcutter blade comes in contact with a solid object.

knock: a general term used to describe various noises occurring in an engine; may be used to describe noises made by loose or worn mechanical parts, preignition, or detonation.

knurl: to indent or roughen a finished surface.

L

lacquer: a solution of solids in solvents that evaporate rapidly, leaving behind a solid residue.

laminate: to build up or construct out of a number of thin sheets.

lands: the full-diameter ridges between the piston grooves.

lanyard: engine shut-off cord on PWC attached to the operator and the stop switch.

lapping: the process of fitting one surface to another by rubbing them together with an abrasive material between the two surfaces.

lapping stick: a stick with a suction cup on the end; used to spin valves during lapping procedures.

lead: a short connecting wire that makes electrical contact between two points.

leadership: the ability to guide and motivate others to complete tasks or achieve goals.

leaf-type feeler gauges: thin metal strips used to measure the gaps between parts.

lean mixture: an air-fuel mixture that contains too much air.

letter of application: a letter that a prospective employee sends to a potential employer to formally apply for a position and request an interview.

letter of recommendation: a letter written by one of the job applicant's references that gives the employer a more in-depth look at applicant's skills.

lifelong learning: the process of continually updating one's knowledge and skills.

liner: usually a thin section placed between two parts, such as a replaceable cylinder liner in an engine.

linkage: any series of rods, yokes, and levers, etc., used to transmit motion from one unit to another.

liquid: any substance that assumes the shape of the vessel in which it is placed without changing volume.

liquid petroleum gas: A normally gaseous hydrocarbon that is usable as a fuel for internal combustion engines. Abbreviation is LPG.

load adjusting needle: a needle valve that regulates the amount of fuel entering the main discharge nozzle.

loaded oil: oil that has reached a level of contamination that prevents it from absorbing more contaminants and functioning as an effective lubricant.

lobe: an off-center or eccentric enlargement on a shaft that converts rotary motion to reciprocating motion. Also called a *cam.*

lock nut: a nut designed to create friction to reduce the tendency for vibration or motion to rotate and loosen the nut.

lock washer: a washer that is designed to prevent loosening of bolts, screws, and nuts.

loop-scavenged engine: engine in which the fuel transfer ports are shaped and located so that the incoming air-fuel mixture swirls.

lost motion: motion between a driving part and a driven part that does not move the driven part. Also see *backlash.*

low-oil shutdown system: a system designed to shut down an engine when the oil level is low.

low-oil warning device: an electrical device that warns the operator when the engine has a low-oil level.

LPG: see *liquid petroleum gas.*

lubrication: the process of reducing friction between sliding surfaces by introducing a slippery or smooth substance between them.

M

machine screw: an externally threaded fastener, typically with a rounded head, that can be used in a threaded bore or with a nut.

magnet (permanent): a piece of hard steel that radiates a magnetic field.

magnetic field: force produced by a magnet and evidenced by lines of force, or magnetic flux, around the magnet.

magneto: an electrical device that generates current when rotated by an outside source of power.

magneto system: a type of ignition system that produces electrical current without an outside primary source of electricity.

major diameter: largest diameter of a bolt's threads.

manifold: a pipe with multiple openings used to connect various cylinders to one inlet or outlet.

manufacturer's technician: an individual who develops prototype engines or engine parts and tests new design theories.

mean effective pressure: the average pressure developed during the power stroke minus the average pressure during the intake, compression, and exhaust strokes. Abbreviated mep.

mechanical breaker point ignition: an ignition system that uses a mechanical switching device (breaker points) to control primary current to the coil. Abbreviated MBI.

mechanical breaker points: mechanical switching device used to control primary current to the coil in MBI systems.

mechanical efficiency: the ratio between the indicated horsepower and the brake horsepower of an engine.

mentor: someone with great experience and knowledge who guides a less experienced worker.

metric (M) series: a type of bolt with threads formed at 60° angles.

micrometer: a measuring instrument for either external or internal measurement in thousandths or ten thousandths of an inch.

mill: to cut or machine with rotating, toothed cutters.

misfiring: failure of proper combustion to occur in one or more cylinders while the engine is running; may be a continuous or intermittent failure.

module: a packaged functional assembly of wired electronic components for use with other such assemblies.

motor: this term should be used in connection with an electric motor and should not be used when referring to an engine.

Motor and Equipment Manufacturer's Association: abbreviation is MEMA.

Motor and Equipment Wholesaler's Association: abbreviation is MEWA.

movable sheave: the movable part of a variable-speed pulley.

muffler: a component installed on the engine's exhaust port to reduce the exhaust noise while still allowing the gases to escape efficiently.

mulching: chopping organic material, such as grass clippings, into very fine particles.

multigrade oil: an oil that meet the viscosity requirements of two or more SAE grades.

multimeter: a measuring instrument that is a combination ammeter, ohmmeter, and voltmeter. See *ammeter, ohmmeter,* and *voltmeter.*

multiviscosity oil: see *multigrade oil.*

N

National Coarse: coarse thread series designation. Abbreviation is NC.

National Fine: fine thread series designation. Abbreviation is NF.

National Standard Parts Association: abbreviaton is NSPA.

natural draft carburetor: a carburetor in which the air flows horizontally through the air horn.

needle bearing: an antifriction bearing using a great number of small, cylindrical rollers. Also known as a *quill-type bearing*.

needle nose pliers: pliers with long thin jaws.

negative pole: the point from which an electrical current flows through the circuit. It is designated by a minus sign (–).

neon tube: an electric bulb or tube filled with a rare gas. Neon tubes are often used on ignition test instruments.

networking: the exchange of information or services among individuals or groups. As a newcomer to the career field, the goal of your networking is to learn about possible job leads.

neutron: an electrically neutral particle found in the nucleus of an atom.

nonferrous metals: this designation includes practically all metals that do not contain iron (or contain very little iron) and, therefore, are not subject to rusting.

north pole: the pole of a magnet where the lines of force start; the opposite of south pole.

nut: a nut holds parts together by squeezing them between the nut on one end and the head of a bolt on the other. See *bolts*.

O

Occupational Safety and Health Administration (OSHA): a governmental organization that establishes rules for safe work practices.

octane number: a number that corresponds with a fuel's ability to resist detonation.

offset screwdriver: a screwdriver with offset shaft, designed to reach obstructed screws.

ohm: a measurement of the resistance to the flow of an electrical current through a conductor.

Ohm's law: formula used to calculate an unknown circuit value when two other values are known.

ohmmeter: an instrument that measures the resistance to the flow of electrical current through a conductor. See *ohm* and *multimeter*.

oil control rings: piston rings designed to remove surplus oil from the cylinder walls.

oil pumping: a term used to describe an engine that is using an excessive amount of lubricating oil.

oil slinger: a device with several blades that pick up oil and splash it onto the internal engine parts. Because the slinger has multiple blades, it provides a more consistent supply of oil to the moving engine parts than a dipper.

oil-wetted air cleaner: an air cleaner that has a filtering element (typically polyurethane foam) that is dampened with engine oil.

open circuit: a break or opening in an electrical circuit that interferes with the passage of the current.

open-circuit voltage: test used to check the general condition of a battery.

open-end wrench: a wrench that grips a nut or bolt head on two sides.

open-loop EFI system: a fuel injection system in which the ECU determines the air-fuel mixture based on a preprogrammed fuel map. This type of system does *not* monitor feedback from an oxygen sensor.

operator presence control: a lever that stops a snow thrower auger from rotating if it is released.

operator presence switch: a switch that stops the engine if the operator leaves the seat while the blades or PTO (power-take-off) is engaged.

optical tachometer: a type of tachometer that uses an optical sensor to measure the rotation of a piece of reflective tape attached to a rotating part of the engine.

oscillate: to swing back and forth like a pendulum.

Otto cycle: an operating cycle, also called *four-stroke cycle*, consisting of intake, compression, power, and exhaust strokes.

out-of-roundness: the oval cylinder shape created by excessive cylinder wear 90° from the crankshaft centerline.

outside diameter: the diameter of the outer circle in a tube or donut shape. Abbreviation is OD.

over square: a cylinder with a bore diameter that is greater than the stroke.

overcharging: charging a battery in excess of what is necessary. Overcharging can severely corrode the positive plate grids, weakening them and causing a loss of electrical conduction.

overhaul: the process of disassembling, cleaning, and replacing parts in an engine or engine component, such as a carburetor.

overhead cam (OHC): a valve train arrangement in which both the camshaft and valve assemblies are located in the cylinder head.

overhead valve (OHV): a valve train arrangement in which the camshaft is installed in the crankcase and the valves are installed in the cylinder head.

owner's manual: a book containing basic maintenance and service information. Typically includes information on maintenance schedules, fluid capacities, and part numbers for maintenance components.

oxidize: to combine an element with oxygen or convert it into its oxide, often through combustion.

oxygen: a odorless, colorless gas that supports combustion. It is produced, along with hydrogen, during battery charging.

oxygenates: additives, such as alcohols and ethers, commonly added to fuels to increase their octane levels.

P

parallel circuit: an electrical circuit in which there is more than one path for the current to flow.

peak inverse voltage (PIV): the amount of voltage a diode can take in the reverse direction without being damaged.

peening: displacing metal just outside the edge of the valve seat insert to lock the insert in place.

performance: a measure of how well an engine works.

personal watercraft: a particular type of popular small boat that is propelled and guided by a high-velocity jet of water. Abbreviation is PWC.

petroleum: a group of liquid and gaseous compounds composed of carbon and hydrogen.

phase separation: the process of ethanol in a fuel blend absorbing water and falling to the bottom of the fuel tank.

Phillips screw: a screw head having a cross instead of a slot for a corresponding type of screwdriver.

Phillips screwdriver: a screwdriver designed to loosen and tighten Phillips screws.

pin: a small metal cylinder used to either retain parts in a fixed position or to preserve alignment of parts.

pin boss: the section of the piston surrounding the piston pin hole. It is thick and often reinforced with cast-in webs.

pinned ring: a piston ring that is held in position by a short pin that fits into the piston ring groove. The pin prevents rotation of the ring around the groove.

pin punch: a punch designed to drive straight pins, tapered pins, and roll pins into and out of holes.

piston: a part that moves up and down in the cylinder in order to draw air-fuel mixture into the cylinder during the intake stroke, compress the mixture during the compression stroke, transfer force to the crankshaft during the combustion stroke, and force exhaust out of the cylinder during the exhaust stroke.

piston collapse: an abnormal reduction in the diameter of the piston skirt due to heat or stress.

piston displacement: the volume of air moved or displaced by moving the piston from one end of its stroke to the other.

piston head: the part of the piston above the rings.

piston lands: those parts of a piston between the piston rings.

piston pin: the journal for the bearing in the small end of an engine connecting rod. The piston pin also passes through the piston walls, holding the piston to the connecting rod.

piston ring: a circular ring that fits into a piston groove and exerts tension on the cylinder wall. Piston rings prevent blowby of exhaust gases into the crankcase and leakage of oil into the combustion chamber.

piston ring expander: a spring placed behind the piston ring in the groove to increase the pressure of the ring against the cylinder wall.

piston ring gap: the clearance between the ends of the piston ring.

piston ring groove: the channel or slots in the piston in which the piston rings are placed.

piston skirt: the part of the piston below the rings and the bosses.

piston slap: a hollow bell-like sound caused by the rocking of a loose-fitting piston in a cylinder.

pitch: the angular relationship of the impeller blades to a line perpendicular to the shaft it is mounted on.

pivot: a pin or short shaft upon which another part rests, turns, rotates, or oscillates.

platinum: an expensive metal having an extremely high melting point and good electrical conductivity. Often used in magneto breaker points.

plunger pump: an outboard engine water pump that consists of a cylinder and a plunger. The plunger is raised and lowered in the cylinder by an eccentric on the propeller shaft.

polarity: the arrangement of positive and negative terminals of a battery, an electric circuit, or a magnet.

polarize: to give polarity to an electric circuit so current will flow in the proper direction.

pop-off pressure: the pressure that lifts the needle from its seat at the carburetor needle valve assembly.

poppet valve: a valve structure consisting of a circular head with an elongated stem attached in the center.

porcelain: general term applied to the material or element used for insulating the center electrode of a spark plug.

port: the openings in the cylinder block for valves, exhaust and inlet pipes, or water connections. In two-cycle engines, the openings for inlet and exhaust purposes. Can also refer to the area to the left of a watercraft's centerline.

porting: system that consists of two holes (ports) in the cylinder wall of some two-stroke engines. One port admits the air-fuel mixture and the other port allows exhaust gases to escape.

positive displacement oil pump: an oil pump commonly used in pressurized lubrication systems.

positive pole: the point to which an electrical current returns after passing through the circuit. This is designated by a plus sign (+).

post: in a battery, the heavy cylindrical part to which the group of plates is attached. The post extends through the cell cover to provide a means of attachment to the adjacent cell or battery cable.

potential: an indication of the amount of energy available.

potential difference: a difference of electrical pressure that sets up a flow of electric current.

pounds per square inch: a unit of pressure measurement. Abbreviation is PSI.

power: the rate at which work is performed.

power stroke: the piston stroke that occurs when both valves are in the closed position and the force of combustion drives the piston downward.

power-take-off: a coupling point between the engine and a driven implement. Abbreviation is PTO.

practical efficiency: an overall measurement of how efficiently an engine uses the fuel supply.

preignition: the burning of the air-fuel mixture before normal ignition occurs.

premium unleaded: a gasoline blend having a higher octane rating than regular unleaded. See also *super unleaded*.

press-fit: a fit accomplished by forcing a shaft into a hole that is slightly smaller in diameter than the shaft. Also known as a *force-fit* or *drive-fit*.

pressure: the measure of the force applied to a given unit of area.

pressure-vacuum water flow system: an outboard engine cooling system in which propeller action and the forward motion of the boat provide water circulation.

pressurized cooling system: a type of cooling system used in some liquid-cooled engines. The major components of a pressurized system include the radiator, water pump, radiator cap, hoses, fan, and thermostat.

pressurized lubrication system: a lubrication sysem used on larger small engines that relies on a positive displacement gear pump, or rotor pump, to supply oil to moving engine parts.

preventive maintenance: regular maintenance performed to prevent engine problems from developing.

primary winding: in an ignition coil or magneto armature, a wire that conducts the low-tension current, which is to be transformed by induction into high-tension current in the secondary winding.

primary wires: the wiring circuit used for conducting the low-tension, or primary, current to the primary windings of the ignition coil and the switching device.

Prony brake: a machine that uses a friction brake for testing the power of an engine while it is running.

propane: a petroleum hydrocarbon compound that has a boiling point of about 44°F and is used as an engine fuel.

proton: a large, heavy, positively (+) charged particle found in the nucleus of an atom.

push mowers: mowers that are propelled by the operator pushing on them.

pushrod: a connecting link in an operating mechanism, such as the rod between the valve lifter and rocker arm on an overhead valve engine.

R

radiator: a water reservoir made from water tanks and many thin copper or aluminum tubes.

radiator cap: a cap that seals the radiator and allows pressure to build in the cooling system. This helps improve cooling efficiency and prevents evaporation of the coolant.

radiator core: a tube-and-fin assembly that is part of a radiator. The fins increase the cooling surface area of the tubes.

rated horsepower: an engine's power rating, typically 80% of its maximum brake horsepower.

ratio: the relation or proportion that one number bears to another.

reach: the length of the spark plug threads. Reach varies with type of spark plug.

ream: to finish a hole accurately with a rotating, fluted tool.

reamer: a cylindrical cutting tool used to shave metal from the walls of a bore to enlarge it to a specific size.

reboring: using a machine tool to precisely enlarge the diameter of a cylinder bore.

reciprocating: a back-and-forth movement, such as the action of a piston in a cylinder.

reciprocating engine: an engine with pistons that move back and forth in cylinders.

recoil start system: a starting system in which a spring-loaded, ratcheting pulley engages a starter clutch on the flywheel when the starting rope is pulled and automatically rewinds the rope when it is released.

rectifier: a device used to convert alternating current to direct current.

reed valve: a flat, springy valve covering the ports between the carburetor and the crank chamber in a two-cycle engine.

reel-type mower: a lawn mower that has helical blades that rotate around a horizontal shaft.

reference: an individual who will provide important information about an applicant to the prospective employer. A reference can be a teacher, school official, previous employer, or any other adult outside the applicant's family.

regulator: an automatic pressure reducing or regulating valve.

relay: a device used as an electrical switch, allowing a relatively low current to be used to control a high current.

reservoir: a space that holds fluid.

resistance: the quality of an electric circuit, or any component in it, to oppose the flow of electrical current.

respirator: a mask that fits over the mouth and nose to protect against the inhalation of hazardous materials.

résumé: a brief written outline of an applicant's education, work experience, and other qualifications for work. A well-written résumé can help secure an interview.

retaining ring: a circular spring steel fastener that fits externally or internally into a groove in a part.

retard: to cause the spark to occur at a later time in the cycle of engine operation.

reverse biased: a term used to describe a diode that is connected in a circuit in such a way that it acts as an insulator.

reverse bucket: a component that causes the jet stream to flow toward the bow of the personal watercraft. A reverse shifting lever is used to engage the reverse bucket over the jet nozzle, causing the craft to back up.

reverse flushing: a method of cleaning radiators and engine coolant passages by forcing clean pressurized water through the block or the radiator in the direction opposite that of normal circulation.

reverse safety switches: safety interlocks that require the cutting deck to be disengaged before the tractor can be shifted into reverse.

revolutions per minute: abbreviation is RPM.

rewind starter assembly: a mechanism mounted above the flywheel on many small engines that spins, or cranks, the engine during starting.

rich mixture: an air-fuel mixture that contains excessive fuel.

ride plate: a plate that covers and protects the jet pump in a personal watercraft.

ridge reamer: an adjustable cutting tool designed to shave away the ridge that forms due to cylinder wear.

ring compressor: a tool that is tightened around a piston to compress the rings so the piston can be installed in the cylinder.

ring expander: a pliers-like tool that expands piston rings without distorting them.

ring spreader: see *ring expander.*

ring tension: the force that a piston ring exerts on the cylinder wall.

rocker arm: a device used in an overhead valve system to transfer the upward motion of the pushrod to a downward force on the valve.

roller bearing: an inner and outer race upon which hardened steel rollers operate.

room temperature vulcanizing sealant: a form-in-place sealant that is also referred to as silicon sealant. Abbreviation is RTV.

rotary mower: a lawnmower that has horizontally rotating blades.

rotary valve: a valve construction in which ported holes move in and out of register with each other to allow fluids or gases to enter and exit.

rotor: a rotating valve or conductor for carrying fluid or electrical current from a central source to the individual outlets as required. Can also refer to the rotating disc in a disc brake system.

rotor-type pump: an outboard engine water pump that has a one-piece vane and rotor. An eccentric gyrates the rotor, causing a pumping action.

rubber: an elastic, vibration-absorbing material of either natural or synthetic origin.

rubber tracks: components found on some heavy-duty snow throwers to provide exceptional traction on ice and snow.

running-fit: sufficient clearance between a shaft and journal to allow free running without overheating.

S

safe file: a file that does not have teeth cut into its edges.

safety data sheet: a sheet containing detailed information about a chemical, including its ingredients and characteristics, the type protective equipment that should be worn when working with the substance, and the procedures to follow in case of an accident.

safety glasses: glasses made from shatterproof plastic that protect the eyes from flying debris.

safety goggles: goggles made from shatterproof plastic that fit tightly to the face, providing more complete protection than safety glasses.

safety shoes: shoes constructed of durable materials that prevent sharp objects from piercing the shoes.

sales manager: an individual who sells or rents implements and vehicles that utilize small gasoline engines.

scale: a flaky deposit occurring on steel and iron or the mineral and metal build-up in a cooling system.

scavenge loss: the portion of the air-fuel charge that flows out through the open exhaust port as it pushes the exhaust gases from the cylinder.

score: a scratch, ridge, or groove marring a finished surface.

scraper bar: a metal bar fastened along the bottom edge of a snow thrower's auger housing intake. The scraper bar adds stiffness to the sheet metal housing and can be replaced when it becomes worn.

screw: a threaded fastener that holds parts together by passing through one part and threading into another.

seat: a surface, usually machined, upon which another part rests.

secondary winding: in an ignition coil or magneto armature, a wire in which a secondary, or high-tension, current is created by induction due to the interruption of current in the adjacent primary winding.

sediment: active material of the battery plates, which is gradually shed and accumulates in a space provided below the plates.

sediment bowl: a component located in a personal watercraft vent hose to prevent water from entering the fuel tank.

seize: to bind or stick.

self-propelled mower: a mower propelled by engine-driven wheels.

self-tapping screw: a screw with a grooved, tapered point that forms threads in the hole as the screw is turned.

semiconductor diode: a two-element solid state electronic device that permits current to flow in only one direction.

semiconductor material: a material that can act as a conductor under certain conditions and an insulator under other conditions. Common semiconductor materials include silicon, germanium, and selenium.

sensitivity: the percent of engine speed change required to cause a governor to produce a corrective movement of the throttle.

separators: sheets of rubber or wood inserted between the positive and negative plates of a cell to keep them out of contact with each other.

series circuit: electrical circuit in which the current passes from the power source to each device in turn and then flows back to the other terminal of the battery.

series-parallel circuit: electrical circuit in which some electrical devices are connected in series and others are connected in parallel.

service manager: an individual who plans and supervises the activities of all service department employees. Responsible for quality workmanship and satisfactory shop operation.

service manual: a book containing detailed service procedures and specifications for a particular model or series of engines.

service representative: an individual who works closely with service managers and mechanics in the field to catch and correct chronic service problems.

set screw: a screw that is made from heat-treated, hardened-alloy steel and used to secure such things as pulleys, gears, and shafts.

shear bolt: a bolt designed to protect a snow thrower's auger and gearbox from serious damage by shearing if something becomes lodged in the auger housing and stops the auger.

shear pin: a pin designed to protect a snow thrower's auger and gearbox from serious damage by shearing if something becomes lodged in the auger housing and stops the auger.

shim: thin sheets used as spacers between two parts, such as the two halves of a journal bearing.

short circuit: to provide a shorter path; often used to indicate an accidental ground in an electrical device or conductor.

shrink-fit: an exceptionally tight fit achieved by the heating and/or cooling of parts. The outer part is heated above its normal operating temperature or the inner part chilled below its normal operating temperature and assembled in this condition.

shroud: a light cover over the flywheel that shields the flywheel and helps direct airflow over the engine to carry away heat.

shunt: to bypass or turn aside. In electrical apparatus, an alternate path for the current.

shunt filter system: an oil filtration system in which part of the oil delivered by the pump is filtered and directed to the engine bearings, and some of the oil is shunted past the filter.

shunt winding: an electric winding or coil of wire that forms a bypass or alternate path for electric current. When applied to electric generators or motors, each end of the field winding is connected to an armature brush.

side clearance: space that allows piston rings to move in and out of the piston ring grooves while maintaining tension on the cylinder walls.

silicon-controlled rectifier: a semiconductor component that conducts electricity only when dc voltage is applied to its gate.

sillment seal: compacted powder that helps ensure permanent assembly of a spark plug and eliminates compression leakage under operating conditions.

single-stage snow throwers: snow throwers that displace snow using only a horizontal auger that gathers and throws the snow through an adjustable deflector.

skid shoes: shoes located at the bottom edges of the snow thrower auger housing to absorb wear during operation and establish the height of the scraper bar above the surface.

slap: side-to-side movement of the piston in the cylinder caused by too much clearance.

sliding-fit: clearance between a shaft and journal that is sufficient to allow free running without overheating.

sliding vane pump: a type of water pump used in an outboard engine. An eccentric cam rotates in the pump, causing the volume between the cam and pump housing to change and drawing water into the pump inlet. The cam then rotates and closes the inlet, pushing the water ahead of it toward the pump outlet.

sludge: a composition of oxidized petroleum products along with an emulsion formed by the mixture of oil and water. This forms a pasty substance, clogs oil lines and passages, and interferes with engine lubrication.

snap rings: fasteners that are compressed and placed in grooves in the piston pin bosses. They prevent the pin from rubbing on the cylinder surface.

Society of Automotive Engineers: abbreviation is SAE.

socket set: a collection of socket wrenches.

socket wrenches: interchangeable cylindrical wrenches that can be attached to a ratchet.

solenoid: an iron core, surrounded by a coil of wire, that moves due to magnetic attraction when an electrical current is fed to the coil. Solenoids are often used to actuate mechanisms by electrical means.

solid state: a term used to describe electrical devices that have no moving parts. These devices are made from semiconductor materials.

solvent: a solution that dissolves some other material.

south pole: the pole of a magnet to which the lines of force flow; the opposite of north pole.

spark: an electrical current possessing sufficient pressure to jump an air gap from one conductor to another.

spark advance: causing the spark to occur at an earlier time in the cycle of engine operation; opposite of retard.

spark arrestor: a device built into the exhaust system to prevent sparks from exiting.

spark gap: the space between the electrodes of a spark plug, across which the spark jumps. Also, a safety device in a magneto that provides an alternate path for the current when it exceeds a safe value.

spark knock: see *preignition.*

spark plug: a device inserted into the combustion chamber of an engine that ignites the compressed air/fuel mixture.

spark plug wire: a heavily insulated wire that connects the output of the ignition coil secondary windings to the spark plug.

spark test: a test performed to verify ignition system operation.

spark tester: a test instrument used to determine whether the ignition system is producing enough voltage to create a spark at the spark plug.

specific gravity: the relative weight of a substance as compared to water.

specific gravity test: a test that measures the density of electrolyte to determine the state of charge of the battery.

speed ranges: the various maximum speeds that can be selected using the speed selector lever. Speed within these ranges are controlled by the speed control pedal.

spiral bevel gears: a gear and pinion wherein the mating teeth are curved and placed at an angle with the pinion shaft.

splash lubrication system: a lubrication system that splashes oil onto various engine components as the engine spins. This type of lubrication system is used in small four-cycle gasoline engines.

spline: a long keyway.

spontaneous combustion: the self-ignition of combustible materials.

spring-loaded check valve: a valve that permits flow in one direction and prevents flow in the opposite direction.

spurt-hole: a hole drilled through a connecting rod and bearing that allows oil under pressure to be squirted out of the bearing for additional lubrication of the cylinder walls.

square: a term used to describe a cylinder with a bore diameter that is equal to the piston stroke.

square foot: abbreviation is sq ft.

square inch: abbreviation is sq in.

square nut: a nut with four sides.

stability: the ability to maintain a desired engine speed without fluctuation.

stamping: a piece of sheet metal cut and formed into the desired shape with the use of dies.

starboard: the area to the right of a watercraft's centerline.

starter: a device that engages and rotates the flywheel to start an engine.

starter clutch wrench: a special tool designed to grip the indentations in a starter clutch so it can be turned.

stator: stationary coils of an alternating current generator.

stator assembly: an alternator component that consists of a series of coils mounted on a circular plate and attached to the engine inside the flywheel.

stator vanes: dividers in the impeller housing that reduce the tendency of the water to revolve as it enters the jet pump venturi of a personal watercraft.

steerable nozzle: a device for directing the stream of water from the jet pump to the left or right. Located at the stern of a PWC.

steering control: the device designed for controlling direction.

stern: the rear of a watercraft.

straight pin: a pin used for alignment. They fit closely, but are not usually an interference fit like dowel pins. See *dowel pin.*

stress: the force or strain to which a material is subjected.

string trimmer: a handheld, engine-powered machine that cuts weeds with a spinning nylon filament.

stroboscope: a term applied to an ignition timing light, which, by being attached to the distributor points, gives the effect of making a mark on a rapidly rotating wheel, such as a flywheel, appear to stand still for observation.

stroke: the movement of a piston in the cylinder from one end of its travel to the other. Also refers to the distance that the piston travels from top dead center to bottom dead center.

stud: a rod with threads cut on both ends.

suction: suction exists in a vessel when the pressure is lower than the atmospheric pressure. Also see *vacuum.*

sulfated: when a battery is improperly charged or allowed to remain in a discharged condition for some length of time, an abnormal amount of lead sulfate will collect on the plates. The battery is then said to be *sulfated.*

sump: the part of the block in a small four-stroke engine that holds and collects the lubricating oil.

super unleaded: a gasoline blend with a higher octane rating than regular unleaded. See also *premium unleaded.*

swash plate: an angled plate attached to rotating shaft; commonly used to operate reciprocating pistons in a pump.

switch: device used to control the flow of current in an electric circuit.

synchronize: to cause two events to occur in unison or at the same time.

systematic troubleshooting: diagnostic method that involves checking and/or testing one component after another component until the problem is located and corrected.

T

tachometer: a device for measuring and indicating the rotational speed of an engine.

tap: to cut threads in a hole with a tapered, fluted, threaded tool.

taper pin: a pin that has a uniform taper of .250″ per foot over the length of the pin and each end rounded slightly. They are generally used to fasten pulleys and gears to shafts to prevent rotation on the shaft.

taper tap: a tap that has a slender taper at the beginning of the tap that makes it start easier in the threads. Used for tapping through holes.

tappet: the adjusting screw for varying the clearance between the valve stem and the cam. May be built into the valve lifter or into the rocker arm on an overhead valve engine.

tapping: the process of cutting threads in a hole.

telescoping gauge: a transfer-type measuring instrument designed to measure the internal diameter of a bore.

tensile strength: the amount of tension, or pulling, force a material can withstand before failing.

tensile stress: a force that creates tension, or pulls on an object.

tension: effort devoted toward elongation or *stretching* of a material.

terminal: in electrical work, a junction point where connections are made, such as the terminal fitting on the end of a wire.

test light: a diagnostic tool used to check for continuity or the presence of voltage in an electrical circuit.

thermal efficiency: a measure of how much of the power produced by the burning air-fuel mixture is actually used to drive the piston downward.

thermostat: a heat-controlled valve used in the cooling system of an engine to regulate the flow of water or used in the electrical circuit to control the current.

thread: the helical portion of a screw or bolt, or the helix in a hole that it fastens into.

thread adhesive: adhesive applied to the threads of nuts, bolts, or screws to prevent them from loosening during service.

thread chaser: a special thread tapping tool used to clean and correct the threads.

threading: the process of making external threads on an external cylindrical surface.

threading tap: a tool used to cut or recut the thread.

thread length: the length of the portion of the fastener with threads.

thread pitch: the number of threads per inch on U.S. customary fasteners; on metric fasteners it is the distance between each thread measured in millimeters.

throttle: a valve that regulates the amount of air-fuel mixture entering the cylinders.

through hole: a threaded hole that goes all the way through material.

throw: with reference to an engine, usually the distance from the centerline of the crankshaft main bearing to the centerline of the connecting rod journal.

thrust surfaces: the sides of the piston forced against the cylinder wall. These surfaces are at right angles (90°) to the centerline of the crankshaft and piston pin.

timing chain: chain used to drive the camshaft and accessory shafts of an engine.

timing gears: any group of gears that are driven from the engine crankshaft to cause the valves, ignition, and other engine-driven apparatus to operate at the desired time during the engine cycle.

tolerance: a permissible variation between the two extremes of specified dimensions.

toothed washer: a stamped sheet metal washer that has internal, external, or external-internal teeth.

top dead center: the point at which the piston is at its upper most position on the compression stroke. Abbreviated TDC.

torque: an effort devoted toward twisting or turning.

torque wrench: a special wrench with a built-in indicator to measure the applied turning force.

transaxle: a combined transmission and rear axle.

transferable skills: skills that can help you succeed in any job you choose. The transferable skills useful in all jobs include reading, writing, speaking, and basic math.

transfer port: in two-cycle engines, an opening in the cylinder wall through which the air/fuel mixture is forced from the crankcase into the cylinder.

transformer: an electrical device designed to increase or decrease voltage or current levels.

transistor: a semiconductor device that is often used for switching applications.

transistor controlled ignition: a type of electronic ignition that uses a transistor as the switching device. Abbreviation is TCI.

troubleshooting: refers to a process of diagnosing or determining the source of trouble or troubles from observation and testing.

tubing wrench: a wrench that is similar to a box-end wrench, but has an opening so the wrench can be used on metal tubing connection fittings.

tune-up: the process of accurate and careful adjustments to obtain maximum engine performance.

tungsten: a hard metal with a high melting temperature.

turbulence: a disturbed or disordered, irregular motion of fluids or gases.

two-cycle engine: see *two-stroke engine.*

two-stage snow blower: see *two-stage snow thrower.*

two-stage snow thrower: a snow thrower in which the auger feeds the snow into a high-speed blower fan that ejects the snow out of the chute.

two-stroke engine: an engine design that produces one power stroke for each revolution of the crankshaft.

U

undercharging: providing an insufficient charge to a battery.

under square: a term used to describe a cylinder with a bore diameter that is less than the stroke.

Unified National Coarse series: a coarse thread series designation. Abbreviation is UNC.

Unified National Fine series: a fine thread series designation. Abbreviation is UNF.

updraft carburetors: a carburetor type in which the mixture flows upward to the engine.

upper cylinder lubrication: a method of introducing a lubricant into the fuel or intake manifold in order to lubricate the upper cylinder, valve guides, and other parts.

V

vacuum: the term ordinarily used to describe a pressure less than atmospheric pressure. See also *suction*.

vacuum carburetor: a simple carburetor that draws fuel directly out of the fuel tank.

vacuum gauge: an instrument designed to measure the amount of vacuum existing in a chamber.

vacuum governor: a type of governor that adjusts throttle position based on intake manifold pressure (vacuum).

valve: a device for alternately opening and sealing an aperture.

valve clearance: air gap allowed between end of valve stem and valve lifter or rocker arm to compensate for heat expansion.

valve face: part of a valve that mates with and rests upon a seating surface.

valve grinding: a process of mating the valve seat and valve face performed with the aid of an abrasive.

valve guide: a hole machined in the engine block to align the valve and ensure accurate raising and lowering in relation to the seat.

valve head: the portion of the valve upon which the valve face is machined.

valve-in-block arrangement: a valve train arrangement in which the camshaft is located in the crankcase and the valves are located in the cylinder block, directly above the camshaft lobes.

valve key or valve lock: the key, washer, or other device that holds the valve spring cup or washer in place on the valve stem.

valve lifter: a rod or plunger that transfers motion from the cam and the other valve train components.

valve margin: the space or rim between the surface of the head and the surface of the valve face.

valve overlap: an interval expressed in degrees where both valves of an engine cylinder are open at the same time.

valve seat: the matched surface on which the valve face rests.

valve seat width: the width of the contact area between the valve seat and valve face.

valve spring: a spring attached to a valve to return it to the seat after it has been released from the lifting or opening operation.

valve spring compressor: a tool that compress a valve spring so the spring retainer can be removed.

valve stem: the portion of a valve that rests within a guide.

valve stem guide: a bushing or hole in which the valve stem is placed.

valve train: all the components that work together to transform the rotation of the crankshaft into the opening and closing of the valves.

vanes: any plate or blade that is moved by or directs the flow of a gas or liquid.

vaporizer: a device for transforming or helping to transform a liquid into a vapor; often includes the application of heat.

vapor lock: a condition in which vaporized gasoline forms bubbles in the fuel line that prevent the proper flow of fuel.

vari-volume pump: an outboard engine water pump that uses a synthetic rubber impeller to force water out into the water jacket.

vented: open to the atmosphere.

venturi: a restriction in a passage, which causes air to move faster (increased velocity).

vibration damper: a device to reduce the torsional or twisting vibration that occurs along the length of the crankshaft used in multiple cylinder engines; also known as a *harmonic balancer*.

vise-grips: locking pliers.

viscosity: the resistance to flow or adhesive characteristics of an oil.

viscosity index: a standard for measureing the relationship between viscosity and temperature.

volatility: the tendency for a fluid to evaporate rapidly or pass off in the form of a vapor.

volt: a unit of electrical force that will cause a current of one ampere to flow through a resistance of one ohm.

voltage regulator: an electrical device for controlling or regulating voltage.

voltmeter: an instrument for measuring the voltage in an electrical circuit. See *volt* and *multimeter*.

volume: the measure of space expressed as cubic inches, cubic feet, or other units of linear measure.

volumetric efficiency: the ratio between the ideal and actual efficiency of an internal combustion engine.

W

washer: a disc that provides a wider bearing surface for a bolt or screw head and/or nut.

water column: a measure of atmospheric pressure based on its ability to displace water.

water inlet screen: a screen that prevents grass and debris from entering the personal watercraft engine cooling system.

water jacket: a passage surrounding the cylinder on liquid-cooled engines. As coolant circulates through the water jacket, it absorbs some of the combustion heat and carries it away from the engine.

water pump: an engine-driven pump that circulates the coolant through a liquid-cooled engine.

watt: a unit of electrical power obtained by multiplying amperes by volts.

welch plug: a stamped steel plug that covers a drilled passage in a carburetor body.

wet bulb primer: a primer that draws fuel from the fuel tank or fuel reservoir in the carburetor and pumps it into the carburetor's air horn.

wet-charged battery: a type of storage battery supplied with the electrolyte already in it.

wide bearing lock washer: a washer that combines the characteristics of a flat washer and a kantlink lock washer.

wing nut: a nut that has smooth, thick flanges molded into two sides so the nut can be tightened or loosened by hand.

wire-type feeler gauges: tools used to check spark plug gap. This type of gauge can be used on both new and used plugs.

wiring diagram: a detailed drawing of all wiring, connections, and components in an electrical circuit.

wrist pin: see *piston pin.*

Z

zerk fitting: see *grease fitting.*

Index